MANUAL OF LAW INDIAN ARMED FORCES

Army, Navy, Air Force, Coast Guard

MANUAL OF LAW INDIAN ARMED FORCES

Army, Navy, Air Force, Coast Guard

Wg Cdr (Dr) U C Jha

Vij Books India Pvt Ltd
New Delhi (India)

Published by

Vij Books India Pvt Ltd

(Publishers, Distributors & Importers)
2/19 (Second Floor), Ansari Road, Darya Ganj
New Delhi - 110002
Phones: 91-11-43596460, 91-9811094883
e-mail : vijbooks@rediffmail.com

ISBN: 978-93-82652-87-8

ISBN ebook: 978-93-82652-88-5

Price : ₹ 2995/-

Printed and bound in India

CONTENTS

ARRANGEMENT OF LEGAL SYSTEMS

PREFACE

Personnel of the armed forces play a crucial role in ensuring the security and peace in any country. The world over, armed forces are governed by a special code of conduct designed to ensure the highest standard of discipline among their members. The Indian Armed Forces, also referred to as the Defence Forces, consist of the army, navy, air force and coast guard. The British military justice system is the progenitor of the Indian military legal system. Before India attained independence, the defence forces were governed by the Indian Army Act 1911, the Indian Navy Discipline Act 1934 and the Indian Air Force Act 1932. After independence, three separate Acts came into force for the governance of the three services – the Army Act 1950, the Air Force Act 1950 and the Navy Act 1957. The Indian Coast Guard came into being on 1 February 1977 as an interim Coast Guard Organization. The service was formally established as an independent organization with the enactment of the Coast Guard Act 1978.

The Army and Air Force Acts were virtually a continuation of the pre-independence Acts, as no procedural or other reforms were made. The Navy Act, however, incorporated a few procedural reforms suggested by the Pilcher Committee appointed in the UK to consider the Administration of Justice under the British Naval Code. The four Acts governing the army, air force, navy and coast guard are not exactly alike. The Army Rules 1954, the Air Force Rules 1969 and the Coast Guard (Discipline) Rules 1983, the Coast Guard (General) Rules 1986, and the Coast Guard (Conditions of Service) Rules 1986 were framed for carrying out the provisions of the Acts governing the respective services. While no rules have been framed for the navy, the Navy (Discipline and Miscellaneous Provisions) Regulations 1965 is statutory in nature and was issued by the government under the power conferred on it by the Navy Act 1957 s 184 and serve the same purpose as the rules in the case of the other services. In 1992, certain amendments were made to the Army Act 1950 and the Army Rules 1954, while the Navy Act was updated in 2005. However, no such exercise has been undertaken in respect of the laws relating to the air force. Under the existing system, pre-trial detention cannot be set off against a sentence of imprisonment passed by a court martial in the air force, though the provision has been incorporated under the Army Act in 1992 and the Navy Act in 2005. Also, 'field punishment' has been omitted under the Army Act in 1992, whereas the Air Force Act has not been updated. The existing naval judicial system has been influenced in many ways by the British judicial system. The Navy Act is considered more progressive than the laws relating to the army and the air force in the sense that the provisions relating to the review of court martial have not been incorporated in it and the judge advocate plays a central role in the administration of justice in a trial by court martial.

The Supreme Court in *Imtiaz Ahmad v The State of UP* (2012) 2 SCC 584 has held: "A person's access to justice is a guaranteed fundamental right under the Constitution and particularly Article 21. Denial of this right undermines public confidence in the justice delivery system and incentivizes people to look for short-cuts and other fora where they feel that justice will be done quicker. In the long run, this also weakens the justice delivery system and poses a threat to Rule of Law....access to justice must not be understood in a purely quantitative dimension. Access to justice in an egalitarian democracy must be understood to mean qualitative access to justice as well."

Article 33 of the Constitution places certain restrictions upon the fundamental rights of a member of the military and paramilitary forces. After its amendment in 1984, Article 33 reads as:

> *Parliament may, by law, determine to what extent any of the rights conferred by this Part shall, in their application to,*
>
> (a) *the members of the armed forces; or*
>
> (b) *the members of the forces charged with the maintenance of public order; or*
>
> (c) *persons employed in any bureau or other organization established by the State for purposes of intelligence or counter intelligence; or*
>
> (d) *person employed in, or in connection with the telecommunication systems set up for the purposes of any force, bureau or organization referred to in clauses (a) to (c),*
>
> *be restricted or abrogated so as to ensure the proper discharge of their duties and maintenance of discipline among them.*

However, all the rights contained in Part III of the Constitution cannot be abrogated even in the case of members of the armed forces. In a recent case (*Major General H M Singh v Union of India* (2014) 3 SCC 670), the Supreme Court held that the denial of promotion to an officer, where vacancy existed, was discriminatory and in violation of Article 16 of the Constitution. A person after enlisting in the armed forces continues to remain entitled to benefits and liberal spirit of the Constitution. Under Article 246 of the Constitution read with Entry 2 of List-1 (Union List) in the Seventh Schedule, the government has established an Armed Forces Tribunal in 2009 for the adjudication of complaints and disputes regarding service matters and appeals arising out of the verdicts of the court martial of members of the army, navy and air force.

This volume covers the laws and subordinate legislations relating to the armed forces. In addition, it analyses the provisions of the Indian Penal Code 1860 and the Code of Criminal Procedure 1973 that apply to the personnel of the armed forces, as well as the Armed Forces Tribunal laws, and the Armed Forces (Special Powers) Act. The corresponding provisions of the army, navy, air force and coast guard laws are presented in a chart at the end of the book.

I am thankful to my wife Ratna for support and wish to thank Vij Books India Pvt Ltd., New Delhi for their cooperation in bringing out this edition.

New Delhi

Wg Cdr (Dr) U C Jha

TABLE OF CASES

I. INRODUCTION

CONTENTS

PARA

[0001] Origin of Military Law The Indian military law owes its origin to the British military legal system made applicable to the guards and afterwards to the European and native troops employed by the East India Company. Guards were enrolled for the protection of the factories or trading posts which were established by the East India Company at Surat, Masulipatam, Armagon, Madras, Hooghly and Balasore in the first half of the seventeenth century. These guards were intended to add to the dignity of the Chief Officials as much as for a defensive purpose. In some cases special restrictions were even placed by treaty on their strength, so as to prevent their acquiring any military importance. Gradually the organization of these guards was improved and from them sprang the East India Company's European and Indian troops. Both these steadily increased in numbers, until in 1857, it numbered over 311,000 officers and men. Statutory provisions were made for the discipline of the East India Company's troops by an Act of 1754[1] for "punishing Mutiny and Desertion of officers and soldiers in the service of the United Company of Merchants of England trading to the East Indies, and for the punishment of offences committed in the East Indies, or at the Island of Saint Helena." The Act empowered the Crown to make Articles of War for the government of these troops, and such articles were accordingly made and published[2]. The terms of the Act were wide enough to cover both European and Indian troops, but the language of the articles showed that they were originally intended for Europeans only. In the absence of any other code, however, the Government of Bengal, Madras, and Bombay seems to have applied these articles, with such modification and omissions as appeared necessary, to the bodies of Indian troops maintained by them, of which the present Indian Army is the descendant.

In 1813, owing to doubts having arisen as to the legal validity of the existing arrangements for the discipline of the Indian troops, provisions were inserted in the Act of 1754 to extend the company's privileges for a further term, which legalised the existing system and gave power to each of the Governments of Fort William, Fort Saint George and Bombay to make, laws, regulations, and Articles of War for the government of all Indian officers and soldiers in their respective services[3]. It was further provided in 1824 that such legislation should apply to the Indian troops of each presidency, wherever serving, and whether within or beyond His Majesty's dominions[4].Under the statutory sanction of these enactments a military code was framed by the government of each presidency and put in force as regards its own troops. These codes followed to a great extent the Articles of War then applicable to the Company's Europeans, but the only punishments award able to Indian officers seem to have been death, dismissal, suspension, and reprimand and to Indian soldiers, death and corporal punishment.

1 27 Geo II, Cap 9.

2 Section 8 of the Act of 1754.

3 53 Geo III, Cap 155 ss. 96 and 97.

4 Geo IV, Cap 81, s. 63.

[0002] The Articles of War Under the Government of India Act 1833[1] the power to legislate for the whole Indian Army was restricted to the Governor General in Council, and laws so made were given general application to all Indian officers and soldiers wherever serving[2]. The Indian Legislature, under the powers conferred upon it by the Act of 1833, for the first time provided a common code for the Indian officers and soldiers. The Governor General in Council enacted the Articles of War as Act XX of 1845. This Act was shortly after repealed and replaced by Act XIX of 1847 which, having been frequently amended[3] in the intervening period, was in its turn repealed by Act XXIX of 1861. This was replaced by the Indian Articles of War by an Act V of 1869. The preamble to this Act for the first time recognised the existence of what are commonly known as "followers" and Act V was equally made applicable to them.

After the First War of Independence, the three armies maintained by the Presidencies were amalgamated into one in 1895 and substantial amendments were made in the Indian Article of War by Act XII of 1894. The Indian Articles of War, as altered by this Act, and by various minor amending Acts, (Acts of Governor-General in Council, XII of 1891, I of 1900, I of 1901, IX of 1901, XIII of 1904, and V of 1905) furnished the statutory basis of the Indian military code until 1911. As time went on, however, and the Indian Army began to take its share in the imperial responsibilities of the British Army, it was found that an Act originally framed for three separate local forces, each serving as a rule in its own Presidency, failed to provide adequately for the discipline and administration of that army under modern conditions. Owing also to the number of amendments superimposed on the original articles, these were often difficult to understand, and sometimes even self-contradictory.

The amendment of the Indian Articles of War was, therefore, again taken up in 1908. Accordingly Indian Army Act, consolidating the existing law as to the Indian Army into one simple and comprehensive enactment was passed into law in March 1911. It came into force on 1st January 1912. All previous Acts dealing with the subject were repealed by s 127 of the said Act. Amendments were subsequently made to this Act by various amending Acts[4]. During the First World War (1914-18) temporary Acts (Acts of Governor General in Council IV of 1917 and XVIII of 1918) were passed to provide for the suspension of sentences. These measures were found to be beneficial, and on 23 March 1920, the Indian Army (Suspension of Sentences) Act 1920[5], a permanent legislation to provide for the suspension of sentences of imprisonment or transportation passed by courts martial on persons subject to the Indian Army Act, which repealed the temporary Acts, came into force. This Act was to be read as one with the Indian Army Act.

After independence, the need for a general revision of the military law was felt[6]. As a result three separate legislations came into force for the governance of the three services – the Army, the Air Force and the Navy. The Army Act 1950 was passed by the Parliament on 22 May 1950 and came into force on 22 July 1950. The Air Force Act 1950 came into force on 22 July 1950. The Navy Act 1957 was passed by Parliament on 27 December 1957, and came into effect from 1 January 1958.

1 Ie the Government of India Act 1833 s 73.

2 3 and 4 Will. IV, Cap 85.

3 Acts of Governor General in Council, VI of 1850, XXXVI of 1850, III of 1854, X of 1856, VIII of 1857, XXII of 1857, and VI of 1860.

4 Acts of Governor General in Council, XV of 1914, X of 1917, XI of 1918, XVIII of 1919, II of 1920, XXXVII of 1920, XXXIII of 1923, VIII of 1930, XXXIII of 1934 and VII of 1935.

5 Act of Governor General in Council XX of 1920.

6 The main objects of the revision were to (1) make the respective Act self-sufficient, (2) adapt the existing provisions to suit the new constitutional set up, (3) bridge the gap between the army and civil laws in the matter of punishment for offences and (4) eliminate the inequalities between the three service Acts. The Statement of Object and Reasons contained in the Army Bill.

[0003] Subordinate Legislations in the Army. The subordinate legislations in the Army include the rules and regulations. The Army Rules 1950 made under the Army Act of 1950 s 191 were subsequently replaced by the Army Rules, 1954. Army Rules are in the nature of procedural laws, somewhat like the Code of Criminal Procedure. The Regulations for the Army 1962, were issued under the authority of the Government of India and replaced the Regulations for the Army in India (reprint 1945) and instructions by His Excellency the Commander-in-Chief (reprint 1945). The Regulations of 1962 were updated and replaced by the Defence Services Regulations, Regulations for the Army, Revised Edition, 1987. Certain provisions of the Regulations of 1987, especially procedures relating to statutory complaints contained in it have been amended in 1997[1]. The Manual of Indian Military Law was compiled by the judge advocate general of the army in India in 1912. The Manual was divided into four parts: (1) part I contained a history of military law and chapters on the laws of evidence applicable to courts-martial, ordinary criminal offences and other legal matters a knowledge of which was considered essential for the officers and soldiers; (2) part II consisted of a reprint of the Indian Army Act, 1911 and statutory rules issued thereunder; (3) part III consisted of the text of certain Acts of the Indian legislatures which were referred to in the earlier parts of the manual; and (4) Part IV contained all notifications issued by the Governor General in Council under the Indian Army Act 1911. The MIML was amended and updated in 1937, and was reprinted in 1961. The reprint incorporated the Army Act 1950 and the Army Rules 1954[2]. In 1983, the Government of India issued an updated and revised bilingual Manual of Military Law (MML) in three volumes: (1) Volume I consisted of eight chapters dealing with a brief history of military law in India (Chapter I), an outline of the Army Act (Chapter II), arrests and investigations of charges (Chapter III), courts martial (Chapter IV), evidence (Chapter V), civil offences (Chapter VI), duties in aid of civil power (Chapter VII) and service privileges (Chapter VIII); (2) Volume II contained the Army Act 1950 and the Army Rules 1954, with explanatory notes, forms and appendices;[3] and (3) Volume III contained certain enactments which are referred to in earlier parts of the Manual. This volume also contains Gazette Notifications issued under the Army Act 1950 by the Government of India and forms of warrants. A new edition of Manual of Military Laws has been issued in the year 2011. The Volume III now contains two new legislations i.e., The Right to Information Act 2005 and the Armed Forces Tribunal Act 2007.

1 Defence Services Regulations, Regulations for the Army 1987, paragraph 364.

2 Further reprints of the Manual of Indian Military Law were brought out in 1967, 1971 and 1976.

3 No power is conferred upon the Central Government of issuing Notes or issuing orders which could have the effect of the Rules made under the Act. Rules and Regulations or administrative instructions can neither be supplemented nor substituted under any provision of the Act or the Rules and Regulations framed thereunder. The administrative instructions issued or the Notes attached to the Rules which are not referable to any statutory authority cannot be permitted to bring about a result which may take away the rights vested in a person governed by the Act. The Government, however, has the power to fill up the gaps in supplementing the rules by issuing instructions if the Rules are silent on the subject provided the instructions issued are not inconsistent with the Rules already framed. The 'notes' issued by the authorities of the Armed Forces are for the guidance of the officers connected with the implementation of the provisions of the Act and the Rules and not with the object of supplementing or superseding the statutory Rules by administrative instructions. *Union of India v Charanjit Singh Gill* (2000) 5 SCC 742.

[0004] Subordinate Legislations in the Air Force In the exercise of the powers conferred by the Air Force Act 1950[1], the Central Government issued the Air Force Act Rules 1950. These rules were further revised and amended vide the Air Force Rules 1969[2]. Under the authority contained in the Air Force Act 1950[3], the Regulations for the Air Force (Revised Edition) 1964, were issued by the Government of India and superseded the "Regulations for the Royal Indian Air Force (Rules) 1942", and "Regulations for the Indian Air Force--Instructions issued by Excellency the Commander-in-Chief of India 1945". In 1988, the Judge Advocate General (Air Force) issued the Manual of Air Force Law under the authority of the Chief of the Air Staff. The manual, which is considered to be an authoritative commentary on the provisions of the Air Force Law, is in two volumes. Volume I of this manual contains the Air Force Act 1950, while Volume II contains the Air Force Rules 1969 and certain appendices containing extracts from the Constitution of India and other related legislations.

1 The Air Force Act 1950 s 189.

2 Vide SRO 310, dated 24 September, 1969, published in the Gazette of India, Extra, Part II, sec (iv).

3 The Air Force Act 1950 s 190. A 'Regulation Cell' formed at the Air Headquarters, New Delhi, in 1980s failed to bring out a revised edition of the Regulations.

[0005] Subordinate Legislations in the Navy and Coast Guard Unlike the Army and the Air Force, the Indian Navy does not have its own rules. The Regulations for the Navy Part I was issued in 1991, under the authority of the Government of India and superseded the corresponding provisions of the Regulations for the Navy Part I, 1965 (non-statutory). It contains 44 chapters on administrative matters. Part II of the Regulations is called the Navy (Discipline and Miscellaneous Provisions) Regulations1965 and is statutory in nature. These were issued by the government under the power conferred under the Navy Act 1957[1]. Part III of the Regulations is called the Naval Ceremonial, Conditions of Service and Miscellaneous Regulations 1963, and is also statutory in nature. Part IV contains the Indian Naval Auxiliary Service Regulations 1973. Certain minor changes were made the Navy Acts in 2005. The Navy (Amendment) Act 2005, amended the Navy Act 1957 ss 3 (16), 79, 94,133, 151, 176 and 184. It inserted a new provision under the Navy Act 1957[2] relating to parole and omitted Chapter XXII from the Act of 1957.

The Coast Guard Act 1978 was passed by the Parliament on 18 August 1978[3]. The subordinate legislation in the Indian Coast Guards includes the Coast Guard (Discipline) Rules 1982, Coast Guard (General) Rules 1986, Coast Guard (Conditions of Service) Rules 1986, Coast Guard (Seniority and Promotion) Rules 1987 and Trail of Persons Subject to Armed Forces Laws of the Union (Exercise of Jurisdiction) Rules 1978[4]. A Coast Guard Manual was issued by the Director General Coast Guard on 1 August 1989[5].

1 The Regulations for the Navy have been made under the provision of the Navy Act 1957 s 184.

2 Ie the Navy Act 1957 s 163A.3.

3 Act No. 30 of 1978. An Act to provide for the constitution and regulation of an Armed Force of the Union for ensuring the security of the maritime zones of India with a view to the protection of maritime and other national interests in such zones and for matters connected therewith.

4 These rules have been issued under the provision of the Coast Guard Act 1978 s 123.

5 Unlike the Manuals issued by the Army and the Air Force, the Coast Guard Manual is not to be cited as an authority, and whenever necessary, reference is to be made to the specific provisions of the Coast Guard Act 1978 or the relevant rules made the Act; Preface to the Coast Guard Manual of 1 August 1989.

II. THE LAW RELATING TO THE ARMY

1. PRELIMINARY

CONTENTS

PARA

A. Introduction

B. Short title and commencement

C. Definitions and Meanings

A. INTRODUCTION

[0006] Introduction The Indian Army Act 1950 constitutes a special law in force conferring a special jurisdiction on the court martial prescribing a special procedure for the trial of the offences under the Act. The Army Act 1950 and the Army Rules 1954 constitute a self-contained code specifying offences and the procedure for detention, custody and trial of the offenders by the court martial. Chapter VI of the Army Act 1950 comprising of sections 34 to 69 specify and define the various offences under the Act[1].

1 *Ranjit Thakur v Union of India* 1987 AIR 2386: 1988 SCR (1) 512: 1987 SCC (4) 611.

B. SHORT TITLE AND COMMENCEMENT

[0007] Short title and commencement This statute covering the Army is the Army Act 1950[1]. It came into force on 22 July 1950 by notification in the Official Gazette[2].

1 The Army Act 1950 s 1(1).

2 The Army Act 1950 s 1(2). See: Government of India notification SRO 120 dated 22 July 1950. Certain amendments were incorporated in the Army Act 1950 in 1955, 1956, 1974, 1975 and 1992.

C. DEFINITIONS AND MEANINGS

Certain words and terms that appear in the Army Act and the Army Rules will need to be understood as they are defined in the Army Act 1950 and the Amy Rules 1954.

[0008] Active service In the Army Act 1950, unless the context otherwise requires, 'active service', as applied to a person subject to the Army Act, means the time during which such person is attached to, or forms part of, a force which is engaged in operations against an enemy[1]; engaged in military operations in, or is on the line of march to, a country or place wholly or partly occupied by an enemy[2]; or attached to or forms part of a force which is in military occupation of a foreign country[3].

1 Army Act 1950 s 3(i)(a).

2 Army Act 1950 s 3(i)(b).

3 Army Act 1950 s 3(i)(c).

[0009] Power to declare persons to be on active service Notwithstanding anything contained in the provisions of the Army Act 1950[1], the central government can, by a notification, declare any person or class of persons subject to the Army Act 1950 shall, with reference to any area in which they may be serving or with reference to any provision of the Army Act 1950 or of any other law for the time being in force, be deemed to be on active service within the meaning of that Act. The term "they may be serving" would cover not only persons actually engaged in performing duties of their respective offices on the date of commission of offence alleged against them but also persons on leave at relevant point of time. 'Serving' would mean holding employment as distinguished from actually performing duties of service. The period of leave will also be included as 'serving'[2] In order to ascertain whether the troops are on 'active service' or not, regard must be had to all the circumstances involved. Where there is any doubt as to whether or not troops are on active service for the purposes of this provision, a declaration should be made under the Army Act 1950[3]. The central government may issue notification under the Army Act 1950 s 9 and declare that any person or class of persons subject to the Army Act, serving in any particular country, place or area shall be deemed to be on active service. The Government of India has issued number of such notifications under the Army Act 1950 s 9[4]. Army person injured in attack by miscreant while going to join duty has to be deemed to have received injury while in active service[5].

1 Ie as contained in the Army Act 1950 s 3 (i): see **[0008]**.

2 Phrase 'they may be serving': *Ajit Singh v State of Punjab* AIR 1970 P&H 351 (FB) : 1970 Cr LJ 1119 : 72 Punj LR 376.

3 Ie under Army Act 1950 s 9.

4 E.g.: Such notification was issued wide SRO 6-E/62 dated 28 November 1962 for the first time to combat Chinese aggression.

5 *Nand Kishore Mishra v Union of India* 2013 AIR SCW 1290.

[0010] Civil offence Unless the context otherwise requires, 'civil offence' means an offence[1] which is triable by a Criminal Court[2].

1 The term 'offence' means any act or omission punishable under the Army Act 1950 and includes a civil offence;

see: Army Act s 3(xvii) **[0028]**.

2 The term 'criminal court' means a court of ordinary criminal justice in any part of India, see: Army Act 1950 s 3 (viii) **[0017]**. Army Act 1950 s 3(ii).

[0011] Civil prison Unless the context otherwise require, 'civil prison' means any jail or place used for the detention of any criminal prisoner under the Prisons Act 1894, or under any other law for the time being in force[1].

1 Army Act 1950 s 3(iii).

[0012] Chief of the Army Staff Unless the context otherwise require, 'chief of the army staff'[1] means the officer commanding the regular army[2].

1 The term 'commander in chief' was replaced by the term 'chief of the army staff' wef 7 May 55; see The commander-in-chief (change of designation) Act 1955 and Government of India, Ministry of Defence Notification SRO 2/E dated 7 May 55.

2 As to the definition of 'regular army' see the Army Act 1950 s 3 (xxi); see **[0034]**. Army Act 1950 s 3 (iv).

[0013] Commanding officer Unless the context otherwise requires, the term 'commanding officer', when used in any provision of the Army Act 1950, with reference to any separate portion of the regular army or to any department thereof, means the officer whose duty it is under the regulations of the army, or by the custom of the service, to discharge with respect to that portion of the regular army or that department, the functions of a commanding officer in regard to matters of the description referred to in that provision[1]. The commanding officer of a person subject to the Army Act 1950 is either: (a) The officer who has been appointed by higher authority to be a commanding officer to exercise his power as such[2]; or (b) Where no appointment has been made, the officer who is, for the time being, in immediate command of: (i) The unit to which the person belongs or is attached to[3]; or (ii) any detachment or a distinct sizeable separate portion of a unit with which the person is for the time being serving, and in respect of which it is the duty of such officer, under the regulations for the army or by the custom of the service, to discharge the functions of a commanding officer[4].

1 Army Act 1950 s 3(v).

2 Defence Services Regulations, Regulations for the Army 1987, Volume I, paragraph 9(a).

3 Defence Services Regulations, Regulations for the Army 1987, Volume I, paragraph 9(b)(i).

4 Defence Services Regulations, Regulations for the Army 1987, Volume I, paragraph 9(b)(ii).

[0014] Officers exercising powers in certain cases Whenever persons subject to the Army Act 1950 are serving under an officer commanding any military organisation not specifically named under the Act and not less than a brigade, the Government may prescribe the officer by whom the powers under the Army Act as regards such persons shall be exercised[1]. The Central Government may confer such powers, either absolutely or subject to certain restrictions and reservations[2].

1 The Army Act 1950 s 8(1).

2 The Army Act 1950 s 8(2).

[0015] Corps Unless the context otherwise requires, 'corps' means any separate body of persons subject to the Army Act 1950, which is prescribed as a corps for the purposes of any of the provisions of the Army Act 1950[1].

(1) Each of the following separate bodies of persons subject to the Army Act 1950 shall be a 'corps' for the purposes of Chapter III and s 43(a) of the Army Act 1950 and of the Army Rules 1954 Chapters II and III of, (except r 13) namely:

(a) President's Body Guard.

(b) The Armoured Corps, Horsed Cavalry Regiments, including Training Centres and non-combatants,

(c) The Regiment of Artillery.

(d) The Corps of Engineers including non-combatants,

(e) The Corps of Signals including non-combatants.

(f) Each regiment or each ungrouped battalion (as the case may be) of Infantry, or in the case of grouped Gorkha Regiments, each group of Infantry including non-combatants.

(g) Each parachute battalion.

(h) The Army Service Corps (including postal).

(i) The Remount, Veterinary & Farm Corps.

(j) The Army Medical Corps.

(k) The Army Dental Corps.

(l) The Army Ordnance Corps.

(m) The Corps of Electrical & Mechanical Engineers.

(n) The Technical Development Establishments.

(o) The Intelligence Corps.

(p) The Corps of Military Police.

(q) The Pioneer Corps.

(r) The Defence Security Corps.

(s) The Army Education Corps.

(r) The Army Physical Training Corps.

(u) The General Service Corps.

(v) The Frontier Defence Corps.

(w) Each Boys Battalion.

(x) Gorkha Boys Company.

(y) Any other separate body of persons subject to the Army Act 1950, employed on any service and not attached to any of the above corps or to any department.

(2) Every unit in which a court-martial book is maintained shall be a 'corps' for the purposes of the Army Act 1950 s 106 and the Army Rules 1954 r 183[2].

(3) For the purposes of every other provision of the Army Act 1950 and of the Army Rules 1954, each of the following separate bodies shall be 'corps':

(a) Every battalion.

(b) Every company which does not form part of battalion.

(c) Every regiment of cavalry, armoured corps or artillery.

(d) Every squadron or battery which does not form part of regiment of cavalry, armoured corps or artillery.

(e) Every school of instruction, training centre, or regimental centre,

(f) Every other separate unit composed wholly or partly of persons subject to the Army Act 1950[3].

1 Army Act 1950 s 3(vi).

2 Ie for the purposes of the Army Act 1950 s 106 of the Army Rules 1954 r 183.

3 The Army Rules 1954 r 187. The effect of this provision is that each of the bodies specified in the Army Rules 1954 r 187 (1) is a 'corps' for the purposes of enrolment, attestation and discharge, except for r 13 of the Army Rules 1954. For all other purposes the bodies mentioned in the Army Rules 1954 r 187 (3) are 'corps'. The expression 'corps' in the Army Rules 1954 is not synonymous with the expression 'army corps' and it must receive a restricted construction with narrow connotation as explained in Army Rules 1954 r 187(3). *PPS Bedi v Union of India* AIR 1982 SC 1413.

[0016] Court martial Unless the context otherwise requires, 'court martial', means a court martial held under the Army Act 1950[1]. A court martial is a criminal court within the meaning of the Code of Criminal Procedure 1973[2]. The trial by court martial under the Army Act, 1950 shall be deemed to be a judicial proceeding within the meaning of the Indian Penal Code 1860 ss 193 and 228 and the court martial shall be deemed to a court within the meaning of the Code of Criminal Procedure 1973 ss 345 and 346[3]. For the purpose of the Army Act 1950, there are four kinds of court martial; general court martial, district court martial, summary general court martial and summary court martial[4]. Court martial are ad hoc bodies constituted every time a trial is to be held. They could be constituted by the central government or senior military officer depending upon the rank of the accused and severity of the offence. Court martial has no civil jurisdiction and it cannot enforce a contract or ward damages in favour of an individual. In a proceeding before court martial rules of natural justice should be observed[5]. However, court martial are not courts in the strict sense of term as understood in relation to implementation of the civil law[6]. Court martial is a substitute of criminal trial; thus principles/law applicable in a criminal trial would apply to it[7].

1 Army Act 1950 s 3(vii).

2 The Code of Criminal Procedure 1973 s 5 includes courts constituted under any law other than the Code, as a class of criminal courts.

3 Army Act 1950 s 152.

4 Army Act 1950 s 108.

5 *S C Patnaik v Union of India* (1969) Cr LJ 930 (Ori).

6 *Union of India v Charanjit S Gill* AIR 2000 SC 3425.

7 *Union of India v Ex-Gnr Ajeet Singh* 2013 AIR SCW 2116 : AIR 2013 SC (Cri) 1041 : 2013 Cri LJ 2215 : 2013 (4) SCC 186.

[0017] Criminal court Unless the context otherwise requires, 'criminal court' means a court of ordinary criminal justice in any part of India[1].

1 Army Act 1950 s 3(viii).

[0018] Customs of the service: Exercise of power vested in holder of military office Any power or jurisdiction given to and any act or thing to be done by; to or before any person holding any military office for the purpose of the Army Rules 1954 may be exercised or done by any other person for the time being authorised in that behalf according to the custom of the service.[1] When commanders, who are empowered to exercise legal powers under the Army Act 1950, are absent from their commands and officiating incumbents are appointed in their places and such appointment s are notified in the formation orders, the legal powers of the formation commanders, in such circumstances may be exercised by the officiating commanders.[2]

1 The Army Rules 1954 r 5.

2 Defence Services Regulations, Regulations for the Army, Volume I, paragraph 53 and 54.

[0019] Department Unless the context otherwise requires, 'department' includes any division or branch of a department[1].

1 Army Act 1950 s 3(ix).

[0020] Enemy Unless the context otherwise requires, 'enemy' includes all armed mutineers, armed rebels, armed rioters, pirates and any person in arms against whom it is the duty of any person subject to military law to act[1]. Militants are undisputedly included in the expression 'enemy' in the Army Act 1950[2]. The term 'enemy' includes a soldier running amok[3].

1 Army Act 1950 s 3(x).

2 *Ratan Singh v Union of India* AIR 1992 SC 415: (1992) Supp 1 SCC 716: (1992) Cr LJ 287: (1992) SCC (Cr) 358.

3 Defence Services Regulations, Regulations for the Army 1987, Volume I, paragraph 351.

[0021] Field Officer Unless the context otherwise requires in the Army Rules 1954, 'field officer' includes an officer, not being a general officer, or any rank (including brevet rank) above the rank of captain[1].

1 The Army Rules 1954 r 2(c).

[0022] The Forces Unless the context otherwise requires, 'the force' means the regular army, navy and air force or any part of any one or more of them[1]. The term 'the Forces' means the armed forces of the Union referred to in art 72(2) of the Constitution of India. The Constitution, Schedule VII List I, includes: (1) Defence of India and every part thereof including preparation for defence and all such acts as may be conclusive in times of war to its prosecution and after its termination to effective demobilization. (2) Naval, military and air forces; any other armed forces of the Union[2]. List II, Entry I, provides for public order and excludes the use of naval, military or air forces or any other forces of the Union in aid of civil power. Entry I of List III provides for criminal law including all matters under the Indian Penal Code 1860 at the commencement of the Constitution, but excluding, inter-alia, the use of the naval, military or air forces or any other forces of the Union in aid of the civil power. Entry 2 of List III provides for the Criminal Procedure Code including all matters of that code at the commencement of the Constitution; but there is no statement in this, excluding the use of the forces of the Union in aid of civil power. The Criminal Procedure Code 1973 ss 129 and 130 contain provision enabling the magistrates to call for assistance of the armed forces to put down a riot.

1 Army Act 1950 s 3(xi).

2 The expression 'other armed forces of the union' includes armed forces other than three well-known forces of the State (viz the naval, military and air forces), such as the Central Reserve Police Force. *Akhilesh v Union Territory*, A. 1981 SC 806 (para 5).

[0023] Junior commissioned officer Unless the context otherwise requires, 'junior commissioned officer' means a person commissioned, gazetted or in pay as a junior commissioned officer in the regular army or the Indian Reserve Forces, and includes a person holding a junior commission in the Territorial Army, who is for the time being subject to the Army Act 1950[1].

1 Army Act 1950 s 3(xii).

[0024] Military custody Unless the context otherwise requires, 'military custody' means the arrest or confinement of a person according to the usages of the service and includes naval or air force custody[1]. The expression 'uses of the service' refers to the mode and manner of arrest and confinement and not usages under which a person can be kept in custody or confinement[2]. Military custody means open or close arrest at the discretion of the superior officer. Open arrest means that person arrested may not leave the barrack or camp but may be required to perform all duties. In close arrest, an officer, junior commissioned officer, warrant officer and non-commissioned officer is put in charge of person of equivalent rank or higher rank, if available, otherwise a person of lower rank may be detailed. Person below the rank of non-commissioned officer are placed under the charge of a guard. The person under close arrest does not go out of his place of arrest or confinement except to take an exercise[3].

1 Army Act 1950 s 3(xiii).

2 *State v KM Nanawati* AIR (1960) Bom 502 (FB).

3 For further details on arrest and custody; see **[0124]**.

[0025] Military reward Unless the context otherwise requires, 'military reward' includes any gratuity or annuity for long service or good conduct, good service pay or pension, and any other military pecuniary reward[1]. A war gratuity is a military reward but a medal or decoration is not. A military reward can be forfeited in the circumstances specified in the rules governing it but not as a court martial sentence.[2]

1 Army Act 1950 s 3(xiv).

2 Manual of Military Law, Volume II, Notes, clause (xiv).

[0026] Non-commissioned officer Unless the context otherwise requires, 'non-commissioned officer' means a person holding a non-commissioned rank or an acting non-commissioned rank in the regular Army or the Indian Reserve Forces, and includes a non-commissioned officer or acting non-commissioned officer of the Territorial Army, who is for the time being subject to the Army Act 1950[1]. Only attested persons are eligible for non-commissioned rank.[2]

1 Army Act 1950 s 3(xv).

2 Manual of Military Law, Volume II, Notes, clause (xv).

[0027] Notification Unless the context otherwise requires, 'notification' means a notification published in the Official Gazette[1].

1 Army Act 1950 s 3(xvi).

[0028] Offence Unless the context otherwise requires, 'offence' means any act or omission punishable under the Army Act 1950 and includes a civil offence.[1]

1 Army Act 1950 s 3(xvii). The offences under the Army Act 1950 are listed in chapter VI under ss 34 to 69.

[0029] Officer Unless the context otherwise requires, 'officer' means a person commissioned, gazetted or in pay as an officer in the regular army, and includes:

(1) an officer of the Indian Reserve Forces[1];

(2) an officer holding a commission in the Territorial Army granted by the President with designation of rank corresponding to that of an officer of the regular army who is for the time being subject to the Army Act 1950[2];

(3) an officer of the Army in India Reserve of Officers who is for the time being subject to the Army Act 1950[3];

(4) an officer of the Indian Regular Reserve of Officers who is for the time being subject to the Army Act 1950[4];

(5) an officer of the navy or air force, in relation to a person subject to the Army Act 1950 when serving under such conditions as may be prescribed.[5]

The term 'officer' does not include a junior commissioned officer, warrant officer, petty officer or non-commissioned officer. The expression 'officer in relation to a person subject to the Army Act 1950', includes a person holding a commission in the Indian navy or the air force, when he is serving under any of the following conditions: (i) When he is a member of a body of the regular army acting with a body of the Indian navy or the air force which is on active service; (ii) When he is being conveyed on any vessel or aircraft employed as a transport or troop ship; (iii) When he is serving in or is a patient in any hospital or medical unit in which any officer of the Indian navy or the air force is on duty or is a patient; (iv) When he is a member of a body of the regular army acting in an emergency with a body of the Indian navy or the air force and an order in writing is made by the officers commanding the bodies concerned stating that an emergency exists and that it is necessary for officers of the Indian navy or the air force to exercise command over persons subject to the Army Act 1950. A copy of every such order shall forthwith be sent to the Central Government; (v) When he is serving in any place in which or with any body of the regular army with which, there is present any officer of the navy or the air force and the Central Government has by special order declared that it is necessary for officers of the Indian navy or the air force to exercise command over persons subject to the Army Act 1950 in that place or with that body of the regular army.[6]

1 Army Act 1950 s 3(xviii)(a).

2 Army Act 1950 s 3(xviii)(b).

3 Army Act 1950 s 3(xviii)(c).

4 Army Act 1950 s 3(xviii)(d).

5 Army Act 1950 s 3(xviii)(f).

6 The Army Rules 1954 r 188.

[0030] Prescribed Unless the context otherwise requires, 'prescribed' means prescribed by rules made under the Army Act 19501.

1 Army Act 1950 s 3(xix). In the Army Act officers have been prescribed under various provisions and these have been specified in the Army Rules 1954 rs 189-204.

[0031] Proper military authority Unless the context otherwise requires in the Army Rules 1954, 'proper military authority', when used in relation to any power, duty, act or matter, such military authority as, in pursuance of the Army Rules 1954 or the Regulations for the Army[1] or the usages of the service, exercises or performs that power or duty or is concerned with the act or matter[2].

1 Ie the Defence Services Regulations, Regulations for the Army 1987 made under the provisions of the Army Act 1950 s 192.

2 The Army Rules 1954 r (2)(d).

[0032] Provost marshal Unless the context otherwise requires, 'provost marshal' means a person appointed as such under the Army Act 1950[1] and includes any of his deputies or assistants or any other person legally exercising authority under him or on his behalf [2]. A provost marshal shall include the one appointed under the Navy Act 1957 or Air Force Act 1950, and any person legally exercising authority under him or on his behalf.[3]

1 Ie appointed under the Army Act 1950 s 107.

2 Army Act 1950 s 3(xx).

3 The Army Act 1950 s 107 (2) and (3).

[0033] Reckonable commissioned service In the Army Rules 1954, unless the context otherwise requires, 'reckonable commissioned service' means service from the date of permanent commission, or the date of seniority for promotion fixed on which furlough rates of pay are drawn and periods of capacity on prisoners of war rates of pay shall be included[1].

1 The Army Rules 1954 r 2 (d-iii).

[0034] Regular Army Unless the context otherwise requires, 'regular army' means officers[1], junior commissioned officers[2], warrant officers[3], non-commissioned officers[4] and other enrolled persons who, by their commission, warrant, terms of enrolment or otherwise, are liable to render continuously for a term military service to the Union in any part of the world, including persons belonging to the Reserve Forces and the Territorial Army when called out on permanent service[5]. The distinction between the regular army and other forces is that persons belonging to the regular army are liable to serve continuously for a term in any part of the world. Reservists or Territorial Army personnel become a part of the regular army only when called on permanent service under the circumstances provided in the Army Act[6].

1 As to the meaning of 'officers'; see **[0029]**.

2 As to the meaning of 'junior commissioned officers'; see **[0023]**.

3 As to the meaning of 'warrant officers'; see **[0037]**.

4 As to the meaning of 'non-commissioned officers'; see **[0026]**.

5 Army Act 1950 s 3(xxi).

6 Ie the Army Act 1950 s 2 (1) (d) and (e).

[0035] Regulations Unless the context otherwise requires, 'regulation' includes a regulation made under the Army Act 1950[1].

1 Ie made under the Army Act s. 192; Army Act 1950 s 3(xxii).

[0036] Superior officer Unless the context otherwise requires, 'superior officer', when used in relation to a person subject to the Army Act 1950, includes a junior commissioned officer, warrant officer and a non-commissioned officer, and, as regards persons placed under his orders, an officer, warrant officer, petty officer and non-commissioned officer of the navy or air force[1]. Although an officer of the Navy or Air Force cannot exercise command in general over persons subject to the Army Act 1950 or be subject to command by such persons unless such officer is serving under prescribed conditions;[2] an officer, warrant officer etc., of the Navy or Air Force is a 'superior officer' as regards person placed under this command.[3]

1 Army Act 1950 s 3(xxiii).

2 Ie under the Army Act s 3(xviii)(f).

3 Manual of Military Law, Volume II, 2011, s 3 notes.

[0037] Warrant officer Unless the context otherwise requires, 'warrant officer' means a person appointed, gazetted or in pay as a warrant officer of the regular army or of the Indian Reserve Forces, and includes a warrant officer of the Territorial Army who is for the time being subject to the Army Act 1950[1].

1 Army Act 1950 s 3(xxiv).

[0038] Words and expression not defined Unless the context otherwise requires, all words (except the word 'India') and expressions used but not defined in the Army Act 1950 and defined in the Indian Penal Code 1860 shall be deemed to have the meanings assigned to them therein[1].

1 Army Act 1950 s 3(xxv).

D. PERSONS SUBJECT TO THE ARMY ACT

[0039] Persons subject to the Army Act The following persons shall be subject to the Army Act 1950 wherever they may be[1], namely:

(1) officers[2], junior commissioned officers[3] and warrant officers[4] of the regular army[5];

(2) persons enrolled under the Army Act[6];

(3) persons belonging to the Indian Reserve Forces[7];

(4) persons belonging to the Indian Supplementary Reserve Forces[8] when called out for service or when carrying out the annual test[9];

(5) officers of the Territorial Army[10], when doing duty as such officers, and enrolled persons of the said Army when called out or embodied or attached to any regular forces, subject to such adaptations and modifications as may be made in the application of the Army Act 1950 to such persons under s 9 (1) of the Territorial Army Act, 1948[11].

(6) persons holding commissions in the army in India Reserve of Officers[12], when ordered on any duty or

service for which they are liable as members of such reserve forces[13];

(7) officers appointed to the Indian Regular Reserve of Officers[14], when ordered on any duty or service for which they are liable as members of such reserve forces[15];

(8) persons not otherwise subject to military law[16] who, on active service[17], in camp, on the march or at any frontier post specified by the central government by notification in this behalf, are employed by, or are in the service of, or are followers of, or accompany any portion of, the regular army[18].

Every person subject to the Army Act under the above mentioned provisions (1) to (7) shall remain so subject until duly retired, discharged, released, removed, dismissed or cashiered from the service[19].

1 The Army Act 1950 is a special law and has extra-territorial application. A person subject to it continues to be so subject at all times irrespective of the place where he is serving e.g. whether he is in India otherwise. His liability to punishment under the Army Act 1950 therefore remains unaffected by the place where he commits the offence.

2 As to the definition of 'officers' see [0029].

3 As to the definition of 'junior commissioned officers' see [0023].

4 As to the definition of 'warrant officers' see [0037].

5 Army Act 1950 s. 2(1)(a). As to the definition of 'regular army' see [0034].

6 Army Act 1950 s. 2(1)(b).

7 Army Act 1950 s. 2(1)(c).

8 Indian Supplementary Reserve force is no more in existence and there is no class of persons who are subject to the Army Act 1950 under this clause.

9 Army Act 1950 s. 2(1)(d).

10 The term 'officers of the Territorial Army' includes junior commissioned officers of the Territorial Army: The Territorial Army Act 1948 s 2(b); see [0040].

11 Army Act 1950 s. 2(1)(e).

12 Army in India Reserve of Officers force is no more in existence and there is no class of officer subject to the Army Act 1950 under this provision.

13 Army Act 1950 s. 2(1)(f).

14 The officers appointed to the Indian Regular Reserve of Officers are subject to the Army Act 1950 only when ordered on duty or service for which they are liable as members of such reserve forces. Officers of the regular Army who retire on pension or gratuity have a liability to serve in the Reserve until they reach the specified age limits.

15 Army Act 1950 s. 2(1)(g).

16 Persons commonly known as 'followers' are not ordinarily subject to the Army Act 1950 unless they have been enrolled under it, but in the interest of discipline and security it is necessary that they and other civilians who accompany any portion of the regular army should be subject to military discipline on active service and in certain other circumstances. This clause provides for such subjection. All persons, including civilian officers and subordinates, who are subject to the Army Act 1950 under this clause are deemed to be of a rank inferior to that of a non-commissioned officer, unless the central government has issued a notification under the Army Act 1950 s.6 (1) regarding the manner in which such persons shall be so subject. The Government of India Notification SRO 325 of 1975 has classified the civilian government servants as officers, JCOs, WOs and NCOs according to their total monthly emoluments. The status so conferred is personal and does not give them power of command over others nor does it make them 'superior officers' within the meaning of the Army Act 1950. The subjection

of civilians in government service to the Army Act 1950 under this clause does not preclude their being dealt with departmentally under their civil, disciplinary regulations but if they are dealt with under military law, the procedure must be in accordance with the Army Act 1950 and the Army Rules 1954.

17 For 'active service' see **[0008]**

18 Army Act 1950 s. 2(1)(i). For 'commanding officer of person subject to military law under this provision'; see: **[0013]**.

19 Army Act 1950 s. 2(2). Subsequent to the promulgation of cashiering, by virtue of this provision, the officer would cease to be subject to the Army Act 1950, and to remove this impediment he would have to be reinstated in the service. *Col AS Dhaliwal v Union of India* (2002) 62 DRJ 854: 2003 (4) SLR 109 (Del).

[0040] Territorial Army The Territorial Army consists of officers and persons enrolled under the Territorial Army Act 1948[1]. Officers in the Territorial Army are of two classes: (1) those holding commissions in the Territorial Army granted by the President with designation of rank corresponding to those of commissioned officers of the regular army; and (2) junior commissioned officers holding commissions in the Territorial Army granted by the President with designation of rank corresponding to those of junior commissioned officers of the regular army [2]. The Territorial Army may be composed of provincial and urban units of the following arms of the service: armoured corps, regiment of artillery, corps of engineers, corps of signals, infantry, army service corps, army medical corps, army ordnance corps, corps of electrical and mechanical engineers, and army postal service. The Central Government may constitute such number of units of the Territorial Army as it thinks fit and may disband or reconstitute any unit so constituted[3].

1 The Territorial Army Act 1948 s 4. All persons enrolled under the Act are governed by the provisions of the Territorial Army Act 1948, Territorial Army Rules 1964 and the Regulations for the Territorial Army 1948. The Territorial Army (TA) is part of Regular Army and its present role is to relieve the Regular Army from static duties and assist civil administration in dealing with natural calamities and maintenance of essential services in situations where life of the communities is affected or the security of the country is threatened. Vide Government of India, Ministry of Defence Gazette Notification No. 6-E dated 28 November 1962 (Army Order 517/62), all persons subject to Army Act 1950, shall wherever they may be serving, be deemed to be active service within the meaning of the Army Act 1950 s 9, read in conjunction with the Army Act s 3 (i). Since the Army Act s 3 and 9 are both applicable in the case of TA personnel, provisions of aforesaid Gazette Notification are equally applicable in the case of TA personnel. TA is an integral part of the armed forces and the members of TA can legitimately be said to be members of the armed forces within the meaning of art 33 of the Constitution.

2 The Territorial Army Act 1948 s 5.

3 The Territorial Army Act 1948 s 3(b).

[0041] Applicability of the Army Act to certain Forces under Central Government

(1) The central government is empowered to apply any of the provisions of the Army Act 1950 to any force raised and maintained in India under its authority and suspend the operation of any other enactment for the time being applicable to the said force[1].

(2) The provisions of the Army Act 1950 so applied shall have effect in respect of persons belonging to the said force as they have effect in respect of persons subject to the Army Act 1950 [2].

(3) When the provisions of the Army Act 1950 are applied to any force under the Army Act 1950, the Central Government can, by notification issued under the Army Act 1950, direct by what authority, the jurisdiction, powers and duties incident to the operation of those provisions shall be exercised or

performed in respect of that force.[3]

1 Army Act 1950 s 4(1). The Army Act 1950 has been applied, with modification to Assam Rifles; and without modification, to the Civil General Transport Companies, General Reserve Engineer Force and Rashtriya Rifles.

2 Army Act 1950 s 4(2).

3 Ie under the Army Act 1950 s 2(1)(i). The Army Act 1950 s 4(4).

[0042] Force The Central Government is empowered to apply any of the provisions of the Army Act 1950 to any force raised or maintained in India under the authority of that government. The word 'force' is not defined anywhere in the Army Act 1950, but the Act[1] clearly contemplates that 'force' referred to in s 4 (1) must be a force organised on similar lines as the army with rank structure. For instance, the General Reserve Engineering Force (GREF) is a force organised on army pattern with units and sub-units and rank structure. The Central Government therefore has the power under the Army Act 1950 [2] to issue notifications applying some of the provisions of the Army Act 1950 and the Army Rules 1954 to the GREF[3].

1 Army Act s 4 (2).

2 Ie under Army Act s 4 (1) and (4).

3 *R Viswan v Union of India* 1983 SCR (3) 60 : 1983 SCC (3) 401 : 1983 SCALE (1)497. In the exercise of power conferred by Army Act 1950 s 4(1) and (4), the Central Government has applied the provisions of the Army Act 1950 to the Rashtriya Rifles, being a Force raised and maintained in India under the authority of the Central Government; and directed that sector commander of Rashtriya Rifles shall exercise the jurisdiction, powers and duties of an officer commanding a brigade in respect of members of the said Force. See SROs 329 and 330 of 23 September 1960. Similarly, the Army Act 1950 was applied with modification to Assam Rifles vide gazette notification SRO 117 of 28 March 1960 and SRO 318 of 6 December 1962 as amended by SRO 325 of 31 August 1977.

[0043] Special provisions as to rank in certain cases The Central Government may by notification, direct that any persons or class of persons subject to the Army Act 1950[1] shall be so subject as officers, junior commissioned officers, warrant officers or non-commissioned officers and may authorize any officer to give a like direction and to cancel such direction[2]. All persons subject to the Army Act 1950 other than officers, junior commissioned officers, warrant officers and non-commissioned officers shall, if they are not persons in respect of whom a notification or direction as stated above is in force, be deemed to be of a rank inferior to that of a non-commissioned officer[3].

1 Ie under the Army Act 1950 s 2 (1)(i).

2 The Army Act 1950 s 6(1).

3 The Army Act 1950 s 6(2).

[0044] Commanding officer of persons subject to military law under the Army Act 1950 s 2 (1)(i)

(a) Every person subject to the Army Act 1950[1] shall, for the purposes of the Army Act 1950 be deemed to be under the commanding officer[2] of the corps, department or detachment, if any, to which he is attached, and, if he is not so attached, under the command of any officer who may for the time being be named as his commanding officer by the officer commanding the force with which such person for the time being is serving, or any other prescribed officer[3] or if, no such officer is named or prescribed under the command of the said officer commanding the force[4].

(b) An officer commanding a force shall not place a person subject to the Army Act 1950[5] under the command of an officer of rank inferior to that of such person, if there is present at the place where such person is any officer of a higher rank under whose command he can be placed[6].

1 Ie under the Army Act 1950 s 2 (1)(i).

2 As to the definition of 'commanding officer' see **[0013]**.

3 Army Rules 1954 r 189: The prescribed officer shall be the officer commanding the army, army corps, division, or brigade or any equivalent formation with which the person subject to the Army Act 1950 under s 2 (1)(i) is for the time being serving.

4 Army Act 1950 s 7(1).

5 Ie under the Army Act 1950 s 2 (1)(i).

6 Army Act 1950 s 7(2).

2. CONSTITUTIONAL PROVISIONS

CONTENTS

[0045] President of India The President of India is the supreme commander of the armed forces and the exercise of this command is to be regulated by law[1]. The President has to act on the advice of the Council of Ministers[2]. It is the duty of the Union to protect every state against external aggression and internal disturbance[3].

1 Constitution of India, art 53 (2): Without prejudices to the generality of the foregoing provision, the supreme command of the Defence Forces of the Union is vested in the President and the exercise of command shall be regulated by law.

2 Constitution of India, art 74 (1).

3 Constitution of India, art 355.

[0046] Power of Parliament to modify fundamental rights Parliament may, by law, determine to what extent any of the rights conferred by the Part III of the Constitution shall, in their application to:

(1) the members of the armed forces[1];

(2) the members of the forces charged with the maintenance of public order[2];

(3) persons employed in any bureau or other organization established by the State for purposes of intelligence or counter intelligence[3]; or

(4) person employed in, or in connection with the telecommunication systems set up for the purposes of any force, bureau or organization referred to above[4],

be restricted or abrogated so as to ensure the proper discharge of their duties and maintenance of discipline among them[5]. Parliament can make a law abrogating or restricting the Fundamental Rights of members of the armed forces or the forces charged with the maintenance of public order only for two reasons. First, 'for ensuring the proper discharge of their duties' and, second, 'for the maintenance of discipline among them'. The Constitution art 33 applies not only to the armed forces but also to other forces such as the police and intelligence bureau[6]. The General Reserve Engineer Force (GREF) is an integral part of the armed forces and the members of GREF are members of the armed forces within the meaning of Article 33 of the Constitution[7]. However, the Constitution art 33 does not apply to other classes of government servants not covered by the provision[8]. Nor does it apply to those who have left military service. The Article gives the power to abridge or abrogate the rights of the personnel covered by its provision only to Parliament and not to the State legislatures or the executive (President)[9]. The extent of restrictions necessary to be imposed on any of the fundamental rights in their application to the armed forces and the forces charged with the maintenance of public order would necessarily depend upon the prevailing situation at a given point of time and it would be inadvisable to encase it in a rigid statutory formula[10]. The Parliament in exercise of its powers under art 33 has enacted the Army Act 1950 and the offences are to be guided by factors like exigencies of service, maintenance of discipline in the army, speedier trial, the nature of offence and person against whom the offence is committed[11]. Denial of promotion to an officer, where vacancy existed, was held to be discriminatory and violative of art 16 of the Constitution of India[12].

1 Constitution of India, art 33 (a).

2 Constitution of India, art 33 (b).

3 Constitution of India, art 33 (c).

4 Constitution of India, art 33 (d).

5 Constitution of India, art 33.

6 Intelligence Bureau Employees' Association v Union of India (1997) 11 SCC 348.

7 R *Viswan v Union of India* 1983 SCR (3) 60 : 1983 SCC (3) 401 : 1983 SCALE (1)497.

8 *Kamleshwar Prasad v State of Bihar* AIR 1962 SC 1166.

9 *Dalbir Singh v State of Punjab* AIR 1962 SC 1106.

10 *Union of India v LD Balam Singh* (2002) 9 SCC 73.

11 *Major GS Sodhi v Union of India* (1991) 2 SCC 382 : AIR 1991 SC 1617 : 1991 AIR SCW 1589.

12 *Major General H M Singh v Union of India* (2014) 3 SCC 670.

[0047] Power to modify certain Fundamental Rights in their application to persons subject to the Army Act 1950 The central government has made rules restricting the right of persons subject to the Army Act 1950:

(1) to be a member of, or to be associated in any way with, any trade union or labour union, or any class of trade or labour unions or any society, institution or association or any class of societies, institutions or associations[1];

(2) to attend or address any meeting or to take part in any demonstration organized by any body of person for any political or other purposes[2];

(3) to communicate with the press or to publish or cause to be published any book, letter or document[3].

The armed forces, entrusted with the defence of a country, need to be highly disciplined and efficient. The government has to make every effort to ensure that its armed forces are capable of guarding the frontiers of the country. The constitution makers therefore placed the need for maintaining discipline among the members of the armed forces above their Fundamental Rights[4]. The Army Act s 21 empowers the central government to make rules restricting 'to such extent and in such manner as may be necessary' three categories of rights of any person subject to the Army Act 1950. These rights are part of the fundamental rights under Article 19(1) cls (a), (b) and (c) and under the constitutional scheme; they cannot be restricted by executive action unsupported by law. But the Army Act 1950 s 21 is saved by Article 33 which carves out an exception in so far as the applicability of fundamental rights to members of the armed forces and the forces charged with the maintenance of public order is concerned[5]. The restrictions imposed under the Army Act 1950 s 21 have been further elaborated under the Army Rules 1954 rs 19 to 21[6].

1 Army Act 1950 s 21(a).

2 Army Act 1950 s 21(b).

3 Army Act 1950 s 21(c).

4 Jha U. C. 2009. *The Military Justice System in India: An Analysis*, Gurgaon: LexisNexis Butterworths Wadhwa Nagpur, p. 30.

5 *R Viswan v Union of India* 1983 SCR (3) 60 : 1983 SCC (3) 401 : 1983 SCALE (1) 497.

6 See **[0048]**, **[0049]** and **[0050]**.

[0048] Unauthorised organization A person subject to the Army Act 1950 shall not, without the express sanction of the central government:

(a) take official cognizance of, or assist or take any active part in, any society, institution or organization, not recognised as part of the armed forces of the Union, unless it be of a recreational or religious nature in which case prior sanction of the superior officer shall be obtained[1];

(b) be a member of, or be associated in any way with, any trade union or labour union[2].

1 The Army Rules 1954 r 19 (i).

2 The Army Rules 1954 r 19 (ii).

[0049] Political and non-military activities A person subject to the Army Act 1950 shall not:

(a) attend, address, or take part in any meeting or demonstration held for a party or political purposes, or belong to or join or subscribe in the aid of, any political association or movement[1].

(b) issue an address to electors or in any other manner publicly announce himself or allow himself to be publicly announced as a candidate or as a prospective candidate for election to the Parliament, the legislature of a state or a local authority, or any public body or act as a member of a candidate's election committee, or in any way actively promote or prosecute a candidate's interest[2].

1 The Army Rules 1954 r 20 (1).

2 The Army Rules 1954 r 20 (2).

[0050] Communications to the press, lectures, etc A person subject to the Army Act 1950 shall not:

(a) publish in any form whatever or communicate directly or indirectly to the press any matter in relation to a political question or on a service subject or containing any service information or publish or cause to be published any book or letter or article or other document on such question or matter containing such information without the prior sanction of the central government, or any officer specified by the central government in this behalf [1]; or

(b) deliver a lecture or wireless address, on a matter relating to a political question or on a service subject or containing any information or views on any service subject without the prior sanction of the central government in this behalf[2].

For the purpose of this provision expression 'service information' and 'service subject' include information or subject, concerning the forces, the defence or the external relation of the Union[3]. The Constitution art 33 requires that Parliament may by law determine the permissible extent to which any of the fundamental rights may be restricted or abrogated in their application to members of the armed forces and other forces charged with the maintenance of public order. Parliament itself is not required to determine the extent of restriction necessary to be imposed on any of the fundamental rights in such cases, in view of the varying requirements of army discipline, prevailing situation at a given point of time and the need for flexibility in this sensitive area[4].

1 The Army Rules 1954 r 21 (i).

2 The Army Rules 1954 r 21 (ii).

3 The Army Rules 1954 r 21 explanation.

4 R *Viswan v Union of India* 1983 SCR (3) 60: 1983 SCC (3) 401: 1983 SCALE (1)497.

3. REGULATION OF SERVICE

CONTENTS

PARA

A. Commission, Appointment and Enrolment

B. Conditions of Service

C. Service Privileges

A. COMMISSION, APPOINTMENT AND ENROLMENT

[0051] Commission and appointment The President may grant, to such person as he thinks fit[1], a commission as an officer[2], or as a junior commissioned officer[3] or appoint any person as a warrant officer[4] of the regular army[5]. The grant of a commission as an officer or junior commissioned officer or appointment as a warrant officer is a formal act, by which such person becomes subject to the Army Act 1950. A commission or appointment is strictly speaking not a contract as its grant or termination or withdrawal is not legally dependent on the consent of the grantee. The use of expression 'a commission' does not mean that commission to be granted should be a permanent regular commission. Granting emergency commission by the President was therefore in no way contrary to the provisions of the Army Act 1950[6]. Where a commission granted to an officer was revoked by notification of the President and subsequently such revocation was invalidated by the Supreme Court, re-commissioning of the officer was not necessary[7].

1 The use of expression 'as he thinks fit' means even an alien may be granted commission as an officer or junior commissioned officer or appointed as a warrant officer.

2 As to the definition of 'officer' see **[0029]**.

3 As to the definition of 'junior commissioned officer' see **[0023]**.

4 As to the definition of 'warrant officer' see **[0037]**.

5 Army Act 1950 s. 10. As to the definition of 'regular army' see **[0034]**.

6 Ie the Army Act 1950 s 10; see: *Tarif Singh Shanti Saroop v Union of India* AIR 1971 Del 233.

7 *Capt Virendra Kumar v Chief of the Army Staff* AIR 1986 SC 1060.

[0052] Ineligibility of aliens for enrolment No person who is not a citizen of India shall except with the consent of the central government, be enrolled in the regular army[1]. This provision, however, does not bar the enrolment of the subjects of Nepal in the regular army[2]. The persons eligible for the enrolment in the regular army are the citizen of India, a subject of Nepal and an alien, with the written consent of the central government. Traditionally, subjects of Nepal are regularly enrolled in the Indian Army and for propose of the Army Act 1950[3], they are not considered aliens.

1 Army Act 1950 s. 11.

2 As to the definition of 'regular army' see **[0034]**.

3 Ie the Army Act 1950 s 10.

[0053] Ineligibility of females for enrolment or employment Women are not eligible for enrolment or employment in the regular army. However, they can be specifically enrolled or employed in certain corps[1], department[2], branch, or attached to any portion of the regular army[3] after notification in the Official Gazette by the central government.[4]. The 'ineligibility of women for enrolment or employment' shall not affect the provisions of any law for the time being in force providing for the raising and maintenance of any service auxiliary to the regular army or any branch of the army in which females are eligible for enrolment or employment[5]. The central government is empowered to waive the bar relating to the ineligibility of women for enrolment or employment in relation to any particular corps or department by a notification in the official gazette. For example, in the army medical corps, women are eligible for employment. In addition, since 1993 women have been commissioned in the regular army in a few other corps and departments. Under the Military Nursing Services (India) Ordinance

(No XXX) of 1943, the Military Nursing Service has been raised and maintained as an auxiliary to the regular army. The provisions of art 14, 15 and 16 of the Constitution of India are not violated by excluding females for short service commission (in judge advocate general branch) in the army. The Army Act 1950 s 12 is not ultra vires the Constitution[6].

1 As to the definition of 'corps' see **[0015]**.

2 As to the definition of 'department' see **[0019]**.

3 As to the definition of 'regular army' see **[0034]**.

4 Army Act 1950 s. 12.

5 Army Act 1950 s. 12 proviso.

6 *Asha Goel v Union of India* Delhi HC Writ Petition No 402 of 1972.

[0054] Procedure before enrolling officer Upon the appearance before the prescribed enrolling officer of any person desirous of being enrolled, the enrolling officer is to read and explain to him, or cause to be read and explained to him in his presence, the conditions of the service for which he is to be enrolled and shall put to him the questions set forth in the prescribed form of enrolment.[1] After having cautioned the individual that if he makes a false answer to any such question he will be liable to punishment under the Army Act 1950[2], the enrolling officer shall record or cause to be recorded his answer to each such question[3].

The following persons shall be the 'enrolling officers' for the purpose of the Army Act 1950[4]:

(1) all recruiting and assistant recruiting officers including officers of the Indian Navy or of the Air Force, who may be appointed as such[5],

(2) the officer commanding a regiment, battalion or training or regimental centre[6], and

(3) any extra assistant recruiting officer or other person who may be appointed as an 'enrolling officer' by the adjutant general[7].

1 Army Rules 1954 appendix I.

2 A false answer to any question set forth in the prescribed form of enrolment is punishable under Army Act 1950 s. 44. See **[0097]**.

3 Army Act 1950 s. 13.

4 Ie for the purpose of the Army Act 1950 s 13.

5 Army Rules 1954 r 7(a).

6 Army Rules 1954 r 7(b).

7 Army Rules 1954 r 7(c).

[0055] Mode of enrolment If, after complying with the provisions of the Army Act 1950[1], the enrolling officer is satisfied that the person desirous of being enrolled fully understands the questions put to him and consents to the conditions of service, and if such officer perceives no impediment he shall sign and shall also-cause such person to sign the enrolment paper. Such person shall thereafter be deemed to be enrolled[2].

1 Ie the Army Act 1950 s 13.

2 Army Act 1950 s 14.

[0056] Validity of enrolment A person enrolled under the Army Act 1950 who has received pay for three months and has been borne on the rolls of any corps[1] or department[2] shall be deemed to have been duly enrolled, and shall not be entitled to claim his discharge on the ground of any irregularity or illegality in his enrolment or on any other ground. Such a person can claim his discharge before the expiry of three months on any ground e.g. illegality or irregularity but that will not affect his being subject to the Army Act 1950 for the period he is so in receipt of pay and borne on the rolls, until his discharge. After the expiry of three months he cannot claim discharge on grounds of illegality or irregularity of enrolment.[3] If a person, whether eligible for enrolment or not, receives pay for three months or more as an enrolled person and has been borne on the rolls of any corps or department, he shall be deemed to be duly enrolled and subject to the Army Act 1950[4].

1 As to the definition of 'corps' see **[0015]**.

2 As to the definition of 'department' see **[0019]**.

3 Army Act 1950 s 15.

4 Manual of Military Law Volume II, 2011, the Army Act 1950 s 15 notes.

[0057] Persons to be attested The following shall be attested:

(1) all persons enrolled as combatants[1];

(2) all persons selected to hold a non-commissioned rank[2]; and

(3) all other persons subject to the Army Act 1950 as may be prescribed by the central government[3].

All combatants and other enrolled persons who may be selected to hold non-commissioned or acting non-commissioned rank shall, when reported fit for duty, be attested in the manner provided in the Army Act 1950[4]. Attestation does not involve further liabilities beyond those assumed at enrolment but confers upon the attested person certain privileges. The discharge of an attested person can, as a rule, only be authorised by higher military authorities, while that of an enrolled person who has not been attested e.g. recruits and followers can be authorised by his commanding officer[5]. Every person required to be attested under the Army Act 1950[6] shall make and subscribe an oath or affirmation in one of the following forms or in such other form to the same purport as the attesting officer ascertains to be in accordance with the religion of the person to be attested, or otherwise binding on his conscience[7].

Form of Oath

> I,..........do swear in the name of God that I will bear true faith and allegiance to the Constitution of India as by the law established and that I will, as in duty bound, honesty and faithfully serve in the regular army of the Union of India and go wherever ordered by land, sea or air, and that I will observe and obey all commands of the President of the Union of India and the commands of any officer set over me even to the peril of my life.

Form of Affirmation

> I,..........do solemnly affirm that I will bear true faith and allegiance to the Constitution of India as by law established and that I will, as in duty bound, honestly and faithfully serve in the regular army of the Union of India and go wherever ordered by land, sea or air, and that I will observe and obey all

commands of the President of the Union of India and the commands of any officer set over me even to the peril of my life.

The aforesaid oath or affirmation shall be administered by the commanding officer of the person to be attested (or in the presence of such commanding officer by a person empowered by him in this behalf) in the manner provided in the Army Act 1950[8]. If it is not so administered, it may be administered by a magistrate or a recruiting officer commanding the station[9].

1 Army Act 1950 s 16 (a).

2 Army Act 1950 s 16 (b). Only attested persons can rise to non-commissioned rank in the regular army.

3 Army Act 1950 s 16 (c).

4 Ie as provided in the Army Act 1950 s 17. Army Rules 1954 r 8.

5 Manual of Military Law Volume II, 2011, the Army Act 1950 s 16 notes.

6 Ie under the Army Act 1950 s 16.

7 Army Rules 1954 r 9(1).

8 Ie as provided in the Army Act 1950 s 17.

9 Army Rules 1954 r 9(2).

[0058] Mode of attestation When a person who is to be attested is reported fit for duty, or has completed the prescribed period of probation, an oath or affirmation shall be administered to him in the prescribed form by his commanding officer[1] in front of his corps[2] or such portion/members of his department[3], as may be present[4]. The form of oath or affirmation prescribed under the Army Act 1950[5] shall contain a promise that the person to be attested will bear true allegiance to the Constitution of India as by law established, and that he will serve in the regular army and go wherever he is ordered by land, sea or air, and that he will obey all commands of any officer set over him, even to the peril of his life[6]. The fact of an enrolled person having taken the oath or affirmation under this provision shall be entered on his enrolment paper, and authenticated by the signature of the officer administering the oath or affirmation[7].

1 As to the definition of 'commanding officer' see **[0013]**.

2 As to the definition of 'corps' see **[0015]**.

3 As to the definition of 'department' see **[0019]**.

4 Army Act 1950 s 17 (1).

5 See Army Rules 1954 r 9.

6 Army Act 1950 s 17 (3).

7 Army Act 1950 s 17 (3).

[0059] Transfer from one corps or department to another Where the central government by any general or special order published in the official Gazette so directs, any person enrolled under the Army Act 1950 may, notwithstanding anything to the contrary contained in the conditions of service for which he is enrolled, be transferred to any corps[1] or department[2] by order of an authority exercising powers not less than those of an officer commanding a division[3]. Enrolment is in the nature of a contract signed by the enrolled person wherein the terms and conditions of his service are specified. By this contract the enrolled person undertakes to serve continuously for a specified period in the particular corps or department in which he is enrolled. Ordinarily he can be transferred from the corps in which he is enrolled to another corps, if the conditions of enrolment so permit. An authority exercising powers not less than of an officer commanding a division may transfer an enrolled to any corps or department, if directed by any general or special order issued by the central government.[4]

1 As to the definition of 'corps'; see **[0015]**.

2 As to the definition of 'department'; see **[0019]**.

3 The Army Rules 1954 r 10.

4 Manual of Military Law, Volume II, 2011, the Army Rules 1954, r 10 notes.

B. CONDITIONS OF SERVICE

[0060] Tenure of service Every person subject to the Army Act 1950 shall hold office during the pleasure of the President[1].

The Army Act 1950 s 18 and art 310 (1) of the Constitution provide that every member of the defence services holds office during the pleasure of the President. The Army Act 1950 s 18 gives the President unfettered power to bring to an end the tenure of service of an employee. The President's powers to terminate the service by way of dismissal, removal or otherwise, of any person subject to the Army Act 1950, under the art 310 (1) of the Constitution are unqualified and unfettered and no show cause notice is necessary. The doctrine of pleasure is not a licence to act with unfettered discretion to act arbitrarily, whimsically, or capriciously. In other words, "at pleasure" doctrine enables the removal of a person holding office at the pleasure of an authority, summarily, without any obligation to give any notice or hearing to the person removed, and without any obligation to assign any reasons or disclose any cause for the removal, or withdrawal of pleasure[2]. The President has to exercise his pleasure according to advise tendered by his council of ministers and need not be exercised by President personally. The executive functions of the President are to be exercised by him as per the provisions of art 74 and 77 of the Constitution. Even those functions which were required by the Constitution to be performed on the subjective satisfaction of the President could be delegated by rules of business made under art 77 (3) to a minister or to a secretary to the Government of India. The President acts on the aid and advice of the Council of Ministers with the Prime Minister at the head in all matters which vests in the executive whether those functions are executive or legislative in character. The President is not required to exercise the executive functions personally[2]. Article 310 (1) of the Constitution is not subject to the provisions of any contract and the government is free to terminate the services of the employee before the expiry of the contractual period and without payment of compensation. For termination of the service under the Army Act 1950 s18 it is not necessary to hold any enquiry. An action to terminate the service may be taken without any inquiry. In all fairness, when no inquiry is held and no opportunity is given to the delinquent to put across his defence, and his service is terminated by invoking the doctrine of pleasure it should be termination simplicitor and not by way of dismissal[4].

There is no dispute that order of termination passed against the army personnel in exercise of 'pleasure doctrine', is subject to judicial review, but while exercising judicial review, the Supreme Court cannot substitute its own conclusion on the basis of materials on record. The Court exercising the power of judicial review has certain limitations, particularly in the cases of serious nature relating to the safety and security of the nation. When the President in exercise of its constitutional power terminates the services of the army officers, whose tenure of services are at the pleasure of the President and such termination is based on materials on record, then the Supreme Court in exercise of powers of judicial review should be slow in interfering with such pleasure of President exercising constitutional power. In a constitutional set up, when office is held during the pleasure of the President, it means that the officer can be removed by the Authority on whose pleasure he holds office without assigning any reason. The Authority is not obliged to assign any reason or disclose any cause for the removal[5].

1 Army Act 1950 s 18. This provision merely reiterates the constitutional position set out in Article 310 (1) of the Constitution of India.

2 *B P Singhal v Union of India* (2010) 6 SCC 331.

3 *Shamsher Singh v State of Punjab* AIR 1974 SC 2192: (1974) 2 SCC 831: 1975 (1) SCR 814.

4 *Hazara Singh v Union of India* 1982 (1) SLR 521.

5 *Union of India v Major SP Singh* 2014 (1) SCALE 484.

[0061] Termination of service by Central Government Subject to the provisions of the Army Act 1950 and the rules and regulations made thereunder the central government may dismiss, or remove from the service, any person subject to the Army Act 1950[1]. The dismissal or removal under this provision may be on account of the reasons of failure to qualify at an examination or course; misconduct; or inefficiency or physical disability. The Central Government is empowered to dismiss or remove from service any person subject to the Army Act 1950 but only in accordance with the provisions of the Army Act 1950 or of any rules or regulations made thereunder. The Army Rules 1954, rs 13-A, 14 and 15 require that a show cause notice to be served upon an officer before his service is terminated on grounds of his failure to qualify at an examination or course, misconduct or inefficiency. Such show cause notice may be dispensed with by the Central Government when it considers it inexpedient or impracticable to do so or when the officer is already convicted by a criminal court for the misconduct. The Army Rules 1954 r 15-A provides for the release of an officer on medical grounds, which is to be carried out on the recommendations of a Medical Board. Dismissal under the Army Act 1950 ss 18 and 19 is not a punishment specified under the Army Act 1950 but merely amounts to termination of a person's commission or service without his consent[2]. Removal from the service is a less grave form of dismissal[3].

1 Army Act 1950 s 19. The exercise of power under this provision read with the Army Rules 1954 r 14 is open to judicial review on well-settled parameters of administrative law governing judicial review of administrative action such as when the exercise of power is shown to have been vitiated by mala fides or is found to be based wholly on extraneous and/or irrelevant grounds or is found to be a clear case of colourable exercise of/or abuse of power or what is sometimes called fraud on power i.e., where the power is exercised for achieving an oblique end; see: *Union of India v Harjeet Singh Sandhu* AIR 2001 SC 1772, (2001) 5 SCC 593, 2001 SCC (L&S) 891. As to the 'persons subject to the Army Act 1950'; see **[0039]**.

2 The Army Act 1950 s 71 contains a list of punishments which could be awarded by a court martial.

3 Manual of Military Law, Volume II, 2011, The Army Act 1950 s 19 notes.

[0062] Termination of service of an officer by the Central Government on his failure to qualify at an examination or course

(a) When an officer[1] does not appear at or, having appeared fails to quality, at the retention examination or promotion examination or any other basic course or examination within the time or extended time specified in respect of that examination or course, the Chief of the Army Staff[2] or the Military Secretary shall call upon the officer to show cause why he should not be compulsorily retired or removed from the service[3].

(b) In the event of the explanation being considered by the Chief of the Army Staff or the Military Secretary to be unsatisfactory, the matter shall be, submitted to the Central Government for order, together with the officer's explanation and the recommendation of the Chief of the Army Staff or the Military Secretary as to whether the officer should be: (i) called upon to retire[4]; or (ii) called upon to resign[5].

(c) The Central Government, after considering the explanation, if any, of the officer and the recommendation of the Chief of the Army Staff or the Military Secretary may call upon the officer to retire or resign, and on his refusing to do so, the officer may be compulsory retired or removed from the service on pension or gratuity, if any, admissible to him[6].

1 For definition of the term 'officer' see **[0029]**.

2 For definition of the term 'chief of the army staff' see **[0012]**.

3 Army Rules 1954 r 13A(1).

4 Army Rules 1954 r 13A(2)(i).

5 Army Rules 1954 r 13A(2)(ii).

6 Army Rules 1954 r 13A(3).

[0063] Termination of service of an officer by the Central Government on account of misconduct

(a) When it is proposed to terminate the service of an officer under the Army Act 1950[1] on account of misconduct, he shall be given an opportunity to show cause in the manner specified in the provisions[2] against such action[3].

(b) However, the above provision shall not apply: (i) where the service is terminated on the ground of conduct which has led to his conviction by a criminal court[4]; or (ii) where the Central Government is satisfied that for reasons, to be recorded in writing, it is not expedient or reasonably practicable to give to the officer an opportunity of showing cause[5].

(c) When after considering the reports on an officer's misconduct, the Central Government or the Chief of the Army Staff is satisfied that the trial of the officer by a court-martial[6] is inexpedient or impracticable, but is of the opinion, that the further retention of the said officer in the service is undesirable, the Chief of the Army Staff shall so inform the officer together with all reports adverse to him and he shall be called upon to submit, in writing, his explanation and defence[7]. However, the Chief of the Army Staff may withhold from disclosure any such report or portion thereof if, in his opinion, its disclosure is not in the interest of the security of the State[8]. In the event of the explanation of the officer being considered unsatisfactory by the Chief of the Army Staff, or when so directed by the Central Government, the case shall be submitted to the Central Government, with the officer's defence and the recommendation of the Chief of the Army Staff as to the termination of the officer's service in the manner specified in the provisions of the Army Rules 1954[9].

(d) Where, upon the conviction of an officer by a criminal court, the Central Government or the Chief of the Army Staff considers that the conduct of the officer which has led to his conviction renders his further retention in service undesirable, a certified copy of the judgment of the criminal court convicting him shall be submitted to the Central Government with the recommendation of the Chief of the Army Staff as to the termination of the officer's service in the manner specified provision stated below[10].

(e) When submitting a case to the Central Government under the above stated provisions[11], the Chief of the Army Staff shall make his recommendation whether the officer's service should be terminated, and if so, whether the officer should be: (i) dismissed from the service[12]; (ii) removed from the service[13]; or (iii) compulsorily retired from the service[14].

(f) The Central Government after considering the reports and the officer's defence, if any, or the judgment of the criminal court, as the case may be, and the recommendation of the Chief of the Army Staff, may: (i) dismiss or remove the officer with or without pension or gratuity[15]; or (ii) compulsory retire him from the service with pension and gratuity, if any, admissible to him[16].

Before initiating action for termination of the services of an officer on the grounds of misconduct, the Central Government or the Chief of the Army Staff should be satisfied that the trial of the officer by court martial is inexpedient or impracticable for reasons other than probable failure to establish the charges against him, and that his further retention in service is undesirable. The dismissal or removal cannot be made retrospective, nor can such valid dismissal or removal be cancelled without the person's consent. Dismissal under Army Rules 1954 r 19 is not a punishment as under the Army Act s 71. It merely amounts to termination of an officer's commission/ service without his consent. Removal is a less grievous form of dismissal. No show cause notice is required to be given to an officer under this rule if his dismissal/removal is sought on grounds of misconduct for which he has already been convicted by a criminal court. The Army Act 1950 s 19 and the Army Rules 1954 r 14 are to be read together and as integral parts of one whole scheme. 'Misconduct' as a ground for terminating the service by way of dismissal or removal, is not to be found mentioned in the Army Act s 19; it is to be read therein by virtue of the Army Rules 1954 r 14. In the context in which then term 'misconduct' has been used in r 14, it is to be given a wider meaning and any wrongful act or any act of delinquency which may or may not involve moral turpitude, would be 'misconduct', and certainly so, if it is subversive of army discipline or high traditions of army and/or if it renders the person unworthy of being retained in service. The language of the Army Rules 1954 r 14(2) employing the expression 'the reports on an officer's misconduct' uses 'reports' in plural and misconduct in singular. Here plural would include singular and singular would include plural. A single report on an officer's misconduct may invite an action under the Army Act 1950s 19 read with the Army Rules 1954 r 14 and there may be cases where there may be more reports than one on a singular misconduct or more misconducts than one in which case it will be the cumulative effect of such reports on misconduct or misconducts, which may lead to the formation of requisite satisfaction and opinion within the meaning of the Army Rules 1954 r 14 (2). The Army Act 1950 ss 19 and 45 being mutually exclusive the removal from service under the Army Act 1950 s 19 read with of the Army Rules 1954 r 19 without a court martial cannot said to be in derogation of the Army Act 1950 s 45. The power under the Army Act 1950 s 19 is an independent power[17].

1 Ie under the under the Army Act 1950 s 19.

2 Ie as specified in the Army Rules 1954 r 14 (2).

3 Army Rules 1954 r 14(1).

4 The Army Rules 1954 r 14(1) proviso (a).

5 The Army Rules 1954 r 14(1) proviso (b).

6 For definition of the term 'court martial' see **[0016]**.

7 Army Rules 1954 r 14(2).

8 Army Rules 1954 r 14(2) proviso.

9 Ie specified in the Army Rules 1954 r 14 (4).

10 Army Rules 1954 r 14(3).

11 Ie under the Army Rules 1954 r 14(2) and (3).

12 Army Rules 1954 r 14(4)(a).

13 Army Rules 1954 r 14(4)(b).

14 Army Rules 1954 r 14(4)(c).

15 Army Rules 1954 r 14(5)(a).

16 Army Rules 1954 r 14(5)(b).

17 *Union of India v. Harjeet Singh Sandhu*, AIR 2001 SC 1772: (2001) 5 SCC 593; 2001 SCC (L&S) 891.

[0064] Termination of Service of an officer by the Central Government on grounds other than misconduct

(a) When the Chief of the Army Staff is satisfied that an officer is unfit to be retained in the service due to inefficiency, or physical disability, the officer: (i) shall be so informed[1], (ii) shall be furnished with the particulars of all matters adverse to him[2], and (iii) shall be called upon to urge any reasons he may wish to put forward in favour of his retention in the service[3].

(b) However, the above stated provisions[4] shall not apply if the Central Government is satisfied that for reasons, to be recorded by it in writing, it is not expedient or reasonably practicable to comply with these provisions. Further, the Chief of the Army Staff or Military Secretary may not furnish to the officer any matter adverse to him, if in his opinion, it is not in the interest of the security of the State to do so[5].

(c) In the event of the explanation being considered by the Chief of the Army Staff or military secretary unsatisfactory, the matter shall be submitted to the Central Government for orders, together with the officer's explanation and the recommendation of the Chief of the Army Staff as to whether the officer should be: (i) called upon to retire[6]; or (ii) called upon to resign[7].

(d) The Central Government after considering the reports, the explanation, if any, of the officer and the recommendation of the Chief of the Army Staff, may call upon the officer to retire or resign, and on his refusing to do so, the officer may be compulsorily retired or removed from the service on pension or gratuity, if any admissible to him[8].

The action under the Army Rules 1954 r 15 is initiated when it is intended to terminate the service of an officer on grounds of inefficiency only. The services of an officer under Army Rules 1954 r 15 cannot be terminated with retrospective effect, nor can such termination be cancelled without the officer's consent[9].

1 Army Rules 1954 r 15(1)(a).

2 Army Rules 1954 r 15(1)(b).

3 Army Rules 1954 r 15(1)(c).

4 Ie the Army Rules 1954(1)(a) (b) and (c).

5 Army Rules 1954 r 15 (1) proviso.

6 Army Rules 1954 r 15(2)(a).

7 Army Rules 1954 r 15(2)(b).

8 Army Rules 1954 r 15(3).

9 Manual of Military Law Volume II, 2011, the Army Rules 1954 r 15(3) notes.

[0065] Release of an officer on medical grounds An officer who is found by a medical board to be permanently unfit for any form of military service may be released from the service in accordance with the procedure as follows[1]. The president of the medical board shall, immediately after the medical board has come to the conclusion that the officer is permanently unfit for any form of military service, issue, a notice specifying the nature of the disease or disability he is suffering from and the finding of the medical board and also intimating him that in view of the finding he may be released from the service; every such notice shall also specify that the officer may, within 15 days of the date of receipt of the notice, prefer a petition against the finding of the medical board to the Chief of the Army Staff through the president of the medical board[2]. Provided that where in the opinion of the medical board the officer is suffering from a mental disease and it is either unsafe to communicate the nature of the disease or disability to the officer or the officer is unfit to look after his interests, the nature of the disease or disability shall be communicated to the officer's next-of-kin who shall have the like right to petition[3]. If no petition is preferred within the time specified above, the officer may be released from the service by an order to that effect by the Chief of the Army Staff or the Adjutant General[4]. If a petition is preferred within the time specified in the above provision, it shall be forwarded to the Central Government together with the records thereof and the recommendation of the Chief of the Army Staff or the Adjutant General. The Central Government may, after considering the petition and the recommendation of the Chief of the Army Staff or the Adjutant General pass such order as it deems fit[5]. The Army Rules 1954 r 15 deals with removal from service and not dismissal. It does not import any culpability. Nevertheless, the procedure laid down in the Army Rules 1954 r 15 must be complied with. The violation of procedure laid down in the Army Rules 1954 r 15 invalidates the termination, even though the delinquent is an emergency commissioned officer. The provisions of Army Rules 1954 r 15 incorporate the principle of natural justice. It requires that when action is proposed to be taken against a person, he should be accorded a reasonable opportunity of being heard by the authority concerned[6]. Decision to prematurely release/discharge of army personnel based on opinion of medical board can be tested by courts/tribunal by examining record of medical board[7].

1 Army Rules 1954 r 15A(1).

2 Army Rules 1954 r 15A(2).

3 Army Rules 1954 r 15A(2) proviso.

4 Army Rules 1954 r 15A(3).

5 Army Rules 1954 r 15A(4).

6 *Union of India v SK Rao Capt* AIR 1972 SC 1173: (1972) 1 SCC 144: [1972] 2 SCR 447.

7 *Veer Pal Singh v Secretary, Ministry of Defence* AIR 2013 SC 2827 (B): 2013 (8) SCALE 686.

[0066] Release A person subject to the Army Act 1950 may be released from the service in accordance with the Release Regulations for the Army or in accordance with any other provision made in that behalf[1].

1 Army Rules 1954 r 16.

[0067] Resignation of commission An officer has no right to resign his commission but may submit an application to the central government to resign his commission. He shall not be relieved of his duties until the central government has accepted his resignation[1]. An officer whose application to resign his commission has been accepted may, before he is relieved of his duties, apply to the central government for withdrawal of the said application. The government may, at its discretion, grant withdrawal of his applications[2]. The employee had no automatic right to be released merely on filing an application for resignation and without laying down any worthwhile basis or foundation for this and the employer had also no power to reject it arbitrarily[3]. A prayer for resignation has to be dealt with on different footing as the discretionary power vests in the authority taking decision on application for resignation is limited and circumscribed[4].

1 Army Rules 1954 r 16C (1).

2 Army Rules 1954 r 16C (2).

3 *Murlidharan CG Lt Col v Union of India*, Delhi High Court CW No 1064 of 2002, decided on 20 December 2002.

4 *Major* R *Ramesh v Union of India*, (2001) 2 MLJ 124 (Mad).

[0068] Dismissal, removal or reduction by Chief of the Army Staff and by other officers The Chief of the Army Staff may dismiss or remove from the service any person subject to the Army Act 1950 other than an officer[1]. The Chief of the Army Staff may reduce to a lower grade or rank or the ranks, any warrant officer or any non-commissioned officer[2]. A brigade commander or equivalent commander or any prescribed officer may dismiss or remove from the service any person serving under his command other than an officer or a junior commissioned officer[3]. Such an officer may also reduce to a lower grade or rank or the ranks, any warrant officer or any non-commissioned officer under his command[4]. However, a warrant officer reduced to the ranks under these provisions shall not be required to serve in the ranks as a sepoy[5]. The commanding officer of an acting non-commissioned officer may order him to revert to his permanent grade as a non-commissioned officer, or if he has no permanent grade above the ranks, to the ranks[6]. The exercise of any power under the above stated provisions shall be subject to the provisions contained in the Army Act 1950 and the Army Rules 1954 and regulations made thereunder[7]. The procedure to be followed for dismissal or removal is contained in the Army Rues 1954[8].

1 Army Act 1950 s 20 (1).

2 Army Act 1950 s 20 (2).

3 Army Act 1950 s 20 (3).

4 Army Act 1950 s 20 (4).

5 Army Act 1950 s 20 (5).

6 Army Act 1950 s 20 (6).

7 Army Act 1950 s 20 (7).

8 Ie in the Army Rues 1954 r 17; see **[0069]**.

[0069] Procedure for dismissal or removal by Chief of the Army Staff and by other officers Except in the case where a person is dismissed or removed from service on the ground of conduct which has led to his conviction by a criminal court or a court martial, no person shall be dismissed or removed under the provisions of the Army Act 1950[1], unless he has been informed of the particulars of the cause of action against him and allowed reasonable time to state in writing any reasons he may have to urge against his dismissal or removal from the service[2]. However, if in the opinion of the officer competent to order the dismissal or removal, it is not expedient or reasonably practicable to comply with the provisions of this provision, he may, after certifying to that effect, order, the dismissal or removal without complying with the procedure set out in the Army Rules 1954[3]. All cases of dismissal or removal where the prescribed procedure has not been complied with shall be reported to the Central Government[4]. It is not necessary to hold a court of inquiry for initiating action under the Army Rules 1954 r 17; action can be taken on the basis of information received from other sources[5].

1 Ie under the Army Act 1950 s 20 (1) or (3).

2 Army Rules 1954 r 17.

3 Ie in the Army Rules 1954 r 17.

4 Army Rules 1954 r 17 proviso. Under this proviso, the Chief of the Army Staff and other officers are competent to order dismissal or removal without complying with the procedure set out in the main part of the Army Rules 1954 r 17 after certifying that it is not expedient or reasonably practicable to comply with the provisions so set out. There is a further requirement that such cases of dismissal or removal shall be reported to the Central Government. *Romesh Kumar Sharma v Union of India* Supreme Court Civil Appeal No 3222 of 2006, decided on 1 August 2006.

5 *VY Thomas v Commandant AOC Centre* 1982 (2) SLR 40 (AP).

[0070] Date from which retirement, resignation, removal, release, discharge or dismissal otherwise than by sentence of court-martial takes effect The dismissal of an officer under the Army Act 1950[1] or the retirement, resignation, release or removal of such officer shall take effect from the date specified in the notification of such dismissal, retirement or removal in the official Gazette[2]. The dismissal of a person subject to the Army Act 1950, other than an officer whose dismissal otherwise than by sentence of a court martial is duly authorised or the discharge of a person so subject whose discharge, if duly authorised, shall be carried out by the commanding officer of such person with all convenient speed. The authority competent to authorise such dismissal or discharge may, when authorising the dismissal or discharge, specify any future date from which it shall take effect[3]. If no such date is specified under the above stated provision, the dismissal or discharge shall take effect from the date on which it was duly authorised or from the date on which the person dismissed or discharged, ceased to perform military duty, whichever is the later date[4]. The retirement, removal, resignation, release, discharge or dismissal of a person subject to the Army Act 1950 shall not be retrospective[5].

1 Ie the Army Act 1950 s 19.

2 Army Rules 1954 r 18 (1).

3 Army Rules 1954 r 18 (2).

4 Army Rules 1954 r 18 proviso.

5 Army Rules 1954 r 18 (3).

[0071] Retirement, release or discharge Any person subject to the Army Act 1950 may be retired, released or discharged from the service by such authority and in such manner as may be prescribed[1].

1 Army Act 1950 s 22. A person subject to the Army Act 1950 continues to be so subject until he is duly retired, released, removed, discharged, dismissed or cashiered from the service. Though the Army Rules 1954 and the Defence Services Regulations, Regulations for the Army 1987 prescribe age limits for compulsory retirement in respect of different ranks, every person subject to the Army Act holds office during the pleasure of the President and has no right to be kept in service till he reaches such age limit. Service personnel becoming due for retirement/ discharge on completion of their engagement period/service tenure or attaining the age of superannuation, shall retire/be discharged from service with effect from the after-noon of the last day of the month in which their date of retirement/discharge falls. Authority: Deputy Secretary to the Government of India No B/33108/AG/PS2(e)/

D(AG) dated 11 Mar 94. Defence Services Regulations, Regulations for the Army 1987, Volume I, paragraph 185.

[0072] Retirement of officer Officers shall be retired from service under the orders of the Central Government, or the authorities specified in the Army Rules 1954[1], with effect from the afternoon of the last date of the month in which they (i) attain the age limit specified in the provisions of the Army Rules 1954[2]; or (ii) complete the tenures of appointment specified under the provisions of the Army Rules 1954[3], whichever is earlier[4]. An officer who has attained the age of compulsory retirement or has become due for such retirement by reason of completing the period of service or tenure allowed to him may be retained in service for a further period at the discretion of Central Government if the exigencies of service so require.[5]

1 Ie specified in the Army Rules 1954 r 16A(2). The authorities specified are (i) the Director General Armed Forces Medical Services in respect of officers of the Army Medical Corps or the Army Dental Corps and Military Nursing Service; (ii) the Additional Director Remount and veterinary Corps in respect of officers of that Corps below the rank of Colonel; (iii) the Deputy Director of Military Farms in respect of officers of the Military Farms below the rank of Colonel; and (iv) the Military Secretary, Army Headquarters, in respect of all other officers.

2 Ie specified in the Army Rules 1954 r 16A(5).

3 Ie specified in the Army Rules 1954 r 16A (5) (f) (ii) and (g) (ii) and r 16A (6).

4 Army Rules 1954 r 16A (1). For further details on the age of retirement of officers and tenures of appointments for the purpose of retirement refer the Army Rules 1954 r 16A (5) and (6).

5 Army Rules 1954 r 16A (4).

[0073] Retirement of an officer at his own request The retirement of an officer at his own request before he becomes liable to retirement under the Army Rules 1954[1] shall require the sanction of the central government[2]. An officer whose request to retire is granted may, before he is retired, may apply to the Central Government for withdrawal of his request. The Central Government may, at its discretion, grant such withdrawal of his application[3]. There is no implicit right of premature retirement from the service[4]. It is open to a person having exercised option of voluntary retirement to withdraw the said offer after its acceptance but before it is made effective. The resignation, in spite of its acceptance, can be withdrawn before the effective date[5].

1 Under Army Rules 1954 r 16A; see **[0072]**. *Bhupinder Singh Brig v Union of India* 1976 (1) SLR 772 (Del): There is no right to hold the post on attaining the age of compulsory retirement.

2 Army Rules 1954 r 16B (1).

3 Army Rules 1954 r 16B (2).

4 *Brig LK Banerjee v Union of India* Bombay High Court WP no 320 of 1989 decided 10 March 1989.

5 *Shashi Kumar v Union of India* TA No 326 of 2009, Armed Forces Tribunal, New Delhi, Principal Bench order dated 28 July 2010.

[0074] Certificate on termination of service Every junior commissioned officer[1], warrant officer[2], or enrolled person who is dismissed, removed, discharged, retired or released from the service shall be furnished by his commanding officer with a discharge certificate[3], in the mother tongue of such person and in the English language. The discharge certificate would state: (i) the authority terminating his service[4]; (ii) the cause for such termination[5]; and (iii) the full period of his service in the regular army[6]. The competent authorities empowered to discharge from service persons subject to the Army Act 1950 have been specified[7].

1 For definition of term 'junior commissioned officer' see **[0023]**.

2 For definition of term 'warrant officer' see **[0037]**.

3 See the Army Rules 1954 r 12. A certificate required to be furnished under the provisions of the army Act 1950 s 23 is called a 'discharge certificate'. A discharge certificate may be furnished either by personal delivery thereof by or on behalf of the commanding officer to the person dismissed, removed, discharged or released, or by the transmission, of the same to such person by registered post. An officer not being an enrolled person is not furnished with a discharge certificate on termination of his commission.

4 Army Act 1950 s 23(a).

5 Army Act 1950 s 23(b).

6 Army Act 1950 s 23(c).

7 Army Rules 1954 r 13. The disciplinary conduct of the individual as reflected in the service record and the requirement of maintaining discipline would decide if services are no longer required. Discharge under the Army Rules 1957 r 13 (3) III (v) for services being no longer required is a consequence of unsatisfactory service record. It is an administrative action resulting from an unsatisfactory record of service and is not a second punishment. *Kulwant Singh v Union of India* TA No. 127 of 2010, the Armed Forces Tribunal, Regional Bench, Chandigarh, decision dated 13 February 2013.

[0075] Discharge or dismissal when out of India Any person enrolled under the Army Act 1950 who is entitled under the conditions of his enrolment to be discharged, or whose discharge is ordered by competent authority, and who, when he is so entitled or ordered to be discharged, is serving out of India, and requests to be sent to India, shall, before being discharged, be sent to India, with all convenient speed[1]. Any person enrolled under the Army Act 1950 who is dismissed from the service and who, when he is so dismissed, is serving out of India, shall be sent to India with all convenient speed[2]. When any such person as stated above (i.e., serving abroad) is sentenced to dismissal combined with any other punishment, such other punishment, or, in the case of a sentence of imprisonment for life or imprisonment, a portion of such sentence may be inflicted before he is sent to India[3]. For the purposes of this provision, 'discharge' shall include release, and the word 'dismissal' shall include removal[4]. When an enrolled person's entitlement to be discharged or released accrues when he is out of India, he must, if he so requests, be sent to India for being discharged or released; in other words, the discharge/ release must then be carried out in India. An enrolled person can, however, be dismissed or removed from the service when serving out of India[5].

1 Army Act 1950 s 24(1).

2 Army Act 1950 s 24(2).

3 Army Act 1950 s 24(3). This provision is permissive and must be read with the Army Act 1950 s 168, 169 and 171 which provide for the infliction of sentence of imprisonment passed by court martial. A prisoner cannot legally be kept abroad to undergo his imprisonment, but must be sent to a civil prison in India where it can be inflicted in accordance with the Army Act 1950. Manual of Military law, Volume II, 2011, s 24 notes.

4 Army Act 1950 s 24(4).

5 Manual of Military law, Volume II, 2011, s 24 notes.

C. SERVICE PRIVILEGES

[0076] Authorized deductions only to be made from pay The pay of every person subject to the Army Act 1950 due to him shall be paid without any deduction other than the deductions authorized under the Army Act 1950[1] or any other Act[2]. The term 'pay' means the rate of pay with increases, if any, for length of service, to which a person subject to the Army Act 1950 is entitled by reason of his rank, appointment, trade, group or classification. It includes additional remuneration such as qualification pay, proficiency pay and the various forms of additional pay. All other emoluments are 'allowances', which are purely discretionary and may be withdrawn at any time. It is illegal to make deductions which are not authorized and the unlawful detention of pay is an offence under the Army Act 1950[3]

1 For deductions authorized by or under the Army Act 1950 s 90 and 91; see **[0384]** and **[0385]** respectively. See the Army Rules 1954 r 205 for other authorised deduction. Authorised Deductions: The following deductions may be made from the pay, non-effective pay and all other emoluments payable to a person subject to the Army Act 1950, namely: (i) upon the general or special order of the Central Government, any sum required to meet any public claim there may be against him, any regimental debt that may be due from him or any regimental claim; and (ii) any sum required to meet compulsory contributions to any provident fund or any benevolent or other fund approved by the Central Government. The term 'public claim' means any public debt or disallowance including any over-issue; or a deficiency or irregular expenditure of public money or store of which, after due investigation, no explanation satisfactory to the Central Government is given by the person who is responsible for the same. The aforesaid deductions shall be in addition to those specified in the Army Act 1950. When a person subject to the Army Act 1950 accepts his liability in respect of regimental dues, it becomes a regimental debt. When he does not so accept his liability, it becomes a regimental claim.

2 Army Act 1950 s 25.

3 Army Act 1950 s 61.

[0077] Remedy of aggrieved persons other than officers A person subject to the Army Act 1950 other than an officer who deems himself wronged by any superior[1] or other officer,[2] may complain[3] to the officer under whose command he is serving[4]. When the officer complained against is the officer to whom a complaint should be preferred, the aggrieved person may complain to such officer's next superior officer[5]. Every officer receiving such complaint shall make an investigation into it for giving full redress to the complainant. When necessary, he will refer the complaint to superior authority[6]. The manner of preferring complaint shall be specified by the proper authority[7]. The Central Government may revise any decision by the Chief of the Army Staff under the Army Act 1950[8], but, subject thereto, the decision of the Chief of the Army Staff shall be final[9].

1 For definition of 'superior officer' see **[0036]**.

2 For definition of 'officer' see **[0029]**.

3 Complaints could be made by a person other than an officer: (a) who deems himself wronged by any superior or other officer; (b) against the decision of an authority disposing of a case under Army Act 1950 ss 80, 83, 84 and 85; and (c) who deems himself wronged by the award of censure (recordable or non recordable). Defence Services Regulations, Regulations for the Army, Volume I, paragraph 364.1(a).

4 Army Act 1950 s 26(1).

5 Army Act 1950 s 26(2).

6 Army Act 1950 s 26(3).

7 Army Act 1950 s 26(4). The manner and channel through which complains must be preferred are specified. See Defence Services Regulations, Regulations for the Army, Volume I, paragraph 364. See: **[0079]**.

8 Ie under the Army Act 1950 s 26(2).

9 Army Act 1950 s 26(5).

[0078] Remedy of aggrieved officers Any officer[1] who deems himself wronged by his commanding officer[2] or any superior officer[3] and who on due application made to his commanding officer does not receive the redress to which he considers himself entitled, may complain to the Central Government [4]. The manner of preferring complaint shall be specified by the proper authority [5]. The complainant must state he has been denied or deprived of something to which he has a military right. An officer who is refused compassionate leave or a compassionate posting has no right of complaint under the Army Act 1950 unless he can produce some evidence of improper motive for the refusal of leave, etc. Complaints may be made respecting such matter, but can be made by an individual only. The combined complaint of several can never be permissible, but should not, if well founded, be treated as mutinous, where it is plain that the only object of those making the complaint is to procure redress of the matter by which they think themselves wronged. A false accusation or false statement made in preferring a complaint under the Army Act 1950 is punishable[6]. The mere fact that a complaint appears to be baseless, or even frivolous, does not render the maker liable to punishment. With a view to stall disciplinary proceedings, a number of army personnel submit statutory complaints under this provision of at various stages of such disciplinary proceedings The complaints under the Army Act 1950 s 27 are not entertainable pertaining to the court martial and disciplinary matters after cognizance of offence has been taken and disciplinary proceedings commenced[7].

1 As to the definition of 'officer' see **[0029]**.

2 As to the definition of 'commanding officer' see **[0013]**.

3 As to the definition of 'superior officer' see **[0036]**.

4 Complaints could be made on three occasions by an officer: (a) who deems himself wronged by his commanding officer or any other superior officer, (b) against the decision of an authority disposing of a case under Army Act ss 83 and 84, (c) who deems himself wronged by the award of censure (recordable or non recordable). Defence Service Regulations, Regulations for the Army, Volume I, paragraph 364.1(a).

5 Army Act 1950 s 27. The manner and channel through which complains must be preferred are specified; see Defence Services Regulations, Regulations for the Army, Volume I, paragraph 364. See **[0079]**.

6 Army Act 1950 s 56(b).

7 *Brig Iqbal Singh (Retd) v Union of India* 119 (2005) DLT 715, 2005 (79) DRJ 492.

[0079] Complaints

(1) **Statutory complaints** Statutory complaints are made under the provision of the Army Act 1950[1] by the following: (a) Any person subject to the Army Act 1950 other than an officer who deems himself wronged by any superior or other officer; (b) Any officer who deems himself wronged by his commanding officer or any other superior officer; (c) Any person subject to the Army Act 1950 against the decision of an authority disposing of a case under the provisions of Army Act 1950[2]; and (d) An officer or a junior commissioned officer who deems himself wronged by the award of censure[3] (recordable or non recordable)[4].

(2) **Number and extent** An officer has the right to complain to the Central Government, junior commissioned officers, warrant officers and other ranks can complaint only to the chief of the army staff and not the Central Government. This right can be exercised only once. A second complaint to these authorities will be allowed only if fresh facts and circumstances have come to light necessitating reconsideration of the case[5].

(3) **Procedure for submission and channel** Statutory complaints are to be addressed to the Central

Government by officers[6]; and to the chief of the army staff by junior commissioned officers, warrant officers and other ranks[7]. All statutory complaints to be made through proper channel [8]. In order to facilitate all intermediary formations and Army Headquarters to closely monitor the progress of statutory complaints, the commanding officer of the complainant shall forward an advance copy of the complaint to all the intermediary formation headquarters and concerned branches of directorates at Army Headquarters immediately. Advance copy of complaints on discipline and vigilance matters will be endorsed to the discipline and vigilance directorate at the army headquarters. The complainant must desist from writing directly to army headquarters or the Central Government with regard to progress of the case. However, if the final decision on the statutory complaint with or without accusations against any superior officer as mentioned hereunder[9], is not taken within a period of 12 months or 09 months respectively, from the date such a complaint is submitted, the complaint will have a right to represent directly to Army Headquarters or the Central Government as the case may be after informing his commanding officer[10]. The following channels will be followed while forwarding statutory complaints: to company commander or other immediate superior, commanding officer, brigade commander or the sub area commander, divisional commander or area commander, general officer commanding corps where applicable, general officer commanding-in-chief command, chief of the army staff, and the central government[11]. Statutory complaints from officers of army medical corps and army dental corps and from all junior commissioned officers, warrant officer and other ranks which pertain to matters relating to promotion, appointment, posting, release and discharge, will be processed through departmental channels, where no departmental channels exists complaints will be processed through respective staff channels[12].

(4) **Layout of complaint** The format for submission of complaints has been laid down by the Army Headquarters and complaints to be submitted in a prescribed standard format[13]. It will be ensured that the complaint is couched in respectful and proper language. A complaint containing a false statement or a false accusation would render the complainant liable for disciplinary action under the Amy Act 1950. If a complaint contains accusations, the complainant will render the following certificate, which will be annexed to complaint: 'I undertake that any false statement or false accusation made by me in this complaint will render me liable for disciplinary action'[14]. If the complaint contains serious accusation(s) against any superior officer pertaining to moral turpitude, maturity or professional competence, the next superior authority to the one against whom such accusation have been made will take necessary steps to conduct investigation, as considered necessary[15].

(5) **Action by the intermediary authority** The immediate superior authority in chain is to offer his detailed para-wise comments on the complaint. He will also ensure that if the following stipulated conditions are not satisfied, he will withhold the complaint to inform the next superior authority and the complainant the reasons for withholding the complaint: (i) that the complaint is complete in all respects and is in correct form[16]; (ii) that the complaint is not couched in discourteous, disrespectful or improper language[17]; or (iii) that the complaint does not contain official documents and correspondence, access to which does not have any formal authority[18]. Where a complaint is withheld on any of the above mentioned grounds, the date of submission of the complaint will count from the date of revised complaint[19]. An intermediary authority will examine the complaints set forth by the complainant and may take any of the following actions: (i) Where the intermediary authorities arrive at the view, after due examination, that only a partial redress will meet the ends of justice, the same may be granted by

the authority concerned. In such cases, the intermediary authority granting such redress will further call upon the complainant to express as to whether he desires to withdraw the complaint, in view of the partial redress granted, within 90 days, and if he gives such occurrence it will be communicated to all concerned and the complaint proceed[20]. (ii) Where the intermediary authority decides to grant full redress sought by the complainant, he shall be suitably informed. The next higher authority to the authority granting such relief will be kept informed of the sought of redress. Such cases will not be forwarded to the authority to whom the complaint is addressed[21]. (iii) Where the redress prayed for is not given at all the intermediary authority will forward the complaint along with his comments and recommendations through normal channels to the authority to whom the complaint is addressed for final disposal[0] Before forwarding the complaint to the next higher authority, the immediate superior authority of the aggrieved individual will endeavour to interview the complainant, if required, and make such investigations as he considers necessary. He will then forward the complaint, along with his detailed para-wise comments and recommendations to the next superior intermediary authority. While forwarding the statutory complaint to the next higher authority, concerned formation headquarters will invariably inform army headquarters about the progress of the case and also inform the complainant through his commanding officer[23].

(6) **Time frame for processing** All complaints will be dealt with expeditiously at all levels. The complaints which do not contain any accusation requiring investigation are to reach the army headquarter within 135 days; whereas complaints containing an accusation requiring investigations are to reach the army headquarters within 180 days; including transaction period[24]. With a view to enable all intermediary formations and army headquarters to closely monitor the progress of statutory complaints mentioned in these provisions[25], all intermediary and higher authorities will be kept informed. All statutory complaints will be accompanied by a delay report, which will be duly filled and initialled, receipt of the complaint as well as before forwarding the complaint to the next higher authority. The format for the report will be laid down by the army headquarters[26]. Whenever a complaint is delayed for any period exceeding the stipulated time frame, reasons for the delay will be annexed to the delay report on a separate sheet of paper. The monitoring of statutory complaints through suitable monitoring schedules and standard operating procedures will be strictly enforced at all levels of the chain of command. The delay apprehended will be projected in time to ensure timely processing and finalisation of complaint. The intermediate formation headquarters will maintain a record and watch the progress of complaints scrupulously, accountability for delays, and action taken against the defaulting officers[27].

(7) **Final disposal of complaints** Orders of the authority disposing of the complaint is to be communicated to the complainant through normal channels. However, a copy of the orders will also be endorsed direct to the complainant by the disposing authority which will be acknowledged by the individual directly to the authority disposing of the complaint. In addition, the formation/unit concerned will also inform the branch concerned at army headquarters, in writing, that copy of the order has been handed over to the individual[28].

(8) **Procedure for processing statutory complaints at Army Headquarters** The Army Act 1950 s 26 confers the powers of decision to the chief of the army staff. All statutory complaints in respect of junior commissioned officer, warrant officer, and other ranks will accordingly be put up to the chief of the army staff for final decision by the concerned directorates through the respective principal staff officer dealing with the subject on which the complaint has been made. In case the subject pertains to

more than one branch, the views of the principal staff officer of those branches should be obtained while projecting the case to the chief of the army staff. Cases involving disciplinary angle should be routed through the adjutant general[29]. The Central Government exercise the powers under Army Act 1950 s 27 and the statutory complaints of officers are processed to the chief of the army staff through CAB (except statutory complaints on discipline and vigilance matters) by the respective directorate/ branches at Army Headquarters. In case the chief of the army staff grants partial or full redress to the complainant, procedure as contained under these provisions will be followed[30]. In other cases the complaint will be forwarded to the Central Government after obtaining the recommendations of the chief of the army staff[31].

(9) **Non-statutory complaints** Non statutory complaints can only be addressed to the immediate superior, company commander or the commanding officer as the case may be. Such complaints will neither be addressed direct to higher authorities nor will copies be endorsed to such authorities[32]. Non statutory complaints are to be dealt with expeditiously[33].

1 Ie the Army Act 1950 ss 26 and 27.

2 Ie under the Army Act 1950 ss 80, 83, 84 or 85.

3 As to the meaning of 'censure' and other details; see **[0158] to [0160]**.

4 Defence Services Regulations, Regulations for the Army, Volume I, paragraph 364.1(a). A petition against the findings and sentence of a court martial will be submitted under Army Act 1950 s 164 read with Regulations for the Army, Volume I, paragraph 365, and not under the paragraph 364.

5 Defence Services Regulations, Regulations for the Army, Volume I, paragraph 364.2.

6 Defence Services Regulations, Regulations for the Army, Volume I, paragraph 364.3 (a).

7 Defence Services Regulations, Regulations for the Army, Volume I, paragraph 364.3 (b).

8 Ie as mentioned in the Defence Services Regulations, Regulations for the Army, Volume I, paragraph 364.5.

9 Ie as mentioned in the Defence Services Regulations, Regulations for the Army, Volume I, paragraph 364.9.

10 Defence Servicse Regulations, Regulations for the Army, Volume I, paragraph 364.4.

11 Defence Services Regulations, Regulations for the Army, Volume I, paragraph 364.5.

12 Defence Services Regulations, Regulations for the Army, Volume I, paragraph 364.6.

13 Defence Services Regulations, Regulations for the Army, Volume I, paragraph 364.7.

14 Defence Services Regulations, Regulations for the Army, Volume I, paragraph 364.8.

15 Defence Services Regulations, Regulations for the Army, Volume I, paragraph 364.9.

16 Defence Services Regulations, Regulations for the Army, Volume I, paragraph 364.10(a).

17 Defence Services Regulations, Regulations for the Army, Volume I, paragraph 364.10(b).

18 Defence Services Regulations, Regulations for the Army, Volume I, paragraph 364.10(c).

19 Defence Services Regulations, Regulations for the Army, Volume I, paragraph 364.11.

20 Defence Services Regulations, Regulations for the Army, Volume I, paragraph 364.12(a).

21 Defence Services Regulations, Regulations for the Army, Volume I, paragraph 364.12(b).

22 Defence Services Regulations, Regulations for the Army, Volume I, paragraph 364.12(c). Though the manner of forwarding the comments with recommendations by the intermediary military authority to the Central Government for final disposal have been provided, non-furnishing of such comments by the said authority to the complainant who lodges the statutory complaint, tantamount to violation of principles of natural justice. This is because, the

comments that are furnished by the intermediary military authority to the Central Government, are essential to the complainant, so as to enable that person to know what has been commented against him by the said military authority, while forwarding the complaint to the Central Government for final disposal. *Union of India v Major General Arun Roye* 2008 CWN (Vol. 112) 528.

23 Defence Servicse Regulations, Regulations for the Army, Volume I, paragraph 364.13.

24 Defence Services Regulations, Regulations for the Army, Volume I, paragraph 364.14.

25 Defence Services Regulations, Regulations for the Army, Volume I, paragraph 364 pararaphs 4,10,11,12 and 13.

26 Defence Services Regulations, Regulations for the Army, Volume I, paragraph 364.15.

27 Defence Services Regulations, Regulations for the Army, Volume I, paragraph 364.16.

28 Defence Services Regulations, Regulations for the Army, Volume I, paragraph 364.17.

29 Defence Servicse Regulations, Regulations for the Army, Volume I, paragraph 364.18.

30 Ie Defence Services Regulations, Regulations for the Army, Volume I, paragraph 364 para 12 and 17 respectively.

31 Defence Services Regulations, Regulations for the Army, Volume I, paragraph 364.19.

32 Defence Services Regulations, Regulations for the Army, Volume I, paragraph 364.20.

33 Defence Servicse Regulations, Regulations for the Army, Volume I, paragraph 364.21. Regulations for the Army, Volume I, paragraph 364.7, 8 and 16 will apply to non statutory complaints.

[0080] Immunity from attachment The arms, clothes, equipment, accoutrements or necessaries of a person subject to the Army Act 1950, or any animal used by him for the discharge of his duty, shall not be seized. The pay and allowances of such person or any part thereof be shall not be attached by direction of any civil or revenue court in satisfaction of any decree or order enforceable against him[1]. The words 'civil or revenue court' do not include a criminal court. If a decree of debt is made against an officer of the Indian Army, whose arms, cloths, equipment, salary and allowance are exempted from attachment under the Army Act 1950 and who is not liable to be arrested[2], he cannot be punished under the Contempt of Court Act 1971 for non compliance of the decree against him[3].

1 Army Act 1950 s 28.

2 Under the Army Act 1950 s 29.

3 *Vrinda Anand v Major Arun Anand* AIR 1987 Del 120.

[0081] Immunity from arrest for debt A person subject to the Army Act 1950 shall not, so long as he belongs to the Forces, be liable to be arrested for debt under any process issued by, or by authority of, any civil or revenue court or revenue officer[1]. The judge of any such court or the said officer may examine into any complaint made by such person or his superior officer of the arrest of such person contrary to the provisions of this section and may, by warrant under his hand, discharge the person, and award reasonable costs to the complainant, who may recover those costs in like manner as he might have recovered costs awarded to him by a decree against the person obtaining the process[2]. For the recovery of such costs no court-fee shall be payable by the complainant[3]. The privilege is from arrest on civil or revenue process. There is no privilege from arrest on any criminal process except as provided in the Criminal Procedure Code 1973[4].

1 Army Act 1950 s 29(1). As to the definition of the term 'Forces'; see **[0022]**.

2 Army Act 1950 s 29(2).

3 Army Act 1950 s 29(3).

4 Ie as provided under the Code Criminal Procedure 1973 ss 45 and 475.

[0082] Immunity of persons attending courts martial from arrest The presiding officer, member of a court martial, judge advocate, a party to any proceeding before a court martial, his legal practitioner or agent, and witness acting in obedience to a summons to attend a court-martial shall not, while proceeding to, attending, or returning from, a court-martial, be liable to arrest under civil or revenue process[1]. If any such person is arrested under any such process, he may be discharged by order of the court martial[2].

1 Army Act 1950 s 30(1).

2 Army Act 1950 s 30(2).

[0083] Privileges of reservists Every person belonging to the Indian Reserve Forces shall, when called out for or engaged in or returning from, training or service, be entitled to all the privileges accorded[1] by the Army Act 1950[2].

1 Under Army Act 1950 ss 28 and 29 only.

2 Army Act 1950 s 31.

[0084] Priority in respect of army personnel's litigation The Government of India, Ministry of Home affairs while listing out the service privileges have issued instructions to the State Governments to accord priority in respect of army personnel's litigation. On the presentation to any court by or on behalf of any person subject to the Army Act 1950 of a certificate from the proper military authority of leave of absence having been granted to him for the purpose of prosecuting or defending any suit or other proceeding in such court, the court shall, on the application of such person, arrange, so far as may be possible, for the hearing and final disposal of such proceeding within the period of the leave so granted[1]. The certificate from the proper military authority shall state the first and last day of the leave or intended leave, and set forth a description of the case with respect to which the leave was granted or applied for[2]. No fee shall be payable to the court in respect of the presentation of any such certificate, or of any application by or on behalf of any such person, for priority for the hearing of his case[3]. Where the court is unable to arrange for the hearing and final disposal of the suit or other proceeding within the period of such leave or intended leave as aforesaid, it shall record its reasons for its inability to do so, and shall cause a copy thereof, to be furnished to such person on his application without any payment whatever by him in respect either of the application for such copy or of the copy itself[4]. If in any case a question arises as to the proper military authority qualified to grant such certificate as aforesaid, such question shall at once be referred by the court to an officer having power not less than a brigade or equivalent commander whose decision shall be final[5].

1 Army Act 1950 s 32(1).

2 Army Act 1950 s 32(2).

3 Army Act 1950 s 32(3).

4 Army Act 1950 s 32(4).

5 Army Act 1950 s 32(5).

[0085] Saving of rights and privileges under other laws The rights and privileges specified in the Army Act 1950[1] shall be in addition to[2], and not in derogation of, any other rights and privileges conferred on persons subject to the Army Act 1950 or on members of the regular Army, Navy and Air Force generally by any other law for the time being in force[3].

1 The rights and privileges under the Army Act 1950 ss 25 to 32.

2 For instance: The Indian Succession Act 1925 ss 65 and 66 provide that a person subject to the Army Act 1950 has a right to make a 'privileged will' which may be made either by word of mouth or by writing without complying with the formalities and signatures and attestation which are required in the case of 'will' made by ordinary persons, if he is employed in an expedition or engaged in actual warfare. Under the Tolls (Army and Air Force) Act 1901 s 3, persons subject to the Army Act 1950 while moving under orders of military authorities are together with the members of their families and belongings exempted from payment of any tolls.

3 Army Act 1950 s 33.

4. OFFENCES

CONTENTS

PARA

[0086] Introduction Chapter VI of the Army Act 1950 classifies various heads and defines the military and civil offences[1]. Chapter IV of the India Penal Code 1860 dealing with general exceptions applies to offences under special laws such as the Army Act 1950[2]. The definition of these offences in the Army Act 1950 must, therefore, be read as subject to the 'general exceptions'[3].

1 The Army Act 1950 ss 34-70. As to the meaning of 'offence' see **[0028]**.

2 The Indian Penal Code 1860 s 40.

3 For example, if a non-commissioned officer charged under the Army Act 1950 s 47 with striking a sepoy proves that he, only, did so in the exercise of right of private defence, he will be entitled to an acquittal under the Indian Penal Code 1860 s 96.

[0087] Offences in relation to enemy and punishable with death Any person subject to the Army Act 1950, who commits any of the following offences:

(1) shamefully abandons or delivers up any garrison, fortress, post, place or guard, committed to his charge, or which it is his duty to defend, or uses any means to compel or induce any commanding officer or other person to commit any of the said acts[1];

(2) intentionally uses any means to compel or induce any person subject to military, naval or air force law to abstain from acting against the enemy[2], or to discourage such person from acting against the enemy[3];

(3) in the presence of the enemy, shamefully casts away his arms, ammunition, tools or equipment or misbehaves in such manner as to show cowardice[4];

(4) treacherously holds correspondence with, or communicates intelligence to the enemy or any person in arms against the Union[5];

(5) directly or indirectly assists the enemy with money, arms, ammunitions; stores or supplies[6];

(6) treacherously or through cowardice sends a flag of truce to the enemy[7];

(7) in time of war or during any military operation, intentionally occasions a false alarm in action, camp,

garrison or quarters, or spreads reports calculated to create alarm or despondency[8];

(8) in time of action leaves his commanding officer or his post, guard, picket, patrol or party without being regularly relieved or without leave[9];

(9) having been made a prisoner of war, voluntarily serves with or aids the enemy[10];

(10) knowingly harbours or protects an enemy not being a prisoner[11];

(11) being a sentry in time of war or alarm, sleeps upon his post or is intoxicated[12]; or

(12) knowingly does any act calculated to imperil the success of the military, naval or air forces of India or any forces co-operating therewith or any part of such forces[13],

shall, upon conviction by court martial[14], be liable to suffer death or such less punishment as mentioned in the Army Act 1950[15].

1 Army Act 1950 s 34(a). The term 'shameful' means a positive and disgraceful dereliction of duty and not merely negligence or misapprehension or error of judgment. 'Shamefully abandons': this offence can only be committed by the person in charge of the garrison, post, etc., and not by the subordinates under his command. The term 'post' includes any point or position (whether fortified or not) which a detachment may be ordered to hold; and the abandonment of a post would also include the abandonment of a siege if there were no circumstances to warrant such a measure. Manual of Military Law, Volume II, 2011, the Army Act 1950 s 34 notes.

2 For definition of the term 'enemy' see **[0020]**.

3 Army Act 1950 s 34(b).

4 Army Act 1950 s 34(c). The term 'misbehaves' means that the accused, from an unsoldier-like regard for his personal safety, in the presence of the enemy, failed in respect of some distinct and feasible duty imposed upon him by a specified order or regulation, or by the well-understood custom of the service, or by the requirements of the case, as applicable to the position in which he was placed at the time. Manual of Military Law, Volume II, 2011, the Army Act 1950 s 34 notes.

5 Army Act 1950 s 34(d). The term 'treacherously' implies an intention to assist the enemy and must be carefully distinguished from 'through cowardice' which occur in this provision. The intention to help the enemy is an essential ingredient of the offence of treachery and must be proved before a conviction can be sustained. Manual of Military Law, Volume II, 2011, the Army Act 1950 s 34 notes.

6 Army Act 1950 s 34(e).

7 Army Act 1950 s 34(f).

8 Army Act 1950 s 34(g).

9 Army Act 1950 s 34(h).

10 Army Act 1950 s 34(i).

11 Army Act 1950 s 34(j). The word harbour includes the supplying a person with shelter, food, drink, money, clothes, arms, ammunition or means of conveyance or the assisting a person by any means to evade apprehension. Indian Penal Code 1860 s 52A.

12 Army Act 1950 s 34(k). The term 'post' as used with respect to an individual in this and other clauses of s. 34, refers to the position or place in which it may be the duty of a person subject to the Army Act 1950 to be, especially when under arms. In determining what, in any particular case, is a 'post' the court martial will use their military knowledge under the Army Act 1950 s. 134. Two or more accused cannot be tried jointly with committing an offence under this clause. Manual of Military Law, Volume II, 2011, the Army Act 1950 s 34 notes.

13 Army Act 1950 s 34(l).

14 As to the meaning of 'courts martial' see **[0016]**. Defence Service Regulations, Regulations for the Army, Volume I, para 451 (a): Any officer, junior commissioned officer, warrant officer or other rank who when in the presence of the enemy, displays a white flag or other symbol in anticipation or in token of surrender will be tried by a general court martial. In relations to the allegations that on militant's opening fire, the delinquent cowardly running away, the charge attracts the Amy Act s 34 (a) and (h), therefore trial should have been held by general court martial and not by a summary court martial. The trial held by summary court martial was without jurisdiction. *Ex-Havildar Ratan Singh v Union of India* AIR 1992 SC 415, (1992) Supp 1 SCC 716, (1992) Cr LJ 287. Offences committed under the Army Act 1950 s 34 should not be dealt with summarily under the Army Act ss 80, 83, 84 or 85. Manual of Military Law, Volume II, 2011, the Army Act 1950 s 34 notes.

15 See the Army Act 1950 s 71.

[0088] Offences in relation to enemy and not punishable with death Any person subject to the Army Act 1950[1] who commits any of the following offences: (1) is taken prisoner, by want of due precaution, or through disobedience of orders, or wilful neglect of duty, or having been taken prisoner, fails to rejoin his service when able to do so[2]; (2) without due authority holds correspondence with or communicates intelligence to the enemy or having come by the knowledge of any such correspondence or communication, wilfully omits to discover it immediately to his commanding or other superior officer[3]; or (3) without due authority sends a flag of truce to the enemy[4], shall, upon conviction by court-martial[5], be liable to suffer imprisonment for a term which may extend to 14 years or such less punishment as mentioned in the Army Act 1950[6].

1 As to the persons subject to the Army Act 1950; see **[0039]**.

2 Army Act 1950 s 35(a). Where the conduct of any person subject to the Army Act 1950 when being taken prisoner by or while in the hands of the enemy is to be inquired into, the chief of the army staff may order a court of inquiry to be held for this purpose and on the basis of the finding of the said court, the pay and allowances of such person may be forfeited by order of the central government. Manual of Military Law, Volume II, 2011, the Army Act 1950 s 35 notes.

3 Army Act 1950 s 35(b). The phrase 'communicates intelligence to', appears to be wide enough to cover the case of intelligence reaching the enemy through the capture or the re-publication (eg, by relatives or newspapers) of letters, sketches, photographs, etc. Everyone connected with the forces should recognize the grave danger of assisting the enemy by gossip, whether verbal or written, as to plans, prospects, operations, numbers, etc. In a charge under this clause, however, it must be proved that the intelligence did in fact reach the enemy. Manual of Military Law, Volume II, 2011, the Army Act 1950 s 35 notes.

4 Army Act 1950 s 35(c). The offence under this clause is less grave in form than the one under the Army Act 195 s. 34(f). As to the meaning of 'enemy' see **[0020]**.

5 Offences committed under the Army Act 1950 s 35 should not be dealt with summarily under the Army Act ss 80, 83, 84 or 85.

6 See Army Act 1950 s 71.

[0089] Offence punishable more severely on active service than at other times Any person subject to the Army Act 1950[1] who commits any of the following offences, that is to say:

(1) forces a safeguard, or forces or uses criminal force to a sentry[2];

(2) breaks into any house or other place in search of plunder[3];

(3) being a sentry sleeps upon his post, or is intoxicated[4];

(4) without orders from his superior officer leaves his guard, picquet, patrol or post[5];

(5) intentionally or through neglect occasions a false alarm in camp, garrison, of quarters; or spreads reports calculated to create unnecessary alarm or despondency[6]; or

(6) makes known the parole, watchword or countersign to any person not entitled to receive it; or knowingly gives a parole, watchword or countersign different from what he received[7],

shall, upon conviction by court-martial[8], if he commits any such offence when on active service, be liable to suffer imprisonment for a term which may extend to 14 years or such less punishment[9]; and if he commits any such offence when not on active service, be liable to suffer imprisonment for a term which may extend to seven years or such less punishment as mentioned in the Army Act 1950[10].

1 As to the persons subject to the Army Act 1950; see **[0039]**.

2 Army Act 1950 s 36(a). The term 'forces' does not necessarily mean use of physical force; passing the sentry when warned by him not to do so will amount to this offence. A 'safeguard' is a party of soldiers detached for the protection of some person or persons, or of a particular village, house, or other property. A single sentry posted from such party is still part of the safeguard, and it is as criminal to force him by breaking into the house or other property under his special care as to force the whole party. A man posted solely to control traffic is not a 'safeguard' for the purposes of this provision. For definition of the term 'uses criminal force' refer the Indian Penal Code 1860 ss 349 and 350. A sentry is posted for protecting some place, property or person and any forcible interference with such protection amounts to an offence under this clause provided the accused was aware that the sentry was in fact acting as such. An accused charged under this clause for using criminal force to a sentry can be found guilty of attempting to use such criminal force under the Army Act s 139(8) or of assaulting the sentry under the Army Act 1950 s 139(3). Similarly, if the charge is laid under the Army Act 1950 s 69 for using criminal force to a sentry, the accused can be convicted of attempting to use such criminal force to or assaulting him under the Army Act 1950 s 139(6). Manual of Military Law, Volume II, 2011, the Army Act 1950 s 36 notes.

3 Army Act 1950 s 36(b). This clause, having regard to special military significance of the term plunder, is applicable only to offences committed on active service. For definition of 'house-breaking' refer the Indian Penal Code 1860 s 445. A house indicates some structure intended for affording some sort of protection to the person dwelling inside it or for the property placed there for custody. Manual of Military Law, Volume II, 2011, the Army Act 1950 s 36 notes.

4 Army Act 1950 s 36(c). A sentry found asleep even a short distance from his post should be charged with leaving his post under the Army Act s 36(d); he cannot properly be charged with being asleep on his post, though he may be charged under the Army Act s 63 with being asleep when on sentry duty. Manual of Military Law, Volume II, 2011, the Army Act 1950 s 36 notes.

5 Army Act 1950 s 36(d). As to the meaning of 'superior officer' see **[0036]**.

6 Army Act 1950 s 36(e).

7 Army Act 1950 s 36(f).

8 As to the meaning of 'courts martial' see **[0016]**.

9 Ie as mentioned in the Army Act 1950 s 71.

10 Ie as mentioned in the Army Act 1950 s 71. Offences under this provision when on active service should not be dealt with summarily under the Army Act 1950 ss 80, 83, 84 or 85. Manual of Military Law, Volume II, 2011, the Army Act 1950 s 36 notes. Army Act 1950 s 36.

[0090] Mutiny Any person subject to the Army Act 1950 who commits any of the following offences: (1) begins, incites, causes, or conspires with any other persons to cause any mutiny in the military, naval or air forces of India or any forces co-operating therewith[1]; or (2) joins in any such mutiny[2]; or (3) being present at any such mutiny, does not use his utmost endeavours to suppress the same[3]; or (4) knowing or having reason to believe in the existence of any such mutiny, or of any intention to mutiny or of any such conspiracy, does not, without delay, give information thereof to his commanding or other superior officer[4]; or (5) endeavours to seduce any person in the military, naval or air forces of India from his duty or allegiance to the Union[5], shall, upon conviction by court-martial, be liable to suffer death or such less punishment as mentioned in the Army Act 1950[6].

The term mutiny has not been defined in the Army Act 1950. Mutiny implies collective insubordination, or a combination of two or more persons to resist, or to induce others to resist or refusal to obey lawful military authority[7]. Collective petitions or representations or the submission of a petition through the medium of any association in respect of military matters are forbidden on this ground. Where there is an actual mutiny or a conspiracy to mutiny, all concerned in the mutiny or conspiracy can be tried under the Army Act 1950 s 37 for causing or conspiring to cause, or joining in, the mutiny, as the case may be. If no mutiny or conspiracy exists, a person can only be tried under the Army Act 1950 s 37 if the charge is one of being present at a mutiny not using his utmost endeavours to suppress the same or of failing to inform his commanding or other superior officer of an intent to cause mutiny or such conspiracy or of endeavouring to seduce any person in the forces from his duty or allegiance to the Union. Offences under the Army Act 1950 s 37 should not be dealt with summarily under the Army Act ss 80, 83, 84 or 85. The limitation of time for the commencement of trial prescribed by the Army Act 1950 s122 does not apply to the offence of mutiny under s 37 of the Army Act 1950[8].

1 Army Act 1950 s 37(a).

2 Army Act 1950 s 37(b).

3 Army Act 1950 s 37(c).

4 Army Act 1950 s 37(d). As to the meaning of 'commanding officer' see **[0013]**; as to the meaning of 'superior officer' see **[0036]**.

5 Army Act 1950 s 37(e). Endeavours to seduce: attempt itself is punishable; it is immaterial whether the attempt succeeds or not.

6 Ie as mentioned in the Army Act 1950 s 71.

7 *Kartar Singh, Sardar Jit Singh v Imperator*, 47 Cri LJ 1946, Vol. 47, p. 100.

8 Manual of Military Law, Volume II, s 37 notes.

[0091] Desertion and aiding desertion Any person subject to the Army Act 1950 who deserts or attempts to desert the service shall, upon conviction by court-martial, if he commits the offence on active service[1] or when under orders for active service, be liable to suffer death or such less punishment as mentioned in the Army Act 1950[2]. Where he commits the offence under any other circumstances, he shall be liable to suffer imprisonment for a term which may extend to seven years or such less punishment as mentioned in the Army Act 1950[3]. Any person subject to the Army Act 1950 who knowingly harbours[4] any such deserter shall, upon conviction by court-martial, be liable to suffer imprisonment for a term which may extend to seven years or such less punishment as mentioned in the Army Act 1950[5]. Any person subject to the Army Act 1950 who, being cognizant of any desertion or attempt at desertion of a person subject to the Army Act 1950, does not forthwith give notice to his own or some other superior officer, or take any steps in his power to cause such person to be apprehended, shall, upon conviction by court-martial, be liable to suffer imprisonment for a term which may extend to two years or such less punishment as mentioned in the Army Act 1950[6].

The terms 'deserter' and 'desertion' have not been defined by the Army Act 1950. Desertion is distinguished from absence without leave under the Army Act s 39; in that desertion or attempt to desert the service implies an intention on the part of the accused either (a) never to return to the service or (b) to avoid some important military duty (commonly known as constructive desertion) e.g., service in a forward area, embarkation for foreign service or service in aid of the civil power and not merely some routine duty or duty only applicable to the accused like a fire picquet duty. A charge under the Army Act 1950 s 38 cannot lie unless it appears from the evidence that one or other such intention existed. It is sufficient if the intention in never to return to the service was formed at the time during the period of absence and not necessarily at the time when the accused first absented himself from unit/duty station. Since every desertion necessarily implies absence without leave, the distinction between desertion and absence without leave must necessarily depend on the animus. Where there is animus deserendi, the absence is straightway desertion[7]. An intention to desert may be inferred from a long absence, wearing of disguise, distance from the duty station and the manner of termination of absence e.g., apprehension but such facts though relevant are only prima facie, and not conclusive, evidence of such intention. Similarly the fact that an accused has been declared an absentee under the Army Act s 106 is not by itself a deciding factor if other evidence suggests the contrary. A person subject to the Army Act 1950 charged with desertion may be found guilty of an attempt to desert or of absence without leave, and such a person charged with attempting to desert may be found guilty of being absent without leave provided evidence was available to prove the absence[8]. When the absence began more than 3 years before the date of trial, the provisions of the Army Act 1950 must be borne in mind and complied with[9]. For instance where an accused person is charged with desertion commencing on a date more than three years before the date of trial, he cannot be found guilty under the Army Act 1950 s 139(1) of absence without leave from that date but such absence must be restricted to a period not exceeding three years immediately prior to the commencement of trial; where such a finding and sentence has been wrongly confirmed, the competent authority under the Army Act 1950 s 163 may substitute a valid finding and pass a sentence for the offence specified or involved in such finding. When a person subject to the Army Act 1950 has been absent from his duty without authority for a period of 30 days, a court of inquiry is mandatory under the Army Act 1950[10] but even after such a court of inquiry has been held, the case can still be disposed of summarily under the Army Act ss 80, 83, 84 or 85 but the charge should be laid for absence without leave under the Army Act 1950 s 39. To establish an attempt to desert, some act which, if completed, would constitute desertion must be proved, e.g., a soldier is arrested in the act of leaving his unit lines without authority, dressed in plain clothes and carrying his personal kit, when the circumstances indicate that he intends to desert. The test is whether the act, or series of acts, in the course of which the offender is apprehended or surrenders, would, if completed, amount to desertion. Attempt to desert is itself made a substantive offence, and a charge for the same should be preferred under the Army Act 1950 s 38 (1) and not under the Army Act 1950 s 65. For an offence of abetment of desertion of a person subject to the Army Act 1950 can be charged under the Army Act 1950 s 66[11]. A person subject to the Army Act 1950, who is declared absent under s 106 of the aforesaid Act does not thereby cease to belong to the corps in which he is enrolled though no longer shown on its returns, and can, if subsequently arrested, be tried by a court martial for desertion. When arrested he will be shown on returns as rejoined from desertion[12].

1 As to the meaning of 'active service' see **[0008]**.

2 Ie as mentioned in the Army Act 1950 s 71.

3 Ie as mentioned in the Army Act 1950 s 71. Army Act s 38(1). An offence under the Army Act s 38 (1) when on active service or under orders for active service should not be dealt with summarily under the Army Act 1950 ss 80, 83, 84 and 85. Two or more persons cannot be tried jointly with committing the offence of desertion under the Army Act 1950 s 38(1). Manual of Military Law, Volume II, s 38 notes.

4 The word 'harbour' includes the supplying a person with shelter, food, drink, money, clothes, arms, ammunition or means of conveyance or the assisting a person by any means to evade apprehension; Indian Penal Code 1860 s 52A.

5 Ie as mentioned in the Army Act 1950 s 71. The Army Act 1950 s 38(2).

6 Ie as mentioned in the Army Act 1950 s 71. The Army Act 1950 s 38(3).

7 *Virendra Kumar v Chief of the Army Staff* AIR 1986 SC 1060, (1986) 2 SCC 217, (1986) SCC (Cr) 149 (the Army Act 1950 ss 38 and 39 make a clear distinction between 'desertion' and 'absence without leave').

8 See the Army Act 1950 s 139 (1) and (2).

9 The Army Act 1950 s 122 which prescribes the limitation of time for the trial of offences expressly excludes desertion; but where a person other than an officer has subsequently to the commission of the offence served continuously in an exemplary manner for not less than three years, he cannot be tried for such offence of desertion which was committed before the commencement of such three years other than desertion on active service. For 'exemplary service' see Defence Service Regulations, Regulations for the Army, Volume I, paragraph 465.

10 Army Act 1950 s 106. As to inquiring into absence see the Army Rules 1954 r 183.

11 Manual of Military Law, Volume II, s 38 notes.

12 The Defence Service Regulations, Regulations for the Army 1987, Volume I, paragraph 376.

[0092] Absence without leave Any person subject to the Army Act 1950 who commits any of the following offences, that is to say:

(1) absents himself without leave[1];

(2) without sufficient cause, overstays leave granted to him[2];

(3) being on leave of absence and having received information from proper authority that any corps, or portion of a corps, or any department to which he belongs, has been ordered on active service, fails without sufficient cause, to rejoin without delay[3];

(4) without sufficient cause, fails to appear at the time fixed at the parade or, place appointed for exercise or duty[4];

(5) when on parade, or on the line of march, without sufficient cause or without leave from his superior officer, quits the parade or line of march[5];

(6) when in camp or garrison or elsewhere, is found beyond any limits fixed, or in any place prohibited, by any general, local or other order, without a pass or written leave from his superior officer[6]; or

(7) without leave from his superior officer or without due cause, absents himself from any school when duly ordered to attend there[7],

shall, upon conviction by court-martial, be liable to suffer imprisonment for a term which may extend to three years or such less punishment as mentioned in the Army Act 1950[8].

The criterion between desertion and absence without leave is intention. Where all the ingredients of the offence of desertion are present except an intention not to return to the service or to avoid some important military duty, the offence will be one of absence without leave or any other offence of this genus e.g., failure to appear at the time fixed at the parade. Absence without leave must not be involuntary absence e.g., due to illness or being taken into civil or military custody, whether on surrender or apprehension. To render an absence involuntary there must be some physical impracticability, outside the control of the offender that prevented his return to his unit. Inability to return to his unit through intoxication which is an offence under the Army Act 1950[9] will not make such absence involuntary nor would an inability which arises through lack of money or loss of his railway or other ticket. Further, where the absence without leave was originally voluntary and has by change of circumstances, subsequently become involuntary the offender may be convicted of absence for the whole period. Similarly, an absence that was originally involuntary becomes voluntary, if the offender fails to return to his unit at the earliest practicable moment e.g., failure to return on release from a civil prison. Where the prosecution proves that the accused was absent and that he had not been granted leave, the court may, in the absence of any satisfactory explanation by the accused, infer that the absence was voluntary. The offence under the Army Act 1950 s 39 is one of absence without leave, and not merely absence. Leave of absence must be notified to the applicant for such leave. A person who has applied for leave, and departs from his unit before it is actually granted, commits the offence of being absent without leave, even though the leave had been granted but not notified to him. When a person has been absent without leave for 30 clear days or has overstayed his leave without sufficient cause for that period, a court of inquiry will be assembled under the Army Act 1950[10].

1 Army Act 1950 s 39(a).

2 Army Act 1950 s 39(b). If it is proved that a person subject to the Army Act 1950 has overstayed his leave, it will be for him to show that he had sufficient cause (e.g., sickness or the unexpected interruption of the ordinary means of transit) for doing so. If, however, any evidence as to the cause of his failure to return is known to the prosecutor, it should be adduced, leaving it to the court to decide as to the sufficiency of such cause. Manual of Military Law, Volume II, 2011, the Army Act 1950 s 39 notes.

3 Army Act 1950 s 39(c). As to the meaning of 'corps' see **[0015]**.

4 Army Act 1950 s 39(d).

5 Army Act 1950 s 39(e). As to the meaning of 'superior officer' see **[0036]**.

6 Army Act 1950 s 39(f). The term 'camp' includes a bivouac and any quarters, shelter, or other place where troops are temporarily lodged. The 'general, local or other orders' are standing orders or orders in writing and applicable continuously over a period of time to persons present in a certain geographical area or in a certain military formation. Ignorance of the order is no excuse if the order is one which the accused ought, in the ordinary course, to know. But a misapprehension reasonably arising from want of clarify in the order is a ground for exculpation. The existence of the order must be proved by producing it or a certified copy where so permissible under the Army Act 1950 s 142(4) on oath or affirmation to the court. A written order cannot be proved by oral testimony. Evidence must also be led to show that the order was duly posted or brought to the notice of the accused, or that he was otherwise in a position to be acquainted with its contents. Manual of Military Law, Volume II, 2011, the Army Act 1950 s 39 notes.

7 Army Act 1950 s 39(g). Two or more accused should not be jointly charged with an offence under the Army Act 1950 s 39. Manual of Military Law, Volume II, 2011, the Army Act 1950 s 39 notes.

8 Ie as mentioned in the Army Act 1950 s 71.

9 Army Act 1950 s 48.

10 Army Act 1950 s 106 and Army Rules 1954 r 183. Manual of Military Law, Volume II, s 39 notes.

[0093] Striking or threatening superior officers Any person subject to the Army Act 1950 who commits any of the following offences, that is uses:

(1) criminal force to or assaults his superior officer[1];

(2) threatening language to such officer[2]; or

(3) insubordinate language to such officer[3],

shall, upon conviction by court-martial, if such officer is at the time in the execution of his office or, if the offence is committed on active service, be liable to suffer imprisonment for a term which may extend to 14 years or such less punishment as mentioned in the Army Act 1950; and in other cases, be liable to suffer imprisonment for a term which may extend to 10 years or such less punishment as mentioned in the Army Act 1950[4]. However, in the case of an offence for using insubordinate language to such officer, the imprisonment shall not exceed five years[5].

An 'assault' is something less than the use of criminal force; the force being cut short before the blow actually falls. It seems to consist in an attempt or offer by a person having present ability, with force to do any hurt or violence to the person of another, and it is committed whenever a well founded apprehension of peril from a force partially or fully put in motion is created, e.g., when a person draws a bayonet or otherwise makes a show of violence against a superior but not when he is behind the bars or at such a distance as to rule out at the moment any actual use of criminal force. An assault is thus included in every use of criminal force, and is an intermediate stage thereof. If the force be used in the exercise of the right of private defence, for instance if it be shown that it was necessary, or that at the moment the accused had reason to believe it was necessary for his actual protection from injury, and that he used no more force than was reasonably necessary for this purpose, he is legally justified in using it and commits no offence. A person charged with using criminal force may be found guilty of an attempt to use criminal force or assault under the Army Act 1950 s 139 (8). The expression 'superior officer' in the Army Act 1950 ss 40 and 41 **[0094]** means not only a superior in rank but also a senior in the same grade where that seniority gives power of command according to the usages of the service, but one sepoy can never be the 'superior officer' of another. Where the accused is charged with an offence against a superior officer who is of the same grade, evidence must be adduced to show that the latter is senior to the accused. If the superior did not wear the insignia of his rank, and was not personally known to the accused, evidence would be necessary to show that the accused was otherwise aware of his being his superior officer, or had reason to believe him, to be this superior officer. If such evidence is not available, the accused should be charged under the Army Act 1950 s 63. The lower the rank of the superior the less is the gravity of the offence[6]. The offence is punishable more severely if such superior officer was at the relevant time in the execution of his office or if the offence is committed on active service. It is difficult accurately to define the words 'in the execution of his office', but the military knowledge and experience of the members of a court-martial will enable them in most instances readily to determine whether the superior officer was or was not in the execution of his office. A superior officer in plain clothes may undoubtedly be in the execution of his office; but where the superior officer is in plain clothes, it becomes necessary to prove some knowledge on the part of the accused at the time of the offence that the person who was assaulted or to whom criminal force was used was a superior officer and that he was known to the accused as such, which is not the case where the superior officer is in uniform. On the other hand, there may be circumstances in which a superior officer in uniform is not in the execution of his office. It may be taken in general that using criminal force to or assaulting any superior officer by a person subject to the Army Act 1950 over whom it is, at the relevant time, the duty of that superior officer to maintain discipline, would be using criminal force to or assaulting him in the execution of his office. When the accused is charged, with using criminal force to or assaulting his superior officer who is at the time in the execution of his office or if the accused is charged with committing the offence on active service and the court is satisfied that the offence was committed but not on active service or that the superior officer was not then in the execution of his office, he may be found guilty under the Army Act 1950 s 139(7)[7] of the same offence as having been committed in circumstances involving a less severe punishment[8].

1 Army Act 1950 s 40(a). As to the meaning of 'force', 'criminal force' and 'assault', see the Indian Penal Code 1860 ss 349, 350 and 351. As to the meaning of 'superior officer' see **[0036]**.

2 Army Act 1950 s 40(b). Threatening language means language from which a person addressed may reasonably infer that criminal force may be used. This may be inferred either from the character of the words used or from the surrounding circumstances. Whereas all threatening language is insubordinate the converse is not true; therefore unless there is no doubt as to his intention an accused should be charged with using insubordinate language rather than threatening. Manual of Military Law, Volume II, 2011, the Army Act 1950 s 40 notes.

3 Army Act 1950 s 40(c). The words must be used with an insubordinate intent. They must be, either in themselves, or in the manner or circumstances in which they are spoken, insulting or disrespectful, and in all cases it must reasonably appear that they were intended to be heard by a superior. The words themselves need not necessarily be discourteous. If they indicate a deliberate intention to be insubordinate or resist lawful authority they may properly be regarded as disrespectful of authority, although courteously expressed. The words need not necessarily be spoken. If an accused writes a letter containing insubordinate expressions and addresses it to a superior officer, intending the letter to be read by the addressee, a charge would lie under this clause. Manual of Military Law, Volume II, 2011, the Army Act 1950 s 40 notes.

4 Ie as mentioned in the Army Act 1950 s 71.

5 Army Act 1950 proviso to s 40.

6 Defence Service Regulations, Regulations for the Army, Volume I, paragraph 450.

7 Army Act 1950 s 139(7): see **[0225]**.

8 Manual of Military Law, Volume II, 2011, the Army Act 1950 s 40 notes.

[0094] Disobedience to superior officer Any person subject to the Army Act 1950 who disobeys in such manner as to show a wilful defiance of authority any lawful command given personally by his superior officer[1] in the execution of his office whether the same is given orally, or in writing or by signal or otherwise, shall, upon conviction by court-martial, be liable to suffer imprisonment for a term which may extend to 14 years or such less punishment as mentioned in the Army Act 1950[2]. Any person subject to the Army Act 1950 who disobeys any lawful command given by his superior officer shall, upon conviction by court-martial, if he commits such offence when on active service, be liable to suffer imprisonment for a term which may extend to 14 years or such less punishment; and if he commits offence when not on active service[3], be liable to suffer imprisonment for a term which may extend to five years or such less punishment as mentioned in the Army Act 1950[4].

For a command being 'lawful', it must be a specific command to an individual i.e., it must be capable of individual execution by the person to whom it is addressed and justified by military, as well as by civil, law and usage, e.g., a command addressed by a superior officer to four persons to 'dismiss' is a lawful military command to each of the four persons so addressed. The command must relate to military duty that is to say disobedience to it must tend to impede, delay or prevent a military proceeding. The disobedience must have reference to the time at which the command is to be obeyed. If the command be a lawful command, and demands a prompt and immediate compliance, hesitation or unnecessary delay in obeying it may be sufficient to constitute an offence under Army Act 1950[5]. An order of superior officer directing the officer charged to attend the recording of evidence before the court of inquiry is perfectly valid and disobedience constitutes an offence under the Army Act 1950 s 41[6]. A disregard of an order to eat food does not by itself amount to a disobedience to a lawful command for purposes of the Army Act s 41 has to be examined in the context of the imperatives of the high and rigorous discipline to be maintained in the armed forces. Every aspect of life of a soldier is regulated by discipline. Rejection of food might, under circumstances, amount to an indirect expression of remonstrance and resentment against the higher authority. To say that, a mere refusal to eat food is an innocent, neutral act might be an over-simplification of the matter. Mere in-action need not always necessarily be neutral. Serious acts of calumny could be done in silence. A disregard of a direction to accept food might assume the complexion of disrespect to, and even defiance of authority. Disobedience of order of superior authority to eat food, sentence of one years' rigorous imprisonment and dismissal from service with added disqualification of being declared unfit for any future civil employment is disproportionately excessive[7].

1 As to the meaning of 'superior officer' see **[0036]**.

2 Ie as mentioned in the Army Act 1950 s 71. Army Act 1950 s 41(1). The essential ingredients of the offence are that the disobedience should show a wilful defiance of authority and should be disobedience of a lawful command given personally in the execution of his office by a superior officer. In order, therefore, to convict an accused of an offence under the Army Act 1950 s 41(1), it must be shown (i) that a lawful command was given by a superior officer, (ii) that it was given personally by such officer; (iii) that it was given by such officer in the execution of his office; (iv) that the accused disobeyed it, not from any misunderstanding or slowness but so as to show a wilful defiance of his superior officer's authority. The disobedience must be wilful and deliberate, and distinguished from disobedience arising from forgetfulness or misapprehension. Manual of Military Law, Volume II, 2011, the Army Act 1950 s 41 notes.

3 As to the meaning of 'active service' see **[0008]**.

4 Ie as mentioned in the Army Act 1950 s 71. Army Act 1950 s 41(2).

5 Ie under the Army Act 1950 s 41(2).

6 *Subhash Chander Sarkar v Union of India* AIR 1973 MP 191.

7 *Ranjit Thakur v Union of India* 1987 AIR 2386, 1988 SCR (1) 512, (1987) 4 SCC 611.

[0095] Insubordination and obstruction Any person subject to the Army Act 1950 who commits any of the following offences, that is to say:

(1) being concerned in any quarrel, affray, or disorder, refuses to obey any officer, though of inferior rank, who orders him into arrest, or uses criminal force to or assaults any such officer[1];

(2) uses criminal force to, or assaults any person, whether subject to the Army Act 1950 or not, in whose custody he is lawfully placed, and whether he is or is not his superior officer[2];

(3) resists an escort whose duty it is to apprehend him or to have him in charge[3];

(4) breaks out of barracks, camp or quarters[4];

(5) neglects to obey any general, local or other order[5];

(6) impedes the provost-marshal[6] or any person lawfully acting on his behalf, or when called upon, refuses to assist in the execution of his duty a provost-marshal or any person lawfully acting on his behalf[7]; or

(7) uses criminal force to or assaults any person bringing provisions or supplies to the forces[8],

shall, upon conviction by court-martial, be liable to suffer imprisonment for a term which may extend, in the case of the offences specified in the provision of the Army Act 1950[9] to two years, and in the case of the offences specified in the other clauses to 10 years, or such less punishment as mentioned in the Army Act 1950[10].

1 Army Act 1950 s 42 (a). As to the meaning of 'affray' see the Indian Penal Code 1960 s 159. An affray differs from assault in that the former cannot be committed in a private place whereas the latter may take place anywhere; further an affray is an offence against the public peace while an assault is an offence against the person of an individual. Manual of Military Law, Volume II, 2011, the Army Act 1950 s 42 notes.

2 Army Act 1950 s 42 (b). As to the meaning of 'criminal force' and 'assault' see the Indian Penal Code 1860 ss 349 to 351. A charge may be laid under this clause for assaulting a civil policeman, if the person committing the assault is subject to military law, and has been lawfully placed in the policeman's custody. Manual of Military Law, Volume II, 2011, the Army Act 1950 s 42 notes.

3 Army Act 1950 s 42(c). Resistance may be direct violence but threatening words and a threatening attitude might amount to resisting an escort, if the threats were sufficient to deter the escort from arresting the accused. Resistance may also be passive, e.g. a person lying down and refusing to move, if physically able to move, could be said to resist. The particulars of the charge should specify the nature of the resistance. The court will use their military knowledge to determine whether it was the duty of the escort to apprehend the accused or to have him in charge. Manual of Military Law, Volume II, 2011, the Army Act 1950 s 42 notes.

4 Army Act 1950 s 42(d). This offence consists of a person quitting barracks, etc., at a time when he had no right to do so, either because he was on duty or under punishment, or because of some regulation or order; and it is immaterial whether the offence was managed by violence, stratagem, disguise, or simply by walking past a sentry unnoticed. The particulars of the charge must show that the absence from barracks etc., was without permission, or otherwise unlawful, and also if the accused was in any way confined to barracks that fact must be alleged in the charge. In a charge for breaking out of barracks, it must be proved that the accused left the confines of the barracks, as charged. A charge of breaking out of quarters would hold good in the case of a person quartered in one part of a barrack and improperly leaving that part for another part where he had no right to be. Manual of Military Law, Volume II, 2011, the Army Act 1950 s 42 notes.

5 Army Act 1950 s 42(e). The orders specified in this clause mean standing orders or orders having a continuous operation or applicable continuously over a period of time to all officers, junior commissioned officers, warrant officer and other ranks present in a certain geographical area, such as command, or station or in a certain military formation. Ignorance of the order is no excuse, if the order is one which the accused ought in the, ordinary course to know. But a misapprehension reasonably arising from want of clarity in the order is a ground for exculpation. The existence of the orders and the fact of the neglect must be proved. A written order cannot be proved by oral testimony. Evidence must also be given to show that the order was duly posted or brought to the notice of the accused, or that he was otherwise in a position to be acquainted with its contents. Manual of Military Law, Volume II, 2011, the Army Act 1950 s 42 notes.

6 As to the meaning of 'provost-marshal' see **[0032]**. A provost-marshal includes a provost-marshal appointed under any law for the time being in force relating to the government of the navy or air force and any person legally exercising authority under him of on his behalf. The court may exercise their military knowledge as to whether a person was a provost-marshal, or a person legally exercising authority under or on behalf of the provost-marshal but it will be open to the accused to show that the person he is charged with impeding was not properly appointed

provost-marshal or was not lawfully acting on his behalf. Manual of Military Law, Volume II, 2011, the Army Act 1950 s 42 notes.

7 Army Act 1950 s 42(f).

8 Army Act 1950 s 42(g).

9 Ie specified in the Army Act 1950 s 42(d) and (e).

10 Ie as mentioned in the Army Act 1950 s 71. Army Act 1950 s 42.

[0096] Fraudulent enrolment Any person subject to the Army Act 1950[1] who commits any of the following offences, that is to say (1) without having obtained a regular discharge from the corps or department to which he belongs, or otherwise fulfilled the conditions enabling him to enrol or enter, enrols himself in, or enters the same or any other corps or department or any part of the naval or air forces of India or the territorial army[2]; or (2) is concerned in the enrolment in any part of the forces[3] of any person when he knows or has reason to believe such person to be so circumstanced[4] that by enrolling he commits an offence against the Army Act 1950[5], shall, upon conviction by court-martial, be liable to suffer imprisonment for a term which may extend to five years or such less punishment as mentioned in the Army Act 1950[6].

A person who leaves one corps or department and enrolls himself in another does not prima facie commit the offence of deserting the service, though he irregularly and improperly exchanges one branch of that service for another. If, however, at the time of leaving his first corps or department, he had no intention of re-enrolling himself, and only did so as an afterthought, or if he absented himself to avoid a particular military service, e.g., service abroad, his offence is desertion, though a convict on a charge framed under the Army Act 1950[7] would also be legal. An offence under the Army Act s 43 could be committed by a person who belongs to a corps or department and enrolls himself again in the same corps or department. Trial in respect of fraudulent enrolment is not barred by the Army Act 1950 except in the case of a person, other than an officer, who has subsequently to the commission of the offence served continuously in an exemplary manner[8] for not less than three years with any portion of the regular army[9].

1 As to the persons subject to the Army Act 1950; see **[0039]**.

2 Army Act 1950 s 43(a). As to the definition of 'corps'; see **[0015]**. As to the definition of 'department'; see **[0019]**. As to the meaning of 'Territorial Army'; see **[0040]**.

3 As to the meaning of 'the Forces'; see **[0022]**.

4 The term 'so circumstanced' implies that where he is subject to the Army Act 1950, so that he is guilty of fraudulent enrolment under s 43 (a) or where, having previously served, he again enrolls without declaring the circumstances of his previous service, so that he commits an offence under s 44.

5 Army Act 1950 s 43(b).

6 Ie as mentioned in the Army Act 1950 s 71. Army Act s 43.

7 Ie Army Act s 43 (a).

8 As to the meaning of 'exemplary manner', see Defence Services Regulations, Regulations for the Army, Volume I, paragraph 466: (a) For the purpose of exemption from trial under Army Act 1950 s 122, a junior commissioned officer, warrant officer or other rank will be considered as having served in an exemplary manner if at any time during his service subsequent to the commission of the offence he has had no red ink entry in his conduct sheet for a continuous period of three years. (b) When exemption from trial on a charge of fraudulent enrolment has been earned by exemplary service in any corps, the commanding officer of that corps will be held responsible for

notifying the fact to the individual's previous corps; Manual of Military Law, Volume II, 2011, the Army Act 1950 s 43 notes.

9 The Army Act 1950 s 122 (4). Manual of Military Law, Volume II, 2011, the Army Act 1950 s 43 notes.

[0097] False answers on enrolment Any person having become subject to[1] the Army Act 1950 who is discovered to have made at the time of enrolment a wilfully[2] false answer to any question set forth in the prescribed form of enrolment which has been put to him by the enrolling officer[3] before whom he appears for the purpose of being enrolled shall, upon conviction by court-martial, be liable to suffer imprisonment for a term which may extend to five years or such less punishment as mentioned in the Army Act 1950[4].

1 The wording of the provision differs from the wording of the other penal sections of the Army Act 1950. This is essential since at the time the offence is committed the person is not actually subject to the Army act 1950; as he does not become so subject until he has signed the enrolment paper under the Army Act s 14. Manual of Military Law, Volume II, 2011, the Army Act 1950 s 44 notes.

2 The expression 'wilfully' means intentionally or deliberately and not by accident or inadvertence: *Ramchandra Narsimha Kullarni v State of Mysore* AIR 1964 SC 1701, [1964] 7 SCR 606, (1964) Cr LJ 609. The answer must be wilfully false; thus where a person might reasonably having been mistaken as to the fact of his having 'served', where, for instance, he was discharged as unfit before he had done duty or worn uniform, a conviction would not be upheld. Where the false answer is as to age, proof must be given by calling someone to prove that the accused is the person referred to in the birth certificate or register; and a mere production of a birth certificate or register is not sufficient. The falsity of the answer must be proved in accordance with the normal rules of evidence. The original enrolment paper must be produced at the trial as evidence under the Army Act 1950 s 141(1). If false answers are given to two or more questions in the enrolment paper, each false answer should be included in a separate charge. Manual of Military Law, Volume II, 2011, the Army Act 1950 s 44 notes.

3 As to the meaning 'enrolling officer' see Army Rules 1954 r 7.

4 Ie as mentioned in the Army Act 1950 s 71; Army Act 1950 s 44.

[0098] Unbecoming conduct Any officer[1], junior commissioned officer[2] or warrant officer[3] who behaves in a manner unbecoming his position and the character expected of him shall, upon conviction by court-martial, if he is an officer, be liable to be cashiered or to suffer such less punishment as mentioned in the Army Act 1950 . Where he is a junior commissioned officer or a warrant officer, he shall be liable to be dismissed or to suffer such less punishment as mentioned in the Army Act 1950[4].

For behaviour to be blameworthy under this provision, it must be unbecoming both the accused's position and the character expected of him as an officer, junior commissioned officer or warrant officer. Where behaviour complained of is not punishable under this provision, a charge may lie under the Army Act 1950 s 63, if such conduct is prejudicial both to good order and military discipline[5]. The offence under this provision[6] must be distinguished from the offence of disgraceful conduct of a cruel, indecent or unnatural kind under the Army Act s 46(a). As a rule a charge should not be preferred under this provision where such behaviour amounts to a specific offence under any other section of the Army Act 1950. The conduct is not brought within the scope of this provision by merely applying to it the statutory language; unless the conduct proved was unbecoming of the accused's position and the character expected of him as an officer etc., having regard to its nature and to the circumstances in which it took place[7]. This provision is invoked in cases where an officer has given stumer cheques, found using unfair means in a promotion examination, or behaving in a riotous manner, etc. There can be no attempt to commit this offence as unbecoming conduct would include the act as well as an attempt to do such act. This provision is not applicable to civilians with relative rank and subject to the Army Act 1950[8]. An offence under this provision should not be dealt with summarily under the Army Act 1950[9].

1 As to the definition of 'officer' see **[0029]**.

2 As to the definition of 'junior commissioned officer' see **[0023]**.

3 As to the definition of 'warrant officer' see **[0037]**.

4 Ie as mentioned in the Army Act 1950 s 71; Army Act 1950 s 45. See *Union of India v S K Rao Capt* AIR 1972 SC 1137, (1972) 1 SCC 144, [1972] 2 SCR 447: for removal from service under the Army Act 1950 s 19 read with the Army Rules 1954 r 14, a court-martial is not necessary. The provisions of the Army Act 1950 ss 19 and 45 are, therefore, mutually exclusive.

5 Manual of Military Law, Volume II, 2011, the Army Act 1950 s 45 notes; see **[0116]**.

6 Ie Army Act 1950 s 45.

7 Manual of Military Law, Volume II, 2011, the Army Act 1950 s 45 notes.

8 Ie under the Army Act 1950 s 2(1)(i).

9 Ie under the Army Act 1950 ss 83, 84 and 85.

[0099] Certain forms of disgraceful conduct Any person subject to the Army Act 1950[1] who commits any of the following offences, that is to say:

(1) is guilty of any disgraceful conduct of a cruel, indecent or unnatural kind[2];

(2) malingers, or feigns, or produces disease or infirmity in himself, or intentionally delays his cure or aggravates his disease or infirmity[3]; or

(3) with intent to render himself or any other person unfit for service, voluntarily causes hurt to himself or that person[4],

shall, upon conviction by court-martial, be liable to suffer imprisonment for a term which may extend to seven years or such less punishment as mentioned in the Army Act 1950[5].

The particulars of a charge of disgraceful conduct under the Army Act s 46 (a) must specify the details of the act or acts alleged to constitute the disgraceful conduct of the kind charged. In the case of an officer accused, the same facts may constitute an offence either of disgraceful conduct under this clause[6] or of unbecoming conduct under the Army Act 1950 s 45. In the absence of any evidence of a definite act of indecency or attempted indecency, mere words that an indecent or unnatural act was committed are not sufficient to constitute an offence under this clause though a charge may probably lie under the Army Act 1950 s 63. Cruelty usually involves the doing of some positive act, such as beating or killing or torturing. In most cases therefore the conduct alleged will amount to an offence under some other section of AA. But there are circumstances in which cruelty can be charged against a person who has culpably failed to do what he ought to have done e.g., where a definite duty was imposed upon a person to do something and he failed to perform that duty. Disgraceful conduct of an unnatural kind ordinarily implies the commission or at least the attempted commission of an offence under the Indian Penal Code 1860 s 377[7]. Therefore, in framing charges under this provision[8], the charge should invariably be laid for disgraceful conduct of an indecent kind unless the evidence permits of the averment in the particulars that an unnatural offence as ordinarily understood was committed or at least attempted. To 'malinger' is to pretend illness or infirmity which does not exist, in order to escape duty. To 'feign' disease or infirmity means that the accused person exhibits appearances resembling the genuine symptoms of disease or infirmity which, to his knowledge, are not due to such disease or infirmity, but have been produced artificially or purposes of deceit; e.g., simulating fits or mental disease. To 'produce' disease is wilfully to cause genuine disease to develop, e.g., by the infection of microbes or poisonous drugs. Similarly a person who refuses to undergo a surgical operation or to be inoculated or vaccinated does not incur any liability under the Army Act 1950 s 45 (b) or s 41 as any puncturing or cutting of the skin, mucuous membrane or tissues amounts to a surgical operation nor can he be punished for refusing to allow anaesthetic to be administered[9].

1 As to the persons subject to the Army Act 1950; see **[0039]**.

2 Army Act 1950 s 46(a).

3 Army Act 1950 s 46(b).

4 Army Act 1950 s 46(c). In a case under this clause evidence must be given of the intent required therein but it would be sufficient to raise a presumption of that intention if the act in question was shown to have been done wilfully and not accidentally. 'Any other person' means any other person subject to the Army Act 1950 and not a civilian. As to the definition of the term 'voluntarily causing hurt' see the Indian Penal Code 1860 ss 319 and 321.

5 Ie as mentioned in the Army Act 1950 s 71; Army Act 1950 s 46.

6 Ie under the Army Act 1950 s 46(a).

7 Manual of Military Law, Volume II, 2011, the Army Act 1950 s 46 notes.

8 Ie under the Army Act 1950 s 46(a).

9 Manual of Military Law, Volume II, 2011, the Army Act 1950 s 46 notes.

[0100] Ill-treating subordinates Any officer[1], junior commissioned officer[2], warrant officer[3] or non-commissioned officer[4] who uses criminal force to or otherwise ill-treats any person subject to the Army Act 1950, being his subordinate in rank or position, shall, upon conviction by court-martial, be liable to suffer imprisonment for a term which may extend to seven years or such less punishment as mentioned in the Army Act 1950[5].

An accused charged under this provision[6] with using criminal force may be convicted of an attempt to use criminal force or assault as a special finding under the Army Act 1950 s 139 (3) and (8). Using criminal force or ill-treatment under this provision need not necessarily be consequent on or connected with the superior status of the accused. The only essentials necessary to constitute an offence under this provision are (i) that the accused used criminal force to or ill-treated a person subject to the Army Act 1950 subordinate to him in rank or position; and (ii) that the accused was acquainted with the identity of the person against whom he used criminal force or whom he ill-treated[7].

1 As to the definition of 'officer' see **[0029]**.

2 As to the definition of 'junior commissioned officer' see **[0023]**.

3 As to the definition of 'warrant officer' see **[0037]**.

4 As to the definition of 'non-commissioned officer' see **[0026]**.

5 Ie as mentioned in the Army Act 1950 s 71; Army Act 1950 s 47. As to the definitions of 'force' and 'criminal force' see the Indian Penal Code 1860 ss 349 and 350.

6 Ie under the Army Act 1950 s 47. A sepoy cannot commit an offence under this provision. Manual of Military Law, Volume II, 2011, the Army Act 1950 s 47 notes.

7 Manual of Military Law, Volume II, 2011, the Army Act 1950 s 47 notes.

[0101] Intoxication Any person subject to the Army Act 1950 who is found in a state of intoxication, whether on duty or not, shall, upon conviction by court-martial[1], if he is an officer, be liable to be cashiered or to suffer such less punishment as mentioned in the Army Act 1950. Where he is not an officer, he shall be liable, subject to the provisions of the Army Act 1950[2], to suffer imprisonment for a term which may extend to two years or such less punishment as mentioned in the Army Act 1950[3]. Where an offence of being intoxicated is committed by a person other than an officer when not on active service or not on duty, the period of imprisonment awarded shall not exceed six months[4].

Intoxication may be induced by opium or any similar drug, as well as by liquor[5]. This provision[6] creates only one single offence, viz. intoxication, and in all cases, whether the act was committed on duty or not on duty, the charge should be 'intoxication'. If the offence was committed on duty, or after; the accused had been warned for duty, the fact that the offence was so committed and the nature of the duty should be specified in the particulars of the charge as the character of the offence, from a military point of view, and therefore its proper punishment is materially affected by the circumstance. Intoxication will be regarded as having the ordinary meaning attached to it in civil life i.e., what an ordinary reasonable person would consider to be such and the fact that an offender is capable or incapable of performing his duty is not a decisive or exclusive test of drunkenness or sobriety. It is, however, one of the tests which should be applied by the court. A person suspected of being intoxicated cannot be put through any drill or test for the purpose of ascertaining his condition[7]. The offence of intoxication cannot be tried jointly[8].

1 As to the definition of 'court martial' see **[0016]**.

2 Ie subject to the Army Act 1950 s 48(2).

3 Ie as mentioned in the Army Act 1950 s 71; Army Act 1950 s 48(1).

4 Army Act 1950 s 48(2).

5 Manual of Military Law, Volume II, 2011, the Army Act 1950 s 48 notes.

6 Ie Army Act 1950 s 48.

7 See: Defence Services Regulations, Regulations for the Army, Volume I, paragraph 393(b). For instructions as to the treatment of a person in arrest for being intoxicated, see: Defence Services Regulations, Regulations for the Army, Volume I, paragraph 393 (b).

8 Manual of Military Law, Volume II, 2011, the Army Act 1950 s 48 notes.

[0102] Permitting escape of person in custody Any person subject to the Army Act 1950 who commits any of the following offences, that is to say (1) when in command of a guard, picquet, patrol or post, releases without proper authority, whether wilfully[1] or without reasonable excuse, any person[2] committed to his charge, or refuses to receive any prisoner or person so committed[3]; or (2) wilfully or without reasonable excuse allows to escape any person who is committed to his charge, or whom it is his duty to keep or guard[4], shall, upon conviction by court-martial, be liable, if he has acted wilfully to suffer imprisonment for a term which may extend to 14 years or such less punishment as mentioned in the Army Act 1950[5]; and if he has not acted wilfully, to suffer imprisonment for a term which may extend to two years or such less punishment as mentioned in the Army Act 1950[6].

There is a difference between the two provisions of the Army Act 1950 s 49. For the purpose of clause (a), the person released must have been committed to the charge of the accused, while for the purpose of clause (b) the person allowed to escape need only have been a person whom the accused was under a duty to keep or guard. The offender under clause (a) must be in the command of the guard, piquet, patrol or post, and previously have had the released person committed to his charge; while under clause (b) the offender who allows a person to escape need not have any such command. Where a doubt exists as to the accused having acted wilfully, he should be charged with having acted without reasonable excuse. An act or omission is wilful if it is done or made by a person with the intention of allowing the escape of a person committed to his charge or whom it is his duty to guard or keep[7]. If the charge is one of wilfully committing the offence, the court martial may, if it is not satisfied that the act was wilful, make a special finding under the Army Act 1950 s 139(7) that the accused acted without reasonable excuse[8].

1 The meaning attached to the word 'wilfully' has to be ascertained on a close examination of the scheme and the nature of the legislation in which the word appears and the context in which it is used; *Ramachandra Narasimha Kulakrni v State of Mysore* AIR 1964 SC 1701: [1964] 7 SCR 606, (1964) Cr LJ 609.

2 The 'person' improperly released or allowed to escape need not be a person subject to the Army Act 1950. Manual of Military Law, Volume II, 2011, the Army Act 1950 s 49 notes.

3 Army Act 1950 s 49(a). The words 'without proper authority' are in the nature of an exception and it will rest on the accused to show that he had the proper authority. The court may use their military knowledge under the Army 1950 s 134 with respect to whether any authority alleged by the accused to exist, was or was not sufficient.

4 Army Act 1950 s 49(b). What constitutes an 'escape' is a question of fact, but before a prisoner can be said to have escaped, it must be shown that he was out of control and reach of his escort.

5 Ie as mentioned in the Army Act 1950 s 71.

6 Ie as mentioned in the Army Act 1950 s 71; Army Act 1950 s 49.

7 Manual of Military Law, Volume II, 2011, the Army Act 1950 s 49 notes.

8 Manual of Military Law, Volume II, 2011, the Army Act 1950 s 139 notes.

[0103] Irregularity in connection with arrest or confinement Any person subject to the Army Act 1950[1] who commits any of the following offences, that is to say: (1) unnecessarily detains a person in arrest or confinement without bringing him to trial, or fails to bring his case before the proper authority[2] for investigation[3]; or (2) having committed a person to military custody fails without reasonable cause to deliver at the time of such committal, or as soon as practicable, and in any case within 48 hours thereafter, to the officer or other person into whose custody the person arrested is committed, an account in writing signed by himself of the offence with which the person so committed is charged[4], shall, upon conviction by court-martial, be liable to suffer imprisonment for a term which may extend to two years or such less punishment as mentioned in the Army Act 1950[5]. The Regulations for the Army provides[6]: Under the Army Act 1952 s 50 (a), serious liability is incurred by an officer who causes any person to be detained in custody for an unnecessarily long period without investigating the case or taking steps to bring him to trial. The Army Rules 1954 prohibits an accused being detained in military custody which includes open arrest for longer than 2 months without the sanction of the chief of the army staff and for longer than 3 months without the approval of the Central Government[7].

1 As to the persons subject to the Army Act 1950 see **[0039]**.

2 As to the meaning of 'proper authority' see the Army Rules 1954 r 2 (d), which states: when used in relation to any power, duty, act or matter, such military authority as, in pursuance of these rules or the regulations made under the Army Act 1950 or the usages of the service, exercises or performs that power or duty or is concerned with the act or matter.

3 Army Act 1950 s 50(a). In support of a charge laid under this provision for either of the offences therein created the prosecutor will have to prove the facts which either show or enable the court to infer that the accused could have brought the person under arrest or in confinement to trial or brought his case before the proper authority for investigation. If these are proved the court may infer that it was unnecessary to keep the person, in question, in custody in the absence of an explanation by the accused. When a guard commander wilfully or without reasonable excuse refuses to receive a person committed to his charge, he commits an offence under this provision in respect of his improper refusal. Manual of Military Law, Volume II, 2011, the Army Act 1950 s 50 notes.

4 Army Act 1950 s 50(b). As to the definition of 'military custody' see **[0024]**. The fact that no account in writing of the type required in under this provision was received by the guard etc., commander from the person committing the person at the time of committal or within 48 hours thereafter would not entitle the guard commander to refuse custody or charge or to effect the subsequent release of any such person. Manual of Military Law, Volume II, 2011, the Army Act 1950 s 50 notes.

5 Ie as mentioned in the Army Act 1950 s 71; Army Act 1950 s 50.

6 Ie the Defence Service Regulations, Regulations for the Army 1987, paragraph 408(b).

7 Ie the Army Rules 1954 r 27(3).

[0104] Escape from custody Any person subject to the Army Act 1950 who, being in lawful custody, escapes or attempts to escape, shall, upon conviction by court-martial, be liable to suffer imprisonment for a term which may extend to five years or such less punishment as mentioned in the Army Act 1950[1]. The term 'lawful custody' under this provision means not only military custody as defined in the Army Act 1950[2] but any lawful custody; so that a person subject to the Army Act 1950 may be convicted under this provision when escaping or attempting to escape from a police officer who has under the Army Act 1950[3] arrested him as a suspected deserter. Similarly when a person is held by the provost marshal or a person legally exercising authority under him or on his behalf under the Army Act 1950[4], he may be charged with an offence under this section. Military custody includes open arrest, and a person escaping or attempting to escape while in open arrest could be charged under this section. A person subject to the Army Act 1950, who escapes from arrest and absents himself without leave, may be charged with, and convicted of, both under this section, and of the subsequent desertion or absence without leave; under the provisions of the Army Act 1950[5]. A prisoner is said to 'escape' when he unlawfully goes out of sight beyond the control of the person in whose custody he is placed. Attempt to escape is itself made a substantive offence and a charge for the same should be preferred under this provision[6].

1 Ie as mentioned in the Army Act 1950 s 71; Army Act 1950 s 51.

2 Ie in the Army Act 1950 s 3(xiii); see **[0024]**.

3 Ie Army Act 1950 s 105(2).

4 Ie under the Army Act 1950 s 107.

5 Ie under the Army Act 1950 s 38(1) or 39(a).

6 Manual of Military Law, Volume II, 2011, the Army Act 1950 s 51 notes.

[0105] Offences in respect of property Any person subject to the Army Act 1950 who commits any of the following offences, that is to say:

(1) commits theft of any property belonging to the government, or to any military, naval or air force mess, band or institution, or to any person subject to military, naval or air force law[1];

(2) dishonestly misappropriates or converts to his own use any such property[2];

(3) commits criminal breach of trust in respect of any such property[3];

(4) dishonestly receives or retains any such property in respect of which any of the offences under the abovestated provisions has been committed, knowing or having reason to believe the commission of such offence[4];

(5) wilfully destroys or injures any property of the government entrusted to him[5]; or

(6) does any other thing with intent to defraud, or to cause wrongful gain to one person or wrongful loss to another person[6],

shall, upon conviction by court-martial, be liable to suffer imprisonment for a term which may extend to 10 years or such less punishment as mentioned in the Army Act 1950[7].

Stealing from a person subject to military law is regarded as a particularly disgraceful military offence, considering that in the daily routine of barrack life, persons must constantly leave exposed their arms, uniform and equipment as well as their private property, such as money, watches, etc., trusting to the honour of their comrades. Persons subject to the Army Act 1950 committing offences involving moral turpitude, fraud, theft, dishonesty and culpable negligence involving financial loss of public or regimental property will be tried by court martial or prosecuted before a civil court. Such cases will not be disposed of summarily or by administrative action; and the punishments in such cases will be deterrent and commensurate with the gravity of the offence[8]. Offences falling within the purview of this provision may be tried both by the ordinary criminal court as also by the court martial both of which have concurrent jurisdiction[9]. If the stolen property has been recovered, it should be produced in court and identified by its owner and by any other witnesses who mention it in their evidence. If it has not been recovered its value or approximate value should be entered in the particulars of the charge and proved in evidence so that the court, if it convicts the accused, may add an award of stoppages to its sentence. where an offender is sentenced by court martial to be placed under stoppages in respect of any property stolen, etc., by him, due allowance must be made, in enforcing such stoppages, for money, or the value of any property found upon him and appropriated by way of restitution under the Army Act 1950[10]. The captured enemy property becomes the property of the Government[11].

1 Army Act 1950 s 52(a). As to the meaning of 'theft' see the Indian Penal Code 1860 s 378. The term 'any property' means any moveable property. For the implication of the term 'possession' see the Indian Penal Code 1860 s 27.

2 Army Act 1950 s 52(b). As to the meaning of 'dishonestly' see the Indian Penal Code 1860 s 24. As to the meaning of 'criminal misappropriation' see the Indian Penal Code 1860 s 403. Converts to his own use: There must be actual conversion of the thing appropriated to the use of some person other than the person entitled thereto. Mere retention of property would not warrant a conviction under this clause; unless there is evidence that the accused used that property; for instance when a clerk received certain sums on various dates but entered them in the accounts on each occasion some days after and it was found that the clerk was not in difficulties and did not use the amount, the mere retention by him of the money for some days would not constitute an offence under this clause. Manual of Military Law, Volume II, 2011, the Army Act 1950 s 52 notes.

3 Army Act 1950 s 52(c). As to the meaning of 'criminal breach of trust' see the Indian Penal Code 1860 s 405. To constitute an offence under this clause, there must be dishonest misappropriation by a person in whom confidence is placed as to the custody or management of the property in respect of which the breach of trust is charged. There must be an entrustment which, in its most general significance, imports a handing over the possession for some purpose which may not imply the conferring of any proprietary right at all. A person is said to be entrusted with

dominion over property when it remains legally in the owner's possession but he is given a limited authority to deal with it. Manual of Military Law, Volume II, 2011, the Army Act 1950 s 52 notes.

4 Army Act 1950 s 52(d). The offence of dishonestly receiving property under this clause has practically the same meaning as under the Indian Penal Code 1860 s 411, except that this clause is only limited to property of the description mentioned in clause (a) of s 52 of the Army Act 1950. Receives or retains: A person cannot be convicted of receiving if he had no guilty knowledge at the time of receipt. But he is guilty of 'retaining' if he subsequently knows or has reason to believe that the property was obtained by theft, criminal misappropriation or criminal breach of trust. The offence of dishonest retention may be completed without any guilty knowledge at the time of receipt. A person who is proved to have stolen etc., property cannot be convicted of retaining it. In clauses (a) to (c) of s 52 of the Army Act 1950, if the property belongs to some person or institution not included in the categories contained in this clause, the accused can only be charged under the Army Act 1950 ss 52(f) or 69 or dealt with by a civil court.

5 Army Act 1950 s 52(e). As to the meaning of 'wrongful gain' and 'wrongful loss' see the Indian Penal Code s 23. Wilfully destroys or injures: A charge for destroying or injuring the property here mentioned must be laid under this provision, and not under the Army Act s 69. The prosecutor must adduce evidence which will either prove, or enable the court to infer, that the injury was not accidental or done by some other person. If the injury appears to be the result of neglect, it will be for the court to determine whether the neglect was wilful and intended to injure the property, or was mere carelessness. In the latter case no offence under this clause would be committed. Manual of Military Law, Volume II, 2011, the Army Act 1950 s 52 notes.

6 Army Act 1950 s 52(f). With intent to defraud: A person is said to do a thing fraudulently if he does that thing with intent to defraud but not, otherwise; see the Indian Penal Code 1860 s 25. The terms 'fraud' and 'defraud' are not found defined in the Indian Penal Code 1860. The word 'defraud' is of double meaning in the sense that it either may or may not imply deprivation. Whenever the words 'fraud' or 'intent to defraud' or 'fraudulently' occur in the definition of a crime two elements at least are essential to the commission of the crime; namely first, deceit or an intention to deceive or in some cases mere secrecy; and secondly, either actual injury or possible injury or an intent to expose some person either to actual injury or to a risk of possible injury by means of that deceit or secrecy. This intent is very seldom the only or the principal intention entertained by; the fraudulent person, whose principal object in nearly every case is his own advantage. As to the meaning of the term 'does any other thing'; an act or omission which would fall under any other clause or any other section of the Army Act 1950 should not be made the subject matter of a charge under this clause. But in doubtful cases, the charge should be laid under this clause. In order to constitute an offence under this clause, it is not sufficient to couple the description of an act which can bear an innocent construction with an averment of intent to defraud. The act alleged to have been committed with intent to defraud must itself appear from the particulars of the charge to be a wrong act though it need not necessarily amount to an offence under the ordinary criminal law. Mere irregularity in accounts, due to incompetence or ignorance of bookkeeping, would not be sufficient under this clause, to constitute an offence as no fraudulent conduct is involved. However acts such as, with intent to defraud, presenting for signature acquaintance rolls, containing entries known to be false; or charging money for railway warrants; tickets, or vouchers, to which a person is entitled free of charge, would all amount to offences of a fraudulent nature for the purposes of this clause. Manual of Military Law, Volume II, 2011, the Army Act 1950 s 52 notes. As to the meaning of 'wrongful loss or wrongful gain' see the Indian Penal Code 1860 s 23.

7 Ie as mentioned in the Army Act 1950 s 71; Army Act 1950 s 52.

8 Defence Service Regulations, Regulations for the Army, Volume I, paragraph 432.

9 *Superintendent & Remembrancer of Legal Affairs v Usha Ranjan Roy Choudhury* AIR 1986 SC 1655, (1986) Supp SCC 190, (1986) Cr LJ 1248.

10 The Army Act 1950 s 151; see **[0237]**.

11 Manual of Military Law, Volume II, 2011, the Army Act 1950 s 52 notes.

[0106] Extortion and corruption A person subject to the Army Act 1950[1] who commits any of the following offences, that is to say, (1) commits extortion[2]; or (2) without proper authority exacts from any person[3] money, provisions or service[4]; shall, upon conviction by court-martial, be liable to suffer imprisonment for a term which may extend to 10 years or such less punishment as mentioned in the Army Act 1950[5].

1 As to the persons subject to the Army Act 1950; see **[0039]**.

2 Army Act 1950 s 53(a). As to the meaning of 'extortion' see the Indian Penal Code 1860 s 383.

3 'Any person' means a person whether subject to the Air Force Act 1950 or not. Manual of Military Law, Volume II, 2011, the Army Act 1950 s 53 notes.

4 Army Act 1950 s 53(b). The court will use their military knowledge under the Army Act 1950 s 134 to judge whether any authority alleged by the accused to exist was or was not sufficient; see **[0220]**.

5 Ie as mentioned in the Army Act 1950 s 71; Army Act 1950 s 53.

[0107] Making away with equipment Any person subject to the Army Act 1950 who commits any of the following offences, that is to say:

(1) makes away with, or is concerned in making away with, any arms, ammunition, equipment, instruments, tools, clothing or any other thing[1] being the property of the government issued to him for his use or entrusted to him[2];

(2) loses by neglect anything mentioned above[3]; or

(3) sells, pawns, destroys or defaces any medal or decoration granted to him[4],

shall, upon conviction by court-martial, be liable to suffer imprisonment for a term which may extend in the case of the offences specified in the first provision to 10 years, and in the case of the offences specified in the other clauses to five years, or such less punishment as mentioned in the Army Act 1950[5].

1. 'Any other thing' should be *ejusdem generis* i.e., part of the accused's kit which he is bound to maintain or his general military equipment supplied by the Government; such 'other thing' should be specified in the statement and particulars of the charge. Manual of Military Law, Volume II, 2011, the Army Act 1950 s 54 notes.

2 Army Act 1950 s 54 (a). Clothing in this clause may include hospital clothing issued to a person subject to the Army Act 1950 or civilian clothing issued from military sources. Manual of Military Law, Volume II, 2011, the Army Act 1950 s 54 notes.

3 Army Act 1950 s 54(b). This provision is not intended to punish a person for a deficiency in his kit occasioned by accident or mere carelessness but for loss by culpable neglect. On the other hand, the fact that a person has not got his arms, service necessaries, etc., at a time when it was his duty to have them (i.e., at a kit inspection), is prima facie evidence of his having lost them by neglect. The onus of proving 'neglect' always remains on the prosecution. But once the loss is proved, the court is entitled to expect the accused to offer some explanation of it, and if he gives none, it is open to the court to conclude that the loss must have been due to his negligence. If he gives an explanation which may reasonably be true and which if true is inconsistent with negligence, even if the court is not convinced of its truth, he must be acquitted, since a reasonable doubt as to his negligence then remains. Manual of Military Law, Volume II, 2011, the Army Act 1950 s 54 notes.

4 Army Act 1950 s 54(c).

5 Ie as mentioned in the Army Act 1950 s 71; Army Act 1950 s 54.

[0108] Injury to property Any person subject to the Army Act 1950 who commits any of the following offences, that is to say:

(1) destroys or injures any property mentioned in the provision of the Army Act 1950[1] or any property belonging to any military, naval or air force mess, band or institution, or to any person subject to military, naval or air force law, or serving with, or attached to, the regular army[2];

(2) commits any act which causes damage to, or destruction of, any property of the government by fire[3]; or

(3) kills, injures, makes away with, ill-treats or loses any animal entrusted to him[4],

shall, upon conviction by court-martial, be liable, if he has acted wilfully, to suffer imprisonment for a term which may extend to 14 years or such less punishment as mentioned in the Army Act 1950; and if he has acted without reasonable excuse to suffer imprisonment for a term which may extend to seven years or such less punishment as mentioned in the Army Act 1950[5].

1 Ie mentioned in the Army Act 1950 s 54(a).

2 Army Act 1950 s 55 (a).

3 Army Act 1950 s 55 (b).

4 Army Act 1950 s 55 (c). To constitute an offence under the above-stated or this clause the act must be either committed wilfully or without reasonable excuse. Manual of Military Law, Volume II, 2011, the Army Act 1950 s 55 notes.

5 Ie as mentioned in the Army Act 1950 s 71; Army Act 1950 s 55.

[0109] False accusations Any person subject to the Army Act 1950 who commits any of the following offences, that is to say:

(1) makes a false accusation against any person subject to the Army Act 1950, knowing or having reason to believe such accusation to be false[1]; or

(2) in making a complaint under the provisions of the Army Act 1950[2] makes any statement affecting the character of any person subject to the Army Act 1950, knowing or having reason to believe[3] such statement to be false or knowingly and wilfully[4] suppresses any material facts[5],

shall, upon conviction by court-martial, be liable to suffer imprisonment for a term which may extend to five years or such less punishment as mentioned in the Army Act 1950[6].

1 Army Act 1950 s 56 (a). This clause implies an accusation being made to some superior authority which would lead to the superior exercising his authority by enquiry or otherwise or the accusation must mean some assertion made publicly or to another person, which, if true, would expose the person respecting whom it is made to punishment or to moral censure. An accusation may be either verbal or in writing. Before an accused can be convicted of a charge under this clause, it must be proved that the accusation was made against the person named in the particulars of the charge, that it was false and that the accused knew or had reason to believe that it was false. Manual of Military Law, Volume II, 2011, the Army Act 1950 s 56 notes. As to the meaning of 'reason to believe' see the Indian Penal Code 1860 s 26.

2 Ie under the Army Act 1950 s 26 or 27.

3 As to the meaning of 'reason to believe' see the Indian Penal Code 1860 s 26.

4 The meaning attached to the word 'wilfully' has to be ascertained on a close examination of the scheme and the nature of the legislation in which the word appears and the context in which it is used; *Ramachandra Narasimha Kulakrni v State of Mysore* AIR 1964 SC 1701: [1964] 7 SCR 606, (1964) Cr LJ 609.

5 Army Act 1950 s 56(b). It is not necessary that the false statement affecting the character of an officer or other person should be directly related to the subject of the complaint. It is sufficient if the false statement is calculated to create prejudice against the officer etc., with reference to whom the complaint is addressed. Manual of Military Law, Volume II, 2011, the Army Act 1950 s 56 notes.

6 Ie as mentioned in the Army Act 1950 s 71; Army Act 1950 s 56.

[0110] Falsifying official documents and false declaration Any person subject to the Army Act 1950 who commits any of the following offences, that is to say:

(1) in any report, return, list, certificate, book or other documents made or signed by him, or of the contents of which it is his duty to ascertain the accuracy, knowingly makes, or is privy to the making of any false or fraudulent statement[1];

(2) in any document of the description mentioned above knowingly makes, or is privy to the making of, any omission, with intent to defraud[2];

(3) knowingly and with intent to injure any person, or knowingly and with intent to defraud, suppresses, defaces, alters or makes away with any document which it is his duty to preserve or produce[3];

(4) where it is his official duty to make a declaration respecting any matter, knowingly makes a false declaration[4]; or

(5) obtains for himself, or for any other person, any pension, allowance or other advantage or privilege by a statement which is false, and which he either knows or believes to be false or does not believe to be true, or by making or using a false entry in any book or record of by making any document containing a false statement, or by omitting to make a true entry or document containing a true statement[5],

shall, upon conviction by court-martial, be liable to suffer imprisonment for a term which may extend to 14 years or such less punishment as mentioned in the Army Act 1950[6].

1 Army Act 1950 s 57(a). A report (which must be in writing), return, certificate or other document mentioned herein must be one executed by the accused in his capacity as a person subject to the Army Act 1950 and not in civil capacity. The 'other document' which should be *ejusdem generis*, should be specified in the statement and particulars of the charge. A trivial error in the report should not, in the absence of fraud or bad faith, be made the ground of a charge under this and the following clause. Manual of Military Law, Volume II, 2011, the Army Act 1950 s 57 notes.

2 Army Act 1950 s 57(b). If a person makes false entries as to payments made in a book which it was his duty to keep in his official capacity he may be charged with knowingly making false statement under clause (a) above or, if it can be shown that he intended to defraud by means of the entries, he may be charged with knowingly making a fraudulent statement. Similarly, if he omits to make in the book entries of payments made by him or to him he may; if the evidence justifies such a course, be charged with knowingly making such omissions with intent to defraud under clause (b). Manual of Military Law, Volume II, 2011, the Army Act 1950 s 57 notes.

3 Army Act 1950 s 57(c).

4 Army Act 1950 s 57(d). The suppression, etc., of a document is not an offence under this clause if it is affected only with intent to deceive and not to defraud. The question as to the duty of the accused to preserve or produce

the document will be determined by the court using their military knowledge. The particulars of a charge under this clause should show the capacity or appointment on account of which it was the accused's duty to produce or preserve the document. Manual of Military Law, Volume II, 2011, the Army Act 1950 s 57 notes.

5 Army Act 1950 s 57(e). Other advantage or privilege must be of a similar kind. Obtaining pension or other such advantage may be for himself or any other person whether subject to the Army Act 1950 or not. Manual of Military Law, Volume II, 2011, the Army Act 1950 s 47 notes.

6 Ie as mentioned in the Army Act 1950 s 71; Army Act 1950 s 57.

[0111] Signing in blank and failure to report Any person subject to the Army Act 1950[1] who commits any of the following offences, that is to say:

(1) when signing any document relating to pay, arms, ammunition, equipment, clothing, supplies or stores, or any property of the government fraudulently[2] leaves in blank any material part for which his signature is a voucher[3]; or

(2) refuses or by culpable neglect omits to make or send a report or return which it is his duty to make or send[4],

shall, upon conviction by court-martial, be liable to suffer imprisonment for a term which may extend to seven years or such less punishment as mentioned in the Army Act 1950[5].

1 As to the persons subject to the Army Act 1950; see **[0039]**.

2 As to the meaning of 'fraudulently' see the Indian Penal Code 1860 s 25.

3 Army Act 1950 s 58 (a).

4 Army Act 1950 s 58 (b). The report must be in writing and the neglect must be culpable, i.e., something more than mere forgetfulness or mistake. Manual of Military Law, Volume II, 2011, the Army Act 1950 s 58 notes.

5 Ie as mentioned in the Army Act 1950 s 71; Army Act 1950 s 58.

[0112] Offences relating to court martial Any person subject to the Army Act 1950 who commits any of the following offences, that is to say:

(1) being duly summoned or ordered to attend as a witness before a court martial[1], wilfully or without reasonable excuse[2], makes default in attending[3];

(2) refuses to take an oath or make an affirmation legally required by a court martial to be taken or made[4];

(3) refuses to produce or deliver any document in his power or control legally required by a court martial to be produced or delivered by him[5];

(4) refuses when a witness to answer any question which he is by law bound to answer[6]; or

(5) is guilty of contempt of court martial by using insulting or threatening language, or by causing any interruption or disturbance in the proceedings of such court[7],

shall, upon conviction by court martial, be liable to suffer imprisonment for a term which may extend to three years or such less punishment as mentioned in the Army Act 1950[8].

There is no restriction, debarring a court-martial from trying any of the offences specified in this provision[9] when committed in respect of itself. However, as a rule, courts should accept an apology sufficient to vindicate their dignity without resorting to extreme measures. The procedure for dealing with similar offences when committed by civilians or persons amenable to naval or air force law is contained in the Army Rules 1954[10].

1 As to the definition of court martial; see **[0016]**. The convening officer, the presiding officer, the judge advocate or the commanding officer of the accused person may, by summons under his hand, require the attendance, at a time and place to be mentioned in the summons, of any person either to give evidence or to produce any document or other thing. The Army Act 1950 s 135 (1).

2 An act or omission is wilful if it is done or made by a person with the intention of allowing the escape of a person committed to his charge or whom it is his duty to guard or keep. Where a doubt exists as to the accused having acted wilfully, he should be charged with having acted without reasonable excuse. If the charge is one of wilfully committing the offence, the court may, if it is not satisfied that the act was wilful, make a special finding under the Army Act 1950 s 139 (7) that the accused acted without reasonable excuse.

3 Army Act 1950 s 59(a).

4 Army Act 1950 s 59(b). A person who for reasons of sincerity of which the court is satisfied, refuses to take an oath, must be given the opportunity of making an affirmation; see the Army Act 1950 s 131(2) and the Army Rules 1954 r 140. The offence is not complete unless there is proof of a refusal both to take the oath and to make an affirmation provided option so to do is given to the accused. The charges of refusing to take an oath legally required by a court-martial to be taken and refusing to make an affirmation legally required by a court-martial to be made; may, therefore, be properly drawn in the alternative. Manual of Military Law, Volume II, 2011, the Army Act 1950 s 59 notes.

5 Army Act 1950 s 59(c). The Indian Evidence Act 1872 ss 123, 124 and 162 deal with privilege of official documents. When a witness is directed by summons to produce a document which is in his possession or power, he must bring it to court, notwithstanding any objection that he may have with regard to its production or admissibility. After this has been done it rests solely with the court to hear the objection or the claim as to privilege, and to decide whether it should be allowed. Manual of Military Law, Volume II, 2011, the Army Act 1950 s 59 notes.

6 Army Act 1950 s 59(d). Because a person is competent to give evidence, he cannot be compelled to answer every question he may be asked when giving evidence and which is relevant to the matter in issue. For instance, on an incriminating question being put to a witness, he is entitled to ask to be excused from answering it, and if after he has asked to be excused, the court compels him to answer (as they are entitled to do) his answer cannot be proved against him at any criminal proceedings except a prosecution for giving false evidence by such answer. Manual of Military Law, Volume II, 2011, the Army Act 1950 s 59 notes.

7 Army Act 1950 s 59(e). A court martial begins to sit from the time the members take their seats for the purposes of trial, even before they are sworn/affirmed, and anything which would be a contempt after the court was sworn/ affirmed would be a contempt once the members have so taken their seats. Manual of Military Law, Volume II, 2011, the Army Act 1950 s 59 notes.

8 Ie as mentioned in the Army Act 1950 s 71; Army Act 1950 s 59.

9 Ie under the Army Act 1950 s 59; see **[0375]**.

10 The Army Rules 1954 r 150.

[0113] False evidence Any person subject to the Army Act 1950 who, having been duly sworn or affirmed before any court martial or other court competent under the Army Act 1950 to administer, an oath or affirmation, makes any statement which is false and which he either knows or believes to be false or does not believe to be true, shall, upon conviction by court-martial, be liable to suffer imprisonment for a term which may extend to seven years or such less punishment as mentioned in the Army Act 1950[1].

The offence specified in this provision is in many respects similar to the offence of giving false evidence under the Indian Penal Code 1860[2]. The courts referred to in this provision are court martial[3], court of inquiry on illegal absence under the Army Act 1950[4], court of inquiry on recovered prisoners of war[5] and any other court of inquiry when the officer assembling the court has directed that the evidence be recorded on oath or affirmation under the Army Act 1950[6]. The proceedings of the court-martial or court of inquiry before which false evidence is alleged to have been given are not admissible as evidence that the accused gave the evidence as charged. The officer who recorded the proceedings, or some other person, who heard the evidence given, must prove by oral evidence this fact and that the accused was duly sworn/affirmed[7].

1 Ie as mentioned in the Army Act 1950 s 71; Army Act 1950 s 60.

2 The Indian Penal Code 1860 s 191.

3 As to the definition of 'court martial' see **[0016]**.

4 Ie under the Army Act 1950 s 106 and the Army Rules 1954 r 181(b).

5 Ie under the Army Act 1950 s 191(2)(d) and the Army Rules 1954 r 181(a).

6 Ie under the Army Act 1950 s 191(2)(d) and the Army Rules 1954 r 181(c).

7 Manual of Military Law, Volume II, 2011, the Army Act 1950 s 60 notes.

[0114] Unlawful detention of pay Any officer[1], junior commissioned officer[2], warrant officer[3] or non-commissioned officer[4] who, having received the pay of a person subject to the Army Act 1950 unlawfully detains or refuses to pay the same when due, shall, upon conviction by court-martial, be liable to suffer imprisonment for a term which may extend to 10 years or such less punishment as mentioned in the Army Act 1950[5]. This provision is a corollary of the Army Act 1950 s 25 which provides that the pay of any person subject to the Army Act 1950 shall be paid without any deductions other than those authorised by or under Army Act 1950[6] or any other Act[7].

1 As to the definition of 'officer' see **[0029]**.

2 As to the definition of 'junior commissioned officer' see **[0023]**.

3 As to the definition of 'warrant officer' see **[0037]**.

4 As to the definition of 'non-commissioned officer' see **[0026]**.

5 Ie as mentioned in the Army Act 1950 s 71; Army Act 1950 s 61.

6 For deductions authorised by or under the Army Act 1950 see ss 90 and 91; see **[0384]** and **[0385]** and the Army Rules 1954 r 205.

7 Manual of Military Law, Volume II, 2011, the Army Act 1950 s 61 notes.

[0115] Offences in relation to aircrafts and flying Any person subject to the Army Act 1950 who commits any of the following offences, that is to say:

(1) wilfully or without reasonable excuse damages, destroys or loses any aircraft or aircraft material belonging to the government[1]; or

(2) is guilty of any act or neglect likely to cause such damage, destruction or loss[2]; or

(3) without lawful authority, disposes of any aircraft or aircraft material belonging to the government[3]; or

(4) is guilty of any act or neglect in flying, or in the use of any aircraft, or in relation to any aircraft or aircraft material, which causes or is likely to cause loss of life or bodily injury to any person[4]; or

(5) during a state of war, wilfully and without proper occasion, or negligently, causes the sequestration by or under the authority of neutral State, or the destruction in a neutral State of any aircraft belonging to the government[5],

shall, upon conviction by court-martial, be liable, if he has acted wilfully, to suffer imprisonment for a term which may extend to 14 years or such less punishment as mentioned in the Army Act 1950 and, in any other case, to suffer imprisonment for a term which may extend to five years or such less punishment as mentioned in the Army Act 1950[6].

If an accused is charged under this provision[7] with wilfully damaging an aircraft he may be found guilty of damaging it without reasonable excuse under the Army Act 1950 s 139(7) if the evidence justifies this course. The terms 'aircraft' and 'aircraft material' have not been defined in the Army Act 1950. They should, be construed in the light of the definitions given in the Air Force Act 1950 which are as follows: 'aircraft' includes aeroplanes, balloons, kite balloons, airships, gliders or other machines for flying; and 'aircraft material' includes any engines, fittings, guns, gear, instruments or apparatus for use in connection with aircraft, and any of its components and accessories and petrol oil, and any other substance used for providing motive power for planes[8].

1 Army Act 1950 s 62(a). The word 'government' denotes the Central Government or the government of a state. As to the meaning of 'government' see General Clauses Act 1897 s 3(8)(b).

2 Army Act 1950 s 62(b). The word 'neglect' in this clause means culpable neglect.

3 Army Act 1950 s 62(c).

4 Army Act 1950 s 62(d).

5 Army Act 1950 s 62(e).

6 Ie as mentioned in the Army Act 1950 s 71; Army Act 1950 s 62.

7 Ie under Army Act 1950 s 62.

8 The Air Force Act 1950 s 4(ii) and (iii); see **[0472]** and **[0473]**.

[0116] Violation of good order and discipline Any person subject to the Army Act 1950 who is guilty of any act or omission[1] which, though not specified in the Army Act 1950, is prejudicial to good order and military discipline shall, upon conviction by court-martial, be liable to suffer imprisonment for a term which may extend to seven years or such less punishment as mentioned in the Army Act 1950[2].

A charge under this provision[3], as a rule, should not be preferred where special provision for the offence is made elsewhere in the Army Act 1950; however, in a proper case an alternative charge may be added under this provision. A charge under this provision must recite its actual words, i.e., there must be charged an 'act' or 'omission' prejudicial to good order and military discipline. An 'omission' to be punishable under this section must amount to neglect which is wilful or culpable. The term 'negligence' has been defined by judicial pronouncements as the omission to do something which a reasonable man, guided upon those considerations which ordinarily regulate the conduct of human affairs, would do, or doing something which a prudent and reasonable man would not do having due regard to the facts and circumstances of the case[4]. The words 'good order' as used in this provision[5] are wide enough to include good order in the sense in which the worlds would be understood in civil life and applicable to civilians in the sense in which they would be understood in military life as applicable to the persons subject to the Army Act 1950. Some of the instances of offences charged under this provision[6] are: negligent performance of duties connected with money or stores resulting in a deficiency and loss; being in improper possession of public property or of property belonging to a comrade (where there is no evidence of actual theft); improperly using government transport and petrol for private purposes; sending an anonymous letter to his commanding officer or other superiors; wearing badges of rank to which the bearer is not entitled; neglect of duty when a sentry, on guard, etc. if an offence is covered under this section, while awarding the punishment the court martial has to keep in view the spirit behind the Army Act 1950[7] and it has to give due regard to the nature and degree of the offence[8].

1 As to the meaning of 'act' and 'omission' see the Indian Penal Code 1860 s 33.

2 Ie as mentioned in the Army Act 1950 s 71; Army Act 1950 s 63.

3 Ie Army Act 1950 s 63.

4 *Padmacharan Naik*, 1982 Cr LJ NOC 192 (Ori).

5 Ie Army Act 1950 s 63.

6 Ie Army Act 1950 s 63.

7 Ie Army Act 1950 s 72.

8 *Ex-Naik Sardar Singh v Union of India* AIR 1992 SC 417: (1991) 3SCC 213.

[0117] Miscellaneous Offences Any person subject to the Army Act 1950 who commits any of the following offences, that is to say:

(1) being in command at any post or on the march, and receiving a complaint that anyone under his command has beaten or otherwise maltreated or oppressed any person, or has disturbed any fair or market, or committed any riot or trespass, fails to have due reparation made to the injured person or to report the case to the proper authority[1];

(2) by defiling any place of worship, or otherwise, intentionally insults the religion or wounds the religious feelings of any person[2];

(3) attempts to commit suicide, and in such attempt does any act towards the commission of such offence[3];

(4) being below the rank of warrant officer, when off duty, appears without proper authority, in or about camp or cantonments, or in or about, or when going to or returning from, any town or bazaar, carrying a rifle, sword or other offensive weapon[4];

(5) directly or indirectly accepts or obtains, or agrees to accept or attempts to obtain, for himself or for any other person, any gratification as a motive or reward for procuring the enrolment of any person, or leave of absence, promotion or any other advantage or indulgence for any person in the service[5]; or

(6) commits any offence against the property or person of any inhabitant of, or resident in, the country in which he is serving[6],

shall, upon conviction by court-martial, be liable to suffer imprisonment for a term which may extend to seven years or such less punishment as mentioned in the Army Act 1950[7].

1 Army Act 1950 s 64(a). The offence under this clause can only be committed by a person who is in command. As to the definition of 'riot' and 'trespass', see the Indian Penal Code 1960 ss 146 and 441.

2 Army Act 1950 s 64(b). The offence under this clause, which is similar to offence under the Indian Penal Code 1860 chapter XV is based on the Fundamental Right to freedom of religion conferred by the Constitution of India, Article 27.

3 Army Act 1950 s 64(c). This offence is the same as the civil offence under the Indian Penal Code 1860 s 309. A person should not be charged with attempted suicide unless the circumstances of the case make it clear that he seriously intended to take his life. Where the action falls short of a deliberate intent to end his life, the accused could be charged under the Army Act 1950 ss 46(c) or 63; the charge alleging that the accused rendered himself temporarily unfit for duty by reason of his conduct.

4 Army Act 1950 s 64(d). This offence can only be committed by the non-commissioned officer or sepoy. The term 'cantonment' is not restricted to those stations which have been declared to be cantonments' for the purposes of the Cantonments Act 1924. The troops are considered to be in a cantonment for the purposes of the Army Act 1950 when they are quartered in any station or locality as a permanent, or semi-permanent, arrangement. Manual of Military Law, Volume II, 2011, the Army Act 1950 s 64 notes.

5 Army Act 1950 s 64(e). This term 'gratification' is not restricted to a pecuniary gratification or a gratification estimable in money. The offence is complete if the gratification is given with the intention indicated, and it is not necessary that the enrolment or other object should be actually procured. An attempt to obtain a gratification (e.g., by asking for it) is punishable equally with the actual receipt of one. An attempt to give a gratification (e.g., an offer of a bribe) is an abetment of the offence by way of instigation and is punishable under the Army act ss 66 or 68 as the case may be. Manual of Military Law, Volume II, 2011, the Army Act 1950 s 64 notes.

6 Army Act 1950 s 64(f). At to the meaning of term 'offence'; see **[0028]**. The word 'offence' here means an offence which would be punishable, if committed in India as a civil offence. Manual of Military Law, Volume II, 2011, the Army Act 1950 s 64 notes.

7 Ie as mentioned in the Army Act 1950 s 71; Army Act 1950 s 64.

[0118] Attempt Any person subject to the Army Act 1950 who attempts to commit any of the offences specified in the provisions of the Army Act 1950[1]; and in such attempt does any act towards the commission of the offence[2], shall, upon conviction by court-martial, where no express provision is made by the Army Act 1950 for the punishment of such attempt, be liable, (1) if the offence attempted to be committed is punishable with death, to suffer imprisonment for a term which may extend to 14 years or such less punishment as mentioned in the Army Act 1950; and (2) if the offence attempted to be committed is punishable with imprisonment, to suffer imprisonment for a term which may extend to one-half of the longest term provided for that offence or such less punishment as mentioned in the Army Act 1950[3].

Attempt consists of the intent to commit a crime, combined with the doing of some act, but falling short of its actual commission. The commission of an offence broadly comprise of four stages (i) forming an intention to commit the crime or offence; (ii) making preparation for its commission; (iii) attempting to commit the crime; and (iv) actual commission of the offence. The first two stages do not attract culpability while the third and fourth stages do. If due to certain reasons, the attempt fails, the crime is not complete but the law punishes for attempting the same and the person is guilty of attempting to commit the offence[4].

1 Ie in the Army Act 1950 ss 34–64. Attempts to commit the offences specified in the Army Act 1950 ss 34 to 64 are, except where such attempts are specifically provided for (e.g., an attempt to desert), triable under the Army Act 1950 s 65. Attempts to commit civil offences are not triable under this section but are triable under the Army Act 1950 s 69 read with the Indian Penal Code 1860 s 511. Manual of Military Law, Volume II, 2011, the Army Act 1950 s 65 notes.

2 'Does any act towards the commission of the offence': There is a difference between the preparation antecedent to an offence and the actual attempt. To constitute an attempt to commit an offence there must be an intent to commit the offence, a commencement of the commission and an act done towards the commission. An act

is said to be done towards the commission of the offence when the offence remains incomplete only because something yet remained to be done, which the person intending to commit the offence is unable to do by reason of circumstances independent of his own volition. These words must not be construed to include all acts, however, remote, which tend towards the commission of the offence. The thing done may be too small or it may proceed too short a way towards the accomplishment of the offence for the law to notice it as an attempt. It must in every case be a question depending upon the circumstances whether a particular act done (with the requisite intention) towards the commission of the offence is sufficiently proximate to its commission to constitute an attempt or is so remote as to merely constitute preparation for its commission. Manual of Military Law, Volume II, 2011, the Army Act 1950 s 65 notes.

3 Ie as mentioned in the Army Act 1950 s 71; Army Act 1950 s 65.

4 *Abhayanand Mishra v State of Bihar* AIR 1961 SC 1698.

[0119] Abetment of offences that have been committed Any person subject to the Army Act 1950 who abets[1] the commission of any of the offences specified in the Army Act 1950[2] shall, upon conviction by court-martial, if the act abetted is committed in consequence of the abetment and no express provision is made by the Army Act 1950 for the punishment of such abetment, be liable to suffer the punishment provided for that offence or such less punishment as mentioned in the Army Act 1950[3].

1 As to the meaning of 'abetment' see the Indian Penal Code 1860 s 107.

2 Ie in the Army Act 1950 ss 34–64.

3 Ie as mentioned in the Army Act 1950 s 71; Army Act 1950 s 66. A person subject to the Army Act 1950 who abets a person not subject to the Army Act 1950 e.g., a civilian or a person subject to the Navy Act 1957 etc., in doing a thing which would have been an offence under the Army Act 1950 had the person doing it been subject thereto is not punishable under the Army Act 1950 s 66 to 68. Such cases will, however, generally fall within the terms of the Army Act 1950 s 69. Manual of Military Law, Volume II, 2011, the Army Act 1950 s 66 notes.

[0120] Abetment of offences punishable with death and not committed Any person subject to the Army Act 1950 who abets[1] the commission of any of the offences punishable with death under the provisions of the Army Act 1950[2], shall, upon conviction by court-martial, if that offence be not committed in consequence of the abetment, and no express provision is made by the Army Act 1950 for the punishment of such abetment, be liable to suffer imprisonment for a term which may extend to 14 years or such less punishment as mentioned in the Army Act 1950[3].

1 As to the meaning of 'abetment' see the Indian Penal Code 1860 s 107.

2 Ie under the Army Act 1950 ss 34, 37 and 38(1).

3 Ie as mentioned in the Army Act 1950 s 71; The Army Act 1950 s 67. The provision deals with punishment for abetment of offences punishable with death where the offence has not been committed in consequence of the abetment and no specific provision for such punishment has been prescribed by the Army Act 1950. Manual of Military Law, Volume II, 2011, the Army Act 1950 s 67 notes.

[0121] Abetment of offences punishable with imprisonment and not committed Any person subject to the Army Act 1950 who abets[1] the commission of any of the offences specified in the Army Act 1950[2] and punishable with imprisonment shall, upon conviction by court-martial, if that offence be not committed in consequence of the abetment, and no express provision is made by the Army Act 1950 for the punishment of such abetment, be liable to suffer imprisonment for a term which may extend to one-half of the longest term provided for that offence or such less punishment as mentioned in the Army Act 1950[3].

1 As to the meaning of 'abetment' see the Indian Penal Code 1860 s 107.

2 Ie as specified in the Army Act 1950 ss 34–64.

3 Ie as mentioned in the Army Act 1950 s 71; Army Act 1950 s 68.

[0122] Civil Offences Subject to the provisions of the Army Act 1950[1], any person subject thereto who at any place in or beyond India, commits any civil offence[2], shall be deemed to be guilty of an offence against the Army Act 1950 and, if charged therewith[3] under this provision, shall be liable to be tried by a court martial. On conviction, such person shall be punishable as follows: (1) if the offence is one which would be punishable under any law in force in India with death or with transportation, he shall be liable to suffer any punishment, other than whipping, assigned for the offence, by the aforesaid law and such less punishment as mentioned in the Army Act 1950[4]; and (2) in any other case, he shall be liable to suffer any punishment, other than whipping, assigned for the offence by the law in force in India, or imprisonment for a term which may extend to 7 years, or such less punishment as mentioned in the Army Act 1950[5].

A person subject to the Army Act 1950 who while stationed in any country other than India commits an act or omission which is an offence under the civil law of that country but which if committed in India would not amount to a 'civil offence' cannot be charged under this provision though a charge may properly be framed under the Army Act 1950[6] if the facts so warrant. For instance, the Official Secrets Act 1923 s 13(3) requires that, before proceedings can be instituted in the criminal courts, the consent of the appropriate government must be obtained. When a member of the armed forces is tried under this provision for an offence under the Narcotic Drugs and Psychotropic Substances Act 1985, the procedural safeguards as contained in that statute would be applicable to him in its entirety, irrespective of the jurisdiction of the general court martial or other courts[7].

1 'Subject to the provisions of the Army Act 1950 s 70': This provision prohibits trial by court martial three civil offences viz., murder, culpable homicide not amounting to murder of a person not subject to military, naval or air force law e.g. a civilian or rape in relation for such a person, unless the said offence was committed (i) while on active service, (ii) at any place outside India, or (iii) at a frontier post specified by the central government, by notification in, this behalf.

2 As to the meaning of 'civil offence' see **[0010]**.

3 The expression 'charged' in the provision has been used in the sense of 'accused' and not in the sense of 'charge-sheeted'. The expression, 'if charged therewith under this provision' occurring in the Army Act 1950 s 69 therefore means, 'if accused of an offence' which in the Army Act is an offence because of the legal friction created by this provision. *Major Gopinathan v State of Madhya Pradesh*, AIR 1963 MP 249; 1963 (2) Cr LJ 161.

4 Ie as mentioned in the Army Act 1950 s 71; Army Act 1950 s 69(a).

5 Ie as mentioned in the Army Act 1950 s 71; Army Act 1950 s 69(b).

6 Ie the Army Act 1950 s 63.

7 *Union of India v L D Balam Singh* (2002) 9 SCC 73.

[0123] Civil offences not triable by courts martial A person subject to the Army Act 1950 who commits an offence of murder or culpable homicide not amounting to murder of a person not subject to military, naval or air force law or of rape[1] in relation to such a person, shall not be tried by a court martial, unless the offence is committed on active service[2] or at any place outside India[3], or at a frontier post specified by the Central

Government by notification[4]. Subject to the above exceptions a court-martial can try all civil offences committed by a person subject to the Army Act 1950[5].

In regard to offences which fall within the purview of the above provision, an offender may be tried only by court martial and there is no concurrent jurisdiction along with ordinary criminal courts[6]. On active service, the offence of rape is triable by court martial also in view of the Army Act 1950 s 70, but the accused not having been detained for court martial, the criminal court is competent to try him[7]. The question whether the court martial has the jurisdiction to try a person who commits an offence has to be adjudged from the provisions of the Army Act 1950 itself and not with reference to the Code of Criminal Procedure 1973[8].

1 The Criminal Law (Amendment) Act, 2013 has made several significant changes to the IPC s. 375, which defines the term rape. Under the new provision, a man is said to commit rape if he penetrates his own penis, or makes another man penetrate his penis, into the vagina, mouth, urethra or anus of a woman, or penetrates any other object, manipulates her body to cause penetration, or applies his own mouth, or makes another man apply his mouth to the vagina, anus or urethra of a woman. Such actions have to be committed in one of seven modes: against her will, without her consent, with her consent which has been obtained through threats, by posing as her husband, with her consent which was taken when she was intoxicated by alcohol or other substances, with/without consent when she is under the age of 18 years, or when she is unable to give her consent. An exception also has been provided for the purpose of medical examination. The punishment for rape is seven years at the least, and may extend up to life imprisonment. Any police officer, public servant, member of armed forces, or medical officer if commits rape, may be imprisoned for at least 10 years, but may be extended to imprisonment for life which shall mean the remainder of that person's natural life and with fine. This applies to rape cases that occur during communal riots, against pregnant women, girls under the age of 16 years. A punishment of life imprisonment, extending to death has been prescribed for situations where the rape concludes with the death of the victim, or the victim entering into a coma.

2 Army Act 1950 s 70(a). The expression 'while on active service' covers persons on 'casual leave'. The expression 'service' cannot be given a restricted meaning and equated with the expression 'on duty'. *Pritam Singh v State* 1980 Cr LJ 296.

3 Army Act 1950 s 70(b).

4 Army Act 1950 s 70(c).

5 Army Act 1950 s 69 and 70.

6 *Superintendent & Remembrancer of Legal Affairs v Usha Ranjan Roy Choudhury* AIR 1986 SC 1655, (1986) Supp SCC 190, (1986) Cr LJ 1248; also see *Joginder Singh v State of Himachal Pradesh* AIR 1971 SC 500, (1971) 3 SCC 86, (1971) Cr LJ 511.

7 *Roshan Law v State* 1971 Cr LJ 554.

8 *Madan Lal v Union of India* (2002) 10 SCC 185. The term 'rape' as defined under the Indian Penal Code 1860 s 375 is different and distinct from attempt to commit rape and hence in respect of an offence of attempt to commit rape, the jurisdiction of the court martial may not be said to be ousted by virtue of the Army Act 1950 s 70.

5. ARREST AND PROCEEDINGS BEFORE TRIAL

CONTENTS

PARA

A. ARREST AND CUSTODY

[0124] Introduction A person subject to Army Act 1950, charged with an offence, may be taken into military custody. The method of arresting a person in the army is informal. The offences under the Army Act are not classified as cognizable or non-cognizable. For arrest no warrant is required. Any senior officer is empowered to place under arrest any person subject to the Army Act 1950 who is accused of an offence. The order for placing the person under arrest can be oral or written. Military custody includes two types of arrests---the 'open arrest' and the 'close arrest'. When arrest is not described by the authority ordering it as open arrest, it means close arrest[1]. The restraint imposed under each type is according to the usages of the service and the regulations. Under closed arrest, a person is usually confined to a room or barracks and remains under the escort of a person of equal rank. Under open arrest, he remains under a moral restraint not to go beyond a certain area, usually the camp. It is not necessary that every person charged with an offence, must be put under close arrest. If the offence is not serious it may be investigated and disposed of without placing the offender under arrest. The following factors to be considered before placing an individual under close arrest: (i) availability of the individual for trial; (ii) individual may not abscond; (iii) individual may not harm to himself; (iv) individual may not temper with evidence or influence prosecution witnesses; and (v) in case the offence is serious like murder, mutiny or the ends of discipline require an immediate arrest to set an example[2]. Whenever a person working in the armed forces is proposed to be arrested, such person shall be provided the cause of arrest in writing for effecting his arrest. If the concerned authority fails to inform the causes in writing, it makes the arrest illegal. The rights guaranteed under art 21 of the Constitution cannot be taken away or abridged completely except according to the procedure established by law[3].

1 Defence Services Regulations, Regulations for the Army 1987, Volume I, paragraph 391(b).

2 Defence Services Regulations, Regulations for the Army 1987, Volume I, paragraph 392.

3 *Ajai Kumar Roy v Union of India* 2003 Cr LJ 3999 (AP).

[0125] Custody of offenders A person subject to the Army Act 1950 who is charged[1] with an offence may be taken into military custody[2] by an order of any superior officer[3]. An officer may order into military custody any officer, though he may be of a higher rank, engaged in a quarrel, affray or disorder[4]. The provisions of the Army Act 1950[5] are not discriminatory in view of art 33 of the Constitution conferring express power on Parliament to make law restricting and/or abrogating fundamental rights of Part III of the Constitution[6].

1 The term 'charge' referred here does not mean the formal written charge as mentioned in the Army Rules 1954 r 28 preferred by the commanding officer when it is decided to send the case for trial but a complaint or accusation that an offence has been committed and which gives rise to the preliminary investigation. Manual of Military Law,

Volume II, 2011, the Army Act 1950 s 101 notes.

2 Army Act 1950 s 101 (1). As to the meaning of 'military custody'; see **[0024]**. This expression is here restricted to the military custody of persons when charged with offences and does not apply to persons in military custody when undergoing sentences. Manual of Military Law, Volume II, 2011, the Army Act 1950 s 101 notes.

3 Army Act 1950 s 101 (2). As to the meaning of 'superior officer' see **[0036]**.

4 Army Act 1950 s 101 (3). As to the meaning of 'officer' see **[0029]**.

5 Ie the Army Act 1950 s 101 and 125.

6 *Gurnam Singh v Union of India* 1984 Cr LJ 718.

[0126] Duty of commanding officer in regard to detention It is the duty of a commanding officer to take care that a person under his command when charged with an offence is not detained in custody for more than 48 hours, without the charge being investigated, unless investigation within that period seems to him to be impracticable having regard to the public service[1]. A commanding officer who unnecessarily detains a person in arrest or confinement renders himself liable to a charge under the Army Act 1950 s 50(a). The case of every person, being detained in custody beyond a period of 48 hours, and the reason thereof, to be reported by the commanding officer to the general or other officer to whom application would be made to convene a general or district court-martial for the trial of the person charged[2]. In reckoning the period of 48 hours[3], Sundays and other public holidays shall be excluded[4]. Subject to the provisions of the Army Act 1950, the Central Government may make rules providing for the manner in which and the period for which any person subject to the Army Act 1950 may be taken into and detained in military custody, pending the trial by any competent authority for any offence committed by him[5].

1 Army Act 1950 s 102 (1). As to the meaning of 'commanding officer'; see **[0013]**. This provision applies in the case of officers as well as junior commissioned officers, warrant officers and other ranks, means that the investigation must be commenced within the time specified, though it may be impossible to complete it within that time. As to exclusion of Sunday and public holidays, see the Army Act 1950 s 102(3).

2 Army Act 1950 s 102 (2). The report should be made by letter and should refer specifically to the case, and state the reasons justifying the detention of the accused in custody without investigation. The absence of an important witness would justify a remand or the accused might be ordered to return to his duty with a specific intimation that his case will be investigated as soon as the absent witness is available. Manual of Military Law, Volume II, 2011, the Army Act 1950 s 102 notes.

3 Ie under the Army Act 1950 s 102 (1).

4 Army Act 1950 s 102 (3). Sundays and other public holidays are excluded when computing the period of 48 hours referred to in the Army Act 1950 s 102(1) though they are not so excluded for any other purpose e.g., time reckoned for the purposes of punishment or of any deduction of pay. Manual of Military Law, Volume II, 2011, the Army Act 1950 s 102 notes.

5 Army Act 1950 s 102 (4). The Army Rules 1954 r 27(3) has been framed under the Army Act 1950 s 102(4)

[0127] Interval between committal and court martial In every case where a person subject to the Army Act 1950[1], who is not on active service, remains in custody for a more than eight days, without a court martial for his trial being ordered to assemble; a special report giving reasons for the delay (i.e., delay report) shall be made by his commanding officer[2]. A similar report shall be forwarded at intervals of every eight days until a court martial is assembled or such person is released from custody[3].

1 Ie as mentioned in the Army Act 1950 s 101: see **[0125]**.

2 For 'special report' and 'form': see the Army Rules 1954, Appendix III, Part IV. For 'delay reports' see **[0128]**.

3 Army Act 1950 s 103. The object of this provision is to bring the accused to trial as soon as possible and to avoid delays in disposing of cases under the Army Act 1950. It is applicable whether the accused is in open or close arrest. The Army Act 1950 does not require these reports to be rendered where the accused is on active service. Manual of Military Law, Volume II, 2011, the Army Act 1950 s 103 notes.

[0128] Delay Reports The delay reports[1] shall be made to the authorities mentioned in the Army Rules 1954 at intervals of every eight days until a court martial is ordered to assemble, or a punishment is awarded under the provision of the Army Act 1950[2], or such person is released from custody[3]. A copy of every such report made on or after the 48 day of such custody shall be sent by the commanding officer direct to the deputy judge advocate general of the command in which such person is held in custody[4]. Detention in military custody beyond two months of a person subject to the Army Act 1950, who is not on active service and in whose case a court martial for trial has not been ordered to assemble, shall require the sanction of the chief of the army staff, or any officer authorized by him in this behalf with the approval of the Central Government. Such an officer, may sanction further detention for a specific period, which he may extend from time to time, subject to a total period of detention of three months[5]. Any such detention beyond a period of three months shall require the approval of the Central Government[6]. Pre-trial detention for a period beyond three months without the approval by the Central Government as required by the Army Rules 1954[7] would be illegal[8].

1 In the form specified in the Army Rules 1954 Appendix III, part IV.

2 Ie under the Army Act 1950 s 80.

3 Army Rules 1954 r 27(1).

4 Army Rules 1954 r 27(2).

5 Army Rules 1954 r 27(3)(i).

6 Army Rules 1954 r 27(3)(ii). Once a court martial has been ordered to assemble, e.g., a convening order is issued, the sanction of the chief of the army staff or the central government will not be necessary. The requirement of the Army Rules 1954 r 27 for obtaining sanction should not be circumvented by issue of a convening order far in advance of the date of trial. If necessary an accused person may be released from arrest without prejudice to his re-arrest, if trial cannot be convened within two or three months. If his detention beyond a period of two or three months is considered necessary, steps should be taken to obtain the sanction well in advance. An accused person should not be kept in such detention in anticipation of a sanction. Detaining an accused in custody beyond two or three months without a sanction, makes such detention illegal and a post-facto sanction obtained would not render such detention legal. Unnecessary detention in custody of an accused without bringing him to trial amounts an offence under the Army Act 1950 s 50(a). Manual of Military Law, Volume II, 2011, the Army Rules 1954 r 27 notes.

7 Ie as required by the Army rules 1954 r 27(3)(ii).

8 The Supreme Court has held: "The basic object of the Army Act 1950 ss 101-103, read with Army Rules 1954 r 27(3)(ii) appears to be to dispose of court martial cases expeditiously and to minimise the period of pre-trial detention so that a person charged under the Army Act should not be unnecessarily deprived of freedom on the ground that he is accused of an offence triable by court martial. The authorities cannot be permitted to deal with the liberty of a person subject to the Army Act 1950, in a casual manner and cannot be allowed by their commission or omission, to frustrate the object of speedy trial as envisaged by the Army Act." The Supreme Court directed that the delinquent shall be entitled to a sum of Rs 30,000 as compensation for his illegal pre-trial detention. *Bhuwneshwar Singh v Union of India* (1993) 4 SCC 327, (1994) SCC (Cr) 1.

[0129] Arrest by civil authorities Whenever any person subject to the Army Act 1950, who is accused of any offence under the Army Act 1950, is within the jurisdiction of any magistrate or police officer, such magistrate or police officer shall aid in the apprehension and delivery to military custody of such person upon receipt of a written application signed by his commanding officer[1].

1 Army Act 1950 s 104. This provision enjoins the civil authorities e.g., a magistrate or a police officer to assist in the arrest and delivery to military custody of a person accused of an offence under the Army Act 1950; Manual of Military Law, Volume II, 2011, the Army Act 1950 s 104 notes. As to the definition of 'commanding officer'; see **[0013]**.

[0130] Capture of deserters Whenever any person subject to the Army Act 1950 deserts, the commanding officer of the corps, department or detachment[1] to which he belongs, shall give written information of the desertion to such civil authorities as, in his opinion, may be able to afford assistance towards the capture of the deserter. The civil authorities are required to take steps for the apprehension of the said deserter in a manner as if he were a person for whose apprehension a warrant had been issued by a magistrate, and shall deliver the deserter, when apprehended, into military custody[2]. A police officer may arrest without warrant any person reasonably believed to be subject to the Army Act 1950, and to be a deserter or to be travelling without authority, and shall bring him without delay before the nearest magistrate, to be dealt with according to law[3].

The desertion or absence without leave of a person subject to the Army Act 1950 will be reported by an express letter[4] by the officer commanding the unit to the civil authorities. In no circumstances communications regarding deserters will be addressed to officials in the foreign countries. When any person including a Gorkha of Nepalese domicile overstays his leave in or deserts, a report will be sent to the Army Headquarters[5].

1 As to the meaning of 'corps', see the Army Rules 1954 r 187 (3); as to the meaning of 'department', see **[0019]**; as to the meaning of 'detachment': the enrolled personnel forming the establishment, for the time being, are examples of a detachment.

2 Army Act 1950 s 105(1). This provision is a special application of the powers granted to the civil authorities under the Army Act 1950 s 104. It lays down the procedure to be followed for apprehending deserters or suspected deserters and for dealing with persons so arrested. Manual of Military Law, Volume II, 2011, the Army Act 1950 s 105 notes.

3 Army Act 1950 s 105(2). The civil or military police will not arrest personnel at railway stations who are apparently on their way to rejoin their units and who are in possession of railway warrants and leave passes unless such leave passes show that they have overstayed their leave by at least 10 days. They will not in any circumstances take away soldiers' leave passes or railway warrants. Deserters/absentees who are apprehended by, or who surrender to the civil police will not be detained in civil jails. The station house officer of the police station who effects the arrest or accepts surrender of a deserter/absentee will arrange his dispatch to the nearest regimental centre or unit specified for the purpose. Information regarding the apprehension/surrender of the deserter/absentee will be given by the station house officer to the regimental centre or unit in advance. See the Defence Services Regulations, Regulations for the Army 1987, Volume 1, paragraph 378.

4 Ie on form IAFD-925.

5 See: The Defence Services Regulations, Regulations for the Army 1987, Volume 1, paragraph 377. As desertion reports invariably reveal the name and location of a deserter's unit, it is essential that such reports should bear the correct security classification. Reports by units in an operational area will be classified Secret, all others will be classified Confidential. The copy of the report sent to the civil police and the railway authorities on IAFD-925

will contain a clear request that on apprehension/surrender of the deserter a completed apprehension certificate (IAFD-910) will be handed over to the regimental centre or unit to whom the police escort hands over the deserter.

[0131] Escorts An officer, junior commissioned officer, warrant officer or non-commissioned officer under close arrest will be placed under the charge of an escort consisting of another officer, junior commissioned officer, warrant officer or non-commissioned officer of the same rank, if possible. The person under arrest, if required, can be placed under the charge of a guard, sentry or provost-marshal[1]. He will not leave his quarters or tent except to take such exercise, under supervision, as the medical officer considers necessary. An officer, JCO or WO under arrest will not wear sash, sword, belt or spurs[2]. A sepoy, on being placed under close arrest, will be placed in confinement under charge of a guard, piquet, patrol, sentry or provost-marshal and will be searched and deprived of knives or other weapons. The accommodation usually available in barracks for the temporary confinement of sepoys under close arrest is the guard detention room attached to a guard room, and similar smaller rooms for the confinement of those who are to be kept apart[3].

A women officer under closed arrest shall all the time remain under an escort of another women officer. Under no circumstances, she will be kept under a male escort. Where another women officer is not available in the unit, a women officer from other unit/stations will be made available under station arrangements. During her visit to other places for purposes of investigation, recording of summary of evidence, attending her trial etc., she shall be escorted by another woman officer who may be assisted by another male officer[4].

1 Defence Services Regulations, Regulations for the Army 1987, Volume I, paragraph 394(c) and 395(a).

2 Defence Services Regulations, Regulations for the Army 1987, Volume I, paragraph 394(b).

3 Defence Services 3Regulations, Regulations for the Army 1987, Volume I, paragraph 395 (b).

4 Army Headquarters AG Branch letter No A/56102/AG/DV-1, dated 26 June 1996.

[0132] Arrest in cases of intoxication A sepoy who is intoxicated will be placed under close arrest alone, if possible, in a guard detention room. He may be deprived of his bedding and boots, except when the weather is cold and he is likely to suffer in consequence. He will be visited, and his condition ascertained, at least every two hours by a non-commissioned officer of the guard and an escort. In case any symptoms of serious illness are observed, a medical officer will be sent for forthwith. A person suspected of being intoxicated will not be put through any drill or test for the purpose of ascertaining his condition. A person charged with intoxication will not be brought before an officer for investigation of the charge until he is sober. For this purpose 24 hours should usually be allowed to elapse before the investigation[1].

1 Defence Services Regulations, Regulations for the Army 1987, Volume I, paragraph 393.

[0133] Release from arrest The release of an officer[1] placed under arrest may be ordered either by the officer who imposed the arrest or by an officer superior to him. Once an arrest has been ordered and the matter has been reported to superior authority, it would not be proper to order the release of person without the sanction of such superior authority. An officer could be released from arrest without prejudice to re-arrest. In such a case, where such re-arrest is considered justified or necessary, it will always be affected by the person ordering the release or by some higher authority. Normally when an officer is released unconditionally, he will not be again be arrested on the same charge unless circumstances had changed and some new conditions arose which justified the action. The general rules applicable to the arrest of officers apply to junior commissioned officers, warrant officer and other ranks also[2].

1 As to the definition of 'officer'; see **[0029]**.

2 See the Defence Services Regulations, Regulations for the Army 1987, Volume I, paragraph 391-397, 401 and 402.

[0134] Restrictions under open arrest An officer, junior commissioned officer or warrant officer[1] under open arrest may take exercise at stated periods and within stated limits, which will usually be the precincts of the barracks or camp of his unit. These limits could be enlarged at the discretion of the commanding officer. He will not appear in any place of amusement or entertainment, or at public assemblies. He will also not appear outside his quarters or tent dressed otherwise than in uniform[2].

1 As to the definition of 'officer', 'junior commissioned officer' and 'warrant officer'; see **[0029], [0023] and [0037].**

2 Defence Services Regulations, Regulations for the Army 1987, Volume I, paragraph 394(d).

[0135] Arrest during the Trial by Court Martial The accused will be placed under close arrest before the commencement of the court martial. During the course of his trial he will remain under close arrest except, where the convening officer or an authority superior to him directs otherwise[1]. Where the sentence awarded in the open court is imprisonment or higher, the accused, if already under close arrest, will remain under close arrest, and if not under close arrest, will be taken into custody, unless the convening or confirming officer or an authority superior to him directs otherwise. Where the sentence announced in open court is lower in the scale of punishments than Imprisonment, the accused, if under arrest, will be released from arrest immediately after the trial without prejudice to re-arrest[2].

1 Defence Services Regulations, Regulations for the Army 1987, Volume I, paragraph 392(k). This provision is merely an administrative instruction. When an accused person is remanded for further investigation, or for trial by court martial, the question of arrest is a matter for the discretion of the commanding officer. It is always his duty to decide whether, having regard to all the circumstances, open or close arrest will best meet the case or whether the accused may be released without prejudice to re-arrest until trial or further orders. The commanding officer will also use his discretion to change the form of arrest from time to time according to the circumstances. Defence Services Regulations, Regulations for the Army 1987, Volume I, paragraph 392(j).

2 Defence Services Regulations, Regulations for the Army 1987, Volume I, paragraph 392(l).

[0136] Provost Marshals Provost marshals[1] may be appointed by the chief of the army staff or by any prescribed officer[2]. The duties of a provost-marshal are to take charge of persons confined for any offence, to preserve good order and discipline, and to prevent breaches of the same by persons serving in, or attached to, the regular army[3]. A provost marshal may at any time arrest and detain for trial any person subject to the Army Act 1950 who commits, or is charged with an offence[4] and may also carry into effect any punishment to be inflicted in pursuance of the sentence awarded by a court-martial, or by an officer exercising authority under the provisions of the Army Act 1950[5], but shall not inflict any punishment on his own authority[6]. However, no officer shall be so arrested or detained otherwise than on the order of another officer[7]. For the purposes of certain provisions of the Army Act 1950[8], a provost marshal shall be deemed to include a provost marshal appointed under any law for the time being in force relating to the government of the navy or air force, and any person legally exercising authority under him or on his behalf[9].

1 As to the definition of 'provost marshal'; see **[0032]**. So far as the duties and powers are concerned, a provost-marshal is also deemed to include a provost marshal appointed under naval and air force law or any person legally exercising authority under him or on his behalf. Manual of Military Law, Volume II, 2011, the Army Act 1950 s 107 notes.

2 Army Act 1950 s 107(1). As to the meaning of 'prescribed officer'; see the Army Rules 1954 r 197. Prescribed officer under the Army Act s 107 (1): The prescribed officer for the purposes of the Army Act 1950 s 107 (1) shall be the officer commanding an army, army corps, division or independent brigade or an officer commanding the forces in the field.

3 Army Act 1950 s 107(2).

4 A provost marshal or any officer working under him may at any time, arrest and detain for trial any person subject to the Army Act 1950 (even though superior in rank) who commits or is charged with an offence. However, an officer can be arrested or detained only on the order of another officer. Similarly, though any member of the Corps of Military Police can legally arrest a junior commissioned officer; he should not be so placed in arrest except under orders of an officer or another junior commissioned officer of the Corps of Military Police. It is an offence under the Army Act 1950 s 42(f) to impede the provost-marshal or any person, lawfully acting on his behalf or to refuse to assist the provost-marshal or person lawfully acting on his behalf. Manual of Military Law, Volume II, 2011, the Army Act 1950 s 107 notes.

5 Ie under the Army Act 1950 s 80: see **[0162]**.

6 Army Act 1950 s 107(3).

7 Army Act 1950 s 107(3) proviso.

8 Ie the Army Act 1950 s 107 (2) and (3).

9 Army Act 1950 s 107(4).

B. INVESTIGATION AND DISPOSAL OF CHARGES

[0137] Introduction In the system of military law, a commander occupies an important position. Unlike a superior in a civilian government organization, a military commander exercises discretion in deciding whether an offence should be charged and how an offender should be punished. One of the most difficult decisions facing a commander concerns the manner in which to dispose of the case. An administrative or disciplinary action may be taken against a military person who fails to meet or uphold the service's standard of conduct. The fundamental purpose of administrative or disciplinary processes is to foster and promote discipline and the type of behaviour required for the maintenance of operational effectiveness. The commander has following options for the resolution of disciplinary problems.

a. No Action: The commander may choose to take no action[1]. The circumstances surrounding an event may warrant that no adverse action be taken. The preliminary inquiry might indicate that the accused is innocent, that the evidence is inadmissible, or the commander may decide that other valid reasons exist for not prosecuting the alleged accused.

b. Administrative Action: The commander may initiate administrative action against a military offender[2]. He might decide that the best disposition for the offence and offender is to take administrative rather than punitive action.

c. Minor Summary Punishment: The commander may dispose of the offence summarily with a minor punishment[3]. The trial is conducted by the commanding officer or a superior officer depending upon the rank of the accused. The maximum punishment depends on the rank of the commander imposing punishment and the rank of the service member being punished. The military accused does not have a right to appeal against the commander's decision to the next higher commander.

d. Court Martial. The commander may dispose of the case with the help of a court martial. If he decides that the offence is serious enough to warrant trial by court martial, he may exercise the fourth option of preferring and forwarding charges. He may choose from four potential levels of court martial[4].

The military chain of command must use its powers appropriately in keeping with the context of the offence/ misconduct and the operational circumstances. The existence of an administrative action regime does not prevent a commander from proceeding directly to disciplinary action where it is more appropriate. Conversely, good management practice may require that certain professional failings be dealt with without recourse to either regime. Such minor transgressions could be corrected more informally and immediately.

1 The Army Rules 1954 r 22 (2): The commanding officer shall dismiss a charge brought before him, if, in his opinion, the evidence does not show that an offence under the Army Act 1950 has been committed, and may do so if, in his discretion he is satisfied that the charge ought not to be proceeded with.

2 Administrative actions could take two forms: (i) Under the Defence Services Regulations, Regulations for the Army 1987, Volume I paragraph 327 an officer or junior commissioned officer can be awarded a minor censure; and (ii) under the provisions of the Army Act 1950 ss 18—20, services of a person subject to the Army Act 1950 can be terminated, he could be administratively dismissed, removed or reduced to a lower rank or grade.

3 Under the provisions of the Army Act 1950 ss 80, 83, 84 and 85; see **[0162], [0166], [0167]** and **[0168]**.

4 The military offender could be tried by an appropriate court martial; see the Army Act 1950 s 108. These courts martial differ in the procedures, rights, and possible punishment that can be adjudged.

[0138] Delivery of Charges It is the duty of a person subject to the Army Act 1950[1], who commits any person into military custody to deliver at the time or within 48 hours thereafter to the officer or other person into whose custody the offender is committed, an account in writing signed by himself of the offence with which the person so committed is charged[2]. In case a charge report is not received within 48 hours, or other evidence sufficient to justify the continued arrest is not forthcoming, the commanding officer will, at the expiration of 72 hours from the time of committal, will order the release of the person in custody (without prejudice to his re-arrest)[3].

1 Under the Army Act 1950 s 50(b), see **[0103]**.

2 Defence Services Regulations, Regulations for the Army 1987, Volume I, paragraph 401(a).

3 Defence Services Regulations, Regulations for the Army 1987, Volume I, paragraph 401(b).

[0139] Guard Report The number, rank, name and offence of every person received into close arrest, and the rank and name of the person by whom he is charged, will be entered by the commander of the guard in his guard report, and the original charge report or its copy will be forwarded to the commanding officer of the person in custody[1]. The commander of the guard will, on the request of any person received into custody, inform him of the rank and name of the person preferring charges against him or ordering his arrest, and give to him a copy of the charge report as soon as he himself receives it[2].

1 Defence Services Regulations, Regulations for the Army 1987, Volume I, paragraph 401(c).

2 Defence Services Regulations, Regulations for the Army 1987, Volume I, paragraph 401(d).

[0140] Hearing of Charge The investigation of charges is to be carried out as prescribed in the Army Rules 1954[1]. Every charge[2] against a person subject to the Army Act 1950 shall be heard by the commanding officer in the presence of the accused. The accused shall have full liberty to cross-examine any witness against him, and to call such witness and make such statement as may be necessary for his defence[3]. However, where the charge against the accused arises as a result of investigating by a court of inquiry, wherein the provisions of the Army Rules 1954 r 180 have been complied with in respect of that accused, the commanding officer may dispense with the procedure described above[4]. The commanding officer shall dismiss a charge brought before him, if, in his opinion, the evidence does not show that an offence under the Army Act 1950 has been committed, and may do so if, in his discretion he is satisfied that the charge ought not to be proceeded with[5]. However, the commanding officer shall not dismiss a charge which he is debarred to try under the provisions of the Army Act 1950[6], without reference to superior authority as specified therein[7]. After compliance of the provisions of the Army Rule 1954 r 22 (1), if the commanding officer is of opinion that the charge ought to be proceeded with, he shall within a reasonable time[8]: (i) dispose of the case under the provisions of the Army Act 1950[9], in accordance with the prescribed manner and form[10]; (ii) refer the case to proper superior military authority[11]; (iii) adjourn the case for the purpose of having the evidence reduced to writing[12]; or (iv) if the accused is below the rank of warrant officer, order his trial by summary court martial[13]. However, the commanding officer shall not order trial by summary court martial without a reference to the officer empowered to convene a district court-martial or on active service a summary general court martial for the trial of the alleged offender unless (i) the offence is one which he can try by a summary court-martial without any reference to that officer[14]; or (ii) he considers that there is grave reason for immediate action and such reference cannot be made without detriment to discipline[15]. Where the evidence taken in accordance with the Army Rules 1954 r 22(3) discloses an offence other than the offence which was the subject of the investigation, the commanding officer may frame suitable charge(s) on the basis of the evidence so taken as well as the investigation of the original charge[16]. Compliance of the Army Rules 1954 r 22-24 is not necessary in the case of officers, unless a request to that effect is made by the officer[17]. Procedure under the Army Rules 1954 r 22 is mandatory in case of persons other than officers. Non-compliance thereto will vitiate the entire enquiry[18].

Where an officer, other than the commanding officer proposes to proceed against an accused under the provisions of the Army Act 1950[19], the provisions of the Army Rules 1954[20], shall, in so far as they are applicable, may be complied with by such officer[21].

1 Ie the Army Rules 1954 r 22. Every charge, whether against a junior commissioned officer, warrant officer or other ranks should be investigated in the first instance by the company commander, at his company orderly room which will be held at such an hour as will allow of an offender remanded for disposal by the commanding officer being ready to go before him at the appointed time. A company commander who has reserved a case for the award of the commanding officer will always attend with the company conduct book, when the offender is brought before the commanding officer. See: Defence Services Regulations, Regulations for the Army 1987, Volume I, paragraphs 402 (c) and 403 (c).

2 The word 'charge' in his rule does not mean a formal written charge contained in a charge sheet. It merely means accusation that a person subject to the Army Act 1950 has committed an offence. It is not mandatory to give any formal written charge sheet to the accused at the time of hearing. *Gyan Chand v Union of India* 1983 Cr LJ 1059 (Del). The charge at this stage are tentative which may be modified after the hearing of or during the procedure as described in the Army Rules 1954 r 22 (3)(c). Where the charge in the initial hearing was preferred under the Army Act 1950 s 63, while the accused was charged under the Army Act 1950 s 52(a), the Supreme Court held that no prejudice was caused to the accused because the hearing on the charge and the trial by general court martial were over the same facts. *Union of India v Nb Sub Baleshwar Ram* SLP No 13625/87 Supreme Court order dated 27

October 1989, unreported.

3 The Army Rules 1954 r 22(1). The civil police and other civilian witnesses may be summoned to attend before a commanding officer if it is considered desirable to compel their attendance by the service of a summons under the provisions of the Army Act 1950 s 135. Military witnesses can be ordered to attend and need not be formally summoned. Witnesses cannot be sworn or affirmed. The right to cross-examine is integral part of natural justice principle. *Ayaaubhkan Noorkhan Pathan v State of Maharashtra* AIR 2013 SC 58.

4 The Army Rules 1954 r 22(1) proviso.

5 The Army Rules 1954 r 22(2). The commanding officer must dismiss the charge if there is no evidence of any offence under the Army Act 1950 having been committed or if the accused has been previously acquitted or convicted of the alleged offence by any court, military or civil, or has been summarily dealt with under the Army Act ss 80, 83, 84 or 85 or the charge has previously been dismissed. See the Amy Act 1950 s 121 and the Army Rules 1954 r 53(1)(a). He may dismiss it, if he considers that the evidence is doubtful or the case is trivial, or, in the exercise of his discretion, for any reason, e.g., the good character of the accused. Manual of Military Law, Volume II, 2011, the Army Rules 1954 r 22 notes.

6 Ie under the Army Act 1950 s 120(2).

7 The Army Rules 1954 r 22(2) proviso.

8 'Within a reasonable time': No particular time is fixed within which a commanding officer must dispose of a case; so that he can always carefully consider a difficult case, but as a rule he should decide immediately, and should never delay for more than a day, unless further evidence is required. Manual of Military Law, Volume II, 2011, the Army Rules 1954 r 22 notes.

9 Ie under the Army Act 1950 s 80. A commanding officer disposes of a case summarily by awarding one of the punishments specified under the Army Act 1950 s 80 and which he can award. A term of imprisonment or detention awarded by a commanding officer should be awarded in days and will commence to run from the day of award. In law (in the absence of any special provision), there is no division of a day, and therefore, however late in the day a prisoner is committed, his term of imprisonment or detention is considered to have commenced at the first minute of that day that is, the first minute after midnight. The sentence will therefore, begin on the first minute of the day of award, and end at sunset of the day it expires. The award is considered final when the accused has been removed from the presence of the commanding officer. The commanding officer can at any time diminish the punishment before its completion, though he cannot add to it. Manual of Military Law, Volume II, 2011, the Army Rules 1954 r 22 notes.

10 Ie in accordance with the Army Rules 1954, Appendix III. Army Rules 1954 r 22 (3)(a).

11 Army Rules 1954 r 22 (3)(b). As to the meaning of 'proper military authority', see the Army Rules 1954 r 2(d): When used in relation to any power, duty, act or matter, such military authority as, in pursuance of the Army Rules 1954 or the regulations made under the Army Act 1950 or the usages of the service, exercises or performs that power or duty or is concerned with the act or matter.

12 Army Rules 1954 r 22 (3)(c). A summary of evidence is to be made in every case where it is intended to remand the accused for trial by a general court martial or district court martial or where the accused is an officer, junior commissioned officer, or warrant officer, for summary disposal of the charge under the Army Act 1950 ss 83, 84 and 85. In the case of summary court martial, a summary of evidence need not be made, if it is intended to try the accused forthwith without reference to superior authority either because the charge admits of this or because of such grave necessity as is referred to in the Army Rules 1954 r 22 (3).

13 Army Rules 1954 r 22 (3)(d).

14 Army Rules 1954 r 22 (3) proviso (a).

15 Army Rules 1954 r 22 (3) proviso (b).

16 Army Rules 1954 r 22(4). Before proceeding with a case, it is the duty of the commanding officer to ascertain that the offender is liable to be proceeded against, having regard to the limitation of tune prescribed by the Army Act 1950. When an other rank (OR) under the age of 21 years is remanded for trial by court martial on a serious charge, his commanding officer will arrange for him to be interviewed with a view to impressing upon him the desirability of keeping his next-of-kin informed. When a boy is remanded for trial by court martial, his commanding officer will inform his parents or legal guardians of the fact at the earliest possible moment, stating the nature of the charge preferred against him. See Defence Services Regulations, Regulations for the Army 1987, Volume I, paragraphs 405(b),(e) and (f).

17 *Lt Col PPS Bedi v Union of India* AIR 1982 SC 1413.

18 *Nb Sub Avtar Singh v Union of India* 1989 (4) SLR 579 (Del).

19 Ie under the Army Act 1950 s 80.

20 Ie the Army Rules 1954 r 22 (1)-(3).

21 The Army Rules 1954 r 22 explanation.

[0141] Identification Parades When circumstances render the identification of an alleged offender necessary, the identification should be carried out in the presence of an officer. It is essential that identification parades are conducted in a manner as to be fair to both the suspect and the witness[1]. Parades for the identification of a person subject to military law by a witness are divided into two categories: (1) Where there is reason to believe that the military person (name unknown) against whom a witness is prepared to give evidence belongs to a particular unit, and other evidence on the charge under investigation has not as yet permitted the singling out of any particular person[2]; and (2) Where the evidence permits of a definite person being singled out, but where it is desired to determine whether a certain witness is, or is not, able to recognise the suspect[3]. As regards parades of the first category, the parade should take place as soon as possible after the offence has been discovered; and all personnel of the unit should be assembled. The witness should be instructed to walk round the ranks, and if he/ she is prepared definitely to identify a particular person, to touch him on the shoulder without speaking. If the witness cannot make any identification, he/she is to be told that he/she can report any suspicions to the officer in charge of the parade. When walking round the ranks, the witness should not be followed too closely nor should he/she be spoken to. When there is more than one witness, each witness will walk round the ranks separately. No witness will be allowed to observe the parade or the actions of any other witness till his/her turn comes[4].

As regard the parade of the second category, the following instructions are to be observed. The parade should take place as soon as possible after the offence has been discovered. The witness or witnesses must not see the suspect under escort or in custody before the parade. Ten to twelve military personnel of similar physique, appearance and turn out will be paraded. Personnel should not be paraded bareheaded. It is up to the witness to ask a particular person in the parade to uncover his head. The suspect should be permitted to choose his own position in the ranks of the parade. No communication which would facilitate identification must be made to any witness who is awaiting his/her turn to identify. The witness should be instructed to walk round the ranks, and if he/she is prepared definitely to identify a particular person, to touch him on the shoulder without speaking. If the witness cannot make any identification, he/she is to be told that he/she can report any suspicions to the officer in charge of the parade. When walking round the ranks, the witness should not be followed too closely nor should he/she be spoken to. When there is more than one witness, each witness will walk round the ranks separately. No witness will be allowed to observe the parade or the actions of any other witness till his/her turn comes. The suspect will be permitted to change his position in the ranks after the departure of each witness and before the arrival of the next. A witness who has completed his/her identification must not be permitted to communicate with one who is awaiting his/her turn to identify[5]. When a person has been identified, his demeanour, and any statement made by him at the time of identification, should be carefully noted[6]. The report of the officer in charge of the identification parade will include the place, date and hour of the parade, the number of persons on parade, the name of each witness and where applicable the name of each person identified[7]. The report of the officer i/c of identification parade is not admissible at a trial by a court-martial but he can be permitted to use the report to refresh his memory[8].

1 Defence Services Regulations, Regulations for the Army 1987, Volume I, paragraphs 406 (a).

2 Defence Services Regulations, Regulations for the Army 1987, Volume I, paragraphs 406 (b)(i).

3 Defence Services Regulations, Regulations for the Army 1987, Volume I, paragraphs 406 (b)(ii).

4 Defence Services Regulations, Regulations for the Army 1987, Volume I, paragraphs 406 (c) and 406 (d) (i), (v) to (vii).

5 Defence Services Regulations, Regulations for the Army 1987, Volume I, paragraphs 406 (c) and 406 (d) (i)-(viii).

6 Defence Services Regulations, Regulations for the Army 1987, Volume I, paragraphs 406 (e).

7 Defence Services Regulations, Regulations for the Army 1987, Volume I, paragraphs 406 (f).

8 Defence Services Regulations, Regulations for the Army 1987, Volume I, paragraphs 406 (g).

[0142] Procedure for taking down the Summary of Evidence[1] Where the case is adjourned for the purpose of having the evidence reduced to writing, evidence of the witnesses who were present and gave evidence before the commanding officer, whether against or for the accused, and of any other person whose evidence appears to be relevant, shall be taken down in writing in the presence and hearing of the accused before the officer recording the summary[2]. The accused may cross-examine any witness and the questions together with the answers thereto shall be added to the evidence recorded[3]. The evidence of each witness after it has been recorded, shall be read over to him, and shall be signed by him, or if he cannot write his name shall be attested by his mark and witnessed as a token of the correctness of the evidence recorded. After all the evidence against the accused has been recorded, the accused will be asked; 'Do you wish to make any statement? You are not obliged to say anything unless you wish to do so, but whatever you say will be taken down in writing and may be given in evidence'. Any statement thereupon made by the accused shall be taken down and read over to him, but he will not be cross-examined upon it. The accused may then call his witnesses, including if he so desires, any witnesses as to character[4]. The evidence of the witnesses and the statement, if any, of the accused shall be recorded in the English language. If the witness or accused, does not understand the English language, the evidence or statement, as recorded, shall be interpreted to him in a language which he understands[5]. If a person cannot be compelled to attend as a witness, or if owing to the exigencies of service or any other grounds (including the expense and loss of time involved), the attendance of any witness cannot in the opinion of the officer taking the summary (to be certified by him in writing), be readily procured, a written statement of his evidence purporting to be signed by him may be read to the accused and included in the summary of evidence[6]. Any witness who is not subject to military law may be summoned to attend by order under the hand of the commanding officer of the accused[7].

1 The record of evidence under the Army Rules 1954 r 23 is called the 'summary of evidence'. It is a written record of evidence for the prosecution and the defence, made by the commanding officer or by another officer on his orders, in relation to a charge against a person subject to the Army Act 1950. It enables the commanding officer to determine whether or not, a prima facie case exists on the alleged charge, and whether the charge be proceeded

with or dismissed. The term 'summary' is sometimes misleading, because a summary of evidence is expected to be as far as possible a complete record of whatever relevant evidence that is available in respect of the charge(s) against the accused. In military law, when a disciplinary case develops into a court martial trial, the only previous record of the evidence that could be used, though to a very limited extent, at the trial is the summary of evidence. A summary of evidence must be in conformity with the rules of evidence. Manual of Military Law, Volume II, 2011, the Army Rules 1954 r notes.

2 Army Rules 1954 r 23 (1). The adjourned hearing for the purpose of reducing the evidence to writing should if possible be held on the same day as the investigation. The commanding officer may record the summary of evidence or direct another officer to take down the evidence, but an officer who has given evidence at the investigation must not be appointed for this purpose. He should be an officer of some experience and with a good knowledge of the vernacular. The summary of evidence can be ordered only by the commanding officer of the accused. When it is recorded under the orders of an officer other than the accused's commanding officer, summary disposal of a charge under the Army act 1950 ss 83, 84 and 85 or the trial of the offender by a general court martial or district court martial on the basis of such a summary of evidence may render the proceedings invalid. Summary of evidence cannot be taken on oath or affirmation. The accused cannot claim to be represented by counsel at the taking of summary of evidence. The evidence, so far as it is relevant and admissible, of every witness who gave evidence before the commanding officer must be taken down unless good reason renders if not reasonably practicable to call him. The evidence of witnesses who did not appear before the commanding officer may also be taken for either prosecution or defence, so long as it appears to be relevant. In reducing the evidence to writing immaterial statements may be omitted and all hearsay and irrelevant matter should be excluded. Manual of Military Law, Volume II, 2011, the Army Rules 1954 r 23 notes.

3 Army Rules 1954 r 23 (2). The accused must be allowed to put any reasonable question to a witness, and especially to put questions respecting any variance between the evidence taken down and that given before the commanding officer. If the accused declines to cross-examine any witness the fact should accordingly be stated. Manual of Military Law, Volume II, 2011, the Army Rules 1954 r 23 notes.

4 Army Rules 1954 r 23 (3). The formal caution provided for in this sub-rule must be given as soon as the evidence for the prosecution is closed. If it is necessary to take additional summary, the accused must again be formally cautioned before he makes any further statement. The fact that he was duly cautioned should be recorded in the summary. It is advisable to have an independent witness present when the accused is cautioned and when he makes the statement. Such independent witness apart from the officer recording the summary would also be competent to prove the statement of the accused at the trial subsequently, if necessary. The statement of an accused person can only be given in evidence at the trial if it is voluntary. If it was made voluntarily, the mere fact that the caution was not given will not prevent it being used as evidence, but in no case must he be authoritatively called on to account for his proceedings, or required to make any statement, or cross examined or asked any questions. Any such statement or the answers to any such questions will not be admissible in evidence against him. The accused may call witnesses on his behalf, and their evidence will be taken down and included in the summary; but he is not bound to call a witness because such witness gave evidence before the commanding officer. Manual of Military Law, Volume II, 2011, the Army Rules 1954 r 23 notes.

5 Army Rules 1954 r 23(4).

6 Army Rules 1954 r 23(5).

7 Army Rules 1954 r 23(6). For the issue of summons see the Army Act 1950 s 135. For form of summons, see the Army Rules 1954, Appendix III Part III.

[0143] Remand of accused The summary of evidence taken down in writing in pursuance of the Army Rules 1954[1], shall be considered by the commanding officer, who thereupon shall either (i) remand the accused for trial by a court martial[2]; or (ii) refer the case to the proper superior military authority[3]; or (iii) if he thinks it desirable, re-hear the case and either dismiss the charge or dispose of it summarily[4]. If the accused is remanded for trial by a court-martial, the commanding officer shall without unnecessary delay either assemble a summary court martial (after referring to the officer empowered to convene a district court martial or on active service a summary general court martial when such reference is necessary) or apply to the proper military authority to convene a court martial, as the case may require[5].

1 Ie under the Army Rules 1954 r 23.

2 Amy Rules 1954 r 24(1)(a).

3 Army Rules 1954 r 24(1)(b)

4 Army Rules 1954 r 24(1)(c). The evidence in the summary may not correspond with that given at the original investigation and the case may appear in a new aspect. The commanding officer may therefore, decide to re-hear the case, and, if he thinks fit, dispose it of summarily or try it by summary court martial, if he has jurisdiction to do so. He can dismiss the case on re-hearing it. Where the commanding officer discovered that no offence has been committed by the alleged accused and dismissed the charge, superior military authority has no jurisdiction to convene general court martial in the case. *Maj VJ Kharod v Union of India* 1987 (5) SLR 630 (Guj).

5 Army Rules 1954 r 24(2). The delay in assembling a summary court martial should be avoided. The accused should be warned for trial at least 96 hours before hand, except on active service when he should be so warned at least 24 hours before the trial commences; see: the Army Rules 1954 r 34. Where precise information as to the locality of the offence is likely to be of use in understanding a case, a plan drawn to scale should accompany a summary of evidence submitted to superior authority. If it is considered necessary that matters of evidence should be shown on this plan, (e.g., place where the body was found in a murder case, or position of accused or a witness) the plan should be in duplicate, and these matters should only appear on one copy, if the plan is subsequently produced at the trial, the unmarked copy will be used, being put in and sworn/affirmed to by the person who made it. These matters of evidence will then (if necessary) be marked on it, in accordance with the evidence given at the trial, and a note to that effect made in the proceedings. Vernacular documents attached to a summary of evidence should be accompanied by a translation in English. Manual of Military Law, Volume II, 2011, the Army Rules 1954 r 25 notes.

[0144] Charge-sheet and charge A charge[1] means an accusation contained in a charge sheet that a person subject to the Army Act 1950 has been guilty of an offence[2]. A charge-sheet shall contain the whole issue(s) to be tried by a court martial at one time[3]. A charge-sheet may contain one charge or several charges[4].

1 The term 'charge' referred to in this provision is the formal written charge upon which the accused is to be tried as distinct from the charge or complaint mentioned in the provisions of the Army Act 1950 s 102 and the Army Rules 1954 r 22, 23 and 25, which give rise to the preliminary investigation. Manual of Military Law, Volume II, 2011, the Army Rules 1954 r 28 notes.

2 The Army Rules 1954 r 28(2).

3 The Army Rules 1954 r 28(1). The charge-sheet is usually prepared by the commanding officer or adjutant of the accused's unit; but in the case of a trial by a general court martial or district court martial the Army Rules 1954 r 37 makes the convening officer equally responsible for its correctness. It must be signed by the officer in actual command of the unit to which the accused belongs. If the accused is attached to another unit, the charge-sheet must be signed by the commanding officer of the unit to which he is so attached. The order for the trial must be endorsed at the foot of the charge-sheet and signed by the convening officer or by a staff officer 'for' him. Charge-sheet cannot be endorsed for trial by a staff officer as such. Manual of Military Law, Volume II, 2011, the Army Rules 1954 r 28 notes.

4 The Army Rules 1954 r 28(3). There may be several charge-sheets, but the court can only deal with one charge-sheet at a time. All charges, includes the alternative charges, must be consecutively numbered. As to insertion of charges in separate charge-sheets see the army Rules 1954 r 79; see **[0282]**. An alternative charge should not be preferred, where a special finding is possible under the provisions of the Army act 1950 s 139 e.g., on a charge of desertion there is no need to prefer a charge of absence without leave as an alternative. As to the forms of charges and specimen charge-sheets, see Army Rules 1954 Appendix II, Part I and II respectively.

[0145] Commencement of charge-sheet Every charge-sheet shall begin with the name and description of the person charged, and state his number, rank, name and the corps or department (if any) to which he belongs. When the accused person does not belong to the regular army, the charge-sheet shall show by the description of him, or directly by an express averment, that he is subject to the Act in respect of the offence charged[1]. If the accused is subject to the Army Act 1950 under specified conditions e.g., an enrolled person of the Territorial Army, the description must contain an averment as to how he is subject to the Army Act 1950. When an accused holding an appointment is brought to trial by a court martial he is to be arraigned in his army rank with his appointment[2].

1 Army Rules 1954 r 29.

2 To be shown as follows: No……Sepoy (Lance Naik)……..Regiment. As to the forms of charges, illustrations, statement of offence and specimen charges, see Army Rules 1954 Appendix II, Part I to IV.

[0146] Contents of charge Each charge shall state one offence only, and in no case shall an offence be described in the alternative in the same charge[1]. Each charge shall be divided into two parts: (i) statement of the offence[2]; and (ii) statement of the particulars of the act, neglect or omission constituting the offence[3]. The offence shall be stated, if not a civil offence, as nearly as practicable, in the words of the Army Act 1950, and if a civil offence, in such words as sufficiently describe in technical words[4]. The particulars shall state such circumstances respecting the alleged offence as will enable the accused to know what act, neglect or omission is intended to be proved against him as constituting the offence[5]. The particulars in one charge may be framed wholly or partly by a reference to the particulars in another charge, and in that case so much of the latter particulars as are so referred to shall be deemed to form part of the first mentioned charge as well as of the other charge[6]. Where it is intended to prove any facts in respect of which any deduction from pay and allowances can be awarded as a consequence of the offence charged, the particulars shall state those facts and the sum of the loss or damage it is intended to charge[7].

The convening officer or in the case of trial by summary court martial, the commanding officer should seek the advice of deputy or assistant judge advocate general of the command concerned in cases where doubt exists as to the manner in which the charge should be framed. Charges for trial by general court martial and for indecency, fraud, theft (except ordinary theft) and civil offences (except simple assaults) should be referred to the deputy judge advocate general or assistant judge advocate general concerned before trial. A single transaction, though technically disclosing more than one offence, should not, as a rule be made the subject of more than one charge[8]. The statement of the particulars must support the statement of the offence[9]. When an offence is punished more severely, when committed under particular circumstances, the particulars should contain an averment about such circumstances[10]. When civil offences are tried by court martial under the Army Act 1950 s 69, although technical terms need not be used in the charge, the essence of the civil offence must be expressed. The statement of particulars should state shortly in ordinary language what the accused is alleged to have done.

All the ingredients necessary to constitute the offence should be specified. Vague statement must be avoided, e.g., in a charge for using insubordinate language to his superior officer or for making a false statement to his commanding officer, it is not sufficient to state that the accused used insubordinate language or made a false statement well knowing the statement to be false; the words alleged to have been spoken or written must be set out in the particulars. The exact or approximate date of the offence should be averred in the particulars. Such averment would show whether or not the trial in respect of the offence is time barred[11]. If for reasons of security it is considered undesirable to disclose the place of offence, the words 'at field' may be averred in the particulars instead of the actual place of offence[12].

1 Army Rules 1954 r 30(1).

2 Army Rules 1954 r 30(2)(a).

3 Army Rules 1954 r 30(2)(b).

4 Army Rules 1954 r 30(3).

5 Army Rules 1954 r 30(4).

6 Army Rules 1954 r 30(5).

7 Army Rules 1954 r 30(6).

8 For instance, where use of criminal force to a superior officer is accompanied by insubordinate language, the use of criminal force alone should be charged (assuming the evidence to be satisfactory), the language being admissible in evidence as to the intent. On the other hand, if it seems desirable, a man can legally be charged in two separate charges with escape from arrest and absence without leave (following such escape). Manual of Military Law, Volume II, 2011, the Army Rules 1954 r notes.

9 For example, if the statement of an offence laid under the Army Act 1950 s 52(a) alleged that the accused committed theft in respect of property of the Government, particulars stating that the accused dishonestly received, or was in unauthorised possession of, the property would not support the statement of the offence and the charge would be a bad charge, and the fact that the accused pleaded guilty to it would not affect the matter. But a merely technical difference, e.g., where the word assault is used in the statement of offence and the particulars disclose the use of criminal force, would not invalidate the charge, if the statement of offence and the particulars taken together supply the court and the accused with sufficient information of the nature of the offence which the court is to try and the accused to meet. Manual of Military Law, Volume II, 2011, the Army Rules 1954 r 30 notes.

10 For example, in a charge under the Army Act 1950 s 41(2) for disobeying a lawful command of his superior officer, an averment to the effect that the offence was committed when on active service, should be made, where necessary, since the said offence when committed on active service is more severely punished than otherwise.

11 See the Army Act 1950 s 122(1).

12 Manual of Military Law, Volume II, 2011, the Army Rules 1954 r 30 notes.

[0147] Signature on charge-sheet The charge-sheet must be signed by the commanding officer of the accused and should contain the place and date of such signature[1].

1 The Army Rules 1954 r 31. As to the meaning of 'commanding officer'; see: **[0013]**. The date of signature is of assistance in ascertaining whether or not provisions of the Army Rules 1954 r 34 regarding warning of the accused for trial, have been complied with. Manual of Military Law, Volume II, 2011, the Army Rules 1954 r 31 notes.

[0148] Validity of charge-sheet A charge-sheet shall not be invalid merely by reason of the fact that it contains any mistake in the name or description of the person charged, provided that he does not object to the charge-sheet during the trial, and that no substantial injustice has been done to the person charged[1]. In the construction of a charge-sheet or charge, there shall be presumed in favour of supporting the same every proposition which may reasonably be presumed to be impliedly included though not expressed therein[2]. The court has power to amend the charge by correcting any mistake in the name or description of an accused person, under the provisions of the Army Rules 1954[3].

1 The Army Rules 1954 r 32 (1).

2 The Army Rules 1954 r 32 (2).

3 Ie under the Army Rules 1954 r 50 or 113.

[0149] Reference to the Judge Advocate General's Department before trial In all cases for trial by general court martial, and all cases under the Army Act 1950, of indecency, fraud, theft, except ordinary theft, and civil offences except simple assaults, the charge sheet and summary of evidence, and all the exhibits will be referred by the convening officer to the deputy judge advocate general of the command or deputy/assistant judge advocate general of the corps, as the case may be, before trial is ordered. The convening officer should also refer for advice any other cases of doubt or difficulty. In all cases the doubts or difficulties and the matters on which advice is required will be specifically stated in the applications[1].

1 Defence Services Regulations, Regulations for the Army 1987, Volume I, paragraph 459.

[0150] The rights of accused to prepare defence Correspondence between the accused and his legal advisers shall not be liable to be censored. The accused shall inform his commanding officer of the names of such advisers and shall also inform him of any distinctive marks that such correspondences will bear[1]. An accused person shall have the right to interview any witnesses whom he may wish to call in his defence. The provisions of the Army Rules 1954[2] shall apply to procuring the attendance of such witnesses[3]. If the accused so desires, the commanding officer of the accused shall take such steps as the circumstances of the case permit to obtain a written statement from a witness whom the accused may wish to call in his defence. The statement shall be obtained in a closed envelope which shall be given to the accused person unopened[4]. If the accused person gives to his commanding officer the name of any person whom he wishes to call in his defence, no person shall interview such witness with reference to the charges against the accused except in the presence of the accused, unless the accused agrees to dispense with his presence in writing. Similarly if the accused wishes to interview a witness whom the prosecutor intends to call, the interview shall be in the presence of an officer detailed by the commanding officer of the accused person[5]. The commanding officer of the accused or the officer responsible for his custody shall take adequate precautions so that no conversation which the accused person may have with his legal advisers or witnesses is liable to be overheard[6]. The accused shall have the right to address an application to the deputy or assistant judge advocate general of the command, if he is kept under arrest longer than 48 days without being brought to trial or is not given full liberty for preparing his defence[7]. As soon as practicable after an accused has been remanded for trial by a general court martial or district court martial, and in any case not less than 96 or on active service 24 hours before his trial, an officer shall give to him free of charge a copy of the summary of evidence and explain to him his rights to preparing his defence and being assisted or presented at the trial. He shall also ask the accused to state in writing whether or not he wishes to have an officer assigned by the convening officer to represent him at the trial. The convening officer shall be informed whether or not the accused so elects[8].

1 The Army Rules 1954 r 33(1).

2 Ie the Army Rules 1954 r 137.

3 The Army Rules 1954 r 33(2).

4 The Army Rules 1954 r 33(3).

5 The Army Rules 1954 r 33(4).

6 The Army Rules 1954 r 33(5). The legislature has provided adequate safeguards for protecting the rights of a person who has been arraigned to stand trial by court martial. The army authorities to abide with and to ensure that valuable rights are not compromised or jeopardised in any manner and the accused is given adequate opportunity to defend himself in accordance with law, uninfluenced by the stature of the personalities involved or the publicity generated in the matter. *Brig Iqbal Singh (Retd) v Union of India* 119 (2005) DLT 715, 2005 (79) DRJ 492.

7 The Army Rules 1954 r 33(6).

8 The Army Rules 1954 r 33(7). The intent of this provision is that an accused must know before 96 hours that he will be tried by the court martial for an offence of which a charge-sheet was given. There is no illegality in serving of tentative charge-sheet. *Ex Gdr Balbir Singh v Chief of the Army Staff* Mil LJ 2005 All 109.

[0151] Warning of accused for trial The accused before he is arraigned shall be informed by an officer of every charge for which he is to be tried and also that, on his giving the names of witnesses whom he desires to call in his defence, reasonable steps will be taken for procuring their attendance, and those steps shall be taken accordingly. The interval between his being so informed and his arraignment shall[1] not be less than 96 hours or where the accused person is on active service less than 24 hours[2]. The officer at the time of so informing the accused shall give him a copy of the charge sheet and shall, if necessary, read and explain to him the charges brought against him. If the accused desires to have it in a language which he understands, a translation thereof shall also be given to him[3]. The officer shall also deliver to the accused a list of the names, rank and corps (if any), of the officers who are to form the court, and where officers in waiting are named, also of those officers in courts martial other than summary courts martial[4]. If it appears to the court that the accused is liable to be prejudiced at his trial by any non-compliance with this provision, the court shall take steps and, if necessary, adjourn to avoid the accused being so prejudiced[5].

1 When the word 'shall' is followed by prohibitive or negative words, the legislative intention of making the provision absolute, peremptory and imperative becomes loud and clear and ordinarily has to be inferred as such. The interval between the accused being informed of charge for which he is to be tried and his arraignment shall not be less than 96 hours is mandatory. Its non observance vitiates the entire proceedings. *Union of India v AK Pandey*, 2009 AIR (SCW) 6354, (2009) 10 SCC 552, 2009 (12) SCALE 617.

2 The Army Rules 1954 r 34 (1). The request of an accused person for witnesses to be called on his behalf should only be refused if it is quite clear that their evidence would be immaterial, or if their attendance cannot be secured within a reasonable time. If the request is refused, the refusal and reasons for it should be communicated to the court, who will deal with the matter under the provisions of the Army Rules 1954 r 138(4). If an essential witness is absent, the court should always adjourn for the purposes of enabling him to attend or of procuring his examination on commission. Manual of Military Law, Volume II, 2011, the Army Rules 1954 r 34 notes.

3 The Army Rules 1954 r 34 (2). A copy and translation of the charge-sheet must always be given, unless this provision has been dispensed with under the Army Rules 1954 r 36. Even where it is so dispensed with, the charges must be clearly explained to the accused, as otherwise he may not have proper opportunity to prepare his defence. Manual of Military Law, Volume II, 2011, the Army Rules 1954 r 34 notes.

4 The Army Rules 1954 r 34 (3). The list of names, rank and corps of the members of the court should normally be delivered to the accused, irrespective of any demand on his part, as soon as the names of the members are known. Manual of Military Law, Volume II, 2011, the Army Rules 1954 r 34 notes.

5 The Army Rules 1954 r 34 (4). The duty of complying with the provisions of the Army Rules 1954 r 34 will usually devolve upon the commanding officer in the case of summary court martial and the prosecutor in the case of other courts martial, who should, in any case, satisfy himself before the trial that it has been properly performed. Even if this rule is dispensed, Ie under the Army Rules 1954 r 36, the accused must have information of the charge and opportunity of calling his witnesses. Manual of Military Law, Volume II, 2011, the Army Rules 1954 r 34 notes.

[0152] Suspension of rules on the ground of military exigencies or the necessities of discipline Where it appears to the officer convening a court martial, or to the senior officer on the spot, that military exigencies, or the necessities of discipline render it impossible or inexpedient to observe any of the provisions contained in the Army Rules 1954[1], he may, by order under his hand, make declaration to that effect specifying the nature of such exigencies or necessities, and thereupon the trial or other proceedings shall be as valid as if the rule mentioned in such declaration had not been contained herein; and such declaration may be made with, respect to any or all of the rules aforesaid in the case of the same court martial[2]. However, the accused shall have full opportunity of making his defence, and shall be afforded every facility for preparing it which is practicable, having due regard to the said exigencies or necessities[3].

The power of suspension of rules on the ground of military exigencies or the necessities of discipline, under the aforesaid provision[4] should rarely be exercised except on active service and then only if absolutely necessary. Occasionally it may be necessary to resort to it in the case of embarkation or on the line of march or possibly in an extreme case where necessities of discipline require speedy trial and punishment. In exercising the powers conferred, as referred above, it is not necessary to dispense with all the provisions mentioned in it[5]. If the Army Rules 1954 r 23 is suspended, steps must be taken to inform the accused before hand of the nature of the charge, the names of the witnesses and the effect of their evidence, and the court must take care that the accused is not prejudiced by reason of the suspension, as, for instance, by not having received a summary of evidence. The power of dispensing with the Army Rules 1954 r 33 is only intended to be exercised where it is necessary to try a person before he can communicate with a witness or friend at a distance. The said rule should never be dispensed with except in extreme cases and even then the accused must be allowed free communication with any witness or friend on the spot. The accused will not have full opportunity of making his defence unless he receive in reasonable time the information mentioned above; and if he requests a reasonable adjournment in order to consider the witnesses evidence, or to acquaint himself with the charge, or requests the postponement of cross-examination of a witness, the court should grant the request, and may adjourn for the purpose. A refusal to do so might be held to be non-compliance with the proviso to the rule and thus to invalidate the trial, For the same reason the court, even in the absence of any such request, must take care that the accused is not prejudiced; by being taken by surprise, either by the charge or the evidence of witnesses. When any of the provisions of the Army Rules 1954 r 33 or 34 have not been complied with, the accused has a right to ask for an adjournment if he has been prejudiced by such non compliance[6].

1 Ie under the Army Rules 1954 r 23, 24, 33, 34 and 95(2).

2 The Army Rules 1954 r 36.

3 The Army Rules 1954 r 36 proviso.

4 Ie by the Army Rules 1954 r 36.

5 For example, it may be expedient to comply with the relevant provisions of the Army Rules 1954 r 23 but not with r 33. Manual of Military Law, Volume II, 2011, the Army Rules 1954 r 36 notes.

6 Manual of Military Law, Volume II, 2011, the Army Rules 1954 r 36 notes.

[0153] Joint trial of several accused persons Any number of accused persons may be charged jointly and tried together for an offence averred to have been committed by them collectively[1]. Any number of accused persons, although not charged jointly, may be tried together for an offence averred to have been committed by one or more of them and to have been abetted by the other or others[2]. Where the accused are so charged under the above mentioned provisions[3], any one or more of them may at the same time be charged with and tried for any other offence averred to have been committed individually or collectively, provided that all the said offences are based on the same facts, or form or are part of a series of offences of the same or similar character[4]. In the cases mentioned above, notice of the intention to try the accused persons together shall be given to each of the accused at the time of his being informed of the charges, and any accused person may claim, either by notice to the authority convening the court or, when arraigned before the court, by notice to the court, that he or some other accused be tried separately on one or more of the charges included in the charge-sheet, on the ground that the evidence of one or more of the other accused persons proposed to be tried together with him, will be material to his defence, or that otherwise he would be prejudiced or embarrassed in his defence. The convening authority or court, if satisfied that the evidence will be material or that the accused may be prejudiced or embarrassed in his defence, and if the nature of the charge admits of this, shall allow the claim. Such an accused, or the other accused person or persons whose separate trial has been claimed, shall be tried separately. Where any such claim has been made and disallowed by the authority convening the court, or by the court, the disallowance of such claim will not be a ground for refusing confirmation of the finding or sentence unless, in the opinion of the confirming authority, substantial miscarriage of justice has occurred by reason of the disallowance of such claim[5].

If two accused persons are charged separately with committing the same offence, they cannot, even at their own request, be tried together, because they have not been charged jointly. The nature of the charge may not admit of a separate trial, e.g., in the case of conspiring to cause or joining in a mutiny, the essence of the charge is combination between the accused persons. Certain offences, on the other hand, cannot from their nature, be committed collectively, e.g., intoxication, sentry sleeping upon or leaving his post; malingering; giving false evidence, cowardice, etc. and speaking generally, all offences where a person's individual state of body or mind is of the essence of the offence. In case of doubt the accused should he tried separately[6].

1 The Army Rules 1965 r 35 (1).

2 The Army Rules 1965 r 35 (2).

3 Ie the Army Rules 1954 r 35(1) and (2).

4 The Army Rules 1965 r 35 (3).

5 The Army Rules 1965 r 35 (4).

6 Manual of Military Law, Volume II, 2011, the Army Rules 1954 r 35 notes.

[0154] Escort for accused An accused person brought before a court martial will, if he is an officer, junior commissioned officer, warrant officer or non-commissioned officer[1] be attended by an officer, junior commissioned officer, warrant officer or non-commissioned officer having him in custody, or, if of lower rank, by an escort. The officer, junior commissioned officer, warrant officer or non-commissioned officer in charge will be responsible for his safe conduct, but will obey the directions of the court while the accused is in court. An accused person will not be handcuffed, unless this is absolutely necessary for the purpose of preventing his escape or rescue, or of restraining his violent conduct[2].

1 As to the definition of 'officer', 'junior commissioned officer', 'warrant officer' and 'non-commissioned officer'; see **[0029]**, **[0023]**, **[0037]** and **[0026]**.

2 Defence Service Regulations, Regulations for the Army 1987, Volume I, paragraph 461.

[0155] Medical Examination before trial An accused person will be examined by a medical officer on the morning of each day the court for his trial is ordered to sit. The commanding officer of the unit is responsible to ensure that the accused is not brought before a court martial if in the opinion of the medical officer he is unfit to undergo his trial[1].

1 Defence Service Regulations, Regulations for the Army 1987, Volume I, paragraph 462.

[0156] Conduct-sheet entries A conduct sheet[1] shall be prepared and maintained for every person subject to the Army Act 1950[2]. The conduct-sheets of officers, junior commissioned officers and warrant officers[3] are will be kept as confidential documents, while those of other ranks will be kept with other service documents[4]. Entries will be made in the conduct-sheets of officers in respect of all convictions by court martial or criminal court or summary punishments awarded under the Army Act 1950[5]. The following entries are made in the conduct sheets of junior commissioned officers, warrant officers and other ranks as red-ink entries: forfeiture of seniority of rank (junior commissioned officers and warrant officers only); conviction by court-martial; conviction by a civil court, except when a fine was the only punishment; reduction of a non-commissioned officer to a lower grade or to the ranks for an offence but not for inefficiency; deprivation of an appointment or of lance or acting rank, for an offence but not for inefficiency; severe reprimand; imprisonment; detention; confinement to the lines exceeding 14 days; and forfeiture of good-service or good-conduct pay[6]. Black-ink entries will be made in the conduct sheets of junior commissioned officers, warrant officers and other ranks in respect of all punishments not included in the list of red-ink entries. These include convictions by civil courts, which in the commanding officer's opinion do not merit a red-ink entry[7]. When the record of a court martial or summary award is ordered to be removed, the entry must be erased and the authority quoted. No entry will be made of any charge on which the accused has been found not guilty[8].

1 Form IAFF 3013.

2 As to the meaning of 'person subject to the Army Act 1950'; see **[0039]**.

3 As to the definition of 'officer', 'junior commissioned officer' and 'warrant officer'; see **[0029]**, **[0023]** and **[0037]**.

4 Defence Services Regulations, Regulations for the Army 1987, Volume I, paragraphs 386.

5 Ie under the Army Act 1950 ss 83 or 84. Defence Services Regulations, Regulations for the Army 1987, Volume I, paragraphs 387(a).

6 Defence Services Regulations, Regulations for the Army 1987, Volume I, paragraphs 387(b).

7 Defence Services Regulations, Regulations for the Army 1987, Volume I, paragraphs 387(c).

8 Defence Services Regulations, Regulations for the Army 1987, Volume I, paragraphs 388(a) (iv) and (v).

6. ADMINISTRATIVE ACTION AND MINOR PUNISHMENTS

CONTENTS

PARA

A. Administrative Action

B. Minor Punishments

A. ADMINISTRATIVE ACTION

[0157] Introduction Administrative action is not punitive in character. It is meant to be corrective and rehabilitative. Administrative actions include measures ranging from reproof or reprimand to dismissal from the service. The factors which need be considered in deciding whether it is appropriate to take administrative action in a particular case are as follows: (i) the context in which the incident occurred and its impact on operational effectiveness; (ii) the likelihood and extent of adverse impact on the individual, unit or service; (iii) the rank of the individual or level of responsibility; (iv) the age and maturity of the individual, (v) the individual's previous conduct and warnings given to him earlier; (vi) any relevant personal circumstances or mitigating factors; and (vii) the individual's response following the discovery of the incident. In the Army, administrative action implies award of reproof or displeasure to officers and junior commissioned officers. It is awarded as an official condemnation by a superior officer for a specific misconduct of minor nature, where disciplinary action by means of a summary disposal or court martial in not considered expedient or necessary.

[0158] Reproof Warning or a minor censure may take the form of reproof and can be administered verbally or in writing to the service personnel by the commanding officer or by an officer superior in command to the commanding officer. A reproof must not take the form of insult or abuse. It may be strong but should be directed to the actual fault committed and the language used should not be intemperate or offensive. A reproof should not be administered in the presence of subordinates unless, for the purpose of making an example, it is necessary that the reproof be public. A warning is not recorded in the service documents of the person concerned. Before administering reproof by way of a warning, the competent authority must ascertain that the ends of justice would be met by closing the case with reproof. Once case has been closed by the administration of a reproof by a competent authority, no superior authority can reopen the case[1].

1 Defence Services Regulations, Regulations for the Army 1987, Volume I, paragraph 327.

[[0159] Severe Displeasure or Displeasure As per customs of service, severe displeasure or displeasure can be awarded to officers and junior commissioned officers by a superior officer for an act, conduct, omission or offence of a minor nature. The award of severe displeasure may be 'recordable' or 'non-recordable'. The authority awarding censure needs to examine the evidence of the inquiry and ensure that a prima facie case exists for issuing of a show cause notice. Reasonable opportunity must be given to the affected person whose character or military reputation is affected to reply to the show cause notice[1]. The reply must then be carefully considered and the censure order must be a speaking order. The award of 'severe displeasure' by the Central Government or the Chief of the Army Staff goes into the service records. If recordable 'severe displeasure' is awarded by the general officer commanding-in-chief command, it is operable for three years from the date of award, and is thereafter is removed from the records. A non-recordable censure does not exist on service records[2]. The award of censure is regulated by 'customs of the services'[3]. Rules of natural justice require that an adjudicating/ administrative authority should afford a reasonable opportunity of being heard to a party[4]. In an adverse remark made against the individual by the chief of the army staff cannot be understood or interpreted as amounting to expression of 'severe displeasure', within the meaning of censure[5]. An award of censure is not barred by limitation under the Army Act 1950[6].

1 The Army Rules 1954 r 180.

2 Army HQ letter No. 32908/AG/DV-1(P) dated 23 April and 19 October 2007.

3 *Union of India v Brigadier JS Sivia* Mil LJ 1996 SC 3. The award of censure is being regulated by 'customs of the service' since the inception of the Indian Army. Section 3 (v) of the Army Act 1950 and the Defence Services Regulations, Regulations for the Army 1987, paragraph 9 recognize the existence of 'customs of the service'. The definition of 'commanding officer' clearly says that in the discharge of his duties as a commanding officer, he has to abide by the 'customs of the service'. Similarly Defence Services Regulations, Regulations for the Army 1987, paragraph 9 which lays down the duties of the commanding officer, specifically says that the commanding officer has to discharge his functions keeping in view the regulations and the 'customs of the service'. It is clear beyond doubt that the award of punishment of censure by way of severe displeasure to an officer or junior commissioned officer is an administrative action.

4 *Union of India v Brigadier JS Sivia* Mil LJ 1996 SC 3. The expression 'reasonable opportunity of being heard' implies that the authority should: (i) give all information as to the nature of the case which the party has to meet; (ii) supply

all information, evidence or material which the authority wishes to use against the party; (iii) receive all relevant materials which the party wishes to produce in support of its case and (iv) give an opportunity to the party to rebut adverse information, evidence or material appearing against such party.

5 *Major General IPS Dewan v Union of India* 1995 SCC (3) 383, AIR 1995 SC 1428, JT 1995 (2) 654.

6 Ie under the Army Act 1950 s 122; *Brig B K Gogna v Union of India* Mil LJ 2001 Delhi 68.

[0160] Grievance against award of Censure Officers and junior commissioned officers who consider that they have been wronged by the award of censure may submit a grievance application which is processed in accordance with the provisions of the Regulations for the Army 1987[1]. An authority superior to the one who awarded the censure may cancel the award, remit a portion or the whole of it, or commute it to a non-recordable censure, if in the opinion of that authority; the censure is unjust, illegal or excessive[2]. While granting redress by mitigating the award, the competent authority must invariably mention the date from which the said order is to be operative[3].

1 Defence Services Regulations, Regulations for the Army 1987, Volume I, paragraph 364.1(a)(iv).

2 The procedure for submission and processing of petitions is contained in the Defence Services Regulations, Regulations for the Army 1987, Volume I, paragraph 364. See **[0079]**.

3 Army HQ letter No. 32908/AG/DV-1(P) dated 23 April and 19 October 2007.

B MINOR PUNISHMENTS

[0161] Introduction Minor punishments may also be inflicted in respect of offences committed by persons subject to the Army Act 1950 without the intervention of a court martial[1] and in the manner stated in the provisions of the Army Act 1950[2].

1 Ie under the Army Act 1950 ss 80, 83, 84 and 85. The proceedings under the Army Act 1950 ss 80, 83, 84 and 85 are summary proceedings. The officer disposing of the case summarily under these sections is not a 'court' nor does the Indian Evidence Act, 1872 apply to such proceedings. Further, unlike a trial by court martial, the accused has no right to be represented by counsel/defending officer or even assisted by the 'friend of the accused'.

2 The Army Act 1950 s 79.

[0162] Punishment of persons other than officers, junior commissioned officers and warrant officers Subject to certain provisions of the Army Act 1950[1], a commanding officer[2] or such other officer as is, with the consent of the Central Government, specified by the Chief of the Army Staff, may, in the prescribed manner[3], proceed against a person subject to the Army Act 1950 otherwise than as an officer, junior commissioned officer or warrant officer who is charged with an offence under the Army Act 1950 and award such person, to the extent prescribed[4], one or more of the following punishments[5]: (1) imprisonment in military custody up to 28 days[6]; (2) detention up to 28 days[7]; (3) confinement to the lines up to 28 days[8]; (4) extra guards or duties[9]; (5) deprivation of a position of the nature of an appointment or of corps or working pay, and in the case of non-commissioned officers, also deprivation of acting rank or reduction to a lower grade of pay[10]; (6) forfeiture of good service and good conduct pay[11]; (7) severe reprimand or reprimand[12]; (8) fine up to 14 days' pay in any one month[13]; and (9) penal deductions under the provision of the Army Act 1950[14].

1 Ie subject to the Army Act 1950 s 81, which imposes certain limitations or restrictions on the powers granted to the commanding officer or other officer under the Army Act 1950 s 80; see **[0163]**.

2 As to the definition of 'commanding officer'; see **[0013]**. For the duties of a commanding officer as to investigation of a charge for an offence and disposal of the charge; see the Army Act s 102 and the Army Rules 1954 r 22-24. A junior commissioned officer commanding a unit or detachment, not being an officer, within the meaning of the Army Act s 3 (xviii), cannot award any of the punishments under this provision; see Manual of Military Law, Volume II, 2011, the Army Act 1950 s 80 notes.

3 In the prescribed manner; see 'offence report' in Part II of Appendix III to the Army Rules 1954.

4 'To the extent prescribed': a commanding officer or other officer specified in this section, if below field rank, cannot award, imprisonment or detention for a period exceeding seven days unless empowered to do so by an officer having power not less than an officer commanding a division; see The Army Rules 1954 r 192. For officers specified by the chief of the army staff, with the consent of the Central Government; see Defence Services Regulations, Regulations for the Army, Volume I, paragraph 443.

5 The following combined punishments under this section are legal: (i) In the case of a non-commissioned officer -one or more of the punishments specified in clauses (d) to (i). In the case of a Sepoy -(i) Imprisonment, detention and confinement to the lines if the total period does not exceed 42 days, but the confinement to the lines will take effect on the expiry of imprisonment and or detention. In addition to the punishments mentioned in clauses (i) and (ii) above, the commanding officer may award one or more of the following punishments e.g., extra guard or duties, deprivation of corps or working pay, reduction to a lower class of pay, forfeiture of good service and good conduct pay, fine and stoppages. A commanding officer cannot increase a punishment after he has once made his award, which is considered complete when the person has quitted his presence. But a commanding officer can at any time before the punishment has been completed, mitigate or remit such punishment. Manual of Military Law, Volume II, 2011, the Army Act 1950 s 80 notes.

6 Army Act 1950 s 80(a). Imprisonment may be rigorous or simple; see the General Clauses Act 1897 s 3(27). The term 'rigorous' or 'simple' should always be used in the award. Imprisonment or detention commences from the date of award and ends at sunset of the day the sentence expires. An award of imprisonment, rigorous or simple, carries with it a minimum of two hours of military instruction daily; see; Defence Services Regulations, Regulations for the Army, Volume I, paragraph 508(a). As to deduction from pay and allowances entailed by an award of imprisonment see the Army Act 1950 s 91(a).

7 Army Act 1950 s 80(b). For detention in military custody; see Defence Services Regulations, Regulations for the Army, Volume I, paragraph 509.

8 Army Act 1950 s 80(c). Defaulter's will be required to answer to their names at uncertain hours throughout the day, and will be employed on working parties to the fullest practicable extent with a view to relieving well-conducted soldiers therefrom. Defaulters will attend parades, and take all duties in regular turn. When the working parties required are not sufficient to keep the defaulters fully employed, the commanding officer may order them to attend extra drill, which will be limited to one hour a day, and will include some form of useful instructions. See item I, column 4 of the Table appended to Defence Services Regulations, Regulations for the Army, Volume I, paragraph 443.

9 Army Act 1950 s 80(d). This punishment is awarded for minor offences on those duties.

10 Army Act 1950 s 80(e). The maximum period for which such forfeiture can be ordered has not been prescribed; see: Pay and Allowances Regulations.

11 Army Act 1950 s 80(f). The commanding officer or other specified officer can forfeit at a time one rate of such pay.

12 Army Act 1950 s 80(g). This punishment can be awarded only to a non-commissioned officer or an acting non-commissioned officer. A lance naik is a non-commissioned officer for the purpose of this clause. An award of

severe reprimand constitutes a red ink entry; see Defence Services Regulations, Regulations for the Army, Volume I, paragraph 387(b).

13 Army Act 1950 s 80(h). The punishment under this clause may be awarded alone or in conjunction with any other punishment under the Army Act 1950 s 80. Recovery can be effected under the Army Act 1950 s 91(h).

14 The Army Act 1950 s 80(i). Under this clause the commanding officer or specified officer is authorised to award stoppages to meet any expenses, loss, damage or destruction caused by the offender to the central government or to any building or property: but the deductions so ordered shall not exceed in any month one half of his pay and allowances for that month. See the Army Act 1950 ss 91(g) and 94.

[0163] Limit of punishments under the Army Act 1950 s 80 In the case of an award of two or more punishments[1], the punishment of confinement to the lines or that of extra guards or duties[2] shall take effect only upon the conclusion of the punishment of imprisonment in military custody or detention up to 28 days[3]. When two or more of the punishments specified in the Army Act 1950 ss 80 (a) to (c) [4] are awarded to a person conjointly, or when already undergoing one or more of the said punishments, the whole extent of the punishments shall not exceed, in the aggregate, 42 days[5]. The punishments specified under the Army Act 1950 s 80(a)-(c) shall not be awarded to any person who is of the rank of a non-commissioned officer or was, at the time of committing the offence for which he is punished, of such rank[6]. The punishment specified under the Army Act 1950 s 80(g) shall not be awarded to any person below the rank of a non-commissioned officer[7].

1 Ie punishments specified in the Army Act 1950 s 80(a)-(d): see **[0162]**.

2 Ie under the Army Act 1950 s 80(c) or (d).

3 Ie as specified under the Army Act 1950 s 80(a) or (b): see the Army Act 1950 s 81(2). Imprisonment, detention, confinement to the lines and extra guards or duties may be awarded separately or conjointly but the carrying out of imprisonment and detention will precede confinement to the lines and extra guards or duties

4 Ie under the Army Act 1950 s 80(a)-(c).

5 Army Act 1950 s 81(3). No award or awards including imprisonment, detention and confinement to the lines shall exceed in the aggregate forty two days

6 The Army Act 1950 s 81(4). As to the meaning of 'non-commissioned officer'; see **[0026]**. A lance naik is a non-commissioned officer for the purpose of this provision. Manual of Military Law, Volume II, 2011, the Army Act 1950 s 81 notes.

7 The Army Act 1950 s 81(5).

[0164] Punishments in addition to those specified The chief of the army staff may, with the consent of the Central Government, specify such other punishments as may be awarded under the provision of the Army Act 1950[1] in addition to or without any of the punishments specified therein, and the extent to which such other punishments may be awarded[2]. The chief of the army staff, with the consent of the Central Government, has specified the certain officers who may exercise the powers of punishments under Army Act 1050 s 80. The maximum punishment includes (i) confinement to the lines for any period not exceeding 15 days; (ii) extra guards or piquets up to a limit of three such duties for any one offence; (iii) reduction to a lower class of pay for 28 days; and (iv) extra drill for two hours a day up to 15 days[3].

1 Ie under the Army Act 1950 s 80: see **[0162]**.

2 Army Act 1950 s 82. This provision empowers the chief of the army staff to add, with the consent of the Central Government, to the punishments awardable under the Army Act 1950 s 80 and to specify the extent of the punishments so added.

3 For details of the authority empowered to award punishment, nature of punishment and the persons liable to punishment see Defence Services Regulations, Regulations for the Army 1987, Volume I, paragraph 443.

[0165] Summary disposal of charges against Officer, Junior Commissioned Officer or Warrant Officer Where an officer, a junior commissioned officer or a warrant officer is remanded for the disposal of a charge against him by an authority empowered under the provisions of the Army Act 1950[1], to deal summarily with that charge, the summary of evidence shall be delivered to him, free of charge, with a copy of the charge as soon as practicable after its preparation and in any case not less than 24 hours before the disposal[2]. Where the authority empowered under the provisions of the Army Act 1950[3], decides to deal summarily with a charge against an officer, junior commissioned officer or warrant officer, he shall unless he dismisses the charge, or unless the accused has consented in writing to dispense with the attendance of the witnesses; hear the evidence in the presence of the accused. The accused shall have full liberty to cross-examine any witness against him, and to call any witnesses and make a statement in his defence[4]. The proceedings shall be recorded as far as practicable in accordance with the provisions contained in the Army Rules 1954[5] and in every case in which punishment is awarded, the proceedings together with the conduct sheet, summary of evidence and written consent to dispense with the attendance of witnesses, if any, of the accused, shall be forwarded through the proper channel to the superior military authority as defined in the Army Act 1950[6].

An authority can dispose of the case summarily not only if asked to do so but also if he is asked to convene a court martial for the trial of the offender. Even if he is asked to deal summarily with a case he can, if he thinks it desirable, convene a court martial. If on perusal of the summary (or abstract) of evidence and other documents, he thinks fit, he can at once, without bringing the accused before him order dismissal of the charge, or order a court martial, or he can decide to hear the evidence with a view to dealing summarily with the case. After hearing the evidence the authority can still dismiss the case or order a court martial or he can deal summarily with it and award a punishment[7].

1 Ie under the Army Act 1950 ss 83, 84 or 85.

2 Army Rules 1954 r 26 (1).

3 Ie under the Army Act 1950 ss 83, 84 or 85.

4 Army Rules 1954 r 26 (2).

5 Ie in Appendix IV to the Army Rules 1954. Form 1 in Appendix IV Part I to be used when the accused has given his consent in writing to dispense with attendance of witnesses at the trial. Form 2 in Appendix IV Part I is to be used when the accused does not consent to dispense with attendance of witnesses at his summary trial.

6 Ie military authority as defined in the Army Act 1950 s 88. Army Rules 1954 r 26 (3).

7 Manual of Military Law, Volume II, 2011, the Army Rules 1954 r 26 notes.

[0166] Punishment of officers, junior commissioned officers and warrant officers by brigade commanders and others An officer having power not less than a brigade, or an equivalent commander or such other officer[1] as is, with the consent of the Central Government, specified by the chief of the army staff may in the prescribed manner[2], proceed against an officer below the rank of field officer[3], a junior commissioned officer[4] or a warrant officer[5], who is charged with an offence under the Army Act 1950, and award one or more of the following punishments, that is to say, (1) severe reprimand or reprimand[6]; and (2) stoppage of pay and allowances until any proved loss or damage occasioned by the offence of which he is convicted is made good[7].

1 An officiating brigade, sub area or equivalent commander, irrespective of his rank, can exercise the powers under the Army Act 1950 s 83.

2 As to the 'prescribed manner' see the Army Rules 1954 r 26, Forms 1 and 2 in Part I of Appendix IV to the Army Rules 1954 and Defence Services Regulations, Regulations for the Army, Volume I, paragraph 444.

3 As to the meaning of 'field officer'; see **[0021]**. An officer of the rank of major or above cannot be dealt with under this provision. Manual of Military Law, Volume II, 2011, the Army Act 1950 s 83 notes.

4 As to the meaning of 'junior commissioned officer'; see **[0023]**.

5 As to the meaning of 'warrant officer'; see **[0037]**.

6 Army Act 1950 s 83(a).

7 Army Act 1950 s 83(b). The sentence of forfeiture of seniority or of service for the purpose of promotion cannot be awarded under this clause. The procedure in this respect is laid down in the Defence Services Regulations, Regulations for the Army 1987, Volume I, Appendix Q.

[0167] Punishment of officers, junior commissioned officers and warrant officers by area commanders and others An officer having power not less than an area commander or an equivalent commander or an officer empowered to convene a general court martial or such other officer[1] as is, with the consent of the Central Government, specified by the chief of the army staff may, in the prescribed manner[2], proceed against an officer below the rank of lieutenant-colonel, a junior commissioned officer or a warrant officer[3], who is charged with an offence under the Army Act 1950, and award one or more of the following punishments that is to say: (1) forfeiture of seniority, or in the case of any of them whose promotion depends upon length of service, forfeiture of service for the purpose of promotion for a period not exceeding 12 months but subject to the right of the accused previous to the award to elect to be tried by a court martial[4]; (2) severe reprimand or reprimand[5]; and (3) stoppage of pay and allowances until any proved loss or damage occasioned by the offence of which he is convicted is made good[6]. Charges against an officer, who at the time of the commission of offence or disposal held the rank of lieutenant colonel (acting or substantive), should not be dealt with summarily, even if he has ceased, to hold that rank at the time the case has been referred to the superior authority by his commanding officer. He should be brought to trial by a court martial or dealt with administratively depending on the merits of the case. Where the accused is specifically asked as to whether he would elect to face the trial by the general court martial or would accept the award passed by the general officer commanding, and he voluntarily opts to accept the award, it is not open to complain that no summary trial as provided for in the Army Rules 1954 was held[7].

1 An officiating area or equivalent commander or other officer specified in this provision, irrespective of his rank, can exercise the powers under the Army Act 1950 s 84. Manual of Military Law, Volume II, 2011, the Army Act 1950 s 84 notes.

2 As to the 'prescribed manner' see the Army Rules 1954 r 26, Forms 1 and 2 in Part I of Appendix IV to the Army Rules 1954 and Defence Services Regulations, Regulations for the Army, Volume I, paragraph 444. For procedure, see the Defence Services Regulations, Regulations for the Army 1987, Volume I, Appendix Q.

3 As to the definition of officer, junior commissioned officer and warrant officer; see **[0029]**, **[0023]** and **[0037]**.

4 Army Act 1950 s 84(a). If the authority dealing summarily with the case proposes to award this punishment he shall ask the accused 'Do you elect to be tried by court-martial or will you accept my award?' Manual of Military Law, Volume II, 2011, the Army Act 1950 s 84 notes.

5 Army Act 1950 s 84(b).

6 Army Act 1950 s 84(c).

7 *Suresh Chand Mehra v Defence Secretary, Union of India* AIR 1991 SC 483, (1991) 2 SCC 198, (1991) SCC (Cr) 452.

[0168] Punishment of junior commissioned officers A commanding officer[1] may, in the prescribed manner[2], proceed against a junior commissioned officer who is charged with an offence under the Army Act 1950 and award one or more of the following punishments, that is to say (1) severe reprimand or reprimand[3]; and (2) stoppage of pay and allowances until any proved loss or damage occasioned by the offence of which he is convicted is made good[4]. However, if the commanding officer or other officer holding the trial is below the rank of colonel, he shall not award the punishment of severe reprimand or reprimand[5].

1 Or other officer, with the consent of the Central Government, and specified by the chief of the army staff can also exercise this power; see the Army Act 1950 s 85.

2 As to the 'prescribed manner' see the Army Rules 1954 r 26, Forms 1 and 2 in Part I of Appendix IV to the Army Rules 1954 and Defence Services Regulations, Regulations for the Army, Volume I, paragraph 444.

3 As to the definition of junior commissioned officer; see **[0023];** The Army Act 1950 s 85(i).

4 Army Act 1950 s 85(ii). For procedure, see the Defence Services Regulations, Regulations for the Army 1987, Volume I, Appendix Q.

5 Army Act 1950 s 85 proviso.

[0169] Transmission of proceedings In every case in which minor punishment as been awarded under the Army Act 1950[1], certified true copies of the proceedings shall be forwarded by the officer awarding the punishment, to a superior military authority as defined in the Army Act 1950[2].

1 Ie under the Army Act 1950 ss 83 to 85; see **[0166], [0167]** and **[0168]** respectively.

2 The Army Act 1950 s 86. Such superior military authority has been defined under the Army Act 1950 s 88. See **[0171]**.

[0170] Review of Proceedings If any punishment awarded under any of the Army Act 1950 ss 83-85 appears to a superior military authority as defined in the Army Act s 88 to be illegal[1], unjust[2] or excessive[3], such authority may cancel, vary or remit the punishment and make such other direction as may be appropriate in the circumstances of the case[4]. Powers to review the proceedings under this provision shall normally be exercised within a period of two years from the date of award of the punishment[5].

1 A punishment is wholly 'illegal' if (i) the finding of guilty cannot be upheld or (ii) the only punishment awarded is of a kind which cannot be awarded for the offence charged (e.g., stoppage of pay and allowances for an offence which is not alleged to have occasioned any loss); or (iii) where the punishment awarded is of a kind which the Authority dealing with the case is not authorized to award. Where the punishment is wholly illegal it must be cancelled and appropriate directions made by the superior military authority. Manual of Military Law, Volume II, 2011, the Army Act 1950 s 87 notes.

2 Where the punishment though not in excess of the punishment authorised appears to be 'unjust' or severe, the superior military authority has the power to remit the whole or part of the punishment. If the whole of the punishment is remitted there will be nothing left except the finding which will stand good and the accused will suffer the forfeitures or penalties which are consequential on conviction. Manual of Military Law, Volume II, 2011, the Army Act 1950 s 87 notes.

3 A punishment is 'excessive' when it is in excess of the punishment authorised by law for the offence i.e., where it is of a kind which the authority dealing with the case is authorised to award for the offence charged but is greater in amount than he is authorised to award e.g., if an authority under the Army Act 1950 ss 83-85 were to award

stoppages greater than the amount of the loss proved to have been occasioned by the offence. In such cases the superior military authority specified in the Army Act 1950 s 88 can vary the punishment by reducing the amount of punishment to an amount which is authorised by law. Manual of Military Law, Volume II, 2011, the Army Act 1950 s 87 notes.

4 The Army Act 1950 s 87. Make such other direction, as may be appropriate in the circumstances of the case: These, words would enable the superior military authority to mitigate or commute the punishment where it is unjust or excessive. Manual of Military Law, Volume II, 2011, the Army Act 1950 s 87 notes.

5 Defence Services Regulations, Regulations for the Army 1987, Volume I paragraph 442.

[0171] Superior Military Authority For the purpose of certain provisions of the Army Act 1950[1], a 'superior military authority' means (1) in the case of punishments awarded by a commanding officer, any officer superior in command to such commanding officer[2]; and (2) in the case of punishments awarded by any other authority, the Central Government, the chief of army staff or other officer specified by the chief of the army staff[3].

1 Ie Army Act s 86 and 87; see **[0169]** and **[0170]**.

2 Army Act 1950 s 88(a). In cases where a detachment commander can exercise the power of a commanding officer within the meaning of the Army Act 1950, the commanding officer of the main unit can be the superior officer of the detachment under this provision. Manual of Military Law, Volume II, 2011, the Army Act 1950 s 88 notes.

3 Army Act 1950 s 88(b). The chief of the army staff has specified the general officer commanding-in-chief of a command as the superior military authority for the purpose of review of punishments awarded to officers, junior commissioned officer and warrant officers under the Army Act 1950 ss 83 and 84. Powers conferred under Army Act s 88 shall normally be exercised within a period of two years from the date of award of the punishment. See: Defence Services Regulations, Regulations for the Army 1987, Volume I paragraph 442.

[0172] Review of Punishment awarded under the Army Act ss 80 and 82 Punishments awarded under Army Act 1950 ss 80 and 82 may be reviewed by an officer superior in command to the officer who awarded the punishment, and if any such punishment appears to such officer to be illegal, unjust or excessive, such officer may cancel, vary or remit the punishment and make such direction as may be appropriate in the circumstances of the case. However, where a punishment is wholly illegal, or is in excess of the punishment authorised by law, it may be cancelled or varied by an officer-in-charge records also. Power of review of punishment shall normally be exercised within a period of two years from the date of award of the punishment[1].

1 Defence Services Regulations, Regulations for the Army 1987, Volume I paragraph 442.

[0173] Collective fines Whenever any weapon or part of a weapon forming part of the equipment of a half squardon, battery, company or other similar unit is lost or stolen, the officer commanding the army, army corps, division or independent brigade to which such units belongs may, after obtaining the report of a court of inquiry impose a collective fine upon the junior commissioned officers, warrant officers, non-commissioned officers and men of such unit, or upon so many of them as in his judgement, should be held responsible for such loss or theft[1]. Such fine shall be assessed as a percentage on the pay of the individuals on whom it falls[2]. The Army Act 1950[3] authorises the imposition of a collective fine on a company or similar unit for the purpose of enforcing collective responsibility. Such a collective fine must be distinguished from a joint fine based on individual responsibility. The intention of this provision is not to permit of the punishment by fine of persons against whom there is suspicion but insufficient proof to warrant their conviction by court martial. This provision is, in a sense, an exception to the general scheme of the Army Act 1950, under which individual responsibility is the basis for punishment or for penal deduction. The powers granted by the Army Act 1950 s 89 are therefore, of an administrative and not judicial character. The imposition of a collective fine under this provision upon persons of a unit is not a bar to trial by court martial of any person of that unit, whose individual act or omission may have contributed to the loss. A collective fine cannot be imposed upon officers[4].

1 Army Act 1950 s 89(1). A collective fine cannot be imposed upon officers.

2 Army Act 1950 s 89(2). Whenever a weapon or part of a weapon referred to in the Army Rules 1954 r 186 is lost or stolen, a court of inquiry is mandatory under the Army Rules 1954 r 185. The amount of the fine to be imposed is regulated by the Army Rules 1954 r 186 and the fine must be assessed as a percentage on the pay of the individuals on whom it falls. Fine cannot be imposed in respect of weapons or parts of weapons not enumerated in the Army Rules 1954 r 186.

3 Army Act 1950 s 89.

4 Manual of Military Law, Volume II, 2011, the Army Act 1950 s 89 notes.

7. COURTS MARTIAL

A. KINDS, COMPOSITION AND POWERS

CONTENTS

PARA

[0174] Introduction Under the provisions of the Army Act 1950, a court martial[1] is an *ad hoc* military court, convened by the military authority or officers to try and punish those members of armed forces who violate the military law. The constitution of the court martial depends upon the nature and gravity of the offence and the rank of the accused. The court martial is a criminal court[2], and has no civil jurisdiction and cannot enforce a contract or award damages in favour of an individual. The proceedings of a court martial are judicial in nature and the rules of natural justice need to be observed. Only a court martial that is properly convened and composed is capable of rendering valid judgments[3].

1 As to the definition of 'court martial'; see **[0016]**.

2 The Code of Criminal Procedure 1973 (Act 2 of 1974) s 5.

3 Army Act, 1950 s 152. Also see: *S C Patnaik v. Union of India*, 1969 Cri LJ 930 (Ori).

[0175] Kinds of courts martial Under the Army Act 1950 there are four kinds of courts martial[1]: general courts martial[2]; district courts martial[3]; summary general courts martial[4]; and summary courts martial[5].

A court martial also has the same responsibility as any court to protect the rights of accused charged before it and to follow the procedural safeguards. Procedure prescribed for court martial is equally fair if not more than a criminal court[6]. A court of inquiry under the provision of the Army Rules 1954[7] is only for the purpose of collection of evidence and is merely in the nature of a preliminary investigation. It may not be equated to a trial and does not amount to a court-martial[8].

1 As to the definition of 'court martial'; see **[0016]**.

2 Army Act 1950 s 108(a).

3 Army Act 1950 s 108(b).

4 Army Act 1950 s 108(c).

5 Army Act 1950 s 108(d).

6 *Mithilesh Kumar v Union of India* Mil LJ 2003 P&H 39.

7 Ie under the Army Rules 1954 r 177.

8 *Suresh Chand Mehra v Defence Secretary, Union of India* AIR 1991 SC 483, (1991) 2 SCC 198, (1991) SCC (Cr) 452.

[0176] Power to convene a general court martial A general court martial may be convened by the Central Government or the Chief of the Army Staff or by any officer empowered in this behalf by warrant of the Chief of the Army Staff[1]. The 'A-1' warrant is at present, issued by the Chief of the Army Staff to officers commanding army, corps, division/area and independent brigade and to officers prescribed by the Central Government under the provisions of the Army Act 1950[2]. A warrant may contain such restrictions, reservations or conditions as the officer issuing it may think fit[3]. When a warrant has been issued and its contents communicated to the addresses, he can act upon it before it actually reaches him. He cannot act after he has received notification that the warrant has been revoked though he may not have received the actual order. In granting a warrant, it should be clearly shown that during the absence of the officer to whom such warrant is issued, the powers therein conferred may be exercised by the officer on whom the command devolves, if he is not under a specified rank. It is, therefore, common to address such a warrant to an officer by designation of his office and not by name.

An officer before convening a general court martial shall first satisfy himself that the charges to be tried by the court are for offences within, the meaning of the Army Act 1950, and that the evidence justifies a trial on those charges, and if not so satisfied, shall order the release of the accused, or refer the case to superior authority[4]. The officer convening a general court martial shall also satisfy himself that the case is a proper one to be tried by the kind of court-martial which he proposes to convene[5]. The officer convening the court martial shall appoint or detail the officers to form the court and, may also appoint or detail such waiting officers as he thinks expedient. He may also, where he considers the services of an interpreter to be necessary appoint or detail an interpreter to the court[6]. The officer convening the court martial shall furnish to the senior member of the court with the original charge-sheet on which the accused is to be tried, and the order for the assembly of the court-martial. He shall also send, to all the other members, copies of the charge sheet and to the judge-advocate, a copy of the charge sheet and a copy of the summary or abstract of evidence[7]. The Army Act 1950 and the Army Rules 1954 show that subjecting an officer to court-martial is a serious step and under the provision of the Army Act 1950[8], such a power conferred on the Central Government may be exercised by the Chief of the Army Staff or any officer empowered in this behalf by warrant of the Chief of the Army Staff. A personal satisfaction is required to be done by the officer who proposes to convene the court martial proceedings[9]. The order of the Chief of the Army Staff empowering the field officer, commanding sub area or the officer on whom his command may devolve during his absence, not under the rank of field officer, from time to time, to convene general court martial for trial of any person under his command, is valid under the Army Act 1950[10]. However, a commanding officer is not competent to convene a general court martial[11].

1 Army Act 1950 s 109.

2 Ie under the Army Act 1950 s 8.

3 Army Act 1950 s 111.

4 Army Rules 1954 r 37(1).

5 Army Rules 1954 r 37(2).

6 Army Rules 1954 r 37(3).

7 Army Rules 1954 r 37(4).

8 Ie under the Army Act 1950 s 109.

9 *Union of India v Gurnam Singh* AIR 2004 SC 2126, (2004) 4 SCC 636, (2004) SCC (Cr) 1372.

10 Ie under the Army Act 1950 s 109; see: *S N Purandare v Union of India* 1988 Cr LJ 714.

11 *Vidya Prakash v Union of India* AIR 1988 SC 705, 1988 SCC (L&S) 603, 1988 (1) SLR 605.

[0177] Power to convene a district court martial A district court-martial may be convened by an officer having power to convene a general court-martial or by any officer empowered in this behalf by warrant of any such officer[1]. The 'B-1' warrant is at present issued which empowers the holder thereof to convene as well as confirm the findings and sentences of district court martial. It is issued to sub-area/brigade commanders by the officers empowered to convene a general court martial. Such a warrant has also been issued to officers prescribed by the Central Government under the provisions of the Army Act 1950[2]. A warrant may contain such restrictions, reservations or conditions as the officer issuing it may think fit[3].

1 Army Act 1950 s 110.

2 Ie under the Army Act 1950 s 8.

3 Army Act 1950 s 111.

[0178] Power to convene a Summary General Court Martial The following authorities shall have power to convene a summary general court martial:

(1) an officer empowered in this behalf by an order of the Central Government or of the Chief of the Army Staff[1];

(2) on active service, the officer commanding the forces in the field, or any officer empowered by him in this behalf[2];

(3) an officer commanding any detached portion of the regular army on active service[3] when, in his opinion, it is not practicable, with due regard to discipline and the exigencies of the service, that an offence should be tried by a general court martial[4].

A summary general court martial can try any offence committed on active service but when troops are not on active service it can only be convened by an officer empowered in this behalf by an order of the Central Government or of the Chief of the Army Staff. The object of the summary general court martial is to provide for the speedy trial of offences committed abroad or on active service in cases where it is not practicable, with due regard to the interests of discipline and of the service, to try such offences by an ordinary general court martial or district court martial[5].

1 Army Act 1950 s 112(1).

2 Army Act 1950 s 112(2).

3 As to the meaning of 'active service' see **[0008]**; also see Army Act 1950 s 9.

4 Army Act 1950 s 112(3). The summary general court martial can be convened by an officer commanding under this provision without a warrant or authorisation. Manual of Military Law, Volume II, 2011, the Army Act 1950 s 112 notes.

5 Manual of Military Law, Volume II, 2011, the Army Act 1950 s 112 notes.

[0179] Composition of general court martial A general court-martial shall consist of not less than five officers[1], each of whom has held a commission for not less than three whole years and of whom not less than four are of a rank not below that of captain[2]. A convening officer can increase beyond the legal minimum the number of officers to sit on a general court-martial, but cannot convene a court with less than the minimum, otherwise the proceedings are void. If a general court martial after the commencement of a trial is reduced below the minimum number of officers required by the Army Act[3], it shall be dissolved. It is desirable that every court should consist of an uneven number of officers. The presiding officer of the general court martial is not detailed in the convening order but the senior member sits as the presiding officer[4]. Whenever an officer of the rank of colonel or above is available to sit as presiding officer of a general court martial, an officer of inferior rank will not be appointed. Whenever a general court martial may have to be so detailed that an officer below the rank of a colonel will be the senior member and consequently its presiding officer, the convening officer must obtain the prior sanction of his next superior authority and state in the order convening the court that such sanction has been obtained[5]. The members and waiting members of the court may be detailed by name or by their ranks and units to which they belong, and in case where units cannot be specified they should be named. When the commanding officer of a corps is to be tried, as many members as possible will be officers who have held or are holding commands equivalent to that held by the accused. When a trial is likely to be prolonged, it will usually be expedient to form the court of a larger number than the legal minimum, and two or four additional members should be detailed. Waiting members should also be detailed to meet reduction by challenge. Each officer serving as a member of a court martial will render a certificate which will be attached by the presiding officer to the proceedings of the court martial[6].

1 As to the definition of 'officer' see **[0029]**.

2 Army Act 1950 s 113.

3 Ie Army Act 1950 s 113; see Army Act 1950 s 117(1).

4 Army Act 1950 s 128.

5 Defence Services Regulations, Regulations for the Army 1987, Volume I, paragraph 460.

6 'Certificate of commissioned service': I, No....Rank....., Name........., Unit...., hereby, certify that I have on the....day of........., held a commission for....years. I understand that any service as a junior commissioned officer or any period of ante-date of commission does not count towards the commissioned service mentioned above, and I have excluded all such periods from the reckoning. A court would have no jurisdiction if each member had not held a commission for the required period, or if its composition differed in any respect from that detailed in the convening order. Any period during which an officer has held a commission in any of the three services shall count as commissioned service for this purpose, but no account shall be taken of an ante-date of seniority. See: Defence Services Regulations, Regulations for the Army 1987, Volume I, paragraph 460(e).

[0180] Ineligibility and disqualification of officers for general court martial An officer is not eligible for serving on a general court martial if he: (i) is not subject to the Army Act 1950[1]; (ii) is an officer who convened the court; (iii) is the prosecutor or a witness for the prosecution; (iv) has investigated the charges before trial, or took down the summary of evidence, or was a member of a court of inquiry respecting the matters on which the charges against the accused are founded, or was the squadron, battery, company, or other commander, who made preliminary inquiry into the case, or was a member of a previous court martial which tried the accused in respect of the same offence; (v) is the commanding officer of the accused, or of the corps to which the accused belongs; or (vi) has a personal interest in the case[2]. The provost-marshal or assistant provost marshal is disqualified from serving on a general court martial[3].

1 Army Rules 1954 r 39(1). The term 'eligible' is used with reference to an officer being subject to the Army Act 1950 and of the necessary standing; i.e., it refers to the status of the officer, and involves no personal considerations. Manual of Military Law, Volume II, 2011, the Army Rules 1954 r 39 notes.

2 Army Rules 1954 r 39(2). The term 'disqualified' is used with reference to the personal qualification of an officer. The term 'personal interest' will extend to even a remote or very small interest, e.g. in a charge relating to the theft of a sum of money, however small, belonging to an officers' mess, or a club, every officer of that mess or club has a personal interest, and is therefore disqualified. A merely technical interest has been held to disqualify a person from holding a judicial position, e. g., a person who holds, as trustee or otherwise on behalf of others money in

which he has no beneficial share himself, nevertheless has a personal interest in any charge relating to that money. Manual of Military Law, Volume II, 2011, the Army Rules 1954 r 39 notes.

3 As to the definition of 'provost marshal' see **[0032]**. Army Rules 1954 r 39(3). The term 'disqualified' is used with reference to the personal qualification of an officer. Manual of Military Law, Volume II, 2011, the Army Rules 1954 r 39 notes.

[0181] Composition of District Court Martial A district court martial shall consist of not less than three officers, each of whom has held a commission for not less than, two whole years[1]. The presiding officer of the district court martial is not detailed in the convening order but the senior member sits as the presiding officer[2]. He should, if possible, be of field rank[3]. The members and waiting members of the court may be detailed by name or by their ranks and units to which they belong, and in case where units cannot be specified they should be named. A district courts martial may be composed wholly of officers, of the corps or department to which the accused belongs; but where possible they should not be so composed. For a district court martial the legal minimum will ordinarily be sufficient; but, if necessary a larger number may be detailed, and waiting members provided. In complicated cases, a district court martial should, when possible, should consist of five officers[4]. Each officer serving as a member of a court martial will render a certificate which will be attached by the presiding officer to the proceedings of the court martial[5].

1 Army Act 1950 s 114.

2 Army Act 1950 s 128.

3 Defence Services Regulations, Regulations for the Army 1987, Volume I, paragraph 460(c).

4 Defence Services Regulations, Regulations for the Army 1987, Volume I, paragraph 460(d).

5 'Certificate of commissioned service': I, No....Rank....., Name........., Unit...., hereby, certify that I have on the....day of........., held a commission for....years. I understand that any service as a junior commissioned officer or any period of ante-date of commission does not count towards the commissioned service mentioned above, and I have excluded all such periods from the reckoning. A court would have no jurisdiction if each member had not held a commission for the required period, or if its composition differed in any respect from that detailed in the convening order. Any period during which an officer has held a commission in any of the three services shall count as commissioned service for this purpose, but no account shall be taken of an ante-date of seniority. See: Defence Services Regulations, Regulations for the Army 1987, Volume I, paragraph 460(e).

[0182] Ineligibility and disqualification of officers for District Court Martial[1]

1 Ineligibility and disqualifications applicable for general courts martial are also applicable for a District Court Martial; see **[0180]**.

[0183] Composition of summary general court martial A summary general court martial shall consist of not less than three officers[1]. The presiding officer of a summary general court martial is not detailed in the convening order but the senior member sits as the presiding officer[2]. A convening officer can increase beyond the legal minimum the number of officers to sit on a court-martial, but cannot decrease the number below the minimum; he must therefore take care to convene a court with not less than the minimum, otherwise the proceedings are void. Though there is no statutory requirement as to the rank or service of a member of a summary general court martial, officers appointed or detailed as members should have held commission for not less than one year. In case officers with commissioned service of not less than three years are available, they should be selected in preference to officers of less service[3]. Any available officer, other than the provost-marshal, assistant provost-marshal, a prosecutor or witness for the prosecution may be appointed a member of the court[4]. For instance, the convening officer can himself be a member of the court, but in that case, he cannot confirm the proceedings of a summary general court martial. Each officer serving as a member of a court martial will render a certificate which will be attached by the presiding officer to the proceedings of the court martial[5].

1 Army Act 1950 s 115.

2 Army Act s 128.

3 Army Rules 1954 r 151(2). It is not mandatory that a member of a summary general court martial must have held a commission for not less than one year. An officer with less than one year's commissioned service can legally sit as a member.

4 Army Rules 1954 r 151(3).

5 'Certificate of commissioned service': I, No....Rank....., Name........., Unit...., hereby, certify that I have on the....day of........., held a commission for....years. I understand that any service as a junior commissioned officer or any period of ante-date of commission does not count towards the commissioned service mentioned above, and I have excluded all such periods from the reckoning. A court would have no jurisdiction if each member had not held a commission for the required period, or if its composition differed in any respect from that detailed in the convening order. Any period during which an officer has held a commission in any of the three services shall count as commissioned service for this purpose, but no account shall be taken of an ante-date of seniority. See: Defence Services Regulations, Regulations for the Army 1987, Volume I, paragraph 460(e).

[0184] Summary court martial A summary court martial may be held by the commanding officer[1] of any corps, department or detachment of the regular army, and he shall alone constitute the court[2]. The proceedings shall be attended throughout by two other persons who shall be officers or junior commissioned officers or one of either, and who shall not as such be sworn or affirmed[3]. In a summary court martial, unless two officers or junior commissioned officers or one of either attend the trial throughout the court will have no jurisdiction. Such officers or junior commissioned officers, who cannot take part in the proceedings as such, need not, however, belong to the unit of the accused. If the commanding officer does not himself take the interpreter's oath, one of the officers or junior commissioned officers attending the trial may be appointed interpreter. He may legally combine this duty with attendance at the trial under the Army Act 1950[4]. The officer holding the trial may clear the court to consider the evidence or to consult with the officers or junior commissioned officers, attending the trial[5]. Under normal circumstances trial by summary court martial for desertion will be held by the commanding officer of the unit of the deserter[6].

1 As to the definition of 'commanding officer'; see **[0013]**. As to the meaning of 'corps', and 'department'; see **[0015]** and **[0019]**. The term 'detachment' means every separate body of persons subject to the Army Act 1950 which is not a corps or department. A medical officer commanding a hospital or other medical unit is the 'commanding officer' of medical personnel under his command. He is also, for the time being the commanding officer of a person subject to the Army Act 1950 not belonging to the medical corps, who is a patient, or is employed in that hospital or medical unit. He may either himself dispose of a charge against such person or refer it for disposal, after the person has left the hospital, to the officer commanding the corps, department or detachment to which such person belongs. However, the medical officer in charge of a regimental medical establishment is not, unless that establishment is detached, the 'commanding officer' of the establishment or of any person who is a patient in, or is employed in, the medical unit to which that establishment belongs. Manual of Military Law, Volume II, 2011, the Army Act s 116 notes.

2 Army Act 1950 s 116(1).

3 Army Act 1950 s 116(2).

4 Ie under the Army Act s 116.

5 Army Rules 1954 r 127(1).

6 For trial of deserter see Defence Services Regulations, Regulations for the Army 1987, Volume I, paragraph 381.

[0185] Dissolution of courts martial A court martial shall dissolve: (i) where after the commencement of a trial, it is reduced below the minimum number of officers required by the Army Act 1950[1]; (ii) where on account of illness of the judge advocate or of the accused before the finding, it is impossible to continue the trial[2]. The officer who convened a court martial may also dissolve such court martial if it appears to him that military exigencies or the necessities of discipline render it impossible or inexpedient to continue the said court martial[3]. Where a court martial is dissolved under these provisions, the accused may be tried again[4].

1 Army Act 1950 s 117(1). 'Shall be dissolved': Apart from the conditions laid down in under this provision, in which the court must be dissolved, a court always has the power to adjourn under the Army Rules 1954 r 82 and report to the convening officer when something has occurred, which, in the option of the court, makes it improper or undesirable that it should continue to hear the case, e.g. if through inadvertence a previous conviction of the accused for a similar offence had been brought to the notice of the court before the finding. In such a case the convening officer, if he agrees with the opinion of the court may dissolve it and convene a fresh court. The members who sat on the dissolved court will be ineligible to sit on the fresh court; see the Army Rules 1954 r 39(2)(c). The trial is for the purposes of this section, held to have commenced when the accused is arraigned; see: the Army Rules 1954 r 48, 85 and 86.

2 Army Act 1950 s 117(2). Illness of the accused or the judge advocate: A medical certificate should always, where possible, be obtained, stating that the illness of the accused/judge advocate renders his presence in court impracticable or dangerous to himself or others; it will also state the medical officer's opinion as to when the accused/judge advocate will be able to be present. See the Army Rules 1954 r 84 and 104.

3 Army Act 1950 s 117(3). 'Impossible to continue': This means to continue within a reasonable time having regard to all the circumstances.

4 Army Act 1950 s 117(4). It may frequently be inexpedient to convene a fresh court for a re-trial under this provision, especially where the accused has been for some time under arrest or in confinement. Manual of Military Law, Volume II, 2011, the Army Act 1950 s 117 notes.

[0186] Powers of general and summary general courts martial A general or summary general court martial shall have power to try any person subject to the Army Act 1950[1] for any offence punishable therein[2] and to pass any sentence authorized[3] thereby[4]. The court martial has no unfettered discretion to impose different punishment to different persons for the same offence when all of them are identically situated in the matter of gravity of offence and the evidence cited in respect of offences against them. It cannot be said that in the matter of court martial, art 14 of the Constitution has no application and the court martial has an absolute and unfettered discretion to pass orders of punishment, which may even appear to be arbitrary and uncalled for in the given circumstances[5].

1 As to the meaning of 'persons subject to the Army Act 1950'; see **[0039]**.

2 As to the 'offences punishable under the Army Act 1950' see ss 34 to 69.

3 As to the 'sentence authorized' see the Army Act 1950 s 71. When the court has a discretion whether to pass sentences of death or not, a sentence of death cannot be so passed by a general court martial without the concurrence of at least two-thirds of the members or by a summary general court martial without the concurrence

of all members of the court; see the Army Act 1950 s 132 (2) and (3).

4 Army Act 1950 s118.

5 R R *Verma v Union of India* 1994 Cri LJ 762.

[0187] Power of district courts martial A district court-martial shall have power to try any person subject to the Army Act 1950 other than an officer[1] or a junior commissioned officer[2] for any offence made punishable therein, and to pass any sentence authorised by the Army Act 1950 other than a sentence of death, imprisonment for life, or imprisonment for a term exceeding two years[3]. However, a district court martial shall not sentence a warrant officer[4] to imprisonment[5].

1 As to the meaning of 'officer'; see **[0029]**.

2 As to the meaning of 'junior commissioned officer'; see **[0023]**.

3 Army Act 1950 s 119. Powers of a district court martial are limited in as much as it has no jurisdiction to try an officer or a JCO nor can it pass a sentence of death, imprisonment for life or imprisonment over two years. If such a court, therefore, passes a sentence of death or imprisonment for life or sentences a WO to imprisonment, it will be wholly illegal and must be sent, back for revision by the confirming officer under the Army Act 1950 s 160 and the Army Rules 1954 r 68; and if wrongly confirmed, action should be taken under the Army Act 1950 s 163 to substitute a valid sentence.

4 As to the meaning of 'warrant officer'; see **[0037]**.

5 Army Act 1950 s 119 proviso.

[0188] Powers of summary courts martial A summary court-martial may try any offence punishable under the Army Act 1950[1]. When there is no grave reason for immediate action and reference can, without detriment to discipline be made to the officer empowered to convene a district court martial or on active service a summary general court martial for the trial of the alleged offender, an officer holding a summary court martial shall not try without such reference any offence punishable under certain provisions of the Army Act 1950[2], or any offence against the officer holding the court[3]. A summary court martial may try any person subject to the Army Act 1950 and under the command of the officer holding the court, except an officer[4]; junior commissioned officer[5] or warrant officer[6]. A summary court martial may pass any sentence which may be passed under the Army Act 1950, except a sentence of death or imprisonment for life or of imprisonment for a term exceeding the limit specified in the following provision[7]. The limit of punishment referred above shall be one year if the officer holding the summary court martial is of the rank of lieutenant colonel and upwards, and three months if such officer is below that rank[8]. The court martial whether summary or general has no unfettered discretion to impose different punishment to different persons for the same offence when all of them are identically situated in the matter of gravity of offence and the evidence cited in respect of offences against them. It cannot be said that in the matter of court martial, art 14 of the Constitution has no application and the court martial has an absolute and unfettered discretion to pass orders of punishment, which may even appear to be arbitrary and uncalled for in the given circumstances[9].

1 Army Act 1950 s 120(1).

2 Ie under the Army Act 1950 ss 34, 37 and 69; see **[0087]**, **[0090]** and **[0122]**.

3 Army Act 1950 s 120(2). The commanding officer is the best and sole judge to decide which case should ordinarily be tried only after reference and sanction. If it subsequently appears to superior authority that his action was not justified, this should merely be viewed as a grave irregularity for which the commanding officer may be held

responsible but it does not affect the legality of the finding or sentence, nor, in ordinary circumstances, furnish reason for setting aside the trial. Where, however, the officer holding the trial loses sight of the law, and tries without considering whether an emergency exists or not, the trial is illegal. See the Army Rules 1954 r 130 for certificate to be attached to the proceedings by the officer holding the trial when he tries, without reference, a case which would ordinarily be referred to the officer empowered to convene a district court martial or, on active service, a summary general court martial. 'Offence against the officer holding the trial': It is difficult to lay down a definite rule in this matter, but generally a consideration of personal interest which would suffice to disqualify an officer to sit as a member of a general court martial or district court martial debars him from holding a summary court martial; save in case of emergency, without previous reference. For instance, offences under the Army Act 1950 ss 40 and 41 when committed towards a commanding officer fall under this category; and should not, except in case of emergency, be tried by summary court martial without previous reference. Manual of Military Law, Volume II, 2011, the Army Act 1950 s 120 notes.

4 As to the meaning of 'officer'; see **[0029]**.

5 As to the meaning of 'junior warrant officer'; see **[0023]**.

6 As to the meaning of 'warrant officer'; see **[0037]**. Army Act 1950 s 120(3).

7 Army Act 1950 s 120(4).

8 Army Act 1950 s 120(5).

9 R R *Verma v Union of India* 1994 Cri LJ 762.

[0189] Prohibition of Second Trial When any person subject to the Army Act 1950 has been acquitted or convicted of an offence by a court-martial or by a criminal court, or has been dealt with under any of the provisions of the Army Act 1950[1], he shall not be liable to be tried again for the same offence by a court martial or dealt with under the said provisions[2]. Where the army authorities opted for a trial of the accused by a court martial but the trial did not proceed because one of the members constituting the said court had retired and a fresh court martial was not available to be constituted as a reference thereto was barred by limitation and the accused was handed over to the civil authorities for being tried by a regular criminal court, the aforesaid provision has no application as the accused was neither acquitted nor convicted by the court martial or by a criminal court nor has he been dealt with under the provisions of the Army Act 1950[3].

1 Ie under the Army Act 1950 ss 80, 83, 84 and 85; see respectively **[0162]**, **[0166]**, **[0167]** and **[0168]**.

2 Army Act 1950 s 121. It is a general principle of law also incorporated as a fundamental right in art 20 of the Constitution that a person cannot be tried twice in respect of the same offence. The findings of a general court martial, summary general court martial or district court martial, if not confirmed, are not valid. In such cases, the accused is not acquitted/convicted, and may legally be tried again. However, re-trials should rarely be resorted to, and only when the needs of discipline and justice demand that an offender shall not escape punishment on account of a legal technicality. Re-trial should not be ordered until the deputy judge advocate general of the command has been consulted and the sanction of superior authority obtained. See the Army Act 1950 s 153. Where a court is not legally constituted and has no jurisdiction, for example, if the convening order is signed by or on behalf of an officer not authorized to convene such a court, or if the number of officers composing the court is below the legal minimum required for that type of court, or if unqualified officers sit; it is no court at all. The accused will not have been really tried, and may be tried again, even though the proceedings of such illegally constituted court have been inadvertently confirmed. See the Army Act 1950 s 117. Where the individual was awarded the punishment of dismissal by the summary court martial and was also supplied with one set of proceedings intimating him that he may submit any appeal against the said order before the appellate authority; and subsequently intimated that the court martial proceedings held against him have been set aside by the competent authority and was directed to

report back and join the unit forthwith. Thereafter, another trial by a summary court martial on the same charges amounted to double jeopardy and was prohibited by the Army Act s 121. The Armed Forces Tribunal Regional Bench Guwahati: *Rfn (Tailor) Bhupal Ram Okesa v. Union of India*, TA No. 49 of 2010 [WP (C) No. 6030 of 2007], decided on June 2011.

3 *Chief of Army Staff v S P Chadha* AIR 1991 SC 460, (1991) 2 SCC 288, (1991) Cr LJ 494.

[0190] Period of limitation for trial Except as provided under the provisions of the Army Act 1950[1], no trial by court-martial of any person subject thereto for any offence shall be commenced after the expiration of a period of three years. Such period shall commence: (i) on the date of the offence[2], (ii) where the commission of the offence was not known to the person aggrieved by the offence or to the authority competent to initiate action, the first day on which such offence comes to knowledge of such person or authority, whichever is earlier[3]; or (iii) where it is not known by whom the offence was committed, the first day on which the identity of the offender is known to the person aggrieved by the offence or to the authority competent to initiate action, whichever is earlier[4]. The above stated limitation[5] shall not apply to a trial for an offence under certain provisions of the Army Act 1950[6]. In the computation of the period of time of three years, as mentioned in the above, time spent by such person as a prisoner of war, or in enemy territory, or in evading arrest after the commission of the offence, shall be excluded[7]. No trial for an offence of desertion other than desertion on active service or of fraudulent enrolment shall be commenced if the person in question, not being an officer, has subsequently to the commission of the offence, served continuously in an exemplary manner for not less than three years with any portion of the regular army[8]. The limitation of three years will run from the date when the competent authority takes a decision to initiate the disciplinary proceeding against the offender[9].

The effect of the above provision is that on the expiration of three years [to be computed in accordance with s 122 (3)] from the commission of the offence, the offender is free from being tried or punished under the Army Act 1950 by a court martial for any offence except those mentioned in the Army Act 1950 s 38 (desertion on active service), s 43 (fraudulent enrolment) or for any of the offences mentioned in s 37 (mutiny). It follows that where an accused person is charged with desertion commencing on a date more than three years before his trial begins, he cannot be found guilty under the Army Act 1950 s 139 (1) of absence without leave from that date, but such absence must, be restricted to a period not exceeding three years immediately prior to the commencement of the trial. Where, however, such a finding and sentence has been wrongly confirmed, the authorities specified in the Army Act 1950 s 163 may substitute a valid finding and pass a sentence for the offence specified or involved in such finding. Once a stay order has been vacated, in spite of the expiry of limitation for commencement of court martial proceedings under the Army Act 1950 s 122, the option to have the delinquent tried by a court martial or to invoke the Army Act 1950 s 19 read with the Army Rules 1954 r 14, depending on the facts and circumstances of an individual case, would still be available to the Central Government or the Chief of the Army Staff[10]. The provision deals with the prohibition of second trial and has no application where the delinquent was neither acquitted nor convicted by the court martial or by a criminal court nor has been dealt with under the Army Act 1950[11].

1 Ie under the Army Act 1950 s 122(2).

2 Army Act 1950 s 122(1)(a).

3 Army Act 1950 s 122(1)(b). Computation of date for limitations under this provision shall start from the date the competent authority initiates action against the individual and it is the date of his knowledge of the commission of the alleged offence and the identity of the alleged offender that is relevant under the Army Act, 1950. *Rajvir Singh*

v Secretary Ministry of Defence, (2012) 3 SCC 167.

4 Army Act 1950 s 122(1)(c).

5 Ie under the Army Act s 122 (1).

6 Army Act 1950 s 122(2); for the offences under the Army Act 1950 ss 38 (desertion on active service), 43 (fraudulent enrolment) or 37 (mutiny); see **[0091]**, **[0096]** and **[0090]** respectively.

7 Army Act 1950 s 122(3).

8 Army Act 1950 s 122(4). Offences mentioned in the Army Act 1950 s 37 (mutiny) and s 38 (desertion on active service) can be tried at any time by a court martial.

9 *Union of India v Hav S P Shukla Mil LJ* 2008 UP 111.

10 *Union of India v Harjeet Singh Sandhu* AIR 2001 SC 1772, (2001) 5 SCC 593 : (2001) Lab IC 1707; *Union of India v Rajbir Singh Khanna* AIR 2001 SC 3327 : (2001) 7 SCC 113.

11 Ie under the Army Act 1950 ss 80, 83, 84 or 85. *Chief of the Army Staff v S P Chadha* AIR 1991 SC 460, 1990 SCR Supl. (3) 691: 1991 SCC (2) 288.

[0191] Liability of offender who ceases to be subject to the Army Act Where an offence under the Army Act 1950 had been committed by any person while subject thereto, and he has ceased to be so subject, he may be taken into and kept in military custody, and tried and punished for such offence as if he continued to be so subject[1]. No such person shall be tried for an offence, unless his trial commences within a period of three years after he had ceased to be subject to the Army Act 1950. In computing such period , the time during which such person has avoided arrest by absconding or concealing himself or where the institution of the proceeding in respect of the offence has been stayed by an injunction or order , the period of the continuance of the injunction or order, the day on which it was issued or made, and the on which it was withdrawn, shall be excluded[2]. However, the above stated provision shall not apply to the trial of any such person for an offence of desertion or fraudulent enrolment or for any of the offences mentioned in the Army Act 1950 s 37 or shall affect the jurisdiction of a criminal court to try any offence triable by such court as well as by a court martial[3]. When a person subject to the Army Act 1950 is sentenced by a court martial to imprisonment for life or imprisonment, the Act shall apply to him during the term of his sentence, though he is cashiered or dismissed from the regular army, or has otherwise ceased to be subject to the Army Act 1950. He may be kept, removed, imprisoned and punished as if he continued to be subject to the Army Act 1950[4]. When a person subject to the Army Act is sentenced by a court martial to death, the Army Act 1950 shall apply to him till the sentence is carried out[5]. Army officer though ceased to be subject to the Army Act 1950 consequent upon his retirement, can be dismissed from the service for committing offence under the Army Act 1950[6].

1 Army Act 1950 s 123(1).

2 Army Act 1950 s 123(2). The words 'trial commences' is required to be understood in the light of the scheme of the Army Act 1950 and the Army Rules 1954. 'Trial' means an act of proving or judicial examination or determination of the issues including its own jurisdiction or authority in accordance with law or adjudging the guilt or innocence of the accused including all steps necessary thereto. The trial commences with the performance of the first act or steps necessary or essential to proceed with the trial. Trial commences the moment the general court martial assembles for proceeding with the trial, consideration of the charge and arraignment of the accused to proceed further with the trial including all preliminaries like objections to the inclusion of the members of the court martial, reading out the charge or charges, amendment thereof and so on. However, where an accused deliberately delays the commencement of the trial, he may not be allowed to take advantage of the same-- *nullus commodum capere protest de injuria sua propria*---no man can take advantage of his own wrong squarely stands in the way of avoidance. *Union*

of India v Madan Lal Yadav AIR 1996 SC 1340 : (1996) 4 SCC 127 : (1996) SCC (Cr) 592.

3 Army Act 1950 s 123 (2) proviso.

4 Army Act 1950 s 123 (3).

5 Army Act 1950 s 123 (4).

6 *Union of India v RKLD Azad* AIR 1996 SC 845.

[0192] Place of Trial Any person subject to the Army Act 1950 who commits any offence against it may be tried and punished for such offence in any place whatever[1]. It is not necessary that person subject to the Army Act 1950 be tried at a place which be within the jurisdiction of a criminal court having jurisdiction over the place where the offence be committed[2]. Procedure prescribed by the Army Act 1950[3] cannot be held unconstitutional on the grounds that it violates art 21 of the Constitution because art 33 of the Constitution provides that the Parliament by law or by an enactment modify the scope of art 21. If the modification stands in derogation of art 21 to that extent art 21 in its application to the armed forces, is modified by enactment of the procedure in the Army Act itself[4].

1 Army Act 1950 s 124. 'Any place whatever' means any place in which the offender may for the time being be and which is within the jurisdiction of an officer authorised to convene a court martial for his trial as if the offence had been committed where the trial takes place and the offender were under the command of the officer convening such court. The provision enables a court martial convened in India to try a person for an offence committed elsewhere and vice versa. Defence Service Regulations, Regulations for the Army 1987, Volume I, paragraph 452 (c) provides: If, in the opinion of a convening officer, a court martial could more conveniently be held at a place other than that where the accused is, he may cause the court to be convened at any place within his command. If it is desired to hold the trial in any place beyond his command, application will be made to the general officer commanding-in-chief, and by him, if necessary to the Adjutant General's Branch, Army Headquarters, with an explanation of the reasons for this course. When the case is to be tried in another command, the court will be convened under the orders, and on the responsibility, of the general officer commanding–in-chief to whose command the accused is removed.

2 *Ram Sarup v Union of India* AIR 1965 SC 247, [1964] 5 SCR 931, (1965) 1 Cr LJ 236.

3 Ie the Army Act 1950 s 124.

4 *Gurung Tham Bahadur v Union of India* 1984 Cr LR (Guj) 250, 1984 (I) Guj LR 429 (DB).

[0193] Choice between Criminal Court and Court Martial When a criminal court[1] and a court martial[2] both have jurisdiction in respect of an offence, it shall be in the discretion of the prescribed officer[3] to decide before which court the proceedings shall be instituted, and if that officer decides that they should be instituted before a court martial, to direct that the accused person shall be detained in military custody[4].

All civil offences can be tried by a court martial (subject to the provisions of the Army Act 1950 s 70), or by a criminal court. An offender who is subject to the Army Act 1950 can either be tried by a criminal court or by a court martial and if the authorities mentioned in the Army Act 1950[5] make a request to the magistrate, the magistrate has either to deliver the offender to the army authorities or refer the matter to the Central Government. The reference would only be there where the magistrate is of the opinion that the offender could not be handed over to the army authorities. Where a criminal court having jurisdiction considers that the accused should be tried before itself, it may, in writing, call upon the officer referred to in the Army Act 1950 to hand over the accused to it for trial, in which case the said officer should either hand over the accused as demanded or suspend the proceedings and refer the case to the central government. An offender is normally handed over to the civil authorities for trial where he is alleged to have committed an offence in collaboration with other persons who are not subject to military law. When an officer, subject to the Army Act 1950, is alleged to have committed a misconduct, in view of the provisions of the Army Act 1950 read with those of the Army Rules 1954[6], the following situation emerges, that is, where the alleged misconduct amounts to an offence including a civil offence, the above-stated provision vests discretion in the officer commanding the army, army corps division or independent brigade in which the accused person is serving or such other officer as may be prescribed, to decide before which court the proceedings must be instituted. Where the decision is to have the delinquent officer tried by a criminal court and if he is acquitted by the criminal court, then that is the end of the matter and the pronouncement of judicial verdict would thereafter exclude any independent disciplinary action being taken against the delinquent officer on the same facts which constituted the misconduct amounting to an offence for which he was charged before the criminal court. In the event of his being convicted, if some further disciplinary action is still proposed to be taken, then it is the conduct of the officer leading to his conviction, as found by the criminal court, which is capable of being taken into consideration by the Central Government or the Chief of the Army Staff under the provisions of the Army Rules 1954[7] for the purpose of such action and those facts alone must form the basis of the formation of opinion as to whether his further retention in service is undesirable whereupon he may be dismissed, removed or compulsorily retired from the service in the manner prescribed by the said provisions. However, on the other hand, where the initial decision was to have the delinquent officer tried not by a criminal court but by a court martial, then it is for the Central Government or the Chief of the Army Staff to arrive at a satisfaction whether the trial of the officer by a court martial is expedient and practicable whereupon the court martial will be convened. The Central Government or the Chief of the Army Staff may arrive at a satisfaction that it is inexpedient or impracticable to have the officer tried by a court martial, the court martial may not be convened and additionally, subject to formation of the opinion as to undesirability of the officer for further retention in the service, the power under the provisions of the Army Act 1950 read with those of the Army Rules 1954[8] may be exercised. Such a decision may be taken either before convening the court martial or even after it has been convened and commenced, subject to satisfaction as to the trial by a court martial becoming inexpedient or impracticable at which stage the Central Government or the Chief of the Army Staff may revert back to the said provisions[9]. It is not that a decision as to inexpediency or impracticability of trial by a court martial may be taken only once and that too at the initial stage only and once taken may not be changed in spite of a change in the fact situation and prevailing circumstances[10]. The ordinary criminal court would have no jurisdiction to take cognizance of the case and to try the accused in a matter where the procedure prescribed by the Army Rules 1954 has not been complied with. The initial lack of jurisdiction to take cognizance and try the case would, of logical necessity, vitiate the trial and the order of conviction and sentence would be liable to be quashed. The question regarding exercise of jurisdiction by the court martial would arise only after the investigation is completed and the police report is available[11]. Merely because the army has directed that the first information report be lodged with the civil police[12] or because the army has called for a detailed report by the police, it may not be said that the army authorities had voluntarily abandoned their option to try the accused person in the court martial[13]. Where the competent military authority has full knowledge of the nature of crime committed by the accused and released him from military custody and handed him over to the civilian authorities, the magistrate is justified in coming to the conclusion that the military officials were not interested in trying the accused in the court martial and, therefore, is in compliance with the provisions of the Army Act 1950. The provisions of the Army Act 1950 relating to choice between a criminal court and a court martial are not discriminatory and do not infringe the provisions of the Constitution of India[14].

1 As to the meaning of 'criminal court' see **[0017]**.

2 As to the meaning of 'court martial' see **[0016]**.

3 Ie the officer commanding the army, army corps, division or independent brigade; or the officers prescribed under the Army Rules 1954 r 197A: The prescribed officer except in cases falling under the Army Act 1950 s 69 in which death is resulted, be the officer commanding the brigade or station in which the accused is serving.

4 The Army Act s 125.

5 Ie under the Army Act 1950 s 125.

6 Ie in view of the Army Act 1950 ss 19 and 125 read with the Army Rules 1954 r 14.

7 Ie under the Army Rules 1954 r 14(3), (4) and (5).

8 Ie under the Army Act 1950 s 19 read with the Army Rules 1954 r 14.

9 *Union of India v Harjeet Singh Sandhu* AIR 2001 SC 1772 : (2001) 5 SCC 593: (2001) Lab IC 1707.

10 *Superintendent & Remembrancer of Legal Affairs v Usha Ranjan Roy Choudhury* AIR 1986 SC 1655 : (1986) Supp SCC 190 : (1986) Cr LJ 1248.

11 *Som Datt Datta v Union of India* AIR 1969 SC 414, [1969] 2 SCR 177 : (1969) Cr LJ 663.

12 *Superintendent & Remembrancer of Legal Affairs v Usha Ranjan Roy Choudhury* AIR 1986 SC 1655 : (1986) Supp SCC 190 : (1986) Cr LJ 1248.

13 *Joginder Singh v State of Himachal Pradesh* AIR 1971 SC 500 : (1971) 3 SCC 86: (1971) Cr LJ 511; *Balbir Singh v State of Punjab* (1995) 1 SCC 90, (1995) SCC (Cr) 202; *Delhi Special Police Establishment v S K Loraiya* AIR 1972 SC 2548 : (1972) 2 SCC 692, [1973] 1 SCR 1010 (The provisions of the Cr PC 1898 s 549(1) must be construed in the light of the Army Act 1950 s 125. Both the provisions have in mind the object of avoiding a collision between the ordinary criminal court and the court martial. Therefore, both of them must receive a similar construction).

14 *Ram Sarup v Union of India* AIR 1965 SC 247 : [1964] 5 SCR 931 : (1965) 1 Cr LJ 236: the persons to whom the provisions of the Army Act 1950 s 125 apply do form a distinct class and they apply to all those persons who are subject to the Army Act 1950 as specified in s 2 thereof.

[0194] Power of Criminal Court to require delivery of Offender When a criminal court having jurisdiction is of opinion that proceedings shall be instituted before itself in respect of any alleged offence, it may, by written notice, require the officer referred to in the Army Act 1950[1] at his option, either to deliver over the offender to the nearest magistrate to be proceeded against according to law, or to postpone proceedings pending a reference to the Central Government[2]. In every such case the said officer[3] shall either deliver over the offender in compliance with the requisition, or shall forthwith refer the question as to the court before which the proceedings are to be instituted for the determination of the Central Government, whose order upon such reference shall be final[4]. The discretion exercised by the military officer is subject to the control of the Central Government[5]. Certain provisions of the Army Act 1950[6] are framed for the purpose of ensuring that there is no conflict between the criminal court and the court martial[7]. The provisions of the Army Act 1950 ss 125 and 126 do not make any difference between the cases where charge sheet is filed and where charge sheet has not been filed. Merely because the police officer conducted inquest of the dead body and sent for chemical examination, does not mean that the competent military authority decided to hand over the case to the criminal court[8]. Although the offence of rape committed on 'active service' is triable by the Army Act 1950, where the military accused was handed over to the police without being detained in the military custody, the criminal court was competent to try him and the Army Act 1950 s 126 need not be invoked[9]. The surrender of the accused to the civil authorities to be dealt by the latter, after being made aware of the nature of the offence against the accused is a clear indication that the military authorities decided not to try him by a court martial. No need for a magistrate to comply with the provisions of the Army Act 1950[10].

1 Ie the Army Act 1950 s 125.

2 Army Act s 126 (1).

3 Ie referred in the Army Act 1950 s 125.

4 Army Act s 126 (2).

5 *Ram Sarup v Union of India* AIR 1965 SC 247, [1964] 5 SCR 931, (1965) 1 Cr LJ 236.

6 Ie under the Army Act 1950 ss 125 and 126.

7 *S K Kashyap v State of Rajasthan* AIR 1971 SC 1120, (1971) 2 SCC 126, (1971) Cr LJ 832.

8 *Som Datt Datta v Union of India* AIR 1969 SC 414, [1969] 2 SCR 177 : (1969) Cr LJ 663.

9 *Roshan Lal v State* 1971 Cr LJ 554.

10 Ie under the Army Act 1950 s 126. *Joginder Singh v State of Himachal Pradesh* AIR 1971 SC 500: (1971) 3 SCC 86: (1971) Cr LJ 511.

[0195] Defence of soldiers charged with criminal offences The following procedure should be followed for the defence of soldiers charged with criminal offences and prosecuted by the government in civil courts: (1) When soldiers are to be tried by a civil court upon any criminal charge, the brigade/sub-area commander should consult the district magistrate, and arrange with him for the selection and remuneration of a pleader, advocate or barrister, as the importance and necessities of the case may require. (2) Except in cases in which the Central Government are interested; the maximum amount that may be paid to the pleader, advocate or barrister is fixed by the government for each day that he appears in the case, on behalf of one or more accused, before a high court, a judicial commissioner's court or sessions court or before any other court. The amounts include expenses of every description which counsel may incur. In a joint trial, when the local military authority is satisfied that the accused require different lines of defence he may authorise the separate payment of fees for each accused so defended. (3) (a) The brigade/sub-area commander is only to appoint a pleader, advocate or barrister in cases where he thinks it desirable. The amount to be paid to counsel will be definitely settled before hand, subject to the maxima laid down by the government. If suitable counsel cannot be obtained for the remuneration admissible under these rules, the case will be reported to superior authority and the orders of government obtained. (b) In high courts in which counsel may not plead unless instructed by a solicitor, a solicitor may be employed and his bill of costs, which should include counsel's fees (subject to the restrictions laid down in clause (2) above) and all other expenses incurred in the case, should be submitted to the legal remembrance of the local government and his certificate obtained that the amount of bill is reasonable before it is submitted for the orders of government. (4) When counsel is provided for the defence of a soldier at the first trial in a civil court, counsel can also be provided when considered necessary on appeal, subject to the limitations laid down in provisions (2) and (3) above. (5) For the purposes of this concession the term 'soldier' used in provision (1) above, includes all junior commissioned officers, warrant officers, non-commissioned officers and sepoys when on duty, and reservists called up for training or called out for service. It does not include junior commissioned officers, warrant officers, non-commissioned officers and sepoys when on leave, enrolled non-combatants or any other classes not mentioned above[1]. The officers commanding units will report to higher authority whenever the trial of a junior commissioned officer, warrant officer, non-commissioned officer and sepoy in a civil court is inordinately delayed[2].

1 Defence Services Regulations, Regulation for the Army 1987, Volume I, paragraph 421.

2 Defence Services Regulations, Regulation for the Army 1987, Volume I, paragraph 422.

[0196] Conviction of officers, junior commissioned officer, warrant officer, non-commissioned officer and sepoy by the civil power The conviction of an officer by the civil power will be reported to the central government and that of a junior commissioned officer to the chief of the army staff for such action as these authorities see fit to take. The conviction of a warrant officer or other ranks will be reported to the brigade/sub-area commander who will decide whether dismissal, discharge or reduction is desirable. The disciplinary authority may, if it comes to the conclusion that an order with a view to imposing a penalty on a government servant on the ground of conduct which had led to his conviction on a criminal charge should be issued, issue such an order without waiting for the period of filing an appeal or, if an appeal has been filed without waiting for the decision in the first court of appeal[1].

1 Defence Services Regulations, Regulation for the Army 1987, Volume I, paragraph 423.

[0197] Concurrent proceedings under the Army Act and the Central Civil Services (Classification, Control and Appeal) Rules 1965 Initiation of concurrent proceedings both under the Army Act 1950 and the Central Civil Services (Classification, Control and Appeal) Rules 1965 is unexceptionable as these two proceedings operate in two different fields though the crime or the misconduct might arise out of the same act. The court martial proceedings deal with the penal aspect of the misconduct while the proceedings under the Central Civil Services (Classification, Control and Appeal) Rules 1965 deal with the disciplinary aspect of the misconduct and the two proceedings do not overlap[1].

1 *Union of India v Sunil Kumar Sarkar* AIR 2001 SC 1092 : (2001) 3 SCC 414 : (2001) Lab IC 1114 (the Notification No SRO-329 dated 23 September 1960 issued under the Central Civil Services (Classification, Control and Appeal) Rules 1965 and under the Army Act 1950 s 4(1) and (4) makes the position clear, that the punishments that might be meted out under the Central Civil Services (Classification, Control and Appeal) Rules 1965 have been taken out of the purview of the court martial proceedings under the Army Act 1950).

[0198] Delivery to commanding officers of persons liable to be tried by court martial The Central Government is empowered to make rules consistent with the Cr PC 1973 and the Army Act, 1950, the Navy Act, 1957, and the Air Force Act, 1950, and any other law relating to the armed forces of the Union, as to cases in which, persons subject to military, naval or air force law, or such other law, shall be tried by a court to which the Cr PC applies or by a court martial[1]. In exercise of the powers conferred by Cr PC 1975, and in supersession of the Criminal Courts and Court-Martial (Adjustment of Jurisdiction) Rules 1952, the Central Government has made the Criminal Courts and Court-Martial (Adjustment of Jurisdiction) Rules 1978[2].

1 Criminal Procedure Code 1973 s 475(1).

2 For details see **[1629]-[1644]**.

B. PROCEDURE AT COURT MARTIAL

CONTENTS

PARA

A. Functionaries connected with court martial

B. Rules as to Evidence

A. FUNCTIONARIES CONNECTED WITH COURT MARTIAL

[0199] Presiding officer At every general, district or summary general court martial, the senior member shall be the presiding officer[1]. The presiding officer of the general, district or summary general court martial is not detailed in the convening order but the senior member sits as the presiding officer. The presiding officer is responsible for the trial being conducted in proper order, and in accordance with the Army Act 1950, rules made thereunder[2] and in a manner befitting a court of justice[3]. It is the duty of the presiding officer to see that justice is administered, that the accused has a fair trial, and that he does not suffer any disadvantage in consequence of his position as a person under trial, or of his ignorance, or of his incapacity to examine or cross-examine witnesses, or otherwise[4]. The presiding officer should be careful to safeguard the dignity of the court and the solemnity of its proceedings. If any person, other than the accused, interrupts the proceedings, he should ordinarily be excluded from the court. The court has, however, further powers under the Army Rules 1954[5] for dealing with persons who interrupt its proceedings. The trial of a person cannot proceed in his absence, even though he interrupts the proceedings. The members of a court martial shall take their seats according to their rank[6].

1 Army Act 1950 s 128.

2 Ie the Army Rules 1954. The court should always have at its disposal the Army Act 1950, the Army Rules 1954, the Defence Services Regulations, Regulations for the Army 1987, and any other official book or orders which are necessary for the purpose of its proceedings.

3 The Army Rules 1954 r 76(1).

4 If the accused is not represented by counsel or defending officer, the presiding officer should assist him in putting forward his defence, and take care that he is not prejudiced by his inability to put proper questions to the witnesses or bring out clearly the points upon which he relies. If a witness gives evidence different from that given by him when the summary of evidence was taken, he should be questioned as to the difference. The presiding officer should always put to the witnesses any questions which appear to him necessary or desirable for the purpose of eliciting the truth. The Army Rules 1954 r 76(1).

5 Ie under the Army Rules 1954 r 150; see **[0375]**.

6 The Army Rules 1954 r 75.

[0200] Judge Advocate The judge advocate general in the army is the superintendent of the administration of military justice and also the adviser the chief of the army staff in legal matters[1]. The judicial department, under the judge advocate general has a selected cadre of officer called judge advocate. Every general court martial shall[2], and every district or summary general court martial may be attended by a judge advocate, who shall be either an officer belonging to the department of the judge advocate general or if no such officer is available, an officer approved of by the judge advocate general or any of his deputies[3]. The accused has no right to object to the judge advocate[4]. A judge advocate plays an important role during the course of trial at a general court martial and he is enjoined to maintain an impartial position. The court martial records its findings after the judge advocate has given his opinion upon the legal bearing of the case[5].

1 Defence Services Regulations, Regulation for the Army 1987, Volume I, paragraph 33.

2 Presence of a judge advocate at a general court martial is a legal necessity and his non-attendance there at will invalidate the proceedings. A court martial, in the absence of a judge advocate if such has been appointed, shall not proceed and shall adjourn. See: The Army Rules 1954 r 82 (4).

3 The Army Act 1950 s 129. Any 'officer' of the judge advocate general's department or, if such officer is not available, an officer approved by the judge advocate general or one of his deputies can attend as judge advocate. Although at a district court martial and summary general court martial appointment of a judge advocate is not legally necessary, in practice a judge advocate is nominated by the deputy judge advocate general command concerned. Invalidity in the appointment of a JA does not vitiate the trial: see the Army Rules 1954 r 103.

4 Under the Army Act 1950 s 130.

5 *SN Mukherjee v Union of India* AIR 1990 SC 1984, (1990) 4 SCC 594, 1990 (5) SLR 8 (SC).

[0201] Disqualification of judge advocate An officer, who is disqualified for sitting on a court martial, shall be disqualified for acting as a judge advocate at that court martial[1]. A judge advocate should be free of all suspicion of bias or prejudice. He should have had experience of the practice and procedure of courts-martial and knowledge of the general principles of law and of the rules of evidence. In a general court martial where a judge advocate was of the rank of lieutenant (with less than three years of service) the entire conclusion and decision as such are vitiated on account of the advice of a person who was neither eligible for nor qualified to sit as judge advocate[2].

1 The Army Rules 1954 r 102; also see Army Rules 1954 r 39(2); see **[0180]**. A combined reading of the provisions of the Army Rules 1954 rs 39, 40 and 102 suggest that an officer who is disqualified to be a part of court martial is also disqualified from acting and sitting as a judge advocate at the court martial. It follows, therefore, that if an officer lower in rank than the officer facing the trial cannot become a part of the court martial, the officer of such rank would be disqualified for acting as a judge advocate at the trial before a general court martial. *Union of India v Charanjit S Gill* (2000) 5 SCC 742, AIR 2000 SC 3425, 2000 (2) SLR 755 (SC).

2 *Ex Sep Ranjit Singh v Union of India* Mil LJ 2002 Delhi 140.

[0202] Invalidity in the appointment of judge advocate A court martial shall not be invalid merely by reasons of any invalidity in the appointment of the judge advocate officiating thereat, in whatever manner appointed, if a fit person has been appointed and the subsequent approval of the judge advocate general or deputy judge advocate general obtained, but this rule shall not relieve from responsibility the person who made the invalid appointment[1]. Where a fit person is not appointed as a judge-advocate, the proceeding and findings of the court martial may not be held to be valid. Such an invalidity in appointing an 'unfit' person as a judge-advocate is not curable[2]. Where a fit person possessing requisite qualifications and otherwise eligible to form part of the general court martial is appointed as a judge-advocate and ultimately some invalidity is found in his appointment, the proceedings of the court martial may not be declared invalid[3].

1 The Army Rules 1954 r 103.

2 Ie under the Army Rules 1954 r 103.

3 *Union of India v Charanjit S Gill* AIR 2000 SC 3425, (2000) 5 SCC 742, (2000) 2 SLR 755.

[0203] Substitute on death, illness or absence of judge advocate If the judge advocate dies, or from illness or from any cause whatever is unable to attend, the court shall adjourn, and the presiding officer shall report the circumstances to the convening authority; and a fit person not disqualified to be judge-advocate may be appointed by that authority, who shall be sworn, or affirmed, and act as judge advocate for the residue of the trial, or until the judge advocate returns[1].

1 The Army Rules 1954 r 104. The court will in no circumstances proceed in the absence of a judge advocate who has been duly appointed. This provision permits substitution of a judge advocate in case of his death or illness, by any other fit person not disqualified to be a judge advocate. Such person may be appointed for the residue of the trial or until return of the judge advocate first appointed. Manual of Military Law, Volume II, 2011, the Army Rules 1954 r 104 notes.

[0204] Powers and duties of judge advocate The powers and duties of a judge advocate[1] are as follows: At a court martial, a judge advocate represents the judge advocate general[2]. The prosecutor and the accused, respectively, are, at all times after the judge advocate is named to act on the court, entitled to his opinion on any question of law relative to the charge or trial, whether he is in or out of court, subject, when he is in court, with the permission of the court[3]. The judge advocate is responsible for informing the court of any informality or irregularity in the proceedings. Whether consulted or not, the judge advocate shall inform the convening officer and the court of any informality or defect in the charge, or in the constitution of the court, and shall give his advice on any matter before the court[4]. Any information or advice given to the court, on any matter before the court shall, if the judge advocate or the court desires it, be entered in the proceedings[5]. At the conclusion of the case, the judge advocate shall sum up the evidence and give his opinion upon the legal bearing of the case, before the court proceeds to deliberate upon its finding[6]. The court, in following the opinion of the judge advocate on a legal point, may record that it has decided in consequence of that opinion[7]. The judge advocate has, equally with the presiding officer, the duty of taking care that the accused does not suffer any disadvantage in consequence of his position as such, or of his ignorance or incapacity to examine or cross-examine witnesses or otherwise, and may, for that purpose, with the permission of the court, call witnesses and put questions to witnesses, which appear to him necessary or desirable to elicit the truth[8]. In fulfilling his duties, the judge advocate must be careful to maintain an entirely impartial position[9].

Upon any point of law or procedure which arises at the trial, the court should be guided by the opinion of the judge advocate, and not disregard it, except for very weighty reasons. The court is responsible for the legality of its decision, but it must consider the grave consequences which may result from its disregard to the advice of the judge advocate on any legal point. If a court martial, acting without jurisdiction or in excess of jurisdiction, convicts a person subject to the Army Act 1950, the members of the court may be held liable in damages by a civil court and such liability—or at least the amount of the damages—may depend upon the question whether they exercised a bona fide judgement, and the fact that they accepted the advice of the judge advocate, even if such advice was held to be wrong, might practically exonerate the members from liability[10].

1 As to the meaning of 'judge advocate' see **[0200]**.

2 The Army Rules 1954 r 105 (2).

3 The Army Rules 1954 r 105 (1).

4 The Army Rules 1954 r 105 (3).

5 The Army Rules 1954 r 105 (4).

6 The Army Rules 1954 r 105 (5).

7 The Army Rules 1954 r 105 (6).

8 The Army Rules 1954 r 105 (7).

9 The Army Rules 1954 r 105 (8).

10 Manual of Militay Law, Volume II, 2011, r 105 notes.

[0205] Reference to the judge advocate general's department before trial In all cases for trial by general court martial, and all cases under the Army Act 1950, of indecency, fraud, theft, except ordinary theft, and civil offences except simple assaults, the charge sheet and summary of evidence, and all the exhibits will be referred by the convening officer to the deputy judge advocate general of the command or deputy/assistant judge advocate general of the corps, as the case may be, before trial is ordered. The convening officer should also refer for advice any other cases of doubt or difficulty. In all cases the doubts or difficulties and the matters on which advice is required will be specifically stated in the applications[1]. The reports by officers of the judge advocate general's department are confidential and will not be communicated directly or indirectly to any authority lower than the authority to whom they are addressed. When proceedings are forwarded to lower formations or to units, such reports will be removed[2]. The opinion of the judge advocate is not exempt from disclosure under the Right to Information Act 2005[3].

1 Defence Services Regulations, Regulations for the Army 1987, Volume I, paragraph 459.

2 Defence Services Regulations, Regulations for the Army 1987, Volume I, paragraph 471.

3 Ie the Right to Information Act 2005 s 8(1)(e). A denial of access to such information to the information seekers, especially in the circumstances that the said information is used admittedly in coming to the conclusion that the delinquent officers were guilty, and in determining the punishment to be accorded to them, would involve a serious breach of principles of natural justice, as non-communication would entail civil consequences and would render such a decision vulnerable to challenge under Article 14 of the Constitution of India provided information is sought and was not given. The right to information is a constitutional right under art 19(1)(a) of the Constitution which, with the enactment of the Right to Information Act 2005 has been given in addition a statutory flavour with the exceptions provided therein. *Union of India v Col VK Shad* ILR (2013) I DELHI 625.

[0206] Defending officer and friend of accused At any general or district court martial, an accused person may be represented by any officer[1] subject to the Army Act 1950 who shall be called 'the defending officer' or assisted by any person whose services he may be able to procure and who shall be called 'the friend of the accused'[2]. It shall be the duty of the convening officer to ascertain whether an accused person desires to have a defending officer assigned to represent him at his trial and, if he does so desire, the convening officer shall use his best endeavours to ensure that the accused shall be so represented by a suitable officer. If owing to military exigencies, or for any other reason, there shall in the opinion of the convening officer, be no such officer available for the purpose, the convening officer shall give a written notice to the presiding officer of the court martial, and such notice shall be attached to the proceedings[3]. The defending officer shall have the same rights and duties as appertain to counsel under these rules and shall be under the like obligations[4]. The friend of the accused may advise the accused on all points and suggest the questions to be put to the witnesses, but he shall not examine or cross-examine the witnesses or address the court[5]. In any summary court martial, an accused person may have a person to assist him during the trial (the friend of the accused), whether a legal adviser or any other person. The friend of the accused may advise him on all points and suggest the questions to be put to witnesses, but shall not examine or cross examine witnesses or address the court[6]. In a summary general court martial, the accused shall be asked what he has to say in defence and shall be allowed to make his defence. He may be allowed to have any person assist to him during the trial[7].

Where an accused had sought the services of any one of seven officers requested for but none could be made available due to the exigencies of military service and an officer nominated by the convening authority was refused by the accused, it was not considered a violation of the Army Rules 1954 r 95[8]. Where an accused had given names of a number of officers out of which anyone could be appointed as defending officer; only some of the officers were not available on the grounds of military exigencies and the convening authority had not certified the non-availability of other officers due to the exigencies of military service, it was held that there was non-compliance with the provisions of the Army Rules 1954 r 95 and the proceedings of court martial were struck down[9]. Friend of accused imposed on the accused against his wish, amounts to denial of right under the Army Rules 1954[10]. Denial to provide 'friend of accused' of accused's choice would vitiate the proceedings[11].

1 As to the definition of 'officer'; see **[0029]**.

2 The Army Rules 1995 r 95 (1).

3 The Army Rules 1995 r 95 (2). Every effort should be made to secure the services of a competent officer as a defending officer, and he should be allowed time and opportunity for properly preparing the defence of the accused. The Army Rules 1954, however, empowers dispensing with this sub-rule in the event of military exigencies, etc. See the Army Rules 1954 r 36.

4 The Army Rules 1995 r 95 (3). As to the duties of defending officer; see the Army Rules 1954, Appendix III paragraphs 39 and 40

5 The Army Rules 1995 r 95 (4).

6 The Army Rules 1954 r 129.

7 The Army Rules 1954 r 159(1).

8 *Nb Ris Rohiteshwar Singh v Union of India* 1982(2) SLR 236.

9 *Lt Col Jagjit Singh v Union of India* CWP No 242 of 1978 decided by Delhi High Court on 26 August 1980.

10 Ie under the Army Rules 1954 r 129. *Union of India v Pritpal Singh* 1984(3) SLR 675.

11 *The Chief of the Army Staff v Ex Sep Dvr (MT) MZH Khan* Mil LJ 2006 All 152.

[0207] Counsel allowed in certain general and district courts martial In every general and district court martial, counsel shall be allowed to appear on behalf of the prosecutor as well as the accused[1]. However, the convening officer may declare that it is not expedient to allow the appearance of counsel thereat and such declaration may be made as regards all general and district courts-martial held in any particular place, or as regards any particular general or district court-martial, and may be made subject to such reservation as to cases on active service, or otherwise, as deemed expedient[2]. There is no restriction as to the number of counsels engaged in a case[3].

1 The Army Rules 1954 r 96.

2 The Army Rules 1954 r 96 proviso.

3 Manual of Military Law, Volume II, 2011, The Army Rules 1954 r 96 notes.

[0208] Requirements for appearance of counsel An accused person intending to be represented by a counsel shall give to his commanding officer or to the convening officer the earliest practicable notice of such intention and, if no sufficient notice has been given, the court may, if it thinks fit, on the application of the prosecutor, adjourn to enable him to obtain, a counsel on behalf of the prosecutor at the trial[1]. If the convening officer so directs, counsel may appear on behalf of the prosecutor, but in that case, unless the notice referred as above has been given by the accused, notice of the direction for counsel to appear shall be given to the accused at such time (not in any case less than seven days) before the trial, as would, in the opinion of the court, have enabled the accused to obtain counsel to assist him at the trial[2]. The counsel, who appears before a court martial on behalf of the prosecutor or accused, shall have the same right as the prosecutor or accused for whom he appears, to call, and orally examine, cross-examine, and re-examine witnesses, to make an objection or statement, to address the court, to put in any plea, and to inspect the proceedings, and shall have the right otherwise to act in the course of the trial in the place of the person on whose behalf he appears, and he shall comply with these rules as if he were that person and in such case that person shall not have the right himself to do any of the aforesaid matters except as regards the statement allowed by the provisions of the Army Rules 1954[3], or except so far as the court permits him so to do[4]. When counsel appears on behalf of the prosecutor; the prosecutor, if called as a witness, may be examined and re-examined as any other witness and certain provisions of the Army Rules 1954[5] shall not apply[6].

1 The Army Rules 1965 r 97 (1). When the convening officer intends to appoint or apply for the services of an officer of the judge advocate general's department or an officer holding legal qualifications to act as prosecutor, similar notice should be given to the accused to enable him, if he so desires, to obtain counsel to represent him at the trial. Manual of Military Law, Volume II, 2011, The Army Rules 1954 r 97 notes.

2 The Army Rules 1965 r 97 (2).

3 Ie the Army Rules 1954 r 58 (2)(2) and r 59.

4 The Army Rules 1965 r 97 (3).

5 Ie the Army Rules 1954 r 56(5) and (6); see **[0215]**.

6 The Army Rules 1965 r 97 (4).

[0209] Counsel for prosecution The counsel appearing on behalf of the prosecutor shall have the same duty as the prosecutor, and is subject to be stopped or restrained by the court as provided[1] in the Army Rules 1954[2].

1 As provided under the Army Rules 1954 r 77(2).

2 The Army Rules 1954 r 98. The counsel appearing on behalf of the prosecutor should always make an opening address, and should state therein the substance of the charge against the accused and the nature and general effect of the evidence which he proposes to adduce in support of it without entering into unnecessary details. Manual of Military Law, Volume II, 2011, The Army Rules 1954 r 98 notes.

[0210] Counsel for accused The counsel appearing on behalf of the accused has the rights and obligations as specified in the Army Rules 1954[1] in the case of the accused[2]. If the court asks counsel for the accused a question as to any witness or matter, he may decline to answer, but he must not give the court any answer or information which is misleading[3].

1 Ie under the Army Rules 1954 r 77 (3).

2 The Army Rules 1954 r 99.

3 Manual of Military Law, Volume II, The Army Rules 1954 r 99 notes.

[0211] Lack of pecuniary resources: provision of defence counsel for accused at court martial trials for offences punishable with death When a person subject to the Army Act 1950 is to be tried by court martial for an offence punishable with death[1] and such person is unable to engage a counsel for his defence at the trial owing to lack of pecuniary resources and the convening officer is satisfied about his inability, a counsel for the defence of the accused at the trial may be employed by the convening officer at government expense in consultation with the deputy judge advocate general concerned[2]. To enable the convening officer to employ a counsel for the defence of an accused the deputy judge advocate general of every command headquarter shall prepare and maintain, in consultation with local government law officers, list of qualified counsels at various stations who are willing to be employed under this provision[3]. The amount payable to a counsel for hearing will be fixed on daily basis in which he appears before a court martial. In addition, he will be given travelling and daily allowances not exceeding those admissible to an officer of the first grade if the trial is held at a place different from the normal place of practice of the counsel[4]. Bills submitted by counsels will be countersigned by the deputy judge advocate general concerned before payment[5]. In a joint trial, when the convening officer is satisfied that the accused persons required different lines of defence he may authorise a separate counsel for each accused[6].

1 Offences contained in the Army Act 1950 ss 34, 37, 38 (desertion of active service), or 69.

2 Defence Services Regulations, Regulations for the Army 1987, Volume I, paragraph 479(a).

3 Defence Services Regulations, Regulations for the Army 1987, Volume I, paragraph 479(b).

4 Defence Services Regulations, Regulations for the Army 1987, Volume I, paragraph 479(c).

5 Defence Services Regulations, Regulations for the Army 1987, Volume I, paragraph 479(d).

6 Defence Services Regulations, Regulations for the Army 1987, Volume I, paragraph 479(e).

[0212] General rules as to counsel Counsel, whether appearing on behalf of the prosecutor or of the accused, shall conform strictly to the provisions contained in Army Rules 1954 and to the rules of criminal courts in India relating to the examination, cross-examination, and re-examination of witnesses, and relating to the duties of a counsel[1]. Counsel should not state as a fact any matter which is not proved, or which he does not intend to prove in evidence, nor should he state what is his own opinion as to any matter of fact before the court. Counsel should treat the court and the judge advocate with due respect, and should, while regarding the exigencies of his case, bear in mind the requirements of military discipline in the respectful treatment of any superior officer of the accused who may attend as a witness[2].

1 The Army Rules 1954 r 100.

2 Manual of Military Law, 2011, Volume II, The Army Rules 1954 r 100 notes.

[0213] Qualifications of counsel Neither the prosecutor nor the accused has any right to object to any counsel if properly qualified[1]. Counsel shall be deemed properly qualified if he is a legal practitioner authorised to practice with right of audience in a court of sessions in India, or if, he is recognised by the convening officer in any other country where the trial is held as having in that part, rights and duties similar to those of such legal practitioner in India and as being subject to punishment or disability for a breach of professional rules[2].

1 The Army Rules 1954 r 101(1).

2 The Army Rules 1954 r 101(2).

[0214] Prosecutor The prosecutor in a court martial is generally an officer detailed by the convening authority or commanding officer[1]. He should be an officer having a working knowledge of the Army Act 1950, the Army Rules 1954 and the laws of evidence. As a rule, he will be the officer who recorded the summary of evidence. In trials by general court martial and in complicated cases a prosecutor should be specially selected for his experience and knowledge of military law, and should be, as far as possible, relieved from ordinary military duty, so that he may be enabled fully to master the case. If such an officer is not available, the convening officer should apply as soon as possible to superior military authority for the services of one[2].

1 The Army Rules 1954 r 43: Appearance of prosecutor and accused—When the court has satisfied itself that the provisions of the Army Rules 1954 r 41 and 42 have been complied with, it shall cause the accused to be brought before the court, and the prosecutor, who must be a person subject to the Army Act 1950, shall take his due place in the court.

2 Defence Services Regulations, Regulations for the Army 1987, Volume I paragraph 458.

[0215] Duty of Prosecutor It is the duly of the prosecutor to assist the court in the administration of justice, to behave impartially, to bring the whole of the transaction before the court, and not to take any unfair advantage of, or suppress any evidence in favour of the accused[1]. In complicated cases the prosecutor should always make an opening address, so that the members of the court may be enabled to understand the general nature of the allegations. The prosecutor shall state the substance of the charge against the accused and the nature and general effect of the evidence which he proposes to adduce in support of it without entering into any unnecessary detail[2]. In case it is necessary for the prosecutor to give evidence for the prosecution on the facts of the case, he shall give it after the delivery of his address (if any), and he must be sworn or affirmed, as the case may be, and give his evidence in detail[3]. The prosecutor may be cross-examined by or on behalf of the accused and afterwards may make any statement which might be made by a witness on re-examination[4]. After the examination of the witnesses, the prosecutor may make a closing address[5]. In case any point of law is raised by the accused, the prosecutor may, with the permission of the court, make his submission with regard to that point[6]. A civilian counsel can also be allowed on behalf of the prosecution at general and district court martial[7].

1 The Army Rules 1954 r 77(1). For example, intoxication is no excuse for the commission of an offence, but if the charges against an accused do not allege intoxication, and he was intoxicated at the time that he committed an offence with which he is charged, the prosecutor should bring out this fact in evidence. Also see Defence Services Regulations, Regulations for the Army 1987, Volume I, paragraph 464. For the duties of prosecutor; see: The Army Rules 1954, appendix III, part IV, paragraphs 36-38.

2 The Army Rules 1954 r 56(3).

3 The Army Rules 1954 r 56(5).

4 The Army Rules 1954 r 56(6).

5 The Army Rules 1954 r 59.

6 The Army Rules 1954 r 59 proviso.

7 The Army Rules 1954 r 96; see **[0209]**.

[0216] Challenges At all trials by general, district or summary general court martial, as soon as the court is assembled, the names of the presiding officer and members shall be read over to the accused, who shall thereupon be asked whether he objects to being tried by any officer sitting on the court[1]. If the accused objects to any such officer, his objection, and also the reply thereto of the officer objected to, shall be heard and recorded, and the remaining officers of the court shall, in the absence of the challenged officer decide on the objection[2]. If the objection is allowed by one-half or more of the votes of the officers entitled to vote, the objection shall be allowed, and the member objected to shall retire, and his vacancy may be filled in the prescribed manner by another officer, subject to the same right of the accused to object[3]. When no challenge is made, or when challenge has been made and disallowed, or the place of every officer successfully challenged has been filled by another officer to whom no objection is made or allowed, the court shall proceed with the trial[4]. The accused has no right to object to the judge advocate or prosecutor[5].

1 The Army Act 1950 s 130(1).

2 The Army Act 1950 s 130(2); *Capt Ram Kumar v COAS* AIR 1985 Del 375.

3 The Army Act 1950 s 130(3).

4 The Army Act 1950 s 130(4).

5 Manual of Military Law, 2011, Volume II, The Army Act 1950 s 130 notes.

[0217] Oaths of member, judge advocate and witness An oath or affirmation in the prescribed manner shall be administered to every member of a court martial and to the judge advocate before the commencement of the trial[1]. Every person giving evidence before a court-martial shall be examined after being duly sworn or affirmed in the prescribed form[2]. However, administering of oath shall not be applicable where the witness is a child under 12 years of age and the court-martial is of opinion that though the witness understands the duty of speaking the truth, he does not understand the nature of an oath or affirmation[3]. The oath/affirmation taken by the members of the court binds them in their capacity of jurors to find a true verdict according to the evidence and in their capacity of judges to administer justice; and to keep secret the votes or opinions of other members[4].

1 The Army Act 1950 s 131(1). For prescribed form/manner of oath or affirmation for a member of the court; see the Army Rules 1954 r 45, 109 and 155. For prescribed form/manner of oath or affirmation for the judge advocate, for the officer attending for the purposes of instruction, shorthand writer and interpreter; see the Army Rules 1954 r 46, 109 and 155. The person to administer oaths or affirmation is prescribed by the Army Rules 1954 r 47. Refusal by a witness subject to the Army Act 1950 to take an oath or make an affirmation is punishable under the Army Act 1950 s 59(b). Giving false evidence on oath/affirmation is an offence under the Army Act 1950 s 60. If a civilian witness refuses to take the oath or make an affirmation or gives false evidence on oath/affirmation, action should be taken by the court as indicated in the Army Rules r 150(3).

2 The Army Act 1950 s 131(2). The prescribed form of oath or affirmation for witness and the person to administer it are prescribed in the Army Rules 1954 r 140.

3 The Army Act 1950 s 131(3). This provision is based on the Oaths Act 1873 s 5 proviso.

4 Manual of Military Law, 2011, Volume II, Army Act 1950 s 131 notes.

[0218] Voting by members Every decision of a court martial, other than the sentence of death, shall be passed by an absolute majority of votes and where there is an equality of votes on either the finding or the sentence, the decision shall be in favour of the accused[1]. No sentence of death shall be passed by a general court martial without the concurrence of at least two-thirds of the members of the court[2]. No sentence of death shall be passed by a summary general court martial without the concurrence of all the members[3]. In matters other than a challenge or the finding or sentence, the presiding officer shall have a casting vote[4]. A certificate to the effect that the death sentence was passed with the concurrence of.....members/unanimously, as the case may be, should be endorsed in the proceedings. In awarding a sentence of death the court must add a direction that the accused shall suffer death by being hanged by the neck until he be dead; or by being shot to death[5]. Mere allegation of an accused that the death sentence was voted by an inadequate majority of the members of the court martial cannot be based on any knowledge as to how the voting went at the consideration of the finding in pursuance of the Army Rules 1954[6].

1 Army Act 1950 s 132(1).

2 Army Act 1950 s 132(2).

3 Army Act 1950 s 132(3).

4 Army Act 1950 s 132(4).

5 See the Army Act 1950 s 166.

6 *Ram Sarup v Union of India* AIR 1965 SC 247: [1964] 5 SCR 931: (1965) 1 Cr LJ 236. See the Army Rules 1954 r 61 and 87: **[0264]** and **[0296]**.

B. RULES AS TO EVIDENCE

[0219] General rule as to evidence The Indian Evidence Act 1872 shall, subject to the provisions of the Army Act 1950[1], apply to all proceedings before a court martial[2].

1 'Subject to the provisions of the Army Act'; see the Army Act 1950 ss 134, 140-144 and the Army Rules 1954 r 134-143.

2 Army Act 1950 s 133.

[0220] Judicial notice A court martial may take judicial notice[1] of any matter within the general military knowledge of the members[2]. The court martial may take judicial notice of the fact that a lower official obeys implicitly the directions of a higher official[3].

1 'Judicial notice' means that the court will recognize a matter without formal evidence. Thus, evidence need not be given as to the relative rank of officers, as to the general duties, authorities and obligations of different members of the service, or generally as to any matters which an officer, as such, may reasonably be expected to know. Manual of Military Law, 2011, Volume II, The Army Act 1950 s 134 notes.

2 Army Act 1950 s 134.

3 *General Court Martial v Aniltej Singh Dhaliwal* AIR 1998 SC 983 : (1998) 1 SCC 756 : (1998) Cr LJ 1402.

[0221] Summoning witnesses The convening officer, the presiding officer of a court martial, the judge advocate or the commanding officer of the accused person may, by summons under his hand, require the attendance, at time and place to be mentioned in the summons, of any person either to give evidence or to produce any document or other thing[1]. In the case of a witness amenable to military authority, the summons shall be sent to his commanding officer, and such officer shall serve it upon him accordingly[2]. In the case of any other witness, the summons shall be sent to the magistrate within whose jurisdiction he may be or reside, and such magistrate shall give effect to the summons as if the witness where required in the court of such magistrate[3]. When a witness is required to produce any particular document or other thing in his possession or power, the summons shall describe it with reasonable precision[4].

1 Army Act 1950 s 135(1). The presiding officer of a court of inquiry is also empowered to summon a witness under this provision.

2 Army Act 1950 s 135(2).

3 Army Act 1950 s 135(3). The words 'such magistrate shall give effect to the summons as if the witness where required in the court of such magistrate' should be understood to mean that the magistrate shall have to issue the summons or warrant of arrest under his hand and seal as if the court itself is issuing the summons or warrant, but however directing the appearance of production before the concerned military authorities. *Union of India v XI Additional Chief Metropolitan Magistrate Bangalore City, Bangalore* Mil LJ 2002 Kar 177.

4 Army Act 1950 s 135(4).

[0222] Documents exempted from production The provision contained in the Army Act 1950[1] shall not affect the operation of the certain part of the Indian Evidence Act 1872[2], or to apply to any letter, postcard, telegram or other document in the custody of the postal or telegraph authorities[3]. If any document in such custody is, in the opinion of any district magistrate, chief presidency magistrate, high court or court of session, wanted for the purpose of any court martial, such magistrate or court may require the postal or telegraph authorities, as the case may be, to deliver such document to such person as such magistrate or court may direct[4]. If any such document is, in the opinion of any other magistrate or of any commissioner of police or district superintendent of police, wanted for any such purpose, he may require the postal or telegraph authorities, as the case may be, to cause search to be made for and to detain such document pending the orders of any such district magistrate, chief presidency magistrate or high court or court of session[5].

1 Ie in the Army Act 1950 s 135; see **[0221]**.

2 Ie of the Indian Evidence Act 1872 ss 123 and 124. These provisions deal with 'affairs of State' and 'official communications'.

3 Army Act 1950 s 136(1).

4 Army Act 1950 s 136(2).

5 Army Act 1950 s 136(3).

[0223] Commissions for examination of witnesses Whenever, in the course of a trial by court martial, it appears to the court that the examination of a witness is necessary for the ends of justice, and that the attendance of such witness cannot be procured without an amount of delay, expense or inconvenience which, in the circumstances of the case, would be unreasonable, such court may address the judge advocate general[1] in order that a commission to take the evidence of such witness may be issued[2]. The judge advocate general may then, if he thinks necessary, issue a commission to any district magistrate or magistrate of the first class, within the local limits of whose jurisdiction such witness resides, to take the evidence of such witness[3]. The magistrate or officer to whom the commission is issued, or, if he is the district magistrate, he or such magistrate of the first class as he appoints in this behalf, shall proceed to the place where the witness is or shall summon the witness before him and shall take down his evidence in the same manner, and may for this purpose exercise the same powers, as in trials of warrant-cases under the Code of Criminal Procedure 1973, or any corresponding law in force in the state of Jammu and Kashmir[4]. Where the witness resides in a tribal area or in any place outside India, the commission may be issued in the manner specified in the provisions of the Code of Criminal Procedure 1973 chapter XXII, or of any corresponding law in force in the state of Jammu and Kashmir[5].

1 The expression 'judge advocate general' includes a deputy judge advocate general; the Army Act 1950 s 137(5).

2 Army Act 1950 s 137(1).

3 Army Act 1950 s 137(2).

4 Army Act 1950 s 137(3). The taking of evidence by commission in courts martial should be most sparingly resorted to, and ought not to be adopted save in extreme cases of delay, expense or in convenience. The following considerations should guide courts martial in this: (i) A complainant, or a witness who practically fills the role of complainant, should never be examined on a commission; as the risk of injustice to the accused is too great. (ii) A material prosecution witness, the value of whose evidence can only be made apparent under full examination and cross-examination in court should very seldom be so examined. (iii) A corroborative witness for either side, or a material witness for the defence, if the accused is fully satisfied by this action, might be examined on a commission.

5 Army Act 1950 s 137(4).

[0224] Examination of a witness on commission The prosecutor and the accused person in any case in which a commission is issued under the provision of the Army Act 1950[1] may respectively forward any interrogatories in writing which the court may think relevant to the issue, and the magistrate or officer executing the commission shall examine the witness upon such interrogatories[2]. The prosecutor and the accused person may appear before such magistrate or officer by counsel or, except in the case of an accused person in custody, in person, and may examine, cross-examine and re-examine, as the case may be, the said witness[3]. After a commission issued under the provision relating to commissions for examination of witnesses in the Army Act 1950[4] has been duly executed, it shall be returned, together with the deposition of the witness examined there-under, to the judge advocate general[5]. Upon receipt of a commission and deposition returned under the above provision, the judge advocate general shall forward the same to the court at whose instance the commission was issued, or if such court has been dissolved, to any other court convened for the trial of the accused person; and the commission, the return thereto and the deposition shall be open to inspection by the prosecutor and the accused person, and may, subject to all just exceptions, be read in evidence in the case by either the prosecutor or the accused, and shall form part of the proceedings of the court[6]. In every case in which a commission is issued under the provision relating to commissions for examination of witnesses in the Army Act 1950[7], the trial may be adjourned for a specified time reasonably sufficient for the execution and return of the commission[8].

1 Ie under the Army Act 1950 s 137: see **[0223]**.

2 Army Act 1950 s 138(1).

3 Army Act 1950 s 138(2).

4 See **[0223]**.

5 Army Act 1950 s 138(3). The expression 'judge advocate general' includes a deputy judge advocate general; see: The Army Act 1950 s 137(5). Evidence taken on commission at the instance of a court martial which has been dissolved is admissible before another court martial assembled for the trial of the accused (only on the same or substantially the same charges).

6 Army Act 1950 s 138(4).

7 Ie under the Army Act 1950 s 137.

8 Army Act 1950 s 138(5).

[0225] Conviction of offence not charged A person charged before a court martial with desertion may be found guilty of attempting to desert or of being absent without leave[1]. A person charged before a court martial with attempting to desert may be found guilty of being absent without leave[2]. A person charged before a court martial with using criminal force may be found guilty of assault[3]. A person charged before a court martial with using threatening language may be found guilty of using insubordinate language[4]. A person charged before a court martial with any one of the offences specified in the provisions of the Army Act 1950[5] may be found guilty of any other of these offences with which he might have been charged[6]. A person charged before a court martial with an offence punishable under the provision of the Army Act 1950[7] may be found guilty of any other offence of which he might have been found guilty if the provisions of the Code of Criminal Procedure 1973, where applicable[8]. A person charged before a court martial with any offence under the Army Act 1950, may, on failure of proof of an offence having been committed in circumstances involving a more severe punishment, be found guilty of the same offence as having been committed in circumstances involving a less severe punishment[9]. A person charged before a court martial with any offence under the Army Act 1950 may be found guilty of having attempted or abetted the commission of that offence, although the attempt or abetment is not separately charged[10].

The object of this provision is to prevent a miscarriage of justice by permitting a person charged with one of the offences mentioned in it to be found guilty of a cognate offence. But a court martial has no power to find a person guilty of offence other than that with which he is charged in the statement of the offence except in the cases specified under this provision[11]. A court may, however, find a person guilty of a charge with the exception of certain words in the particulars of the charge or with certain immaterial variations, and this finding will be valid as long as in its reduced or varied form it discloses the offence which forms the subject of the charge[12].

1 Army Act 1950 s 139(1).

2 Army Act 1950 s 139(2).

3 Army Act 1950 s 139(3).

4 Army Act 1950 s 139(4).

5 Ie in the Army Act 1950 s 52(a), (b), (c) and (d): see **[0105].**

6 Army Act 1950 s 139(5).

7 Ie under the Army Act 1950 s 69: see **[0122]**.

8 Army Act 1950 s 139(6). For special findings see Cr PC 1973 ss 221 and 20

9 Army Act 1950 s 139(7). For example, a person charged with using criminal force to his superior officer in the execution of his office may be convicted of using criminal force to his superior officer; or a person charged with an offence committed on active service may be found guilty of the same offence committed not on active service; or a person charged with wilfully allowing the escape of a person in his charge may be found guilty of allowing his escape without reasonable excuse. Manual of Military Law, Volume II, 2011, the Army Act 1950 s 139 notes.

10 Army Act 1950 s 139(8). Where a person charged with an offence is found guilty of having attempted or abetted the commission of that offence and no express provision has been made for the punishment for such attempt or abetment, the punishment will be laid in as specified in the Army act 1950 s 65 for attempt and ss 66-68 for abetment.

11 Ie under the Army Act 1950 s 139.

12 Manual of Military Law, Volume II, 2011, the Army Act 1950 s 138 notes.

[0226] Presumption as to signatures In any proceeding under the Army Act 1950, any application, certificate, writ petition, reply or other document purporting to be signed by an officer in the service of the government shall, on production, be presumed to have been duly signed by the person by whom and in the character in which it purports to have been signed, until the contrary is shown[1]. The presumption only relates to the signature and the character by whom and in which it purports to have been signed and not to the contents of the document[2].

1 Army Act 1950 s 140.

2 Manual of Military Law, 2011, Volume II, The Army Act 1950 s 140 notes.

[0227] Enrolment paper Any enrolment paper purporting to be signed by an enrolling officer shall, in proceedings under the Army Act 1950, be evidence of the person enrolled having given the answers to questions which he is therein represented as having given[1]. The enrolment of such person may be proved by the production of the original or a copy of his enrolment paper purporting to be certified to be a true copy by the officer having the custody of the enrolment paper[2]. On the trial of a person subject to the Army Act 1950 for making a false answer on enrolment or for fraudulent enrolment, the answer made or the fact of enrolment can be proved by the production of his enrolment paper. The fact of the enrolment (but not any answer made on enrolment) may also be proved by a certified true copy of the enrolment paper. The enrolment paper, or when admissible the true copy of it, must be produced by a witness on oath or affirmation and the accused identified as the person referred to. Where a certified true copy of the enrolment paper is admissible, it must purport to be so certified by the officer having custody of the enrolment paper and not by a subordinate officer 'for' him[3].

1 Army Act 1950 s 141(1).

2 Army Act 1950 s 141(2).

3 Manual of Military Law, 2011, Volume II, The Army Act 1950 s 140 notes.

[0228] Presumption as to certain documents A letter, return or other document respecting the service of any person in, or the cashiering, dismissal or discharge of any person from, any portion of the regular army, or respecting the circumstances of any person not having served in, or belonged to any portion of the forces, if purporting to be signed by or on behalf of the Central Government or the Chief of the Army Staff or by any prescribed officer[1], shall be evidence of the facts stated in such letter, return or other document[2]. An army, navy or air force list of gazette purporting to be published by authority shall be evidence of the status and rank of the officers, junior commissioned officers or warrant officers therein mentioned, and of any appointment held by them and of the corps, battalion or arm or branch of the services to which they belong[3]. Where a record is made in any regimental book in pursuance of the Army Act 1950 or the Army Rules 1954 or otherwise in pursuance of military duty, and purports to be signed by the commanding officer or by the officer whose duty it is to make such record, such record shall be evidence of the facts therein stated[4]. A copy of any record in any regimental book purporting to be certified to be a true copy by the officer having custody of such book shall be evidence of such record[5].

Where any person subject to the Army Act 1950[6] is being tried on a charge of desertion or of absence without leave, and such person has surrendered himself into the custody of any officer or other person subject to the Army Act 1950, or has been apprehended by such officer or person, a certificate purporting to be signed by such officer, or by the commanding officer of the portion of the regular army, or by the commanding officer of the corps, department or detachment to which such person belongs, as the case may be, and stating the fact, date and place of such surrender or apprehension, and the manner in which he was dressed, shall be evidence of the matters so stated[7]. Where any person subject to the Army Act 1950 is being tried on a charge of desertion or of absence without leave, and such person has surrendered himself into the custody of, or has been apprehended by, a police officer not below the rank of an officer in charge of a police station, a certificate purporting to be signed by such police officer and stating the fact, date and place of such surrender or apprehension and the manner in which he was dressed, shall be evidence of the matters so stated[8]. Any document purporting to be a report under the hand of any chemical examiner to government or any of the government scientific experts, namely, the chief inspector of the explosive, the director of finger print bureau, the director, Haffkeine Institute, Bombay; director of a central forensic science laboratory or a state forensic science laboratory and serologist to the government upon any matter or thing duly submitted to him for examination or analysis and report may be used as evidence in any proceeding under the Army Act 1950[9].

1 As to the meaning of 'prescribed officer', see: the Army Rules 1954 r 198. Prescribed officer under the Army Act 1950 s 142(1): The prescribed officer for the purposes of the Army Act 1950 s 142(1) shall be the officer commanding the corps, department or detachment to which the person appears to have belonged or alleges that he belongs or had belonged.

2 Army Act 1950 s 142(1).

3 Army Act 1950 s 142(2).

4 Army Act 1950 s 142(3).

5 Army Act 1950 s 142(4).

6 As to the persons subject to the Army Act 1950; see **[0039].**

7 Army Act 1950 s 142(5). The certificate should only state the fact, date and place of surrender or apprehension and the manner in which the offender was dressed; it can only be admitted as evidence of those facts and then only cases of desertion of absence without leave. If it is necessary to prove the circumstances of the surrender or apprehension, a witness must be called. If the deserter or absentee surrenders to or is apprehended by any officer, the certificate must purport to be signed by that officer. But if the offender surrenders himself to a junior commissioned officer, warrant officer, non-commissioned officer or sepoy of any unit, department or detachment, or if the offender is apprehended by a junior commissioned officer, warrant officer, non-commissioned officer or sepoy, the certificate must purport to be signed by the commanding officer of such junior commissioned officer etc., of that unit, department or detachment. The certificate must be signed by the officer indicated and not by another officer 'for' him. Manual of Military Law, 2011, Volume II, The Army Act 1950 s 142 notes.

8 Army Act 1950 s 142(6). The certificate should only state the fact, date and place of surrender or apprehension and the manner in which the offender was dressed; it can only be admitted as evidence of those facts and then only cases of desertion of absence without leave. If it is necessary to prove the circumstances of the surrender or apprehension, a witness must be called. It is essential that the certificate should be actually signed by a police officer not below the rank of officer-in-charge of a police station. It is, however, not necessary that it must be signed by the police officer-in-charge of the police station concerned. The certificate should be on IAFD-910. Manual of Military Law, 2011, Volume II, The Army Act 1950 s 142 notes.

9 Army Act 1950 s 142(7).

[0229] References by accused to government officers If at any trial for desertion or absence without leave, overstaying leave or not rejoining when warned for service, the person tried states in his defence any sufficient or reasonable excuse for his unauthorised absence, and refers in support thereof to any officer in the service of the government, or if it appears that any such officer is likely to prove or disprove the said statement in the defence, the court shall address such officer and adjourn the proceedings until his reply is received[1]. The written reply of such an officer, if signed by him be received in evidence and have the same effect as if made on oath before the court[2]. Where the court is dissolved before the receipt of such reply, or if the court omits to comply with these provisions, the convening officer may, at this direction, annul the proceedings and order a fresh trial[3].

1 Army Act 1950 s 143(1).

2 Army Act 1950 s 143(2). The written reply is prima facie evidence not only of the signature of the writer and the

character in which it was signed but also of the truth of the facts stated therein. Manual of Military Law, 2011, Volume II, The Army Act 1950 s 143 notes.

3 Army Act 1950 s 143(3).

[0230] Evidence of previous convictions and general character Where any person subject to the Army Act 1950 has been convicted by a court martial of any offence, such court martial may inquire into, and receive and record evidence of any previous convictions of such person, either by a court martial or by a criminal court, or any previous award of punishment under certain provisions of the Army Act 1950[1], and may further inquire into and record the general character of such person and such other matters as may be prescribed[2]. Evidence received under this provision may be either oral, or in the shape of entries in, or certified extracts from, court martial books or other official records and it shall not be necessary to give notice before trial to the person tried that evidence as to his previous convictions or character will be received[3]. At a summary court martial the officer holding the trial may, if he thinks fit, record any previous convictions against the offender, his general character, and such other matters as may be prescribed, as of his own knowledge, instead of requiring them to be proved under the foregoing provisions[4].

1 Ie under the Army Act 1950 ss 80, 83, 84 and 85; see **[0162]**, **[0166]**, **[0167]** and **[0168]**.

2 Army Act 1950 s 144(1). This provision should be read with the Army Rules 1954 r 64 and 123. Character includes both reputation and disposition but apart from previous conviction, evidence of character, where admissible, may only be given of general reputation and general disposition and not of particular acts by which reputation or disposition were shown. Manual of Military Law, 2011, Volume II, The Army Act 1950 s 144 notes.

3 Army Act 1950 s 144(2).

4 Army Act 1950 s 144(3).

[0231] Lunacy of accused Whenever, in the course of a trial by a court martial, it appears to the court that the person charged is by reason of unsoundness of mind incapable of making his defence, or that he committed the act alleged but was by reason of unsoundness of mind incapable of knowing the nature of the act or knowing that it was wrong or contrary to law, the court shall record a finding accordingly[1]. The presiding officer of the court, or, in the case of a summary court martial, the officer holding the trial, shall forthwith report the case to the confirming officer, or to the authority empowered to deal with its finding under the provision of the Army Act 1950[2], as the case may be[3]. The confirming officer to whom the case is so reported may, if he does not confirm the finding, take steps to have the accused person tried by the same or another court martial for the offence with which he was charged[4]. The authority to whom the finding of a summary court martial is reported under the provision of the Army Act 1950[5], and a confirming officer confirming a finding in any case so reported to him shall order the accused person to be kept in custody in the prescribed manner[6] and shall report the case for the orders of the Central Government[7]. Upon receipt a report under the above stated provision, the Central Government may order the accused person to be detained in a lunatic asylum or other suitable place of safe custody[8].

An application that the accused is of unsound mind and consequently incapable of making his defence should be made before arraignment. The application will normally be made by counsel for the defence or the defending officer, but should, if necessary, be made by the prosecutor. Evidence in support of the application must be given[9]. In cases where personnel are arraigned before court martial on a capital charge and insanity is pleaded on their behalf, the accused shall be examined by two specialists on mental diseases, one of whom may be a civilian or an officer of the army medical corps in civil employ. If it appears during the investigation of such cases that a defence of insanity is likely to be raised, the examination will be carried out before trial[10].

1 Army Act 1950 s 145(1).
2 Ie under the Army Act 1950 s 162.
3 Army Act 1950 s 145(2).
4 Army Act 1950 s 145(3).
5 Ie under the Army Act 1950 s 145(2).
6 As to the meaning of 'in prescribed manner'; see the Army Rules 1954 r 199(3). For the purposes of the Army Act 1950 s 145(4) the manner in which an accused person shall be kept in custody shall be as follows: The accused shall be confined in such manner as may in the opinion of the proper military authority, be best calculated to keep him securely without unnecessary harshness, as he is not to be considered as a criminal but as a person labouring under a disease.
7 Army Act 1950 s 145(4).
8 Army Act 1950 s 145(5). As to the meaning of 'other suitable place': in view of the provisions of Cr PC 1973, s 337, the place of safe custody must, if it is not a lunatic asylum, be a jail.
9 Manual of Military Law, 2011, Volume II, The Army Act 1950 s 145 notes.
10 See: Defence Services Regulations, Regulations for the Army 1987, Volume I, paragraph 463.

[0232] Subsequent fitness of lunatic accused for trial Where any accused person, having been found by reason of unsoundness of mind to be incapable of making his defence, is in custody or under detention under the provision of the Army Act 1950[1], the prescribed officer[2], may if such person is:

(1) in custody under the provision of the Army Act 1950[3], on the report of a medical officer that he is capable of making his defence[4]; or

(2) detained in a jail under the provision of the Army Act 1950[5], on a certificate of the Inspector General of Prisons, and if such person is detained in a lunatic asylum under the said provision, on a certificate of any two or more of the visitors of such asylum that he is capable of making his defence[6],

take steps to have such person tried by the same or another court martial for the offence with he was originally charged or, if the offence is a civil offence, by a criminal court[7].

1 Ie under the Army Act 1950 s 145; see **[0231]**.
2 Ie the officer commanding the army, army corps, division or brigade within the area of whose command the accused is in custody or is detained, or any other prescribed officer. For other 'prescribed officer'; see the Army Rules 1954 r 199(1). The prescribed officer for the purposes of the Army Act 1950 s 146 shall be (i) in the case of trial by summary court martial, the commanding officer of the corps, department or detachment to which the accused person belongs, or any authority superior to the commanding officer; and (ii) in the case of trial by any other court martial, the convening officer or any authority superior to him.
3 Ie under the Army Act 1950 s 145(4).
4 Army Act 1950 s 146(a).
5 Ie under the Army Act 1950 s 145(5).
6 Army Act 1950 s 146(b).
7 Army Act 1950 s 146.

[0233] Transmission to Central Government of orders under s 146 A copy of every order made by an officer under the provisions of the Army Act 1950[1] for the trial of the accused shall forthwith be sent to the Central Government[2].

1 Ie under the Army Act 1950 s 146; see **[0232]**.

2 Army Act 1950 s 147.

[0234] Release of lunatic accused Where any person is in custody[1] or under detention[2] under the provision of the Army Act 1950:

(1) if such person is in custody, on the report of a medical officer[3]; or

(2) if such person is detained on a certificate from any of the authorities mentioned in the provision of the Army Act 1950[4] that, in the judgment of such officer or authority such person may be released without danger of his doing injury to himself or to any other person[5],

the Central Government may order that such person be released or detained in custody, or transferred to a public lunatic asylum if he has not already been sent to such an asylum[6].

1 Ie under the Army Act 1950 s 145(4): see **[0231]**.

2 Ie under the Army Act 1950 s 145(5).

3 Army Act 1950 s 148(a).

4 Ie under the Army Act 1950 s 146(b).

5 Army Act 1950 s 148(b).

6 Army Act 1950 s 148.

[0235] Delivery of lunatic accused to relatives Where any relative or friend of any person who is in custody[1] or under detention[2] under the provision of the Army Act 1950 desires that he should be delivered to his care and custody, the Central Government may, upon application by such relative or friend and on his giving security to the satisfaction of that government that the person delivered shall be properly taken care of and prevented from doing injury to himself or any other person, and be produced for the inspection of such officer, and at such times and places, as the Central Government may direct, order such person to be delivered to such relative or friend[3].

1 Ie under the Army Act 1950 s 145(4); see **[0231]**.

2 Ie under the Army Act 1950 s 145(5).

3 Army Act 1950 s 149.

[0236] Order for custody and disposal or property pending trial Where any property regarding which any offence appears to have been committed, or which appears to have been used for the commission of any offence, is produced before a court martial during a trial, the court may make such order as it thinks fit for the proper custody of such property pending the conclusion of the trial. If the property is subject to speedy or natural decay, the court may after recording such evidence as it thinks necessary, order it to be sold or otherwise disposed of[1].

1 Army Act 1950 s 150.

[0237] Order for disposal of property regarding which offence is committed After the conclusion of a trial before any court martial, the court or the officer confirming the finding or sentence of such court martial, or any authority superior to such officer, or, in the case of a court martial whose finding or sentence does not require confirmation, the officer commanding the army, army corps, division or brigade within which the trial was held, may make such order as it or he thinks fit for the disposal by destruction, confiscation, delivery to any person claiming to be entitled to possession thereof, or otherwise, of any property or document produced before the court or in its custody, or regarding which any offence appears to have been committed or which has been used for the commission of any offence[1]. Where any order has been so made under the above stated provision in respect of property regarding which an offence appears to have been committed, a copy of such order signed and certified by the authority making the same may, whether the trial was held within India or not, be sent to a magistrate within whose jurisdiction such property for the time being is situated, and such magistrate shall thereupon cause the order to be carried into effect as if it were an order passed by him under the provisions of the Code of Criminal Procedure 1973, or any corresponding law in force in the state of Jammu and Kashmir[2]. The term 'property' includes, in the case of property regarding which an offence appears to have been committed, not only such property as has been originally in the possession or under the control of any person, but also any property into or for which the same may have been converted or exchanged, and anything acquired by such conversion or exchange whether immediately or otherwise[3].

Theft or misappropriation of property does not alter the ownership, and therefore, prima facie the person from whom property has been stolen or misappropriated is the lawful owner of it, and can recover it from the holder. Where stolen property has not been recovered, the value of the property should be stated in the particulars of the charge and proved in evidence. Stoppages may then be awarded to recoup the owner[4]. In a case of theft followed by sale to an innocent purchaser, stoppages may be awarded to recoup the purchaser on a charge of theft, provided that charge contains an additional averment informing the accused of the further liability he has incurred in respect of the innocent purchaser[5].

1 Army Act 1950 s 151(1).

2 Army Act 1950 s 151(2).

3 Army Act 1950 s 151(3).

4 See the Army Rules 1954 r 30(6).

5 Manual of Military Law, 2011, Volume II, the Army Act 1950 s 151 notes.

[0238] Powers of courts martial in relation to proceedings under the Army Act 1950 Any trial by a court martial under the provisions of the Army Act 1950 shall be deemed to be judicial proceeding within the meaning of the provisions of the Indian Penal Code 1860[1], and the court martial shall be deemed to be a court within the meaning of the Code of Criminal Procedure 1973[2].

1 Ie within the meaning of the Indian Penal Code 1860 ss 193 and 228.

2 Ie within the meaning of the Code of Criminal Procedure 1973 ss 345 and 346. The Army Act 1950 s 152.

C. PROCEDURE AT TRIAL

(i) General and District Court Martial

CONTENTS

PARA

(E) Finding and sentence

(F) Confirmation and Revision

(G) Proceedings of General and District Court-Martial

(A) *Convening the Court*

[0239] Convening of general and district court martial An officer before convening a general or district court martial shall first satisfy himself that the charges to be tried by the court are for offences within the meaning of the Army Act 1950 and that the evidence justifies a trial on those charges. If he is not so satisfied, shall order the release of the accused or refer the case to superior authority[1]. The officer convening the court martial shall also satisfy himself that the case is a proper one to be tried by the kind of court martial which he proposes to convene[2]. He shall appoint or detail the officers to form the court and, may also appoint or detail such waiting officers as he thinks expedient. He may also, where he considers the services of an interpreter to be necessary, appoint or detail an interpreter to the court[3]. The officer convening a court-martial shall furnish to the senior member of the court with the original charge-sheet on which the accused is to be tried and, where no judge-advocate has been appointed, also with a copy of the summary of evidence and the order for the assembly of the court martial. He shall also send, to all the other members, copies of the charge sheet and to the judge-advocate when one has been appointed, a copy of the charge sheet and a copy of the summary of evidence[4].

The convening authority must look into the evidence himself and satisfy that the evidence justifies the trial of the accused on the proposed charges[5]. He need not personally satisfy himself that the charges framed against the accused are within the purview of the Army Act 1950 and that the evidence justifies a trial by court martial on such charges. The above satisfaction can be entered by an officer empowered under the provisions of the Army Act 1950[6] before the actual convening of the court martial. In other words, the officer who finds that the charges are coming within the meaning of the Army Act 1950 and the evidence justifies a trial by court martial need not necessarily convene the court martial. His successor who is very well competent to do so can convene the court martial. The officer who records the satisfaction[7] and the officer, who convenes the court martial[8], can be two different officers, but both must be competent under the Army Act 1950[9].

The convening officer must ensure that he holds the necessary court martial warrant empowering him to convene the description of court martial that he considers appropriate. A court martial convened by an officer who is not empowered to do so will lack jurisdiction. Where the convening officer finds it impracticable to follow the ordinary rules as to appointing members from different corps, or as to the rank of members, he should state his opinion in the convening order[10]. Where several persons are to be tried separately by the same court, a copy of convening order should be prepared for each accused[11]. In addition to the restrictions in the rank of officers appointed to serve on courts martial which are prescribed by the Army Act 1950 and the Army Rules 1954, the following rules will be observed: (i) Whenever an officer of the rank of colonel or above is available to sit as presiding officer of a general court martial, an officer of inferior rank will not be appointed. Whenever a general court martial may have to be so detailed that an officer below the rank of a colonel will be the senior member and consequently its presiding officer, the convening officer must obtain the prior sanction of his next superior authority and state in the order convening the court that such sanction has been obtained[12]. When the commanding officer of a corps is to be tried, as many members as possible will be officers who have held or are holding commands equivalent to that held by the accused[13]. In the case of a general court martial, when a trial is likely to be prolonged, it will usually be expedient to form the court of a larger number than the legal minimum, and two or four additional members should be detailed. Waiting members should also be detailed to meet reduction by challenge[14]. The presiding officer of a district court martial should, if possible, be of field rank[15]. For a district court martial the legal minimum will ordinarily be sufficient; but, if necessary a larger number may be detailed, and waiting members provided. For the trial of doubtful or complicated cases, a district court martial should when possible, consist of five officers[16].

1 The Army Rules 1954 r 37 (1). The declaration as to military exigencies dispensing with certain rules should he in a separate order; see the Army Rules 1954 r 36. For form of declaration see Army Rules 1954 Appendix III. As to the duties of the convening officer, see the Army Rules 1954 Appendix III, Part IV, paragraphs 10-13. Under this provision, the convening officer has to apply his mind to satisfy himself that the charge to be tried by the court are for offences within the meaning of the Army Act 1950 and that evidence justifies the trial of those charges. *Union of India v Harish Chandra Goswami* AIR 1999 SC 1940, 1999 Cri LJ 2877.

2 The Army Rules 1954 r 37 (2). The convening officer has also to satisfy himself that the case is a proper one to be tried by the kind of court martial which he proposes to convene. *Union of India v Harish Chandra Goswami* AIR 1999 SC 1940, 1999 Cri LJ 2877.

3 The Army Rules 1954 r 37 (3).

4 The Army Rules 1954 r 37 (4). The object of this provision is to enable the presiding officer and members of the court martial to have an idea of the charge/charges on which the accused is to be arraigned. If any amendment to the charge(s) is considered necessary by the presiding officer, he should communicate his views to the convening officer before the trial begins. Only when a judge advocate is not appointed, a copy of the summary of evidence and convening order is to be sent to the presiding officer. A copy of the summary of evidence sent to the presiding officer should have the portions of evidence which, being inadmissible or irrelevant, are not being led at the trial, completely expurgated. The judge advocate is responsible to inform the convening officer of any informality or defect in the charge or in the constitution of the court; see: the Army Rules 1954 r 105(3). Members of the court must take care that they are not unduly influenced by any statement appearing in the summary of evidence, though they will naturally have regard in testing the credibility of a witness, to the fact that his evidence given at the trial is contradictory to his statement at the summary. Manual of Military Law, 2011, Volume II, the Army Rules 1954 r 37 notes.

5 *Murli Manohar Pathak v Union of India* Mil LJ 1997 Raj 114.

6 Ie under the Army Act 1950 s 109.

7 Ie under the Army Rules 1954 r 37(1),

8 under the Army Rules 1954 r 37(3)

9 Ie under the Army Act 1950 s 109. *Union of India v Gurnam Singh* AIR 2004 SC 2126: 2004 (3) SLR 756: (2004) 4 SCC 636: (2004) SCC (Cr) 1372.

10 See the Army Rules 1954 r 40 (1) and (2).

11 Manual of Military Law, 2011, Volume II, the Army Rules 1954 r 37 notes.

12 Defence Services Regulations, Regulations for the Army 1987, Volume I, paragraph 460 (a).

13 Defence Services Regulations, Regulations for the Army 1987, Volume I, paragraph 460 (b).

14 Defence Services Regulations, Regulations for the Army 1987, Volume I, paragraph 460 (d).

15 Defence Services Regulations, Regulations for the Army 1987, Volume I, paragraph 460 (c).

16 Defence Services Regulations, Regulations for the Army 1987, Volume I, paragraph 460 (d).

[0240] Adjournment for insufficient number of officers If, before the accused is arraigned, the full number of officers detailed are not available to serve, by reason of non-eligibility, disqualification, challenge or otherwise, and if there are not a sufficient number of officers in waiting to take the place of those unable to serve, the court shall ordinarily adjourn for purpose of fresh members being appointed. If the court is of opinion that in the interests of justice, and for the good of the service, it is inexpedient so to adjourn, it may, if not reduced in number below the legal minimum, proceed, after recording their reasons for so doing[1]. If the court adjourns for the purpose of the appointment of fresh members, whether under this provision or otherwise the convening officer may, if he thinks fit, convene another court[2]. After the trial has once begun, fresh members cannot be appointed in any circumstances[3]. The trial is said to have commenced when the accused is arraigned[4].

1 The Army Rules 1954 r 38(1). A general court martial for which, say seven members have been detailed, should not ordinarily begin the trial with less than seven. It may be assumed that the convening officer, in detailing seven members when five would have legally sufficed, had in view the possible prolongation of the trial or the desirability, in the circumstances of the case, of submitting the issues to be decided to the arbitration of a larger tribunal. But under this provision, the court martial may proceed, unless reduced below the legal minimum. Manual of Military Law, 2011, Volume II, the Army Rules 1954 r 38 notes.

2 The Army Rules 1954 r 38(2).

3 See: the Army Act 1950 s 117 (1); see **[0185]**.

4 Manual of Military Law, 2011, Volume II, the Army Rules 1954 r 38 notes.

[0241] Ineligibility and disqualification of officers for court martial An officer is not eligible for serving on a court martial if he is not subject to the Army Act 1950[1]. A judge advocate appointed with the court martial should not be an officer of a rank lower than the officer facing the trial unless the officer of such rank is not available (having due regards to the exigencies of public service) and the opinion regarding non-availability is specifically recorded in the convening order[2].

1 For other ineligibility and disqualifications applicable for General Court Martial, District Court Martial and Summary General Court Martial; see **[0180]**, **[0182]** and **[0183]**.

2 *Union of India v Charanjit Singh Gill* 2000 (2) SLR 755 SC.

[0242] Composition of general court martial A general court martial shall be composed, as far as practicable, of officers of different corps or departments, and in no case exclusive of officers of the corps or department to which the accused belongs[1]. The members of a court-martial for the trial of an officer shall be of a rank not lower than that of the officer unless, in the opinion of the convening officer, officers of such rank are not (having due regard to the exigencies of the public service) available. Such opinion shall be recorded in the convening order[2]. In no case shall an officer below the rank of captain be a member of a court martial for the trial of a field officer[3].

1 The Army Rules 1954 r 40(1). This sub-rule by its very language in not mandatory. *Lt Col PPS Bedi v Union of India* AIR 1982 SC 1413. This provision can be departed if the convening officer finds that it is not 'practicable' to comply with it. *Capt Ram Kumar v Chief of the Army Staff* AIR 1985 Delhi 374.

2 The Army Rules 1954 r 40(2). The expression of the convening officer's opinion justifying a departure from general rule should be inserted in the convening order. A High Court is competent to probe into the justification of constitution of court martial under the writ jurisdiction. It can quash the proceedings if the constitution of court martial is not justified under the Army Act 1950 s 109 and the Army Rules 1954 r 40(2). *Lt Col AS Bhadury v Union of India* 1986 (4) SLR 791.

3 The Army Rules 1954 r 40(3). As to the definition of 'field officer' see **[0021]**.

(B) *Procedure of Trial: Constitution of Court*

[0243] Inquiry by court as to legal constitution On the court assembling, the order convening the court shall be laid before it together with the charge sheet and the summary of evidence or a true copy thereof, and also the ranks, names, and corps of the officers appointed to serve on the court; and the court shall satisfy itself that it is legally constituted; that is to say (i) that, so far as the court can ascertain, the court has been convened in accordance with the provisions of the Army Act 1950 and the Army Rules 1954[1]; (ii) that the court consists of a number of officers, not less than the minimum required by law and, as mentioned in provisions of the Army Rule 1954[2], not less than the number detailed[3]; (iii) that each of the officers so assembled is eligible and not disqualified for serving on that court-martial[4]; and (iv) that in the case of general court martial, the officers are of the required rank[5]. The court shall, further, if it is a general or district court martial to which a judge advocate has been appointed, ascertain that the judge advocate is duly appointed and is not disqualified for sitting on that court martial[6]. The court, if not satisfied with regard to the compliance with the aforesaid provisions shall report its opinion to the convening authority, and may adjourn for that purpose[7]. The inquiries necessitated by this provision should be conducted in closed court. The court is not 'open' at this stage, and the accused has not yet been brought before it[8].

1 The Army Rules 1954 r 41(1)(a).

2 Ie as mentioned in the Army Rules 1954 r 38.

3 The Army Rules 1954 r 41(1)(b).

4 The Army Rules 1954 r 41(1)(c).

5 The Army Rules 1954 r 41(1)(d).

6 The Army Rules 1954 r 41(2).

7 The Army Rules 1954 r 41(3).

8 Manual of Military Law, 2011, Volume II, the Army Rules 1954 r 41 notes.

[0244] Inquiry by court as to amenability of accused and validity of charge If the court is satisfied that the requirements of the Army Rules 1954[1] have been complied with, it shall further satisfy itself in respect of each charge about to be brought before it that (i) it appears to be laid against a person subject to the Army Act 1950, and subject to the jurisdiction of the court[2], and (ii) each charge discloses an offence under the Army Act 1950 and is framed in accordance with the provisions of the Army Rules 1954, and is so explicit as to enable the accused readily to understand what he has to answer[3]. The court, if not satisfied on the above matters, shall report its opinion to the convening authority and may adjourn for that purpose[4].

1 Ie the Army Rules 1954 r 41 see **[0243]**.

2 The Army Rules 1954 r 42(1)(a).

3 The Army Rules 1954 r 42(1)(b).

4 The Army Rules 1954 r 42(2). As to the validity of charge; see the Army Rules 1954 rs 28-32.

(C) *Procedure at Trial: Challenge and Swearing*

[0245] Appearance of prosecutor and accused When the court has satisfied itself that the provisions of the Army Rules 1954[1] have been complied with, it shall cause the accused to be brought before the court, and the prosecutor, who must be a person subject to the Army Act 1950, shall take his due place in the court[2].

1 Ie the Army Rules 1954 r 41 and 42.

2 The Army Rules 1954 r 43.

[0246] Proceedings for challenges of members of court The order convening the court and the names of the presiding officer and the members of the court shall then be read over to the accused and he shall be asked, as required by the provisions of the Army Act 1950[1], whether he has any objection to being tried by any officer sitting on the court. Any such objection shall be disposed of in accordance with the provisions of the Army Act 1950[2]. However, (i) the accused shall state the names of all the officers constituting the court in respect of whom he has objection, before any objection is disposed of[3]; (ii) the accused may call any person to give evidence in support of his objection and such person may be questioned by the accused and by the court[4]; (iii) if more than one officer is objected to, the objection to each officer shall be disposed of separately, and the objection in respect of the officers of the lowest in rank shall be disposed of first; and on an objection to an officer, the remaining officers of the court shall, in the absence of the challenged officer, vote on the disposal of such objection, not withstanding that objections have also been made to any of those officers[5]; (iv) when an objection in respect of an officer is allowed, that officer shall forthwith retire, and take no further part in the proceedings[6]; (v) when an officer so retires or is not available to serve owing to any cause, which the court may deem to be sufficient, and there are any officers in waiting detailed as such, the presiding officer shall appoint one of such officers to fill the vacancy. If there is no officer in waiting available, the court shall proceed as required by the provisions of the Army Rules 1954[7]; (vi) the eligibility, absence of disqualification, and freedom from objection of an officer filling a vacancy shall be ascertained by the court, as in the case of other officers appointed to serve on the court[8]. The accused has no right to object to the prosecutor or judge advocate[9].

1 Ie under the Army Act 1950 s 130; see **[0216]**.

2 Ie under the provisions of the Army Act 1950 s 130. Each member should answer to his name as it is called, so that the accused can identify each member who is to try him. The Army Rules 1954 r 44.

3 The Army Rules 1954 r 44 proviso (a): The accused must make each objection separately: he cannot object to the court collectively, except upon a plea to the jurisdiction.

4 The Army Rules 1954 r 44 proviso (b). The witnesses called by the accused in support of his plea cannot be examined on oath or affirmation since the court is not yet sworn or affirmed, but provisions of the Army Rules 1954 r 141 will substantially apply.

5 The Army Rules 1954 r 44 proviso (c). If the accused persists in objecting to the court collectively, the court should treat the objection as made to all the members individually, and the procedure contained under this provision should be strictly followed. In practice an objection to a member may be equivalent to a plea to the jurisdiction, as for example when on the trial of a field officer one of the members is objected to because he is below the rank of captain. In such a case the objection should be dealt with under this rule. An officer objected to on the ground of personal enmity, prejudice, or malice or for having formed and expressed an opinion on the case, should, unless the objection is obviously groundless, request and be permitted to retire. The court may be closed to consider each objection. Manual of Military Law, 2011, Volume II, the Army Rules 1954 r 44 notes.

6 The Army Rules 1954 r 44 proviso (d). The officer objected to must not be present in the closed court when the objection in his respect is being considered by the court, but all the other members present, i.e. who have not retired upon objections to them being allowed, must vote on the disposal of the abjection. Manual of Military Law, 2011, Volume II, the Army Rules 1954 r 44 notes.

7 Ie under the Army Rules 1954 r 38. The Army Rules 1954 r 44 proviso (e). Where any waiting members are detailed, it is the duty of the presiding officer to appoint one of those members to fill a vacancy. He is not required to take the first on the list; ordinarily he should select one of corresponding rank to the retiring or absent officer. If the presiding officer is himself successfully objected to the senior remaining member will take his place and will then proceed to fill the vacancy in the court in the manner indicated above. See: The Army Act 1950 s 128.

8 The Army Rules 1954 r 44 proviso (f). If there is no officer in waiting available and the court is reduced in number below the legal minimum, it must adjourn for the purpose of appointment of fresh members; and though not so reduced, it should ordinarily adjourn unless it is of opinion that, in the interests of justice and for the good of the service, it is not expedient to do so. Manual of Military Law, 2011, Volume II, the Army Rules 1954 r 44 notes.

9 Manual of Military Law, 2011, Volume II, the Army Rules 1954 r 44 notes.

[0247] Oaths of member, judge advocate and witness An oath or affirmation in the prescribed manner shall be administered to every member of every court martial and to the judge advocate before the commencement of the trial[1]. Every person giving evidence before a court martial shall be examined after being duly sworn or affirmed in the prescribed form[2]. The above stated provision shall not apply where the witness is a child under 12 years of age and the court-martial is of opinion that though the witness understands the duty of speaking the truth, he does not understand the nature of an oath or affirmation[3].

1 The Army Act 1950 s 131 (1). The oath/affirmation taken by the members of the court binds them in their capacity of jurors to find a true verdict according to the evidence (discarding from their minds any private knowledge or information they may happen to possess, and in their capacity of judges to administer justice; and to keep secret the votes or opinions of other members. For prescribed form of oath/affirmation see the Army Rules 1954 rs 45, 46 and 47 at **[0248]**, **[0249]**, and **[0250]**.

2 The Army Act 1950 s 131 (2).

3 The Army Act 1950 s 131 (3).

[0248] Swearing or affirming of members As soon as the court is constituted with the proper number of officers who are not objected to, or objections in respect of whom have been over-ruled, an oath or affirmation shall be administered to every member in one of the following forms or in such other form to the same purport as the court ascertains to be according to his religion or otherwise binding on his conscience[1]. Christians and Sikhs are generally sworn, the former on the New Testament or some book containing it and the latter on the Guru Granth. Hindus and Muslims are generally affirmed. Jews are sworn on the Old Testament. A person taking the oath will hold the book (New Testament, Old Testament or Guru Granth) in his uplifted hand and will say or repeat the oath after the person administering it. The oath must be administered and taken with solemnity. It is not necessary to kiss the book. Members may be sworn separately or collectively. If a person desires to be sworn in the Scottish form, no question as to his religious belief is to be asked nor is he required to hold or kiss the Bible while being sworn. He will be sworn standing and holding up his right hand, and the oath will commence in these terms 'I swear by Almighty God as I shall answer to God at the Great Day of Judgement………'. In addition to providing a prescribed form of oath or affirmation, the rule permits an oath or affirmation to be administered to the person to be sworn or affirmed in such form to the same purport as the court ascertains to be according to his religion or otherwise, binding on his conscience[2].

Form of Oath

I………swear by Almighty God that I will well and truly try the accused (or accused persons) before the court according to the evidence, and that I will duly administer justice according to the Army Act 1950 without partiality, favour or affection and if any doubt shall arise, then, according to my conscience, the best of my understanding and the custom of war in the like cases; and I do further swear that I will not on any account at any time, whatsoever, disclose, or discover the vote or opinion of any particular member of this court martial, unless required to give evidence thereof by a court of justice or a court martial in due course of law.

Form of Affirmation

I………do solemnly, sincerely and truly declare and affirm that I will well and truly try the accused (or accused persons) before the court according to the evidence, and that I will duly administer justice according to the Army Act 1950 without partiality, favour or affection; and if any doubt shall arise, then, according to my conscience, the best of my understanding, and the custom of war in the like cases; and I do further solemnly, sincerely and truly declare and affirm that I will not, on any account at any time, whatsoever, disclose or discover the vote or opinion of any particular member of this court martial, unless required to give evidence thereof by a court of justice or a court martial in due course of law.

1 The Army rules 1954 r 45. The oath or affirmation taken by the members implies that, as a general rule, the opinions of the individual members ought not to be stated, and consequently the court ought, not to disclose whether the decision was unanimous or by a majority. The decision is the decision of the court as a whole, and the fact of its being unanimous or not is usually immaterial. The qualification at the end of the oath or affirmation, 'unless required to give evidence thereof', only applies to such cases where members of the court are changed individually with partiality or bribery, and thus in a court of justice or a court martial it would, or might, be necessary to make disclosures regarding individual votes to the court trying the members so charged. As to the person to administer the oath or affirmation, see provisions of the Army Rules 1954 r 47.

2 Manual of Military Law, 2011, Volume II, the Army Rules 1954 r 45 notes.

[0249] Swearing or affirming of judge advocate and other officers After the members of the court are all sworn or have made affirmation, an oath or affirmation shall be administered to the following persons or such of them as are present at the court martial, in such of the following forms as shall be appropriate, or in such other form to the same purport as the court ascertains to be according to the religion or otherwise binding on the conscience of the person to be sworn or affirmed[1]. Christians and Sikhs are generally sworn, the former on the New Testament or some book containing it and the latter on the Guru Granth. Hindus and Muslims are generally affirmed. Jews are sworn on the Old Testament. A person taking the oath will hold the book (New Testament, Old Testament or Guru Granth) in his uplifted hand and will say or repeat the oath after the person administering it. The oath must be administered and taken with solemnity. It is not necessary to kiss the book. Members may be sworn separately or collectively. If a person desires to be sworn in the Scottish form, no question as to his religious belief is to be asked nor is he required to hold or kiss the Bible while being sworn. He will be sworn standing and holding up his right hand, and the oath will commence in these terms 'I swear by Almighty God as I shall answer to God at the Great Day of Judgement.........'. In addition to providing a prescribed form of oath or affirmation, the rule permits an oath or affirmation to be administered to the person to be sworn or affirmed in such form to the same purport as the court ascertains to be according to his religion or otherwise, binding on his conscience[2].

(A) Judge Advocate

Form of Oath

> I.........swear by Almighty God that I will to the best of my ability carry out the duties of judge advocate in accordance with the Army Act 1950, and the rules made thereunder and without partiality, favour or affection, and I do further swear that I will not on any account at any time whatsoever, disclose or discover the vote or opinion on any matter of any particular member of this court martial, unless required to give evidence thereof by a court of justice or, a court martial in due course of law.

Form of Affirmation

> I.........do solemnly, sincerely and truly declare and affirm that I will to the best of my ability carry out the duties of judge advocate in accordance with the Army Act 1950 and the rules made thereunder and without partiality, favour or affection, and I do further solemnly, sincerely and truly declare and affirm that I will not on any account at any time, whatsoever, disclose or discover the vote or opinion on any matter of any particular member of this court martial, unless required to give evidence thereof by a court of justice or a court martial in due course of law.

(B) Officer attending for the purposes of instruction

Form of Oath

> I.........swear by Almighty God that I will not on any account, at any time whatsoever, disclose or discover the vote or opinion of any particular member of this court-martial unless required to give evidence thereof by a court of justice or a court-martial, in due course of law.

Form of Affirmation

I.........do solemnly, sincerely and truly declare and affirm that I will not on any account, at any time whatsoever, disclose or discover the vote or opinion of any particular member of this court-martial; unless required to give evidence thereof by a court of justice or a court martial, in due course of law.

(C) Shorthand Writer

Form of Oath

I.........swear by Almighty God that I will truly take down to the best of my power the evidence to be given before this court martial and such other matters as I may be required, and will, when required, deliver to the court a true transcript of the same.

Form of Affirmation

I.........do solemnly, sincerely and truly declare and affirm that I will truly take down to the best of my power the evidence to be given before this court martial and such other matters as I may be required, and will, when required deliver to the court a true transcript of the same.

(D) Interpreter

Form of Oath

I.........swear by Almighty God that I will faithfully interpret and translate, as I shall be required to do, touching the matter before this court-martial.

Form of Affirmation

I.........do solemnly, sincerely and truly declare and affirm that I will faithfully interpret and translate, as I shall be required to do, touching the matter before this court-martial.

1 The Army rules 1954 r 46. The accused has a right of objection to the shorthand writer or interpreter, who may be sworn/affirmed at any time during the trial; see: the Army Rules 1954 r 90. However he has no right of objection to the judge advocate or to the officers under instruction.

2 Manual of Military Law, 2011, Volume II, the Army Rules 1954 r 46 notes.

[0250] Persons to administer oaths and affirmations All oaths and affirmations shall be administered by the judge advocate (if any), a member of the court, or some other person empowered by the court to administer such oath or affirmation[1].

1 The Army Rules 1954 r 47. Oaths and affirmations may be administered by any of the persons mentioned in this provision. Their being of the same religion as the person affirmed or sworn is immaterial. It will generally be convenient for the judge advocate to administer the oath or affirmation to the presiding officer and members, or if there is no judge advocate, for the presiding officer to first administer the oath and affirmation to the members and then be himself sworn or affirmed by one of them. The oath or affirmation to the judge advocate may be administered by the presiding officer. Manual of Military Law, 2011, Volume II, the Army Rules 1954 r 47 notes.

(D) *Prosecution, Defence and Summing-up*

[0251] Arraignment of accused After the members of the court and other persons are sworn or affirmed the accused shall be arraigned on the charges against him[1]. The charges upon which the accused is arraigned shall be read and, if necessary, translated to him, and he shall be required to plead separately to each charge[2].

1 The Army Rules 1954 r 48(1). The accused should be arraigned by the presiding officer or judge advocate, if any. Arraignment consists of: (i) calling upon the accused by his number (if any), rank, name and description as given in the charge-sheet and asking him 'Is that your number, rank, name and unit (or description)?' (ii) reading the charge to him; and (iii) asking him whether he is guilty or not guilty. Where two or more persons are jointly charged and tried for the same offence, each is separately arraigned. Manual of Military Law, 2011, Volume II, the Army Rules 1954 r 48 notes.

2 The Army Rules 1954 r 48(2). The plea of the accused must be taken on all the charges in a charge-sheet. This applies to alternative charges if the accused has been arraigned upon them. See the Army Rules 1954 r 52(3): **[0255]**.

[0252] Objection by accused to charge The accused, when required to plead to any charge, may object to the charge on the ground that it does not disclose an offence under the Army Act 1950, or is not in accordance with the Army Rules 1954. The court after hearing any submission which may be made by the prosecutor or by or on behalf of the accused, shall consider the objection in closed court and shall either disallow it and proceed with the trial, or allow it and adjourn to report to the convening authority or, if it is in doubt, it may adjourn to consult the convening authority[1].

1 The Army Rules 1954 r 49.

[0253] Amendment of charge At any time during the trial, if it appears to the court that there is any mistake in the name or description of the accused in the charge-sheet, the court may amend the charge-sheet so as to correct that mistake[1]. If, on the trial of any charge, it appears to the court at any time before it has begun to examine the witnesses, that in the interest of justice any addition to, omission from, or alteration in, the charge is required, it may report its opinion to the convening authority, and may, adjourn and the convening authority may either direct the new trial to be commenced, or amend the charge, and order the trial to proceed with such amended charge after due notice to the accused[2].

1 The Army Rules 1954 r 50(1). A mistake in name or description will only be amended, if it is clear to the court that the accused is the person intended to be charged in the charge-sheet, and that, he is not prejudiced in his defence by the mistake having been made. The court may act whether the objection to the charge is taken by the accused or by the judge advocate or by a member of the court, and either before or after the arraignment of the accused. See the Army Rules 1954 rs 42 and 49; see **[0244]** and **[0252]**.

2 The Army Rules 1954 r 50(2). The witnesses referred to in sub-rule are the ones on the substance of the charge and not those who are called as to objections to the members, or with respect to a special plea to the jurisdiction, under the Army Rules 1954 r 51.

[0254] Special plea to the jurisdiction The accused, before pleading to a charge, may offer a special plea to the general jurisdiction of the court, and if he does so, and the court considers that anything stated in such plea shows that the court has no jurisdiction it shall receive any evidence offered in support, together with any evidence offered by the prosecutor in disproof or qualification thereof[1], and any address by or on behalf of the accused and reply by the prosecutor in reference thereto[2]. If the court overrules the special plea, it shall proceed with the trial[3]. If the court allows the special plea, it shall record its decision, and the reasons for it, and report it to the convening authority and adjourn; such decision, shall not require any confirmation, and the convening authority shall either forthwith convene another court for the trial of the accused, or order the accused to be released[4]. If the court is in doubt as to the validity of the plea, it may refer the matter to the convening authority, and may adjourn for that purpose or may record a special decision with respect to such plea, and proceed with the trial[5].

1 Evidence must be taken on oath or affirmation. Manual of Military Law, 2011, Volume II, the Army Rules 1954 r 51 notes.

2 The Army Rules 1954 r 51(1).

3 The Army Rules 1954 r 51(2). The confirmation of the finding, after a plea to the jurisdiction has been overruled, will have the effect of confirming the decision of the court in over-ruling the plea. If, however, the confirming officer is of opinion that the plea is valid and should have been allowed, he must refuse to confirm the finding of the court, and another court may legally be convened. Manual of Military Law, 2011, Volume II, the Army Rules 1954 r 51 notes.

4 The Army Rules 1954 r 51(3). If the court allows the plea, the decision of the court cannot be over-ruled, but another court may legally be convened. Manual of Military Law, 2011, Volume II, the Army Rules 1954 r 51 notes.

5 The Army Rules 1954 r 51(4).

[0255] General plea of 'guilty' or 'not guilty' If no special plea to the general jurisdiction of the court is offered, or if such plea being offered, is overruled, or is dealt with by a special decision under the Army Rules 1954[1], the accused person's plea of 'guilty' or 'not guilty' (or if he refuses to plead or does not plead intelligibly either one or the other a plea of 'not guilty') shall be recorded on each charge[2]. If an accused person pleads 'guilty', that plea shall be recorded as the finding of the court; but before it is recorded, the presiding officer or judge advocate, on behalf of the court, shall ascertain that the accused understands the nature of the charge to which he has pleaded guilty and shall inform him of the general effect of that plea, and in particular of the meaning of the charge to which he has pleaded guilty, and of the difference in procedure which will be made by the plea of guilty, and shall advise him to withdraw that plea if it appears from the summary of evidence that the accused ought to plead 'not guilty'[3]. Where an accused pleads 'guilty', such plea and the factum of compliance of above stated provision[4] shall be recorded by the court in the following manner: "Before recording the plea of 'guilty' of the accused, the court explained to the accused the meaning of the charge(s), to which he had pleaded guilty and ascertained that the accused had understood the nature of the charge(s) to which he had pleaded guilty. The court also informed the accused the general effect of the plea and the difference in procedure which will be followed consequent to the said plea. The court having satisfied itself that the accused understands the charge(s) and the effect of the plea of 'guilty', accepts and records the same. The provisions of Army Rules 1954[5] are thus complied with[6]." Where an accused person pleads 'guilty' to the first of two or more charges laid in the alternative, the prosecutor may, after the provisions of Army Rules 1954[7] has been complied with by the court and before the accused is arraigned on the alternative charge or charges, withdraw such alternative charge or charges without requiring the accused to plead thereto and a record to that effect shall be made upon the proceedings of the court[8]. A plea of 'guilty' shall not be accepted in cases where the accused is liable, if convicted to be sentenced to death, and where such plea is offered, a plea of 'not guilty' shall be recorded and the trial shall proceed accordingly[9].

1 Ie under the Army Rules 1954 r 51(4).

2 The Army Rules 1954 r 52(1). If the accused pleads in some language not understood by the court, or inarticulately, he will not have pleaded intelligibly, and a plea of 'not guilty' will be entered. Manual of Military Law, 2011, Volume II, the Army Rules 1954 r 52 notes.

3 The Army Rules 1954 r 52(2). The object of this provision is to prevent the accused from pleading guilty under a misapprehension; e. g., a man charged with wilfully injuring government property may, under a misapprehension, plead 'guilty' because the property has been actually injured, though not willfully; or a man charged with receiving property, knowing it to have been stolen may, under a misapprehension, plead 'guilty' because the property was in fact stolen, though when he received it, he did not know it to have been stolen. In such cases the presiding officer must explain to the accused that he must plead 'not guilty'. Manual of Military Law, 2011, Volume II, the Army Rules 1954 r 52 notes.

4 Ie the Army Rules 1954 r 52(2).

5 Ie the Army Rules 1954 r 52(2).

6 The Army Rules 1954 r 52(2A). If the accused pleads guilty, a statement that the requirements of this provision have been complied with must be recorded. In a case where the certificate appended to the confession revealed that the judge advocate assumed automatic compliance of the Army Rules 1954 r 52(2) on the accused pleading guilty to charge; and the documents failed to show; (i) whether charges framed in English were explained to the accused, who was not at all conversant with the language; (ii) whether the judge advocate had satisfied himself that the petitioner had understood the charge before pleading guilty to them; it was held that the judge advocate committed an error. *Bhagwan Singh v Union of India* 1983 Cr LJ 1386.

7 Ie the Army Rules 1954 r 52(2)

8 The Army Rules 1954 r 52(3).

9 The Army Rules 1954 r 52(4). This provision intended to ensure that a person charged with an offence for which death penalty can be awarded shall not be convicted without a full trial. Manual of Military Law, 2011, Volume II, the Army Rules 1954 r 52 notes.

[0256] Plea in bar The accused, at the time of his general plea of 'guilty' or 'not guilty' to a charge for an offence, may offer a plea in bar of trial on the ground that: (i) he has been previously convicted or acquitted of the offence by a competent criminal court or by a court martial, or has been dealt with summarily under the provisions of the Army Act 1950[1], for the offence, or that a charge in respect of the offence has been dismissed as provided under the Army Rules 1954[2]; (ii) the offence has been pardoned or condoned by competent military authority[3]; or (iii) the period of limitation for trial as laid down in the Army Act 1950[4] has expired[5]. If he offers such plea in bar, the court shall record it as well as his general plea, and if it considers that any fact or facts stated by him are sufficient to support the plea in bar, it shall receive any evidence offered, and hear any address made by or on behalf of the accused and the prosecutor in reference to the plea[6]. If the court finds that the plea in bar is proved, it shall record its finding, and notify it to the confirming authority, and shall either adjourn, or if there is any other charge against the accused, whether in the same or in a different charge-sheet, which is not affected by the plea in bar, may proceed to the trial of the accused on that charge[7]. If the finding that the plea in bar is proved is not confirmed, the court may be re-assembled by the confirming authority, and proceed as if the plea had been found not proved[8]. If the court finds that the plea in bar is not proved, it shall proceed with the trial, and the said findings shall be subject to confirmation like any other finding of the court[9].

1 Ie under the Army Act 1950 ss 80, 83, 84 and 85 as the case may be.

2 Ie as provided in the Army Rules 1954 r 22(2). The Army Rules 1954 r 53(1)(a).

3 The Army Rules 1954 r 53(1)(b). It has long been recognised as a custom of the service that a military offence can be condoned. For the purpose of barring a trial condonation means such conduct on the part of a competent authority i.e., an authority having power to determine that the charge should not be proceeded with—as is inconsistent with subsequently trying the offender, and as would make it inequitable to do so; it must be a deliberate and intentional act, done with full knowledge of all material facts. If, with full knowledge of the facts, competent authority removes an officer, or allows him to resign, he should not afterwards be tried by court martial for his offence. The fact that after trial, but before confirmation, the accused has been employed in active operations does not effect the legal validity of the sentence, but affords ground for pardon. Manual of Military Law, 2011, Volume II, the Army Rules 1954 r 53 notes.

4 Ie under the Army Act 1950 s 122.

5 The Army Rules 1954 r 53(1)(c). The Army Act 1950 provides that a person shall not be liable to trial for an offence of which he has been convicted or acquitted by a court-martial or by a criminal court, or for which he has been dealt with summarily, or which was committed more than three years before the date of his trial, unless the offence was mutiny, desertion or fraudulent enrolment. Mutiny or desertion on active service, may be tried at any time. Desertion at other times or fraudulent enrolment is not to be tried, if the offender, not being an officer, has served for 3 years subsequently in an exemplary manner in any portion of regular Army. See: The Army Act 1950 ss 121 and 122: **[0189]** and **[0190]**.

6 The Army Rules 1954 r 53(2). The evidence on the plea is to be taken on oath or affirmation.

7 The Army Rules 1954 r 53(3).

8 The Army Rules 1954 r 53(4).

9 The Army Rules 1954 r 53(5). If the finding on the plea, where the court allows it is confirmed, it amounts to an acquittal and is final. Manual of Military Law, 2011, Volume II, the Army Rules 1954 r 53 notes.

[0257] Procedure after plea of 'Guilty' Upon the record of the plea of 'guilty', if there are other charges in the same charge-sheet to which the plea is 'not guilty', the trial shall first proceed with respect to the latter charges. After the finding on 'not guilty' charges, the trial shall proceed with the charges on which a plea of 'guilty' has been entered. If there are alternative charges, the court may either proceed with respect to all the charges as if the accused had not pleaded 'guilty' to any charge or may subject to the following provision[1], instead of trying him record a finding of 'guilty' upon any one of the alternative charges to which he has pleaded 'guilty' and a finding of 'not guilty' upon all the other alternative charges[2]. Where alternative charges are preferred and the accused pleads 'not guilty' to the charge which alleges the more serious offence and 'guilty' to the other, the court shall try him as if he had pleaded 'not guilty' to all the charges[3]. After the record of the plea of 'guilty' on a charge (if the trial does not proceed on any other charges) the court shall receive any statement which the accused desires to make in reference to the charge, and shall read the summary of evidence, and annex it to the proceedings, or if there is no such summary shall take and record sufficient evidence to enable it to determine the sentence and the confirming officer to know all the circumstances connected with the offence. This evidence shall be taken in the manner provided in the Army Rules 1954 in the case of plea of 'not guilty'[4].

After evidence has been so taken, or the summary of evidence has been read, as the case may be, the accused may make a statement in mitigation of punishment, and may call witnesses as to his character[5]. If from the statement of the accused or from the summary of evidence, or otherwise, it appears to the court that the accused did not understand the effect of his plea of 'guilty', the court shall alter the record and enter a plea of 'not guilty', and proceed with the trial accordingly[6]. If a plea of 'guilty' is recorded, and the trial proceeds with respect to other charges in the same charge-sheet, the proceedings under the provisions of the Army Rules

1954[7], shall take place when the findings on the other charges in the same charge sheet are recorded[8]. When the accused states anything in mitigation of punishment which in the opinion of the court requires to be proved, and would, if proved, affect the amount of punishment, the court may permit the accused to call witnesses to prove the same[9].

1 Ie the Army Rules 1954 r 54(2).

2 The Army Rules 1954 r 54(1). The accused will always be asked, in case of a plea of 'guilty', whether he desires to call witness to character. Manual of Military Law, 2011, Volume II, the Army Rules 1954 r 54 notes.

3 The Army Rules 1954 r 54(2).

4 The Army Rules 1954 r 54(3).

5 The Army Rules 1954 r 54(4).

6 The Army Rules 1954 r 54(5).

7 Ie under the Army Rules 1954 r 54 (3) and (4).

8 The Army Rules 1954 r 54(6).

9 The Army Rules 1954 r 54(7).

[0258] Withdrawal of plea of 'not guilty' subject to compliance with the Army Rules[1] The accused may, if he thinks fit, at any time during the trial, withdraw his plea of 'not guilty', and plead 'guilty', and in such case the court will at once, subject to a compliance with the provisions of the Army Rules 1954[2], record a plea and finding of 'guilty' and shall proceed as directed by the provisions of the Army Rules 1954[3].

1 The Army Rules 1954 r 52 (2) and (4).

2 Ie the Army Rules 1954 r 52 (2) and (4).

3 Ie the Army Rules 1954 r 54; see **[0257]**. The Army Rules 1954 r 55. If the accused proposes to withdraw his plea of not guilty, the court must inform him of the general effect of his withdrawal, and of the difference in the procedure, in the same manner as if he pleaded guilty under the Army Rules 1954 r 52; see **[0255]**.

[0259] Plea of 'not guilty', application for adjournment, and case for the prosecution After the plea 'not guilty' to any charge is recorded, the trial shall proceed as follows: (i) The court shall ask the accused whether he wishes to apply for an adjournment on the ground that any of the provisions relating to trial have not been complied with, and that he has been prejudiced thereby or on the ground that he has not had sufficient opportunity for preparing his defence, and shall record his answer[1]; (ii) If the accused shall make any such application, the court shall hear any statement of evidence which he may desire to adduce in support thereof, and any statement of the prosecutor or evidence in answer thereto; and if it shall appear to the court that the accused has been prejudiced by any non-compliance with any of such rules relating to procedure or that he has not had sufficient opportunity of preparing his defence, it may grant such adjournment as may appear to it in the circumstances to be proper[2]; (iii) The prosecutor may, if he desires, and shall, if so required by the court make an opening address, and shall state therein the substance of the charge against the accused and the nature and general effect of the evidence which he proposes to adduce in support of it without entering into any unnecessary detail[3]; (iv)The evidence for the prosecution shall then be taken[4]; (v) If it should be necessary for the prosecutor to give evidence for the prosecution on the facts of the case, he shall give it after the delivery of his address (if any), and he must be sworn or affirmed, as the case may be, and give his evidence in detail[5]; and (vi) the prosecutor may be cross-examined by or on behalf of the accused and afterwards may make any statement which might be made by a witness on re-examination[6]. In case of complexity the prosecutor should always make an opening address, so that the members of the court may be enabled to understand the general nature of the allegations. He must be careful to refrain from making any assertions which he does not propose to substantiate by evidence. The address of the prosecutor may be in writing, in such a case it should be read by him and handed to the court for attachment to the proceedings[7].

1 The Army Rules 1954 r 56(1). As to the right of the accused to prepare his defence; see the Army Rules 1954 r 33 at **[0150]**.

2 The Army Rules 1954 r 56(2). The court must adjourn if it appears to it that the accused is likely to be prejudiced by non-compliance with any of the rules relating to procedure before trial or that he did not have sufficient time to prepare his defence.

3 The Army Rules 1954 r 56(3).

4 The Army Rules 1954 r 56(4).

5 The Army Rules 1954 r 56(5). When counsel appears on behalf of the prosecutor, this provision does not apply.

6 The Army Rules 1954 r 56(6). When counsel appears on behalf of the prosecutor, this provision does not apply.

7 Manual of Military Law, 2011, Volume II, the Army Rules 1954 r 56 notes.

[0260] Plea of no case At the close of the case for prosecution, the accused may offer a plea that evidence given on behalf of the prosecution in respect of any one or more charges, has not established a prima-facie case against him and that he should not, therefore, be called upon to make his defence to that charge or charge(s)[1]. Where the accused takes such a plea, the prosecutor may address the court in answer thereto and the accused may reply[2]. The court shall consider the plea in closed court and shall not allow plea unless satisfied that (i) the prosecution has not established a prima facie case on the charge or charges of laid[3]; and (ii) it is not open to it on the evidence adduced to make a special finding under provisions of the Army Act 1950 or the Army Rules 1954[4]. If the court allows the plea, it shall record the finding of 'not guilty' on the charge or charges, to which the plea relates, and shall announce the finding forthwith in open court as subject to confirmation[5]. If the court over rules the plea, it shall proceed with the trial[6]. If the court has any doubt as to the validity of the plea, it may refer the matter to the convening authority, and adjourn for that purpose[7]. The court may, of its own motion, after the close of the case for the prosecution, and after hearing the prosecutor find the accused 'not guilty' of the charge, and announce the finding forthwith in open court as subject to confirmation[8]. The court shall record brief reasons while arriving at the finding of the plea, in accordance with the provisions of the Army Rules 1954[9].

1 The Army Rules 1954 r 57(1).

2 The Army Rules 1954 r 57(2).

3 The Army Rules 1954 r 57(3)(a).

4 Ie under the Army Act 1950 s 139 or the Army Rules 1954 r 62 (4). The Army Rules 1954 r 57(3)(b).

5 The Army Rules 1954 r 57(4).

6 The Army Rules 1954 r 57(5).

7 The Army Rules 1954 r 57(6).

8 The Army Rules 1954 r 57(7).

9 Ie the Army Rules 1954 r 62(1). The Army Rules 1954 r 57(8).

[0261] Examination of the accused and defence witnesses In a trial, for the purpose of enabling the accused to explain any circumstances appearing in evidence against him, the court, or the judge advocate: (i)) may at any stage, without previously warning the accused, put such questions to him as considers necessary[1]; (ii) shall, after the close of the case for prosecution or before he is called on for his defence, question him generally on the case[2]. No oath shall be administered to the accused when he is examined under this provision[3]. The accused shall not render himself liable to punishment by refusing to answer questions referred above, or by giving answers to the them which knows not to be true[4]. After the close of the case for prosecution, the presiding officer or the judge advocate shall explain to the accused that he may make an unsworn statement, orally or in writing, giving his account of subject of the charge(s), against him or if he wishes, he may give evidence as a witness, on oath or affirmation, in disproof of the charge(s) against him or any person charged together with him at the same trial[5]. However, (i) the accused shall not be called as a witness except on his own request in writing[6]; and (ii) his failure to give evidence shall not be made the subject of any comment by any of the parties of the court or give rise to any presumption against himself or any person charged together with him at the same trial[7]; (iii) if he gives evidence on oath or affirmation, he shall be examined as first witness for defence and shall be liable to be cross-examined by the prosecutor and to be questioned by the court[8]. The accused then may call his witnesses including, if he so desire, any witnesses as to character. If the accused intends to call witnesses as to the facts of the case other than himself, he may make an opening address before the evidence for defence is given[9].

1 The Army Rules 1954 r 58 (1)(a). The presiding officer or the judge advocate may question the accused for the purpose of enabling the accused to explain any circumstance appearing in his statement or in the evidence against him. Such questions may be put even though the accused has made no statement. The questions and the accused's answers thereto should, as far as possible, be recorded verbatim. The questions should not be put in the way of cross-examination or for testing his defends or for supplementing the prosecution case. The accused does not render himself liable to punishment for refusing to answers such questions or giving answers to them which he knows not to be true. The court may draw such inference from the refusal of the accused or the answers given by him as it thinks just. Manual of Military Law, Volume II, 2011 the Army Rules 1954 r 58 notes.

2 The Army Rules 1954 r 58 (1)(b).

3 The Army Rules 1954 r 58 (2). The accused has the privilege of making statements which are unsupported by evidence. Any statement of the facts, though not on oath, upon which the accused relies for his defence, must be taken into consideration by the court, who may draw its inferences from it. If made orally, it should be taken down verbatim, so far as it states facts which are within the personal knowledge of the accused and upon which he relies for his defence. If made in writing it shall be read and attached to the proceedings. Manual of Military Law, Volume II, 2011 the Army Rules 1954 r 58 notes.

4 The Army Rules 1954 r 58 (1)(c).

5 The Army Rules 1954 r 58 (2).

6 The Army Rules 1954 r 58 (2) proviso (a).

7 The Army Rules 1954 r 58 (2) proviso (b).

8 The Army Rules 1954 r 58 (2) proviso (c).

9 The Army Rules 1954 r 58 (3).

[0262] Closing Addresses After the examination of the witnesses, the prosecutor may make a closing address and the accused or his counsel or the defending officer, as the case may be, shall be entitled to reply[1]. However, where any point of law is raised by the accused, the prosecutor may, with the permission of the court, make his submission with regard to that point[2].

1 The Army Rules 1954 r 59.

2 The Army Rules 1954 r 59 proviso.

[0263] Summing up by the judge advocate The judge advocate (if any) shall sum up in open court the evidence and advise the court upon the law relating to the case[1]. After the summing up of the judge advocate, no other address shall be allowed[2].

1 The Army Rules 1954 r 60(1). A summing up by judge advocate is obligatory and may be given orally or in writing; but in practice it should invariably be in writing. In his summing up the judge advocate should explain the charges and the law relating to them, the issues raised by the charges and briefly recapitulate the evidence on such issues. He must be careful not to indicate to the court any opinion he may have formed regarding the facts of the case. See: the Army Rules 1954 r 144.

2 The Army Rules 1954 r 60(2).

(E) *Finding and sentence*

[0264] Consideration of finding The court shall deliberate on its finding in closed court in the presence of the judge advocate[1]. The opinion of each member of the court as to the finding shall be given by word of mouth on each charge separately[2].

1 The Army Rules 1954 r 61 (1). The presiding officer should initiate the deliberations of the court by a statement of the questions to be considered and the order in which they should be considered. Manual of Military Law, Volume II, 2011 the Army Rules 1954 r 58 notes.

2 The Army Rules 1954 r 61 (2). If the court is doubtful whether the actual offence charged is proved or whether the particulars of the charge have been satisfactorily established in evidence, they must consider their powers of making a special finding, either under the provisions of the Army Act 1950 s 139 or under the Army Rules 1954 r 62(4). The members of courts martial must consider that (i) it is a fundamental maxim of law that an accused person is presumed to be innocent until he has been proved to be guilty, and (ii) that their finding must be based upon the evidence given before them. The opinions of members must be given orally. As to taking opinions; see: the Army Rules 1954 r 87 see **[0291]**.

[0265] Form, record and announcement of finding

(a) The finding on every charge upon which the accused is arraigned shall be recorded and, except as provided in the following provisions shall be recorded as finding of 'guilty' or of 'not guilty'. After recording the finding on each charge the court shall give brief reasons in support thereof. The judge advocate or, if there is none, the presiding officer shall record such brief reasons in the proceedings. The above record shall be signed and dated by the presiding officer and the judge advocate, if any[1].

(b) Where the court is of opinion as regards any charge that the facts proved do not disclose the offence charged or any offence of which he might under the Army Act 1950 legally be found guilty on the charge as laid, the court shall acquit the accused of that charge[2].

(c) If the court doubts as regards any charge whether the facts proved show the accused to be guilty or not of the offence charged or of any offence of which he might under the Army Act 1950 legally be found guilty on the charge as laid, may, before recording a finding on that charge, refer to the confirming authority for an opinion, setting out the facts which it finds to be proved, and if necessary, adjourn for that purpose[3].

(d) Where the court is of opinion as regards any charge that the facts which it finds to be proved in evidence differ materially from the facts alleged in the statement of particulars in the charge, but are nevertheless sufficient to prove the offence stated in the charge, and that the difference is not so material as to have prejudiced the accused in his defence, it may, instead of a finding of 'not guilty', record a special finding[4].

(e) The special finding may find the accused guilty on a charge subject to the statement of exceptions or variations specified therein[5].

(f) Where there are alternative charges, and the facts proved appear to the court not to constitute the offence mentioned in any of those alternative charges, the court shall record a finding of 'not guilty' on that charge[6].

(g) The court shall not find the accused guilty on more than one of two or more charges laid down in the alternative, even if conviction upon the charge necessarily connotes guilty upon the alternative charge or charges[7].

(i) If the court thinks that the facts proved constitute one of the offences stated in two or more of the alternative charges, but doubts which of those offences the facts do at law constitute, it may, before recording a finding on those charges, refer to the confirming authority for an opinion, setting out the facts which it finds to be proved and stating that it doubts whether those facts constitute in law the offence stated in such one or other of the charges and may, if necessary, adjourn for that purpose[8].

(j) In any case where the court is empowered by the provisions of the Army Act 1950[9] to find the accused guilty of an offence other than that charged, or guilty of committing an offence in circumstances involving a less degree of punishment, or where it could, after hearing the evidence, have made a special finding of guilty subject to exceptions or variations in accordance with the provisions of the Army Rules 1954[10], it may, if it is satisfied of the justice of such course, and if the concurrence of the convening officer is signified by the prosecutor, accept and record a plea of guilty of such other offences or of the offence as having been committed in circumstances involving such less degree of punishment or of the offence charged subject to such exceptions or variations[11]. However, the failure to obtain the concurrence of the convening officer shall not invalidate the proceedings when confirmed[12].

(k) The finding on each charge shall be announced forthwith in open court as subject to confirmation[13].

1 The Army Rules 1954 r 62(1).

2 The Army Rules 1954 r 62(2).

3 The Army Rules 1954 r 62(3). Before referring to the confirming authority the court must have arrived at a decision as to the facts which it finds to be proved and the opinion of the confirming authority will be sought as to whether, upon the facts so found to be proved, the accused can legally be found guilty. The court cannot refer to the confirming authority for any opinion as to the facts, as to which it is the sole judge. The reason for the reference should be recorded. The opinion of the confirming officer should be read upon re-assembly of the court and attached to the proceedings. Manual of Military Law, Volume II, 2011 the Army Rules 1954 r 62 notes.

4 The Army Rules 1954 r 62(4). The special finding relates only to the particulars of the charge, and not to the

statement of the offence. Before recording a special finding the court must be satisfied that the facts which it finds to be proved, subject to certain exceptions and variations, amount to the substance of the charge; otherwise they must acquit. For example; on a charge against a sepoy for losing by neglect a great coat and a waist belt; the court may properly find the accused "guilty of the charge except that he did not lose a waist belt, but it cannot legally find him 'guilty of the charge' except that he made away with and did not lose the articles in question'. Manual of Military Law, Volume II, 2011 the Army Rules 1954 r 62 notes.

5 The Army Rules 1954 r 62(5).

6 The Army Rules 1954 r 62(6).

7 The Army Rules 1954 r 62(7).

8 The Army Rules 1954 r 62(8).

9 Ie the Army Act 1950 s 139.

10 The Army Rules 1954 r 62 (4) and (5).

11 The Army Rules 1954 r 62(9).

12 The Army Rules 1954 r 62(9) proviso.

13 The Army Rules 1954 r 62(10).

[0266] Procedure on acquittal If the finding on all the charges is 'not guilty' the presiding officer shall date and sign the finding and authenticate the whole of the proceedings. The proceedings thereafter shall be signed by the judge advocate, if any, and shall be transmitted for confirmation[1].

1 The Army Rules 1954 r 63.

[0267] Procedure on conviction If the finding on any charge is 'guilty' then, for the guidance of the court in determining its sentence, and of the confirming authority in considering the sentence, the court, before deliberating on its sentence; shall, whenever possible, take evidence of and record the general character, age, service, rank and any recognised acts of gallantry or distinguished conduct of the accused, any previous convictions of the accused either by a court martial or a criminal court, any previous punishments awarded to him by an officer exercising authority under the provisions of the Army Act 1950[1], the length or time he has been in arrest or in confinement on any previous sentence, and any military decoration, or military reward, of which he may be in possession or to which he is entitled[2]. Evidence on the above matters may be given by a witness verifying a statement which contains a summary of the entries in the regimental books respecting the accused and identifying the accused as the person referred to in that summary[3]. The accused may cross-examine any such witness, and may call witnesses to rebut such evidence; and if the accused so requests, the regimental books, or a duly certified copy of the material entries therein, shall be produced; and if the accused alleges that the summary is in any respect not in accordance with the regimental books, or such certified copy, as the case may be, the court shall compare the summary with those books or copy, and if it finds it is not in accordance therewith, shall cause the summary to be corrected[4]. When all the evidence on the above matters has been given, the accused may address the court, thereon and in mitigation of punishment[5].

1 Ie under the Army Act 1950 ss 80, 83, 84 or 85.

2 The Army Rules 1954 r 64(1). The court cannot take oral evidence that the accused is of bad character; but oral evidence of good character is always permissible. If the accused calls witnesses as to his good character, they may be cross-examined by the prosecutor with a view to testing their veracity and thereby indirectly bringing out evidence of bad character. Witnesses as to character can also be called during the hearing of the case for the

defence and before the finding. Manual of Military Law, Volume II, 2011 the Army Rules 1954 r 64 notes. As to the meaning of 'military reward'; see **[0025]**.

3 The Army rules 1954 r 64(2).

4 The Army rules 1954 r 64(3). The term 'regimental books' includes departmental books maintained by corps, e.g., sheet roll of a 'court martial book', but does not include departmental business books. The copy of the material entries in the regimental book must be certified by the officer having custody of the original book. The witness producing the extract from the regimental, books and the statement as to age, service, rank, etc., of the accused should be the adjutant or some other officer, and there is no objection to the prosecutor giving such evidence. He must be sworn as any other witness and may be cross-examined by the accused and questioned by the court. Manual of Military Law, Volume II, 2011 the Army Rules 1954 r 64 notes.

5 The Army rules 1954 r 64(4).

[0268] Sentence The court shall award a single sentence in respect of all the offences of which the accused is found guilty, and such sentence shall be deemed to be awarded in respect of the offence in each charge in respect of which if can be legally given and not to be awarded in respect of any offence in a charge in respect of which it cannot be legally given[1].

1 The Army rules 1954 r 65. The sentence must be a sentence authorised by the Army Act 1950 under ss 71-76. For example; a court-martial cannot award a sentence of confinement to lines, or sentence an offender to restore stolen property. But a court martial may under the Army Act 1950 s 151(1) make a separate order for the disposal of property. Such an order should be recorded below the signature of the presiding officer to the sentence and should be separately dated and signed by the presiding officer. Sentences, unless for one or more years exactly, should if for one month or upwards, be recorded in months. Sentences consisting of partly of months and partly of days should be recorded in months and days. A month means a calendar month. Manual of Military Law, Volume II, 2011 the Army Rules 1954 r 65 notes.

[0269] Recommendation to mercy If the court makes a recommendation to mercy, it shall give its reasons for its recommendation[1]. The number of opinions by which the recommendation to mercy mentioned in this rule, or any question relative thereto, is adopted or rejected, may be entered in the proceedings[2].

1 The Army rules 1954 r 66(1). A recommendation to mercy will be appended to the sentence; it forms part of the proceedings of the court. In view of the discretion of the court in the matter of awarding sentence, a recommendation to mercy will be exceptional. It will usually be made only when the court, though unwilling to pass a lenient sentence least the offence should be considered as venial one, thinks that, owing to the offender's character or other exceptional circumstances, he should not suffer the full penalty which the offence would ordinarily demand. As a rule the court will be able to adjust the sentence according to what, in its judgment, the offender should suffer having regard to the attendant circumstances. It is indisputable that offences are more effectually prevented by certainty than by severity of punishment. Manual of Military Law, Volume II, 2011 the Army Rules 1954 r 66 notes.

2 The Army rules 1954 r 66(2). As a recommendation to mercy is part of the proceedings, any expression of opinion in it in relation to the finding must be read with, and as part of the finding. Manual of Military Law, Volume II, 2011 the Army Rules 1954 r 66 notes.

[0270] Announcement of sentence and signing and transmission of proceedings The sentence together with any recommendation to mercy and the reasons for any such recommendation will be announced forthwith in open court. The sentence will be announced as subject to confirmation[1]. Upon the court awarding the sentence, the presiding officer shall date and sign the sentence and such signature shall authenticate the whole of the proceedings and the proceedings upon being signed by the judge advocate (if any), shall at once be transmitted for confirmation[2].

1 The Army rules 1954 r 67(1).

2 The Army Rules 1954 r 67(2). It is essential that the date of sentence should be inserted as under the provisions of the Army Act 1950 s 167 a term of imprisonment is reckoned to commence on the day on which the sentence and proceedings were signed by the presiding officer. When, however, the presiding officer after recording the finding and sentence, omits to either sign or date the proceedings, he can, even after confirmation, sign them and date his signature as of the true date of the decision. The proceedings must not be signed by the members of the court other than the presiding officer. The signature authenticates the whole of the proceedings, including the documentary evidence produced at the trial. Manual of Military Law, Volume II, 2011 the Army Rules 1954 r 67 notes.

(F) *Confirmation and Revision*

[0271] Revision[1]

1. The Army Rules 1954 r 68; see **[0407] and [0408]**.

[0272] Review of court martial proceedings[1]

1. The Army Rules 1954 r 69; see **[0395]**.

[0273] Confirmation[1]

1. The Army Rules 1954 r 70; see **[0396]**.

[0274] Promulgation[1]

1. The Army Rules 1954 r 71; see **[0411]**.

[0275] Mitigation of punishment on partial confirmation[1]

1. The Army Rules 1954 r 72; see **[0404]**.

[0276] Confirmation notwithstanding informality in, or excess of punishment[1]

1. The Army Rules 1954 r 73; see **[0406]**.

[0277] Members or prosecutor not to confirm proceedings[1]

1. The Army Rules 1954 r 74; see **[0397]**.

(G) *Proceedings of General and District Court-Martial*

[0278] Seating of members The members of a court-martial shall take their seats according to their army rank[1].

1 The Army Rules 1954 r 75.

[0279] Responsibility of presiding officer The presiding officer of a court martial is responsible for the trial being conducted in proper order, and in accordance with the Army Act 1950, the Army Rules 1954 and in a manner befitting a court of justice[1]. It is his duty to see that justice is administered, that the accused has a fair trial, and he does not suffer any disadvantage in consequence of his position as a person under trial, or of his ignorance, or of his incapacity to examine or cross-examine witnesses, or otherwise[2].

The presiding officer should be careful to safeguard the dignity of the court and the solemnity of its proceedings. If any person, other than the accused, interrupts the proceedings, he should ordinarily be excluded from the court. The court has, however, further powers under the Army Rules 1954[3] for dealing with persons who interrupt its proceedings. The trial of a person cannot proceed in his absence, even though he interrupts the proceedings. If the accused is not represented by counsel or defending officer, the presiding officer should assist him in putting forward his defence, and take care that he is not prejudiced by his inability to put proper questions to the witnesses or bring out clearly the points upon which he relies. If there is a judge advocate, he has a similar duty, but the presence of a judge advocate does not relieve the presiding officer of his responsibility under this provision. If a witness gives evidence different from that given by him when the summary of evidence was taken, he should be questioned as to the difference. The presiding officer should always put to the witnesses any questions which appear to him necessary or desirable for the purpose of eliciting the truth[4].

1 The Army Rules 1954 r 76 (1).

2 The Army Rules 1954 r 76 (2).

3 Ie the Army Rules 1954 r 150; see **[0375]**.

4 See the Army Rules 1954 r 143.

[0280] Power of court over address of prosecutor and accused It is the duly of the prosecutor to assist the court in the administration of justice, to behave impartially, to bring the whole of the transaction before the court, and not to take any unfair advantage of, or suppress any evidence in favour of, the accused[1]. The prosecutor is not to refer matter not relevant to the charge(s). It is the duty of the court to stop him from so doing and also restrain any undue violence of language or want of fairness or moderation on the part of the prosecutor[2]. The court shall allow great latitude to the accused in making his defence; he must abstain from any remarks contemptuous or disrespectful towards the court, and from coarse and insulting language towards others, but he may for the purposes of his defence impeach the evidence and the motives of the witnesses and the prosecutor, and charge other persons with blame and even criminality, subject, if he does so, to any liability which he may thereby incur. The court may caution the accused as to the irrelevance of his defence, but shall not, unless in special cases[3], stop his defence solely on ground of such irrelevance[4].

1 The Army Rules 1954 r 77(1). The prosecutor is an officer whose duty, it is to see, that justice is done and not a partisan intent on securing a conviction independently of the justice of the case. He should, therefore, put before the court facts which show the true character of the offence, and must be careful to prove affirmatively any facts tending to show the innocence of the accused or extenuate his offence, e.g., he should himself produce any available evidence of provocation which might mitigate punishment. The prosecutor must not introduce matters of aggravation into the evidence against the accused unless they are relevant to the charge against him. Generally speaking, anything which tends to show that the accused committed the offence charged, or to show the true character of the offence, is relevant. Manual of Military Law, 2011, Volume II, the Army Rules 1954 r 77 notes.

2 The Army Rules 1954 r 77(2).

3 The case must be very special to justify the court in stopping the accused in his defence, or in excluding on the ground of irrelevancy, evidence offered by him, or to justify any further proceedings against him on account of his defence. Manual of Military Law, 2011, Volume II, the Army Rules 1954 r 77 notes.

4 The Army Rules 1954 r 77(3).

[0281] Procedure on trial of accused persons together Where two or more accused persons are tried together and any evidence as to the facts of the case is tendered by any one or more of them, the evidence and addresses on the part of or on behalf of all the accused persons shall be taken before the prosecutor replies, and the prosecutor shall make one address only in reply as regards all the accused persons[1].

1 The Army Rules 1954 r 78.

[0282] Separate charge-sheets

(A) The convening officer may direct any charges against an accused person to be inserted in different charge-sheets, and when he so directs, the accused shall be arraigned and until after the finding tried, upon each charge-sheet separately, and the procedure in the Army Rules 1954[1], shall, until after finding, be followed in respect of each charge-sheet, as if it contained the whole of the charges against the accused[2].

(B) The trials upon the several charge-sheets shall be in such order as the convening officer directs[3].

(C) When the court have tried the accused upon all the charge-sheets they shall, in the case of the finding being 'not guilty' on all the charges, proceed as directed by the Army Rules 1954[4], and in case of the finding on any one or more of the charges being 'guilty' proceed as directed by provisions of the Army Rules 1954[5], in like manner in each case as if all the charges in the different charge-sheets had been contained in one charge-sheet, and the sentence passed shall be of the same effect as if all the charges had been contained in one charge-sheet[6].

(D) If the convening officer directs that, in the event of the conviction of an accused person upon a charge in any charge-sheet, he need not be tried upon the subsequent charge-sheets, the court in such event may, without trying the accused upon any of the subsequent charge-sheets, proceed as provided in the above-stated provision[7].

(E) Where a charge-sheet contains more than one charge, the accused may, before pleading, claim to be tried separately in respect of any charge or charges in that charge-sheet, on the ground that he will be embarrassed in his defence if he is not so tried separately; and in such case the court, unless they think his claim unreasonable, shall arraign and try the accused in like manner as if the convening officer had inserted the said charge or charges in different charge-sheets[8].

(F) If a plea of 'guilty', to any charge in a charge-sheet has been recorded as the finding of the court, certain provisions of the Army Rules 1954[9] shall not be complied with until after the court had arrived at its findings on all the charge-sheets[10].

1 Ie in the Army Rules 1954 rs 48-62.

2 The Army Rules 1954 r 79 (1).

3 The Army Rules 1954 r 79 (2).

4 Ie the Army Rules 1954 r 63.

5 Ie the Army Rules 1954 r 54 and 64-67.

6 The Army Rules 1954 r 79 (3).

7 The Army Rules 1954 r 79 (4). The powers given to the convening officer under this provision cannot be exercised by the prosecutor on his own initiative or by the court.

8 The Army Rules 1954 r 79 (5).

9 The Army Rules 1954 r 54 (3) and (4).

10 The Army Rules 1954 r 79 (6). Under this provision where an accused has pleaded guilty to a charge entered in one of several charge-sheets, the summary evidence relating thereto and any statement which he may make in reference to the charge or in mitigation of punishment will not be read or recorded until after the finding of the court on all the charge-sheets has been arrived at. But for this provision, the fair trial of the accused upon the other charge-sheets might be prejudiced, especially if he stated, in mitigation of punishment, anything which might point to his guilt on any charge in a charge-sheet which has not yet been tried. Manual of Military Law, 2011, Volume II, the Army Rules 1954 r 79 notes.

[0283] Court Martial to be public Subject to certain provisions of the Army Rules 1954[1], the place in which court martial is held for the purpose of trying an offence under the Army Act 1950 shall be deemed to an open court to which the public generally may have access, so far as the same can conveniently contain them[2]. However, if the court is satisfied that it is necessary or expedient in the public interest or for the ends of justice so to do, the court may at any stage of the trial of any particular case order that the public generally or any portion thereof or any particular person shall not have access to, or be or remain in the place in which the court held[3].

1 Ie the Army Rules 1954 r 80; see **[0284]**.

2 Army Rules 1954 r 80A.

3 The Army Rules 1954 r 80A proviso.

[0284] Sitting in closed court A court martial shall, where it is so directed by the Army Rules 1954, and may in any other case on any deliberation amongst the members, sit in closed court[1]. No person shall be present in closed court except the members of the court, the judge advocate (if any) and any officers under instruction[2]. For the purpose of giving effect to the foregoing provisions of this rule, the court-martial may either retire or cause the place where they sit to be cleared of all other persons not entitled to be present[3]. Except as provided in the above-stated provisions, all proceedings, including the view of any place, shall be in open court and in the presence of the accused subject to the following provision[4]. The court shall have the power to exclude from the court any witness who has yet to give evidence or any other person, other than the accused, who interferes with its proceedings[5].

1 The Army Rules 1954 r 80 (1).

2 The Army Rules 1954 r 80(2). All the members of the court, and the judge advocate, where one is appointed, must be present in the closed court. The officers under instructions should also be present. If for any reason an officer under instruction is not present to attend the deliberations in closed court, his absence will not affect the validity of such deliberations. Manual of Military Law, 2011, Volume II, the Army Rules 1954 r 80 notes.

3 The Army Rules 1954 r 80(3).

4 The Army Rules 1954 r 80(4).

5 The Army Rules 1954 r 80(5). This provision does not affect the power of the court to exclude any person, other than the accused, who interferes with the proceedings; a power which every court possesses for the proper conduct

of its proceedings. A court martial has inherent power to sit 'in camera' if necessary for the proper administration of justice. A court martial may sit 'in camera' if evidence of a secret or top secret nature is led at the trial. Manual of Military Law, 2011, Volume II, the Army Rules 1954 r 80 notes.

[0285] Hours of sitting

(a) A court martial may sit at such times and for such period between the hours of six in the morning and six in the afternoon as may be directed by the proper superior military authority, and so far as no such direction extends, as the court from time to time determines but no court shall sit for more than six hours in any one day[1].

(b) If the court considers it necessary to continue the trial after six in the noon or to sit for more than six hours in any one day, it may do so but if it does so should record in the proceedings the reason for so doing[2].

(c) In cases requiring an immediate example or when the convening officer certifies under his hand that it is expedient for the public service, trials may be held at any hour[3].

(d) If the court or the convening officer or other superior military authority thinks that military exigencies or the interests of discipline require the court to sit on Sunday or on any other day declared as a holiday in army or command orders, the court may sit accordingly, but otherwise the court shall not sit on any of those days[4].

1 The Army Rules 1954 r 81(1). Reasons for longer sittings of the court or for sittings outside the hours specified should be recorded in the proceedings; Manual of Military Law, 2011, Volume II, the Army Rules 1954 r 81 notes.

2 The Army Rules 1954 r 81(2).

3 The Army Rules 1954 r 81(3).

4 The Army Rules 1954 r 81(4). When the court sits on a Sunday or a gazetted holiday, the reasons for so doing should also be recorded in the proceedings; Manual of Military Law, 2011, Volume II, the Army Rules 1954 r 81 notes.

[0286] Continuity of trial and adjournment of court When a court is once assembled and the accused has been arraigned the court shall continue the trial from day to day, in accordance with the provisions of the Army Rules 1954[1], unless it appears to the court that an adjournment is necessary for the ends of justice or that such continuance is impracticable[2]. A court may adjourn from time to time and from place to place and may, when necessary, view any place[3]. The senior officer on the spot may also, for military exigencies adjourn or prolong the adjournment of the court[4]. A court martial, in the absence of a judge advocate (if such has been appointed for that court-martial) shall not proceed, and shall adjourn[5]. If the time to which an adjournment is made is not specified, the adjournment shall be until further orders from the proper military authority; and, if the place to which an adjournment is made is not specified, the adjournment shall be to the same place or to such other place as may be specified in further orders from the proper military authority[6]. The provision does not empower the court martial to adjourn hearing sine die[7]. The reasons for any adjournment must be entered in the proceedings, and either announced in court in presence of the accused, or communicated to the prosecutor and accused[8].

1 Ie the Army Rules 1954 r 81.

2 The Army Rules 1954 r 82 (1).

3 The Army Rules 1954 r 82 (2).

4 The Army Rules 1954 r 82 (3).

5 The Army Rules 1954 r 82 (4).

6 The Army Rules 1954 r 82 (5).

7 *RS Bhagat v Union of India* AIR 1982 Delhi 191.

8 Manual of Military Law, 2011, Volume II, the Army Rules 1954 r 82 notes.

[0287] Suspension of trial Where, in consequence of anything arising while the court is sitting, the court is unable by reason of dissolution as specified in the Army Act 1950[1], or otherwise, to continue the trial, the presiding officer or, in his absence, the senior member, present, will immediately report the facts to the convening authority[2]. Where a court martial is dissolved before the finding, or, in case of a finding of guilty, before award of the sentence, the entire proceedings before the court martial shall be null and the accused may be tried before another court martial[3].

1 Ie in the Army Act 1950 s 117

2 The Army Rules 1954 r 83(1).

3 The Army Rules 1954 r 83 (2). When a court is dissolved under this provision, every member thereof will be disqualified to sit as a member of the fresh court convened for the trial of the accused; see the Army Rules 1954 r 39 (2)(c).

[0288] Proceedings on death or illness of accused In case of the death of the accused, or of such illness of the accused as renders it impossible to continue the trial, the court shall ascertain the fact of the death or illness by evidence, and record the same and adjourn, and transmit the proceedings to the convening authority[1].

1 The Army Rules 1954 r 84. 'Impossible to continue' means to continue within a reasonable time having regard to all the circumstances; see the Army Act 1950 s 117 (2). Oral evidence of the fact of the death or illness will be taken on oath or affirmation. Also, a medical certificate should always, where possible, be obtained, stating that the illness of the accused renders his presence in court impracticable, or dangerous to himself or others, and also the time when, in the opinion of the medical officer, the accused will be able to be present. Manual of Military Law, 2011, Volume II, the Army Rules 1954 r 84 notes.

[0289] Death, retirement or absence of presiding officer In the case of the death, retirement on challenge or unavoidable absence of the presiding officer, the next senior officer shall take the place of the presiding officer and the trial shall proceed if the court is still composed of not less than the minimum number of officers of which it is required by law to consist[1].

1 The Army Rules 1954 r 85.

[0290] Presence throughout of all members of court A member of a court who has absent while any part of the evidence on the trial of an accused person is taken, shall take no further part in the trial by that court of that person, but the court will not be affected unless it is reduced below the legal minimum[1]. An officer shall not be added to a court martial after the accused has been arraigned[2].

1 The Army Rules 1954 r 86 (1). The trial need not be postponed due to the short-time absence of judge advocate, if not prejudice to the accused. *Maj Balram Ali v Union of India* 2003 (5) SLR (Delhi) DB 541.

2 The Army Rules 1954 r 86 (2).

[0291] Taking of opinions of members of court Every member of a court must give his opinion by word of mouth on every question which the court has to decide, and must give his opinion as to the sentence, notwithstanding that he has given his opinion in favour of acquittal[1]. The opinion of the members of the court shall be taken in succession, beginning with the member lowest in rank[2].

1 The Army Rules 1954 r 87(1). Opinions must be given orally. All decisions to be passed by an absolute majority, except in the case of a sentence of death passed by a general court martial which requires a two-thirds majority and a sentence of death passed by summary general court martial which requires the concurrence of all the members. As to the Army Act 1950 s 132; see **[0218]**. The presiding officer has no second or casting vote in the case of a sentence of death; nor where there is an equality of votes on a challenge, finding or sentence. In order to obtain an absolute majority in respect of the sentence, every member must vote, even if he had voted for an acquittal on the finding. It is desirable that the nature, of the punishment to be awarded should first be considered. The procedure to be adopted could be illustrated by the following example: At a general court martial consisting of seven members, three are in favour of a sentence of imprisonment for life, two in favour of imprisonment, and two in favour of dismissal (without imprisonment). The most lenient punishment will be first put to the vote and will be rejected by 5 votes to 2. The next most lenient punishment will then be put to the vote, viz., imprisonment. All seven members must vote again and the two members who had previously voted in favour of dismissal will naturally give their votes for imprisonment rather than imprisonment for life. The result will be an absolute majority of 4 votes to 3 in favour of imprisonment. The quantum or length of the imprisonment to be awarded will be arrived at in the same manner, the most lenient proposal being put to the vote first. It is improper to strike an average between the various sentences suggested by the members of the court, but it may often happen that, in the course of further discussion, members who had originally made different proposals will arrive at a unanimous decision as to the proper sentence to be awarded. The opinion of each member on the finding must be taken separately upon each charge upon which the accused is arraigned. Manual of Military Law, Volume II, the Army Rules 1954 r 87 notes.

2 The Army Rules 1954 r 87(2). The term 'lowest in rank' means lowest in the rank in which members take their seats. Manual of Military Law, Volume II, the Army Rules 1954 r 87 notes.

[0292] Procedure on incidental questions If any objection is raised on any matter of law, evidence, or procedure by the prosecutor or by or on behalf of the accused during the trial, the prosecutor or the accused or counsel or the defending officer (as the case may be) shall have a right to answer the same and the person raising the objection shall have a right of reply[1].

1 The Army Rules 1954 r 88. This provision will apply to such questions as the admissibility of evidence, the propriety of any question or the recalling of a witness. It will also apply to a submission, which may always be made by or on behalf of the accused at the close of the case for the prosecution that no case has been made out justifying the court in putting the accused upon his defence. Manual of Military Law, 2011, Volume II, the Army Rules 1954 r 88 notes.

[0293] Swearing of court to try several accused persons A court may be sworn or affirmed at one time to try any number of accused persons then present before it, whether those persons are to be tried collectively or separately, and each accused person shall have power to object to the members of the court, and shall be asked separately whether he objects to any member[1]. In the case of several accused persons to be tried separately, the court, upon one of those persons objecting to a member, may, according as it thinks fit, proceed to determine that objection or postpone the case of that person and swear or affirm the members of the court for the trial of the others alone[2]. In the case of several accused persons to be tried separately, the court when sworn or affirmed, shall proceed with one case postponing the other cases, and taking them afterwards in succession[3]. Where several accused persons are tried separately by the same court upon charges arising out of the same transaction, the court may, if it considers it to be desirable in the interests of justice, postpone consideration of any sentence to be awarded to any one or more of such accused persons until the trials of all such accused persons have been completed[4].

1 The Army Rules 1954 r 89 (1).

2 The Army Rules 1954 r 89 (2).

3 The Army Rules 1954 r 89 (3).

4 The Army Rules 1954 r 89 (4).

[0294] Swearing of interpreter and shorthand writer At any time during the trial an impartial person may, if the court thinks it necessary and shall, if either the prosecutor or the accused requests it on any reasonable ground, be sworn or affirmed to act as interpreter[1]. An impartial person may at any time of the trial, if the court thinks it desirable, be sworn or affirmed to act as a shorthand writer[2]. Before a person is sworn or affirmed as an interpreter or shorthand writer the accused shall be informed of the person who is proposed to be sworn or affirmed, and may object to the person as not being impartial or for any reasonable course; and the court, if it thinks that the objection is reasonable, shall not swear or affirm that person as interpreter or shorthand writer[3].

1 The Army Rules 1954 r 90(1). A member or judge advocate should not normally act as an interpreter where the trial is likely to be prolonged. Manual of Military Law, 2011, Volume II, the Army Rules 1954 r 90 notes.

2 The Army Rules 1954 r 90(2). An interpreter or shorthand writer is usually sworn or affirmed at the commencement of the trial. For the occasions when an interpreter must be employed; see the Army Rules 1954 r 91: **[0295]**.

3 The Army Rules 1954 r 90(3). The accused has a right to object to the shorthand writer or the interpreter. When such an objection is raised, the same procedure will be followed as in the case of an objection to a member of the court. Manual of Military Law, 2011, Volume II, the Army Rules 1954 r 90 notes.

[0295] Evidence when to be translated When any evidence is given in a language which any of the officers composing the court, the judge advocate, the prosecutor or the accused, or his defending officer or counsel does not understand, that evidence shall be interpreted to such officer or person in a language which he does understand. If an interpreter in such language has been appointed by the convening officer, and duly sworn or affirmed, the evidence shall be interpreted by him. If no such interpreter has been appointed and sworn or affirmed, an impartial person shall be sworn or affirmed by the court as required by the Army Rules 1954[1]. When documents are put in for purpose of formal proof, it shall be in the discretion of the court to cause as much to be interpreted as appears necessary[2].

1 Ie the Army Rules 1954 r 90.

2 The Army Rules 1954 r 91.

[0296] Record in proceedings of transactions of court martial

(a) At a court martial the judge-advocate, or, if there is none, the presiding officer shall record, or cause to be recorded all transactions of the court in the Hindi or English language, and shall be responsible for the accuracy of the record. If the judge-advocate is called as a witness by the accused, the presiding officer shall be responsible for the accuracy of the record in the proceedings of the evidence of the judge advocate[1].

(b) The evidence shall be taken down in a narrative form in as nearly as possible the words used, but in any case where the prosecutor, the accused person, the judge-advocate, or the court considers it material, the question and answer shall be taken down verbatim[2].

(c) Where an objection has been taken to any question or to the admission of any evidence or to the procedure of the court, such objection shall, if the prosecutor or accused so requests or the court thinks fit be entered upon the proceedings together with the grounds of the objection and the decision of the court thereon[3].

(d) Where any address by, or on behalf of, the prosecutor or the accused,is not in writing, it shall not be necessary to record the same in the proceedings further or otherwise than the court thinks proper, except that (i) the court shall in every case make such record of the defence made by the accused as will enable the confirming officer to judge of the reply made by, or on behalf of, the accused to each charge against him[4]; and (ii) the court shall also record any particular matters in the address by or on behalf of, the prosecutor or the accused which the prosecutor or the accused, as the case may be, may require[5].

(e) The court shall not enter in the proceedings any comment or anything not before the court, or any report of any fact not forming part of the trial, but if any such comment or report seems to the court necessary, the court may forward it to the proper military authority in a separate document, signed by the presiding officer[6].

1 The Army Rules 1954 r 92(1). The record, where no shorthand writer is employed, must be taken in a clear and legible hand and should be typed. Interlineations and corrections must be avoided as much as possible; if made they should be initialled by the presiding officer or judge advocate, if any. If desired, a typed copy may be substituted for the original manuscript record; if so substituted it must be checked with the original by the officer responsible for the accuracy of the proceedings. The pages should be numbered and the various sheets fastened together, sheets not used being removed. Sufficient space must be left below the signature of the presiding officer for the decision of the confirming authority. The place and date of the signing of the sentence by the presiding officer must be inserted. No corrections or additions may be made to the proceedings of a court martial after promulgation. If a shorthand writer is employed the evidence is usually taken down verbatim by him. If the evidence of a witness is not given in English, the material effect of question and answer interpreted in English will be recorded. Manual of Military Law, 2011, Volume II, the Army Rules 1954 r 92 notes.

2 The Army Rules 1954 r 92(2). The provision applies to questions and answers given in cross-examination and re-examination as well as in examination-in-chief. While recording evidence in the narrative form, the material effect of the question and answer will be written down: e.g., where the question is 'What did the accused do next'; and the answer is 'He left the room'. The evidence as recorded, would read, 'The accused then left the room'. Documentary evidence will be read by the presiding officer or judge advocate, if any; it should then be marked with a distinguishing letter or figure and attached to the proceedings. In many cases it will be sufficient to attach copies of documents which must, however, be compared with the originals by the court and certified under the hand of the presiding officer to be true copies. Manual of Military Law, 2011, Volume II, the Army Rules 1954 r 92 notes.

3 The Army Rules 1954 r 92(3).

4 The Army Rules 1954 r 92 (4)(a).

5 The Army Rules 1954 r 92(4)(b).

6 The Army Rules 1954 r 92(5). The court can make in a separate document any remark it thinks proper on the conduct of any person who appeared before it, or on the manner in which a particular witness has given his

evidence, or on the manner in which the prosecution has been conducted; also, if it thinks the evidence shows that the accused has committed some offence not charged; e.g., if he is charged with desertion in January, and the evidence shows that he deserted in December, it must acquit him, but may report separately the offence of December. Manual of Military Law, 2011, Volume II, the Army Rules 1954 r 92 notes.

[0297] Custody and inspection of proceedings The proceedings shall be deemed to be in the custody of the judge advocate; or, if there is none, of the presiding officer. The proceedings may, with proper precaution for their safety, be inspected by the members of the court, the prosecutor and accused, respectively, at all reasonable time before the court is closed to consider the finding[1].

1 The Army Rules 1954 r 93.

[0298] Transmission of proceedings after findings The proceedings shall be at once sent by the person having the custody thereof to such person as may be directed by the order convening the court, or, in default of any such direction, to the confirming officer[1].

1 The Army Rules 1954 r 94.

(H) *Defending officer, friend of accused and counsel*

[0299] Defending officer and friend of accused[1]

1 The Army Rules 1954 r 95; see **[0206]**.

[0300] Counsel allowed in certain general and district courts martial[1]

1 The Army Rules 1954 r 96; see **[0207]**.

[0301] Requirements for appearance of counsel[1]

1 The Army Rules 1954 r 97; see **[0208]**.

[0302] Counsel for prosecution[1]

1 The Army Rules 1954 r 98; see **[0209]**.

[0303] Counsel for accused[1]

1 The Army Rules 1954 r 99; see **[0210]**.

[0304] General rules as to counsel[1]

1 The Army Rules 1954 r 100; see **[0212]**.

[0305] Qualifications of counsel[1]

1 The Army Rules 1954 r 101; see **[0213]**.

(I) Judge Advocate

[0306] Disqualification of judge advocate[1]

1 The Army Rules 1954 r 102; see **[0201]**.

[0307] Invalidity in the appointment of judge advocate[1]

1 The Army Rules 1954 r 103; see **[0202]**.

[0308] Substitute on death, illness or absence of judge advocate[1]

1 The Army Rules 1954 r 104; see **[0203]**.

[0309] Powers and duties of judge advocate[1]

1 The Army Rules 1954 r 105; see **[0204]**.

(ii) Summary Court Martial

CONTENTS

[0310] Introduction Summary court martial are peculiar to the Indian Army; similar system does not exist in the Navy and the Air Force. Summary court martial were established in the British Indian Army during 1860s[1]. When a person subject to the Army Act 1950, has committed an offence which can be tried by summary court martial, officers commanding units when determining by what court the accused will be tried, will bear in mind that the legislature, in conferring upon them the powers of summary court-martial, intends that they will exercise these powers[2]. The purpose of summary court martial is to maintain discipline by means of prompt disposal and effective punishment to the offenders. The commanding officers are expected to exercise their powers of trial by summary court martial judiciously. Holding of summary court martial is an exception and not the rule[3].

1 The Indian Articles of War (Act v of 1869) Article 93; Rules of Procedure (Native Army) paragraph 12 provided: The discipline of the Native Army depends in great measure on the summary court martial. When a soldier or other native amenable to the Indian Articles of War has committed an offence which is ordinarily triable by summary court martial, commanding officer, when determining by what court the prisoner is to be tried, are to bear in mind that the legislature, in conferring upon them the powers of a summary court martial, intends that they shall exercise these powers. The Rules of Procedure further clarified: "It will be seen from the definition of commanding officer in Part I of the Indian Articles of War that a 'commanding officer' is defined as a British officer, and as, by Article 93 a summary court martial may only be held by a commanding officer, no native officer, even though in command of a detachment, may hold a summary court martial." Indian Articles of War (Act V of 1869); Rules of Procedure (Native Army) paragraph 28.

2 The provision contained in the Indian Articles of War 1869, Article 93, now find place in the Defence Services Regulations, Regulations for the Army 1987, Volume I, as paragraph 447.

3 *Ex L/Nk Vishav Priya Singh v Union of India* 147 (2008) DLT 202.

[0311] Proceedings The officer holding the trial (hereinafter called the court), shall record, or cause to be recorded the transactions of every summary court martial in the Hindi or English language[1]. The evidence shall be taken down in a narrative form in as nearly as possible the words used; but in any case where the court considers it material, the question and answer shall be taken down verbatim[2]. Certain provisions of the Army Rules 1954 shall be applicable mutatis mutandis while recording proceedings of a summary court martial[3].

1 The Army Rules 1954 r 106(1).

2 The Army Rules 1954 r 106(2).

3 Ie the Army Rules 1954 r 92; see: **[0296]**.

[0312] Evidence when to be translated When any evidence is given in a language which the court or the accused does not understand, that evidence shall be interpreted to the court or officers or junior commissioned officers attending the proceedings in accordance with the provisions of the Army Act 1950[1] or the accused as the case may be in language which it or he does understand. The court, for this purpose, shall either appoint an interpreter, or itself take the oath or affirmation prescribed for an interpreter at a summary court-martial. When documents are put in for the purpose of formal proof, it shall be in the discretion of the court to cause as much to be interpreted as appears necessary[2].

1 The Army Act 1950 s 116(2).

2 The Army Rules 1954 r 107. The commanding officer should, as a general rule, take the interpreter's oath or affirmation himself, in addition to the oath or affirmation prescribed in the Army Rules 1954 r 109 for the court. In the rare cases where the commanding officer does not know the language of the accused he should appoint a competent interpreter. Whoever interprets any evidence must be sworn or affirmed as an interpreter before his doing so; also see: the Army Rules 1954 r 149.

[0313] Assembly When the court, the interpreter (if any), and the officers or junior commissioned officers attending the trial are assembled, the accused shall be brought before the court, and the oaths or affirmation prescribed in the Army Rules 1954[1] taken by the persons therein mentioned[2].

1 Ie the Army Rules 1954 r 109. See: **[0314]**.

2 The Army Rules 1954 r 108.

[0314] Swearing or affirming of court and interpreter The court[1] shall make oath or affirmation in one of the following forms or in such other form to the same purport as may be according to its religion or otherwise binding on its conscience[2].

Form of oath

> I........., swear by Almighty God that I will well and truly try the accused (or accused persons) before the court according to the evidence, and that I will duly administer justice according to the Army Act 1950 without partiality, favour or affection; and if any doubt shall arise, then, according to my conscience, the best of my understanding, and the custom of war in the like cases.

Form of affirmation

> I.........., do solemnly, sincerely and truly declare and affirm that I will well and truly try the accused (or accused persons) before the court according to the evidence, and that I will duly administer justice according to the Army Act without partiality, favour or affection; and if any doubt shall arise, then according to my conscience the best of my understanding, and the custom of war in the like cases.

After which the court, or some person empowered by it, shall administer to the interpreter (if any), an oath or affirmation in one of the following forms, or in such other form to the same purport as the court ascertains to be according to his religion or otherwise binding on his conscience[3].

Form of oath

I.........., swear by Almighty God that I will faithfully interpret and translate, as I shall be required to do, touching the matter before this court-martial.

Form of affirmation

I........., solemnly, sincerely and truly declare and affirm that I will faithfully interpret and translate, as I shall be required to do, touching the matter before this court-martial.

After the oaths and affirmations have been administered, all witnesses shall withdraw from the court[4].

1 The 'court' is the officer holding the trial. Two other offers or junior commissioned officers or one of either must attend the trial, but they do not form part of the court and are not as such sworn or affirmed; see the Army Act 1950 s 116(2).

2 The Army Rules 1954 r 109(1).

3 The Army Rules 1954 r 109(2).

4 The Army Rules 1954 r 109(3).

[0315] Swearing of court to try several accused persons A summary court martial may be sworn or affirmed at one time to try any number of accused persons then present before it whether those persons are to be tried collectively or separately[1]. In the case of several accused persons to be tried separately, the court, when sworn or affirmed, shall proceed with one case postponing the other cases and taking them afterwards in succession[2]. Where several accused persons are tried separately upon charges arising out of the same transaction, the court may, if it considers it to be desirable in the interests of justice, postpone consideration, of any sentence to be awarded to any one or more such accused persons until the trials of all such accused persons have been completed[3].

1 The Army Rules 1954 r 110(1).

2 The Army Rules 1954 r 110(2).

3 The Army Rules 1954 r 110(3).

[0316] Arraignment of accused After the court and interpreter (if any) are sworn or affirmed[1], the accused shall be arraigned on the charges against him[2]. The charges on which the accused is arraigned shall be read and, if necessary, translated to him, and he shall be required to plead separately to each charge[3].

1 Under the Army Rules 1954 r 109 and 110; see: **[0314]** and **[0315]**.

2 The Army Rules 1954 r 111(1).

3 The Army Rules 1954 r 111(2). Arraignment consists of (i) calling upon the accused by his number, rank, name, and description as given in the charge-sheet and asking him 'Is that your number, rank, name and unit (or description)?' (ii) reading the charge to him; and (iii) asking him whether he is guilty or not guilty. Where two or more persons are jointly charged and tried for the same offence, each is separately arraigned. Where there are more charge-sheets than one against an accused, he must be arraigned and tried upon the first charge-sheet before arraignment upon the second or subsequent charge-sheets; see the Army Rules 1954 rs 79 and 126. The charge-sheet, after being read to the accused, will be annexed to the proceedings. The plea of the accused must be taken on all the charges in a

charge sheet. The plea on each charge should be recorded as 'guilty' or 'not guilty'. Manual of Military Law, 2011, Volume II, the Army Rules 1954 r 111 notes.

[0317] Objection by accused to charge The accused, when required to plead to any charge, may object to the charge on the ground that it does not disclose an offence under the Army Act 1950, or is not in accordance with the Army Rules 1954[1].

1 The Army Rules 1954 r 112.

[0318] Amendment of charge At any time during the trial if it appears to the court that there is any mistake in the name or description of the accused in the charge-sheet, it may amend the charge-sheet so as to correct that mistake[1]. If on the trial of any charge it appears to the court at any time before it has begun to examine the witnesses, that in the interests of justice any addition to, omission from, or alteration in, the charge is required, it may amend such charge and may, after due notice to the accused, and with the sanction of the officer empowered to convene a district court martial or on active service a summary general court martial for the trial of the accused if the amended charge requires such sanction, proceed with the trial on such amended charge[2].

1 The Army Rules 1954 r 113(1).

2 The Army Rules 1954 r 113(2). If the amended charge is one requiring reference to superior authority [see the Army Act 1950 s 120(2)] and the officer holding the trial considers that there is grave reason for immediate action and that such reference cannot be made without detriment to discipline, he should attach an explanatory Memorandum to the proceedings and after giving the accused sufficient notice of the amendments, proceed with the trial. See: the Army Rules 1954 r 130.

[0319] Special pleas If a special plea to the general jurisdiction of the court, or a plea in bar of trial, is offered by the accused, the procedure laid down for general and district courts martial[1] when disposing of such pleas shall be followed. In the case of finding by a summary court-martial on either of such pleas, no confirmation is required[2].

1 For 'special plea of the general jurisdiction of the court' and 'plea in bar of trial'; see **[0254]** and **[0256]**.

2 The Army Rules 1954 r 114.

[0320] General plea of 'guilty' or 'not guilty' The accused person's plea of 'guilty' or 'not guilty' (or if he refuses to plead, or does not plead intelligibly either one or the other, a plea of 'not guilty') shall be recorded on each charge[1]. If an accused person pleads 'guilty', that plea shall be recorded as the finding of the court; but before it is recorded, the court shall ascertain that the accused understands the nature of the charge to which he has pleaded guilty and shall inform him of the general effect of that plea, and in particular of the meaning of the charge to which he has pleaded guilty, and of the difference in procedure which will be made by the plea of guilty, and shall advise him to withdraw that plea if it appears from the summary of evidence (if any) or otherwise that the accused ought to plead not guilty[2]. Where an accused pleads 'guilty', such plea and the factum of compliance of the above provision[3], shall be recorded by the court in the following manner: "Before recording the plea of 'guilty' of the accused, the court explained to the accused the meaning of the charge(s) to which he had pleaded 'guilty' and ascertained that the accused had understood the nature of the charge(s) to which he had pleaded 'guilty'. The court also informed the accused the general effect of the plea and the difference in procedure, which will be followed consequent to the said plea. The court having satisfied itself that the accused understands the charge(s) and the effect of his plea of 'guilty' accepts and records the same. The provisions of the Army Rule 115(2) are thus complied with[4]."

Where an accused person pleads guilty to the first of two or more charges laid in the alternative, the court may, after certain provision of the Army Rules 1954[5] has been complied with and before the accused is arraigned on the alternative charge or charges, withdraw such alternative charge or charges without requiring the accused to plead thereto, and a record to that effect shall be made upon the proceedings of the court[6]. The court (i.e., the high court) cannot appreciate the evidence but will certainly look into the procedure which is adopted by summary court martial and examine it on touchstone of the rules in general and the Army Rules 1954 r 115 and 129 in particular. Any order which is made to the detriment of the accused must be made after due compliance with the procedure laid down in the Army Rules 1954. If there is a violation of the procedural safeguards that would be violative of art 14 of the Constitution because it is now settled that one of the attributes of the principles of natural justice is to ensure fairness during enquiries, trials so that the decisions are arrived in such a manner which are free from arbitrariness and bias[7].

1 The Army Rules 1954 r 115(1).

2 The Army Rules 1954 r 115(2). This is a mandatory provision and the court is required to ascertain, before it records 'plea of guilty' of the accused, as to whether the accused undertakes the nature of the charge to which he has pleaded guilty and shall inform him of the general effect of that plea and in particular of the meaning of charge to which he has pleaded guilty. The court is further required under this provision of law to advise the accused to withdraw that plea if it appears from summary of evidence or otherwise that the accused ought to plead not guilty. In a summary court martial, 'plea of guilty' is necessarily required to be signed by the accused to give authenticity to it. In the absence of such signatures, the proceedings do not inspire any confidence and it is, therefore, to be presumed that the accused did not plead guilty during the summary court martial proceedings. *Ex Naik Rohtas v Union of India*, TA No 1 of 2011, WP (C) No 5054 of 1993, decided by the Armed Forces Tribunal Principal Bench, New Delhi on 30 May 2012.

3 Ie the Army Rules 1954 r 115(2).

4 The Army Rules 1954 r 115(2A).

5 Ie the Army Rules 1954 r 115(2).

6 The Army Rules 1954 r 115(3).

7 *Prithpal Singh v Union of India* 1984 (3) SLR J&K High Court.

[0321] Procedure after plea of 'guilty' Upon the record of the plea of 'guilty', if there are other charges in the same charge-sheet to which the plea is 'not guilty', the trial shall first proceed with respect to the latter charges, and, after the finding of those charges, shall proceed with the charges on which a plea of 'guilty' has been entered; but if there are alternative charges, the court may either proceed with respect to all the charges as if the accused had not pleaded 'guilty' to any charge, or may, instead of trying him, record a finding upon any one of the alternative charges to which he has pleaded 'guilty' and a finding of 'not guilty' upon all the other alternative charges[1]. After the record of the plea of 'guilty' on a charge (if the trial does not proceed on any other charges), the court shall read the summary of evidence, and annex it to the proceedings or if there is no such summary, shall take and record sufficient evidence to enable it to determine the sentence, and the reviewing officer to know all the circumstances connected with the offence. The evidence shall be taken in like manner as is directed by the Army Rules 1954[2] in case of a plea of 'not guilty'[3]. After such evidence has been taken, or the summary of evidence has been read, as the case may be, the, accused may address the court in reference to the charge and in mitigation of punishment and may call witnesses as to his character[4]. If from the statement of the accused, or from the summary of evidence, or otherwise, it appears to the court that the accused did not understand the effect of his plea of 'guilty', the court shall alter the record and enter a plea of 'not guilty', and proceed with the trial accordingly[5]. If a plea of 'guilty' is recorded and the trial proceeds with respect to other charges in the same charge-sheet, the proceedings under the provisions of the Army Rules 1954[6] shall take place when the findings on the other charges in the same charge-sheet are recorded[7]. When the accused states anything in mitigation of punishment which in the opinion of the court requires to be proved, and would, if proved, affect the amount of punishment, the court may permit the accused to call witnesses to prove the same[8]. In cases where the court is empowered under the Army Act 1950[9] to find the accused guilty of an offence other than that charged, or guilty of committing an offence in circumstances involving a less degree of punishment, or where it could, after hearing the evidence, have made a special finding of guilty subject to exceptions or variations in accordance with the provisions of the Army Rules 1954[10], it may if it is satisfied of the justice of such course, accept and record a plea of guilty of such other offence, or of the offence as having been committed in circumstances involving such less degree of punishment, or of the offence charged subject to such exceptions or variations[11].

1 The Army Rules 1954 r 116(1).

2 See the Army Rules 1954 r 118.

3 The Army Rules 1954 r 116(2).

4 The Army Rules 1954 r 116(3).

5 The Army Rules 1954 r 116(4).

6 Ie the Army Rules 1954 r 116 (2) and (3).

7 The Army Rules 1954 r 116(5).

8 The Army Rules 1954 r 116(6).

9 Ie the Army Act 1950 s 139.

10 Ie the Army Rules 1954 r 121 (3).

11 The Army Rules 1954 r 116(7).

[0322] Withdrawal of plea of 'not guilty' The accused may, if he thinks fit, at any time during the trial, withdraw his plea of 'not guilty' and plead 'guilty', and in such case the court shall at once, subject to a compliance with the provisions of the Army Rules 1954[1], record a plea and finding of 'guilty', and shall, so far as may be, proceed in the manner provided in the Army Rules 1954[2].

1 The Army Rules 1954 r 115(2).

2 Ie under the Army Rules 1954 r 116. The Army Rules 1954 r 117.

[0323] Procedure after plea of 'not guilty' After the plea of 'not guilty' to any charge is recorded, the evidence for the prosecution shall be taken[1]. At the close of the evidence for the prosecution, the accused shall be asked if he has anything to say in his defence, and may address the court in his defence, or may defer such address until he has called his witnesses. The court may question the accused on the case for the purpose of enabling him to explain any circumstances appearing in his statement or in the evidence against him. The accused shall not render himself liable to punishment by refusing to answer such questions, or by giving answers to them which he knows not to be true. No oath shall be administered to the accused. The accused may then call his witnesses, including also witnesses to character[2].

1 As to the 'calling of all prosecutor's witnesses' and 'calling of witness whose evidence is not contained in summary'; see; the Army Rules 1954 r 145 and 134 respectively. The court shall, in the case of trials by summary court martial, take proper steps to procure the attendance of the witnesses whom the accused desires to call and whose

attendance can reasonably be procured, but the accused may be required to undertake to defray the cost (if any) of their attendance. See: The Army Rules 1954 r 137(2).

2 The Army Rules 1954 r 118. The evidence will be taken by question and answer, or the witness may be asked to tell his own version, questions being subsequently asked to make good any omissions. It will, as a rule, be recorded in a narrative form; but where the accused or the court considers it material, the question and answer will be taken down verbatim. The material effect only of the question and answer will be written down, e.g., where the question is 'what did the accused do next?' and the answer is 'he left the room', the evidence as recorded would read 'the accused then left the room'. Documentary evidence after being read should be marked with a distinguishing letter or figure and attached to the proceedings. An accused cannot give evidence on oath and therefore any statement made by him must be carefully considered. Though not given on oath and subject to the test of cross-examination, it will often be of value, particularly if it is in any respect corroborated by evidence from other sources. It is open to the accused, at the close of the case for the prosecution, to submit that the evidence given for the prosecution has not established a prima facie case against him and that he should not, therefore be called upon for his defence. If the court is satisfied that it is well founded, the accused must be acquitted. Manual of Military Law, Volume II, 2011, the Army Rules 1954 r 118 notes.

[0324] Witnesses in reply to defence The court may, if it thinks it necessary in the interest of justice, call witnesses, in reply to the defence[1].

1 The Army Rules 1954 r 119. This is an extreme measure and should only be resorted to when the accused has made or elicited from his witnesses some statement material to the defence, which could not reasonably have been foreseen when the case for the prosecution was being investigated. Manual of Military Law, Volume II, 2011, the Army Rules 1954 r 119 notes.

[0325] Verdict After all the evidence, both for prosecution and defence, has been heard, the court shall give its opinion as to whether the accused is guilty or not guilty of the charges[1].

1 The Army Rules 1954 r 120. The court need not be closed and the finding may be pronounced at once. On the other hand the officer holding the trial may clear the court to consider the evidence, or to discuss any point with the officers /junior commissioned officers attending the trial, or may adjourn the court to allow himself time for further consideration or reference as to any doubtful point. Manual of Military Law, Volume II, 2011, the Army Rules 1954 r 120 notes.

[0326] Form and record of finding The finding on every charge upon which the accused is arraigned shall be recorded, and except as mentioned in following provisions, such finding shall be recorded simply as a finding of 'guilty', or of 'not guilty'[1]. When the court is of opinion as regards any charge that the facts proved do not disclose the offence charged or any offence of which he might under the Army Act 1950 legally be found guilty on the charge as laid, the court shall acquit the accused of that charge[2]. When the court is of opinion as regards any charge that the facts found to be proved in evidence differ materially from the facts alleged in the statement of particulars in the charge, but are nevertheless sufficient to prove the offence stated in the charge, and that the difference is not so material as to have prejudiced the accused in his defence, it may, instead of a finding of 'not guilty' record a special finding[3]. The special finding may find the accused guilty on a charge subject to the statement of exceptions or variations specified therein[4]. The court shall not find the accused guilty on more than one of two or more charges laid down in the alternative, even if conviction upon one charge necessarily connotes guilty upon the alternative charge or charges[5].

1 The Army Rules 1954 r 121(1).
2 The Army Rules 1954 r 121(2).
3 The Army Rules 1954 r 121(3).
4 The Army Rules 1954 r 121(4).
5 The Army Rules 1954 r 121(5).

[0327] Procedure on acquittal If the finding on each of the charges in a charge-sheet is 'not guilty', the court shall date and sign the proceedings, the findings shall be announced in open court, and the accused will be released in respect of those charges[1].

1 The Army Rules 1954 r 122.

[0328] Procedure on conviction If the finding on any charge is 'guilty', the court may record of its own knowledge, or take evidence of and record, the general character, age, service, rank, and any recognised acts of gallantry or distinguished conduct of the accused, and previous convictions of the accused either by a court martial, or a criminal court, any previous punishments awarded to him by an officer exercising authority under the provision of the Army Act 1950[1], the length of time he has been in arrest or in confinement on any previous sentence, and any military decoration, or military reward, of which he may be in possession or to which he is entitled[2]. If the court does not record the matters mentioned under this provision of its own knowledge, evidence on these matters may be taken in the manner provided in the Army Rules 1954[3] for similar evidence at general and district court martial[4].

1 Ie under the provision of the Army Act 1950 s 80.
2 The Army Rules 1954 r 123(1).
3 Ie in the Army Rules 1954 r 64; see **[0267]**.
4 The Army Rules 1954 r 123(2).

[0329] Sentence The court shall award one sentence in respect of all the offences of which the accused is found guilty[1].

Trials held under the summary court martial have been criticized by the Supreme Court, high courts and the armed forces tribunal on the grounds of awarding excessive and harsh punishments[2], denial of procedural rights guaranteed under art 14 of the Constitution[3], lack of evidence[4], being arbitrary and violative of art 14 of the Constitution[5], retrial without jurisdiction[6], biased, punishment disproportionate to the gravity of the misconduct[7], non-compliance with the provisions of the Army Rules 1954[8], trial without jurisdiction[9], and violative of art 20 (2) of the Constitution and the Army Act 1950 s 121[10].

1 The Army Rules 1954 r 124. Sentences, unless for one year exactly, should, if for one month or upwards, be recorded in months. Sentences consisting partly of months and partly of days should be recorded in months and days. A month means a calendar month. When a summary court martial awards a sentence of imprisonment for a period not exceeding three months, to which no sentence of dismissal is added, the court should enter a direction, which should form part of the sentence, that the imprisonment will be carried out by confinement in military custody; see the Army Act 1950 s 169(3). Unless such a direction is given, the offender has to be committed to a civil prison, which is most undesirable in the case of a person who is to return to duty after undergoing his punishment. On active service, however, the officer commanding the forces in the field can, under, the Army

Act 1950 s 169(4), appoint places in which sentence of imprisonment of any length may be carried out. For the date a sentence of dismissal awarded by a court-martial takes effect, see the Army Rules 1954 r 168. Sentences of imprisonment combined with dismissal should, as a rule, be carried out by confinement in a civil prison. As to the scale punishments awardable by summary courts martial; see the Defence Services Regulations, Regulations for the Army 1987, Volume I, paragraph 448; see [0330].

2 *Ravinder Singh v Union of India* 97 (2002) Del LT 756 (DB), *Ex-Naik Sardar Singh v Union of India* AIR 1992 SC 417: (1991) 3 SCC 213, *Sep Veer Bhan v Chief of the Army Staff* 2005 (7) SLR (Delhi) (DB) 281.

3 *Ex Hav Prithpal Singh v Union of India* 1984 (3) SLR 675 J&K High Court.

4 *Lance Naik Mirza Nazir Ahmed v Union of India* WP No 317 of 1981, J&K High Court.

5 *R R Verma v Union of India* 1994 Cr LJ 762.

6 *Surinder Singh v Union of India* Misc Petition No 2323 of 1991, MP High Court.

7 *Ranjit Thakur v Union of India* (1987) 4 SCC 611, 1988 SCC (L&S)1. Punishment must be commensurate with the gravity of offence. If it is excessively harsh and vindictive it is open to judicial review.

8 *Uma Shankar Pathak v Union of India* 1989 (3) SLR 405, *Ex-Hav Ratan Singh v Union of India* AIR 1992 SC 415, (1992) Supp 1 SCC 716: (1992) Cr LJ 287, *Chief of Army Staff v MZH Khan* 2007 (6) SLR 351.

9 *Ex Havildar Mahipal Singh v Union of India* 55 (1994) DLT 176.

10 *Ex Signalman Sunil Kumar v Union of India* TA No 382 of 2009, WP (C) No 198 of 2008 of Delhi High Court, decided on 29 September 2009 by the Armed Forces Tribunal Principal Bench (Court No 3) New Delhi.

[0330] Scale of punishments awardable by summary courts martial The following general instructions are issued for the guidance of officers holding summary courts martial in passing sentence[1]. However, these provisions should not be considered as limiting the discretion of the court to pass any legal sentence, whether in accordance with these instructions or not, if in its opinion, there is good reason for doing so: (i) When passing sentence, courts will have regard not only to the nature and degree of the offence and the previous character of the accused but also to his status and rank and to the legal consequences of the sentence proposed to be awarded. A punishment which is suitable or even lenient in the case of a young sepoy may have an extremely severe effect in the case of a non-commissioned officer of some years' service who has earned a pension; (ii) Imprisonment for any term exceeding three months will be undergone in a civil or military prison[2]. In practice this entails dismissal, or discharge, from the service, as it is usually inexpedient for a man who has been the inmate of a civil jail to return to the service. Three months rigorous imprisonment or less to be undergone in military custody should, therefore, be looked upon as the normal punishment for most first offences and for most purely military offences except those of a grave nature or where the offender already has a bad character. A sentence of imprisonment combined with dismissal should be carried out in a civil prison; (iii) The award of imprisonment in a civil jail coupled with dismissal from the service must never be used merely as a means of getting rid of a man from the service but should be imposed only when the offence by itself, or the offence and the man's previous record taken together, actually merits such a punishment. In other cases in which removal is considered desirable in the interest of the service, the discharge of the individual under the appropriate item of Army Rules 1954 r 13 should be applied for by the commanding officer and authorised by the brigade or superior commander; (iv) In the table of normal punishments shown below, offences which cannot be tried by a summary court martial, except after reference under Army Act 1950 s 120(2), and the less common offences have not been included. Such offences if tried by summary court martial must be dealt with according to the merits of each case.

Table of Punishments

(A) **Normal punishment: rigorous imprisonment for three months or less to be undergone in military custody**. Offences: disobedience, not of a grave nature; insubordination, not of a grave nature; first desertion or fraudulent enrolment; absence without leave or overstaying leave; failing to appear at parade; quitting parade, guard, etc., without leave; absence from camp or after tattoo; intoxication; releasing or suffering prisoner to escape; escaping from custody; losing by neglect, arms, etc; false answer on enrolment; minor contempt of court martial; neglect of orders; act prejudicial, etc., not of a grave nature; sentry plundering, etc., not of a grave nature; sentry sleeping on or quitting post in peace time; use of force to superior, not of a grave nature; failing to rejoin for active service, not of a grave nature; making away with, under the Army Act 1950 s 54(a), other than arms and ammunition; false accusations and complaints, not of a grave nature; striking or ill-treating a subordinate, not of a grave nature; and first offences not of a grave nature.

(B) **Normal punishment: rigorous imprisonment for six months or less and dismissal from the service**. Offences: disobedience of a grave nature or studied insubordination; malingering, feigning or producing disease; use of force to superior, grave cases; contempt of court martial, grave cases; giving false evidence; ordinary theft; frauds; indecency or cruelty; and act prejudicial, etc., of a grave nature than under (A) above.

(C) **Normal punishment: rigorous imprisonment for one year and dismissal from the service**. Offences: making away with arms or ammunition; repeated disobedience or insubordination; desertion, grave cases and second or subsequent convictions; thefts, grave cases; frauds, grave cases; causing hurt to render unfit for service; unnatural offences; failing to rejoin for active service of grave and deliberate nature; and act prejudicial, etc., of a grave nature[3].

1 When a person subject to the Army Act has committed an offence which can be tried by summary court martial, the officers commanding units when determining by what court the accused will be tried, will bear in mind that the legislature, in conferring upon them the powers of summary court martial, intends that they will exercise these powers. Defence Services Regulations, Regulation for the Army 1987, Volume I, paragraph 447.

2 The Army Act 1950 s 169.

3 Defence Services Regulations, Regulation for the Army 1987, Volume I, paragraph 448.

[0331] Signing of proceedings The court shall date and sign the sentence and such signature shall authenticate the whole of the proceedings.

1 The Army Rules 1954 r 125. It is essential that the date of sentence should be inserted, as under the Army Act 1950 s 167 a term of imprisonment is reckoned to commence on the day on which the sentence and proceedings were signed by the court.

[0332] Finding and sentence of a summary court martial The finding and sentence of a summary court martial shall not require to be confirmed and may be carried out forthwith;[1] however, if the officer holding the trial is of less than five years service, he shall not, except on active service, carry into effect any sentence until it has received the approval of an officer commanding not less than a brigade[2].

1 The Army Act 1950 s 161 (1).

2 The Army Act 1950 s 161 (2).

[0333] Charges in different charge-sheets When the charges at a trial by summary court martial are contained, in different charge-sheets, the procedure laid down for general and district courts martial when trying charges contained in different charge-sheets shall, so far as may be applicable, be followed[1].

1 The Army Rules 1954 r 126. As to insertion of charges in separate charge-sheets and procedure, see the Army Rules 1954 r 79.

[0334] Clearing the court The officer holding the trial may clear the court to consider the evidence or to consult with the officers or junior commissioned officers, attending the trial[1]. Except as above-mentioned, all the proceedings, including the view of any place, shall be in open court, and in the presence of the accused[2].

1 The Army Rules 1954 r 127(1).

2 The Army Rules 1954 r 127 (2).

[0335] Adjournment A summary court martial may adjourn from time to time and from place to place, and may, when necessary, view any place[1].

1 The Army Rules 1954 r 128.

[0336] Friend of accused In any summary court martial, an accused person may have a person (called the friend of the accused), to assist him during the trial, whether a legal adviser or any other person. A person so assisting him may advise him on all points and suggest the questions to be put to witnesses, but shall not examine or cross examine witnesses or address the court[1]. Where the accused had not opted, but a 'friend of accused' was imposed to assists him; the High Court held that it cannot appreciate the evidence but will certainly look into the procedure which is adopted by summary court martial and examine it on touchstone of the rules in general and the Army Rules 1954 r 129 in particular. Any order which is made to the detriment of the accused must be made after due compliance with the procedure laid down in the Army Rules 1954. If there is a violation of the procedural safeguards that would be violative of art 14 of the Constitution because it is now settled that one of the attributes of the principles of natural justice is to ensure fairness during enquiries, trials so that the decisions are arrived in such a manner which are free from arbitrariness and bias[2].

1 The Army Rules 1954 r 129.

2 *Prithpal Singh v Union of India* 1984 (3) SLR, J&K High Court.

[0337] Memorandum to be attached to proceedings An explanatory memorandum is to be attached to the proceedings when a summary court martial tries, without reference, an offence which should not ordinarily be so tried[1].

1 The Army Rules 1954 r 130. This explanation should invariably be attached. If the officer holding the trial loses sight of the law and tries without reference any of the offences mentioned in the Army Act 1950 s 120(2) without considering whether grave reasons for immediate action exist or not, the trial is illegal.

[0338] Promulgation The sentence of a summary court martial shall, except as provided in the Army Rules 1954[1], be promulgated at the earliest opportunity after it has been pronounced and shall be carried out without delay after promulgation[2].

1 Ie the Army Rules 1954 r 132; see **[0339]**.

2 The Army Rules 1954 r 131. The charge(s), finding and sentence of the proceedings of summary court martial will be promulgated in all cases to the accused in the manner stated below. The details of proceedings will be read out to the accused by his commanding officer in the presence of the adjutant and the senior junior commissioned officers of the unit. The commanding officer may order the promulgation to be carried out at a parade. If the accused has been sentenced to dismissal or to be reduced to the ranks or to a lower rank or grade he will be stripped of his badges of rank and other regimental insignia. The date of promulgation with be recorded on the proceedings. The result of courts martial will be published in the orders of all formations in which the notice of the convening of the court appeared. In every case such results will be published in the orders of the unit concerned, in Part II Orders. See: Defence Services Regulations, Regulations for the Army 1987, Volume I, paragraph 473.

[0339] Promulgation to be deferred in certain circumstances When the officer holding the trial has less than five years service, the sentence of a summary court martial shall not (except on active service) be carried out until approved by superior authority as provided in the Army Act 1950[1].

1 Ie as provided in the Army Act 1950 s 161(2); see **[0232]**. The Army Rules 1954 r 132. The officer to whom the sentence is referred cannot in any way alter the finding or remit, mitigate, or commute the sentence, but if he considers the sentence too severe he should inform the officer holding the trial of his views and direct him to modify the sentence, which order should be obeyed as a matter of discipline. The original sentence must not be carried out until the case is finally settled. The provisions of this rule do not affect the date from which the sentence takes effect; see the Army Act 1950 s 167 and the Army Rules 1954 r 168.

[0340] Review of proceedings The proceedings of a summary court martial shall, immediately on promulgation, be forwarded through the deputy judge advocate general of the command in which the trial is held to the officer authorised to deal with them in pursuance of the provisions of the Army Act 1950[1]. After review by him, they will be returned to the accused person's corps for preservation in accordance with the provisions of the Army Rules 1954[2].

1 Ie the Army Act 1950 s 162.

2 Ie the Army Rules 1954 r 146(2). The Army Rules 1954 r 133.

[0341] Transmission of proceedings of summary court martial The proceedings of every summary court martial shall without delay be forwarded to the officer commanding the division or brigade within which the trial was held, or to the prescribed officer[1]; and such officer, or the Chief of the Army Staff, or any officer empowered in this behalf by the Chief of the Army Staff may, for reasons based on the merits of the case, but not any merely technical grounds, set aside the proceedings or reduce the sentence to any other sentence which the court might have passed[2]. An express provision has been made for recording reasons based on merits of the case in relation to the proceedings of the summary court martial in cases where said proceedings are set aside or the sentence is reduced[3].

1 As to the meaning of 'prescribed officer'; see the Army Rules 1954 r 200. The prescribed officer for the purposes of the Army Act 1950 s 162 shall, whenever any division or brigade is temporarily withdrawn from its territorial area, be the officer, not being below the rank of field officer, commanding the corresponding divisional or brigade area, within which the trial is held. However, when the officer who held the trial is himself the commander of such area, he shall forward the proceedings to superior authority. when the trial is held on board a ship the prescribed officer shall be the officer commanding the troops on board the ship, or the officer who would, have had power to deal with the proceedings had the trial been held at the port of disembarkation. However, when the officer who held the trial is himself the officer commanding the troops on board the ship, he shall forward the proceedings to

the authority at the port of disembarkation.

2 The Army Act 1950 s 162.

3 *SN Mukherjee v Union of India* AIR 1990 SC 1984, (1990) 4 SCC 594, 1990 (5) SLR 8 (SC).

(iii) Summary General Court Martial

CONTENTS

[0342] Introduction The object of the summary general court martial is to provide for the speedy trial of offences committed abroad or on active service[1] in cases where it is not practicable, with due regard to the interests of discipline and of the service, to try such offences by an ordinary general court martial or district court martial. A summary general court martial can try any offence committed on active service but when troops are not on active service it can only be convened by an officer empowered in this behalf by an order of the Central Government or of the chief of the army staff[2].

1 As to the definition of 'active service'; see **[0008]**.

2 Manual of military Law, 2011, Volume II, the Army Act 1950 s112 notes.

[0343] Convening the court and record of proceedings The summary general court martial may be convened and the proceedings of the court recorded in accordance with the form in the Army Rules 1954 Appendix III, with such variations as the circumstances of each case may require[1]. The officer convening the court shall appoint or detail the officers to form the court, and may also appoint or detail such officers as waiting members as he thinks expedient. Such officers should have held commissions for not less than one year, but, if any officers are available who have held commissions for not less than three years, they should be selected in preference to officers of less service[2]. The provost-marshal, an assistant provost marshal, or an officer who is prosecutor or witness for the prosecution shall not be appointed a member of the court, but subject to the above stated provision any other available officer may be appointed to sit[3].

1 The Army Rules 1954 r 151 (1). As to the power to convene and composition of summary general court martial; see **[0178]** and **[0183]**. The convening order must be signed personally by the convening officer. In the convening order, members and waiting members (if any) may be appointed by name, or only their ranks and units may be mentioned. In the latter event, the ranks, names, etc., of the members of the court as constituted, will be recorded in the proceedings. Manual of Military Law, 2011, Volume II, the Army Rules 1954 r 151 notes.

2 The Army Rules 1954 r 151 (2). It is not mandatory that a member of a summary general court martial must have held a commission for not less than one year. An officer with less than one year's commissioned service can legally sit as a member. Manual of Military Law, 2011, Volume II, the Army Rules 1954 r 151 notes.

3 The Army Rules 1954 r 151 (3).

[0344] Charge The statement of an offence may be made briefly in any, language sufficient to describe or disclose an offence under the Army Act 1950[1].

1 The Army Rules 1954 r 152.

[0345] Trial of several accused persons The court may be sworn at the same time to try any number of accused persons then present before it, but except as provided in the Army Rules 1954[1] the trial of each accused person shall be separate[2].

1 Ie the Army Rules 1954 r 35; see **[0153]**.

2 The Army Rules 1954 r 153.

[0346] Challenges The names of the presiding officer and members of the court shall be read over to the accused who shall thereupon be asked if he objects to be tried by any of these officers[1]. Any objection shall be decided as provided for in the Army Act 1950 and the Army Rules 1954[2]; the vacancies being filled from among the waiting members (if any), or by fresh members being appointed by the convening officer[3].

1 The Army Rules 1954 r 154(1).

2 Ie the Army Act 1950 s 130 and the Army Rules 1954 r 44.

3 The Army Rules 1954 r 154(2).

[0347] Swearing or affirming the court, judge advocate, etc The provisions of the Army Rules 1954[1] relating to administering and taking of oaths and making of affirmations shall apply to every summary general court martial[2].

1 The Army Rules 1954 rs 45-47; see: **[0248]**, **[0249]**, and **[0250]**.

2 The Army Rules 1954 r 155.

[0348] Arraignment When the court is sworn or affirmed, the judge advocate (if any) or the presiding officer shall state to the accused then to be tried, the offence with which he is charged with, if necessary, an explanation giving him full information of the act or omission with which he is charged and shall ask the accused whether he is guilty or not guilty of the offence[1].

1 The Army Rules 1954 r 156. As to objection by accused to charge, see the Army Rules 1954 r 49, which by r 164 is applied, so far as practicable, to a summary general court martial. As to responsibility of presiding officer, see: the Army Rules 1954 r 76. As to general plea of 'guilty' or 'not guilty'; see: the Army Rules 1954 r 52. As to procedure after plea of 'guilty'; see: the Army Rules 1954 r 54. Both these provisions are, by the Army Rules 1954 r 164 are applied, so far as practicable, to a summary general court martial. A plea of 'guilty' will not be accepted by the court if the charge or charges upon which an accused is arraigned render him, liable, on conviction, to be sentenced to death. If such plea is offered, the court will enter a plea of 'not guilty' and proceed with the trial accordingly. Manual of Military Law, 2011, Volume II, the Army Rules 1954 r 156 notes.

[0349] Plea of jurisdiction If a special plea to the general jurisdiction is offered by the accused, and is considered by the court to be proved, the court shall report the same to the convening officer[1].

1 The Army Rules 1954 r 157. See the Army Rules 1954 r 51 which by r 164 is applied, so far as practicable, to a summary general court martial.

[0350] Evidence The witnesses for the prosecution will be called and the accused shall be allowed to cross-examine them and to call any available witnesses for his defence[1]. An oath or affirmation as laid down in the Army Rules 1954[2] shall be administered to every witness, if so required by the Army Act 1950, before he gives his evidence, by one of the persons specified in the Army Rules 1954[3].

1 The Army Rules 1954 r 158(1)

2 The Army Rules 1954 r 140.

3 The Army Rules 1954 r 158(2).

[0351] Defence The accused shall be asked what he has to say in his defence, and shall be allowed to make his defence. He may be allowed to have any person to assist him during the trial, whether a legal adviser or any other person[1]. The court or the judge-advocate, if any, may question the accused on the case for the purpose of enabling him to explain any circumstances appearing in his statement or in the evidence against him. The accused shall not render himself liable to punishment by refusing to answer such questions or by giving answers to them, which he knows not to be true[2].

1 The Army Rules 1954 r 159(1). As to rights of the accused to prepare his defence, see the Army Rules 1954 r 33 which by the Army Rules 1954 r 164 is applied, so far as practicable, to a summary general court martial.

2 The Army Rules 1954 r 159(2).

[0352] Record of the Evidence and Defence The judge advocate (if any), or the presiding officer shall take down or cause to be taken down a brief record of the evidence of the witnesses at the trial and of the defence of the accused; the record so taken down shall be attached to the proceedings[1]. If it appears to the convening officer that military exigencies or other circumstances prevent compliance with the above stated provision, he may direct that the trial will be carried on without any such brief record being taken down[2]. If the accused pleads 'guilty' the summary of evidence, if any, may be read and attached to the proceedings, and it shall not be necessary for the court to hear witnesses for the prosecution, respecting matters contained in the summary of evidence so read[3].

1 The Army Rules 1954 r 160(1).

2 The Army Rules 1954 r 160(2).

3 The Army Rules 1954 r 160(3).

[0353] Finding and sentence The court shall then be closed to consider its finding. If the finding on any charge is 'guilty', the court may receive any evidence as to previous convictions and character which is available. The court shall then deliberate in closed court as to its sentence[1].

1 The Army Rules 1954 r 161. As to voting of members, see the Army Act 1950 s 132 (1) and (4). For votes required before a sentence of death can be passed; see: the Army Act 1950 s 132 (3). The provisions of the Army Rules 1954 rs 61 Consideration of finding), 62 (form, record and announcement of finding), 64 (recommendation to mercy) and 67 (announcement of sentence) are applied by the Army Rules 1954 rs 164, so far as practicable, to trials by summary general court martial.

[0354] Signing and transmission of proceedings Upon the court arriving at a finding of 'not guilty', or awarding the sentence in case of having arrived at a finding of 'guilty', the, presiding officer shall date and sign the finding or sentence, as the case may be. The signature shall authenticate the whole of the proceedings and the proceedings upon being signed by the judge-advocate, if any, shall at once be transmitted to the confirming officer, for confirmation[1].

1 The Army Rules 1954 r 162. Every finding and sentence of a summary general court martial is subject to confirmation; see the Army Act 1950 s 153.

[0355] Adjournment A summary general-court-martial may adjourn from time to time and from place to place and may when necessary view any place[1]. The proceedings shall be held in open court, in the presence of the accused except on any deliberation among the members when the count may be closed[2].

1 The Army Rules 1954 r 163(1).

2 The Army Rules 1954 r 163(2).

[0356] Application of rules The following provisions of the Army Rules 1954, namely rs 22 (hearing of charge), see **[0140]**; 23 (procedure for taking down the summary of evidence), see **[0142]**; 24 (remand of accused), see **[0143]**; 27 (delay report), see **[0128]**; 33 (rights of accused to prepare defence), see **[0150]**; 34 (warning of accused for trial), see **[0151]**; 36 (suspension of rules on grounds of military exigencies or the necessities of discipline), see **[0152]**; 38 (adjournment for insufficient number of officers), see **[0240]**; 49 (objection by accused to charge), see **[0252]**; 51 (special plea to the jurisdiction), see **[0254]**; 52 (general plea of 'guilty' or 'not guilty'), see **[0255]**; 53 (plea in bar), see **[0256]**; 54 (procedure after plea of 'guilty'), see **[0257]**; 55 (withdrawal of plea of 'not guilty'), see **[0258]**; 61 (consideration of finding), see **[0264]**; 62 (form, record and announcement of finding), see **[0265]**; 64 (procedure on conviction), see **[0267]**; 65 (sentence), see **[0268]**; 66 (recommendation of mercy), see **[0269]**; 67 (announcement of sentence), see **[0270]**; 71 (promulgation), see **[0411]**; 72 (mitigation of sentence on partial confirmation), see **[0404]**; 73 (confirmation notwithstanding informality in, or excess of, punishment), see **[0406]**; 74 (member or prosecutor not to confirm proceedings), see **[0397]**; 76 (responsibility of presiding officer), see **[0279]**; 77 (power of court over address of prosecutor and accused), see **[0280]**; 78 (procedure on trial of accused persons together), see **[0281]**; 80 (sitting in closed court), see **[0284]**; 80-A (court-martial to the public), see **[0283]**; 84 (proceedings on death or illness of accused), see **[0288]**; 85 (death, retirement or absence of presiding officer), see **[0289]**; 86 (presence throughout of all members of the court), see **[0290]**; 94

(transmission of proceedings after-finding), see **[0298]**; 95 (defending officer and friend of accused), see **[0206]**; 96 (counsel allowed in certain general and district court martial), see **[0207]**; 97 (requirement for appearance of counsel), see **[0208]**; 98 (counsel for prosecution), see **[0209]**; 99 (counsel for accused), see **[0210]**; 100 (general rules as to counsel), see **[0212]**; 101 (qualification for counsel), see **[0213];** 102 (disqualification of judge-advocate), see **[0201]**; 103 (invalidity in the appointment of judge-advocate), see **[0202]**; 104 (substitute on death, illness, or absence of judge-advocate), see **[0203]**; 105 (powers and duties of judge-advocate), see **[0204]**; 145 (finding of insanity), see **[0369]**; 146 (preservation of proceedings), see **[0370]**; 147 (right of person tried to copies of proceedings), see **[0371]**; 148 (loss of proceedings), see **[0373]**; 149 (validity of irregular procedure in certain cases), see **[0374]**; shall, so far as practicable, apply as if a summary general court martial were a district court martial[1].

1 The Army Rules 1954 r 164.

[0357] Evidence of opinion of convening officer Any statement in an order convening a summary general court-martial as to the opinion of the convening officer shall be conclusive evidence of that opinion, but this provision shall not prejudice the proof at any time of any such opinion when not so stated[1].

1 The Army Rules 1954 r 165.

D. COURT MARTIAL: GENERAL PROVISIONS

CONTENTS

PARA

(A) Witnesses and evidence

(B) Addresses

(C) Insanity

(D) Preservation of proceedings

(E) Irregular procedure when no injustice is done

(F) Offences of witnesses and others

(A) *Witnesses and evidence*

[0358] Calling of all prosecutor's witnesses The prosecutor or, in the case, of a trial by summary court martial, the court is not bound to call all the witnesses for the prosecution whose evidence is in the summary of evidence or whom the accused has been informed he or it intends to call, but he or it should ordinarily call such of them as the accused desires, in order that he may cross-examine them, and shall, for this reason, so far as practicable, secure the attendance of all such witnesses[1].

1 The Army Rules 1954 r 134. The prosecutor is not required to call any witness at the trial who was called by the accused at the taking of summary of evidence. It is not necessary for the prosecutor to examine at length a witness for the prosecution called at the request of the accused and tendered for cross-examination under this provision. Manual of Military Law, Volume II, 2011, the Army Rules 1954 r 134 notes.

[0359] Calling of witness whose evidence is not contained in summary If the prosecutor, or, in the case of a summary court martial, the court intends to call a witness whose evidence is not contained in any summary of evidence given to the accused, notice of the intention shall be given to the accused, a reasonable time before the witness is called together with an abstract of his proposed evidence; and if such witness is called without such notice having been given the court shall, if the accused so desires it, either adjourn after taking the evidence of the witness, or allow the cross-examination of such witness to be postponed and the court shall inform the accused of his right to demand such adjournment or postponement[1].

1 The Army Rules 1954 r 135. This provision applies only in the case of witnesses called for the prosecution and not in the case of witnesses called by the accused or by the court under the Army Rules 1964 r 143 (4).

[0360] List of witnesses of accused The accused shall not be required to give to the prosecutor or court a list of the witnesses whom he intends to call, but it shall rest with the accused alone to secure the attendance of any witness whose evidence is not contained in the summary and for whose attendance the accused has not requested steps to be taken as provided by the provisions of the Army Rules 1954[1].

1 Ie the Army Rules 1954 r 34(1). The Army Rules 1954 r 136. A member of the court, judge advocate and prosecutor are competent witnesses for the defence, and may be sworn or affirmed at any stage of the proceedings, but an officer should not be detailed to serve as a member of, or act as prosecutor or judge advocate at, a court-martial if his evidence is likely to be required. A witness for the prosecution cannot serve as a member of the court or act as judge advocate at the trial of the case in which he is a witness; see the Army Rules 1954 r 39(2)(b) and 102.

[0361] Procuring attendance of witnesses In the case of trials by general or district court martial, the commanding officer of the accused, the convening officer or, after the assembly of the court, the presiding officer, shall take proper steps to procure the attendance of the witnesses whom the prosecutor or accused desires to call, and whose attendance can reasonably be procured, but the person requiring the attendance of a witness may be required to undertake to defray the cost (if any) of their attendance[1]. The court shall, in the case of trials by summary court martial, take proper steps to procure the attendance of the witnesses whom the accused desires to call and whose attendance can reasonably be procured, but the accused may be required to undertake to defray the cost (if any) of their attendance[2].

1 The Army Rules 1954 r 137(1). As to summoning civilian witnesses; see the Army Act 1950 s 135. For form of summons, see the Army Rules 1954 Appendix III, Part III. If a civilian witness had in his possession or under his control any books, accounts, letters, returns, papers, or other documents which are considered necessary for the trial, care must be taken in summoning him to require him to bring them with him; the witness would be justified in declining to acknowledge a mere oral request. Witnesses who are subject to AA should be ordered by the proper authority to attend without the issue of a formal summons. The appropriate naval or air force authorities should be approached for the attendance of witnesses subject to naval or air force law. For action where a civilian witness, who has been duly summoned and whose expenses have been tendered, makes default in attending; see the Army Rules 1954 r 150(3). As to privilege from arrest under civil or revenue process of a witness summoned to attend before a court-martial; see the Army Act 1950 s 30.

2 The Army Rules 1954 r 137(2). An accused person can have no technical ground of complaint if the attendance of a witness from distant parts cannot be procured, but it is the duty of the commanding officer or convening officer, or after the assembly of the court, the presiding officer, or, in the case of trial by summary court martial, the court, to take all reasonable steps to secure the attendance of any witness whom there is any ground to suppose to be material to the defence. The Army Rules 1954 r 138 makes provision for the adjournment of the court if the attendance of such witness is essential. Manual of Military Law, Volume II, 2011, the Army Rules 1954 r 137 notes.

[0362] Procedure when essential witness is absent If such proper steps as mentioned in the preceding provision have not been taken as to any witness, or if any witness whose attendance could not be reasonably procured before the assembly of the court is essential to the prosecution or defence, the court shall (i) take steps to procure the issue of a commission for the examination of such witness[1]; or (ii) if it is a general or district court martial, adjourn and report the circumstances to the convening officer[2]; or (iii) if it is a summary court martial, adjourn to enable the witness to attend, or adopt such other course as appears to the officer holding the trial best calculated to do justice[3].

1 The Army Rules 1954 r 138(a). Only the judge advocate general or deputy judge advocate general of a command can issue a commission and then only when action is initiated by a court martial. An assistant judge advocate general cannot issue a commission. See: the Army Act 1950 s 137 and 138; **[0223]** and **[0224]**.

2 The Army Rules 1954 r 138(b).

3 The Army Rules 1954 r 138(c). At a summary court martial the court may, for instance, acquit the accused forthwith, or order his release without prejudice to his subsequent trial should the witness become available. Manual of

Military Law, Volume II, 2011, the Army Rules 1954 r 138 notes.

[0363] Withdrawal of witnesses from court During the trial a witness, other than the prosecutor, shall not, except by special leave of the court, be permitted to be present in court while not under examination and if, while he is under examination, a discussion arises as to the allowance of a question, or the sufficiency of his answers, or otherwise as to his evidence, he may be directed to withdraw[1].

1 The Army Rules 1954 r 139. It is customary to have all witnesses present in court while the members of the count are being sworn or affirmed, but they should withdraw before the arraignment. This does not, of course, apply to the prosecutor if he is a witness. Permission to remain in court while not under examination may reasonably be given, e.g., to expert or professional witnesses, provided that no objection is made by or on behalf of the accused. Manual of Military Law, Volume II, 2011, the Army Rules 1954 r 139 notes.

[0364] Oath or affirmation to be administered to witnesses An oath or affirmation shall, if so required by the Army Act 1950, be administered to every witness before he gives his evidence by the judge advocate (if any), a member of the court, or some other person empowered by the court in one of the following forms or in such other form to the same purport as the court ascertains to be according to the religion or otherwise binding on the conscience of the witness[1].

Form of oath

I.........., swear by almighty God that what I shall state shall be the truth, the whole truth, and nothing but the truth.

Form of Affirmation

I..........., do solemnly, sincerely and truly declare and affirm that what I shall state shall be the truth, the whole truth, and nothing but the truth.

The following is a translation into Hindi of the above oath and affirmation.

Form of oath

Main.........., Parmeshwar ki shapath leta hun, kih main jo kuchh kahunga vah satya, purna satya, aur kewal satya hoga.

Form of affirmation

Main.........., satya nishtha, shudh hridaya tatha sachhai se ghoshana karta hun aur partigya karta hun ki main jo kuchh kahunga vah satya, purna satya aur kewal satya hoga.

1 The Army Rules 1954 r 140.

[0365] Mode of questioning witness Every question shall be put to a witness orally by the officer holding the trial, by the prosecutor, by or on behalf of the accused, or by the judge advocate and the witness will forthwith reply, unless an objection is made by the court, judge advocate, prosecutor, or accused, in which case he shall not reply until the objection is disposed of. The witness shall address his reply to the court[1]. The evidence of a witness as taken down shall be read to him if he so requests before he leaves the court, and shall, if necessary, be corrected. If he makes any explanation or correction, the prosecutor and accused or counsel or the defending officer may respectively examine him respecting the same[2]. If the witness denies the correctness of any part of the evidence when the same is read over to him, the court may instead of correcting the evidence, record the objection made to it by the witness[3]. If the evidence is not given in English and the witness does not understand that language, the evidence as recorded shall be interpreted to him in the language in which it was given, or in a language which he understands if he so requests before he leaves the court[4]. Where evidence is recorded by shorthand writer, it shall not be necessary to read the evidence of the witness to him under the provisions of the Army Rules 1954[5], if, in the opinion of the court and the judge advocate, if any (such opinion to be recorded in the proceedings), it is unnecessary so to do[6].

1 The Army Rules 1954 r 141(1). The court and judge advocate must carefully listen to the actual questions put by the prosecutor and by or on behalf of the accused, as well as to the form in which such questions are put, and they must intervene before the witness replies if in their opinion, any question is improper or 'leading'. If either the prosecutor or the accused, or the officer or counsel representing him, considers that a particular question about to be put by him may be objected to, he should submit the propriety of the question to the decision of the court, having first informed the witness that he must not make his reply until the decision of the court has been given. A witness is first examined by the person calling him, then cross-examined by the opposite party, after which he may be re-examined by the party calling him on matters raised in the cross-examination. The court should, if requested by either party, allow the cross-examination of a witness by that party to be postponed, especially if his evidence comes as a surprise; see also the Army Rules 1954 r 135 where a witness is called whose evidence is not contained in the summary of evidence. A request for postponement should not be acceded to, if, in the opinion of the court, it is made for purposes of obstruction. Manual of Military Law, Volume II, 2011, the Army Rules 1954 r 141 notes.

2 The Army Rules 1954 r 141(2). When the evidence of a witness has been read to him, he should be asked whether it is correct. Any material alteration or explanation should be inserted at the end of the record of his evidence, and not by way of interlineations or erasure. If the witness makes any explanation or correction, the prosecutor and accused or counsel or defending officer may respectively examine him respecting the same. The fact that the witness was informed of his right under this provision should be recorded in the proceedings, if he declines to have his statement read over or translated to him. Manual of Military Law, Volume II, 2011, the Army Rules 1954 r 141 notes.

3 The Army Rules 1954 r 141(3).

4 The Army Rules 1954 r 141(4). After a witness has given his evidence every effort should be made to keep him separate from other witnesses who have not given their evidence before the court. Manual of Military Law, Volume II, 2011, the Army Rules 1954 r 141 notes.

5 Ie under the Army Rules 1954 r 141 (2) or (4).

6 The Army Rules 1954 r 141(5).

[0366] Questions to witnesses by court or judge advocate The presiding officer, the judge advocate (if any), or the officer holding the trial and, with the permission of the court, any member of the court may address a question to a witness while such witness is giving his original evidence and before he withdraws[1]. Upon any such question being answered, the presiding officer, the judge advocate (if any), or the officer holding the trial, shall also put to the witness any question relative to that answer which the prosecutor or the accused or counsel or the defending officer may request him to put and which the court deem reasonable[2].

1 The Army Rules 1954 r 142(1).

2 The Army Rules 1954 r 142(2). The presiding officer, judge advocate or officer holding the trial should always, under this provision, put any question which they are requested by the prosecutor, or by or on behalf of the accused, to put and which does not seem unreasonable. Manual of Military Law, Volume II, 2011, the Army Rules 1954 r 142 notes.

[0367] Re-calling of witnesses and calling of witnesses in reply At the request of the prosecutor or of the accused, a witness may, by leave of the court, be recalled at any time before the closing address of or on behalf of the accused (or at a summary court martial at any time before the finding of the court for the purpose of having any question put to him through the presiding officer, the judge-advocate (if any), or the officer holding the trial[1]. The court may, if it considers it expedient, in the interests of justice, so to do allow a witness to be called or recalled by the prosecutor, before the closing address of or on behalf of the accused, for the purpose of rebutting any material statement made by a witness for the defence or for the purpose of giving evidence on any new matter which the prosecutor could not reasonably have foreseen[2]. Where the accused has called witnesses to character, the prosecutor before the closing address of or on behalf of the accused, may call or re-call witnesses for the purpose of proving a previous conviction or entries in the defaulters' book against the accused[3]. The court may call or re-call any witness at any time before the finding, if it considers that it is necessary for the ends of justice[4].

1 The Army Rules 1954 r 143(1). If a witness is recalled, he should not be sworn or affirmed again, but reminded of his previous oath or affirmation. The fact of his being so reminded should be recorded in the proceedings. Manual of Military Law, Volume II, 2011, the Army Rules 1954 r 143 notes.

2 The Army Rules 1954 r 143(2). This provision is not applicable in a trial by summary court martial. Manual of Military Law, Volume II, 2011, the Army Rules 1954 r 143 notes.

3 The Army Rules 1954 r 143(3). This provision is not applicable in a trial by summary court martial. Manual of Military Law, Volume II, 2011, the Army Rules 1954 r 143 notes.

4 The Army Rules 1954 r 143(4). The power under this provision of calling or recalling a witness should only be exercised in exceptional circumstances, e.g., where it appears for the first time from the evidence given at the trial that a person, who has not been called either by the prosecutor or on behalf of the defence, was present at, and probably witnessed the occurrence which forms the subject of the charge which is being tried. Witnesses should not be called or recalled under this provision in order to supplement any negligent conduct on the part of the prosecution. If witnesses are called or recalled under this provision, the prosecutor and the accused should be invited to put or suggest any relevant questions which in their opinion should be put by the court. If new evidence is given after the closing address by or on behalf of the accused, the court should permit the accused or his representative to make a further address upon the new matter which has been elicited, if any. Manual of Military Law, Volume II, 2011, the Army Rules 1954 r 143 notes.

(B) *Addresses*

[0368] Addresses All addresses by the prosecutor and the accused and the summing up of the judge advocate may either be given orally or in writing, and if in writing shall be read in open court[1].

1 The Army Rules 1954 r 144. The summing up of the judge advocate should invariably in writing. Manual of Military Law, Volume II, 2011, the Army Rules 1954 r 142 notes.

(C) *Insanity*

[0369] Finding of insanity Where the court finds either that the accused by reason of unsoundness of mind, is incapable of making his defence; or that he committed the act alleged but was by reason of unsoundness of mind, incapable of knowing the nature of the act or that it was wrong or contrary to the law, the court shall give brief reasons in support thereof. The judge advocate, if any, or the presiding officer or in the case of summary court martial, the officer holding the trial shall record or cause to be recorded such brief reasons in the proceedings[1]. The presiding officer or in the case of summary court martial, the officer holding the trial shall date and sign the above record, and the proceedings upon being signed by the judge advocate, if any, shall at once be transmitted to the confirming officer or the authority empowered to deal with its finding under the Army Act 1950[2], as the case may be[3].

1 The Army Rules 1954 r 145(1).

2 Ie under the Army Act 1950 s 162.

3 The Army Rules 1954 r 145(2). Also see the Army Act 1950 s 145 and 146; **[0231]** and **[0232]**.

(D) *Preservation of proceedings*

[0370] Preservation of proceedings The proceedings of a court martial (other than a summary court martial) shall, after promulgation, be forwarded, as circumstances require, to the office of the judge-advocate general, and there preserved for not less, in the case of a general court martial, than seven years, and, in the case of any other court martial, than three years[1]. The proceedings of a summary court martial shall be preserved for not less than three years, with the records of the corps or department to which the accused belonged[2].

1 The Army Rules 1954 r 146(1).

2 The Army Rules 1954 r 146(2)4

[0371] Right of person tried to copies of proceedings Every person tried by a court martial (other than summary court martial) shall, after the proceedings have been signed by the presiding officer and in the case of summary court martial the officer holding the trial, and before they are destroyed, on request made by such a person in writing to the court or the officer holding the trial of the person having the custody of his proceedings, be entitled for the supply of the copy of such proceedings, within the reasonable time and free of cost, including the proceedings upon revision if any[1].

1 The Army Rules 1954 r 147. An accused in entitled to a copy of the proceedings of his trial free of charge. In case of a joint trial by summary court martial the officer holding the trial or in case of a joint trial by general court martial, district court martial, or summary general the convening officer, should ensure that sufficient copies of the proceedings are prepared to facilitate delivery of the same to the accused on demand. The application for a copy of the proceedings should be made personally by the accused. Manual of Military Law, Volume II, 2011, the Army Rules 1954 r 147 notes.

[0372] Copy of proceedings not to be given in certain cases Notwithstanding anything contained in the provisions of the Army Rules 1954[1], if the Central Government certifies that it is against the interests of the security of the State or friendly relations with foreign States to supply a copy of the proceedings or any part thereof under the said provisions, he shall not be furnished with such copy[2]. However, if the Central Government is satisfied that the person demanding the copy is desirous of submitting a petition in accordance with the Army Act 1950 or instituting any action in a court of law in relation to the finding or sentence, it shall permit inspection of the proceedings to such person or his legal adviser, if any, on the following conditions, namely (a) the inspection shall be made at such times and such places as the Central Government or any authority authorised by it may direct[3]; and (b) The person allowed to inspect the proceedings shall, before such inspection, furnish: (i) an undertaking, in writing, that he shall not make copies of the proceedings or any part thereof and that the information or documents contained in such proceedings shall not be used by him, for any purpose whatsoever other than for the purpose of submitting a petition in accordance with the Army Act 1950 or instituting an action in a court of law in relation to the said finding or sentence[4]; and (ii) a certificate that he is aware that he may render himself liable to prosecution under the provisions of the Indian Official Secrets Act 1923[5], if he commits any act specified in the said provisions in relation to the documents or information contained in the said proceedings[6]. The above stated provision shall be deemed always to have been inserted in the Army Rules 1954[7].

1 Ie in the Army Rules 1954 r 147; see **[0371]**.

2 The Army Rules 1954 r 147A.

3 The Army Rules 1954 r 147A proviso (a).

4 The Army Rules 1954 r 147A proviso (b) (i).

5 Ie the Indian Official Secrets Act 1923 s 3 and 5.

6 The Army Rules 1954 r 147A proviso (b) (ii). The accused or his legal adviser will be liable to be prosecuted for contravening the Official Secrets Act 1923 s 3 or 5, if they communicate any information obtained during the inspection of the proceedings to unauthorised persons or make unauthorised use of such information.

7 The Army Rules 1954 r 147A note. Ministry of Defence Gazette Notification No, E-7 dated 17 June 1960 published in Extra-ordinary Gazette Part I, s 3 dated 20 June 1960, refers.

[0373] Loss of proceedings If, before confirmation, the original proceedings of a court martial which require confirmation or any part thereof, are lost, a copy thereof, if any, certified by the presiding officer of or the judge advocate at the court martial may be accepted in lieu of the original[1]. If there is no such copy, and sufficient evidence of the charge, finding, sentence, and transactions of the court can be procured, that evidence may, with the assent of the accused, be accepted in lieu of the original proceedings, or part thereof, which have been lost[2]. In the cases mentioned above, the finding and sentence may be confirmed, and shall be as valid as if the original proceedings, or part thereof, had not been lost[3]. If the accused refuses the assent the provisions referred in the Army Rules 1954[4], he may be tried again, and the finding and sentence of the previous court of which the proceedings have been lost shall be void[5]. If, after confirmation or in any case where confirmation is not required, the original proceedings of a court martial or any part thereof are lost, and there is sufficient evidence of the charge, findings, sentence, and transactions of the court and of the confirmation (if required) of the finding and sentence, that evidence shall be a valid and sufficient record of the trial for all purposes[6].

1 The Army Rules 1954 r 148(1).

2 The Army Rules 1954 r 148(2). As soon as it is known that the proceedings have been lost; steps should be taken to obtain and preserve the best evidence available. The evidence may be obtained by the presiding officer or some member of the court writing out from memory the substance of the charge, finding, sentence and transactions of the court, which should be authenticated by the signatures of the members. A copy of the charge, however, should always be procured if possible. Manual of Military Law, Volume II, 2011, the Army Rules 1954 r 148 notes.

3 The Army Rules 1954 r 148(3).

4 Ie under the Army Rules 1954 r 148(2).

5 The Army Rules 1954 r 148(4).

6 The Army Rules 1954 r 148(5).

(E) *Irregular procedure when no injustice is done*

[0374] Validity of irregular procedure in certain cases Whenever, it appears that a court martial had jurisdiction to try any person and make a finding and that there is legal evidence or a plea of guilty to justify such finding, such finding and any sentence which the court martial had jurisdiction to pass thereon may be confirmed, and shall, if so confirmed and in the case of a summary court martial where confirmation is not necessary, be valid, notwithstanding any deviation from the Army Rules 1954 or notwithstanding that the charge sheet has not been signed by the commanding officer or the convening officer, provided that the charges have, in fact, before trial been approved by the commanding officer and the convening officer or notwithstanding any defect or objection, technical or other, unless it appears that any injustice has been done to the offender, and where any finding and sentence are otherwise valid they shall not be invalid by reason only of a failure to administer an oath or affirmation to the interpreter or shorthand writer. However, nothing in this provision shall relieve an officer from any responsibility for any willful or negligent disregard of any of the provisions contained in the Army Rules 1954[1].

This provision is intended to prevent a miscarriage of justice in consequence of defects usually of a technical nature, in matters of procedure which do not affect the real merits of the case; but before acting upon this provision the confirming officer must be satisfied that the accused has not suffered any injustice through any deviation from the Army Rules 1954 or through any defect or objection. Whether or not a deviation, etc., is of a substantial nature will often depend upon the circumstances. The court should not allow any technicality to interfere with the accused in the making of his defence. The confirming officer should always direct the attention of all officers concerned to deviations and defects which have been observed and for which they are responsible. Whenever after confirmation, the charges or findings thereon are declared to be invalid, the trial must be treated as null, the conviction set aside, the person convicted relieved of all consequences of his trial and the record of conviction erased[2].

1 The Army Rules 1954 r 149.

2 Manual of Military Law, Volume II, 2011, the Army Rules 1954 r 149 notes.

(F) *Offences of witnesses and others*

[0375] Offences of witnesses and others When any court martial is of opinion that there is ground for inquiring into any offence specified in the Army Act 1950[1] and committed before it or brought under its notice in the course of its proceedings, or into any act done before it or brought under its notice in the course of its proceedings, which would, if done by a person subject to the Army Act 1950, have constituted such an offence, such court martial may proceed as follows: If the person who appears to have committed the offence is subject to the Army Act 1950, the court may bring his conduct to the notice of the proper military authority, and may also order him to be placed in military custody with a view to his punishment by an officer exercising authority under the provisions of the Army Act 1950[2] or to his trial by a court martial[3]. If the person who appears to have done the act is amenable to naval or air force law, the court may bring his conduct to the notice of the proper naval or air force authority, as the case may be[4]. If the person who appears to have done the act is not subject to military, naval or air force law, then in the case of acts which would, if done by a person subject to the Army Act 1950, have constituted an offence under the certain provisions of the Army Act 1950[5], the officer who summoned the witness to appear or the presiding officer or officer holding the court, may forward a written complaint to the nearest Magistrate of the first class having jurisdiction, and in the case of acts which would, if done as aforesaid, have constituted an offence under certain provisions of the Army Act 1950[6] the court, after making any preliminary inquiry that may be necessary, may send the case to the nearest Magistrate of the first class having jurisdiction for inquiry or trial in accordance with the Code of Criminal Procedure 1973[7].

A trial by court martial is deemed to be a judicial proceeding within the meaning of the Indian Penal Code 1860[8]. A court martial is deemed to be a court within the meaning of the Criminal Procedure Code 1973[9]. When a person subject to the Army Act 1950 commits an offence under the Army Act 1950[10] or when a corresponding offence is committed by a person subject to naval or air force law or by a civilian, court martial should act wisely in accepting an apology sufficient to vindicate their dignity instead of resorting to the more severe measures here indicated. Courts martial should exercise the greatest discretion in instituting proceedings or in taking measures which may result in the institution of proceedings, against a person subject to the Army Act 1950 for the offence specified in the Army Act 1950[11], or against a person subject to naval or air force law, or a civilian for corresponding offence. In the case of a person subject to the Army Act 1950, the court martial may, in its discretion, either merely report his conduct to the proper military authority, or may in addition order him into military custody pending disposal of his case. If a person is so ordered into custody this fact should be mentioned in the report; and it then becomes the duty of the officer receiving the report to see that the case is promptly investigated in accordance with the Army Act 1950[12]. The report should be in sufficient detail to place the officer in full possession of the facts and enable him to exercise his discretion whether to order trial by court martial if he is competent to do so, or to direct summary disposal[13].

1 Ie under the Army Act 1950 ss 59 and 60.

2 Ie under the Army Act 1950 ss 80, 83, 84 or 85.

3 The Army Rules 1954 r 150(1).

4 The Army Rules 1954 r 150(2).

5 Ie under the Army Act 1950 ss 59 (a), (b), (c) or (d).

6 Ie under the Army Act 1950 s 59 (e) or s 60.

7 Ie under the Code of Criminal Procedure 1973 s 340. The Army Rules 1954 r 150(3). A court's decision to institute proceedings under this provision must be a judicial one, i.e., either based on what the court has itself heard or seen and considered, or on evidence taken before it and considered. Similarly an officer's decision to institute proceedings must be a reasonable one, based on sufficient grounds. The report to the magistrate may be in letter form, and should be sufficiently detailed to place him in full possession of all the materials on which the decision to prosecute was based. It should set forth the name and identity of the person accused and of the witnesses who can substantiate the accusation. A narrative of the events complained of, should be included in the report and a record of the evidence taken in preliminary inquiry (if any) attached. Manual of Military Law, Volume II, 2011, the Army Rules 1954 r 150 notes.

8 The Indian Penal Code 1860 ss 193 and 228.

9 The Criminal Procedure Code 1973 ss 345 and 346.

10 Ie under the Army Act 1950 s 59.

11 Ie specified in the Army Act 1950 s 60.

12 Ie the Army Act 1950 s 102(1).

13 Manual of Military Law, Volume II, 2011, the Army Rules 1954 r 150 notes.

E. PUNISHMENTS AND PENAL DEDUCTIONS

CONTENTS

PARA

(A) Punishments

(B) Penal Deductions

(A) *Punishments*

[0376] Punishments awardable by court martial Punishments may be inflicted in respect of offences committed by persons subject to the Army Act 1950 and convicted by courts martial, according to the scale following: (1) death[1]; (2) imprisonment for life[2, 3]; (3) imprisonment, either rigorous or simple, for any period not exceeding 14 years[4]; (4) cashiering, in case of officers[5]; (5) dismissal from the service[6]; (6) reduction to the ranks or to a lower rank or grade or place in the list of their rank, in the case of warrant officers and reduction to the ranks or to a lower rank or grade, in the case of non-commissioned officers[7], provided that a warrant officer reduced to the ranks shall not be required to serve in the ranks as a sepoy[8]; (7) forfeiture of seniority of rank in the case of officers, junior commissioned officers, warrant officers and non-commissioned officers and forfeiture of all or any part of their service for the purpose of promotion, in the case of any of them whose promotion depends upon length of service[9]; (8) forfeiture of service for the purpose of increased pay, pension or any other prescribed purpose[10]; (9) severe reprimand or reprimand, in the case of officers, junior commissioned officers, warrant officers and non-commissioned officers[11]; (10) forfeiture of pay and allowances for a period not exceeding three months for an offence committed on active service[12]; (11) forfeiture in the case of a person sentenced to cashiering or dismissal from the service of all arrears of pay and allowances and other public money due to him at the time of such cashiering or dismissal[13]; (12) stoppage of pay and allowances until any proved loss or damage occasioned by the offence of which he is convicted is made good[14].

Some of the punishments provided by the above provision as awardable by court martial are not necessarily punishments, in the sense of the term as ordinarily known to criminal jurisprudence, but are penalties as known to service jurisprudence. Such penalties have been treated as punishments awardable by court martial under the above-stated provision of the Army Act 1950[15]. In cases of charges under the Army Act 1950 s 69, a court martial can also award any punishment, assigned for the offence under any law in force in India. For instance, a fine is not specified as a punishment under the Army Act 1950[16] but a court martial exercising jurisdiction under s 69 can award a fine and such fine is recoverable under the provisions of the Army Act 1950[17], if the civil offence in question is punishable with a fine under the law in force in India. An officer will not introduce or adopt any system of punishment that is in any respect at variance with the Army Act 1950, the Army Rules 1954 or the Defence Services Regulations, Regulations for the Army 1987, Volume I[18].

1 Army Act 1950 s 71(a). A sentence of death can only be passed by a general court martial with the concurrence of at least two-thirds of the members or by a summary general court martial with the concurrence of all the members; see the army Act 1950 ss 132(2) and (3). A certificate to the effect that the death sentence was passed with the concurrence of ....members/unanimously, as the case may be, should be endorsed in the proceedings. In awarding a sentence of death the court must add a direction that the accused shall suffer death by being hanged by the neck until he be dead; or by being shot to death; see the Army Act 1950 s 166. A person who is sentenced by a court martial to death continues to be subject to the Army Act 1950 till the sentence is executed: see the Army Act 1950 s 123 (4). An officer sentenced to death or imprisonment must first be sentenced to be cashiered: see the Army Act 1950 s 74.

2 The term 'transportation for life' has been replaced by 'imprisonment for life'. See: The Indian Penal Code 1860 s 53A: Any reference to 'transportation for life' in any other law for the time being in force or in any instrument or order having effect by virtue of any such law or any enactment repealed shall be construed as a reference to 'imprisonment for life'. Where the accused was awarded imprisonment for life under the Army Act 1950 s 69 and the Indian Penal Code 1869 s 302, had spent 11 years and 1 month in actual custody, 1 year 7 months and 29 days in pre-trail custody and has earned 4 years' remission in the jail; it was held that cannot be released from imprisonment on grounds that he has undergone imprisonment exceeding 14 years. He has to undergo actual imprisonment for 14 years excluding remission earned in jail. *Union of India v Sadha Singh* AIR 1999 SC 3833.

3 Army Act 1950 s 71(b). Imprisonment for life is a punishment which a general court martial or summary general court martial can award only in cases of charges under the Army Act 1950 s 69 where such a punishment is assigned for that offence under the law in force in India or where the offence is punishable with death as under the Army Act 1950 ss 34, 37 or 38(1) and the court considers that sentence to be too severe in the circumstances of the case. Imprisonment for life cannot be awarded for any of the remaining offences as the maximum punishment laid down for such offences is imprisonment for fourteen years or cashiering/dismissal. For calculating fractions of terms of punishment imprisonment for life is to be reckoned as equivalent to imprisonment for 20 years (see

the Indian Penal Code 1860 s 57), though for other purposes it is treated as imprisonment for the whole of the remaining period of the convicted man's natural life. In practice, the sentence of imprisonment for life is treated as a sentence for a certain number of years only. In case of officers, a sentence of cashiering must precede sentence of imprisonment for life. Manual of Military Law, Volume II, 2011, the Army Act 1950 s 71 notes.

4 Army Act 1950 s 71(c). Imprisonment is either (i) rigorous, that is, with hard labour; or (ii) simple. The terms 'rigorous' and 'simple' should invariably be used in sentences passed under the Army Act 1950. If a court inadvertently passes a sentence of 'imprisonment' without specifying whether it is rigorous or simple, the sentence is treated as one of 'simple imprisonment'. An officer sentenced to imprisonment must first be sentenced to be cashiered. As to execution of sentences of imprisonment see the Army Act 1950 ss 169-171. Sentences of imprisonment, unless for one or more years exactly, should, if for one month or upwards, be recorded in months. Sentences consisting partly of months and partly of days should be recorded in months and days. Manual of Military Law, Volume II, 2011, the Army Act 1950 s 71 notes.

5 Army Act 1950 s 71(d). Cashiering is the more ignominious form of dismissal; and normally an officer who has been cashiered cannot hold an appointment under the Government. In case of an officer, a sentence of cashiering must precede the sentence of death, imprisonment for life or imprisonment. For the date on which sentences of cashiering and dismissal take effect, see the Army Rules 1954 r 168. The decision whether a cashiered or dismissed officer shall receive a pension or gratuity, is in the discretion of the Central Government. The Defence Services Regulations, Regulations for the Army, Volume I, paragraph 703 (a) makes provision for the forfeiture of gallantry decorations, campaign and commemorative medals clasps in the event of a person subject to the Army Act 1950 being cashiered. Manual of Military Law, Volume II, 2011, the Army Act 1950 s 71 notes. The accused was found guilty by the general court martial and sentenced to rigorous imprisonment for 14 years and dismissal from service. It was held by the Delhi High Court that a sentence of dismissal and imprisonment awarded to an officer without a sentence of cashiering is invalid. See: *M R Saini v Union of India* 1985 Cr LJ 1263.

6 Army Act 1950 s 71(e). Dismissal under this provision is a punishment awardable by a court martial where as dismissal under the Army Act 1950 s 19 is an administrative measure. The Defence Services Regulations, Regulations for the Army, Volume I, paragraph 703 (a) makes provision for the forfeiture of gallantry decorations, campaign and commemorative medals clasps in the event of a person subject to the Army Act 1950 being dismissed. Manual of Military Law, Volume II, 2011, the Army Act 1950 s 71 notes.

7 Army Act 1950 s 71(f). Service in the lower rank, grade or class will reckon from the date of signing the original sentence, whether the original sentence in question was a revised sentence or mitigated by the confirming officer from a more severe sentence. Reduction of a warrant officer or non-commissioned officer under this clause to the ranks or to a lower rank or grade is a punishment awardable by a court-martial whereas a similar reduction under the Army Act s 20(4) is an administrative measure resorted to on grounds of inefficiency or unsuitability. See Defence Services Regulations, Regulations for the Army, Volume I, paragraphs 172 and 173. The term 'grade' in this provision means 'rank'. Manual of Military Law, Volume II, 2011, the Army Act 1950 s 71 notes.

8 Army Act 1950 s 71(f) proviso.

9 Army Act 1950 s 71(g). A sentence of forfeiture of seniority may be combined with a sentence of forfeiture of service for the purpose of promotion. The effect of a sentence of forfeiture of a seniority of rank is that the seniority of the person in his rank alone is affected, not the period of the service in the rank. The sentence of forfeiture of service for the purpose of promotion can be awarded in respect of all or any part of his service. The forfeiture does not affect the seniority of the officer etc., in the rank he holds at the time the sentence is passed. The effect of this sentence would be that all future promotions depending upon length of service will be retarded by the period forfeited under this clause. This would not preclude a court martial from awarding the punishment of forfeiture of seniority of rank in the form of sentencing an officer to take precedence in the rank held by him in his corps as if his name had appeared a specified number of places lower in the list of his corps, in cases where

dates of appointment of a large number of officers are identical and the forfeiture of even one day's service for the purposes of promotion might in its effect constitute too severe a punishment for the offence which nevertheless would not be adequately met by a severe reprimand. Manual of Military Law, Volume II, 2011, the Army Act 1950 s 71 notes.

10 Army Act 1950 s 71(h).

11 Army Act 1950 s 71(i). Although acting rank is not cognisable in the sentence of a court martial, a sepoy holding any such rank, being a non-commissioned officer, may nevertheless be sentenced by a court martial to be severely reprimanded or reprimanded. Severe reprimand constitutes a 'red ink' entry; see Defence Services Regulations, Regulations for the Army, Volume I, paragraph 387(b).

12 Army Act 1950 s 71(j). This punishment can only be awarded by a court martial where anoffence is committed on active service. This sentence may be awarded in addition to other punishments. Care must be taken in awarding a sentence of forfeiture of pay and allowances in days to ensure that the total period in days does not exceed three calendar months e.g., when February intervenes. Manual of Military Law, Volume II, 2011, the Army Act 1950 s 71 notes. As to the meaning of 'active service' see **[0008]**.

13 Army Act 1950 s 71(k). As cashiering or dismissal takes effect from the date specified in the Army Rules 1954 r 168, this punishment will hardly be effective unless action has already been taken under the Army Act 1950 s 93 for withholding the pay and allowances of the accused in which case the pay and allowances so withheld will automatically be forfeited under the Army Act 1950 s 91(b), if the accused was in custody. Forfeiture under this provision will then cover only arrears of pay and allowances prior to the date the accused was placed in custody as well as any public money due to him. Manual of Military Law, Volume II, 2011, the Army Act 1950 s 71 notes.

14 Army Act 1950 s 71(l). An award to compensate for loss or damage is termed 'stoppages'. Such an award can only be made if the particulars of the charge allege that the act or omission of the accused occasioned a loss or damage and, is proved on record; see the Army Rules 1954 r 30(6). Irrespective of the currency in which the wording of a charge may assess the loss or damage, any stoppage that is imposed by a court martial must be awarded in the Indian currency. The only exception to this provision is where the accused's rate of pay is expressed in any regulations or instructions in any other currency. If a court wishes to award compensation to the injured party as well as to cause the offender to lose all arrears of pay and allowances, etc, it should sentence him to stoppages under this provision and to forfeiture of all arrears of pay and allowances, etc. under s 71 (k). The stoppages will first be satisfied from any pay and allowances or other public money due to him, and the remainder (if any) will be forfeited to the State under the sentence. A court martial acting under this provision will simply sentence the offender to stoppages to a certain extent. The recovery which is automatic will take place under the provisions of the Army Act 1950 ss 90 or 91, whichever is applicable. The officer enforcing the sentence will be guided by the provisions of the Army Act 1950 ss 94 and 95 i.e., he will (unless the offender is sentenced to dismissal or is an officer) stop half his pay and allowances in any one month and the whole of any gratuity or other public money (not pay and allowances) due to him, until the compensation awarded in the sentence is complete. No portion of the pay and allowances of a person sentenced to dismissal is protected and the whole of such a person's pay and allowances can, if necessary be withheld. Manual of Military Law, Volume II, 2011, the Army Act 1950 s 71 notes.

15 Ie under the Army Act 1950 s 71: see *Union of India v Harjeet Singh Sandhu* AIR 2001 SC 1772 : (2001) 5 SCC 593 : (2001) SCC (L&S) 891. The power conferred by the Army Act 1950 s 19 on the Central Government and that conferred on the court martial by the Army Act 1950 s 71 are clearly distinguishable from each other.

16 Ie under the Army Act 1950 s 71.

17 Ie under the Army Act 1950 ss 90(f), 91(h) or 174.

18 The Defence Services Regulations, Regulations for the Army 1987, Volume I, paragraph 353.

[0377] Alternative punishments awardable by courts martial A court martial may, on convicting a person subject to the Army Act 1950 of any of the service offences[1], award either the particular punishment prescribed by the section or in lieu thereof, any one of the punishments lower in the scale set out in the Army Act 1950[2], regard being had to the nature and degree of the offence[3]. This provision does not set out that in all cases, a lesser punishment must be awarded. In other words, merely because a lower punishment is not granted, it would not mean that the punishment was violative of the provision of the Army Act 1950[4].

1 Ie under the Army Act 1950 ss 34–68.

2 Army Act 1950 s 71. See **[0376]**.

3 Army Act 1950 s 72. *Sardar Singh v Union of India* AIR 1992 SC 417, (1991) 3 SCC 213 : (1991) SCC (Cr) 503.

4 Ie violative of the Army Act 1950 s 72: see *Union of India v R K Sharma* AIR 2001 SC 3053, (2001) 9 SCC 592 (dismissal from service provided under the Army Act 1950 s 71(e) is a lesser punishment than imprisonment for either seven or 14 years as contemplated under the Army Act 1950 ss 57 and 63).

[0378] Combination of punishments A sentence awarded by a court martial may have combination of punishments. A court martial may award in addition to, or without any one other punishment, the punishment specified in the Army Act 1950[1] and any one or more of the punishments specified[2] thereunder[3].

1 Ie in the Army Act 1950 s 71(d) and (e). See **[0376]**.

2 Ie in the Army Act 1950 s 71(f)–(l). See **[0376]**.

3 The Army Act 1950 s 73. The following combined sentences are legal: (i) Cashiering, imprisonment, stoppages and forfeiture of pay and allowances in the case of an officer. (ii) Imprisonment, dismissal, reduction (warrant officer and non-commissioned officer), stoppages and forfeiture. (iii) dismissal, reduction (non-commissioned officers), stoppages and forfeiture; (iv) forfeiture of seniority of rank, forfeiture of service for promotion (when applicable), severe reprimand, forfeitures and stoppages, in the case of an officer, junior commissioned officers, warrant officers or non-commissioned officers. Manual of Military Law, Volume II, 2011, the Army Act 1950 s 73 notes.

[0379] Cashiering of officers An officer shall be sentenced to be cashiered[1] before he is awarded any of the punishments specified in the provisions[2] of the Army Act 1950[3].

1 Cashiering can be awarded only to the officers. Cashiering is not defined in statutes, but is a form of dismissal where a person is stripped of his ranks and medals because of a serious misdemeanor. Manual of Military Law, Volume II, 2011, the Army Act 1950 s 74 notes.

2 Ie under the Army Act 1950 s 71(a)–(c). While sentencing an officer to death, imprisonment for life or imprisonment, the court martial must take care to ensure that the sentence of cashiering precedes the sentence of death, imprisonment for life or imprisonment. A sentence of dismissal and imprisonment awarded to an officer without a sentence of cashiering is invalid; *M R Saini v Union of India* 1985 Cr LJ 1263.

3 The Army Act 1950 s 74.

[0380] Result of certain punishments in case of warrant officers or non-commissioned officers A warrant officer or a non-commissioned officer sentenced by a court martial to imprisonment for life, imprisonment, or dismissal from the service, shall be deemed to be reduced to the ranks[1].

1 Army Act 1950 s 77. Although under this provision a warrant officer or non-commissioned officer holding

substantive rank, when sentenced to imprisonment for life, imprisonment, or dismissal is, ipso facto, reduced to the ranks it is desirable to specify the reduction in the sentence. A court martial cannot sentence a person holding an acting rank to reduction to the ranks; but an acting non-commissioned officer, being a non-commissioned officer in terms of the Army Act 1950 s 3 (xv) loses his acting rank under this provision upon being sentenced to any of the punishments mentioned therein. Manual of Military Law, Volume II, 2011, the Army Act 1950 s 74 notes.

[0381] Sentence: Proportional to offence committed The court martial shall award a single sentence in respect of all the offences of which the accused is found guilty, and such sentence shall be deemed to be awarded in respect of the offence in each charge in respect of which if can be legally given and not to be awarded in respect of any offence in a charge in respect of which it cannot be legally given[1]. The sentence must be a sentence authorised by the Army Act 1950[2]. However, a court martial may under the Army Act 1950[3] make a separate order for the disposal of property. Such an order should be recorded below the signature of the presiding officer to the sentence and should be separately dated and signed by the presiding officer. The question of the choice and quantum of punishment is within the jurisdiction and discretion of the court martial. However, the sentence has to suit the offence and the offender. It must not be vindictive or unduly harsh. It must not be so disproportionate to the offence as to shock the conscience and amount if itself to conclusive evidence of bias. The doctrine of proportionality, as part of the concept of judicial review, would ensure that even on an aspect which is, otherwise, within the exclusive province of the court martial, if the decision of the court even as to sentence is an outrageous defiance of logic, then the sentence would not be immune from correction. Irrationality and perversity are recognised grounds of judicial review[4]. Sentences, unless for one or more years exactly, should if for one month or upwards, be recorded in months. Sentences consisting of partly of months and partly of days should be recorded in months and days. A month means a calendar month[5].

1 The Army Rules 1954 r 65.

2 See the Army Act ss 71 to 76.

3 Ie under the Army Act 1950 s 151(1)

4 *Ranjit Thakur v Union of India* AIR 1987 SC 2386, (1987) 4 SCC 611, (1988) SCC (L&S) 1; *Sardar Singh v Union of India* AIR 1992 SC 417, (1991) 3 SCC 213, (1991) SCC (Cr) 503.

5 Defence Services Regulations, Regulations for the Army 1987, Volume I, paragraph 468 (e).

[0382] Guiding Principles for awarding sentence A court martial is to observe the following principles in awarding sentence:

(1) When passing sentence, a court martial will have regard not only to the nature and degree of the offence and the previous character of the accused, as proved in evidence, but also to the nature and amount of any such consequences as, by virtue of any statute, rule, order or regulation, are involved in their finding, or entailed by their sentence, in addition to the punishment awarded by the court. Where attention has been called in local orders to the unusual prevalence of the offence of which the accused has been found guilty, the court will also pay regard to the fact that such warning has been issued[1].

(2) All convictions, whether by courts-martial or by civil courts, for offences committed by an officer, junior commissioned officer, warrant officer, or other ranks during his military service, including any time passed in a state of desertion, will be given in evidence against him. The court will consider if any circumstances have been disclosed by the evidence in extenuation or aggravation of the offence. Sentences must vary according to the requirements of discipline, but in ordinary circumstances, and for

the first offence, a sentence should be light. Care must be taken to discriminate between offences due to youth, temper, sudden temptation, grave and sudden provocation or unaccustomed surroundings, and those due to premeditated misconduct[2].

(3) Persons who are convicted by court martial of certain offence under the Army Act 1950[3] should ordinarily be sentenced to imprisonment and should undergo their sentence in a civil prison[4].

(4) When an offender is convicted on two or more charges, the sentence should be that which is considered adequate for the gravest of the offences, with some addition for each of the other charges[5].

(5) A court martial in framing sentences will observe the following rules: (a) Terms of imprisonment unless for one or more years exactly, should if for one month or upwards be recorded in months[6]; and (b) Sentences consisting partly of months and partly of days should be recorded in months and days[7].

(6) When a soldier has been convicted by court martial of theft, misappropriation or receiving with guilty knowledge, the Army Act 1950[8] provides for the restitution of the stolen property in certain cases. If the soldier has been sentenced to be placed under stoppages in respect of the property stolen or unlawfully obtained, and any sum of money that may have been found on him has been appropriated to the above use, he should be placed under stoppages for the balance only of the stoppage awarded by the court[9].

These provisions should be treated as a guide only. The court must always award such punishment as the members consider being just and proper and must not presume that the convening authority, in sending the case for trial, took a more serious view of the facts[10].

1 Defence Services Regulations, Regulations for the Army 1987, Volume I, paragraph 468(a).

2 Defence Services Regulations, Regulations for the Army 1987, Volume I, paragraph 468(b).

3 Ie under the Army Act 1950 s 52 or 69.

4 Defence Services Regulations, Regulations for the Army 1987, Volume I, paragraph 468(c).

5 Defence Services Regulations, Regulations for the Army 1987, Volume I, paragraph 468(d).

6 Defence Services Regulations, Regulations for the Army 1987, Volume I, paragraph 468(e)(1).

7 Defence Services Regulations, Regulations for the Army 1987, Volume I, paragraph 468(e)(ii).

8 Ie the Army Act 1950 s 151; see **[0237]**.

9 Defence Services Regulations, Regulations for the Army 1987, Volume I, paragraph 468(f).

10 Manual of Military Law, Volume I, 2011, Chapter IV para 84.

[0383] Retention in ranks of persons convicted on active service When, on active service, any enrolled person[1] has been sentenced by a court martial to dismissal, or to life imprisonment or imprisonment whether combined with dismissal or not, the prescribed officer[2] may direct that such person may be retained to serve in the ranks, and such service shall be reckoned as part of his term of his imprisonment for life or imprisonment, if any[3].

1 The words 'any enrolled person' means a person subject to the Army Act 1950 s 2(1). Junior commissioned officers and warrant officers, though originally enrolled are not liable to be retained to serve in the ranks under the Army Act 1950 s 78.

2 As to the meaning of 'prescribed officer' the Army Rules 1954 r 191 provides: The prescribed officer for the

purposes of the Army Act s 78 shall be the officer commanding the forces in the field, or, in the case of a sentence which he confirms or could have confirmed or which did not require confirmation, the officer commanding the army corps, division, brigade or any detached portion of regular army within which the trial was held.

3 Army Act 1950 s 78. A person can only be retained to serve in the ranks under this section while he is on active service, and the order must be made before the sentence of merely suspended so long as the person is retained to serve in the ranks. If it is subsequently desired to retain the person in the service, the dismissal must be remitted. Manual of Military Law, Volume II, 2011, the Army Act 1950 s 78 notes.

(B) *Penal Deductions*

[0384] Deduction from pay and allowances of officers The following penal deductions may be made from the pay and allowances[1] of an officer[2]:

(1) all pay and allowances due to an officer for every day he absents himself without leave, unless a satisfactory explanation has been given to his commanding officer and has been approved by the Central Government[3];

(2) all pay and allowances for every day while he is in custody[4] or under suspension from duty[5] on a charge for an offence for which he is afterwards convicted by a Criminal Court or a court-martial or by an officer exercising authority under the Army Act 1950[6];

(3) any sum required to make good the pay of any person subject to the Army Act 1950 which he has unlawfully retained or unlawfully refused to pay[7];

(4) any sum required to make good such compensation for any expenses, loss[8], damage or destruction occasioned by[9] the commission of an offence as may be determined by the court-martial by whom he is convicted of such offence, or by an officer exercising authority under the Army Act 1950[10];

(5) all pay and allowances ordered by a court martial to be forfeited or stopped[11];

(6) any sum required to pay a fine awarded by a criminal court or a court martial exercising jurisdiction under the Army Act s 69[12];

(7) any sum required to make good any loss, damage, or destruction of public or regimental property[13] which, after due investigation, appears to the Central Government to have been occasioned by the wrongful act or negligence on the part of the officer[14];

(8) all pay and allowances forfeited by order of the Central Government if the officer is found by a court of inquiry constituted by the chief of the army staff in this behalf, to have deserted to the enemy, or while in enemy hands, to have served with, or under the orders of, the enemy, or in any manner to have aided the enemy, or to have allowed himself to be taken prisoner by the enemy through want of due precaution or through disobedience of orders or wilful neglect of duty, or having been taken prisoner by the enemy, to have failed to rejoin his service when it was possible to do so[15];

(9) any sum required by order of the Central Government or any prescribed officer, to be paid for the maintenance of his wife or his legitimate or illegitimate child or towards the cost of any relief given by the, said Government to the said wife or child[16].

1 The Army Act 1950 s 25 enjoins that the pay of any person subject to the Army Act 1950 due to him as such under

any regulation for the time being in force shall be paid without any deduction other than the deductions authorised by or under the Army Act 1950 or any other Act. The term 'pay' means the rate of pay with increases, if any, for length of service, to which a person subject to the Army Act 1950 is entitled by reason of his rank, appointment, trade group or trade classification, and includes additional remuneration such as qualification pay, proficiency pay and various forms of additional pay which is admissible only on fulfillment of certain conditions. The regulations may provide for the withdrawal of such additional remuneration if the conditions governing them are not fulfilled. All other emoluments are 'allowances'. It is illegal to make deductions which are not authorised and the unlawful withholding of pay is an offence under the Army Act 1950 s 61. The Army Act 1950 s 90 enunciate the penal deductions that may be made from the pay and allowances of an officer and by implication exclude other penal deductions but they do not prohibit deductions not penal e.g., in respect of rations, or stoppages to meet a public claim or regimental debt or claim etc., under the Army Rules 1954 r 205. As to remission of penal deductions, see the Army Act 1950 s 97 and the Army Rules 1954 r 195.

2 As to the meaning of the term 'officer' see **[0029]**.

3 Army Act 1950 s 90 (a). If pay has been discontinued under the Pay and Allowances Regulations or has not been drawn during a period of absence without leave, such pay is liable to be forfeited under this clause on the issue of an order by the Central Government. If pay has been drawn during such a period, the issue constitutes an over-issue and the amount is recoverable as a public claim under the Army Rules 1954 r 205. It is unnecessary for an officer to be found guilty of absence by any tribunal before any deductions for the period of absence can be enforced under this provision. Manual of Military Law, Volume II, 2011, the Army Act 1950 s 90 notes.

4 The term 'custody' includes custody by the civil authorities.

5 'Suspension from duty': valid deductions under this provision can only be made if the officer is subsequently convicted of the offence for which he was suspended or kept in custody; see Defence Services Regulations, Regulations for the Army 1987, Volume I, paragraph 346.

6 Ie under the Army Act 1950 ss 83 and 84; see respectively **[0166]** and **[0167]**. Army Act 1950 s 90 (b). Pay and allowances are issuable to an officer though he is in custody or under suspension from duty on a charge for an offence unless such pay and allowances or any part thereof are directed to be withheld under the Army Act 1950 s 93, in which case they can be forfeited on his subsequent conviction for that offence. Even though pay and allowances are not so withheld, their issue during such period may constitute an over-issue and the amount may be recovered as a public claim under the Army Rules 1954 r 205. Manual of Military Law, Volume II, 2011, the Army Act 1950 s 90 notes.

7 Army Act 1950 s 90 (c). It is an offence under the Army Act 1950 s 61 to detain pay unlawfully, etc., but it would not appear necessary for an officer to be convicted of an offence under that section before a deduction may be made under this clause.

8 The term 'expenses' and 'losses' etc., are not limited to public and regimental funds and property but would also extend to e.g., loss of wages and doctor's expenses incurred by an individual (servicemen or a civilian), as the direct result of the offence of which the delinquent is convicted. Manual of Military Law, Volume II, 2011, the Army Act 1950 s 90 notes.

9 'Occasioned by': in order to put an officer under stoppages by way of penal deductions, under either this clause it is not sufficient to show merely that the loss, etc., was facilitated or made possible by his offence, act, or neglect. It is necessary to show that the loss etc., was 'occasioned by' in the sense of being the natural and reasonable consequence of the particular offence of which he is convicted. In the case, however, of the continuing wrongful act of improperly using government property, e.g., a motor vehicle, any loss or damage happening to such property during the continuance of such user may be held to be occasioned thereby. Where the loss etc, was merely facilitated or made possible by the offence, it is possible to effect its recovery as a public etc., claim under the Army Rules 1954 r 205 where appropriate. Manual of Military Law, Volume II, 2011, the Army Act 1950 s 90 notes.

10 Ie under the Army Act 1950 ss 83 and 84. Army Act 1950 s 90 (d). A person is not liable for the ordinary expenses of his prosecution, capture or conveyance or indirect expenses of a similar kind. Nor would he be liable under this clause for damage to a policeman's clothes, because the policeman fell down and damaged them while in pursuit of the person endeavouring to escape. Where a person refuses to march, being able to do so, and a taxi has to be hired for his conveyance, he may be held liable for the expense thus incurred by his contumacy; but he would not be liable if intoxicated and incapable of walking. The principle is that stoppages are intended, not for punishment, but to compensate for the loss etc, sustained. Where an officer has been convicted for an offence by a court martial which did not award any stoppages, no penal deductions can subsequently be ordered under this clause administratively for compensation for damage caused through that offence. As regards averment in the particulars of the charge of the amount of the loss etc., see the Army Rule 1954 r 30(6).

11 Army Act 1950 s 90 (e). A court martial can award both forfeiture of pay and allowances or arrears thereof and stoppages under the Army Act 1950 s 71 clauses (j), (k) and (1) respectively. However, an officer exercising authority under the Army Act 1950 ss 83 and 84 can award stoppages and not forfeiture.

12 Army Act 1950 s 90 (f). Fine is not one of the punishments specified in the Army Act 1950 s 71 and is only awardable by a court martial when exercising jurisdiction under the Army Act 1950 s 69. When the fine awarded by court martial cannot be recovered wholly by deductions from the pay and allowances of an officer, action may also be taken for its recovery under the Army Act 1950 s 174.

13 'Public property' in this clause means not only property of the government, but also any property belonging to the community at large as distinct from that which is private property. Captured enemy property becomes public property. The words 'of public or regimental property' qualify 'loss' and 'damage' as well as destruction. Furniture etc., hired by the military authorities for military use may be treated as 'public' or 'regimental' property. Manual of Military Law, Volume II, 2011, the Army Act 1950 s 90 notes.

14 Army Act 1950 s 90 (g). It must be shown to the satisfaction of the central government that there has been a loss etc., occasioned by some wrongful act or negligence on the part of the officer; and as a general rule an officer is first afforded an opportunity of advancing any reasons why a deduction should not be made from his pay and allowances. The central government can legally impose a penal deduction on an officer under this clause notwithstanding that he has been previously dealt with under the Army Act 1950 s 83 or 84 or by a court martial for the wrongful act or neglect but they may not increase a penal deduction awarded by court martial or other authority, or order such deduction where the loss etc., was averted in the particulars but the court martial or other authority did not award any stoppages. A mere invitation to an officer to make a payment towards any loss or damage occasioned by his wrongful act or neglect, however, does not bar the central government from making an order under this provision. Manual of Military Law, Volume II, 2011, the Army Act 1950 s 90 notes.

15 Army Act 1950 s 90 (h). An officer does not automatically forfeit his pay and allowances while a prisoner of war. When there is reason to believe that an officer has been taken prisoner by his own voluntary action or willful neglect of duty or that he has served with or under or has aided the enemy, etc., a provisional court of inquiry will be assembled at the earliest moment to investigate the circumstances: see Defence Services Regulations, Regulations for the Army 1987, Volume I paragraph 524. The chief of the army staff or any officer authorised by him may then under the Army Act 1950 s 96 order the pay and allowances of such person to be withheld pending the result of such inquiry. A court of inquiry respecting a prisoner of war still absent and not known to have died in captivity will be provisional, to be followed later by another court of inquiry when the individual returns to service or is recovered. If the officer's conduct is found by the court of inquiry (provisional or otherwise) to be blameworthy, the central government may, on the basis of such finding, order forfeiture of the pay and allowances of the officer. When a court of inquiry is assembled on a prisoner of war, evidence shall be recorded on oath or affirmation; see the Army Rules 1954 r 178 and 181(a). As to provision for dependents of prisoners of war from remitted deductions or from his pay and allowances; see the Army Act 1950 ss 98 and 99 and the Army Rules 1954 r 196. For the duration for which a person is deemed to be a prisoner of war; see the Army Act 1950 s 100.

16 Army Act 1950 s 90 (i). This provision was enacted mainly in order to prevent any financial hardship being caused to the wife or children by the provisions of the Army Act 1950 s 28 under which the pay and allowances of a person subject to the Army Act cannot be attached in satisfaction of any decree of a civil court. In other words, if in a suit for maintenance or payment of alimony a civil court grants a decree in favour of the wife or children, the amount decreed can be deducted from the pay and allowance of a person and paid to the wife or children under this provision. Such being the intention, deductions should not, as a rule, be ordered under this provision except to give effect to a decree for maintenance granted by a civil court. Manual of Military Law, Volume II, 2011, the Army Act 1950 s 90 notes. In cases where parentage of child is in controversy for grant of maintenance, defendant alleged father can be directed by the court to submit to DNA test; *Mrs Kanchan Bedi v Gurpreet Singh Bedi* AIR 2003 Delhi 446. The word 'maintenance' used in this provision includes past as well as future maintenance; *Mrs Vrinda Anand v Dr (Maj) Arun Anand* AIR 1987 Delhi 120.

[0385] Deduction from pay and allowances of persons other than officers Subject to the provisions of the Army Act 1950[1] the following penal deductions may be made from the pay and allowances[2] of a person subject to the Army Act 1950 other than an officer[3]:

(1) all pay and allowances for every day of absence either on desertion or without leave, or as a prisoner of war, and for every day of imprisonment for life or imprisonment awarded by a criminal court, a court-martial or an officer exercising authority under the provisions of the Army Act 1950[4];

(2) all pay and allowances for every day while he is in custody on a charge for an offence of which he is afterwards convicted by a criminal court or a court martial, or on a charge of absence without leave for which he is afterwards awarded imprisonment by an officer exercising authority under the provisions of the Army Act 1950[5];

(3) all pay and allowances for every day on which he is in hospital on account of sickness certified by the medical officer attending on him to have been caused by an offence under the Army Act 1950 committed by him[6];

(4) for every day on which he is in hospital on account of sickness certified by the medical officer attending on him to have been caused by his own misconduct or imprudence, such sum as may be specified by order of the central government or such officer as may be specified by that government[7];

(5) all pay and allowances ordered by a court martial or by an officer exercising authority under the Army Act 1950 ss 80, 83, 84 and 85 to be forfeited or stopped[8];

(6) all pay and allowances for every day between his being recovered from the enemy and his dismissal from the service in consequence of his conduct when being taken prisoner by, or while in the hands of the enemy[9];

(7) any sum required to make good such compensation for any expenses, loss, damage or destruction caused by him to the central government or to any building or property as may be awarded by his commanding officer[10];

(8) any sum required to pay a fine awarded by a criminal court, a court martial exercising jurisdiction under the Army Act 1950[11] or an officer exercising authority under any provision of the Army Act 1950[12];

(9) any sum required by order of the Central Government or any prescribed officer to be paid for the maintenance of his wife or his legitimate or illegitimate child or towards the cost of any relief given by the said government to the said wife or child[13].

1 Ie the Army Act 1950 s 94.

2 The Army Act 1950 s 25 enjoins that the pay of any person subject to the Army Act 1950 due to him as such shall be paid without any deduction other than the deductions authorised under the Army Act 1950 or any other Act. The term 'pay' means the rate of pay with increases, if any, for length of service, to which a person subject to the Army Act 1950 is entitled by reason of his rank, appointment, trade group or trade classification, and includes additional remuneration such as qualification pay, proficiency pay and various forms of additional pay which is admissible only on fulfillment of certain conditions. The regulations may provide for the withdrawal of such additional remuneration if the conditions governing them are not fulfilled. All other emoluments are 'allowances'. It is illegal to make deductions which are not authorised and the unlawful withholding of pay is an offence under the Army Act 1950 s 61. The Army Act 1950 s 91 enunciate the penal deductions that may be made from the pay and allowances of an officer and by implication exclude other penal deductions but they do not prohibit deductions not penal e.g., in respect of rations, or stoppages to meet a public claim or regimental debt or claim etc., under the Army Rules 1954 r 205. As to remission of penal deductions, see the Army Act 1950 s 97 and the Army Rules 1954 r 195.

3 The term 'persons other than officer', includes junior commissioned officers, warrant officers, non-commissioned officers and sepoys.

4 Ie the Army Act 1950 s 80. Army Act 1950 s 91 (a): Penal deductions under this provision has been made mandatory and the pay and allowances are to be forfeited automatically and no discretion is given to the commanding officer to decide whether or not to enforce wholly or partially the forfeiture. It is unnecessary for a junior commissioned officer, warrant officer or other ranks to be found guilty of absence by a court martial or by his commanding officer before a forfeiture of pay and allowances for the period of absence can be enforced under this clause. A sepoy who has been sentenced by his commanding officer to undergo detention or confinement to the lines under the Army Act 1950 s 80 does not suffer deductions under this provision. A junior commissioned officer, warrant officer or other ranks automatically forfeits his pay and allowances while a prisoner of war and such pay and allowances cannot as a rule be restored to him unless a court of inquiry assembled to inquire into his conduct finds that he was not taken prisoner through neglect or misconduct on his part or that he was otherwise blameless and the authority prescribed in the Army Rules 1954 r 195(c) remits the forfeiture; see the Army Act 1950 ss 98-100, the Army Rules 1954 r 178, 181 and 196 and the Defence Services Regulations, Regulations for the Army 1987, Volume I paragraph 50 When the sentence of imprisonment for life or imprisonment is suspended by competent authority under the Army Act 1950 s 182, no forfeiture under this provision can take place for the period it is so suspended. Manual of Military Law, Volume II, 2011, the Army Act 1950 s 91 notes.

5 Ie the Army Act 1950 s 80. Army Act 1950 s 91 (b): The pay and allowances are to be forfeited automatically and no discretion is given to the commanding officer to decide whether or not to enforce wholly or partially the forfeiture. Effect cannot be given to this clause unless the pay and allowances of a person in custody on a charge for an offence have been ordered to be withheld under the Army Act 1950 s 93. Once they have been so withheld the deductions are carried out automatically on conviction for that offence. If pay and allowances are not so withheld, their issue during such period constitutes an over-issue and the amount is recoverable as a public claim under the Army Rules 1954 r 205. Junior commissioned officers and non-commissioned officers under 'close arrest' but not in confinement will incur no forfeiture of pay and allowances. For persons below that rank 'close arrest' is the same thing as 'confinement' and they will forfeit pay and allowances for every day of 'close arrest'. The term 'custody' includes custody by the civil authorities. A non-commissioned officer or sepoy who has been sentenced to any punishment other than imprisonment under the Army Act s 80 for the offence of absence without leave or a sepoy who is awarded imprisonment under the Army Act s 80 for an offence other than that of absence without leave does not forfeit his pay and allowances while in custody under this clause. Upon a charge for desertion or absence without leave, a finding that the accused did the act charged but was insane at the time when he did the same, does not amount to a conviction, as it negatives 'intention', and no forfeiture of pay and allowances results. The Army

Act 1950 s 192 prescribes how days of absence etc., are to be calculated for the purposes of this clause. Manual of Military Law, Volume II, 2011, the Army Act 1950 s 91 notes.

6 Army Act 1950 s 91 (c). A penal deduction under this provision has been made mandatory. The deduction is only authorised where the sickness is caused by an offence of which a person has been found guilty. It, therefore, does not extend to sickness caused by immorality or intemperance, when there is no conviction (either by a court martial or the officer disposing of the case summarily) for an offence by which the sickness was caused. The medical officer must attend the investigation of the offence, whether before the court martial or the officer disposing of the case summarily, and give evidence in substantiation of the facts contained in his certificate. Manual of Military Law, Volume II, 2011, the Army Act 1950 s 91 notes. Also see the Defence Services Regulations, Regulations for the Army 1987, Volume I, paragraph 1228.

7 Army Act 1950 s 91 (d). The amount to be deducted is specified in the Pay and Allowance Regulations.

8 Army Act 1950 s 91 (e). Forfeiture of Pay and allowances or of arrears of pay and any public money due at the time of dismissal can only be awarded by a court martial under the Army Act 1950 s 71 (j) and (k). A commanding officer or specified officer can, however, award deprivation of corps or working pay, forfeiture of good service and good conduct pay or a fine under the Army Act 1950 s 80. Stoppages or compensation cannot be awarded by a court-martial unless the grounds for awarding it are stated in the particulars of the charge and the loss etc., are proved in evidence; see the Army Rules 1954 r 30(6). A deduction cannot be effected in anticipation of stoppages. As to the limit of deductions: see the Army Act 1950 s 94; see **[0388]**.

9 Army Act 1950 s 91 (f). A penal deduction under this provision has been made mandatory. A person subject to the Army Act 1950 other than an officer forfeits his pay and allowances while a prisoner of war. This provision authorizes forfeiture of pay and allowances due to such person between the date of his being recovered from the enemy and the date of his dismissal from the service if the court of inquiry assembled under the Army Act 1950 s 96 and the Defence Services Regulations, Regulations for the Army 1987, Volume I paragraph 524 to inquire into his conduct finds that he was taken prisoner through neglect or misconduct on his part. Also see the Army Act 1950 s 100. As to the meaning of 'enemy' see **[0020]**.

10 Army Act 1950 s 91 (g). 'Public property' in this provision means not only property of the government, but also any property belonging to the community at large as distinct from that which is private property. Captured enemy property becomes public property. The words 'of public or regimental property' qualify 'loss' and 'damage' as well as destruction. Furniture etc., hired by the military authorities for military use may be treated as 'public' or 'regimental' property. The word compensation have also been held to include loss of wages and doctor's fee when a person's negligence has occasioned personal injury to a third person. The words 'any building or property' include the buildings or property of persons subject to the Army Act 1950 or of civilians, whether there is any claim against the public or not. Thus, a commanding officer may order a person to pay damages for a broken window, or such other minor damage done by him. Where a person has been convicted by a court martial for an offence, his commanding officer cannot subsequently award compensation for damage caused through that offence. The penal deductions under this clause are purely executory following the commanding officer's award under the Army Act 1950 s 80(i). A JCO may be awarded stoppages by his CO under this clause; see the Army Act 1950 s 85. Manual of Military Law, Volume II, 2011, the Army Act 1950 s 91 notes. As to the limit of deductions; see the Army Act 1950 s 94.

11 Ie under the Army Act 1950 s 69.

12 Ie under the Army Act 1950 ss 80 and 89. Army Act 1950 s 91 (h): The deductions permissible on account of fine under this clause cannot, except where the accused is sentenced to dismissal, exceed in any one month one half of his pay and allowances for that month; see the Army Act 1950 s 94. In addition to deduction under this provision, a fine awarded by a court-martial can also be recovered under the Army Act 1950 s 174.

13 Army Act 1950 s 91 (i). This provision was enacted to prevent any financial hardship being caused to the wife or

children by the provisions of the Army Act 1950 s 28 under which the pay and allowances of a person subject to the Army Act 1950 cannot be attached in satisfaction of any decree of a civil court. In other words, if in a suit for maintenance or payment of alimony a civil court grants a decree in favour of the wife or children, the amount decreed can be deducted from the pay and allowance of a person and paid to the wife or children under this clause. Such being the intention, deductions should not, as a rule, be ordered under this clause except to give effect to a decree for maintenance granted by a civil court. Manual of Military Law, Volume II, 2011, the Army Act 1950 s 91 notes. As to the limit of deductions; see the Army Act 1950 s 94; see **[0388]**.

[0386] Computation of time of absence or custody For the purposes of the Army Act 1950 s 91(a) and (b):

(1) no person shall be treated as absent or in custody for a day unless the absence or custody has lasted, whether wholly in one day, or partly in one day and partly in another, for six consecutive hours or upwards[1];

(2) any absence or custody for less than a day may be reckoned as absence or custody for a day if such absence or custody prevented the absentee from fulfilling any military duty which was thereby thrown upon some other person[2];

(3) absence or custody for twelve consecutive hours or upwards may be reckoned as absence or custody for the whole of each day during any portion of which the person was absent or in custody[3];

(4) a period of absence or imprisonment, which commences before, and ends after, midnight may be reckoned as a day[4].

1 Army Act 1950 s 92(a). This provision prescribes six hours as the minimum period of absence that will count as a day of absence unless two conditions are fulfilled, first, that the absentee was prevented by his absence from fulfilling a military duty, and second, that the duty was thrown upon some other person. Six clear hours must, therefore, elapse, and they must be reckoned consecutively. For instance, if a person absented himself from 0900pm on 1 July 2013 and returned at 0245am on 2 July 2013, he would forfeit no pay as his absence did not amount to six hours or upwards, but he was bound to go on guard or perform some other military duty and in consequence of his absence some other person had to go on guard or perform that duty, then he would forfeit one day's pay Manual of Military Law, Volume II, 2011, the Army Act 1950 s 92 notes.

2 Army Act 1950 s 92(b). If the absence or custody amounts to six hours but not to twenty four hours, one day's pay is forfeited unless the absence exceeds twelve consecutive hours and falls partly on one natural day (reckoned from midnight to midnight) and partly on another, in which case such absence or custody is reckoned for the whole of each natural day during any portion of which the person was absent or in custody. Manual of Military Law, Volume II, 2011, the Army Act 1950 s 92 notes.

3 Army Act 1950 s 92(c).

4 Army Act 1950 s 92(d).

[0387] Pay and allowances during trial In the case of any person subject to the Army Act 1950 who is in custody or under suspension from duty on a charge for an offence, the prescribed officer[1] may direct that the whole or any part of the pay and allowance of such person shall be withheld, pending the result of his trial on the charge against him, in order to give effect to the provisions of the Army Act 1950[2].

1 The prescribed officer is in the case of an officer is the chief of the army staff, and in the case of a person other than an officer, the officer empowered to convene a court martial for his trial. See the army Rules 1954 r 194.

2 Ie Army Act 1950 s 90(b) and 91(b); see respectively **[0384]** and **[0385]**. The Army Act 1950 s 93.

[0388] Limit of certain deductions The total deductions from the pay and allowances of a person made under the Army Act 1950[1] shall not, except where he is sentenced to dismissal, exceed in any one month one-half of his pay and allowances for that month[2].

1 Ie under the Army Act s 91(e) and (g) to (i).

2 Army Act 1950 s 94. The intention of this provision is to leave a certain minimum proportion of his monthly emoluments to a person, other than an officer, for his subsistence. The restriction imposed, however does not apply (i) to deductions under the Army Act 1950 s 90 from the pay and allowances of an officer; (ii) to deductions under the Army Act 1950 s 91 (a),(b),(c),(d), and (f);or (iii) where the offender has been sentenced to dismissal. Manual of Military Law, Volume II, 2011, the Army Act 1950 s 94 notes.

[0389] Deduction from public money due to a person Any sum authorised by the Army Act 1950 to be deducted from the pay and allowances of any person may, without prejudice to any other mode of recovering the same, be deducted from any public money due to him other than a pension[1].

1 Army Act 1950 s 95. The words 'any public money due to him other than a pension' allow the amount to be deducted from a gratuity or other sums earned by but not paid to a person subject to the Army Act 1950. It would not include money lodged in a fund of whatever description, nor ration or lodging etc., or allowance. A pension is excluded because being granted as an act or grace it is non-justifiable and the government can take away or modify its grant. Further, a pensioner not being subject to the Army Act 1950 is outside the scope thereof. Manual of Military Law, Volume II, 2011, the Army Act 1950 s 95 notes.

[0390] Pay and allowances of prisoner of war during inquiry into his conduct Where the conduct of any person subject to the Army Act 1950[1] when being taken prisoner by, or while in the hands of, the enemy, is to be inquired into under the Army Act 1950 or any other law, the chief of the army staff or any officer authorised by him may order that the whole or any part of the pay and allowances of such person shall be withheld pending the result of such inquiry[2].

1 As to the meaning of 'person subject to the Army Act 1950'; see **[0039]**.

2 Army Act 1950 s 96. A junior commissioned officer, warrant officer or other rank automatically forfeits his pay and allowances for the period he is a prisoner of war unless a court of inquiry assembled under the Defence Services Regulations, Regulations for the Army 1987, Volume I, paragraph 524 finds that he was not taken prisoner through neglect or misconduct on his part and the forfeiture has been remitted by the competent military authority specified in the Army Rules 1954 r 195(3). In the case of a person other than an officer, therefore, the pay and allowances which may be withheld under this provision will relate to the period after he returns or is apprehended. However, an officer does not automatically forfeit his pay and allowances while a prisoner of war. The pay and allowances of an officer, being prisoner of war, may be withheld by the chief of the army staff or other officer authorised by him, pending the result of an inquiry into the officer's conduct. If the court of inquiry finds him to be blameworthy, his pay and allowance can then be forfeited by the central government. This section was enacted to give effect to the provisions of the Army Act s 90(h) and 91(f) and thus supplements those provisions. Manual of Military Law, Volume II, 2011, the Army Act 1950 s 96 notes.

[0391] Remission of Deductions Any deduction from pay and allowances authorised by the Army Act 1950 may be remitted in such manner and to such extent[1], and by such authority, as may from time to time be prescribed[2].

1 The words 'and to such extent' means the remission may be partial, but there is nothing to prevent a further remission made subsequently. Manual of Military Law, Volume II, 2011, the Army Act 1950 s 97 notes.

2 Army Act 1950 s 97. As to the term 'prescribed' see the Army Rules 1954 r 195. Prescribed Authorities under the Army Act s 97: Any penal deduction from the pay and allowances of a person subject to the Army Act 1950 made under Chapter VIII thereof (ss 90-100), may be remitted as hereinafter provided, that is to say: (a) A penal deduction from the pay and allowances of any such person may be remitted by the Central Government; (b) The commanding officer of any such person, other than an officer, who has been absent without leave for a period not exceeding five days may, unless the person is convicted by a court-martial on a charge for such absence, remit the forfeiture of pay and allowances to which that absence renders him liable; (c) A forfeiture of pay and allowances incurred by any such person owing to his absence as a prisoner of war may, (unless it shall have been proved before a court of inquiry that he was taken prisoner through his own willful neglect of duty, or that he served with or under, or aided, the enemy or that he did not, as soon as possible, return to the service) be remitted by the chief of the army staff, by the officer commanding an army, army corps, division or independent brigade, or by the officer commanding the forces in the field. Manual of Military Law, Volume II, 2011, the Army Act 1950 s 90 notes.

[0392] Provision for dependents of prisoner of war from remitted deductions In the case of all persons subject to the Army Act 1950 being prisoners of war, whose pay and allowances have been forfeited under the Army Act 1950[1], but in respect of whom a remission has been made under s 97, it shall be lawful for proper provision to be made by the prescribed authorities[2] out of such pay and allowances for any dependants of such persons. Such remission shall deem to apply only to the balance thereafter remaining of such pay and allowances[3].

1 Ie under the Army Act 1950 s 90(h) or s 91(a).

2 The 'prescribed authorities' for the purposes of the Army Act s 98 shall be: (i) In the case of officers of the army medical corps, director general armed forces medical services. (ii) In the case of all other officers, the director of personal services, and (iii) in all other cases, the officer not below the rank of lieutenant colonel commanding a training battalion, training centre, depot or record office who maintains the accounts of the individual or any superior authority. The Army Rules 1954 r 196.

3 Army Act 1950 s 98.

[0393] Provision for dependants of prisoner of war from his pay and allowances It shall be lawful for proper provision to be made by the prescribed authorities[1] for any dependants of any person subject to the Army Act 1950 who is a prisoner of war or is missing, out of his pay and allowances[2].

1 The 'prescribed authorities' under the Army Act 1950 s 99 shall be: (i) In the case of officers of the army medical corps, director general armed forces medical services. (ii) In the case of all other officers, the director of personal services, and (iii) in all other cases, the officer not below the rank of lieutenant colonel commanding a training battalion, training centre, depot or record office who maintains the accounts of the individual or any superior authority. The Army Rules 1954 r 196.

2 Army Act 1950 s 99. This provision applies where the pay and allowances of a person who is a prisoner of war or is missing have not been forfeited e.g., in the case of a person, other than an officer, who is missing or in the case of an officer who is a prisoner of war or is missing and in whose case a court of inquiry under the Defence Services Regulations, Regulations for the Army 1987, Volume I, has not been held or a court of inquiry has been held but the court found the officer blameless. Manual of Military Law, Volume II, the Army Act 1950 s 99 notes.

[0394] Period during which a person is deemed to be a prisoner of war For the purposes of certain provisions of the Army Act 1950[1], a person shall be deemed to continue to be a prisoner of war until the conclusion of any inquiry into his conduct such as is referred to in the Army Act 1950[2], and if he is cashiered or dismissed from the service in consequence of such conduct, until the date of such cashiering or dismissal[3].

1 Ie for the purposes of the Army Act 19501 ss 98 and 99: see respectively **[0392]** and **[0393]**.

2 Ie under the Army Act 1950 s 96: see **[0390]**.

3 The Army Act 1950 s 100.

F. CONFIRMATION AND REVISION

CONTENTS

PARA

[0395] Review of court martial proceedings All general court martial proceedings and district court martial proceedings where the sentence awarded is dismissal or above are required to be reviewed by judge advocate general or his deputies[1]. The proceedings of a general court martial shall be submitted by the judge advocate at the trial for review to the deputy or assistant judge advocate general of the command who shall then forward it to the confirming officer. The proceedings of a district court martial shall be sent by the presiding officer or the judge advocate direct to the confirming officer who must, in all cases, where the sentence is dismissal or above, seek advice of the deputy or assistant judge advocate general of the command before confirmation[2].

1 Manual of Military Law, Volume II, the Army Rules 1954 r 69 notes.

2 The Army Rules 1954 r 69.

[0396] Confirmation Upon receiving the proceedings of a general or district court martial, the confirming authority may confirm or refuse confirmation, or, reserve confirmation for superior authority, and the confirmation, non-confirmation, or reservation shall be entered in and form part of the proceedings[1].

1 The Army Rules 1954 r 70.

[0397] Finding and sentence not valid, unless confirmed No finding or sentence of a general, district or summary general court martial shall be valid unless confirmed[1]. A member of a court martial, or an officer who has acted as a prosecutor at a court martial, shall not confirm the finding or sentence of that court martial, and where such member or prosecutor becomes confirming officer, he shall refer the finding the sentence of the court martial to a superior authority competent to confirm the findings and sentences of the like description of court martial[2]. In the absence of any confirmation, whether original finding or on revision, the finding of court martial is not valid[3]. The findings and sentence of a summary court martial do not require confirmation, but may be carried out forthwith. However, if the officer holding the trial has less than five years service, he shall not, except on active service, carry into effect any sentence until it has received the approval of an officer commanding not less than a brigade[4].

1 Ie as provided by the Army Act 1950 s 153. As regards the authorities/officers empowered to confirm findings and sentences of courts martial see the Army Act 1950 ss 154-157. Confirmation ought to be withheld in certain case, for example: (i) Where the provisions of the Army Act 1950 relating to jurisdiction have been contravened; (ii) Where evidence of a nature prejudicial to the accused has been wrongly admitted; (iii) Where the accused has been unduly restricted in his defence; (iv) where a finding of 'guilty' has been come to with the exception of certain words of the charge, and these words so far describe the essence of the offence, that the finding with the words omitted fails to disclose an offence of which the court could legally have convicted; (v) Where a special finding of 'guilty' fails to disclose an offence of which the court could have legally convicted; (vi) Where the charge is bad in law, even though the accused has pleaded guilty; or (vii) Where there has been such a deviation from the Army Rules 1954 that injustice has been done to the accused. Manual of Military Law, Volume II, 2011, the Army Act 1950 s 153 notes. Also see the Army Rules 1954 r 70; **[0396]**.

2 The Army Rules 1954 r 74.

3 *Chief of Army Staff v Dharam Pal Kukrety* AIR 1985 SC 703 : (1985) 2 SCC 412 : (1985) Cr LJ 913.

4 The Army Act 1950 s 161.

[0398] Power to confirm finding and sentence of general court martial The findings and sentences of general courts martial may be confirmed by the Central Government, or by any officer empowered in this behalf by warrant of the Central Government[1].

1 The Army Act 1950 s 154.

[0399] Power to confirm finding and sentence of district court martial The findings and sentences of district courts martial may be confirmed by any officer having power to convene a general court martial or by any officer empowered in this behalf by warrant of such officer[1].

1 The Army Act 1950 s 155.

[0400] Limitation of powers of confirming authority A warrant issued under the provisions of the Army Act 1950[1] may contain such instructions, reservations or conditions as the authority issuing it may think fit[2].

1 Ie issued under the Army Act 1950 s 154 or 155. See respectively **[0398]** and **[0399]**.

2 The Army Act 1950 s 156.

[0401] Power to confirm finding and sentence of summary general court martial The findings and sentences of summary general courts martial may be confirmed by the convening officer or if he so directs, by an authority superior to him[1].

1 The Army Act 1950 s 157. In the case of a summary general courts martial, the convening officer can confirm the finding and sentence thereof, if he so desires. Manual of Military Law, Volume II, 2011, the Army Act 1950 s 157 notes.

[0402] Restrictions of Power: Confirmation of court marital proceedings The powers of officers to confirm the proceedings of a general court martial or summary general court martial are restricted as follows.

(1) The proceedings, of a general court martial or summary general court martial where any of the sentences specified under column I below, except death sentences, is passed will be reserved for confirmation by the authority specified opposite under column II below[1]:

S. No.	I	II
(i)	Death sentence	Central Government
(ii)	Sentences passed on officers who hold or held the rank of Brigadier or above at the time of commission of the offence or at the time of cognizance of offence.	Chief of the Army Staff
(iii)	All sentences passed on officers not required to be reserved for confirmation by COAS under item (ii) above	General Officer Commanding-in-Chief
(iv)	Sentences passed on junior commissioned officers of dismissal or higher in the scale of punishment set out in the Army Act 1950 s 71.	General Officer Commanding-in-Chief

(2) In cases where sentence of death has been awarded, the proceedings will be forwarded to Army Headquarters in accordance with the provisions of the Defence Service Regulations[2], for submission to the Central Government. No minute reserving confirmation will be entered in such proceedings since the Central Government is the only authority competent to confirm them. The recommendations of each forwarding authority will, however, be annexed to the proceedings. Other proceedings in respect of officers which require confirmation, by the chief of the army staff, will be forwarded together with the minute reserving confirmation and the recommendations of each forwarding authority[3].

(3) The restrictions with regard to the powers to confirm general court martial or summary general court martial proceedings, specified in the Defence Service Regulations[4], also apply to the non-confirmation of any such proceedings[5].

(4) In the event of finding of 'not guilty' by a court martial the powers of officers to confirm or non-confirm the proceedings will be restricted as under: (a) When the offence charged against any officer is punishable with death --by the chief of the army staff[6]; (b) If the accused officer holds or held the rank of Brigadier or above at the time of commission of the offence, or at the time of cognizance of the offence --by the chief of the army staff[7]; and (c) All cases of officers other than those mentioned at (a)

and (b) above—general officer commanding-in-chief[8]. A commanding officer who has investigated a case in his capacity as commanding officer, will not, except on board the ship, subsequently confirm the proceedings of a court martial arising out of the same matter. If he purports so to act in a case outside the exception, the proceedings are not void but must be confirmed by a properly 'qualified authority'[9].

1 The Defence Service Regulations, Regulations for the Army 1987, Volume I, paragraph 472(a).

2 Ie in accordance with the Defence Service Regulations, Regulations for the Army 1987, Volume I, paragraph 477.

3 The Defence Service Regulations, Regulations for the Army 1987, Volume I, paragraph 472(b).

4 Ie the Defence Service Regulations, Regulations for the Army 1987, Volume I, paragraph 472(a).

5 The Defence Service Regulations, Regulations for the Army 1987, Volume I, paragraph 472(c).

6 The Defence Service Regulations, Regulations for the Army 1987, Volume I, paragraph 472(d)(i).

7 The Defence Service Regulations, Regulations for the Army 1987, Volume I, paragraph 472(d)(ii).

8 The Defence Service Regulations, Regulations for the Army 1987, Volume I, paragraph 472(d)(iii).

9 The Defence Service Regulations, Regulations for the Army 1987, Volume I, paragraph 472.

[0403] Power of confirming authority to mitigate, remit or commute sentence Subject to such restrictions, reservations or conditions, as may be contained in any warrant issued under the Army Act 1950[1], a confirming authority may, when confirming the sentence of a court martial, mitigate or remit the punishment thereby awarded, or commute that punishment for any punishment or punishments lower in the scale laid down in the Army Act 1950[2].

1 Ie under the Army Act 1950 s 154 or 155.

2 Ie under the Army Act 1950 s 71. The Army Act 1950 s 158. The powers conferred by this provision may be exercised by the confirming officer, as such, only when confirming the sentence. After promulgation, when the confirmation is complete the power of the confirming officer in that capacity ceases and the above powers can only be exercised by one of the authorities mentioned in the Army Act 1950 s 179. 'Mitigation' is awarding a less amount of the same species of punishment, as, for example, by reducing the length of imprisonment to which an offender has been sentenced; and is in effect equivalent to a remission of part of the sentence. The power to mitigate etc, cannot be exercised whilst execution of the sentence is suspended. 'Remission' may be remission of the whole or of part of the sentence; thus a sentence of imprisonment may be remitted altogether, or a portion of the term may be remitted. 'Commutation' is changing the description of punishment by awarding a punishment lower in the scale of punishments in the Army Act 1950 s 71, as imprisonment in lieu of imprisonment for life, or dismissal in lieu of cashiering, or forfeiture of seniority in lieu of reduction in rank. Manual of Military Law, Volume II, 2011, the Army Act 1950 s 158 notes.

[0404] Mitigation of sentence on partial confirmation Where a sentence has been awarded by a court martial in respect of offences in several charges, and the confirming authority confirms the finding on some but not on all of such charges, that authority shall take into consideration the fact of such non confirmation, and shall, if it seems just, mitigate, remit, or commute the punishment awarded according as it seems just, having regard to the offences in the charges in respect of the findings which are confirmed[1]. Where a sentence has been awarded by a court martial in respect of offences in several charges and has been confirmed, and any one of such charges or the finding thereon is found to be invalid, the authority having power to mitigate, remit, or commute the punishment awarded by the sentence shall take into consideration the fact of such invalidity, and if it seems just, mitigate, remit or commute the punishment awarded according as it seems just, having regard to the offences in the charges which with the findings thereon are not invalid, and the punishment as so modified shall be as valid as if it had been originally awarded only in respect of those offences[2].

1 The Army Rules 1954 r 72 (1). Where a sepoy has been convicted of (i) desertion on active service under the Army Act 1950 s 38(1) and (ii), of theft of government property under the Army Act 1950 s 52 (a), and has been sentenced to rigorous imprisonment for 14 years; and the confirming officer confirms the finding on the second charge but not that on the first charge, which alone justified the sentence of 14 years rigorous imprisonment , he is bound under this rule to remit the sentence at least to rigorous imprisonment for 10 years, which is the maximum sentence under the Army Act 1950 s 52 (a). If, however, the confirming officer confirms the finding of the first charge and not that on the second, he may mitigate or commute it to some less punishment, if he considers that a sentence of rigorous imprisonment for 14 years on the first charge alone is in the circumstances, too severe. Manual of Military Law, Volume II, 2011, the Army Rules 1954 r 72 notes.

2 The Army Rules 1954 r 72 (2). This provision gives to the authority prescribed under the Army Act 1950 s 179 similar powers to do after confirmation that which under the above-stated provision the confirming officer may do before confirmation. As to substitution of a valid for an invalid sentence, see the Army Act 1950 s 163.

[0405] Confirming of findings and sentences on board a ship When any person subject to the Army Act 1950[1] is tried and sentenced by a court martial while on board a ship, the finding and sentence so far as not confirmed and executed on board the ship, may be confirmed and executed in like manner as if such person had been tried at the port of disembarkation[2].

1 As to the meaning of 'person subject to the Army Act 1950'; see **[0039]**.

2 The Army Act 1950 s 159.

[0406] Confirmation notwithstanding informality in or excess of punishment If the sentence of a court martial is informally expressed, the confirming authority may, in confirming the sentence, vary the form so that it shall be properly expressed. If the punishment awarded by the sentence is in excess of the punishment authorised by law, the confirming authority may vary the sentence so that the sentence shall not be in excess of the punishment authorised by law; and the confirming authority may confirm the finding and the sentence, as so varied, of the court martial[1].

The object of this provision is to prevent the proceedings of courts martial from being rendered invalid when they cannot be sent back for revision without great inconvenience to the public service. It will not exonerate from blame the presiding officers and members of courts martial who award sentences which are informal or in excess of their powers. If confirming officer decides to act under this provision, instead of ordering a revision of the sentence, he should call the attention of the members of the court to the informality or irregularity of the sentence. The confirming authority cannot under this provision vary a sentence which is illegal in its character and therefore null e.g., a sentence of imprisonment awarded by a district court martial a warrant officer or a sentence of reduction awarded to a lance naik or a sentence of confinement to lines awarded to a sepoy. In such cases the court must be reassembled for the purpose of passing a valid sentence[2].

1 The Army Rules 1954 r 73.

2 Manual of Military Law, Volume II, 2011, the Army Rules 1954 r 73 notes.

[0407] Revision of finding or sentence Any finding or sentence of a court martial which requires confirmation[1] may be once revised by order of the confirming authority and on such revision, the court, if so directed by the confirming authority, may take additional evidence[2]. The court, on revision, shall consist of the same officers as were present when the original decision was passed, unless any of those officers are unavoidably absent[3]. In case of such unavoidable absence the cause thereof shall be duly certified in the proceedings, and the court shall proceed with the revision, provided that, if a general court martial, it still consists of five officers, or, if a summary general or district court martial, of three officers[4]. Revisional jurisdiction of the confirming authority is not confined to giving the directions for recoding additional evidence but extends analyzing the evidence on record for indicating where the court martial could have erred in appreciation of evidence[5].

1 The term 'which requires confirmation' denotes that the finding or sentence of a summary court martial can never be revised. See the Army Act 1950 s 161: **[0409]**.

2 The Army Act 1950 s 160(1).

3 The Army Act 1950 s 160(2).

4 The Army Act 1950 s 160(3).

5 *Union of India v Capt AP Bajpai* (1998) 4 SCC 245. *Capt Harish Uppal v Union of India* (1973) 3 SCC 319 : 1973 SCC (Cri) 268 : (1973) 2 SCR 1025.

[0408] Revision: procedure Where the finding is sent back for revision under the Army Act 1950[1] the court shall reassemble in open court, the revision order shall be read, and if the court is directed to take fresh evidence, such evidence shall also be taken in open court[2]. Except where the court is directed to take fresh-evidence, no fresh evidence shall be adduced[3]. The court may, on a request from the prosecutor, in the interest of justice, allow a witness to be called or re-called for the purpose of rebutting any material statement made by a witness for the defence during revision[4]. After the revision order has been read in open court whether the revision is of finding or sentence and the evidence, if any, in accordance with the above-stated provisions has been taken, the prosecutor and the accused shall be given a further opportunity to address the court in the order as laid down in the Army Rules 1954[5]. If necessary, the judge advocate, if any, may sum up the (additional) evidence and advise the court upon the law relating to the case. The court shall then deliberate on its finding or the sentence, as the case may be, in closed court[6]. Where the finding is sent back for revision and the court does not adhere to its former finding, it shall revoke the finding and sentence, and record the new finding, in the manner laid down in the manner laid down in the Army Rules 1954[7], and if such new finding involves a sentence, pass sentence afresh, after complying with the provisions of the Army Rules 1954[8]. Where the sentence alone is sent back for revision, the court shall not revise the finding[9]. After the revision, the presiding officer shall date and sign the decision of the court, and the proceedings, upon being signed by the judge-advocate, if any, shall at once be transmitted for confirmation[10]. The object of revision is generally to cure defects in the finding or sentence, or both. The confirming officer, however, by partial confirmation or by exercising his powers under the Army Rules 1954[11] can often correct mistakes made by the court, and thus obviate the inconvenience of reassembling the court for revision. For instance, if the sentence originally awarded by the court martial is wholly illegal, e.g., a sentence of rigorous imprisonment awarded to a warrant officer by a district court martial; and the court on revision, may award a legal sentence. A court cannot be re-assembled more than once for revision, whether of finding or of sentence[12]. A confirming officer cannot send back part of a finding or sentence: if he thinks that a part only requires revision, he must return the whole, pointing out the part which, in his opinion, requires revision. Where the finding is sent back for revision and the court adheres to the finding, it can nevertheless revise the sentence[13].

1 Ie the Army Act 1950 s 160; see **[0407]**.

2 The Army Rules 1954 r 68(1).

3 The Army Rules 1954 r 68(2).

4 The Army Rules 1954 r 68(3).

5 Ie the Army Rules 1954 r 59.

6 The Army Rules 1954 r 68(4).

7 Ie the Army Rules 1954 r 62.

8 Ie the Army Rules 1954 r 64. The Army Rules 1954 r 68(5).

9 The Army Rules 1954 r 68(6).

10 The Army Rules 1954 r 68(7).

12 Ie under the Army Rules 1954 r 72(1) or 73.

12 The Army Act 1950 s 160 (1).

13 Manual of Military Law, Volume II, 2011, the Army Rules 1954 r 68 notes.

[0409] Finding and sentence of a summary court martial The finding and sentence of a summary court-martial shall not require to be confirmed, but may be carried out forthwith[1]. However, if the officer holding the trial is of less than five years service, he shall not, except on active service[2], carry into effect any sentence until it has received the approval of an officer commanding not less than a brigade[3].

1 'Carried out forthwith': The officer holding the trial when passing sentence may, if a sentence of imprisonment be awarded, direct under the provisions of the Army Act 1950 s 183(2) that the offender be not committed until the orders of the authority/officer specified in the Army Act 1950 s 182 are obtained. The Army Act 1950 s 161(1).

2 As to the definition of 'active service'; see **[0008]**.

3 The Army Act 1950 s 161(2).

[0410] Alteration of finding or sentence in certain cases Where a finding of guilty by a court martial, which has been confirmed, or which does not require confirmation, is found for any reason to be invalid or cannot be supported by the evidence, the authority which would have had power under the provisions of the Army Act 1950[1] to commute the punishment awarded by the sentence, if the finding had been valid, may substitute a new finding and pass a sentence for the offence specified or involved in such finding[2]. However, no such substitution shall be made unless such finding could have been validly made by the court martial on the charge and unless it appears that the court martial must have been satisfied of the facts establishing the said offence[3].

Where a sentence passed by a court-martial which has been confirmed, or which does not require confirmation, not being a sentence passed in pursuance of a new finding substituted under the above provision, is found for any reason to be invalid, the authority referred therein may pass a valid sentence[4]. The punishment awarded by a sentence passed under the above provisions shall not be higher in the scale of punishments than, or in excess of the punishment awarded by, the sentence for which a new sentence is substituted under this provision[5]. Any finding substituted, or any sentence passed, under this provision shall, for the purposes of the Army Act 1950 and the Army Rules 1954, have effect as if it were a finding or sentence, as the case may be, of a court martial[6].

1 Ie under the Army Act 1950 s 179.

2 The Army Act 1950 s 163(1). This provision enables any of the authorities mentioned in the Army Act 1950 s 179; see **[0434]**, to substitute a new finding for an invalid finding or for one which cannot be supported by the evidence, which have been confirmed and which are thus not open to revision and to pass a sentence in respect

of the new finding, It also gives these authorities similar powers in regard to a finding not requiring confirmation, i.e., any finding of a summary court martial. The confirming officer himself has no power to substitute or change the finding; if in his opinion the court has arrived at a wrong finding, he can only send it back for revision or not confirm it. Manual of Military Law, Volume II, 2011, the Army Act 1950 s 163 notes.

3 The Army Act 1950 s 163(1) proviso.

4 The Army Act 1950 s 163(2). This provision enables the authorities mentioned in the Army Act 1950 s 179 to substitute a valid sentence for an invalid sentence not being a sentence passed in pursuance of a new finding under the Army Act 1950 s 163(1).

5 The Army Act 1950 s 163(3). This provision requires that the new sentence substituted for an invalid sentence must not be higher in scale than, or in excess of, the original sentence. The words 'invalid sentence' are used to mean a sentence which is authorised under the Army Act 1950 but which is inapplicable in relation to the accused or to the offence with which he is charged, as distinct from an illegal sentence or a sentence which is unknown to the Army Act 1950 e.g., reproof. Manual of Military Law, Volume II, 2011, the Army Act 1950 s 163 notes.

6 The Army Act 1950 s 163(4). The substituted finding and/or sentence will have the same effect as if it were the original finding and/or sentence. Manual of Military Law, Volume II, 2011, the Army Act 1950 s 163 notes.

[0411] Promulgation The charge, finding, and sentence, and any recommendation to mercy shall, together with the confirmation or non-confirmation of the proceedings, be promulgated in such manner as the confirming authority may direct; and if no direction is given, according to the custom of the service. Until promulgation has been effected, confirmation is not complete and the finding and sentence shall not be held to have been confirmed until they have been promulgated[1].

In the absence of any direction by the confirming authority, the usual custom of the service as to promulgation will be followed, but a written notice to the offender of the charge, etc., will be sufficient promulgation under this provision. The charge(s), finding, sentence, recommendations to mercy, if any, and confirmation, or non-confirmation of the proceedings shall be promulgated in the manner stated below and the date of promulgation with be recorded on the proceedings[2]. In the case of officers, the details of the proceedings will be read out to the accused by his formation commander in the presence of his commanding officer and such other officers of his staff as he considers necessary. If he has been sentenced to cashiering or dismissal, he will be stripped of his badges of rank and all regimental insignia[3]. In the case of junior commissioned officers, warrant officers or other ranks, the details of proceedings will be read out to the accused by his commanding officer in the presence of the adjutant and the senior junior commissioned officers of the unit. If he has been sentenced to dismissal or to be reduced to the ranks or to a lower rank or grade he will be stripped of his badges of rank and other regimental insignia[4]. The promulgation of general and district courts martial proceedings in units commanded by officers below the rank of major will be done by formation commanders. If the confirmation authority thinks fit, he may order the promulgation to take place at a place at a parade in such form as he decides. In cases of summary courts martial, the commanding officer of the unit may order the promulgation to be carried out at a parade. The result of all courts martial will be published in the orders of all formations in which the notice of the convening of the court appeared. In every case such results will be published in the orders of the unit concerned, in Part I Orders in the case of officers and in Part II Orders in the case of junior commissioned officers, warrant officers or other ranks[5]. If, subsequent to conviction but before promulgation can be effected, an accused absents himself, and a declaration by a, court of inquiry under the Army Act 1950[6] is made in respect thereof, the proceedings of the court martial may be promulgated by the publication of the foregoing particulars, in the case of an officer in Part

I Orders and in the case of a junior commissioned officer, warrant officer or other rank in Part II Orders of the unit. They will, however, forthwith be communicated to the accused on his apprehension (if liable for further service) or surrender[7].

1 The Army Rules 1954 r 71.

2 Defence Services Regulations, Regulations for the Army 1987, Volume I, paragraph 473(a).

3 Defence Services Regulations, Regulations for the Army 1987, Volume I, paragraph 473(a)(i).

4 Defence Services Regulations, Regulations for the Army 1987, Volume I, paragraph 473(a)(ii).

5 Defence Services Regulations, Regulations for the Army 1987, Volume I, paragraph 473(b).

6 Ie under the Army Act 1950 s 106.

7 Defence Services Regulations, Regulations for the Army 1987, Volume I, paragraph 473(c).

[0412] Remedy against order, finding or sentence of court martial Any person subject to the Army Act 1950 who considers himself aggrieved by any order passed by any court martial may present a petition to the officer or authority empowered to confirm any finding or sentence of such court-martial, and the confirming authority may take such steps as may be considered necessary to satisfy itself as to the correctness, legality or propriety of the order passed or as to the regularity of any proceeding to which the order relates[1]. Any person subject to the Army Act 1950 who considers himself aggrieved by a finding or sentence of any court martial which has been confirmed, may present a petition to the Central Government, the chief of the army staff or any prescribed officer superior in command to the one who confirmed such finding or sentence, and the Central Government the chief of the army staff or other officer, as the case may be, may pass such order thereon as it or he thinks fit[2]. Where the Central Government itself has exercised the power of confirmation of the sentence awarded by the general court martial, it being the highest authority mentioned in the Army Act 1950 s 164(2), there can be no occasion for further appeal to any other body[3]. There is no express obligation imposed on the confirming authority or the Central Government to give reasons in support of its decision to confirm the proceedings of the court martial under this provision of the Army Act 1950[4].

Petitions by persons still in service will be addressed to the officer or authority empowered to confirm the finding and sentence of that court martial (before confirmation); and to the Central Government, the chief of the army staff or any authority superior in command to the confirming authority (after confirmation). Unless the redress asked for is granted by a subordinate authority, the petition will be forwarded to the addressee with the remarks of all the intermediate commanders concerned. A person, who addressed a petition to the confirming officer before confirmation, will have the right to address another petition, i.e., post confirmation petition to the concerned authorities.) The above provisions must be explained to every convicted person at the time of promulgation of the finding and sentence of a court martial[5]. A petition can only be addressed by an aggrieved person either personally or through a representative appointed by a power of attorney. A petition received from a person, other than the aggrieved one, or his duly constituted attorney, or a petition from an aggrieved person which has already been finally disposed of will be returned to the petitioner explaining the correct legal position to him. The orders of the officer or authority to whom the petition is addressed will be final and will exhaust the legal rights of redress under the Army Act 1950. A petition against the order, decision, finding or sentence of a court martial (except a summary court martial wherein punishment of imprisonment of three months or less has been awarded) can also be filed in the Armed Forces Tribunal under the provisions of the Armed Forces Tribunal Act 2007[6].

1 The Army Act 1950 s 164(1). The use of the expression 'order' under this provision and the expression 'finding or sentence' in the Army Act 1950 s 164 (2) indicates that the scope of this provision and sub-section (2) is not the same. The expression 'order' under this provision cannot be construed to include a 'finding or sentence'. In other words in so far as the finding and sentence of the court martial is concerned the only remedy that is available to a person aggrieved by the same is under s 164 (2) and the same remedy can be invoked only after the finding or sentence has been confirmed by the confirming authority and not before the confirmation of the same. Though a person aggrieved by the finding or sentence of a court martial has no right to make a representation before the confirmation of the same by the confirming authority, but in case such a representation is made by a person aggrieved by the finding or sentence of a court martial it is expected that the confirming authority shall give due consideration to the same while confirming the finding and sentence of the court martial. *Brig RP Singh VSM v Union of India* 14 (2004) DLT 792, 2004 (77) DRJ 480.

2 The Army Act 1950 s 164(2).

3 *Ram Sarup v Union of India* AIR 1965 SC 247, 1965(I) Cr LJ 236.

4 *Som Datt Dutta v Union of India* AIR 1969 SC 414, 1969 Cr LJ 663, (1968) 2 SCR 177.

5 Defence Services Regulations, Regulations for the Army 1987, Volume I, paragraph 365(m). As to the filing of petitions against the orders, findings and sentence of court martial; see Defence Services Regulations, Regulations for the Army 1987, Volume I, paragraph 365.

6 The Armed Forces Tribunal Act 2007 s 15; see: **[1728]**.

[0413] Annulment of proceedings The Central Government, the chief of the army staff or any prescribed officer[1] may annul the proceedings of any court-martial on the ground that they are illegal or unjust[2].

1 The 'prescribed officer' under the Army Act 1950 s 165 shall be the officer commanding an army, army corps, division or brigade in respect of proceedings confirmed by him or by a person under his command. The Army Rules 1954 r 202.

2 The Army Act 1950 s 165. Before passing orders under this provision the advice of the deputy judge advocate general of the command concerned must be taken.

G. EXECUTION OF SENTENCE

CONTENTS

PARA

[0414] Form of sentence of death In awarding a sentence of death a court martial shall, in its discretion, direct that the offender shall suffer death by being hanged by the neck until he be dead, or shall suffer death by being shot to death[1].

1 The Army Act 1950 s 166. A person sentenced by a court martial to death remains subject to the Army Act 1950 until the sentence is carried out; see: the Army Act 1950 s 123(4).

[0415] Custody of person under sentence of death When a person is sentenced by a court martial to suffer death, the commanding officer of such person may, if he thinks fit, by a warrant in one of the forms in the Army Rules 1954 Appendix V, commit the said person for safe custody in a civil prison pending confirmation or the carrying out of the sentence[1].

1 The Army Rules 1954 r 169.

[0416] Opportunity for petition against sentence of death While confirming the sentence of death, the confirming authority shall specify the period within which the person sentenced may, after the sentence has been promulgated to him, submit a petition against the finding or sentence against him of the court martial[1]. The person against whom the sentence of death has been confirmed, shall at the time of promulgation, be informed of his rights under the Army Act 1950[2] and of the period specified by the confirming authority within which, he may, if he so wishes to do, submit a petition against the finding or sentence of the court martial[3]. Every petition against a finding or sentence submitted by such a person, and every order in respect of such petition shall be transmitted through the Adjutant General at the army headquarters.[4] A sentence of death shall not be carried into effect until the expiry of the period specified by the confirming authority under the above stated provision[5] or if, within the period so specified, the person under sentence submits a petition against the finding or sentence of the court martial, until the authority legally competent to dispose of such petition finally, after considering the petition, orders that sentence of death may be carried into effect[6].

1 The Army Rules 1954 r 170(1).

2 Ie under the Army Act 1950 s 164 (2).

3 The Army Rules 1954 r 170(2).

4 The Army Rules 1954 r 170(3). The confirming officer in cases of death sentences in the Central Government. Defence Service Regulations, Regulations for the Army, Volume I, paragraph 472; see **[0402]**.

5 Ie under the Army Rules 1954 r 170(1).

6 The Army Rules 1954 r 170(4).

[0417] Death warrant The officer commanding the army, army corps or division or an officer commanding forces in the field shall nominate a provost marshal or other officer not below the rank of lieutenant colonel who shall be responsible for the due execution of the sentence of death passed under the Army Act 1950, and shall issue to such officer the death warrant in the relevant form[1]. The officer specified in the above provision shall not issue the death warrant until he is satisfied that having regard to the provisions of the Army Rules 1954[2], the sentence of death may be carried into effect[3]. No sentence of death passed under the Army Act 1950 shall be carried into effect until the death warrant has been received by the provost marshal or other officer mentioned under the above stated provision[4]. If the authority specified in the above provision[5] is of the opinion that the sentence of death be carried out in a civil prison, he shall forward a warrant in one of the forms contained in the Army Rules 1954 Appendix V together with an order of the confirming authority certifying the confirmation of the sentence, to the civil prison for the execution of the sentence[6].

1 Ie as contained in the Army Rules 1954 Appendix V; The Army Rules 1954 r 170A(1).

2 Ie the Army Rules 1954 r 170.

3 The Army Rules 1954 r 170A (2).

4 Ie under the Army Rules 1954 r 170A (1).The Army Rules 1954 r 170A (3).

5 Ie the officer commanding the army, army corps or division or an officer commanding forces in the field; The Army Rules 1954 r 170A (1).

6 The Army Rules 1954 r 170A (4).

[0418] Execution of sentence of death On receipt of death warrant the provost marshal or other officer, nominated under the Army Rules 1954[1] shall: (i) inform the person sentenced as soon as possible of the date on which the sentence will be carried out[2]; (ii) if the person sentenced has been committed to a civil prison under the Army Rules 1954[3], obtain the custody of his person by issuing a warrant in one of the forms in the Army Rules 1954 Appendix V[4]; and (iii) proceed to carry out the sentence as required by the death warrant and in accordance with any general or special instructions which may from time to time be given by or under the authority of the Chief of the Army Staff [5]. During the execution of the sentence of death passed under the Army Act 1950, no person except those specified below, shall attend the execution of sentence of death: (i) the provost marshal or other officer who is responsible for the due execution of the sentence in accordance with these provisions[6]; (ii) a commissioned medical officer of the armed forces of the Union[7]; (iii) an officer nominated by the officer who issued the death warrant, who is able to identify the person under sentence as the person described in the death warrant and as the person who was tried and sentenced by the court martial mentioned therein[8]; (iv) such non-commissioned officers as may be detailed by the provost martial or other officer aforesaid for escort or security purpose or to assist in the execution[9]; and (v) if execution is carried out in effect in an army unit, the officer for the time being in command of such unit[10]. After the sentence of death has been carried into effect, the provost marshal or other officer nominated the Army Rules 1954 stated above[11], or the superintendent of the civil prison, as the case may be, shall complete or cause to be completed parts II and III of the death warrant, and shall without unnecessary delay return the completed death warrant to the officer who had issued the same[12].

1 Ie under the Army Rules 1954 r 170A (1); see **[0417]**.

2 The Army Rules 1954 r 170B (1) (a).

3 Ie under the Army Rules 1954 r 169.

4 The Army Rules 1954 r 170B (1) (b).

5 The Army Rules 1954 r 170B (1) (c).

6 The Army Rules 1954 r 170B (2) (a).

7 The Army Rules 1954 r 170B (2) (b).

8 The Army Rules 1954 r 170B (2) (c).

9 The Army Rules 1954 r 170B (2) (d).

10 The Army Rules 1954 r 170B (2) (e).

11 Ie under the Army Rules 1954 r 170A (1).

12 The Army Rules 1954 r 170B (3).

[0419] Procedure on commutation of sentence of death If a sentence of death is commuted under the Army Act 1950 or if the person sentenced to death is pardoned, and (i) if he has been committed to a civil prison under a warrant issued under the Army Rules 1954[1] a further warrant in one of the forms given in the Army Rules 1954 Appendix V shall be issued by the commanding officer of such person[2]; (ii) if he has been detained in military custody, any warrant which may be necessary to give effect to the sentence as so commuted, shall be issued in one of the forms given in the Army Rules 1954 Appendix IV[3].

1 Ie under the Army Rules 1954 r 169.

2 The Army Rules 1954 r 171 (a).

3 The Army Rules 1954 r 171 (b).

[0420] Commencement of sentence of imprisonment for life or imprisonment Whenever any person is sentenced by a court martial under the Army Act 1950 to imprisonment for life or imprisonment, the term of his sentence shall, whether it has been revised or not, be reckoned to commence on the day on which the original proceedings were signed[1] by the presiding officer or, in the case of a summary court martial by the court[2].

1 'Original proceedings were signed': Means the day on which the first verdict and sentence, if any, was announced. For example, on his trial by a court martial, 'A' was found not guilty on 15 May 2013. On revision, on 15 June 2013, he was convicted and awarded 3 months rigorous imprisonment. The term of his sentence shall reckon to commence wef 15 May 2013. It is, therefore, essential that the proceedings be dated as well as signed. When, however, a presiding officer or officer holding the trial omits either to sign or date the proceedings, he can even after confirmation sign them and date his signature as of the true date. Manual of Military Law, Volume II, 2011, the Army Act 1950 s 167 notes.

2 The Army Act 1950 s 167. A term of imprisonment for life or imprisonment cannot be made to commence at the expiration of a previous term, but must commence on the day on which the original proceedings are signed. If, therefore, the court desires to inflict, e.g., six months' additional imprisonment on a prisoner already undergoing six months prisoner, of which three months are unexpired, the court must award nine months. Manual of Military Law, Volume II, 2011, the Army Act 1950 s 167 notes. A term of imprisonment for life or imprisonment awarded by way of commutation must commence on the date of the signing of original proceedings even though such sentence was one of a different character. A court martial in framing sentences will observe the following rules: (a) Terms of imprisonment unless for one or more years exactly, should if for one month or upwards be recorded in months.(b) Sentences consisting partly of months and partly of days should be recorded in months and days. See: Defence Services Regulations, Regulations for the Army 1987, Volume I, paragraph 468 (e).

[0421] Execution of sentence of imprisonment for life Whenever, any sentence of imprisonment for life is passed under the Army Act 1950 or whenever, any sentence of death is commuted to imprisonment for life, the commanding officer of the person under sentence or a prescribed officer shall forward a warrant in the prescribed form to the officer in charge of the civil prison in which such person is to be confined and shall arrange for his dispatch to such prison with the warrant[1]. A warrant for the committal of a person sentenced by a court martial to a prison[2] shall be in one of the forms given in the Army Rules 1954[3]. Such warrant shall be signed and dispatched by the commanding officer of the prisoner or by any higher authority or his staff officer and forwarded to proper prison authority[4].

1 The Army Act 1950 s 168.

2 Ie under the provisions of the Army Act 1950 s 168 and 169(2).

3 See the Army Rules 1954 Appendix IV.

4 The Army Rules 1954 r 166.

[0422] Execution of sentence of imprisonment Whenever any sentence of imprisonment is passed under the Army Act 1950 by a court martial or whenever any sentence of death or imprisonment for life is commuted to imprisonment, the confirming officer or in case of a summary court martial the officer holding the court or such other officer as may be prescribed[1], shall, save as otherwise provided in the provisions of the Army Act 1950[2], direct either that the sentence shall be carried out by confinement in a military prison or that it shall be carried out by confinement in a civil prison[3]. When a direction has been made under the abovestated provision, the commanding officer of the person under sentence or such other officer as may be prescribed shall forward a warrant in the prescribed form to the officer in charge of the prison in which such person is to be confined and shall arrange for his dispatch to such prison with the warrant[4]. In the case of a sentence of imprisonment for a period not exceeding three months and passed under the Army Act 1950 by a court martial, the appropriate officer states above may direct that the sentence shall be carried out by confinement in military custody instead of in a civil or military prison[5]. On active service, a sentence of imprisonment may be carried out by confinement in such place as the officer commanding the forces in the field may from time to time appoint[6]. A warrant for the committal of a person sentenced by court martial to a civil prison by an officiating commanding officer of the unit to which the appellant is attached is valid[7].

1 The 'prescribed officer' under the Army Act 1950 s 169 (1), for the purposes of directing whether the sentence shall be carried out by confinement in a civil prison or by confinement in a military prison, shall be, in the case of a sentence which has been confirmed, any higher authority than the confirming officer, and in the case of a sentence which does not require confirmation, any higher authority to the officer holding the trial; the Army Rules 1954 r 203. Sentence of imprisonment combined with dismissal should, as a rule, be carried out by confinement in a civil prison. Sentences of imprisonment not exceeding three months, to which no sentence of dismissal has been added, should be carried out by confinement in military custody, or, if sufficient accommodation in cells does not exist, in a military prison. Where an offender has been sentenced to imprisonment exceeding three months (but not exceeding nine months) and circumstances exist which justify the turn of the offender to military service, the competent authority should give a direction that he should be committed to a military prison. When the power of directing imprisonment to be undergone in military custody or a military prison vests in the confirming officer, the direction should be part of the confirmation minute, but when, as in the case of a summary court martial, it vests in the court, the direction should form part of the sentence. The direction may also be given by an authority having power, under the provisions of the Army Act 1950 ss 162 or 179 to mitigate the sentence. Manual of Military Law, Volume II, 2011, the Army Act 1950 s 169 notes.

2 The Army Act 1950 s 169 (3) and (4).

3 The Army Act 1950 s 169(1).

4 The Army Act 1950 s 169(2).

5 The Army Act 1950 s 169(3).

6 The Army Act 1950 s 169(4). The officer commanding the forces in the field on active service can establish military prisons in the field in which sentences of imprisonment of any length may be carried out. This enables a sentence of imprisonment to be carried out locally on active service and the prisoner, unless he is dismissed, to be sent back to duty on its expiration. The officer commanding the forces in the field can also appoint a local civil prison as a place in which such sentences may be carried out, if he considers the civil prison to be a suitable place and accommodation is available. Manual of Military Law, Volume II, 2011, the Army Act 1950 s 169 notes.

7 *Bhuwneshwar Singh v Union of India* (1993) 4 SCC 327, (1994) SCC (Cr) 1.

[0423] Sentence of Cashiering or Dismissal A sentence of cashiering or dismissal awarded by a court martial shall take effect from the date on which the sentence is promulgated to the person under sentence, or except in the case of an officer, from such subsequent date as may be specified by the commanding officer at the time of such promulgation[1]. When dismissal is combined with imprisonment which is to be carried out in a military prison or in military custody, the dismissal shall not take effect until the date on which the prisoner is released from a military prison or from military custody[2]. When cashiering or dismissal is combined with imprisonment for life or with imprisonment which is to be carried out in a civil prison, the cashiering or dismissal shall not take effect until the date on which the prisoner is received into a civil prison[3].

1 The Army Rules 1954 r 168(1). A sentence of cashiering or dismissal awarded by a court martial to an officer takes effect from the date of promulgation, or when combined with imprisonment, from the date on which the prisoner is received into a civil prison. The sentence is notified in the Gazette of India. It may sometimes be expedient for a commanding officer, in order to keep a person sentenced to dismissal (other than an officer) subject to the Army Act 1950 for a short period, to specify a date subsequent to the date of promulgation. If he considers such action desirable he must do so at the time of the promulgation of the sentence to the person and he should record the date he specifies in the minute of promulgation. When a commanding officer exercises this option of specifying a subsequent date, the date specified must be strictly limited by the requirements of the case. For instance, in the case of a person sentenced out of India to dismissal alone, or to dismissal combined with imprisonment which is carried out locally either in military custody or for special reasons in local civil custody, the subsequent date might be 'date of disembarkation' or 'date of embarkation' according to whether the intention is to despatch the person to India on a transport or by a private vessel. It is obviously desirable to keep the person subject to military discipline while travelling on a transport or until he can be despatched to India. If the person is to be sent by a transport, the commanding officer can enter in the discharge certificate 'date of disembarkation' as the date from which the dismissal takes effect. Manual of Military Law, Volume II, 2011, the Army Rules 1954 r 168 notes.

2 The Army Rules 1954 r 168(2).

3 The Army Rules 1954 r 168(3). A prisoner under sentence of cashiering or dismissal combined with imprisonment which is carried out in a civil prison remains subject to the Army Act 1950 until he is received into a civil prison. The commanding officer should enter on the discharge certificate the date of admission into a civil prison as the date from which the dismissal takes effect, or in the case of an officer, report the date of admission to the proper military authority. Manual of Military Law, Volume II, 2011, the Army Rules 1954 r 168 notes.

[0424] Period of Custody undergone by the officer or person to be set off against the imprisonment When a person or officer subject to the Army Act 1950[1] is sentenced by a court martial to a term of imprisonment, not being an imprisonment in default of payment of fine, the period spent by him in civil or military custody during investigation, inquiry or trial of the same case, and before the date of order of such sentence, shall be set off against the term of imprisonment imposed upon him. The liability of such person to undergo imprisonment on such order of sentence shall be restricted to the remainder of the term of imprisonment imposed upon him[2]. The benefit of this provision is not available to persons who were sentenced to suffer the imprisonment before the Army (Amendment) Act 1992 came into force[3].

1 As to the definition of 'officer' and 'person subject to the Army Act 1950'; see **[0029]** and **[0039]**.

2 The Army Act 1950 s 169A.

3 *Union of India v Sunil Kumar Sarkar* AIR 2001 SC 1092 : (2001) 3 SCC 414 : (2001) SCC (L&S) 600.

[0425] Temporary custody of offender Where a sentence of imprisonment for life or imprisonment is directed to be undergone in a civil prison the offender may be kept in a military custody or in any other fit place, till such time as it is possible to send him to a civil prison[1].

1 The Army Act 1950 s 170.

[0426] Execution of sentence of imprisonment in special cases Whenever, in the opinion of an officer commanding an army, army corps, division or independent brigade, any sentence or portion of a sentence of imprisonment cannot for special reasons, conveniently be carried out in a military prison or in military custody in accordance with the provisions of the Army Act 1950[1] such officer may direct that such sentence or portion of sentence shall be carried out by confinement in any civil prison or other fit place[2].

1 Ie the Army Act 1950 s 169.

2 The Army Act 1950 s 171. The power conferred under this provision might be of use in an emergency, such as an epidemic. It will also admit of local arrangements being made for the execution of a sentence of rigorous imprisonment passed in any place outside India when it is, for any reason, inconvenient or undesirable that an offender should be sent to India to undergo his sentence. In such a case, the warrant of commitment in Form B (the Army Rules 1954 Appendix IV Part II) must be suitably varied and must cite the order made under this section. When the prisoner is to be despatched to India he should be demanded by a warrant in Form G in the above said Appendix and must be committed to the civil prison in India on a fresh warrant of commitment. This provision differs from the Army Act 1950 s 169(4) in that (i) the direction may be made by the specified authorities even though the troops are not on active service, and (ii) the direction can be made only when the imprisonment is to be carried out in a military prison or military custody. Manual of Military Law, Volume II, 2011, the Army Act 1950 s 171 notes.

[0427] Conveyance of prisoner from place to place A person under sentence of imprisonment for life or imprisonment may during his conveyance from place to place, or when on board ship, aircraft, or otherwise, be subjected to such restraint as is necessary for his safe conduct and removal[1].

1 The Army Act 1950 s 172.

[0428] Communications of certain orders to prison officers Whenever an order is duly made under the Army Act 1950 setting aside or varying any sentence, order or warrant under which any person is confined in a civil or military prison, a warrant in accordance with such order shall be forwarded by the officer making the order or his staff officer or a prescribed person[1] to the officer in charge of the prison in which such person is confined[2].

1 The 'prescribed person' under the Army Act 1950 s 173: the officer making the order in pursuance of which such warrant, or his staff officer, or the commanding officer of the unit to which the person undergoing sentence belonged. Any warrant issued under the provisions of the Army Act 1950 s 173 shall be in one of the forms given in the Army Rules 1954 Appendix IV. See the Army Rules 1954 r 167.

2 The Army Act 1950 s 173. For form of warrants under this provision; see the Army Rules 1954 Appendix IV, Part II, Forms D to G.

[0429] Execution of sentence of fine When a sentence of fine is imposed by a court martial under the provisions of the Army Act 1950[1] whether the trial was held within India or not, a copy of such sentence, signed and certified by the confirming officer, or where no confirmation is required, by the officer holding the trial may be sent to any magistrate in India. Such magistrate shall cause the fine to be recovered in accordance with the provisions of the Code of Criminal Procedure 1973 or any corresponding law in force in the State of Jammu and Kashmir for the levy of fines as if it were a sentence of fine imposed by such magistrate[2].

1 Ie under the Army Act 1950 s 69.

2 The Army Act 1950 s 174. This provision should be used when the fine imposed by sentence of a court martial is not recoverable under the Army Act 1950 ss 90(f) or 91(h).

[0430] Establishment and regulation of military prisons The Central Government may set apart any building or part of a building, or any place under its control, as a military prison for the confinement of persons sentenced to imprisonment under the Army Act 1950[1].

The rules in respect of the military prisons[2] made under Army Act 1950[3] are contained in the Military Prison Rules 1962[4]. Before dispatching a prisoner to military prison, the officer commanding unit will enquire by signal from the commandant of the prison about the availability of accommodation thereat. Till the confirmation is received the prisoner will not be dispatched to the military prison[5]. The strength of the escorts will not normally exceed one non-commissioned officer and one sepoy per prisoner. When escorting more than one prisoner, the strength of the escort may be increased at the scale of one non-commissioned officer and one other rank per prisoner at the discretion of the dispatching authority. The prisoner and escort will travel on warrant[6] and ration money at usual rates will be admissible to them during the journey. Dispatch of the prisoner will be notified to the commandant of the prison by signal[7]. An escort is responsible for the safety of a prisoner entrusted to its charge. If the commanding officer considers that a prisoner is likely to escape or be violent he may order him to be handcuffed throughout the journey. Otherwise, handcuffs may be used at the discretion of the non-commissioned officer-in-charge escort, if the prisoner shows violence or attempts to escape[8]. A prisoner should be committed to the prison between 0900hrs and 1700hrs. In exceptional circumstances a prisoner may be admitted outside these hours. No prisoner will be committed on a Sunday or other public holiday[9]. A prisoner committed to the military prison will be accompanied by the appropriate warrant of commitment (the Army Rules 1954 Appendix IV, Part II Form C). The nature of the offence will be entered in the warrant and where the offence is under Army Act 1950[10], a brief statement of the offence will be attached to the Warrant of Commitment. It will be ensured that the division recommended by the confirming officer/court, as the case may be, for military prisoners while undergoing their sentences in civil jails is also mentioned in the warrant of commitment in accordance with the relevant army order[11]. Every commitment will be accompanied by a medical certificate of the state of health of the soldier. When the medical officer considers the soldier unfit for ordinary work or training he will state the grounds on which his opinion is based[12]. On a soldier's committal to the prison his character roll, medical history sheet, dental card, clothing and equipment record (IAFF 957 B) and the last ration certificate will be sent with him and on his release they will be returned to his commanding officer[13]. A prisoner at the military prison will be regarded as under special report. At the end of every three months commandant of the prison will render a report on the prisoner showing whether his conduct in the prison has been such as to merit suspension of the balance of the sentence. The report will be forwarded to the commander/general officer commanding sub area/area in which the prison is situated and will be considered by authorities competent to suspend the sentence under Army Act 1950[14]. In exceptional circumstances where a prisoner's early return to the service is considered undesirable, his commanding officer should attach to the warrant of commitment his recommendations relating to the question of suspension of the sentence. Such recommendations will be submitted to the appropriate authority by the commandant of the prison when he submits the special report[15]. Well in advance of a prisoner becoming due for release on completion of sentence or otherwise, the commandant of the prison will ask the regimental centre concerned for instructions regarding the disposal of the prisoner on release from the prison. The prisoner, on release, will be dispatched, accordingly, on a warrant. Similar action will also be taken when the sentence of a prisoner is suspended[16].

1 The Army Act 1950 s 175.

2 The military prisons constituted under the Army Act 1950 were situated at Trimulgherry and Golconda. At present military does not have any prison under the Army Act 1950.

3 The Army Act 1950 s 177.

4 Defence Service Regulations, Regulations for the Army 1987, Volume I, paragraph 496.

5 Defence Service Regulations, Regulations for the Army 1987, Volume I, paragraph 497.

6 Issued under the Travel Regulations para 379(i).

7 Defence Service Regulations, Regulations for the Army 1987, Volume I, paragraph 498.

8 Defence Service Regulations, Regulations for the Army 1987, Volume I, paragraph 499.

9 Defence Service Regulations, Regulations for the Army 1987, Volume I, paragraph 500.

10 The Army Act 1950 s 63.

11 Defence Service Regulations, Regulations for the Army 1987, Volume I, paragraph 501.

12 Defence Service Regulations, Regulations for the Army 1987, Volume I, paragraph 502.

13 Defence Service Regulations, Regulations for the Army 1987, Volume I, paragraph 503.

14 Ie under Army Act 1950 s 182(1).

15 Defence Service Regulations, Regulations for the Army 1987, Volume I, paragraph 505.

16 Defence Service Regulations, Regulations for the Army 1987, Volume I, paragraph 506.

[0431] Informality or error in the order or warrant Whenever any person is sentenced to imprisonment for life or imprisonment under the Army Act 1950, and is undergoing the sentence in any place or manner in which he might be confined under a lawful order or warrant in pursuance of the aforesaid Act, the confinement of such person shall not be deemed to be illegal only by reason of any informality or error in the order, warrant or other document, or the authority by which, such person was brought into or is confined in any such place. Any such order, warrant or document may be amended accordingly[1].

1 The Army Act 1950 s 176.

[0432] Power to make rules in respect of prisons and prisoners The Central Government may make rules providing for the following, namely:

(1) the government, management and regulation of military prisons[1];

(2) the appointment, removal and powers of inspectors, visitors, governors and officers thereof[2];

(3) the labour of prisoners undergoing confinement therein, and for enabling persons to earn, by special industry and good conduct, a remission of a portion of their sentence[3];

(4) the safe custody of prisoners and the maintenance of discipline among them and the punishment, by personal correction, restraint or otherwise, of offences committed by prisoners[4];

(5) the application to military prisons of any of the provisions of the Prisons Act 1894, relating to the duties of officers of prisons and the punishment of persons not being prisoners[5]; and

(6) the admission into any prison, at proper times and subject to proper restrictions, of persons with whom prisoners may desire to communicate, and for the consultation by prisoners under trial with their legal advisers without the presence as far as possible of any third party within hearing distance[6].

1 The Army Act 1950 s 177(a).

2 The Army Act 1950 s 177(b).

3 The Army Act 1950 s 177(c).

4 The Army Act 1950 s 177(d).

5 The Army Act 1950 s 177(e).

6 The Army Act 1950 s 177(f).

[0433] Restriction of rule-making power in regard to corporal punishment Rules made under the provisions of the Army Act 1950[1] shall not authorise corporal punishment to be inflicted for any offence, nor render the imprisonment more severe than it is under the law for the time being in force relating to civil prisons[2].

1 Ie under the Army Act 1950 s 177.

2 The Army Act 1950 s 178.

H. PARDON, REMISSION AND SUSPENSIONS

CONTENTS

PARA

[0434] Pardon and Remission When any person subject to the Army Act 1950 has been convicted by a court martial[1] of any offence, the prescribed authority[2] may:

(1) either with or without conditions which the person sentenced accepts, pardon the person or remit the whole or any part of the punishment awarded[3]; or

(2) mitigate the punishment awarded[4]; or

(3) commute such punishment for any less punishment or punishments mentioned in the Army Act 1950[5]; or

(4) either with or without conditions which the person sentenced accepts, release the person on parole[6].

Any order made under this provision should, after promulgation, be sent to the judge advocate general, army headquarters, for attachment to the court martial proceedings. The powers conferred under this provision should not be exercised by an officer holding a command inferior to that of the authority confirming the sentence unless such officer is authorised by such confirming authority or an authority superior to the confirming authority to exercise such power. Similarly, the powers conferred under this provision shall not be exercised by an officer mentioned therein if such officer holds a command inferior to that of the authority/officer who has already once taken action under this section, without reference to such latter authority/officer[7].

1 As to the definition of 'court martial'; see **[0016]**.

2 Ie the Central Government or the Chief of the Army Staff[1] or, in the case of a sentence, which he could have confirmed or which did not require confirmation, the officer commanding the army, army corps, division or independent brigade in which such person at the time of conviction was serving or the prescribed officer; The Army Act 1950 s 179. As to the meaning of 'prescribed officer'; see: the Army Rules 1954 r 204. Prescribed officer under the Army Act 1950 s 179: The prescribed officer for the purposes of the Army Act 1950 s 179 shall be (i) as regards persons undergoing sentence in a civil prison or any other place, the officer commanding the army, army corps, division, or independent brigade within the area of whose command the prisoner subject to such punishment may for the time be; (ii) as regards persons convicted on active service, the officer commanding the forces in the field.

3 The Army Act 1950 s 179(a). A sentence of dismissal might be remitted on the conditions that the person sentenced shall not receive pay in respect of or count service for any purpose during the period spent under dismissal. The conditions, if any, must be clearly stated and the written acceptance of the person obtained. A 'pardon' takes away the conviction, and when a pardon has been granted the record of the conviction must be removed from the pardoned persons' conduct sheet and will not be provable against him should he be again tried by a court martial and convicted of any offence. The remission granted under the Army Act 1950 s 179 is different from the 'remission' earned under a Jail Manual. Under the Army Act 1950 s 179(a), it is an act of grace or charity on the

part of the authorities concerned being extended in favour of a particular convict and cannot be demanded as of right, whereas the remission which are earned during the detention in the prison under Jail Manual, the convict has a vested interest which cannot be forfeited or taken away by any authority except in accordance with the provision laid down in the said Manual. *State of Himachal Pradesh v Ex Capt AK Rana* 1989 Cr LJ NOC 58.

4 The Army Act 1950 s 179(b). Mitigation cannot be made conditional. Manual of Military Law, Volume II, 2011, the Army Act 1950 s 179 notes.

5 The Army Act 1950 s 179(c). Commutation cannot be made conditional. Manual of Military Law, Volume II, 2011, the Army Act 1950 s 179 notes.

6 The Army Act 1950 s 179(d). Release on parole with conditions has, like suspension, no effect on the finding but merely suspends the execution of the sentence. Unconditional release on parole is tantamount to remission of the unexpired portion of the sentence. Parole is a part of penal and prison reform with a view to humanise the prison system and release of parole is a wing of reformative process and is expected to provide opportunity to the prisoner to transform himself to be a useful citizen. *Kashmir Singh v State of Haryana* Mil LJ 1998 P&H 188, *Indira Singh v State (Delhi Administration)* AIR 1978 SC 1091.

7 Manual of Military Law, Volume II, 2011, the Army Act 1950 s 179 notes.

[0435] Cancellation of conditional pardon, release on parole or remission If any condition on which a person has been pardoned or released on parole or a punishment has been remitted is, in the opinion of the authority which granted the pardon, release or remission, not fulfilled, such authority may cancel the pardon, release or remission and thereupon the sentence of the court shall be carried into effect as if such pardon, release or remission had not been granted[1]. A person whose sentence of imprisonment of life or imprisonment is carried into effect under the above stated provisions shall undergo only the unexpired portion[2] of his sentence[3].

1 The Army Act 1950 s 180(1).

2 As to the meaning of 'unexpired portion': This is the period of the sentence less the period the person was in custody in consequence of the sentence i.e., less the period from the effective date of sentence to date of release in consequence of the remission. Manual of Military Law, Volume II, 2011, the Army Act 1950 s 180 notes.

3 The Army Act 1950 s 180(2).

[0436] Reduction of warrant officer or non-commissioned officer When under the provisions of the Army Act 1950[1] a warrant officer[2] or a non-commissioned officer[3] is deemed to be reduced to the ranks, such reduction shall, for the purpose of the Army Act 1950[4], be treated as a punishment awarded by a sentence of a court martial[5].

1 Ie under the Army Act 1950 s 77.

2 As to the meaning of 'warrant officer'; see **[0037]**.

3 As to the meaning of 'non-commissioned officer'; see **[0026]**.

4 Ie for the purpose of the Army Act 1950 s 179.

5 The Army Act 1950 s 181. A non-commissioned officer sentenced by a court martial to imprisonment etc., is *ipso facto* reduced to the ranks, and the suspension of his sentence does not cancel or suspend the reduction. There is, however, no legal bar to a person receiving promotion or an appointment whilst under a suspended sentence. Manual of Military Law, Volume II, 2011, the Army Act 1950 s 181 notes.

[0437] Suspension of sentence of imprisonment for life or imprisonment Where a person subject to the Army Act 1950 is sentenced by a court martial to imprisonment for life or imprisonment, the competent authority or officer[1] may suspend the sentence whether or not the offender has already been committed to prison or to military custody[2]. Such authority or officer may in the case of an offender so sentenced direct that until the orders of such authority or officer have been obtained the offender shall not be committed to prison or to military custody[3]. The powers conferred by above provision[4] may be exercised in the case of any such sentence which has been confirmed, reduced or commuted[5]. The power of suspension must be exercised reasonably and expeditiously, and such action was not immune from challenge under the art 14 and 21 of the Constitution[6].

1 Ie the Central Government, the Chief of the Army Staff or any officer empowered to convene a general court martial or a summary general court martial; The Army Act 1950 s 182(1).

2 The Army Act 1950 s 182(1). The authority/officer specified under this provision may in his discretion, issue a general direction that no person under his command sentenced to imprisonment for life or imprisonment is to be committed to prison or to military custody until his orders have been obtained. Sentence of imprisonment exceeding two years will, since only a general court martial or summary general court martial can pass such a sentence, always require confirmation by an officers who will himself be one of the authorities under this provision. Manual of Military Law, Volume II, 2011, the Army Act 1950 s 182 notes.

3 The Army Act 1950 s 182 (2).

4 Ie by the Army Act 1950 s 182(1) and (2).

5 The Army Act 1950 s 182(3).

6 *Jandel Singh v Union of India* 1987 MPLJ 100 (DB).

[0438] Orders pending suspension Where the sentence referred to in the provisions of the Army Act 1950[1] is imposed by a court martial other than a summary court martial, the confirming officer may, when confirming the sentence, direct that the offender be not committed to prison or to military custody until the orders of the authority or officer specified in that provision have been obtained[2]. Where a sentence of imprisonment is imposed by a summary court martial, the officer holding the trial or the officer authorised to approve of the sentence under the Army Act 1950[3] may make such direction[4].

1 Ie in the Army Act 1950 s 182; see **[0437]**.

2 The Army Act 1950 s 183 (1). The direction under this provision may be given by the authority/officer specified in the Army Act s 182(1); or by the confirming officer in the case of any sentence awarded by a district court martial unless the confirming officer happens to be one of the authorities specified in the Army Act s 182(1).

3 Ie in the Army Act 1950 s 161 (2).

4 The Army Act 1950 s 183 (2). The direction under this provision may be given by the officer holding the trial; or the officer authorised to approve the sentence under the army Act 1950 s 161(2).

[0439] Release on suspension Where a sentence is suspended under the provisions of the Army Act 1950[1] the offender shall forthwith be released from custody[2].

1 Ie under the Army Act 1950 s 182.

2 The Army Act 1950 s 184. Suspension does not affect the finding or the continuity of the sentence but the offender is released from custody and if in service can carry his duties. Manual of Military Law, Volume II, 2011, the Army Act 1950 s 184 notes.

[0440] Computation of period of suspension Any period during which the sentence is under suspension shall be reckoned as part of the term of such sentence[1].

1 The Army Act 1950 s 185. Suspension of a sentence does not affect its continuity. Under the provisions of the Army Act 1950 s 167, a sentence of imprisonment for life or imprisonment, whether suspended or not, commences on the date on which the original proceedings of the court were signed and runs continuously until it expires. Manual of Military Law, Volume II, 2011, the Army Act 1950 s 185 notes.

[0441] Order after suspension The authority or officer specified in the Army Act 1950[1] may, at any time while a sentence is suspended, order that: the offender be committed to undergo the unexpired portion of the sentence[2]; or the sentence be remitted[3].

1 Ie in the Army Act 19501 s 182; see **[0437]**.

2 The Army Act 1950 s 186(a).

3 The Army Act 1950 s 186(b).

[0442] Reconsideration of case after suspension Where a sentence has been suspended, the case may at any time, and shall at intervals of not more than four months, be reconsidered by the authority or officer specified in the Army Act 1950[1], or by any general or other officer not below the rank of field officer duly authorised by the authority or officer specified in that provision[2]. Where on such reconsideration by the officer so authorised it appears to him that the conduct of the offender since his conviction has been such as to justify a remission of the sentence, he shall refer the matter to the authority or officer specified in the provisions of the Army Act 1950[3].

1 Ie in the Army Act 1950 s 182; see **[0437]**.

2 The Army Act 1950 s 187 (1). Failure to reconsider a suspended sentence at the proper date has no effect upon the sentence; it can be subsequently reconsidered, and a further suspension or a committal may then be ordered. Manual of Military Law, Volume II, 2011, the Army Act 1950 s 187 notes.

3 Ie under the Army Act 1950 s 182. The Army Act 1950 s 187 (2).

[0443] Fresh sentence after suspension Where an offender, while a sentence on him is suspended under the Army Act 1950, is sentenced for any other offence, then if the further sentence is:

(1) also suspended under the Army Act 1950, the two sentences shall run concurrently[1];

(2) for a period of three months or more and is not suspended under the Army Act 1950, the offender shall also be committed to prison or military custody for the unexpired portion of the previous sentence, but both sentences shall run concurrently[2]; and

(3) if the further sentence is for a period of less than three months and is not suspended under the Army Act 1950, the offender shall be so committed on that sentence only, and the previous sentence shall, subject to any order which may be passed under the Army Act 1950[3], continue to be suspended[4].

1 The Army Act 1950 s 188(a).

2 The Army Act 1950 s 188(b). Under this provision, the offender is committed to undergo the unexpired portion of the previous sentence from the date the further sentence is effective. An order by a competent military authority under the Army Act 1950 s 182(1) is not required. Committal warrants must, in order to comply with the provisions of the Prisoners Act 1900, be forwarded to the authorities of the prison to which the offender is sent. It will generally be convenient to prepare separate warrants; in preparing the warrant in respect of the former sentence care must be taken to state the unexpired portion which the offender has to undergo. Manual of Military Law,

Volume II, 2011, the Army Act 1950 s 188 notes.

3 Ie under the Army Act 1950 ss 186 or 187.

4 The Army Act 1950 ss 188(c). If dismissal has been added to the further, unsuspended sentence and no order has been passed under the Army Act 1950 s 169, that the imprisonment is to be undergone in military custody, the offender should not be committed to a civil prison until the competent authority under the Army Act 1950 s 182(1) has had an opportunity to order the unexpired portion of the former sentence into execution. Manual of Military Law, Volume II, 2011, the Army Act 1950 s 188 notes.

[0444] Scope of power of suspension The powers conferred by the Army Act 1950[1] s 182 and 186 shall be in addition to and not in derogation of the power of mitigation, remission and commutation[2].

1 Ie under the provisions of the Army Act 1950 ss 182 and 186; see respectively **[0437]** and **[0441]**.

2 The Army Act 1950 s 189.

[0445] Effect of suspension and remission or dismissal Where in addition to any other sentence the punishment of dismissal has been awarded by a court-martial, and such other sentence is suspended under the Army Act 1950[1], then, such dismissal shall not take effect until so ordered by the authority or officer specified in that provision[2]. If such other sentence is remitted under the provisions of the Army Act 1950[3], the punishment of dismissal shall also be remitted[4].

1 Ie under the Army Act 1950 s 182.

2 The Army Act 1950 s 190(1). In the case of a sentence of dismissal combined with imprisonment for life or imprisonment which is suspended the dismissal does not take effect until so ordered by the competent authority under the provisions of the Army Act 1950 s 182(1). This is so even if the sentence is subsequently ordered into execution by the competent authority or is automatically put into execution under the provisions of the Army Act 1950 s 188(b). A competent authority who orders into execution a sentence of imprisonment for life or of imprisonment other than imprisonment to be undergone in a military prison or military custody should, if dismissal has been added to such sentence, as a rule, order the dismissal to take effect when the offender is received into a civil prison. If the dismissal accompanies a sentence of imprisonment for life or imprisonment which is not suspended, it takes effect as provided in the Army Rules 1954 r 168, that is, when the sentence is one of imprisonment for life or of imprisonment which has to be undergone in a civil prison it takes effect immediately on the offender being received into such a prison and he therefore, ceases to be subject to the Act. In such a case, therefore, the dismissal must be remitted before the sentence of imprisonment for life or imprisonment can be suspended. Manual of Military Law, Volume II, 2011, the Army Act 1950 s 190 notes.

3 Ie under the Army Act 1950 s 186,

4 The Army Act 1950 s 190(2). The effect of this provision is that whenever dismissal has been added to a sentence of imprisonment for life or imprisonment and such sentence is remitted under the provisions of the Army Act 1950 s 186, the dismissal is also automatically remitted. The remission of a sentence of imprisonment for life or imprisonment under the Army Act 1950 s 179 does not operate so as to remit a sentence of dismissal, which accompanied such sentence. If a suspended sentence to which dismissal has been added runs out whilst still under suspension the dismissal should as a rule, be formally remitted under the Army Act 1950 s 179 by one of the authorities/officers empowered as this provision does not automatically remit such dismissal. Manual of Military Law, Volume II, 2011, the Army Act 1950 s 190 notes.

8. COURTS OF INQUIRY

CONTENTS

[0446] Courts of Inquiry A court of inquiry is an assembly of officers[1] or of junior commissioned officers[2] or of officers and junior commissioned officers, warrant officers[3], or non-commissioned officers[4] directed to collect evidence, and, if so required, to report with regard to any matter which may be referred to them[5]. The court may consist of a Presiding Officer, who will either be an officer or a junior commissioned officer, and one or more members. The presiding officer and members of the court may belong to any Regt or Corps of the service according to the nature of the investigation[6]. A court of inquiry may be assembled by the officer in command of any body of troops, whether belonging one or more corps[7]. The court of inquiry should normally have three members. The courts of inquiry are primarily fact finding bodies which are required to collect evidence and to make a report[8]. This is merely in the nature of a preliminary investigation, a fact finding body[9], and cannot be equated with a trial[10].

The convening officer is responsible that a court of inquiry or station board is composed of members whose experience and training best fit them to deal with the matter at issue. The personnel detailed to constitute the court of inquiry should have no personal interest or involvement, direct or indirect, in the subject matter of the investigation. When the character or military reputation of an officer is likely to be a material issue, the presiding officer of the court of inquiry wherever possible, will be senior in rank and other members at least equivalent in rank to that officer. When investigating damages to service equipment, the evidence of a technical officer who is experienced and fully conversant with the technical details of the equipment should be recorded[11]. An officer of the defence accounts department may be appointed to assist at any military court of inquiry assembled in connection with financial irregularities so that he may properly guide the investigations of the court. He may, however, not sit as a member of such a court. In the event of the officer of the defence accounts department finding himself unable to agree with the conclusions of the court, it will be open to him to record a note of dissent[12].

1 As to the definition of 'officers' see **[0029]**.

2 As to the definition of 'junior commissioned officers' see **[0023]**.

3 As to the definition of 'warrant officers' see **[0037]**.

4 As to the definition of 'non-commissioned officers' see **[0026]**.

5 The Army Rules 1954 r 177 (1).

6 The Army Rules 1954 r 177 (2).

7 The Army Rules 1954 r 177 (3).

8 *Gian Chand v Union of India* 1983 Cr LJ 1059 (Del).

9 *Major General Inder Jit Singh v Union of India* (1997) 9 SCC 1, AIR 1997 SCW 1916.

10 *Maj SC Mehra v Union of India* (1991) 2 SCC 198 : AIR 1991 SC 483 : 1991 (1) SLR 187.

11 Defence Services Regulations, Regulations for the Army 1987, Volume I, paragraph 518.

12 Defence Services Regulations, Regulations for the Army 1987, Volume I, paragraph 519.

[0447] Members of Court not to be sworn or affirmed The members of the court shall not be sworn or affirmed, but when the court is a court of inquiry on recovered prisoners of war, the members shall make the following declaration:

> I do declare upon my honour that I will duly and impartially inquire into and give my opinion as to the circumstances in which...... became a prisoner of war, according to the true spirit and meaning of the regulations of the regular army; and I do further declare, upon my honour that I will not on any account, or at any time disclose or discover my own vote or opinion or that of any particular member of the court, unless required to do so by competent authority[1].

1 The Army Rules 1954 r 178.

[0448] Procedure: Court of Inquiry

(a) The court shall be guided by the written instructions of the authority who assembled the court. The instructions shall be full and specific and shall state the general character of the information required. They shall also state whether a report is required or not[1].

(b) The officer who assembled the court shall, when the court is held on a returned prisoner of war or on a prisoner of war who is still absent, direct the court to record its opinion whether the person concerned was taken prisoner through his own willful neglect of duty, or whether he served with or under, or aided the enemy; he shall also direct the court to record its opinion in the case of a returned prisoner of war; whether he returned as soon as possible to the service and in the case of a prisoner of war still absent whether he failed to return to the service when it was possible for him to do so. The officer who assembled the court shall also record his own opinion on these points[2].

(c) Previous notice should be given of the time and place of the meeting of a court of inquiry, and of all adjournments of the court, to all persons concerned in the inquiry except a prisoner of war who is still absent[3].

(d) The count may put such questions to a witness as it thinks desirable for testing the truth or accuracy of any evidence he has given and otherwise for eliciting the truth[4].

(e) The court may be re-assembled as often as the officer who assembled the court may direct, for the purpose of examining additional witnesses, or further examining any witness, or recording further information[5].

(f) Any witness may be summoned to attend by order under the hand of the officer assembling the court. The summons shall be in the form provided in the Army Rules 1954 Appendix III[6].

(g) The whole of the proceedings of a court of inquiry shall be forwarded by the presiding officer to the officer who assembled the court[7].

1 The Army Rules 1954 r 179(1).

2 The Army Rules 1954 r 179(2).

3 The Army Rules 1954 r 179(3).

4 The Army Rules 1954 r 179(4).

5 The Army Rules 1954 r 179(5). This provision is a source of power of the officer who assembled the court to re-assemble for the purpose of examining additional witness or recording further information. The second inquiry is not bad if it is composed of different set of officers. *Lt Col Ramesh Mohan v Union of India* Mil LJ 2002 J&K 166.

6 The Army Rules 1954 r 179(5A). A witness can also be summoned to attend the court by order under the hand of the presiding officer of a court of inquiry; see the Army Act 1950 s 135(1).

7 The Army Rules 1954 r 179(6).

[0449] Court of Inquiry: Prisoners of War

(1) Whenever persons subject to the Army Act 1950 are taken prisoners by an enemy, a court of inquiry under the Army Rule 1954[1] will be assembled under local arrangements to enquire into their conduct[2].

(2) The court of inquiry will be held as soon as possible after the return of the prisoner or prisoners but when there is reason to believe that a person has been taken prisoner by his own voluntary action or wilful neglect of duty, or that he has served with or under, or has aided, the enemy, a provisional court of inquiry will be assembled at the earliest possible moment to investigate the circumstances[3].

(3) The proceedings will be forwarded by the officer who assembled the court to the general officer commanding-in-chief command, the division/area commander or the commander of the forces in the field, who will, unless full remission of the forfeiture of pay and allowances incurred by a prisoner of war has already been made, issue such orders as he may think fit regarding the remission of such forfeiture[4]. An officer does not forfeit pay and allowances while a prisoner of war[5].

(4) A remission of forfeiture of pay and allowances may be partial or full[6].

(5) A court of inquiry under the Army Rule 1954[7] on the conduct of a prisoner of war who is still absent

may be assembled as and when necessary, and in particular to assist the authority empowered to remit the forfeiture of pay and allowances incurred by such prisoner of war in deciding what remission, if any, should be made in order that provision may be made for the dependants of the prisoner of war[8]. Such remission may also be made on the written report on the prisoner's conduct by an officer who has personal knowledge of the case or has been deputed to investigate it, or on the personal knowledge, regarding such conduct, of the authority having power to make the remission[9].

(6) A court of inquiry in respect of a prisoner of war still absent and not know to have died in captivity will be provisional[10].

(7) Where an authority, who has power under Army Act 1950 and the Army Rules 1954[11], to make provision for the dependants of a prisoner of war, considers that such provision should be made but is unable to make it owing to no remission of the forfeiture of pay and allowances of the prisoner of war having been made, he will, if not himself empowered to make the remission, refer the matter to the authority who has that power[12].

1 Ie under the Army Rule 1954 r 177.

2 Defence Services Regulations, Regulations for the Army 1987, Volume I, paragraph 524 (a).

3 Defence Services Regulations, Regulations for the Army 1987, Volume I, paragraph 524(b).

4 Ie under the Army Rule 1954 r 195.

5 Defence Services Regulations, Regulations for the Army 1987, Volume I, paragraph 524 (c).

6 Defence Services Regulations, Regulations for the Army 1987, Volume I, paragraph 524 (d). See: the Army Act 1950 s 97.

7 Ie the Army Rule 1954 r 177.

8 See the Army Act 1950 s 98 and theArmy Rules 1954 r 196.

9 Defence Services Regulations, Regulations for the Army 1987, Volume I, paragraph 524(e).

10 Defence Services Regulations, Regulations for the Army 1987, Volume I, paragraph 524(f).

11 Ie under the Army Act 1950 s 98 and the Army Rule 1954 r 196.

12 Defence Services Regulations, Regulations for the Army 1987, Volume I, paragraph 524(g).

[0450] Procedure when character of a person subject to the Army Act 1950 is involved Except in the case of a prisoner of war who is still absent whenever any inquiry affects the character or military reputation of a person subject to the Army Act 1950, full opportunity must be afforded to such person of being present throughout the inquiry and of making any statement, and of giving any evidence he may wish to make or give, and of cross-examining any witness whose evidence, in his opinion, affects his character or military reputation and producing any witnesses in defence of his character or military reputation. The presiding officer of the court shall take such steps as may be necessary to ensure that any such person so affected and not previously notified receives notice of and fully understands his rights, under this provision[1].

The Army Rules 1954 is framed under the Army Act 1950 and has a statutory force and its provisions[2] are binding on the authorities as also on the person who is brought before the court of inquiry. The procedural safeguards envisaged under the rule are not only fair but just also. It ensures fairness in action and affords equality before law and equal protection of law to a person who is subject to the Army Act 1950 and who is brought before the court of inquiry. The language of the rule is certain and unambiguous, capable of only one interpretation i.e., that to afford a full opportunity in terms of this provision is the responsibility of the competent authority[3]. The expression 'full opportunity' leaves no manner of doubt that if no opportunity is afforded or if the opportunity is not full, the same would not meet the requirements of the provision. The illegality attached a court of inquiry would render even the punishment awarded as illegal[4]. The provision is mandatory[5] and gives adequate protection to the person affected even at the stage of the court of inquiry[6]. Where the basis of the punishment awarded to the delinquent is based on the findings of the court of inquiry which on account of non-compliance of Army Rules 1957 r 180 cannot be sustained[7].

1 The Army Rules 1954 r 180. Whenever it appears possible that the character or military reputation of a person subject to the Army Act 1950 may be affected as the result of the court of inquiry, the authority who assembles the court of inquiry will take all necessary steps to secure that these provisions are observed. The ultimate responsibility of ensuring that they are observed in every case will, however, rest upon the presiding officer of the court of inquiry, and should it transpire during the sitting of the court that the character or military reputation of any person subject, to Army Act 1950 is affected by the evidence put forward, the presiding officer, will immediately arrange for such person to be afforded the full facilities of the rule, adjourning the court if necessary for the purpose of securing his, attendance. The Manual of Military Law Volume II, 2011, the Army Rules 1954 r 180 notes.

2 Ie the Army Rules 1954 r 180.

3 *Lt Gen Surendra Kumar Sahni v Chief of the Army Staff* (2008) 3 SLR 39.

4 *Lt Gen SK Dahiya v Union of India* Mil LJ 2007 Del 151.

5 *RP Dwivedi v Chief of the Army Staff* MP High Court WP No 4430 of 1997.

6 *Major General Inder Jit Singh v Union of India* (1997) 9 SCC 1, AIR 1997 SCW 1916. It is fundamental facet of natural justice that in the case of quasi-judicial proceedings the authority empowered to decide a dispute between the contesting parties has to be free from bias. The test of bias is whether a reasonable intelligent man, fully appraised of all the circumstances, would feel a serious apprehension of bias; *Union of India v Sanjay Jethi* 2013 (13) SCALE.

7 *Naib Subedar Manjit Singh v Union of India*, WP (C) 6614 of 2007, Delhi High Court decided on 5 September 2008.

[0451] Evidence when to be taken on oath or affirmation Evidence in a court of inquiry shall be recorded on oath or affirmation when it is assembled: (i) on a prisoner of war[1]; (ii) to inquire into illegal absence under the provisions of the Army Act 1950[2]; or (iii) in any other case when so directed by officer assembling the court[3]. The court shall administer the oath or affirmation to witnesses as if the court were a court martial[4].

1 The Army Rules 1954 r 181(a).

2 Ie under the Army Act 1950 s 106. The Army Rules 1954 r 181(b).

3 The Army Rules 1954 r 181(c).

4 The Army Rules 1954 r 181 explanation. As to the form of oath or affirmation, see the Army Rules 1954 r 140; see **[0365]**.

[0452] Proceeding of court of inquiry not admissible in evidence The proceedings of a court of inquiry, or any confession, statement, or answer to a question, made or given at a court of inquiry, shall not be admissible in evidence against a person subject to the Army Act 1950, nor shall any evidence respecting the proceedings of the court be given against any such person except upon the trial of such person for willfully giving false evidence before that court[1]. However, nothing under this provision shall prevent the proceeding from being used by the prosecution or the defence for the purpose of cross-examining any witness[2].

1 The Army Rules 1954 r 182

2 The Army Rules 1954 r 182 proviso

[0453] Inquiry into absence without leave When any person subject to the Army Act 1950 has been absent from his duty without due authority for a period of 30 days[1], a court of inquiry[2] shall, as soon as practicable, be assembled, and such court shall, as soon as practicable, be assembled, and such court shall, on oath or affirmation administered in the prescribed manner[3] inquire respecting the absence of the person, and the deficiency, if any, in the property of the government entrusted to his care, or in any arms, ammunition, equipment, instruments, clothing or necessaries; and if satisfied of the fact of such absence without due authority or other sufficient cause, the court shall declare such absence and the period thereof, and the said deficiency[4], if any, and the commanding officer of the corps or department to which the person belongs shall enter in the court martial book[5] of the corps or department a record of the declaration[6]. If the person declared absent does not afterwards surrender or is not apprehended, he shall, for the purposes of the Army Act 1950, be deemed to be a deserter[7].

1 In calculating the period of 30 days, the day on which the person became absent and the day on which the court of inquiry assembles must both be excluded. If the court of inquiry assembles a day too soon, the record of its declaration is not admissible in evidence, as an entry has not made in the regimental books in accordance with the army Act s 142(3). The person, however, should be declared illegally absent and charged with absence as from the day on which absence commences. Manual of Military Law, Volume II, 2011, the Army Act 1950 s 106 notes.

2 The term 'court of inquiry' has been defined under the Army Rules 1954, r 177 (1); see **[0446]**. For procedure of courts of inquiry to be held under the Army Act 1950 s 106; see the Army Rules 1954 r 183; **[0454]**.

3 Evidence in the court of inquiry must be taken on oath or affirmation. As to the meaning of 'prescribed manner' see the Army Rules 1954 r 183 and 140; **[0454]** and **[0365]** respectively.

4 Before declaring any deficiency of arms, etc., the court of inquiry will satisfy itself by evidence that the absentee was in possession of the missing articles within a reasonable period before the date of absenting himself. It will record the values of the unexpired wear of all articles of government property including arms, equipment, public clothing, etc., found to be deficient. The property of government entrusted to his care i.e., government property issued to him for his use or entrusted to his care for military purposes. Manual of Military Law, Volume II, 2011, the Army Act 1950 s 106 notes.

5 Court martial book: A court martial book is a book maintained by every unit of the army containing the record of all declarations made by court of inquiry under the Army Act 1950 s 106 about the illegal absence of person subject the Army Act 1950 and belonging to that unit. The declaration of the court of inquiry contains the date and place from which the person absented himself, the date of the deficiency, if any, of arms, equipments, clothing, etc., and the place where it occurred. The commanding officer of the unit to which the person belongs is to enter the record of the declaration in the court-martial book. This record of declaration is admissible in evidence under the Army Act 1950 s 142 (4).

6 Army Act 1950 s 106 (1). The declaration of the court of inquiry should contain the date and place from which the person absented himself, the date of the deficiency (if any) of clothing, etc., and the place where it occurred. Manual of Military Law, Volume II, 2011, the Army Act 1950 s 106 notes.

7 Army Act 1950 s 106 (2). The actual proceedings of the court of inquiry are not admissible in evidence. Under the provisions of the Army Rules 1954 r 183, the court of inquiry proceedings are to be destroyed as soon as its declaration is recorded in the regimental books. The record of the finding of the court of inquiry will be admissible in evidence, notwithstanding that the person had already surrendered or been apprehended, provided that such surrender or apprehension had not come to the knowledge of his commanding officer when the court of inquiry assembled. As soon as the declaration of illegal absence has been made and recorded the person is struck off the

strength of the unit as a deserter, but he does not thereby cease to belong to the corps in which he is enrolled; see the Defence Services Regulations, Regulations for the Army 1987, Volume 1, paragraph 376. When a person, who has been 'struck off' as a deserter rejoins, the commanding officer, if satisfied that the evidence does not justify a charge of desertion, may legally deal with the case as one of absence without leave. Manual of Military Law, Volume II, 2011; the Army Act 1950 s 106 notes.

[0454] Court of inquiry as to illegal absence: declaration

(a) A court of inquiry under the Army Act 1950[1], when assembled, require the attendance of such witnesses as it thinks sufficient to prove the absence and other facts specified as matters of inquiry in that section[2].

(b) It shall take down the evidence given it in writing and at the end of the proceedings shall make a declaration of the conclusions at which it has arrived in respect of the facts it is assembled to inquire into[3].

(c) The commanding officer of the absent person shall enter in the court martial book of the corps or department a record of the declaration of the court, and the original proceedings will be destroyed[4].

(d) The court of inquiry shall examine all witnesses who may be desirous of coming forward on behalf of the absentee, and shall put such questions to them as may be desirable for testing the truth or accuracy of any evidence they have given and otherwise for eliciting the truth, and the court in making its declaration shall give due weight to the evidence of all such witnesses[5].

(e) An oath or affirmation shall be administered to the witnesses in the manner specified in the Army Rules 1954[6].

1 Ie under the Army Act 1950 s 106; see **[0453]**.

2 The Army Rules 1954 r 183(1).

3 The Army Rules 1954 r 183(2).

4 The Army Rules 1954 r 183(3). The court of inquiry declares that (number, rank, name) illegally absented himself for a period of 30 clear days, excluding the day on which the absence commenced and that on which the court of inquiry assembles. The court of inquiry in making its declaration will follow the wording as shown below. An exact reproduction of the declaration will be entered in the court martial book. It should be free from alteration or erasure. When the declaration is to be produced in evidence at a court martial, a copy will be made on IAFD-918 which is admissible under the army act 1950 s 142(4), and will be produced instead of the court martial book. IAFD-918 must be a correct extract from the court-martial book and free from alteration or erasure.

DECLARATION

The court declares that (number, rank, name and unit).........illegally absented himself without leave (or other sufficient cause) at.........(station or place) on the........., that he is still so absent, and that on the (date on which the inventory of kit was taken).........he was deficient, and that he is still deficient of the following articles (value of equipment and clothing to be stated).

..................Value Rs..........

..................Value Rs..........

Name of the Presiding Officer and Members	Presiding Officer
	Members

5 The Army Rules 1954 r 183(4).

6 Ie under the Army Rules 1954 r 181. The Army Rules 1954 r 183(5).

[0455] Right of certain persons to copies of statements and documents Any person subject to the Army Act 1950 who is tried by the court martial shall be entitled to copies of such statements and documents contained in the proceedings of a court of enquiry, as are relevant to his prosecution or defence at his trial[1]. Any person subject to the Army Act 1950 whose character or military reputation is affected by the evidence before a court of enquiry shall be entitled to copies of such statements and documents as have a bearing on his character or military reputation as aforesaid, unless the Chief of Army Staff for reasons recorded by him in writing, orders otherwise[2]. Though the Army Rule 1954[3] provide that the person who is tried by a court martial is entitled to copies of such statements and documents contained in the proceedings of a court of inquiry as are relevant to his prosecution or defence at his trial, yet there is no provision for supplying the accused with a copy of the report of court of inquiry. The court of inquiry and participation in court of inquiry is at a stage prior to the trial by court martial[4].

1 The Army Rules 1954 r 184(1).

2 The Army Rules 1954 r 184(2). This provision only allows the delinquent whose character or military reputation is affected by the evidence recorded by the court of enquiry to have copies of such statements and documents as have a bearing on his character or military reputation. It no where says that copy of opinion and findings of the court of enquiry should be supplied to the delinquent officers. *Major General Inder Jit Singh v Union of India* (1997) 9 SCC 1, AIR 1997 SCW 1916.

3 Ie the Army Rule 1954 r 184.

4 *Major General Inder Jit Singh v Union of India* (1997) 9 SCC 1, AIR 1997 SCW 1916.

[0456] Court of inquiry when rifles, etc., are lost or stolen Whenever any weapon or part of a weapon, which forms part of the equipment of a squadron, battery, company or other similar unit, and in respect of the loss or theft of which a fine may be imposed under the provisions of the Army Rules 1954[1] is lost or stolen, a court of enquiry shall be assembled, under the orders of the officer commanding the army, army corps, division or independent brigade, to investigate the circumstances under which the loss or theft occurred[2]. The officer who assembled the court shall direct it to record an opinion as to the circumstances of the loss or theft[3].

1 Ie under the Army Rules 1954 r 186.

2 The Army Rules 1954 r 185(1).

3 The Army Rules 1954 r 185(2).

[0457] Court of inquiry: Loss of secret documents Immediately the loss of a top secret, secret or confidential document or key is brought to his notice, the formation commander concerned will convene a court of inquiry, presided over by a senior officer not belonging to the unit or headquarters where the loss has occurred, and including not less than two other officers, to investigate the matter and to advise what further steps should be taken. Any individual subject to the Army Act 1950 who is implicated in any way in the loss of the document forming the subject of the court of inquiry, will be afforded full opportunity of being present throughout the inquiry, and of making any statement, and of giving any evidence he may wish to make or give, and of cross examining any witness, whose evidence in his opinion affects his character or military reputation, and of producing any witness in defence of his character or military reputation.[1] The court will sit 'in camera'. Every witness will be cautioned that any disclosure by him of any matters forming part of the proceedings of the court may be treated as an offence against the Official Secrets Act 1923. A copy of the proceedings of the court will be forwarded to the army headquarters, general staff branch, MI directorate, MI-11 through staff channels[2].

1 See the Army Rules 1954 r 180: **[0450]**.

2 Defence Services Regulations, Regulations for the Army 1987, Volume I, paragraph 525.

[0458] Collective fines may be imposed The officer commanding the army, army corps, division or independent brigade shall then record his opinion on the circumstances of the loss or theft, and may impose for each weapon or part of a weapon lost or stolen collective fines to the extent of the current official prices of such weapons or part of weapons on the junior commissioned officers, warrant officers, non-commissioned officers, and men of such unit or upon so many of them as he considers should be held responsible for the occurrence[1]. Such fine will be assessed as a percentage on the pay of the individuals on whom it falls[2].

1 The Army Rules 1954 r 186(1).

2 The Army Rules 1954 r 186(2).

[0459] Courts of Inquiry—Incidents and offences The following incidents and offences will also be investigated by courts of inquiry: (A) Assault and affrays between persons subject to the Army Act 1950 and to other services Acts (whether on duty or on leave) or with civilians[1]; (B) Breaches of discipline: (i) Collective insubordination[2]; (ii) Mechanical transport accidents resulting in death or serious injury[3]; (iii) Suicide, attempted or suspected suicide[4]; and (iv) Murder and rape, only when the offence has been committed against a person subject to the Army Act 1950, Navy Act 1957 or Air Force Act 1950, or in any of the circumstances mentioned in the Army Act 1950[5]. Courts of inquiry held on cases of suicide will record their opinion and reasons therefor, as to the motive and the condition of the mind of the deceased prior to the death wherever possible. Certified true copies or translations of all papers relevant to the case such as the private correspondence of the deceased will be attached to the courts of inquiry proceedings[6].

1 Defence Services Regulations, Regulations for the Army 1987, Volume I, paragraph 522(a).

2 Defence Services Regulations, Regulations for the Army 1987, Volume I, paragraph 522 (b)(i).

3 Defence Services Regulations, Regulations for the Army 1987, Volume I, paragraph 522 (b)(ii).

4 Defence Services Regulations, Regulations for the Army 1987, Volume I, paragraph 522 (b)(iii).

5 Ie the Army Act 1950 s 70 (a),(b) and (c). Defence Services Regulations, Regulations for the Army 1987, Volume I, paragraph 522(b)(iv).

6 Defence Services Regulations, Regulations for the Army 1987, Volume I, paragraph 50

[0460] Courts of Arbitration Courts of arbitration (panchayats) may be held in units with the consent of the parties concerned, for the settlement of private disputes. The officer commanding unit will see that the record contains the substance of the matter, the names of the arbitrators appointed by the disputants, and that of the umpire appointed by himself, and the agreement of those concerned, to abide by the decision of the majority. The award, which, in the case of pecuniary damages, shall not exceed six months' pay and allowances, will be signed by the presiding officer. The officer commanding may not set aside a permissible award because he dissents from it[1].

1 Defence Services Regulations, Regulations for the Army 1987, Volume I, paragraph 527.

[0461] Courts of Inquest

(1) Under the Criminal Procedure Code 1973[1], the responsibility for holding an inquest in cases of unnatural deaths, i.e. deaths due to suicide, violence, accident or under suspicious circumstances devolves on the

local civil authorities. Written information regarding cases of such deaths of persons subject to the Army Act 1950 or of those not subject the said Act which occurs within the unit lines will be conveyed by officer commanding unit immediately on occurrence, by hand, to the local civil police officer. Where the civil authorities are not easily accessible as for instance in operational areas and it is not practicable for them to hold an inquest before the dead body may become putrefied, a general approval for conducting military courts of inquest may be obtained in advance from the state governments concerned. The funeral or cremation will take place in such cases only after the concurrence of the presiding officer and of the medical member of the court of inquest has been obtained[2].

(2) Where a court of inquest has been held by civil authorities a court of inquiry where necessary should be held to investigate the circumstances of death and ascertain the military aspect of attributability for the purpose of pensionary benefits and allied matters[3].

(3) Where the sanction in writing has been obtained from the civil authorities to carry out the inquest under the aegis of the military authorities, a military court of inquest with comprehensive terms of reference should be held. The procedure to be followed in such cases will be as stated below[4].

(4) In operational areas, where civil authorities are not in a position to hold the post-mortem and the court of inquest, the military authorities should hold a court of inquest with medical officer as a member of the court, with comprehensive terms of reference. The court of inquest after having given permission to dispose of the dead body should further proceed to investigate the circumstances of occurrence of death, the aspect of attributability and related matters by following the procedure for a court of inquiry. In the subsequent proceedings the attendance of the medical member may not be insisted upon depending upon the circumstances of the case because of the nature of his employment[5].

(5) When post-mortem is decided to be carried out by the police authorities, they may have the dead body sent to the nearest civil surgeon or other qualified medical officer appointed in this behalf by the state government. A service pathologist should be made available if a suitable medical officer is not available with the civil authorities to carry out a post-mortem examination whether outside or inside an operational area[6].

(6) If the civil police authorities do not intend sending the dead body for a post-mortem examination and decide not to hold an inquest, the concerned military authorities will obtain a declaration in writing[7].

(7) When a military court of inquest is held, a post-mortem examination may be carried out by military medical officers in all cases where such examination is necessary. Service pathologist in such cases shall not be entitled to any remuneration as this is a part of his military duty[8].

(8) Military courts of inquest will follow the same procedure as for courts of inquiry. The convening officer will, as soon as practicable, forward a copy of the court's proceedings (only up to inquest stage) to the magistrate of the area concerned having authority to hold an inquest[9].

1 Ie the Code of Criminal Procedure 1973 s 174.

2 Defence Services Regulations, Regulations for the Army 1987, Volume I, paragraph 529 (a).

3 Defence Services Regulations, Regulations for the Army 1987, Volume I, paragraph 529 (b).

4 Defence Services Regulations, Regulations for the Army 1987, Volume I, paragraph 529(c).

5 Defence Services Regulations, Regulations for the Army 1987, Volume I, paragraph 529(d).

6 Defence Services Regulations, Regulations for the Army 1987, Volume I, paragraph 529(e).

7 Defence Services Regulations, Regulations for the Army 1987, Volume I, paragraph 529(f).

8 Defence Services Regulations, Regulations for the Army 1987, Volume I, paragraph 529(g).

9 Defence Services Regulations, Regulations for the Army 1987, Volume I, paragraph 529(h).

9. RULES

CONTENT

PARA

[0462] Generally The central government is empowered to make rules for the purpose of carrying into effect of the provisions of the Army Act 1950. The rules so made must not contain anything contrary to or inconsistent with any provision of the Army Act 1950 itself. Consequently, if any rule is found to conflict with any provision of the Army Act 1950, the Act shall prevail. The Army Rules 1954 have been made in pursuant of the Army Act 1950 s 191[1]. In regard to any matter not specifically provided for in the Army Rules 1954, it shall be lawful for the competent authority to do such thing or take such action as appears to it to be just and proper[2].

1 Manual of Military Law, Volume II, 2011, r 191 notes.

2 The Army Rules 1954 r 6.

[0463] Power to make rules The Central Government may make rules for the purpose of carrying into effect the provisions of the Army Act 1950[1]. The rules may provide for the following:

(1) the removal, retirement, release or discharge from the service of persons subject to the Army Act 1950[2];

(2) the amount and incidence of fines to be imposed under the Army Act 1950[3];

(3) the assembly and procedure of courts of inquiry, the recording of summaries of evidence and the administration of oaths or affirmations by such courts[4];

(4) the convening and constituting of courts-martial and the appointment of prosecutors at trials by courts martial[5];

(5) the adjournment, dissolution and sitting of courts martial[6];

(6) the procedure to be observed in trials by courts martial and the appearance of legal practitioners thereat[7];

(7) the confirmation, revision and annulment of, and petitions against, the findings and sentences of courts martial[8];

(8) the carrying into effect of sentences of courts martial[9];

(9) the forms of orders to be made under the provisions of the Army Act 1950 relating to courts martial, transportation and imprisonment[10];

(10) the constitution of authorities to decide for what persons, to what amounts and in what manner, provision should be made for dependants under the Army Act 1950[11], and the due carrying out of such decisions[12];

(11) the relative rank of the officers, junior commissioned officers, warrant officers, petty officers and non-commissioned officers of the regular army, navy and air force when acting together[13];

(12) any other matter directed by the Army Act 1950 to be prescribed[14].

1 The Army Act s 191 (1).

2 The Army Act s 191 (2) (a).

3 Ie under the Army Act s 89. The Army Act s 191 (2) (b).

4 The Army Act s 191 (2) (d).

5 The Army Act s 191 (2) (e).

6 The Army Act s 191 (2) (f).

7 The Army Act s 191 (2) (g).

8 The Army Act s 191 (2) (h).

9 The Army Act s 191 (2) (i).

10 The Army Act s 191 (2) (j).

11 Ie under the Army Act 1950 s 99.

12 The Army Act s 191 (2) (k).

13 The Army Act s 191 (2) (l).

14 The Army Act s 191 (2) (m).

[0464] Power to make regulations The Central Government may make regulations for all or any of the purposes of the Army Act 1950 other than those specified in the Act[1]. Under this provision[2], the Central Government is empowered to make regulations for all or any of the purposes of the Army Act 1950 other than those specified in s 191 of the Act. The Defence Services Regulations, Regulations for the Army 1987 have not been published in the official gazette[3] and on account of operation of the statute the same have not attained the force of law, and are not statutory in nature. Therefore, such regulations, in any case, cannot have overriding effect over statutory provisions. The regulations cannot supplant specific statutory provisions but are intended only to supplement existing relevant statutory provisions. It is trite that the Central Government cannot amend or supersede statutory provision by administrative instructions[4].

1 Ie specified in the Army Act s 191. The Army Act s 192. The regulations made under this provision may cover a wider field than that the limited purposes for which the Army Rules 1954 have been framed under the Army Act 1950. Manual of Military Law, Volume II, 2011, Rules 191 comments.

2 Ie the Army Act 1950 s 192.

3 Ie under the Army Act 1950 s 193A.

4 *Brig RP Singh VSM v Union of India* 14 (2004) DLT 792, 2004 (77) DRJ 480.

[0465] Publication of rules and regulations in Gazette All rules and regulations made under the Army Act 1950 shall be published in the Official Gazette and on such publication, shall have effect as if enacted in the Army Act 1950[1].

1 The Army Act s 193. The Defence Services Regulations, Regulations for the Army 1987 have not been published in the official gazette.

[0466] Rules and regulations to be laid before Parliament Every rule and every regulation made by the Central Government under the Army Act 1950 shall be laid, as soon as may be after it is made, before each House of Parliament while it is in session, for a total period of thirty days which may be comprised in one session or in two or more successive sessions. If, before the expiry of the session immediately following the session, or the successive sessions aforesaid, both Houses agree in making any modification in the rule or regulation should not be made the rule or regulation on shall thereafter have effect only in such modified form or be of no effect, as the case may be; so, however that any such modification or annulment shall be without prejudice to the validity of anything previously done under that rule or regulation[1].

1 The Army Act 1950 s 193A.

III. THE LAW RELATING TO THE AIR FORCE

1. PRELIMINARIES

CONTENTS

PARA

A. INTRODUCTION

[0467] Introduction Before India attained independence the Indian Air Force Act 1932 governed the functioning of the British Indian Air Force. The need for revision became imperative after India became independent. It was therefore decided to revise the British Act to make it self sufficient and complete code in itself. The object was to make it similar to the Army Act in form and arrangement of matter, but keep the specific provisions as per the specific requirement of the air force. Accordingly the Indian Air Force Bill 1949 was introduced in the Parliament. The Air Force Act 1950 and the Air Force Rules 1969 constitute a self-contained code specifying offences and the procedure for detention, custody and trial of the offenders by the court martial.

Though certain amendments have been made by the Parliament under the Army Act 1950 (s 169A) and the Navy Act 1957 (s 151 (3)), yet no such amendment has been incorporated in the Air Force Act 1950. The aforesaid provisions have been incorporated in both the statutes to avoid hardship to persons convicted by the court martial. Similar hardship is suffered by the persons who are sentenced to imprisonment under various provisions of the Air Force Act 1950. Keeping in view the aforesaid amendment in the Army Act 1950 and the Navy Act 1957 and regard being had to the purpose of the amendment and the totality of the circumstances, the Union of India must seriously consider to bring an amendment in the Air Force Act 1950 so that the hardships faced by the persons convicted by the court martial are avoided[1].

1 *Samrendra Beura v Union of India* 2013 AIR SCW 3080 (A) : AIR 2013 SC 2414 : AIR 2013 SC (Cri) 1415.

B. SHORT TITLE AND COMMENCEMENT

[0468] Short title and commencement This stature covering the Air Force is the Air Force Act 1950[1]. It came into force on 22 July 1950 by notification in the Official Gazette[2].

1 The Air Force Act 1950 s 1(1).

2 The Air Force Act s 1(2); Notification Number SRO 124, dated 22 July 1950, Gazette of India, Part II, Sec. 4, p. 87. The Air Force Act 1950 has been extended to Goa, Daman and Diu by Regulation 12 of 1962, s. 3 and Sch., to Dadra and Nagar Haveli (wef 1 July 1955) by Regulation 6 of 1963, s. 2 and Sch. I; to Pondicherry (wef 1 October 1963) by Regulation 7 of 1963, s. 3 and Sch. I. and to the State of Sikkim vide Notification No. SRO 25 (E), dated 20 April 1976 (wef 1 May 1976).

C. DEFINITIONS AND MEANINGS

[0469] Introduction The definitions do not take away the ordinary and natural meaning of the word and phrase. The definition determines the application of the word or phrase defined; but the definition itself must first be interpreted before it is applied. When the definition of a word gives it an extended meaning, the word is not to be interpreted by its extended meaning every time it is read, for the meaning ultimately depends on the context. Definitions are to be applied only when there is nothing repugnant in the context or subject: this is particularly so when such a qualification as 'unless the context otherwise requires' is expressly stated in the Air Force Act 1950[1]. Certain words and terms that appear in the Air Force Act and the Air Force Rules will need to be understood as they are defined in the Air Force Act 1950 and the Air Force Rules 1969.

1 Ie as expressly stated in the Air Force Act 1950 s 4. Manual on Air Force Law, volume I, Air Force Act 1950 s 4 notes.

[0470] Active service In the Air Force Act 1950, unless the context otherwise requires, 'active service', as applied to a person subject to the Air Force Act 1950, means the time during which such person is attached to, or forms part of, a force which is engaged in operations against an enemy[1]; engaged in air force operations in, or is on the line of march to, a country or place wholly or partly occupied by an enemy[2]; or attached to, or forms part of, a force which is in military occupation of any foreign country[3]. The Central Government may, by notification[4], declare that any person subject to the Air Force Act shall be deemed to be on active service within the meaning of the Air Force Act 1950[5].

1 Air Force Act 1950 s 4 (i)(a).

2 For definition of 'enemy'; see **[0488]**. Air Force Act 1950 s 4 (i)(b).

3 Air Force Act 1950 s 4 (i)(c).

4 As to issue of notification; see **[0471]**.

5 As to the provision relating to the power to declare persons on active service under the Air Force Act 1950 s 9; see **[0512]**.

[0471] Active service: Notification The Central Government has issued three notifications declaring persons subject to Air Force Act 1950 on active service : SRO 8E dated 5 December 1962[1], SRO 34 E dated 6 December 1971[2] and SRO 5E dated 17 March 1978[3].

1 SRO 8E is no longer in force.

2 SRO 34 E has been superseded.

3 According to SRO 5E, those serving in J&K , Manipur, Nagaland, Tripura, Sikkim A&N Island, Arunachal Pradesh and Mizoram are deemed to be on active service for the purpose of Air Force Act 1950. Accordingly civilians working with the air force in the areas where persons subject to the Air Force Act 1950 are to be on active service would be subject to Air Force Act 1950. See: Manual on Air Force Law, volume I, notes to Air Force Act 1950 s 4 and 9. The notification issued under this provision shall cover not only persons actually engaged in duties but also persons on leave at the relevant time. *Ajit Singh v State of Punjab* AIR 1970 P&H 351 (FB): 1970 Cr LJ 1119.

[0472] Aircraft In the Air Force Act 1950, unless the context otherwise requires, 'aircraft' includes aeroplanes, balloons, kite balloons, airships, gliders or other machines for flying[1].

1 Air Force Act 1950 s 4 (ii).

[0473] Aircraft material In the Air Force Act 1950, unless the context otherwise requires, 'aircraft material' includes any engines, fittings, guns, gear, instruments or apparatus for use in connection with aircraft, and any of its components and accessories and petrol oil, and any other substance used for providing motive power for planes[1].

1 Air Force Act 1950 s 4 (iii).

[0474] Air force In the Air Force Act 1950, unless the context otherwise requires, 'air force' means officers[1] and airmen[2] who by their commission, warrant, terms of enrolment or otherwise, are liable to render continuously for a term air force service to the Union in every part of the world or any specified part of the world, including persons belonging to any Air Force Reserve or the Auxiliary Air Force when called out on permanent service[3].

1 As to the meaning of 'officer'; see **[0494]**.

2 As to the meaning of 'airmen'; see **[0478]**.

3 Air Force Act 1950 s 4 (iv).

[0475] Air force custody In the Air Force Act 1950, unless the context otherwise requires, 'air force custody' means the arrest or confinement[1] of a person according to the usages of the service and includes military or naval custody[2].

1 Confinement would include confinement in unit guard room or detention cell while undergoing a sentence of imprisonment under the Air Force Act 1950 s 166(3) of detention awarded under the Air Force Act 1950 s 82 or by a court martial. Manual of Air Force Law, volume I, Air Force Act 1950 s 4 notes.

2 Air Force Act 1950 s 4 (v).

[0476] Air force law In the Air Force Act 1950, unless the context otherwise requires, 'air force law' means the law enacted by the Air Force Act 1950, the rules made thereunder[1] and includes the usages of the service[2].

1 Air Force Rules 1969 have been made under the authority of the Air Force Act 1950 s 189.

2 Air Force Act 1950 s 4 (vi).

[0477] Air force reward In the Air Force Act 1950, unless the context otherwise requires, 'air force reward' includes any gratuity or annuity for long service or good conduct, badge pay or pension, and any other air force pecuniary reward[1].

1 Air Force Act 1950 s 4 (vii). Medals or decoration, not being a pecuniary reward is not an air force reward. Manual of Air Force Law, volume I, Air Force Act 1950 s 4 notes.

[0478] Airman In the Air Force Act 1950, unless the context otherwise requires, 'airman' means any person subject to the Air Force Act 1950 other than an officer[1].

1 Air Force Act 1950 s 4 (viii). As to the definition of 'officer'; see **[0494]**.

[0479] Air officer In the Air Force Act 1950, unless the context otherwise requires, 'air officer' means any officer[1] of the air force above the rank of group captain[2].

1 As to the definition of 'officer'; see **[0494]**.

2 Air Force Act 1950 s 4 (ix).

[0480] Air signal In the Air Force Act 1950, unless the context otherwise requires, 'air signal' means any signal intended for the guidance of aircraft[1], whether given by flag, ground signal, light, wind indicator or in any manner whatsoever[2].

1 As to the definition of 'aircraft'; see **[0472]**.

2 Air Force Act 1950 s 4 (x).

[0481] Chief legal adviser In the Air Force Act 1950, unless the context otherwise requires, 'chief legal adviser' means a person appointed as such by the chief of the air staff[1] to give advice on matters relating to air force law and to perform such other duties of a legal character as may arise in connection therewith[2].

1 As to the definition of chief of the air staff; see **[0484]**.

2 Air Force Act 1950 s 4 (xi). In the Regulations for the Air Force and for certain official purposes the chief legal advisor is also referred as judge advocate general (Air). Manual of Air Force Law, volume I, Air Force Act 1950 s 4 notes.

[0482] Civil offence In the Air Force Act 1950, unless the context otherwise requires, 'civil offence' means an offence[1] which is triable by a criminal court[2].

1 As to the definition of 'offence'; see **[0493]**.

2 As to the definition of 'criminal court'; see **[0487]**. Air Force Act 1950 s 4 (xii).

[0483] Civil prison In the Air Force Act 1950, unless the context otherwise requires, 'civil prison' means any jail or place used for the detention of any criminal prisoner under the Prisons Act 1894 or under any other law for the time being in force[1].

1 Air Force Act 1950 s 4 (xiii).

[0484] Chief of the air staff In the Air Force Act 1950, unless the context otherwise requires, 'chief of the air staff' means the officer commanding the air force[1].

1 Air Force Act 1950 s 4 (xiv).

[0485] Commanding officer In the Air Force Act 1950, unless the context otherwise requires, 'commanding officer' used in relation to a person subject to the Air Force Act 1950, means the officer for the time being in command of the unit or detachment to which such person belongs or is attached[1].

1 Air Force Act 1950 s 4 (xv). A commanding officer may be called by other terms as commandant, president, assistant provost marshal or officer commanding. However, in all legal documents, such as charge sheets, he should be described only as commanding officer. Manual of Air Force Law, volume I, notes to Air Force Act 1950 s 4.

[0486] Court martial In the Air Force Act 1950, unless the context otherwise requires, 'court martial' means a court martial held under the Air Force Act 1950[1].

1 Air Force Act 1950 s 4 (xvi).

[0487] Criminal court In the Air Force Act 1950, unless the context otherwise requires, 'criminal court' means a court of ordinary criminal justice in any part of India[1].

1 Air Force Act 1950 s 4 (xvii).

[0488] Enemy In the Air Force Act 1950, unless the context otherwise requires, 'enemy' includes all armed mutineers, armed rebels, armed rioters, pirates and any person in arms against whom it is the duty of any person subject to air force law to act[1].

1 Air Force Act 1950 s 4 (xviii). The term 'enemy' includes an armed airman running amuck. Manual of Air Force Law, volume I, notes to Air Force Act 1950 s 4. The Regulations for the Air Force 1964, paragraph 575.

[0489] The Force In the Air Force Act 1950, unless the context otherwise requires, 'the force' means the regular army, navy and air force or any part of any one or more of them[1].

1 Air Force Act 1950 s 4 (xix).

[0490] Minor punishment The term 'minor punishment' means punishment inflicted without the intervention of the court martial under the Air Force Act 1950[1].

1 Ie under the Air Force Act 1950 s 82 or 86. Air Force Rules 1969 r 2 (c).

[0491] Non-commissioned officer In the Air Force Act 1950, unless the context otherwise requires, 'non-commissioned officer' means a person holding a non- commissioned rank or an acting non-commissioned rank in the air force, and includes any person holding a non-commissioned rank or an acting non- commissioned rank in any Air Force Reserve or the Auxiliary Air Force when subject to the Air Force Act 1950[1].

1 Air Force Act 1950 s 4 (xx).

[0492] Notification In the Air Force Act 1950, unless the context otherwise requires, 'notification' means a notification published in the Official Gazette[1].

1 Air Force Act 1950 s 4 (xxi).

[0493] Offence In the Air Force Act 1950, unless the context otherwise requires, 'offence' means any act or omission punishable under the Air Force Act 1950, and includes a civil offence, as hereinbefore defined[1].

1 Ie 'Civil Offences' as defined under Air Force Act 1950 s 4 (xii); see: **[0482]**. Air Force Act 1950 s 4 (xxii).

[0494] Officer In the Air Force Act 1950, unless the context otherwise requires, 'officer' means a person commissioned, gazetted or in pay as an officer in the air force and includes:

(1) an officer of any Air Force Reserve or the Auxiliary Air Force who is for the time being subject to the Air Force Act 1950[1];

(2) in relation to a person subject to Air Force Act 1950 when serving under such conditions as may be prescribed[2], an officer of the regular army or the navy, but does not include a junior commissioned officer[3], warrant officer[4], petty officer[5] or non-commissioned officer[6].

1 Air Force Act 1950 s 4 (xxiii)(a).

2 As to the meaning of the term 'condition prescribed' see the Air Force Rules 1969 r 158; **[0495]**.

3 As to the definition of junior commissioned officer; see **[0023]**.

4 As to the definition of warrant officer; see **[0504]**.

5 As to the definition of petty officer; see the Navy Act 1957 s 3 (17): **[0928]**.

6 As to the definition of non-commissioned officer; see **[0491]**. Air Force Act 1950 s 4 (xxiii)(b).

[0495] Conditions prescribed under the Air Force Act 1950 s 4 (xxiii) (b) For the purposes of the Air Force Act 1950 and the Air Force Rules 1969, the expression 'officer', in relation to a person subject to the aforesaid Act, includes a person gazetted, commissioned or in pay as an officer of the regular Army or the Navy, when the person subject to the Act is serving under any of the following conditions: (i) When he has been placed under the orders of such officer[1]; (ii) When he is being conveyed in or is on board a vehicle, vessel or aircraft which is being commanded by such officer[2]; (iii) When he is serving in or is a patient in a hospital or medical establishment in which such officer is on duty[3]; (iv) When he forms part of or is serving with a body of the Air Force which is acting with a body of the regular Army or the Navy, and any one of these bodies is on active service[4]; (v) When he forms part of or is serving with a body of the Air Force acting in an emergency with a body of the regular Army or the Navy and an order[5] in writing is made by the officer commanding that body of the Air Force that an emergency exists and it is necessary for the officers of the regular Army or the Navy, as the case may be, to exercise command over persons subject to the Act[6]; (vi) When he is serving in any place in which or with any body of the Air Force with which, there is present any officer of the regular Army or the Navy and the Central Government has by special order declared that it is necessary for the officers of the regular Army or the Navy to exercise command over persons subject to the Act in that place or with that body of the Air Force[7].

1 The Air Force Rules 1969 r 158 (a).

2 The Air Force Rules 1969 r 158 (b).

3 The Air Force Rules 1969 r 158 (c).

4 The Air Force Rules 1969 r 158 (d).

5 A copy of every such order shall for with be sent to the Central Government; the Air Force Rules 1969 r 158, notes.

6 The Air Force Rules 1969 r 158 (e).

7 The Air Force Rules 1969 r 158 (f).

[0496] Prescribed In the Air Force Act 1950, unless the context otherwise requires, 'prescribed' means prescribed by the rules[1] made under the Air Force Act 1950[2].

1 Air Force Rules 1969 have been made under the authority of the Air Force Act 1950 s 189.

2 Air Force Act 1950 s 4 (xxiv).

[0497] Proper air force authority The term 'proper air force authority' when used in relation to any power, duty, act or matter means such air force authority as, in pursuance of the Air Force Act 1950 or the Army Rules 1969 or the regulations for the air force or the usages of the service, exercises or performs that power or duty or is concerned with the act or matter[1].

1 Air Force Rules 1969 r 2 (d).

[0498] Provost marshal In the Air Force Act 1950, unless the context otherwise requires, 'provost marshal' means a person appointed as such under the Air Force Act 1950[1] and includes any of his deputies or assistants or any other person legally exercising authority under him or on his behalf[2].

1 Ie appointed under the Air Force Act 1950 s 108.

2 Air Force Act 1950 s 4 (xxv).

[0499] Regulations In the Air Force Act 1950, unless the context otherwise requires, 'regulation' includes a regulation made[1] under Air Force Act 1950[2].

1 Ie the Regulations for the Air Force 1964 made under the authority of the Air Force Act 1950 s 190.

2 Air Force Act 1950 s 4 (xxvi).

[0500] Schedule The term 'schedule' means a schedule appended to the Air Force Rules 1969[1].

1 The Air Force Rules 1969 r 2 (e). The forms contained in the 'Schedule' are (i) First Schedule-Forms as to enrolment, attestation etc, (A1to A5); (ii) Second Schedule- Delay Report Form; (iii) Third Schedule-Forms of Summon (C1, C2); (iv) Fourth Schedule- Forms for Summary Disposal of Charges under the Air Force Act 1950 s 86 (D1, D2); (v) Fifth Schedule-Charge Sheet; (vi) Sixth Schedule-Forms as to Court Martial (F1 to F3); and (vii) Seventh Schedule-Forms of Warrant (G1 to G14.). The Air Force Rules 1969 r 4 and Manual of Air Force Law, volume II, r 4 notes.

[0501] Superior officer In the Air Force Act 1950, unless the context otherwise requires, 'superior officer', when used in relation to a person subject to the Air Force Act 1950, includes a warrant officer and a non-commissioned officer, and as regards persons serving under such conditions as may be prescribed[1], an officer, junior commissioned officer, warrant officer, petty officer and non-commissioned officer of the regular army or the navy[2].

1 As to the meaning of 'condition prescribed' see the Air Force Rules 1969 r 159; **[0502]**.

2 Air Force Act 1950 s 4 (xxvii).

[0502] Conditions prescribed under the Air Force Act 1950 s 4 (xxvii) When a person subject to the Air Force Act 1950 has been placed under the orders of an officer, junior commissioned officer, warrant officer, petty officer or non-commissioned officer of the regular Army or the Navy, such officer, junior commissioned officer, warrant officer, petty officer or non-commissioned officer, as well as those other officers, junior commissioned officers, warrant officers, petty officers or non-commissioned officers of the regular Army or the Navy who are directly superior in command to such officer, junior commissioned officer, warrant officer, petty officer or non-commissioned officer shall for the purposes of the aforesaid Act and the Air Force Rules 1969 be superior officers in relation to such persons[1].

1 The Air Force Rules 1969 r 159.

[0503] Unit In the Air Force Act 1950, unless the context otherwise requires, 'unit' includes: (i) any body of officers and airmen for which a separate authorised establishment exists[1]; (ii) any separate body of persons subject to the Air Force Act 1950 employed on any service and not attached to a unit as aforesaid[2]; (iii) any other separate body of persons composed wholly or partly of persons subject to the Air Force Act 1950, and specified as a unit by the Central Government[3].

1 Air Force Act 1950 s 4 (xxviii) (a).

2 Air Force Act 1950 s 4 (xxviii) (b).

3 Air Force Act 1950 s 4 (xxviii) (c).

[0504] Warrant officer In the Air Force Act 1950, unless the context otherwise requires, 'warrant officer' means a person appointed, gazetted or in pay as a warrant officer of the Air Force and includes an acting warrant officer, a master warrant officer, and a warrant officer of any Air Force Reserve or the Auxiliary Air Force who is for the time being subject to the Air Force Act 1950[1].

1 Air Force Act 1950 s 4 (xxix).

[0505] Words and expressions In the Air Force Act 1950, unless the context otherwise requires, all words (except the word 'India') and expressions used herein and defined in the Indian Penal Code 1860, and not hereinbefore defined, shall be deemed to have the meanings respectively assigned to them by that Code[1].

1 Air Force Act 1950 s 4 (xxx).

D. PERSONS SUBJECT TO THE AIR FORCE ACT 1950

[0506] Persons subject to the Air Force Act The following persons shall be subject to the Air Force Act 1950 wherever they may be[1]: (i) officers and warrant officers of the Air Force[2]; (ii) persons enrolled[3] under the Air Force Act 1950[4]; (iii) persons belonging to the Regular Air Force Reserve or the Air Defence Reserve or the Auxiliary Air Force, in the circumstances specified[5] in the Reserve and Auxiliary Air Forces Act 1952[6]; and (iv) persons not otherwise subject to air force law[7], who on active service[8], in camp, on the march, or at any frontier post specified by the Central Government by notification in this behalf, are employed by, or are in the service of, or are followers of, or accompany any portion of the air force[9].

1 'Wherever they may be': The Air Force Act, being a special law has extra-territorial application in as much as a person subject to it continues to be so at all times irrespective of the place where he is serving, e.g., whether he/she is in India or elsewhere. The subjection to the Air Force Act 1950 and hence the liability to punishment under the aforesaid Act is unaffected by the place where the person is stationed or the place where the offence is committed. Manual of Air Force Law, volume I, s 2 notes.

2 The Air Force Act 1950 s 2 (a). As to the definition of 'officers', 'warrant officers' and 'air force'; see **[0494]**, **[0504]** and **[0474]** respectively.

3 'Non-combatant (Enrolled)' commonly known as NC (E), is subject to the Air Force Act 1950 under this provision. As to the procedure and mode of enrolment; see the Air Force Act 1950 s 13-15; see **[0524]** and **[0525]**.

4 The Air Force Act 1950 s 2 (b).

5 Ie as specified in the Reserve and Auxiliary Air Forces Act 1952 s 26.

6 The Air Force Act 1950 s 2 (c).

7 As to the meaning of 'air force law'; see **[0476]**.

8 As to the meaning of 'active service'; see **[0470]**.

9 The Air Force Act 1950 s 2 (d).

[0507] Termination of application of the Air Force Act 1950 Every person subject to the Air Force Act 1950[1] shall remain so subject until duly retired, discharged, released, removed, dismissed or cashiered[2] from the service[3].

1 Ie under the Air Force Act 1950 s 2 (a) to (c).

2 Cashiering can only be awarded to officers by a court martial. It is a disgraceful form of dismissal. Manual of Air Force Law, Volume I, s 3 notes.

3 The Air Force Act 1950 s 3. A person subject to the Air Force Act 1950 cannot terminate his subjection unilaterally; cessation of subjection must take place in one of the ways mentioned under this provision. There is no provision in the Air Force Act 1950 under which a person can resign. Manual of Air Force Law, Volume I, s 3 notes.

E. SPECIAL PROVISIONS FOR THE APPLICATION OF THE AIR FORCE ACT IN CERTAIN CASES

[0508] Application of the Air Force Act to certain forces under the central government

1 The Central Government may, by notification, apply, with or without modifications, all or any of the provisions of the Air Force Act 1950 to any force raised and maintained in India and suspend the operation of any other enactment for the time being applicable to the said force[1].

2 The provisions of the Air Force Act 1950 so applied shall have effect in respect of persons belonging to the said force as they have effect in respect of persons subject to the aforesaid Act holding in the Air Force the same or equivalent rank as the aforesaid persons hold for the time being in the said force[2].

3 The provisions of the Air Force Act 1950 so applied shall also have effect in respect of persons who are employed by, or are in the service of, or are followers of, or accompany any portion of the said force as

they have effect in respect of persons subject to certain provisions[3] of the aforesaid Act[4].

4 While any of the provisions of the Air Force Act 1950 apply to the said force, the Central Government may, by notification, direct by what authority any jurisdiction, powers or duties incident to the operation of these provisions shall be exercised or performed in respect of the said force[5].

1 The Air Force Act 1950 s 5 (1).

2 The Air Force Act 1950 s 5 (2).

3 Ie under the Air Force Act 1950 s 2 (d).

4 The Air Force Act 1950 s 5 (3).

5 The Air Force Act 1950 s 5 (4).

[0509] Special provisions as to rank in certain cases The Central Government may, by notification, direct that any persons or class of persons subject to the Air Force Act 1950[1], shall be so subject as officers, warrant officers or non-commissioned officers[2], and may authorise any officer to give a like direction and to cancel such direction[3]. All persons subject to the Air Force Act 1950 other than officers, warrant officers and non-commissioned officers shall, if they are not persons in respect of whom notification or direction under the aforesaid provision is in force, be deemed to be of rank inferior to that of a non-commissioned officer[4].

1 Ie under the Air Force Act 1950 s 2 (d).

2 As to the definition of 'officers', 'warrant officers' and 'non-commissioned officers'; see **[0494]**, **[0504]** and **[0491]** respectively.

3 The Air Force Act 1950 s 6 (1).

4 The Air Force Act 1950 s 6 (2).

[0510] Commanding officer of persons subject to air force law under the Air Force Act 1950 s 2 (d) Every person subject to certain provision of the Air Force Act 1950[1] shall, for the purposes of the Act, be deemed to be under the commanding officer of the unit, or detachment, if any, to which he is attached. If he is not so attached under the command of any officer who may for the time being be named as his commanding officer, he shall deemed to be under the officer commanding the force with which such person may for the time being be serving, or of any other prescribed officer[2], or, if no such officer is named or prescribed, under the command of the said officer commanding the force[3]. An officer commanding a force shall not place a person subject to certain provisions of the Air Force Act 1950[4] under the command of an officer of official rank inferior to that of such person if there is present at the place where such person is any officer of higher rank under whose command he can be placed[5].

1 Ie under the Air Force Act 1950 2 (d).

2 As to the meaning of 'prescribed officer' see the Air Force Rules 1969 r 160. Prescribed officer under the Air Force Act 1950 s 7(1): The prescribed officer for the purposes of the Air Force Act 1950 s 7(1) shall be the officers commanding a station wing, squadron or unit, nominated in this behalf by the Air or other officer commanding the command or group in which the person is for the time being serving.

3 The Air Force Act 1950 s 7 (1).

4 Ie under the Air Force Act 1950 2 (d).

5 The Air Force Act 1950 s 7 (2).

[0511] Officers exercising powers in certain cases Whenever persons subject to the Air Force Act 1950 are serving under an officer commanding any air force formation not specifically named under the provision, and being, in the opinion of the Central Government, not less than a squadron, the Government may prescribe the officer by whom the powers which, under the Air Force Act 1950, may be exercised by air officers in charge of commands, and officers commanding groups, wings and squadrons shall, as regards such persons, be exercised[1]. The Central Government may confer such powers either absolutely, or subject to such restrictions, reservations, exceptions and conditions as it may think fit[2].

1 The Air Force Act 1950 s 8 (1).

2 The Air Force Act 1950 s 8 (2).

[0512] Power to declare persons to be on active service Notwithstanding anything contained in the Air Force Act 1950[1], the Central Government may, by notification, declare that any person or class of persons subject to the Air Force Act shall, with reference to any area in which they may be serving or with reference to any provision of the Air Force Act or of any other law for the time being in force, be deemed to be on active service within the meaning of the Air Force Act 1950[2].

1 Ie as contained in the Air Force Act 1950 s 4 (i).

2 Air Force Act 1950 s 9. Also see **[0471]**.

[0513] Exercise of power vested in holder of air force appointment Any power or jurisdiction conferred on, and any act or thing to be done by, or before any person holding any air force appointment may be exercised by, or done by, or before any other person for the time being authorised in that behalf according to the usages of the service[1].

1 The Air Force Rules 1969 r 5.

[0514] Cases un-provided for In any case not provided for by the Air Force Rules 1969 such course shall be adopted as appears best calculated to justice[1].

1 The Air Force Rules 1969 r 6.

2. CONSTITUTIONAL PROVISIONS

CONTENTS

PARA

[0515] President of India The President of India is the supreme commander of the armed forces and the exercise of this command is to be regulated by law[1]. The President has to act on the advice of the Council of Ministers[2]. It is the duty of the Union to protect every state against external aggression and internal disturbance[3].

1 Constitution of India, art 53 (2): Without prejudices to the generality of the foregoing provision, the supreme command of the Defence Forces of the Union shall be vested in the President and the exercise thereof shall be regulated by law.

2 Constitution of India, art 74 (1).

3 Constitution of India, art 355.

[0516] Power of Parliament to modify fundamental rights Parliament may, by law, determine to what extent any of the rights conferred by the Part III of the Constitution shall, in their application to the members of the armed forces[1]; the members of the forces charged with the maintenance of public order[2]; persons employed in any bureau or other organization established by the State for purposes of intelligence or counter intelligence[3]; or person employed in, or in connection with the telecommunication systems set up for the purposes of any force, bureau or organization referred to above[4]; be restricted or abrogated so as to ensure the proper discharge of their duties and maintenance of discipline among them[5].

1 Constitution of India, art 33 (a).

2 Constitution of India, art 33 (b).

3 Constitution of India, art 33 (c).

4 Constitution of India, art 33 (d).

5 Constitution of India, art 33. For more details, see **[0046]**.

[0517] Power to modify certain Fundamental Rights in their application to persons subject to the Air Force Act 1950 Subject to the provisions of any law for the time being in force relating to the air force or to any branch thereof, the central government may, by notification, make rules restricting in such manner and to such extent as may be specified the right of any person subject to the Air Force Act 1950:

(1) to be a member of, or to be associated in any way with, any trade union or labour union, or any class of trade or labour unions or any society, institution or association or any class of societies, institutions or associations[1];

(2) to attend or address any meeting or to take part in any demonstration organized by any body of person for any political or other purposes[2];

(3) to communicate with the press or to publish or cause to be published any book, letter or document[3].

1 The Air Force Act 1950 s 21(a).

2 The Air Force Act 1950 s 21(b).

3 The Air Force Act 1950 s 21(c). This provision empowers the Central Government to make rules restricting certain fundamental rights contained in art 19 of the Constitution. The restrictions imposed under this provision have been further elaborated under the Air Force Rules 1969 rs 19 to 21. For more details on the subject see **[0047]**.

[0518] Membership of organisations No person subject to the Air Force Act 1950 shall, without the express sanction of the Central Government: (i) Be a member of, or associated in any way with, any society, institution, association or organisation that is not recognised as part of the armed forces of the Union or is not of a purely social, recreational, educational, or religious nature[1]. In case any question arises as to whether any society, institution, association or organisation is of a purely social, recreational, educational or religious nature, the decision of the Central Government thereon shall be final[2]. (ii) Be a member of or be associate in any way with any trade union or labour union, or any class of trade or labour unions[3].

1 The Air Force Rules 1969 r 19 (a).

2 The Air Force Rules 1969 r 19 (a) explanation.

3 The Air Force Rules 1969 r 19 (b). The provision is similar to one contained in the Army Rules 1954 r 19; see **[0048]**.

[0519] Political and other activities No person subject to the Air Force Act 1950 Act shall attend address, or take active part in, any meeting or demonstration held for party or political purposes, or belong to or join, or subscribe in aid of, any political association or movement[1]. No person subject to the Air Force Act 1950 shall issue an address to electors or in any other manner publicly announce himself or allow himself to be publicly announced as a candidate or as a prospective candidate for election or Parliament, Legislature of a State, local authority, or other public body, or act as a member of a candidate's election committee, or in any way actively prosecute a candidate's interest[2].

1 The Air Force Rules 1969 r 20 (a).

2 The Air Force Rules 1969 r 20 (b). The provision is similar to one contained in the Army Rules 1954 r 20; see **[0049]**.

[0520] Communications to press, lectures etc. No person subject to the Air Force Act 1950 shall: (i) Publish in any form whatever or communicate directly or indirectly to the press any matter on a service subject or containing any service information, or publish or cause to be published any book or letter or article or other document on such matter or containing such information, without the previous sanction of the chief of the air staff or any other officer specified by him in this behalf[1]; or (ii) Deliver a lecture or wireless address on a service subject or containing any information or views on any service subject without the previous sanction of the chief of the air staff or any other officer specified by him in this behalf[2]. For the purpose of this provision, service information and service subject mean information or subject, as the case may be, concerning the forces, the defence or the external relation of the Union[3].

1 The Air Force Rules 1969 r 21 (a).

2 The Air Force Rules 1969 r 21 (b).

3 The Air Force Rules 1969 r 21 explanation. The provision is similar to one contained in the Army Rules 1954 r 21; see **[0050]**.

3. REGULATION OF SERVICE

CONTENTS

PARA

A. Commission, Appointment and Enrolment

B. Conditions of service

C. Service Privileges

A. COMMISSION, APPOINTMENT AND ENROLMENT

[0521] Commission and appointment The President may grant, to such person as he thinks fit[1] a commission as an officer or appoint any person as a warrant officer[2] of the Air Force[3].

1 The expression 'such person as he thinks fit' will include an alien or a female. Manual of Air Force Law, volume I, s 10 notes.

2 As to the definition of 'officer' and 'warrant officer'; see **[0494]** and **[0504]**.

3 The Air Force Act 1950 s 10. The grant of commission or appointment confers a legal status on the grantee/ appointee and entitles him to the rights as well as privileges under the Constitution of India, the Air Force Act 1950 and other relevant statutes. Manual of Air Force Law, Volume I, s 10 notes.

[0522] Ineligibility of aliens for enrolment No person who is not a citizen of India shall, except with the consent of the Central Government signified in writing, be enrolled in the Air Force[1]. However, nothing contained in this provision shall bar the enrolment of the subjects of Nepal in the Air Force[2].

1 As to the definition of 'air force'; see **[0474]**. The Air Force Act 1950 s 11.

2 The Air Force Act 1950 s 11 proviso.

[0523] Ineligibility of females for enrolment or employment No female shall be eligible for enrolment or employment in the Air Force, except in such corps, department, branch or other body forming part of, or attached to any portion of, the Air Force as the Central Government may, by notification, specify in this behalf. However, nothing contained in this provision shall affect the provisions of any law for the time being in force providing for the raising and maintenance of any service auxiliary to the Air Force or any branch thereof in which females are eligible for enrolment or employment[2].

1 The Air Force Act 1950 s 12.

2 The Air Force Act 1950 s 12 proviso. This provision is similar to one contained in the Army Act 1950 s 12; see **[0053]**.

[0524] Procedure before enrolling officer Upon the appearance before the prescribed enrolling officer[1] of any person desirous of being enrolled, the enrolling officer shall read and explain to him, or cause to be read and explained to him in his presence, the conditions of the service for which he is to be enrolled; and shall put to him the questions set forth in the prescribed form of enrolment[2], and shall, after having cautioned him that if he makes a false answer to any such question he will be liable to punishment under the Air Force Act 1950, record or cause to be recorded his answer to each such question[3].

1 For 'prescribed enrolling officer'; see the Air Force rules 1969 r 7 **[0526]**.

2 For 'prescribed form of enrolment' see first schedule to the Air Force Rules 1969 (Forms A1 and A2).

3 The Air Force Act 1950 s 13. Giving wilfully false answer to a question set forth in the prescribed enrolment form is an offence under the Air Force Act 1950 s 44.

[0525] Mode of enrolment If, after complying with the provisions of the Air Force Act 1950[1], the enrolling officer is satisfied that the person desirous of being enrolled fully understands the questions put to him and consents to the conditions of service, and if such officer perceives no impediment, he shall sign and shall also cause such person to sign the enrolment paper, and such person shall thereupon be deemed to be enrolled[2].

1 Ie the Air Force Act 1950 s 13.

2 The Air Force Act 1950 s 14

[0526] Enrolling officers and form of enrolment The following officers shall be enrolment officers for the purposes of the Air Force Act 1950[1]: all recruiting officers[2]; all assistant recruiting officers[3]; and the officer commanding a unit of the air force[4]. The Form of enrolment set forth in the Air Force Rules 1969 (First Schedule) is prescribed for the purposes of the enrolment under the Air Force Act 1950[5].

1 Ie the Air Force Act 1950 s 13 and 14.

2 The Air Force Rules 1969 r 7 (1) (a).

3 The Air Force Rules 1969 r 7 (1) (b).

4 The Air Force Rules 1969 r 7 (1) (c).

5 Ie the Air Force Act 1950 s 13 and 14. The Air Force Rules 1969 r 7 (2).

[0527] Validity of enrolment Every person who has for the period of three months been in receipt of pay as a person enrolled under the Air Force Act 1950 and been borne on the rolls of any unit shall be deemed to have been duly enrolled. He shall not be entitled to claim his discharge on the ground of any irregularity or illegality in his enrolment or on any other ground whatsoever. If any person, in receipt of such pay and borne on the rolls as aforesaid, claims his discharge before the expiry of three months from his enrolment, no such irregularity or illegality or other ground shall, until he is discharged in pursuance of his claim, affect his position as an enrolled person under the Air Force Act 1950 or invalidate any proceedings, act or thing taken or done prior to his discharge[1].

1 The Air Force Act 1950 s 15. This provision is similar to one contained in the Army Act 1950 s 15; see **[0056]**.

[0528] Persons to be attested The following combatants when reported fit for the duties of their trade shall be attested[1]: persons enrolled as combatants[2]; persons selected to hold a non-commissioned or acting non-commissioned rank[3]; and other persons subject to the Air Force Act 1950 as may be prescribed by the Central Government[4].

1 The Air Force Rules 1969 r 8.

2 The Air Force Act 1950 s 16 (a).

3 The Air Force Act 1950 s 16 (b).

4 The Air Force Act 1950 s 16 (c).

[0529] Mode of attestation When a person who is to be attested is reported fit for duty, or has completed the prescribed period of probation, an oath or affirmation shall be administered to him in the prescribed form by his commanding officer in front of his unit or such portion thereof as may be present, or by any other prescribed person[1]. The form of oath or affirmation prescribed under this provision[2] shall contain a promise that the person to be attested will bear true allegiance to the Constitution of India as by law established, and that he will serve in the Air Force and go wherever he is ordered by land, sea of air, and that he will obey all commands of any officer set over him, even to the peril of his life[3]. The fact of an enrolled person having taken the oath or affirmation directed by this provision to be taken shall be entered on his enrolment paper, and authenticated by the signature of the officer administering the oath or affirmation[4]. The refusal to get attested indicates lack of allegiance to the Constitution of India and the person who refuses to get attested is liable to be released, dismissed, removed or discharged from service[5].

1 The Air Force Act 1950 s 17 (1).

2 As prescribed in the Air Force Rules 1969 r 9. See **[0530]**.

3 The Air Force Act 1950 s 17 (2).

4 The Air Force Act 1950 s 17 (3). The refusal to get attested is to be viewed seriously in view of the provisions of Air Force Act 1950 s 17.

5 *Ex LAC Ravinder Singh v Union of India*, OA No 63 of 2009, decided by the Armed Forces Tribunal, Principal Bench, New Delhi on 20 December 2010.

[0530] Oath or affirmation to be taken on attestation The oath or affirmation to be taken on attestation shall be in the following forms or in such other forms to be same purport as the attesting officer ascertains to be in accordance with the religion of the person to be attested or otherwise binding on his conscience[1]. The oath or affirmation prescribed under this provision shall, whenever practicable be administered by the commanding officer of the person to be attested or in the presence of such commanding officer by a person empowered by him to administer it in the manner described in the provisions of the Air Force Act 1950[2]. If it is not so administered, it may be administered by a magistrate, a recruiting officer or an assistant recruiting officer[3].

Form of Oath

> I..........do swear in the name of God that I will bear true faith and allegiance to the Constitution of India as by law established and that I will as in duty bound honestly and faithfully serve in the Air Force of the Union of India, and go wherever ordered by air, land or sea, and that I will observe and obey all commands of the President of the Union of India and the commands of any officer set over me even to the peril of my life.

Form of Affirmation

> I..........do solemnly affirm that I will bear true faith and allegiance to the Constitution of India as by law established and that I will as in duty bound, honestly and faithfully serve in the Air Force of the Union of India and go wherever ordered by air, land or sea, and that I will observe and obey all commands of the President of the Union of India and the commands of any officer set over me even to the peril

of my life.

1 The Air Force Rules 1969 r 9 (1).

2 Ie the Air Force Act 1950 s 17.

3 The Air Force Rules 1969 r 9 (2).

B. CONDITIONS OF SERVICE

[0531] Tenure of service under the Air Force Act Every person subject to the Air Force Act 1950 shall hold office during the pleasure of the President[1]. A person subject to the Air Force Act 1950 continues to be so subject until duly retired, discharged, released, removed, dismissed or cashiered from the service[2].

1 The Air force Act 1950 s 18. This provision merely reiterates the doctrine of pleasure envisaged under Article 310 (1) of the Constitution. The President's power to terminate the service by way of dismissal, removal or otherwise, of any person subject to the Air Force Act 1950 is unqualified and unfettered. The President's power under Article 310 can be delegated to the executive; *Major Diwan Singh v Union of India* 1973 AISLJ 173. The President's power in relation to defence services being wholly untrammelled could not possibly be subjected to an constraints other than those found in the Constitution itself; *Wg Cdr Hazara Singh v Union of India* 1976 (1) SLR 340 Del. An order under this provision need not be a speaking order; *Wg Cdr Hazara Singh v Union of India* 1982 (1) SLR 623, (1982) Lab IC 208 (Del). Also see **[0060]**.

2 The Air Force Act 1950 s 3.

[0532] Termination of service by Central Government Subject to the provisions of the Air Force Act 1950 and the rules and regulations made thereunder[1], the Central Government may dismiss, or remove from the service any person subject to the aforesaid Act[2].

1 Exercise of power under this provision is subject to the other provisions of the Air Force Act 1950, the Air Force Rules 1969 and the Regulations for the Air Force 1964, made under the Air Force Act 1950 s 189 and 190.

2 The Air Force Act 1950 s 19. The Air Force Rules 1969 r 16 and 17 lay down the procedure, which provide for reasonable safeguard against arbitrary or improper exercise of power under this provision. Both, the Air Force Rules 1969 r 16 and 17 require that the affected person be furnished with all matters adverse against him before he is called upon to show cause why action under the Air Force Act 1950 s 19 should not be taken. Failure to do so would be bad in law. Dismissal or removal under this provision is not a punishment for the purposes of the Air Force Act 1950 s 73. Manual of Air Force Law, volume I s 19 notes. Merely because the Air Force Act 1950 provides two modes for termination of service under s 18 and 19 of the Act respectively; the one harsher and the other more beneficial to the servants, the provision would not be discriminatory under art 14 of the Constitution. *Wg Cdr Hazara Singh v Union of India* (1982) 1 SLR 623, (1982) Lab IC 208 (Del).

[0533] Dismissal or removal of officers for misconduct

1 An officer may be dismissed or removed from service for misconduct by the Central Government but before doing so and subject to the following provision, he shall be given an opportunity to show cause against such action[1].

2 Where the dismissal or removal of an officer is proposed on ground of misconduct which has led to his conviction by a criminal court, or where the Central Government is satisfied that for reasons to be

recorded in writing, it is not expedient or reasonably practicable to do so, it shall not be necessary to give an opportunity to the officer of show in cause against his dismissal or removal[2].

3 Where an officer has been convicted by a criminal court and the Central Government after examining the judgment of the criminal court in his case and considering the recommendation about him of the Chief of the Air Staff, is of opinion that further retention of such officer in the service is undesirable, that Government may dismiss or remove such officer from the service[3].

4 In any case not falling under the aforesaid provision, when the Chief of the Air Staff after considering the reports on an officer's misconduct, is of opinion that the trial of the officer by a court-martial is inexpedient or impracticable but the further retention of the officer in the service is undesirable, he shall so inform the officer and subject to certain provisions of the Air Force Rules 1969[4] furnish to the officer all reports adverse to him calling upon him to submit in writing within a reasonable period to be specified, his explanation in defence and any reasons which he may wish to put forward against his dismissal or removal[5].

5 The Chief of the Air Staff may withhold from disclosure any report adverse to an officer or any portion thereof, if in his opinion its disclosure is not in the interests of the security of the State[6].

6 If no explanation is received from the officer within the specified period or if the explanation received is considered to be not satisfactory or, when so directed by the Central Government, the reports against the officer as well as his explanation if any, shall be submitted to the Central Government by the Chief of the Air Staff together with his recommendation as to the dismissal or removal of the officer from the service[7].

7 The Central Government may, after considering the reports against the officer and his defence, if any, and the recommendations of the Chief of the Air Staff, dismiss or remove the officer from service[8].

8 In this as well as the following provision[9] the Chief of the Air Staff while submitting a case to the Central Government may recommend that instead of removing an officer from service, he may be compulsorily retired or that he should be called upon to resign his commission, and the Central Government in passing orders may instead of removing an officer from service, compulsorily retire him or give the officer an option to submit his resignation, and if he refuses to do so, remove him from the service[10].

1 The Air Force Rules 1969 r 16 (1). Dismissal under the Air Force Act 1950 s 19 and this provision is not a punishment in term of the Air Force Act 1950 s 73. It merely amounts to termination of an officer's commission/service without his consent.

2 The Air Force Rules 1969 r 16 (2).

3 The Air Force Rules 1969 r 16 (3).

4 Ie the Air Force Rules 1969 r 16 (5).

5 The Air Force Rules 1969 r 16 (4).

6 The Air Force Rules 1969 r 16 (5).

7 The Air Force Rules 1969 r 16 (6).

8 The Air Force Rules 1969 r 16 (7).

9 Ie the Air Force Rules 1969 r 17.

10 The Air Force Rules 1969 r 16 (8). In case where the trial by court martial was not expedient and impracticable, the recourse to the Air Force Rules 1969 r 16 for dismissal of an officer was considered valid. The file noting showed

that there was consultation, examination and only thereafter it was decided that the officer had indulged in gross-misconduct leading to death of an individual and, therefore, in terms of the Air Force Rules 1969 r 16 the officer was dismissed from service. *Union of India v Ex Sqn Ldr R Sood*, LPA No. 545 of 1999 and CM No. 3803 of 1999, decided by the Delhi High Court on 11 January 2008.

[0534] Removal from service of officers on grounds other than misconduct

1 When the Chief of the Air Staff is satisfied that an officer is unfit to be retained in service due to inefficiency, physical disability or other ground other than misconduct, the officer shall be: (i) so informed[1]; (ii) furnished with the particulars of all matters adverse to him[2]; and (iii) called upon to submit in writing, within a reasonable period, any reasons he may wish to urge for not being removed from the service[3]. However, all or any of the aforesaid provisions (i), (ii) and (iii) shall not apply if the Central Government is satisfied that for reasons, to be recorded by it in writing, it is not expedient or reasonably practicable to comply with the provisions thereof[4]. In addition, the Chief of the Air Staff may not disclose any matter adverse to the officer, or any portion thereof, if in his opinion, its disclosure is not in the interests of the security of the State[5].

2 If no reply is received from the officer within the specified period, or the reasons submitted by him are considered not satisfactory by the Chief of the Air Staff, the matter shall be submitted to the Central Government for orders, together with the explanation of the officer, if any, and the recommendation of the Chief of the Air Staff for the removal of the officer from the service[6].

3 The Central Government may, after considering the explanation, if any, of the officer and the recommendations of the Chief of the Air Staff, and after satisfying itself that the failure, where applicable, to disclose matters adverse to the officer was in the interests of the security of the State, may remove or compulsorily retire the officer from the service[7].

1 The Air Force Rules 1969 r 17 (1) (a).

2 The Air Force Rules 1969 r 17 (1) (b).

3 The Air Force Rules 1969 r 17 (1) (c).

4 The Air Force Rules 1969 r 17 (1) proviso.

5 The Air Force Rules 1969 r 17 (1) second proviso.

6 The Air Force Rules 1969 r 17 (2).

7 The Air Force Rules 1969 r 17 (3). The Chief of the Air Staff while submitting a case to the Central Government may recommend that instead of removing an officer from service, he may be compulsorily retired or that he should be called upon to resign his commission, and the Central Government in passing orders may instead of removing an officer from service, compulsorily retire him or give the officer an option to submit his resignation, and if he refuses to do so, remove him from the service. The Air Force Rules 1969 r 16 (8). Removal from service for not passing promotion examination under this provision was held legal. *Flt Lt VK Jetly v Union of India* 1988 (2) SLJ 131.

[0535] Dismissal, removal or reduction by Chief of the Air Staff and other officers

1 The Chief of the Air Staff may dismiss or remove from the service any person subject to the Air Force Act 1950 other than an officer[1].

2 The Chief of the Air Staff may reduce to a lower grade or rank or the ranks, any warrant officer or any non-commissioned officer[2].

3 An officer having power not less than an air officer in charge of a command or equivalent commander or any prescribed officer[3] may dismiss or remove from the service any person serving under his command other than an officer or a warrant officer[4].

4 On active service[5], an officer commanding the air forces in the field may reduce to a lower rank or to the ranks any warrant officer or non-commissioned officer under his command[6].

5 The Chief of the Air Staff or an officer specified in certain provision of the Air Force Act 1950[7] may reduce to a lower class in the ranks any airman other than a warrant officer or non-commissioned officer[8].

6 The commanding officer of an acting non-commissioned officer may order him to revert to his substantive rank as a non-commissioned officer, or if he has no such substantive rank, to the ranks[9].

7 The exercise of any powers under this provision shall be subject to the other provisions contained in the Air Force Act 1950 and the rules and regulations[10] made thereunder[11].

1 The Air force Act 1950 s 20 (1). A person who has been administratively dismissed/ removed/reduced under this provision has a statutory right to submit a petition under the Air Force Act 1950 s 26 or 27, if he considered himself aggrieved by such order. Manual of Air Force Law, volume I, s 20 notes.

2 As to the definition of 'warrant officer' and 'non-commissioned officer' see **[0504]** and **[0491]**. The Air force Act 1950 s 20 (2).

3 For 'prescribed officer' under this provision; see Air Force Rules 1960 r 160A. Prescribed officer under the Air Force Act 1950 s 20 (3): The prescribed officer for the purposes the Air Force Act 1950 s 20 (3) shall be the air or other officer commanding a group and is respect of airmen serving at air headquarters or unit directly under the air headquarters, the air officer in-charge administration.

4 The Air force Act 1950 s 20 (3). Power granted under this provision is not unfettered and unguided. *NN Chakravarthy v Union of India* 1980 SLJ 545 All, 1980 Lab LJ 869; *P Sammual v Union of India* WP (C) 709, 757, 612 and 696 of 1976, High Court of Rajasthan at Jodhpur.

5 As to the definition of 'active service'; see **[0470]**.

6 The Air Force Act 1950 s 20 (4).

7 Ie the Air Force Act 1950 s 20 (3).

8 The Air force Act 1950 s 20 (5). Power granted under this provision is not unfettered and unguided. *NN Chakravarthy v Union of India* 1980 SLJ 545 All, 1980 Lab LJ 869.

9 The Air force Act 1950 s 20 (6).

10 Exercise of power under this provision is subject to the other provisions of the Air Force Act 1950, the Air Force Rules 1969 and the Regulations for the Air Force 1964, made under the Air Force Act 1950 s 189 and 190.

11 The Air force Act 1950 s 20 (7).

[0536] Dismissal or removal of a person subject to the Air Force Act 1950 other than an officer Except in a case where a person subject to the Air Force Act 1950 other than an officer is dismissed or removed from the service on the ground of conduct which had led to his conviction by a criminal court or a court martial, no such person shall be dismissed or removed under the provisions of the aforesaid Act[1] unless he has been informed of the particulars of the cause of action against him and allowed reasonable time to state in writing any reasons he may have to urge against his dismissal or removal from the service[2]. Notwithstanding anything contained in the aforesaid provision[3], if in the opinion of the officer competent to order the dismissal or removal or such person, it is not expedient or reasonably practicable to comply with the aforesaid provisions, he may, after certifying to that effect, order the dismissal or removal[4]. All cases of dismissal or removal without complying with the procedure prescribed in the aforesaid provision[5] shall, without delay, be reported to the Central Government[6].

1 Ie the Air Force Act 1950 s 20 (1) or (3).

2 The Air Force Rules 1969 r 18 (1).

3 Ie the Air Force Rules 1969 r 18 (1).

4 The Air Force Rules 1969 r 18 (2).

5 Ie under the Air Force Rules 1969 r 18 (1).

6 The Air Force Rules 1969 r 18 (3).

[0537] Retirement, release or discharge Any person subject to the Air Force Act 1950 may be retired, released or discharged from the service by such authority and in such manner as may be prescribed[1].

1 The Air force Act 1950 s 22.

[0538] Discharge not to be delayed Every person enrolled under the Air Force Act 1950 shall, as soon as he becomes entitled under the conditions of his enrolment to be discharged, be so discharged with all convenient speed[1]. However, a person shall not be so entitled to be discharged during the period during which the central Government, by a notification in this behalf, suspends the entitlement to discharge in respect either of all the persons enrolled under the Air Force Act 1950 or to any class of such persons to which he belongs[2].

1 The Air Force Rules 1969 r 10. For prescribed authorities competent to authorize discharge; see the Air Force Rules 1969 r 15 and table annexed thereto. Any power conferred by the Air Force Rules 1969 r 15 on any of the prescribed authorities competent to authorize discharge may also be exercised by any other authority superior to it.

2 The Air Force Rules 1969 r 10 proviso. As regards date from which discharge takes place; see the Air Force Rules 1969 r 12 **[0539]**.

[0539] Date from which retirement discharge, release, removal or dismissal otherwise than by sentence of a court martial takes effect The dismissal of a person subject to the Air Force Act 1950, whose dismissal otherwise than by sentence of court martial is duly authorised, or the retirement, discharge, release or removal of a person so subject, whose retirement discharge, release or removal as the case may be, is duly authorised, shall be carried out by the commanding officer of such person with all convenient speed. The competent authority may, when authorising the dismissal retirement, discharge, release or removal, specify any further date from which it shall take effect[1]. However, if no such date is specified, it shall take effect from the date on which it was duly authorised, or from the date on which the dismissed, retired, discharged, released or removed person ceased to do air force duty, whichever is later[2]. The retirement, removal, release discharge or dismissal of a person subject to the Air Force Act 1950 shall not be retrospective[3].

1 The Air Force Rules 1969 r 12 (1).

2 Air Force Rules 1969 r 12 (1) proviso.

3 The Air Force Rules 1969 r 12 (2).

[0540] Discharge or dismissal when out of India Any person enrolled under the Air Force Act 1950 who is entitled under the conditions of his enrolment to be discharged, or whose discharge is ordered by competent authority, and who, when he is so entitled or ordered to be discharged, is serving out of India, and requests to be sent to India, shall, before being discharged, be sent to India with all convenient speed[1]. Any person enrolled under the Air Force Act who is dismissed from the service and who, when he is so dismissed, is serving out of India, shall be sent to India with all convenient speed[2]. Where any such person as is mentioned in the aforesaid provision is sentenced to dismissal combined with any other punishment, such other punishment, or, in the case of a sentence of transportation, imprisonment or detention, a portion of such sentence, may be inflicted before he is sent to India[3]. For the purposes of this provision, the word 'discharge' shall include release, and the word 'dismissal' shall include removal[4].

1 The Air Force Act 1950 s 24 (1).

2 The Air Force Act 1950 s 24 (2).

3 The Air Force Act 1950 s 24 (3).

4 The Air Force Act 1950 s 24 (3).

[0541] Release A person subject to the Air Force Act 1950 may be released from the air force in accordance with the provisions of the Air Force Rules 1969, or in accordance with any orders or instructions made in that behalf by or under the authority of the Central Government[1].

1 The Air Force Rules 1969 r 13.

[0542] Retirement Subject to the other provisions of the Air Force Rules 1969, a person subject to the Air Force Act 1950 may be retired in accordance with the terms and conditions of his service by or under the authority of the Central Government[1].

1 The Air Force Rules 1969 r 14.

[0543] Certificate on termination of service Every warrant officer, or enrolled person who is dismissed, removed, discharged, retired or released from the service shall be furnished by his commanding officer with a certificate[1], in the language which is the mother tongue of such person and also in the English language setting forth: (i) the authority terminating his service[2]; (ii) the cause for such termination[3]; and (iii) the full period of his service in the Air Force[4].

1 Called discharge certificate; see **[0544]**.

2 The Air force Act 1950 s 23 (a)

3 The Air force Act 1950 s 23 (b).

4 The Air force Act 1950 s 23 (c).

[0544] Discharge certificate A certificate furnished in accordance with the provisions of the Air Force Act 1950[1], is called 'discharge certificate'. All airmen who are discharged or dismissed will be given a discharge certificate IAFF (P) 53[2]. A discharge certificate may be so furnished either by personal delivery thereof by or on behalf of the commanding officer of the person dismissed, removed, discharged, retired or released or by its transmission by registered post to such person[3].

1 Ie the Air Force Act 1950 s 23.

2 Regulations for the Air Force 1964, paragraph 353.

3 The Air Force Rules 1969 r 11.

C. SERVICE PRIVILEGES

[0545] Authorised deductions only to be made from pay The pay of every person subject to the Air force Act 1950 due to him as such under any regulation, for the time being in force, shall be paid without any deduction other than the deductions authorised by or under the Air force Act 1950 or any other Act[1].

1 The Air force Act 1950 s 25. The provision is similar to as contained in the Army Act 1950 s 25, for more details see: **[0076]**.

[0546] Remedy of aggrieved airmen Any airman who deems himself wronged by any superior or other officer[1] may complain to the officer under whose command or orders he is serving[2]. When the officer complained against is the officer to whom the complaint should be preferred, the aggrieved airman may complain to such officer' s next superior officer, and if he thinks himself wronged by such superior officer, he may complain to the Chief of the Air Staff[3]. Every officer receiving such complaint shall make as complete an investigation into it as may be possible for giving full redress to the complainant; or, when necessary, refer the complaint to superior authority[4]. Every such complaint shall be preferred in such manner as may from time to time be specified by the proper authority[5]. The Central Government may revise any decision by the Chief of the Air Staff made under certain provision of the Air Force Act 1950[6], but subject thereto, the decision of the Chief of the Air Staff shall be final[7].

1 As to the definition of 'airman', 'officer' and 'superior officer' see **[0478]**, **[0494]** and **[0501]**.

2 The Air force Act 1950 s 26 (1).

3 The Air force Act 1950 s 26 (2).

4 The Air force Act 1950 s 26 (3).

5 The Air force Act 1950 s 26 (4)

6 Ie under the Air force Act 1950 s 26 (2).

7 The Air force Act 1950 s 26 (5). The provision is similar to as contained in the Army Act 1950 s 26; see **[0077]**.

[0547] Procedure: Remedy for aggrieved airmen

1 Every complaint made under the Air Force Act 1950 s 26 must show that a service wrong has been done to the complaint in that he has been deprived of a service right or privilege. An airman may make a complaint on matters not arising from the service, but such complaints will not be deemed to have been made under this provision. Joint, collective, or anonymous petitions of any kind are forbidden. Collective petitions or representations include separate petitions or representations prepared by separate airmen in consultation with each other.

2 Any application for redress, be it for service wrong or on personal matters affecting morale and welfare, must in the first instance, be addressed by an airman to his commanding officer and be submitted through proper channels as mentioned in the succeeding provisions. The practice of bypassing the normal service channels and making direct representations to higher authorities except as provided in these provisions is prohibited. Airmen will render themselves liable to severe disciplinary/administrative action for any violation of these provisions. No notice will be taken of a representation on service matters submitted by relatives of airmen.

3 An airman's application for redress of grievance will be submitted through proper channels as given below and, except as provided in certain provisions of the Air Force Act 1950[1], will always be submitted to his section commander in the first instance. Advance copies of the application will not be sent to any higher authority. The application shall be submitted to section commander, and then forwarded to the unit or detachment commander; station commander; group headquarters, where applicable; command headquarters; and then to the air headquarters.

4 On receipt of the application, the section commander will investigate the case, and if possible, redress the grievance of the airman. If however, he is unable to do so, the application together with a report from him on the points raised in the application will be forwarded to the unit or detachment commander, and the airman concerned informed of the fact in writing. The application will continue to be forwarded to the next higher authority in the chain mentioned in stated in the aforesaid provision in a similar manner, until such time as the grievance of the airman is redressed or a final decision on the case is given by air headquarters.

5 It is of utmost importance that application for redress of grievances by airmen are dealt with expeditiously so as to reach the authority competent to redress the grievance not later than four days from its date of submission by the aggrieved person. No intermediate authority will hold up the application for more than 10 days. In the event of any longer delay a report indicating the reasons will be made to the next higher authority.

6 If an aggrieved airman feels that his application has not received due consideration in a reasonable period of time, he may seek an interview with the station commander or with an inspecting officer, i.e., the chief of the air staff or the air officer commanding-in-chief. When it is desired to seek an interview with an inspecting officer, the following action will be taken: (i) The airman will make a request to his commanding officer through his section commander for such an interview; (ii) If the time permits, full details of the case will be forwarded to the inspecting officer in advance; (iii) If, however, the notice for the inspection is short, the commanding officer will apprise the inspecting officer of the facts of the case before interview. It is entirely at the discretion of the inspecting officer to grant or refuse the interview.

7 Any method other than those specified in the aforesaid provisions for seeking a remedy of grievance by airman, is not possible[2].

8 A person can complain only once under this provisions in respect of any such matter. Repetitive complaint may be summarily rejected unless the applicant has brought out new facts, occurring subsequently or which come to the knowledge of the complainant subsequently. Rejection of a complaint under the Air Force Act 1950 s 26 need not be by a speaking order, and the applicant has no right to demand that a speaking order should be issued in the event of rejection of the application[3].

1 The Air Force Act 1950 s 26 (2). Complaints or applications for redress of grievances may be addressed direct to next higher authorities only when the commanding officer or next higher authority refuses to give legitimate redress asked for or unnecessarily delays the forwarding of the complaints to higher authorities. Under such circumstances the complainant will inform the intermediate authority of his action.

2 Regulations for the Air Force 1964, paragraph 621. A false accusation or false statement made in preferring a complaint under the Air Force Act 1950 s 26 is punishable under the aforesaid Act s 56 (b).

3 Manual of Air Force Law, Volume I, s 26 and 27 notes. Non-furnishing of comments of the intermediate

authorities to the complainant who lodged the statutory complaint is tantamount to violation of the principles of natural justice. *Union of India v Maj Gen Arun Roye* 2008 CWN 528, the Calcutta High Court further opined: "This is because the comments that are furnished by the intermediate authorities to the Central Government are essential to the complainant, so as to enable that person to know what has been commented against him/her by the said military authority while forwarding the complaint to the Government".

[0548] Remedy of aggrieved officers Any officer who deems himself wronged by his commanding officer or any superior officer[1] and who on due application made to his commanding officer does not receive the redress to which he considers himself entitled, may complain to the Central Government in such manner as may from time to time be specified by the proper authority[2].

1 As to the definition of 'officer', 'commanding officer' and 'superior officer' see **[0494]**, **[0485]** and **[0501]**.

2 The Air force Act 1950 s 27. The provision is similar to as contained in the Army Act 1950 s 27; for more details see **[0478] and [0479]**.

[0549] Procedure: Remedy for aggrieved officers

1 Complaints made by the officer under the provisions of the Air Force Act 1950[1] must show that a service wrong has been done to the complainant in that he has been deprived of a service right or privilege. An officer may make a complaint on matters not arising from the service, but such complaints will not be deemed to have been made under the aforesaid provisions of the Air Force Act 1950. In applications for redress of grievances criticism of superiors should be scrupulously avoided[2].

2 Joint or collective or anonymous petitions of any kind are forbidden. Collective petitions or representations include separate petitions or representations prepared by separate officers in combination with each other.

3 An officer's application for redress be it for service wrongs or on personal matters affecting morale and welfare, must in the first instance be submitted by a service officer to his commanding officer. The practice of bypassing the normal service channels and making direct representations to higher authorities, except as provided in the following provisions are prohibited. Officers will render themselves liable to severe disciplinary or administrative action for any violation of these provisions. Further, no notice will be taken of a representation on service matters submitted by relatives of officers.

4 An officer's application, except as stated in the succeeding provisions, is to be addressed to his commanding officer and copies of the application are not to be forwarded to higher authorities. On receipt of the application, the commanding officer will investigate the case, and if possible, redress the grievance of the officer locally. In case the commanding officer redresses the grievance, he will inform the applicant and obtain from him in writing a statement to the effect that his grievance has been redressed. If however, the commanding officer is not in a position to redress the grievance locally, the application together with a report from the commanding officer will be forwarded to the next higher formation in the chain of command, and the officer concerned informed of this fact in writing.

5 On receipt of the application, higher formation will take similar action as mentioned in the aforesaid provisions and the application will continue to be forwarded to higher authority until it reaches air headquarters, unless the grievance is redressed. The applicant is to be informed of the fact that his application has been forwarded to the next higher authority. After due consideration at air headquarters,

the officer will be informed through the normal channels about the action taken on his grievance. If the officer is not satisfied with the redress granted by air headquarters, his application will be forwarded to the Central Government for a decision.

6 Complaints/ applications for redress of grievance may be addressed to next higher authorities only when the commanding officer or the intermediate authority refuses to give a legitimate redress asked for or unnecessarily delays forwarding of the complaints to higher authorities. Under such circumstances, the complaint will inform the intermediate authority of his action.

7 If an aggrieved officer feels that his application has not received due consideration in a reasonable period of time, he may seek an interview with an inspecting officer, i.e., the chief of Air staff, air officer commanding-in-chief or air officer commanding as the case may be. When it is desired to seek an interview with the inspecting officer, the following action will be taken: (i) The officer will make a request to his commanding officer in writing for such an interview; (ii) If the time permits, full details of the case will be forwarded to the inspecting officer in advance; and (iii) If, however, the notice for the inspection is short, the commanding officer will apprise the inspecting officer of the facts of the case before interview. It is entirely at the discretion of the inspecting officer to grant or refuse an interview.

8 It is of utmost importance that applications for redress of grievance by officers are dealt with expeditiously so as to reach the authority competent to redress the grievance not later than 45 days from its date of submission by the aggrieved person. No intermediate authority will hold up the application for more than 10 days. In the event of such a delay a report indicating the reasons for the delay will be made to the next higher authority.

9 Any method other than those specified in this rule for seeking a remedy of grievances by officers is not permissible[3].

10 A person can complain only once under this provisions in respect of any such matter. Repetitive complaint may be summarily rejected unless the applicant has brought out new facts, occurring subsequently or which come to the knowledge of the complainant subsequently. Rejection of a complaint under the Air Force Act 1950 s 27 need not be by a speaking order, and the applicant has no right to demand that a speaking order should be issued in the event of rejection of the application[4].

1 Ie under the Air Force Act 1950 s 27.

2 Remarks or criticisms of superiors: Except as specifically permitted by the Regulations for the Air Force 1964, no officer or other person shall make remarks or pass criticisms on the orders or conduct of his superiors which may tend to bring them into contempt; and no officer shall say or do anything which, if heard or seen by or reported to those under him, might discourage them or render them dissatisfied with their condition or with the service on which they are or may be employed. Regulations for the Air Force 1964, paragraph 569.

3 Regulations for the Air Force 1964, paragraph 60. A false accusation or false statement made in preferring a complaint under the Air Force Act 1950 s 27 is punishable under the aforesaid Act s 56 (b).

4 Manual of Air Force Law, volume I, s 26 and 27 notes. Non-furnishing of comments of the intermediate authorities to the complainant who lodged the statutory complaint is tantamount to violation of the principles of natural justice. In *Union of India v Maj Gen Arun Roye* 2008 CWN 528, the Calcutta High Court further opined: "This is because the comments that are furnished by the intermediate authorities to the Central Government are essential to the complainant, so as to enable that person to know what has been commented against him/her by the said military authority while forwarding the complaint to the Government."

[0550] Immunity from attachment The arms, clothes, equipment, accoutrements or necessaries of a person subject to the Air Force Act 1950 shall not be seized, and the pay and allowances of such person shall not be attached, by direction of any civil or revenue court or any revenue officer, in satisfaction of any decree or order enforceable against him[1].

1 The Air force Act 1950 s 28.The term 'civil or revenue court' in this provision do not include a criminal court. The provision is similar to as contained in the Army Act 1950 s 28, for more details; see **[0080]**.

[0551] Immunity from arrest for debt No person subject to the Air force Act 1950 shall, so long as he belongs to the Forces, be liable to be arrested for debt under any process issued by, or by the authority of, any civil or revenue court or revenue officer[1]. The judge of any such court or the said officer may examine into any complaint made by such person or his superior officer of the arrest of such person contrary to the provisions of this section, and may, by warrant under his hand, discharge the person, and award reasonable costs to the complainant, who may recover those costs in like manner as he might have recovered costs awarded to him by a decree against the person obtaining the process[2]. For the recovery of such costs no court fee shall be payable by the complainant[3]. There is no privilege from arrest on any criminal process except as provided in the Criminal Procedure Code 1973[4].

1 The Air force Act 1950 s 29 (1).

2 The Air force Act 1950 s 29 (2)

3 The Air force Act 1950 s 29 (3). The provision is similar to as contained in the Army Act 1950 s 29; see **[0081]**.

4 Ie as under the Code Criminal Procedure 1973 ss 45 and 475.

[0552] Immunity of persons attending courts martial from arrest No presiding officer or member of a court martial[1], no judge advocate, no party to any proceeding before a court martial, or his legal practitioner or agent, and no witness acting in obedience to a summons to attend a court martial shall, while proceeding to, attending, or returning from, a court martial, be liable to arrest under civil or revenue process[2]. If any such person is arrested under any such process, he may be discharged by order of the court martial[3].

1 As to the definition of 'court martial' see **[0486]**.

2 The Air force Act 1950 s 30 (1).

3 The Air force Act 1950 s 30 (2). The provision is similar to as contained in the Army Act 1950 s 3; see **[0082]**.

[0553] Privileges of reservists Every person belonging to any Air Force Reserve or the Auxiliary Air Force shall, when called out for, or engaged in, or returning from, training or service, be entitled to all the privileges accorded under the the Air Force Act 1950[1] to a person subject to the aforesaid Act[2].

1 Ie the Air Force Act 1950 s 28 and 29.

2 The Air force Act 1950 s 31.

[0554] Priority in respect of Air Force personnel's litigation

1 On the presentation any court by or on behalf of any person subject to the Air Force Act 1950 of a certificate, from the proper air force authority[1], of leave of absence having been granted to or applied for by him for the purpose of prosecuting or defending any suit or other proceeding in such court, the court shall, on the application of such person, arrange, so far as may be possible, for the hearing and

final disposal of such suit or other proceeding within the period of the leave so granted or applied for[2].

2 The certificate from the proper air force authority shall state the first and last day of the leave or intended leave, and set forth a description of the case with respect to which the leave was granted or applied for[3].

3 No fee shall be payable to the court in respect of the presentation of any such certificate, or of any application by or on behalf of any such person, for priority for the hearing of his case[4].

4 Where the court is unable to arrange for the hearing and final disposal of the suit or proceeding within the period of such leave or intended leave, it shall record its reasons for its inability to do so, and shall cause a copy to be furnished to such person on his application without any payment[5].

5 If in any case a question arises as to the proper air force authority qualified to grant such certificate as aforesaid, such question shall be at once referred by the court to an officer having power not less than a group commander or equivalent commander whose decision shall be final[6].

1 As to the definition of 'proper air force authority'; see **[0497]**.

2 The Air force Act 1950 s 32 (1)

3 The Air force Act 1950 s 32 (2).

4 The Air force Act 1950 s 32 (3).

5 The Air force Act 1950 s 32 (4).

6 The Air force Act 1950 s 32 (5). The provision is similar to as contained in the Army Act 1950 s 32, for more details; see **[0084]**.

[0555] Saving of rights and privileges under other laws The rights and privileges specified in the Air force Act 1950 s 25-32 shall be in addition to any others conferred on persons subject to the Air force Act 1950 or on members of the regular Army, Navy and Air Force generally by any other law for the time being in force[2].

1 Ie in the Air force Act 1950 s 25-32.

2 The Air force Act 1950 s 33. The provision is similar to one contained in the Army Act 1950 s 33; see **[0085]**.

4. OFFENCES

CONTENTS

PARA

[0556] Offence in relation to the enemy[1] and punishable with death Any person subject to the Air Force Act 1950[2] who commits any of the following offences, that is to say:

(1) shamefully abandons or delivers up any garrison, fortress, post, place or guard, committed to his charge, or which it is his duty to defend, or uses any means to compel or induce any commanding officer or other person to commit the said act[3];

(2) intentionally uses any means to compel or induce any person subject to military, naval or air force law to abstain from acting against the enemy, or to discourage such person from acting against the enemy[4];

(3) in the presence of the enemy, shamefully casts away his arms, ammunition, tools or equipment or misbehaves in such manner as to show cowardice[5];

(4) treacherously holds correspondence with, or communicates intelligence to, the enemy or any person in arms against the Union[6];

(5) directly or indirectly assists the enemy with money, arms, ammunition, stores or supplies[7];

(6) treacherously or through cowardice sends a flag of truce to the enemy[8];

(7) in time of war or during any air force operation, intentionally occasions a false alarm in action, camp or quarters or spreads reports calculated to create alarm or despondency[9];

(8) in time of action leaves his commanding officer or his post, guard, piquet, patrol or party without being regularly relieved or without leave[10];

(9) having been made a prisoner of war, voluntarily serves with or aids the enemy[11];

(10) knowingly harbours or protects an enemy not being a prisoner[12];

(11) being a sentry in time of war or alarm, sleeps upon his post or is intoxicated[13];

(12) knowingly does any act calculated to imperil the success of the military, naval or air forces of India or any forces cooperating therewith or any part of such forces[14];

(13) treacherously or shamefully causes the capture or destruction by the enemy of any aircraft belonging to the Forces[15];

(14) treacherously uses any false air signal[16] or alters or interferes with any air signal[17]; or

(15) when ordered by his superior officer or otherwise under orders to carry out any air force operations, treacherously or shamefully fails to use his utmost exertions to carry such orders into effect[18];

shall, on conviction by court martial, be liable to suffer death or such less punishment as mentioned in the Air Force Act 1950[19].

1 As to the definition of 'enemy'; see **[0488]**.

2 As to the meaning of 'person subject to Air Force Act 1950'; see **[0506]**.

3 The Air Force Act 1950 s 34 (a).

4 The Air Force Act 1950 s 34 (b).

5 The Air Force Act 1950 s 34 (c).

6 The Air Force Act 1950 s 34 (d).

7 The Air Force Act 1950 s 34 (e).

8 The Air Force Act 1950 s 34 (f).

9 The Air Force Act 1950 s 34 (g).

10 The Air Force Act 1950 s 34 (h).

11 The Air Force Act 1950 s 34 (i).

12 The Air Force Act 1950 s 34 (j).

13 The Air Force Act 1950 s 34 (k).

14 The Air Force Act 1950 s 34 (l).

15 The Air Force Act 1950 s 34 (m).

16 As to the meaning of 'air signal'; see **[0480]**.

17 The Air Force Act 1950 s 34 (n).

18 The Air Force Act 1950 s 34 (o).

19 Ie as mentioned in the Air Force Act 1950 s 73. The Air Force Act 1950 s 34.

[0557] Offences in relation to the enemy and not punishable with death Any person subject to the Air Force Act 1950 who commits any of the following offences, that is to say:

(1) is taken prisoner, by want of due precaution, or through disobedience of orders, or wilful neglect of duty, or having been taken prisoner, fails to rejoin his service when able to do so[1];

(2) without due authority holds correspondence with or communicates intelligence to the enemy; or having come by the knowledge of any such correspondence or communication wilfully omits to discover it immediately to his commanding or other superior officer[2];

(3) without due authority sends a flag of truce to the enemy[3];

(4) negligently causes the capture or destruction by the enemy of any aircraft belonging to the Government[4]; or

(5) when ordered by his superior officer, or otherwise under orders to carry out any warlike operations in the air, negligently or through other default fails to use his utmost exertions to carry such orders into effect[5];

shall, on conviction by court martial, be liable to suffer imprisonment for a term which may extend to fourteen years or such less punishment as mentioned in the Air Force Act 1950[6].

1 The Air Force Act 1950 s 35 (a).

2 The Air Force Act 1950 s 35 (b).

3 The Air Force Act 1950 s 35 (c).

4 The Air Force Act 1950 s 35 (d).

5 The Air Force Act 1950 s 35 (e).

6 Ie as mentioned in the Air Force Act 1950 s 73. The Air Force Act 1950 s 35.

[0558] Offences punishable more severely on active service[1] than at other times Any person subject to the Air Force Act 1950 who commits any of the following offences, that is to say:

(1) forces a safeguard, or forces or uses criminal force to a sentry[2];

(2) breaks into any house or other place in search of plunder[3];

(3) being a sentry sleeps upon his post, or is intoxicated[4];

(4) without orders from his superior officer[5] leaves his guard, piquet, patrol or post[6];

(5) intentionally or through neglect occasions a false alarm in camp or quarters; or spreads reports calculated to create unnecessary alarm or despondency[7];

(6) makes known the parole, watchword or countersign to any person not entitled to receive it; or knowingly gives a parole, watchword or countersign different from what he received[8]; or

(7) without due authority alters or interferes with any air signal[9];

shall, on conviction by court martial,

if he commits any such offence when on active service, be liable to suffer imprisonment for a term which may extend to 14 years or such less punishment as mentioned in the Air Force Act 1950[10]; and

if he commits any such offence when not on active service, be liable to suffer imprisonment for a term which may extend to seven years or such less punishment as mentioned in the Air Force Act 1950[11].

1 As to the meaning of 'active service'; see: **[0470]**.

2 The Air Force Act 1950 s 36 (a).

3 The Air Force Act 1950 s 36 (b).

4 The Air Force Act 1950 s 36 (c).

5 As to the definition of 'superior officer'; see: **[0501]**.

6 The Air Force Act 1950 s 36 (d).

7 The Air Force Act 1950 s 36 (e).

8 The Air Force Act 1950 s 36 (f).

9 The Air Force Act 1950 s 36 (g).

10 Ie as mentioned in the Air Force Act 1950 s 73.

11 Ie as mentioned in the Air Force Act 1950 s 73. The Air Force Act 1950 s 36.

[0559] Mutiny Any person subject to the Air Force Act 1950 who commits any of the following offences, that is to say:

(1) begins, incites, causes, or conspires with any other persons to cause, any mutiny in the military, naval or air forces of India or any forces cooperating therewith[1];

(2) joins in any such mutiny[2];

(3) being present at any such mutiny, does not use his utmost endeavours to suppress the same[3];

(4) knowing or having reason to believe in the existence of any such mutiny, or of any intention to commit such mutiny or any such conspiracy, does not, without delay, give information thereof to his commanding[4] or other superior officer[5]; or

(5) endeavours to seduce any person in the military, naval or air forces of India from his duty or allegiance to the Union[6];

shall, on conviction by court martial, be liable to suffer death or such less punishment as mentioned in the Air Force Act 1950[7].

1 The Air Force Act 1950 s 37 (a).

2 The Air Force Act 1950 s 37 (b).

3 The Air Force Act 1950 s 37 (c).

4 As to the definition of 'commanding officer'; see: **[0485]**.

5 As to the definition of 'superior officer'; see: **[0501]**. The Air Force Act 1950 s 37 (d).

6 The Air Force Act 1950 s 37 (e).

7 Ie as mentioned in the Air Force Act 1950 s 73. The Air Force Act 1950 s 37.

[0560] Desertion and aiding desertion Any person subject to the Air Force Act 1950, who:

(1) deserts[1] or attempts to desert the service shall on conviction by court martial,

if he commits the offence on active service or when under orders for active service, be liable to suffer death or such less punishment as mentioned in the Air Force Act 1950; and

if he commits the offence under any other circumstances, be liable to suffer imprisonment for a term which may extend to seven years or such less punishment as mentioned Air Force Act 1950[2].

(2) knowingly harbours any such deserter shall, on conviction by court martial, be liable to suffer imprisonment for a term which may extend to seven years or such less punishment as mentioned in the Air Force Act 1950[3].

(3) being cognizant of any desertion or attempt at desertion of a person subject to the Air Force Act 1950, does not forthwith give notice to his own or some other superior officer, or take any steps in his power to cause such person to be apprehended, shall, on conviction by court martial, be liable to suffer imprisonment for a term which may extend to two years or such less punishment as mentioned in the Air Force Act 1950[4].

1 The expression 'desertion' has not been defined in the Air Force Act 1950. A person is said to desert, who (i) leaves the service or, when it is his duty to join or rejoin the service, fails to do so, with (in either case) the intention subsisting at the time of the leaving or failure, or formed thereafter of remaining permanently absent from his duty; or (ii) absents himself without leave with intent to avoid some important air force service, for example, to avoid proceeding on active service or for an air force operation. Manual of Air Force Law, Volume I, notes to s 38.

2 Ie as mentioned in the Air Force Act 1950 s 73. The Air Force Act 1950 s 38 (1), As to the meaning of 'active service'; see [0470].

3 Ie as mentioned in the Air Force Act 1950 s 73. The Air Force Act 1950 s 38 (2).

4 Ie as mentioned in the Air Force Act 1950 s 73. The Air Force Act 1950 s 38 (3). Also see **[0091]**.

[0561] Absence without leave Any person subject to the Air Force Act 1950 who commits any of the following offences, that is to say:

(1) absents himself without leave[1];

(2) without sufficient cause overstays leave granted to him[2];

(3) being on leave of absence and having received information from proper authority that the unit or detachment, to which he belongs, has been ordered on active service[3], fails, without sufficient cause, to rejoin without delay[4];

(4) without sufficient cause fails to appear at the time fixed, at the parade or place appointed for exercise or duty[5];

(5) when on parade, or on the line of march, without sufficient cause or without leave from his superior officer, quits the parade or line of march[6];

(6) when in camp or elsewhere, is found beyond any limits fixed, or in any place prohibited, by any general, local or other order, without a pass or written leave from his superior officer[7]; or

(7) without leave from his superior officer or without due cause, absents himself from any school when duly ordered to attend there[8];

shall, on conviction by court martial, be liable to suffer imprisonment for a term which may extend to three years or such less punishment as mentioned in Air Force Act 1950[9].

1 The Air Force Act 1950 s 39 (a).

2 The Air Force Act 1950 s 39 (b).

3 As to the meaning of 'active service'; see **[0470]**.

4 The Air Force Act 1950 s 39 (c).

5 The Air Force Act 1950 s 39 (d).

6 The Air Force Act 1950 s 39 (e).

7 The Air Force Act 1950 s 39 (f).

8 The Air Force Act 1950 s 39 (g).

9 Ie as mentioned in the Air Force Act 1950 s 73. The Air Force Act 1950 s 39.

[0562] Striking or threatening superior officer Any person subject to the Air Force Act 1950 who commits any of the following offences, that is uses: criminal force to, or assaults his superior officer[1]; threatening language to such officer[2]; or insubordinate language to such officer[3]; shall, on conviction by court martial, if such officer is at the time in the execution of his office or, if the offence is committed on active service, be liable to suffer imprisonment for a term which may extend to fourteen years or such less punishment as mentioned in the Air Force Act 1950; and in other cases, be liable to suffer imprisonment for a term which may extend to ten years or such less punishment as mentioned in the Air Force Act 1950[4]. However, in case the offence relates to the use of insubordinate language[5], the imprisonment shall not exceed five years[6].

1 The Air Force Act 1950 s 40 (a).

2 The Air Force Act 1950 s 40 (b).

3 The Air Force Act 1950 s 40 (c).

4 Ie as mentioned in the Air Force Act 1950 s 73. The Air Force Act 1950 s 40.

5 Ie under the Air Force Act 1950 s 40 (c).

6 The Air Force Act 1950 s 40 proviso.

[0563] **Disobedience to superior officer**

(a) Any person subject to the Air Force Act 1950 who disobeys in such manner as to show a wilful defiance of authority any lawful command given personally by his superior officer[1] in the execution of his office whether the same is given orally or in writing or by signal or otherwise shall, on conviction by court martial, be liable to suffer imprisonment for a term which may extend to 14 years or such less punishment as mentioned in the Air Force Act 1950[2].

(b) Any person subject to the Air Force Act 1950 who disobeys any lawful command given by his superior officer shall, on conviction by court martial, if he commits such offence when on active service[3], be liable to suffer imprisonment for a term which may extend to 14 years or such less punishment as mentioned in the Air Force Act 1950; and if he commits such offence when not on active service, be liable to suffer imprisonment for a term which may extend to five years or such less punishment as mentioned in the Air Force Act 1950[4].

1 As to the meaning of 'superior officer'; see **[0501]**.

2 Ie as mentioned in the Air Force Act 1950 s 73. The Air Force Act 1950 s 41 (1).

3 As to the meaning of 'active service'; see **[0470]**.

4 Ie as mentioned in the Air Force Act 1950 s 73. The Air Force Act 1950 s 41(2).

[0564] Insubordination and obstruction Any person subject to the Air Force Act 1950 who commits any of the following offences, that is to say:

(1) being concerned in any quarrel, affray or disorder, refuses to obey any officer, though of inferior rank, who orders him into arrest, or uses criminal force to or assaults any such officer[1];

(2) uses criminal force to, or assaults any person, whether subject to the Air Force Act 1950 or not, in whose custody he is lawfully placed, and whether he is or is not his superior officer[2];

(3) resists an escort whose duty it is to apprehend him or to have him in charge[3];

(4) breaks out of barracks, camp or quarters[4];

(5) neglects to obey any general, local or other order[5];

(6) impedes the provost marshal[6] or any person lawfully acting on his behalf or, when called upon, refuses to assist in the execution of his duty a provost marshal or any person lawfully acting on his behalf[7]; or

(7) uses criminal force to or assaults any person bringing provisions or supplies to the Forces[8];

shall, on conviction by court martial, be liable to suffer imprisonment for a term which may extend, in the case of the offences specified in clauses (4) and (5) above to two years, and in the case of the offences specified in the other clauses to 10 years, or such less punishment as mentioned in the Air Force Act 1950[9].

1 The Air Force Act 1950 s 42 (a).

2 The Air Force Act 1950 s 42 (b).

3 The Air Force Act 1950 s 42 (c).

4 The Air Force Act 1950 s 42 (d).

5 The Air Force Act 1950 s 42 (e).

6 As to the meaning of 'provost marshal'; see **[0498]**.

7 The Air Force Act 1950 s 42 (f).

8 The Air Force Act 1950 s 42 (g).

9 Ie as mentioned in the Air Force Act 1950 s 73. The Air Force Act 1950 s 42.

[0565] Fraudulent enrolment Any person subject to the Air Force Act 1950 who commits any of the following offences, that is to say, without having obtained a regular discharge from the Air Force[1] or otherwise fulfilled the conditions enabling him to enrol or enter, enrols himself in, or enters the said force or any part of the military or the naval forces of India[2]; or is concerned in the enrolment in any part of the Forces[3], of any person when he knows or has reason to believe such person to be so circumstanced that by enrolling he commits an offence against the Air Force Act 1950[4]; shall, on conviction by court martial, be liable to suffer imprisonment for a term which may extend to five years or such less punishment as mentioned in the Air Force Act 1950[5].

1 As to the meaning of 'air force'; see **[0474]**.

2 The Air Force Act 1950 s 43 (a).

3 As to the meaning of 'the Forces'; see **[0489]**.

4 The Air Force Act 1950 s 43 (b).

5 Ie as mentioned in the Air Force Act 1950 s 73. The Air Force Act 1950 s 43.

[0566] False answers on enrolment Any person having become subject to the Air Force Act 1950 who is discovered to have made at the time of enrolment a wilfully false answer to any question set forth in the prescribed form of enrolment which has been put to him by the enrolling officer before whom he appears for the purpose of being enrolled, shall, on conviction by court martial, be liable to suffer imprisonment for a term which may extend to five years or such less punishment as mentioned in the Air Force Act 1950[1].

1 Ie as mentioned in the Air Force Act 1950 s 73. The Air Force Act 1950 s 44.

[0567] Unbecoming conduct Any officer[1] or warrant officer[2] who behaves in a manner unbecoming his position and the character expected of him shall, on conviction by court martial, if he is an officer, be liable to be cashiered or to suffer such less punishment as is mentioned is in the Air Force Act 1950; and if he is a warrant officer, be liable to be dismissed or to suffer such less punishment as mentioned in the Air Force Act 1950[3].

1 As to the meaning of 'officer'; see **[0494]**.

2 As to the meaning of 'warrant officer'; see **[0504].**

3 Ie as mentioned in the Air Force Act 1950 s 73. The Air Force Act 1950 s 45.

[0568] Certain forms of disgraceful conduct Any person subject to the Air Force Act 1950 who commits any of the following offences, that is to say:

(1) is guilty of any disgraceful conduct of a cruel, indecent or unnatural kind[1];

(2) malingers, or feigns, or produces disease or infirmity in himself, or intentionally delays his cure or

aggravates his disease or infirmity[2]; or

(3) with intent to render himself or any other person unfit for service, voluntarily causes hurt to himself or that person[3];

shall, on conviction by court martial, be liable to suffer imprisonment for a term which may extend to seven years or such less punishment as mentioned in the Air Force Act 1950[4].

1 The Air Force Act 1950 s 46 (a).

2 The Air Force Act 1950 s 46 (b).

3 The Air Force Act 1950 s 46 (c)

4 Ie as mentioned in the Air Force Act 1950 s 73. The Air Force Act 1950 s 46.

[0569] Ill- treating a subordinate Any officer[1], warrant officer[2] or non- commissioned officer[3] subject to the Air Force Act 1950, who uses criminal force to or otherwise ill-treats any person subject to the said Act, being his subordinate in rank or position, shall, on conviction by court martial, be liable to suffer imprisonment for a term which may extend to seven years or such less punishment as mentioned in the Air Force Act 1950.

1 As to the meaning of 'officer'; see **[0494]**.

2 As to the meaning of 'warrant officer'; see **[0504]**.

3 As to the meaning of 'non-commissioned officer'; see **[0491]**.

4 Ie as mentioned in the Air Force Act 1950 s 73. The Air Force Act 1950 s 47.

[0570] Intoxication Any person subject to the Air Force Act 1950 who is found in a state of intoxication, whether on duty or not, shall, on conviction by court martial, if he is an officer[1], be liable to be cashiered or to suffer such less punishment as mentioned in the Air Force Act 1950[2]; and if he is not an officer, be liable to suffer imprisonment for a term which may extend to two years or such less punishment as mentioned in the Air Force Act 1950[3]. However, where an offence of being intoxicated is committed by a person other than an officer when not on active service[4] or not on duty, the period of imprisonment awarded shall not exceed six months[5].

1 As to the meaning of 'officer'; see **[0494]**.

2 Ie as mentioned in the Air Force Act 1950 s 73.

3 Ie as mentioned in the Air Force Act 1950 s 73. The Air Force Act 1950 s 48 (1).

4 As to the meaning of 'active service'; see **[0470]**.

5 The Air Force Act 1950 s 48 (2).

[0571] Permitting escape of person in custody Any person subject to the Air Force Act 1950 who commits any of the following offences, that is to say: (i) when in command of a guard, picquet, patrol or post, releases without proper authority, whether wilfully or without reasonable excuse, any person committed to his charge or refuses to receive any prisoner or person so committed[1]; or (ii) wilfully or without reasonable excuse allows to escape any person who is committed to his charge, or whom it is his duty to keep or guard[2]; shall, on conviction by court martial, be liable, if he has acted wilfully, to suffer imprisonment for a term which may extend to 14 years or such less punishment as mentioned in the Air Force Act 1950[3]; and if he has not acted wilfully, to suffer imprisonment for a term which may extend to two years or such less punishment as mentioned in the aforesaid provision[4].

1 The Air Force Act 1950 s 49 (a).

2 The Air Force Act 1950 s 49 (b).

3 Ie as mentioned in the Air Force Act 1950 s 73.

4 The Air Force Act 1950 s 49.

[0572] Irregularity in connection with arrest or confinement Any person subject to the Air Force Act 1950 who commits any of the following offences, that is to say: (i) unnecessarily detains a person in arrest or confinement without bringing him to trial, or fails to bring his case before the proper authority for investigation[1]; or (ii) having committed a person to air force custody[2] fails without reasonable cause to deliver at the time of such committal, or as soon as practicable, and in any case within 48 hours thereafter, to the officer[3] or other person into whose custody the person arrested is committed, an account in writing signed by himself of the offence with which the person so committed is charged[4]; shall, on conviction by court martial, be liable to suffer imprisonment for a term which may extend to two years or such less punishment as mentioned in the Air Force Act 1950[5].

1 The Air Force Act 1950 s 50 (a).

2 As to the definition of 'air force custody'; see **[0475]**.

3 As to the definition of 'officer'; see **[0494]**.

4 The Air Force Act 1950 s 50 (b).

5 Ie as mentioned in the Air Force Act 1950 s 73. The Air Force Act 1950 s 50.

[0573] Escape from custody Any person subject to the Air Force Act 1950 who, being in lawful custody, escapes or attempts to escape, shall, on conviction by court martial, be liable to suffer imprisonment for a term which may extend to five years or such less punishment as mentioned in the Air Force Act 1950[1].

1 Ie as mentioned in the Air Force Act 1950 s 73. The Air Force Act 1950 s 51.

[0574] Offences in respect of property Any person subject to the Air Force Act 1950 who commits any of the following offences, that is to say:

(1) commits theft[1] of any property belonging to the Government, or to any military, naval or air force mess, band or institution, or to any person subject to military, naval or air force law[2];

(2) dishonestly[3] misappropriates or converts to his own use any such property[4];

(3) commits criminal breach of trust[5] in respect of any such property[6];

(4) dishonestly receives or retains any such property in respect of which any of the offences under above-stated provisions (1), (2) and (3) has been committed, knowing or having reason to believe the commission of such offence[7];

(5) wilfully destroys or injures any property of the Government entrusted to him[8]; or

(6) does any other thing with intent to defraud, or to cause wrongful gain to one person or wrongful loss[9] to another person[10];

shall, on conviction by court martial, be liable to suffer imprisonment for a term which may extend to 10 years or such less punishment as mentioned in the Air Force Act 1950[11].

1 As to the definition of 'theft'; see Indian Penal Code 1860 s 378.

2 The Air Force Act 1950 s 52 (a).

3 As to the definition 'dishonestly'; see Indian Penal Code 1860 s 24.

4 The Air Force Act 1950 s 52 (b).

5 As to the definition 'criminal breach of trust'; see Indian Penal Code 1860 s 405.

6 The Air Force Act 1950 s 52 (c).

7 The Air Force Act 1950 s 52 (d).

8 The Air Force Act 1950 s 52 (e).

9 As to the meaning of 'wrongful gain or wrongful loss'; see Indian Penal Code 1860 s 23.

10 The Air Force Act 1950 s 52 (f).

11 Ie as mentioned in the Air Force Act 1950 s 73. The Air Force Act 1950 s 52.

[0575] Extortion and corruption Any person subject to the Air Force Act 1950 who commits any of the following offences, that is to say: (i) commits extortion[1]; or (ii) without proper authority exacts from any person money, provisions or service[2]; shall, on conviction by court martial, be liable to suffer imprisonment for a term which may extend to ten years or such less punishment as mentioned in the Air Force Act 1950[3].

1 As to the definition of 'extortion'; see the Indian Penal Code 1860 s 383. The Air Force Act 1950 s 53 (a).

2 The Air Force Act 1950 s 53 (b).

3 Ie as mentioned in the Air Force Act 1950 s 73. The Air Force Act 1950 s 53.

[0576] Making away with equipment Any person subject to the Air Force Act 1950 who commits any of the following offences, that is to say: (i) makes away with, or is concerned in making away with, any arms, ammunition, equipment, instruments, tools, clothing or any other thing being the property of the Government issued to him for his use or entrusted to him[1]; (ii) loses by neglect anything stated above in clause (i)[2]; or (iii) sells, pawns, destroys or defaces any medal or decoration granted to him[3]; shall, on conviction by court martial, be liable to suffer imprisonment for a term which may extend, in the case of the offences specified in clause (i) to ten years, and in the case of the offences specified in clauses (ii) and (iii) to five years, or such less punishment as mentioned in the Air Force Act 1950[4].

1 The Air Force Act 1950 s 54 (a).

2 The Air Force Act 1950 s 54 (b).

3 The Air Force Act 1950 s 54 (c).

4 Ie as mentioned in the Air Force Act 1950 s 73. The Air Force Act 1950 s 54.

[0577] Injury to property Any person subject to the Air Force Act 1950 who commits any of the following offences, that is to say: (i) destroys or injures any property mentioned in the Air Force Act 1950[1], or any property belonging to any military, naval or air force mess, band or institution, or to any per son subject to military, naval or air force law, or serving with, or attached to, the Air Force[2]; or (ii) commits any act which causes damage to, or destruction of, any property of the Government by fire[3]; or (iii) kills, injures, makes away with, ill-treats or loses any animal entrusted to him[4]; shall, on conviction by court martial, be liable, if he has acted wilfully, to suffer imprisonment for a term which may extend to 14 years or such less punishment as mentioned in the provisions of the Air Force Act 1950[5]; and if he has acted without reasonable excuse to suffer imprisonment for a term which may extend to seven years or such less punishment as mentioned in the above-stated provision[6].

1 Ie as mentioned in the Air Force Act 1950 s 54 (a); see **[0576]**.

2 The Air Force Act 1950 s 55 (a).

3 The Air Force Act 1950 s 55 (b).

4 The Air Force Act 1950 s 55 (c).

5 As mentioned in the Air Force Act 1950 s 73.

6 As mentioned in the Air Force Act 1950 s 73. The Air Force Act 1950 s 55.

[0578] False accusation Any person subject to the Air Force Act 1950 who commits any of the following offences, that is to say: (i) makes a false accusation against any person subject to the Air Force Act 1950, knowing or having reason to believe such accusation to be false[1]; or (ii) in making a complaint under the provisions of the Air Force Act 1950[2], makes any statement affecting the character of any person subject to above-stated Act, knowing or having reason to believe such statement to be false, or knowingly and wilfully suppresses any material facts[3]; shall, on conviction by court martial, be liable to suffer imprisonment for a term which may extend to five years or such less punishment as mentioned in the Air Force Act 1950[4].

1 The Air Force Act 1950 s 56 (a).

2 Ie under provisions of Air Force Act 1950 s 26 or 27.

3 The Air Force Act 1950 s 56 (b).

4 As mentioned in the Air Force Act 1950 s 73. The Air Force Act 1950 s 56.

[0579] Falsifying official documents and false declaration Any person subject to the Air Force Act 1950 who commits any of the following offences, that is to say:

(1) in any report, return, list, certificate, book or other document[1] made or signed by him, or of the contents of which, it is his duty to ascertain the accuracy, knowingly makes, or is privy to the making of, any false or fraudulent statement[2];

(2) in any document of the description mentioned in the above-stated provision, knowingly makes, or is privy to the making of, any omission, with intent to defraud[3];

(3) knowingly and with intent to injure any person, or knowingly and with intent to defraud, suppresses, defaces, alters or makes away with any document which it is his duty to preserve or produce[4];

(4) where it is his official duty to make a declaration respecting any matter, knowingly makes a false declaration[5]; or

(5) obtains for himself, or for any other person, any pension, allowance or other advantage or privilege by a statement which is false, and which he either knows or believes to be false or does not believe to be true, or by making or using a false entry in any book or record, or by making any document containing a false statement, or by omitting to make a true entry or document containing a true statement[6];

shall, on conviction by court martial, be liable to suffer imprisonment for a term which may extend to 14 years or such less punishment as mentioned in the Air Force Act 1950[7].

1 As to the meaning of 'document'; see the Indian Penal Code 1860 s 29.

2 The Air Force Act 1950 s 57 (a).

3 The Air Force Act 1950 s 57 (b).

4 The Air Force Act 1950 s 57 (c).

5 The Air Force Act 1950 s 57 (d).

6 The Air Force Act 1950 s 57 (e).

7 As mentioned in the Air Force Act 1950 s 73. The Air Force Act 1950 s 57.

[0580] Signing in blank and failure to report Any person subject to the Air Force Act 1950 who commits any of the following offences, that is to say: (i) when signing any document relating to pay, arms, ammunition, equipment, clothing, supplies or stores, or any property of the Government fraudulently leaves in blank any material part for which his signature is a voucher[1]; or (ii) refuses or by culpable neglect omits to make or send a report or return which it is his duty to make or send[2]; shall, on conviction by court martial, be liable to suffer imprisonment for a term which may extend to seven years or such less punishment as mentioned in the Air Force Act 1950[3].

1 The Air Force Act 1950 s 58 (a).

2 The Air Force Act 1950 s 58 (b).

3 As mentioned in the Air Force Act 1950 s 73. The Air Force Act 1950 s 58.

[0581] Offences relating to courts martial Any person subject to the Air Force Act 1950 who commits any of the following offences, that is to say:

(1) being duly summoned or ordered to attend as a witness before a court martial, wilfully or without reasonable excuse, makes default in attending[1];

(2) refuses to take an oath[2] or make an affirmation legally required by a court martial to be taken or made[3];

(3) refuses to produce or deliver any document in his power or control legally required by a court martial to be produced or delivered by him[4];

(4) refuses when a witness to answer any question which he is by law bound to answer[5]; or

(5) is guilty of contempt of court martial by using insulting or threatening language, or by causing any interruption or disturbance in the proceedings of such court[6];

shall, on conviction by court martial, be liable to suffer imprisonment for a term which may extend to three years or such less punishment as mentioned in the Air Force Act 1950[7].

1 The Air Force Act 1950 s 59 (a).

2 As to the definition of 'oath'; see the Indian Penal Code 1860 s 51.

3 The Air Force Act 1950 s 59 (b).

4 The Air Force Act 1950 s 59 (c).

5 The Air Force Act 1950 s 59 (d).

6 The Air Force Act 1950 s 59 (e).

7 As mentioned in the Air Force Act 1950 s 73. The Air Force Act 1950 s 59.

[0582] False evidence Any person subject to the Air Force Act 1950 who, having been duly sworn or affirmed before any court martial or other court competent under the aforesaid Act to administer an oath or affirmation, makes any statement which is false, and which he either knows or believes to be false or does not believe to be true, shall, on conviction by court martial, be liable to suffer imprisonment for a term which may extend to seven years or such less punishment as mentioned in the Air Force Act 1950[1].

1 As mentioned in the Air Force Act 1950 s 73. The Air Force Act 1950 s 60. The offence specified under this provision is in many respects similar to the offence of giving false evidence under the Indian Penal Code 1860 s 191. The courts referred in this provision are (i) court martial, (ii) court of inquiry on illegal absence under the Air Force Act 1950 s 107, (iii) court of inquiry on recovered prisoners of war under the Air Force Act 1950 s 189 (2)(d) and the Air Force Rules 1969 r 156 (3), and (iv) any other court of inquiry when the commanding officer assembling the court has directed that the evidence be recorded on oath or affirmation. Manual of Air Force Law, Volume I, the Air Force Act 1950 s 60 notes.

[0583] Unlawful detention of pay Any officer[1], warrant officer[2] or noncommissioned officer[3] who, having received the pay of a person subject to the Air Force Act 1950 unlawfully detains or refuses to pay the same when due, shall, on conviction by court martial, be liable to suffer imprisonment for a term which may extend to 10 years or such less punishment as mentioned in the Air Force Act 1950[4].

1 As to the definition of 'officer'; see **[0494]**.

2 As to the definition of 'warrant officer'; see **[0504]**.

3 As to the definition of 'non-commissioned officer'; see **[0491]**.

4 Ie as mentioned in the Air Force Act 1950 s 73. The Air Force Act 1950 s 61.

[0584] Offences in relation to aircraft and flying Any person subject to the Air Force Act 1950 who commits any of the following offences, that is to say:

(1) wilfully or without reasonable excuse damages, destroys or loses any aircraft[1] or aircraft material[2] belonging to the Government[3];

(2) is guilty of any act or neglect likely to cause such damage, destruction or loss[4];

(3) without lawful authority disposes of any aircraft or aircraft material belonging to the Government[5];

(4) is guilty of any act or neglect in flying, or in the use of any aircraft, or in relation to any aircraft or aircraft material, which causes or is likely to cause loss of life or bodily injury to any person[6]; or

(5) during a state of war, wilfully and without proper occasion, or negligently, causes the sequestration, by or under the authority of a neutral State, or the destruction in a neutral State, of any aircraft belonging to the Government[7];

shall, on conviction by court martial, be liable, if he has acted wilfully, to suffer imprisonment for a term which may extend to 14 years or such less punishment as mentioned in the Air Force Act 1950[8], and, in any other case, to suffer imprisonment for a term which may extend to five years or such less punishment mentioned aforesaid Act[9].

1 As to the definition of 'aircraft'; see **[0472]**.

2 As to the definition of 'aircraft material'; see **[0473]**.

3 The Air Force Act 1950 s 62 (a).

4 The Air Force Act 1950 s 62 (b).

5 The Air Force Act 1950 s 62 (c).

6 The Air Force Act 1950 s 62 (d).

7 The Air Force Act 1950 s 62 (e).

8 Ie as mentioned in the Air Force Act 1950 s 73.

9 Ie as mentioned in the Air Force Act 1950 s 73. The Air Force Act 1950 s 62.

[0585] Other offences relating to aircraft and flying Any person subject to the Air Force Act 1950 who commits any of the following offences, that is to say:

(1) signs any certificate in relation to an aircraft[1] or aircraft material[2] belonging to the Government without ensuring the accuracy thereof[3];

(2) being the pilot of an aircraft belonging to the Government, flies it at a height less than such height as may be specified by the Chief of the Air Staff, except while taking off or landing, or in such other circumstances as may be specified by the Chief of the Air Staff[4]; or

(3) being the pilot of an aircraft belonging to the Government, flies it so as to cause, or to be likely to cause, unnecessary annoyance to any person[5];

shall, on conviction by court martial, be liable to suffer imprisonment for a term which may extend to two years or such less punishment as mentioned in the Air Force Act 1950[6].

1 As to the definition of 'aircraft'; see **[0472]**.

2 As to the definition of 'aircraft material'; see **[0473]**.

3 The Air Force Act 1950 s 63 (a).

4 The Air Force Act 1950 s 63 (b).

5 The Air Force Act 1950 s 63 (c).

6 Ie as mentioned in the Air Force Act 1950 s 73. The Air Force Act 1950 s 63.

[0586] Disobedience of lawful command of captain of aircraft Any person subject to the Air Force Act 1950 who, whatever his rank, commits any of the following offences, that is to say:

(1) while he is in an aircraft disobeys any lawful command given by the captain of the aircraft, whether such captain is subject to the Air Force Act 1950 or not, as respects all matters relating to the flying or handling of the aircraft, or affecting the safety thereof[1]; or

(2) being the captain of a glider aircraft towed by another aircraft disobeys any lawful command given by the captain of the towing aircraft, whether the latter is subject to the Air Force Act 1950 or not, as respects all matters aforesaid[2];

shall on conviction by court martial, be liable to suffer imprisonment for a term which may extend to 14 years or such less punishment as mentioned in the Air Force Act 1950[3].

1 The Air Force Act 1950 s 64 (a).

2 The Air Force Act 1950 s 64 (b).

3 Ie as mentioned in the Air Force Act 1950 s 73. The Air Force Act 1950 s 64.

[0587] Violation of good order and air force discipline Any person subject to the Air Force Act 1950 who is guilty of any act or omission which though not specified in the Air Force Act 1950, is prejudicial to good order and air force discipline shall, on conviction by court martial, be liable to suffer imprisonment for a term which may extend to seven years or such less punishment as mentioned in the Air Force Act 1950[1].

1 Ie as mentioned in the Air Force Act 1950 s 73. The Air Force Act 1950 s 65. A charge under this provision must recite its actual words, i.e., the accused must be for an 'act' or an 'omission' which is 'prejudicial to good order and air force discipline'. The word 'act' denotes as well a series of acts as a single act; and word 'omission' denotes as well a series of omissions as a single omission. See: the Indian Penal Code 1860 s 32 and 33. An 'omission' to be punishable under this provision must amount to neglect which is willful and culpable. The Manual of Air Force Law, Volume I, Air Force Act 1950 s 65 notes.

[0588] Miscellaneous offences Any person subject to the Air Force Act 1950 who commits any of the following offences, that is to say:

(1) being in command at any post or on the march, and receiving a complaint that anyone under his command has beaten or otherwise maltreated or oppressed any person, or has disturbed any fair or market, or committed any riot or trespass, fails to have due reparation made to the injured person or to report the case to the proper authority[1];

(2) by defiling any place of worship, or otherwise, intentionally insults the religion or wounds the religious feelings of any person[2];

(3) attempts to commit suicide, and in such attempt does any act towards the commission of such offence[3];

(4) being below the rank of warrant officer, when off duty, appears, without proper authority, in or about camp or cantonments, or in or about, or when going to or returning from, any town or bazar, carrying a rifle, sword or other offensive weapon[4];

(5) directly or indirectly accepts or obtains, or agrees to accept or attempts to obtain, for himself or for any other person, any gratification as a motive or reward for procuring the enrolment of any person, or leave of absence, promotion or any other advantage or indulgence for any person in the service[5]; or

(6) commits any offence against the property or person of any inhabitant of, or resident in, the country in which he is serving[6];

shall, on conviction by court martial, be liable to suffer imprisonment for a term which may extend to seven years or such less punishment as mentioned in the Air Force Act 1950[7].

1 The Air Force Act 1950 s 66 (a). The offence under this provision can be committed only by a person who is in command. As to the definition of 'riot' and 'trespass'; see the Indian Penal Code s 146 and 441.

2 The Air Force Act 1950 s 66 (b).

3 The Air Force Act 1950 s 66 (c).

4 The Air Force Act 1950 s 66 (d). The term 'cantonment' is not restricted to those stations which have been declared to be cantonment for the purposes of the Cantonment Act 1934. Airmen are considered to be in cantonment for the purpose of the Air Force Act 1950 when they are quartered in any station or locality as a permanent or semi-

permanent arrangement. The Manual of Air Force Law, Volume I, Air Force Act 1950 s 66 notes.

5 The Air Force Act 1950 s 66 (e).

6 The Air Force Act 1950 s 66 (f).

7 Ie as mentioned in the Air Force Act 1950 s 73. The Air Force Act 1950 s 66.

[0589] Attempt Any person subject to the Air Force Act 1950 who attempts to commit any of the offences specified in the provisions of the Air Force Act 1950[1], and in such attempt does any act towards the commission of the offence shall, on conviction by court martial, where no express provision is made by the Air Force Act 1950 for the punishment of such attempt, be liable, if the offence attempted to be committed is punishable with death, to suffer imprisonment for a term which may extend to 14 years or such less punishment as is in the aforesaid Act mentioned[2]; and if the offence attempted to be committed is punishable with imprisonment, to suffer imprisonment for a term which may extend to one-half of the longest term provided for that offence or such less punishment as mentioned in the Air Force Act 1950[3].

1 Ie in the Air Force Act 1950 ss 34-66.

2 Ie as mentioned in the Air Force Act 1950 s 73.

3 Ie as mentioned in the Air Force Act 1950 s 73. The Air Force Act 1950 s 67.

[0590] Abetment of offences that have been committed Any person subject to the Air Force Act 1950 who abets the commission of any of the offences specified in the provisions of the Air Force Act 1950[1], shall, on conviction by court martial, if the act abetted is committed in consequence of the abetment and no express provision is made by the aforesaid Act for the punishment of such abetment, be liable to suffer the punishment provided for that offence or such less punishment as mentioned in the Air Force Act 1950[2].

1 Ie in the Air Force Act 1950 ss 34-66.

2 Ie as mentioned in the Air Force Act 1950 s 73. The Air Force Act 1950 s 68.

[0591] Abetment of offences punishable with death and not committed Any person subject to the Air Force Act 1950 who abets the commission of any of the offences punishable with death under the provisions of the Air Force Act 1950[1], shall, on conviction by court martial, if that offence be not committed in consequence of the abetment, and no express provision is made by the aforesaid Act for the punishment of such abetment, be liable to suffer imprisonment for a term which may extend to 14 years or such less punishment as mentioned in the Air Force Act 1950[2].

1 Ie under the Air Force Act 1950 ss 34, 37 and 38 (1).

2 Ie as mentioned in the Air Force Act 1950 s 73. The Air Force Act 1950 s 69.

[0592] Abetment of offences punishable with imprisonment and not committed Any person subject to the Air Force Act 1950 who abets the commission of any of the offences specified in the provisions of the Air Force Act 1950[1], and punishable with imprisonment shall, on conviction by court martial, if that offence be not committed in consequence of the abetment, and no express provision is made by the aforesaid Act for the punishment of such abetment, be liable to suffer imprisonment for a term which may extend to one-half of the longest term provided for that offence or such less punishment as mentioned in the Air Force Act 1950[2].

1 Ie in the Air Force Act 1950 ss 34-66.

2 Ie as mentioned in the Air Force Act 1950 s 73. The Air Force Act 1950 s 70.

[0593] Civil offences Subject to the provision contained in the Air Force Act[1], any person subject to the Air Force Act 1950 who at any place in or beyond India commits any civil offence[2] shall be deemed to be guilty of an offence against the Air Force Act 1950 and, if charged therewith under this provision shall be liable to be tried by a court martial and, on conviction, be punishable as follows, that is to say:

(1) if the offence is one which would be punishable under any law in force in India with death, or with imprisonment for life, he shall be liable to suffer any punishment, other than whipping, assigned for the offence by the aforesaid law and such less punishment as mentioned in the Air Force Act 1950[3]; and

(2) in any other case, he shall be liable to suffer any punishment other than whipping, assigned for the offence by any law in force in India, or imprisonment for a term which may extend to seven years or such less punishment as mentioned in the Air Force Act 1950[4].

1 Ie as contained in the Air Force Act 1950 s 72.

2 As to the meaning of 'civil offence'; see **[0482]**.

3 Ie as mentioned in the Air Force Act 1950 s 73. The Air Force Act 1950 s 71 (a).

4 Ie as mentioned in the Air Force Act 1950 s 73. The Air Force Act 1950 s 71 (b).

[0594] Civil offences not triable by court martial A person subject to the Air Force Act 1950 who commits an offence of murder[1] against a person not subject to military, naval or air force law, or of culpable homicide[2] not amounting to murder against such a person or of rape[3] in relation to such a person, shall not be deemed to be guilty of an offence against the Air Force Act 1950 and shall not be tried by a court martial, unless he commits any of the said offences: (i) while on active service[4], or (ii) at any place outside India[5], or (iii) at a frontier post specified by the said Government by notification in this behalf[6].

1 As to the definition of 'murder'; see the Indian Penal Code 1860 s 300.

2 As to the definition of 'culpable homicide'; see the Indian Penal Code 1860 s 299.

3 As to the definition of 'rape'; see the Indian Penal Code 1860 s 375.

4 The Air Force Act 1950 s 72 (a).

5 The Air Force Act 1950 s 72 (b).

6 The Air Force Act 1950 s 72 (c). The Air Force Act 1950 s 72.

5. ARREST AND PROCEEDINGS BEFORE TRIAL

CONTENTS

PARA

A. Arrest and Custody

B. Investigation and disposal of charges and remand for trial

C. Preparation of defence by the accused persons

D. Exemption from Air Force Rules 1969

A. Arrest and Custody

[0595] Introduction Arrest in its natural sense means the apprehension or restraints or the deprivation of one's personal liberty. In the legal sense arrest consists in taking into custody of another person under authority empowered by law for the purpose of holding or detaining him to answer a charge. The term 'custody' and 'arrest' are not synonymous. In every arrest there is custody but the converse is not true. Custody may amount to arrest in certain cases but not in all. The expression 'air force custody' is restricted to the air force custody of persons when charged with offences[1] and does not apply to persons in air force custody when undergoing sentence[2]. Arrest is either close or open arrest. When arrest is not described as open arrest, it means close arrest[3].

1 As to the meaning of terms 'air force custody' and 'offences', see **[0475]** and **[0493]**.

2 Manual of Air Force Law, Volume I, s 102 notes.

3 Regulations for the Air Force 1964, paragraph 641 (b).

[0596] Custody of offenders Any person subject to the Air Force Act 1950 who is charged with an offence may be taken into air force custody[1]. Any such person may be ordered into air force custody by any superior officer[2]. Any officer may order into air force custody any officer, though he may be of a higher rank, engaged in a quarrel, affray or disorder[3].

1 The Air Force Act 1950 s 102 (1).

2 As to the meaning of 'superior officer'; see **[0501]**. The Air Force Act 1950 s 102 (2).

3 The Air Force Act 1950 s 102 (3).

[0597] Officer: when to be placed in arrest An officer may be placed in arrest by a competent authority without previous investigation when circumstances so require, but a commanding officer on receiving a complaint, or learning of circumstances tending to incriminate an officer, will not ordinarily place him in arrest, until he has satisfied himself by inquiry that it will be necessary to proceed with the case and to report it to superior authority. He will invariably place in arrest an officer against whom he prefers a charge[1].

1 Regulations for the Air Force 1964, paragraph 643.

[0598] Officers/Warrant officers under arrest When an officer or warrant officer is placed under arrest the commanding officer, unless he dismisses the case, will report the matter without delay to the next superior authority under whose command the unit may be. When an officer is placed under arrest a report shall be made by the fastest means to Air Headquarters. Subsequently, reports regarding the progress of investigation shall be submitted in the manner laid down by the controlling station, command and Air Headquarters through staff channels. An officer or warrant officer under close arrest will be placed under the charge of an escort consisting of another officer or warrant officer of the same or senior rank, if possible, and will not leave his quarters or tent except to take such exercise under supervision as the medical officer considers necessary. An officer or warrant officer may, however, if circumstances so require, be placed for custody under the charge of a guard, piquet, patrol, sentry or member of the service police. An officer or warrant officer under open arrest may take exercise at stated periods and within stated limits, which will usually be the precincts of the barracks or camp of his unit; these limits may be enlarged at the discretion of the officer commanding of the station. He will not appear in any place of amusement or entertainment, or at public assemblies. He will not appear outside his quarters or tent dressed otherwise than in uniform. An officer or warrant officer in open arrest may, under strict orders as to his conduct, be directed to proceed from one station to another, or be permitted to leave the station for a particular purpose.

An offender in close arrest will not be required to perform any duty, other than such duties as may be necessary to relieve him from the charge of any cash, equipment, stores, accounts, or office of which he may have charge, or for which he is responsible. If by error, or in emergency, he has been ordered to perform any duty, he is not thereby absolved from liability to be proceeded against for the offence for which he is under arrest. On active service[1], however, an offender may be ordered to bear arms, attend parades and perform all his ordinary duties, provided that care is taken to ensure that he is called upon to perform no duties in addition to those performed by airmen who are not in arrest or undergoing punishment. An offender, while in open arrest, may be ordered by his commanding officer to carry out such flying or other duties as may be necessary in the course of his training or such part of his ordinary duties as his commanding officer may consider advisable that he should perform. An offender, when in close arrest, is not to bear arms except by order of his commanding officer in an emergency or as stated in the aforesaid provisions[2].

1 As to the meaning of 'active service' see **[0470]**.

2 Regulations for the Air Force 1964, paragraph 644.

[0599] Airman under arrest A warrant officer or a non-commissioned officer[1] charged with a serious offence will be placed in arrest forthwith but if the offence alleged does not appear to be serious, it may be investigated and disposed of without previous arrest. An airman other than a warrant officer or non-commissioned officer[1] or apprentice charged with a serious offence will be placed in arrest on the commission or discovery of the offence, but if the offence alleged appears not to be serious it may be investigated and disposed of without previous arrest. He will not be placed in close arrest for offences unaccompanied by intoxication, violence or insubordination, unless confinement is necessary to ensure his safe custody or for the maintenance of discipline. An airman or apprentice, who disobeys an order distinctly given or resists the authority of a warrant officer, or non-commissioned officer will be placed in close arrest without altercation and the fact immediately reported to his subordinate commander or to the adjutant. When a warrant officer or non-commissioned officer has to place an airman or apprentice in close arrest, he will obtain the assistance of one or more airmen to conduct the offender to the guard room and will himself avoid coming in contact with him. When an airman makes confession of desertion or of having committed an offence in relation to enrolment, and the investigation cannot immediately be completed, he need not be placed in arrest pending inquiry. But if at the time of confession or subsequently, he is charged with any other offence, he may be placed in arrest and the investigation and trial may proceed for that offence independently of the confession. When an airman has been placed in close arrest for more than two days the fact will be notified in personnel occurrence reports forthwith. In such cases release from close arrest will also be promulgated in personnel occurrence reports. The cause of release (e.g., dealt with by commanding officer, charge dismissed, charge not proceeded with, etc.) should be stated. When an airman is convicted, either by court martial or by a civil court, or by his commanding officer of an offence, for which he has been placed in close arrest, and deduction of all pay and allowances under the Pay and Allowances Regulations for the Air Force is involved as a result of such conviction, the notification in personnel occurrence reports of the conviction should also state the period in custody in order that the airman may forfeit pay and allowances accordingly[2].

A non-commissioned officer in close arrest will not be required to perform any duty, other than such duties as may be necessary to relieve him from the charge of any cash, equipment, stores, accounts, or office of which he may have charge, or for which he is responsible. If by error, or in emergency he has been ordered to perform any duties, he is not thereby absolved from liability to be proceeded against for the offence for which he is under arrest. On active service, however, a non-commissioned officer may be ordered to bear arms, attend parades, and perform all his ordinary duties provided that care is taken to ensure that he is called upon to perform no duties in addition to those performed by airmen who are not in arrest or undergoing punishment. A non-commissioned officer while in open arrest, may he ordered by his commanding officer to carry out such flying or other duties as may be necessary in the course of his training, or such part of his ordinary duties as his commanding officer may consider advisable that he should perform. A non-commissioned officer when in close or open arrest will not bear arms except by order of his commanding officer in an emergency or during active service[3].

An aircraftman or apprentice on being placed in close arrest will be placed in confinement under charge of a picquet, patrol, sentry or member of the service police and will be searched and deprived of knives, other weapons and any article that can be used as missile during the investigation and the trial. A receipt containing the list of articles recovered will be given to him. An aircraftman/apprentice in close arrest will be allowed his bedding and will take sufficient exercise for the preservation of his health. An aircraftman/apprentice in close arrest will not bear arms except by order of his commanding officer in an emergency or during active service[4].

1 As to the definition of 'warrant officer' and 'non-commissioned officer' see **[0504]** and **[0491]**.

2 Regulations for the Air Force 1964, paragraph 645.

3 Regulations for the Air Force 1964, paragraph 646 (a).

4 Regulations for the Air Force 1964, paragraph 646 (b).

[0600] Release from arrest It is not desirable, except when it appears that the arrest has been made through error, that an officer should be released from arrest by the officer who ordered his arrest without the sanction of Air Headquarters. Whenever possible, the sanction of the highest authority to whom the case may have been referred should be obtained before an officer or warrant officer is released from arrest. An officer or airman has no right to claim trial by court martial, except in the circumstances mentioned in the Air Force Act 1950[1], or to claim a court of inquiry, or after he has been released by proper authority, to persist in considering himself under the restraint of arrest or to refuse to return to duty. Where an officer is released from arrest without being dealt with summarily or tried by court martial a report of the circumstances will be sent to the chief of the air staff by the officer who orders the release. An air or other officer who awards a summary punishment will report the matter to the chief of the air staff forwarding a copy of the charge sheet and summary of evidence and giving particulars of the punishment awarded. Care will also be taken that an appropriate entry is made on the accused's record of service[2].

1 Ie the Air Force Act 1950 s 86.

2 Regulations for the Air Force 1964, paragraph 647.

[0601] Duty of commanding officer in regard detention It shall be the duty of every commanding officer[1] to take care that a person under his command when charged with an offence is not detained in custody for more than 48 hours after the committal of such person into custody is reported to him, without the charge being investigated[2], unless investigation within that period seems to him to be impracticable with due regard to the public service[3]. Every case of a person being detained in custody beyond a period of 48 hours, and the reason thereof shall be reported by the commanding officer to the air or other officer to whom application would be made to convene a general or district court martial for the trial of the person charged[4]. In reckoning the period of 48 hours specified in the aforesaid provisions, Sundays and public holidays shall be excluded[5]. Subject to the provisions of the Air Force Act 1950, the Central Government may make rules providing for the manner in which and the period for which any person subject to the aforesaid Act may be taken into and detained in air force custody, pending the trial by any competent authority for any offence committed by him[6].

1 As to the definition of 'commanding officer'; see **[0485]**.

2 The phrase 'without the charge being investigated' means hearing of a charge under the Air Force Rules 1969 r 24, whether or not the commanding officer has ordered any other type of investigation, such as court of inquiry. Manual of Air Force Law, Volume I, s 104 notes.

3 The Air Force Act 1950 s 103 (1). A commanding officer who unnecessarily detains a person under arrest or confinement, renders himself liable to a charge under the Air Force Act 1950 s 50 (a).

4 The Air Force Act 1950 s 103 (2).

5 The Air Force Act 1950 s 103 (3).

6 The Air Force Act 1950 s 103 (4). See the Air Force Rules 1969 r 22 and 23; **[0602]** and **[0604]**.

[0602] Manner and extent of custody pending trial or confirmation of court martial proceedings

1 Any person subject to the Air Force Act 1950 who has been ordered into air force custody by a competent authority may be taken into such custody in accordance with the usages of the service[1]. However, while being held for trial or after trial pending confirmation of the proceedings, the arrest or confinement imposed upon him shall not be more rigorous than the circumstances require to ensure his physical fitness and security[2].

2 Detention in air force custody beyond a total period of 60 whether continuously or in broken periods, of a person subject to the Air Force Act 1950, who is not on active service and for whose trial a court martial has not assembled, shall require the sanction of the Chief of the Air Staff or any other officer duly authorised, with the approval of the Central Government, by the Chief of the Air Staff in that behalf[3].

3 The Chief of the Air Staff or such other officer may sanction further detention of such person as is described in the aforesaid provision for a specific period, which he may extend from time to time, provided that the total period of detention, whether continuous or broken, shall not exceed 90 days[4].

4 No such person as is described in the aforesaid provisions[5] shall be detained in air force custody beyond a period of 90 days, whether continuously or in broken periods except with the approval of the Central Government[6].

5 As soon as the proceedings of a court martial have been received by an officer having powers to confirm them, that officer shall, as soon as may be, order the release (without prejudice to re-arrest) of the accused if the finding of the court-martial is 'not guilty' on the charge, or where there are more charges them one, on all the charges, on which he was tried[7].

6 Where the sentence awarded by a court martial is lower in the scale of punishments set out in the Air Force Act 1950[8], than dismissal, the officer referred to in the aforesaid provision shall either order the release of the accused person without prejudice to re-arrest or at his discretion, order that the accused person shall be kept under open arrest[9].

7 No person shall be detained in air force custody pending confirmation of the proceedings of a court martial, for a period in excess of the term of imprisonment or detention to which the court martial has sentenced him[10].

1 The Air Force Rules 1969 r 22 (1).

2 The Air Force Rules 1969 r 22 (1) proviso.

3 The Air Force Rules 1969 r 22 (2).

4 The Air Force Rules 1969 r 22 (3).

5 Ie the Air Force Rules 1969 r 22 (2).

6 The Air Force Rules 1969 r 22 (4).

7 The Air Force Rules 1969 r 22 (5).

8 Ie the Air Force Act 1950 s 73.

9 The Air Force Rules 1969 r 22 (6).

10 The Air Force Rules 1969 r 22 (7).

[0603] Interval between committal and court martial In every case where any such person as is mentioned in the Air Force Act 1950[1] and as is not on active service remains in such custody for a longer period than eight days, without a court martial for his trial being ordered to assemble, a special report giving reasons for the delay shall be made by his commanding officer in the manner prescribed[2]; and a similar report shall be forwarded every eight days until a court martial is assembled or such person is released from custody[3].

1 Ie the Air Force Act 1950 s 102; see **[0596]**.

2 As to the meaning of 'special report' and 'in the manner prescribed'; see the Air Force Rules 1969 r 23: **[0604]**.

3 Air Force Act 1950 s 104.

[0604] Delay report In every case where a person subject to the Air Force Act 1950, who is not on active service, is in air force custody for a period longer than eight days, whether continuously or in broken periods, without a court martial for his trial hearing been assembled, or without a punishment having been awarded to him under the provisions of the Air Force Act 1950[1], the Commanding officer shall make a report in the delay report form contained in the Air Force Rules 1969[2], to the officer empowered to convene a general or district court martial for the trial of such person. Such report shall be made at interval of every eight days until a court martial is assembled or the case is disposed under the aforesaid provisions of the Air Force Act 1950[3] or such person is released from custody, as the case may be[4]. A copy of each of the third and subsequent reports submitted under the aforesaid provision will be forwarded directly to the deputy chief legal adviser of the command concerned, or in the case of persons belonging or attached to the Air Headquarters or a unit directly under Air Headquarters, to the chief legal adviser[5].

1 Ie the Air Force Act 1950 s 82 or 86.

2 Ie the Air Force Rules 1969 Second Schedule.

3 Ie the Air Force Act 1950 s 82 or 86.

4 The Air Force Rules 1969 r 23 (1).

5 The Air Force Rules 1969 r 23 (2).

[0605] Arrest by civil authorities Whenever any person subject to the Air Force Act 1950, who is accused of any offence under the aforesaid Act, is within the jurisdiction of any magistrate or police officer, such magistrate or police officer shall aid in the apprehension and delivery to air force custody of such person upon receipt of a written application to that effect signed by his commanding officer[1].

1 Air Force Act 1950 s 105.

[0606] Capture of deserters Whenever any person subject to the Air Force Act 1950 deserts, the commanding officer of the unit or detachment to which he belongs, shall give written information of the desertion to such civil authorities to afford assistance towards the capture of the deserter; and such authorities shall thereupon take steps for the apprehension of the said deserter in like manner as if he were a person for whose apprehension a warrant had been issued by a magistrate, and shall deliver the deserter, when apprehended, into air force custody[1]. Any police officer may arrest without warrant any person reasonably believed to be subject to the Air Force Act 1950, and to be a deserter or to be travelling without authority, and shall bring him without delay before the nearest magistrate, to be dealt with according to law[2].

1 The Air Force Act 1950 s 106 (1).

2 The Air Force Act 1950 s 106 (2).

[0607] Inquiry into absence without leave[1]

1 The Air Force Act 1950 s 107; see **[0896]**.

[0608] Provost Marshal Provost marshal may be appointed by the Chief of the Air Staff, or by any prescribed officer[1]. The duties of a provost marshal are to take charge of persons confined for any offence, to preserve good order and discipline, and to prevent breaches of the same by persons serving in, or attached to, the air force[2]. A provost marshal may at any time arrest and detain for trial any person subject to the Air Force Act 1950 who commits, or is charged with, an offence, and may also carry into effect any punishment to be inflicted in pursuance of the sentence awarded by a court martial, or by an officer exercising authority under the provisions of the aforesaid Act[3] s 82 but shall not inflict any punishment on his own authority[4]. However, no officer shall be so arrested or detained otherwise than on the order of another officer[5]. For the purposes of certain provisions of the Air Force Act 1950[6], a provost marshal shall be deemed to include a provost marshal appointed under the Army Act 1950 or the Navy Act 1957 and any person legally exercising authority under him or on his behalf[7].

1 As to the meaning of 'prescribed officer'; see the Air Force Rules 1969 r 166. Prescribed officers under the Air

Force Act 1950 s 108(1): The following shall be the prescribed officers for the purposes of the Air Force Act 1950 s 108(1): (i) An air or other officer commanding a command may appoint any person subject to the Air Force Act 1950 and serving under him, to exercise the powers of a provost marshal in relation to the persons serving under his command; (ii) The Air Officer in-charge Administration may appoint any person subject to the Air Force Act 1950 serving in the air headquarters or the units directly under the air headquarters to exercise the powers of a provost marshal in relation to all persons serving in the air headquarters and such units; and (iii) An officer commanding the air forces in the field may appoint any person subject to the Air Force Act 1950 and serving under him to exercise the powers of a provost marshal in relation to such air forces.

2 The Air Force Act 1950 s 108 (2).

3 Ie under the Air Force Act 1950 s 82.

4 The Air Force Act 1950 s 108 (3).

5 The Air Force Act 1950 s 108 (3) proviso.

6 Ie the Air Force Act 1950 s 108 (2) and (3).

7 The Air Force Act 1950 s 108 (4).

B. Investigation and Disposal of charges and Remand for trial

[0609] Introduction A commanding officer has a number of options for the resolution of disciplinary problems. He may: (i) take no action i.e., dismiss the charge; (ii) initiate administrative action; (iii) award punishment summarily; and (iv) take up matter for trial by a court martial.

[0610] Disposal of the charge of adjournment for taking down the summary of evidence

1 Every charge against a person subject to the Air Force Act 1950 shall be heard in the presence of the accused. The accused shall have full liberty to cross-examine any witness against him, and to call any witnesses and made any statement in his defence[1].

2 The commanding officer shall dismiss a charge brought before him if, in his opinion, the evidence does not show that some offence under the Air Force Act 1950 has been committed, and may do so if, in his discretion, he thinks the charge ought not to be proceeded with[2].

3 At the conclusion of the hearing of a charge, if the commanding officer is of opinion that the charge ought to be proceeded with, he shall, without unnecessary delay, either: (i) Dispose of the case summarily[3]; or (ii) Refer the case to the proper superior air force authority for sanction under the Air Force Act 1950[4]; or (iii) Adjourn the case for the purpose of having the evidence reduced to writing[5].

4 Where the case is adjourned for the purpose of having the evidence reduced to writing, at the adjourned hearing the evidence of the witnesses who gave evidence before the commanding officer, whether against or for the accused, and of any other person whose evidence appears to be relevant shall be taken down in writing in the presence and hearing of the accused before the officer recording the evidence[6].

5 The accused may put questions in cross-examination to any witness, and the questions with the answers shall be added in writing to the evidence taken down[7].

6 The evidence of each witness when taken down[8], shall be read over to him, and shall be signed by

him, or if he cannot write his name, shall be attested by his mark and witnessed. Any statement of the accused shall be added in writing and read over to him[9].

7 The evidence of the witnesses and the statement, if any, of the accused shall be recorded in the English language. If the witness or accused does not understand English the evidence or statement; as recorded; shall be interpreted to him in a language which he understands[10].

8 If a person cannot be compelled to attend as a witness, or if owning to the exigencies of service or any other grounds, including the expense and loss of time involved; the attendance of any witness cannot be readily procured, a written statement of his evidence purporting to be signed by him may be read to the accused and included in the summary of evidence[11].

9 Any witness who is not subject to the air force law may be summoned by order under the hands of the commanding officer of the accused to attend the hearing of the charge or to attend the adjourned hearing for the purpose of having the evidence reduced to writing under the Air Force Rules 1969[12]. The summons shall be in Form C1 as provided in the Air Force Rules 1969 Third Schedule[13].

1 The Air Force Rules 1969 r 24 (1). The charge against an officer or airman in arrest will be disposed of daily (except on Sundays and holidays) and when practicable, in the morning. Every charge against an airman will be investigated in the first instance by the subordinate commander at such hour as will allow an airman remanded for disposal by the commanding officer to be ready to go before him at the appointed time. Regulations for the Air Force 1964 paragraph 661 (c) and (d).

2 The Air Force Rules 1969 r 24 (2).

3 The Air Force Rules 1969 r 24 (3) (a).

4 Ie the Air Force Act 1950 s 83. The Air Force Rules 1969 r 24 (3) (b).

5 The Air Force Rules 1969 r 24 (3) (c).

6 The commanding officer himself can record the evidence, or he may direct any other officer for the same. The Air Force Rules 1969 r 24 (4).

7 The Air Force Rules 1969 r 24 (5). As soon as it appears probable that it will be necessary for an accused person to be remanded for trial by court martial, the commanding officer will proceed to have the evidence for and against the accused reduced to writing in accordance the provision. If the commanding officer does not himself conduct the proceedings he will be careful to ensure that the officer whom he details for the duty is one who is unlikely to be called as a witness. Regulations for the Air Force 1964, paragraph 691 (a).

8 Ie the Air Force Rules 1969 r 24 (4) and (5).

9 The Air Force Rules 1969 r 24 (6).

10 The Air Force Rules 1969 r 24 (7).

11 The commanding officer or the officer recording the summary must certify in writing that the attendance of such witness cannot be readily procured. The Air Force Rules 1969 r 24 (8).

12 Ie to attend the hearing of the charge under the Air Force Rules 1969 r 24 (1), or to attend the adjourned hearing under the Air Force Rules 1969 r 24 (4). The Air Force Rules 1969 r 24 (9) (a).

13 The Air Force Rules 1969 r 24 (9) (b).

[0611] Accused remanded to station commander When a subordinate commander remands a case for disposal by the station commander, he will submit charge report[1] to that officer for entry in the guard report of the unit, before the hour fixed for the disposal of offenders by the station commander. A subordinate commander who has reserved a charge for the decision of the station commander will attend the trial of the airman, if instructions to that effect are issued in the station standing orders. While attending, he will have with him the airman's sheet roll. The disposal of the offence will be entered by the station commander in the guard report, and charge report will be duly completed. This form will be returned to the subordinate commander who will then complete his minor offence report[2] and the conduct sheet. The charge report may then be destroyed. Charges initiated by naval, military, air force or other public authorities in respect of offences committed by airmen away from their units/stations, will, after investigation, be remanded to the station commander for disposal. If an airman is remanded for further enquiry the charges against him will be brought forward daily and the order for remand will be entered daily in the guard report or minor offence report by the investigating officer. Guard report will be posted daily in a guard book and will be kept for one year[3].

1 Ie form IAFF (P) 13.

2 Ie form IAFF (P) 24.

3 Regulations for the Air Force 1964, paragraph 664.

[0612] Remand of accused The evidence and statement, if any, taken down in writing in pursuance of the provisions of the Air Force Rules 1969[1] (i.e., the summary of evidence) shall be considered by the commanding officer, who shall either: (i) Remand the accused for trial by court martial[2]; or (ii) Refer the case to the proper superior air force authority for sanction under the Air Force Act 1950 s 83 or disposal of case under s 86[3]; or (iii) If he thinks it desirable, re-hear the case and dispose it of summarily[4]. If the accused is remanded for trial by court martial, the commanding officer shall without delay apply to the proper air force authority to convene a court martial[5]. The summary of evidence, or its true copy, shall be furnished to the convening authority with the application to convene a court martial, and shall be laid before the court martial before which the accused is tried on the assembly of the court[6].

1 Ie the Air Force Rules 1969 r 24.

2 The Air Force Rules 1969 r 25 (1) (a).

3 The Air Force Rules 1969 r 25 (1) (b).

4 The Air Force Rules 1969 r 25 (1) (c). After considering the summary of evidence, a commanding officer may, if he thinks that the trial of the accused by court martial is not, justified, rehear the case and dispose of it summarily, provided it is within his competence to do so. Regulations for the Air Force 1964, paragraph 691(b).

5 The Air Force Rules 1969 r 25 (2).

6 The Air Force Rules 1969 r 25 (3).

[0613] Application of the provisions of the Air Force Rules 1969 r 24 and 25 to officers exercising powers of a commanding officer The provisions of the Air Force Rules 1969 r 24 and 25 shall, so far as practicable, also apply to an officer exercising the powers of a commanding officer[1].

1 For Air Force Rules 1969 r 24 and 25; see **[0610]** and **[0612]**. The Air Force Rules 1969 r 26.

[0614] Accused person remanded When an accused person is remanded for further investigation or for trial by court martial, the commanding officer must consider whether, having regard to all the circumstances, the accused should or should not be released from close or open arrest; and either placed in open arrest or released without prejudice until further orders. If, on the investigation of a charge, sufficient evidence is not forthcoming, as to whether the accused has, or has not, committed the offence, and there is no opportunity of carrying the investigation further at the time, the accused, if the offence charged is not of a serious nature, may be released from arrest without prejudice to his re-arrest. The accused may be ordered to do duty till further evidence is forthcoming and the matter can be further inquired into[1].

1 Regulations for the Air Force 1964, paragraph 665.

[0615] Disposal by commanding officer and sending before a court martial A commanding officer should consider each case on its merits. He should not summarily dispose of a case which obviously warrants a more severe punishment than he is empowered to award. In respect of offences specified under certain provisions of the Air Force Act 1950[1], a commanding officer may after hearing the charge and the evidence produced before him, acquit the offender, but he cannot award any punishment except with the previous sanction in writing of an officer having power to convene a district court martial. Before proceeding with a case, it is the duty of the commanding officer to see that the offender is liable to be proceeded against, having regard to certain provisions of the Air Force Act 1950[2]. Except where it is important that the guilt or innocence of the accused should be definitely decided, it is undesirable to send a case before a court martial when it appears doubtful whether the, evidence will lead to a conviction. In such a case the charge should ordinarily be dismissed under the provisions of the Air Force Rules 1969. When an airman or apprentice under the age of 21 years is remanded for trial by court martial on a serious charge, his commanding officer will interview him and impress upon him the desirability of keeping his next of kin informed. When any such person is awaiting trial on a serious charge by a civil court, similar action will be taken by the commanding officer. When an apprentice is remanded for trial by court martial, his commanding officer will inform his parents or legal guardians of the fact at the earliest moment, stating the nature of the charge preferred against him. In cases where an airman is charged with one offence, another offence comes to light and the investigation cannot be completed immediately or proceeded with, the investigation and trial in respect of the original offence may proceed independently and the charge for the second offence may be dealt with as prescribed[3]. When a person already under sentence of court martial is charged with an offence for which it is necessary to arraign him before a court martial the trial should take place at once[4].

1 Ie the Air Force Act 1950s 83.

2 Ie the Air Force Act 1950 s 121.

3 Ie as prescribed in the Regulations for the Air Force 1964, paragraph 665.

4 Regulations for the Air Force 1964, paragraph 666.

[0616] Action by officer having power to convene a district court martial An officer having power to convene a district court martial to whom an application for the convening of a court martial is made or to whom a case is referred under the certain provision of the Air Force Rules 1969[1] may, at his discretion either: (i) authorise in writing the commanding officer or other officer exercising the powers of a commanding officer to dismiss the charge or dispose of the case summarily[2], (ii) refer the case to a superior authority[3], or (iii) order the assembly of a district court-martial for the trial of the accused person[4].

1 Ie the Air Force Rules 1969 r 25 (1) (b).

2 The Air Force Rules 1969 r 27 (a).

3 The Air Force Rules 1969 r 27 (b).

4 The Air Force Rules 1969 r 27 (c).

[0617] Action by officer having power to convene a general court martial An officer having power to convene a general court martial to whom application for the convening of a court martial is made, or to whom a case is referred under the certain provisions of the Air Force Rules 1969[1] may, at his discretion either: (i) return the case to the commanding officer or other officer exercising the powers of a commanding officer authorising such officer in writing to dismiss the charge or dispose of the case summarily[2]; (ii) deal with the case summarily, as provided in the Air Force Rules 1969 r 31[3], or (iii) order the assembly of a court-martial for the trial of the accused person[4]; or (iv) refer the case to a superior authority[5].

1 Ie the Air Force Rules 1969 r 25 (1) (b) or r 27 (b).

2 The Air Force Rules 1969 r 28 (a).

3 The Air Force Rules 1969 r 28 (b)

4 The Air Force Rules 1969 r 28 (c).

5 The Air Force Rules 1969 r 28 (d).

[0618] Framing of charge-sheet and charge A charge-sheet shall, so far as practicable, conform to the form of charge-sheet specified in the Air Force Rules 1969[1] and shall contain the whole issue or issues to be tried by a court martial at one time[2]. A charge means an accusation contained in a charge-sheet that a person subject to the Act has been guilty of an offence[3]. A charge-sheet may contain one charge or several charges[4].

1 Ie the Air Force Rules 1969 Fifth Schedule.

2 The Air Force Rules 1969 r 34 (1). The charge sheet referred in this provision is the formal written charge sheet upon which the accused is to be tried. It is a distinct from the charge or complaint contained in the Air Force Act 1950 s 102 and the Air Force Rules 1969 r 24. Manual of Air Force Law, volume II, r 34 notes.

3 The Air Force Rules 1969 r 34 (2).

4 The Air Force Rules 1969 r 34 (3). For more details see: **[0619] to [0622]**.

[0619] Commencement of charge-sheet Every charge-sheet shall begin with the name and description of the person charged, and state, in the case of an officer[1], his rank, name, number, and unit, and in the case of a warrant officer[2], or other enrolled person, his number, rank, name and unit. When the accused person does not belong to the regular air force, the charge-sheet shall show by the description of him, or directly by an express averment, that he is subject to the Air Force Act 1950 in respect of the offence charged[3].

1 As to the definition of 'officer'; see **[0494].**

2 As to the definition of 'warrant officer'; see **[0504]**.

3 The Air Force Rules 1969 r 35.

[0620] Contents of charge

1 Each charge shall state one offence only, and in no case shall an offence be described in the alternative in the same charge[1].

2 Each charge shall be divided into two parts: the statement of the offence[2]; and the statement of the particulars of the act, neglect, or omission constituting the offence[3].

3 The offence shall be stated, if not a civil offence, as nearly as practicable, in the words of the Air Force Act 1950, and if a civil offence, in such words as sufficiently describe that offence, but not necessarily

in technical words[4].

4 The particulars shall state such circumstances respecting the alleged offence as will enable the accused to know what act, neglect or omission is intended to be proved against him as constituting the offence[5].

5 The particulars in one charge may be framed wholly or partly by a reference to the particulars in another charge, and in that case so much of the latter particulars as are so referred to shall be deemed to form part of the first mentioned charge as well as of the other charge[6].

6 Where it is intended to prove any facts in respect of which any deduction from pay and allowances can be awarded as a consequence of the offence charged, the particulars shall state those facts, and the sum of the loss or damage it is intended or charge[7].

1 The Air Force Rules 1969 r 36 (1).

2 The Air Force Rules 1969 r 36 (2)(a).

3 The Air Force Rules 1969 r 36 (2)(b).

4 The Air Force Rules 1969 r 36 (3).

5 The Air Force Rules 1969 r 36 (4).

6 The Air Force Rules 1969 r 36 (5).

7 The Air Force Rules 1969 r 36 (6).

[0621] Signature on charge-sheet The charge-sheet must be signed by the commanding officer of the accused and must contain the place and date of such signature[1].

1 The Air Force Rules 1969 r 37.

[0622] Validity of charge-sheet A charge-sheet shall not be invalid by reason only of any mistake in the name or description of the person charged, if he does not object to the charge-sheet during the trial, and it is not shown that injustice has been done to the person charged[1]. A court martial or an authority dealing with the case summarily under the Air Force Act 1950 s 82 or 86 may presume matters which, though not stated in the charge, and necessary to support its validity, can reasonably implied from it[2].

1 The Air Force Rules 1969 r 38 (1).

2 In the construction of a charge-sheet or charge, there shall be presumed in favour of supporting the same every proposition which may reasonably be presumed to be impliedly included though not expressed therein; The Air Force Rules 1969 r 38 (2).

C. Preparation of defence by the accused persons

[0623] Opportunity for accused to prepare defence An accused person for whose trial a court martial has been ordered to assemble shall be afforded proper opportunity of preparing his defence. He shall be allowed free communication with his witnesses, friend or legal adviser whom he may wish to consult[1].

1 The Air Force Rules 1969 r 39.

[0624] Warning of accused for trial

1 The accused before he is arraigned shall be informed by an officer of every charge on which he is to be tried; and also that, on his giving the names of witnesses whom he desires to call in his defence, reasonable steps will be taken for procuring their attendance, and those steps shall be taken accordingly. The interval between his being so informed of the charges against him and his arrangement must be such as to allow him to have his witnesses present, and to consider his defence[1].

2 The officer at the time of so informing the accused shall give him a copy of the charge-sheet, and, if the summary of evidence has not been dispensed with under the provisions of the Air Force Rules 1969[2], a copy of the summary of evidence, and if he so desires it, vernacular translation of the same, and shall, if necessary, read and explain to him the charges brought against him[3].

3 If he desires it, a list of the names, ranks, and units of the officers who are to form the court, and where officers in waiting are names, also of these officers, will be given to the accused[4].

4 If it appears to the court that the accused is liable to be prejudiced at his trial by any non-compliance with this provision, the court shall take steps and, if necessary, adjourn to avoid the accused being so prejudiced[5].

1 The Air Force Rules 1969 r 40 (1).

2 Ie the Air Force Rules 1969 r 42.

3 The Air Force Rules 1969 r 40 (2).

4 The Air Force Rules 1969 r 40 (3).

5 The Air Force Rules 1969 r 40 (4). Also see **[0151]** and **[0702]**.

[0625] Joint trial of Several Accused Persons

1 Any number accused persons may be charged jointly and tried together for an offence averred to have been committed by them collectively[1].

2 Any number of accused persons, whether charged jointly or not, may be tried together for an offence averred to have been committed by one or more of them and to have been abetted by the other or others[2].

3 Where the accused persons are so charged under the aforesaid provisions, any one or more of them may at the same time be charged with and tried for any other offence averred to have been committed individually or collectively[3]. However, it will be necessary all the said offences are based on the same facts, or form, or any part of, a series of offences of same or similar character[4].

4 In the cases mentioned above, notices of intention to try the accused the persons together shall be given to each of the accused persons at the time of being informed of the charge. Any accused person may claim, by giving notice to the convening authority, or to the court, that he or some other accused person be tried separately on the charge(s), on the grounds that the evidence of one or more of the other accused persons proposed to be tried together with him will material to his defence or that otherwise he would be prejudiced or embarrassed in his defence. The convening authority or court, if satisfied that the accused may be prejudices or embarrassed in his defence as aforesaid, and if the nature of the charge admits of this, shall allow the claim, and such accused person or as the case may be, the other

accused person or persons, whose separate trial has been claimed, shall be tried separately[5].

5 Where any such claim as referred in the aforesaid provision has been made and disallowed by the authority convening the court or by the court, the disallowance of such claim shall not be a ground for refusing, confirmation of the finding or sentence unless, in the opinion of the confirming authority, substantial miscarriage of justice has occurred by reason of disallowance of such claim[6].

6 Where proceedings of any court-martial in respect of any charge against an accused person are not confirmed on the ground stated in the aforesaid provision, such accused person may be tried again on that charge[7].

It is the discretion of the court martial to amalgamate the cases against the accused persons if they relate to the same incident, provided their interest is not inconsistent with each other. The only requirement that the court martial has to satisfy is that the accused is not prejudicially affected and that it is expedient to amalgamate the cases[8].

1 The Air Force rules 1969 r 41 (1).

2 The Air Force rules 1969 r 41 (2).

3 The Air Force rules 1969 r 41 (3).

4 The Air Force rules 1969 r 41 (3) proviso.

5 The Air Force rules 1969 r 41 (4).

6 The Air Force rules 1969 r 41 (5).

7 The Air Force rules 1969 r 41 (6).

8 The Armed Forces Tribunal New Delhi (Principal Bench in *Ex Sepoy Mahender Singh v Union of India*, in TA No. 239 of 2009 [WP (C) No. 3134 of 1989], decided on 15 January 2010, considered the provisions of joint trial by a general court martial under the Army Rules 1954 r 35 (= Air Force Rules 1969 r 41).

D. Exemption from Air Force Rules 1969

[0626] Suspension of rules on the ground of the exigencies of the service or the necessities of discipline Where it appears to the officer convening a court martial, or to the senior officer on the spot, that exigencies of the service or the necessities of discipline render it impossible or inexpedient to observe certain provisions of the Air Force Rules 1969[1] he may, by order under his hand, make a declaration to that effect specifying the nature of such exigencies or necessities, and thereupon the trial or other proceedings shall be as valid as if the rule mentioned in such declaration had not been contained herein; and the declaration may be made with respect to all or any of the provisions of the rules aforesaid mentioned[2]. However, the accused shall have full opportunity of making his defence, and shall be afforded every facility for preparing it which is practicable, having due regard to the said exigencies or necessities[3].

1 Ie the Air Force Rules 1969 r 24 (4), (5), (6) and (7) and r 25, 39 and 40.

2 The Air Force Rules 1969 r 42.

3 The Air Force Rules 1969 r 42 proviso.

6. ADMINISTRATIVE ACTION AND MINOR PUNISHMENTS

CONTENTS

PARA

A. Administrative Action

B. Minor Punishments

A. ADMINISTRATIVE ACTION

[0627] Reproof of officers and warrant officers

1 A commanding officer or any superior air force officer may reprove an officer or warrant officer[1] under his command for an offence which, in his opinion, is not of such a serious nature as to merit disciplinary action under the Air Force Act 1950. The reproof of an officer or warrant officer is not a recognised punishment under the aforesaid Act, and will not be entered in the officer's or warrant officer's record. In order to avoid any confusion with a 'reprimand' under the Air Force Act 1050, it is

not to be referred to by any terms other than 'reprove' or 'reproof'[2].

2 Care must be taken to ensure that the procedure stated in the aforesaid provision is not adopted when superior authority is likely to consider that the offence calls for disciplinary action under the Air Force Act 1950, as the reproof might be held to amount to a condonation of the offence barring disciplinary action under the Air Force Act 1950[3].

3 The censure is a matter of custom of service awarded for offences/lapses, which are not of serious nature as to merit disciplinary action under the Air Force Act 1950 or where disciplinary action is inexpedient. Censure may take the form of 'Reproof', 'Displeasure' or 'Severe Displeasure'. The award of 'Displeasure' or 'Severe Displeasure' carries negative marks for the consideration of the promotion board depending on the period for which it is expressed. The award of 'Displeasure' or 'Sever Displeasure' would be considered only once by that promotion board before which the officer's case first comes for consideration irrespective of the pendency of the Censure[4].

1 As to the definition of 'officer' and 'warrant officer'; see **[0494]** and **[0504]**.

2 Regulations for the Air Force 1964, paragraph 712 (a). Censure should not to be awarded without giving opportunity to the officer or warrant officer to explain his conduct, act or omission. Censure shall not be awarded unless the affected person has been given an opportunity to explain his conduct, act or omission at a court of inquiry or formal investigation by proper application of the Regulations for the Air Force 1964, paragraph 790. If the incident was not investigated, or if investigated, the aforesaid provisions of the Regulations for the Air Force could not be applied, then a 'Show Cause' notice listing the facts on account of which the award of censure is contemplated, will be served on the officer. The Air Force Order 227 of 1977 paragraph 23.

3 Regulations for the Air Force 1964, paragraph 712 (b).

4 *Air Commodore SK Mishra v Union of India* 1998 IAD Delhi 609 : 1998 (44) DRJ 328, decided 28 November 1997.

[0628] Severe displeasure / displeasure Severe displeasure / displeasure may be awarded to an officer by the central government or the chief of the air staff, or the air officer commanding-in-chief command under whom the officer is serving or was serving at the time of the commission/omission of the impugned act/omission or misconduct. It can also be awarded by the air officer-in-charge administration, if the officer is serving, or at the time of the commission/omission of the impugned act, was serving in Air Headquarters or in a unit under the direct administrative control of Air Headquarters. Severe displeasure/displeasure of the central government is normally conveyed in the form of a letter and is kept permanently in the personal file of the officer. Severe displeasure by the chief of the air staff or the air officer commanding-in-chief command or air officer-in-charge administration will be expressed in terms of a period, not exceeding 36 months in the case of award by the chief of the air staff, and not exceeding 18 months in the case of award by the air officer commanding-in-chief command or air officer-in-charge administration. There will be no period of award for displeasure. Censure is not to be awarded without giving an opportunity to the officer to explain his conduct, act or omission. Censure awarded to an officer will be considered while deciding his suitability or otherwise his promotion to the next higher rank only[1]. Severe displeasure/displeasure may be awarded to an airman by the chief of the air staff, or the air officer commanding-in-chief command under whom the airman is serving or was serving at the time of the commission/omission of the impugned act/omission or misconduct or by the air officer-in-charge administration, if the airman is serving, or at the time as aforesaid, was serving in air headquarters or in a unit under the direct administrative control of air headquarters. Severe displeasure by the chief of the air staff or the air officer commanding-in-chief command or air officer-in-charge administration will be expressed in terms of a period, not exceeding 36 months in the case of award by the chief of the air staff, and not exceeding 18 months in the case of award by the air officer commanding-in-chief command or air officer-in-charge administration. Censure is not to be awarded without giving an opportunity to the airman to explain his conduct, act or omission. Censure awarded to an airman will be considered while deciding his suitability or otherwise his promotion to the next higher rank only[2]. Review of an award of censure to an officer or airman may be carried out by any authority superior to the one by whom such censure was awarded. Request for review of the award of censure is to be made within six months from the date of receipt of letter conveying the award[3].

1 Air Force Order 03 of 2008 paragraphs 18, 20 and 26.

2 Air Force Order 03 of 2008 paragraphs 30, 31 and 35.

3 Air Force Order 03 of 2008 paragraphs 42 and 43.

B. Minor Punishment

[0629] Punishments otherwise than by court martial Punishments may also be inflicted in respect of offences committed by persons subject to the Air Force Act 1950 without the intervention of a court martial[1].

1 Ie as stated in the Air Force Act 1950 ss 82 and 86. The Air Force Act 1950 s 81.

[0630] Minor Punishments Minor punishments are those which are inflicted without the intervention of a court martial under the provisions of the Air Force Act 1950 s 82 or 861.

1 The Air Force Rules 1969 r 2 (c); see **[0490]**.

[0631] Punishment of persons other than officers and warrant officers Subject to certain the provisions of the Air Force Act 1950[1], a commanding officer[2] may, in the prescribed manner[3], proceed against a person subject to the Air Force Act 1950 otherwise than as an officer or warrant officer who is charged with an offence under the aforesaid Act and award such person, to the extent prescribed[4], one or more of the following punishments: detention up to 28 days[5]; confinement to the camp up to 14 days[6]; extra guards or duties not exceeding three in number[7]; deprivation of acting rank[8]; forfeiture of badge pay[9]; severe reprimand or reprimand[10]; fine up to 14 days' pay in any one month[11]; penal deductions under the Air Force Act 1950 s 92 (g)[12]; admonition[13]; and any prescribed field punishment up to 28 days, in the case of a person on active service[14].

1 Ie the Air Force Act 1950 s 84. It imposes certain restrictions and limits as regards the exercise of powers under the Air Force Act 1950 s 82.

2 The power can be exercised by other officers as specified by the Chief of the Air Staff, with the consent of the Central Government. For definition of 'commanding officer'; see **[0485]**.

3 As to the meaning of 'prescribe manner'; see the Air Force Rules 1969 r 22 and the Regulations for the Air Force 1964, paragraphs 661-680.

4 As to the meaning of 'to the extent prescribed'; see the Air Force Rules 1969 r 29 and 30.

5 The Air Force Act 1950 s 82 (a).

6 The Air Force Act 1950 s 82 (b).

7 The Air Force Act 1950 s 82 (c).

8 The Air Force Act 1950 s 82 (d).

9 The Air Force Act 1950 s 82 (e).

10 The Air Force Act 1950 s 82 (f).

11 The Air Force Act 1950 s 82 (g).

12 The Air Force Act 1950 s 82 (h).

13 The Air Force Act 1950 s 82 (i).

14 The Air Force Act 1950 s 82 (j).

[0632] Execution of punishment of detention A sentence of detention awarded by a court martial or by an officer exercising authority under the Air Force Act 1950[1] may be carried out in a military or air force detention barrack. However, on active service, when the unit is halted at any place where there is a provost marshal, under the orders of such officer[2].

1 Ie under the Air Force Act 1950 s 82.

2 The Air Force Rules 1969 r 153; see **[0872]**.

[0633] Requirement of sanction in certain cases Subject to certain the provisions of the Air Force Act 1950[1], the punishments mentioned in the Air Force Act 1950 s 82 shall not be inflicted in respect of an offence committed under the Air Force Act 1950 ss 34, 35 and 36 when committed on active service or under the Air Force Act 1950 ss 37, 38, 40, 42 (f) and (g), 43, 47, 52, 60, 62, 63, 64, 66 (a), (b) and (c) and 71 except with the previous sanction in writing of an officer having power to convene a district court martial[2]. The said punishments may be awarded without such sanction in the case of any offence, other than an offence under the Air Force Act 1950 ss 34 or 71, committed by persons who have not been enrolled as combatants[3].

1 Ie the Air Force Act 1950 s 83 (2).

2 The Air Force Act 1950 s 83 (1). This provision imposes restrictions on the award of minor punishments by a commanding officer exercising power under the Air Force Act 1950 s 82. The restrictions apply only to offences under any of the provisions mentioned under the Air Force Act 1950 s 83 (1). In all such cases, the punishing authority has to obtain previous sanction in writing of the officer having power to convene a district court martial. As regards NCs (E) the restriction applies only if the offence was under the Air Force Act 1950 ss 34 or 71, not otherwise. The Manual of Air Force Law, Volume I, s 83 notes.

3 The Air Force Act 1950 s 83 (2).

[0634] Limit of punishments under the Air Force Act 1950 s 82 An award of punishment under the Air Force Act 1950[1] shall not include field punishment in addition to one or more of the punishments specified in the Air Force Act 1950 s 82 (a) and (b)[2]. In the case of an award of two or more of the punishments specified in the Air Force Act 1950 s 82 (a), (b) and, (c), the punishment specified in (b) or (c) shall take effect only at the end of the punishment specified in clause (a)[3]. When two or more of the punishments specified in the Air Force Act 1950 s 82 (a) and (b) are awarded to a person conjointly, or when already undergoing one or more of the said punishments, the whole extent of the punishments shall not exceed in the aggregate 42 days[4]. The punishments specified in the Air Force Act 1950 s 82 (a), (b), (c), (e), (g) and (j) shall not be awarded to any person who is of the rank of non-commissioned officer or was, at the time of committing the offence for which he is punished, of such rank[5]. The punishment specified in the Air Force Act 1950 s 82 (f) shall not be awarded to any person below the rank of a non-commissioned officer[6].

1 Ie under the Air Force Act 1950 s 82.

2 The Air Force Act 1950 s 84 (1). Field punishment has been abolished under the Army Act 1950.

3 The Air Force Act 1950 s 84 (2).

4 The Air Force Act 1950 s 84 (3).

5 The Air Force Act 1950 s 84 (4).

6 The Air Force Act 1950 s 84 (5).

[0635] Punishments in addition to those specified in the Air Force Act 1950 s 82 The Chief of the Air Staff may, with the consent of the Central Government, specify such other punishments which may be awarded under the Air Force Act 1950 s 82 in addition to those specified in the said provision[1].

1 The Air Force Act 1950 s 85. No other punishment has been specified so far under this provision; the Manual of Air Force Law, Volume I, s 85 notes.

[0636] Limitation of powers of minor punishment according to rank

1 A commanding officer or other officer exercising the powers of a commanding officer, if of the rank of squadron leader or above, may, without the intervention of a court martial, award the minor punishments specified in the provisions of the Air Force Act 1950[1].

2 A commanding officer, or other officer exercising the powers of commanding officer, of the rank of flight lieutenant, shall have the powers of punishment specified in the aforesaid provision, provided that he shall not award detention or field punishment for a period exceeding seven days[2].

3 A commanding officer, or other officer exercising the powers of a commanding officer who is below the rank of flight lieutenant shall have the powers of imposing punishment specified in the aforesaid provision, except the following in the case of non-commissioned officers: (i) Severe reprimand[3]; (ii) Deprivation of acting rank[4]; and (iii) Penal deduction under the Air Force Act s 92 (g); and in the case of persons below non-commissioned ranks, forfeiture of badge pay[5]. However, such officer shall not award detention or field punishment for a period exceeding seven days, or confinement to the camp for a period exceeding ten days[6].

4 Notwithstanding anything contained in aforesaid provisions[7], where a commanding officer or other officer exercising the powers of a commanding officer is below the rank of squadron leader, an officer superior in command to such commanding or other officer, may, if he considers desirable, restrict the powers under the said provision of such commanding officer or other officer to any extent that he thinks fit[8].

1 Ie the Air Force Act 1950 s 82. The Air Force Rules 1969 r 29 (1).

2 The Air Force Rules 1969 r 29 (2).

3 The Air Force Rules 1969 r 29 (3)(a).

4 The Air Force Rules 1969 r 29 (3)(b).

5 The Air Force Rules 1969 r 29 (3)(c).

6 The Air Force Rules 1969 r 29 (3) (c) proviso.

7 Ie the Air Force Rules 1969 r 29 (2) and (3).

8 The Air Force Rules 1969 r 29 (4).

[0637] Powers of minor punishment of subordinate commanders

1 Subject to the following provision, an officer other than a commanding officer, who has with the consent of the Central Government been specified by the chief of the air staff as a 'subordinate commander', may award such minor punishments and to such extent as specified under this provision[1].

2 The subordinate commanders specified in the column 1 of the Table below if authorised in this behalf by the commanding officer or other officer exercising the powers of a commanding officer, may award to the persons specified in column 2 the minor punishments specified in the column 3 thereof. However, when an officer of the rank of Flight Lieutenant is officiating in an appointment normally held by an officer of higher rank, or when no subordinate commander of the rank of squadron leader or above is available, an officer of the rank of flight lieutenant shall not be authorised to award the punishment of fine[2].

1.Authority competent to award punishment	2. Person who may be punished	3. Punishment
1. Officer of the rank of Flight Lieutenant or above	(a) Non-commissioned Officer (b) Airmen below non-commissioned rank	(i) Reprimand. (ii) Admonition (i) Confinement to the camp for a period not exceeding 7 days. (ii) Extra Guards or duties no exceeding 3 in number. (iii) Admonition. (iv) Fine not exceeding 4 days pay provided that an airman shall not be fined more than 7 days pay in any one month
(2) Officer Below the rank of Flight Lieutenant.	(a) Non-commissioned Officer (b) Airmen below non-commissioned rank.	Admonition (i) Confinement to the camp for a period not exceeding 3 days. (ii) Extra Guards or duties not exceeding 3 in number. (iii) Admonition

1 The Air Force Rules 1969 r 30 (1).

2 The Air Force Rules 1969 r 30 (2).

[0638] Revision of minor punishment awarded under the Air Force Act 1950 s 82

1 If a minor punishment awarded under the Air Force Act 1950[1], appears to the Central Government, the chief of the air staff, or any officer superior in command to the officer who awarded the punishment, to be wholly illegal, such authority shall direct that the award can be cancelled and the entry in the records of the accused be expunged[2].

2 If such minor punishment appears to the authority specified in the aforesaid provision to be in excess of the punishment authorised by law, such authority may vary the punishment awarded so that it shall

not be in excess of the punishment authorised by law, and the entry in the records of the accused shall be varied accordingly[3].

3 If such minor punishment appears to the authority specified in the aforesaid provision to be unjust or too severe having regard to all circumstance of the case, such authority may mitigate or remit the punishment awarded or commute the punishment for any other punishment(s) lower in the scales laid down in the the Air Force Act 1950[4], which the commanding officer or other officer exercising powers under that provision could have validly awarded. Such mitigation, remission or commutation shall be entered in the records of the accused[5]. However, for the purpose of this provision, the punishment of field punishment shall be deemed to be higher in scale than detention[6]. Further, the field punishment shall not be commuted for punishment of detention for a term exceeding term of such field punishment and the field punishment or detention shall not be commuted for a punishment of confinement to the camp for a term exceeding the term of such field punishment or detention[7].

4 Any authority specified under this provision[8] may, in addition to or without any order passed under the aforsaid provisions[9], issue such direction in any case as may appear to such authority to be necessary for doing justice in the matter[10].

5 The power to review the minor punishment should be exercised by a superior air force authority within a period of two years from the date of the award[11].

1 Ie under the Air Force Act 1950s 82. As to the meaning of 'minor punishment'; see **[0490]**.

2 The Air Force Rules 1969 r 33 (1).

3 The Air Force Rules 1969 r 33 (2).

4 Ie under the Air Force Act 1950s 82.

5 The Air Force Rules 1969 r 33 (3).

6 The Air Force Rules 1969 r 33 (3) proviso.

7 The Air Force Rules 1969 r 33 (3) additional proviso.

8 Ie as specified under the Air Force Rules 1969 r 33 (1).

9 Ie under the Air Force Rules 1969 r 33 (1), (2) or (3).

10 The Air Force Rules 1969 r 33 (4).

11 Regulations for the Air Force 1964, paragraph 711.

[0639] Punishment of officers and warrant officers An officer having power to convene a general court martial or other officers[1] may, in the prescribed manner[2], proceed against an officer[3] below the rank of squadron leader or a warrant officer[4], who is charged with an offence under the Air Force Act 1950, and award one or more of the following punishments:

(a) Forfeiture of seniority, or in the case of any of them whose promotion depends upon length of service, forfeiture of service for the purpose of promotion for a period not exceeding 12 months, but subject to the right of the accused previous to the award to elect to be tried by a court martial[5].

(b) Severe reprimand or reprimand[6].

(c) Stoppage of pay and allowance until any proved loss or damage occasioned by the offence of which he is convicted is made good but subject to the right of the accused previous to the award to elect to be tried by a court martial[7].

(d) Forfeiture of pay and allowances for a period not exceeding three months for an offence under certain provisions of the Air Force Act 1950[8] in so far as it consists of neglect to obey flying orders or under certain other provisions[9] of the aforesaid Act[10].

1 'Other officer': under the provisions of the Air Force Act 1950 s 86, the chief of the air staff has, with the consent of the central government, specified that any air officer in command of a unit or formation may proceed under the said provision against an officer below the rank of squadron leader or a warrant officer, who is for the time being serving under the command of that air officer and award one or more of the punishments as stated in the Air Force Act s 86. The Manual of Air Force Law, Volume I, s 86 notes.

2 As to the meaning of 'prescribed manner'; see the Air Force Rules 1969 r 31 and forms D1, D2 in fourth schedule to the Air Force Rules 1969. The Manual of Air Force Law, Volume I, s 86 notes.

3 As to the definition of 'officer'; see **[0494]**.

4 As to the definition of 'warrant officer'; see **[0504]**.

5 The Air Force Act 1950 s 86 (a).

6 The Air Force Act 1950 s 86 (b).

7 The Air Force Act 1950 s 86 (c).

8 Ie under the Air Force Act 1950 s 42 (e).

9 Ie under the Air Force Act 1950 ss 62 or 63.

10 The Air Force Act 1950 s 86 (d).

[0640] Summary disposal of charge against officers and warrant officers

1 When a charge against an officer or warrant officers[1] is to be summarily disposed under the Air Force Act 1950[2] a copy of the summary of evidence shall be delivered to him free of charge as soon as practicable after its preparation, and in any case not less than 48 hours before such disposal[3].

2 The officer dealing with the case summarily under the aforesaid provision shall hear the witnesses, if any, in the presence of the accused, but may dispense with the hearing of any or all witnesses, if the accused person consents in writing thereto[4].

3 If the accused person demands the evidence be taken of oath, the officer dealing with the case summarily shall administer to each witness before he gives his evidence, the oath or affirmation as prescribed[5] but the accused person shall not be sworn[6].

4 The accused may put questions in cross-examination to any witness, call any witness and make a statement in his defence[7].

5 The proceeding shall be recorded in the forms used for summary disposal of charges against officers and warrants officers[8] and in every case in which a punishment is awarded, the original and certified true copy of the proceedings together with the summary of evidence shall be forwarded through the proper channel to the superior air force authority as defined in the provisions of the Air Force Act 1950[9].

1 As to the definition of 'officer' and 'warrant officer'; see **[0494]** and **[0504]**.

2 Ie the Air Force Act 1950 s 86.

3 The Air Force Rules 1969 r 31 (1).

4 The Air Force Rules 1969 r 31 (2).

5 As prescribed under the Air Force Rules 1969 r 118.

6 The Air Force Rules 1969 r 31 (3).

7 The Air Force Rules 1969 r 31 (4).

8 As for as practicable in accordance with the Air Force Rules 1969 Fourth Schedule (Form D 1 or Form D 2), as appropriate.

9 Ie the Air Force Act 1950 s 89. The Air Force Rules 1969 r 31 (5).

[0641] Summary award of punishment by commanding or other officer When a commanding officer, or other officer having power to dispose of an offence summarily, has once awarded a punishment for that offence, he cannot afterwards increase the punishment for that offence[1].

1 The Air Force Rules 1969 r 32.

[0642] Transmission of proceedings In every case in which punishment has been awarded under certain provisions of the Air Force Act 1950[1], certified true copies of the proceedings shall be forwarded by the officer awarding the punishment to a superior air force authority[2].

1 Ie the Air Force Act 1950 s 86.

2 As to the definition of superior air force authority; see the Air Force Act 1950 s 89; **[0644]**. The Air Force Act 1950 s 87.

[0643] Review of proceedings If any punishment awarded under the the Air Force Act 1950[1] appears to a superior air force authority as defined in the Air Force Act 1950[2] to be illegal, unjust or excessive, such authority may cancel, vary or remit the punishment and make such other direction as may be appropriate in the circumstances of the case[3].

A punishment is wholly 'illegal' if (i) the finding of guilty cannot be upheld; or (ii) the only punishment awarded is of a kind which cannot be awarded for the offence charged (e.g., stoppage of pay and allowances for an offence which is not alleged to have occasioned any loss); or (iii) where the punishment awarded is of a kind which the authority dealing with the case is not authorized to award. Where the punishment is wholly illegal it must be cancelled and appropriate direction made by the superior authority. A punishment is 'excessive' when it is in excess of the punishment authorized by the law for the offence i.e., where it is of a kind which authority dealing with the case is authorized to award for the offence charged but is greater in amount than he is authorized to award. For example, if an authority under the Air Force Act 1950 s 86 were to award stoppage greater than the amount of loss proved to have been occasioned by the offence or forfeiture of seniority of rank for a period in excess of 12 months. In such cases the superior air force authority can vary the punishment by reducing the amount of punishment to an amount which is authorized by the law. Where the punishment though not excess of the punishment authorized, appears to be unjust or severe, the superior air force authority has the power to remit the whole or part of the punishment[4].

1 Ie the Air Force Act 1950 s 86.

2 Ie as defined in the Air Force Act 1950 s 89; see **[0644]**.

3 The Air Force Act 1950 s 88. 'Make such other directions, as may appropriate in the circumstances of the case': these words would enable the superior air force authority to mitigate or commute the punishment where it is unjust or excessive. The Manual of Air Force Law, Volume I, s 88 notes.

4 The Manual of Air Force Law, Volume I, s 88 notes.

[0644] Superior air force authority For the purposes of certain provisions of the Air Force Act 1950[1], a 'superior air force authority' means: (i) in the case of punishments awarded by a commanding officer, any officer superior in command to such commanding officer[2]; and (ii) in the case of punishments awarded by any other authority, the Central Government, the Chief of the Air Staff or other officer specified by the Chief of the Air Staff[3].

1 Ie for the Air Force Act 1950 ss 87 and 88.

2 The Air Force Act 1950 s 89 (a).

3 The Air Force Act 1950 s 89 (b). No other authority has been specified by the chief of the air staff under this provision. The Manual of Air Force Law, Volume I, s 89 notes.

[0645] Collective fines Whenever any weapon or part of a weapon forming part of the equipment of a unit or detachment is lost or stolen, the officer commanding[1] such unit or detachment may, after obtaining the report of a court of inquiry, impose a collective fine upon the warrant officers[2], non-commissioned officers[3] and men of such unit, or upon so many of them as, in his judgment, should be held responsible for such loss or theft[4]. Such fine shall be assessed as a percentage on the pay of the individuals on whom it falls[5].

1 As to the definition of 'commanding officer'; see **[0485]**.

2 As to the definition of 'warrant officer'; see **[0504]**.

3 As to the definition of 'non-commissioned officer'; see **[0491]**.

4 The Air Force Act 1950 s 90 (1). The power granted under this provision is of an administrative and not judicial character. The Manual of Air Force Law, volume I, s 90 notes.

5 The Air Force Act 1950 s 90 (2).

[0646] Imposition of collective fines under the Air Force Act 1950 s 90 (1) A collective fine imposed under the Air Force Act 1950[1] shall not exceed the current official price of the weapon or part of the weapon, the loss or theft of which was reported upon by the court of inquiry, or where more than one such weapon or parts of weapons were so reported upon, the aggregate of the current official prices of such weapons or parts of weapons[2].

1 Ie under the Air Force Act 1950 s 90 (1).

2 The Air Force Rules 1969 r 157.

7. COURT MARTIAL

CONTENTS

PARA

A. Court Martial: kinds, power and composition

B. Functionaries Connected with Court Martial

C. Rules as to Evidence

A. Court Martial

[0647] Different kinds of courts martial There are three kinds of court martial[1] under the Air Force Act 1950: (i) general court martial[2], (ii) district court martial[3] and (iii) summary general court martial[4].

1 As to the definition of 'court martial'; see **[0486]**.

2 The Air Force Act 1950 s 109 (a).

2 The Air Force Act 1950 s 109 (b).

3 The Air Force Act 1950 s 109 (c).

[0648] Power to convene a general court martial A general court martial may be convened by the Central Government or the Chief of the Air Staff[1], or by any officer[2] empowered in this behalf by warrant of the Chief of the Air Staff[3].

1 As to the definition of the 'chief of the air staff'; see **[0484]**.

2 As to the definition of the 'officer'; see **[0494]**. An officer cannot convene a court martial outside the jurisdictional limits of his command. Manual of Air Force Law, Volume I, s 110 notes.

3 The Air Force Act 1950 s 110. The Form of warrant is at present issued by the chief of the air staff to the air officers commanding-in-chief of command and to the air officer in-charge administration. Manual of Air Force Law, Volume I, s 110 notes.

[0649] Power to convene a district court martial A district court martial may be convened by an officer having power to convene a general court martial, or by any officer empowered in this behalf by warrant of any such officer[1].

1 The Air Force Act 1950 s 111.Power to convene district court martial is exercised by the air officers commanding-

in-chief of command by virtue of power to convene a general court martial. No warrant has so far been issued under this provision. Manual of Air Force Law, Volume I, s 111 notes.

[0650] Contents of warrants issued under the Air Force Act 1950 s 110 and 111 A warrant issued under the Air Force Act 1950[1] may contain such restrictions, reservations or conditions as the officer issuing it may think fit[2].

1 Ie under the Air Force Act 1950 s 110 and 111.

2 The Air Force Act 1950 s 112. One usual form of restriction is to limit the power of an officer not below a specific rank. Manual of Air Force Law, volume I, s 112 notes.

[0651] Power to convene a summary general court martial The following authorities shall have the power to convene a summary general court martial: (i) an officer empowered in this behalf by an order of the Central Government or of the Chief of the Air Staff[1]; (ii) on active service, the officer commanding the forces in the field, or any officer empowered by him in this behalf[2]; and (iii) an officer commanding any detached portion of the Air Force on active service when, in his opinion, it is not practicable, with due regard to discipline and the exigencies of the service, that an offence should be tried by a general court martial[3]. The object of this provision is to provide for the speedy trial of offence committed abroad or on active service where is not practicable with due regard to the interest of discipline and of the service, to try such offences by an ordinary general or district court martial. A summary general court martial can try any offence committed on active service but when not on active service it can only be convened by an officer empowered in this behalf by an order of the central government or of the chief of the air staff[4].

1 The Air Force Act 1950 s 113 (a).

2 The Air Force Act 1950 s 113 (b). The power under this provision can be exercised only during active service. As to the meaning of 'active service'; see **[0470]**.

3 The Air Force Act 1950 s 113 (c). The power under this provision can be exercised only during active service.

4 Manual of Air Force Law, Volume I, s 113 notes.

[0652] Description of the Court In deciding the description of court before which a charge shall be tried, the convening officer will bear in mind that there are few offences which cannot effectively be dealt with by a district court martial. In cases, however, of very aggravated offences, when the state of discipline in a unit or command a serious example expedient, or when the offender bears a bad character, a general court martial may be assembled[1].

1 Regulations for the Air Force 1964, paragraph 735.

[0653] Composition of general court martial A general court martial shall consist of not less than five officers[1], each of whom has held a commission for not less than three whole years and of whom not less than four are of a rank not below that of flight lieutenant[2].

1 As to the definition of 'officer' see **[0494]**.

2 The Air Force Act 1950 s 114. Even though the definition of the term 'officer' includes an officer of the regular army or the navy under certain prescribed condition, the members of a court martial convened under the Air Force Act 1950 normally are to consist only of air force officers. The stipulation of minimum rank as 'flight lieutenant' in this provision and the absence of the words 'or equivalent' and also in the Air Force Rules 1969 rs 46-48, clearly

reveal the intention that only air force officers are to be appointed members of a court martial convened under the Air Force Act 1950. Manual of Air Force Law, Volume I, s 114 notes. Additional provisions as regard to composition of a general court martial are: In addition to the restrictions in the rank of the officers, appointed to serve on courts martial which are prescribed by the Air Force Act 1950 and the Air Force Rules 1969, the following rules will be observed: (i) Whenever a group captain or above is available to sit as presiding officer of a general court martial, an officer of lower rank will not be appointed; (ii) When a trial is likely to be prolonged it will usually be expedient to form the court of a larger number than the minimum prescribed under the Air Force Act, 1950 and two to four additional members should be detailed; (iii) Waiting members should also be detailed to meet reduction by challenge; (iv) For a general court martial the minimum will ordinarily be sufficient; but if necessary, the larger number may be detailed; and (v) The members of the court should, wherever possible, be at least one substantive rank higher than the accused. The Regulations for the Air Force 1964, paragraph 737.

[0654] Composition of district court martial A district court martial shall consist of not less than three officers, each of whom has held a commission for not less than two whole years[1].

1 The Air Force Act 1950 s 115. There is no statutory requirement of a minimum rank for a member of district court martial. Additional provisions as regard to composition of a district court martial: In addition to the restrictions in the rank of the officers, appointed to serve on courts martial which are prescribed by the Air Force Act 1950 and the Air Force Rules 1969, the following rules will be observed: (i) The presiding officer of a district court martial shall not be of a rank lower than a squadron leader; (ii) When a trial is likely to be prolonged it will usually be expedient to form the court of a larger number than the minimum prescribed under the Air Force Act 1950 and two additional members should be detailed; (iii) Waiting members should also be detailed to meet reduction by challenge; (iv) For the trial of doubtful or complicated cases, a district court martial should, when possible, consist of five officers; (iv) In a district court martial, the members of the court will not be below the rank of flight lieutenant. The Regulations for the Air Force 1964, paragraph 737.

[0655] Composition of summary general court martial A summary general court martial shall consist of not less than three officers[1].

1 As to the definition of 'officer'; see **[0494]**. Though there is no statutory requirement as to the rank or service of a member of a summary general court martial, officers appointed or detailed as members should have held commission for not less than one year and if any officer with commissioned service of not less than three years are available, they should be selected in preference to officers of less service. See the Air Force Rules 1969 r 130 (2). The Air Force Act 1950 s 116.

[0656] Dissolution of court martial A court martial shall be dissolved, if: (i) after the commencement of a trial[1] is reduced below the minimum number of officers required by the Air Force Act 1950[2], (ii) on account of the illness of the judge advocate or of the accused[3] before the finding, it is impossible to continue the trial[4], (iii) it appears to the officer who convened a court martial that the exigencies of the service or the necessities of discipline render it impossible or inexpedient to continue the said court martial[5]. Where a court martial is dissolved under this provision, the accused may be tried again[6].

1 For the purpose of this provision, the trial is held to have commenced when the accused is arraigned; see the Air Force Rules 1969 r 59, 92 and 93.

2 The Air Force Act 1950 s 117 (1).

3 A medical certificate should where possible, be obtained, stating that the illness of the accused/judge advocate renders his presence in court impracticable or dangerous to himself or others; it will also state the medical officer's

opinion as to when the accused/judge advocate will be able to be present; see the Air Force Rules 1969 r 91. Manual of Air Force Law, volume I, s 117 notes.

4 The Air Force Act 1950 s 117 (2).

5 The Air Force Act 1950 s 117 (3).

6 The Air Force Act 1950 s 117 (4).

[0657] Powers of general and summary general courts martial A general or summary general court martial shall have power to try any person subject to the Air Force Act 1950[1] for any offence punishable[2] therein and to pass any sentence authorised[3] thereby[4].

1 As to the 'person subject to the Air Force Act 1950'; see **[0506]**.

2 As to the 'offences punishable' see the Air Force Act 1950 ss 34-71.

3 Ie the sentence authorised under the Air Force Act 1950 ss 73-79.

4 The Air Force Act 1950 s 118. In addition the following points must be considered by the court while awarding a sentence: (i) When passing a sentence, a court martial will have regard not only to the nature and degree of offence and the previous character of the accused, as provided by evidence, but also to the nature and amount of any consequences, which under regulations, are involved in their finding or entailed by their sentence, in addition to the punishment it awards; (ii) The court will also consider if any circumstances have been disclosed by the evidence in extenuation, or aggravation of the offence; (iii) Where it is proved after conviction that attention has been called in local orders to the usual prevalence of the offence of which the accused has been found guilty, the court will pay regard to the fact that such warning has been issued; (iv) Sentences must necessarily vary according to the requirements of discipline but in ordinary circumstances, and for a first offence, a sentence should be light; (v) Care must be taken to discriminate between offences due to youth, temper, sudden temptation, or unaccustomed surroundings, and those due to premeditated misconduct; (vi) If an accused airman, being of the rank of warrant officer, has elected to be tried by court martial instead of submitting to the jurisdiction of an officer having power to convene and confirm general courts martial, his punishment should not on that ground be increased; (vii) In ordinary circumstances court should not award a heavier sentence than that which the officer referred to above has power to award; (viii) In awarding imprisonment or detention the court will keep in view the locality and climate in which the accused will have to undergo his sentence; (ix) An airman who is convicted by a court martial of an offence under the Air Force Act 1950 ss 46 (a), 52 or 67, ought, unless in the opinion of the court there are special reasons to the contrary, to be sentenced to imprisonment; and (x) When an offender is convicted on two or more charges, the sentence should be that which is considered adequate for the gravest of the offences, with some addition for each of the other charges. Regulations for the Air Force 1964, paragraph 754.

[0658] Powers of district court martial A district court martial shall have power to try any person subject to the Air Force Act 1950 other than an officer[1] or warrant officer[2] for any offence made punishable therein, and to pass any sentence authorised by this Act other than a sentence of death, imprisonment for life, or imprisonment for a term exceeding two years[3].

1 As to the definition of 'officer'; see **[0494]**.

2 As to the definition of 'warrant officer'; see **[0504]**.

3 The Air Force Act 1950 s 119. In addition, certain points must be considered by the district court martial while awarding a sentence; see notes 4 of the aforesaid provision: **[0657]**.

[0659] Prohibition of second trial When any person subject to the Air Force Act 1950 has been acquitted or convicted of an offence by a court martial[1] or by a criminal court[2], or has been dealt with under certain provisions of the aforesaid Act[3], he shall not be liable to be tried again for the same offence by a court martial or dealt with under the said provisions[4]. Even if a finding of conviction is recorded by a court martial is not confirmed and no action has been taken on that basis, it does not affect the fact that the accused has been tried and convicted by a court martial. In such a case, the provision of the Air Force Act 1950 s 120 will fully apply and bar a retrial of the accused by another court martial[5].

1 As to the definition of 'court martial'; see **[0486]**.

2 As to the definition of 'criminal court'; see **[0487]**.

3 Ie the Air Force Act 1950 s 82 or 86.

4 The Air Force Act 1950 s 120.

5 *Sqn Ldr G B Singh v Union of India* 1973 Cr LJ 485 (All).

[0660] Period of limitation for trial No trial by court martial of any person subject to the Air Force Act 1950 for any offence shall be commenced after the expiration of a period of three years from the date of such offence[1]. However, the aforesaid provision shall not apply to a trial for an offence of desertion or fraudulent enrolment or certain other offences mentioned in the Air Force Act 1950 s 37[2]. In the computation of the period of three years[3], anytime spent by such person as a prisoner of war, or in enemy territory, or in evading arrest after the commission of the offence, shall be excluded[4]. No trial for an offence of desertion, other than desertion on active service or of fraudulent enrolment shall be commenced if the person in question, not being an officer has, subsequently to the commission of the offence, served continuously in an exemplary manner for not less than three years with any portion of the Air Force[5].

1 The Air Force Act 1950 s 121 (1).

2 The Air Force Act 1950 s 121 (2). This provision relates to the offence of mutiny; see **[0559]**.

3 Ie under the Air Force Act 1950 s 121 (1).

4 The Air Force Act 1950 s 121 (3).

5 The Air Force Act 1950 s 121 (4).

[0661] Liability of offender who ceases to be subject to the Air Force Act 1950

1 Where an offence under the Air Force Act 1950 had been committed by any person while subject to the aforesaid Act, and he has ceased to be so subject, he may be taken into and kept in air force custody, and tried and punished for such offence as if he continued to be so subject[1].

2 Except as provided by the following two provisions[2], any such person shall not be tried for an offence, unless his trial commences within six months after he had ceased to be subject to the Air Force Act 1950[3].

3 The aforesaid provision shall not apply to the trial of any such person for an offence of desertion or fraudulent enrolment or for any of the offences, mentioned in the Air Force Act 1950 s 37[4].

4 The aforesaid provision[5] shall not affect the jurisdiction of a civil court to try any offence triable by such court as well as by a court martial[6].

5 When a person subject to the Air Force Act 1950 is sentenced by a court martial to imprisonment for life or imprisonment, the provisions of the aforesaid Act shall apply to him during the term of his sentence, though he is cashiered or dismissed from the Air Force, or has otherwise ceased to be subject

to the Air Force Act 1950, and he may be kept, removed, imprisoned and punished as if he continued to be subject to the aforesaid Act[7].

6 When a person subject to the Air Force Act 1950 is sentenced by a court martial to death, the provisions of the Air Force Act 1950 shall apply to him till the sentence is carried out[8].

1 The Air Force Act 1950 s 122 (1).

2 Ie the Air Force Act 1950 s 122 (3) and (4).

3 The Air Force Act 1950 s 122 (2).

4 The Air Force Act 1950 s 122 (3)

5 Ie the Air Force Act 1950 s 122 (2).

6 The Air Force Act 1950 s 122 (4).

7 The Air Force Act 1950 s 122 (5).

8 The Air Force Act 1950 s 122 (6).

[0662] Place of trial Any person subject to the Air Force Act 1950 who commits any offence against it may be tried and punished for such offence in any place whatever[1].

1 The Air Force Act 1950 s 123. The term 'any place whatever' means any place in which the offender may for the time being be and which is within the jurisdiction of an officer authorised to convene a court martial for his trial as if the offence had been committed where the trial takes pace and the offender were under the command of the officer convening such court. This provision enables a court martial convened in India to try a person for an offence committed elsewhere and vice versa. Manual for the Air Force, Volume I, s 123 notes.

[0663] Choice between criminal court and court martial When a criminal court and a court martial[1] have each jurisdiction in respect of an offence, it shall be in the discretion of the chief of the air staff, the officer commanding any wing or station in which the accused prisoner is serving or such other officer as may be prescribed[2] to decide before which court the proceedings shall be instituted. If that officer decides that they should be instituted before a court martial, to direct that the accused person shall be detained in air force custody[3].

1 As to the definition of 'criminal court' and 'court martial'; see **[0487]** and **[0486]**.

2 'Other officer as may be prescribed': see the Air Force Rules 1969 r 167. Prescribed officers under the Air Force Act 1950 s 124: The prescribed officers for the purposes of the Air Force Act 1950 s 124 shall be the air or other officer commanding the command or the officer commanding the Forces or the air forces in the field, under whom the accused person is serving.

3 The Air Force Act 1950 s 124. This provision should be read with the provisions contained in the Air Force Act 1950 s 71, 72 and 125. All civil offences can be tried by a court martial (subject to the provisions of the Air Force Act 1950 s 72) or by a criminal court. Manual for the Air Force, Volume I, s 124 notes.

[0664] Procedure in cases of civil offences committed by persons subject to the air force law All civil offences except those specified the Air Force Act 1950 s 72 can be tried either by court martial or by a criminal court. Similarly, some of the offences in Chapter VI of the Air Force Act 1950 are triable both by court martial and criminal court. Criminal proceedings against persons subject to the Air Force Act 1950 may be initiated by: (i) The police on the complaint of a private individual or on arrest by them for a cognizable offence; (ii) The air force authorities on a report to the police, or to a magistrate that a civil offence has been committed; or (iii) A magistrate taking cognizance suo moto or on the complaint of a private individual. In cases (i) and (iii) stated above, the air force authorities may decline to interfere with the course of the criminal law, may claim the accused for trial or if the offender is already in air force custody order trial by court martial, if the accused is legally liable thereto. In a case falling under (ii) above, the air force authorities will not take any further action unless in their opinion the complaint is wrongly dismissed or the accused is wrongly discharged by the criminal court; or the accused is acquitted by the criminal court but is liable on the same alleged facts to be tried for a purely air force offence for which he could not have been tried by the criminal court. In any of these cases it will be open to air force authorities to bring the accused to trial before court martial. Whenever there is concurrent jurisdiction and the appropriate air force authorities decide to claim the offender for trial by court martial the provisions of the Air Force Act 1950 s 124 and 125, and the Criminal Courts and Court-Martial (Adjustment of Jurisdiction) Rules 1978 as amended from time to time will be adhered to[1]. In those cases falling under the Air Force Act 1950 s 71, in which death has resulted, the decision as to whether the offender is to be tried by criminal court or court martial will rest with the chief of the air staff. If the case is one that must or should be tried by criminal court, the offender should be handed over to the civil power at the earliest possible stage[2].

1 See **[1643]** and **[1644]**.

2 Regulations for the Air Force 1964, paragraph 683. In cases where an airman is charged before a civil court; see Regulations for the Air Force 1964, paragraph 682.

[0665] Power of criminal court to require delivery of offender When a criminal court[1] having jurisdiction is of opinion that proceedings shall be instituted before itself in respect of any alleged offence, it may by, written notice, require the officer referred to in the provisions of the Air Force Act 1950[2] at his option, either to deliver over the offender to the nearest magistrate to be proceeded against according to law, or to postpone proceedings pending a reference to the Central Government[3]. In such case the said officer shall either deliver the offender in compliance with the requisition, or shall refer the question as to the court before which the proceedings are to be instituted for the determination of the Central Government whose order upon such reference shall be final[4].

1 As to the definition of 'criminal court'; see **[0487]**.

2 Ie the Air Force Act 1950 s 124; see **[0663]**.

3 The Air Force Act 1950 s 125 (1).

4 The Air Force Act 1950 s 125 (2). This provision to be read with the Air Force Act 1950 s 124.

[0666] Successive trials by a criminal court and a court martial A person convicted or acquitted by a court martial may, with the previous sanction of the Central Government, be tried again by a criminal court for the same offence, or on the same facts[1]. If a person sentenced by a court martial or punished under certain other provisions of the Air Force Act 1950[2] is afterwards tried and convicted by a criminal court for the same offence, or on the same facts, that court shall, in awarding punishment shall give due regard to the punishment he may already have undergone for the said offence[3].

This provision violates art 20 of the Constitution, which lays down that no person shall be prosecuted and punished for the same offence more than once. Similar provision contained in the Army Act 1950 s 127 has been omitted[4].

1 The Air Force Act 1950 s 126 (1).

2 Ie under the Air Force Act 1950 s 82 or 86.

3 The Air Force Act 1950 s 126 (2).

4 Ie by the Act 37 of 1992, with effect from 6 September 1992. Also see: *Samrendra Beura v Union of India* 2013 AIR SCW 3080 (A): AIR 2013 SC 2414, AIR 2013 SC (Cri), 2013 Cri LJ 3040, 2013 (7) SCALE 378.

B. Functionaries connected with Court Martial

[0667] Presiding officer At every general, district or summary general court martial the senior member shall be the presiding officer[1].

1 The Air Force Act 1950 s 127. For responsibility of presiding officer see the Air Force Rules 1969 r 83; **[0740]**.

[0668] Judge advocate The Air Force Act 1950 defines the term 'chief legal adviser'[1] who is appointed as such by the chief of the air staff to give advice on matters relating to air force law and to perform such other duties of a legal character as may arise in connection therewith[1]. The office of chief legal adviser (or judge advocate general) is not statutory in the Indian Air Force. Every general court martial shall, and every district or summary general court martial may, be attended by a judge advocate, who shall be either an officer belonging to the department of the chief legal adviser or if no such officer is available, an officer approved by the chief legal adviser or any of his deputies[2].

1 The Air Force Act 1950 s 4 (xi); see **[0481]**.

2 The Air Force Act 1950 s 128. As to power and duties of judge advocate see the Air Force Rules 1969 r 111; see **[0769]**.

[0669] Challenges

1 At all trials by general, district or summary general courts martial, as soon as the court is assembled, the names of the presiding officer and members shall be read over to the accused, who shall thereupon be asked whether he objects to being tried by any officer sitting on the court[1].

2 If the accused objects to any such officer, his objection, and also the reply thereto of the officer objected to, shall be heard and recorded, and the remaining officers of the court shall, in the absence of the challenged officer, decide on the objection[2].

3 If the objection is allowed by one- half or more of the votes of the officers entitled to vote, the objection shall be allowed, and the member objected to shall retire, and his vacancy may be filled in the prescribed manner by another officer, subject to the same right of the accused to object[3].

4 When no challenge is made, or when challenge has been made and disallowed, or the place of every officer successfully challenged has been filled by another officer to whom no objection is made or allowed, the court shall proceed with the trial[4].

1 The Air Force Act 1950 s 129 (1).

2 The Air Force Act 1950 s 129 (2).

3 The Air Force Act 1950 s 129 (3).

4 The Air Force Act 1950 s 129 (4).

[0670] Oaths of member, judge advocate and witness An oath or affirmation in the prescribed manner[1] shall be administered to every member of every court martial and to the judge advocate before the commencement of the trial[2]. Every person giving evidence before a court martial shall be examined after being duly sworn or affirmed in the prescribed form[3]. The aforesaid provisions shall not apply where the witness is a child under 12 years of age and the court martial is of opinion that though the witness understands the duty of speaking the truth, he does not understand the nature of an oath or affirmation[4].

1 For 'prescribed manner', of oath affirmation: see (i) Members of court martial-the Air Force Rules 1969 r 53 and 134; and (ii) Judge advocate, officers attending for the purposes of instruction, shorthand writers and interpreters-the Air Force Rules 1969 r 54 and 134.

2 The Air Force Act 1950 s 130 (1).

3 The Air Force Act 1950 s 130 (2). For 'prescribed manner', of oath affirmation of witness; see the Air Force Rules 1969 r 118.

4 The Air Force Act 1950 s 130 (3).

[0671] Voting by members Subject to certain the provisions of the Air Force act 1950[1], every decision of a court martial shall be passed by an absolute majority of votes; and where there is an equality of votes on either the finding or the sentence, the decision shall be in favour of the accused[2]. No sentence of death shall be passed by a general court martial without the concurrence of at least two-thirds of the members of the court[3]. No sentence of death shall be passed by a summary general court martial without the concurrence of all the members[4]. In matters other than a challenge or the finding or sentence, the presiding officer shall have a casting vote[5].

1 Ie the Air Force act 1950 s 131 (2) and (3).

2 The Air Force Act 1950 s 131 (1).

3 The Air Force Act 1950 s 131 (2).

4 The Air Force Act 1950 s 131 (3).

5 The Air Force Act 1950 s 131 (4).

C. Rules as to Evidence

[0672] General rule as to evidence The Indian Evidence Act 1872, shall, subject to the provisions of the Air Force Act 1950[1], apply to proceedings before a court martial[2].

1 As to 'subject to the provisions of the Air Force Act 1950'; see ss 133, 139 to 143 and Air Force Rules 1969 rs 112 to121.

2 The Air Force Act 1950 s 132.

[0673] Judicial notice A court martial may take judicial notice of any matter within the general air force knowledge of the members[1].

1 The Air Force Act 1950 s 133.

[0674] Summoning witnesses The convening officer, the presiding officer of a court martial, the judge advocate or the commanding officer of the accused person, may, by summons under his hand, require the attendance, at a time and place to be mentioned in the summons, of any person either to give evidence or to produce any document or other thing[1]. In the case of a witness amenable to air force authority, the summons shall be sent to his commanding officer, and such officer shall serve it upon him accordingly[2]. In the case of any other witness, the summons shall be sent to the magistrate within whose jurisdiction he may be or reside, and such magistrate shall give effect to the summons as if the witness were required in the court of such magistrate[3]. When a witness is required to produce any particular document or other thing in his possession or power, the summons shall describe it with reasonable precision[4]. The forms of summon are contained in the Air Force Rules 1969[5].

1 The Air Force Act 1950 s 134 (1).

2 The Air Force Act 1950 s 134 (2).

3 The Air Force Act 1950 s 134 (3).

4 The Air Force Act 1950 s 134 (4).

5 Ie the Air Force Rules 1969, Forms C1 and C2.

[0675] Documents exempted from production The provision contained in the Air Force Act 1950[1] shall not affect the operation of the certain parts of the Indian Evidence Act 1872[2], or to apply to any letter, postcard, telegram or other document in the custody of the postal or telegraph authorities[3]. If any document in such custody is, in the opinion of any district magistrate, chief presidency magistrate, high court or court of session, wanted for the purpose of any court martial, such magistrate or court may require the postal or telegraph authorities, as the case may be, to deliver such document to such person as such magistrate or court may direct[4]. If any such document is, in the opinion of any other magistrate or of any commissioner of police or district superintendent of police, wanted for any such purpose, he may require the postal or telegraph authorities, as the case may be, to cause search to be made for and to detain such document pending the orders of any such district magistrate, chief presidency magistrate or high court or court of session[5].

1 Ie in the Air Force Act 1950 s 134: see **[0674]**.

2 Ie the Indian Evidence Act 1872 ss 123 and 124. These provisions deal with 'affairs of State' and 'official communications'.

3 The Air Force Act 1950 s 135 (1).

4 The Air Force Act 1950 s 135 (2).

5 The Air Force Act 1950 s 135 (3).

[0676] Commissions for examination of witnesses

1 Whenever, in the course of a trial by court martial, it appears to the court that the examination of a witness is necessary for the ends of justice, and that the attendance of such witness cannot be procured without an amount of delay, expense or inconvenience which, in the circumstances of the case, would be unreasonable, such court may address the Chief Legal Adviser in order that a commission to take the evidence of such witness may be issued[1].

2 The Chief Legal Adviser may then, if he thinks necessary, issue a commission to any district magistrate or magistrate of the first class, within the local limits of whose jurisdiction such witness resides, to take

the evidence of such witness[2].

3 The magistrate or officer to whom the commission is issued, or, if he is the district magistrate, he or such magistrate of the first class as he appoints in this behalf, shall proceed to the place where the witness is or shall summon the witness before him and shall take down his evidence in the same manner, and may for this purpose exercise the same powers, as in trials of warrant cases under the Code of Criminal Procedure, 1973 or any corresponding law in force in the State of Jammu and Kashmir[3].

4 When the witness resides in a tribal area or in any place outside India, the commission may be issued in the manner specified in Chapter XXII of the Code of Criminal Procedure 1973 or of any corresponding law in force in the State of Jammu and Kashmir[4].

5 In this and the next succeeding section, the expression Chief Legal Adviser includes a Deputy Chief Legal Adviser[5].

1 The Air Force Act 1950 s 136 (1).

2 The Air Force Act 1950 s 136 (2).

3 The Air Force Act 1950 s 136 (3).

4 The Air Force Act 1950 s 136 (4).

5 The Air Force Act 1950 s 136 (5).

[0677] Examination of a witness on commission

1 The prosecutor and the accused person in any case in which a commission is issued under the aforesaid provision[1] may respectively forward any interrogatories in writing which the court may think relevant to the issue, and the magistrate or officer executing the commission shall examine the witness upon such interrogatories[2].

2 The prosecutor and the accused person may appear before such magistrate or officer by counsel or except in the case of an accused person in custody, in person, and may examine, cross-examine and re-examine, as the case may be, the said witness[3].

3 After a commission issued under the aforesaid provision[4] has been duly executed, it shall be returned, together with the deposition of the witness examined thereunder to the chief legal adviser[5].

4 On receipt of a commission and deposition returned under the aforesaid provision[6], the chief legal adviser shall forward the same to the court at whose instance the commission was issued or, if such court has been dissolved, to any other court convened for the trial of the accused person; and the commission, the return thereto and the deposition shall be open to inspection by the prosecutor and the accused person, and may, subject to all just exceptions, be read in evidence in the case by either the prosecutor or the accused, and shall form part of the proceedings of the court[7].

5 In every case in which a commission is issued under the provisions of the Air Force Act 1950[8], the trial may be adjourned for a specified time reasonably sufficient for the execution and return of the commission[9].

1 Ie the Air Force Act 1950 s 136.

2 The Air Force Act 1950 s 137 (1).

3 The Air Force Act 1950 s 137 (2).

4 Ie the Air Force Act 1950 s 136.

5 The Air Force Act 1950 s 137 (3).

6 Ie the Air Force Act 1950 s 137 (3).

7 The Air Force Act 1950 s137 (4).

8 Ie the Air Force Act 1950 s 136.

9 The Air Force Act 1950 s 137 (5).

[0678] Conviction of offence not charged In a trial before court martial, a person charged with: (i) desertion may be found guilty of attempting to desert or of being absent without leave[1]; (ii) attempting to desert may be found guilty of being absent without leave[2]; (iii) using criminal force may be found guilty of assault[3]; (iv) using threatening language may be found guilty of using insubordinate language[4]; (v) any one of the offences specified in the Air Force Act 1950[5] may be found guilty of any other of these offences with which he might have been charged[6]; (vi) an offence punishable under the Air Force Act 1950[7] s 71 may be found guilty of any other offence of which he might have been found guilty if the provisions of the Code of Criminal Procedure 1973 were applicable[8]; (vii) any offence under the Air Force Act 1950 may, on failure of proof of an offence having been committed in circumstances involving a more severe punishment, be found guilty of the same offence as having been committed in circumstances involving a less severe punishment[9]; (viii) with any offence under the Air Force Act 1950 may be found guilty of having attempted or abetted the commission of that offence, although the attempt or abetment is not separately charged[10].

1 The Air Force Act 1950 s 138 (1).

2 The Air Force Act 1950 s 138 (2).

3 The Air Force Act 1950 s 138 (3).

4 The Air Force Act 1950 s138 (4).

5 Ie Air Force Act 1950 s 52 (a), (b), (c) and (d).

6 The Air Force Act 1950 s 138 (5).

7 Ie the Air Force Act 1950 s 71.

8 The Air Force Act 1950 s 138 (6).

9 The Air Force Act 1950 s 138 (7).

10 The Air Force Act 1950 s 138 (8).

[0679] Presumption as to signatures In any proceeding under the Air Force Act 1950, any application, certificate, warrant, reply, or other document purporting to be signed by an officer in the service of the Government shall, on production, be presumed to have been duly signed by the person by whom and in the character in which it purports to have been signed, until the contrary is shown[1].

1 The Air Force Act 1950 s 139. The expression 'purporting' means that if the paper appears to be signed, as mentioned in these provisions, it can be accepted without calling a witness to prove that it has been so signed, unless indeed some evidence is given to contrary. Manual of Air Force Law, Volume I, s 139 notes.

[0680] Enrolment paper Any enrolment paper purporting to be signed by an enrolling officer[1] shall, in proceedings under the Air Force Act 1950, be evidence of the person enrolled having given the answers to questions which he is therein represented as having given[2]. The enrolment of such person may be proved by the production of the original or a copy of his enrolment paper purporting to be certified to be a true copy by the officer having the custody of the enrolment paper[3].

1 As to the meaning of 'enrolling officer'; see The Air Force Rules 1969 r 7 (1): **[0526]**.

2 The Air Force Act 1950 s 140 (1).

3 The Air Force Act 1950 s 140 (2).

[0681] Presumption as to certain documents

1 A letter, return or other document respecting the service of any person in, or the cashiering, dismissal or discharge of any person from, any portion of the Air Force, or respecting the circumstance of any person not having served in, or belonged to, any portion of the Forces, if purporting to be signed by or on behalf of the central government or the chief of the air staff, or by any prescribed officer[1], shall be evidence of the facts stated in such letter, return or other document[2].

2 An army, navy or air force list or gazette purporting to be published by authority shall be evidence of the status and rank of the officers or warrant officers therein mentioned, and of any appointment held by them and of the unit or branch of the services to which they belong[3].

3 Where a record is made in any service book in pursuance of the Air Force Act 1950 or the Air Force Rules 1969 or otherwise in pursuance of air force duty, and purports to be signed by the commanding officer or by the officer whose duty it is to make such record, such record shall be evidence of the facts therein stated[4].

4 A copy of any record in any service book purporting to be certified to be a true copy by the officer having custody of such book shall be evidence of such record[5].

5 Where any person subject to the Air Force Act 1950 is being tried on a charge of desertion or of absence without leave, and such person has surrendered himself into the custody of any officer or other person subject to the aforesaid Act, or has been apprehended by such officer or person, a certificate purporting to be signed by such officer, or by the commanding officer of the unit, or detachment to which such person belongs, and stating the fact, date and place of such surrender or apprehension, and the manner in which he was dressed, shall be evidence of the matters so stated[6].

6 Where any person subject to the Air Force Act is being tried on a charge of desertion or of absence without leave, and such person has surrendered himself into the custody of, or has been apprehended by, a police officer not below the rank of an officer-in-charge of a police station, a certificate purporting to be signed by such police officer and stating the fact, date and place of such surrender or apprehension and the manner in which he was dressed shall be evidence of the matters so stated[7].

7 Any document purporting to be a report under the hand of any Chemical Examiner or Assistant Chemical Examiner to Government upon any matter or thing duly submitted to him for examination or analysis and report may be used as evidence in any proceeding under the Air Force Act 1950[8].

1 As to the meaning of 'prescribed officer' see the Air Force Rules 1969 r 168. Prescribed officer under the Air Force Act 1950 s 141(1): The prescribed officer for the purposes of the Air Force Act 1950 s 141(1) shall be the officer commanding the unit to which the person appears to have belonged, or alleges that he belongs or had belonged. However, (i) in the case of officers, the Director of Personnel (Officers); and (ii) in the case of airmen, Officer Commanding, Air Force Record Office, shall also be the prescribed officer.

2 The Air Force Act 1950 s 141 (1).

3 The Air Force Act 1950 s 141 (2).

4 The Air Force Act 1950 s 141 (3).

5 The Air Force Act 1950 s 141 (4).

6 The Air Force Act 1950 s 141 (5).

7 The Air Force Act 1950 s 141 (6).

8 The Air Force Act 1950 s 141 (7).

[0682] Reference by accused to government officer If at any trial for desertion or absence without leave, overstaying leave or not rejoining when warned for service, the person tried states in his defence any sufficient or reasonable excuse for his unauthorised absence, and refers in support thereof to any officer in the service of the government, or if it appears that any such officer is likely to prove or disprove the said statement in the defence, the court shall address such officer and adjourn the proceedings until his reply is received[1]. The written reply of any officer so referred to shall, if signed by him, be received in evidence and have the same effect as if made on oath before the court[2]. If the court is dissolved before the receipt of such reply, or if the court omits to comply with the provisions of this provision, the convening officer may, at his discretion, annul the proceedings and order a fresh trial[3].

1 The Air Force Act 1950 s 142 (1).

2 The Air Force Act 1950 s 142 (2).

3 The Air Force Act 1950 s 142 (3).

[0683] Evidence of previous convictions and general character When any person subject to the Air Force Act 1950 has been convicted by a court martial of any offence, such court martial may inquire into, and receive and record evidence of any previous convictions of such person, either by a court martial or by a criminal court, or any previous award of punishment under the Air Force Act 1950[1] and may further inquire into and record the general character of such person and such other matters as may be prescribed[2]. Evidence received under this provision may be either oral, or in the shape of entries in, or certified extracts from, court martial books or other official records, and it shall not be necessary to give notice before trial to the person tried that evidence as to his previous convictions or character will be received[3].

1 Ie the Air Force Act 19501 s 82 or 86.

2 The Air Force Act 1950 s 143 (1).

3 The Air Force Act 1950 s 143 (2).

[0684] Lunacy of accused Whenever, in the course of a trial by a court martial, it appears to the court that the person charged is by reason of unsoundness of mind incapable of making his defence, or that he committed the act alleged but was by reason of unsoundness of mind incapable of knowing the nature of the act or knowing that it was wrong or contrary to law, the court shall record a finding accordingly[1]. The presiding officer of the court shall forthwith report the case to the confirming officer[2]. The confirming officer may, if he does not confirm the finding, take steps to have the accused person tried by the same or another court martial for the offence with which he was charged[3]. A confirming officer confirming a finding in any case so reported to him under the aforesaid provision[4] shall order the accused person to be kept in custody in the prescribed manner and shall report the case for the orders of the Central Government[5]. On receipt of a report under the above-stated provision the Central Government may order the accused person to be detained in a lunatic asylum or other suitable place of safe custody[6].

1 The Air Force Act 1950 s 144 (1).

2 The Air Force Act 1950 s 144 (2).

3 The Air Force Act 1950 s 144 (3).

4 Ie under the Air Force Act 1950 s 144 (2).

5 The Air Force Act 1950 s 144 (4).

6 The Air Force Act 1950 s 144 (5).

[0685] Subsequent fitness of lunatic accused for trial Where any accused person, having been found by reason of unsoundness of mind to be incapable of making his defence, is in custody or under detention under the provisions of the Air Force Act 1950[1], the officer commanding a unit or detachment within the area of whose command the accused is in custody or is detained, or any other officer prescribed[2] in this behalf, may: (i) if such person is in custody under the provisions of the Air Force Act 1950[3], on the report of a medical officer that he is capable of making his defence[4], or (ii) if such person is detained in a jail under certain provisions of the Air Force Act 1950[5], on a certificate of the Inspector General of Prisons and if such person is detained in a lunatic asylum under the said provision on a certificate of any two or more of the visitors of such asylum that he is capable of making his defence; take steps to have such person tried by the same or another court martial for the offence with which he was originally charged, or, if the offence is a civil offence, by a criminal court[6].

1 Ie under the Air Force Act 1950 s 144.

2 As to the meaning of 'prescribed officer' see the Air Force Rules 1969 r 170. Prescribed officer under the Air Force Act 1950 s 145: The prescribed officer for the purposes of the Air Force Act 1950 s 145 shall be the Chief of the Air Staff or the air or other officer who has powers to convene a court martial for the trial of the accused person.

3 Ie under the Air Force Act 1950 s 144 (4).

4 The Air Force Act 1950 s 145 (a).

5 Ie under the Air Force Act 1950 s 144 (5).

6 The Air Force Act 1950 s 145 (b).

[0686] Transmission to central government of orders under the Air Force Act 1950 s 145 A copy of every order made by an officer under the Air Force Act 1950[1] for the trial of the accused shall forthwith be sent to the Central Government[2].

1 Ie the Air Force Act 1950 s 145.

2 The Air Force Act 1950 s 146.

[0687] Release of lunatic accused Where any person is in custody or detention under the Air Force Act 1950[1]: (i) if such person is in custody under the aforesaid provision, on the report of a medical officer[2], or (ii) if such person is detained under the aforesaid provision, on a certificate from any of the authorities mentioned in the Air Force Act 1950[3] that, in the judgment of such officer or authority such person may be released without danger of his doing injury to himself or to any other person; the Central Government may order that such person be released, or detained in custody, or transferred to a public lunatic asylum if he has not already been sent to such an asylum[4].

1 Ie in custody under the Air Force Act 1950 s 144 (4), or detention under the Air Force Act 1950 s 144 (5).

2 The Air Force Act 1950 s 147 (a).

3 Ie the Air Force Act 1950 s 145 (b).

4 The Air Force Act 1950 s 147 (b).

[0688] Delivery of lunatic accused to relatives Where any relative or friend of any person who is in custody or detention[1] desires that he should be delivered to his care and custody, the Central Government may upon application by such relative or friend and on his giving security to the satisfaction of that Government that the person delivered shall be properly taken care of and prevented from doing injury to himself or any other person, and be produced for the inspection of such officer, and at such times and places, as the Central Government may direct, order such person to be delivered to such relative or friend[2].

1 Ie in custody under the Air Force Act 1950 s 144 (4), or detention under the Air Force Act 1950 s 144 (5).

2 The Air Force Act 1950 s 148.

[0689] Order for custody and disposal of property pending trial When any property regarding which any offence appears to have been committed, or which appears to have been used for the commission of any offence, is produced before a court martial during a trial, the court may make such order as it thinks fit for the proper custody of such property pending the conclusion of the trial, and if the property is subject to speedy or natural decay may, after recording such evidence as it thinks necessary, order it to be sold or otherwise disposed of[1].

1 The Air Force Act 1950 s 149.

[0690] Order for disposal of property regarding which offence is committed

1 After the conclusion of a trial before any court martial, the court or the officer confirming the finding or sentence of such court martial or any authority superior to such officer, may make such order as it or he thinks fit for the disposal by destruction, confiscation, delivery to any person claiming to be entitled to possession thereof, or otherwise of any property or document produced before the court or in its custody, or regarding which any offences appears to have been committed or which has been used for the commission of any offence[1].

2 Where any order has been made under the aforesaid provision in respect of property regarding which an offence appears to have been committed, a copy of such order signed and certified by the authority making the same may, whether the trial was held within India or not, be sent to a magistrate within whose jurisdiction such property for the time being is situated, and such magistrate shall thereupon cause the order to be carried into effect as if it were an order passed by him under the provisions of the Code of Criminal Procedure 1973 or any corresponding law in force in the State of Jammu and Kashmir[2].

3 In this provision the term 'property' includes, in the case of property regarding which an offence appears to have been committed, not only such property as has been originally in the possession or under the control of any person, but also any property into or for which the same may have been converted or exchanged, and anything acquired by such conversion or exchange whether immediately or otherwise[3].

1 The Air Force Act 1950 s 150 (1).

2 The Air Force Act 1950 s 150 (2).

3 The Air Force Act 1950 s 150 (3).

[0691] Powers of courts martial when certain offences are committed by persons not subject to the Air Force Act 1950 Any trial by a court martial under the provisions of the Air Force Act 1950 shall be deemed to be a judicial proceeding within the meaning of the Indian Penal Code 1860[1], and the court martial shall be deemed to be a court within the meaning of the Code of Criminal Procedure 1973[2].

1 Ie the Indian Penal Code 1860 s 193 and 228.

2 Ie the Code of Criminal Procedure 1973 s 345 (1) and 346. The Air Force Act 1950 s 151.

D. Procedure at Trial

(i) General and District Courts Material

CONTENTS

PARA

(A) Convening of court martial

(D) Form of oath

(E) Prosecution, defence and summing up

(F) Finding and sentence

(G) Confirmation and Revision

(H) General provisions as to proceedings of general and district court martial

(I) Defending Officer, Counsel and Friend of Accused

(J) Witnesses and Evidence

(A) *Convening of court martial*

[0692] Convening of general and district court-martial

1 An officer before convening a general or district court martial shall first satisfy himself that the charges to be tried by the court martial are for offences within the meaning of the Air Force Act 1950, and framed in accordance with law, and that the evidence justifies a trial on those charges. He may amend the charge if deems fit, and if not so satisfied order the release of the accused, or refer the case to superior authority[1].

2 He shall also satisfy himself that the case is a proper one to be tried by the description of court martial he proposes[2] to convene[3].

3 The officer convening a court martial shall appoint or detail the officers to form the court, and such waiting officers as he thinks expedient. He may also, where he considers the services of an interpreter to be necessary, appoint or detail an interpreter to the court[4].

4 After the convening officer has appointed or detailed the officer to form a court martial under the aforesaid provision[5], the convening order of the court martial and endorsement on the charge sheet for trial of the accused by court martial may either be signed by convening officer or by a staff officer on his behalf. The charge sheet on which the accused to be tried, the summary of evidence and the convening order for assembly of court martial shall then be sent to the senior member of the court-martial and the judge advocate, if appointed[6].

The convening officer should satisfy himself that (i) each charge and the attendant circumstances have been carefully examined; (ii) advise of the judge advocate general or command judge advocate have been obtained and considered; (iii) a prima facie case exists with respect to each charge; (iv) he holds the necessary court martial warrant empowering him to convene the description of court martial that he considers appropriate; (v) the court is composed in accordance the Air Force Act 1950 and the Air Force Rules 1969; (vi) no officer who is ineligible or disqualified is appointed as a member or judge advocate; and (vii) if the accused does not understand English, an interpreter in the language of the accused person has been detailed[7].

1 The Air Force Rules 1969 r 43 (1).

2 In deciding the description of court before which a charge shall be tried, the convening officer will bear in mind that there are few offences which cannot effectively be dealt with by a district court-martial. In cases, however, of very aggravated offences when the state of discipline in a unit or command a serious example expedient, or when the offender bears a bad character, a general court martial may be assembled. Regulations for the Air Force 1964, paragraph 735.

3 The Air Force Rules 1969 r 43 (2).

4 The Air Force Rules 1969 r 43 (3).

5 Ie the Air Force Rules 1969 r 43 (3).

6 The Air Force Rules 1969 r 43 (4). The object of this provision is to enable senior member of the court martial to have an idea of the charge(s) on which the accused is to be arraigned. Manual of Air Force Law, Volume II, r 43 notes.

7 Manual of Air Force Law, Volume II, r 43 notes.

[0693] Convening Orders The presiding officer of a court martial must be named in the convening order for the assembly of the court. The members and waiting members will be mentioned by name or the number and ranks and the units from which they are drawn. Where members are detailed not by name but by rank and unit an officer detailed from the named unit must be of the rank specified. There shall be no alteration or erasure in the portion of the convening order relating to the officers named and detailed to constitute the court. Where alterations in the constitution of the court are necessary at any time after the order has been prepared, the order shall be replaced by a new order. This procedure is not necessary when a waiting member is directed to serve on a court martial[1].

1 Regulations for the Air Force, 1964 paragraph 739.

[0694] Adjournment for insufficient number of officers If, before the accused is arraigned, the full number of officers detailed are not available to serve by reason of non eligibility, disqualification, challenge or otherwise, and if there are not a sufficient number of officers in waiting to take the place of those unable to serve, the court shall ordinarily adjourn for the purpose of fresh members being appointed; but if the court is of opinion that in the interests of justice, and for the good of the service, it is inexpedient so to adjourn it may, if not reduced in number below the required minimum, proceed recording their reasons for so doing[1]. If the court adjourns for the purpose of the appointment of fresh members whether under these rules or otherwise, the convening officer may, if he thinks fit, convene another court[2].

1 The Air Force Rules 1969 r 44 (1).

2 The Air Force Rules 1969 r 44 (2). If another court is convened, a member of the previous court martial which tried the accused is ineligible to serve as member in the subsequently convened court. Manual of Air Force Law, volume II, r 44 notes.

[0695] Ineligibility and disqualification of officers for court martial An officer[1] is not eligible to serve on a court martial unless he is subject to air force law[2]. An officer is disqualified for serving on a general or district court martial if he: (i) Is the officer who convened the court[3]; (ii) Is the prosecutor, or a witness for the prosecution[4]; (iii) Investigated the charges before trial, or took down the summary of evidence or was a member of a court of inquiry respecting the matters on which the charges against the accused are founded, or was the flight, squadron, station, unit, or other commander who made preliminary inquiry into the case, or was a member or previous court martial which tried the accused in respect of the same offence[5]; (iv) Is the commanding officer of the accused or of the unit to which the accused is attached or belongs[6]; or (v) Has a personal interest in the case[7]. The provost marshal[8] or assistant provost marshal is disqualified from serving on a general or district court martial[9].

1 As to the definition of 'officer'; see **[0494]**.

2 The Air Force Rules 1969 r 45 (1).

3 The Air Force Rules 1969 r 45 (2) (a).

4 The Air Force Rules 1969 r 45 (2) (b).

5 The Air Force Rules 1969 r 45 (2) (c).

6 The Air Force Rules 1969 r 45 (2) (d).

7 The Air Force Rules 1969 r 45 (2) (e).

8 As to the definition of 'provost marshal'; see **[0498]**.

9 The Air Force Rules 1969 r 43 (3).

[0696] Composition of general court martial The senior member of a general court martial shall be of a rank not below that of a group captain, unless in the opinion of the convening officer, to be stated in the order convening the court and to be conclusive, an officer of that rank is not available, having due regard to the public service[1]. All members of a general court martial for the trial of an officer shall be of equal if not superior rank to the accused, unless in the opinion of the convening officer, to be stated in the order convening the court and to be conclusive, offices of the required rank are not available, having due regard to the public service[2]. However, in no case shall an officer below the rank of flight lieutenant be appointed a member of a court martial for the trial of an officer of or above the rank of squadron leader[3].

1 The Air Force Rules 1969 r 46 (1). The expression of the convening officer's opinion justifying a departure from the general rule should be inserted in the convening order. Manual of Air Force Law, volume II, r 46 notes.

2 The Air Force Rules 1969 r 46 (2). The judge advocate junior to the accused was appointed and on conclusion of general court martial, dismissal order was passed. The question of seniority of judge advocate was not raised during

the trial, moreover no senior judge advocate was available. No injustice caused to the accused. High court wrongly interfered with the findings of general court martial. *Union of India v SPS Rajkumar* 2007 (3) SLR, SC 547.

3 The Air Force Rules 1969 r 46 proviso.

[0697] Composition of a district court martial The senior member of a district court martial shall be of a rank not below that of squadron leader, unless in the opinion of the convening officer, to be stated in the order convening the court and to be conclusive, an officer of that rank is not (having due regard to the public service) available[1].

1 The Air Force Rules 1969 r 47.

[0698] Composition of courts martial In addition to the restrictions in the rank of the officers, appointed to serve on courts martial which are prescribed by the Air Force Act 1950 and the Air Force Rules 1969[1], the following rules will be observed: (i) Whenever a group captain or above is available to sit as presiding officer of a general court martial, an officer of lower rank will not be appointed; (ii) The presiding officer of a district court martial shall not be of a rank lower than a squadron leader; (iii) When a trial is likely to be prolonged it will usually be expedient to form the court of a larger number than the minimum prescribed under the Air Force Act 1950 and two or four additional members should be detailed; (v) Waiting members should also be detailed to meet reduction by challenge; (vi) For a general court martial the minimum will ordinarily be sufficient; but if necessary, the larger number may be detailed; (vii) For the trial of doubtful or complicated cases, a district court martial should, when possible, consist of five officers; (viii) In a general court martial, the members of the court should, wherever possible, be at least one substantive rank higher than the accused; and (ix) In a district court martial, the members of the court will not be below the rank of flight lieutenant[2].

1 See **[0695]** to **[0697]**.

2 Regulations for the Air Force 1964, paragraph 737.

[0699] Units of members of court martial A general or district court martial shall not be composed exclusively of officers of the same unit, unless the convening officer states in the order convening the court that in his opinion other officers are not available, having due regard to the public service, and in no case shall it consist exclusively of officers belong to the same unit as the accused[1].

1 The Air Force Rules 1969 r 48. This provision is not applicable to summary general court martial; see the Air Force Rules 1969 r 142.

(B) *Procedure at Trial: Constitution of Court*

[0700] Inquiry by court as to legal constitution On the court assembling, the order convening and the names, rank and unit of the officers appointed to serve on the court shall be read. It shall be the first duty of the court to satisfy itself that: (i) it has been convened in accordance with the Air Force Act 1950 and the Air Force Rules 1969[1]; (ii) it consists of a number of officers not less than the required minimum, and, except as mentioned in the Air Force Rules 1969[2], not less than the number detailed[3]; (iii) each of the officers so assembled is eligible and not disqualified for serving on that court martial[4]. The court shall, further, if it is a general or district court martial to which a judge advocate has been appointed, ascertain that the judge advocate is duly appointed and is not disqualified for acting at that court martial[5]. The court, if not satisfied on the above matters, shall report its opinion to the convening authority, and may adjourn for that purpose[6].

1 The Air Force Rules 1969 r 49 (1) (a).

2 Ie the Air Force Rules 1969 r 44

3 The Air Force Rules 1969 r 49 (1) (b).

4 The Air Force Rules 1969 r 49 (1) (c).

5 The Air Force Rules 1969 r 49 (2).

6 The Air Force Rules 1969 r (3). The inquiries necessitated by this provision should be conducted in closed court. The court is not yet 'open' at this stage and the accused is not brought before the court yet. Manual of Air Force Law, Volume II, r 49 notes.

[0701] Inquiry by court as to amenability of accused and validity of charge The court, when satisfied on the matters stated in the aforesaid provisions, shall satisfy itself in respect of each charge about to be brought before them: (i) That it appears to be laid against a person subject to the Air Force Act 1950 and to the jurisdiction of the court[1]; and (ii) That each charge discloses an offence under the Air Force Act 1950 Act and is framed in accordance with the Air Force Rules 1969, and is so explicit as to enable the accused readily to understand what he has to answer[2]. The court, if not satisfied on the above stated matters, shall report its opinion as the convening authority and may adjourn for that purpose[3].

1 The Air Force Rules 1969 r 50 (1) (a).

2 The Air Force Rules 1969 r 50 (1) (b).

3 The Air Force Rules 1969 r 50 (2). The inquiries necessitated by this provision should be conducted in closed court. The court is not yet 'open' at this stage and the accused is not brought before the court yet. Manual of Air Force Law, Volume II, r 49 notes.

[0702] Action before trial Before trial, the commanding officer will ensure that the following requirements are complied with: (i) The accused is informed by an officer, of every charge on which he is to be tried; (ii) If he so desires, the accused must be informed of the rank, name and unit of the officer, who are to form the court, as well as the waiting members; (iii) The accused must be informed that on his giving the names of ally of the witnesses for the defence, reasonable steps will be taken to procure their attendance; (iv) The accused is afforded proper opportunity for preparing his defence; (v) The accused person for trial will be examined in respect of fitness for trial by a medical officer on the morning of each day the court is ordered to sit for his trial; and that no accused person is brought before a court martial if, in the opinion of the medical officer, he is unfit to undergo trial. The requirements of the aforesaid provisions (i), (ii), (iii) and (iv) will be complied with 96 hours before a trial and if the accused is on active service, 24 hours before trial[1].

1 Regulations for the Air Force 1964, paragraph 740. Also see **[0151]** and **[0264]**

(C) *Procedure at Trial: challenges and swearing*

[0703] Appearance of accused and prosecutor When the court is satisfied as to the facts mentioned in the aforesaid provisions, it shall cause the accused to be brought before the court, and the prosecutor who must be a person subject to air force law, shall take his place[1].

1 The Air Force Rules 1969 r 51. The presiding officer should cause the court orderly to announce that the court is open, whereupon the accused, defending officer (or defence counsel and/or the friend of the accused) and prosecutor take their places and members of the public take their seats. The accused is marched in with his escorts, and if an officer or warrant officer, may be marched in by the escort himself. The witness may be brought in at this stage to hear the court sworn, but their attendance is not compulsory and may, if there is a large number, be dispensed with. They must leave the court before the accused is arraigned. Manual of Air Force Law, Volume II, r 51 notes.

[0704] Choice of Prosecutor In a difficult case the convening officer will select a specifically qualified officer to act as prosecutor. If such an officer is not available, he would apply as soon as possible to superior authority for the services of one. In command headquarters, if no such officer is available locally, application should be made to the Air Headquarters[1].

1 Regulations for the Air Force 1964, paragraph 738.

[0705] Proceedings for challenges of members of court The order convening the court and the names of the presiding officer and members of the court shall then be read over to the accused and he shall be asked, as required by the Air Force Act 1950[1], whether he objects to be tried by any officer sitting on the court. Any such objections shall be disposed of in accordance with the aforesaid provisions of the Air Force Act 1950[2]. However: (i) The accused shall state the names of all the officers to whom he object before any objection is disposed of[3]; (ii) The accused may call any person to give evidence in support of his objection, and such person may be questioned by the accused and by the court[4]; (iii) If more than one officer is objected to, the objection to each officer shall be disposed of separately, and the objection in respect of that officer lowest in rank shall be disposed of first; and on an objection to an officer, the remaining officers of the court shall in the absence of the challenged officer, vote on the disposal of such objection notwithstanding that objections have also been to any of them officers[5]; (iv) When an objection to an officer is allowed that officer shall forthwith retire, and take no further part in the proceedings[6]; (v) When an officer objected to retires, and there are any officers in waiting, the vacancy shall be forthwith filled by one of the officers in waiting being directed by the presiding officer to serve in lieu of the retiring officer. If there is no officer in waiting available, the court shall proceed as directed by the provisions of the Air Force Rules 1969[7]; (vii) The eligibility, absence of disqualification, and freedom from objection of an officer filling a vacancy shall be ascertained by the court, as in the case of other officers appointed to serve on the court[8]. The requirement of asking the accused under this provision, whether he objects to any member sitting on the court martial was mandatory[9].

1 Ie the Air Force Act 1950 s 129; see **[0670]**.

2 Ie the Air Force Act 1950 s 129. The Air Force Rules 1969 r 52. The accused has no right to object to the prosecutor or judge advocate. Manual of Air Force Law, Volume II, r 52 notes.

3 The Air Force Rules 1969 r 52 proviso (a).

4 The Air Force Rules 1969 r 52 proviso (b).

5 The Air Force Rules 1969 r 52 proviso (c).

6 The Air Force Rules 1969 r 52 proviso (d).

7 Ie the Air Force Rules 1969 r 44. The Air Force Rules 1969 r 52 proviso (e).

8 The Air Force Rules 1969 r 52 proviso (f).

9 *Lt Col PPS Bedi v Union of India* AIR 1982 SC 1413.

(D) *Form of oath*

[0706] Swearing or affirming of members As soon as the court is constituted with the proper number of officers who are not objected to, or objections in respect of whom have been over-ruled, an oath or affirmation shall be administered to every member in one of the following forms or in such other form to the same purport as the court ascertains to be according to his religion or otherwise binding on his conscience[1].

Form of oath

I.........do swear by Almighty God that I will well and truly try the accused (or accused persons) before the court according to the evidence, and that I will duly administer justice according to the Air Force Act 1950, without partiality, favour or affection; and if any doubt shall arise, then, according to my conscience, the best of my understanding and the custom of war in the like cases; and I do further swear that I will not, on any account at any time, whatsoever, disclose, or discover the vote or opinion of any particular member of this court-martial, unless required to give evidence thereof by a court of justice or a court martial in due course of law[2].

Form of affirmation

I.........do solemnly, sincerely and truly declare and affirm that I will well and truly try the accused (or accused persons) before the court according to the evidence, and that I will duly administer justice according to the Air Force Act 1950, without partiality, favour or affection; and if any doubt shall arise, then, according to my conscience, the best of my understanding, and the custom of war in the like cases; and I do further solemnly, sincerely and truly declare and affirm that I will not, on any account at any time, whatsoever, disclose, or discover the vote or opinion of any particular member of this court-martial, unless required to give evidence thereof by a court of justice or a court martial in due course of law[3].

1 The Air Force Rules 1969 r 53. Christians and Sikhs are generally sworn, the former on the New Testament or some book containing it and the latter on the *Guru Granth*. Hindus and Muslims are generally affirmed. Jews are sworn on the Old Testament. A person taking the oath will hold the book (New Testament, Old Testament or *Guru Granth*) in his uplifted hand and will say or repeat the oath after the person administering it. The oath must be administered and taken with solemnity. In addition to providing a prescribed form of oath or affirmation, the rule permits an oath or affirmation to be administered to the person to be sworn or affirmed in such form to the same purpose as the court ascertains to be according to his religion or otherwise, binding on his conscience. These provisions must be strictly complied with, otherwise the court martial may be invalid. Manual of Air Force Law, Volume II, r 53 notes.

2 Form of oath for members. The Air Force Rules 1969 r 53.

3 Form of affirmation for members. The Air Force Rules 1969 r 53.

[0707] Swearing or affirming of judge advocate and others After the members of the court are all sworn or have made affirmation, an oath or affirmation shall be administered to the following persons or such of them as are present at the court martial, in such of the following forms as shall be appropriate, or in such other form to the same purport as the court ascertains to be according to the religion or otherwise binding on the conscience of the person to be sworn or affirmed[1].

(A) Judge Advocate

Form of Oath

I..........do swear by Almighty God that I will to the best of my ability carry out the duties of judge advocate in accordance with the Air Force Act 1950, and the rules made thereunder and without partiality, favour or affection, and I do further swear that I will not on any account at any time whatsoever, disclose or discover the vote or opinion on any matter of any particular member of this court martial unless required to give evidence thereof by a court of justice or a court martial in due course of law.

Form of Affirmation

I.........do solemnly, sincerely and truly declare and affirm that I will to the best of my ability carry out the duties of judge advocate in accordance with the Air Force Act 1950, and the rules made thereunder and without partiality favour or affection, and I do further solemnly, sincerely and truly declare and affirm that I will not on any account at any time whatsoever disclose or discover the vote or opinion on any matter of any matter of any particular member of this court martial, unless required to give evidence thereof by a court of justice or a court martial, in due course of law.

(B) Officer attending for the purposes of instructions

Form of oath

I.........do swear by Almighty God that I will not on any account at any time whatsoever disclose or discover the vote or opinion of any particular member of this court martial unless required to give evidence thereof by a court of justice or a court martial, in due course of law.

Form of affirmation

I.........do solemnly, sincerely and truly declare and affirm that I will not on any account, at any time whatsoever, disclose or discover the vote or opinion of any particular member of this court-martial unless required to give evidence thereof by a court of justice or a court martial, in due course of law.

(C) Shorthand writer

Form of Oath

I.........swear by Almighty God that I will truly take down to the best of my power the evidence to be given before this court martial and such other matters as I may be required, and will, when required, deliver to the court a true transcript of the same.

Form of Affirmation

I.........do solemnly, sincerely and truly declare and affirm that I will truly take down to the best of my power the evidence to be given before this court martial and such other matters as I may be required, and will, when required deliver to the court a true transcript of the same.

(D) Interpreter

Form of oath

I.........do swear by Almighty God that I will faithfully interpret and translate, as I shall be required to do, touching the matter before this court martial.

Form of affirmation

I.........do solemnly, sincerely and truly declare and affirm that I will faithfully interpret and translate, as I shall be required to do so, touching the matter before this court martial.

1 The Air Force Rules 1969 r 54. These provisions must be strictly complied with, otherwise the court martial may be invalid. Manual of Air Force Law, Volume II, r 53 notes.

[0708] Persons to administer oaths and affirmations All oaths and affirmations shall be administered by a member of the court, the judge advocate, or some other person empowered by the court to administer such oath or affirmation[1].

1 The Air Force Rules 1969 r 55.

(E) *Prosecution, defence and summing up*

[0709] Arraignment of accused After the members of court and other persons are sworn or affirmed as mentioned in the aforesaid provisions, the accused shall be arraigned, on the charges against him[1]. The charges upon which the accused is arraigned shall be read and, if necessary translated to him, and he shall be required to plead separately to each charge[2]. The trial of an accused person by a court martial commences upon his arraignment and not prior to that[3].

1 The Air Force Rules 1969 r 56 (1).

2 The Air Force Rules 1969 r 56 (2). The accused should be arraigned by the presiding officer or judge advocate, if any. Arraignment consists of: (i) calling upon the accused by his number (if any), rank, name and description as given in the charge-sheet and asking him 'Is that your number, rank, name and unit?' (ii) reading the charge to him; and (iii) asking him whether he is guilty or not guilty. Where two or more persons are jointly charged and tried for the same offence, each is separately arraigned. Manual of Air Force Law, Volume II, r 56 notes.

3 Manual of Air Force Law, Volume II, r 56 notes.

[0710] Objection by accused to charge The accused, when required to plead to any charge, may object to the charge on the ground that it does not disclose an offence under the Air Force Act 1950 or is not in accordance with the provisions of the Air Force Rules 1969[1].

1 The Air Force Rules 1969 r 57.

[0711] Amending of charge At any time during the trial, if it appears to the court that there is any mistake in the name or description of the accused in the charge-sheet, the court may amend the charge-sheet so as to correct that mistake[1]. If on the trial of any charge it appears to the court at any time before they have begun to examine the witnesses, that in the interests of justice any addition to, omission from, or alteration in the charge is required, they may report their opinion to the convening authority, and may adjourn, and the convening authority may either direct a new trial to be commenced, or amend the charge and order the trial to proceed with such amended charge after due notice to the accused[2].

1 The Air Force Rules 1969 r 58 (1). A mistake in the name or description will only be amended, if it is clear to the court that the accused is the person intended to be charged in the charge-sheet, and that, he is not prejudiced in his defence by the mistake having been made. Any amendment in the statement of the particulars of offence can be done only by the convening authority and not the court. Manual of Air Force Law, volume II, r 58 notes.

2 The Air Force Rules 1969 r 58 (2).

[0712] Special plea to the jurisdiction The accused, before pleading to a charge may offer a special plea to the general jurisdiction of the court; and if he does so and the court considers that anything stated in such plea shows that the court has no jurisdiction, they shall receive any evidence offered in support, together with any evidence offered by the prosecutor in disproof or qualification thereof, and any address by the accused and reply by the prosecutor in reference thereto[1]. If the court overrules the special plea, they shall proceed with trial[2]. If the court allows the special plea, it shall record its decision and the reasons for it, and report it to the convening authority and adjourn; such decision shall not require any confirmation, and the convening authority shall either forthwith convene another court for the trial of the accused, or order the accused to be released[3]. If the court is in doubt as to the validity of the plea, it may refer the matter to the convening authority, and may adjourn for that purpose, or may record a special decision with respect to such plea, and proceed with the trial[4].

1 The Air Force Rules 1969 r 59 (1). The evidence on special plea to jurisdiction must be taken on oath or affirmation. Manual of Air Force Law, Volume II, r 59 notes.

2 The Air Force Rules 1969 r 59 (2).

3 The Air Force Rules 1969 r 59 (3).

4 The Air Force Rules 1969 r 59 (4).

[0713] General plea of 'guilty' or 'not guilty' If no special plea to the general jurisdiction of the court is offered, or if such plea being offered, is overruled or is dealt with by a special decision under the Air Force Rules 1969[1], the accused person's plea---'guilty' or 'not guilty' (or if he refuses to plead, or does not plead intelligibly either one or the other, a plea of 'not guilty')---shall be recorded on each charge[2]. If an accused person pleads 'guilty', that plea shall be recorded as the finding of the court; but, before it is recorded, the officer conducting the proceedings, on behalf of the court, shall ascertain that the accused understands the nature of the charge to which he has pleaded guilty, and shall inform him of the general effect of that plea, and in particular of the meaning of the charge to which he has pleaded guilty, and of the difference in procedure which will be made by the plea of guilty, and shall advise him to withdraw that plea if it appears from the summary of evidence that the accused ought to plead 'not guilty'[3]. When an accused person pleads 'guilty' to the first of two or more charges laid in the alternative, the prosecutor may, after the aforesaid provisions have been complied with by the court and before the accused is arraigned on the alternative charge or charges, withdraw such alternative charge or charges without requiring the accused to plead thereto and a record to that effect shall be made upon the proceedings of the court[4]. A plea of 'guilty' shall not be accepted in cases where the accused is liable, if convicted, to the sentenced to death and where such plea is offered, a plea of 'not guilty' shall be recorded and the trial shall proceed accordingly[5].

1 Ie the Air Force Rules 1969 r 59 (4); see **[0712]**.

2 The Air Force Rules 1969 r 60 (1).

3 The Air Force Rules 1969 r 60 (2).

4 The Air Force Rules 1969 r 60 (3).

5 The Air Force Rules 1969 r 60 (4).

[0714] Plea in bar The accused, at the time of his general plea of 'guilty' or 'not guilty' to a charge for an offence, may offer a plea in bar of trial on the ground that: (i) He has been previously convicted or acquitted of the offence by a competent criminal court or by a court martial or has been dealt with summarily under the Air Force Act 1950[1] for the offence or a charge in respect of the offence has been dismissed as provided in the Air Force Rules 1969[2]; (ii) The offence has been pardoned or condoned by competent air force authority[3]; or (iii) The time which has elapsed between the commission of the offence and the commencement of the trial is more than three years, and the limit of time for trial is not extended under the provisions of the Air Force Act 1950[4]. If he offers such plea in bar, the court shall record it as well as his general plea, and if it considers that any fact or facts stated by him are sufficient to support the plea in bar it shall receive and evidence offered, and hear any address made by the accused and the prosecutor in reference to the plea[5]. If the court find that the plea in bar is proved, it shall record its finding, and notify it to the confirming authority, and shall either adjourn, or if there is any other charge against the accused, whether in the same or in a different charge-sheet, which is not affected by the plea in bar, may proceed with the trial of the accused on that charge[6]. If the finding that the plea in bar is proved is not confirmed, the court may be reassembled by the confirming authority, and proceed as if the plea had been found not proved[7]. If the court finds that the plea in bar is not proved; it shall proceed with the trial, and the said finding, shall be subject to confirmation like any other finding of the court[8].

1 Ie the Air Force Act 1950 s 82 and 86.

2 Ie the Air Force Rules 1969 r 24 (2). The Air Force Rules 1969 r 61 (1)(a).

3 The Air Force Rules 1969 r 61 (1)(b).

4 Ie under the Air Force Act 1950 s 121. The Air Force Rules 1969 r 61 (1)(c).

5 The Air Force Rules 1969 r 61 (2).

6 The Air Force Rules 1969 r 61 (3).

7 The Air Force Rules 1969 r 61 (4).

8 The Air Force Rules 1969 r 61 (5).

[0715] Procedure after plea of 'guilty'

1 Upon the record of the plea of 'guilty', if there are other charges in the same charge-sheet to which the plea is 'not guilty', the trial shall first proceed with respect to those other charges, and after findings on those charges, shall proceed with the charges on which a plea of 'guilty' has been entered; but if they are alternative charges, the court may either proceed with respect to all the charges as if the accused had not pleaded 'guilty' to any charge, or may, subject to the following provision[1], instead of so trying him, proceed as stated under the provisions of the Air Force Rules 1969[2] in respect of the charges to which he has pleaded 'guilty'[3].

2 Where alternative charges are preferred and the accused pleads 'not guilty' to the charge which alleges the more serious offence and 'guilty' to the other, the court shall try the accused person as if he had pleaded 'not guilty' to all the charges[4]. However, this provision shall not apply if the concurrence of the

convening officer has been signified by the prosecutor[5].

3 The procedure of the court in respect of a charge on which a plea of 'guilty' has been recorded, shall be as follows: (i) the court shall receive any statement which the accused desires to make in reference to the charge, and shall read the summary of evidence, and annex it to the proceedings, or if there is no such summary, shall take and record sufficient evidence to enable them to determine the sentence, and the confirming officer to know all the circumstances connected with the offence. This evidence will be taken in like manner as is directed by these provisions in the case of a plea of 'not guilty'[6]; (ii) After evidence has been so taken, or the summary of evidence has been read, as the case may be, the accused may make a statement in mitigation of punishment, and may call witnesses as to his character. If the accused at any court martial states anything in mitigation of punishment which, in the opinion of the court, requires to be proved, affect the amount of punishment, the court may permit the accused to call witnesses to prove the same[7]; (iii) If from the statement of the accused or from the summary of evidence or otherwise it appears to the court that the accused did not understand the effect of his plea of 'guilty' the court shall alter the record its opinion and proceed with the trial as on a plea of 'not guilty'; otherwise the court shall subject to the provision of the Air Force Rules 1969[8], record a finding of 'guilty' on the charge[9]; (iv) when a court has recorded an opinion as referred in the aforesaid provision[10] and proceeds with the trial as on a plea of 'not guilty', they shall, if there was a charge laid in the alternative which the prosecutor withdrew under the Air Force Rules 1969[11], reinstate such alternative charge, arraign the accused thereon and proceed with the trial as if such charge had never been withdrawn[12].

4 If a plea of 'guilty' is recorded on any charge, and the trial proceeds with respect to other charges in the same charge sheet, the proceedings under the aforesaid provision shall take place when the findings on the other charges in the same charge-sheet have been recorded[13].

1 Ie subject to The Air Force Rules 1969 r 62 (2)

2 Ie as stated under the Air Force Rules 1969 r 62 (3).

3 The Air Force Rules 1969 r 62 (1).

4 The Air Force Rules 1969 r 62 (2).

5 The Air Force Rules 1969 r 62 (2) proviso.

6 The Air Force Rules 1969 r 62 (3) (a).

7 The Air Force Rules 1969 r 62 (3) (b).

8 Ie the Air Force Rules 1969 r 71.

9 The Air Force Rules 1969 r 62 (3) (c). The form of record in the proceedings, when the court acts under this provision would be as follows: "The court being satisfied that the accused does not understand (the effect of his plea of guilty to) (the nature of) the charge, enter a plea of not guilty thereto." If the court fails to act under this provision, the confirming officer should refuse confirmation and can order a new trial. If he confirms, the finding will be set aside. Manual of Air Force Law, Volume II, r 62 notes.

10 Ie the Air Force Rules 1969 r 62 (3) (c).

11 Ie under the Air Force Rules 1969 r 60.

12 The Air Force Rules 1969 r 62 (3) (d).

13 The Air Force Rules 1969 r 62 (4).

[0716] Withdrawal of plea of 'not guilty' The accused may, if he thinks fit, at any time during the trial, withdraw his plea of 'not guilty', and plead 'guilty', and in such case the court will at once, subject to a compliance with the provisions of the Air Force Rules 1969[1], record a plea and finding of 'guilty', and shall, so far as is necessary, proceed in the manner directed by the Air Force Rules 1969[2].

1 Ie the Air Force Rules 1969 r 60 (2) and (4).

2 Ie the Air Force Rules 1969 r 62. The Air Force Rules 1969 r 63.

[0717] Plea of 'not guilty' and case for prosecution After the plea of not-guilty to any charge is recorded, the prosecutor may, if he desires, make an opening address[1]. The evidence for the prosecutor shall then be taken[2]. If it is necessary for the prosecutor to give evidence for the prosecution on the facts of the case, he shall give it after the delivery of his address, and he must be sworn and give his evidence[3]. The prosecutor may be cross-examined by the accused and afterwards may make any statement, which might be made by a witness on re-examination[4].

1 The Air Force Rules 1969 r 64 (a).

2 The Air Force Rules 1969 r 64 (b).

3 The Air Force Rules 1969 r 64 (c). When counsel appears on behalf of the prosecutor, this provision shall not apply.

4 The Air Force Rules 1969 r 64 (d). When counsel appears on behalf of the prosecutor, this provision shall not apply.

[0718] Plea of no case At the close of the case for prosecution, the accused may offer a plea that the evidence given on behalf of the prosecution, in respect of any one or more charges, has not established a prima-facie case[1] against him and that he should not, therefore, be called upon for his defence as respects such charge or charges[2]. The court shall hear the address by the accused it support of such plea and the reply by the prosecutor there to, and shall consider the plea in closed court and if its satisfied that the plea is well-founded in respect of any one or more charges to which it relates, it shall record finding of 'not-guilty' in respect of such charge or charges, and the accused shall thereafter be called upon for his defence on, in respect of the remaining charges, if any, in the charge-sheet[3].

1 A prima facie case does not mean a case should be proved to the hilt but a case which can be said to be established if the evidence which is led in support of the same was believed. While determining whether a prima facie case has been made out, the relevant consideration is whether on the evidence led, it was possible to arrive at the conclusion which could be arrived at on that evidence. *Martin and Brown Ltd v RN Banerjee* AIR 1958 SC 79.

2 The Air Force Rules 1969 r 65 (1).

3 The Air Force Rules 1969 r 65 (2).

[0719] Procedure for defence At the close of the evidence for the prosecution if the plea for 'no case' is not offered by the accused, or if offered is overruled the accused may, if he so desires, make an opening address[1]. The accused shall be asked if he has anything to say in his defence and may make a statement in his defence[2]. Any statement allowed under this provision, may be made either orally or in writing; but the accused making the statement shall not be sworn[3]. The court or the judge advocate, if any, may question the accused for the purpose of enabling, him to explain any circumstances appearing in his statement or in the evidence against him. The accused shall not render himself liable to punishment by refusing to answer such questions or by giving answers to them which he knows not to be true, but the court may draw such inference from such refusal or answers as it thinks fit[4]. The accused shall then be asked if he intends to call any witness to the facts of the case. If the accused does not state that he intends to call witnesses to the facts of the case, the procedure specified in the Air Force Rules 1969 r 67, and if he states that the intends to call witnesses to the facts of the case, the procedure as specified in the Air Force Rules 1969 r 68 shall be followed[5].

1 The Air Force Rules 1969 r 66 (1).

2 The Air Force Rules 1969 r 66 (2). This provision is merely a paraphrase of art 20 (3) of the Constitution and the bar of administering oath to an accused is imposed by law.

3 The Air Force Rules 1969 r 66 (3).

4 The Air Force Rules 1969 r 66 (4).

5 See: **[0721]** and **[0722]** respectively. The Air Force Rules 1969 r 66 (5).

[0720] Accused competent witness for defence A person accused of an offence before a court martial shall be a competent witness for the defence and may give evidence on oath or affirmation in disproof of the charges as made against him or any person charged together with him at the same trial[1]. However, (i) he shall not be called as witness except on his own request in writing[2]; or (ii) his failure to give evidence shall not be made the subject of any comment by any of the parties; or the court; or give rise to any presumption against himself or any person charged together with him at the same trial[3].

1 The Air Force Rules 1969 r 66A.

2 The Air Force Rules 1969 r 66A proviso (a).

3 The Air Force Rules 1969 r 66A proviso (b).

[0721] Procedure where accused does not call witnesses to the facts of the case The accused may call witnesses as to character[1]. The prosecutor may, in reply to the witnesses as to character, produce proof of formal conviction either by a court martial or by a criminal court and entries in the service conduct sheets[2]. The prosecutor may address the court for the purpose of summing up the evidence for the prosecution[3]. The accused may then address the court in his defence. The time at which such address is allowed is in the Air Force Rules 1969 referred to as the time for the second address of the accused[4]. The fact that the accused has stated that he does not intend to call any witness to the facts of the case does not prevent him from doing so before the evidence of the defence is completed. For example, unexpected witnesses may become available[5].

1 The Air Force Rules 1969 r 67 (1).

2 The Air Force Rules 1969 r 67 (2).

3 The Air Force Rules 1969 r 67 (3).

4 The Air Force Rules 1969 r 67 (4).

5 Manual of Air Force Law, Volume II, Air Force Rules 1969 r 67 notes.

[0722] Procedure where accused calls witnesses to the facts of the case The accused may call witnesses, including witnesses as to character[1]. The prosecutor may with the permission of the court, call witnesses in reply[2]. The accused may again address the court. The time at which such second address is allowed is in these rules referred to as the time for the second address of the accused[3]. The prosecutor shall be entitled to address the court in reply[4].

1 The Air Force Rules 1969 r 68 (1).

2 The Air Force Rules 1969 r 68 (2).

3 The Air Force Rules 1969 r 68 (3).

4 The Air Force Rules 1969 r 68 (4).

[0723] Summing up by judge advocate The judge advocate, if any, shall unless both he and the court think summing up necessary, sum up in open court the whole case[1]. After the summing up of the judge advocate, no other address shall be allowed[2]. However, summing up by judge advocate is not mandatory in all cases[3].

1 The Air Force Rules 1969 r 69 (1).

2 The Air Force Rules 1969 r 69 (2).

3 Manual of Air Force Law, Volume II, Air Force Rules 1969 r 69 notes.

(F) *Finding and sentence*

[0724] Consideration of finding The court shall deliberate on its finding in closed court[1]. The opinion of each member of the court shall be taken separately on each charge[2].

1 The Air Force Rules 1969 r 70 (1).

2 The Air Force Rules 1969 r 70 (2).

[0725] Form, Record and announcement of finding

1 The finding , on every charge which the accused is charged, shall be recorded and except as provided in these provisions, shall be recorded as finding of 'guilty' or of 'not guilty'[1]. After recording the finding on each charge, the court shall give brief reasons in support of it[2]. The judge advocate or, if there is none, the presiding officer, shall record or cause to be recorded such brief reasons in the proceedings[3]. The above record shall be signed with indicating date by the presiding officer and the judge advocate, if any[4].

2 Where the court is of opinion as regards any charge that the facts proved do not disclose the offence charged or any offence of which he might under the Air Force Act 1950 be found guilty on the charge as laid, the court shall acquit the accused of that charge[5].

3 If the court doubts as regards any charge whether the facts proved show the accused to be guilty or not of the offence charmed, or of any offence of which he might under the Air Force Act 1950 be found guilty on the charge as laid, it may, before recording a finding on that charge, refer to the confirming authority for an opinion setting out the facts which it finds to be proved, and may, if necessary, adjourn for that purpose[6].

4 Where the court is of opinion as regards any charge that the facts which it find to be proved in evidence differ materially from the facts alleged in the statement of particulars in the charge, but are nevertheless sufficient to prove the offence stated in the charge, and that the difference is not so material as to have prejudiced the accused in his defence, it may, instead of a finding or 'not guilty', record a special finding[7].

5 The special finding may find the accused guilty on a charge subject to the statement of exceptions or variations specified therein[8].

6 Where there are alternative charges and the facts proved appears to the court not to constitute the offence mentioned in any of those alternative charges, the court shall record a finding of 'not guilty' on that charge. If the court thinks that the facts proved constitute one of the offences stated in two or more of the alternative charges, but doubts which of those offences the facts do at law constitute, then it may, before recording a finding on those charges, refer to the confirming authority for an opinion, setting out the facts which it finds to be proved, and stating that it doubts whether those facts constitute in law the offence in such one or another of the alternative charges and may, if necessary, adjourn for the purpose[9].

7 The court shall not find the accused guilty on more than one of two or more charges laid in the alternative, given if conviction upon one charge necessarily connotes guilt upon the alternative charge or charges[10].

8 In any case where the court is empowered by the provisions of the Air Force Act 1950[11], to find the accused guilty of an offence other than that charged, or guilty of committing an offence in circumstances involving a less degree of punishment or where it could after hearing the evidence have made a special finding of guilty subject to exceptions or variations in accordance with the provisions of the Air Force Rules 1969[12], it may, if it is satisfied of the justice of such course, and if the concurrence of the convening officer is signified by the prosecutor, accept and record a plea of guilty of such other offence as having been committed, in circumstances involving such less degree of punishment, or of the offence charged subject to such exceptions or variations[13].

9 The finding on each charge shall be announced forthwith in open court as sub to confirmation[14].

1 The Air Force Rules 1969 r 71 (1). The provision has been substituted vide the Air Force (Amendment) Rules, 2012; published in the Gazette of India on 31 March 2012.

2 The Air Force Rules 1969 r 71 (1A). The provision has been added vide the Air Force (Amendment) Rules, 2012; published in the Gazette of India on 31 March 2012.

3 The Air Force Rules 1969 r 71 (1B). The provision has been added vide the Air Force (Amendment) Rules, 2012; published in the Gazette of India on 31 March 2012.

4 The Air Force Rules 1969 r 71 (1C). The provision has been added vide the Air Force (Amendment) Rules, 2012; published in the Gazette of India on 31 March 2012.

5 The Air Force Rules 1969 r 71 (2).

6 The Air Force Rules 1969 r 71 (3).

7 The Air Force Rules 1969 r 71 (4).

8 The Air Force Rules 1969 r 71 (5).

9 The Air Force Rules 1969 r 71 (6).

10 The Air Force Rules 1969 r 71 (7).

11 Ie the Air Force Act 1950 s 138. See **[0678]**.

12 Ie the Air Force Rules 1969 71 (4) and (5).

13 The Air Force Rules 1969 r 71 (8).

14 The Air Force Rules 1969 r (9).

[0726] Procedure on acquittal If the finding on all the charges in 'not guilty' the presiding officer shall date and sign the finding and such signature shall authenticate the whole of the proceedings, and the proceedings, upon being signed by the judge advocate, if any, shall be at once transmitted for confirmation to the person specified in the Air Force Rules 1969[1].

1 Ie as specified in the Air Force Rules 1969 r 101. The Air Force Rules 1969 r 72.

[0727] Procedure on conviction If the finding on any charge is 'guilty, then for the guidance of the court in determining its sentence, and of the confirming authority in considering the sentence, the court, before deliberating on its sentence shall whenever possible, take evidence of and record certain details about the accused[1]. Evidence on the above matters may be given by a witness verifying a statement, which contains a summary of the entries in the service records respecting the accused and identifying the accused as the person referred to in that summary[2]. The accused may cross-examine any such witness, and may call witnesses to rebut such evidence; and if the accused so requests, the service records or a duly certified copy of the material entries therein, shall be produced; and if the accused alleges that the summary is in any respect not in accordance with the service records or such certified copy, as the case may be, the court shall compare the summary with those records or copy, and if it finds it is not in accordance therewith, shall caused the summary to be corrected accordingly[3]. When all the evidence on the above matters has been given the accused may address the court thereon[4].

1 This includes general character, age, service, rank and any recognised acts of gallantry or distinguished conduct of the accused, any previous convictions of the accused either by a court martial or a criminal court, any previous punishments awarded to him by an officer exercising authority under Air Force Act 1950 s 82 or 86, the length of time he has been in arrest or in confinement on any previous sentence, censure awarded by superior authority in accordance with the Air Force Order (AFO) on the subject and any military or air force decoration or military or air force reward, of which he may be in possession or to which he is entitled. The Air Force Rules 1969 r 73 (1). The provision relating to 'censure awarded by superior authority in accordance with the Air Force Order (AFO)', has been inserted vide the Air Force (Amendment) Rules, 2012; published in the Gazette of India on 31 March 2012.

2 The Air Force Rules 1969 r 73 (2).

3 The Air Force Rules 1969 r 73 (3).

4 The Air Force Rules 1969 r 73 (4).

[0728] Sentence The court shall award one sentence in respect of all the offences of which the accused is found guilty, and such sentence shall be deemed to be awarded in respect of the offence in each charge in respect of which it can be given, and not to be awarded in respect of any offence in a charge in respect of which it cannot be given[1].

1 The Air Force Rules 1969 r 74. The sentence must be sentence authorized by the Air Force Act 1950 s 73-79.

[0729] Consideration of sentences by court When passing a sentence, a court martial will have regard not only to the nature and degree of offence and the previous character of the accused, as provided by evidence, but also to the nature and amount of any consequences, which under regulations, are involved in their finding or entailed by their sentence, in addition to the punishment it awards. The court will also consider if any circumstances have been disclosed by the evidence in extenuation, or aggravation of the offence. Where it is proved after conviction that attention has been called in local orders to the usual prevalence of the offence of which the accused has been found guilty, the court will pay regard to the fact that such warning has been issued. Sentences must necessarily vary according to the requirements of discipline but in ordinary circumstances, and for a first offence, a sentence should be light. Care must be taken to discriminate between offences due to youth, temper, sudden temptation, or unaccustomed surroundings, and those due to premeditated misconduct. If an accused airman, being of the rank of warrant officer, has elected to be tried by court martial instead of submitting to the jurisdiction of an officer having power to convene and confirm general courts martial, his punishment should not on that ground be increased. In ordinary circumstances court should not award a heavier sentence than that which the officer referred to above has power to award. In awarding imprisonment or detention the court will keep in view the locality and climate in which the accused will have to undergo his sentence. An airman, who is convicted by a court martial of an offence under certain provisions of the Air Force Act 1950[1], ought, unless in the opinion of the court there are special reasons to the contrary, to be sentenced to imprisonment. When an offender is convicted on two or more charges, the sentence should be that which is considered adequate for the gravest of the offences, with some addition for each of the other charges[2].

1 Ie the Air Force Act 1950 ss 46 (a), 52 or 67.

2 The Regulations for the Air Force 1964, paragraph 754.

[0730] Imprisonment and detention---how awarded A court martial, in framing sentences of imprisonment or detention will observe the following rules: (i) Terms of imprisonment or detention not amounting to one month, will be awarded in days, and a month means a calendar month; (ii) Terms of imprisonment or detention, of one year or more years, will be awarded in years; and (iii) Other terms of imprisonment or detention will be awarded in months, or, if required in months and days[1].

1 The Regulations for the Air Force 1964, paragraph 755.

[0731] Recommendation to mercy If the court makes a recommendation to mercy it shall give its reasons for its recommendation[1]. The number of opinions by which a recommendation to mercy is adopted or rejected, may be entered in the proceedings[2].

1 The Air Force Rules 1969 r 75 (1).

2 The Air Force Rules 1969 r 75 (2). In view of the discretion of the court in the matter of awarding sentence and the very wide range of punishments which can be awarded, a recommendation of mercy will be exceptional. The procedure contained in the Air Force Rules 1969 r 94 to be followed by the court for making recommendation to mercy; see **[0752]**. Manual of Air Force Law, Volume II, r 75 notes.

[0732] Announcement of sentence, signing, and transmission of proceedings The sentence together with any recommendation to mercy and the reasons for any such recommendation shall be announced in open court as subject to confirmation[1]. After the sentence has been awarded, the presiding officer shall date and sign the sentence and such signature shall authenticate the whole of the proceedings and the proceedings upon being signed by the judge advocate, if any, shall at once be transmitted for confirmation[2].

1 The Air Force Rules 1969 r 76 (1).

2 The Air Force Rules 1969 r 76 (2). The dating of the record is essential, as the term of imprisonment or detention awarded is reckoned to commence on the day on which the original proceedings are signed by the presiding officer. Manual of Air Force Law, Volume II, r 75 notes.

[0733] Revision In order to cure defects in the finding or sentence, the confirming officer can send back to proceedings to the court for revision. Where the finding or sentence is sent back for revision under the Air Force Act 1950[1], the court shall re-assemble in 'open court', the revision order shall be read and if the court is directed to take fresh evidence, such evidence shall also be taken in open court. The court shall then deliberate on its finding in closed court[2]. Where the finding is sent back for revision and the court does not adhere to its former finding it shall revoke the finding and sentence, and record a new finding, and if such new finding involves a sentences, pass sentence afresh[3]. Where the sentence alone is sent back for revision the court shall not revise the finding[4]. The accused shall, if he so desires, be allowed to address the court before the court closes for deliberating on its finding or the sentence[5]. After revision, the presiding officer shall date and sign the decision of the court, and the proceedings, upon signed by the judge advocate, if any, shall be at once transmitted for confirmation[6]. The revision order containing the direction of the confirming officer should be attached as an exhibit. A court cannot re-assemble more than once for revision, whether finding or sentence[7].

1 Ie under the Air Force Act 1950 s 159.

2 The Air Force Rules 1969 r 77 (1).

3 The Air Force Rules 1969 r 77 (2).

4 The Air Force Rules 1969 r 77 (3).

5 The Air Force Rules 1969 r 77 (3A).

6 The Air Force Rules 1969 r 77 (4).

7 Manual of Air Force Law, Volume II, r 77 notes.

[0734] Promulgation Promulgation is the process of formal communication to the accused of the details of the trial after its conclusion. The charge, finding, sentence, and any recommendations to mercy shall, together with the confirmation or non-confirmation of the proceedings, are promulgated in such manner as the confirming authority may direct; and if no direction is given, according to the custom of the service[1].

1 The Air Force Rules 1969 r 78. For mode of promulgation; see **[0735]**.

[0735] Mode of promulgation During promulgation, the charges, findings, sentence, recommendation to mercy (if any) and confirmation or non-confirmation, is communicated to the accused. Promulgation by reading out of the particulars detailed above on parade will be done only when the confirming authority specially directs that the promulgation shall take place in that manner. The date of promulgation will be recorded on the proceedings[1]. At the conclusion of promulgation, the commanding officer or other staff officer is to inform the accused the rights available under the Air Force Act 1950[2].

1 The Regulations for the Air Force 1964, paragraph 766.

2 Ie under the Air Force Act 1950 s 161. Manual of Air Force Law, Volume II, r 79 notes. For more details on record of promulgation; see: **[0849]**.

[0736] Mitigation of sentence on partial confirmation Where a sentence has been awarded by a court martial in respect of offences in several charges, and the confirming authority confirms the finding on some but not on all of such charges, that authority shall take into consideration the fact of such non-confirmation and shall if it seems just, mitigate, remit, or commute the punishment awarded according as seems just, having regard to the offences in the charges the findings on which are confirmed[1]. Where a sentence has been awarded by a court martial in respect of offences in several charges and has been confirmed, and any one of such charges or the finding thereon is found to be invalid, the authority having power to mitigate, remit or commute the punishment awarded by the sentence shall take into consideration the fact of such invalidity, and if it seems just, mitigate remit or commute the punishment awarded according as seems just having regard to the offences in the charges which with the findings thereon are not invalid, and the punishment as to modified shall be as valid as if it had been originally awarded only in respect of those offences[2].

1 The Air Force Rules 1969 r 79 (1).

2 The Air Force Rules 1969 r 79 (2).

[0737] Confirmation notwithstanding informality in, or excess of punishment If the sentence of a court martial is informally expressed, the confirming authority may, in confirming the sentence, vary the form so that it shall be properly expressed. If the punishment awarded by the sentence is in excess of the punishment authorised by law, the confirming authority may vary the sentence so that the punishment shall not be in excess of the punishment authorized by law; and the confirming authority may confirm the finding and the sentence, as so varied, of the court martial[1].

1 The Air Force Rules 1969 r 80.

[0738] Member or prosecutor not to confirm proceedings A member of a court martial or a prosecutor at a court martial, shall not confirm the finding or sentence of that court martial. In cases, where such member or prosecutor becomes the confirming officer, he shall refer the finding and sentence of the court martial to a superior authority competent to confirm the findings and sentences[1]. If the proceedings are confirmed in error by an officer not having power to confirm, his act and the subsequent promulgation will be null, and it will be open to the proper authority to confirm them[2].

1 The Air Force Rules 1969 r 81.

2 Manual of Air Force Law, Volume II, r 81 notes.

(H) *General provisions as to proceedings of general and district court martial*

[0739] Seating of members The members of a court martial shall take their seats according to their rank[1].

1 The Air Force Rules 1969 r 82. Amongst officer of same rank, they will take their seats according to their inter-se seniority. Manual of Air Force Law, volume II, r 82 notes.

[0740] Responsibility of presiding officer The presiding officer is responsible that the trial is conducted in proper order, and in accordance with the Air Force Act 1950 and the Air Force Rules 1969, and will take care that everything is conducted in a manner befitting a court of justice[1]. It is the duty of the presiding officer to see that justice is administered and the accused has a fair trial. Further the accused does not suffer any disadvantage or consequence of his position as a person under trial, or of his ignorance, or of his incapacity to examine or cross-examine witnesses or otherwise[2].

1 The Air Force Rules 1969 r 83 (1).

2 The Air Force Rules 1969 r 83 (2).

[0741] Power of court over address of prosecutor and accused It shall be the duty of the prosecutor to assist the court in the administration of justice, to behave impartially, to bring the whole of the transaction before the court, and not to take any unfair advantage of or suppress any evidence in favour of the accused[1]. The prosecutor may not refer to any matter which is not relevant to the charge(s) before the court and it is the duty of the court to stop him from so doing and also to restrain any undue violence of language or want of fairness or moderation on the part of the prosecutor[2]. The court shall allow great latitude to the accused in marking his defence; he must abstain from any remarks contemptuous or disrespectful towards the court, and from coarse and insulting language towards others, but he may for the purpose of his defence impeach the evidence and the motives of witnesses and prosecutor, and charge other persons with blame and even criminality, subject, if he does so, to any liability to further proceedings to which he would otherwise be subject. The court may caution the accused as to the irrelevance of his defence, but shall not, unless in special cases, stop his defence solely on ground of such irrelevance[3].

1 The Air Force Rules 1969 r 84 (1).

2 The Air Force Rules 1969 r 84 (2).

3 The Air Force Rules 1969 r 84 (3).

[0742] Procedure on trial of accused persons together Where two or more accused persons are tried together and any evidence as to the facts of the case is tendered by any one or more of them, the evidence and addresses on the past of all accused persons shall be taken before the prosecutor replies, and the prosecutor shall make one address only in reply as regards all the accused persons[1].

1 The Air Force Rules 1969 r 85.

[0743] Separate charge-sheets

1 When the convening officer directs any charges against an accused persons to be inserted in different charge-sheets, the accused shall be arraigned and until after the finding tried, upon each charge-sheet separately, and accordingly the procedure as contained in the Air Force Rules 1969[1] shall until after the finding, be followed in respect of each charge-sheet, as if it contained the whole of the charges against the accused[2].

2 The trials upon the several charge-sheets shall be in such order as the convening officer directs[3].

3 When the court has tried the accused upon all the charge-sheets it shall, in the case of the finding being 'not guilty' on all the charges, proceed as directed by the Air Force Rules 1969[4] and in case of the finding on any one or more of the charges being 'guilty' proceed as directed by certain provisions of the Air Force Rules 1969[5], in the manner in each case as if all the charges in the different charge-sheets had been contained in one charge-sheet, and the sentence passed shall be of the same as if all the charges had been contained in one charge-sheet[6].

4 If the convening officer directs that, in the event of the conviction of the accused person upon a charge in any charge-sheet, he need not be tried upon the subsequent charge sheets, the court in such event may, without trying the accused upon any of the subsequent charge-sheets, proceed as before directed

by the aforesaid provision[7].

5 Where a charge-sheet contains more than one charge, the accused may, before pleading, claim to be tried separately in respect of any charge or charges in that charge-sheet, on the ground that he will be embarrassed in his defence if he is not so tried separately; and in such case the court, unless it thinks his claim unreasonable, shall arraign and try the accused in like manner as if the convening officer had inserted the said charge or charges in different charge-sheets[8].

6 If the accused pleads 'guilty' to a charge in a charge-sheet, and the trial does not proceed as mentioned in the Air Force Rules 1969[9] with respect to the other charges in that charge-sheet the court shall, subject to the directions of the convening officer, proceed to try the accused on the charges in the next charge-sheet before it proceeds as directed by certain provisions of the Air Force Rules 1969[10].

1 Ie in the Air Force Rules 1969 rs 56 to 71.

2 The Air Force Rules 1969 r 86 (1).

3 The Air Force Rules 1969 r 86 (2).

4 Ie the Air Force Rules 1969 r 72.

5 Ie the Air Force Rules 1969 rs 62 and 73 to76.

6 The Air Force Rules 1969 r 86 (3).

7 Ie the the Air Force Rules 1969 r 86 (3). The Air Force Rules 1969 r 86 (4).

8 The Air Force Rules 1969 r 86 (5).

9 Ie in the Air Force Rules 1969 r 62 (1).

10 Ie the Air Force Rules 1969 r 62 (3) and (4). The Air Force Rules 1969 r 86 (6).

[0744] Sitting in closed court When a court martial sits in closed court on any deliberation amongst the members or otherwise, no person shall be present except the members of the court, the judge advocate, officers under instruction, and interpreter (if appointed and the court considers his presence necessary). The court may either retire, or may cause the place to be cleared of all other persons not entitled to be present[1]. Except as mentioned above, all the proceedings, including the view of any place, shall be in open court and in the presence of the accused[2].

1 The Air Force Rules 1969 r 87 (1).

2 The Air Force Rules 1969 r 87 (2).

[0745] A court martial to be public Subject to the provisions of the Air Force Rules 1969[1] , the place in which a court martial is held for the purpose of trying an offence under the Air Force Act 1950 shall be deemed to be an open court to which the public generally may have access, so far as the same can conveniently contain them[2]. However, if the court is satisfied that it is necessary or expedient in the public interest or for the ends of justice so to do, the court may at any stage of the trial of any particular case order that the public generally or any portion thereof or any particular person shall not have access to, or be or remain in place in which the court is held[3].

1 Ie the Air Force Rules 1969 r 87; see **[0744]**.

2 The Air Force Rules 1969 r 87A.

3 The Air Force Rules 1969 r 87A proviso.

[0746] Hours of sitting A court martial may sit at such times and for such period between the hours of six in the morning and six in the afternoon as may be directed by the proper air force authority or, in the absence of any such direction, as the court-martial may, from time to time, determine[1]. However no court martial shall, subject to certain provisions of the Air Force Rules 1969[2], sit for more than six hours in any one day[3]. Where the court martial considers it necessary to continue the trial after six in the afternoon or to sit for more than six hours in any one day, it may do so but if it does so, the court-martial shall record in the proceedings the reasons for so doing[4]. In cases requiring an immediate disposal or when the convening officer certifies under his hand that it is expedient in public interest, trials may be held at any hour[5]. Where the court martial or the convening officer or the senior officer on the spot is of the opinion that service exigencies or the interests of discipline require the court-martial to sit on Sunday or any other day declared as a holiday, the court-martial may sit accordingly but in no other case the court martial shall sit on any of these days[6].

1 The Air Force Rules 1969 r 88 (1).

2 Ie the Air Force Rules 1969 r 88 (2) and (3).

3 The Air Force Rules 1969 r 88 (1) proviso.

4 The Air Force Rules 1969 r 88 (2).

5 The Air Force Rules 1969 r 88 (3).

6 The Air Force Rules 1969 r 88 (4).

[0747] Continuity of trial and adjournment of court It is necessary that a trial, once begun must proceed without interruption to its conclusion. When a court is assembled and the accused has been arraigned the court shall, subject to the provisions of the Air Force Rules 1969[1], continue the trial from day to day unless it appears to the court that an adjournment is necessary for the ends of justice, or that such continuance is impracticable[2]. A court may adjourn from time to time, and from place to place, and may, when necessary, view any place[3]. A court martial, in the absence of a judge advocate (if such has been appointed for that court-martial), shall not proceed, and, if necessary shall adjourn[4]. The senior officer on the spot may also, for exigencies of the service adjourn or prolong the adjournment of the court[5]. If the time to which an adjournment is made is not specified, the adjournment shall be until further orders from the proper air force authority[6]; and if the place to which an adjournment is made is not specified, the adjournment shall be to the same place or to such other place as may be specified in further orders from the proper air force authority[7].

1 Ie the Air Force Rules 1969 r 88.

2 The Air Force Rules 1969 r 89 (1).

3 The Air Force Rules 1969 r 89 (2).

4 The Air Force Rules 1969 r 89 (3).

5 The Air Force Rules 1969 r 89 (4).

6 As to the meaning of 'proper air force authority'; see the Air Force Rules 1969 r 2 (d) **[0497]**.

7 The Air Force Rules 1969 r 89 (5).

[0748] Suspension of trial Where, in consequence of anything arising while the court is sitting, the court is unable by reason of dissolution, as specified in the Air Force Act 1950[1], or otherwise, to continue the trial, the presiding officer, or in his absence, the senior member present shall immediately report the facts to the convening authority[2]. Where a court martial is dissolved before the finding, or, in case of a finding of guilty, before award of the sentence, the proceedings of the court martial, shall be null, and the accused may be tried by another court martial[3].

1 Ie in the Air Force Act 1950 s 117.

2 The Air Force Rules 1969 r 90 (1).

3 The Air Force Rules 1969 r 90 (2). When a court martial is dissolved under this provision, every member thereof shall be disqualified to sit as a member of the fresh court martial, if convened for the trial of the accused; see the Air Force Rules 1969 r 45 (2)(c); see **[0695]**.

[0749] Proceedings on death or illness of the accused In case of the death of the accused, or of such illness of the accused as renders it impossible to continue the trial, the court shall ascertain the fact of the death or illness by evidence and record the same, and adjourn, and transmit the proceedings to the convening authority[1].

1 The Air Force Rules 1969 r 91. Also see the Air Force Act 1950 s 117 (2); see **[0656]**.

[0750] Death, retirement or absence of presiding officer In the case of the death, retirement on challenge or unavoidable absence of the presiding officer, the next senior officer shall take the place of the presiding officer and the trial shall proceed if the court is still composed of not less than the minimum number of officers of which it is required by law to consist[1].

1 The Air Force Rules 1969 r 92. Also see the Air Force Act 1950 s 117 (1); see **[0656]**.

[0751] Presence of members during trial A member of a court, who has been absent while any part of the evidence on the trial of an accused person is taken, shall take no further part in the trial by that court of that person. However, the proceedings of the court shall not be invalid unless reduced below the required minimum[1]. An officer shall not be added to a court martial after the accused has been arraigned[2].

1 The Air Force Rules 1969 r 93 (1).

2 The Air Force Rules 1969 r 93 (2).

[0752] Taking of opinions of members of court Every member of a court must give his opinion on every question, which the court has to decide, and must give his opinion as to the sentence, notwithstanding that he has given his opinion in favour of acquittal[1]. The opinions of the members of the court shall be taken in succession beginning with the member lowest in rank[2].

1 The Air Force Rules 1969 r 94 (1).

2 The Air Force Rules 1969 r 94 (2).

[0753] Procedure on incidental question If any question arises incidentally during the trial, the person, whether prosecutor or accused, requesting the opinion of the court, is to speak first; the other person is then to answer, and the first person is to be allowed to reply[1].

1 The Air Force Rules 1969 r 95.

[0754] Swearing of court to try several accused persons

1 A court may be sworn or affirmed at one time to try any number of accused persons then present

before it, whether those persons are to be tried together or separately and each accused person shall have power to object to the members of the court, and shall be asked separately whether he objects to any member[1].

2 In the case of several accused persons to be tried separately, the court, upon one of those persons objecting to a member, may, according as it thinks fit proceed to determine that objection or postpone the case of that person and swear or affirm the members of the court for the trial of the others alone[2].

3 In the case of several accused persons to be tried separately, the court, when sworn or affirmed, shall proceed with one case, postponing the other cases and taking them afterwards in succession[3].

4 Where several accused persons are tried separately by the same court martial upon charges arising out of the same transaction, the court may, if it considers it desirable in the interests of justice, postpone consideration of sentence to be awarded to any one or more of such accused persons until the trials of all such accused persons have been completed[4].

1 The Air Force Rules 1969 r 96 (1).

2 The Air Force Rules 1969 r 96 (2).

3 The Air Force Rules 1969 r 96 (3).

4 The Air Force Rules 1969 r 96 (4).

[0755] Swearing of interpreter and shorthand writer At any time during the trial an impartial person may, if the court thinks it necessary, and shall if either the prosecutor or the accused request it on any reasonable ground, be sworn or affirmed to act as interpreter[1]. An impartial person may, at any time of the trial, if the court thinks it desirable, be sworn or affirmed to act as a shorthand writer[2]. Before a person is sworn or affirmed as interpreter or shorthand writer, the accused shall be informed of the person who is proposed to be sworn or affirmed and may object to the person as not being impartial or for any reasonable cause; and the court, if it thinks that the objection is reasonable, shall not swear or affirm that person as interpreter or shorthand writer[3].

1 The Air Force Rules 1969 r 97 (1). An interpreter may be appointed under this provision by the convening authority or by the court. Manual of Air Force Law, Volume II, r 97 notes.

2 The Air Force Rules 1969 r 97 (2).

3 The Air Force Rules 1969 r 97 (3).

[0756] Evidence, when to be translated When any evidence is given in a language which any of the officers composing the court, the judge advocate, the prosecutor or the accused or his defending officer or counsel does not understand that evidence shall be interpreted to such officer or person in a language which he understands. If an interpreter in such language has been appointed by the convening officer, and duly sworn or affirmed, the evidence shall be interpreted by him. If no such interpreter has been appointed and sworn or affirmed an impartial person shall be sworn or affirmed by the court as required by the Air Force Rules 1969[1]. When documents are put in for the purpose of formal proof, it shall be in the discretion of the court to cause as much to be interpreted as appears necessary[2].

1 Ie the Air Force Rules 1969 r 97; see **[0755]**.

2 The Air Force Rules 1969 r 98.

[0757] Record in proceedings of transactions of courts martial

1 At a court martial the judge advocate, or, if there is none, the presiding officer, shall record, or cause to be recorded in the English language, all transactions of that court, and shall be responsible for the accuracy of the record (in the Air Force Rules 1969 referred to as the proceedings); and if the judge advocate is called as a witness by the accused, the presiding officer shall be responsible for the accuracy of the record in the proceedings of the evidence of the judge advocate[1].

2 The evidence shall be taken down in a narrative form in as nearly as possible the words used; but any case where the prosecutor, the accused person, judge advocate or the court consider it material, the question and answer shall be taken down verbatim[2].

3 The question which has been objected to, and the tender of any evidence which has been objected to, shall, if the prosecutor or accused so requests, or the court thinks fit, be entered with the grounds of the objection, and the decision of the court thereon[3].

4 Where any address by, or on behalf of, the prosecutor or the accused person is not in writing, it shall not be necessary to record the same in the proceedings further or otherwise than the court thinks proper, except that: (i) The court shall in every case make such record of the defence made by the accused as will enable the confirming officer to judge of the reply made by, or on behalf, of the accused to each charge against him[4]; and (ii) The court shall also record any particular matters in the address by, or on behalf of, the prosecutor or accused person, which the prosecutor or accused person, as the case may be, requires[5].

5 The court shall not enter in the proceedings any comment or anything not before the court, or any report of any fact not forming part of the trial; but if any such comment or report seems to the court necessary, the court may forward in to the proper air force authority in a separate document, signed by the presiding officer[6].

1 The Air Force Rules 1969 r 99 (1).

2 The Air Force Rules 1969 r 99 (2).

3 The Air Force Rules 1969 r 99 (3).

4 The Air Force Rules 1969 r 99 (4) (a).

5 The Air Force Rules 1969 r 99 (4) (b).

6 As to the meaning of 'proper air force authority' see: **[0497]**. The Air Force Rules 1969 r 99 (5).

[0758] Custody and inspection of proceedings The proceedings shall be deemed to be in the custody of the judge advocate (if any), or of the presiding officer. The proceedings may, with proper precaution for their safety, be inspected by the members of the court, the prosecutor and accused, respectively, at all reasonable times before the court is closed, to consider the finding[1].

1 The Air Force Rules 1969 r 100.

[0759] Transmission of proceedings after finding The proceedings shall, as required under the Air Force Rules 1969[1] be at once sent by the person having the custody to person as may be directed by the order convening the court, or, a default of any such direction, to the confirming officer[2].

1 Ie the Air Force Rules 1969 r 72 or 76.

2 The Air Force Rules 1969 r 101.

(I) *Defending Officer, Counsel and Friend of Accused*

[0760] Defending officer and friend of accused At any court-martial an accused person may be represented by any officer subject to air force law who shall be called 'the defending officer' or assisted by any person whose services he may be able to procure and who shall be called 'the friend of the accused'[1]. It shall be the duty of the convening officer to ascertain whether an accused person desires to have a defending officer assigned to represent him at his trial and, if he does so desire, the convening officer shall use his best endeavours to ensure that the accused shall be so represented by suitable officer. If owning to service exigencies or for any other reason, there shall in the opinion of the convening officer be no such officer available for the purpose the convening officer shall give a written notice to the presiding officer of the court martial, and such notice shall be attached to the proceedings[2]. The defending officer shall have the same rights and duties as appertain to counsel under the Air Force Rules 1969 and shall be under the like obligations[3]. The friend of the accused may advise the accused on all points and suggest the questions to be put to the witnesses, but he shall not examine or cross-examine the witnesses or address the court[4].

1 The Air Force Rules 1969 r 102 (1).

2 The Air Force Rules 1969 r 102 (2).

3 The Air Force Rules 1969 r 102 (3). Also see **[0761]**.

4 The Air Force Rules 1969 r 102 (4).

[0761] Counsel allowed in certain general and district courts martial In every general and district courts martial counsel shall be allowed to appear on behalf of the prosecutor and accused. However, the chief of the air staff, or the convening officer may declares that it is not expedient to allow the appearance of counsel, and such declaration may be made as regards all general and district courts martial held in any particular place, or as regards any particular general or district court martial, and may be made subject to such reservation as to cases on active service[1] or otherwise, as deemed expedient[2]. Except as provided in the Air Force Rules 1969[3], the rules with respect to counsel shall apply only to the courts martial under this provision[4].

1 As to the definition of 'active service'; see **[0470]**.

2 The Air Force Rules 1969 r 103 (1).

3 Ie the Air Force Rules 1969 r 102 (3); see note 3: **[0760]**.

4 The Air Force Rules 1969 r 103 (2).

[0762] Requirements for appearance of counsel

1 Where an accused person gives notice of his intention to have counsel to assist him during the trial either on the day on which is informed of the charge or at any time not being less than seven days before the trial, or such shorter time before the trial as in the opinion of the court would have enabled the prosecutor to obtain, if he had thought fit, counsel to assist him during the trial or where such notice is given to the accused on the part of the prosecution, counsel may appear at the court martial to assist the accused[1].

2 If the convening officer so directs, counsel may appear on behalf of the prosecutor, but in that case, unless the notice under the aforesaid provision has been given by the accused, notice of the direction for counsel to appear shall be given the accused at such time (not in any case less than seven days) before the trial, as would, in the opinion of the court, have enabled the accused to obtain counsel to assist him at the trial[2].

3 The counsel, who appears before a court martial on behalf of the prosecutor or accused, shall have the same right as the prosecutor or accused for whom he appears, to call and orally examine, cross-examine and re-examine witnesses, to make an objection or statement, to address the court, to put in any plea and to inspect the proceedings and shall have the right otherwise to act in the course of the trial in the place of the person on whose behalf he appears, and be shall comply with these provisions as if he were that person, and in such case that, person shall not have the right himself to do any of the above matters except as regards the statement allowed by the provisions of the Air Force Rules 1969[3] or except so far as the court permits him so to do[4].

4 When counsel appears on behalf of the prosecutor, the prosecutor, if called as a witness may be examined and re-examined as any other witness and certain provisions of the Air Force Rules 1969[5] shall not apply[6].

1 The Air Force Rules 1969 r 104 (1).

2 The Air Force Rules 1969 r 104 (2).

3 Ie the Air Force Rules 1969 r 62 (3) or r 66 (2).

4 The Air Force Rules 1969 r 104 (3).

5 Ie the Air Force Rules 1969 r 64 (c) and (d).

6 The Air Force Rules 1969 r 104 (4).

[0763] Counsel for prosecution The counsel appearing on behalf of the prosecution shall have the same duty as the prosecutor, and is subject to be stopped and restrained by the court in the manner provided by the Air Force Rules 1969[1].

1 Ie by the Air Force Rules 1969 r 84 (2). The Air Force Rules 1969 r 105

[0764] Counsel for accused The counsel appearing on behalf of the accused has the like rights and is under the like obligations as are specified by the provisions of the Air Force Rules 1969[1] in the case of accused[2].

1 Ie the Air Force Rules 1969 r 84 (3).

2 The Air Force Rules 1969 r 106.

[0765] General rules as to counsel A counsel, whether for the prosecution or for the accused, shall conform strictly to the provisions of the Air Force Rules 1969 and to the rules of criminal courts in India relating to the examination, cross-examination and re-examination of witnesses, and relating to the duties of counsel[1].

1 The Air Force Rules 1969 r 107. Counsel should treat the court and judge advocate with due respect and should bear in mind the requirements of service discipline in the respectful treatment of any superior officer of the accused who may attend as witness. Counsel, whether for prosecution or defence, should wear robes when appearing before court martial. Manual of Air Force Law, Volume II, r 107 notes.

[0766] Qualifications of counsel Neither the prosecutor nor the accused has any right to object to any counsel if properly qualified[1]. A counsel shall be deemed to be properly qualified if he is a legal practitioner authorized to practise with right of audience in a court of sessions in India, or if he is recognised by the convening officer in any other country where the trial is held as having in that country rights and duties similar to those of such a legal practitioner in India and as being subject to punishment or disability for a breach of professional rules[2]. A counsel who has been found guilty of contempt of court by a court of justice in India shall be disqualified to appear, act or plead on behalf of the prosecutor and accused at general and district court martial, unless he has purged himself of the contempt[3]. When the trial is held in any country other than India, a counsel shall be disqualified if he has been found guilty of contempt of court in that country, unless he has purged himself of the contempt[4].

1 The Air Force Rules 1969 r 108 (1).

2 The Air Force Rules 1969 r 108 (2).

3 The Air Force Rules 1969 r 108 (3). The provision has been inserted vide the Air Force (Amendment) Rules, 2012; published in the Gazette of India on 31 March 2012.

4 The Air Force Rules 1969 r 108 (3A). The provision has been inserted vide the Air Force (Amendment) Rules, 2012; published in the Gazette of India on 31 March 2012.

[0767] Statement by accused when defended by counsel or officer Notwithstanding the fact that an accused is represented at the trial by a counsel or an officer subject to air force law, the accused may, if he thinks fit, make a statement[1] giving his own account of the subject of the charges against him[2].

1 Ie as provided in the Air Force Rules 1969 r 62 (3) and r 66 (2).

2 The Air Force Rules 1969 r 109.

[0768] Disqualifications of judge advocate An officer, who is disqualified for sitting as a court martial, shall be disqualified for acting as judge advocate at that court martial[1].

1 The Air Force Rules 1969 r 110. Omission to appoint a judge advocate will invalidate the proceedings. As to the power and duties of judge advocate, see the Air Force Rules 1969 r 111; **[0769]**.

[0769] Powers and duties of judge advocate The powers and duties of a judge advocate are as follows:

1 The prosecutor or the accused, is at all times, after the judge-advocate is named to act on the court, entitled to his opinion on any question of law relative to the charge or trial, whether he is or out of court, subject, when he is in court to the permission of the court[1].

2 At a court martial he represents the chief legal advisor[2].

3 He is responsible for informing the court of any informality or irregularity in the proceedings. Whether consulted or not, he shall inform the convening officer and the court of any informality or defect in the charge, or in the constitution of the court, and shall give his advice on any matter before the court[3].

4 Any information or advice given to the court on any matter before the court shall, if he or the court desires if, be entered in the proceedings[4].

5 At the conclusion of the case he shall, unless both he and the court consider it unnecessary, sum up the evidence and give his opinion upon the legal bearing of the case before the court proceeds to deliberate upon its finding[5].

6 The court, in following the opinion of the judge advocate on a legal point may record that it has decided in consequence of that opinion[6].

7 The judge advocate has, equally with the presiding officer, the duty of taking, care that the accused does not suffer any disadvantage in consequence of his position as such, or of his ignorance or incapacity to examine or cross-examine witnesses or otherwise, and may, for that purpose, with the permission of the court, call witnesses and put questions to witnesses, which appear to him necessary or desirable to elicit the truth[7].

8 In fulfilling his duties, the judge advocate must be careful to maintain an entirely impartial position[8].

1 The Air Force Rules 1969 r 111 (a).

2 As to the definition of 'chief legal advisor' see Air Force Act 1950 s 4 (xi); **[0481]**. The Air Force Rules 1969 r 111 (b).

3 The Air Force Rules 1969 r 111 (c).

4 The Air Force Rules 1969 r 111 (d).

5 The Air Force Rules 1969 r 111 (e).

6 The Air Force Rules 1969 r 111 (f).

7 The Air Force Rules 1969 r 111 (g).

8 The Air Force Rules 1969 r 111 (h).

(J) *Witnesses and Evidence*

[0770] Calling of all prosecutor's witnesses The prosecutor is not bound to call all the witnesses for the prosecution whose evidence is in the summary of evidence or whom the accused has been informed it is intended to call, but should ordinarily call such of them as the accused desires in order that he may cross-examine them and shall, for this reason, so far as practicable, secure the attendance of all such witnesses[1].

1 The Air Force Rules 1969 r 112.

[0771] Calling of witnesses whose evidence is not contained in summary If the prosecutor intends to call a witness whose evidence is not contained in any summary given to the accused notice of the, intention shall be given to the accused, a reasonable time before the witness is called, and if such witness is called without such notice having been given, the court shall, if the accused to desires it, either adjourn after taking the evidence of the witness, or allow the cross-examination of such witness to be postponed, and the court shall inform the accused of his right to demand such adjournment or postponement[1].

1 The Air Force Rules 1969 r 113.

[0772] List of witnesses for accused The accused shall not be required to give to the prosecutor or court a list of the witnesses whom he intends to call. However, it shall rest with the accused to secure the attendance of any witness whose evidence is not contained in the summary, and for whose attendance the accused has not requested[1].

1 Ie as provided by the Air Force Rules 1969 r 40 (1). The Air Force Rules 1969 r 114.

[0773] Procuring attendance of witnesses The commanding officer of the accused, the convening officer, or after the assembly of the court, the presiding officer, shall take proper steps to procure the attendance of the witnesses whom the prosecutor or accused desires to call and whose attendance can reasonably be procured, but the person requiring the attendance of a witness may be required to undertake to defray the cost, if any, of their attendance[1].

1 The Air Force Rules 1969 r 115. Also see the Air Force Rules 1969 r 116 [0774]. For the form of summon, see Form C 2, in the Third schedule to the Air Force Rules 1969. If a civilian witness is required to attend a court martial, the summons will be served in accordance with the Air Force Act 1950 s 134(3).

[0774] Procedure when essential witness is absent If proper steps as mentioned in the preceding provision[1] have not been taken as to any witness, or if any witness whose attendance could not reasonably be procured before the assembly of the court is essential to the prosecution or defence, the court shall (i) take steps to procure the issue of a commission for the examination of such witness[2]; or (ii) adjourn and report the circumstances to the convening officer[3].

1 Ie under the Air Force Rules 1968 r 115; see **[0773]**.

2 The Air Force Rules 1969 r 116 (a). As to issue of commission; see **[0676]** and **[0677]**.

3 The Air Force Rules 1969 r 116 (b).

[0775] Withdrawal of witnesses from court During the trial, a witness shall not, except by special leave of the court, be permitted to be present in court while not under examination. While the witness is under examination, if a discussion arises as to the sufficiency of his answers or otherwise as to his evidence, he may be directed by the court to withdraw[1]. This provision does not apply to a prosecutor, if he is a witness[2].

1 The Air Force Rules 1969 r 117.

2 Manual of Air Force Law, Volume II, r 117 notes.

[0776] Oath or affirmation to be administered to witnesses An oath or affirmation shall, if so required by the Air Force Act 1950, be administered to every witness, before the gives his evidence, by a member of the court, the judge advocate, or some other person empowered by the court, in one of the following forms or in such other form to the same purport as the court ascertains to be according to the religion or binding on the conscience of the witness[1].

Form of oath

> I.........do swear in the name of God that what I shall state shall be the truth, the whole truth, and nothing but the truth.

Form of affirmation

> I.........do solemnly affirm that what I shall state shall be the truth, the whole truth, and nothing but the truth.

1 The Air Force Rules 1969 r 118.

[0777] Mode of questioning witnesses Every question shall be put to witness orally by the presiding officer, the judge advocate, the prosecutor or the accused person and the witness will forthwith reply, unless an objection is made by the court, judge advocate, prosecutor, or accused, in which case he shall not reply until the objection is disposed of. The witness shall address his reply to the court[1]. The evidence of a witness as taken down shall be read to him after he has given all his evidence and before the leaves the court, and shall, if necessary, be corrected[2]. If the witness denies the correctness of any part of the evidence when the same is read over to him, the court may instead of correcting the evidence, record the objection made to it by the witness[3]. If the evidence is not given in English and the witness does not understand that language the evidence as recorded shall be interpreted to him in the language in which it was given or in a language which he understands[4].

1 The Air Force Rules 1969 r 119 (1).

2 The Air Force Rules 1969 r 119 (2).

3 The Air Force Rules 1969 r 119 (3).

4 The Air Force Rules 1969 r 119 (4).

[0778] Question to witness by court or judge advocate At any time before the time for the second address of the accused the presiding officer, the judge advocate and with the permission of the court, any member of the court may address any question to a witness[1]. Upon any such question being answered, the officer conducting the proceeding shall also put to the witness any question relative to that answer which he may be requested to put by the prosecutor or the accused, and which the court deems reasonable[2].

1 The Air Force Rules 1969 r 120 (1).

2 The Air Force Rules 1969 r 120 (2).

[0779] Recalling of witnesses and calling of witnesses in reply At the request of the prosecutor or accused person, a witness may, by leave of the court, be recalled at any time before the time for the second address of the accused, for the purpose of having any question put to him through the officer conducting the proceedings[1]. A witness may, in special cases, be allowed by the court to be called or recalled by the prosecutor before the time for the second address of the accused, for the purpose of rebutting any material statement made by a witness for the defence upon his examination by the accused on any new matter which the prosecutor could not reasonably have foreseen[2]. Where the accused has called witnesses to character, the prosecutor, before the time for the second address of the accused, may call or recall witnesses for the purpose of proving a previous conviction or entries in the service records against the accused[3]. The court may call or recall any witness at any time before finding if it considers that it is necessary for the ends of justice[4].

1 The Air Force Rules 1969 r 121 (1).

2 The Air Force Rules 1969 r 121 (2).

3 The Air Force Rules 1969 r 121 (3).

4 The Air Force Rules 1969 r 121 (4).

(K) *Addresses*

[0780] Addresses may be in writing Addresses by the prosecutor and the accused and the summing tip of the judge advocate may either be given orally or be in writing. If the address is in writing, it shall be read in open court[1].

1 The Air Force Rules 1969 r 10

(L) *Insanity*

[0781] Provisions as to finding of insanity Where the court finds either that the accused is of unsound mind and consequently incapable of making his defence or that he committed the act alleged but was by reason of unsoundness of mind incapable of knowing the nature of the act or that it was wrong or contrary to law, the presiding officer shall date and sign the finding and the proceedings. The proceedings after being signed by the judge advocate if any, shall be transmitted to be confirming officer[1].

1 The Air Force Rules 1969 r 123.

(M) *Preservation of Proceedings*

[0782] Preservation of Proceedings The proceedings of a court martial shall after promulgation be forwarded to the office of the chief legal advisor (judge advocate general) and there preserved for not less, in the case of a general court martial, than seven years, and in the case of any other court martial, than three years[1].

1 The Air Force Rules 1969 r 124.

[0783] Court martial proceedings where evidence is of a secret nature If any evidence against a person subject to the Air Force Act 1950, remanded for trial by court martial is of a secret nature, the commanding officer will ensure that summary of evidence is treated as a secret document. No extra copies will be made and all the copies of summary of evidence will be collected after trial from the individuals to whom they have been issued. This includes copies of any exhibits produced at the trial which contain secret matter. If after trial the accused applies for his copy in order that he may petition, it may be reissued to him on a temporary basis. The proceedings of all courts martial which contain any matter involving security will be passed under secret cover. In all cases where an officer or airman is charged with an offence which relates to communicating or attempting to communicate secret information to an unauthorised person a copy of the summary of evidence will be sent for information to Air Headquarters (Directorate of Intelligence) as early as possible after recording the summary of evidence[1].

1 Regulations for the Air Force 1964, paragraph 726.

[0784] Right of person tried to copies of proceedings Every person tried by a court martial shall be entitled on demand, at any time after the confirmation of the finding and sentence and before the proceedings are destroyed, to obtain free of cost from the officer or person having the custody of the proceedings, a copy thereof, including the proceedings upon revision, if any[1].

1 The Air Force Rules 1969 r 125. This provision is subject to the Air Force Rules 1969 r 126; see **[0785]**.

[0785] Copy of proceedings not to be given in certain cases Notwithstanding anything contained in the aforementioned provision[1], if the Central Government certifies that it is against the interest or the security of the State or friendly relations with foreign States to supply a copy of the proceedings or any part thereof under the said rule, he shall not be furnished with such copy[2]. However, if the Central Government is satisfied that the person demanding the copy is desirous of submitting a petition in accordance with the Air Force Act 1950 or instituting any action in a court of law in relation to a finding or sentence, if shall permit inspection of the proceedings by such person or his legal adviser, if any, on the following conditions: (a) The inspection shall be made at such times and such places as the Central Government or any authority authorised by it may direct[3], and (b) The person allowed to inspect the proceedings shall, before such inspection furnish: (i) An undertaking, in writing, that he shall not make copies of the proceedings or any part thereof and that the information or documents contained in such proceedings shall not be used by him, for any purpose whatsoever other than for the purpose of submitting a petition in accordance with the Air Force Act 1950 or instituting any action in a court of law in relation to the said finding or sentence[4]; and (ii) A certificate that he is aware that he may render himself liable to prosecution under the Indian Official Secrets Act 1923[5], if he commits any act specified in the said sections in relation to the documents or information contained in the said proceedings[6].

1 Ie under the Air Force Rules 1969 r 125; see **[0784]**.

2 The Air Force Rules 1969 r 126.

3 The Air Force Rules 1969 r 126 proviso (a).

4 The Air Force Rules 1969 r 126 proviso (b) (i).

5 Ie under the Indian Official Secrets Act 1923 s 3 and 5.

6 The Air Force Rules 1969 r 126 proviso (b) (ii).

[0786] Loss of proceeding

1. If before confirmation the original proceedings of a court martial, or its part are lost, a copy thereof, if any certified by the presiding officer of or the judge advocate at the court martial may be accepted in lieu of the original[1].
2. If there is no such copy, and sufficient evidence of the charge, finding sentence, and transactions of the court can be procured, that evidence may, with the consent of the accused, be accepted in lieu of the original proceedings, or part thereof lost[2].
3. In above mentioned cases the finding and sentence may be confirmed, and shall be as valid as if the original proceedings, or part thereof, had not been lost[3].
4. If the proceedings, or part thereof, were lost before confirmation, and there is no such copy or evidence, or the accused refuses such consent as mentioned above, the accused may be tried again, and the finding and sentence of the previous court, of which the proceedings were so lost, shall be null[4].
5. If, after confirmation, the original proceedings of a court martial of any part thereof are lost and there is sufficient evidence of the charge, finding sentence, and transactions of the court, and of the confirmation of the finding and sentence, that evidence shall be valid and sufficient record of the trial for all purposes[5].

1 The Air Force Rules 1969 r 127 (1).

2 The Air Force Rules 1969 r 127 (2).

3 The Air Force Rules 1969 r 127 (3).

4 The Air Force Rules 1969 r 127 (4).

5 The Air Force Rules 1969 r 127 (5).

(N) *Irregular procedure when no injustice is done*

[0787] Validity or irregular procedure in certain cases Whenever it appears that a court martial had jurisdiction to try any person and make a finding and that there is legal evidence or a plea of guilty to justify such finding, such finding and sentence which the court martial had jurisdiction to pass thereon may be confirmed, and shall, if so confirmed, be valid notwithstanding any deviation from the Air Force Rules 1969. However, before confirming the finding and sentence, the confirming officer must satisfy that the accused has not suffered any injustice through any deviation from the Air Force Rules or through any defect or objection. Where any finding and sentence are otherwise valid they shall not be invalid only because of failure to administer an oath or affirmation to the interpreter or shorthand writer. However, this provision shall not relieve an officer from any responsibility for any wilful or negligent disregard of any of the provisions of the Air Force Rules 1969[1].

1 The Air Force Rules 1969 r 128. This provision is intended to prevent a miscarriage of justice in consequence of defects, usually of technical nature, in matters of procedure which do not affect the real merits of the case. Manual of Air Force Law, Volume II, r 128 notes.

(O) *Offences of witnesses and others*

[0788] Offences of witnesses and others When any court martial is of opinion that there is ground for inquiring into any offence specified in the provisions of the Air Force Act 1950[1] and committed before it or brought under its notice in the course of its proceedings, which would if done by a person subject to the Air Force Act 1950, have constituted such an offence, such court martial may proceed as follows: (i) If the person who appears to have committed the offence is subject to the Air Force Act 1950, the court may bring his conduct to the notice of the proper air force authority and may also order him to be placed in air force custody for his trial by an officer exercising authority under the Air Force Act 1950[2] or by court martial[3]; (ii) If the person who appears to have done the act is subject to the Army Act 1950 or the Navy Act 1957, the court may bring his conduct to the notice of the proper military or naval authority[4]; (iii) If the person who appears to have done the act is not subject to military, naval or air force law, than in the case of acts which would, if done by a person subject to the Air Force Act 1950, have constituted an offence under the aforesaid Act[5] the officer who summoned the witness to appear or the presiding officer of the court martial, may forward a written complaint to the nearest Magistrate of the first class having jurisdiction. In the case of acts which would, if done, have constituted an offence other provisions of the Air Force Act 1950[6], the court, after making necessary preliminary inquiry, may send the case to the nearest Magistrate of the first class having jurisdiction for inquiry or trial in accordance with the Code of Criminal Procedure 1973 s 340[7].

1 Ie the Air Force Act 1950 s 59 and 60.

2 Ie under the Air Force Act 1950 s 82 or 86.

3 The Air Force Rules 1969 r 129 (a).

4 The Air Force Rules 1969 r 129 (b).

5 Ie under the Air Force Act 1950 s 59 (a), (b), (c) or (d).

6 Ie under the Air Force Act 1950 s 59 (e) and s 60.

7 The Air Force Rules 1969 r 129 (c).

(ii) Summary General Court Martial

CONTENTS

PARA

Summary General Court martial

Summary General Court martial

[0789] Convening the court and record of proceedings Summary general court martial may be convened and the proceedings of the court recorded in accordance the provisions contained in the Air Force Act 1950[1], with such variations as the circumstances of each case may require[2]. The officer convening the court shall appoint or detail the officers to form the court, and may also appoint or detail officers as waiting members. Such officers should have held commissions for not less than one year, but if any officers, who have held commission for not less than three years, are available they shall be selected in preference to officers of less service[3]. A provost martial, assistant provost marshal or officer who is a prosecutor or witness for prosecution shall not be appointed a member of the court[4].

1 Ie as contained in the Air Force Rules 1969 Form F 3 in the Sixth Schedule.

2 The Air Force Rules 1969 r 130 (1). The convening order for a summary general court martial is to be signed personally by the officer convening the court. Another officer cannot sign it on his behalf. Manual of Air Force Law, Volume II, r 130 notes.

3 The Air Force Rules 1969 r 130 (2).

4 The Air Force Rules 1969 r 130 (3). For definition of 'provost marshal'; see **[0498]**.

[0790] Charge The statement of an offence to be made briefly in any language sufficient to describe or disclose an offence under the Air Force Act 1950[1].

1 The Air Force Rules 1969 r 131. A formal charge-sheet is not a legal necessity at a trial by summary general court martial. Manual of Air Force Law, Volume II, r 131 notes.

[0791] Trial of several accused persons The court may be sworn at the same time to try any number of accused persons present before it, but, except as contained in the provisions of the Air Force Rules 1969[1], the trial of each accused person shall be separate[2].

1 Ie the Air Force Rules 1969 r 41 dealing with joint trials of several accused persons. See: **[0625]**.

2 The Air Force Rules 1969 r 132.

[0792] Challenges The names of the presiding officer and members of the court shall be read over to the accused who shall be asked if he objects to the tried by any of these officers[1]. Any objection shall be decided as provided for in the Air Force Act 1950 and the Air Force Rules 1969[2], the vacancies being filled from among the waiting members, if any, or by fresh members being appointed by the convening officer[3].

1 The Air Force Rules 1969 r 133 (1).

2 Ie as provided in the Air Force Act 1950 s 129 and the Air Force Rules 1969 r 52. See: **[0669]** and **[0705]**.

3 The Air Force Rules 1969 r 133 (2).

[0793] Swearing or affirming the court, judge advocate etc The provisions of the Air Force Rules 1969[1] relating to administering and taking of oaths and making of affirmations shall apply to every summary general court martial[2].

1 Ie the Air Force Rules 1969 rs 53, 54 and 55. See: **[0706]**, **[0707]** and **[0708]** respectively.

2 The Air Force Rules 1969 r 134.

[0794] Arraignment[1] When the court is sworn or affirmed, the judge advocate, if any, or the presiding officer shall inform the accused then to be tried, the offence with which he is charged, if necessary, with an explanation giving him full information of the act or omission with which he is charged, and shall ask of the accused whether he is guilty or not[2] of the offence[3].

1 Arraignment consists of calling upon the accused by his number, rank, name and description as given in the charge sheet and asking him 'Is that your number, rank, name and unit (or description)? Each charge is read separately and the accused is called upon to plead, i.e., to say whether he is 'guilty' or 'not guilty' of each charge separately as it is read out. Manual of Air Force Law, volume II, the Air Force Rules 1969 r 135 notes.

2 As to the general plea of 'guilty' or 'not guilty' see the Air Force Rules 1969 r 60: **[0713]**; and as to the procedure after plea of 'guilty' see the Air Force Rules 1969 r 62: **[0715]**. Both these provisions are applicable in a trial by a summary general court martial. A plea of guilty will not be accepted by the court if the charge or charges upon which an accused is arraigned render him liable, on conviction, to be sentenced to death. If such a plea is offered, the court will enter a plea of 'not guilty' and proceed with the trial accordingly. See: the Air Force Rules 1969 r 60 (4). Manual of Air Force Law, Volume II, the Air Force Rules 1969 r 135 notes.

3 The Air Force Rules 1969 r 135.

[0795] Plea to jurisdiction If a special plea to the general jurisdiction is offered by the accused, it is to be dealt according to the provisions of the Air Force Rules 1969[1]. If the plea is considered by the court to be proved, it shall report the same to the convening officer[1].

1 Ie according to the Air Force Rules 1969 r 59 and 61 respectively; see **[0712]** and **[0714]**.

2 The Air Force Rules 1969 r 136.

[0796] Evidence The witnesses for the prosecution will be called. The accused shall be allowed to cross-examine them and to call any witnesses for his defence[1]. An oath or affirmation as laid down in the Air Force Rules 1969[2] shall be administered to every witness, if required by the Air Force Act 1950, by one of the person specified[3].

1 The Air Force Rules 1969 r 137 (1).

2 Ie in the Air Force Rules 1969 r 118. For form of oath; see **[0776]**.

3 Ie as specified in the Air Force Rules 1969 r 118. The Air Force Rules 1969 r 137 (2).

[0797] Defence The accused shall be asked what he has to say in his defence and shall be allowed to make his defence[1]. He may be allowed to have any person to assist him during the trial[2], whether a legal adviser or any other person[3]. The court, or the judge advocate (if any), may question the accused for the purpose of enabling him to explain any circumstances appearing in his statement or in the evidence against him. The accused shall not render himself liable to punishment by refusing to answer such questions or by giving answers to them which he knows not to be true, but the court may draw such inference from such refusal or answers as it thinks fit[4].

1 As to the right of accused to prepare his defence, see the Air Force Rules 1969 r 39; see: **[0623]**. This provision is applicable to a summary general court martial also. Manual of Air Force Law, Volume II, the Air Force Rules 1969 r 138 notes.

2 There is no provision for appearance of a civilian defence counsel at summary general court martial. The legal advisor or other person permitted to assist the accused will not have the right of appearance. However, the accused is permitted to have a defending officer as the provisions of the Air Force Rules 1969 r 102 are applicable to summary general court martial. Manual of Air Force Law, Volume II, the Air Force Rules 1969 r 138 notes.

3 The Air Force Rules 1969 r 138 (1).

4 The Air Force Rules 1969 r 138 (2).

[0798] Record of the evidence and defence The judge advocate (if any), or the presiding officer shall take down a brief record of the evidence of the witnesses at the trial and of the defence of the accused. The record shall be attached to the proceedings[1]. However, if it appears to the convening officer that exigencies of the service or other circumstances prevent compliance of the above provision, he may direct that the trial may be carried on without any such brief record being taken down[2]. If the accused pleads 'guilty', the summary of evidence, if any, may be read and attached to the proceedings. It shall not be necessary for the court to hear witnesses for the prosecution respecting matters contained in the summary of evidence so read[3].

1 The Air Force Rules 1969 r 139 (1).

2 The Air Force Rules 1969 r 139 (1) proviso.

3 The Air Force Rules 1969 r 139 (2). The record of the evidence under this provision will be made separately, signed by the presiding officer and judge advocate (if any), and shall be attached to the Appendix to form F3, Section III, Sixth Schedule to Air Force Rules 1969. Manual of Air Force Law, Volume II, the Air Force Rules 1969 r 139 notes.

0799] Finding and sentence The court shall then be closed to consider its finding. If the finding on any charge is 'guilty' the court may receive any evidence as to previous convictions and character, which is available. The court shall then deliberate in closed court as to its sentence[1].

1 The Air Force Rules 1969 r 140. As to the voting of members of summary general court martial; see the Air Force Act 1950 s 131 (1) and (4). No sentence of death shall be passed by a summary general court martial without the concurrence of all the members; see the Air Force Act 1950 s 131 (3).

[0800] Adjournment A summary general court martial may adjourn from time to time and from place to place and may when necessary inspect any place[1]. The proceedings shall be held in open court, in the presence of the accused, except on any deliberation among the members, when the court may be closed[2].

1 The Air Force Rules 1969 r 141 (1). The restrictions contained in the Air Force Rules 1969 r 88 are not applicable to summary general court martial. Even then the court should not deny the accused reasonable rest or adequate time to prepare his defence, as the circumstances permit. Manual of Air Force Law, volume II, the Air Force Rules 1969 r 141 notes.

2 The Air Force Rules 1969 r 141 (2).

[0801] Application of rules Certain provisions of Air Force Rules 1969[1] shall, so far as practicable; apply to summary general courts martial as if summary general court martial were district courts martial[2].

1 The Air Force Rules 1969 r 24 (disposal of the charge or adjournment for taking down the summary of evidence), see **[0610]**; r 25 (remand of accused)), see **[0612]** ; r 26 (application of the Air Force Rules 1969 r 24 and 25 to officers exercising powers of a commanding officer); r 39 (opportunity for accused to prepare defence), see **[0623]**; r 40 (warning of accused for trial), see **[0624]**; r 42 (suspension of rules on the grounds of the exigencies of the service or the necessary of discipline), see **[0626]**; r 44 (adjournment for insufficient number of officers), see **[0694]**; r 57 (objection by accused to the charge, see **[0710]**; r 59 (special plea to the jurisdiction), see **[0712]**; r 60 (general plea of guilty or not guilty), see **[0713]**; r 61(plea in bar), see **[0714]**; r 62 (procedure after plea of guilty), see **[0715]**; r 63 (withdrawal of plea of not guilty), see **[0716]**; r 70 (consideration of finding), see **[0724]**; r 71 (form and record of finding), see **[0725]**; r 72 (procedure on acquittal), see **[0726]**; r 73 (procedure on conviction), see **[0727]**; r 74 (sentence), see **[0728]**; r 75 (recommendation to mercy), see **[0731]**; r 76 (signing and transmission of proceedings), see **[0732]**; r 77 (revision), see **[0733]**; r 78 (promulgation), see **[0734]**; r 79 (mitigation of sentence on partial confirmation), see **[0736]**; r 80 (confirmation notwithstanding informality in or excess of punishment), see **[0737]**; r 81 (member or prosecutor not to confirm proceedings), see **[0738]**; r 83 (responsibility of presiding officer), see **[0740]**; r 84 (power of court over address of prosecutor and accused), see [0741]; r 85 (procedure on trial of accused persons together), see **[0742]**; r 87 (sitting in closed court), see **[0744]**; r 87A (court martial to be public), see **[0745]**; r 90 (suspension of trial), see **[0748]**; r 91 (proceedings on death or illness of the accused), see **[0749]**; r 92 (death, retirement or absence of presiding officer), see **[0750]**; r 93 (present of members during trial), see **[0751]**; r 100 (custody and inspection of proceedings), see **[0758]**; r 101 (transmission of proceedings after finding), see **[0759]**; r 102 (defending officer and friend of accused), see **[0760]**; r 110 (disqualification of judge-advocate), see **[0768]**; r 111 (powers and duties of judge-advocate), see **[0769]**; r 123 (provisions as to finding of insanity), see **[0781]**; r 124 (preservation of proceedings), see **[0782]**; r 125 (rights of person fried to copies of proceedings), see **[0784]**; r 126 (copy of proceedings not to be given in certain cases), see **[0785]**; r 127 (loss of proceedings), see **[0786]**; r 128 (validity of irregular procedure in certain cases), see **[0787]**; and r 129 (offences of witnesses and others), see **[0788]**.

2 The Air Force Rules 1969 r 142.

[0802] Evidence of opinion of convening officer Any statement in an order convening a summary general court martial as to the opinion of the convening officer shall be conclusive evidence[1] of that opinion, but this provision shall not prejudice the proof at any time of any such opinion when not so stated[2].

1 As to the meaning of 'conclusive evidence' see the Indian Evidence Act 1872 s 4.

2 The Air Force Rules 1969 r 143.

E. Punishments and Penal Deductions

CONTENTS

PARA

(i) Punishments

(ii) Penal Deductions

(i) Punishments

[0803] Punishments awardable by courts martial The following punishments may be inflicted by court martial[1] in respect of offences specified in the Air Force Act 1950 ss 34-70 and committed by persons subject to the Act:

(1) death[2];

(2) imprisonment for life[3];

(3) imprisonment, either rigorous or simple, for any period not exceeding fourteen years[4];

(4) detention for a term not exceeding two years in the case of airmen[5];

(5) cashiering, in the case of officers[6];

(6) dismissal from service[7];

(7) reduction to the ranks or to a lower rank or classification, in the case of warrant officers and non-commissioned officers[8]. However, a warrant officer reduced to the ranks shall not be required to serve in the ranks as an airman[9];

(8) forfeiture of seniority of rank, in the case of officers, warrant officers and non- commissioned officers; and forfeiture of all or any part of their service for the purpose of promotion, in the case of any of them whose promotion depends upon length of service[10];

(9) forfeiture of service for the purpose of increased pay, pension or any other prescribed purpose[11];

(10) severe reprimand or reprimand, in the case of officers, warrant officers and non-commissioned officers[12];

(11) forfeiture of pay and allowances for a period not exceeding three months for an offence committed on active service[13];

(12) forfeiture in the case of a person sentenced to cashiering or dismissal from the service of all arrears of pay and allowances and other public money due to him at the time of such cashiering or dismissal[14];

(13) stoppage of pay and allowances until any proved loss or damage occasioned by the offence of which he is convicted is made good[15].

1 As to the definition of 'court martial'; see **[0486]**.

2 The Air Force Act 1950 s 73 (a). A sentence of death can only be passed by a general court martial with the concurrence of at least two-thirds of the members or by a summary general court martial with the concurrence of all the members; see the Air Force Act 1950 s 131 (2) and (3). A certificate to that effect that the death sentence was passed with the concurrence of ....members/unanimously, as the case may be must be endorsed in the proceedings. In awarding a sentence of death the court must add a direction that the accused shall suffer death by being hanged by the neck until he be dead, or by being shot to death; see the Air Force Act 1950 s 163. The Manual of Air Force Law, Volume I, s 73 notes.

3 The Air Force Act 1950 s 73 (b). The term 'transportation for life' has been replaced by 'imprisonment for life'. See: The Indian Penal Code 1860 s 53A.

4 The Air Force Act 1950 s 73 (c). Imprisonment is either (i) rigorous, that is, with hard labour; or (ii) simple. The terms 'rigorous' and 'simple' should invariably be used in sentences passed under the Army Act 1950. If a court

inadvertently passes a sentence of 'imprisonment' without specifying whether it is rigorous or simple, the sentence is treated as one of 'simple imprisonment'. An officer sentenced to imprisonment must first be sentenced to be cashiered. Conversion of rigorous imprisonment into simple imprisonment is commutation. The Manual of Air Force Law, Volume I, s 73 notes.

5 The Air Force Act 1950 s 73 (d). Cashiering is the more ignominious form of dismissal; and normally an officer who has been cashiered cannot hold an appointment under the Government. In case of an officer, a sentence of cashiering must precede the sentence of death, imprisonment for life or imprisonment. The Manual of Air Force Law, volume I, s 73 notes.

6 The Air Force Act 1950 s 73 (e).

7 The Air Force Act 1950 s 73 (f).

8 The Air Force Act 1950 s 73 (g). A warrant officer or non-commissioned officer who is reduced to the rank by sentence of a court martial shall be reduced to the classification of Leading Aircraftman. The reduction by or as a consequence of the sentence of a court martial shall take effect from the date on which the original court martial proceedings were signed by the presiding officer. Regulations for the Air Force 1964, paragraph 293 (b).

9 The Air Force Act 1950 s 73 (g) proviso.

10 The Air Force Act 1950 s 73 (h). Punishment under this provision cannot be awarded to an airman below the rank of corporal. The Manual of Air Force Law, Volume I, s 73 notes.

11 The Air Force Act 1950 s 73 (i).

12 The Air Force Act 1950 s 73 (j). Punishment under this provision cannot be awarded to an airman below the rank of corporal. The Manual of Air Force Law, Volume I, s 73 notes.

13 The Air Force Act 1950 s 73 (k). This punishment can only be awarded by a court martial where an offence is committed on active service. For definition of 'active service'; see **[0470]**. The Manual of Air Force Law, Volume I, s 73 notes.

14 The Air Force Act 1950 s 73 (l).

15 The Air Force Act 1950 s 73 (m).

[0804] Alternative punishments awardable by court martial Subject to the provisions of the Air Force Act 1950, a court martial may, on convicting a person subject to the aforesaid Act of any of the offences specified[1], award either the particular punishment with which the offence is stated in the said provision to be punishable, or, in lieu thereof, any one of the punishments lower in the scale set out in the Act[2], regard being had to the nature and degree of the offence[3].

1 Ie specified in the Air Force Act 1950 ss 34-70.

2 Ie set out in the Air Force Act 1950 s 73; see **[0803]**.

3 The Air Force Act 1950 s 74.

[0805] Combination of punishments Combination of punishment is legal and permissible under the Air Force Act 1950. A court martial may award in addition to the punishment specified in the Air Force Act 1950[1], any one or more of the punishments as specified in other provisions[2] of the Act[3].

1 Ie as specified in the Air Force Act 1950[1] s 73 (e) or (f).

2 Ie as specified in the Air Force Act 1950[1] s 73 (g) to (m).

3 The Air Force Act 1950 s 75. Combination of punishment is legal and permissible under the Air Force Act 1950. This provision vests a power in court martial to choose and award a combination of the punishment enumerated in

the Air Force Act 1950 s 73 depending upon the nature and degree of offence and subject to the limitations imposed by this provision. For example, following punishment is legal in the case of an officer: cashiering, imprisonment, stoppage and forfeiture of all arrears of pay and allowances. The Manual of Air Force Law, Volume I, s 75 notes.

[0806] Cashiering of officers An officer shall be sentenced to be cashiered before he is awarded any of the punishments specified under the provisions of the Air Force Act 1950[1]. While sentencing an officer to death, imprisonment for life or imprisonment, the court martial must ensure that the sentence of cashiering precedes the sentence of death, imprisonment for life or imprisonment[2].

1 Ie as specified under the Air Force Act 1950 s 73 (a) to (c). The Air Force Act 1950 s 76. Cashiering can be awarded only to the officers. Cashiering is not defined in statutes, but is a form of dismissal where a person is stripped of his ranks and medals because of a serious misdemeanour. The Manual of Air Force Law, Volume I, s 75 notes.

2 The Manual of Air Force Law, Volume I, s 76 notes.

[0807] Field punishment Where any person subject to the Air Force Act 1950 and under the rank of warrant officer commits any offence on active service[1], it shall be lawful for a court martial to award for that offence any such punishment as is prescribed as a field punishment. Field punishment shall be of the character of personal restraint or of hard labour but shall not be of a nature to cause injury to life or limb and shall not include flogging[2].

1 As to the meaning of 'warrant officer' and 'active service'; see **[0504] and [0470]**.

2 The Air Force Act 1950 s 77. Field punishment can only be awarded to a non-commissioned officer or aircraftman. A non-commissioned officer awarded field punishment by a court martial is deemed to be reduced to the ranks. Field punishment should always be awarded in days or months. However, a court cannot award field punishment for more than three months. For prescribed form of field punishment; see the Air Force Rules 1969 r 152. The Manual of Air Force Law, Volume I, s 77 notes.

[0808] Execution: Field Punishment[1]

1 See: **[0871]**. Field punishment has been abolished under the Army Act 1950.

[0809] Position of field punishment in scale of punishments Field punishment shall for the purpose of commutation be deemed to stand next below dismissal in the scale of punishments specified in Air Force Act 1950[1].

1 Ie as specified in the Air Force Act 1950 s 73. The Air Force Act 1950 s 78. Only sentences of death, imprisonment for life, imprisonment or dismissal can be commuted to field punishment, provided the offender is under the rank of warrant officer and the offence is committed on active service. The Manual of Air Force Law, Volume I, s 78 notes. Field punishment has been abolished under the Army Act 1950 in 1993.

[0810] Result of certain punishments in the case of a warrant officer or a non-commissioned officer A warrant officer[1] or a non-commissioned officer[2] sentenced by a court martial to imprisonment for life, imprisonment, detention, field punishment or dismissal from the service shall be deemed to be reduced to the ranks[3].

1 As to the definition of 'warrant officer'; see **[0504]**.

2 As to the definition of 'non-commissioned officer'; see **[0491]**.

3 The Air Force Act 1950 s 79. A warrant officer or non-commissioned officer who is deemed to be reduced to the ranks under this provision shall be reduced to the classification of Leading Aircraftman. The reduction by or as a consequence of the sentence of a court martial shall take effect from the date on which the original court martial proceedings were signed by the presiding officer; see: Regulations for the Air Force 1964, paragraph 293 (b).

[0811] Retention in the ranks of a person convicted on active service When, on active service[1], any enrolled person[2] has been sentenced by a court martial to dismissal, imprisonment for life, imprisonment or detention, whether combined with dismissal or not, the prescribed officer[3] may direct that such person may be retained to serve in the ranks and such service shall be reckoned as part of his term of imprisonment for life, imprisonment or detention, if any[4].

1 As to the definition of 'active service'; see **[0470]**.

2 The term 'any enrolled person' means a person subject to the Air Force Act 1950 s 2(b). Warrant officers and non-commissioned officers though originally enrolled are not liable to be retained to serve in the ranks under this provision. The Manual of Air Force Law, Volume I, s 80 notes.

3 For 'prescribed officer'; see **[0812]**.

4 The Air Force Act 1950 s 80.

[0812] Prescribed officer under the Air Force Act 1950 s 80 The prescribed officer for the purposes of certain provisions of the Air Force Act 1950[1] shall be the officer commanding the Forces in the field, or the air or other officer commanding the command, or in the field any detached portion of the air force, in which the trial was held, or any officer superior in command to such air or other officer[2].

1 Ie the Air Force Act 1950 s 80; see **[0811]**.

2 The Air Force Rules 1969 r 161.

(ii) Penal Deductions

[0813] Introduction The air force law enjoins that that the pay of any person subject to the Air Force Act 1950 due to him as such under any regulations shall be paid without any deductions other than those authorised under the aforesaid Act or any other Act[1]. It is illegal to make deductions which are not authorised and unlawful withholding of pay is an offence under the Air Force Act 1950[2]. However, there are certain deductions which are authorised and can be made from the pay and allowances of persons subject to the Air Force Act 1950[3].

1 The Air Force Act 1950 s 25; see **[0545]**.

2 The Air Force Act 1950 s 61; see **[0583]**.

3 The Air Force Act 1950 s 91-101.

[0814] Deductions from pay and allowances of officers The following penal deductions may be made from the pay and allowances of an officer:

1 All pay and allowances due to an officer for every day he absents himself without leave, unless a satisfactory explanation has been given to his commanding officer and has been approved by the Central Government[1].

2 All pay and allowances for every day while he is in custody or under suspension from duty on a charge

for an offence of which he is afterwards convicted by a criminal court or a court martial or by an officer exercising authority under certain provisions of the Air Force Act 1950[2].

3 Any sum required to make good the pay of any person subject to the Air Force Act 1950 which he has unlawfully retained or unlawfully refused to pay[3].

4 Any sum required to make good such compensation for any expenses, loss, damage or destruction occasioned by the commission of an offence as may be determined by the court martial by whom he is convicted of such offence, or by an officer exercising authority under certain provisions of the Air Force Act 1950[4].

5 All pay and allowances ordered by a court martial or an officer exercising authority under certain provisions of the Air Force Act 1950[5] to be forfeited or stopped[6].

6 Any sum required to pay a fine awarded by a criminal court or a court martial exercising jurisdiction under certain provisions of the Air Force Act 1950[7].

7 Any sum required to make good any loss, damage, or destruction of public or service property which, after due investigation, appears to the Central Government to have been occasioned by the wrongful act or negligence on the part of the officer[8].

8 All pay and allowances forfeited by order of the Central Government if the officer is found by a court of inquiry constituted by the Chief of the Air Staff in this behalf, to have deserted to the enemy, or while in enemy hands, to have served with, or under the orders of, the enemy or in any manner to have aided the enemy, or to have allowed himself to be taken prisoner by the enemy through want of due precaution or through disobedience of orders or wilful neglect of duty, or having been taken prisoner by the enemy, to have failed to rejoin his service when it was possible to do so[9].

9 Any sum required by order of the Central Government to be paid for the maintenance of his wife or his legitimate or illegitimate child or towards the cost of any relief given by the said Government to the said wife or child[10].

1 The Air Force Act 1950 s 91 (a).

2 The Air Force Act 1950 s 91 (b). The term 'custody' includes custody by the civil authorities. Manual of Air Force Law, Volume I, s 91 notes.

3 The Air Force Act 1950 s 91 (c).

4 Ie the Air Force Act 1950 s 86; The Air Force Act 1950 s 91 (d).

5 Ie the Air Force Act 1950 s 86.

6 The Air Force Act 1950 s 91 (e).

7 Ie the Air Force Act 1950 s 71; The Air Force Act 1950 s 91 (f).

8 The Air Force Act 1950 s 91 (g). The term 'public property in this provision means not only property of the government but also any property belonging to the community at large. Captured enemy property will also amount to public property. Manual of Air Force Law, Volume I, s 91 notes.

9 The Air Force Act 1950 s 91 (h).

10 The Air Force Act 1950 s 91 (i).

[0815] Deductions from pay and allowances of airmen Subject to the certain provisions of the Air Force Act 1950[1], the following penal deductions may be made from the pay and allowances of an airman:

1 All pay and allowances for every day of absence either on desertion or without leave, or as a prisoner of war, and for every day of imprisonment for life or imprisonment awarded by a criminal court, or a court martial, or of detention, or field punishment awarded by a court martial or an officer exercising authority under the Air Force Act 1950[2].

2 All pay and allowances for every day while he is in custody on a charge for an offence of which he is afterwards convicted by a criminal court or a court martial, or on a charge of absence without leave for which he is afterwards awarded detention or field punishment by an officer exercising authority under the Air Force Act 1950[3].

3 All pay and allowances for every day on which he is in hospital on account of sickness certified by the medical officer attending on him to have been caused by an offence under the Air Force Act 1950 committed by him[4].

4 For every day on which he is in hospital on account of sickness certified by the medical officer attending on him to have been caused by his own misconduct or imprudence, such sum as may be specified by order of the Central Government or by such officer as may be specified by that Government[5].

5 All pay and allowances ordered by a court martial or by an officer exercising authority under the Air Force Act 1950[6] to be forfeited or stopped[7].

6 All pay and allowances for every day between his being recovered from the enemy and his dismissal from the service in consequence of his conduct when being taken prisoner by, or while in the hands of, the enemy[8].

7 Any sum required to make good such compensation for any expenses, loss, damage or destruction caused by him to the Central Government or to any building or property as may be awarded by his commanding officer[9].

8 Any sum required to pay a fine awarded by a criminal court, a court martial exercising jurisdiction under the Air Force Act 1950[10], or an officer exercising authority under certain provisions of the Air Force Act 1950[11].

9 Any sum required by order of the Central Government or any prescribed officer to be paid for the maintenance of his wife or his legitimate or illegitimate child or towards the cost of any relief given by the said Government to the said wife or child[12].

1 Ie the Air Force Act 1950 s 95; see **[0818]**.

2 Ie the Air Force Act 1950 s 82; The Air Force Act 1950 s 92 (a).

3 Ie the Air Force Act 1950 s 82; The Air Force Act 1950 s 92 (b).

4 The Air Force Act 1950 s 92 (c).

5 The Air Force Act 1950 s 92 (d).

6 Ie the Air Force Act 1950 s 82 or 86.

7 The Air Force Act 1950 s 92 (e).

8 The Air Force Act 1950 s 91 (f).

9 The Air Force Act 1950 s 91 (g).

10 Ie the Air Force Act 1950 s 71.

11 Ie under the Air Force Act 1950 s 82 or 90; see **[0631]** and **[0645]**. The Air Force Act 1950 s 92 (h).

12 The Air Force Act 1950 s 92 (i).

[0816] Computation of time of absence or custody For the purposes of certain provisions of the Air Force Act 1950[1]: no person shall be treated as absent or in custody for a day a unless the absence or custody has lasted, whether wholly in one day, or partly in one day and partly in another, for six consecutive hours or upwards[2]; any absence or custody for less than a day may be reckoned as absence or custody for a day if such absence or custody prevented the absentee from fulfilling any air force duty which was thereby thrown upon some other person[3]; absence or custody for twelve consecutive hours or upwards may be reckoned as absence or custody for the whole of each day during any portion of which the person was absent or in custody[4]; and a period of absence, or imprisonment, which commences before and ends after, midnight may be reckoned as a day[5].

1 Ie the Air Force Act 1950 s 92 (a) and (b).

2 The Air Force Act 1950 s 93 (a). This provision prescribes six hours as the minimum period of absence that will count as a day of absence unless two conditions are fulfilled; first that the absentee was prevented by his absence from fulfilling any air force duty, and second, that the duty was thereby thrown upon some other person. Six clear hours must, therefore, elapse, and they must be reckoned consequently. Manual of Air Force Law, Volume I, s 93 notes.

3 The Air Force Act 1950 s 93 (b).

4 The Air Force Act 1950 s 93 (c).

5 The Air Force Act 1950 s 93 (d).

[0817] Pay and allowances during trial In the case of any person subject to the Air Force Act 1950 who is in custody or under suspension from duty on a charge for an offence, the prescribed officer[1] may direct that the whole or any part of the pay and allowances of such person shall be withheld, pending the result of his trial on the charge against him, in order to give effect to the certain provisions of the Air Force Act 1950[2].

1 As to the meaning of 'prescribed officer'; see the Air Force Rules 1969 r 163. Prescribed officer under the Air Force Act 1950 s 94: The prescribed officer for purposes of the Air Force Act 1950 s 94 shall, in the case of an officer or a warrant officer, be the Chief of the Air Staff and, in the case of a person other than an officer or a warrant officer, be the officer empowered to convene a court martial for his trial.

2 Ie the Air Force Act 1950 s 91 (b) and 92; The Air Force Act 1950 s 94.

[0818] Limit of certain deductions The total deductions from the pay and allowances of a person made under certain provisions of the Air Force Act 1950[1] shall not, except where he is sentenced to dismissal, exceed in any one month one-half of his pay and allowances for that month[2].

1 Ie the Air Force Act 1950 s 92 (e) and (g) to (i).

2 The Air Force Act 1950 s 95.

[0819] Deduction from public money due to a person Any sum authorised by the Air Force Act 1950 to be deducted from the pay and allowances of any person may, without prejudice to any other mode of recovering the same, be deducted from any public money due to him other than a pension[1].

1 The Air Force Act 1950 s 96.

[0820] Pay and allowances of prisoner of war during inquiry into his conduct Where the conduct of any person subject to the Air Force Act 1950 when being taken prisoner by, or while in the hands of, the enemy[1], is to be inquired into under the aforesaid Act, an authorized officer[2] may order that the whole or any part of the pay and allowances of such person shall be withheld pending the result of such inquiry[3].

1 As to the definition of 'enemy'; see **[0488]**.

2 Ie the Chief of the Air Staff or any officer authorised by him.

3 The Air Force Act 1950 s 97.

[0821] Remission of deductions Any deduction from pay and allowances authorised by the Air Force Act 1950 may be remitted in such manner, and to such extent, and by such authority[1], as may from time to time be prescribed[2].

1 As to the 'prescribed authority' see the Air Force Rules 1969 r 164. The prescribed authority under the Air Force Act 1950 s 98: Any penal deduction from the pay and allowances of a person subject to the Air Force Act 1950, made under chapter VIII thereof, may be remitted as follows: (a) The Central Government may remit to any extent any penal deduction from the pay and allowances of any person; (b) Where an airman absents himself without leave for a period not exceeding five days, the officer who is in command of the unit, for which he absented himself, at the time when such absence terminates, or the Chief of the Air Staff may, if a satisfactory explanation is given by such airman, remit in whole or in part the forfeiture of pay and allowances to which that absence renders him liable provided that the airman is not convicted by a court-martial on a charge for such absence; (c) A forfeiture of pay and allowances incurred by any person subject to the Act owing to his absence as a prisoner of war may in whole or in part be remitted by the Chief of Air Staff or by the officer commanding the air forces in the field, except when such forfeiture has been ordered by the Central Government under the air Force Act 1950 s 91 (h).

2 The Air Force Act 1950 s 98.

[0822] Provision for dependants of prisoner of war from remitted deductions In the case of persons subject to the Air Force Act 1950, being prisoners of war, whose pay and allowances have been forfeited under the aforesaid Act[1], but in respect of whom a remission has been made under the Air Force Act 1950[2], it shall be lawful for proper provision to be made by the prescribed authorities[3] out of such pay and allowances for any dependants of such persons. Such remission shall apply only to the balance thereafter remaining of such pay and allowances[4].

1 Ie the Air Force Act 1950 s 91 (h) or 92 (a).

2 Ie the Air Force Act 1950 s 98.

3 As to the meaning of 'prescribed authorities'; see the Air Force Rules 1969 r 165. Prescribed officer under the Air Force Act 1950 s 99: Prescribed authorities under the Air Force Act s 99: (1) The prescribed authorities for the purposes of the Air Force Act 1950 s 99 shall be the officer commanding the air forces in the field under whom the person was serving at the time he became a prisoner of war or was found missing, or the Director of Personal Services, Air Headquarters, or any authority superior either to the said officer commanding or the said Director. (2) Any such authority may, in its discretion and subject to a maximum of 50 percent of the pay and allowances of the prisoner of war or the person missing, make such provisions from time to time for the dependents of the prisoner of war or the person missing, as the case may be, for whom in its judgment such provision should be made.

4 The Air Force Act 1950 s 99.

[0823] Provision for dependants of prisoner of war from his pay and allowances It shall be lawful for proper provision to be made by the prescribed authorities[1] for any dependants of any person subject to the Air Force Act 1950, who is a prisoner of war or is missing, out of his pay and allowances[2].

1 The term 'prescribed authorities' under the Air Force Act 1950 s 100 means the officer commanding the air forces in the field under whom the person was serving at the time he became a prisoner of war or was found missing, or the Director of Personal Services, Air Headquarters, or any authority superior either to the said officer commanding or the said Director. Any such authority may, in its discretion and subject to a maximum of 50 percent of the pay and allowances of the prisoner of war or the person missing, make such provisions from time to time for the dependents of the prisoner of war or the person missing, as the case may be, for whom in its judgment such provision should be made. The Air Force Rules 1969 r 165.

2 The Air Force Act 1950 s 100.

[0824] Period during which a person is deemed to be a prisoner of war For the purposes of certain provisions of the Air Force Act 1950[1], a person shall be deemed to continue to be a prisoner of war until the conclusion of any inquiry into his conduct such as is referred to in the provisions of the aforesaid Act[2], and if he is cashiered or dismissed from the service in consequence of such conduct, until the date of such cashiering or dismissal[3].

1 Ie the Air Force Act 1950 s 99 and 100. See **[0822]** and **[0823]**.

2 Ie the Air Force Act 1950 s 97. See **[0820]**.

3 The Air Force Act 1950 s 101.

F. CONFIRMATION AND REVISION

CONTENTS

PARA

[0825] Finding and sentence not valid, unless confirmed The finding or sentence of a general, district or summary general court martial shall not be valid unless confirmed under the provisions of the Air Force Act 1950[1].

1 The Air Force Act 1950 s 152. Confirmation is complete when the proceedings are promulgated. A commanding officer who has investigated the case cannot subsequently confirm the proceedings of a court martial arising out of the same matter. Manual of Air Force Law, Volume I, s 152 notes.

[0826] Power to confirm finding and sentence of general court martial The findings and sentences of general courts martial may be confirmed by the Central Government, or by any officer empowered in this behalf by warrant of the Central Government[1]. The chief of the air staff is the competent authority for confirming the findings and sentence of a general court martial[2].

1 The Air Force Act 1950 s 153. Warrant under this provision have been issued by the Central Government to the chief of the air staff, air officer commanding-in-chief of command and the air officer-in-charge-administration. Manual of Air Force Law, Volume I, s 153 notes.

2 *Pilot Officer SPN Sharma v Union of India* AIR 1968 Del 156.

[0827] Power to confirm finding and sentence of district court martial The findings and sentences of district courts martial may be confirmed by any officer having power to convene a general court martial or by any officer empowered in this behalf by warrant of such officer[1].

1 The Air Force Act 1950 s 154. No officer has been empowered under this provision. Manual of Air Force Law, Volume I, s 154 notes.

[0828] Limitation of powers of confirming authority A warrant issued under the provisions of the Air Force Act 1950[1] may contain restrictions, reservations or conditions as the authority issuing it may think fit[2].

1 Ie the Air Force Act 1950 s 153 or 154.

2 The Air Force Act 1950 s 155.

[0829] Power to confirm finding and sentence of summary general court martial The findings and sentences of summary general courts martial may be confirmed by the convening officer or if he so directs, by an authority superior to him[1].

1 The Air Force Act 1950 s 156.

[0830] Restriction on powers of officers to confirm court martial proceedings The powers of officers to confirm the proceedings of court martial are restricted as follows. (1) In the case of general court martial: (a) In all cases where a sentence of death has been awarded, the proceedings will be confirmed by the central government. In such cases, the proceedings will be forwarded to the air headquarters for submission to the Central Government. No minutes reserving confirmation will be entered in such proceedings. The recommendation of each forwarding authority will be annexed to the proceedings. (b) In cases where sentence of dismissal/cashiering/imprisonment has been awarded against an officer, the proceedings will be forwarded to the air headquarters for confirmation by the chief of the air staff, together with the minutes reserving confirmation entered in the proceedings and recommendations of the forwarding authority, if any, annexed separately. (2) In the cases of summary general court martial, the proceedings together with the minutes reserving confirmation and recommendation of the forwarding authority, if any, annexed separately be forwarded to the authorities for confirmations as follows: (a) death sentence—to the central government; (b) sentences upon officers down to and including dismissal under the provision of the Air Force Act 1959 s 73—to the chief of the air staff; (c) sentences not included in the aforesaid provisions (a) and (b) in respect of officer—to the air officer commanding-in-chief command; and (d) sentences upon warrant officers down to and including dismissal—to the air officer commanding-in-chief command[1]. In all cases in which proceedings of the court martial are referred for confirmation by higher authorities, the report on trial by command judge advocate of the command is also to be dispatched to air headquarters along with the recommendations of the forwarding authority, annexed separately[2].

1 As to the definition of 'officer' and 'warrant officer'; see: **[0494]** and **[0504]**. Air Force Order 03 of 2008, paragraph 120.

2 Air Force Order 03 of 2008, paragraph 121.

[0831] Power of confirming authority to mitigate, remit or commute sentences Subject to such restrictions, reservations or conditions as may be contained in any warrant issued under the Air Force Act 1950[1] and the following provisions[2]; a confirming authority when confirming the sentence of a court martial, may mitigate or remit the punishment, or commute that punishment for any punishment or punishments lower in the scale laid down in the Air Force Act 1950[3]. A sentence of transportation shall not be commuted for a sentence of imprisonment or detention for a term exceeding the term of transportation awarded by the court[4]. A sentence of imprisonment shall not be computed for a sentence of detention for a term exceeding the term of imprisonment awarded by the court[5].

1 Ie the Air Force Act 1950 s 153 or 154.

2 Ie the Air Force Act 1950 s 157 (2) and (3).

3 Ie the Air Force Act 1950 s 73. The Air Force Act 1950 s 157 (1).

4 In view of the Indian Penal Code 1860 s 53A any reference to transportation for life is to be construed to a reference to imprisonment for life. The Air Force Act 1950 s 157 (2).

5 The Air Force Act 1950 s 157 (3). This provision is similar to the Army Act 1950 s 158; see **[0403]**.

[0832] Confirming of findings and sentences on board a ship When any person subject to the Air Force Act 1950 is tried and sentenced by a court martial while on board a ship, the finding and sentence so far as not confirmed and executed on board the ship, may be confirmed and executed in like manner as if such person had been tried at the port of disembarkation[1].

1 The Air Force Act 1950 s 158.

[0833] Comments of confirming authority When the confirming authority finds it necessary to comment on the proceedings of a court martial whether original or revised, his remarks will be will be made separately and will not form part of the proceedings. They will be communicated in a separate minute to the members of the court. In exceptional cases, in the interests of discipline, a more public instruction is required, they will be made known in the orders of the command. Great care will however be taken not to interfere with the discretion with which the courts are vested in the exercise of their judicial functions[1].

1 Regulations for the Air Force 1964, paragraph 767.

[0834] Revision of finding or sentence Any finding or sentence of a court martial may be once revised by order of the confirming authority and on such revision, the court, if so directed by the confirming authority, may take additional evidence[1]. The court, on revision, shall consist of the same officers as were present when the original decision was passed, unless any of those officers are unavoidably absent[2]. In case of such unavoidable absence the cause thereof shall be duly certified in the proceedings, and the court shall proceed with the revision, provided that, if a general court martial, it still consists of five officers, or, if a summary general or district court martial, of three officers[3].

1 The Air Force Act 1950 s 159 (1).

2 The Air Force Act 1950 s 159 (2).

3 The Air Force Act 1950 s 159 (3). The confirming officer cannot go on ordering retrial by another court martial until he obtains a verdict or finding of his own liking. *Sqn Ldr G B Singh v Union of India* 1977 Cri LJ 485 (All).

[0835] Alteration of finding or sentence in certain cases Where a finding of guilty by a court martial, which has been confirmed, or which does not require confirmation, is found for any reason to be invalid or cannot be supported by the evidence, the authority which would have had power under the provisions of the Air Force Act 1950[1] to commute the punishment awarded, if the finding had been valid, may substitute a new finding and pass a sentence for the offence specified in such finding[2]. However, no such substitution shall be made unless such finding could have been validly made by the court martial on the charge and unless it appears that the court martial must have been satisfied of the facts establishing the said offence[3]. Where a sentence passed by a court martial which has been confirmed, or which does not require confirmation, not being a sentence passed in pursuance of a new finding substituted under the above-stated provision, is found for any reason to be invalid, the authority referred therein may pass a valid sentence[4]. The punishment awarded by a sentence passed under the above-stated provisions shall not be higher in the scale of punishments than, or in excess of the punishment awarded by, the sentence for which a new sentence is substituted under this provision[5]. Any finding substituted, or any sentence passed, under this provision shall, for the purposes of the Air Force Act 1950 and the Air Force Rules 1969, have effect as if it were a finding or sentence, as the case may be, of a court martial[6].

1 Ie under the Air Force Act 1950 s 177.

2 The Air Force Act 1950 s 160 (1).

3 The Air Force Act 1950 s 160 (1) proviso.

4 The Air Force Act 1950 s 160(2).

5 The Air Force Act 1950 s 160 (3).

6 The Air Force Act 1950 s 160(4). The provision is similar to the Army Act 1950 s 163; see **[0410]**.

[0836] Remedy against order, finding or sentence of court martial Any person subject to the Air Force Act 1950 who considers himself aggrieved by any order passed by a court martial may present a petition to the officer or authority empowered to confirm any finding or sentence of such court martial. The confirming authority may take such steps as may be considered necessary to satisfy itself as to the correctness, legality or propriety of the order passed or as to the regularity of any proceeding to which the order relates[1]. Any person subject to the Air Force Act 1950 who considers himself aggrieved by a finding or sentence of a court martial which has been confirmed, may present a petition to the Central Government, the chief of the air staff or any prescribed officer[2] superior in command to the one who confirmed such finding or sentence. The Central Government, the chief of the air staff or other officer, as the case may be, may pass such order thereon as it or he thinks fit[3]. A petition against the order, decision, finding or sentence of a court martial under the Air Force Act 1950 can also be filed in the Armed Forces Tribunal under the provisions of the Armed Forces Tribunal Act 2007[4].

In the existing system of justice under the Air Force Act 1950 and the Air Force Rules 1969, there can be no scintilla of doubt that the pre-trial detention cannot be set off against the sentence of imprisonment passed by the court-martial for the offence under the Air Force Act 1950 s 39 (a) which has been affirmed under the aforesaid Act s 161(1) and the period of sentence shall commence from the date when the original proceeding was signed by the presiding officer. The Parliament has amended the Army Act 1950 by incorporating s 169-A to avoid hardship to the persons convicted by the court-martial. The said provision provides that when a person subject to the Act is sentenced by a court martial to a term of imprisonment, not being an imprisonment in default of payment of fine, the period spent by him in civil or military custody during investigation, inquiry or trial of the same case and before the date of order of such sentence, shall be set off against the term of imprisonment imposed upon him, and the liability of such person or officer to undergo imprisonment on such order of sentence shall be restricted to the remainder, if any, of the term of imprisonment imposed upon him. Similarly, the Navy Act 1957 has also been amended in 2005 by incorporating s 151 (3) which deals with commencement of sentence. It states whenever any offender is sentenced by a court-martial to a term of imprisonment, in pursuance of the Act, not being imprisonment in default of payment of fine, the period spent by him in civil or naval custody during investigation, inquiry or trial of the same case, and before the date of order of such sentence, shall be set off against the terms of imprisonment imposed upon him, and the liability of such offender to undergo imprisonment on such order of sentence shall be restricted to the remainder, if any, of the term of imprisonment imposed upon him. Though such amendments have been made by the Parliament in the Army Act 1950 and the Navy Act 1957, yet no such amendment has been incorporated in the Air Force Act 1950. The aforesaid provisions have been incorporated in both the statutes to avoid hardship to persons convicted by the court-martial. Keeping in view the aforesaid amendment in the Army Act 1950 Act and the Navy Act 1957 and regard being had to the purpose of the amendment and the totality of the circumstances, we think it apt to recommend the Union of India to seriously consider to bring an amendment in the Air Force Act 1950 so that the hardships faced by the persons convicted by the court-martial are avoided[5].

1 The Air Force Act 1950 s 161(1).

2 The 'prescribed officer' under the Air Force Act 1950 s 161(2) shall be any officer superior in command to the officer who confirmed the proceedings, provided that he has powers not less than that of an air officer commanding a command. The Air Force Rules 1969 r 171.

3 The Air Force Act 1950 s 161(1). The provision is similar to the Army Act 1950 s 164; for more details; see **[0412]**.

4 The Armed Forces Tribunal Act 2007 s 15; see: **[1728]**.

5 *Samrendra Beura v Union of India*, 2013 AIR SCW 3080 (A): AIR 2013 SC 2414 : AIR 2013 SC (Cri) 1415 : 2013 Cri LJ 3040 : 2013 (7) SCALE 378.

[0837] Annulment of proceedings The Central Government, the chief of the air staff or any prescribed officer[1] may annul the proceedings of any court martial on the ground that they are illegal or unjust[2].

1 The 'prescribed officer' under the Air Force Act 1950 s 162 shall be any officer superior in command to the officer who confirmed the proceedings. The proceedings of a court martial may be annulled after considering the advice of the Chief Legal Adviser or Deputy Chief Legal Adviser. The Air Force Rules 1969 r 172.

2 The Air Force Act 1950 s 162.

[0838] Mode of promulgation The proceedings of a court martial including the charges, findings, sentence, recommendation to mercy (if any) and confirmation or non-confirmation, will be promulgated by communication to the accused[1]. Promulgation by reading out of the particulars detailed above on parade will be done only when the confirming authority specially directs that the promulgation shall take place in that manner[1].

1 Regulations for the Air Force 1964, paragraph 766 (a). Also see the Air Force Rules 1969 r 78; **[0734]**.

[0839] Record of promulgation The date of promulgation will be recorded on the court martial proceedings. After promulgation to the accused, the proceedings (original and copies) will be sent to Directorate of Personal Services, Air Headquarters, through concerned command headquarters[1]. The result of every court-martial, will be published as follows: (i) In the unit/ wing/ station routine orders of the concerned unit/ wing/ station; (ii) In the personnel occurrence reports by the concerned unit/ wing/ station; and (iii) In Air Headquarters Routine Orders Part I. If, subsequent to conviction but before promulgation can be effected, an accused absents himself and a declaration by a court of inquiry under the Air Force Act 1950[2] is made in respect thereof, or in the case of air officer if the commanding officer furnishes a certificate (to be annexed to the court martial proceedings) that the accused has been absent without leave for a period of 30 clear days, the proceedings of the court martial may be promulgated in accordance with the aforesaid provision. The will, however, be communicated forthwith to the accused on his apprehension (if liable for further service) or surrender[3].

1 Regulations for the Air Force 1964, paragraph 757 (b).

2 Ie the Air Force Act 1950 s 107.

3 Regulations for the Air Force 1964, paragraph 766 (b).

[0840] Annulment of illegal proceedings after promulgation The proceedings of a court martial may be annulled by the Chief of the Air Staff, or, on the advice of the judge advocate general or his deputy, by the confirming officer. The authority thus annulling a finding and sentence will direct that the record of the conviction be removed and that the accused be relieved from the consequence of his trial. Where the finding and sentence have been confirmed, and it afterwards appears to the confirming officer that the proceedings of the court-martial were illegal, or that circumstances have arisen which show that substantial injustice has been done, the confirming officer may order the release of the person under sentence pending reference to the judge advocate general or his deputy[1].

1 Regulations for the Air Force 1964, paragraph 769.

[0841] Court martial Proceedings On conclusion of a trial the proceedings of court martial (original and two copies) will be submitted by the judge advocate or the presiding officer when there is no judge advocate, to the authority specified in this behalf in the convening order. Where there is more than one accused one additional copy of court martial proceedings will be prepared for each additional accused person. The confirming officer will seek the advice of the judge advocate general or command judge advocate[1] as applicable before confirmation. The Proceedings will finally be deposited with the judge advocate general for retention[2].

1 The reports by officers of the chief legal adviser (judge advocate general) department will be treated as confidential and will not be communicated directly or indirectly to any authority lower than the authority to whom they are addressed. When proceedings are forwarded to lower formations or to units, such reports will be removed. Regulations for the Air Force 1964, paragraph 761.

2 Regulations for the Air Force 1964, paragraph 757.

G. Execution of Sentences

CONTENTS

PARA

[0842] Committal warrant A warrant for the committal of a person to a civil prison[1], or to a military prison or to detention barracks under the provisions of the Air Force Act 1950[2] shall be in the relevant Form given in the Seventh Schedule to the Air Force Rules 1969. Such warrant shall be signed and forwarded by the commanding officer[3] of the prisoner or by an officer superior in command to such commanding officer or by any staff officer of such superior officer[4].

1 As to the definition of 'civil prison'; see **[0483]**.

2 Ie the Air Force Act 1950 ss 165, 166 or 170.

3 As to the definition of 'commanding officer'; see **[0485]**.

4 The Air Force Rules 1969 r 144.

[0843] Form of sentence of death In awarding a sentence of death, a court martial shall, in its discretion, direct that the offender shall suffer death by being hanged by the neck until he be dead, or shall suffer death by being shot to death[1].

1 The Air Force Act 1950 s163.

[0844] Custody of person under sentence of death Notwithstanding anything contained in the Air Force Rules 1969[1], when a person is sentenced by court martial to suffer death, the commanding officer may, if he thinks fit, by a warrant in the relevant form in the Air Force Rules 1969[2], commit the said person for safe custody in an air force, military or civil prison or in air force or military detention barracks pending confirmation or the carrying out of the sentence[3].

1 Ie the Air Force Rules 1969 r 22; see **[0602]**.

2 Ie in the Air Force Rules 1969 Seventh Schedule.

3 The Air Force Rules 1969 r 147 (1).

[0845] Person under death sentence: restrictions Where a person under sentence of death is in air force custody, or in detention barracks, the following provisions governing such custody shall apply to him: (i) He shall be deprived of every article, which it might be dangerous or inexpedient to leave in his possession[1]; (ii) He shall be confined in a separate cell and kept apart from all other persons under sentence of death, imprisonment or detention or in custody[2]; (iii) He shall be kept by day and by night in the constant charge, of two officers, warrant officers or non-commissioned officers[3]; (iv) He shall not be requested to perform any duties other than to keep clean his person and cell[4]; (v) He shall be allowed daily physical exercise[5]; (vi) He shall be granted facilities to correspond with his relatives, friends and legal advisers[6]; (vii) He shall be permitted to smoke[7]; (viii) He shall be visited once daily by the commanding officer or the commandant of the unit, prison or detention barracks as well as by the medical officer[8]; (ix) He shall not be visited by any person other than a member of the staff on duty unless prior permission in writing has been given by the confirming authority or an authority specified by the confirming authority in his behalf[9]; and (x) Where the confirming authority or the officer specified by it in this behalf has given a written permission to any person other than a member of the staff on duty to visit the person sentenced to death the visit shall take place in the sight of a member of the staff, and unless the confirming authority or the specified officer orders otherwise, in the hearing of a member of the staff[10]. In this provision reference to 'a member of the staff' means a member of the staff of the air force unit, prison or detention barracks in which the person under sentence has been held in custody[11].

1 The Air Force Rules 1969 r 147 (2) (a).

2 The Air Force Rules 1969 r 147 (2) (b).

3 The Air Force Rules 1969 r 147 (2) (c).

4 The Air Force Rules 1969 r 147 (2) (d).

5 The Air Force Rules 1969 r 147 (2) (e).

6 The Air Force Rules 1969 r 147 (2) (f).

7 The Air Force Rules 1969 r 147 (2) (g).

8 The Air Force Rules 1969 r 147 (2) (h).

9 The Air Force Rules 1969 r 147 (2) (i).

10 The Air Force Rules 1969 r 147 (2) (j).

11 The Air Force Rules 1969 r 147 (2) explanation.

[0846] Opportunity for petition against sentence of death While confirming a sentence of death, the confirming authority shall specify the period within which the person sentenced may, after the sentence has been promulgated to him, submit a petition against the finding or sentence against him of the court martial[1]. The person against whom a sentence of death has been confirmed shall, at the time of promulgation, be informed of his rights under the Air Force Act 1950[2] and of the period specified by the confirming authority within which he may, if he so wishes to do, submit a petition against the finding or sentence against him of the court martial[3]. Every petition against a finding or sentence submitted by a person against whom a sentence of death has been confirmed, and every order in respect of such petition shall be transmitted, where the confirming authority is the Chief of the Air Staff or the Central Government, through the air officer in-charge administration at the air headquarters and in any other case, through the confirming officer[4]. A sentence of death shall not be carried into effect until the expiry of the period specified by the confirming authority under the aforesaid provision[5] or if, within the period so specified, the person under sentence submits a petition against the finding or sentence of the court martial, until the authority legally competent to dispose of such petition finally, after considering the petition, orders that the sentence of death may be carried into effect[6].

1 The Air Force Rules 1969 r 148 (1).

2 Ie the Air Force Act 1950 s 161 (2).

3 The Air Force Rules 1969 r 148 (2).

4 The Air Force Rules 1969 r 148 (3).

5 Ie the Air Force Rules 1969 r 148 (1).

6 The Air Force Rules 1969 r 148 (4).

[0847] Death warrant The officer commanding the air force station to which the person sentenced belongs or is attached, or where there is no such air force station, the air or other officer commanding the command or the group to which such person belongs or is attached shall nominate a provost marshal or other officer not below the rank of squadron leader who shall be responsible for the due execution of the sentence of death passed under the Air Force Act 1950, and shall issue to such officer the death warrant in the relevant form contained in the Air Force Rules 1969 Seventh Schedule[1]. The officer specified in the aforesaid provision shall not issue the death warrant until he is satisfied that having regard to the certain provisions of the Air Force Rules 1969[2], the sentence of death may be carried into effect[3]. No sentence of death passed under the Air Force Act 1950 shall be carried into effect until the death warrant has been received by the provost marshal or other officer nominated under the aforesaid provision[4].

1 The Air Force Rules 1969 r 149 (1).

2 Ie the Air Force Rules 1969 r 148

3 The Air Force rules 1969 r 149 (2).

4 Ie under the Air Force Rules 1969 r 149 (1); The Air Force Rules 1969 r 149 (3).

[0848] Execution of sentence of death On receipt of the death warrant, the provost marshal or other officer, nominated under the Air Force Rules 1969[1] shall: (i) Inform the person sentenced as soon as possible of the date on which the sentence will be carried out[2]; (ii) If the person sentenced has been committed to an air force, military or civil prison or to air force or military detention barracks, obtain the custody of his person by issuing a warrant in the relevant form contained in the Air Force Rules 1969 Seventh Schedule[3]; (iii) Proceed to carry out the sentence as required by the death warrant and in accordance with any general or special instructions, which may from time to time be given by or under the authority of the Chief of the Air Staff[4].

1 Ie the Air Force Rules 1969 r 149 (1).

2 The Air Force Rules 1969 r 150 (1) (a).

3 The Air Force Rules 1969 r 150 (1) (b).

4 The Air Force Rules 1969 r 150 (1) (c).

[0849] Execution of death sentence: witnessing During the execution of a sentence of death passed under the Air Force Act 1950, no person, except those specified below, shall be present without the authority of the officer who issued the death warrant. The following persons shall attend the execution of the sentence of death: (i) The provost marshal or other officer who is responsible for the due execution of the sentence in accordance with the Air Force Rules 1969[1]; (ii) A commissioned medical officer of the armed forces of the Union[2]. (iii) An officer nominated by the officer who issued the death warrant, who is able to identify the person under sentence as the person described in the death warrant and as the person who was tried and sentenced by the court-martial mentioned therein[3]; (iv) Such non-commissioned officers as may be detailed by the provost marshal or the other officer aforesaid for escort and security purposes or to assist at the execution[4]; and (v) If the execution is carried into effect in an air force unit or station, the officer for the time being in command of such station or unit[5].

1 The Air Force Rules 1969 r 150 (2) (a).

2 The Air Force Rules 1969 r 150 (2) (b).

3 The Air Force Rules 1969 r 150 (2) (c).

4 The Air Force Rules 1969 r 150 (2) (d).

5 The Air Force Rules 1969 r 150 (2) (e).

[0850] Execution of death sentence: return of warrant After the sentence of death has been carried into effect, the provost-marshal or other officer nominated under the Air Force Rules 1969[1] shall complete or cause to be completed parts II and III of the death warrant and shall, without unnecessary delay return the completed death warrant to the officer who had issued the same to him[2].

1 Ie the Air Force Rules 1969 r 149 (1).

2 The Air Force Rules 1969 r 150 (3).

[0851] Procedure on pardon or where proceedings are set aside or where sentence of death is commuted or remitted Where a person sentenced to death is pardoned, or where the proceedings against him are set aside under the Air Force Act 1950 or where the sentence of death is not confirmed or is commuted or remitted under the aforesaid Act, then: (i) If the person sentenced is in custody in an air force, military or civil prison, or in an air force or military detention barracks under a warrant issued under the Air Force Rules 1969[1], a further warrant in the relevant form given in the Air Force Rules 1969 Seventh Schedule shall be issued by the commanding officer of such person[2]; or (ii) If he has been detained in air force custody he shall be released or, as the case may be, any warrant which may be necessary to give effect to the sentence as so commuted or remitted shall be issued by such commanding officer[3].

1 Ie the Air Force Rules 1969 r 147.

2 The Air Force Rules 1969 r 151 (a).

3 The Air Force Rules 1969 r 151 (b).

[0852] Commencement of sentence of imprisonment for life or imprisonment Whenever any person is sentenced by a court martial under the Air Force Act 1950 to imprisonment for life, imprisonment or detention the term of his sentence shall, whether it has been revised or not, be reckoned to commence on the day on which the original proceedings were signed, by the presiding officer[1].

1 The Air Force Act 1950 s 164.

[0853] Pre-trial custody Pre-trial period of custody are not set-off against sentence of imprisonment or detention warded by a court martial under the Air Force Act 1950. The Code of Criminal Procedure 1973 s 4 excludes applicability of the Code in respect of proceedings under the special law. The provision of set off contained in the Code of Criminal Procedure 1973 s 428 can never be attracted in the case of persons convicted and sentenced by court martial[1].

1 *Ajmer Singh v Union of India* JT 1987 (2) SC 290. The Army Act 1950 was subsequently amended in 1992 and s 169A now provides that the custody undergone by a person subject to the Army Act 1950 to be set off against the term of imprisonment awarded by a court martial. The Navy Act s 151 (3) has also incorporated similar provision by an amendment in 2005. The Supreme Court has commented against this shortcoming in the Air Force Act 1950 and asked the government to incorporate the provision of set off in the Air Force Act. *Samrendra Beura v Union of India* 2013 AIR SCW 3080 (A): AIR 2013 SC 2414 : AIR 2013 SC (Cri) 1415 : 2013 Cri LJ 3040 : 2013 (7) SCALE 378.

[0854] Execution of sentence of imprisonment for life Whenever any sentence of imprisonment for life is passed under the Air Force Act 1950 or whenever any sentence of death be commuted to the imprisonment for life, the commanding officer of the person under sentence or such other officer as may be prescribed[1] shall forward a warrant in the prescribed form to the officer-in-charge of the civil prison in which such person is to be confined and shall arrange for his despatch to such prison with the warrant[2]. A warrant for the committal of a person to a civil prison, or to a military or to detention barracks under the provisions of the Air Force Act 1950[3] shall be in the relevant Form and shall be signed and forwarded by the commanding officer of the prisoner[4].

1 'Prescribed officer', no officer has been prescribed under this provision. Manual of Air Force Law, Volume I, s 165 notes.

2 The Air Force Act 1950 s 165.

3 Ie the Air Force Act 1950 s 165, 166 or 170.

4 Warrant can be signed by the commanding officer of the prisoner or by an officer superior in command to such commanding officer or by any staff officer of such superior officer. The Air Force Rules 1969 r 144. See **[0842]**.

[0855] Execution of sentence of imprisonment Whenever any sentence of imprisonment is passed under the Air Force Act 1950 or whenever any sentence of death or imprisonment for life is commuted to imprisonment, the confirming officer or such other officer as may be prescribed, shall, except as provided in the following provisions[1], direct either that the sentence shall be carried out by confinement in a military or air force prison or that it shall be carried out by confinement in a civil prison[2]. When a direction has been made under the aforesaid provision the commanding officer of the person under sentence or such other officer as may be prescribed shall forward a warrant in the prescribed form to the officer-in-charge of the prison in which such person is to be confined and shall arrange for his despatch to such prison with the warrant[3]. In the case of a sentence of imprisonment for a period not exceeding three months, the officers referred to in the aforesaid provision[4] may direct that the sentence shall be carried out by confinement in air force custody instead of in a civil or military or air force prison[5]. On active service[6], a sentence of imprisonment may be carried out by confinement in such place as the officer commanding the forces in the field may from time to time appoint[7]. A warrant for the committal of a person to a civil prison, or to a military or to detention barracks under the provisions of the Air Force Act 1950[8] shall be in the relevant Form and signed by the commanding officer of the prisoner[9].

1 Ie the Air Force Act 1950 s 166 (3) and (4).

2 The Air Force Act 1950 s 166 (1).

3 The Air Force Act 1950 s 166 (2).

4 Ie the Air Force Act 1950 s 166 (1).

5 The Air Force Act 1950 s 166 (3). There is no air force prison in existence now. Manual of Air Force Law, Volume I, s 166 notes.

6 As to the definition of 'active service'; see **[0470]**.

7 The Air Force Act 1950 s 166 (4).

8 Ie the Air Force Act 1950 s 165, 166 or 170.

9 The Air Force Rules 1969 r 144; see **[0842]**.

[0856] Temporary custody of offender Where a sentence of imprisonment for life or imprisonment is directed to be undergone in a civil prison, the offender may be kept in any fit place[1], till such time as it is possible to send him to a civil prison[2].

1 Ie in military or air force custody or any other fit place. The Air Force Act 1950 s 167.

2 The Air Force Act 1950 s 167.

[0857] Execution of sentence of imprisonment in special cases Whenever, in the opinion of an air officer or air officer commanding a command, any sentence or portion of a sentence of imprisonment cannot for special reasons, conveniently be carried out in a military prison or in air force custody in accordance with the provisions of the Air Force Act 1950[1] such officer may direct that such sentence or portion of sentence shall be carried out by confinement in any civil prison or other fit place[2].

1 Ie the Air Force Act 1950 s 166.

2 The Air Force Act 1950 s 168. Direction under this provision may be made by the specified authorities even when not on active service. Further, a direction can only be made when imprisonment, cannot for special reasons conveniently, be carried out in a military prison or air force custody. Manual of Air Force Law, volume I, s 168 notes.

[0858] Conveyance of prisoner from place to place A person under sentence of imprisonment for life or imprisonment may, during his conveyance from place to place, or when on board ship, aircraft, or otherwise, be subjected to such restraint as is necessary for his safe conduct and removal[1].

1 The Air Force Act 1950 s 169.

[0859] Execution of sentence of detention Whenever any sentence of detention is passed under the Air Force Act 1950, or whenever any sentence of death, imprisonment for life or imprisonment is commuted to detention, the sentence shall be carried out by detaining the offender in any military or air force detention barracks/cells or other military or air force custody. When the sentence is to be carried out by detention in any military or air force detention barracks, the commanding officer of the person under sentence shall forward a warrant in the prescribed form to the officer-in-charge of the detention barracks in which the person under sentence is to be detained. The commanding officer shall send the person under sentence to such detention barracks with the warrant[1].

1 As to the warrant for the committal of a person to a civil prison; see Air Force Rules 1969 r 144: **[0842]**. The Air Force Act 1950 s 170.

[0860] Communication of certain orders to prison officers Whenever an order is made under the Air Force Act 1950 setting aside or varying any sentence, order or warrant under which any person is confined in a civil, military or air force prison or detained in a military or air force detention barracks; a warrant in accordance with such order shall be forwarded by the officer making the order, to the officer-in-charge of the place where such person is confined[1].

1 The warrant can be signed by any prescribed under the Air Force Rules 1969 r 145; see **[0861]**. The Air Force Act 1950 s 171.

[0861] Warrants under the Air Force Act 1950 s 171 Every warrant issued under the Air Force Act 1950[1] shall be in the relevant Form given in the Seventh Schedule, and shall be signed by the officer making the order in pursuance of which such warrant is issued, or by his staff officer[2]. The prescribed officer for the purpose of forwarding the warrant under the aforesaid provision of the Act shall be officer commanding the unit or detachment to which the person belongs or is attached[3].

1 Ie under the Air Force Act 1950 s 171.

2 The Air Force Rules 1969 r 145 (1). See the Air Force Rules 1969, Seventh Schedule, Forms G8 to G10, G13 and G14. Manual of Air Force Law, Volume I, s 171 notes.

3 The Air Force Rules 1969 r 145 (2).

[0862] Execution of sentence of fine When a sentence of fine is imposed by a court martial[1] whether the trial was held within India or not, a copy of such sentence, signed and certified by the confirming officer may be sent to any magistrate in India. Such magistrate shall thereupon cause the fine to be recovered in accordance with the provisions of the Code of Criminal Procedure 1973 or any corresponding law in force in the State of Jammu and Kashmir for the levy of fines as if it were a sentence of fine imposed by such magistrate[2].

1 Ie under the Air Force Act 1950 s 71.

2 The Air Force Act 1950 s 172. This provision should be used when the fine imposed by sentence of a court martial is not recoverable under the Air Force Act 1950 s 91 (f) or 92 (h). When a minor punishment of fine is awarded under the Air Force Act 1950 s 82 (g), the same can only be recovered under the Air Force Act 1950 s 92 (h). Manual of Air Force Law, Volume I, s 172 notes.

[0863] Establishment and regulation of air force prisons The Central Government may set apart any building or part of a building, or any place under its control, as an air force prison or detention barracks for the confinement of persons sentenced to imprisonment or detention under the Air Force Act 1950[1].

1 The Air Force Act 1950 s 173. No air force prison has so far been established. Manual of Air Force Law, Volume I, s 173 notes.

[0864] Informality or error in the order or warrants Whenever a person is sentenced to imprisonment for life, imprisonment or detention under the Air Force Act 1950, and is undergoing the sentence in any place or manner in which he might be confined under a lawful order or warrant in pursuance of the aforesaid Act, the confinement of such person shall not be deemed to be illegal only by reason of any informality or error in any order, warrant or other document. Such order, warrant or document may be amended accordingly[1].

1 The Air Force Act 1950 s 174.

[0865] Power to make rules in respect of prisons and prisoners The Central Government may make rules providing for: (i) the government, management and regulation of air force prisons and detention barracks[1]; (ii) the appointment, removal and powers of inspectors, visitors, governors and officers thereof[2]; (iii) the labour of prisoners undergoing confinement therein, and for enabling such prisoners or persons to earn by special industry and good conduct, a remission of a portion of their sentence[3]; (iv) the safe custody of such prisoners or persons and the maintenance of discipline among them and the punishment, by personal correction, restraint or otherwise, of offences committed by them[4]; (v) the application to air force prisons or detention barracks of any of the provisions of the Prisons Act 1894 relating to the duties of officers of prisons and the punishment of persons not being prisoners[5]; and (vi) the admission into any prison, at proper times and subject to proper restrictions, of persons with whom prisoners may desire to communicate, and for the consultation by prisoners under trial with their legal advisers without the presence as far as possible of any third party within hearing distance[6].

1 The Air Force Act 1950 s 175 (a). No air force prison has so far been established. Manual of Air Force Law, volume I, s 175 notes.

2 The Air Force Act 1950 s 175 (b).

3 The Air Force Act 1950 s 175 (c).

4 The Air Force Act 1950 s 175 (d).

5 The Air Force Act 1950 s 175 (e).

6 The Air Force Act 1950 s 175 (f).

[0866] Restriction of rule-making power in respect to corporal punishment Rules made under certain provision of the Air Force Act 1950[1] shall not authorise corporal punishment to be inflicted for any offence, nor render the imprisonment more severe than it is under any law for the time being in force relating to civil prisons in India[2].

1 Ie the Air Force Act 1950 s 175; see **[0865]**.

2 The Air Force Act 1950 s 176. No rules have been made under this provision so far. Manual of Air Force Law, volume I, s 176 notes.

[0867] Sentence of cashiering A sentence of cashiering awarded by a court martial shall take effect from the date on which the sentence is promulgated to the person under sentence[1]. When cashiering is not combined with imprisonment or death and the confirming officer has specified a date for cashiering to take effect, the cashiering shall take effect from the date of promulgation or from the date so specified, whichever is later[2]. If cashiering has been combined with imprisonment, then it will take effect from the date on which the prisoner is received into a civil prison[3].

1 The Air Force Rules 1969 r 146 (1).

2 The Air Force Rules 1969 r 146 (1) proviso.

3 Manual of Air Force Law, volume II, r 147 notes.

[0868] Cashiering: promulgation The promulgation parade for the sentence of cashiering includes the convict being stripped off has badges of rank and other regimental insignia, by his formation commander in the presence of his commanding officer and other officers[1].

1 Vidhu Rama. 2011. *Court Martial Process: Empirically Studied*, New Delhi: Vij Books India Pvt Ltd, p. 63. The punishment is an ignoble form of dismissal from the service under the Air Force Act 1950 and the Army Act 1950. It can be equated with 'dismissal with disgrace' awarded under the Navy Act 1957.

[0869] Sentence of dismissal: not combined with imprisonment A sentence of dismissal awarded by a court martial, not combined with dismissal shall take effect from the date on which the sentence is promulgated to the person under the sentence, or from such subsequent date as may be specified by the commanding officer at the time of such promulgation[1].

1 The Air Force Rules 1969 r 146 (2).

[0870] Sentence of dismissal: combined with imprisonment or detention In cases where the sentence of dismissal is combined with imprisonment or detention which is carried out in a military or air force detention barracks, detention cells or air force custody, the dismissal shall not take effect until the date on which the prisoner is duly released from such military or air force detention barracks or custody[1]. In addition, when dismissal is combined with imprisonment, which is carried out in a civil prison, the dismissal shall not take effect until the date on which the prisoner is received in the civil prison[2].

1 The Air Force Rules 1969 r 146 (2) proviso.

2 The Air Force Rules 1969 r 146 (2) additional proviso.

[0871] Field Punishment: Execution A court martial or an officer exercising authority under the provisions of the Air Force Act 1950[1], may, for the purpose of awarding field punishment, sentence an offender for a period not exceeding, in the case of a court martial three months, and in the case of such an officer, 28 days, to one of the following punishments, namely: (i) Field punishment No. 1, or (ii) Field punishment No. 2 Where an offender is sentenced to field punishment No. 1, he may, during the continuance of his sentence unless the court martial or the officer, as the case may be, otherwise directs, be punished as follows: (i) He may be kept in irons, that is to say, in fetters or hand-cuffs or both fetters and hand-cuffs, and may be secured so as to prevent his escape[3], (ii) When in irons, he may he attached for a period or periods not exceeding two hours in any one day to a fixed object, but he must not be so attached during more than three out of any four consecutive days nor during more than twenty-one days in all[4].

The offenders must be attached so as to be standing firmly on his feet which, if tied, must not be more than twelve inches apart and it must be possible for him to move each foot at least three inches. If he is tied round the body there must be no restriction of his breathing. If his arms or wrists are tied, there must be six inches of play between them and the fixed object. His arms must hang either by the side of his body or behind his back[5]. For the purpose of this punishment, irons should be used when available, but straps or ropes may be used in lieu of them when necessary. Any straps or ropes used for the purpose must be of sufficient width to inflict no bodily harm, and leave no permanent mark on the offender[6].

The offender may be subjected to the like labour, employment and restraint and dealt with in like manner as if he were undergoing a sentence of rigorous imprisonment[7]. Where an offender is sentenced to field punishment No. 2, the certain provisions with respect to field punishment No. 1[8] shall apply in his case except that he shall not be liable to be attached to a fixed object[9]. Every portion of a field punishment shall inflicted in such a manner as is calculated not to cause injury or leave any permanent mark on the offender; and a portion of a field punishment must be discontinued upon a report by a responsible medical officer that the continuance of that portion would be prejudicial to the offender's health[10]. Field punishment shall be carried out within the unit to which the offender belongs or is attached so long as that unit is actually on the move, but when the unit is halted at any place where there is a provost marshal or any other officer appointed by the commander of the forces or the air forces in the field to execute such punishment, the punishment shall be carried out under the orders of such officer[11]. When the unit to which the offender belongs or is attached is actually on the move, an offender awarded field punishment No. 1 shall be exempt from the operation of certain provision of punishment[12], but all offenders awarded field punishment shall march with their unit, carry their arms and equipment, perform all their air force duties as well as extra fatigue duties, and be treated as defaulters[13].

1 Ie under the Air Force Act 1950 s 82.

2 The Air Force Rules 1969 r 152 (1).

3 The Air Force Rules 1969 r 152 (2)(a).

4 The Air Force Rules 1969 r 152 (2)(b).

5 The Air Force Rules 1969 r 152 (2) (b) explanation 1.

6 The Air Force Rules 1969 r 152 (2) (b) explanation 2.

7 The Air Force Rules 1969 r 152 (2)(c).

8 As provided under the Air Force Rules 1969 r 152 (2).

9 The Air Force Rules 1969 r 152 (3).

10 The Air Force Rules 1969 r 152 (4).

11 The Air Force Rules 1969 r 152 (5).

12 Ie as provided under the Air Force Rules 1969 r 152 (2) (b).

13 The Air Force Rules 1969 r 152 (6). The field punishment has been abolished under the Army Act 1950.

[0872] Nature of punishment of detention A sentence of detention awarded by a court martial or by an officer exercising authority under the Air Force Act 1950[1] may be carried out: (i) In a military or air force detention barrack[2]; (ii) In a barrack detention room under the control of a military or air force unit[3]; or (iii) On active service, when the unit is halted at any place where there is a provost marshal, under the orders of such officer[4].

1 Ie under the Air Force Act 1950 s 82.

2 The Air Force Rules 1969 r 153 (a)

3 The Air Force Rules 1969 r 153 (b)

4 The Air Force Rules 1969 r 153 (c).

H. Pardons, Remissions and Suspensions

CONTENTS

PARA

[0873] Pardon and remission When any person subject to the Air Force Act 1950 has been convicted by a court martial of any offence, the prescribed authority or officer[1], may: (i) either with or without conditions which the person sentenced accepts, pardon the person or remit the whole or any part of the punishment awarded[2]; or (ii) mitigate the punishment awarded[3]; or (iii) commute such punishment for any less punishment or punishments mentioned in the Air Force Act 1950[4]; (iv) either with or without conditions which the person sentenced accepts, release the person on parole[5].

1 Ie the Central Government, the Chief of the Air Staff, or air officer commanding a command. In relation to persons convicted on active service, the officer commanding the air forces in the field shall also be prescribed officer. The Air Force Rules 1969 r 174.

2 The Air Force Act 1950 s 177 (a).

3 The Air Force Act 1950 s 177 (b).

4 The Air Force Act 1950 s 177 (c). A proviso to this sub-section stating: 'a sentence of transportation shall not be commuted for a sentence of imprisonment for a term exceeding the term of transportation awarded by the court; and a sentence of imprisonment shall not be com- muted for a sentence of detention for a term exceeding the term of imprisonment so awarded', has not been included in view of the Indian Penal Code 1860 s 53A. Similar provision contained in the Army Act 1950 s 179 (c) has been omitted.

5 The Air Force Act 1950 s 177 (d).

[0874] Remission, mitigation and commutation of sentence The powers conferred by the Air Force Act 1950[1] will not be exercised by an officer holding a command inferior to that of the authority confirming the sentence, unless such officer is authorised by such confirming authority or other superior air force authority to exercise such power. In cases where an order has already been passed by a competent authority under the aforesaid provision, an officer inferior in command will not exercise any powers under that provision without prior approval of such authority. Similarly, in cases where a person undergoing sentence of imprisonment has been moved outside the command in which he was convicted, the authorities in whose command the prison or other place in which he is undergoing the sentence is situated will not exercise any powers under the aforesaid provision of the Air Force Act 1950, in respect of such person without reference to the air or other officer commanding of the command in which such person was convicted. When remission, mitigation or commutation of a court martial sentence is ordered under the aforesaid provisions, the order will be recorded in writing. The written order will be sent to the unit of the person for promulgation to him and completion of his service records. After completion of his records the order will be sent through the same channels as the original proceedings of the court-martial for attachment to them. In every case in which a sentence of imprisonment which a person is undergoing is mitigated under the aforesaid provision of the Air Force Act 1950, such authority will be responsible for immediately forwarding direct to the officer in charge prison in which that person is undergoing sentence formal notice of such mitigation, commutation or remission for promulgation to offender[2].

1 Ie the Air Force Act 1950 s 177; see **[0873]**.

2 Regulations for the Air Force 1964, paragraph 765 (a), (b) and (c).

[0875] Cancellation of conditional pardon, release on parole or remission If any condition on which a person has been pardoned or released on parole or a punishment has been remitted is, in the opinion of the authority which granted the pardon, release or remission, not fulfilled, such authority may cancel the pardon, release or remission. Thereupon, the sentence of the court shall be carried into effect as if such pardon, release or remission had not been granted[1]. A person whose sentence of imprisonment for life, imprisonment or detention is carried into effect under the aforesaid provision shall undergo only the unexpired portion of his sentence[2].

1 The Air Force Act 1950 s 178 (1).

2 The Air Force Act 1950 s 178 (2).

[0876] Reduction of warrant officer or non-commissioned officer When under the provisions of the Air Force Act 1950[1] a warrant officer or a non-commissioned officer is deemed to be reduced to the ranks, such reduction shall, for the purpose of the Air Force Act 1950 s 177 be treated as a punishment awarded by a sentence of a court martial[2].

1 Ie the Air Force Act 1950 s 79. As to the definition of 'warrant officer' and 'non-commissioned officer'; see: **[0504]** and **[0491]**.

2 The Air Force Act 1950 s 179.

[0877] Suspension of sentence of imprisonment for life, imprisonment or detention Where a person subject to the Air Force Act 1950 is sentenced by a court martial to imprisonment for life, imprisonment or detention, any authority or officer[1], may suspend the sentence whether or not the offender has already been committed to prison or to air force custody[2]. The authority or officer specified in the aforesaid provision may in the case of an offender so sentenced direct that, until the orders of such authority or officer have been obtained, the offender shall not be committed to prison or to air force custody[3]. The powers conferred the aforesaid provisions[4] may be exercised in the case of any such sentence which has been confirmed, reduced or commuted[5].

1 Ie the Central Government, the Chief of the Air Staff, or any officer empowered to convene a general or a summary general court martial; The Air Force Act 1950 s 180 (1).

2 The Air Force Act 1950 s 180 (1).

3 The Air Force Act 1950 s 180 (2).

4 Ie the Air Force Act 1950 s 180 (1) and (2).

5 The Air Force Act 1950 s 180 (3).

[0878] Orders pending suspension A confirming officer may, when confirming any sentence referred to in the Air Force Act 1950[1], direct that the offender be not committed to prison or to air force custody until the orders of the authority or officer specified in the aforesaid provision have been obtained[2].

1 Ie the Air Force Act 1950 s 180.

2 The Air Force Act 1950 s 181.

[0879] Release in suspension Where a sentence is suspended under the provisions of the Air Force Act 1950[1], the offender shall forthwith be released from custody[2].

1 Ie the Air Force Act 1950 s 180; see **[0877]**.

2 The Air Force Act 1950 s 182.

[0880] Computation of period of suspension Any period during which the sentence is under suspension shall be reckoned as part of the term of such sentence[1].

1 The Air Force Act 1950 s 183. Suspension of a sentence does not affect its continuity. A sentence of imprisonment for life, or imprisonment or detention, whether suspended or not, commences on the date on which the original proceedings were signed by the presiding officer of the court martial and runs continuously until it expires. Manual of Military Law, Volume I, s 183 notes.

[0881] Order after suspension The authority or officer specified in the Air Force Act 1950[1] may, at any time while a sentence is suspended, order (i) that the offender be committed to undergo the unexpired portion of the sentence[2], or (ii) that the sentence be remitted[3].

1 Ie the Air Force Act 1950 s 180; see **[0877]**.

2 The Air Force Act 1950 s 184 (a).

3 The Air Force Act 1950 s 184 (b).

[0882] Reconsideration of case after suspension Where a sentence has been suspended, the case may at any time, and shall, at intervals of not more than four months, be reconsidered by the authority or officer specified in the Air Force Act 1950[1]. Where on such reconsideration by the officer so authorised it appears to him that the conduct of the offender since his conviction has been such as to justify a remission of the sentence, he shall refer the matter to the authority or officer specified[2].

1 Ie the Air Force Act 1950 s 180; see **[0877]**. It can also be considered or by any air or other officer not below the rank of squadron leader duly authorised by the authority or officer specified in the Air Force Act 1950 s 180. The Air Force Act 1950 s 185 (1).

2 Ie specified in the Air Force Act 1950 s 180; the Air Force Act 1950 s 185 (2).

[0883] Fresh sentence after suspension Where an offender, while a sentence on him is suspended under the Air Force Act 1950, is sentenced for any other offence, then: (i) if the further sentence is also suspended under the aforesaid Act, the two sentences shall run concurrently[1]; (ii) if the further sentence is for a period of three months or more and is not suspended under the aforesaid Act, the offender shall also be committed to prison or air force custody for the unexpired portion of the previous sentence, but both sentences shall run concurrently[2]; and (iii) if the further sentence is for a period of less than three months and is not suspended under the aforesaid Act, the offender shall be so committed on that sentence only, and the previous sentence shall, subject to any order which may be passed under certain provisions of the Air Force Act 1950[3], continue to be suspended[4].

1 The Air Force Act 1950 s 186 (a).

2 The Air Force Act 1950 s 186 (b).

3 Ie the Air Force Act 1950 s 184 or 185.

4 The Air Force Act 1950 s 186 (c).

[0884] Scope of power of suspension The powers conferred by certain provisions of the Air Force Act 1950[1] shall be in addition to and not in derogation of, the power of mitigation, remission and commutation[2].

1 Ie the Air Force Act 1950 s 180 and 184.

2 The Air Force Act 1950 s 187.

[0885] Effect of suspension and remission on dismissal Where in addition to any other sentence the punishment of dismissal has been awarded by a court martial, and such other sentence is suspended under the Air Force Act 1950[1], then, such dismissal shall not take effect until so ordered by the authority or officer specified in the aforesaid provision[2]. If such other sentence is remitted under the Air Force Act 1950[3], the punishment of dismissal shall also be remitted[4].

1 Ie the Air Force Act 1950 s 180.

2 The Air Force Act 1950 s 188 (1).

3 Ie the Air Force Act 1950 s 184.

4 The Air Force Act 1950 s 188 (2).

8. COURTS OF INQUIRY

CONTENTS

[0886] General A court of inquiry is an assembly of officers or of officers and warrant officers[1] directed to collect evidence and if so required, to report with regard to any matter which may be referred to them[2]. A court of inquiry may be assembled by the officer in command of any unit or portion of the Air Force[3]. Except in the cases where the assembly of a court of inquiry has been made mandatory by the law, regulations or orders, the competent authority has the discretion to assemble a court of inquiry or not[4]. The court may consist of any number of officers of any rank or of one or more officers together with one or more warrant officers. The members of the court may belong to any branch or department of the service, according to the nature of the investigation[5]. Previous notice shall be given of the time and place of the meeting of a court of inquiry, and of all adjournments of the court, to all persons concerned in the inquiry (except a prisoner of war who is still absent)[6]. It is the duty of a court of inquiry to put such questions to a witness as it thinks desirable for testing the truth or accuracy of any evidence he has given and otherwise for eliciting the truth[7]. The whole of the proceedings of a court of inquiry shall be forwarded by the presiding officer to the officer who assembled the court[8]. The court may be reassembled as often as the officer who assembled the court may direct, for the purpose of examining additional witnesses, or further examining any witnesses, or recording further information[9].

1 As to the definition of 'officer' and 'warrant officer'; see **[0494]** and **[0504]**.

2 The Air Force Rules 1969 r 154 (1).

3 The Air Force Rules 1969 r 154 (2).

4 Manual of Air Force Law, Volume II, r 154 notes.

5 The Air Force Rules 1969 r 154 (3).

6 The Air Force Rules 1969 r 154 (4).

7 The Air Force Rules 1969 r 154 (5).

8 The Air Force Rules 1969 r 154 (6).

9 The Air Force Rules 1969 r 154 (7).

[0887] Composition of a court of inquiry If an officer, requiring to assemble a court of inquiry, is unable to provide for the constitution of the court in accordance with the provision of the regulations for the Air Force 1964[1], he will refer the matter to higher authority. The assembling authority will detail an officer by name to act as presiding officer and one or more officers junior to him, or warrant officers as members. The rank of the presiding officer should not normally be below that of flight lieutenant, and where the court is directed to express an opinion which may bear upon the conduct, character, or professional reputation of an officer, the presiding officer must not be junior in rank and seniority to that officer. Where, however, a court is assembled to investigate a fatal flying accident or where the forecasts of the loss in a flying accident is expected to exceed Rs 10 lakhs, the rank of the presiding officer will not be less than that of a wing commander provided the services of an officer of that rank can be made available without undue delay. The personnel detailed to constitute the court should have no direct or indirect interest in the subject matter of the investigation, and where the investigation may involve technical or professional knowledge or skill of any description e.g., equipment and accounts, etc., at least one officer or warrant officer having appropriate qualifications will be included on the court either as a, member or in attendance. In the case of fires, except where the outbreak is small and insignificant, the court will consist of members drawn from unit, other than that at which the outbreak occurred, and a representative of the military engineering services will be invited to be present at the inquiry. In the case of explosion, arrangements shall be made, whenever possible, for an ordnance officer or an officer of the army supply corps as appropriate to be present at the court, and assist in investigating the cause of the accident. If a court is to investigate losses, deficiencies or damage connected with medical, surgical or dental stores, or foodstuff or barrack equipment on the charge of a medical officer, a medical officer should be detailed as one of the members of the court. The assembling authority will exercise his discretion as to when a warrant officer can with advantage be detailed to act as a member of a court. A warrant officer will not be appointed on a court the main business of which is to report on the conduct, character, or professional reputation of a commissioned officer, nor will he be detailed as a member of a court of inquiry assembled to deal with a returned prisoner of war. Where the subject to be investigated is likely to involve criticism of the station commander, the circumstances calling for inquiry will be reported to higher authority who will convene an independent court[2].

1 Ie the Regulations for the Air Force 1964, paragraph 783 (a).

2 Regulations for the Air Force 1964, paragraph 783.

[0888] Terms of Reference In order that a court of inquiry can properly inquire into any matter, it is essential that assembling authority provides the court with suitable and precise terms of reference pointing out the exact aspect of the case on which the court's findings and recommendations, if any, are required. The terms of reference should also clearly state if the evidence is required to be taken on oath[1].

1 Regulations for the Air Force 1964, paragraph 784. When a court of inquiry is held on prisoners of war and in any other case in which assembling authority so directs, the evidence shall be taken on oath or affirmation. The court shall administer the same oath/affirmation to witness as if it were a court martial. However, the members of the court shall not themselves be sworn or affirmed. Regulations for the Air Force 1964, paragraph 789.

[0889] Assembly of a court of inquiry The date, time and place of assembly of a court of inquiry will be notified to all persons concerned or directed to be in attendance. Notice to persons who are not subject to the Air Force Act 1950 will be given in writing, and a copy of the notice will be annexed to the proceedings. The assembly of a court will be arranged so as to interfere as little as possible with the ordinary duties of officers and airmen. A court may adjourn from time to time and from place to place as may be found convenient due notice of the date, time and place of re-assembly being given to those concerned[1].

1 Regulations for the Air Force 1964, paragraph 785. A court of inquiry may be re-assembled as often as the officer who assembled the court may direct for the purpose of examining additional witnesses, for further examining any witness or for recording further evidence. Regulations for the Air Force 1964, paragraph 794.

[0890] Attendance of witnesses The presiding officer of a court of inquiry will, as far as possible, obtain beforehand details of the witnesses whose evidence appears to be necessary. The court shall also record the evidence of any other witness whose statement may be material to the investigation. A court of inquiry cannot compel the attendance of civilian witnesses; if, after being invited to attend, a civilian witness declines to do so, the court will invite him to make a statement in writing. Applications for attendance of witnesses other than those serving the station where the court of inquiry has been convened will be made as follows, in writing, stating the date, time and place where the witnesses will be required: (i) For witnesses belonging to any branch of the armed forces- to the headquarters of the command, formation or department concerned; (ii) For civilian police witnesses-to the officer-in-charge of the local police station or the superintendent of police of the civil district to which the witness belongs; and (iii) For other civilian witnesses- to the witness personally and, if considered/ advisable, to his employer also; if there is, difficulty in tracing the address of such a witness, the assistance of the local civil police may be requested[1].

1 Regulations for the Air Force 1964, paragraph 786.

[0891] Proceedings of a court of inquiry and recording of evidence A court of inquiry is not a public court and should normally sit in private. Except as provided in certain provisions of the Regulations for the Air Force 1964[1], a witness will be excluded from the sittings of a court unless he himself is under examination or cross-examination. As far as possible, evidence should be recorded in chronological order. Each witness should be given a serial number and his statement should begin with brief details of his service particulars if he is a service witness, or his name, address, etc., if he is a civilian witness, followed by a brief description of his duties or his position. The evidence of witnesses in examination and cross-examination should be recorded in first person narrative form and not in the form of questions and answers unless the court thinks fit to record any particular question or answer as such. Each witness should sign his evidence on every page on the original copy of the proceedings. Corrections, if any, on original copy should be initialled by the witness. When witness is illiterate, his statement should be read out to him, if necessary through an interpreter. The witness should then put down his thumb impression at the end of each page of his evidence, the thumb impression being attested by a member of the court[2].

1 Ie Regulations for the Air Force 1964, paragraph 790; see **[0892]**.

2 Regulations for the Air Force 1964, paragraph 788.

[0892] Action when character or professional reputation of persons is affected

1 As soon as it appears to the court that the character or professional reputation of an officer or airman

is affected by the evidence recorded, or that he is to blame, the affected person is to be so informed by the court. All the evidence recorded up to that stage is to be read over to the affected person, and the court is to explain to the person, if so required by him, how, in its opinion, it appears that the officer's or airman's character or professional reputation is adversely affected, or how he appears to be to blame[1].

2 From the time an officer or airman is so informed, in accordance with the aforesaid provision he has the right to be present during all the ensuing proceedings, except when the court is deliberating privately. The fact that an officer or airman to whom this provision applies is or is not present will be recorded in the proceedings[2].

3 The affected officer or airman may, if he so desires, cross-examine any witness whose evidence was recorded prior to the action taken under the aforesaid provision[3]. He may, likewise, cross-examine subsequent witnesses after their statements have been recorded. He may also request the court to record the evidence of any witness in his defence. The officer or airman may make any statement in his defence[4].

4 In case the officer or airman affected cannot, for any reason be present to exercise his privilege under the aforesaid provisions[5], the court is to inform him by letter (or otherwise as may be convenient) of the reasons why, in the opinion of the court, his character or professional reputation appears to be affected, or he appears to be to blame. The affected person may make a statement in writing in denial, exculpation, or explanation. This statement is to be attached to the proceedings, and the court is to endeavour, by examining or recalling witnesses, to accord, to the affected person, such protection as is intended in the aforesaid provisions[6].

5 If, after recording all the evidence, and after taking such action under the aforesaid provisions[7] as may be called for in the circumstances the court is of the opinion that an officer or airman is to blame, or that his character or professional reputation, is affected, the entire proceedings are to be shown to the affected person, and he is to be asked whether he desires any further statement to make. Any such statement is to be recorded, and fresh points are to be fully investigated by the court[8].

6 The findings, and recommendations, if called for, of the court may then be made in accordance with the terms of reference[9].

7 An officer or airman to whom certain provisions of the Regulations for the Air Force 1964[10] applies does not have the right to demand that the evidence be taken on oath or affirmation, or, except so far as the assembling authority or the court may permit, to be represented by a solicitor or other agent[11].

8 If the assembling authority attributes blame to an officer or, an airman other than the officer or airman held to blame by the court, or attributes blame in a way substantially different from that of the court, the proceedings will be returned to the presiding officer of the court (without any endorsement on the proceedings) by the assembling authority together with a statement from the assembling authority as to why that authority considers that blame should be attributed to such officer or airman or in a way substantially different from that of the court. This statement will form part of the court of inquiry proceedings. The court of inquiry will be reconvened and the court will show to the affected person the entire proceedings and statement of the assembling authority. The court will then obtain from the person any statement that he may wish to make and record the evidence of any witnesses he may wish to call in cross-examination or of any fresh witnesses. When complete, the proceedings will be

forwarded to the assembling authority together with any additional findings and or recommendations that the court may wish to record. The assembling authority will endorse its remarks on the proceedings only after completion of action under this provision[12].

9 If blame is attributed by any authority higher than the assembling authority to an officer or airman other than the officer or airman held to blame by the court or the assembling authority, the proceedings will be returned to the assembling authority together with such authority's statement for action under the aforesaid provision. The concerned higher authority will endorse its remarks on the proceedings, only after the proceedings are received back from the assembling authority after completion of action. When forwarding the proceedings to higher authority after taking action under this provision, the assembling authority or any other intermediary authority may append remarks on any additional findings recommendations made[13].

10 The same court which originally investigated the particular occurrence will, as far as possible, be reconvened for purposes of the aforesaid provisions[14]. A fresh court is to be assembled only in exceptional circumstances[15].

1 Regulations for the Air Force 1964, paragraph 790 (a). This provision is similar to the one contained in the Army Rules 1954 r 180; for more details; see **[0450]**.

2 Regulations for the Air Force 1964, paragraph 790 (b).

3 Ie the Regulations for the Air Force 1964, paragraph 790 (a).

4 Regulations for the Air Force 1964, paragraph 790 (c).

5 Ie the Regulations for the Air Force 1964, paragraph 790 (a), (b) and (c).

6 Ie the Regulations for the Air Force 1964, paragraph 790 (a), (b) and (c); Regulations for the Air Force 1964, paragraph 790 (d).

7 Ie under the Regulations for the Air Force 1964, paragraph 790 (a), (b), (c) and (d).

8 Regulations for the Air Force 1964, paragraph 790 (e).

9 Regulations for the Air Force 1964, paragraph 790 (f).

10 Regulations for the Air Force 1964, paragraph 790 (a), (b), (c) and (d).

11 Regulations for the Air Force 1964, paragraph 790 (g).

12 Regulations for the Air Force 1964, paragraph 790 (h).

13 Regulations for the Air Force 1964, paragraph 790 (j).

14 Ie the Regulations for the Air Force 1964, paragraph 790 (h) and (j).

15 Regulations for the Air Force 1964, paragraph 790 (k).

[0893] Findings The court of inquiry will, in every case where it is so required, record its findings on the proceedings, and will be careful to ensure that such findings are supported by evidence and cover the points upon which it is required by the terms of reference, or by regulation, to report. It will note any particular point on which it is unable to record a complete finding and the reasons for the same. The courts should endeavour in their findings to differentiate between incidents caused by error of judgement not involving disregard of orders, etc., and incidents due to disregard of orders or other causes directly within the control of the personnel involved. The court should not regard itself as debarred from making the required differentiation even if it is impossible, on account of the death of the personnel involved or from other cause to obtain evidence or a statement in defence. In determining the degree of responsibility of any persons for a loss, damage, etc., the court will endeavour to determine: (i) whether the person was directly or indirectly to blame, (ii) whether the loss, damage, etc., was due to culpable negligence or to negligence or to irregularity on the part of that person. The court will draw attention to any irregularity disclosed in the course of the investigation even though, in its opinion, it was not a contributing factor to the incident under investigation and is outside its terms of reference. When the court is of opinion that compensation should be paid by any person or persons deemed to be responsible, it will state the amount that it considers should be paid by such persons, but any recommendation made by it will be considered as being made without prejudice to any action that may be taken by higher authority. The findings will be signed by the presiding officer and all the members of the court, but any member of the court may, if he thinks that he should do so, sign subject to any reservations which he desires to make, or may express his dissent from any findings of fact or recommendation arrived at by the other members[1].

1 Regulations for the Air Force 1964, paragraph 791.

[0894] Liability A court of inquiry, or any member thereof, must not make any admission of liability in respect of any matter being investigated by it, or give any undertaking to satisfy any claim, or to initiate or defend any legal proceedings, or negotiate or accept any settlement of any claim made by or on behalf of, or against the air forces or any unit or member thereof[1].

1 Regulations for the Air Force 1964, paragraph 795.

[0895] Inquiry into absence without leave When any person subject to the Air Force Act 1950 has been absent from his duty without due authority for a period of 30 days, a court of inquiry shall, as soon as practicable, be assembled, and such court shall, on oath or affirmation administered in the prescribed manner, inquire respecting the absence of the person, and the deficiency, if any, in the property of the government entrusted to his care, or in any arms, ammunition, equipment, instruments, clothing or necessaries, and if satisfied of the fact of such absence without due authority or other sufficient cause, the court shall declare such absence and the period thereof, and the said deficiency, if any; and the commanding officer of the unit to which the person belongs shall enter in the court martial book of the unit a record of declaration[1]. If the person declared absent does not afterwards surrender or is not apprehended, he shall, for the purposes of the Air Force Act 1950, be deemed to be a deserter[2].

1 The Air Force Act 1950 s 107 (1). In calculating the period of 30 days, the day on which the person became absent and the day on which the court of inquiry assembles must both be excluded. Manual of Air Force Law, Volume I, s 107 notes.

2 The Air Force Act 1950 s 107 (2).

[0896] Courts of Inquiry under the Air Force Act 1950 s 107 for the purpose of determining the illegal absence of persons subject to the Air Force Act A court of inquiry under the provisions of the Air Force Act 1950[1] shall, when assembled, require the attendance of such witnesses as it thinks sufficient to prove the absence and other facts specified as matter of inquiry in that section[2]. The court of inquiry shall take down the evidence given by them in writing and at the end of proceedings shall make a declaration of the conclusions at which it has arrived in respect of the facts it is assembled to inquire into[3]. The court of inquiry shall examine all witnesses who may be desirous of coming forward on behalf of the absentee, and shall put such questions to them as may be desirable for testing the truth or accuracy of any evidence they have given, and otherwise for eliciting the truth, and the court in making its declaration shall give weight to the evidence of all such witnesses[4].

The court of inquiry shall administer the same oath or affirmation to the witnesses as if the court were a court martial, but the members of such court shall not themselves be sworn or affirmed[5]. The commanding officer of the unit to which the absent person belongs shall enter in the court martial book of the unit a record of the declaration of the court, and the original proceedings will be destroyed[6]. Any person, the subject of the inquiry, shall be entitled to a copy of the declaration of the court, to be supplied by the person having custody of the court martial book, on payment at the rate laid down in the Air Force Rules 1969[7].

1 Ie the Air Force Act 1950 s 107.

2 The Air Force Rules 1969 r 155 (1).

3 The Air Force Rules 1969 r 155 (2).

4 The Air Force Rules 1969 r 155 (3).

5 The Air Force Rules 1969 r 155 (4).

6 The Air Force Rules 1969 r 155 (5).

7 Ie the Air Force Rules 1969 r 156 (9); the Air Force Rules 1969 r 155 (6).

[0897] Courts of inquiry other than those held under the Air Force Act 1950 s 107

1 The court shall be guided by the written instructions of the authority which assembled the court. The instructions shall be full and specific, and shall state the general character of the information required. They shall also state whether a report is required or not[1].

2 Except in the case of a prisoner of war who is still absent, whenever any inquiry affects the character or service reputation of a person subject to the Air Force Act 1950, full opportunity must be afforded to such person of being present throughout the inquiry and of making any statements and or giving any evidence he may wish to make or give, and of cross-examining any witness whose evidence, in his opinion, affects his character or service reputation, and producing any witnesses in defence of his character or service reputation[2].

3 When a court of inquiry is held on prisoners of war, and in any other case in which the officer who assembled the court has so directed, the evidence shall be taken on oath or affirmation, in which case the court shall administer the same oath or affirmation, to witnesses as if the court were a court martial[3].

4 The officer who assembled the court shall, when the court is held on a returned prisoner of war or on a prisoner of war who is still absent, direct the court to record its opinion whether the person concerned was taken prisoner through his own wilful neglect of duty, or whether he served with or under, or he aided the enemy; he shall also direct the court to record its opinion in the case of a returned prisoner of war, whether he returned as soon as possible to the service, and in the case of prisoner of war still absent, whether he failed to return to the service when it was possible for him to do so. The officer who assembled the court shall also record his own opinion on these points. In other cases, the court shall give no opinion on the conduct of any person unless so directed by the officer who assembled the court[4].

5 The members of the court shall not themselves be sworn or affirmed but when the court is a court of inquiry on recovered prisoners of war, the members shall make the following declaration:

I........., do declare upon my honour that I will duly and impartially inquire into and give my opinion as to the circumstances in which.........become a prisoner of war, according to the true spirit and meaning of the rules and regulations made under the Air Force 1950, and I do further declare, upon my honour, that I will not on any account, or at any time, disclose or discover my own vote or opinion, or that of any particular member of the court, unless required to do so by competent authority[5].

6 The proceeding of a court of inquiry, or any confession or statement or answer to a question made or given at a court of inquiry, shall not be admissible in evidence against a person subject to Air Force Law, nor shall any evidence respecting the proceedings of the court be given against any such person except upon the trial of such person for wilfully giving false evidence before that court[6].

7 Any person subject to the Air Force Act 1950 whose character or service reputation is in the opinion of the Chief of the Air Staff, affected by anything in the evidence before or in the report of a court of inquiry shall be entitled to a copy of the proceedings of such court unless the Chief of the Air Staff sees reason to order otherwise[7].

8 Any person subject to the Air Force Act 1950 who is tried by a court martial in respect of any matter or thing which has been reported on by a court of inquiry shall be entitled to a copy of the proceedings of such court, including any report made by the court[8]. However, if the Chief of the Air Staff considers that it is against the interests or the security of the State or friendly relations with a foreign State to supply a copy of proceedings or any part thereof, such person shall not be furnished with such copy, but in such cases he shall, subject to suitable precautions as to security, be permitted inspection of such portions of the proceedings of the court of inquiry on the basis of which the charges, on which he is arraigned before the court-martial, have been framed[9].

9 A copy of the proceedings of the court of inquiry shall be furnished under the aforesaid provisions[10] on payment for the same of a sum calculated at the rates of fifty paise for every two hundred words of part thereof[11].

10 A person subject to the Air Force Act 1950 before he is, furnished with a copy of the proceedings of the court of inquiry under the aforesaid provisions or he is permitted to inspect any portion of the proceedings shall be required to render a certificate that he is aware that he may render himself liable to prosecution under the Official Secrets Act 1923 for any breach of the provisions of the said Act in relation to such proceedings or portion thereof[12].

1 The Air Force Rules 1969 r 156 (1).

2 The Air Force Rules 1969 r 156 (2). Certain provisions relating to court of inquiry are as follows: (i) Investigation of personal injuries and accidental deaths: Regulations for the Air Force 1964, paragraph 796; (ii) Unnatural death/ death under suspicious circumstances: Regulations for the Air Force 1964, paragraph 798; (iii) Flying Accidents: Regulations for the Air Force 1964, paragraph 799; (iv) Mechanical transport accidents: Regulations for the Air Force 1964, paragraph 802; (v) Incidents of fire: Regulations for the Air Force 1964, paragraph 803; (vi) Loss of public money: Regulations for the Air Force 1964, paragraph 805; (vii) Loss of secret documents: Regulations for the Air Force 1964, paragraph 808; (viii) Action when a penal deduction is recommended under the Air Force Act 1950 s 91 and 92: Regulations for the Air Force 1964, paragraph 810.

3 The Air Force Rules 1969 r 156 (3). See the Regulations for the Air Force 1964, paragraph 809 on court of inquiry in case of a prisoner of war.

4 The Air Force Rules 1969 r 156 (4).

5 The Air Force Rules 1969 r 156 (5).

6 The Air Force Rules 1969 r 156 (6).

7 The Air Force Rules 1969 r 156 (7).

8 The Air Force Rules 1969 r 156 (8).

9 The Air Force Rules 1969 r 156 (8) proviso.

10 Ie under the Air Force Rules 1969 r 156 (7) and (8).

11 The Air Force Rules 1969 r 156 (9).

12 The Air Force Rules 1969 r 156 (10).

[0898] Court of Inquest Under the provisions of the Criminal Procedure Code 1973 s 174, the responsibility for holding an inquest in cases of unnatural deaths, that is, death due to suicide, violence, accident or under suspicious circumstances devolves on the local civil authorities. Information regarding such cases of death of persons subject to the Air Force Act 1950 or any deaths within unit lines will, therefore, be given immediately on occurrence, in writing and conveyed by hand of an officer to the senior local civil police officer. If the civil police authorities do not intend sending the dead body for a post mortem examination and decide not to hold an inquest, the air force officer conveying the information of death will obtain a declaration in writing to that effect. A service court of inquest consisting of three officers, of which one must be a medical officer will then be convened under the orders of the station commander or superior officer. In case of death of service personnel occurring at a place outside India, not including the state of Jammu and Kashmir, unless the local law requires otherwise, it is not necessary to inform the local civil police authorities and the inquest may be held by the officer commanding the unit to which the deceased belonged. The cremation/funeral will take place only after concurrence of the presiding officer and the medical member of the court of inquest has been obtained. Service courts of inquest will follow the procedure laid down in the Air Force Rules 1969[1]. A copy of the court of inquest proceedings will be forwarded to Air Headquarters through proper channel[2].

1 Ie the Air Force Rules 1969 r 154 and 155; see **[0886]** and **[0896]**.

2 Regulations for the Air Force 1964, paragraph 797.

9. POWER TO MAKE RULES

CONTENTS

PARA

[0899] Power to make rules The Central Government may make rules for the purpose of carrying into effect the provisions of the Air Force Act 1950[1]. The rules made may provide for:

(1) The removal, retirement, release or discharge from the service of persons subject to the Air Force Act 1950[2].

(2) The amount and incidence of fines to be imposed under Air Force Act 1950 s 90[3].

(3) The specification of the punishment which may be awarded as field punishments under the Air Force Act 1950 s 77 and 82[4].

(4) The assembly and procedure of courts of inquiry, the recording of summaries of evidence and the administration of oaths or affirmations by such courts[5].

(5) The convening and constituting of courts martial and the appointment of prosecutors at trials by courts martial[6].

(6) The adjournment, dissolution and sitting of courts martial[7].

(7) The procedure to be observed in trials by courts martial and the appearance of legal practitioners thereat[8].

(8) The confirmation, revision and annulment of, and petitions against the findings and sentences of courts martial[9].

(9) The carrying into effect of sentences or courts martial[10].

(10) The forms of orders to be made under the provisions of Air Force Act 1950 relating to courts martial, imprisonment for life, imprisonment and detention[11].

(11) The constitution of authorities to decide for what persons, to what amounts and in what manner, provision should be made for dependants of prisoners of war under the Air Force Act 1950 s 100 and the due carrying out of such decisions[12].

(12) The relative rank of the officers, junior commissioned officers, warrant officers, petty officers and non-commissioned officers of the regular Army, Navy and Air Force when acting together[13].

(13) Any other matter directed by the Air Force Act 1950 to be prescribed[14].

1 The Air Force Act 1950 s 189 (1). The Air Force Rules 1969 have been made under this provision.

2 The Air Force Act 1950 s 189 (2) (a).

3 The Air Force Act 1950 s 189 (2) (b).

4 The Air Force Act 1950 s 189 (2) (c).

5 The Air Force Act 1950 s 189 (2) (d).

6 The Air Force Act 1950 s 189 (2) (e).

7 The Air Force Act 1950 s 189 (2) (f).

8 The Air Force Act 1950 s 189 (2) (g).

9 The Air Force Act 1950 s 189 (2) (h).

10 The Air Force Act 1950 s 189 (2) (i).

11 The Air Force Act 1950 s 189 (2) (j).

12 The Air Force Act 1950 s 189 (2) (k).

13 The Air Force Act 1950 s 189 (2) (l).

14 The Air Force Act 1950 s 189 (2) (m).

[0900] Power to make regulations The Central Government may make regulations for all or any of the purposes of the Air Force Act 1950 other than those specified in the Act[1].

1 Ie under the Air Force Act 1950 s 189; the Air Force Act 1950 s 190. The Regulations for the Air Force 1964 have been made under this provision.

[0901] Publication of rules and regulations in Gazette All rules and regulations made under the Air Force Act 1950 shall be published in the Official Gazette and, on such publication, shall have effect as if enacted in the aforesaid Act[1].

1 The Air Force Act 1950 s 191. The Regulations for the Air Force 1964 have not been published in the gazette.

[0902] Laying of rules and regulations before Parliament Every rule and every regulation made under the Air Force Act 1950 shall be laid, as soon as may be after it is made, before each House of Parliament, while it is in session, for a total period of 30 days which may be comprised in one session or in two or more successive sessions. If, before the expiry of the session immediately following the session or the successive sessions aforesaid, both Houses agree in making any modification in the rule or regulation or both Houses agree that the rule or regulation should not be made, the rule or regulation shall thereafter have effect only in such modified form or be of no effect. However, any such modification or annulment shall be without prejudice to the validity of anything previously done under that rule or regulation[1].

1 The Air Force Act 1950 s 191A. This provision was inserted vide the Delegated Legislation Provisions (Amendment) Act 1985 s 2 to implement the recommendations of the Committee on Subordinate Legislation regarding publication and laying of rules and other delegated legislations. The Manual of Air Force Law, volume I, s 191A notes.

IV. THE LAW RELATING TO THE NAVY

1. PRELIMINARIES

CONTENTS

PARA

A. Introduction

[0903] Introduction Before independence, the law relating to the governance of the Navy was contained in the Indian Navy (Discipline) Act 1934. This Act was passed pursuant to the Government of India Act 1919 s 66. The Act empowered the then Indian Legislature to apply the provisions of the UK's Naval Discipline Act to the naval forces raised in India. Accordingly the UK's Naval Discipline Act 1934, was modified and set forth in the First Schedule to the Indian Navy (Discipline) Act 1934, and made applicable to the Indian naval forces. This Act dealt largely with disciplinary provisions. There were no statutory provisions concerning the matters relating to administration, enrolment, grant of commission, etc. In 1950, the revised Army Act and the Air Force Act were passed by the Parliament. It was not possible at that time to draft a revised navy Bill, as the present Act was modelled mainly on the corresponding British Act. In the UK, a special committee[1] had been appointed for the revision of the British Naval Code. It was thought that it would be an advantage to await the report of that Committee. The Bill for the Indian Navy was made taking into consideration the report of the Committee. It was passed by both the Houses of Parliament and received the assent of the President on 27 December 1957 and came into force on 1 January 1958 as the Navy Act 1957[2]. No rules have been framed under the Navy Act 1957.

The Navy Act 1957 and the Regulations for the Navy Part II, 1965 prescribes the procedure to be followed in case it is decided that an offender should be tried by court martial. The Act also provides sufficient safeguard by way of further appeal to the chief of the naval staff and then ultimately to the central government[3].

1 The Committee appointed to consider the Administration of Justice under the Naval Discipline Act 1949, commonly known as the Pilcher Committee. Jha U.C. 2009. *The Military Justice System in India: An Analysis*, New Delhi: LexixNexis, p. 22.

2 The main objects of the Bill was to make the law self sufficient by incorporating the necessary provisions of certain other related enactments and regulations and to adapt the existing provisions to suit the new constitutional set-up and present day requirement. The Statement of Objects and Reasons, the Navy Bill 1957.

3 *Union of India v Himmat Singh Chahar* AIR 1999 SC1980; 1999 Cri LJ 2894; (1999) 4 SCC 521.

B. Short title and commencement

[0904] Short title and commencement This statute covering the Navy is called the Navy Act 1957[1]. It came into force on 1 January 1958[2] by notification in the Official Gazette[3].

1 The Navy Act 1957 s 1 (1).

2 Vide SRO 11 (E), dated 31 December 1957, published in the Gazette of India, Ext., Part II, S. 4, p. 81.

3 The Navy Act 1957 s 1 (2).

C. Definitions and meanings

Certain words and terms that appear in the Navy Act and the Regulations for the Navy, will need to be understood as they are defined in the Navy Act 1957 and the Regulations for the Navy 1965, Part II.

[0905] Active service In the Navy Act 1957, unless the context otherwise requires, 'active service' means the service or duty (i) during the period of operation of a Proclamation of Emergency issued under the Constitution of India[1]; or (ii) during any period declared by the Central Government by notification in the Official Gazette as a period of active service with reference to any area in which any person or class of persons subject to naval law[2] may be serving[3].

1 Ie under the Constitution of India Article 352 (1).

2 As to the meaning of 'persons subject to naval law'; see **[0941]**.

3 The Navy Act 1957 s 3 (1).

[0906] Administrative authority In the Regulations for the Navy 1965 Part II unless the context otherwise requires, 'administrative authority' in relation to any provision of the Regulations means the authority which is designated as such in the Navy Orders[1].

1 As to the meaning of 'navy orders'; see **[0926]**. The Regulations for the Navy 1965, Part II, (Discipline and Miscellaneous Provisions), regulation 2 (b).

[0907] Chief of the Naval Staff In the Navy Act 1957, unless the context otherwise requires, 'chief of the naval staff' means the flag officer appointed by the President as chief of the naval staff or in his absence on leave or otherwise an officer appointed by the central government to officiate as such or in the absence of such officiating appointment the officer on whom the command devolves in accordance with regulations[1] made under the Navy Act 1957[2].

1 Ie the Regulations for the Navy 1965, Part II, (Discipline and Miscellaneous Provisions).

2 The Navy Act 1957 s 3 (2).

[0908] Exercise of powers of the Chief of the Naval Staff in his absence from Naval Headquarters Any power vested in the chief of the naval staff by the Regulations for the Navy 1965, Part II, may be exercised when he is absent from naval headquarters on duty or otherwise by the vice chief of the naval staff and in the absence of both, by the senior principal staff officer present in the naval headquarters. The chief of the naval staff under a general or special order may reserve to himself the exercise of the any specific power[1].

1 The Regulations for the Navy 1965, Part II, regulations 5.

[0909] Civil court In the Regulations for the Navy 1965 Part II unless the context otherwise requires, 'civil court' means a court of ordinary criminal jurisdiction in India[1].

1 The Regulations for the Navy 1965, Part II, regulations 2 (d).

[0910] Civil offence In the Navy Act 1957, unless the context otherwise requires, 'civil offence' means an offence triable by a court of ordinary criminal jurisdiction in India[1].

1 The Navy Act 1957 s 3 (3).

[0911] Civil prison In the Navy Act 1957, unless the context otherwise requires, 'civil prison' means any jail or place used for the detention of any criminal prisoner under the Prisons Act 1894 or under any other law for the time being in force[1].

1 The Navy Act 1957 s 3 (4).

[0912] Commanding officer In the Regulations for the Navy 1965 Part II unless the context otherwise requires, 'commanding officer' means the officer or other person in actual command of a ship or establishment[1].

1 The Regulations for the Navy 1965, Part II, regulations 2 (dd).

[0913] Commanding Officers: General Instructions The commanding officer shall (i) at all times and in all circumstances show an example of respect and obedient to his superiors[1]; (ii) see that all the officers obey the several instructions which are addressed to them, or which, though of general purport, concern them[2]; (iii) correct or report to his superiors any reprehensible conduct on the part of those under his command[2]; (iv) notice the conduct and abilities of those under his command in order that he may give them the testimonials they deserve, or, if called on, to make correct reports of their merits[2]; and (v) while upholding the legitimate authority of all the officers under his command, check by timely reproofs any tendency he may notice to abuse of power, showing by his example that a firm but conciliatory manner of conducting duty is the surest way to gain the respect and confidence of sailors[5].

1 Regulations for the Navy 1965, Part II, regulation 213 (i).

2 Regulations for the Navy 1965, Part II, regulation 213 (ii).

3 Regulations for the Navy 1965, Part II, regulation 213 (iii).

4 Regulations for the Navy 1965, Part II, regulation 213 (iv).

5 Regulations for the Navy 1965, Part II, regulation 213 (v).

[0914] Commissioned officer In the Navy Act 1957, unless the context otherwise requires, 'commissioned officer' means a person holding a commission from the President in the Indian Navy or the Indian Naval Reserve Force[1].

1 As to the definition of 'Indian Naval Reserve Forces'; see **[0918]**. The Navy Act 1957 s 3 (5).

[0915] Court martial In the Navy Act 1957, unless the context otherwise requires, 'court-martial' means a court martial constituted under the Navy Act[1].

1 The Navy Act 1957 s 3 (6).

[0916] Enemy In the Navy Act 1957, unless the context otherwise requires, 'enemy' includes all armed rebels, armed mutineers, armed rioters and pirates and any person in arms against whom it is the duty of any person subject to Naval law[1] to act[2].

1 As to the meaning of 'person subject to Naval law'; see **[0941]**.

2 The Navy Act 1957 s 3 (7).

[0917] Flag officer In the Navy Act 1957, unless the context otherwise requires, 'flag officer' means an officer of the rank of Admiral of the Fleet, Admiral, Vice Admiral or Rear-admiral[1].

1 The Navy Act 1957 s 3 (8).

[0918] Indian Naval Reserve Forces In the Navy Act 1957, unless the context otherwise requires, 'Indian Naval Reserve Forces' mean the naval reserve forces raised and maintained by the Central Government[1].

1 The Navy Act 1957 s 3 (9).

[0919] Indian Navy In the Navy Act 1957, unless the context otherwise requires, 'Indian Navy' means the regular Naval forces raised and maintained by the Central Government[1].

1 The Navy Act 1957 s 3 (10).

[0920] Indian waters In the Navy Act 1957, unless the context otherwise requires, 'Indian waters' for the purpose of certain provisions of the aforesaid Acts[1], means the seas extending from the shores of India to such limits as may be prescribed[2].

1 Ie the Navy Act 1957 s 31, 97 and 99.

2 The Navy Act 1957 s 3 (11).

[0921] Naval custody In the Navy Act 1957, unless the context otherwise requires, 'naval custody' means the arrest or confinement of a person in the prescribed manner or in accordance with the usages of the naval service, and includes military or air force custody[1].

There is no provision in the Navy Act 1957, which provides for the detention in a naval jail or naval custody of person subject to naval law, who has been convicted for the offence of murder by an ordinary criminal court. The expression 'trial' is used in the sense of proceedings before a court martial and it ends when these proceedings come to an end. The word 'trial' is well understood in criminal law and it ends when the proceedings in the trial came to an end[2].

1 The Navy Act 1957 s 3 (12).

2 *State v KM Nanavati*, (1960) 62 Bom LR 383; 1960 Cri LJ 1558.

[0922] Naval establishment In the Navy Act 1957, unless the context otherwise requires, 'naval e stablishment' means an establishment belonging to, or under the control of, the Indian Navy whether within or without India[1].

1 The Navy Act 1957 s 3 (12A).

[0923] Naval offence In the Navy Act 1957, unless the context otherwise requires, 'naval offences' means any of the offences under the aforesaid Act ss 34 to 76[1].

1 The Navy Act 1957 s 3 (13).

[0924] Naval service In the Navy Act 1957, unless the context otherwise requires, 'naval service' means the naval organization of India[1].

1 The Navy Act 1957 s 3 (14).

[0925] Naval tribunal In the Navy Act 1957, unless the context otherwise requires, 'naval tribunal' means (i) a court martial constituted under the aforesaid Act s 97, (ii) a disciplinary court constituted under s 96, or (iii) a commanding officer or other officer or authority exercising powers of punishment under the Navy Act 1957[1].

1 The Navy Act 1957 s 3 (15).

[0926] Navy orders In the Regulations for the Navy 1965 Part II unless the context otherwise requires, 'navy orders' means the general orders of the Chief of the Naval Staff issued in the publication entitled 'navy orders' and includes confidential navy orders[1].

1 The Regulations for the Navy 1965, Part II, regulations 2 (e). Navy Order 16 of 1981 issued pursuant to this provision which delegated power to the chief of the naval staff to issue such orders, is not be violative of the provisions of the Navy Act 1957 or the Navy Regulations 1965. Navy Order 16 of 1981 is valid and has statutory backing and is not ultra-vires of the aforesaid Act or the Regulations. *Commodore CP George v Chief of Naval Staff* 58 (1995) DLT 578.

[0927] Officer In the Navy Act 1957, unless the context otherwise requires, 'officer' means a commissioned officer[1] and includes (i) a subordinate officer other than a petty officer[2]; (ii) a commissioned officer re-employed as such[3].

1 As to the meaning of 'commissioned officer'; see **[0914]**.

2 As to the meaning of 'petty officer'; see **[0928]**. The Navy Act 1957 s 3 (16) (a).

3 The Navy Act 1957 s 3 (16) (b).

[0928] Petty officer In the Navy Act 1957, unless the context otherwise requires, 'petty officer' means a sailor rated as such and includes a chief petty officer and a master petty officer[1].

1 The Navy Act 1957 s 3 (17). The discipline of the ships and establishments and the comfort of the men is dependent in a great measure on the manner in which petty officers carry out their duties and maintain their position. Is is essential that the importance of their position and of the influence which they should exercise on the discipline, efficiency and morale of the service as a whole should be realized throughout the service. All petty officers shall be granted every reasonable indulgence and shall be made to feel that confidence is reposed in them and shall be treated with the consideration which is due to the position of trust which they hold. The prefix 'master chief sahib' or 'chief petty officer' or 'petty officer' or the corresponding prefix in the case of non-seaman sailors shall be used by all ranks when addressing or speaking of sailors holding those ranks. Petty officers shall be shown in the ship's book distinct from lower ranks. The separation is to be made by classes (seaman, artificers and the like) and the petty officers shall be shown on separate sub-divisions of their respective lists. It shall be the duty of petty officers to preserve order and regularity wherever the crew or any part of it may be employed and this responsibility rests upon them whenever they are with the men, whether on duty or not. For more details on the duties and privileges of petty officers, see the Regulations for the Navy 1965, Part II, regulation 20

[0929] Prescribed In the Navy Act 1957, unless the context otherwise requires, 'prescribed' means prescribed by regulations[1] made under the aforesaid Act[2].

1 Ie the Regulations for the Navy 1965.

2 The Navy Act 1957 s 3 (18).

[0930] Prescribed form In the Regulations for the Navy 1965 unless the context otherwise requires, 'prescribed form', means an appropriate form in the Regulations for the Navy 1965, Part II, Appendix I applicable to the relevant provision of the Navy Act 1957 or Regulations for the Navy 1965 Part II[1].

1 The Regulations for the Navy 1965, Part II, regulation 2 (f).

[0931] Proper superior authority In the Regulations for the Navy 1965 Part II unless the context otherwise requires, 'proper superior authority' when used in relation to any power, duty, act or matter means such authority as in pursuance of the aforesaid Regulations or Navy Orders or any other orders issued by the Chief of the Naval Staff or usages or custom of the naval service exercises or performs that power or duty or is concerned with that act or matter[1].

1 The Regulations for the Navy 1965, Part II, regulation 2 (g).

[0932] Provost marshal In the Navy Act 1957, unless the context otherwise requires, 'provost-marshal' means a person appointed as such under the provisions of the aforesaid Act[1] and includes any of his deputies or assistants or any other person lawfully exercising authority under him or on his behalf[2].

1 Ie under the Navy Act 1957 s 89; see **[1046]**.

2 The Navy Act 1957 s 3 (19).

[0933] Sailor In the Navy Act 1957, unless the context otherwise requires, 'sailor' means a person in the naval service other than an officer[1].

1 As to the meaning of 'officer'; see **[0927]**. The Navy Act 1957 s 3 (20). All leading sailors shall be granted every reasonable indulgence and they shall be made to feel that confidence is reposed in them and shall be treated with the consideration which is due to the position of trust which they hold. On all occasions of sailors falling in, leading sailors shall do so separately from other sailors except on ceremonial parades, when leading sailors may be included in the ranks. Leading sailors dressed in the established uniform shall be allowed to pass dockyard gates and may also pass out parties of men. It shall be the duty of leading sailors to preserve order and regularity wherever the crew or any part of it may be employed and this responsibility rests upon them whenever they are with the sailors whether on duty or not. For more details on the duties and privileges of leading sailors, see the Regulations for the Navy 1965, Part II, regulation 223.

[0934] Ship In the Navy Act 1957, unless the context otherwise requires, 'ship' except in the expression 'on board a ship' includes an establishment of the Indian Navy commissioned as a ship in accordance with the custom of the navy[1].

1 The Navy Act 1957 s 3 (21).

[0935] Subject to the naval law In the Navy Act 1957, unless the context otherwise requires, 'subject to the naval law' means liable to be arrested and tried under the Navy Act 1957 for any offence[1].

1 The Navy Act 1957 s 3 (22).

[0936] Subordinate officer In the Navy Act 1957, unless the context otherwise requires, 'subordinate officer' means a person appointed as an acting sub-lieutenant, a midshipman or a cadet in any branch of the Indian Navy or the Indian Naval Reserve forces, but does not include a cadet whilst under training in a joint service institution[1].

1 The Navy Act 1957 s 3 (23).

[0937] Superior officer In the Navy Act 1957, unless the context otherwise requires, 'superior officer', when used in relation to a person subject to naval law, means any officer or petty officer who is senior to that person under Regulations for the Navy and any officer or petty officer, who though not senior to that person, is entitled under the aforesaid Act or the Regulations to give a command to that person. The term 'superior officer', when such person is serving under prescribed conditions, includes an officer, junior commissioned officer, warrant officer, non-commissioned officer of the regular army or the air force of higher relative rank to that person or entitled under the Navy Act 1957 or the Regulations to give a command to that person[1].

1 The Navy Act 1957 s 3 (24).

[0938] Words and expressions not defined In the Navy Act 1957, all words and expression used but not defined, but defined in the Indian Penal Code 1860, shall have the meaning respectively assigned to them in that code[1].

1 The Navy Act 1957 s 3 (25).

[0939] Cases un-provided for In regard of any matter not specifically provided for in the Regulations for the Navy 1965, Part II, it shall be lawful for the competent authority to do such thing or take action as it appears to be just and proper[1].

1 The Regulations for the Navy 1965, Part II, regulations 6.

D. Naval Forces and persons subject to Naval Law

[0940] Power of Central Government to raise and maintain naval forces The Central Government may raise and maintain a regular naval force and also reserve and auxiliary naval forces[1].

1 The Navy Act 1957 s 5.

[0941] Persons subject to naval law

1 The following persons shall be subject to naval law[1] wherever they may be: (a) every person belonging to the Indian Navy[2] during the time that he is liable for service under the Navy Act 1950[3]; (b) every person belonging to the Indian Naval Reserve Forces[4] when he is: (i) on active service[5], (ii) in or on any property of the naval service including naval establishments[6], ships[7] and other vessels, aircraft, vehicles and armories[8], (iii) called up for training or undergoing training in pursuance of regulations made under the aforesaid Act, until he is duly released from his training[9], (iv) called up into actual service in the Indian Navy in pursuance of regulations made under the aforesaid Act, until he is duly released there from[10], or (v) in uniform[11]; (c) members of the regular army and air force when embarked on board any ship or aircraft of the Indian Navy, to such extent and subject to such conditions as may be prescribed[12]; (d) every person not otherwise subject to naval law, who enters into an agreement with the Central Government under certain provision of the Navy Act 1957[13]; (e) every person belonging to any auxiliary forces raised under the aforesaid Act, to such extent and subject to such conditions as may be prescribed[14]; and (f) every person who, although he would not otherwise be subject to Naval law, is by any other Act or during active service by regulations made under the aforesaid Act in this behalf made subject to naval law, to such extent and subject to such conditions as many be prescribed[15].

2 The following persons shall be deemed to be persons subject to naval law: (a) every person ordered to be received, or being a passenger, on board any ship or aircraft of the Indian Navy, to such extend and subject to such conditions as may be prescribed[16]; (b) every person sentenced under the Navy Act 1957 to imprisonment or detention, during the term of his sentence, notwithstanding that he is discharged or dismissed with or without disgrace from the naval service or would otherwise but for this provision cease to be subject to naval law[17].

1 As to the meaning of 'subject to naval law'; see **[0941]**.

2 As to the meaning of 'Indian Navy'; see **[0919]**.

3 The Navy Act 1957 s 2 (1) (a).

4 As to the definition of 'Indian Naval Reserve Forces'; see **[0918]**.

5 As to the definition of 'active service'; see **[0905]**. The Navy Act 1957 s 2 (1) (b) (i).

6 As to the definition of 'naval service'; see **[0924]**.

7 As to the definition of 'naval establishment'; see **[0922]**.

8 The Navy Act 1957 s 2 (1) (b) (ii).

9 The Navy Act 1957 s 2 (1) (b) (iii).

10 The Navy Act 1957 s 2 (1) (b) (iv).

11 The Navy Act 1957 s 2 (1) (b) (v).

12 The Navy Act 1957 s 2 (1) (c).

13 Ie under the Navy Act 1957 s 6; see **[0943]**. The Navy Act 1957 s 2 (1) (d).

14 The Navy Act 1957 s 2 (1) (e).

15 The Navy Act 1957 s 2 (1) (f).

16 The Navy Act 1957 s 2 (2) (a).

17 The Navy Act 1957 s 2 (2) (b).

[0942] Provisions as to existing naval forces, appointments, etc. The Indian Navy in existence at the commencement of the Navy Act 1957 shall be deemed to be the regular naval force raised under the aforesaid Act[1]. The Indian Naval Reserve, the Indian Naval Volunteer Reserve and the Indian Fleet Reserve in existence at the commencement of the Navy Act 1957 shall be deemed to be the Indian Naval Reserve Forces raised under the aforesaid Act[2]. Officers in the Indian Navy or the Indian Naval Reserve Forces at the commencement of the Navy Act 1957 shall be deemed to have been appointed as such under the aforesaid Act[3]. The person holding office as judge advocate of the feet at the commencement of the Navy Act 1957 shall on such commencement be deemed to have been appointed as the judge advocate general of the navy under the aforesaid Act[4]. Sailors in the Indian Navy or in the Indian Naval Reserve Forces at the commencement of the Navy Act 1957 shall be deemed to have been dully enrolled as such under the aforesaid Act[5].

1 The Navy Act 1957 s 187 (1).

2 The Navy Act 1957 s 187 (2).

3 The Navy Act 1957 s 187 (3).

4 The Navy Act 1957 s 187 (4).

5 The Navy Act 1957 s 187 (5).

[0943] Provisions respecting disciplines of persons under engagements to serve Central Government

1 If any person not otherwise subject to Naval law[1] enters to into a engagement with the Central Government to serve: (i) in a particular ship[2]; or (ii) in such particular ship or in such ships as the Central Government, the Chief of the Naval Staff, or the prescribed officer may from time to time, determine[3]; and agrees to become subject to naval law upon entering into the engagement, that person shall, so long as the engagement remains in force and notwithstanding that for the time being he may not be serving in any ship, be subject to naval law[4].

2 The Central Government may, by order, direct that subject to such exceptions as may in particular cases be made by or on behalf of the Chief of the Naval Staff[5], persons of any such class as may be specified in the order shall, while being subject to naval law by virtue of this provision, be officer[6], petty officers[7], or other sailors[8], for the purposes of the Navy Act 1957 or of such provisions of the aforesaid Act as may be so specified[9].

1 As to the meaning of 'person subject to naval law'; see **[0941]**.

2 The Navy Act 1957 s 6 (1) (a).

3 The Navy Act 1957 s 6 (1) (b).

4 The Navy Act 1957 s 6 (1).

5 As to the meaning of 'chief of the naval staff'; see **[0907]**.

6 As to the meaning of 'officer'; see **[0927]**.

7 As to the meaning of 'petty officer'; see **[0928]**.

8 As to the meaning of 'sailor'; see **[0933]**.

9 The Navy Act 1957 s 6 (2).

[0944] Relationship between the members of the Navy, Army and Air Force acting together When members of the regular army and the air force or either of these forces are serving with members of the Indian navy or Indian naval reserve forces under prescribed conditions, then those members of the regular army or the air force shall exercise such command, and be subject to such discipline as may be prescribed[1]. However, the aforesaid provision does not authorize the exercise of powers of punishment by members of the regular army or the air force over members of the Indian navy or the Indian naval reserve forces, except as provided in certain provisions of the Navy Act 1957[2], or in such cases and subject to such conditions as may be prescribed[3].

1 The Navy Act 1957 s 7 (1).

2 Ie the Navy Act 1957 s 93 (3) (e).

3 The Navy Act 1957 s 7 (2).

[0945] Provision respecting discipline of master of merchant vessel under convoy Every master or other person for the time being in command of any merchant or other vessel comprised in a convey under the command of an officer of the Indian navy shall obey, in all matters relating to the navigation or security of the convey, any directions which may be given by such officer, and shall take such precautions for avoiding the enemy as may required by any such direction[1]. If any such directions are not obeyed, any such officer or any person acting under his orders may compel obedience by force of arms without being liable for any injury or loss of life or any danger to or loss of property resulting there from[2].

1 The Navy Act 1957 s 8 (1). As to the definition of 'enemy'; see **[0916]**.

2 The Navy Act 1957 s 8 (2).

2. CONSTITUTIONAL PROVISIONS

CONTENTS

PARA

[0946] President of India The President of India is the supreme commander of the armed forces and the exercise of this command is to be regulated by law[1]. The President has to act on the advice of the Council of Ministers[2]. It is the duty of the Union to protect every state against external aggression and internal disturbance[3].

1 Constitution of India, art 53 (2): Without prejudices to the generality of the foregoing provision, the supreme command of the Defence Forces of the Union shall be vested in the President and the exercise thereof shall be regulated by law.

2 Constitution of India, art 74 (1).

3 Constitution of India, art 355.

[0947] Power of Parliament to modify fundamental rights Parliament may, by law, determine to what extent any of the rights conferred by the Part III of the Constitution shall, in their application to:

(1) the members of the armed forces[1];

(2) the members of the forces charged with the maintenance of public order[2];

(3) persons employed in any bureau or other organization established by the State for purposes of intelligence or counter intelligence[3]; or

(4) person employed in, or in connection with the telecommunication systems set up for the purposes of any force, bureau or organization referred to above[4],

be restricted or abrogated so as to ensure the proper discharge of their duties and maintenance of discipline among them[5].

1 Constitution of India, art 33 (a).

2 Constitution of India, art 33 (b).

3 Constitution of India, art 33 (c).

4 Constitution of India, art 33 (d).

5 Constitution of India, art 33. For more details, see **[0046]**.

[0948] Fundamental rights to apply to persons subject to naval law with modification The rights conferred by Part III of the Constitution in their application to persons subject to naval law[1] shall be restricted or abrogated to the extent provided in the Navy Act 1957[2].

1 As to the meaning of 'persons subject to naval law'; see **[0941]**.

2 Ie as provided in the Navy Act 1957 s 19; see **[0949]**; The Navy Act 1957 s 4.

[0949] Restrictions respecting right to form associations, freedom of speech, etc.

1 No person subject to Naval law[1] shall, without the express sanction of the Central Government: (i) be a member of, or be associated in any way with, any trade union, labour union, political association or with any class of trade unions, labour unions or political association[2], or (ii) be a member of, or be associated in any way with, any other society, institution, association or organization that is not recognized as part of the Armed Forces of the Union or is not of a purely social, recreational or religious nature[3]. If any questions arise as to whether any society, institution, association or organization is of a purely social, recreational or religious nature, the decision of the Central Government thereon shall be final[4].

2 No person subject to naval law shall attend or address any meeting or take any part in any demonstration organized by any body of persons for any political purposes or for such other purposes as may be specified in this behalf by Central Government[5].

3 No person subject to naval law shall communicate with the press or publish or cause to be published in any book, letter or other document having bearing on any naval, army or air force subject or containing any Act or opinion calculated to embarrass the relations between the government and the people or any section thereof or between the Government and any foreign country, except with the previous sanction of the Central Government[6].

4 No person subject to naval law shall whilst he is so subject practice any profession or carry on any other occupation, trade or business without the previous sanction of the Chief of the Naval Staff[7].

1 As to the meaning of 'persons subject to naval law'; see **[0941]**.

2 The Navy Act 1957 s 19 (1) (a).

3 The Navy Act 1957 s 19 (1) (b).

4 The Navy Act 1957 s 19 explanation.

5 The Navy Act 1957 s 19 (2).

6 The Navy Act 1957 s 19 (3).

7 The Navy Act 1957 s 19 (4).

3. REGULATIONS OF SERVICE

CONTENTS

PARA

A. Commission, Appointment and Enrolments

B. Conditions of service

A. Commission, Appointment and Enrolments

[0950] Eligibility for appointment or enrolment No person who is not a citizen of India shall be eligible for appointment or enrolment in the Indian navy or the Indian naval reserve force except with the consent of the Central Government[1]. However, nothing in this provision shall render a person ineligible for appointment or enrolment in the Indian navy or the Indian naval reserve forces on the ground that he is a subject of Nepal[2].

No woman shall be eligible for appointment or enrolment in the Indian navy or the Indian naval reserve force except in such department, branch or other body forming part thereof or attached thereto and subject to such conditions as the Central Government may, by notification in the official Gazette, specify in this behalf[3].

1 As to the definition of 'Indian Navy' and 'Indian Naval Reserve Force; see **[0919]** and **[0918]**. The Navy Act 1957 s 9 (1). This provision is similar to the Army Act 1950 s 11; see **[0052]**.

2 The Navy Act 1957 s 9 (1) proviso.

3 The Navy Act 1957 s 9 (2).

[0951] Commissions and appointments Officers[1] other than subordinate officers shall be appointed by commission granted by the President[2]. The grant of commission shall be notified in the official gazette and such notification shall be conclusive proof of the grant of such commission[3]. Subordinate officers shall be appointed in such manner and shall hold such rank as may be prescribed[4].

1 As to the definition of the term 'officer'; see **[0927]**.

2 The Navy Act 1957 s 10 (1).

3 The Navy Act 1957 s 10 (2).

4 The Navy Act 1957 s 10 (3).

[0952] Enrolment The terms and conditions of service of sailors[1], the person authorised to enroll, for service as sailors and the manner and procedure of such enrolment shall be as prescribed[2]. No person shall be enrolled as a sailor in the Indian navy for a period exceeding 20 years in the first instance[3]. However, in the case of a minor, the said period of 20 years shall be reckoned from the date on which he attains the age of 17[4]. Notwithstanding anything contained in any other law for the time being in force: (i) the enrolment of any person under the Navy Act 1957 shall be binding on him both during his minority and after he attains majority[5]; (ii) neither the parent or guardian of a minor duly enrolled under the aforesaid Act nor any other person shall be entitled to claim custody of the said minor as against the central government or any of its officers or other person set over him[6].

1 As to the definition of the term 'sailor'; see **[0933]**.

2 The Navy Act 1957 s 11 (1).

3 The Navy Act 1957 s 11 (2).

4 The Navy Act 1957 s 11 (2) proviso.

5 The Navy Act 1957 s 11 (3) (a).

6 The Navy Act 1957 s 11 (3) (b). Also see: *Anuj Kumar Dey v Union of India* Mil LJ 1998 SC.

[0953] Validity of enrolment Where a person after his enrolment has for a period of three months from the date of such enrolment been in receipt of pay as a sailor[1], he shall be deemed to have been duly enrolled and shall not thereafter be entitled to claim his discharge on the ground of any irregularity or illegality in his engagement or any other ground whatsoever; and if within the said three months such person claims his discharge, no such irregularity or illegality or other ground shall, until such person is discharged in pursuance of his claim affect his position as a sailor in the naval service or invalidate any proceedings, act or thing taken or done prior to his discharge[2].

1 As to the definition of the term 'sailor'; see **[0933]**.

2 The Navy Act 1957 s 12.

[0954] Oath of allegiance Every officer[1] and every sailor[2] shall, as soon as may be, after appointment or enrolment make and subscribe before the commanding officer[3] of the ship[4] to which he belongs, or the prescribed officer an oath or affirmation in the following form:

> I,.........do swear in the name of God/solemnly affirm, that I will bear true faith and allegiance to the Constitution of India as by law established and that I will, as in duty bound, honestly and faithfully serve in the naval service and go wherever ordered by sea, land or air, and that I will, observe and obey all commands of the President and the commands of any superior officer set over me, even to the peril of my life[5].

1 As to the definition of the term 'officer'; see **[0927]**.

2 As to the definition of the term 'sailor'; see **[0933]**.

3 As to the definition of the term 'commanding officer'; see **[0912]**.

4 As to the definition of the term 'ship'; see **[0934]**.

5 The Navy Act 1957 s 13. Where an applicant had joined the Indian navy as sailor and immediately after his enrolment he was made to take an oath which every officer and sailor is bound to take under this provisions of the Navy Act 1957, it was held that the training period will be included in the computation of the qualifying period of service for earning pension. *Anuj Kumar Dey v Union of India* Mil LJ 1998 SC.

B. Conditions of service

[0955] Liability of service of officers and sailors Subject to certain provision of the Navy Act 1957[1], officers[2] and sailors[3] shall be liable to serve in the Indian navy or the Indian naval reserve forces, until they are duly discharged, dismissed with disgrace, retired, permitted to resign, or released[4]. No officer shall be at liberty to resign his office except with the permission of the central government and no sailor shall be at liberty to resign his post except with the permission of the prescribed officer[5]. The acceptance of any resignation shall be a matter within the discretion of the central government or the officer concerned[6]. Officers retired or permitted to resign shall be liable to recall to naval service in an emergency in accordance with Regulations for the Navy made under the Navy Act 1957, and on such recall shall be liable to serve until they have been duly discharged, dismissed, dismissed with disgrace, retired, permitted to resign or released[7].

1 Ie the Navy Act 1957 s 14 (4).

2 As to the definition of the term 'officer'; see **[0927]**.

3 As to the definition of the term 'sailor'; see **[0933]**.

4 The Navy Act 1957 s 14 (1).

5 The Navy Act 1957 s 14 (2).

6 The Navy Act 1957 s 14 (3).

7 The Navy Act 1957 s 14 (4).

[0956] Tenure of service officers and sailors Every officer[1] and sailor[2] shall hold office during the pleasure of the President[3]. Subject to certain provisions of the Navy Act 1957 and the Regulations for the Navy: (i) the central government may dismiss or discharge or retire from the naval service any officer or sailor[4], (ii) the chief of the naval staff or any prescribed officer may dismiss or discharge from the naval service any sailor[5].

1 As to the definition of the term 'officer'; see **[0927]**.

2 As to the definition of the term 'sailor'; see **[0933]**.

3 The Navy Act 19571 s 15 (1). For procedure to be followed for termination of service; see **[1120]** and **[1121]**.

4 The Navy Act 19571 s 15 (2) (a).

5 The Navy Act 19571 s 15 (2) (b).

[0957] Discharge on expiry of engagements Subject to certain provisions of the Navy Act 1957[1], a sailor[2] shall be entitled to be discharged at the expiration of the term of service for which he is engaged unless: (i) such expiration occurs during active service in which case he shall be liable to continue to serve for such further period as may be required by the chief of the naval staff[3]; or (ii) he is re-enrolled in accordance with the Regulations for the Navy[4].

1 Ie the Navy Act 1957 s 18; see **[0960]**.

2 As to the definition of the term 'sailor'; see **[0933]**.

3 As to the definition of 'active service'; see **[0905]**. The Navy Act 19571 s 16 (a).

4 The Navy Act 19571 s 16 (b)

[0958] Provisions as to discharge A sailor entitled to be discharged under the Navy Act 1957 s 16 shall be discharged with all convenient speed and in any case within one month of his becoming so entitled[1]. However, where a sailor is serving overseas at the time he becomes entitled to be discharged, he shall be returned to India for the purpose of being discharged with all convenient speed and in any case within three months of his becoming so entitled[2]. Further, where such enrolled person serving overseas does not desire to return to India, he may be discharged at the place where he is at the time[3]. Every sailor discharged shall be entitled to be conveyed free of cost from any place he may be at the time to any place in India to which he may desire to go[4]. Notwithstanding anything contained in the preceding provisions, an enrolled person shall remain liable to serve until he is duly discharged[5]. Every sailor who is dismissed, discharged, retired, permitted to resign or released from service shall be furnished by the prescribed officer with a certificate in the language which is the mother tongue of such sailor and also in the English language setting fourth: (i) the authority terminating his service[6], (ii) the cause for such termination[7]; and (iii) the full period of his service in the Indian navy and the Indian naval reserve forces[8].

1 The Navy Act 1957 s 17 (1).

2 The Navy Act 1957 s 17 (1) proviso.

3 The Navy Act 1957 s 17 (1) additional proviso.

4 The Navy Act 1957 s 17 (2).

5 The Navy Act 1957 s 17 (3).

6 The Navy Act 1957 s 17 (4) (a).

7 The Navy Act 1957 s 17 (4) (b).

8 The Navy Act 1957 s 17 (4) (c).

[0959] Date from which dismissal, discharge, retirement, resignation takes effect The dismissal or discharge of an officer under the Navy Act 1957[1] or the retirement, resignation or release of such officer shall take effect from the date specified in the order of dismissal, discharge, retirement, resignation or release, and shall be notified in the official Gazette[2]. The dismissal, discharge, retirement, resignation or release of persons subject to naval law shall not be retrospective[3].

1 Ie the Navy Act 1957 s 15.

2 The Regulations for the Navy 1965, Volume II, regulation 219 (1).

3 The Regulations for the Navy 1965, Volume II, regulation 219 (2).

[0960] Saving of powers of dismissal by naval tribunals The provisions contained in the Navy Act 1950[1] shall not affect the award of the punishment of dismissal with disgrace or dismissal from the naval service under the Navy Act 1957 by a naval tribunal[2].

1 Ie as contained in Chapter V of the Navy Act 1957 s 14 to 17.

2 As to the definition of 'naval tribunal'; see **[0925]**. The Navy Act 1957 s 18.

[0961] Re-instatement of persons belonging to the Indian Naval Reserve Forces on termination of period of training or actual service with the Indian Navy

1 If a person belonging to the Indian naval reserve forces is, during the period of his employment under an employer called up for training or called up into actual service with the Indian navy in pursuance of his liability under any regulations made under the Navy Act 1957, it shall be the duty of every such employer to reinstate the person in his employment on the termination if the period of his training or service with the Indian navy in an occupation and under conditions not less favourable to him than those which would have been applicable to him had his employment not been so interrupted[1]. However, if the employer refuses to reinstate such person or denies his liability to reinstate such person, or if for any reason reinstatement of such person is represented by the employer to be impracticable, either party may refer the matter to the authority prescribed in this behalf and that authority shall, after considering all matters which may be put before it and after making such further inquiry into the matters as may be prescribed, pass an order: (i) exempting the employer from the application of this provisions[2], (ii) requiring the employer to re-employ such person on such terms as the authority thinks suitable[3], or (iii) requiring the employer to pay to such person by way of compensation for failure or inability to re-employ a sum not exceeding an amount equal to six months' remuneration at the rate at which his last remuneration was payable to him by the employer[4].

2 If any employer fails to obey the order of any such authority as is referred to in the aforesaid provision[5], he shall be punishable with fine which may be extended to Rs 1,000/-, and the court by which an employer is convicted under this provision shall order him (if he has not already been so required by the authority) to pay to the person whom he has failed to re-employ a sum equal to six months' remuneration at the rate at which his last remuneration was payable to him by the employer, and any amount so required to be paid either by the said authority or by the court shall be recoverable as if it were a fine imposed by such court[6].

3 In any proceeding under this provision it shall be a defence for an employee to prove that the person formerly employed did not apply to the employer for re-instatement within a period of two months from the termination of the period of his training or service with the Indian navy[7].

4 The duty imposed by the provision of the Navy Act 1957[8] upon an employer to reinstate in his employment a person such as is described in that provision shall attach to an employer who, before such

person is actually called up for training, or called up into actual service with the Indian navy, terminates his employment in circumstance such as to indicate an intention to evades the duty imposed by that provision, and such intention shall be presumed until the contrary is proved, if the termination takes place after the issue of orders calling him up for training or service with the Indian navy under the Navy Act 1957[9].

1 The Navy Act 1957 s 19A (1).

2 The Navy Act 1957 s 19A (1) proviso (a).

3 The Navy Act 1957 s 19A (1) proviso (b).

4 The Navy Act 1957 s 19A (1) proviso (c).

5 Ie the Navy Act 1957 s 19A (1) proviso.

6 The Navy Act 1957 s 19A (2).

7 The Navy Act 1957 s 19A (3).

8 Ie the Navy Act 1957 s 19A (1).

9 The Navy Act 1957 s 19A (4).

[0962] Preservation of service rights belonging to the Indian Naval Reserve Forces when called up for training or actual service with the Indian Navy When any person belonging to the Indian Naval Reserve Force and called up for training or actual service with the Indian navy in pursuance of his liability under any the Regulations for the Navy, has any rights under any provident fund or superannuating fund or other scheme for the benefit of employees maintained in connection with the employment he relinquishes, he shall continue, so long as he is engaged in training or service with the Indian navy and if he is reinstated, until such reinstatement under the Navy Act 1957, to have in respect of such fund or scheme such rights as may be prescribed[1].

1 The Navy Act 1957 s 19B.

C. Provisions as to Pay, Pension and Maintenance of Families

[0963] Deductions from pay, etc., not to be made unless authorised No deductions other than those authorized by or under the Navy Act 1957 or any other Act shall be made from the pay, pensions, gratuities, allowances and other benefits due to officers[1] and sailors[2] under any regulations for the time being in force[3].

1 As to the definition of the term 'officer'; see **[0927]**.

2 As to the definition of the term 'sailor'; see **[0933]**.

3 The Navy Act 1957 s 27.

[0964] Deductions from pay and allowances of officers The following deductions may be made from the pay and allowances of an officer without recourse to trial by a naval tribunal[1]: (i) all pay and allowance for everyday of absence without leave unless an explanation is given to the satisfaction of the commanding officer for such absence and approved by the chief of the naval staff[2]. However, the officer is not dealt with by a naval tribunal for the said absence[3]; (ii) all pay and allowance for everyday while he is in civil or naval custody or under suspension from duty on charge for an offence of which he is afterwards convicted by a competent naval tribunal or criminal court and sentenced to imprisonment[4]; (iii) all pay and allowance for everyday while he is in hospital on account of sickness certified by the prescribed medical officer to have been caused by an act amounting to an offence punishable under the Navy Act 1957, provided that such certificate is accepted by the chief of naval staff[5]. (iv) any sum required to make good the pay and allowances of any person subject to naval law which he has unlawfully retained or refused to pay[6]; (v) any sum required to make good any loss, damage or destruction of government property or property belonging to a naval mess, band or institution which after due investigation appears to the central government, the chief of the naval staff or the prescribed officer to have been occasioned by the wrongful act or negligence on the part of the officer[7]; (vi) any sum required to be paid for the maintenance of his wife or legitimate or illegitimate children under the provisions of the Navy Act 1957[8]; (vii) any sum which after due investigation appears to the prescribed officer to be due to a service mess or canteen[9].

1 As to the definition of the term 'officer' and 'naval tribunal'; see **[0927] and [0925].**

2 The Navy Act 1957 s 28 (1).

3 The Navy Act 1957 s 28 (1) proviso.

4 The Navy Act 1957 s 28 (2).

5 The Navy Act 1957 s 28 (3).

6 The Navy Act 1957 s 28 (4).

7 The Navy Act 1957 s 28 (5).

8 Ie under the Navy Act s 31; The Navy Act 1957 s 28 (6).

9 The Navy Act 1957 s 28 (7).

[0965] Deductions from pay and allowances of sailors The following deductions may be made from the pay and allowances of a sailor without recourse to trial by a naval tribunal[1]: (i) all pay and allowances for every day of absence without leave unless an explanation is given to the satisfaction of the commanding officer for such absence[2]; (ii) all pay and allowances for everyday he is in confinement on a charge for an offence of which he is afterwards convicted by a competent naval tribunal or criminal court[3]; (iii) all pay and allowance for everyday he is in hospital on account of sickness certified by the prescribed medical officer to have been caused by an act amounting to an offence punishable under the Navy Act 1957[4]; (iv) any sum required to make good any loss, damage or destruction of any property which after due investigation appears to be central government or the chief of the naval staff or the prescribed officer to have been occasioned by the wrongful act or negligence on the part of the sailor[5]; (v) any sum required to be paid for the maintenance of his wife or legitimated or illegitimate children under the provision of the Navy Act 1957[6].

From a plain reading of the Navy Act 1957 s 29 and Regulations for the Navy 1965, part II, regulations 118 and 119(1), it clearly transpires that the intent of these provisions is that forfeiture should follow after the conviction of the incumbent[7].

1 As to the definition of the term 'sailor' and 'naval tribunal'; see **[0933]** and **[0925].**

2 The Navy Act 1957 s 29 (1).

3 The Navy Act 1957 s 29 (1).

4 The Navy Act 1957 s 29 (1).

5 The Navy Act 1957 s 29 (1).

6 Ie under the Navy Act s 31; The Navy Act 1957 s 29 (5).

7 *Chand Kumar Prasad v Union of India*, OA No 78 of 2013, decided by the Armed Forces Tribunal, principal bench, New Delhi on 6 August 2013.

[0966] Deductions awarded by the naval tribunals Deductions may be made from the pay and allowances of an officer[1] or sailor[2] in respect of any sentence of fine, forfeiture or mulcts of pay and allowances awarded by a naval tribunal[3].

1 As to the definition of the term 'officer'; see **[0927]**.

2 As to the definition of the term 'sailor'; see **[0933]**.

3 As to the definition of 'naval tribunal'; see **[0925].** The Navy Act 1957 s 30.

[0967] Liability of maintenance of wife and children

1 A person subject to naval law[1] shall be liable to maintain his wife and his legitimate or illegitimate children to the same extent as if he were not so subject; but the execution or enforcement of any decree or order for maintenance passed or made against such person shall not be directed against his person, pay, arms, ammunition, equipments instruments or clothing[2].

2 Notwithstanding anything contained in the aforesaid provision: (i) where it appears to the satisfaction of the prescribed authority[3] that a person subject to naval law has without reasonable cause deserted or left in destitute circumstance his wife or any legitimate child unable to maintain himself or has by reason of contracting a second marriage become liable to provide separate maintenance to his first wife[4]; (ii) where any decree or order is passed under any law against a person who is, or subsequently becomes, subject to naval law for the maintenance for his wife or his legitimate or illegitimate children and a copy of the decree or order is sent to the prescribed authority, such authority may direct a portion of the pay of the person so subject to naval law to be deducted from such pay and appropriated in the prescribed manner towards the maintenance of his wife or children. The amount deducted shall not exceed the amount fixed by the decree or order (if any) and shall not be at a higher rate than the rate fixed by the Regulations for the Navy[5]. However, in the case of a decree or order for maintenance referred to in the aforesaid provision no deduction from pay shall be directed unless the prescribed authority is satisfied with the person against whom such decree or order has been passed or made has had a reasonable opportunity of appearing or has actually appeared either in person or through a duly appointed legal practitioner, to defend the case before the court by which the decree or order was passed or made[6].

3 Where arrears of maintenance under a decree or order referred to in the aforesaid provision[7] have accumulated while the person against whom the decree or order has been made is subject to the naval law whether or not deductions in respect thereof have been made from his pay under these provisions, no step for the recovery of those arrears shall be taken in any court after such person has ceased to be so subject unless the court is satisfied that he has, since he ceased to be subject to naval law, the ability to pay the arrears or any part thereof and has failed to do so[8].

4 Notwithstanding anything contained in any other law, where a proceeding for obtaining a decree or order for maintenances is started against a person subject to naval law: (i) the court may send the process for service on that person to the commanding officer[9] of the ship[10] on the such person is serving or on the books of which he is borne[11], (ii) if, by reason of the ship being at sea or otherwise, it is impracticable for the court to send the process to the commanding officer, the court may, after

not less than three weeks, notice to the central government send it to a secretary to that government for transmission to the commanding officer for service on that person[12]. However, such service shall not be valid unless there is sent along with the process such of money as may be prescribed to enable that person to attend the hearing of the proceeding and to return to his ship or quarters after such attendance[13].

5 If a decree or order is passed or made in the proceeding against the person on whom the process is served, the sum sent along with the process shall be awarded as costs of the proceeding against that person[14].

6 No process in any proceeding under these provisions shall be valid against a person subject to naval law if served on in after he is under orders for service at a foreign station or beyond Indian waters[15].

7 The production of certificate of the receipt of the process purporting to be signed by such commanding officer as aforesaid shall be evidence that the process has been duly served, unless contrary is proved[16].

8 Where by a decree or order a copy whereof has been sent to the central government or the chief of the naval staff or the prescribed authority under the Navy Act 1957[17], the person against whom the decree or order has been passed or made is directed to pay as costs any sum sent along with the process referred to in the aforesaid Act[18], the central government may pay to the person entitled an amount in full satisfaction of that sum and the amount so paid by the central government shall be deemed to be a public demand recoverable from the person against whom the decree or order has been passed or made, and without prejudice to any other mode of recovery, may be recovered by deduction from his pay, in addition to the deductions authorized by the Navy Act 1957[19].

9 Where any person subject to naval law has made an allotment of any part of his pay and allowances for the benefit of his wife, that allowance shall not be discontinued or reduced until the prescribed authority is satisfied that the allotment should no longer be made or should be reduced[20].

10 In these provisions the expression 'pay' includes all the sums payable to a person subject to naval law in respect of his services other than allowance in lieu of lodgings, rations, provisions clothing and travelling allowances[21].

1 As to the meaning of the term 'persons subject to naval law'; see **[0941]**.

2 The Navy Act 1957 s 31 (1).

3 The central government, the chief of the naval staff or any other prescribed authority may take cognizance under this provision.

4 The Navy Act 1957 s 31 (2) (a).

5 The Navy Act 1957 s 31 (2) (b).

6 The Navy Act 1957 s 31 (2) (b) proviso.

7 The Navy Act 1957 s 31 (2).

8 The Navy Act 1957 s 31 (3).

9 As to the definition of 'commanding officer'; see **[0912]**.

10 As to the definition of 'ship'; see **[0934]**.

11 The Navy Act 1957 s 31 (4) (a).

12 The Navy Act 1957 s 31 (4) (b).

13 The Navy Act 1957 s 31 (4) proviso.

14 The Navy Act 1957 s 31 (5)

15 The Navy Act 1957 s 31 (6)

16 The Navy Act 1957 s 31 (7)

17 Ie under the Navy Act 1957 s 31 (2) (b).

18 As referred to in the Navy Act 1957 s 31 (4) proviso.

19 Ie under the Navy Act 1957 s 31 (2); The Navy Act 1957 s 31 (8).

20 The Navy Act 1957 s 31 (9).

21 The Navy Act 1957 s 31 (10).

[0968] Limit of certain deductions Except when the deductions are made under certain provisions of the Navy Act 1957[1], the total deductions from the pay and allowances of an officer or sailor shall not exceed in any one month one-half of his pay and allowances for that month[2].

1 Ie under the Navy Act 1957 s 28 (1), (2) and (4) or s 29 (1) and (2).

2 The Navy Act 1957 s 32.

[0969] Remission of deductions Any deduction from the pay and allowances authorized by or under the Navy Act 1957 may be remitted by the chief of the naval staff in his discretion[1]. Such deduction may also be remitted in such manner and to such extent and by such other authority as may be prescribed[2].

1 The Navy Act 1957 s 33 (1).

2 The Navy Act 1957 s 33 (2).

D. Service Privileges

[0970] Immunity from attachment The arms, cloths equipments, accoutrements or necessaries of any person in the Naval service, while subject to Naval law[1], shall not be seized, nor shall the pay and allowances of such person be attached under any process or direction issued by, or by the authority of, any court or public servant in respect of any claim decree or order enforceable against him[2].

1 As to the meaning of 'person subject to naval law'; see the Navy Act 1957 s 3 (22): **[0941].**

2 The Navy Act 1957 s 20.

[0971] Immunity from arrest or debt No person in the naval service shall, so long as he is subject to naval law[1], be liable to be arrested for debt under any process or direction issued by, or by the authority of, any court or public servant[2]. If any such person is arrested in contravention of the provision of the aforesaid provision the court or public servant by whom or by whose or by whose authority such process or direction was issued shall on complaint by the person arrested or by his superior officer enquires into the case and if satisfied that the arrest was made in contravention of aforesaid provision, shall make an order for the immediate discharge of the person arrested and may award to the complainant the costs of the complaint to be recoverable in the same manner as if such costs were awarded to him by a decree against the person at whose instance such process or direction was issued[3]. No court fee shall be payable on a complaint made under the aforesaid provision[4] or for recovery of the costs that may be awarded under that provision[5].

1 As to the meaning of 'person subject to naval law'; see the Navy Act 1957 s 3 (22): **[0941].**

2 The Navy Act 1957 s 21 (1)

3 The Navy Act 1957 s 21 (2).

4 Ie the Navy Act 1957 s 21 (2).

5 The Navy Act 1957 s 21 (3).

[0972] Immunity of person attending court martial or disciplinary court from arrest President or other member of a court martial[1] or disciplinary court[2], judge advocate, party to any proceeding before a court martial or disciplinary court or advocate or agent of such party, and witness acting in obedience to a summons to attend a court martial or disciplinary court, while proceeding to, attending or returning form, a court martial or disciplinary court shall not be be liable to arrest under any civil or revenue process[3]. If any such person is arrested under any such process, he may be discharged by order of the court-martial or disciplinary court[4].

1 As to the meaning of 'court martial'; see the Navy Act 1957 s 3 (6): **[0915]**.

2 Ie the 'disciplinary court' held under the Navy Act 1957 s 95: see **[1228] to [1230]**.

3 The Navy Act 1957 s 22 (1).

4 The Navy Act 1957 s 22 (2).

[0973] Remedy of aggrieved person If an officer or sailor[1] thinks that he has suffered any personal oppression injustice or other ill treatment at the hands of any superior officer[2], he may make a complaint in accordance with the Regulations for the Navy 1965, Part II[3]. If the complainant is not satisfied with the decision on his complaint, it should be forwarded to the Central Government[4].

1 As to the definition of 'officer' and 'sailor'; see **[0927]** and **[0933]**.

2 As to the definition of 'superior officer'; see **[0937]**.

3 Ie the Regulations for the Navy 1965, Part II, statutory. The Navy Act 1957 s 23 (1).

4 As provided in the Regulations for the Navy 1965, Part II statutory, regulations 234-241. The Navy Act 1957 s 23 (2).

[0974] Representation affecting conditions of service

1 Any sailor who wishes to make a representation affecting his welfare or who has any suggestion to make connected with the service, shall bring the subject to the notice of his divisional officer through his divisional petty officer[1]. Whether the matter affects one individual or more than one individual, the procedure prescribed in the aforesaid provision shall invariably be followed[2]. If the representation is one with which the divisional officer cannot himself deal, he shall bring it to the notice of the executive officer (through the departmental officer, where applicable) and subsequently, if necessary, through him to the commanding officer, and so to higher authority as the circumstances may require[3]. It shall be the duty of every chief petty officer, petty officer or leading sailor to keep himself informed of any cause of complaint or dissatisfaction among the sailors and to inform his divisional officer so that the matter may be investigated[4]. A copy of the aforesaid provisions[5] in English and Hindi shall be kept permanently posted on a notice board in all chief petty officer's and petty officer's messes[6].

2 The aforesaid provisions shall not affect: (i) the procedure by which sailor may bring requests before inspecting officers at inspection in accordance with the custom of the service[7]; (ii) the custom by which any sailor is allowed to request, through his divisional officer, to see the commanding officer with regard to matters of private nature[8]; (iii) the custom by which complaints of an immediate nature other than those about food, may be taken before the officer of the watch[9]; (iv) the customary procedure by which complaints of an immediate nature about food in ships and establishments under the general mess system, are in the first instance, taken to the senior cook sailor in the galley, or in ships and establishments organized for centralized messing, to the sailor in charge of the dining hall[10].

1 The Regulations for the Navy 1965, Part II statutory, regulation 234 (1). As to the definition of 'sailor' and 'petty officer'; see **[0933]** and **[0928]**.

2 The Regulations for the Navy 1965, Part II statutory, regulation 234 (2).

3 The Regulations for the Navy 1965, Part II statutory, regulation 234 (3).

4 The Regulations for the Navy 1965, Part II statutory, regulation 234 (4).

5 The Regulations for the Navy 1965, Part II statutory, regulation 234 (1), (2), (3) and (4).

6 The Regulations for the Navy 1965, Part II statutory, regulation 234 note.

7 The Regulations for the Navy 1965, Part II statutory, regulation 234 (5) (a).

8 The Regulations for the Navy 1965, Part II statutory, regulation 234 (5) (b).

9 The Regulations for the Navy 1965, Part II statutory, regulation 234 (5) (c).

10 The Regulations for the Navy 1965, Part II statutory, regulation 234 (5) (d).

[0975] Complaints to higher authority If an officer or a sailor thinks that he has suffered any personal oppression, injustice or other ill-treatment or that he has been treated unjustly in any way, he may make complaint in accordance with the Regulations for the Navy 1965[1]. Any other method of seeking a redress from a superior authority, except as mentioned in the Regulations for the Navy 1965, Part II, statutory, is forbidden[2].

1 The Regulations for the Navy 1965, Part II statutory, regulation 235 (1). Also see **[0973]**.

2 The Regulations for the Navy 1965, Part II statutory, regulation 235 (2).

[0976] To whom the complaint shall be made If the complainant be a commanding officer[1] of an Indian naval ship, his complaint shall be in writing and addressed to his immediate superior[2]. If the complainant be an officer[3] serving in one of Indian naval ship, his complaint shall be made orally to the commanding officer, in accordance with the service custom whereby a complainant is to make an oral request to see the commanding officer for that purpose. If the complainant is an officer below the rank of captain, such request shall be made through the executive officer, and if the complainant is not the head of department, the request shall be made in the first place to the head of the department[4]. If the complaint is serving in a naval establishment[5] not commissioned as a ship and not under the command of a commanding officer of one of Indian naval ship, the complaint shall be made orally to his immediate superior[6]. If the complainant is an officer who is not serving in a naval establishment, he shall submit his complaint to his immediate superior, either orally or in writing as may be practicable[7]. If the complainant is a sailor[8], his complaint shall be made orally to the commanding officer. A request to see the commanding officer shall be made to the executive officer through the complainant's divisional officer and of head of the department. A sailor[8] detached from his ship or establishment shall make his complaint to the officer under whose command he may be at this time[9].

1 As to the definition of 'commanding officer' and 'ship'; see **[0912] and [0934]**.

2 The Regulations for the Navy 1965, Part II statutory, regulation 236 (1).

3 As to the definition of 'officer'; see **[0927]**.

4 The Regulations for the Navy 1965, Part II statutory, regulation 236 (2).

5 As to the definition of 'naval establishment'; see **[0922]**. However, for the purpose of this provision the term 'naval establishment' shall, in addition to naval headquarters and naval dockyard, include offices of administrative authorities, naval officer-in-charge and resident naval officers of ports and naval advisers to Indian missions abroad. The Regulations for the Navy 1965, Part II statutory, regulation 236 (3) explanation.

6 The Regulations for the Navy 1965, Part II statutory, regulation 236 (3).

7 The Regulations for the Navy 1965, Part II statutory, regulation 236 (4).

8 As to the definition of 'sailor'; see **[0933]**.

9 The Regulations for the Navy 1965, Part II statutory, regulation 236 (5).

[0977] Assistance to complainant If the complainant be an officer of junior rank or a sailor, he may request any officer in his to advise and assist him in the statement of his case at all stages. If no such request is made, it shall be the duty of the divisional officer, or such other officer as the commanding officer may detail, to give his assistance, such officer shall point out to the complainant the rules to be observed under certain provisions of the Regulations for the Navy 1965, Part II, statutory[1].

1 Ie the Regulations for the Navy 1965, Part II statutory, regulation 238. As to the definition of 'sailor', and 'officer'; see **[0933] and [0927]**. The Regulations for the Navy 1965, Part II statutory, regulation 237.

[0978] Rules to be observed by the complainant Complainant shall be confined to a statement of facts complained of and to the alleged consequences to the complainant himself[1]. Joint complainants by two or more persons are not allowed; each individual shall make his own complaint[2]. It shall be an offence against good order and naval discipline to make a complaint, either oral or written, which includes a statement of fact which is untrue to the knowledge of the complainant[3]. It shall be an offence against good order and naval discipline to make a complaint in terms, which comprise language or comments that are disrespectful or insubordinate or subversive of discipline, except in so far as such language or comments are necessary for an adequate statement of the facts[4].

1 The Regulations for the Navy 1965, Part II statutory, regulation 238 (1).

2 The Regulations for the Navy 1965, Part II statutory, regulation 238 (2).

3 The Regulations for the Navy 1965, Part II statutory, regulation 238 (3). As to the offence of 'good order and naval discipline'; see the Navy Act 1957 s 74: **[1030]**.

4 The Regulations for the Navy 1965, Part II statutory, regulation 238 (4).

[0979] How the complaint shall be dealt with On receipt of any complaint, the commanding officer or other officer receiving the same shall satisfy himself that the complaint is made in accordance with the Regulations for the Navy 1965, Part II statutory. He shall then deal with it in the exercise of his discretion as may seem to him right, and cause the complainant to be informed of his decision[1]. If the commanding officer or the other officer receiving the complaint refuses or is unable to remedy the complaint so made, the complainant may respectfully ask that he may be allowed to make his complaint in writing, and on receiving such request, the commanding officer or the other officer shall give the complainant 24 hours to reconsider the matter. The complainant, while still having the assistance of the officer referred to in the Regulations for the Navy 1965, Part

II statutory[2], may then address his complaint to the commanding officer or the other officer in writing, who shall then forward the complaint to his next superior officer, together with his own remarks thereon, to be dealt with in accordance with the aforesaid provision[3]. If the complainant is not satisfied with the decision on his complaint, or if he does not get the redress asked for within a period of one month from the date of submission of his complaint or the date of its dispatch to the next superior authority, as the case may be, he may request that his complaint be forwarded to the next superior authority and so on to the chief of the naval staff to be dealt with in accordance with the aforesaid provisions[4] and finally to the Central Government and all such requests shall be complied with. The complainant shall be justified in appealing direct to the next superior authority if he does not receive the final reply within a period of six months from the date of submission of his complaint[5]. No officer or sailor shall be penalized for having made a complaint in accordance with these provisions[6].

1 The Regulations for the Navy 1965, Part II statutory, regulation 239 (1).

2 Ie the Regulations for the Navy 1965, Part II statutory, regulation 237.

3 Ie the Regulations for the Navy 1965, Part II statutory, regulation 239 (1); the Regulations for the Navy 1965, Part II statutory, regulation 239 (2).

4 Ie the Regulations for the Navy 1965, Part II statutory, regulation 239 (1) and (2).

5 The Regulations for the Navy 1965, Part II statutory, regulation 239 (3).

6 The Regulations for the Navy 1965, Part II statutory, regulation 239 (4).

[0980] Remarks or criticism on superiors Except as specifically permitted in the Regulations for the Navy 1965, Part II, no officer or sailor shall make remarks or pass criticism on the conduct or orders of his superiors which may tend to bring them into contempt. No officer shall say or do anything which, if heard or seen by or reported to those under him, might discourage them or render them dissatisfied with their condition or with the service on which they are or may be employed[1].

1 As to the definition of 'officer' and 'sailor'; see **[0927] and [0933]**. The Regulations for the Navy 1965, Part II statutory, regulation 240.

[0981] Combinations All combinations of officers or sailors for the purpose of bringing about alteration in the existing regulations or custom of the service, whether affecting their interests individually or collectively, are contrary to the tradition and practice of the service and injurious to its welfare and discipline[1]. Every officer or sailor shall be entitled individually to make known to his superior any proper cause of complaint, but individual officers or sailors shall not combine, either by the appointment of committees or in any other manner; nor shall they sign collectively memorials, petitions or applications, nor obtain signatures to such documents[2].

1 As to the definition of 'officer' and 'sailor'; see **[0927] and [0933]**. The Regulations for the Navy 1965, Part II statutory, regulation 241 (1).

2 The Regulations for the Navy 1965, Part II statutory, regulation 241 (2).

[0982] Priority of hearing of cases concerning persons in the naval service On the presentation to any civil or revenue court by or on behalf of any person in the Naval service while subject to Naval law[1] of a certificate from the proper Naval authority of leave of absence having been granted to or applied for by him for the purpose of prosecuting or defending any suit or other proceedings in such court , the court shall , on the application of such person, arrange, so far as may be possible, for the hearing and final disposal of such suit or other proceeding within the period the leave so granted or applied for[2]. The certificate from the proper Naval authority shall state the first and last day of the leave granted or applied for and set forth a description of the case with respect to which the leave has been granted or applied for, and shall be duly signed and authenticated by such authority[3]. No fee shall payable to the court in respect of the presentation of any such certificate, or in respect of any application by or on behalf of any such person for priority for the hearing of his case and every such certificate duly signed and authenticated as aforesaid shall be conclusive evidence of the correctness of the contents thereof[4]. Where the court is unable to arrange for the hearing and final disposal of the suit or proceeding with in the period of the leave granted or applied for as aforesaid, it shall records its reasons for having been unable to do so, and shall cause a copy thereof to be furnished to such person on his application, without any payment whatever by him in respect either of the application for such copy of the copy itself[5]. Every criminal court before which a case is pending against a person in the Naval service shall, so far as may be possible arrange for the early hearing and final disposal of such case[6].

1 As to the meaning of 'persons subject to naval law'; see the Navy Act 1957 s 3 (22): **[0941].**

2 The Navy Act 1957 s 24 (1).

3 The Navy Act 1957 s 24 (2).

4 The Navy Act 1957 s 24 (3).

5 The Navy Act 1957 s 24 (4).

6 The Navy Act 1957 s 24 (5). This provision is similar to the Army Act 1950 s 32; see **[0084]**.

[0983] Rights of Chief of the Naval Staff or commanding officer to obtain copies of judgments or orders made by a criminal court A criminal court before which any proceedings have been taken against a person in the naval service[1] while subject to naval law shall, on application by the Chief of the Naval Staff or the commanding officer of that person, grant copies of the judgment and final orders in the case free of cost and without delay[2].

1 As to the definition the 'chief of the naval staff', 'commanding officer' and 'naval service'; see **[0907], [0912]** and **[0924]**.

2 The Navy Act 1957 s 25.

[0984] Saving of rights and privileges under other laws The rights and privileges specified in the preceding provisions[1] shall be in addition to, and not in derogation of, any other rights and privileges conferred on persons in the Naval service while subject to Naval law or on members of the regular army, navy air force generally by any other law for the time being in force[2].

1 Ie as specified in the Navy Act 1957, chapter VI, ss 20-26.

2 The Navy Act 1957 s 26. For more details; see **[0085]**.

4. ARTICLES OF WAR

CONTENTS

PARA

A. Articles of war

A. Articles of War

[0985] Misconduct of officers or persons in command Every flag officer, captain of or other person subject to naval law[1] who, being in command on ship[2], vessel or aircraft of the Indian navy or any naval establishment[3]: (i) fails to use his utmost exertions to bring into action any such ship, vessel or aircraft which it is his duty to bring into action[4]; (ii) surrenders any such ship, vessel or aircraft to the enemy[5] when it is capable of being successfully defended or destroyed[6]; (iii) fails to pursue the enemy whom it is his duty to pursue or to assist to the utmost of his ability any friend whom it is his duty to assist[7]; (iv) in the course of any action by or against the enemy improperly withdraws from the action or from his station or fails in his own person and according his rank to encourage the persons under the command to fight courageously[8]; or (v) surrenders any such naval establishment or any part of such an establishment to the enemy when it is capable of being successfully defended or when it is his duty to cause it to be destroyed[9]; shall (i) if such act is committed with the intend to assist the enemy or from cowardice, be punished with death or such other punishment as is hereinafter mentioned[10]; and (ii) in any other case, be punished with imprisonment for a term, which may extend up to seven years or such other punishment as mentioned in the Navy Act 1957[11].

1 As to the meaning of 'flag officer' and 'persons subject to naval law'; see **[0917] and [0941]**.

2 As to the meaning of 'ship'; see **[0934]**.

3 As to the meaning of 'naval establishment'; see **[0922]**.

4 The Navy act 1957 s 34 (a).

5 As to the meaning of 'enemy'; see **[0916]**.

6 The Navy Act 1957 s 34 (b).

7 The Navy Act 1957 s 34 (c).

8 The Navy Act 1957 s 34 (d).

9 The Navy Act 1957 s 34 (e).

10 Ie as mentioned in the Navy Act 1957 s 81; The Navy Act 1957 s 34 punishment clause (a).

11 Ie as mentioned in the Navy Act 1957 s 81; The Navy Act 1957 s 34 punishment clause (b).

[0986] Misconduct by persons other than those in command Every person subject to naval law[1] who, not being in command of any naval establishment or any ship, vessel or aircraft of the Indian navy, fails when ordered to prepare for action by or against the enemy, or during any such action to use his utmost exertions to carry the lawful orders of his superior officers into executions shall: (i) if such act is committed with the intent to assist the enemy, be punished with death or such other punishment as is hereinafter mentioned[2]; and (ii) in any other case, be punished with imprisonment for a term which may be extended to seven years or such other punishment as mentioned in the Navy Act 1957[3].

1 As to the meaning of 'persons subject to naval law'; see **[0941]**.

2 Ie as mentioned in the Navy Act 1957 s 81; The Navy Act 1957 s 35 (a).

3 Ie as mentioned in the Navy Act 1957 s 81; The Navy Act 1957 s 35 (b).

[0987] Delaying or discouraging action or service command Every person subject to naval law[1] who willfully delays or discourages upon any pretext whatsoever; any action or service which has been commanded on the part of the navy, regular army, or air force or any forces co-operating therewith shall, (i) if such act is committed with intent to assist the enemy[2], be punished with death or other punishment[3]; and (ii) in any other case, be punished with imprisonment which may extend to seven years or such other punishment as mentioned in the Navy Act 1957[4].

1 As to the meaning of 'persons subject to naval law'; see **[0941]**.

2 As to the meaning of 'enemy'; see **[0916]**.

3 Ie as mentioned in the Navy Act 1957 s 81; The Navy Act 1957 s 36 (a).

4 Ie as mentioned in the Navy Act 1957 s 81; The Navy Act 1957 s 36 (b).

[0988] Penalty for disobedience in action Every person subject to naval law[1] who, being in the presence or vicinity of the enemy or having been ordered to be prepared for action by or against the enemy: (i) deserts his post[2]; or (ii) sleeps upon his watch[3]; shall be punished with death or such other punishment as mentioned in the Navy Act 1957[4].

1 As to the meaning of 'persons subject to naval law'; see **[0941]**.

2 The Navy Act 1957 s 37 (a).

3 The Navy Act 1957 s 37 (b).

4 Ie as mentioned in the Navy Act 1957 s 81; The Navy Act 1957 s 37.

[0989] Penalty for spying Every person not otherwise subject to naval law[1] who is or acts as a spy for the enemy shall be punished under the Navy Act 1957 with death or such other punishment as mentioned in the Navy Act 1957[2] as if he were a person subject to naval law[3].

1 As to the meaning of 'person subject to naval law'; see **[0941]**.

2 Ie as mentioned in the Navy Act 1957 s 81.

3 The Navy Act 1957 s 38.

[0990] Correspondence, etc., with the enemy Every person subject to naval law[1], who: (i) traitorously holds correspondence with the enemy[2] or gives intelligence to the enemy[3]; (ii) fails to make known to the proper authorities any information he may have received from the enemy[4]; (iii) assists the enemy with any supplies[5]; or (iv) having been made a prisoner of war, voluntarily serves with or aids to enemy[6]; shall be punished with death or such other punishment as mentioned in the Navy Act 1957[7].

1 As to the meaning of 'persons subject to naval law'; see **[0941]**.

2 As to the meaning of 'enemy'; see **[0916]**.

3 The Navy Act 1957 s 39 (a).

4 The Navy Act 1957 s 39 (b).

5 The Navy Act 1957 s 39 (c).

6 The Navy Act 1957 s 39 (d).

7 Ie as mentioned in the Navy Act 1957 s 81; The Navy Act 1957 s 39.

[0991] Improper communication with the enemy Every person subject to naval law[1] who without any traitorous intention holds any improper communication with the enemy[2] shall be punished with imprisonment for a term which may be extend to 14 years or such other punishment as mentioned in the Navy Act 1957[3].

1 As to the meaning of 'persons subject to naval law'; see **[0941]**.

2 As to the meaning of 'enemy'; see **[0916]**.

3 Ie as mentioned in the Navy Act 1957 s 81; The Navy Act 1957 s 40.

[0992] Deserting post and neglect of duty Every person subject to Naval law[1], who: (i) deserts his post[2]; (ii) sleep upon his watch[3]; (iii) fails to perform or negligently performs the duty imposed on him[4]; or (iv) willfully conceals any words, practice or design tending to the hindrance of the naval service[5]; shall be punished with imprisonment for a term, which may be extended to two years or such other punishment as mentioned in the Navy Act 1957[6].

1 As to the meaning of 'persons subject to naval law'; see **[0941]**.

2 The Navy Act 1957 s 41 (a).

3 The Navy Act 1957 s 41 (b).

4 The Navy Act 1957 s 41 (c).

5 The Navy Act 1957 s 41 (d).

6 Ie as mentioned in the Navy Act 1957 s 81; The Navy Act 1957 s 41.

[0993] Mutiny defined Mutiny means any assemble or combination of two or more persons subject to naval law[1], the Army Act, 1950, the Air Force Act 1950, or between persons two at least of whom are subject to naval law or any such Act: (i) to overthrow or resist lawful authority in the navy, regular army, regular air force or any part of any one or more of them or any forces co-operating therewith or any part thereof[2]; (ii) to disobey such authority in such circumstances as to make the disobedience subversive of discipline or with the object of avoiding any duty or service against, or in connection with operations against, the enemy[3]; (iii) to show contempt to such authority in such circumstance as to make such conduct subversive of discipline[4]; or (iv) to impede the performance of any duty or service in the navy, regular army, or air force or any part of any one or more of them or any forces co-operating therewith or any part thereof[5].

1 As to the meaning of 'persons subject to naval law', 'persons subject to the Army Act 1950', and 'persons subject to the Air Force Act 1950'; see **[0941], [0039] and [0506]**. The Army Act 1950 and the Air Force Act 1950 do not define the term 'mutiny'.

2 The Navy Act 1957 s 42 (a).

3 The Navy Act 1957 s 42 (b).

4 The Navy Act 1957 s 42 (c).

5 The Navy Act 1957 s 42 (d).

[0994] Punishment for mutiny Every person subject to naval law[1], who: (i) joins in a mutiny[2]; (ii) begins, incites, causes or conspires with any other persons to cause a mutiny[3]; (iii) endeavors to incite any person to join in a mutiny or to commit an act of mutiny[4]; (iv) endeavors to seduce any person in the regular army, navy or air force from his allegiance to the constitutions or loyalty to the State or duty to his superior officers[5] or uses any means to compel or induce any such person to abstain from acting against the enemy[6] or discourages such person from acting against the enemy[7]; (v) does not use his utmost exertions to suppress or prevent a mutiny[8]; (vi) willfully conceals any traitorous or mutinous practice or design or any traitorous words spoken against the State[9]; (vii) knowing or having reason to believe in the existence of any mutiny or of any intention to mutiny does not without delay give information thereof to the commanding officer[10] of his ship or other superior officer[11]; or (viii) utters words of sedition or mutiny[12]; shall be punished with death or such other punishment as mentioned in the Navy Act 1957[13].

1 As to the meaning of 'person subject to naval law'; see **[0941]**.

2 The Navy Act 1957 s 43 (a).

3 The Navy Act 1957 s 43 (b).

4 The Navy Act 1957 s 43 (c).

5 As to the meaning of 'superior officer'; see **[0937]**.

6 As to the meaning of 'enemy'; see **[0916]**.

7 The Navy Act 1957 s 43 (d).

8 The Navy Act 1957 s 43 (e).

9 The Navy Act 1957 s 43 (f).

10 As to the meaning of 'commanding officer'; see **[0912]**.

11 The Navy Act 1957 s 43 (g).

12 The Navy Act 1957 s 43 (h).

13 Ie as mentioned in the Navy Act 1957 s 81; The Navy Act 1957 s 43.

[0995] Persons on board ships or aircrafts seducing navel personal from allegiance Every person not otherwise subject to naval law[1] who being on board any ship or aircraft of the Indian navy or on board any ship in the service of the government endeavours to seduce from his allegiance to the Constitution or loyalty to the state or duty to superior officers[2] any person subject to naval law shall be punished under the Navy Act 1957 with death or such other punishment as mentioned in the Navy Act 1957[3] as if he were a person subject to naval law[4].

1 As to the meaning of 'persons subject to naval law'; see **[0941]**.

2 As to the meaning of 'superior officer'; see **[0937]**.

3 Ie as mentioned in the Navy Act 1957 s 81.

4 The Navy Act 1957 s 44.

[0996] Offences by passengers Any person although not belonging to the Indian navy or the regular army or air force who is ordered to be received or is a passenger on board any ship or aircraft of the Indian navy shall be subject to naval law[1] to the extend and subject to the following conditions:

1 Any such person who while on board a ship[2] or an aircraft of the Indian navy commits any offence against the good order and discipline of the service[3] may be placed under such restraint by the officer in command of the ship or aircraft in which he has embarked as the offence(s) committed by him may appear to justify or render necessary. The officer who has occasion to place any such passenger under arrest shall take the earliest opportunity that presents itself of reporting the circumstances to the first senior officer he may fall in with, in order that it may be determined, after due investigation. Whether the alleged offender shall be released from arrest or continue under arrest until the termination of the voyage for which he has embarked or whether he shall be transferred to some other ship or aircraft of the Indian navy[4].

2 If any such person while on board a ship or aircraft of the Indian navy commits any criminal offence punishable by the law of India he may be kept under such restraint as is necessary until an opportunity shall offer of delivering him over to a civil court competent to try him for the same[5].

3 Nothing in the Regulations for the Navy 1965 shall preclude any person on board a ship or aircraft of the Indian navy or on board any ship in the service of the government to be proceeded against for an offence punishable under the Navy Act 1957[6].

4 Officers and sailors who, upon being invalided or discharged, may be ordered or permitted to take passage in any Indian naval ship or aircraft and persons sentenced under the Navy Act 1957 so long as they are on board the ship in which they are embarked as passengers shall be subject to naval law[7].

1 As to the meaning of 'subject to naval law'; see **[0935]**.

2 As to the meaning of 'ship'; see **[0934]**.

3 As to the 'offence against the good order and discipline'; see the Navy Act 1957 s 74.

4 The Regulations for the Navy 1965, volume II, regulation 232 (a).

5 The Regulations for the Navy 1965, volume II, regulation 232 (b). As to the meaning of 'civil court'; see **[0909]**.

6 Ie under the Navy Act 1957 s 44; The Regulations for the Navy 1965, volume II, regulation 232 (c).

7 The Regulations for the Navy 1965, volume II, regulation 232 (d). As to the meaning of 'officer' and 'sailor'; see **[0927] and [0933]**.

[0997] Striking superior officers Every person subject to naval law[1] who commits any of the following offences: (i) strikes or attempts to strike his superior officer[2]; (ii) draws or lifts up any weapon against such officer[3]; or (iii) uses or attempts to use any violence against such officer[4]; shall be punished, if the offence is committed on active service with imprisonment for a term which may extend to 10 years or other punishment[5]; and in any other case with imprisonment for a term which may extend to five years or such other punishment as mentioned in the Navy Act 1957[6].

1 As to the meaning of 'persons subject to naval law'; see **[0941]**.

2 As to the meaning of 'superior officer'; see **[0937]**; The Navy Act 1957 s 45 (a).

3 The Navy Act 1957 s 45 (b).

4 The Navy Act 1957 s 45 (c).

5 Ie as mentioned in the Navy Act 1957 s 81.

6 Ie as mentioned in the Navy Act 1957 s 81; The Navy Act 1957 s 45.

[0998] Ill-treating subordinates Every person subject to naval law[1] who is guilty of ill-treating any other person subject to such law, being his subordinates in rank or position, shall be punished with imprisonment for a term which may extend to seven years or such other punishment as mentioned in the Navy Act 1957[2].

1 As to the meaning of 'person subject to naval law'; see **[0941]**.

2 Ie as mentioned in the Navy Act 1957 s 81; The Navy Act 1957 s 46. For the purposes of prosecution for ill-treating subordinates, the accused should be charged under this provision and not under the Navy Act 1957 s 74. *Commander Ranvir Kumar Sinha v Union of India* 1991 Cr LJ 1729 (DB) (Bom).

[0999] Disobedience and insubordination Every person subject to naval law[1], who: (i) willfully disobeys any lawful command of his superior officer[2]; (ii) in the presence of his superior officer, or otherwise shows or express his intention to disobey a lawful command given by such superior officer[3]; (iii) uses insubordinate, threatening or insulting language to his superior officer[4]; or (iv) behaves with contempt to his superior officer[5]; shall, if the offence is committed on active service[6] or in a manner to show willful defiance of authority, be punished with imprisonment for a term which may extent to 10 years or such other punishment as is hereinafter mentioned[7] and in other cases, be punished with imprisonment for a term which may extend to three years or such other punishment as mentioned in the Navy Act 1957[8].

1 As to the meaning of 'person subject to naval law'; see **[0941]**.

2 As to the meaning of 'superior officer'; see **[0937]**; The Navy Act 1957 s 47 (a).

3 The Navy Act 1957 s 47 (b).

4 The Navy Act 1957 s 47 (c).

5 The Navy Act 1957 s 47 (d).

6 As to the meaning of 'active service'; see **[0905]**;

7 Ie as mentioned in the Navy Act 1957 s 81.

8 The Navy Act 1957 s 47.

[1000] Quarreling, fighting and disorderly behaviour Every person subject to naval law[1], who (i) quarrels, fights with or strikes any other person, whether such person is or is not subject to naval law[2]; (ii) uses reproachful or provoking speeches or gestures tending to make a quarrel or disturbance[3]; or (iii) behaves in a disorderly manner[4];

shall be punished with imprisonment for a term, which may extend to two years or such other punishment as mentioned in the Navy Act 1957[5].

1 As to the meaning of 'persons subject to naval law'; see **[0941]**.

2 The Navy Act 1957 s 48 (a).

3 The Navy Act 1957 s 48 (b).

4 The Navy Act 1957 s 48 (c).

5 Ie as mentioned in the Navy Act 1957 s 81; The Navy Act 1957 s 48.

[1001] Desertion Every person subject to naval law[1] who absents himself from his ship or from the place where his duty requires him to be, with an intention of not returning to such ship or place, or who at any time and under any circumstance when absent from his ship or place of duty does any act which shows that he has an intention of not returning to such ship or place is said to desert[2].

Every person who deserts shall, (i) if he deserts to the enemy, be punished with death or such other punishment as mentioned[3]; or (ii) if he deserts under any other circumstance, be punished with imprisonment for a term which may extend to 14 years or such other punishment as mentioned in the Navy Act 1957[4]. In every such case the deserter shall forfeit all pay, head money, bounty salvage, prize money and allowances that have been earned by him and all annuities, pensions, gratuities, medals and decorations that may have been granted to him and also all clothes and effects which he may have left on board the ship or the place from which he deserted, unless otherwise directed by the tribunal by which he is tried, the central government or the chief of the naval staff[5].

1 As to the meaning of 'persons subject to naval law'; see **[0941]**.

2 The Navy Act 1957 s 49 (1).

3 Ie as mentioned in the Navy Act 1957 s 81; The Navy Act 1957 s 49 (2) (a).

4 Ie as mentioned in the Navy Act 1957 s 81; The Navy Act 1957 s 49 (2) (b).

5 The Navy Act 1957 s 49.

[1002] Seducing person to desert Every person subject to naval law[1] who endeavours to seduce any other person subject to naval law to desert shall be punished with imprisonment for a term, which may extend to two years or such other punishment as mentioned in the Navy Act 1957[2].

1 As to the meaning of 'persons subject to naval law'; see **[0941]**.

2 Ie as mentioned in the Navy Act 1957 s 81; The Navy Act 1957 s 50.

[1003] Breaking out of ship and absence without leave Every person subject to naval law[1] who without being guilty of desertion improperly leaves his ship[2] or place of duty or any place where he is required to be or is absent without leave shall be punished with imprisonment for a term which may extend to two years or such other punishment as is hereinafter mentioned[3] and shall also be punished by such mulcts of pay and allowances as may be prescribed[4].

1 As to the meaning of 'person subject to naval law'; see **[0941]**.

2 As to the meaning of 'ship'; see **[0934]**.

3 Ie as mentioned in the Navy Act 1957 s 81.

4 The Navy Act 1957 s 51.

[1004] Drunkenness Every person subject to naval law[1] who is guilty of drunkenness shall, if the offence is committed on active service[2] be punished with imprisonment for a term which may extend to two years or other punishment as mentioned in the Navy Act 1957[2]. In other case such person shall be punished with imprisonment up to six months or other punishment as mentioned in the Navy Act 1957[4]. For the purpose of aforesaid provision, a person shall be deemed to be guilty of drunkenness if owing to the influence of alcohol or any drug whether alone or in combination with any other circumstance, he is unfit to be entrusted with his duty or with any duty which he may be called upon to perform or behaves in a disorderly manner or in a manner likely to bring discredit to the naval service[5].

1 As to the meaning of 'person subject to naval law'; see **[0941]**.

2 As to the meaning of 'active service'; see **[0905]**.

3 Ie as mentioned in the Navy Act 1957 s 81.

4 The Navy Act 1957 s 52 (1).

5 As to the meaning of 'naval service'; see **[0924]**. The Navy Act 1957 s 52 (2).

[1005] Uncleanness or indecent acts Every person subject to naval law[1] who is guilty of (i) uncleanness[2]; or (ii) any indecent act[3]; shall be punished with imprisonment for a term which may be extend to two years or such other punishment as mentioned in the Navy Act 1957[4].

1 As to the meaning of 'person subject to naval law'; see **[0941]**.

2 The Navy Act 1957 s 53 (a).

3 The Navy Act 1957 s 53 (b).

4 Ie as mentioned in the Navy Act 1957 s 81; The Navy Act 1957 s 53.

[1006] Cruelty and conduct unbecoming the character of an officer Every officer[1] subject to naval law[2] who is guilty of cruelty shall be punished with imprisonment for a term which may extend to seven years or such other punishment as is hereinafter mentioned[3]. Every officer subject to naval law who is guilty of any scandalous or fraudulent conduct or of any conduct unbecoming the character of an officer shall be punished with imprisonment for a term, which may extend to two years or such other punishment as mentioned in the Navy Act 1957[4].

1 As to the meaning of 'officer'; see **[0927]**.

2 As to the meaning of 'subject to naval law'; see **[0935]**.

3 Ie as mentioned in the Navy Act 1957 s 81; The Navy Act 1957 s 54(1).

4 Ie as mentioned in the Navy Act 1957 s 81; The Navy Act 1957 s 54 (2).

[1007] Losing ship or aircraft Every person subject to naval law[1] who willfully loses, strands or hazards or suffers to be lost, stranded or hazarded any ship[2] of the Indian navy or in the service of the Government, or loses or suffers to be lost any aircraft of the Indian navy or in the service of the Government shall be punished with imprisonment for a term which may extend to 14 years or such other punishment as mentioned in the Navy Act 1957[3]. Every person subject to naval law who negligently or by any default loses, strands or hazards or suffers to be lost, stranded or hazarded any ship of the Indian navy or in the service of the Government or loses or suffers to be lost any aircraft of the Indian navy or in the service of the Government shall be punished with imprisonment for a term which may extend to two years or such other punishment as mentioned in the Navy Act 1957[4].

1 As to the meaning of 'person subject to naval law'; see **[0941]**.
2 As to the meaning of 'ship'; see **[0934]**.
3 Ie as mentioned in the Navy Act 1957 s 81; The Navy Act 1957 s 55 (1).
4 Ie as mentioned in the Navy Act 1957 s 81; The Navy Act 1957 s 55 (2).

[1008] Dangerous authorized flying Every person subject to naval law[1], who is guilty of any act or neglect in flying or in the use of any aircraft of the Indian navy or in relation to any such aircraft or aircraft material , which causes or is likely to cause loss of life or bodily injury to any person shall, if he acts willfully or with willful neglect, to be punished with imprisonment for a term which may extend to 14 years or other punishment[2]; and in any other case, be punished with imprisonment for a term which may extend to five years or such other punishment as mentioned in the Navy Act 1957[3].

1 As to the meaning of 'person subject to naval law'; see **[0941]**.
2 Ie as mentioned in the Navy Act 1957 s 81; The Navy Act 1957 s 55A (a).
3 Ie as mentioned in the Navy Act 1957 s 81; The Navy Act 1957 s 55A (b).

[1009] Inaccurate certificate Every person subject to naval law[1] who signs any certificate in relation to an aircraft or aircraft material belonging to or in the service of the government without ensuring the accuracy thereof, shall be punished with imprisonment for a term which may extend to two years such other punishment as mentioned in the Navy Act 1957[2].

1 As to the meaning of 'person subject to naval law'; see **[0941]**.
2 Ie as mentioned in the Navy Act 1957 s 81; The Navy Act 1957 s 55B.

[1010] Low flying and annoyance by flying Every person subject to naval law[1] being the pilot of an aircraft of the Indian navy, who, flies it a height less than the minimum height authorized by his commanding officer or appropriate service authority except while taking off or landing[2]; or flies it so as to cause or likely to cause unnecessary annoyance to any person, shall be punished with imprisonment for a term which may extent to two years or such other punishment as mentioned in the Navy Act 1957[3].

1 As to the meaning of 'person subject to naval law'; see **[0941]**.
2 The Navy Act 1957 s 55C (a).
3 Ie as mentioned in the Navy Act 1957 s 81; The Navy Act 1957 s 55C (b).

[1011] Disobedience of lawful command of captain of an aircraft Every person subject to naval law[1], who, while he is in an aircraft belonging to or in the use of the Government, disobeys any lawful command given by the captain of the aircraft, whether such captain is subject to naval law or not, in relation to all matters relating to flying or handling or the aircraft or affecting the safety thereof shall be punished with imprisonment for a term which may extent to 14 years or such other punishment as mentioned in the Navy Act 1957[2].

1 As to the meaning of 'person subject to naval law'; see **[0941]**.
2 Ie as mentioned in the Navy Act 1957 s 81; The Navy Act 1957 s 55 D.

[1012] Offences by officers in charge of convoy All officers[1] appointed for the convoy and protection of any ships[2] or vessels shall diligently perform their duty without delay according to their instruction[3]. Every such officer subject to naval law[4], who (i) does not defend the ships and goods under his convey without deviation to any other objects[5]; (ii) refuses to fight their defence if they are assailed[6]; (iii) cowardly abandons and exposes the ships in his convoy to hazard[7]; (iv) demands or extracts any money or other reward from any merchant or master for conveying any ships or vessels entrusted to his care[8]; or (v) misuses the masters or mariners thereof[9]; shall be punished with death or other punishment[10], and shall also make such reparation in damages to the merchants owners and others as a civil court of competent jurisdiction may adjudge[11].

1 As to the meaning of 'officer'; see **[0927]**.

2 As to the meaning of 'ship'; see **[0934]**.

3 The Navy Act 1957 s 56 (1).

4 As to the meaning of 'subject to naval law'; see **[0935].**

5 The Navy Act 1957 s 56 (2) (a).

6 The Navy Act 1957 s 56 (2) (b).

7 The Navy Act 1957 s 56 (2) (c).

8 The Navy Act 1957 s 56 (2) (d).

9 The Navy Act 1957 s 56 (2) (e).

10 Ie such other punishments as mentioned in the Navy Act 1957 s 81.

11 The Navy Act 1957 s 56.

[1013] Taking unauthorized goods on board ship Every officer[1] subject to naval law[2] in command of any ship[3] of the Indian navy who receives on board or permits to be received on board such ship any goods or merchandise whatsoever other than for the sole use of the ship or persons belonging to the ship, except goods and merchandise on board any ship which may be ship-wrecked or in imminent danger either on the high seas or in some port creek, or harbour, for the purpose of preserving them for their proper owners, or except such goods or merchandise as he may at any time be ordered to take or receive on board by order of the Central Government or his superior officer[4], shall be punished with dismissal from the naval service or other punishment as mentioned in the Navy Act 1957[5].

1 As to the meaning of 'officer'; see **[0927]**.

2 As to the meaning of 'subject to naval law'; see **[0935]**.

3 As to the meaning of 'ship'; see **[0934]**.

4 As to the meaning of 'superior officer'; see **[0937]**.

5 Ie as mentioned in the Navy Act 1957 s 81; The Navy Act 1957 s 57.

[1014] Offences in respect of property Every person subject to naval law[1] who wastefully expends or fraudulently buys, sells or receives any property of government or property belonging to a naval, military or air force mess, band or institution, and every person who knowingly permits any such wasteful expenditure, or any such fraudulent purchase, sale or receipt, shall be punished with imprisonment for a term which may extend to two years or other punishment as mentioned in the Navy Act 1957[2].

1 As to the meaning of 'person subject to naval law'; see **[0941]**.

2 Ie as mentioned in the Navy Act 1957 s 81; The Navy Act 1957 s 58.

[1015] Arson Every person subject to naval law[1] who unlawfully sets fire to any dockyard or other property[2], not being the property of an enemy, shall be punished with death or such other punishment as mentioned in the Navy Act 1957[3].

1 As to the meaning of 'person subject to naval law'; see **[0941]**.

2 Ie victualling yard or steam factory yard, arsenal, magazine, building stores or to any ship, vessel, hoy, barge, boat, aircraft, or other craft or furniture. See; the Navy Act 1957 s 59.

3 Ie as mentioned in the Navy Act 1957 s 81; The Navy Act 1957 s 59.

[1016] Falsifying official documents and false declarations Every person subject to naval law[1]: (i) who knowingly makes or signs a false report, return, list, certificate, book, muster or other document to be used for official purpose[2]; (ii) who commands, counsels or procures the making or singing thereof[3]; (iii) who aids or abets any other person in the making or singing thereof[4]; or (iv) who knowingly makes, commands, counsels or procures the making of, a false or fraudulent statement or a fraudulent omission in any such document[5]; shall be punished with imprisonment for a term which may extend to seven years or such other punishment as mentioned in the Navy Act 1957[6].

1 As to the meaning of 'person subject to naval law'; see **[0941]**.

2 The Navy Act 1957 s 60 (a).

3 The Navy Act 1957 s 60 (b).

4 The Navy Act 1957 s 60 (c).

5 The Navy Act 1957 s 60 (d).

6 Ie as mentioned in the Navy Act 1957 s 81; The Navy Act 1957 s 60.

[1017] Malingering, etc. Every person subject to naval law[1]: (i) who willfully does any act or willfully disobeys any orders whether in hospital or elsewhere with intent to produce or to aggravate any disease or infirmity or to delay is cure[2]; or (ii) who feigns any disease, infirmity or inability to perform his duty[3]; shall be punished with imprisonment for term which may extend to five years or other punishment as mentioned in the Navy Act 1957[4].

1 As to the meaning of 'person subject to naval law'; see **[0941]**.

2 The Navy Act 1957 s 61 (a).

3 The Navy Act 1957 s 61 (b).

4 Ie as mentioned in the Navy Act 1957 s 81; The Navy Act 1957 s 61.

[1018] Penalty for endeavouring to stir up disturbance on account of unwholesomeness of victuals or other just grounds Every person subject to naval law[1] who has any cause of complaint either of the unwholesomeness of the victuals or upon any other just ground shall quietly make the same known to his superior or captain or to the Chief of the Naval Staff, in accordance with the prescribed channels of communication. The said superior captain or Chief of the Naval Staff shall, as far as he is able, cause the same to be presently remedied. Every person subject to naval law who upon any pretence whatever attempts to stir up any disturbance shall be punished with imprisonment for a term which may extend to 14 years or such other punishment as mentioned in the Navy Act 1957[2].

1 As to the meaning of 'person subject to naval law'; see **[0941]**.

2 Ie as mentioned in the Navy Act 1957 s 81; The Navy Act 1957 s 62.

[1019] Offences in respect of papers relating to prize All the papers, charter-parties, bills of lading, passports and other writings whatsoever that shall be taken, seized, or found aboard any ships which are taken as prize shall be dully preserved. The commanding officer[1] of the ship which takes such prize shall send the originals entire and without fraud to the court of competent jurisdiction or such other court or commissioners as shall be authorised to determine whether such prize be lawful capture, there to be viewed, made use of and proceeded upon according to law[2]. Every commanding officer who willfully fails to send the papers, charter parties, bills of lading, passports or other writings whatsoever that shall be taken, seized or found aboard any ships which are taken as prize to the proper court or other authority shall be punished with dismissal from the naval service or such other punishment as mentioned in the Navy Act 1957[3] and in addition shall forfeit and lose any share of the capture[4].

1 As to the meaning of 'commanding officer'; see **[0912]**.

2 The Navy Act 1957 s 63 (a).

3 Ie as mentioned in the Navy Act 1957 s 81.

4 The Navy Act 1957 s 63 (b).

[1020] Offences in respect of prize Every person subject to naval law[1] who takes out of any prize or ship seized for prize, any money, plate, or goods, unless it is necessary of the better securing thereof or for the necessary use and service of any ships of war of the Indian navy, before the same be adjudged lawful prize in a court of competent jurisdiction, shall be punished with imprisonment for a term which may extend to two years or other punishment as mentioned in the Navy Act 1957[2], and in addition shall forfeit and lose his share of capture[3].

1 As to the meaning of 'person subject to naval law'; see **[0941]**.

2 Ie as mentioned in the Navy Act 1957 s 81.

3 The Navy Act 1957 s 64.

[1021] Offences in respect of persons on board prize ship Every person subject to naval law[1] who in any sort pillages, beats, or ill-treats officers, mariners or other persons on board a ship or vessel taken as a prize or who unlawfully strips them of their cloths shall be punished with imprisonment for a term which may extend to two years or such other punishment as mentioned in the Navy Act 1957[2].

1 As to the meaning of 'person subject to naval law'; see **[0941]**.

2 Ie as mentioned in the Navy Act 1957 s 81; The Navy Act 1957 s 65.

[1022] Unlawful taking or ransoming or prize Every commanding officer[1] of ship[2] of the Indian navy subject to naval law[3], who, (i) by collusion with the enemy takes as prize any vessel, goods or thing[4]; (ii) unlawfully agrees with any person for the ransoming of any vessel, goods or thing taken as prize[5]; or (iii) in pursuance of any unlawful agreement for ransoming or otherwise by collusion actually quits or restores any vessel, goods or thing taken as prize[6]; shall be punished with imprisonment for a term which may be extend to two years or such other punishment as mentioned in the Navy Act 1957[7].

1 As to the meaning of 'commanding officer'; see **[0912]**.

2 As to the meaning of 'ship'; see **[0934]**.

3 As to the meaning of 'subject to naval law'; see **[0935]**.

4 The Navy Act 1957 s 66 (a).

5 The Navy Act 1957 s 66 (b).

6 The Navy Act 1957 s 66 (c).

7 Ie as mentioned in the Navy Act 1957 s 81; The Navy Act 1957 s 66.

[1023] Breaking bulk on board a prize ship Every person subject to naval law[1] who breaks bulk on board any vessel taken as prize, or detained in the exercise of any belligerent right or under any law relating to piracy or to the slave trade or to the customs, with intent dishonestly to misappropriate anything therein or belonging thereto, shall be punished with imprisonment for a term which may extend to two years or other punishment as mentioned in the Navy Act 1957[2].

1 As to the meaning of 'person subject to naval law'; see **[0941]**.

2 Ie as mentioned in the Navy Act 1957 s 81; The Navy Act 1957 s 67.

[1024] Violation of the Navy Act, regulations and orders Every person subject to naval law[1] who neglected to obey or contravenes any provisions of the Navy Act 1957 or the Regulations for the Navy[2] or any general or local order, shall, unless other punishment is provided in the aforesaid Act for such neglect or contravention, be punished with imprisonment for a term which may extend to two years or such other punishment as mentioned in the Navy Act 1957[3].

1 As to the meaning of 'person subject to naval law'; see **[0941]**.

2 The Regulations for the Navy 1965, Part II (Discipline and Miscellaneous Provisions), statutory.

3 Ie as mentioned in the Navy Act 1957 s 81; The Navy Act 1957 s 68.

[1025] Offences in relation to court martial Every person subject to naval law[1] who (i) being duly summoned or ordered to attend as a witness before a court martial willfully or without reasonable excuse fails to attend[2]; (ii) refuses to take an oath or make an affirmation legally required by a court martial to be taken or made[3]; (iii) being sworn, refuses to answer any questions which he is in law bound to answer[4]; (iv) refuses to produce or deliver up a document in his power which the court may legally demand[5]; or (v) is guilty of contempt of court martial[6]; shall be punished with imprisonment for a term which may be extend to three years or such other punishment as mentioned in the Navy Act 1957[7].

1 As to the meaning of 'person subject to naval law'; see **[0941]**.

2 The Navy Act 1957 s 69 (a).

3 The Navy Act 1957 s 69 (b).

4 The Navy Act 1957 s 69 (c).

5 The Navy Act 1957 s 69 (d).

6 The Navy Act 1957 s 69 (e).

7 Ie as mentioned in the Navy Act 1957 s 81; The Navy Act 1957 s 69.

[1026] Fraudulent entry Every person who upon entry into or offering himself to enter the naval service willfully makes or give any false statement whether orally or in writing to any officer or person authorised to enter or enroll sailors[1] or others in or for such naval service, shall, if he has become subject to naval law[2] be punished with imprisonment for a term which may extend to five years or such other punishment as mentioned in the Navy Act 1957[3].

1 As to the meaning of 'naval service', 'officer', and 'sailor'; see **[0924], [0727] and [0933]**.

2 As to the meaning of 'subject to naval law'; see **[0935]**.

3 Ie as mentioned in the Navy Act 1957 s 81; The Navy Act 1957 s 70.

[1027] Escape from custody Every person subject to naval law[1] who being in lawful custody escapes or attempts to escape from such custody shall be punished with imprisonment for a term, which may extend to five years or such other punishment as mentioned in the Navy Act 1957[2].

1 As to the meaning of 'person subject to naval law'; see **[0941]**.

2 Ie as mentioned in the Navy Act 1957 s 81; The Navy Act 1957 s 71.

[1028] Failure to assist in detention of offenders Every person subject to naval law[1], who (i) does not use his utmost endeavors to detect, apprehend or bring punishment all offenders against the Navy Act 1957[2]; or (ii) does not assist the officers appointed for that purpose[3]; shall be punished with imprisonment for a term which may be extend to two years or such other punishment as mentioned in the Navy Act 1957[4].

1 As to the meaning of 'person subject to naval law'; see **[0941]**.

2 The Navy Act 1957 s 72 (a).

3 The Navy Act 1957 s 72 (b).

4 Ie as mentioned in the Navy Act 1957 s 81; The Navy Act 1957 s 72.

[1029] Penalty for failure to attend by members of reserve forces when called up Every member of the Indian Naval Reserve Forces[1] and every person belonging to any auxiliary forces raised under the Navy Act 1957 who, when called up for training or when called up into actual service with the Indian navy in pursuance of the regulations made under the aforesaid Act[2], and required by such call to join any ship[3] or attend at any place, fails without reasonable excuse to comply with such requirement, shall be punished with imprisonment for a term which may extend to three years or such other punishment as mentioned in the Navy Act 1957[4].

1 As to the meaning of 'Indian Naval Reserve Forces'; see **[0918]**.

2 Ie the Regulations for the Navy 1965.

3 As to the meaning of 'ship'; see **[0934]**.

4 Ie as mentioned in the Navy Act 1957 s 81; The Navy Act 1957 s 73.

[1030] Offences against good order and naval discipline Every person subject to naval law[1] who is guilty of an act, disorder, or neglect to the prejudice of good order and naval discipline, not hereinbefore specified, shall be punished with imprisonment for a term which may extend to three years or such other punishment as mentioned in the Navy Act 1957[2]. *Mens rea* seems to be implied in the words used in this provision. However, it is not possible to infer an inclusion of the element of *mens rea*[3].

1 As to the meaning of 'person subject to naval law'; see **[0941]**.

2 The Navy Act 1957 s 74.

3 *Commander Ranvir Kumar Sinha v Union of India* 1991 Cri LJ 1729 (Bom).

[1031] Attempts Every person subject to naval law[1] who attempts to commit any of the offences specified in the Navy Act 1957[2] and in such attempt does any act towards the commission of the offences shall, where no express provision is made by the aforesaid Act for the punishment of such attempt, be punished (i) if the offences attempted to be committed is punishable with death, with imprisonment for a term which may extend to 14 years or other punishment as mentioned[3]; and (ii) if the offence attempted to be committed is punishable with imprisonment, with one-half of the maximum punishment provided for the offence or with such other punishment as mentioned in the Navy Act 1957[4].

1 As to the meaning of 'person subject to naval law'; see **[0941]**.

2 Ie the Navy Act 1957 ss 34-74 and 76.

3 Ie as mentioned in the Navy Act 1957 s 81; The Navy Act 1957 s 75 (a).

4 Ie as mentioned in the Navy Act 1957 s 81; The Navy Act 1957 s 75 (b).

[1032] Abetment of offences Any person subject to naval law[1] who abets the commission of any of the offence specified in certain provisions of the Navy Act 1957[2] shall, whether the act abetted is committed or not in consequence of the abetment, and where no express provision is made by the aforesaid Act for the punishment of such abetment, be punished with the punishment provided for that offence[3].

1 As to the meaning of 'person subject to naval law'; see **[0941]**.

2 Ie the Navy Act 1957 ss 34-74.

3 The Navy Act 1957 s 76.

[1033] Civil offences Every person subject to naval law[1] who commits a civil offence[2] punishable with death or with imprisonment for life shall be punished with the punishment assigned for that offence[3]. Every person subject to naval law who commits any other civil offence shall be punished either with the punishment assigned for the offence or with imprisonment for a term which may extend to three years or such other punishment as mentioned in the Navy Act 1957[4].

1 As to the meaning of 'person subject to naval law'; see **[0941]**.

2 As to the meaning of 'civil offence'; see **[0910]**.

3 The Navy Act 1957 s 77 (1).

4 Ie as mentioned in the Navy Act 1957 s 81; The Navy Act 1957 s 77 (2).

[1034] Jurisdiction as to place and offences

1 Subject to certain provisions of the Navy Act 1957[1], every person subject to navy law[2] who is charged with a naval offence[3] or a civil offence[4] may be tried and punished under the Navy Act 1957 regardless of where the alleged offence was committed[5].

2 A person subject to naval law who commits an offence of murder against a person not subject to army, naval, or air force law or an offence of culpable homicide not amounting to murder against such person or an offence of rape in relation to such person shall not be tried and punished under the Navy Act 1957 unless he commits any of the said offence: (i) while on active service[6]; (ii) at any place outside India[7]; or (iii) at any place specified by the Central Government by notification in this behalf[8].

3 If a person subject to naval law commits murder of a civilian, and that person is not subject to army, naval or air force law, at any place other than that referred to in the Navy Act 1957 s 78 (2)(a), (b) or (c), he cannot be tried under the Navy Act, but must be tried in a criminal court[9].

1 Ie the Navy Act 1957 s 78 (2).

2 As to the meaning of 'person subject to naval law'; see **[0941]**.

3 As to the meaning of 'naval offence'; see **[0923]**.

4 As to the meaning of 'civil offence'; see **[0910]**.

5 The Navy Act 1957 s 78 (1).

6 The Navy Act 1957 s 78 (2) (a).

7 The Navy Act 1957 s 78 (2) (b).

8 The Navy Act 1957 s 78 (2) (c).

9 *State v KM Nanavati* (1960) 62 Bom LR 383; 1960 Cri LJ 1558.

[1035] Jurisdiction as to time No person unless he is an offender who has avoided apprehension or fled from justice or committed the offence of desertion or fraudulent entry or the offence of mutiny shall be tried or punished in pursuance of the Navy Act 1957 or any offence committed by him unless such trial commences within three years from the commission of such offence[1]. However, in the computation of the period of three years any time during which an offender was outside India or any time during which he was a prisoner of war shall be deducted[2]. In computation of the period of three years, any time during which: (i) the commission of the offence was not known to the person aggrieved by the offence or to the authority competent to initiate action, the first day on which such offence comes to the knowledge of such person or authority, whichever is earlier[3]; (ii) it was not known by whom the offence was committed, the first day on which the identity of the offender is known to the person aggrieved by the offence or to the authority investigating into the offence, whichever is earlier, shall be excluded[4]. Further, where the institution of the prosecution in respect of an offence has been stayed by an injunction or order, then in computing the period of three years, the period of the continuance of the injunction or order, the day on which it was issued or made and the day on which it was withdrawn shall be excluded[5]. In addition, no trial for an offence of desertion other than desertion on active service or fraudulent entry shall be commenced if the person in question not being an officer has subsequently to the commission of the offence served continuously in an exemplary manner for not less than three years in the Indian Navy[6].

1 The Navy Act 1957 s 79.

2 The Navy Act 1957 s 79 proviso.

3 The Navy Act 1957 s 79 second proviso (a).

4 The Navy Act 1957 s 79 third proviso (b).

5 The Navy Act 1957 s 79 fourth proviso.

6 The Navy Act 1957 s 79 fifth proviso.

[1036] Trial after a person ceases to be subject to naval law When any offence mentioned in the Navy Act 1957[1] has been committed by any person while subject to naval law[2] and such person has since the commission of the offence ceased to be subject to naval law, he may be taken into and kept in custody, tried and punished under the Navy Act for such offence in like manner as he may have been taken into and kept in custody, tried and punished of he had continued subject to naval law[3]. However, he shall not be tried for such offence except in the case of an offence of mutiny or desertion, unless the trial against him commences within six months after he has ceased to be so subject[4].

1 Ie in the Navy Act 1957 chapter VIII.

2 As to the meaning of 'subject to naval law'; see **[0935]**.

3 The Navy Act 1957 s 80.

4 The Navy Act 1957 s 80 proviso.

B. Offences in Relation to court martial, disciplinary court and prisons

[1037] Offences by person not subject to naval law in relation to courts martial and disciplinary courts
Every person not subject to naval law[1], who (i) being duly summoned or ordered to attend as a witness before a court martial or disciplinary court fails to attend without due cause[2], (ii) refuses to take an oath or make an affirmation legally required by a court martial or disciplinary court to be taken or made[3], (iii) being sworn or affirmed, refuses to answer any questions put by or before a court martial or disciplinary court, which he is law bound to answer[4], (iv) refuses to produce or deliver up a document in his power which the court martial or disciplinary court may legally demand[5], or (v) is guilty of contempt of court martial or disciplinary court[6]; shall be punished with imprisonment for a term which may extend to two years, or with fine, or with both[7].

1 As to the meaning of 'person subject to naval law'; see **[0941]**.

2 The Navy Act s 165 (a).

3 The Navy Act s 165 (b).

4 The Navy Act s 165 (c).

5 The Navy Act s 165 (d).

6 The Navy Act s 165 (e).

7 The Navy Act s 165.

[1038] Penalties for aiding escape or attempt to escape of prisoners and for breach of prison regulations

1 Every person, who (i) conveys or causes to be conveyed into any naval prison or naval detention quarters any arms, tools or instruments, or any mask or other disguise to facilitate the escape of any prisoner or person undergoing detention[1], or (ii) by any means whatever aids any prisoner or person undergoing detention to escape or in an attempt to escape from such prison or naval detention quarters whether an escape be actually made or not[2]; shall be punished with imprisonment for a term which may extend to 14 years[3].

2 Every person who brings or attempts to bring into a naval prison or naval detention quarters, in contravention of the Regulations for the Navy, spirituous or fermented liquor; shall for every such offence be punished with a fine not exceeding Rs 200 and not less than Rs 100/-[4].

3 Every person, who (i) brings into a naval prison or naval detention quarters or for any prisoner or person undergoing detention, without the knowledge of the officer-in-charge of prison or detention quarters,

any money, clothing, provision, tobacco, letters, papers, or other articles not allowed by the rules of the prison or naval detention quarters, to be in the possession of a prisoner or person undergoing detention[5], or (ii) throws into said prison or naval detention quarters, any such articles, or by desire of any prisoner or person undergoing detention, without the sanction of the said officer carries out of the prison or naval detention quarters any of the such articles[5]; shall for every such offence be punished with a fine not exceeding Rs 200/-[7].

4 Every person, who (i) interrupts any officer of a naval prison or naval detention quarters in the execution of his duty[8], or (ii) aids or abets any person to assault, resist, or interrupt any such officer[9]; shall for every such offence be punished with imprisonment which may extend to two years, or with fine, or both[10].

5 Every fine recovered under the forgoing provisions shall be applied as the central government may direct notwithstanding any law, charter, or custom to the contrary[11].

1 The Navy Act 1957 s 166 (1) (a).

2 The Navy Act 1957 s 166 (1) (b).

3 The Navy Act 1957 s 166 (1).

4 The Navy Act 1957 s 166 (2).

5 The Navy Act 1957 s 166 (3) (a).

6 The Navy Act 1957 s 166 (3) (b).

7 The Navy Act 1957 s 166 (3).

8 The Navy Act 1957 s 166 (4) (a).

9 The Navy Act 1957 s 166 (4) (b).

10 The Navy Act 1957 s 166 (4).

11 The Navy Act 1957 s 166 (5).

[1039] Penalty as regards gaolers, etc. Every governor, gaoler, and keeper of any prison, gaol, or house of correction or of any naval detention quarters, and every person having the charge or command of any place, ship, or vessel for imprisonment, who shall without lawful excuse, refuse or neglect to receive or confine, remove, discharge, or deliver up any offender against the provisions of the Navy Act 1957, or any of them, shall incur for every such refusal or neglect a penalty not exceeding Rs 1,000/- and every such penalty shall be applied as the central government may direct notwithstanding any law, charter, or custom to the contrary[1].

1 The Navy Act 1957 s 167.

5. PRE-TRIAL PROCEDURE

CONTENTS

PARA

A. Arrest

B. Charge

C. Investigation

A. Arrest

[1040] Power to issue warrants of arrest The chief of the naval staff, every officer in command of a fleet or squadron of ships of the Indian navy or of any ship of the Indian navy or the senior officer present at a port or an officer having by virtue of certain provision of the Navy Act 1957[1] power to try offences, may by warrant under his hand, authorize any person to arrest any offender subject to naval law[2] for any offence triable under the Navy Act 1957 mentioned in such warrant and any such warrant may include the names of more persons than one in respect of several offence of the same nature[3]. Any person named in any such warrant as aforesaid may forthwith on his arrest, if the warrant so directs, be taken to the ship of the Indian navy to which he belongs or some other ship of the Indian navy[4]. A person authorized to arrest an offender may use such force as may be necessary for the purpose affecting such arrest[5]. Where a warrant under the Navy Act 1957[6] is issued to a police officer, the police officer shall take steps to execute the warrant and arrest the offender in like manner as if such warrant had been issued by a magistrate of competent jurisdiction and shall, as soon as may be, deliver the person when arrested into naval custody[7].

1 Ie the Navy Act 1957 s 93 (2) and (3).

2 As to the meaning of 'subject to naval law'; see **[0935]**.

3 The Navy Act 1957 s 83 (1).

4 The Navy Act 1957 s 83 (2).

5 The Navy Act 1957 s 83 (3).

6 Ie the Navy Act 1957 s 83 (1).

7 As to the meaning of 'naval custody'; see **[0921]**; The Navy Act 1957 s 83 (4).

[1041] Arrest without warrant Any person subject to naval law[1] may be ordered into custody by any superior officer[2] for any offence triable under the Navy Act 1957[3]. Every person subject to naval law may arrest without warrant any other person subject to naval law though he may be of a higher rank who in his view commits an offence punishable with death, or imprisonment for life for a term which may extend to 14 years[4]. A provost marshal[5] may arrest any person subject to naval law in accordance with the provisions of the Navy Act 1957[6]. It shall be lawful for the purpose of effecting arrest, or taking a person into custody, without warrant to use such force as may be necessary for the purpose[7]

1 As to the meaning of 'person subject to naval law'; see **[0941]**.

2 As to the meaning of 'superior officer'; see **[0937]**.

3 The Navy Act 1957 s 84 (1).

4 The Navy Act 1957 s 84 (2).

5 As to the definition of 'provost marshal'; see **[0932]**.

6 Ie the Navy Act 1957 s 89; The Navy Act 1957 s 84 (3).

7 The Navy Act 1957 s 84 (4).

[1042] Procedure and conditions of naval custody No person subject to naval law[1] who is arrested under the Navy Act 1957 shall be detained in naval custody[2] without being informed of the grounds for such arrest[3]. Every person subject to naval law who is arrested and detained in naval custody shall be produced before his commanding officer[4] or other prescribed officer within a period of 48 hours of such arrest excluding the time necessary for the journey from the place of arrest to such officer. No such person shall be detained in custody beyond the period of 48 hours without the authority of such commanding or other officer[5].

1 As to the meaning of 'person subject to naval law'; see **[0941]**.

2 As to the meaning of 'naval custody'; see **[0921]**.

3 The Navy Act 1957 s 85 (1).

4 As to the meaning of 'commanding officer'; see **[0912]**.

5 The Navy Act 1957 s 85 (2).

[1043] Investigation after arrest The charge made against any person subject to naval law[1] taken into custody shall without any unnecessary delay be investigated by the proper authority and as soon as may be either proceedings shall be taken for the trial or such person shall be discharged from custody[2].

1 As to the meaning of 'person subject to naval law'; see **[0941]**.

2 The Navy Act 1957 s 86.

[1044] Duty to receive or keep in custody The commanding officer[1] shall be responsible for the safe custody of every person who is in naval custody[2] on board his ship or in his establishment[3]. The officer or sailor in charge of guard, or a provost marshal[4] shall receive and keep any person who is duly committed to his custody[5].

1 As to the meaning of 'commanding officer'; see **[0912]**.

2 As to the meaning of 'naval custody'; see **[0921]**;

3 The Navy Act 1957 s 87 (1).

4 As to the definition of 'officer', 'sailor' and 'provost marshal'; see **[0927]**, **[9033]** and **[0932]**.

5 The Navy Act 1957 s 87 (2).

[1045] Procedure before trial Subject to the provisions of the Navy Act 1957, the procedure before trial and the manner of investigation shall be as prescribed under the Regulations for the Navy[1].

1 Ie as prescribed under the Regulations for the Navy 1965, Part II, statutory. The Navy Act 1957 s 88; also see: **[1050]** and **[1053]**.

[1046] Provost marshals Provost marshals[1] may be appointed by the chief of the naval staff or the prescribed officer[2]. The duties of a provost marshal are to take charge of persons in naval custody[3], to preserve good order and discipline and to prevent breaches of the same by persons subject to naval law[4] or to the law in force relating to the government of the regular army or the air force[5]. A provost marshal may at any time arrest and detain for trial any person subject to naval law who commits or is charged with, an offence and may also carry into effect any punishment to be inflicted in pursuance of sentence passed under the Navy Act 1957, but shall not inflict any punishment on his own authority[6]. However, no officer shall be so arrested or detained otherwise than on the order of another officer[7]. For the purpose of certain provisions of the Navy Act 1957[8] a provost marshal shall be deemed to include and any of his assistants appointed under the law in force relating to the government of the regular army or air force[9].

1 As to the definition of 'provost marshal'; see **[0932]**.

2 The Navy Act 1957 s 89 (1).

3 As to the definition of 'naval custody'; see **[0921]**.

4 As to the meaning of definition of 'persons subject to naval law'; see **[0941]**.

5 The Navy Act 1957 s 89 (2).

6 The Navy Act 1957 s 89 (3). The accused, subject to the Navy Act 1957 could not be detained in a naval jail under this provision after his trial. There is also no other provision in the Navy Act 1957, which authorizes the accused's

detention in a naval jail after his conviction. *State v KM Nanavati* (1960) 62 Bom LR 383; 1960 Cri LJ 1558.

7 The Navy Act 1957 s 89 (3) proviso.

8 Ie the Navy Act 1957 s 89 (2) and (3).

9 The Navy Act 1957 s 89 (4).

B. Charge

[1047] Joinder of charges For every distinct offence of which any person is accused, there shall be separate charge but except as otherwise provided by Regulations for the Navy, all separate charges may be tried together[1].

1 The Navy Act 1957 s 90. Also see [1049].

[1048] Acts amounting to different offences If a single act or series of acts is of such a nature that it is doubtful which of several offences the facts which can be proved will constitute, the accused may be charged with having committed all or any of such offences, and any number of such charges may be tried at one trial; or he may be charged in the alternative with having committed some of the said offences[1].

1 The Navy Act 1957 s 91.

[1049] Joinder of accused persons The following persons may be charged and tried together: (i) persons accused of the same offence committed in the course of the same transaction[1]; (ii) persons accused of an offence and persons accused of abetment of or an attempt to commit, such offence[2]; and (iii) persons accused of different offences committed in the course of the same transaction[3]. However, in a trial by a court martial, the trial judge advocate may, on the application made in this behalf by any accused, direct that each of the accused be tried separately by the same court martial[4].

1 The Navy Act 1957 s 92 (i).

2 The Navy Act 1957 s 92 (ii).

3 The Navy Act 1957 s 92 (iii).

4 The Navy Act 1957 s 92 proviso.

C. Investigation

[1050] Investigation of departmental offences If a sailor[1] commits a departmental or a divisional offence, the offence shall be investigated by his departmental or divisional officer as the case may be, and he may be summarily tried and punished by his departmental officer or his divisional officer provided that the offence can be adequately punished with in the powers of punishment delegated to such officer[2]. If the departmental or the divisional officer decides not to deal with the case himself, he shall refer the case to the executive officer[3]. Where a sailor commits any other offence such offence may be investigated and the sailor may be tried and punished by the officer of the watch or the officer of the day provided that the offence can be adequately punished within the powers of punishment delegated to the officer of the watch or the officer of the day[4]. If the officer of the watch or the officer of the day decides not to deal with the case himself, he shall refer it to the executive officer[5]. The executive officer may investigate and try and punish summarily any offence referred to him provided it can be adequately punished within the powers of punishment delegated to him[6]. If the executive officer decides not to deal with the case himself, he shall refer it to the commanding officer[7].

1 As to the definitions of 'sailor'; see **[0933]**.
2 The Regulations for the Navy 1965, part II, regulation 22 (1).
3 The Regulations for the Navy 1965, part II, regulation 22 (2).
4 The Regulations for the Navy 1965, part II, regulation 22 (3).
5 The Regulations for the Navy 1965, part II, regulation 22 (4).
6 The Regulations for the Navy 1965, part II, regulation 22 (5).
7 As to the definitions of 'commanding officer'; see **[0912]**. The Regulations for the Navy 1965, part II, regulation 22 (6).

[1051] Offences by sailors on board tenders Offences committed by sailors[1] belonging to a tender shall be similarly investigated and tried and if ultimately the offence is one which cannot be adequately dealt with by the commanding officer[2] of the tender he shall refer it to the commanding officer of the parent ship[3].

1 As to the definitions of 'sailor'; see **[0933]**.
2 As to the definitions of 'commanding officer'; see **[0912]**.
3 As to the definitions of 'ship'; see **[0934]**. The Regulations for the Navy 1965, part II, regulation 23.

[1052] Modification in case of training establishments In training establishments where an officer-in-charge of a school has been delegated powers of awarding punishment, the officer of the day if he decides not to deal with the case himself, shall refer the case of any sailor[1] belonging to a school to the officer-in-charge of that school, who may deal with the case provided it can be adequately punished within his powers of punishment[2]. If the officer-in-charge of the school decides not to deal with the case himself, he shall refer it to the commanding officer[3].

1 As to the definitions of 'sailor'; see **[0933]**.
2 The Regulations for the Navy 1965, part II, regulation 24 (1).
3 As to the definitions of 'commanding officer'; see **[0912]**. The Regulations for the Navy 1965, part II, regulation 24 (2).

[1053] Investigation of other offences The preliminary investigation of offences by the officer of the watch or officer of the day shall take place as soon as possible after the commission of the offence while witnesses' memory is still fresh[1]. The formal investigation of offences shall, when the service and circumstances admit, be deferred until the day following that of the commission of the offence[2]. Hasty charges shall not be made and as far as practicable there shall not be any delay in the investigation of the charge and the decision of the case and, when the accused is found guilty in the award of the punishment[3]. The fact that an offender's service documents are not available shall not normally delay the investigation of an offence though there may be some delay in the infliction of punishment if the said documents are expected within a reasonable time[4]. All charges shall be investigated fully on the quarterdeck or other suitable place, in the presence of the complainant and the accused and the complainant, accused and the witnesses shall be heard fully and with impartiality[5]. The accused, the divisional officer or other defending officer, the complainant and the master-at-arms (or the person performing his duties) shall be present throughout the investigation[6]. The witnesses shall be kept apart and out of earshot so that they cannot hear what other witnesses are saying when giving evidence and they shall withdraw after they have given evidence[7]. The investigating officer shall, in every case consider whether the case is sufficiently serious to warrant the recording of the evidence and whether is desirable to record it as a precaution against a witness changing his evidence[8]. Inconsiderate punishments, as well as needlessly protracted punishments, shall be avoided and in awarding punishment regard shall be had to: (i) the necessity for prevention of crime or offences and for the maintenance of proper order and discipline[9]; (ii) the gravity of the offence and the previous character of the offender[10]; and (iii) any consequences which may arise indirectly as a result of the offence or of the award, particularly in regard to the charges against the offender's pay for offences of absence or desertion, or for damage to or loss of stores and such other matters[11]. In cases of repeated offences the effect of gradually increasing the degree of punishment until the maximum is reached shall be tried before awarding the maximum punishment[12]. All altercations with excited or drunken men shall be avoided; no man under the influence of temper or drink shall be placed in a situation likely to excite him further and thereby lead him to acts of violence or insubordination[13].

1 The Regulations for the Navy 1965, part II, regulation 25 (1).
2 The Regulations for the Navy 1965, part II, regulation 25 (2).
3 The Regulations for the Navy 1965, part II, regulation 25 (3).
4 The Regulations for the Navy 1965, part II, regulation 25 (4).
5 The Regulations for the Navy 1965, part II, regulation 25 (5).
6 The Regulations for the Navy 1965, part II, regulation 25 (6).
7 The Regulations for the Navy 1965, part II, regulation 25 (7).
8 The Regulations for the Navy 1965, part II, regulation 25 (8).
9 The Regulations for the Navy 1965, part II, regulation 25 (9) (i).
10 The Regulations for the Navy 1965, part II, regulation 25 (9) (ii).
11 The Regulations for the Navy 1965, part II, regulation 25 (9) (iii).
12 The Regulations for the Navy 1965, part II, regulation 25 (10).
13 The Regulations for the Navy 1965, part II, regulation 25 (11).

[1054] Assistance to the accused If the alleged offence is one which may be brought before the commanding officer[1], the accused may request and shall be afforded at the earliest stage at which this is practicable, the assistance of any officer or other person in his ship whose assistance is reasonably available[2]. If no such request is made, it shall be the duty of the divisional officer or such other officer as the commanding officer may detail, to advise the accused at all stages[3]. The officer or person advising the accused may be changed at any stage either at the request of the accused or on account of exigencies of service[4].

1 As to the definition of 'commanding officer'; see **[0912]**.
2 The Regulations for the Navy 1965, part II, regulation 26 (1).
3 The Regulations for the Navy 1965, part II, regulation 26 (2).
4 The Regulations for the Navy 1965, part II, regulation 26 (3).

[1055] Procedure at investigation in general During investigations the evidence in support of the charge shall be heard first[1]. Immediately after the charge has been read out, the investigating officer shall warn the accused that he should not make any statement or give any evidence on his own behalf until all the evidence against him has been heard[2]. On conclusion of the evidence in support of the charge, the investigating officer shall decide whether a case has been made out against the accused[3]. If there is no case, the investigating officer shall either dismiss the case or, if further evidence is likely to become available, stand it over and if there is a prima facie case, and it is a simple one with which the investigating officer thinks he can deal with himself, he shall ask the accused if he admits the charge[4]. If the accused does not admit the charge and the matter is one within the investigating officer's powers of punishment, he shall inform the accused that he will proceed to try the case, giving him an opportunity of making a statement and calling witnesses[5].

1 The Regulations for the Navy 1965, part II, regulation 27 (1).

2 The Regulations for the Navy 1965, part II, regulation 27 (2).

3 The Regulations for the Navy 1965, part II, regulation 27 (3). The meaning of 'on conclusion of the evidence in support of the charge', under this provision is that the chief-examination must be followed by cross-examination. *RS Singh v Union of India*, TA No. 171 of 2010, decided by the Armed Forces Tribunal, Regional Bench, Chennai on 22 October 2010.

4 The Regulations for the Navy 1965, part II, regulation 27 (4).

5 The Regulations for the Navy 1965, part II, regulation 27 (5).

[1056] Investigation by the officer of the watch, the officer of the day, or the executive officer

1 If, after hearing the evidence in support of the charge, the officer of the watch, the officer of the day or the executive officer is of opinion that the charge, if proved, would be beyond his power to punish, he must bear in mind that a confession made before him by the accused will not be admissible in evidence at any further proceedings unless the accused has been cautioned, before he speaks, that he is not obliged to say anything unless he wishes to do so, and that any statement he may make may be given in evidence. Care should be taken to avoid any suggestion that the accused's answers can only be used in evidence against him, as this may discourage an innocent person from making a statement which might help to clear him of the charge. The investigating officer must also bear in mind that in case beyond his power of punishment his functions are to see whether there is a prima facie case, to collect evidence when it is important that evidence be collected immediately, and, to give the accused a chance to make a statement. If the alleged offence is one which is likely in itself to lead at least to a warrant punishment (as distinct from one which may lead to a warrant punishment because it is the culminating offence in a series of minor offences), the investigating officer should address the accused in the following words after hearing the evidence in support of the charges:

"Do you wish to say anything in answer to the charge? You are not obliged to say anything unless you wish to do so; but whatever you say will be taken down in writing and may be given in evidence.[1]"

2 The officer of the watch or officer of the day need not use these words unless he decides to hear then defence before sending the case to the executive officer[2].

3 If the accused makes a statement, it should be taken down in writing, On conclusion of this statement the investigating officer should not ask any question save to point out any ambiguity and ask if the accused wishes to clear it up or to point out that no reference has been made to some charge and ask if the accused wishes to say anything about it. In particular, nothing must be said which indicates that the accused is expected to make any further statement[3].

4 If he has not already done so, the investigating officer must then make up his mind whether the case

against the accused has been made out. If he decides that no case has been made out, he is to dismiss the charge[4].

5 If the investigating officer decides to refer the case to higher authority, the accused is to be informed accordingly, the customary terminology 'commander's report' or 'captain's report', as the case may be, being used[5].

1 The Regulations for the Navy 1965, part II, regulation 28 (1).

2 The Regulations for the Navy 1965, part II, regulation 28 (2).

3 The Regulations for the Navy 1965, part II, regulation 28 (3).

4 The Regulations for the Navy 1965, part II, regulation 28 (4).

5 The Regulations for the Navy 1965, part II, regulation 28 (5).

[1057] Investigation by the commanding officer The investigation of any offence by the commanding officer[1] shall also be regulated by the preceding provision[2]. If, after hearing the evidence in support of the charge, the commanding officer is of opinion that there is a prima facie case and that the charge, if proved, would be within his power to punish, he shall proceed to try the case[3]. If the commanding officer decides to apply for trial by court-martial, or to give a warrant punishment, the accused shall be told that the case is 'remanded'[4]. If the punishment to be awarded is likely o be a warrant punishment requiring approval of superior authority, a summary of evidence given by the witnesses shall be recorded[5].

1 As to the definition of 'commanding officer'; see **[0912]**.

2 Ie the Regulations for the Navy 1965, part II, regulation 28. The Regulations for the Navy 1965, part II, regulation 29 (1).

3 The Regulations for the Navy 1965, part II, regulation 29 (2). Once the commanding officer has come to a definite conclusion that a prima facie case has been made out and the charge has been proved, before awarding any punishment to the accused it is the duty of the commanding officer to try the case. Non-adherence to the mandatory provision of the Regulations for the Navy 1965, part II, r 29 (2) will vitiate the summary trial. *Smt Neelam Mishra v Union of India*, TA No. 197 of 2010, decided by the Armed Forces Tribunal, Regional Bench, Chennai on 29 April 2011.

4 The Regulations for the Navy 1965, part II, regulation 29 (3).

5 The Regulations for the Navy 1965, part II, regulation 29 (4).

[1058] Right to elect trial by court martial If a chief petty officer[1] or petty officer is charged with an offence which, proved would justify his being summarily reduced in lower rank, the following procedure shall be adopted: (i) A formal and public investigation shall be held by the commanding officer[2], a careful summary of the evidence of the witnesses for and against being made at the time in such a way that it could, if necessary, be incorporated in the appropriate form in due course as a summary evidence[3]; (ii) Both before and during the investigation the accused shall be afforded the assistance under the provisions of the Regulations for the Navy 1965[4]; (iii) At the conclusion of the investigation, the commanding officer, if he thinks that the offences if proved, would deserve summary reduction in rank, shall inform the accused that he can, if he desires, be tried by court martial and that a rank taken away by sentence of court martial cannot be regained without submitting it to the chief of the naval staff for approval, but the commodore bureau of sailor or the commanding officer would have the power to restore it if the reduction in rank is summarily effected by warrant[5]; (iv) If the accused, within 24 hours of such information indicates that he does not wish to be tried by court martial and the commanding officer decides that reduction in rank is the appropriate punishment, necessary steps shall be taken to obtain the approval on the warrant, of a flag officer or commodore to whom reference can most conveniently be made, the warrant being accompanied by a summary of the evidence. Each of the witness shall sign the summary of the evidence he has given. The warrant shall be signed, but neither dated nor read until the necessary approval has been obtained, but if such approval cannot be obtained within a reasonable period, the commanding officer may award the sentence himself, reporting the circumstances without delay to the appropriate administrative authority[6]; (v) Should the accused elect to be tried by court martial, the necessary steps for the purpose shall be taken[7]; (vi) Should the exigencies of service, such as a single ship being on detached service, not permit a court martial to be assembled within a reasonable period the senior officer present may, if he considers it necessary, direct the commanding officer to deal with the case summarily and if in these circumstances, the commanding officer reduces a chief petty officer or petty officer to a lower rank, the appropriate administrative authority shall order a board of enquiry to assemble at the earliest possible date; if the report of board of enquiry indicates that a lighter punishment would have been sufficient, the said authority may restore the rank from a date to be fixed by it. The accused and the complainant together with the defending officer shall be present during the whole of the time that witnesses are being examined before the board of enquiry. A report, including the minutes of the enquiry, and a copy of warrant shall be forwarded by the administrative authority to the chief of the naval staff[8].

1 As to the definitions of 'petty officer'; see **[0927]**.

2 As to the definitions of 'commanding officer'; see **[0912]**.

3 The Regulations for the Navy 1965, part II, regulation 30 (a).

4 Ie the Regulations for the Navy 1965, part II, regulation 26. The Regulations for the Navy 1965, part II, regulation 30 (b); see **[1054]**.

5 The Regulations for the Navy 1965, part II, regulation 30 (c).

6 The Regulations for the Navy 1965, part II, regulation 30 (d).

7 The Regulations for the Navy 1965, part II, regulation 30 (e).

8 The Regulations for the Navy 1965, part II, regulation 30 (f).

[1059] Identification of suspect When an offence has been committed and it is possible that witnesses may not be certain of the identity of the person apprehended, an identity parade shall be held[1]. The suspect (accused) shall be fall in with, if possible, at least eight other persons of the same or similar height, age, appearance and rig as himself[2]. The suspect (accused) shall be allowed to stand where he pleases and shall be asked whether he has any objection to the arrangements[3]. The suspect's (accused's) divisional officer or the person who may have been appointed to advice and assist him shall attend the parade, but other spectators shall not be allowed to do so[4]. The witnesses shall be admitted one by one and each witness shall be asked to identify the suspect and his reaction shall be recorded[5]. If a witness desires it, all the persons on the parade shall be ordered to remove or replace their caps, speaks, walk or do anything else that would assist in identification; all such actions are to be recorded[6]. After each witness has withdrawn, the accused shall be given an opportunity to change his position in the rank[7]. Witnesses who have inspected the parade shall be segregated from those who have not and steps shall be taken to ensure that no witness sees the suspect before he is fallen in with others in the position of his choice, and that no witness sees photographs or is given any description of the suspect before the parade[8].

1 The Regulations for the Navy 1965, part II, regulation 31 (1).

2 The Regulations for the Navy 1965, part II, regulation 31 (2).

3 The Regulations for the Navy 1965, part II, regulation 31 (3).

4 The Regulations for the Navy 1965, part II, regulation 31 (4).

5 The Regulations for the Navy 1965, part II, regulation 31 (5).

6 The Regulations for the Navy 1965, part II, regulation 31 (6).

7 The Regulations for the Navy 1965, part II, regulation 31 (7).

8 The Regulations for the Navy 1965, part II, regulation 31 (8).

[1060] Postponement of investigation Where the accused is on the sick list, the investigation may, at the discretion of the commanding officer[1] be postponed until the accused is fit for duty[2].

1 As to the definitions of 'commanding officer'; see **[0912]**.

2 The Regulations for the Navy 1965, part II, regulation 32.

[1061] Scrutiny of service documents The service documents of the accused shall not be scrutinsed by the commanding officer[1] or investigating officer until the accused has made his statement or stated that he does not intend to make a statement[2]. The commanding officer or the investigating officer, having decided whether or not the case against the accused has been made out, may examine the accused's service record in order to decide whether to deal with the case himself or refer it to higher authority; and such examination shall not be deemed to form a conviction of the accused[3].

1 As to the definitions of 'commanding officer'; see **[0912]**.

2 The Regulations for the Navy 1965, part II, regulation 33 (1).

3 The Regulations for the Navy 1965, part II, regulation 33 (2).

6. SUMMARY PUNISHMENTS AND TERMINATION OF SERVICE

CONTENTS

PARA

A. Powers of Punishment

[1062] Powers of punishment of commanding officer Under the Navy Act 1957, a commanding officer[1] may summarily try and punish any offence committed by a sailor[2] other than a capital offence and may award several punishments specified in the Regulations for the Navy 1965[3]. However: (i) If the offence is alleged to have been committed by a sailor who is entitled under the Regulations to elect trial by court martial, the procedure described in the Regulations shall be followed[4]; (ii) Except as provided in the Regulations for the Navy 1965[5], a chief petty officer, a petty officer, a sailor holding a leading rank or a sailor holding a good conduct badge shall not be summarily sentenced to imprisonment or detention[6]; (iii) A commanding officer shall not try summarily an offence where the chief of the naval staff has by general or special order directed that it shall be dealt with by court martial[7]. If the commanding officer, in cases within his jurisdiction considers that the offence cannot be adequately punished within his powers of punishment or where for other reasons he considers it desirable, he shall apply for a court martial[8]. The officer next in command is to assume the powers of trial and punishment of the commanding officer only if the commanding officer has ceased to exercise command through sickness or for any other reason or because of absence on duty or leave during which he will be absent from the ship for over 48 hours[9].

1 As to the definition of 'commanding officer'; see **[0912]**.

2 As to the definition of 'sailor'; see **[0933]**.

3 Ie the Regulations for the Navy 1965, part II, regulation 13; see **[1069]**. The Regulations for the Navy 1965, part II regulation 7 (1). See the power of court martial and commanding officers to try offences, The Navy Act 1957 s 93 (2)-(4); **[1123]**.

4 The Regulations for the Navy 1965, part II, regulation 7 (1) proviso (a).

5 Ie the Regulations for the Navy 1965, part II, regulation 36; see **[1075]**.

6 The Regulations for the Navy 1965, part II, regulation 7 (1) proviso (b).

7 The Regulations for the Navy 1965, part II, regulation 7 (1) proviso (c).

8 The Regulations for the Navy 1965, part II, regulation 7 (2).

9 The Regulations for the Navy 1965, part II, regulation 7 (3).

[1063] Punishments applicable to master chief petty officers A master chief petty officer may be tried and punished summarily by the commanding officer[1] of the rank of commander and above, and may then be awarded certain punishments contained in the Regulations for the Navy 1965[2]. In ships[3] commanded by officers below the rank of commander, the punishments referred to in the aforesaid provision may, subject to the exceptions provided for in the Regulations for the Navy 1965[4],in respect of emergency and with the previous approval of an officer of the rank of commander or above, be awarded by the commanding officer[5]. When being tried summarily, a master chief petty officer shall have no right to elect trial by court martial[6]. As master chief petty officer charged with offences which, if proved, will merit more severe punishment, is to be tried by court martial and in the event of such master chief petty officer being reduced to a rank below chief petty officer, he shall be given the option of release from the naval service[7].

1 As to the definition of 'commanding officer'; see **[0912]**.

2 Ie the Regulations for the Navy 1965, part II, regulation 13, punishment No. 3, 3A, 3B, 5, 6, 10, 12 and 14; The Regulations for the Navy 1965, part II, regulation 7A (1).

3 As to the definition of 'ship'; see **[0934]**.

4 Ie the Regulations for the Navy 1965, part II, regulation 12; see **[1068]**.

5 The Regulations for the Navy 1965, part II, regulation 7A (2).

6 The Regulations for the Navy 1965, part II, regulation 7A (2).

7 The Regulations for the Navy 1965, part II, regulation 7A (2).

[1064] Powers of officers in command of tenders absent from ship or boat detached Subject to the provisions of the Regulations for the Navy 1965, part II, the powers of trial and punishment of a commanding officer may, as respects sailors on board a tender to the ship, be exercised in the case of a single tender absent from the parent ship by the officer in command of the tender. In the case of two or more tenders absent from the parent ship in company or acting together, by the officer in immediate command of such tenders and as respects sailors on board any boat belonging to the ship be exercised when such boat is absent on detached service by the officer in command of the boat, provided that the commanding officer of the parent ship may at his discretion restrict powers to be exercised under the Regulations for the Navy 1965, according to the circumstances including the time that the tender or boat will be away and the seniority and experience of the officer who is to be in command[1].

1 The Regulations for the Navy 1965, part II, regulation 8.

[1065] Power of officers in immediate command of sailors on detached service The powers of trial and punishment of the commanding officer[1] may be exercised as respects sailors on detached service on shore or otherwise, by the officer in immediate command[2]. However, (i) the commanding officer of the ship to which the sailors on detached service belong may restrict the powers exercisable under these regulations and should in every case consider whether it is desirable to do so[3]; (ii) where sailors belonging to different ship are on detached service together, the proper superior authority may restrict the powers exercisable under the Regulations for the Navy 1965[4]; (iii) notwithstanding anything herein before contained, the chief of the naval staff may, by special or general order provide for the regulation of the powers on the officer in immediate command of sailors on detached service and where such a special or general order is in force, no other directions shall be given by the commanding officer or other superior authority[5].

1 As to the definition of 'commanding officer'; see **[0912]**.

2 The Regulations for the Navy 1965, part II, regulation 9.

3 The Regulations for the Navy 1965, part II, regulation 9 proviso (a).

4 The Regulations for the Navy 1965, part II, regulation 9 Proviso (b).

5 The Regulations for the Navy 1965, part II, regulation 9 proviso (c).

[1066] Powers of punishment of officers in command of naval barracks not commissioned as a ship The powers of trial and punishment of the commanding officer[1] may as respects sailors[1] quartered in naval barracks be exercised by the officer in command of the naval barracks provided that a proper superior authority may at its discretion restrict the powers of punishment to such extent as it may consider desirable[2].

1 As to the definition of 'commanding officer' and 'sailor'; see **[0912] and [0933]**.

2 The Regulations for the Navy 1965, part II, regulation 10.

[1067] Other officers empowered to deal with offences Offences may also be summarily tried and punished by officers to whom the commanding officer[1] has delegated powers of trial and punishment as provided in certain provision of the Regulations for the Navy 1965[2].

1 As to the definition of 'commanding officer'; see **[0912]**.

2 Ie the Regulations for the Navy 1965, part II, regulation 21; The Regulations for the Navy 1965, part II, regulation 11.

[1068] Restriction on powers of officers below the rank of commander Notwithstanding anything contained in certain provisions of the Regulations for the Navy 1965[1], a punishment requiring a warrant which would not otherwise require the approval of a superior authority, shall not be awarded by an officer below the rank of commander without the approval of an officer of or above that rank except in the case of extreme urgency like period of war, or in the case of ship on detached service abroad for a long period, subject always in such a case to any directions he may have received in his behalf from his superior authority[2].

1 Ie the Regulations for the Navy 1965, part II, regulations 7-11; see **[1062]-[1067]**.

2 The Regulations for the Navy 1965, part II, regulation 12.

B. Summary punishment to sailors

[1069] Summary Punishments The following punishments may be awarded summarily to sailors other than artificer apprentices and boys under training subject to the provisions of the Navy Act 1957 and the Regulations for the Navy 1965, Part II, and may be referred to by the numbers prefixed to each of them[1].

No. 1	Imprisonment for a period not exceeding three months
No. 2	Detention for a period not exceeding three months
No. 3	Dismissal from the Naval service
No. 3A	Forfeiture of seniority in rank of not more than 12 months in case of master chief petty officer
No. 3B	Forfeiture of time for promotion of not more than 12 months in case of master chief petty officer
No. 4	Reduction in rank
No. 5	Fine in respect of civil offences
No. 6	Mulcts of pay and allowances
No. 8	Solitary confinement in a cell or under a canvas screen for a period not exceeding fourteen days
No. 9	Deprivation of Good Conduct Badge and Good Conduct Medal
No. 10	Reprimand by the captain
No. 11	Extra work and drill for a period not exceeding 14 days
No. 12	Stoppage of leave for a period not exceeding 60 days
No. 13	Extra work or drill for not more than two hours in a day for a period not exceeding seven days
No. 14	Admonition

The punishments which may be awarded to artificer apprentices and boys under training are contained in the Regulations for the Navy 1965, Part II, Chapter III, regulations 74 to 88[2].

1 The Regulations for the Navy 1965, Part II, regulation 13 (1).

2 See regulations 74 to 88 at **[1097]** to **[1108]**; The Regulations for the Navy 1965, Part II, regulation 13 (2).

[1070] Warrant Punishment Punishments mentioned in the Regulations for the Navy 1965, Part II, regulation 13 (1), No. 1 to 5 and 8 and 9 are known as warrant punishments and shall not have effect unless a warrant is made out in the prescribed form[1].

1 The Regulations for the Navy 1965, Part II, regulation 14.

[1071] Punishments requiring approval of superior authority Punishment No. 3, dismissal from the naval service, and where any other punishment accompanies it, the whole of the punishment proposed to be awarded shall require the approval of the chief of the naval staff[1]. Punishment No. 1, imprisonment, and punishment No. 2, detention, Punishment No. 3A, forfeiture of seniority in rank in case of master chief petty officer and Punishment No. 3B, forfeiture of time for promotion in case of master chief petty officer, shall require the approval of the administrative authority[2]. Punishment No. 4, 5 and punishment No. 9 (the deprivation of a good conduct medal) shall require the approval of a flag officer or commodore[3].

1 The Regulations for the Navy 1965, Part II, regulation 15 (1).

2 The Regulations for the Navy 1965, Part II, regulation 15 (2).

3 The Regulations for the Navy 1965, Part II, regulation 15 (3).

[1072] Delegated authority to punish

1 In pursuance of certain provisions of the Navy Act 1957[1], the commanding officer[2] may delegate in writing powers of awarding punishments[3].

2 The executive officer, if he is of the rank of commander may be delegated the power to award the following punishments: (i) extra work and drill for a period not exceeding 14 days (No. 11)[4]; (ii) stoppage of leave for a period not exceeding 24 days (No. 12)[5]; (iii) extra work or drill for not more than two hours a day for a period not exceeding seven days (No. 13)[6]; (iv) admonition (No. 14)[7]; (v) mulcts of pay and allowances for a first offence of leave breaking up to 36 hours (No. 6)[8]; (vi) mulcts of pay and allowances for first offence of returning from leave drunk or drunkenness on shore (No. 6)[9].

3 The executive officer, if he is of the rank of lieutenant commander or lieutenant, may be delegated the power to award the following punishments: (i) extra work and drill for a period not exceeding seven days (No. 11)[10]; (ii) stoppage of leave for a period not exceeding 24 days but not to chief petty officer and petty officers (No. 12)[11]; (iii) extra work or drill for a period not exceeding seven days (No. 13)[12]; (iv) admonition (No. 14)[13].

4 The commander of an air squadron, if he is of or above the rank of lieutenant may be delegated the power to award the following punishments to sailors of the air squadron for offences connected with the work of the squadron but not for offences connected with the general duties of the ship: (i) extra work and drill for a period not exceeding seven days (No. 11)[14]; (ii) stoppage of leave for a period not exceeding 24 days but not to chief petty officers and petty officers (No. 12)[15]; (iii) extra work or drill for a period not exceeding seven days (No. 13)[16]; (iv) admonition (No. 14)[17].

5 The officer of the watch or officer of the day if he is of the rank of lieutenant or above may be delegated the power to award the following punishments: (i) extra work or dill for one day (No. 13)[18];

(ii) admonition (No. 14)[19].

6 Any of the following officers may, if he is of or above the rank of lieutenant, be delegated the power to award the punishments of extra work or drill for one day (No. 13) and admonition (No. 14) to any sailor of his department for an offence connected with the duties of his department but not connected with the general duties of the ship: (i) lieutenant commander (flying)[20]; (ii) lieutenant commander (air)[21]; (iii) the officer of the engineering department below the engineer officer in seniority or if there is only one officer or there is no other officer of the prescribed rank, the engineer officer[22]; (iv) at a naval air station, the officer of the engineering department next below the air engineer officer or if there is only one officer or there is no other officer of the prescribed rank in the department, the air engineer officer[23]; (v) the officer of then logistics department next below the logistics officer in seniority or if there is only one officer and there is no other officer of the prescribed rank, the logistics officer[24]; (vi) the officer of the electrical department next below the electrical officer in seniority or if there i only one officer or there is no other officer of the prescribed rank in the department, the electrical officer[25].

7 Any divisional officer of or above the rank of lieutenant may be delegated the power to award the punishments of extra work or drill for one day (No. 13) and admonition (No. 14) to any sailor of his division for offences connected with the division but not with the general duties of the ship or establishment[26].

8 The medical officer in charge of a ward may be authorised to award the punishment of extra work or drill for one day (No. 13) or admonition (No. 14)[27].

9 The commanding officer of a tender in company with the parent ship may be authorized to award the following punishments: (a) if he is of the rank of captain, any punishment referred to in the Regulations for the Navy 1965, Part II, regulation 13 other than imprisonment, detention or dismissal[28]; (b) if he is of the rank of commander: (i) reprimand by captain (No. 10)[29]; (ii) extra work and drill for a period not exceeding fourteen days (No. 11)[30]; (iii) stoppage of leave not exceeding twenty-four days (No. 12)[31]; (iv) extra work or drill not exceeding seven days (No. 13)[32]; (v) admonition (No. 14)[33]; (vi) mulcts of pay and allowances for leave breaking offences up to seventy-two hours absence (No. 6)[34]; (vii) Mulcts of pay and allowances for a first offence of returning from leave drunk or drunkenness on shore (No. 6)[35]; (c) if he is of the rank of lieutenant commander or below (i) mulcts of pay and allowances for first and un-aggravated offence of leave breaking up to 36 hours absence or first offence of returning from leave drunk or drunkenness on shore[36]; (ii) extra work and drill for a period not exceeding seven days (No. 11)[37]; (iii) stoppage of leave for a period not exceeding 24 days but not to chief petty officers and petty officers (No. 12)[38]; (iv) extra work or drill for not more than two hours in a day for a period not exceeding seven days (No. 13)[39]; (v) admonition (No. 14)[40].

10 The executive officer of a tender may, if he is of or above the rank of lieutenant, be authorised to award the same punishment as may be delegated to the executive officer if he is lieutenant commander or a lieutenant[41].

11 The officer-in-charge of a school at a training establishment may be delegated the power to award to sailors in the school the same punishments as may be delegated to the executive officer of corresponding rank[42].

12 In pursuance of certain provisions of the Navy Act 1957[43] the commanding officer of barracks may

delegate in writing to executive officer of barrack and officer of the day the same powers of punishments as may be delegated by the commanding officer under the foregoing provisions to the executive officer and officer of the day respectively[44].

13 The punishments under certain provisions of the Regulations for the Navy 1965, part II[45], shall be duly entered in the daily record of offences and punishments and the punishments under certain other provisions of the aforesaid Regulations[46] shall be entered in a special minor punishments book signed by the officer awarding them[47].

14 The minor punishments book shall be examined and initialed by the executive officer daily and signed by the commanding officer weekly[48].

15 The record of all punishments awarded under the Regulations for the Navy 1965, part II[49], shall be examined weekly by the commanding officer of the depot ship or establishment[50].

1 Ie the Navy Act 1957 s 93 (4).

2 As to the definition of 'commanding officer'; see **[0912]**.

3 The Regulations for the Navy 1965, part II, regulation 21 (1).

4 The Regulations for the Navy 1965, part II, regulation 21 (2) (a).

5 The Regulations for the Navy 1965, part II, regulation 21 (2) (b).

6 The Regulations for the Navy 1965, part II, regulation 21 (2) (c).

7 The Regulations for the Navy 1965, part II, regulation 21 (2) (d).

8 The Regulations for the Navy 1965, part II, regulation 21 (2) (e).

9 The Regulations for the Navy 1965, part II, regulation 21 (2) (f).

10 The Regulations for the Navy 1965, part II, regulation 21 (3) (a).

11 The Regulations for the Navy 1965, part II, regulation 21 (3) (b).

12 The Regulations for the Navy 1965, part II, regulation 21 (3) (c).

13 The Regulations for the Navy 1965, part II, regulation 21 (3) (d).

14 The Regulations for the Navy 1965, part II, regulations 21 (4) (a).

15 The Regulations for the Navy 1965, part II, regulation 21 (4) (b).

16 The Regulations for the Navy 1965, part II, regulation 21 (4) (c).

17 The Regulations for the Navy 1965, part II, regulation 21 (4) (d).

18 The Regulations for the Navy 1965, part II, regulation 21 (5) (a).

19 The Regulations for the Navy 1965, part II, regulation 21 (5) (b).

20 The Regulations for the Navy 1965, part II, regulation 21 (6) (i).

21 The Regulations for the Navy 1965, part II, regulation 21 (6) (ii).

22 The Regulations for the Navy 1965, part II, regulation 21 (6) (iii).

23 The Regulations for the Navy 1965, part II, regulation 21 (6) (iv).

24 The Regulations for the Navy 1965, part II, regulation 21 (6) (v).

25 The Regulations for the Navy 1965, part II, regulation 21 (6) (vi).

26 The Regulations for the Navy 1965, part II, regulation 21 (7).

27 The Regulations for the Navy 1965, part II, regulation 21 (8).

28 The Regulations for the Navy 1965, part II, regulation 21 (9) (a).

29 The Regulations for the Navy 1965, part II, regulation 21 (9) (b) (i).

30 The Regulations for the Navy 1965, part II, regulation 21 (9) (b) (ii).

31 The Regulations for the Navy 1965, part II, regulation 21 (9) (b) (iii).

32 The Regulations for the Navy 1965, part II, regulation 21 (9) (b) (iv).

33 The Regulations for the Navy 1965, part II, regulation 21 (9) (b) (v).

34 The Regulations for the Navy 1965, part II, regulation 21 (9) (b) (vi).

35 The Regulations for the Navy 1965, part II, regulation 21 (9) (b) (vii).

36 The Regulations for the Navy 1965, part II, regulation 21 (9) (c) (i).

37 The Regulations for the Navy 1965, part II, regulation 21 (9) (c) (ii).

38 The Regulations for the Navy 1965, part II, regulation 21 (9) (c) (iii).

39 The Regulations for the Navy 1965, part II, regulation 21 (9) (c) (iv).

40 The Regulations for the Navy 1965, part II, regulation 21 (9) (c) (v).

41 The Regulations for the Navy 1965, part II, regulation 21 (10).

42 The Regulations for the Navy 1965, part II, regulation 21 (11).

43 Ie the Navy Act 1957 s 93 (4).

44 The Regulations for the Navy 1965, part II, regulation 21 (12).

45 Ie the Regulations for the Navy 1965, part II, regulation 21 (2), (3), (4), (9), (10) and (11).

46 Ie the Regulations for the Navy 1965, part II, regulation 21 (5), (6), (7) and (8).

47 The Regulations for the Navy 1965, part II, regulation 21 (13).

48 The Regulations for the Navy 1965, part II, regulation 21 (14).

49 Ie the Regulations for the Navy 1965, part II, regulation 21 (9), (10) and (11).

50 The Regulations for the Navy 1965, part II, regulation 21 (15).

C. Regulation for Individual Punishments

(i) Imprisonment and Detention (Nos. 1 and 2)

[1073] A. When to be awarded Sentence of imprisonment should normally be confined to sailors[1] who have already undergone several sentences of detention without effect, and to other sailors who are also to be dismissed from service[2]. Imprisonment may, however, be awarded in lieu of detention when there is no detention accommodation available in naval detention quarters in which case a note to that effect shall be made on the punishment warrant and on the advancement and conduct record sheet[3]. Notwithstanding the above provisions, persons below the age of 21 shall not be summarily sentenced to imprisonment except for grave civil offences and (in such cases) detention may be awarded even though they have not to be retained in service[4]. A sentence of 90 days shall not be awarded if that period exceeds three calendar months[5]. Detention shall not be awarded for a period of less than 10 days[6]. In addition to the consequential punishment provided in the Navy Act 1950[7], a sentence of imprisonment or detention shall carry with it deprivation of good conduct medal and badges[8]. Whenever a sentence shall be passed by a commanding officer[9] on an offender already under sentence of detention or imprisonment under the Regulations for the Navy 1965, part II, for former offence, the commanding officer may award sentence of detention or imprisonment for the offence, for which he is under trial, to commence at the expiration of the sentence of detention or imprisonment to which he has been previously sentenced[10]. However, any term of detention or imprisonment awarded to a person in pursuance of this provision as will prolong the total term of detention or imprisonment beyond the maximum period of three months as specified in the Regulations for the Navy 1965, part II[11], shall be deemed to be remitted[12].

1 As to the definition of 'sailor'; see **[0933]**.

2 The Regulations for the Navy 1965, part II, regulation 34 (1).

3 The Regulations for the Navy 1965, part II, regulation 34 (2).

4 The Regulations for the Navy 1965, part II, regulation 34 (3).

5 The Regulations for the Navy 1965, part II, regulation 34 (4).

6 The Regulations for the Navy 1965, part II, regulation 34 (5).

7 Ie in the Navy Act 1950 s 82 (9).

8 The Regulations for the Navy 1965, part II, regulation 34 (6).

9 As to the definition of 'commanding officer'; see **[0912]**.

10 The Regulations for the Navy 1965, part II, regulation 34 (7).

11 Ie the Navy 1965, part II, regulation 13 (1).

12 The Regulations for the Navy 1965, part II, regulation 34 (7) proviso.

[1074] B. Imprisonment The sentence of imprisonment may be rigorous or simple, or partly rigorous and partly simple[1]. The commanding officer[2], in awarding sentence of imprisonment, shall not direct that the prisoner shall be kept in solitary confinement during any period of his imprisonment[3]. A sentence of simple imprisonment shall not be ordinarily awarded except in cases where the proper medical officer certifies that the offender is not in a fit physical condition to undergo rigorous imprisonment[4].

1 The Regulations for the Navy 1965, part II, regulation 35 (1).

2 As to the definition of 'commanding officer'; see **[0912]**.

3 The Regulations for the Navy 1965, part II, regulation 35 (2).

4 The Regulations for the Navy 1965, part II, regulation 35 (3).

[1075] C. Restriction in the case of certain sailors Chief petty officers and petty officers who can be reduced to lower rank shall not be sentenced summarily to imprisonment or detention except for desertion and they shall not be sentenced summarily to imprisonment or detention and reduction in rank at the same time unless their offence includes desertion[1]. Chief petty officers and petty officers who cannot be reduced to lower rank, leading sailors and sailors wearing Good Conduct Badges shall not be sentenced summarily to imprisonment or detention except for the following offences, namely: highly insubordinate conduct[2], desertion, or deserting post[3], sleeping on watch[4], smuggling[5], quitting ship, boat, or working party, without leave[6], drunkenness on duty[7], violent assault[8], aggravated or repeated leave breaking[9], flagrant contravention of the censorship regulations[10], flagrant contravention of gasoline, ammunition, or damage control regulations, which endanger life, the ship aircraft or establishment[11].

1 As to the definition of 'petty officer'; see **[0928]**; as to the offence of 'desertion'; see **[0992]**. The Regulations for the Navy 1965, part II, regulation 36 (1).

2 The Regulations for the Navy 1965, part II, regulation 36 (2) (a).

3 The Regulations for the Navy 1965, part II, regulation 36 (2) (b).

4 The Regulations for the Navy 1965, part II, regulation 36 (2) (c).

5 The Regulations for the Navy 1965, part II, regulation 36 (2) (d).

6 The Regulations for the Navy 1965, part II, regulation 36 (2) (e).

7 The Regulations for the Navy 1965, part II, regulation 36 (2) (f).

8 The Regulations for the Navy 1965, part II, regulation 36 (2) (g).

9 The Regulations for the Navy 1965, part II, regulation 36 (2) (h).

10 The Regulations for the Navy 1965, part II, regulation 36 (2) (i).

11 The Regulations for the Navy 1965, part II, regulation 36 (2) (j).

(ii) Dismissal from the naval service (No. 3)

[1076] Dismissal from the naval service (No. 3) An offender considered unworthy of retention may be punished with summary dismissal from naval service. However, dismissal shall not be awarded (i) before the various punishments to which he has rendered himself liable have been inflicted upon him and found to have no effect, and (ii) if the chief of the naval staff considers that the individual is likely to reform if transferred to another ship[1]. A sailor who has committed an offence deserving imprisonment shall, if his past record clearly shows that he is unworthy of retention, be punished with imprisonment and dismissal[2]. Imprisonment followed by discharge 'SNLR' (services no longer required), shall not be normally appropriate[3]. A sentence of dismissal shall not normally be accompanied by a sentence of detention except in the case offender below the age of 21 years[4]. The punishment of dismissal does not automatically entail any other punishment except deprivation of good conduct medal. The punishment of reduction in rank or the deprivation of good conduct badge(s) shall be included in the sentence, if appropriate[5]. An order for dismissal of a person from naval service, whether accompanied by other punishments or not shall be made only by the chief of the naval staff, and no punishment shall be inflicted on a person until a decision has been obtained on the question whether such person should be dismissed from naval service or not[6]. If a person dismissed from naval service desires it and there is no objection on the part of the local authorities to his landing, he may be dismissed abroad, and where such person desires to return home, he may be sent at the first opportunity by a navy ship or merchant vessel[7]. Where such person is sent in a naval ship under the aforesaid provision, its commanding officer shall be informed of his offence, and the commanding officer shall not order him to work except in emergency and on arrival in India such person shall be immediately discharged to shore[8].

1 The Regulations for the Navy 1965, part II, regulation 37 (1).

2 The Regulations for the Navy 1965, part II, regulation 37 (2).

3 The Regulations for the Navy 1965, part II, regulation 37 (2) note (A).

4 The Regulations for the Navy 1965, part II, regulation 37 (2) note (B).

5 The Regulations for the Navy 1965, part II, regulation 37 (3).

6 The Regulations for the Navy 1965, part II, regulation 37 (4).

7 The Regulations for the Navy 1965, part II, regulation 37 (5).

8 The Regulations for the Navy 1965, part II, regulation 37 (6).

(iii) Forfeiture of seniority (No. 3A) and Forfeiture of time for Promotion (No. 3B)

[1077] Forfeiture of seniority (No. 3A) and Forfeiture of time for Promotion (No. 3B) A master chief petty officer may summarily be awarded punishment of forfeiture of seniority in rank or forfeiture of time for promotion for a period not exceeding 12 months[1]; with the approval of the administrative authority[2]. Wherever a master chief petty officer has summarily been punished with forfeiture of seniority in rank or time for promotion, a notation shall be made in the conduct record sheet, of the service certificate and at other necessary places[3]. The punishment of forfeiture of seniority shall have the effect as laid down in the Navy Act 1957[4]. The punishment of forfeiture of time for promotion shall delay the promotion by the time specified[5].

1 As to the definition of 'petty officer'; see **[0928]**. The Regulations for the Navy 1965, part II, regulation 37A (1).

2 The Regulations for the Navy 1965, part II, regulation 37A (2).

3 The Regulations for the Navy 1965, part II, regulation 37A (3).

4 Ie the Navy Act 1957 s 82 (11) and (12); The Regulations for the Navy 1965, part II, regulation 37A (4).

5 The Regulations for the Navy 1965, part II, regulation 37A (5).

(iv) Reduction in Rank (No. 4)

[1078] A. Summary reduction in rank A sailor[1] may be reduced to any lower rank in his own category or to any lower class in his rank, provided that no sailor shall be reduced in rank: (i) below the limits laid down in the regulations for the time being in force governing the advancement of sailors[2], (ii) below, either actually or relatively, the rank in which he first entered or re-entered, if service in the latter event was not continuous and re-entry was under a fresh engagement[3]. Whenever a sailor is summarily reduced to a lower rank for misconduct or is reduced to lower rank following conviction by a civil authority under the Regulations for the Navy 1965, Part II, regulation 119 (6), a written note giving the offences shall be attached to the sailor's service certificate which shall remain there until he is re-instated in his former rank[4]. If a chief petty officer is reduced in rank summarily he shall be given the option of release from the naval service[5].

1 As to the definition of 'sailor'; see **[0933]**.

2 The Regulations for the Navy 1965, part II, regulation 38 (1) (a).

3 The Regulations for the Navy 1965, part II, regulation 38 (1) (b).

4 The Regulations for the Navy 1965, part II, regulation 38 (2).

5 As to the definition of 'petty officer'; see **[0928]**. The Regulations for the Navy 1965, part II, regulation 38 (3).

[1079] B. Acting rank A sailor[1] holding an acting rank may be reduced to a lower rank by warrant as a punishment in accordance with the procedure and the reductions in rank shall have the effect on assessment of character, good conduct badges and the like[2]. If such sailor commits an offence which, though indicating an unfitness for the higher rank is not considered sufficiently serious to merit reduction in rank by warrant, and if his general conduct is otherwise unsatisfactory, he may be reverted by his commanding officer for unsuitability in which case the penalties which follow reduction in rank by warrant shall not be applicable[3].

1 As to the definition of 'sailor'; see **[0933]**.

2 The Regulations for the Navy 1965, part II, regulation 39 (1).

3 The Regulations for the Navy 1965, part II, regulation 39 (1).

(v) Fine in respect of civil offences (No. 5)

[1080] Fine in respect of civil offences (No. 5) A fine not exceeding Rs 250/- may be imposed summarily when a sailor[1] is found guilty of a civil offence and the amount of fine shall be credited to the ship's imprest account[2]. The commanding officer[3] may, while passing the sentence of fine the aforesaid provision, order the whole or any part of the fine recovered to be applied in the payment to any aggrieved person as compensation for any loss or injury caused to him by the said offence[4].

1 As to the definition of 'sailor'; see **[0933]**.

2 The Regulations for the Navy 1965, part II, regulation 40 (1).

3 As to the definition of 'commanding officer'; see **[0912]**.

4 The Regulations for the Navy 1965, part II, regulation 40 (2).

(vi) Mulcts of pay and allowance (No. 6) for improper absence

[1081] A. Scale of mulcts Except as provided in the Regulations for the Navy 1965, part II, every sailor[1] who is found guilty of absence without leave or improperly leaving his ship[2] or place of duty shall be punished with mulcts of pay and stoppage of leave in accordance with the following scale: (i) where the period of absence does not exceed three hours, one day's pay and one day's leave[3]; (ii) where the period of absence exceeds three hours but does not exceed 36 hours, one day's pay and one days leave for every three hours absence or part thereof[4]; (iii) where the period of absence exceeds 36 hours, one day's pay and one day's leave for every three hours of absence up to 36 hours and one day's pay and one day's leave for each subsequent period of six hours or part of six hours, so, however, that the stoppage of leave shall in no case exceed 60 days[5]. If the period of absence is trivial or if there are extenuating circumstances and the period of improper absence does not exceed 36 hours the commanding officer[6] may, at his discretion, reduce the mulcts by such an amount as he may consider reasonable; the stoppage of leave being reduced to a corresponding extent[7]. The aforesaid provision shall apply to leave breaking up to 36 hours dealt with in conjunction with other offences[8]. If the period of absence exceeds 36 hours or the offence is aggravated or repeated, any other punishment permitted by the Regulations for the Navy 1965, part II, may be awarded according to the degree of offence, in addition to the mulcts of pay and stoppage of leave on the scale in the aforesaid provision[9] and if there are mitigating circumstances justifying exceptional treatment, the commanding officer may at his discretion, reduce the mulcts, provided that the actual mulcts (i.e. excluding detention or confinement in cell) shall not be reduced to less than one day's pay for each day's absence and where the stoppage of leave according to the said scale would amount to 30 days or less it may also be correspondingly reduced[10]. Stoppage of leave for any period in excess of the scale shall not be awarded as a punishment for leave breaking, except in aggravated or repeated cases[11].

1 As to the definition of 'sailor'; see **[0933]**.

2 As to the definition of 'ship'; see **[0934]**.

3 The Regulations for the Navy 1965, part II, regulation 41 (1) (a).

4 The Regulations for the Navy 1965, part II, regulation 41 (1) (b).

5 The Regulations for the Navy 1965, part II, regulation 41 (1) (c).

6 As to the definition of 'commanding officer'; see **[0912]**.

7 The Regulations for the Navy 1965, part II, regulation 41 (2).

8 The Regulations for the Navy 1965, part II, regulation 41 (3).

9 Ie the Regulations for the Navy 1965, part II, regulation 41 (1).

10 The Regulations for the Navy 1965, part II, regulation 41 (4).

11 The Regulations for the Navy 1965, part II, regulation 41 (5).

[1082] B. Remission of mulcts over 60 days If the number of days mulcts in accordance with the Regulations of the Navy 1965[1], or if the period of sentence to which a leave breaker is confined by reason of the punishment of detention or solitary confinement in a cell plus the number of days mulcts, would amount to a total of more than 60 days, any excess mulcts shall be remitted provided that in no case shall the actual mulcts (i.e. excluding the punishment of detention or confinement in cell) be reduced to less than one day's pay for each day's absence[2]. The aforesaid provision shall also be applicable to cases where imprisonment is awarded owing to lack of detention accommodation and such provisions shall not apply to cases where on other grounds, imprisonment is awarded in preference to detention, or where on the same occasion, the offender is also convicted of any offence other than leave breaking[3]. If, however, exceptional hardship is involved, the circumstances should be submitted to the chief of the naval staff for consideration[4]. In all cases where a sailor has been sentenced to stoppage of leave exceeding 30 days, he shall be allowed ashore leave once a week, after the expiration of the 30 days[5]. This provision shall not fetter the discretion of the commanding officer to reduce the mulcts to the extent provided in the Regulations for the Navy 1965[6].

1 Ie the Regulations for the Navy 1965, part II, regulation 41 (1); see **[1081]**.

2 The Regulations for the Navy 1965, part II, regulation 42 (1).

3 The Regulations for the Navy 1965, part II, regulation 42 (2).

4 The Regulations for the Navy 1965, part II, regulation 42 (3).

5 The Regulations for the Navy 1965, part II, regulation 42 (4).

6 Ie as provided in the Regulations for the Navy 1965, part II, regulation 41; see **[1081]**. The Regulations for the Navy 1965, part II, regulation 42 (5).

(vii) Solitary confinement in a cells or under a canvas screen (No. 8)

[1083] Physical conditions A sailor[1] sentenced to cells shall be confined under a canvas screen or in a cell approved by the chief of the naval staff of a period not exceeding 14 days and any such sentence shall require a warrant[2]. A cell shall measure not less than two metres in length and one metre in breadth and shall be as high as the space between decks, and shall be ventilated properly. No cell shall be made or altered without the authority of the chief of the naval staff[3]. No sailor shall be confined in which the temperature exceeds 30^{0}C unless the commanding officer[4] is satisfied that there is adequate ventilation[5]. No sailor shall undergo a cell punishment unless a medical officer has examined him and certified that he is in a fit physical condition to undergo that punishment and such certificate shall be recorded on the punishment warrant[6].

1 As to the definition of 'sailor'; see **[0933]**.

2 The Regulations for the Navy 1965, part II, regulation 55 (1).

3 The Regulations for the Navy 1965, part II, regulation 55 (2).

4 As to the definition of 'commanding officer'; see **[0912]**.

5 The Regulations for the Navy 1965, part II, regulation 55 (3).

6 The Regulations for the Navy 1965, part II, regulation 55 (4).

[1084] Restriction regarding sailors holding leading ranks Sailors[1] holding leading ranks who can be reduced in rank shall not be sentenced to cell and sailors holding leading ranks who cannot be reduced in rank may be awarded cell, punishment but only for the following offences: gross insubordination[2]; desertion and deserting post[3]; sleeping on watch[4]; dishonesty[5]; smuggling[6]; quitting ship, boat or working party without leave[7]; drunkenness on duty[8]; aggravated or fourth (or later) repeated offences of absence without leave[9]; flagrant contravention of the censorship regulations[10]; gross misconduct on shore when not dealt with by civil authority[11]; and continued neglect of duty[12].

1 As to the definition of 'sailor'; see **[0933]**.

2 The Regulations for the Navy 1965, part II, regulation 56 (a).

3 The Regulations for the Navy 1965, part II, regulation 56 (b).

4 The Regulations for the Navy 1965, part II, regulation 56 (c).

5 The Regulations for the Navy 1965, part II, regulation 56 (d).

6 The Regulations for the Navy 1965, part II, regulation 56 (e).

7 The Regulations for the Navy 1965, part II, regulation 56 (f).

8 The Regulations for the Navy 1965, part II, regulation 56 (g).

9 The Regulations for the Navy 1965, part II, regulation 56 (h).

10 The Regulations for the Navy 1965, part II, regulation 56 (i).

11 The Regulations for the Navy 1965, part II, regulation 56 (j).

12 The Regulations for the Navy 1965, part II, regulation 56 (k).

[1085] General rules for cell punishment Every sailor sentenced to cells shall be deprived of any good conduct medal or badges he may hold and such punishment shall carry with it forfeiture of time and pay for the period of the confinement[1]. A sentence of cells shall not be postponed or suspended[2]. A sentence of cells may, at the discretion of the senior officer present, be carried out in a ship or naval establishment other than that in which it was awarded[3].

1 The Regulations for the Navy 1965, part II, regulation 57 (1).

2 The Regulations for the Navy 1965, part II, regulation 57 (2).

3 The Regulations for the Navy 1965, part II, regulation 57 (3).

[1086] Routine to be followed The day on which the warrant is read shall count as a complete day of the sentence irrespective of the actual time at which confinement commences[1]. The offender shall pick on all days other than Sundays either 90 grams of tarred hemp or 2.70 kg sisal, which shall be weighed when given to him and again when received from him. Alternatively, the offender may be given productive and useful task already learnt by him or which he can easily pick-up[2]. The offender shall not be allowed the use of his bedding for the first four nights, but in cold weather he may be allowed to use a blanket if considered necessary and he shall be deprived of tobacco, knives, razors, writing material, and all books and papers, except suitable books of instruction[3].

However, the offender may be allowed to read religious books[4]. The offender shall keep himself and his cell clean and after the third day's confinement he shall be brought on deck under a sentry's charge for two hours a day, one hour in the morning and one hour in the afternoon and he may be given the normal forums of arms drill during these exercise periods[5]. A medical officer shall visit the offender night and morning in hot climate and once a day in other cases. The officer of the watch or officer of the day shall visit the offender in his cell once in each watch[6]. Subject to the aforesaid provision an offender shall not be permitted to hold communication with any person, except when authorized by the commanding officer[7]. A sailor in cell may be permitted to receive letters addressed to him, but such letters shall be opened by him in the presence of one of the regulating staff to ensure that nothing undesirable is enclosed and such sailor shall be permitted to write letters only in exceptional circumstances[8]. If the commanding officer is of opinion, on the advice of the medical officer or otherwise, that strict adherence to these provisions would permanently affect the health of any offender, the commanding officer may, for reasons to be recorded in writing, read all or any of such provisions with respect to that offender[9].

1 The Regulations for the Navy 1965, part II, regulation 58 (1).
2 The Regulations for the Navy 1965, part II, regulation 58 (2).
3 The Regulations for the Navy 1965, part II, regulation 58 (3).
4 The Regulations for the Navy 1965, part II, regulation 58 (3) proviso.
5 The Regulations for the Navy 1965, part II, regulation 58 (4).
6 The Regulations for the Navy 1965, part II, regulation 58 (5).
7 The Regulations for the Navy 1965, part II, regulation 58 (6).
8 The Regulations for the Navy 1965, part II, regulation 58 (7).
9 The Regulations for the Navy 1965, part II, regulation 58 (8).

(viii) Deprivation of Good Conduct Medal or Badge (No. 9)

[1087] Deprivation of good conduct medal Any sailor to whom a good conduct medal has been awarded may be deprived of it summarily by warrant for misconduct and thereupon the medal shall be returned to the commodore, bureau of sailors, Bombay[1]. No person shall be deprived of this medal nor shall any punishment entailing the forfeiture of this medal be awarded without the previous approval of a flag officer of commodore[2]. A sailor[3] may be deprived of his medal without being deprived of any good conduct badge[4]. The commanding officer[5] may at his discretion take away one badge, but not more, without depriving the sailor of his medal, if his conduct has been in all other respect satisfactory notwithstanding that the deprivation of a badge may necessitate the award of the entry 'Good' at the annual assessment of character provided that such discretion shall be exercised in favour of any sailor only once[6]. If a badge should be taken away without loss of the medal, the medal shall not be worn until the badge is regained[7]. A sailor who receives any of the following punishments shall be deprived of the medal, namely: imprisonment[8]; dismissal[9]; detention[10]; reduction in rank[11]; cells[12]; deprivation of two or more good conduct badges[13]; deprivation of a badge on a second occasion after the award of the medal; such deprivation shall be noted on the warrant, both in the heading and in the appropriate column[14]. The medal shall be forfeited when a sailor holding it: deserts[15]; is awarded a character assessment inferior to 'VG'[16]; is deprived of a badge and it is not restored to him within 12 months from the date of deprivation[17]. Forfeiture under the Regulations for the Navy 1965, part II, regulation 59(7)(a) shall be implemented on conviction and noted on the punishment warrant and forfeiture under regulation 59(7)(b) and (c) shall be implemented immediately after the character has been assessed or the period of 12 months expires whichever is earlier[18]. A warrant shall not be required for the forfeiture of the medal but the sailor shall be informed formally of the forfeiture and when he appears before the commanding officer for this purpose, he shall not be treated as a defaulter, and shall be dealt with after requestment[19]. Deprivation or forfeiture of the medal shall be noted on the sailor's service certificate[20].

1 The Regulations for the Navy 1965, part II, regulation 59 (1).

2 The Regulations for the Navy 1965, part II, regulation 59 (2).

3 As to the definition of 'sailor'; see **[0933]**.

4 The Regulations for the Navy 1965, part II, regulation 59 (3).

5 As to the definition of 'commanding officer'; see **[0912]**.

6 The Regulations for the Navy 1965, part II, regulation 59 (4).

7 The Regulations for the Navy 1965, part II, regulation 59 (5).

8 The Regulations for the Navy 1965, part II, regulation 59 (6) (a).

9 The Regulations for the Navy 1965, part II, regulation 59 (6) (b).

10 The Regulations for the Navy 1965, part II, regulation 59 (6) (c).

11 The Regulations for the Navy 1965, part II, regulation 59 (6) (d).

12 The Regulations for the Navy 1965, part II, regulation 59 (6) (f).

13 The Regulations for the Navy 1965, part II, regulation 59 (6) (g).

14 The Regulations for the Navy 1965, part II, regulation 59 (6) (h).

15 The Regulations for the Navy 1965, part II, regulation 59 (7) (a).

16 The Regulations for the Navy 1965, part II, regulation 59 (7) (b).

17 The Regulations for the Navy 1965, part II, regulation 59 (7) (c).

18 The Regulations for the Navy 1965, part II, regulation 59 (8).

19 The Regulations for the Navy 1965, part II, regulation 59 (9).

20 Ie on the page 4 of the sailor's service certificate; The Regulations for the Navy 1965, part II, regulation 59 (10).

[1088] Restoration of medals When a sailor[1] has been deprived of the good conduct medal or has forfeited it for misconduct, the medal may, with the approval of the chief of the naval staff, be restored: (i) at any time, if the sailor has rendered some special service[2]; (ii) on completion of 5 years service with continuous 'VG' character[3]. When a sailor is discharged before completing 5 years 'VG' service required for restoration of the medal and subsequently re-enters, any further service with 'VG' character may be allowed to count for the purpose of qualifying for restoration[4].

1 As to the definition of 'sailor'; see **[0933]**.

2 The Regulations for the Navy 1965, part II, regulation 60 (1) (a).

3 The Regulations for the Navy 1965, part II, regulation 60 (1) (b).

4 The Regulations for the Navy 1965, part II, regulation 60 (2).

(ix) Deprivation of Good Conduct Badges

[1089] Deprivation of Badges A sailor[1] who receives any of the following punishments shall be deprived of any badge he may hold: imprisonment[2], detention[3], reduction in rank[4], and cells[5]. Deprivation of two or more badges or deprivation of one badge for the second time the award of long service and good conduct medal or meritorious service medal shall involve deprivation of the medal[6]. Any sailor holding one or more badges may be deprived of them by warrant, except as provided in the Regulations for the Navy 1965, part II, regulation 119[7]. One badge so lost may regained by six months 'VG' conduct, and additional badges by further period of six months, reckoned in each case from the date of the preceding restoration[8]. If, however, a sailor has been sentenced to deprivation a second time within three years of actual service, the qualification for restoration shall be 12 months for the first restoration, and six months for each subsequent restoration[9]. Time, which does not count for purpose of award shall not be reckoned towards restoration of badges[10]. Sailors serving in non-badge ranks shall be eligible for the restoration of badges, although not eligible for the award of further badges[11]. Restorations shall be made when they become due whether the sailor prefers his claim or not[12].

1 As to the definition of 'sailor'; see **[0933]**.

2 The Regulations for the Navy 1965, part II, regulation 63 (1) (a).

3 The Regulations for the Navy 1965, part II, regulation 63 (1) (b).

4 The Regulations for the Navy 1965, part II, regulation 63 (1) (c).

5 The Regulations for the Navy 1965, part II, regulation 63 (1) (d).

6 The Regulations for the Navy 1965, part II, regulation 63 (2).

7 The Regulations for the Navy 1965, part II, regulation 63 (3).

8 The Regulations for the Navy 1965, part II, regulation 63 (4).

9 The Regulations for the Navy 1965, part II, regulation 63 (5).

10 The Regulations for the Navy 1965, part II, regulation 63 (6).

11 The Regulations for the Navy 1965, part II, regulation 63 (7).

12 The Regulations for the Navy 1965, part II, regulation 63 (8).

(x) Reprimand by the Captain (No. 10)

[1090] Reprimand by the Captain The punishment of reprimand by the captain shall be awarded only to leading ranks and above and such punishment shall always be recorded[1].

1 The Regulations for the Navy 1965, part II, regulation 64.

(xi) Extra work and drill

[1091] Routine to be followed Sailors[1] below leading ranks may be awarded the punishment of extra work and drill up to 14 days when they are to be subject to the following routine: (i) leave to be stopped[2]; (ii) to turn out half an hour before the hands[3]; (iii) to do extra work during non-working hours, from half an hour before the hands turn to until 2100, one hour of which during the dog-watch, to be if possible, drill or boat pulling[4]; (iv) to be mustered frequently[5]; (v) to have full time for meals except dinner for which half an hour will be allowed; to be employed for the remainder of dinner hour at drill or work[6]; (vi) drill is to be performed wearing correct drill only[7].

1 As to the definition of 'sailor'; see **[0933]**.

2 The Regulations for the Navy 1965, part II, regulation 65 (a).

3 The Regulations for the Navy 1965, part II, regulation 65 (b).

4 The Regulations for the Navy 1965, part II, regulation 65 (c).

5 The Regulations for the Navy 1965, part II, regulation 65 (d).

6 The Regulations for the Navy 1965, part II, regulation 65 (e).

7 The Regulations for the Navy 1965, part II, regulation 65 (f).

[1092] Other instructions Extra work shall be substituted drill would have to be carried out in sight of civilian on-lookers[1]. When possible, extra work shall be done in the department to which the offender belongs[2]. If a sailor[3] has to keep a night watch either in harbour or at sea, this punishment shall cease at 2000 and he shall not be turned out before the usual time[4]. When a sailor is under this punishment, he shall be allowed to leave the ship or establishment only on duty though he may be allowed to proceed on long leave at the discretion of the commanding officer[5].

1 The Regulations for the Navy 1965, part II, regulation 66 (1).

2 The Regulations for the Navy 1965, part II, regulation 66 (2).

3 As to the definition of 'sailor'; see **[0933]**.

4 The Regulations for the Navy 1965, part II, regulation 66 (3).

5 The Regulations for the Navy 1965, part II, regulation 66 (4).

(xii) Stoppage of Leave (No. 12)

[1093] Stoppage of leave When stoppage of leave[1] is awarded for leave breaking, it shall not exceed the scale laid down except for aggravated or repeated offences[2]. Stoppage of leave may also be awarded in appropriate cases for any other offence either as the only punishment or with another punishment[3]. While under stoppage of leave, a sailor[4] shall not be allowed to leave the ship or establishment except on duty, he may, however, be allowed to proceed on long leave at the discretion of the commanding officer[5]. The punishment of stoppage of leave shall not involve any other penalties except mustering with sailors under punishment[6].

1 As stoppage of leave, in common with other punishments, commences from the date on which it is awarded and runs continuously from that date and as it may not be awarded for more than 60 days, stoppage of leave should be considered ineffective if given in conjunction with the sentence of imprisonment or detention of 60 days or more. The Regulations for the Navy 1965, part II, regulation 67 (1).

2 The Regulations for the Navy 1965, part II, regulation 67 (2).

3 The Regulations for the Navy 1965, part II, regulation 67 (3).

4 As to the definition of 'sailor'; see **[0933]**.

5 As to the definition of 'commanding officer'; see **[0912]**; the Regulations for the Navy 1965, part II, regulation 67 (4).

6 The Regulations for the Navy 1965, part II, regulation 67 (5).

(xiii) Extra Work or Drill (No. 13)

[1094] Extra work or drill Extra work or drill for not more than 2 hours a day may be awarded for any period not exceeding 7 days to sailors[1] below leading ranks[2]. Drill shall be performed wearing correct drill order only and when drill would have to be carried out in sight of civilian onlookers, extra work shall be substituted[3].

1 As to the definition of 'sailor'; see **[0933]**.

2 The Regulations for the Navy 1965, part II, regulation 68.

3 The Regulations for the Navy 1965, part II, regulation 69.

(xiv) Admonition (No. 14)

[1095] Admonition When a sailor is found guilty of an offence which, of itself or in view of the mitigating circumstances, it not considered to deserve any more serious punishment, he shall be awarded the punishment of admonition[1]. The offence and the punishment shall be recorded[2].

1 The Regulations for the Navy 1965, part II, regulation 70 (1).

2 The Regulations for the Navy 1965, part II, regulation 70 (2).

[1096] Special directions In regard to all summary punishments, the following sdditional directions shall be observed, namely: (i) suspension on Sunday: summary punishments which are carried out on board, except confinement in cells or under a canvas screen, and stoppage of leave, shall be suspended on Sunday, but that day shall count as part of the period for which any sentence is awarded[1]; (ii) night's rest: sailors shall not be deprived of their night's rest at sea as a punishment[2]; (iii) iron and handcuffs: the use of irons or handcuffs shall, except for the purpose of ensuring the safe custody of a prisoner, or for mutinous conduct, be avoided as far as possible[3]; (iv) gags shall not be used and sailors who are noisy or violent shall be confined in a cell for such time as may be necessary[4]; (v) stoppage of pay: pay shall not be forfeited nor shall any stoppage of pay and allowances be made for misconduct, except in cases expressly authorised by the Navy Act 1957, or by the Regulations for the Navy 1965, part II[5]; (vi) applicable punishment: every punishment must be applicable to the offence, and to offender at the time he committed the offence of which he stands convicted[6].

1 The Regulations for the Navy 1965, part II, regulation 71 (a).

2 The Regulations for the Navy 1965, part II, regulation 71 (b).

3 The Regulations for the Navy 1965, part II, regulation 71 (c).

4 The Regulations for the Navy 1965, part II, regulation 71 (d).

5 The Regulations for the Navy 1965, part II, regulation 71 (e).

6 The Regulations for the Navy 1965, part II, regulation 71 (f).

D. Summary Punishments for Artificer Apprentices and Boys

[1097] Scale of punishments The following punishments may be awarded summarily to the artificer apprentices and boys:

No. 1 Imprisonment not exceeding three months

No. 2 Detention not exceeding three months

No. 3 Dismissal from the naval service

No. 4 Confinement in cells not exceeding 14 days

No. 5 Isolation not exceeding 14 days

No. 6 Blank

No. 7 To have meals at the defaulters' table; to stand on deck for half an hour during the dinner hour; to do half an hour's drill during recreation time; to turn out half an hour earlier and stand on deck; leave to be stopped. This punishment should not be awarded for the period exceeding 14 days

No. 8 Stoppage of leave for a period not exceeding 28 days

No. 9 Mulcts of pay for improper absence and for unfitness for duty form drinking on shore

No. 10 Extra work for a period not exceeding 14 days

No. 11 Reduction in rank of instructor, petty officer or leading boys[1]

1 The Regulations for the Navy 1965, part II, regulation 74.

[1098] Suspension of punishment on Sundays Punishments which are carried out on board, other than cells and stoppage of leave shall be suspended on Sunday but that day shall count as part of the period for which any sentence is awarded[1].

1 The Regulations for the Navy 1965, part II, regulation 75.

[1099] Delegation of powers Commanding officer[1] of training establishments and training ships may delegate to the executive officer, of or above the rank or relative rank of lieutenant, power to impose the following punishments mentioned in the Regulations for the Navy 1965, part II, regulation 74 to the extent mentioned against each: No. 7- in full; No. 10 - not exceeding seven days[2]. The Commanding office may, by written authority delegate to the under mentioned officers whenever and so long as he may deem fit, the power to award the following punishments mentioned in the Regulations for the Navy 1965, part II, regulation 74 to the extent mentioned against each: (i) training commander of or above the rank of lieutenant or relative rank of lieutenant: No. 7 - for seven days; No. 10 - for seven days[3]; (ii) the officer of the day or officer-in-charge of workshop of the rank of lieutenant or relative rank of lieutenant: No. 10 - for one day[4]. All such punishments shall be recorded in a special book kept for the purpose and such power shall be confined to cases of misconduct on the part of individual apprentices or boys, and shall not be exercised with respect to case of misconduct on the part of a group of apprentices or boys[5].

1 As to the definition of 'commanding officer'; see **[0912]**.

2 The Regulations for the Navy 1965, part II, regulation 76 (1).

3 The Regulations for the Navy 1965, part II, regulation 76 (2) (a).

4 The Regulations for the Navy 1965, part II, regulation 76 (2) (b).

5 The Regulations for the Navy 1965, part II, regulation 76 (2).

[1100] General regulations applicable to punishments In administering punishments to artificer apprentices and boys, the general regulations contained in the Regulations for the Navy 1965, part II, chapter III and IV shall be adhered to wherever applicable and so far as they are not inconsistent with the Regulations[1].

1 The Regulations for the Navy 1965, part II, regulation 77.

[1101] Punishment of Instructors, petty officers and leading boys Instructors, petty officers and leading boys and apprentices shall be reduced a lower rank before being awarded certain punishments mentioned in the Regulations for the Navy 1965, part II[1], and any higher punishment[2].

1 Ie contained in the Navy 1965, part II, regulation 74, No. 7.

2 The Regulations for the Navy 1965, part II, regulation 78.

[1102] Confinement in cell (No. 4) Confinement in a cell shall be awarded only in exceptional circumstances like short term of imprisonment or detention[1].

1 The Regulations for the Navy 1965, part II, regulation 79.

[1103] Isolation (No. 5) Apprentices and boys who have been awarded the punishment of isolation shall be subject to the following restrictions and conditions: (i) they shall attend all instruction[1]; (ii) when not undergoing instructions, they shall be confined in a suitable place set aside for the purpose[2]; (iii) they shall be allowed the use of bedding[3]; (iv) they shall keep themselves and their place of confinement clean[4]; (v) they shall be allowed the use of religious and instructional books[5]; (vi) they shall be deprived of tobacco, knives and all books, papers or writing material, except for instructional purposes[6]. However, they may be allowed to write letters to their homes, the number of such letters not exceeding one per week or a total of two during the period of punishment[7]; (vii) they shall wear a distinctive dress to indicate that are undergoing isolation punishment and when blue uniform is worn, it shall consist of a broad white duck band and, when white uniform is born, of a broad blue band and the band shall be attached securely to the sleeve of each arm and shall be worn continuously during the period of punishment[8]; (viii) they shall undergo one hour's physical drill daily to be performed in the open air whenever practicable[9].

1 The Regulations for the Navy 1965, part II, regulation 80 (a).

2 The Regulations for the Navy 1965, part II, regulation 80 (b).

3 The Regulations for the Navy 1965, part II, regulation 80 (c).

4 The Regulations for the Navy 1965, part II, regulation 80 (d).

5 The Regulations for the Navy 1965, part II, regulation 80 (e).

6 The Regulations for the Navy 1965, part II, regulation 80 (f).

7 The Regulations for the Navy 1965, part II, regulation 80 (f) proviso.

8 The Regulations for the Navy 1965, part II, regulation 80 (g).

9 The Regulations for the Navy 1965, part II, regulation 80 (h).

[1104] Stoppage of leave (No. 8) Apprentices and boys undergoing punishment of stoppage of leave[1] shall be employed for a maximum of one hour daily during their recreational period on any work[2].

1 Great care should be exercised before awarding stoppage of leave for a period in excess of 14 days. The Regulations for the Navy 1965, part II, regulation 82 (1).

2 The Regulations for the Navy 1965, part II, regulation 82 (2).

[1105] Extra Drill (No. 10) Extra drill shall be done as squad drill with arms and up to one hour per day[1].

1 The Regulations for the Navy 1965, part II, regulation 83.

[1106] Reduction in lower rank (No. 11) Reduction in lower rank shall be compulsory for leave breaking for over 12 hours[1].

1 The Regulations for the Navy 1965, part II, regulation 84.

[1107] Previous offences When an offence is being dealt with under certain provisions of the Regulations for the Navy 1965[1], all previous offences committed by the person concerned shall be taken into consideration when award in punishment[2].

1 Ie the Regulations for the Navy 1965, part II, chapter III.

2 The Regulations for the Navy 1965, part II, regulation 87.

[1108] Charge for theft Charge for theft shall not be made except when there is clear evidence of criminal intent[1].

1 The Regulations for the Navy 1965, part II, regulation 88. When a Apprentice or boy is found in possession of an article belonging to another, the apprentice or boy concerned shall not be punished for theft unless the commanding officer is satisfied that when it was taken there was an intention to cause wrongful loss to a person or wrongful gain to himself or another person. Unless the commanding officer is satisfied of this, or if he is satisfied that the apprentice or the boy, as the case may be, really found the article lying about, he should be charged with being guilty of neglect to the prejudice of good order and naval discipline in not handing over to the proper authority the articles which, to his knowledge, had come into his possession without the consent of the owners. The Regulations for the Navy 1965, part II, regulation 88, illustration.

E. Summary Punishment of officers below the rank of commander

[1109] Award of summary punishment under the Navy Act 1957 s 94 The central government or the chief of the naval staff[1] or the flag officer[2] commanding-in-chief of a naval command or the commanding officer[3] of a ship[4] or the officer-in-charge of naval academy may impose summary punishment on any office below the rank of commander as provided in the Navy Act 1957[5].

1 As to the definition of 'chief of the naval staff'; see **[0907]**.

2 As to the definition of 'flag officer'; see **[0917]**.

3 As to the definition of 'commanding officer'; see **[0912]**.

4 As to the definition of 'ship'; see **[0934]**.

5 Ie the Navy Act 1957 s 94; see **[1110]**.

[1110] Power of Central Government, Chief of the Naval Staff and other officers to impose forfeiture of time or seniority

1 The Central Government may impose on any officer below the rank of commander one or more of the following punishments: (i) forfeiture of seniority in rank of not more than 12 months[1]; (ii) forfeiture of time for promotion of not more than twelve months[2]; (iii) mulcts of pay and allowances[3].

2 The chief of the naval staff may impose on any officer below the rank of the commander one or more

of the following punishments: (i) forfeiture of seniority in rank of not more than six months[4]; (ii) forfeiture of time for promotion of not more than six months[5]; (iii) mulcts of pay and allowances[6].

3 The flag officer commanding-in-chief of a naval command may, subject to the Regulations for the Navy 1965, part II, made under the Navy Act 1957, impose on any officer below the rank of commander one or more of the following punishments: (i) forfeiture of seniority in rank of not more than three months[7]; (ii) forfeiture of time for promotion of not more than three months8; (iii) severe reprimand or reprimand[9]; (iv) mulcts of pay and allowances[10].

4 The commanding officer[11] of a ship[12] may, subject to the Regulations for the Navy 1965, part II, impose on any subordinate officer one or more of the following punishments: (i) forfeiture of seniority in rank of not more than three months[13]; (ii) for feature of time for promotion of not more than three months[14]; (iii) mulcts of pay and allowances[15].

5 In imposing punishment under certain aforesaid provisions[16], it shall not be necessary for the central government or the chief of the naval staff, to hear the accused in person or by any friend or counsel[17].

6 The commanding officer of a ship or the officer-in-charge of a naval academy may impose on any subordinate officer whilst under training such minor punishments not higher than the punishment of severe reprimand, as may be prescribed[18].

1 The Navy Act 1957 s 94 (1) (a). For more details see the Regulations for the Navy 1965, part II, regulation 147I; see **[1118]**.

2 The Navy Act 1957 s 94 (1) (b).

3 The Navy Act 1957 s 94 (1) (c).

4 The Navy Act 1957 s 94 (2) (a). For more details see the Regulations for the Navy 1965, part II, regulation 147H; see **[1117]**.

5 The Navy Act 1957 s 94 (2) (b).

6 The Navy Act 1957 s 94 (2) (c).

7 The Navy Act 1957 s 94 (2A) (a).

8 The Navy Act 1957 s 94 (2A) (b).

9 The Navy Act 1957 s 94 (2A) (c).

10 The Navy Act 1957 s 94 (2A) (d). For more details see the Regulations for the Navy 1965, part II, regulation 147E; see **[1114]**.

11 As to the definition of 'commanding officer'; see **[0912]**.

12 As to the definition of 'ship'; see **[0934]**.

13 The Navy Act 1957 s 94 (1) (3).

14 The Navy Act 1957 s 94 (1) (3).

15 The Navy Act 1957 s 94 (1) (3). For more details see the Regulations for the Navy 1965, part II, regulation 147C; see **[1116]**.

16 Ie the Navy Act 1957 s 94 (1), (2) and (2A).

17 The Navy Act 1957 s 94 (4).

18 The Navy Act 1957 s 94 (5). As prescribed in the Regulations for the Navy 1965, part II, regulation 147B; see **[1111]**.

[1111] Award of minor punishment by commanding officer of ship or officer-in-charge of naval academy The commanding officer of a ship or officer-in-charge of the naval academy may impose on any subordinate officer whilst under training, the following punishments under the Navy Act 1957[1]: (i) severe reprimand[2]; (ii) reprimand[3]; (iii) stoppage of leave for a period not exceeding 14 days[4]; (iv) extra work and or drill for period not exceeding 10 days[5]. For imposing of punishment under the aforesaid provision, it shall not be necessary for the commanding officer of a ship or officer-in-charge of the naval academy to serve a show cause notice to the accused officer or hear the accused officer in person or by any friend or counsel[6].

1 Ie under the Navy Act 1957 s 94 (5). As to the definition of 'commanding officer' and 'ship'; see **[0912]** and **[0934]**.

2 The Regulations for the Navy 1965, part II, regulation 147B (1) (a).

3 The Regulations for the Navy 1965, part II, regulation 147B (1) (b).

4 The Regulations for the Navy 1965, part II, regulation 147B (1) (c).

5 The Regulations for the Navy 1965, part II, regulation 147B (1) (d).

6 The Regulations for the Navy 1965, part II, regulation 147B (2).

[1112] Imposition of punishment by the commanding officer When commanding officer proposes to award a punishment of forfeiture of seniority in rank or time for promotion to a subordinate officer under the Navy Act 1957[1], the accused officer may be given an opportunity to show cause in the manner specified in the following provision[2]. When after considering the report on a subordinate officer's misconduct, a commanding officer is of the opinion that the misconduct of the officer deserves to be punished he shall so inform the officer together with all reports adverse to him and call upon him to submit in writing his explanation in defence[3]. However, the commanding officer may withhold from disclosure any such report if its disclosure is not in the public interest[4]. On receipt of the officer's explanation if any, the commanding officer shall consider it and if the same is found unsatisfactory, may impose the punishment of forfeiture of seniority in the rank or time for promotion as empowered under the Navy Act 1957 s 94 (3). Where the punishment awarded involves forfeiture of seniority in the rank, the same shall require approval of the chief of the naval staff, or the flag officer commanding-in-chief of a naval command if the accused is serving in a command[5].

1 Ie the Navy Act 1957 s 94 (3). As to the definition of 'commanding officer'; see **[0912]**.

2 The Regulations for the Navy 1965, part II, regulation 147C (1).

3 The Regulations for the Navy 1965, part II, regulation 147C (2).

4 The Regulations for the Navy 1965, part II, regulation 147C (2) proviso.

5 The Regulations for the Navy 1965, part II, regulation 147C (3).

[1113] Action by the flag officer commanding-in-chief of a naval command on misconduct report If on a perusal of the record, the flag officer commanding-in-chief is of the opinion that there is a prima facie case and that the charges if proved would be within his powers to punish, he shall proceed to try the case as provided in the Regulations for the Navy 1965[1]. However, if he is of the opinion that the charge, if proved would be beyond his power to punish, he shall: (i) make a report in this behalf and submit the same together with all the relevant records to the chief of the naval staff for being dealt with under the Navy Act 1957 s 94[2]; or (ii) proceed to convene a court martial for the trial of the accused[3]. Before proceeding with the action as contemplated in the aforesaid provision[4], the flag officer commanding-in-chief shall ask the accused as follows: "Do you consent to accept a summary award under the Navy Act 1957 s 94 or do you elect to be tried by court martial"[5]. If the accused officer elects to be tried by the court martial, necessary steps will be taken for that purpose[6]. If the accused officer does not elect to be tried by court martial and consent to be tried summarily under the Navy Act 1957 s 94, a notation to that effect shall be made in the proceeding of the case to be forwarded to the chief of the naval staff for disposal[7].

1 Ie as provided under the Regulations for the Navy 1965, part II, regulation 147E and 147F; The Regulations for the Navy 1965, part II, regulation 147D (1).

2 The Regulations for the Navy 1965, part II, regulation 147D (1) (a).

3 The Regulations for the Navy 1965, part II, regulation 147D (1) (b).

4 Ie the Regulations for the Navy 1965, part II, regulation 147D (1) (a).

5 The Regulations for the Navy 1965, part II, regulation 147D (2).

6 The Regulations for the Navy 1965, part II, regulation 147D (3).

7 The Regulations for the Navy 1965, part II, regulation 147D (4).

[1114] Imposition of punishment by flag officer commanding-in-chief of a naval command When the flag officer commanding-in-chief of a naval command proposes to award punishment under the Navy Act 1957[1], the accused officer may be given an opportunity to show cause in the manner as mentioned below[2]. When after considering the report on the misconduct of an officer, the flag officer commanding-in-chief of a naval command if of the opinion that the misconduct of the officer is deserves to be punished, he shall so inform the officer together with all reports adverse to him and call upon him to submit in writing his explanation in defence[3]. However, the flag officer commanding-in-chief may withhold from disclosure any such report if its disclosure is not the public interest[4]. On receipt of the officer's explanation, if any the flag officer commanding-in-chief shall consider it and, if the same is found unsatisfactory, may: (i) impose the punishment of forfeiture of seniority in the rank or time for promotion, severe reprimand in case subordinate officer[5]; (ii) impose the punishment of severe reprimand or reprimand in case officer other than subordinate officers[6]; or (iii) remand the accused officer for trial by court martial[7]. Where in case of an officer other than a subordinate officer, the flag officer commanding-in-chief of a naval command considers that the charges if proved would justify the accused officer being awarded punishment of forfeiture of seniority in the rank or time for promotion, before proceeding further with the said charge, the flag officer commanding-in-chief shall ask the accused officer as follow: "Do you consent to accept summary award by me or do you elect to be tried by court-martial?" If the accused officer elects to be tried by court martial. The necessary steps for that purpose shall be taken[8]. If the accused officer does not elect trial by court martial and consents to the summary trial under the Navy Act 1957 s 94, representation to this effect shall be made in the proceedings and the officer proceeded with summarily[9].

1 Ie the Navy Act 1957 s 94 (2A).

2 The Regulations for the Navy 1965, part II, regulations 147E (1).

3 The Regulations for the Navy 1965, part II, regulations 147E (2).

4 The Regulations for the Navy 1965, part II, regulations 147E (2) proviso.

5 The Regulations for the Navy 1965, part II, regulations 147E (3) (a).

6 The Regulations for the Navy 1965, part II, regulations 147E (3) (b).

7 The Regulations for the Navy 1965, part II, regulations 147E (3) (c).

8 The Regulations for the Navy 1965, part II, regulations 147E (4) (a).

9 The Regulations for the Navy 1965, part II, regulations 147E (4) (b).

[1115] Imposition of punishment of forfeiture of seniority or time for promotion on an officer other than subordinate officer When the flag officer commanding-in-chief proceeds with trial of the accused officer, he shall read out the charge against the accused officer and ask him whether he pleads guilty or not[1]. If the accused officer pleads guilty, the plea of guilty shall be so recorded and if there no further charge to be read, the accused may be permitted to make a statement in mitigation of punishment. If the accused officer makes an oral statement, its gist or the statement, if in writing shall be attached to the proceedings[2]. The flag officer commanding-in-chief shall then consider the whole case and award such punishment as he consider just and proper[3]. Where an accused officer pleads not guilty to the charges, the flag officer commanding-in-chief shall proceed further with the trial[4]. After the statements of witnesses received along with the report have been made part of the proceedings the flag officer commanding-in-chief shall inform the accused officer that he is not obliged to make any statement, but if he wishes to make a statement orally or in writing, he may do so. The statement of the accused officer may deal with the facts of the case, with his character and with matters in mitigation of punishment. If the accused officer makes an oral statement its gist or the statement, if in writing, shall from part of the proceedings[5]. In the course of a trial wherever it appears desirable, the flag officer commanding-in-chief, may call and examine any witness whom be considers essential for proper proposal of the case. The witness so called may be cross-examined by the accused officer and if necessary by the presenting officer[6]. The evidence of such a witness shall be recorded in brief in narrative form on a separate sheet and attached to proceedings[7]. If on consideration of the whole case, the finding of the flag officer commanding-in-chief on any charge is not guilty, he shall acquit the officer of that charge. If the accused officer is acquitted of all the charges, the flag officer commanding-in-chief shall record the finding of not guilty and acquit the officer[8]. If after considering the whole case, the flag officer commanding-in-chief finds the accused officer guilty on any or all of the charges, he may award proper punishment empowered under the Navy Act 1957 s 94[9].

1 The Regulations for the Navy 1965, part II, regulations 147F (1).
2 The Regulations for the Navy 1965, part II, regulations 147F (2).
3 The Regulations for the Navy 1965, part II, regulations 147F (3).
4 The Regulations for the Navy 1965, part II, regulations 147F (4).
5 The Regulations for the Navy 1965, part II, regulations 147F (5).
6 The Regulations for the Navy 1965, part II, regulations 147F (6).
7 The Regulations for the Navy 1965, part II, regulations 147F (7).
8 The Regulations for the Navy 1965, part II, regulations 147F (8).
9 The Regulations for the Navy 1965, part II, regulations 147F (9).

[1116] Procedure in respect of trial of officer other than subordinate officers The proceedings of the trial of an officer other than a subordinate officer by the flag officer commanding-in-chief of a naval command, where the charges if proved would justify an award of forfeiture of seniority in rank or time for promotion, shall be recorded as far as possible, with such variations as are necessitated by the circumstances of each case in the prescribed form. The report submitted to the flag officer commanding-in-chief repeating to the misconduct of an accused officer shall, inter alia contain the statement of witness duly signed and a list of charges of which the accused officer is assigned[1]. The trial of an accused officer may take place at a venue, date and time convenient to the flag officer commanding-in-chief[2]. The commanding officer or any other suitable officer nominated by him, shall present the case of the prosecution before the flag officer commanding-in-chief and act as the presenting officer during the trial[3]. An officer appointed by the flag officer commanding-in-chief shall make a report of the proceedings of the trial under his directions[4]. The accused shall defend himself and shall not be entitled to be defended by any other officer or counsel[5]. The flag officer commanding-in-chief shall decide all questions arising in the course of the trial[6].

1 The Regulations for the Navy 1965, part II, regulations 147G (1).
2 The Regulations for the Navy 1965, part II, regulations 147G (2).
3 The Regulations for the Navy 1965, part II, regulations 147G (3).
4 The Regulations for the Navy 1965, part II, regulations 147G (4).
5 The Regulations for the Navy 1965, part II, regulations 147G (5).
6 The Regulations for the Navy 1965, part II, regulations 147G (6).

[1117] Imposition of punishment by the chief of the naval staff On receipt of a report, when the chief of the naval staff proposes to award a punishment of forfeiture of seniority in the rank or time for promotion under certain provisions of the Navy Act 1957[1] on account of misconduct of an officer, the officer may be given an opportunity to show cause, in the manner specified in the following provision against that action[2]. When after considering the report of officer's misconduct, the chief of the naval staff is of the opinion that the officer deserves to punished, he shall so inform the officer together with all reports adverse to him and call upon him to submit in writing, his explanation and defence together with his opinion, if the same has not been exercised by him earlier, whether he consents to accept summary award under the Navy Act 1957 s 94 or elects to be tried by court martial[3]. However, the chief of the naval staff may withhold from disclosure any such report if its disclosure is not in the public interest[4]. On receipt of the officer's explanation, if any and if the officer has not elected to be tried by court martial, the chief of the naval staff shall consider it and if the same is found unsatisfactory: (i) may impose the punishment of forfeiture of seniority in the rank or time promotion as empowered under the Navy Act 1957 s 94 (2)[5]; or (ii) if he considers that the punishment within his power shall not be adequate, submit a report of the case together with all the relevant records to the central government for being dealt with under the Navy Act 1957 s 94 (1) or take steps to bring the accused officer to trial by court martial[6].

1 Ie the Navy Act 1957 s 94 (2); see **[1110]**.
2 The Regulations for the Navy 1965, part II, regulations 147H (1).
3 The Regulations for the Navy 1965, part II, regulations 147H (2).
4 The Regulations for the Navy 1965, part II, regulations 147H (2) proviso.
5 The Regulations for the Navy 1965, part II, regulations 147H (3) (a).
6 The Regulations for the Navy 1965, part II, regulations 147H (3) (b).

[1118] Imposition of punishment by the central government On receipt of a report of misconduct of an officer, when the central government proposes to award a punishment of forfeiture of seniority in the rank or time for promotion under certain provisions of the Navy Act 1957[1], he may be given an opportunity to show cause, if not already done so by the flag officer commanding-in-chief or chief of the naval staff, in the manner specified in the following provision[2]. Where forfeiture of seniority is proposed to be awarded for misconduct, the Central Government is of the opinion that the officer deserves to be punished, it shall so inform the officer together with all records adverse to him and call upon him to submit in writing his explanation in defence together with his opinion, if the same has not been exercised by him earlier, whether he consents to accept summary award under the Navy Act 1957 s 94 or elects to be tried by court martial[3]. However, the officer's explanation, if any, and if the officer has not elected to be tried by court martial, the Central Government shall consider it and the same is found unsatisfactory, may impose the punishment of forfeiture of seniority in the rank or time for promotion as empowered under the Navy Act 1957[4].

1 Ie the Navy Act 1957 s 94 (1); see **[1110]**.

2 The Regulations for the Navy 1965, part II, regulations 147I (1).

3 The Regulations for the Navy 1965, part II, regulations 147I (2).

4 Ie under the Navy Act s 94 (1); The Regulations for the Navy 1965, part II, regulations 147I (2) proviso.

[1119] Effect of punishment of forfeiture of seniority in the rank or time for promotion The punishment of forfeiture of seniority and forfeiture of time which may be awarded to officers under certain provision of the Navy Act 1957[1] shall be two distinct and separate[2]. Where forfeiture of seniority is awarded the forfeiture shall be noted in the navy list by the post-dating of the seniority of the officer and where forfeiture of time is awarded it shall result only in the delay of promotion to the extent specified in the order of forfeiture[3]. Forfeiture of seniority under the Navy Act 1957 s 94 shall be imposed only for very serious misconduct and the normal punishment under that provision shall be forfeiture of time[4].

1 Ie the Navy Act 1957 s 94; see **[1110]**.

2 The Regulations for the Navy 1965, part II, regulations 147J (1).

3 The Regulations for the Navy 1965, part II, regulations 147J (1).

4 The Regulations for the Navy 1965, part II, regulations 147J (1).

F. Termination of Service

[1120] Termination of service of the officers by the government on grounds of misconduct

1 When it is proposed to terminate the service of an officer under the Navy Act 1957[1] on account of misconduct, he shall be given an opportunity to show cause in the manner specified below[2]. However, this provision shall not apply: (i) where the service is terminated on the ground of misconduct which has led to his conviction by a civil court[3]; or (ii) where the Government is satisfied that for reasons, to be recorded in writing, it is not expedient or reasonably practicable to give to the officer an opportunity of showing cause[4].

2 When after considering the reports on an officer's misconduct, the government or the chief of the naval staff is satisfied that the trial of the officer by a court martial is inexpedient or impracticable, but is of the opinion that the further retention of the said officer in the service is undesirable, the chief of the naval staff shall so inform the officer together with all reports adverse to him and he shall be called upon to submit, in writing, his explanation and defence[5]. However, the chief of the naval staff may withhold from disclosure any such report or portion thereof it, in his opinion, its disclosure is not in the interest of the security of the State[6].

3 In the event of the explanation of the officer being considered unsatisfactory by the chief of the naval staff, or when so directed by the government, the case shall be submitted to the government with the

officer's defence and the recommendation of the chief of the naval staff as to the termination of the officer's service in the manner specified in the following provision[7].

4 When submitting a case to the government under the aforesaid provision[8], the chief of the naval staff shall make his recommendation whether the officer's service should be terminated and if so, whether the officer should be: (i) dismissed from the naval service[9]; (ii) discharged from the service[10]; (iii) called upon to retire[11]; or (iv) called upon to resign[12].

5 The government after considering the reports and the officer's defence, if any, as the case may be, and the recommendation of the chief of the naval staff, may dismiss or discharge the officer with or without pension or call upon him to retire or resign and on his refusing to do so, the officer may be compulsorily retired or discharged from the service on pension or gratuity, if any, admissible to him[13].

1 Ie under the Navy Act 1957 s 15; see **[0956]**.

2 The Regulations for the Navy 1965, Part II, regulation 216 (1).

3 The Regulations for the Navy 1965, Part II, regulation 216 (1) proviso (a).

4 The Regulations for the Navy 1965, Part II, regulation 216 (1) proviso (b).

5 The Regulations for the Navy 1965, Part II, regulation 216 (2).

6 The Regulations for the Navy 1965, Part II, regulation 216 (2) proviso.

7 The Regulations for the Navy 1965, Part II, regulation 216 (3).

8 Ie the Regulations for the Navy 1965, Part II, regulation 216 (3).

9 The Regulations for the Navy 1965, Part II, regulation 216 (5) (a).

10 The Regulations for the Navy 1965, Part II, regulation 216 (5) (b).

11 The Regulations for the Navy 1965, Part II, regulation 216 (5) (c).

12 The Regulations for the Navy 1965, Part II, regulation 216 (5) (d).

13 The Regulations for the Navy 1965, Part II, regulation 216 (6).

[1121] Termination of service of officers by the government on grounds other than misconduct When the chief of the naval staff is satisfied that an officer[1] is unfit to be retained in the service due to inefficiency or physical disability, the officer: (i) shall be so informed[2], (ii) shall be furnished with the particulars of all matters adverse to him[3], and (iii) shall be called upon to urge any reasons he may wish to put toward in favour of his retention in the service[4]. However, the aforesaid provisions (i) (ii) and (iii) shall not apply if the chief of the naval staff is satisfied that for reasons to be recorded by him in writing, it is not expedient practicable to comply with the provisions thereof[5]. Further, the chief of the naval staff may not furnish to the officer any matter adverse to him if, in his opinion, it is not in the interest of the security of the State to do so[6]. In the event of the explanation being considered by the chief of the naval staff unsatisfactory, the matter shall be submitted to the government for orders, together with the officer's explanation and recommendation of the chief of the naval staff as to whether the officer should be: (i) called upon to retire[7]; or (ii) called upon to resign[8]. The government after considering the explanations, if any, of the officer and the recommendation of the chief of the naval staff, may call upon the officer to retire or resign, and on his refusing to do so, the officer may be compulsorily retired or discharged from the service on pension or gratuity, if any, admissible to him[9].

1 As to the definition of the term 'officer' see; **[0927]**.

2 The Regulations for the Navy 1965, Part II, regulation 217 (1) (a).

3 The Regulations for the Navy 1965, Part II, regulation 217 (1) (b).

4 The Regulations for the Navy 1965, Part II, regulation 217 (1) (c).

5 The Regulations for the Navy 1965, Part II, regulation 217 (1) proviso.

6 The Regulations for the Navy 1965, Part II, regulation 217 (1) additional proviso.

7 The Regulations for the Navy 1965, Part II, regulation 217 (2) (a).

8 The Regulations for the Navy 1965, Part II, regulation 217 (2) (b).

9 The Regulations for the Navy 1965, Part II, regulation 217 (3).

[1122] Release on medical grounds An officer[1] who is found by a medical board to be permanently unfit for any form of naval service may be released from the service in accordance with the procedure laid down in the is the Regulations for the Navy 1965[2]. The president of the medical board shall, immediately after the medical board has come to the conclusion that the officer is permanently unfit for any form of naval service, issue a notice specifying the nature of the disease or disability he is suffering from and the finding of the medical board and also intimating him that in view of the finding he may be released from the services[3]. However, where in the opinion of the medical board the officer is suffering from a mental disease and it is either unsafe to communicate the nature of the disease or disability to the officer or the officer is unfit to look after his interest, the nature of the disease or disability shall be communicated to the officer's next-of-kin who shall also have the right to petition under the following provision[4]. Every such notice shall also specify that the officer may, within 15 days of the date of receipt of the notice prefer a petition against the finding of the medical board to the chief of the naval staff through the president of the medical board[5]. If no petition is preferred within the time specified in the aforesaid provision the officer may be released from the service by an order to that effect by the chief of the naval staff[6]. If a petition is preferred within the time specified in the Regulations[7], it shall be forwarded to the government together with the records thereof and the recommendation of the chief of the naval staff and the government may, after considering the petition and the recommendation of the chief of the naval staff, pass such order as it deems fit[8].

1 As to the definition of the term 'officer' see; **[0927]**.

2 The Regulations for the Navy 1965, Part II, regulation 218 (1).

3 The Regulations for the Navy 1965, Part II, regulation 218 (2)

4 The Regulations for the Navy 1965, Part II, regulation 218 (2) proviso.

5 The Regulations for the Navy 1965, Part II, regulation 218 (3).

6 The Regulations for the Navy 1965, Part II, regulation 218 (4).

7 Ie the Regulations for the Navy 1965, Part II, regulation 218 (3).

8 The Regulations for the Navy 1965, Part II, regulation 218 (5).

7. COURT MARTIAL

A. PRELIMINARIES

CONTENT

PARA

(i) Court Martial: Power and Application

[1123] Power of court martial and commanding officers to try offences

1 An offence triable under the Navy Act 1957 may be tried and punished by court martial[1].

2 An offence not capital which is triable under Navy Act 1957 and which is committed by a person other than an officer (and in cases by the Navy Act 1957 expressly provided for when committed by an officer), may, subject to the Regulations for the Navy be summarily tried and punished by the commanding officer[2] of the ship[3] to which the offender belongs, subject to the restriction that the commanding officer shall not have power to award imprisonment or detention for more than three months or to award dismissal with disgrace from the naval service[4]. However, no sentence of imprisonment or dismissal shall be carried into effect until approved by the prescribed authorities[5].

3 The power vested in a commanding officer of a ship under this provision may, subject to the Regulations for the Navy, be exercised as follows: (i) as respects sailors on board a tender to the ship, be exercised in the case of a single tender absent from the ship, by the officer in command of such tender and in the case of two or more tenders absent from the ship in company or acting together by the officer in immediate command of such tenders[6]; (ii) as respects sailors on board any boat belonging to the ship, be exercised when such boat is absent on detached service by the officer in command of the boat[7]; (iii) as respects sailors on detached service either on shore or otherwise, be exercised by the officer in immediate command of the boat[8]; (iv) as respects sailors quartered in Naval barracks, be exercised by the officer in command of the barracks[9]; (v) as respects sailors attached to or serving with any body of the regular army, or the air force under prescribed conditions, be exercised by the commanding officer of any such body of the regular army or air force[10].

4 The commanding officer of a ship or barracks may delegate the power of awarding punishments inferior in scale to dismissal, to the officers under his command in accordance with the regulations made under the Navy Act 1957[11].

1 The Navy Act 1957 s 93 (1).

2 As to the definition of 'commanding officer'; see **[0912]**.

3 As to the definition of 'ship'; see **[0934]**.

4 The Navy Act 1957 s 93 (2).

5 The Navy Act 1957 s 93 (2) proviso.

6 The Navy Act 1957 s 93 (3) (a).

7 The Navy Act 1957 s 93 (3) (b).

8 The Navy Act 1957 s 93 (3) (c).

9 The Navy Act 1957 s 93 (3) (d).

10 The Navy Act 1957 s 93 (3) (e).

11 The Navy Act 1957 s 93 (4).

[1124] Constitution of court martial

1 Court martial[1] shall be constituted and convened subject to the following provisions of the Navy Act

1957[2].

2 The President, the chief of the naval staff, or any officer empowered in his behalf by commission from the chief of the naval staff shall have the power to order court martial for the trial of offences under the Navy Act 1957[3].

3 Unless otherwise prescribed in respect of any specified port or station, an officer holding a commission from the chief of the naval staff to order court martial shall not be empowered to do so if there is present at the place where such court martial is to be held an officer superior in rank to himself and in command of one or more of the ships of the Indian navy although such last mentioned officer may not hold a commission to order court martial and in such a case such last mentioned officer may order a court martial although he does not hold a commission for the purpose[4].

4 If an officer holding a commission from the chief of the naval staff to order courts martial, having the command of a fleet or squadron and being outside Indian waters die, be recalled, leave his station or be removed from his command, the officer upon whom the command of the fleet or squadron devolves and so from time to time the officer who shall have the command of the fleet or squadron, shall without any commission from the chief of the naval staff have the same power to order courts martial as the first mentioned officer was invested with[5].

5 If an officer holding a commission from the chief of the naval staff to order courts martial and having the command of any fleet or squadron of the Indian navy outside Indian waters shall detach any part of such fleet or squadron, or separate himself from any part of such fleet or squadron he may be commission under his hand empower in the first mentioned case, the commanding officer[6] of the squadron or detachment ordered on such separate service and in the case of death or ceasing so to command the officer to whom the command of such separate squadron or detachment shall belong. In the second mentioned case, the senior officer of the ships of the Indian navy on the division of the station from which he is absent, to order courts martial during the time of such separate service or during his absence from that division of the station. Every such authority shall continue in force until revoked or until the officer holding it returns to India or until he comes into the presence of a superior officer empowered to order courts martial in the same squadron, detachment or division of station but so that such authority shall revive on the officer holding it ceasing to be in the presence of such a superior officer and so from time to time as often as the case so requires[7].

6 A court martial shall consist of not less than five nor more than nine officers[8].

7 No officer shall be qualified to sit on the court martial unless: (i) he is subject to naval law[9]; (ii) he is an officer of the Indian navy of the rank of lieutenant or higher rank[10], and (iii) he is of or over 21 years of age[11].

8 A prosecutor shall not be qualified to sit on the court martial as member[12].

9 The persons disqualified to sit on a court martial are: (i) the officer who ordered the court martial, (ii) the officer who was the commanding officer of the ship to which the accused belonged at the time of the commission of the alleged offence, and (iii) the officer investigated the offence[13].

10 Subject to certain provisions of the Navy Act 1957[14] officers of the Indian navy shall be eligible to sit as members of a court martial irrespective of the branch of the Naval service to which they belong[15]. However, (i) the majority of the members of the court martial, including the president, shall be officers

of the executive branch of the naval service[16], and (ii) at trials of certain offences under the Navy Act 1957[17], officers other than officers of the executive branch of the naval service shall not be eligible to sit[18].

11 A court martial shall not be deemed to be duly constituted unless the members thereof are drawn from at least two ships not being tenders, and commanded by officers of the rank of lieutenant or higher rank[19].

12 The president of a court martial shall be named by the authority ordering the court martial[20].

13 No court martial for the trial of a flag officer shall be duly constituted unless the president is a flag officer and the other officers composing the court are of the rank of captain or of higher rank[21].

14 No court martial for the trial of a captain shall be duly constituted unless the president is a captain or of higher rank and the other officers composing the court are commanders or officers of higher rank[0]

15 No court martial for the trial of a commander shall be duly constituted unless the president is a commander or have higher rank and two other members are commanders or officers of higher rank[23].

16 No court martial for the trial of a person below the rank of commander shall be duly constituted unless the president is a substantive or acting commander or of higher rank[24].

17 No commander or lieutenant commander or lieutenant shall be required to sit as a member of a court martial when four officers of higher rank and junior to the president can be assembled at the place where the court martial is to be held, but the regularity or validity of any court martial or of the proceedings thereof shall not be affected by any commander, lieutenant commander or lieutenant being required to sit or sitting thereon under any circumstance and when any commander, lieutenant commander or lieutenant sits on any court martial, the members of it shall not exceed five[25].

18 Members of the court martial other than the president shall be appointed subject to the aforesaid provisions, in the manner provided in the Navy Act 1957[26].

19 Subject to certain provisions of the Navy Act 1957[27], the president shall summon all officers except such as are exempted under the following provisions, next in seniority to himself present at the place where the court martial shall be held to sit thereon until the number of nine or such other number not less than five as is attainable is complete[28].

20 The officer convening the court martial or the senior naval officer present at the place where the court martial is to be held, may exempt by writing under his hand conveyed to the president of the court martial any officer from attending as member on ground of sickness or urgent public duty[29].

21 In these provisions[30] reference to specified ranks of officers shall, unless otherwise stated, be deemed to be reference to substantive ranks and to include reference to equivalent rank in all branches of the naval service[31].

22 When the naval forces are on active service[32], officers of the Indian naval reserve forces[33] subject to naval law[34] shall be eligible to sit as members of court martial on the same basis and under the same conditions as officers of the Indian navy[35].

1 As to the definition of 'court martial'; see **[0915]**.

2 The Navy Act 1957 s 97 (1).

3 The Navy Act 1957 s 97 (2).
4 The Navy Act 1957 s 97 (3).
5 The Navy Act 1957 s 97 (4).
6 As to the definition of 'commanding officer'; see **[0912]**.
7 The Navy Act 1957 s 97 (5).
8 The Navy Act 1957 s 97 (6).
9 The Navy Act 1957 s 97 (7) (a).
10 The Navy Act 1957 s 97 (7) (b).
11 The Navy Act 1957 s 97 (7) (c).
12 The Navy Act 1957 s 97 (8).
13 The Navy Act 1957 s 97 (9).
14 Ie the Navy Act 1957 s 97 (7) to (9).
15 The Navy Act 1957 s 97 (10).
16 The Navy Act 1957 s 97 (10) proviso.
17 Ie under the Navy Act 1957 ss 34, 35, 55, 55A, 55C and 56.
18 The Navy Act 1957 s 97 (10) additional proviso.
19 The Navy Act 1957 s 97 (11).
20 The Navy Act 1957 s 97 (12).
21 The Navy Act 1957 s 97 (13)
22 The Navy Act 1957 s 97 (14).
23 The Navy Act 1957 s 97 (15).
24 The Navy Act 1957 s 97 (16)
25 The Navy Act 1957 s 97 (17).
26 Ie the Navy Act 1957 s 97 (19); The Navy Act 1957 s 97 (18).
27 Ie the Navy Act 1957 s 97 (11).
28 The Navy Act 1957 s 97 (19). Also see the Regulations for the Navy 1965, part II, regulation 174 (1).
29 The Navy Act 1957 s 97 (20).
30 Ie the Navy Act 1957 s 97.
31 The Navy Act 1957 s 97 (21).
32 As to the definition of 'active service'; see **[0905]**.
33 As to the definition of 'Indian Naval Reserve Forces'; see **[0918]**.
34 As to the definition of 'subject to naval law'; see **[0934]**.
35 The Navy Act 1957 s 97 (22).

[1125] When application for court martial be made The commanding officer[1] shall make an application for the trial of an offender by court martial in the following cases: (i) when an offence has been committed by a sailor[2], which it is beyond his power to try[3]; (ii) when the commanding officer considers that an offence has been committed by a sailor which is beyond his powers to punish adequately[4]; (iii) when any offence has been committed which he considers ought to be tried by court martial[5]; (iv) if the accused has exercised his option in accordance with the Regulations for the Navy 1965, to be tried by court martial[6]; or (v) when so directed by his superior authority[7]. If a commanding officer himself is to be tried, an application for trial shall be made by his superior authority[8]. In the case of an officer serving in naval headquarters, the application for trial shall be made by an officer designated in this behalf by the chief of the naval staff[9]. In the case of an officer on the staff of an administrative authority, the application for trial shall be made by such officer as may be designated by the administrative authority[10]. In the case of an officer serving a naval establishment not commissioned as a ship, the application for trial shall be made by the head of that establishment, unless such establishment is under the command of a commanding officer of one of Indian naval ships[11]. Where an officer other than a commanding officer is required to make an application for trial by court martial, references hereinafter to the commanding officer shall include references to such other officer[12].

1 As to the definition of 'commanding officer'; see **[0912]**.

2 As to the definition of 'sailor'; see **[0933]**.

3 The Regulations for the Navy 1965, part II, regulation 148 (1) (a).

4 The Regulations for the Navy 1965, part II, regulation 148 (1) (b).

5 The Regulations for the Navy 1965, part II, regulation 148 (1) (c).

6 The Regulations for the Navy 1965, part II, regulation 148 (1) (d).

7 The Regulations for the Navy 1965, part II, regulation 148 (1) (e).

8 The Regulations for the Navy 1965, part II, regulation 148 (2)

9 The Regulations for the Navy 1965, part II, regulation 148 (3)

10 The Regulations for the Navy 1965, part II, regulation 148 (4)

11 The Regulations for the Navy 1965, part II, regulation 148 (5)

12 The Regulations for the Navy 1965, part II, regulation 148 (6)

(ii) Summary of Evidence

[1126] Procedure for investigation and taking down summary of evidence Before a commanding officer[1] proceeds to make an application for trial by court martial he shall either investigate the case himself or appoint a suitable person to investigate the case and to record a summary of evidence[2]. The investigating officer shall take down in writing the evidence of any person whose appears to be relevant and the evidence of each witness after it has been recorded shall be read over to him and shall be signed by him or if he cannot write, his name shall be attested by his mark and witnessed by the investigating officer as a token of the correctness of the evidence recorded[3]. The evidence of the witness shall be recorded in the English language and if the witness does not understand the English language, the statement as recorded shall be interpreted to him in the language, which he understands and a notation shall be made to the effect[4]. If owing to the exigencies of service or any other grounds including the expense and the loss of time involved the attendance of any witness cannot in the opinion of the investigating officer be readily procured, some other officer may be directed by the commanding officer to take the evidence of the witness, or a written statement of the witness relating to the charge shall be obtained and such statement shall be included in the summary of evidence[5].

1 As to the definition of 'commanding officer'; see **[0912]**.

2 The Regulations for the Navy 1965, part II, regulation 149 (1).

3 The Regulations for the Navy 1965, part II, regulation 149 (2)

4 The Regulations for the Navy 1965, part II, regulation 149 (3)

5 The Regulations for the Navy 1965, part II, regulation 149 (4)

[1127] Summoning of witness before investigating officer A witness whose attendance cannot otherwise be attained, may be summoned under the provisions of the Regulations for the Navy 1965[1].

1 Ie the Regulations for the Navy 1965, part II, regulation 233; see **[1215]**. The Regulations for the Navy 1965, part II, regulation 150.

[1128] Statement of accused When the investigating officer has completed recording the evidence he shall, if he himself is not the commanding officer[1], forward it to the commanding officer[2]. The commanding officer shall formulate the charges and he shall charge the accused with having committed the offences listed in the charge sheet. The commanding officer shall there upon caution the accused as follows: "Do you wish to make any statement? You are not obliged to say anything unless you wish to do so, but whatever you say will be taken down in writing and may be given as evidence[3]." Any statement made by the accused shall be taken down, read over to him and signed by him but he shall not be cross-examined upon it[4].

1 As to the definition of 'commanding officer'; see **[0912]**.

2 The Regulations for the Navy 1965, part II, regulation 151 (1).

3 The Regulations for the Navy 1965, part II, regulation 151 (2). Non-supply of the copies of the charge sheet and statement of witness supporting the charge-sheet was voilative of the Regulations for the Navy 1965, part II, regulation 151 and vitiated the trial. *Union of India v BN Jha* [2003] 2 SCR 721.

4 The Regulations for the Navy 1965, part II, regulation 151 (3).

[1129] Remand of accused The evidence recorded by the investigating officer and the statement of the accused (the summary of evidence), shall be considered by the commanding officer[1] who thereupon shall either: (i) remand the accused for trial by court martial[2], (ii) refer the case to his superior authority for directions[3], or (iii) in the case of a sailor if it is within his jurisdiction to try the offences charged, then, unless he has received directions to the contrary from his superior authority, dispose of the case summarily[4]. When the case is referred to a proper superior authority for directions, such authority shall given directions, as it considers appropriate provided that where investigation has been carried out for the purpose of giving effect to any directions of any higher authority, the case shall be submitted to him[5]. Where in accordance with the directions of a superior authority given under the aforesaid provision, the commanding officer has been directed as apply for trial by court martial the commanding officer shall remand the accused for trial by court martial[6]. When the accused has been remanded for trial by court martial, the commanding officer shall proceed to make an application to the proper convening authority in the manner here in after provided[7].

1 As to the definition of 'commanding officer'; see **[0912]**.

2 The Regulations for the Navy 1965, part II, regulation 152 (1) (a).

3 The Regulations for the Navy 1965, part II, regulation 152 (1) (b).

4 The Regulations for the Navy 1965, part II, regulation 152 (1) (c). As to the definition of 'sailor'; see **[0933]**.

5 The Regulations for the Navy 1965, part II, regulation 152 (2).

6 The Regulations for the Navy 1965, part II, regulation 152 (3).

7 The Regulations for the Navy 1965, part II, regulation 152 (4).

[1130] Application for trial: circumstantial letter An application for the trial by court martial of any person shall be made as follows. 'Circumstantial letter' shall be forwarded to the convening authority through the usual channels, reporting the circumstances on which the charge or charges are founded in the order of their occurrence, and in sufficient detail to show the real nature and extent of the offence. The letter shall not refer to the previous character, conduct or conviction of the accused, or contain any reference to facts prejudicial to him other than such as bear directly on the charges[1]. When a charge is drawn under the certain provision of the Navy Act 1950[2] the circumstantial letter shall contain specific details of every respect in which it is alleged that the accused was at fault[3]. Any statement made by the accused in the course of enquiries or during investigation or after he had been charged shall not be included in the circumstantial letter unless it constitutes an essential part of the alleged offence[4]. If the commanding officer[5] desires to enter into further explanations as to his reasons for asking for a court martial which would necessarily refer to the previous conduct or antecedent of the accused he shall do so orally or by separate letter to the convening authority[6].

1 The Regulations for the Navy 1965, part II, regulation 153 (1).

2 Ie the Navy Act 1950 s 55.

3 The Regulations for the Navy 1965, part II, regulation 153 (2).

4 For instance in a charge of perjury such statement shall be forwarded as an annexure to the circumstantial letter in a separate document and reference shall be made in the circumstantial letter itself to the fact that such statement was made and to its inclusion in the annexure. The Regulations for the Navy 1965, part II, regulation 153 (3)

5 As to the definition of 'commanding officer'; see **[0912]**.

6 The Regulations for the Navy 1965, part II, regulation 153 (4).

[1131] Documents to accompany circumstantial letter A letter enclosing following documents will accompany circumstantial letter: (i) the charge sheet drawn in accordance with the Regulations for the Navy 1965[1]; (ii) a list of witnesses for the prosecution[2]; (iii) a summary of evidence in support of the charges[3]; (iv) a list of the exhibits which the prosecutor proposes to put in evidence[4]. When the offender is below the rank of an officer: (v) a certified extract of all entries of offences and punishments in the record of offences sheet prior to the date of the offence charged but subsequently to his joining his present ship, with his character assessed from the previous 31 December to the date of the offence with which he may be charged but excluding all consideration of that offence[5]; (vi) a certified copy of the accused's certificate of service[6].

1 The Regulations for the Navy 1965, part II, regulation 154 (a). See the Regulations for the Navy 1965, part II, regulation 155; **[1132]**.

2 The Regulations for the Navy 1965, part II, regulation 154 (b).

3 The Regulations for the Navy 1965, part II, regulation 154 (c).

4 The Regulations for the Navy 1965, part II, regulation 154 (d).

5 The Regulations for the Navy 1965, part II, regulation 154 (e).

6 The Regulations for the Navy 1965, part II, regulation 154 (f).

[1132] The charge-sheet The charge shall contain the list of charges**,** on which it is proposed to try the accused[1]. Subject to the provisions of the Navy Act 1957, a charge sheet may contain one or more charges[2]. Every charge sheet shall begin with the name and description of the person charged and shall state his rank, the number and the ship to which he belongs[3]. Each charge shall deal with a distinct offence and in no case shall an offence be described in the alternative in the same charge[4]. If the law which creates the offence gives it any specific name, the offence may be described in the charge by that name only[5]. If the law which creates an offence does not give it any specific name, so much of the definition of the offence must be stated so as to give the accused notice of the matter with which he is charged[6]. The law and the section of the law against which an offence is said to have been committed shall be mentioned in the charge[7]. The fact that the charge is made is equivalent to a statement that every legal condition required by law to constitute the offence charged with is fulfilled in the particular case[8]. The charge shall contain such particulars as to time and place of the alleged offence and of the person, if any against whom or the thing, if any, in respect of which it was committed, as are reasonably sufficient to give the accused notice of the matter with which he is charged[9]. When the nature of the case is such that the particulars mentioned in the foregoing sub-regulation do not give the accused sufficient notice of the matter with which he is charged, the charge shall also contain such particulars of the manner in which the alleged offence was committed as will be sufficient for that purpose, unless such particulars are stated in the circumstantial letter[10].

When the accused is charged with criminal breach of trust or dishonest misappropriation of money or stores, it shall be sufficient to specify the gross sum or the aggregate of all items of stores in respect of which the offence is alleged to have been committed, and the dates between which the offence is alleged to have been committed without specifying particular items or exact dates, and the charge so framed shall be deemed to be a charge for one offence, provided that the time included between the first and last of such dates shall not exceed one year[11]. Where an accused person is believed to have committed an offence of being absent without leave in addition to some other offences, a charge of absence without leave shall also be included in the charge sheet in order that the court may have the power to sentence the accused to mulcts of pay and allowances[12]. Where it is intended to prove any facts in respect of which any mulcts of pay and allowances may be awarded to make good any proved loss or damage occasioned by the offence charged, the charge shall contain particulars of these facts and the sum of the loss or damage it is intended to charge[13]. In every charge, words used in describing an offence shall be deemed to have been used in the sense attached to them respectively by the law under which such offence is punishable[14]. A charge sheet shall be in the prescribed form or in form as near to as circumstances admit[15].

1 The Regulations for the Navy 1965, part II, regulation 155 (1).
2 The Regulations for the Navy 1965, part II, regulation 155 (2).
3 The Regulations for the Navy 1965, part II, regulation 155 (3).
4 The Regulations for the Navy 1965, part II, regulation 155 (4).
5 The Regulations for the Navy 1965, part II, regulation 155 (5).
6 The Regulations for the Navy 1965, part II, regulation 155 (6).
7 The Regulations for the Navy 1965, part II, regulation 155 (7).
8 The Regulations for the Navy 1965, part II, regulation 155 (8).
9 The Regulations for the Navy 1965, part II, regulation 155 (9).
10 The Regulations for the Navy 1965, part II, regulation 155 (10).
11 The Regulations for the Navy 1965, part II, regulation 155 (11).
12 The Regulations for the Navy 1965, part II, regulation 155 (12).
13 The Regulations for the Navy 1965, part II, regulation 155 (13).
14 The Regulations for the Navy 1965, part II, regulation 155 (14).
15 The Regulations for the Navy 1965, part II, regulation 155 (15).

Duties of Convening Authority

[1133] Examination of charges and evidence When the convening authority has received the circumstantial letter and other documents, he shall, before he orders a court martial to assemble, satisfy himself that the charges are correct and sufficient and that they are properly framed and carefully drawn up[1]. The convening authority shall not convene a court martial unless he has satisfied himself that the evidence if un-contradicted or unexplained will probably suffice to ensure a conviction[2].

1 The Regulations for the Navy 1965, part II, regulation 156 (1).

2 The Regulations for the Navy 1965, part II, regulation 156 (2).

[1134] Amendment of charges The convening authority may amend the charges submitted to him and thereupon a fresh charge sheet shall be drawn up and signed by the convening authority and the charge sheet so amended shall stand substituted for the original charge sheet[1]. Where the charge sheet has not been amended, it shall be countersigned by the convening authority[2].

1 The Regulations for the Navy 1965, part II, regulation 157 (1).

2 The Regulations for the Navy 1965, part II, regulation 157 (2).

[1135] Amendment to circumstantial letter The convening authority may make such amendments in the circumstantial letters as may appear to be necessary on the basis of the charges framed and the summary of evidence. In such a case, a notation 'as amended by the convening authority' shall be made on top of the first page of the circumstantial letter as well as all amendments shall be authenticated by the convening authority with his signature. The circumstantial letter as finally approved shall be signed by the convening authority to indicate his approval[1].

1 The Regulations for the Navy 1965, part II, regulation 158.

[1136] Convening of court martial When the convening authority is satisfied that all the documents are in order and that a court martial ought to be convened, he shall issue a warrant in the prescribed form together with a copy of the charge sheet to the officer nominated by him as president of the court martial directing him to assemble a court martial at the place and on the date mentioned in the warrant[1]. The circumstantial letter shall not be communicated to the president or to the other members of the court until the court assembles and is duly sworn[2]. The summary of evidence shall on no account be given to the president or the other members of the court at any stage of the proceedings[3].

1 The Regulations for the Navy 1965, part II, regulation 159 (1).

2 The Regulations for the Navy 1965, part II, regulation 159 (2).

3 The Regulations for the Navy 1965, part II, regulation 159 (3).

[1137] Convening of court martial at Delhi/New Delhi An officer empowered by a admission from the chief of the naval staff to order court martial in Delhi or New Delhi shall be entitled to convene such court martial even in the presence of an officer superior in rank to him and in command of one or more of the ships of the Indian navy[1].

1 The Regulations for the Navy 1965, part II, regulation 159A.

[1138] Selection of president Should the rank of the person to be tried, or the character of the offence charged, be such as to require that the court should be composed of officers of standing and experience, the convening authority shall take care to select as president an officer of such seniority as may ensure the attendance of the officers of the highest rank who may be present at the place where the court martial may be ordered to assemble; but should the nature of the offence be such as may be properly dealt with by officers of less experience, he may select any eligible officer to preside whom he may consider most desirable, with reference to the convenience of the service[1].

1 The Regulations for the Navy 1965, part II, regulation 160.

[1139] Appointment of the trial judge advocate Where a judge advocate in the department of the judge advocate general of the navy is on the staff of convening authority, that judge advocate shall ordinarily be the trial judge advocate for all courts martial convened by the convening authority[1]. When there are two or more judge advocates on the staff, the convening authority shall select one of them in consultation with the senior judge advocate[2]. Where a convening authority does not have a judge advocate in the department of the judge advocate general of the navy on his staff, he shall ordinarily make a request to the services of a judge advocate being made available and where a judge advocate has been so nominated in this behalf, he shall be the trial judge advocate at the court martial to be convened[3]. If the services of a judge advocate in the department of the judge advocate general of the navy are not available, the convening authority may appoint any fit person as the trial judge advocate[4]. However, in the case of a court martial for the trial of a capital offence, reference shall be made to the judge advocate general of the navy to nominate a trial judge advocate[5]. Further, if such trial is held outside the Indian waters, the convening authority shall obtain the directions of the chief of the naval staff[6]. Where the trial judge advocate is a judge advocate in the department of the judge advocate general of the navy, it shall not be necessary to issue to him any special warrant to act[7]. A trial judge advocate who is not a judge advocate in the department of the judge advocate general of the navy, shall be appointed by warrant in the prescribed form[8].

1 The Regulations for the Navy 1965, part II, regulation 161 (1).

2 The Regulations for the Navy 1965, part II, regulation 161 (2).

3 The Regulations for the Navy 1965, part II, regulation 161 (3).

4 The Regulations for the Navy 1965, part II, regulation 161 (4).

5 The Regulations for the Navy 1965, part II, regulation 161 (4) proviso.

6 The Regulations for the Navy 1965, part II, regulation 161 (4) additional proviso.

7 The Regulations for the Navy 1965, part II, regulation 161 (5).

8 The Regulations for the Navy 1965, part II, regulation 161 (6).

[1140] Notice of trial to trial judge advocate The convening authority shall transmit to the trial judge advocate a copy of the warrant issued to the president of the court martial together with the original and sufficient copies of the circumstantial letter and documents mentioned in Regulation for the Navy 1965, part II[1], to enable the trial judge advocate to give them to each accused[2].

1 Ie the Regulations for the Navy 1965, part II, regulation 154; see **[1131]**.

2 The Regulations for the Navy 1965, part II, regulation 162.

[1141] Appointment of prosecutor The convening authority shall by warrant under his hand in the prescribed form, appoint a suitable person to prosecute and notify such appointment to the trial judge advocate[1]. Where an officer is appointed as prosecutor, it shall be his duty to obtain from the convening authority such papers as may be necessary for the purpose of the prosecution[2]. Where a counsel is appointed to conduct the prosecution, an officer shall also be appointed to assist him. In such cases, it shall be the duty of that officer to obtain from the convening authority such papers as may be necessary[3]. A counsel shall not be engaged for conducting the prosecution at court martial without the prior approval of the chief of the naval staff[4]. The recommendation for engagement of counsel shall not be made unless the convening authority is satisfied that it is essential in the interests of adequate prosecution and when approval of the chief of naval staff is given, the counsel shall be engaged in consultation with the judge advocate general of the navy. The fees for counsel shall be fixed in consultation with the judge advocate general, subject to any restrictions regarding the maximum amount payable as may be laid down by the government[5].

1 The Regulations for the Navy 1965, part II, regulation 163 (1).
2 The Regulations for the Navy 1965, part II, regulation 163 (2).
3 The Regulations for the Navy 1965, part II, regulation 163 (3).
4 The Regulations for the Navy 1965, part II, regulation 163 (4).
5 The Regulations for the Navy 1965, part II, regulation 163 (5).

[1142] Appointment of provost marshal The convening authority, or such officer as he may direct, shall by warrant under his hand in the prescribed form appoint a provost marshal[1] to take the accused into his custody and safely keep him until he shall be delivered in due course of law[2].

1 As to the definition of 'provost marshal'; see **[0932]**.
2 The Regulations for the Navy 1965, part II, regulation 164.

[1143] Appointment of officer of the court The convening authority shall also by warrant under his hand in the prescribed form, appoint an officer of the court to perform the duties mentioned in Regulations for the Navy 1965[1], and such other duties as he may be directed by the president of the court martial or the trial judge advocate to perform for the due transaction of the administrative business of the court[2].

1 Ie under the Regulations for the Navy 1965, part II, regulation 166; see **[1144]**.
2 The Regulations for the Navy 1965, part II, regulation 165.

[1144] Duties of the officer of the court The officer of the court appointed under the aforesaid provision[1] shall perform the following duties: (i) he shall serve the accused with a notice of trial issued by the trial judge advocate and other papers and shall obtain his signature[2]; (ii) he shall serve the prosecutor with the papers ordered to be delivered by the trial judge advocate[3]; (iii) when so directed, he shall serve the summons issued by the trial judge advocate upon any witness[4]; (iv) he shall be responsible for making due arrangements for the sitting of the court under the directions of the trial judge advocate and shall obtain from the proper source the furniture and fittings and supply stationery required for use of the court[5]; (v) he shall muster the witnesses outside the courtroom and as soon as the court is assembled, he shall report to the president that they are in attendance[6]; (vi) when so directed by the president, he shall cause the accused to be brought in and to admit the prosecutor and audience[7]; (vii) he shall ensure that no witness enters the court unless called to give evidence, except by the permission of the court[8]; (viii) he shall ensure that each witness leaves the court as soon as he has been examined and is not allowed to communicate with those witnesses who have yet to give evidence[9]; (ix) he shall ensure that no witness duly summoned leaves the vicinity of the court[10]; and (x) when the court is cleared for deliberations, he shall ensure that no one is allowed to remain within the court's vicinity[11].

1 Ie the Regulations for the Navy 1965, part II, regulation 165; see **[1143]**.

2 The Regulations for the Navy 1965, part II, regulation 166 (a).

3 The Regulations for the Navy 1965, part II, regulation 166 (b).

4 The Regulations for the Navy 1965, part II, regulation 166 (c).

5 The Regulations for the Navy 1965, part II, regulation 166 (d).

6 The Regulations for the Navy 1965, part II, regulation 166 (e).

7 The Regulations for the Navy 1965, part II, regulation 166 (f).

8 The Regulations for the Navy 1965, part II, regulation 166 (g).

9 The Regulations for the Navy 1965, part II, regulation 166 (h).

10 The Regulations for the Navy 1965, part II, regulation 166 (i).

11 The Regulations for the Navy 1965, part II, regulation 166 (j).

[1145] General notice of court martial Whenever a court martial is ordered, a general notice of assembly, which shall not be less than 96 hours, or on active service[1], not less than 24 hours, shall be given by general orders or by signal to the ships present so that the proper officers may be prepared to attend at the place and hour appointed[2]. The names of the president and of the officers whose presence is anticipated will be announced. After the announcement, no officer junior to the president of a rank eligible to sit as a member shall proceed on leave of absence without the express authority of the convening authority or the senior naval officer[3].

1 As to the definition of 'active service'; see **[0905]**.

2 The Regulations for the Navy 1965, part II, regulation 167 (1).

3 The Regulations for the Navy 1965, part II, regulation 167 (2).

[1146] Transmission to president of list of officers eligible to sit on court martial As soon as practicable but not later than the morning of the day appointed for the court martial, the convening authority, or in his absence the senior naval officer present shall send to the president a list of the officers who are eligible and may be required to sit as members notifying if there be any whose attendance is not attainable on ground of sickness or as being exempted on ground of urgent public duty[1]. Such list shall also give the names of the officers absent on leave[2].

1 The Regulations for the Navy 1965, part II, regulation 168 (1).

2 The Regulations for the Navy 1965, part II, regulation 168 (2).

(iii) Judge Advocate General and his Duties

[1147] Appointment of the Judge Advocate General of the Navy and his subordinate officers

1 The judge advocate general of the navy and other judge advocates for his department, as deemed necessary, are appointed by Central Government[1].

2 Out of the judge advocates so appointed, the Central Government may designate any one to be the deputy judge advocate general of the navy[2].

3 A person shall not be qualified for appointment as judge advocate general of the navy unless he: (i) is a citizen of India[3], and (ii) has for at least ten years held a judicial office in the territory of India[4], or (iii) has for at least 10 years been an advocate of a high court or two or more such courts in succession[5]. However, the Central Government may, if it is of opinion that it is necessary or expedient so to do in the exigencies of service, relax, for reasons to be recorded in writing, the qualification specified under the aforesaid provision (ii) or (iii) in respect of any person[6].

4 A person shall not be qualified for appointment as deputy judge advocate general of the navy unless he: (i) is a citizen of India[7], and (ii) has for least seven years held a judicial office in the territory of India[8], or (iii) has for at least seven years been an advocate of a high court or two or more such courts in succession[9]. However, the Central Government may, if it is of opinion that it is necessary or expedient so to do in the exigencies of service, relax, for reasons to be recorded in writing, the qualification specified under the aforesaid provision (ii) or (iii) in respect of any person[10].

5 A person shall not be qualified for appointment as judge advocate unless he: (i) is a citizen of India[11], and (ii) is qualified for enrolment as an advocate or a pleader of a high court[12].

6 For the purpose of the aforesaid provisions: (i) in computing the period during which a person has been an advocate of a high court, the period during which the person has held judicial office after he became a advocate, shall be included[13]; (ii) the expression 'judicial office' shall be deemed to include the office of the judge advocate of the fleet or any of his deputies or assistants and any other legal or judicial office in the department of the judge advocate of the fleet held before the commencement of the Navy Act 1957, and the office of the judge advocate general of the navy or of a judge advocate held after the commencement of the aforesaid Act[14].

1 The Navy Act 1957 s 168 (1).

2 The Navy Act 1957 s 168 (2).

3 The Navy Act 1957 s 168 (3) (a).

4 The Navy Act 1957 s 168 (3) (b).

5 The Navy Act 1957 s 168 (3) (c).

6 The Navy Act 1957 s 168 (3) proviso.

7 The Navy Act 1957 s 168 (4) (a).

8 The Navy Act 1957 s 168 (4) (b).

9 The Navy Act 1957 s 168 (4) (c).

10 The Navy Act 1957 s 168 (4) proviso.

11 The Navy Act 1957 s 168 (5) (a).

12 The Navy Act 1957 s 168 (5) (b).

13 The Navy Act 1957 s 168 explanation (a).

14 The Navy Act 1957 s 168 explanation (c).

[1148] Functions of the judge advocate general of the navy The judge advocate general of the navy shall perform such duties of a legal and judicial character pertaining to the Indian navy as may from time to time be referred or assigned to him by the central government or the chief of the naval staff, and to discharge the functions conferred on him by or under the Navy Act 1957, or any other law in force[1].

1 The Navy Act 1957 s 169.

[1149] Discharge of functions of the judge advocate general of the navy in his absence The functions of the judge advocate general of the navy shall in his absence on leave or otherwise, be performed by such one of the judge advocates in his department as may be designated by the chief of the naval staff[1].

1 The Navy Act 1957 s 170.

(iv) Duties of trial judge advocate

[1150] Notice of trial to the accused The trial judge advocate shall: (i) give timely notice to the accused of the time and date of the trial[1]; (ii) cause the accused to be furnished with copies of the charge sheet, the circumstantial letter, the summary of evidence and the list of exhibits proposed to be exhibited at the trial by the prosecution[2]; (iii) inform thee accused that any witness whom he may desire to call and whose attendance can reasonably be procured shall be summoned on his behalf[3]; (iv) inform the accused that he may, if he so desires and if he makes an application in writing, give evidence on his own behalf[4]. The notice to the accused shall be in the prescribed form[5].

1 The Regulations for the Navy 1965, part II, regulation 169 (1) (a).

2 The Regulations for the Navy 1965, part II, regulation 169 (1) (b). Non-supply of the copies of the charge sheet and statement of witness supporting the charge-sheet was voilative of the Regulations for the Navy 1965, part II, vitiated the trial. *Union of India v BN Jha* (2003) 2 SCR 721.

3 The Regulations for the Navy 1965, part II, regulation 169 (1) (c).

4 The Regulations for the Navy 1965, part II, regulation 169 (1) (d).

5 The Regulations for the Navy 1965, part II, regulation 169 (2).

[1151] Notice to prosecutor The trial judge advocate shall inform the prosecutor of the time and date of the court martial issuing him with a notice in the prescribed form and request the prosecutor to forward to him certified copies of the documents mentioned in the Navy Act 1957[1].

1 Ie the Navy Act 1957 s 119; The Regulations for the Navy 1965, part II, regulation 170.

[1152] Attendance of witnesses The trial judge advocate shall take necessary steps to procure the attendance of witnesses, whom the prosecutor or the accused may desire to call and whose attendance can reasonably be procured, serving them with summons in the prescribed from[1].

1 The Regulations for the Navy 1965, part II, regulation 171.

(v) Preparation of defence by the accused

[1153] Rights of accused to prepare defence An accused for whose trial an application has been made shall be afforded full opportunity as is consistent with the exigencies of the service for preparing his defence[1]. Any correspondence between the accused and his legal advisers shall not be liable to be censored. The accused shall inform the commanding officer of the names of such persons and shall also inform him of any distinctive marks that such correspondences will bear[2]. The accused shall have the right to interview any witness whom he may wish to call in his defence[3]. If the accused so desires, the commanding officer of the accused shall take such steps as the circumstances of the case permit to obtain a written statement in a closed envelope from a witness whom the accused may wish to call in his defence and such statement shall be given to the accused unopened[4]. If the accused gives to his commanding officer the name of any person whom he wishes to call in his defence, no person shall interview such witness with reference to the charges against the accused except in the presence of the accused, unless the accused agrees to dispense with his presence in writing. If the accused wishes to interview a witness whom the prosecutor intends to call, the interview shall be in the presence of an officer detailed by the commanding officer of the accused person[5].

1 The Regulations for the Navy 1965, part II, regulation 172 (1).
2 The Regulations for the Navy 1965, part II, regulation 172 (2).
3 The Regulations for the Navy 1965, part II, regulation 172 (3).
4 The Regulations for the Navy 1965, part II, regulation 172 (4).
5 The Regulations for the Navy 1965, part II, regulation 172 (5).

[1154] Defending officer and defence counsel Except where the accused defends himself, he may be defended by an officer who shall be called the defending officer or by a qualified defence counsel[1]. A counsel shall be deemed to be properly qualified, if he is an advocate within the meaning of the Advocate Act 1961[2]. The accused may request and shall be afforded at the earliest opportunity the assistance of any officer in his ship whose assistance is reasonably available and in case the accused is unable to obtain such assistance and he desires to have a defending officer assigned to represent him, the convening authority shall appoint a suitable officer[3].

1 The Regulations for the Navy 1965, part II, regulation 173 (1).
2 The Regulations for the Navy 1965, part II, regulation 173 (2).
3 The Regulations for the Navy 1965, part II, regulation 173 (3).

(vi) Duties of the President

[1155] Summoning of members The president shall by signal summon the officers junior to himself present at the place where the court martial shall be held to sit there on which signal shall be deemed to be a compliance with certain provisions of the Navy Act 1957[1]. When issuing the signal, provision shall be made for the attendance of spare members who would be eligible to sit if any objection to a member of the court is allowed[2].

1 Ie the Navy Act 1957 s 97 (19); The Regulations for the Navy 1965, part II, regulation 174 (1).
2 The Regulations for the Navy 1965, part II, regulation 174 (2).

[1156] Responsibilities for conduct of court The president shall be responsible together with the trial judge advocate for ensuring that the trial is conducted in accordance with the provisions of the Navy Act 1957 and the Regulations for the Navy 1965, part II, and that the customary ceremonial set forth in Regulations for the Navy 1965, part II, appendix III is observed[1].

1 The Regulations for the Navy 1965, part II, regulation 175.

[1157] Order in which members shall sit Officers whose duty it may be to attend as members of court martial shall sit only in the confirmed rank they hold; but commodores when not acting in conjunction with senior captains shall sit as commodores otherwise as captains only[1]. The members of the court shall sit in order of seniority, the officer next senior to the president sitting on his right, the next senior on his left and so on[2].

1 The Regulations for the Navy 1965, part II, regulation 176 (1).

2 The Regulations for the Navy 1965, part II, regulation 176 (2).

[1158] When accused pleads guilty Before the court accepts a plea of guilty and there are no other charges to be tried, the court shall call upon the prosecutor to read the circumstantial letter[1].

1 As to the 'circumstantial letter'; see **[1130]**. The Regulations for the Navy 1965, part II, regulation 177.

Provisions concerning procedure

[1159] Provisions as to witnesses for the prosecution and the defence The prosecutor shall not be bound to call all the witnesses whose names are in the list given to the accused, but he shall call such of them as the accused may desire to be called in order that the accused may cross-examine them if he wishes to do so and such witnesses, shall be called before the prosecution is finally closed[1]. The accused shall not be required to give to the prosecutor or the court a list of witnesses whom he intends to call, but should he desire assistance in the matter of securing the attendance of witnesses, he shall inform the trial judge advocate in the prescribed form[2]. The prosecutor is a competent witness[3]. A member of the court, whether previously objected to or not by either side, shall not be disqualified from being examined as a witness should it be found in the course of the proceedings that he may give material evidence, but thereafter he shall be disqualified from acting as a member of the court, unless his evidence has been given after conviction, and has been directed to the good character of the accused[4]. When the accused is called on for his defence, he shall, on his application, be granted a reasonable time for the preparation of the defence. The court may adjourn from time to time on the application of the accused, if he shall satisfy the court that the time granted to him has not been sufficient for the due preparation of his defence[5].

1 The Regulations for the Navy 1965, part II, regulation 178 (1).

2 The Regulations for the Navy 1965, part II, regulation 178 (2).

3 The Regulations for the Navy 1965, part II, regulation 178 (3).

4 The Regulations for the Navy 1965, part II, regulation 178 (4).

5 The Regulations for the Navy 1965, part II, regulation 178 (5).

[1160] Mode of questioning witness Every question shall be put to a witness orally and the witness shall forthwith reply, unless an objection is made, in which case he shall not reply to the court until the objection is decided by the trial judge advocate[1]. The evidence of a witness as taken down shall be read to him if he so requests before he leaves the court, and shall, if necessary, be corrected and if he makes any explanation or correction. The prosecutor and the defence may respectively examine him regarding the same[2]. If the witness denies the correctness of any part of the evidence when the same is read over to him, the trial judge advocate may, instead of correcting the evidence, record the objection made by the witness[3]. If the evidence is not given in English and the witness does not understand that language, the evidence as recorded shall be interpreted to him in the language in which it was given, or in a language which he understands if he so requests before he leaves the court[4]. On application of the accused the court shall allow his cross-examination of a witness to be postponed, unless it appears that the request has been made for the purpose of obstruction[5].

1 The Regulations for the Navy 1965, part II, regulation 179 (1).

2 The Regulations for the Navy 1965, part II, regulation 179 (2).

3 The Regulations for the Navy 1965, part II, regulation 179 (3).

4 The Regulations for the Navy 1965, part II, regulation 179 (4).

5 The Regulations for the Navy 1965, part II, regulation 179 (5).

[1161] Questions to witness by court or judge advocate The president, the trial judge advocate, or with the permission of the president, any member of the court may address a question to a witness while such witness is giving his original evidence and before he withdraws[1].

1 The Regulations for the Navy 1965, part II, regulation 180.

[1162] Recalling of witness and calling of witness in reply Without prejudice to certain provisions of the Navy Act 1957[1], the trial judge advocate, if he considers it expedient in the interest of justice, so to do, allow a witness to be called or recalled by the prosecutor, before the closing address of or on behalf of the accused, for the purpose of rebutting any material statement made by a witness for the defence or for the purpose of giving evidence on any new matter which the prosecutor could not reasonably have foreseen[2]. Where the accused has called witnesses to character, the prosecutor before the closing address of or on behalf of the accused, may call or recall witnesses for the purpose of proving a previous conviction or entries in the defaulter's book against the accused[3].

1 Ie the Navy Act 1957 s 137.

2 The Regulations for the Navy 1965, part II, regulation 181 (1).

3 The Regulations for the Navy 1965, part II, regulation 181 (2).

[1163] Amendment of charges during the trial If at any time in the course of the trial after the court has been sworn and before the finding, the trial judge advocate is satisfied that there is a variance in unessential details between the charge or charges and the evidence adduced in support thereof, the trial judge advocate may amend the charge or charges accordingly provided that: (i) no evidence which could not have been given in support of the original charge shall be given in support of the substituted charge[1]; (ii) the accused shall not be substantially prejudiced by the making of such amendment in the conduct of his defence[2]; and (iii) the court shall, if so requested by the accused adjourn for a reasonable time to enable him to meet the charge or charges as so amended[3]. All such amendments shall be noted in the minutes at the point at which such amendments shall be made, and shall be verified on the original documents by the signature of the trial judge advocate[4].

1 The Regulations for the Navy 1965, part II, regulation 182 (1) (a).

2 The Regulations for the Navy 1965, part II, regulation 182 (2) (b).

3 The Regulations for the Navy 1965, part II, regulation 182 (1) (c).

4 The Regulations for the Navy 1965, part II, regulation 182 (2).

(vii) Evidence on Navigational Matter

[1164] Documents to be made available in navigational cases At all trials at which evidence is to be given on the navigation of one of Indian naval ships or vessels, the prosecutor on opening his case shall lay before the court the following documents as apply to the case: (i) the ship's log[1]; (ii) the rough and fair engine room registers[2]; (iii) control room log[3]; (iv) the chart or charts and sailing directions by which the ship was navigated[4]; (v) the last table of compass deviations[5]; (vi) the navigational data book and the gyro-compass log[6]; (vii) the Captain's night order book[7]; and (viii) the Navigating officer's note book and work book[8]. After the prosecutor has opened his case, the president shall, unless he considers the circumstances so exceptional that such procedure would be a waste of time, order the documents referred to in the aforesaid provision to be handed to one or more navigation direction or other competent officers who shall work up the ship's reckoning throughout the material time; the result, together with such other details as may be required, being delivered to the court in the prescribed form completed in all relevant respects and attested by the signature of the officer(s) so directed. The such officer(s) shall be sworn and be subject to cross-examination by both persecution and defence as to its accuracy[9]. The president shall endorse such report as approved, if the court concurs, and if not, an expression of its dissent shall be added, signed by the president, showing in what respects and for what reason it dissents[10]. With the said report such officer(s) shall also deliver to the court a copy or tracing of the chart by which the ship was navigated on which the position of the ship so determined have been laid off, and also the determined position when ashore or in danger, as noted in the log book[11]. The rule and direction of the current and of the tidal stream and the state of the tide should also, if possible, be ascertained, stated, and verified on oath[12]. The report in the prescribed form and the prepared chart, as well as an attested copy of the ship's log book and the engine room register or of the control room log, commencing from at least 48 hours before the ship took the ground or was endangered, if so long from a known anchorage, shall accompany the minutes[13]. At trials at which evidence may be required on the navigation of an aircraft such documents as exist and may be available to serve a similar purpose to those set out in the aforesaid provision[14] shall be made available by the commanding officer[15] of the aircraft and the court may follow, with such variation as may be necessary or desirable, the procedure prescribed under this provision[16].

1 The Regulations for the Navy 1965, part II, regulation 183 (1) (a).

2 The Regulations for the Navy 1965, part II, regulation 183 (1) (b).

3 The Regulations for the Navy 1965, part II, regulation 183 (1) (c).

4 The Regulations for the Navy 1965, part II, regulation 183 (1) (d).

5 The Regulations for the Navy 1965, part II, regulation 183 (1) (e).

6 The Regulations for the Navy 1965, part II, regulation 183 (1) (f).

7 The Regulations for the Navy 1965, part II, regulation 183 (1) (g).

8 The Regulations for the Navy 1965, part II, regulation 183 (1) (h).

9 The Regulations for the Navy 1965, part II, regulation 183 (2).

10 The Regulations for the Navy 1965, part II, regulation 183 (3).

11 The Regulations for the Navy 1965, part II, regulation 183 (4).

12 The Regulations for the Navy 1965, part II, regulation 183 (5).

13 The Regulations for the Navy 1965, part II, regulation 183 (6).

14 Ie the Regulations for the Navy 1965, part II, regulation 183 (1).

15 As to the definition of 'commanding officer, see **[0912]**.

16 The Regulations for the Navy 1965, part II, regulation 183 (7).

[1165] Absence of documents Should the absence of any of the documents mentioned in the aforesaid provision[1] be likely to render it difficult for the officer(s) mentioned therein to complete their task to the satisfaction of the court, it shall be permissible for the prosecution to call an expert witness, if possible a qualified Navigation Direction Officer, to assist the court[2]. Such a witness shall not be called under the Regulations for the Navy 1965[3] and shall, with the permission of the court, be present to hear the evidence and shall then lay out the resulting courses on the chart[4]. Such witness shall be subject to unrestricted cross-examination[5].

1 Ie the Regulations for the Navy 1965, part II, regulation 183; see **[1164]**.

2 The Regulations for the Navy 1965, part II, regulation 184 (1).

3 Ie the Regulations for the Navy 1965, part II, regulation 183.

4 The Regulations for the Navy 1965, part II, regulation 184 (2).

5 The Regulations for the Navy 1965, part II, regulation 184 (3).

[1166] Navigation direction officers: examination and cross-examination The examination and cross-examination of the officer(s) who leave been directed to perform the duty mentioned in the Regulations for the Navy 1965[1], shall be limited to ascertaining the accuracy or inaccuracy of the documents laid before the court[2]. However, if no other navigational experts are reasonably available and it is desired to have further evidence from such officer(s), the court may recall such officer(s) and permit him to be questioned on other navigational matters by both the prosecution and the defence[3].

1 Ie under the Regulations for the Navy 1965, part II, regulation 183; see **[1164]**.

2 The Regulations for the Navy 1965, part II, regulation 185 (1).

3 The Regulations for the Navy 1965, part II, regulation 185 (2).

[1167] Reason for finding in navigational cases The reasons for finding of 'guilty' or 'not guilty' including cases where the court accepts the 'plea of no case to answer' on charges under certain provisions of the Navy Act 1957[1] shall be recorded[2].

1 Ie the Navy Act 1957 s 55 and 55A; see **[1007]** and **[1008]**.

2 The Regulations for the Navy 1965, part II, regulation 185A.

[1168] Evidence of negligence not alleged in circumstantial letter If the court, at any time during the trial, considers that the accused has been negligent in any way not specifically detailed in the circumstantial letter or the charges, the court shall formulate a fresh allegation against the accused, inform the accused about the allegation and invite him to deal with the fresh allegation in his defence, adjourning if necessary to give him time to meet it[1]. Any witness for whom the accused asks shall, if practicable, be called or recalled and if he is a prosecution witness, he shall be cross-examined by the defence and re-examined by the prosecutor. If he is a defence witness, he shall be examined by the defence, cross-examined by the prosecutor and re-examined by the defending officer[2]. If the charge is found proved, any such additional heading indicating a form of negligence, if finally established to the satisfaction of the court, shall be included in the finding[3].

1 The Regulations for the Navy 1965, part II, regulation 186 (1).

2 The Regulations for the Navy 1965, part II, regulation 186 (2).

3 The Regulations for the Navy 1965, part II, regulation 186 (3).

(viii) Court martial: General

[1169] Period of sitting Ordinarily the court martial shall sit five hours a day and its sittings shall not be protracted without specific reasons[1].

1 The Regulations for the Navy 1965, part II, regulation 187.

[1170] Ascertaining the opinion of the court In ascertaining the opinion of the court in accordance with certain provisions of the Navy Act 1957[1], the votes of members of the court shall be taken in succession beginning with the member lowest in rank[2].

1 Ie the Navy Act 1957 s 124; see **[1204]**.

2 The Regulations for the Navy 1965, part II, regulation 188.

[1171] The minutes of proceedings The proceedings of the court martial shall be recorded as far as possible in the prescribed form[1]. The questions and answers shall be recorded verbatim and serially numbered throughout and all exhibits shall be fastened together in the order in which they were produced in the court. A list shall be made of exhibits showing the precise question and answer at which the document was exhibited[2]. The records referred to in the aforesaid provision shall be accompanied by an index of questions put to each witness and the pages of the minutes shall be serially numbered[3]. Whenever a question proposed to be asked by either party is objected to by the other party, the trial judge advocate shall decide whether the question is to be admitted or not and the fact of the objection having been made, the ground thereof and the decision of the trial judge advocate shall be recorded in the minutes, if the trial judge advocate or either of the parties so desires[4].

1 The Regulations for the Navy 1965, part II, regulation 190 (1).

2 The Regulations for the Navy 1965, part II, regulation 190 (2).

3 The Regulations for the Navy 1965, part II, regulation 190 (3).

4 The Regulations for the Navy 1965, part II, regulation 190 (4).

[1172] Responsibilities of trial judge advocate for preparing minutes The trial judge advocate shall be responsible for ensuring that the minutes are duly recorded and prepared[1]. The transcript made by the shorthand writer shall be made under the directions of the trial judge advocate and both the shorthand writer and the trial judge advocate shall certify that the transcript is a faithful record of the proceedings[2].

1 The Regulations for the Navy 1965, part II, regulation 191 (1).

2 The Regulations for the Navy 1965, part II, regulation 191 (2).

[1173] Number of copies In addition to the original proceedings, sufficient copies of the proceedings shall be made to enable one to be sent to the convening authority and one supplied to each of the accused in the event of an application being made pursuant to the provisions of the Navy Act 1957[1]. The trial judge advocate shall transmit the original proceedings directly to the judge advocate general of the navy and shall submit a copy thereof to the convening authority[2]. Where an officer produces certificate or other documents of character under the provisions of the Navy Act 1957[3], a certificate shall be extracted on the prescribed form and it shall not be necessary to exhibit the original certificates unless it is otherwise decided by the trial judge advocate[4].

1 Ie the Navy Act 1957 s 129; see **[1209]**. The Regulations for the Navy 1965, part II, regulation 192 (1).

2 The Regulations for the Navy 1965, part II, regulation 192 (2).

3 Ie the Navy Act 1957 s 119 (1) (a) (iii); see **[1199]**.

4 The Regulations for the Navy 1965, part II, regulation 192 (3).

[1174] Report by president of court martial to convening authority As soon as the court has been dissolved, the president shall inform the convening authority or the senior naval officer present, the finding and the sentence of the court martial[1]. If the court desires to draw attention to the conduct or manner of giving evidence of any witness, an entry regarding such conduct or manner may be made in its proceedings, after the sentence and, except in cases where such witness is also sentenced under the Navy Act 1957[2], such entry shall not form part of its proceedings[3]. All other representations which the court may desire to make with reference to matters arising out of the court martial shall be made the subject of a separate letter signed by the president before the court has been dissolved, and shall not form part of the recorded proceedings of the court[4].

1 The Regulations for the Navy 1965, part II, regulation 193 (1).

2 Ie the Navy Act 1957 s 139 or 140; see **[1220]** and **[1221]**.

3 The Regulations for the Navy 1965, part II, regulation 193 (2).

4 The Regulations for the Navy 1965, part II, regulation 193 (3).

[1175] Powers of the court martial to award minor punishments Without prejudice to the minor punishments as may be inflicted according to the custom of the Navy, a court martial may award the following punishments in accordance with the provisions of the Regulations for the Navy 1965: (i) solitary confinement in a cell or under a canvas screen for a period not exceeding 14 days (No. 8)[1]; (ii) deprivation of good conduct badge and good conduct medal (No. 9)[2]; (iii) extra work and drill for a period not exceeding 14 days (No. 11)[3]; (iv) stoppage of leave for a period not exceeding 60 days (No. 12)[4]; and (v) extra work or drill for not more than two hours in a day for a period not exceeding seven days (No. 13)[5].

1 The Regulations for the Navy 1965, part II, regulation 193A (a).

2 The Regulations for the Navy 1965, part II, regulation 193A (b).

3 The Regulations for the Navy 1965, part II, regulation 193A (c).

4 The Regulations for the Navy 1965, part II, regulation 193A (d).

5 The Regulations for the Navy 1965, part II, regulation 193A (e).

[1176] Execution of sentence It shall be the responsibility of the convening authority to take necessary steps to give effect to the sentence[1]. The convening authority shall not give effect to a sentence if he considers that an error has occurred in the conduct of the court martial. If he doubts the correctness of the finding in fact or in law or the legality or the propriety of the sentence, he shall not put the sentence into effect until a decision has been obtained from the chief of the naval staff[2]. Where an officer is sentenced to imprisonment, the convening authority shall not put the sentence into effect until he has communicated with and received the directions of the chief of the naval staff[3].

1 The Regulations for the Navy 1965, part II, regulation 194 (1).

2 The Regulations for the Navy 1965, part II, regulation 194 (2).

3 The Regulations for the Navy 1965, part II, regulation 194 (3).

[1177] Custody until commitment A person sentenced to imprisonment or detention may be detained in naval custody[1] until he has been committed to prison or detention quarters or until other orders have been received from the proper superior authority[2].

1 As to the meaning of 'naval custody'; see **[0921]**.

2 The Regulations for the Navy 1965, part II, regulation 195.

B. Procedure

CONTENT

PARA

(i) Procedure of Court Martial

(i) Procedure of Court Martial

[1178] Where court martial to be held A court martial may be held ashore or afloat[1].

1 The Navy Act 1957 s 98.

[1179] Trial Judge Advocate Every court martial shall be attended by a person (the trial judge advocate) who shall be either a judge advocate in the department of the judge advocate general of the navy or any fit person appointed by the convening officer[1]. However, in the case of a court martial for the trial of a capital offence the trial judge advocate shall be a person nominated by the judge advocate general of the navy unless such trial is held outside Indian waters[2]. The trial judge advocate shall administer oath to every witness at the trial and shall perform such other duties as are provided in the Navy Act 1957 and as may be prescribed[3].

1 The Navy Act 1957 s 99 (1).

2 The Navy Act 1957 s 99 (1) proviso.

3 The Navy Act 1957 s 99 (2).

[1180] Court martial to be public The place in which a court martial is held for the purpose of trying an offence under the Navy Act 1957 shall be deemed to be an open court to which the public generally may have access so far as the same can conveniently contain them[1]. However, if the court is satisfied that it is necessary or expedient in the public interest, for the ends of justice so to do, the court may at any stage of the trial of any particular case order that the public generally or any portion thereof or any particular person shall not have access to or be or remain in, the place in which the court is held[2].

1 The Navy Act 1957 s 100.

2 The Navy Act 1957 s 100 proviso.

[1181] Commencement of proceedings As soon as the court has been assembled the accused the accused shall be brought before it and the prosecutor the person or persons, if any, defending the accused and the audience admitted[1]. Except where the accused defends himself, he may be defended by such person or persons as may be prescribed[2]. The trial judge advocate shall read out the warrant for assembling the court and the names of officers who are exempted from attending under the Navy Act 1957[3] together with the reasons for such exemption[4]. The trial judge advocate shall read out the names of the officers composing the court and shall ask the prosecutor whether he objects to any of them[5]. If the prosecutor shall have made no objection or after any objection made by the prosecutor has been disposed of, the trial judge advocate shall ask the accused if he objects to any member of the court[6].

1 The Navy Act 1957 s 101 (1).

2 The Navy Act 1957 s 101 (2).

3 Ie the Navy Act 1957 s 97 (20); see **[1224]**.

4 The Navy Act 1957 s 101 (3).

5 The Navy Act 1957 s 101 (4).

6 The Navy Act 1957 s 101 (5).

[1182] Objection to members The following provisions shall apply to the disposal of objections raised by the prosecutor as well as the accused: (i) Any member may be objected to on the ground which affects his competency to act as an impartial Judge; and the trial judge advocate may reject summarily without reference to the members of the court any objection not made on such grounds[1]. (ii) Objections to members shall be decided separately, those to the officer lowest in rank being taken first[2]. However, if the objection is to the president, such objection shall be decided first and all the other members whether objected to or not shall vote as to the disposal of the objection[3]. (iii) On an objection being allowed by one-half or more of the officers entitled to decide the objection, the member objected to shall at once retire and his place shall be filled up before an objection against another member is taken up[4]. (iv) Should the president be objected to and the objection be allowed, the court shall adjourn until a new president has been appointed by the convening authority or by the officer empowered in this behalf by the convening authority[5]. (v) Should a member be objected to on the ground of being summoned as a witness, and should it be found that the objection has been made in good faith and that the officer is to give evidence as to facts and not merely as to character the objection shall be allowed[6].

The objection of an accused to a court member which affected their competency to act as an impartial judge can only be decided by the members of the court martial in accordance with the provisions of the Navy Act 1957[7]. A trial judge advocate cannot usurp the jurisdiction of the court and reject summarily the objection of the accused holding that the objections were not sustainable. In doing so he clearly over stepped the limitations of his jurisdiction and decided a matter which the court alone, and not he, was empowered to. The jurisdiction of the trial judge advocate under the Navy Act 1957[8] is limited to the extent of finding out whether the objection is on the ground specified in the first part of the aforesaid provision[9].

1 The Navy Act 1957 s 102 (a).

2 The Navy Act 1957 s 102 (b).

3 The Navy Act 1957 s 102 (b) proviso.

4 The Navy Act 1957 s 102 (c).

5 The Navy Act 1957 s 102 (d).

6 The Navy Act 1957 s 102 (e).

7 Ie the Navy Act 1957 s 102 (b) to (e).

8 Ie the Navy Act 1957 s 102 (a).

9 *Union of India v Shivendra Bikaram Singh* 2003 Cri LJ 3028.

[1183] Future objections The trial judge advocate shall then ask the accused whether he has any further objections to make respecting the constitution of the court; and should the accused raise any such objection, it shall then be decided by the court, which decision shall be final and the constitution of the court martial shall not be afterwards impeached and it shall be deemed in all respects to have been duly constituted[1]. If the accused should have no further objection to make to the constitution the court or if any objection is disallowed, the members and the trial judge advocate shall then make an oath or affirmation in the form set out in the provisions of the Navy Act 1957[2].

1 The Navy Act 1957 s 103 (1).

2 Ie in the Navy Act 1957 s 104; The Navy Act 1957 s 103 (2).

[1184] Administrating oath or affirmation Before the court shall proceed to try the person charged, an oath or affirmation in the following form and manner shall be administrated to the president and every member of the court martial in the order of their seniority by the trial judge advocate[1]:

> I.........do swear in the name of God/solemnly affirm, that I will duly and faithfully and to the best of my ability, knowledge and judgment perform the duties of my office according to law, without fear or favour, affection or ill-will, and that I will not upon any account at any time whatsoever disclose or discover the vote or opinion of any particular member of this court martial unless thereunto required in due course of law.

The trial judge advocate shall then be sworn or affirmed by the president in the following form[2]:

> I.........do swear in the name of God/solemnly affirm, that I will duly and faithfully and to the best of my ability, knowledge and judgment perform the duties of my office according to law, without fear or favour, affection or ill-will, and that I will not upon any account at any time whatsoever disclose or discover the vote or opinion of any particular member of this court martial unless thereunto required in due course of law.

1 The Navy Act 1957 s 104 (1).

2 The Navy Act 1957 s 104 (2).

[1185] Arraignment When the court is ready to commence the trial, the trial judge advocate shall readout the charges and shall ask the accused whether he pleads guilty or not guilty[1]. If the accused pleads guilty, then before such plea is recorded, the trial judge advocate shall ensure that the accused understands the charge to which he has pleaded guilty and the difference of procedure, which will result the plea of guilty[2]. If appears from the accused's replies or from the summary of evidence prepared in the prescribed manner that he should not plead guilty, the trial judge advocate may advice the accused to withdraw his plea[3]. If the court accepts the plea of guilty, it shall be recorded as the finding of the court and the court shall proceed to take steps to pass sentence unless there are other charges to be tried in which event the sentence shall be deferred until after the findings on such charges are given[4].

1 The Navy Act 1957 s 105 (1).

2 The Navy Act 1957 s 105 (2).

3 The Navy Act 1957 s 105 (3).

4 The Navy Act 1957 s 105 (4).

[1186] Opening of prosecution case If the accused pleads not guilty or refuses to, or does not plead or if he claims to be tried or if in the circumstance mentioned in certain provisions of the Navy Act 1957[1], withdraws the plea of guilty or if the court does not accept the plea of guilty, the court shall proceed to try the accused[2]. The prosecutor shall open his case by reading the circumstantial letter prepared in accordance with the provisions of the Regulations for the Navy[3], reading from the Navy Act 1957 or the Indian Penal Code or other law the description of the offence charged and stating shortly by what evidence he expects to prove the guilt of the accrued[4]. The prosecutor shall then examine his witnesses[5].

1 Ie the Navy Act 1957 s 105 (3); see **[1185]**.

2 The Navy Act 1957 s 106 (1).

3 Ie the Regulations for the Navy 1965, part II, regulation 153; see **[1130]**.

4 The Navy Act 1957 s 106 (2).

5 The Navy Act 1957 s 106 (3).

[1187] Calling of prosecution witness not in the original list No witness whose name was not included in the original list of witnesses supplied to the trial judge advocate and the accused in accordance with the Regulations for the Navy[1], shall be called by the prosecutor unless the trial judge advocate has given notice to the accused of the prosecutor's intention to call such witness and has supplied the accused with the summary of the evidence of such witness[2].

1 Ie the Regulations for the Navy 1965, part II, regulation 154; See [1131].

2 The Navy Act 1957 s 107.

[1188] Swearing of interpreter and shorthand-writer At any time during the trial, should the court think that necessary, an impartial person may be employed to serve as an interpreter and sworn or affirmed as such in the following manner[1]:

> I.........do swear in the name of God/solemnly affirm, that I will to the best of my ability truly interpret and translate as I will be required to touching the matter before this court martial.

During the trial, an impartial person shall be employed as a shorthand-writer and duly sworn or affirmed as such in the following manner[2]:

> I.........do swear in the name of God/solemnly affirm that I will truly take down to the best of my power the evidence to be given before this court martial and such other matters as I will be required, and when required, will deliver to the court a true transcript of the same.

1 The Navy Act 1957 s 108 (1).

2 The Navy Act 1957 s 108 (2).

[1189] Objection to interpreter or shorthand-writer Before any person is sworn or affirmed as an interpreter or a shorthand-writer, the accused shall be asked if he objects to such person as not being impartial and the court shall decide the objection[1]. The evidence given by a witness shall be read over to him by shorthand-writer before the witness leaves the court, if so requires by the court or the witness[2].

1 The Navy Act 1957 s 109 (1).

2 The Navy Act 1957 s 109 (2).

[1190] Swearing of witnesses No witness shall be examined until he has been duly sworn or affirmed in the following manner[1]:

> I.........do swear in the name of God/solemnly affirm that the evidence which I shall give before this court shall be the truth, the whole truth and nothing but the truth.

Every person giving evidence on oath or affirmation before a court martial shall be bound to state the truth[2].

1 The Navy Act 1957 s 110 (1).

2 The Navy Act 1957 s 110 (2).

[1191] Plea of no case and defence of accused When the examination of the witness for the prosecution is concluded, the accused shall be called on for his defence[1]. Before entering on his defence, the accused may raise a plea of no case[2]. If such a plea is raised the court will decide the plea after hearing the accused and the prosecutor and the advice of the trial judge advocate[3]. If the court accepts the plea, the accused shall be acquitted on the charge or charges in respect whereof the plea has been accepted[4]. If the court overrules the plea, the accused shall be called upon to enter on his defence[5]. The trial judge advocate shall then inform the accused that he may give evidence as a witness on his own behalf should he desire to do so and should he make a request in writing to do so, but that he will thereby render himself liable to cross-examination[6]. If the accused does not apply to give evidence, he may make a statement as to the facts of the case and if he has no defene witnesses to examine as to facts the prosecutor may sum up his case and the accused shall be entitled to reply[7]. If the accused or any one of the several accused applies to give evidence and there are no other witness in the case for the defense, other than witnesses as to character, then the evidence of such accused shall be recorded and if the accused so desires the witnesses as to character shall be examined and the prosecutor shall then sum up his case and the accused may reply[8]. If the accused or any one of the accused adduces any oral evidence as to facts other than his own evidence, if any, the accused may then sum up his case on the conclusion of that evidence and the prosecutor shall be entitled to reply[9].

1 The Navy Act 1957 s 111 (1).
2 The Navy Act 1957 s 111 (2).
3 The Navy Act 1957 s 111 (3).
4 The Navy Act 1957 s 111 (4).
5 The Navy Act 1957 s 111 (5).
6 The Navy Act 1957 s 111 (6).
7 The Navy Act 1957 s 111 (7).
8 The Navy Act 1957 s 111 (8).
9 The Navy Act 1957 s 111 (9).

[1192] Adjournment to view Whenever the court thinks that it should view the place in which the offence charged is alleged to have been committed or any other place in which any other transaction material to the trial is alleged to have occurred, the court shall make an order to that effect and may then adjourn to the place to be viewed, along with the prosecutor and the accused and the person, if any, by whom the accused is represented[1]. The court on completion of the view shall adjourn and reassemble in the courtroom[2].

1 The Navy Act 1957 s 112 (1).
2 The Navy Act 1957 s 112 (2).

[1193] Summing up by the trail judge advocate When the case for the defence and the prosecutor's reply are concluded, the trial judge advocate, in open court shall sum up the evidence for the prosecution and defence and lay down the law by which the court is to be guided[1].

1 The Navy Act 1957 s 113.

[1194] Duties of the trial judge advocate At all trials by court martial it is the duty of the trial judge advocate to decide all questions of law arising in the course of the trial, and specially all questions as to the relevancy of facts which it is proposed to prove and the admissibility of evidence or the propriety of the questions asked by or on behalf of the parties; and in his discretion to prevent the production of inadmissible evidence whether it is or is not objected to by the parties[1]. Whenever in the course of a trial it appears desirable to the trial judge advocate that arguments and evidence as to the admissibility of evidence or arguments in support of an application for separate trials or on any other points of law should not be heard in the presence of the court, he may advice the president of the court accordingly and the president shall thereupon make an order for the court to retire or direct the trial judge advocate to here the arguments in some other convenient place[2]. Where the trial judge advocate produced an already typed order which was read out, it was held that the trial judge advocate had prejudiced the issue before hearing the arguments and read out the order which had already been dictated[3].

1 The Navy Act 1957 s 114 (1). Also see **[1150]** to **[1152]**.

2 The Navy Act 1957 s 114 (2).

3 *Commander V S Batra v Chief of the Naval Staff*, Mil LJ 1998 Delhi 205.

[1195] Duties of the court It is the duty of the court to decide which view of the facts is true and then arrive at the finding, which under such view ought to be arrived at[1].

1 The Navy Act 1957 s 115.

[1196] Retirement to consider finding After the trial judge advocate has finished his summing up, the court will be cleared to consider the finding[1]. The trial judge advocate shall not sit with the court when the court is considering the finding and no person shall speak to or hold any communication with the court while the court is considering the finding[2].

1 The Navy Act 1957 s 116 (1).

2 The Navy Act 1957 s 116 (2).

[1197] Announcement of the finding When the court has considered the finding, the court shall be reassembled and the president shall inform the trial judge advocate in open court what is the finding of the court as ascertained in accordance with the provisions of the Navy Act 1957[1]. The court shall give its finding on all the charges on which the accused is tried[2].

1 Ie the Navy Act 1957 s 124; The Navy Act 1957 s 117 (1).

2 The Navy Act 1957 s 117 (2).

[1198] Drawing of the finding The trial judge advocate shall then draw up the finding as announced by the court[1]. The finding shall be signed by all the members of the court by way of attestation notwithstanding any difference of opinion there may have been among the members and shall be countersigned by the trial judge advocate[2]. Where the finding on any charge is one of not guilty the court shall acquit the accused of that charge[3]. If the accused is acquitted of all the charges, the court shall after signing the finding[4], be dissolved[5]. Neither the court nor the trial judge advocate shall announce in open court whether the finding was unanimous or not but the president shall make a record of the division of voting on each finding without disclosing the vote or opinion of any particular member of the court martial and such record shall be communicated to the trial judge advocate for transmission to the judge advocate general of the navy[6].

1 The Navy Act 1957 s 118 (1).

2 The Navy Act 1957 s 118 (2).

3 The Navy Act 1957 s 118 (3).

4 Ie as provided in the Navy Act 1957 s 118 (2).

5 The Navy Act 1957 s 118 (4).

6 The Navy Act 1957 s 118 (5).

[1199] Evidence of character and previous convictions If the accused is found guilty on any or all of the charges, the court before awarding punishment may call evidence as to the previous character and qualifications of the accused. In addition to any oral evidence of general character of the accused that may be adduced, the court shall take into consideration the following documents which shall be read by the trial judge advocate in open court: (a) for an officer (i) any entries against him relating to his previous convictions in the list of officers who have been tried by court martial[1]; (ii) any previous entries against him in the log of the ship to which he may have belonged when the offence(s) for which he is being tried were committed; (iii) any documents, other than such entries in the log, of the nature of a definite censure by superior authority, which log and documents the prosecution is to produce[2]; and (iv) any certificate or other documents of character which the accused may produce[3]; (b) for a sailor (i) the entries against him in the conduct and offences record sheets prior to the date of the offence charged, but subsequent to his joining his present ship, with character assessed from the previous 31st day of December to the date of the offence for which he may be under trial but excluding all consideration of the later[4]; (ii) his certificate of service[5]; and (iii) any entries against him relating to his previous conviction in the list of those who have been tried by court martial[6]. The accused may then make a statement in mitigation of punishment and lead any evidence of character if he has not already done so before the finding[7].

1 The Navy Act 1957 s 119 (1) (a) (i). As to the definition of officer; see **[0927]**.

2 The Navy Act 1957 s 119 (1) (a) (ii).

3 The Navy Act 1957 s 119 (1) (a) (iii).

4 The Navy Act 1957 s 119 (1) (b) (i). As to the definition of sailor; see **[0933]**.

5 The Navy Act 1957 s 119 (1) (b) (ii).

6 The Navy Act 1957 s 119 (1) (b) (iii).

7 The Navy Act 1957 s 119 (2).

[1200] Consideration of the sentences The court shall then retire and consider and determine on the punishment proper to be inflicted in conformity with the finding. All the members of the court whether they have voted for an acquittal or not, shall vote on the question of proper punishment to be awarded to the accused for the offence of which he has been found guilty[1]. The trial judge advocate shall sit with the court while they are considering the sentence and assist the court in the determination of the sentence but shall not vote thereon[2].

1 The Navy Act 1957 s 120 (1).

2 The Navy Act 1957 s 120 (2).

[1201] Announcement of the sentence When the court has decided on the sentence whether unanimously or by majority, the trial judge advocate shall draw up the sentence in the prescribed form which shall be signed by every member of the court by way of attestation notwithstanding any difference of opinion there may have been among the members and shall be countersigned by the trial judge advocate[1]. The court shall then be reassembled and the accused brought in and the trial judge advocate shall by direction of the court pronounce the sentence[2]. The accused shall then be removed and the court dissolved[3].

1 The Navy Act 1957 s 121 (1).

2 The Navy Act 1957 s 121 (2).

3 The Navy Act 1957 s 121 (3).

[1202] Adjournment A court martial may, if it appears to the court that an adjournment is desirable, be adjourned accordingly, but except where such an adjournment is ordered shall sit from day to day with the exception of Sundays until the trial is concluded, unless prevented from so doing by stress of weather or unavoidable accident[1]. The proceedings of a court martial shall not, after the commencement of a trial, be delayed by the absence of a member;[2] provided not less than four members are present[3]. If any member is absent from any part of the trial, he shall not thereafter take any part in the proceedings[4].

1 The Navy Act 1957 s 122 (1).

2 The Navy Act 1957 s 122 (2).

3 The Navy Act 1957 s 122 (2) proviso.

4 The Navy Act 1957 s 122 (2) additional proviso.

[1203] Provisions relating to dissolution of court martial A court martial assembled under the Navy Act 1957 shall be dissolved: (i) when the number of members comprising the court is after the commencement of a trial reduced below for[1]; (ii) by the prolonged illness of the president, trial judge advocate or the accused[2]; (iii) by the death of the president or the trial judge advocate[3]; (iv) on the making of a report under certain provisions of the Navy Act 1957[4]. Whenever a court martial is dissolved by virtue of the aforesaid provisions, the accused may be retried[5].

1 The Navy Act 1957 s 123 (1) (a).

2 The Navy Act 1957 s 123 (1) (b).

3 The Navy Act 1957 s 123 (1) (b).

4 Ie the Navy Act 1957 s 143 (2). The Navy Act 1957 s 123 (1) (d).

5 The Navy Act 1957 s 123 (2).

[1204] Ascertaining the opinion of the court Subject to certain provisions of the Navy Act 1957[1], every question for determination by a court martial shall be decided by the vote of majority[2]. However, where there is an equality of votes, the decision most favourable to the accused shall prevail[3].

The sentence of death shall not be passed on any offender unless four at least of the members present at the court martial where the member does not exceed five, and in all other cases a majority of not less than two thirds of the members present, concur in the finding[4]. Where in respect of an offence, the only punishment which may be awarded is death, a finding that a charge for such offence is proved shall not be given unless four at lest of the members present at the court martial where the number does not exceed five, and in all other cases a majority of not less than two-thirds of the members present, concur in the finding[5].

1 Ie the Navy Act 1957 s 124 (2) and (3).

2 The Navy Act 1957 s 124 (1). In ascertaining the opinion of the court, the votes of members of the court shall be taken in succession beginning with the member lowest in rank. The Regulations for the Navy 1965, part II, regulation 188.

3 The Navy Act 1957 s 124 (1) proviso.

4 The Navy Act 1957 s 124 (2).

5 The Navy Act 1957 s 124 (3).

[1205] Finding that the offence was committed with intent involving less degree of punishment Where the amount of punishment for any offence depends upon the intent with which it has been committed and any person is charged with having committed such an offence with an intent involving a greater degree of punishment, a court martial may find that the offence was committed with an intent involving less degree of punishment and award such punishment accordingly[1].

1 The Navy Act 1957 s 125.

[1206] Alternative findings If the accused is charged with one offence and it appears in evidence that he committed a different offence for which he might have been charged under the Navy Act 1957[1], he may be convinced of the offence, which he is shown to have committed although he was not charged with it[2].

1 Ie under the Navy Act 1957 s 91; see **[1048]**.

2 The Navy Act 1957 s 126.

[1207] Finding lesser offence proved on charge of greater offence When a person is charged with an offence consisting of several particulars, a combination of some only of which constitutes a complete minor offence and such combination is proved, but the remaining particulars are not proved, he may be convicted of the minor offences although he was not charged with it[1]. When a person is charged with an offence and facts are proved which reduce it to a minor offence, he may be convicted of the minor offence, he may be convicted of the minor offence although he was not charge with it[2]. When a person is charged with an offence, he may be convicted of an attempt to commit such an offence, although the attempt is not separately charged[3].

1 The Navy Act 1957 s 127 (1).

2 The Navy Act 1957 s 127 (2).

3 The Navy Act 1957 s 127 (3).

[1208] Transmission of proceeding to the judge advocate general of the navy The trial judge advocate shall transmit in accordance with the prescribed procedure with as much expedition as may be, the original proceeding or a complete and authenticated copy thereof and the original sentence of every court martial attended by him to the judge advocate general of the navy to be dealt with by him in accordance with the provisions of the Navy Act 1957[1].

1 Ie under the Navy Act 1957 ss 160 and 161, for judicial review; see **[1233]** and **[1234]**. The Navy Act 1957 s 128.

[1209] Right of accused to copy of proceedings and sentence Every person tried by a court martial and convicted shall be entitled on demand to one copy of the proceeding and sentence of such court martial free of cost but no such demand shall be allowed after the lapse of one year from the date of the final decision of such court[1].

1 The Navy Act 1957 s 129. See the Regulations for the Navy 1965, part II, regulation 192; see **[1173]**.

(ii) Rules as to Evidence

[1210] Application of the Evidence Act Subject to the provisions of the Navy Act 1957, the Indian Evidence Act 1872 shall apply to all proceedings before a court martial[1].

1 The Navy Act 1957 s 130.

[1211] Accused competent witness for defence A person accused of an offence before a court martial shall be a competent witness for the defence and may give evidence on oath in disproof of the charges made against him or any person charged together with him at the same trial[1]. However: (i) he shall not be called as a witness except on his own request in writing[2]; or (ii) his failure to give evidence shall not be made the subject of any comment by any of the parties or the court or give rise to any presumption against himself or any person charged together with him at the same trial[3].

1 The Navy Act 1957 s 131.

2 The Navy Act 1957 s 131 proviso (a).

3 The Navy Act 1957 s 131 proviso (b).

[1212] Judicial notice A court martial may take judicial notice of any matter within the general naval, army or air force experience and knowledge of the members[1].

1 The Navy Act 1957 s 132.

[1213] Presumption as to certain documents

1 Whenever it is necessary for the purpose of either the prosecution or the defence to prove the contents of any voucher, receipt, account, muster, ship's book, letter, signal, telegram or other document made or kept in pursuance of any Act, the Regulations for the Navy or of the custom of the service a copy of the same purporting to be signed and certified as a correct copy by the officer for the time being commanding the ship in which the same was made or kept or by a secretary to the central government, may be received as evidence of such document and of the matters, transactions and accounts therein recorded[1].

2 A navy list or Gazette or other official document purporting to be published by authority of the central government or the chief of the naval staff shall be evidence of the status and rank of officers therein mentioned and of any appointment held by such officers until the contrary is proved[2].

3 Where it is shown that a person is born on the 'books of a ship' of the Indian navy, such fact shall be evidence that such person is subject to naval law[3] until the contrary is proved[4]. In this provision, the term 'books of a ship' shall include any official book, document or list purporting to contain the name or names of person appointed to the ship[5].

4 Where any person subject to naval law is being tried on a charge of desertion, improperly leaving his ship, or absence without leave and such person has surrendered himself into custody of or has been apprehended by any person subject to naval law or by a person subject to the law relating to the government of the regular army or the air force, a certificate purporting to be signed by such person and stating the fact, date and place of such surrender or apprehension shall be evidence of the matters so stated unless the contrary is proved[6].

5 Where any person subject to naval law is being tried on a charge of desertion, improperly leaving his ship or absence without leave and such person has on arrest or surrender been taken to a police station, a certificate purporting to be signed by the officer-in-charge of the station and stating the fact, date and place of such surrender or apprehension shall be evidence of the matters stated unless the contrary is proved[7].

6 Any document purporting to be a report, under the hand of: (i) any Chemical Examiner or Assistant Chemical Examiner to the Government[8]; (ii) the Chief Inspector of Explosives[9]; (iii) the Director of Finger Print Bureau[10]; (iv) the Director of Haffkein Institute, Bombay[11]; (v) the Director, Deputy Director or Assistant Director of a Central Forensic Science Laboratory or a State Forensic Science Laboratory[12]; (vi) the Serologist to the Government[13]; upon any matter or thing duly submitted to him for examination or analysis, may be used as evidence in any proceedings under the Navy Act 1957[14].

7 The statement of naval, army or air force medical officer taken and attested by the commanding officer of a ship or establishment may be given evidence in any proceeding under the Navy Act 1957[15]. However, that the court may, if it thinks fit, and shall if so required by the prosecutor or the accused, summon and examine such medical officer as the subject matter of his statement[16].

8 If it is proved that an offender under the Navy Act 1957 has absconded and that there is no immediate prospect of arresting him, the commanding officer or other prescribed person may, in his absence examine any persons who might appear to him to be acquainted with the case and record their depositions on oath. Any deposition may on the arrest of such person be used in evidence against him in any proceeding under the Navy Act 1957, if the deponent is dead or incapable of giving evidence or his attendance cannot be procured without an amount of delay, expense or inconvenience[17].

1 The Navy Act 1957 s 133 (1).

2 The Navy Act 1957 s 133 (2).

3 As to the meaning of 'persons subject to naval law'; see **[0941]**.

4 The Navy Act 1957 s 133 (3).

5 The Navy Act 1957 s 133 (3) explanation.

6 The Navy Act 1957 s 133 (4).

7 The Navy Act 1957 s 133 (5).

8 The Navy Act 1957 s 133 (6) (a).

9 The Navy Act 1957 s 133 (6) (b).

10 The Navy Act 1957 s 133 (6) (c).

11 The Navy Act 1957 s 133 (6) (d).

12 The Navy Act 1957 s 133 (6) (e).

13 The Navy Act 1957 s 133 (6) (f).

14 The Navy Act 1957 s 133 (6).

15 The Navy Act 1957 s 133 (7).

16 The Navy Act 1957 s 133 (7) proviso.

17 The Navy Act 1957 s 133 (8).

[1214] Summoning of witnesses

1 Every person who may be required to give evidence or produce a document before a court martial shall be summoned in the prescribed manner[1] in writing under the hand of the judge advocate general of the navy or the trial judge advocate[2].

2 Every person who may be required to give evidence before a commanding officer or the officer preparing a summary of evidence in accordance with the regulations made under the Navy Act 1957 or before a

board of inquiry shall be summoned in the prescribed manner by writing under the hand of the judge advocate general of the navy or the senior officer in the station or such other officer prescribed in this behalf[3].

3 In the case of a witness, subject to naval law[4] or to the law relating to the government of the regular army or the air force the summons shall be served in the manner prescribed[5].

4 In the case of any other witness, the summons shall be served either in the prescribed manner, or it shall be sent to the magistrate within whose jurisdiction the witness may be or resides and such magistrate shall give effect to the summons as if the witness were required in the court of such magistrate[6].

5 When a witness is required to produce any particular document or thing in his possession or power, the summons shall describe it with reasonable precision[7].

6 Every person not subject to naval law who may be summoned as aforesaid shall be allowed and paid such reasonable expenses as may be prescribed[8].

7 Nothing in aforesaid provisions shall be deemed to affect the operation of certain provisions of the Indian evidence Act 1872[9], or to apply any document in the custody of the postal or telegraph authorities[10].

1 As to the meaning of 'prescribed manner' see the Regulations for the Navy 1965, Part II, regulation 233; see **[1215]**.

2 The Navy Act 1957 s 134 (1).

3 The Navy Act 1957 s 134 (2).

4 As to the meaning of 'subject to naval law'; see **[0935]**.

5 The Navy Act 1957 s 134 (3).

6 The Navy Act 1957 s 134 (4).

7 The Navy Act 1957 s 134 (5).

8 The Navy Act 1957 s 134 (6).

9 Ie the Indian evidence Act 1872 s 123 and 124.

10 The Navy Act 1957 s 134 (7).

[1215] Summoning of witnesses: procedure

1 When the presence of a witness, required to give evidence before a commanding officer or an officer preparing the summary of evidence or before a board of inquiry or before a court martial cannot otherwise be obtained, summons may be issued in accordance with the following provisions: (i) the summons shall be in the prescribed form[1]; (ii) in the case of a witness subject to naval law or a law relating to the government of the regular army or air force, the summons shall be served upon the individual through his commanding officer or other superior authority as may be most convenient and in the case of any other witness who is a government servant, the summons may be served upon the head of the office in which he is serving[2]; (iii) in the case of every witness the summons shall be served by causing it to be delivered personally or sending it by registered post or it may, in accordance with the provisions of the Navy Act 1957[3], be sent to the magistrate in whose jurisdiction the witness may be or resides[4].

2 The prescribed officers under the Navy Act 1957[5] relating to the summoning of witnesses before

a commanding officer or the officer preparing a summary of evidence shall be the administrative authority or the judge advocate. The prescribed officers for summoning of the witnesses before a board of inquiry, shall be the convening authority or the president of the board[6].

3 A civilian witness in government service not subject to naval law, who is summoned under the aforesaid provision of the Navy Act 1957 to attend a court martial, disciplinary court, board of inquiry or before the commanding officer or other officer preparing a summary of evidence, shall be entitled to receive travelling allowances under civil rules or travel regulations according to whether he is serving in a civil department or in the defence services, provided that the facts as to which he is to give evidence have come to his knowledge in the discharge of his public duties[7].

4 A civilian witness, not subject to naval law and not in government service, when called to appear before a court martial, disciplinary court, board of inquiry or before the commanding officer or other officer preparing a summary of evidence shall be entitled to travelling and subsistence allowances at the rates fixed by the local government, high courts or administrations for non-official witness appearing before the courts of law under their jurisdiction. Such rates of allowances shall be ascertained and paid through the magistrate where witnesses are called through him and in other cases, the rates of the allowances shall be ascertained from the magistrate in whose jurisdiction the witness resides at the time he is summoned to give evidence and paid by the summoning authority[8].

5 It shall be the duty of summoning authority to advance to the witness, through the magistrate if he is called through a magistrate, otherwise direct, a sufficient sum to cover his travelling expenses and arrange payment to him of the subsistence allowance expenses on account of return conveyance before he leaves the station to which he is summoned[9].

6 Civilian witnesses, not subject to naval law and not in government service, when called upon to give expert evidence shall, in addition, be paid fees for their expert evidence or service subject to the approval of the competent financial authority under whose powers the amount at issue falls[10].

7 Private individuals employed as interpreters and shorthand writers before a court martial, disciplinary court or board of Inquiry shall be paid out of pocket expenses for their services at the discretion of the president of the court-martial, disciplinary court or board of inquiry subject to the approval of the competent financial authority under whose powers the amount at issue falls[11].

1 The Regulations for the Navy 1965, Part II, regulation 233 (1) (a).

2 The Regulations for the Navy 1965, Part II, regulation 233 (1) (b).

3 Ie the Navy Act 1957 s 134(4).

4 The Regulations for the Navy 1965, Part II, regulation 233 (1) (c).

5 Ie the Navy Act 1957 s 134(4).

6 The Regulations for the Navy 1965, Part II, regulation 233 (2).

7 The Regulations for the Navy 1965, Part II, regulation 233 (3).

8 The Regulations for the Navy 1965, Part II, regulation 233 (4).

9 The Regulations for the Navy 1965, Part II, regulation 233 (5).

10 The Regulations for the Navy 1965, Part II, regulation 233 (6).

11 The Regulations for the Navy 1965, Part II, regulation 233 (7).

[1216] Commissions for examination of witnesses Whenever in the course of a trial by court martial, it appears to the trial judge advocate that the examination of a witness is necessary for the ends of justice and that the attendance of such witness cannot be procured without an amount of delay expense or inconvenience which under the circumstance of the case would be unreasonable, the trial judge advocate may dispense with such attendance and may apply to the judge advocate general of the navy to issue a commission to any metropolitan magistrate or judicial magistrate of the first class within the local limits of whose jurisdiction such witness resides, to take the evidence of such witness[1]. The trial in such an event may be adjourned for a specified time reasonably sufficient for the execution and return of the commission[2]. The judge advocate general of the navy on receipt of an application under the aforesaid provision[3] may, if he thinks fit, issue a commission to the metropolitan magistrate or judicial magistrate of the first class or an authority exercising the powers equivalent to those of a judicial magistrate of the first class under the Code of Criminal Procedure 1973, for the examination of the witness[4]. The magistrate or authority to whom the commission is issued or if he is chief metropolitan magistrate or chief judicial magistrate, he or such metropolitan magistrate or judicial magistrate of the first class as is appointed by him in this behalf shall proceed to such place where the witness is or shall summon the witness before him and shall take down his evidence in the same manner and may for this purpose exercise the same powers as in the trials of warrant cases under the Code of Criminal Procedure 1973, or of any corresponding law in force at the place where the evidence is recorded[5].

1 The Navy Act 1957 s 135 (1).

2 The Navy Act 1957 s 135 (2).

3 Ie the Navy Act 1957 s 135 (1).

4 The Navy Act 1957 s 135 (3).

5 The Navy Act 1957 s 135 (4).

[1217] Examination of witness on commission Where a commission is issued under the aforesaid provision[1], the prosecutor and the accused may respectively forward any interrogatories in writing which the trial judge advocate may think relevant to the issue and the magistrate or authority to whom the commission is directed or to whom the duty of executing such commission has been delegated shall examine the witness upon such interrogatories[2]. The prosecutor and the accused may appear before such magistrate or authority by counsel or, except in the case of an accused person in custody, in person and may examine, cross-examine and re-examine, as the case may be, the said witness[3]. After a commission issued under the aforesaid provision has been duly executed, it shall be returned together with the deposition of the witness examined there under to the judge advocate general of the navy who issued the commission[4]. On receipt of the commission and the deposition returned under the aforesaid provision, the judge advocate general of the navy shall forward the same to the trial judge advocate at whose instance the commission was issued[5]. The commission the return thereto and the deposition shall be open to inspection by the prosecutor and the accused and may subject to all just exceptions be read in evidence in the case by either the prosecutor or the accused and shall form part of the proceedings of the trial[6]. Any deposition so taken shall be received in evidence at any subsequent stage of the trial whether before the same court or, if the said court is dissolved meanwhile, before another court convened for the trial of the accused in respect of the same charges[7].

1 Ie the Navy Act 1957 s 135.

2 The Navy Act 1957 s 136 (1).

3 The Navy Act 1957 s 136 (2).

4 The Navy Act 1957 s 136 (3).

5 The Navy Act 1957 s 136 (4).

6 The Navy Act 1957 s 136 (5).

7 The Navy Act 1957 s 136 (6).

[1218] Power to summon and examine material witness The trial Judge advocate may, at any stage of the trial, summon any person as a witness or examine any person in attendance, though not summoned as a witness, or recall and re-examine any person already examined; and the trial judge advocate shall summon and examine or recall and re-examine any such person if his evidence appears to the court or to the trial judge advocate as essential to the just decision of the case[1]. Summons to the witnesses shall be issued as provided under the Navy Act 1957[2].

1 The Navy Act 1957 s 137 (1).

2 The Navy Act 1957 s 137 (2).

(iii) Compensation to aggrieved persons out of fine

[1219] Power of court to pay compensation out of fine Whenever a court martial imposes a fine as a punishment, the court may when passing judgment order the whole or any part of the fine recovered to be applied: (i) in the payment to any person aggrieved as compensation for any loss or injury caused by the offence[1]; (ii) when any person is convicted of any civil offence which includes theft, criminal misappropriation, criminal breach of trust or cheating or of having dishonestly received or retained, or of having voluntarily assisted in disposing of stolen property knowing or having reason to believe the same to be stolen property, in compensating any *bona fide* purchaser of the property for the loss of the same if such property is restored to the possession of the person entitled thereto[2]. However, no such payment or compensation shall be made before the expiry of 15 days from the date the sentence, and when a petition is presented against the conviction or sentence until the said petition is disposed of[3].

1 The Navy Act 1957 s 138 (1) (a).

2 The Navy Act 1957 s 138 (1) (b).

3 The Navy Act 1957 s 138 (2).

(iv) Power of Court Martial respecting Contempt

[1220] Summary punishment for contempt of court by person subject to naval law When any person subject to naval law[1] commits an offence under the Navy Act 1957[2] in the presence of or in relation to proceeding before a court martial, such court martial may punish the offender summarily by imprisonment for a term which may extent to three months or such other less punishment under authorized under the Navy Act1957[3].

1 As to the meaning of 'person subject to naval law'; see **[0941]**.

2 Ie the Navy Act 1957 s 69, o**ffences in relation to court martial; see [1025].**

3 The Navy Act 1957 s 139.

[1221] Summary punishment for contempt of court by person not subject to naval law When any person not subject to naval law commits an offence as is described in certain provisions of the Navy Act 1957[1] in the presence of a court martial, such court martial may take such person into custody and at any time before the rising of then court on the same day, if it thinks fit, take cognizance of the offences and sentence the offender to fine not exceeding Rs 200/- or in default of payment to simple imprisonment for a term which may be extend to one, month unless such fine shall be sooner paid[2].

1 Ie the Navy Act 1957 s 165.

2 The Navy Act 1957 s 140.

[1222] Power of court martial when certain offences are committed by persons not subject to naval law When any such offence as is described in the Navy Act 1957[1] or the Indian Penal Code 1860[2] is committed by any person not subject to naval law in or in relation to a proceeding before a court martial, such court martial or the officer ordering the same if such court martial is dissolved, may exercise the powers under the Code of Criminal Procedure 1973[3], as if it or he were a criminal court within the meaning of that provision[4].

1 Ie the Navy Act 1957 s 165; see **[1037]**.

2 Ie the Indian Penal Code 1860 ss 193-196, 199, 200, 228, 463 or 471.

3 Ie under the Code of Criminal Procedure 1973 s 340.

4 The Navy Act 1957 s 141.

[1223] Powers of court martial and disciplinary courts in relation to proceeding under the Navy Act 1957 Any trial by a court martial or disciplinary court under the provisions of the Navy Act 1957 shall be deemed to be a judicial proceedings within the meaning of the Indian Penal Code 1860[1], and the court martial or disciplinary court shall be deemed to be a court within the meaning of certain provisions of the Code of Criminal Procedure 1973[2].

1 Ie the Indian Penal Code 1860 s 193 and 228.

2 Ie under the Code of Criminal Procedure 1973 s 345 and 346; The Navy Act 1957 s 142.

(v) Lunacy of the Accused

[1224] Accused found insane during trial Where it appears in the course of the trial by court martial of any person charged with an offence that such person is insane, the court shall find specially the fact of his insanity and shall order such person to be kept in strict custody in such place and in such manner as the court may deem fit until the directions of the Central Government thereupon are known[1]. Every such case shall be reported by the court to the convening authority for orders of the Central Government and it shall be lawful for the Central Government to give orders for the safe custody of such person in such place and in such manner as the Central Government may deem fit[2]. Whenever on the receipt of report from the Central Government or otherwise the convening authority considers that such person is capable of making his defence, the convening authority may take steps to convene a court martial for the trial of such person[3].

1 The Navy Act 1957 s 143 (1).

2 The Navy Act 1957 s 143 (2).

3 The Navy Act 1957 s 143 (3).

[1225] Lunacy of the accused at the time of offence Whenever any person subject to naval law[1] is acquitted upon the ground that, at the time at which he is alleged to have committed an offence, he was by reason of unsoundness of mind, incapable of knowing the nature of the act alleged as constituting the offence, or that it was wrong or contrary to law, the finding shall specifically state whether he committed the act or not[2]. Whenever the finding made under the aforesaid provision states that the accused person committed the act alleged, the court martial shall, if such act would, but for the incapacity found, have constituted an offence, order such person to be detained in safe custody in such place and in such manner as may be prescribed and shall report the action taken to the officer convening the court[3]. The officer convening the court shall then report the case for the orders of the Central Government and shall take necessary steps to detain the said person in safe custody pending receipt of such orders[4]. The Central Government may on receipt of a report under the aforesaid provision order the accused person to be detained in a mental hospital or other suitable place of safe custody[5].

1 As to the meaning of 'person subject to naval law'; see **[0941]**.

2 The Navy Act 1957 s 144 (1).

3 The Navy Act 1957 s 144 (2).

4 The Navy Act 1957 s 144 (3).

5 The Navy Act 1957 s 144 (4).

(vi) Disposal of Property

[1226] Disposal of property pending trial When any property regarding which an offence appears to have been committed or which appears to have been used for the commission of an offence is produced before a court martial, the court may make such order as it thinks fit for the proper custody of such property pending the conclusion of the trial and if the property is subject to speedy or natural decay may after recording such evidence as it thinks necessary order it to be sold or otherwise disposed of[1].

1 The Navy Act 1957 s 145.

[1227] Disposal of property regarding which offence is committed When the trial before any court martial is concluded, the court may make such order as it thinks fit for the disposal by destruction, confiscation or delivery to any person claiming to be entitled to possession thereof or otherwise of any property or document produced before it or in its custody or regarding which an offence appears to have been committed or which has been used for the commission of any offence[1]. However, except in the case of property which is subject to speedy or natural decay such property or document shall, if so required by regulations, made under the Navy Act 1957, be kept in custody until the orders or the chief of the naval staff are known[2]. An order under the aforesaid provision[3] shall not be carried out for one month, unless the property is subject to speedy or natural decay[4]. When an order under this provision cannot be conveniently carried out by persons in the naval service, a copy of such order certified by the Chief of the Naval Staff or an officer prescribed in this behalf, may be sent to a magistrate within whose jurisdiction the property is for the time being situated and such magistrate shall thereupon take steps to cause the order to be carried into effect as if it were an order passed by him[5]. In this provision, the term 'property' includes, in the case of property regarding which an offence appears to have been committed, not only such property as has been originally in the possession or under the control of any person, but also any property into or for which the same may have been converted or exchanged and anything acquired by such conversion or exchange whether immediately or otherwise[6].

1 The Navy Act 1957 s 146 (1).

2 The Navy Act 1957 s 146 (1) proviso.

3 Ie under the Navy Act 1957 s 146 (1).

4 The Navy Act 1957 s 146 (2).

5 The Navy Act 1957 s 146 (3).

6 The Navy Act 1957 s 146 explanation.

C. Disciplinary Courts

CONTENT

[1228] Disciplinary courts when may be constituted Under the Navy Act 1957, a disciplinary court can be constituted in time of war or during active service[1], in respect of certain specified offences[2] committed by officers and punishable in lesser degree. The officer having the power to order a court martial may, if he considers the offences to be of such a character as not to necessitate trial by court martial, in lieu of ordering a court martial may order a disciplinary court to be constituted[3].

1 As to the definition of 'active service'; see **[0905]**.

2 Ie the offence contained in the Navy Act 1957 ss 41, 47, 48, 49, 51, 52, 68, and 74 or of any of these offences read with the Navy Act 1957 ss 75 or 76.

3 The Navy Act 1957 s 95. As to the constitution of disciplinary court, see the Navy Act 1957 s 96; **[1229]**.

[1229] Constitution and procedure of disciplinary courts A disciplinary court is composed of not less than three nor more than five officers[1]. However, the majority of the officers including the president shall be officers of the executive branch of the naval service[2]. At least one of these officers composing the court shall be superior in rank to the officer under trial and in any case shall be of the rank of substantive or acting commander or of higher rank[3]. A disciplinary court shall have power to impose any punishment inferior to detention in the scale as contained in the Navy Act 1957[4], but no greater punishment[5]. The officers composing the disciplinary court shall be named by the authority ordering the same or by an officer empowered in this behalf by such authority[6]. Subject to the aforesaid provisions[7], the procedure and practice of courts martial followed under the Navy Act 1957 shall apply to the procedure and practice of disciplinary courts subject to such modification as may be prescribed[8].

1 The Navy Act 1957 s 96 (1).

2 The Navy Act 1957 s 96 (1) proviso.

3 The Navy Act 1957 s 96 (2).

4 Ie as contained in the Navy Act 1957 s 81; see **[1231]**.

5 The Navy Act 1957 s 96 (3).

6 The Navy Act 1957 s 96 (4).

7 Ie the Navy Act 1957 s 96 (1), (2), (3) and (4).

8 Ie as prescribed in the Regulations for the Navy 1965, Part II, regulation 196; see **[1230]**. The Navy Act 1957 s 96 (5).

[1230] Disciplinary court applicability of provisions Subject to certain provisions of the Navy Act 1957[1], the procedure and practice of court martial provided by the Navy Act or by the Regulations for the Navy 1965, Part II, shall apply to the disciplinary courts with the following modifications: (i) such of the provisions as are inconsistent with the Navy Act 1957[2] shall not apply[3]; (ii) the provisions of the Navy Act 1957 s 122 shall apply as if for the word 'four' the word 'two' were substituted in the first proviso to s 122 (2)[4]; (iii) the provisions of the Navy Act 1957 s 123 shall apply as if for clause (a) thereof, the following clause was substituted: '(a) where the number of members comprising the court is after the commencement of a trial reduced below two'[5]; (iv) the provisions relating to the award of punishments not within the jurisdiction of a disciplinary court shall not apply[6].

1 Ie the Navy Act 1957 s 96; see **[1229]**.

2 Ie the Navy Act 1957 s 96 (1) to (4).

3 The Regulations for the Navy 1965, Part II, regulation 196 (a).

4 Ie not less than two members are present. The Regulations for the Navy 1965, Part II, regulation 196 (b).

5 The Regulations for the Navy 1965, Part II, regulation 196 (c).

6 The Regulations for the Navy 1965, Part II, regulation 196 (d).

D. Punishment

CONTENT

PARA

[1231] Punishment The following punishments may be inflicted under the Navy Act 1957: death[1]; imprisonment which may be for the term of life or any other lesser term[2]; dismissal with disgrace from the naval service[3]; detention[4]; dismissal from the naval service[5]; forfeiture of seniority in rank in the case of officers and master chief petty officers[6]; forfeiture of time for promotion in the case of officers below the rank of commander and master chief petty officers[7]; dismissal from the ship to which the offender belongs[8]; reduction in rank, in the case of petty officers and persons holding leading rank[9]; fine, in respect of civil offences[10]; mulcts of pay and allowances[11]; severe reprimand or reprimand[12]; forfeiture of pay, head money, bounty, salvage, prize money and allowances earned by, and all annuities, pensions, gratuities, medals and decorations granted to, the offender or of any one or more of the above particulars; also in the case of desertion, of all cloths and effects left by the deserter in the ship to which he belongs[13]; and such minor punishments as are inflicted according to the custom of the navy or may from time to time be prescribed[14]. Each of the punishments specified in the aforesaid provision shall be deem to be inferior in degree to every punishment preceding it in the above scale[15].

1 The Navy Act 1957 s 81 (1) (a).

2 The Navy Act 1957 s 81 (1) (b).

3 The Navy Act 1957 s 81 (1) (c).

4 The Navy Act 1957 s 81 (1) (d).

5 The Navy Act 1957 s 81 (1) (e).

6 The Navy Act 1957 s 81 (1) (f).

7 The Navy Act 1957 s 81 (1) (g).

8 The Navy Act 1957 s 81 (1) (h).

9 The Navy Act 1957 s 81 (1) (i).

10 The Navy Act 1957 s 81 (1) (j).

11 The Navy Act 1957 s 81 (1) (k).

12 The Navy Act 1957 s 81 (1) (l).

13 The Navy Act 1957 s 81 (1) (m). In a case where punishment is imposed under this provision forfeiting pension and/or gratuity, need for passing an order forfeiting pension under the Navy (Pension) Regulations regulation 15 (2) may not arise. *Union of India v P D Yadav* (2002) 1 SCC 405.

14 The Navy Act 1957 s 81 (1) (n). Award of censure to an officer was permissible in view of the provisions of the Navy Act 1957 s 81(n) read with s 82(20). *Commodore CP George v Chief of Naval Staff* 58 (1995) DLT 578.

15 The Navy Act 1957 s 81 (2).

[1232] Provisions as to award of punishment

1 The punishments that may be inflicted under the Navy Act 1957 shall be awarded in accordance with the following provisions[1].

2 Except in the case of mutiny in time of war or on active service, the punishment of death shall not be inflicted on any offender until the sentence has been confirmed by the central government[2].

3 The punishment of imprisonment for a term exceeding two years shall in all cases be accompanied by a sentence of dismissal with disgrace from the naval service[3].

4 The punishment of imprisonment for a term not exceeding two years may in all cases be accompanied by a sentence of dismissal with disgrace or dismissal from the naval service[4]. However, in the case of officers, unless the sentence of dismissal with disgrace is also awarded such sentence of imprisonment shall involve dismissal from the naval service[5].

5 The sentence of imprisonment may be rigorous or simple, partly rigorous and partly simple[6].

6 The sentence of dismissal with disgrace shall involve in all cases forfeiture of all pay, head money, bounty, salvage, prize money and allowances that have been earned by and of all annuities, pensions, gratuities, medals and decorations that may have been granted to the offender and an in capacity to serve government again in a defence service, or a civil services, or to hold any post connected with defence or any civil post under the government[7]. However, the forfeiture of moneys shall not apply except in the case of deserters to moneys which should have been paid on the last payday preceding conviction[8].

7 The punishment of dismissal from the naval service shall in the case of persons who hold any lien on appointments in the regular army or air force, involve dismissal from such army or air force service[9].

8 The punishment of detention may be inflicted for any term not exceeding two years, but no sentence

of detention shall be awarded unless naval detention quarters or army or air force detention barracks are in existence[10].

9 The punishment or imprisonment or detention whether on board ship or on shore shall, subject to certain provisions of the Navy Act 1957[11] involve reduction in rank in the case of a petty officer or person holding a leading rank and shall in all cases be accompanied by stoppage of pay and allowances during the term of imprisonment or detention[12]. However, where the punishment awarded is detention for a term not exceeding 14 days, the sentence may direct that the punishment shall not be accompanied by stoppage of pay and allowances during the term of detention[13].

10 No officer shall be subject to detention[14].

11 The punishment of forfeiture of seniority shall be imposed in the substantive rank held at the date of the sentence, and shall involve a corresponding forfeiture of seniority in every higher Acting rank subject always to the condition that forfeiture of seniority in any rank shall in no case exceed the seniority in that rank at the date of the sentence[15].

12 The punishment of forfeiture of seniority shall involve the loss of the benefit of service included in the seniority forfeited for the purposes of pay, pension, gratuity, promotion and such other purpose, as may be prescribed, provided that such pay, pension, gratuity and promotion and other purpose depend upon such service[16].

13 No master chief petty officer shall be subject to the punishment of forfeiture of seniority of more than 12 months[17].

14 The punishment of forfeiture of time for promotion shall delay promotion by the time specified[18].

15 No master chief petty officer shall be subject to the punishment of forfeiture of time for promotion of more than 12 months[19].

16 No person shall be reduced in rank below the limits prescribed, or lower either actually or relatively than the rank in which he entered or was appointed in the naval service[20].

17 Mulcts of pay and allowances shall not be awarded except as provided in certain provisions of the Navy Act 1957[21].

18 Mulcts of pay and allowances shall be awarded in accordance with the provisions of the Regulations for the Navy 1965, Part II, on conviction of offences under the Navy Act 1957 s 51[0]

19 Mulcts of pay may also be awarded to make good any proved loss or damage occasioned by the offence on which there is a conviction, and for the offence of drunkenness by sailors[23].

20 The punishment of fine may be awarded in respect of civil offences in addition to, or in lieu of, other punishments specified in the Navy Act 1957[24].

21 The forfeiture of money under certain provisions of the Navy Act 1957[25] s 81 (1) (m) shall not, except in case of desertion, apply to moneys which should have been paid on the last payday preceding conviction[26].

22 All other punishments authorised by the Navy Act 1957 may be inflicted in such manner as is heretofore in use in the naval service or as may be prescribed[27].

23 Subject to the foregoing provisions, where any punishment is specified by the Navy Act 1957 as the

penalty for an offence and it is further declared that 'such other punishment as is hereinafter mentioned' may be awarded in respect of the same offence, the expression 'such other punishment' shall be deemed to comprise any one or more of the punishments inferior in degree to the specified punishment according to the scale of punishments laid down in the Navy Act 1957 s 81(1)[28].

1 The Navy Act 1957 s 82 (1).

2 The Navy Act 1957 s 82 (2).

3 The Navy Act 1957 s 82 (3).

4 The Navy Act 1957 s 82 (4). Where a naval officer is sentenced to imprisonment less than two years, discretion is vested in the disciplinary authority as to why it should or not award the dismissal with disgrace. Dismissal from naval service with disgrace and with grace is quite different. Consequent dismissal with disgrace is more serious than the dismissal from the service, simpliciter. *Ex-surgeon Commander Bhaskar Roy v Union of India* 1998 (1) Mh LJ 220.

5 The Navy Act 1957 s 82 (4) proviso.

6 The Navy Act 1957 s 82 (5).

7 The Navy Act 1957 s 82 (6).

8 The Navy Act 1957 s 82 (6) proviso.

9 The Navy Act 1957 s 82 (7).

10 The Navy Act 1957 s 82 (8).

11 Ie the Navy Act 1957 s 82 (14).

12 The Navy Act 1957 s 82 (9).

13 The Navy Act 1957 s 82 (9) proviso.

14 The Navy Act 1957 s 82 (10).

15 The Navy Act 1957 s 82 (11).

16 The Navy Act 1957 s 82 (12). Forfeiture of seniority in rank involves loss of service. Period for which seniority is forfeited has to be excluded in calculation of pensionable service. *Lt Cdr Malkiat Singh v Union of India* AIR 2013 SC 1776 : 2013 (2) SCALE 541.

17 The Navy Act 1957 s 82 (12A).

18 The Navy Act 1957 s 82 (13).

19 The Navy Act 1957 s 82 (13A).

20 The Navy Act 1957 s 82 (14).

21 Ie the Navy Act 1957 s 82 (16) and (17). The Navy Act 1957 s 82 (15).

22 The Navy Act 1957 s 82 (16).

23 The Navy Act 1957 s 82 (17).

24 The Navy Act 1957 s 82 (18).

25 Ie the Navy Act 1957 s 81 (1) (m).

26 The Navy Act 1957 s 82 (19).

27 The Navy Act 1957 s 82 (20).

28 The Navy Act 1957 s 82 (21).

E. Judicial Review

CONTENT

PARA

[1233] Judicial review by the judge advocate general of the navy All proceedings of trials by court martial or discipline courts shall be reviewed by the judge advocate general of the navy either on his motion or on application made to him within the prescribed time by any person aggrieved by any sentence or finding. The judge advocate general shall transmit the report of such review together with such recommendations as may appear just and proper to the chief of the naval staff for his consideration and for such action as the chief of the naval staff may think fit[1]. Where any person aggrieved has made an application under the aforesaid provision, the judge advocate general may, if the circumstances of the case so require, give him an opportunity of being heard either in person or through a legal practitioner or an officer of the Indian navy[2].

Under the Navy Act 1957[3], it is the duty of the judge advocate general to perform such duties of a legal and judicial character pertaining to the Indian navy as may from time to time be referred or assigned to him by the central government or the chief of the naval staff. Thus the presence of judge advocate general, and the specific powers of review conferred on him are capable of pointing out that his opinion and view are of paramount importance, and it cannot be ignored[4].

1 The Navy Act 1957 s 160 (1).

2 The Navy Act 1957 s 160 (2).

3 Ie the Navy Act 1957 s 169; see **[1148]**.

4 *Lt Cdr KN Surendran v Union of India* Kerala High Court decided on 2 August 2002.

[1234] Consideration by the chief of the naval staff On receipt of the report and recommendations if any, from the judge advocate general[1], the chief of the naval staff shall in all cases of capital sentence and in all cases where the court martial is ordered by the President, and may in other cases transmit proceedings and the report to the central government together with such recommendations as he may deem fit to make[2]. Nothing under provisions of the Navy Act 1950[3] shall authorize the judge advocate general or the chief of the naval staff to make any recommendation for setting aside or the central government to set aside, an order of acquittal passed under the Navy Act 1957[4].

1 Ie under the Navy Act 1957 s 160; see **[1233]**.

2 The Navy Act 1957 s 161 (1).

3 Ie the Navy Act 1950 s 160 or 161.

4 The Navy Act 1957 s 161 (2).

F. Execution of Sentence

CONTENT

PARA

(i) Execution of sentence

(i) Execution of sentence

[1235] Form of sentence of death In awarding a sentence of death, a court martial shall in its discretion direct that the offender shall suffer death by being hanged by the neck until he be dead or shall suffer death by being shot to death[1].

1 The Navy Act s1957 s 147.

[1236] Interim custody until execution of sentence of death A person sentenced to death may be detained in naval custody or may be removed to a civil prison to be kept in custody until further orders be received from the central government, the chief of the naval staff or the officer ordering court martial by which he was sentenced to death or other prescribed officer. The order in the prescribed form of the central government, the chief of the naval staff or the convening authority or such officer shall be sufficient warrant for detaining the person in custody[1].

1 The Navy Act s1957 s 148.

[1237] Execution of sentence of death When a sentence of death is to be executed, the chief of the naval staff or convening authority or the prescribed officer shall give directions as to the time, place and manner in which such sentence is to be carried out and the order of such officer or authority in the prescribed form shall be sufficient warrant for the execution of such sentence[1]. There shall be attached to the prescribed form an order of the central government certifying the confirmation of the sentence by the central government in all cases where such confirmation is necessary; and where such confirmation is not necessary, a certificate of the chief of the naval staff or other prescribed officer stating that such confirmation is not necessary[2].

1 The Navy Act s1957 s 149 (1).

2 The Navy Act s1957 s 149 (2).

[1238] Place of imprisonment and detention Every term of imprisonment whether imprisonment was awarded as an original or commuted punishment may be served in a naval prison, naval detention quarters or in any civil prison, house of correction or military or air force prison or detention barracks[1]. Every term of detention whether the detention was awarded as an original or commuted punishment may be served in any naval detention quarters or army or air force detention barracks[2]. Where in pursuance of the Navy Act 1950, a person is sentenced to imprisonment or detention or has his sentence commuted to imprisonment or detention, the order in the prescribed form of the authority or officer[3] shall be a sufficient warrant for the sending of such person to the place of imprisonment or detention, to undergo the sentence according to law, or until he reaches such place of imprisonment or detention for detaining him in naval custody or in the case of a person sentenced to imprisonment, in any civil prison or place of confinement[3].

1 The Navy Act s1957 s 150 (1).

2 The Navy Act s1957 s 150 (2).

3 Ie the order of the central government or the chief of the naval staff or the officer ordering the court martial by which such person was sentenced or the senior officer present in port or if he was sentenced by the commanding officer of a ship, or other officer empowered under the Navy Act 1957 to exercise like powers, the order in the prescribed form of such commanding officer or other officer; The Navy Act s1957 s 150 (3).

4 The Navy Act s1957 s 150 (3).

[1239] Commencement of sentences

1 Subject to certain provisions of the Navy Act 1950[1], every term of imprisonment or detention awarded in pursuance of the aforesaid Act shall be reckoned as commencing on the day on which the sentence was awarded[2].

2 Where by reason of a ship being at sea or off a place at which there is no proper prison or naval

detention quarters a sentence of imprisonment or detention cannot be duly executed, then subject as hereinafter mentioned, an offender under the sentence, may be sent with all reasonable speed to some place at which there is a proper prison or naval detention quarters or in the case of an offender under sentence of detention to some place at which there are some naval detention quarters in which the sentence can be duly executed. On arrival there, the offender shall undergo his sentence in like manner as if the date of such arrival were the day on which the sentence was awarded and not withstanding that in the meanwhile he has returned to his duty or become entitled to his discharge. The term of imprisonment or detention, shall be reckoned accordingly subject to the deduction of any time during which he has been kept in confinement in respect of the said offence[3].

3 Whenever any offender is sentenced by a court martial to a term of imprisonment, in pursuance of the Navy Act 1957, not being imprisonment in default of the payment of fine, the period spent by him in civil or naval custody during investigation, inquiry or trial of the same case, and before the date of order of such sentence, shall be set off against the terms of imprisonment imposed upon him, and the liability of such offender to undergo imprisonment on such order of sentence shall be restricted to the remainder, of the term of imprisonment imposed on him[4].

1 Ie the Navy Act 1950 s 151 (2) and (3).

2 The Navy Act 1950 s 151 (1).

3 The Navy Act 1950 s 151 (2).

4 The Navy Act 1950 s 151 (3).

[1240] Imprisonment of offender already under sentence Whenever a sentence is passed by a court martial on an offender already under sentence either of detention or imprisonment passed upon him under the Navy Act 1957 for a former offence, the court may award a sentence of detention or imprisonment for the offence for which he is under trial to commence at the expiration of the sentence of detention or imprisonment to which he has been previously sentenced[1]. However, the term of detention imposed on a person by a sentence in pursuance of this provision will prolong the total term of detention beyond two years shall be deemed to be remitted[2].

1 The Navy Act 1950 s 152.

2 The Navy Act 1950 s 152 proviso.

[1241] Change of place of confinement Whenever it is deemed expedient, it shall be lawful for the central government, the chief of the naval staff or senior officer present, by an order in writing in the prescribed form, from time to time to change the place of confinement of any offender imprisoned or sentenced to be imprisoned or detained in pursuance of the Navy Act 1957 or of any offender undergoing or sentenced to undergo detention. The gaoler or other person having the custody of such offender shall immediately on the receipt of such order remove such offender to the gaol, prison or house of correction or, in the case of an offender undergoing or sentenced to undergo detention, to the naval detention quarters mentioned in the said order, or shall deliver him over to naval custody for the purpose of the offender being removed to such prison or naval detention quarters. Every gaoler or keeper of prison, house of correction or naval detention quarters shall, upon being furnished with such order of removal, receive into his custody and shall confine pursuant to such sentence or order every such offender[1].

1 The Navy Act 1950 s 153.

[1242] Discharge or removal of prisoners Whenever any offender is undergoing imprisonment or detention in pursuance of the Navy Act 1957, it shall be lawful for the authority of officer[1], to give an order in writing in the prescribed form directing that the offender be discharged[2]. It shall also be lawful for the central government and the chief of the naval staff by order in writing in the prescribed form, to direct that any such offender be delivered over to naval custody for the purpose of being brought before a court martial, either as a witness or for trial or otherwise. On production of such order, the offender shall be discharged, or be delivered over to such custody[3].

1 Ie the central government or the chief of the naval staff or where an offender is undergoing imprisonment or detention by orders of his commanding officer; The Navy Act 1950 s 154. As to the definition of 'commanding officer'; see **[0912]**.

2 As to the provision of discharge under this provision, see the Regulations for the Navy 1965, Part II, regulation 226; **[1243]**.

3 The Navy Act 1950 s 154.

[1243] Discharge from prison or detention If a prisoner or a person under detention should be discharged under the provisions of the Navy Act 1957[1], such discharge shall have the effect of remitting any portion of his sentence that may be unexpired at the date of such discharge, except in the case of his delivery to naval custody for the purpose specified in the latter part of the said provision[2]. The power under this provision shall be exercised with great discretion and shall not be exercised except where the services of offenders are required in emergency[3].

1 Ie under the Navy Act 1957 s 154.

2 Ie the later part of the Navy Act 1950 s 154; The Regulations for the Navy 1965, Part II, regulation 226.

3 The Regulations for the Navy 1965, Part II, regulation 226 explanation.

[1244] Time of detention in naval custody The time during which any offender under sentence of imprisonment or detention is detained in naval custody shall be reckoned as imprisonment or detention under his sentence for whatever purpose he is so detained; and the governor, gaoler, keeper or superintendent who shall deliver over any such offender shall again receive him from naval custody, so that he may undergo the remainder of his punishment[1].

1 The Navy Act 1950 s 155.

[1245] Removal of insane prisoners If any person imprisoned or undergoing detention by virtue of the Navy Act 1957 shall become insane, and certificate to that effect shall be given by two physicians or surgeons, the central government shall by warrant in the prescribed form, direct the removal of such person to such asylum or other proper receptacle for insane persons in India as it may judge proper for the unexpired term of his imprisonment or detention. If such person is again certified to be of sound mind, the central government may issue a warrant in the prescribed form for his being removed to such prison or place of confinement or in the case of a person sentenced to detention, such naval detention quarters as may be deemed expedient, to undergo the remainder of his punishment, and every gaoler or keeper of any prison, gaol, or house of correction shall receive him accordingly[1].

1 The Navy Act 1950 s 156.

[1246] Naval prisoners and naval detention quarters The central government may set apart any buildings or vessels or any parts thereof as naval prisons or naval detention quarters. Such buildings, vessels or parts of buildings or vessels so set apart as naval prisons or naval detention quarters, shall be deemed to be naval prisons or naval detention quarters respectively within the meaning of the Navy Act 1957[1].

1 The Navy Act 1950 s 157.

[1247] Execution of sentence of fine When a sentence of fine is imposed under the Navy Act 1957 by a court martial or disciplinary court, the officer ordering the court martial or disciplinary court may transmit a copy of the order imposing the fine duly certified under his hand to any magistrate in India. Such magistrate shall thereupon cause the fine to be recovered in accordance with the provisions of the Code of Criminal Procedure 1973, or any law corresponding thereto in force in the state of Jammu and Kashmir as if it were a sentence of fine imposed by such magistrate[1].

1 The Navy Act 1950 s 158.

[1248] Power to make regulation in respect of naval prisons and detention quarters The central government may, by notification in the official gazette make regulations providing: (i) for the government, management and regulation of naval prisons and detention quarters[1]; (ii) for the appointment and removal and powers of inspector, visitors and officers thereof[2]; (iii) for the food, bedding and clothing of prisoners or persons undergoing detention therein[3]; (iv) for the labour of such prisoners or persons therein and for enabling such prisoners or persons to earn by special industry and good conduct remission of a portion of their sentence[4]; and (v) for the care of such prisoners or persons, their safe custody and the maintenance of good order and discipline among them and the punishment by personal correction, restraint or otherwise of offences committed by such prisoners or persons[5]. The regulations to be made under this provision may apply to naval prisons or detention quarters any of the provisions of the Prisons Act 1894, and rules made there under, imposing punishments on any persons not being prisoners or relating to the duties of gaolers, medical officers and other officers of the prisons[6]. The regulation to be made under this provision shall not authorize corporal punishment to be inflicted for any offence[7].

1 The Navy Act 1950 s 159 (1) (a). See the Regulations for the Navy 1965, Part II, regulations 106-114; **[1249] – [1257]**.

2 The Navy Act 1950 s 159 (1) (b).

3 The Navy Act 1950 s 159 (1) (c).

4 The Navy Act 1950 s 159 (1) (d).

5 The Navy Act 1950 s 159 (1) (e).

6 The Navy Act 1950 s 159 (2).

7 The Navy Act 1950 s 159 (3).

(ii) Provisions concerning prisons and detention quarters

[1249] Selection of place of confinement The space provided on the warrant for the insertion of the name of the jail or detention establishment to which the prisoner is to be sent, shall be completed in accordance with the local standing orders or in the absence of such orders in accordance with the directions of the officer approving the warrant[1].

1 The Regulations for the Navy 1965, Part II, regulation 106.

[1250] Visiting Jails The Administrative authorities shall obtain information as to the state of jails in which Indian naval personnel normally serve terms of imprisonment, by directing an officer or officers of the rank of commander or above to visit them for time to time, with the permission of the civil authorities and report on them[1].

1 The Regulations for the Navy 1965, Part II, regulation 107.

[1251] Medical examination A medical officer shall examine the offender prior to his commitment to a prison or detention establishment, to ascertain whether he is physically capable of undergoing a sentence, and again on his return to the ship[1].

1 The Regulations for the Navy 1965, Part II, regulation 108.

[1252] Committal order The order for imprisonment or detention, being the authority for the superintendent of a jail or for the officer in command of the detention establishment to receive and detain an offender, and to release him at the expiration of his sentence, shall be made out on the prescribed form[1].

1 The Regulations for the Navy 1965, Part II, regulation 109.

[1253] Persons sentenced, how borne Persons sentenced summarily or by court martial to imprisonment shall be borne on ship's book unless will be discharged direct from the prison to civil life, when they are to be discharged from ship's book from the time of arrival at the prison or from the time the order for discharge from the service is received[1].

1 The Regulations for the Navy 1965, Part II, regulation 110.

[1254] Civil custody Sailors convicted by the civil authority, whether sentenced to imprisonment or not, shall continue to be borne on the books of the ship to which they belong[1] unless they will not return to that ship, when they shall be dealt with as directed in the Regulations for the Navy 1965, Part II, regulation 110[2].

1 See **[1253]**.

2 The Regulations for the Navy 1965, Part II, regulation 111.

[1255] Sailors from ships about to sail Sailors undergoing imprisonment or detention awarded summarily may, at the discretion of the senior naval officer present, be removed from confinement for the purpose of rejoining their ships before sailing, if a very few days of the sentence remain unexpired, or at any time, if the completion of the sentence will involve any serious inconvenience to the service[1]. If the commanding officer considers it advisable that sailors should be so released, he shall report the matter at least three days before hand to the senior naval officer present and, with his approval, may issue an order in writing for the release of the offender[2].

1 The Regulations for the Navy 1965, Part II, regulation 112 (1).

2 The Regulations for the Navy 1965, Part II, regulation 112 (2).

[1256] Dismissal after confinement When a sailor has been dismissed or discharged from the service, notice thereof shall be given by the commanding officer to the authorities at the place of confinement to which he is sent in order that he may be set at liberty at the expiration of his sentence[1].

1 The Regulations for the Navy 1965, Part II, regulation 113.

[1257] Escorts A sufficient escort shall accompany each offender sent to confinement[1]. The commanding officer of a ship on whose books a sailor is borne on the date of release shall make arrangements for persons to be at the place of confinement at the exact time when the sailor may be entitled to his release, to receive and conduct the offender on board. When the sentence expires on a Sunday the offender is entitled to be released on the preceding Saturday[2].

1 The Regulations for the Navy 1965, Part II, regulation 114 (1).

2 The Regulations for the Navy 1965, Part II, regulation 114 (2).

G. Modification of Finding and Sentences, Pardon and Commutation, Remission and Suspension of Sentence

CONTENT

PARA

[1258] Petitions to the Central Government or Chief of the Naval Staff against finding or sentences Any person subject to naval law[1] who considers himself aggrieved by finding or sentence of any court-martial may present a petition to the central government or to the chief of the naval staff. The central government or the chief of the naval staff may pass order on the petition as considered fit[1].

1 The Navy Act 1950 s 162. As to the power of the central government and the chief of the naval staff in respect of findings and sentences of a court martial; see **[1259].**

[1259] Powers of central government and the chief of the naval staff in respect of findings and sentences Where any person is tried under the provisions of the Navy Act 1950, the central government or the chief of the naval staff, may in the case of a conviction: (i) set aside the finding and sentence and acquit or discharge the accused or order him to be retried[1], (ii) alter the finding, maintaining the sentence, provided that such sentence may be legally passed on the altered finding[2], (iii) with or without altering the finding, reduce the sentence or commute the punishment awarded for any punishment inferior in scale[3], or (iv) either with or without conditions, pardon the person or remit the whole or any part of the punishment awarded[4]. However, a sentence of imprisonment shall not be commuted for a sentence of detention for a term exceeding the term of imprisonment awarded, and a sentence of dismissal with disgraces not accompanied by a sentence of imprisonment shall not be commuted for a sentence of detention[5]. Further, the central government or the chief of the naval staff are not authorized to enhance the sentence[6]. Any sentence modified under the aforesaid provision[7] shall be carried into execution as if it had been originally passed[8]. If any condition on which a person has been pardoned or released on parole or a punishment has been remitted is in the opinion of the authority which granted the pardon, or release or remission not fulfilled such authority may cancel the pardon or release or remission and thereupon the sentence awarded shall be carried into effect as if such pardon, release or remission had not been granted[9]. However, in the case of a person sentenced to imprisonment or detention such person shall undergo only the unexpired portion or the sentence[10].

1 The Navy Act 1950 s 163 (1)(a).

2 The Navy Act 1950 s 163 (1)(b).

3 The Navy Act 1950 s 163 (1)(c).

4 The Navy Act 1950 s 163 (1)(d).

5 The Navy Act 1950 s 163 (1) proviso.

6 The Navy Act 1950 s 163 (1) additional proviso.

7 Ie under the Navy Act 1950 s 163 (1).

8 The Navy Act 1950 s 163 (2).

9 The Navy Act 1950 s 163 (3).

10 The Navy Act 1950 s 163 (3) proviso.

[1260] Provision relating to parole Where any person is tried under the provisions of the Navy Act 1957, the competent authority[1] may in the case of conviction either with or without conditions release the person on parole[2].

1 Ie the central government or the chief of the naval staff or the flag officers commanding-in-chief of the naval commands; The Navy Act 1950 s 163A.

2 The Navy Act 1950 s 163A.

[1261] Suspension of sentences

1 Where a person has been sentenced to imprisonment or detention, the central government or the officer having the power to issue an order of committal (the committing authority)[1] may, in lieu of issuing such an order, order that the sentence be suspended until an order of committal is issued. In such case: (i) the term of the sentence shall not be reckoned as commencing until an order of committal is issued[2]; (ii) the case may at any time, and shall at interval of not more than three months, be reconsidered by

the authority[3], and if on any such reconsideration it appears to such authority that the conduct of the offender since his conviction has been such as to justify a remission of the sentence, the shall remit the whole or any part of it[4]; (iii) subject to the Regulations for the Navy 1965, Part II, the authority may at any time whilst the sentence is suspended issue an order of committal and thereupon the sentence shall cease to be suspended[5]; (iv) where a person subject to naval law, whilst a sentence on him is so suspended, is sentenced to imprisonment or detention for any other offence then, if he is at any time committed either under the suspended sentence or under any such subsequent sentence, and whether or not any such subsequent sentence has also been suspended, the committing authority may direct that the two sentences shall run either concurrently or consecutively; so, not to cause a person to undergo detention for a period exceeding the aggregate of two consecutive years[6].

2 When a person has been sentenced to imprisonment or detention and an order of committal has been issued, the authority[7] may order the sentence to be suspended. In such case the person whose sentence is suspended shall be discharged and the currency of the sentence shall be suspended until he is again committed under the same sentence, and certain provisions of the Navy Act 1957[8] shall apply in like manner as in the case where a sentence has been suspended before an order of committal has been issued[9].

3 Where a sentence is suspended under this provision, whether before or after committal the central government or, subject to the Regulations for the Navy 1965, Part II, the committing authority or officer by whom the sentence is suspended, may direct that any penalty which is involved by the punishment of imprisonment or detention either shall be or shall not be remitted or suspended[10].

1 Ie under the Navy Act 1957 s 163 or s 150 (3).

2 The Navy Act 1957 s 164 (1) (a).

3 Ie the central government or committing authority or any prescribed officer; the Navy Act 1957 s 164 (1) (b).

4 The Navy Act 1957 s 164 (1) (b).

5 The Navy Act 1957 s 164 (1) (c).

6 The Navy Act 1957 s 164 (1) (d).

7 Ie the central government or committing authority or any prescribed officer; the Navy Act 1957 s 164 (2).

8 Ie the Navy Act 1957 s 164 (1) (b), (c) and (d).

9 Navy Act 1957 s 164 (2).

10 The Navy Act 1957 s 164 (3).

[1262] Power of suspending a sentence The power of suspending a sentence of imprisonment or detention under the provisions of the Navy Act 1957[1] maybe exercised when a sailor of good reputation has committed himself because of some long continued strain, or in circumstances which lead the commanding officer or superior authority to believe that he will retrieve his good name, or when the sailor's services are required for a dangerous or arduous duty which would otherwise be avoided, or to enable a deserter or persistent leave breaker who is considered to be capable of reformation to be transferred to sea, so that he may be removed from the temptation to repeat his offence[2]. Officers shall, as far as possible, use this power freely whenever they can do so without detriment to discipline, and when the offender is likely by his conduct, to justify the confidence placed in him; but a sentence shall never be suspended when it is intended that the offender shall not return to the service[3].

1 Ie the Navy Act 1957 s 164; see [1261].

2 The Regulations for the Navy 1965, Part II, regulation 96 (1).

3 The Regulations for the Navy 1965, Part II, regulation 96 (2).

[1263] Suspension of court martial sentence If the officer who ordered the court martial or any other officer having power to suspend a sentence considers, either upon a perusal of the minutes or upon receiving recommendation from the court that the sentence should be suspended, he shall instead of issuing a committal order, give an order in writing that the sentence is to be suspended until an order of committal is issued[1]. When an order suspending a court martial sentence has been made under the aforesaid provision, the accused shall be: (i) informed by his commanding officer that it has been decided to suspend his sentence, that his case will be reviewed periodically, and that, if his subsequent conduct is such as to justify a remission of the sentence, it will be remitted[2], (ii) warned that, if the continuity of his 'VG' conduct is broken or if his behaviour is in any way unsatisfactory while he is on probation, the sentence may be enforced[3]; and (iii) released from custody[4]. In all cases where a sentence passed by court martial is suspended, the intimation shall be sent immediately to the chief of the naval staff together with a statement of the reasons for suspension of the sentence[5].

1 The Regulations for the Navy 1965, Part II, regulation 97 (1).

2 The Regulations for the Navy 1965, Part II, regulation 97 (2) (i).

3 The Regulations for the Navy 1965, Part II, regulation 97 (2) (ii).

4 The Regulations for the Navy 1965, Part II, regulation 97 (2) (iii).

5 The Regulations for the Navy 1965, Part II, regulation 97 (3).

[1264] Suspension of summary punishment With the concurrence of the authority who approves a punishment warrant for imprisonment or detention, the commanding officer may, instead of issuing a committal order, give an order in writing that the sentence shall be suspended until an order of committal is issued and if such authority is not present at the place, the commanding officer shall use his discretion in the matter[1]. At any time after a committal order has been issued, the officer who signed committal order may order the residue of the sentence to be suspended[2]. When the commanding officer suspends a sentence, he shall make a report thereof when the punishment return is forwarded[3]. When a sentence has been suspended, either before or after an order of committal has been issued, the offender shall be released from custody and informed by his commanding officer that his case will be reviewed periodically, and that the enforcement or remission of the remaining portion of the sentence will depend on his conduct remaining 'VG'[4]. When a sailor whose sentence has been suspended is transferred to another ship or establishment, the fact that a sentence is under suspension shall be notified immediately by letter to his new commanding officer, who should also be informed whether the sailor's conduct to-date has been such as to deserve remission in due course[5].

1 The Regulations for the Navy 1965, Part II, regulation 98 (1).

2 The Regulations for the Navy 1965, Part II, regulation 98 (2).

3 The Regulations for the Navy 1965, Part II, regulation 98 (3).

4 The Regulations for the Navy 1965, Part II, regulation 98 (4)

5 The Regulations for the Navy 1965, Part II, regulation 98 (5).

[1265] Period of suspension A sentence which has been suspended, either before or after a committal order has been issued, shall remain suspended until such an order has been issued or the sentence has been finally remitted[1]. A sentence may remain suspended for 12 months, unless the sailor commits himself in the meantime.

Under no circumstances the sentence shall remain suspended for a longer period except when the issue of a committal order has not been possible because the sailor has deserted or been absent without leave[2].

1 The Regulations for the Navy 1965, Part II, regulation 99 (1).

2 The Regulations for the Navy 1965, Part II, regulation 99 (2).

[1266] Reconsideration of court martial sentence A court martial sentence which has been suspended may be reconsidered at intervals of not more than three months, unless it has been put into execution in the meantime. On these occasions the individual shall be brought before the commanding officer, who should take the opportunity of reviewing the circumstances and warning him that he is still under probation[1]. The commanding officer shall make a report on the sailor's conduct, recommending whether the sentence should remain suspended or be remitted, to the chief of the naval staff who shall, if he considers that the offender' conduct justifies remission, remit the sentence accordingly[2]. If at any time during the probationary period the continuity of a sailor's 'VG' conduct is broken or behaviour is in any way unsatisfactory, the sentence may be enforced and the commanding officer shall forward a report and a committal order shall be issued by the chief of the naval staff or by the officer ordering the court martial by which the sailor was sentenced[3]. It is the responsibility of the administrative authorities that the reconsideration of suspended sentence is carried out at intervals of not more than three months[4].

1 The Regulations for the Navy 1965, Part II, regulation 100 (1).

2 The Regulations for the Navy 1965, Part II, regulation 100 (2).

3 The Regulations for the Navy 1965, Part II, regulation 100 (3).

4 The Regulations for the Navy 1965, Part II, regulation 100 (4).

[1267] Reconsideration of summary sentence The commanding officer of the ship to which the sailor for the time being belongs shall reconsider the sentence as in the foregoing provision and decide whether the rest of the sentence shall be finally remitted or remain suspended, informing the sailor of his decision[1]. If during the probationary period the continuity of the sailor's 'VG' conduct is broken or his behaviour is in any way unsatisfactory, the commanding officer shall enforce the sentence by issuing the committal order[2]. The review, remission or enforcement of a suspended sentence shall be reported when the punishment return is forwarded[3].

1 The Regulations for the Navy 1965, Part II, regulation 101 (1).

2 The Regulations for the Navy 1965, Part II, regulation 101 (2).

3 The Regulations for the Navy 1965, Part II, regulation 101 (3).

[1268] Offences during suspension If a person whose sentence has been suspended commits a further offence for which he is sentenced to imprisonment or detention, any officer having power to issue a committal order in respect of the second sentence or any officer having power to issue or re-issue committal order in respect of the first may, subject to any recommendations to the contrary made by the court or officer who tried him for the second offence, order the sentence to run concurrently or consecutively. If two sentences of detention amount in the aggregate to more than two years, the excess shall be remitted and where the second sentence is awarded under the Navy Act 1957 and is one of imprisonment, a previous sentence of detention shall be remitted[1]. A sentence of detention shall not be awarded if the offender is already under sentence of imprisonment[2].

1 The Regulations for the Navy 1965, Part II, regulation 102 (1).

2 The Regulations for the Navy 1965, Part II, regulation 102 (2).

[1269] Consequential penalties If a sentence is suspended before a committal order is issued, any consequential penalties which would be entailed by the infliction of the suspended punishment shall also be regarded as suspended unless and until the committal order is issued. Any additional punishments which accompany a sentence of imprisonment or detention, like mulcts of pay, stoppage of leave, but are not consequential thereon, shall not be suspended[1]. If a committal order is issued and the sentence is subsequently suspended, or if a sentence is suspended but a committal order is subsequently issued all the consequential penalties and other consequences, namely: (i) reduction in rank[2]; (ii) deprivation of badges and medal[3]; (iii) effect upon character[4]; and (iv) loss of pay and time[5]; shall be enforced in respect of so much of the sentence as is actually served[6]. If a sentence which has been suspended is subsequently carried out, reduction in rank, deprivation of badges and medal, loss of pay and time shall take effect from the date of committal[7]. When a sentence of imprisonment or detention is suspended after committal, reduction in rank and deprivation of badges and medal shall take effect from the date of sentence and loss of pay and time from the date of committal[8]. For all sentences, effect upon character shall operate from the date of sentence[9].

1 The Regulations for the Navy 1965, Part II, regulation 103 (1).

2 The Regulations for the Navy 1965, Part II, regulation 103 (2) (i).

3 The Regulations for the Navy 1965, Part II, regulation 103 (2) (ii).

4 The Regulations for the Navy 1965, Part II, regulation 103 (2) (iii).

5 The Regulations for the Navy 1965, Part II, regulation 103 (2) (iv).

6 The Regulations for the Navy 1965, Part II, regulation 103 (2).

7 The Regulations for the Navy 1965, Part II, regulation 103 (3).

8 The Regulations for the Navy 1965, Part II, regulation 103 (4).

9 The Regulations for the Navy 1965, Part II, regulation 103 (5).

[1270] Other consequential effects A sentence of imprisonment or detention, even if suspended shall automatically cause a break in 'VG' conduct[1]. If, at the time of assessment of character, an offender's sentence, or a portion thereof, is under suspension, the only penalties which shall be taken into consideration are the portion of such sentence and the consequential penalties (if any) which have actually been enforced. If the suspended sentence or the suspended portion thereof is subsequently enforced, the character previously assessed shall be altered to that which is appropriate to the full sentence[2]. All alterations in character under the aforesaid provision shall be reported to the Commodore, Bureau of Sailors, Bombay[3]. Where a suspended sentence or the suspended portion of a sentence is carried out in the year following that in which the sentence was awarded, together with the sentence of imprisonment or detention, only the latter sentence shall be taken into account in assessing character at the end of the year, whether such sentence run consecutively or concurrently[4]. If an offender under a suspended sentence deserts and is not recovered, or is not claimed for further service, his character shall be assessed as if the sentence has been carried out[5].

1 The Regulations for the Navy 1965, Part II, regulation 104 (1).

2 The Regulations for the Navy 1965, Part II, regulation 104 (2).

3 The Regulations for the Navy 1965, Part II, regulation 104 (3).

4 The Regulations for the Navy 1965, Part II, regulation 104 (4).

5 The Regulations for the Navy 1965, Part II, regulation 104 (5).

[1271] Record of suspension, etc. of sentence The suspension of a sentence in whole or in part shall be recorded with full particulars of the offence and sentence on the promotion and conduct record sheet[1]. The following notations shall be made in the service certificate[2], each notation being authenticated by the commanding officer's signature, with the date on which the sentence was either suspended, remitted or enforced[3]. Care shall be taken that the original notation which is ruled through is not obliterated[4].

S. No.	Sentence	Notation
(a)	Suspension of sentence before committal	Put 'suspended' alongside the notation of the number of days awarded.
(b)	Suspension of sentence after committal	Insert in the appropriate column the number of days served, adding 'residue suspended'.
(c)	Remission of sentence	Rule through the notation 'suspended' or residue suspended and insert notation 'remitted' or residue remitted.
(d)	Committal or re-committal following suspension of sentence or of residue of sentence.	Rule through the notation 'suspended' or 'residue suspended' and insert notation 'committed' or 'recommitted' as requisite.

1 The Regulations for the Navy 1965, Part II, regulation 105 (1).

2 Notations shall be made in the 'time forfeited' column on page 4 of the service certificate; the Regulations for the Navy 1965, Part II, regulation 105 (2).

3 The Regulations for the Navy 1965, Part II, regulation 105 (2).

4 The Regulations for the Navy 1965, Part II, regulation 105 (3).

8. DISPOSAL OF PRIVATE PROPERTY OF PERSONS DECEASED AND MISSING

CONTENTS

PARA

[1272] Disposal of property of deceased sailors

1 On the death of a sailor[1] while subject to naval law[2], the commanding officer[3] of the ship[4] to which the sailor belonged shall as soon as may be: (i) secure all movable property belonging to the deceased that is in the ship or quarters and cause an inventory thereof to be made[5]; (ii) draw the pay and allowance due to such persons[6]; (iii) if he thinks fit, and subject to any regulations made in this behalf , collect all moneys left by the deceased in any bank, post office saving bank, co-operative bank or society, or any other institution receiving deposits in money, and for that purpose may require the agent, manager or proper authority of such bank or other institution to pay the moneys to the commanding officer; and such agent, manager or authority shall, notwithstanding anything contained in any other law, be bound to comply with the requisition[7].

2 Where any money has been paid by the banking company, society or other institution in compliance with the requisition under the aforesaid provision, no person shall have any claim against the said bank, society, or other institution in respect of such money[8].

3 The commanding officer shall, if in his opinion it is necessary for the purpose of securing the payment of the ship and service debts and other debts in the ship or quarters of the deceased and the expenses, if any, incurred by the commanding officer in respect of the estate of the deceased, cause the movable property of the deceased to be sold or converted into money[9].

4 If the representative of the deceased is on the spot and either pays or gives security for the payment of the ship and service debts and other debts in ship or quarters due from the deceased the commanding officer shall not take action under certain aforesaid provisions[10].

5 The commanding officer shall, out of the moneys so received, collected or realised under certain provisions of the Navy Act 1957[11], pay the ship and service debts and other debts in ship or quarters of the deceased, and the expenses incurred in connection with the realization of the assets of the deceased[12].

6 Any property left over after meeting the expenditure indicated in the aforesaid provision, or where the representative had paid or given security for the payment of the ship and service debts and other debts in ship or quarters the entire property of the deceased, shall be delivered over by the commanding officer to the representative of the deceased, whereupon his responsibility for the administration of the estate of the deceased shall cease[13].

7 If no claim is made in respect of the said surplus by a representative of the deceased within 12 months of the death, the commanding officer shall take steps to hand over the property to the prescribed person who shall continue the administration of the estate of the deceased as provided for in the Navy Act 1957[14].

1 As to the meaning of 'sailor'; see **[0933]**.

2 As to the meaning of 'subject to naval law'; see **[0935]**.

3 As to the meaning of 'commanding officer'; see **[0912]**.

4 As to the meaning of 'ship'; see **[0934]**.

5 The Navy Act 1957 s 171 (1) (a).

6 The Navy Act 1957 s 171 (1) (b).

7 The Navy Act 1957 s 171 (1) (c).

8 The Navy Act 1957 s 171 (2).

9 The Navy Act 1957 s 171 (3).

10 Ie under The Navy Act 1957 s 171 (1)(c) or 171 (3); The Navy Act 1957 s 171 (4).

11 The Navy Act 1957 s 171 (1) and (3).

12 The Navy Act 1957 s 171 (5)

13 The Navy Act 1957 s 171 (6)

14 Ie as provided under the Navy Act 1957 s 176; The Navy Act 1957 s 171 (7).

[1273] Disposal of property of deceased officers The aforesaid provisions of the Navy Act 1957[1] shall also apply to the disposal of the property of an officer[2] who dies while subject to naval law[3], but with the following modifications: (i) the functions of the commanding officer[4] under the aforesaid provision[5] shall be performed by a committee of adjustment constituted in this behalf in the prescribed manner[6]; and (ii) the surplus, if any, after the payment of debts and expenses specified in the Navy Act 1957[7] shall be paid to the person prescribed in this behalf[8].

1 Ie the Navy Act 1957 s 171.

2 As to the meaning of 'officer'; see **[0927]**.

3 As to the meaning of 'subject to naval law'; see **[0935]**.

4 As to the meaning of 'commanding officer'; see **[0912]**.

5 Ie as stated in the Navy Act 1957 s 171.

6 The Navy Act 1957 s 172 (i).

7 Ie as specified in the Navy Act 1957 s 171 (3); see **[1272]**.

8 The Navy Act 1957 s 172 (ii).

[1274] Decision of questions as to ship and service debts and other debts in ship or quarters If in any case a doubt or difference arises as to what are the ship or service debts and the debts in ship or quarters of a deceased officer or sailor or as to the amount payable in respect thereof, the decision of the prescribed persons shall be final and shall be binding on all person for all purposes[1].

1 The Navy Act 1957 s 173.

[1275] Nature of the powers of commanding officer or committee of adjustments For the purpose of the exercise of duties under the provisions of the Navy Act 1957[1], the commanding officer[2] or the committee of adjustment, shall, to the exclusion of all other persons and authorities have the same rights and powers as if the commanding officer or the committee had taken out representation to the estate of the deceased, and any receipt given by such commanding officer or the committee, shall have effect accordingly[3]. The term 'representation' in the aforesaid provision includes probate, letters of administration with or without the will annexed and a succession certificate issued by a court of competent jurisdiction constituting a person executor or administrator of the estate of the deceased person or authorizing him to receive or realize the assets of the deceased person[4].

1 Ie under the Navy Act 1957 s 171 or 172; see **[1272]** and **[1273]**.

2 As to the meaning of 'commanding officer'; see **[0912]**.

3 The Navy Act 1957 s 174.

4 The Navy Act 1957 s 174 explanation.

[1276] Powers of central government to hand over estate of deceased persons to the administrator general

1 Notwithstanding anything contained in the Administrator General's Act 1963, an administrator general shall not interpose in any manner in relation to any property of a deceased which has been dealt with under the provisions of the Navy Act 1957[1] except in so far as he is expressly required or competent to do so by or under the provisions of the Navy Act 1957[2].

2 The central government may, at any time and in such circumstance as it thinks fit, direct that the estate of a deceased sailor or officer shall be handed over by the commanding officer or the committee of adjustment, to the administrator general of a State for administration and thereupon such commanding officer or the committee shall make over the estate to such administrator general[3].

3 Where any estate is handed over to the administrator general, the later shall administer such estate in accordance with the provisions of the Administrator General's Act 1963[4]. However, where the estate is handed over to the administrator general before the ship and service debts in ship or quarters of the deceased are paid, it shall be the duty of the administrator general to pay these debts in priority to any other debts due by the deceased[5].

4 The administrator general shall pay the surplus, if any, remaining in his hands after discharging all debts and charges, to the heirs of the deceased and if no heir is traceable, shall make over the surplus to the person prescribed in this behalf[6].

5 The administrator general shall not charge in respect of his duties under this provision any fee exceeding three percent of the total amount coming to or remaining in his hands after payment of the ship and service debts and the other debts in ship or quarters[7].

1 Ie the Navy Act 1957 s 171 or 172; see **[1272]** and **[1273]**.

2 The Navy Act 1957 s 175 (1).

3 The Navy Act 1957 s 175 (2).

4 The Navy Act 1957 s 175 (3).

5 The Navy Act 1957 s 175 (3) proviso.

6 The Navy Act 1957 s 175 (4).

7 The Navy Act 1957 s 175 (5).

[1277] Disposal of surplus by prescribed persons On receipt of the surplus referred to in the aforesaid provisions of the Navy Act 1957[1], the prescribed person shall: (i) if he knows of a legal representative of the deceased, pay the surplus to that representative[2]; (ii) if the surplus does not exceed the prescribed amount not exceeding Rs 100,000/- in value and if he thinks fit, pay or deliver to any person appearing to him to be entitled to receive the same, without requiring such person to produce any probate, letters of administration, succession certificate or other conclusive evidence of title[3]; (iii) if the prescribed person does not know of any such representative to whom the surplus could be paid under certain provision[4], or if the surplus has not been disposed of under certain other provision[5], publish every year a notice in the prescribed form and manner for six consecutive years; and if no claim to the surplus is made by the legal representative of the deceased within six months even after the publication of the last of such notices, the prescribed person shall deposit the surplus together with any income or accumulation of income accrued there from, to the credit of the central government[6]. However, such deposit shall not prejudice the claims of any person to such surplus or any part thereof, if he is otherwise entitled to it[7].

1 Ie under the Navy Act 1957 s 171 (7), s 172 (ii) or s 175 (4).

2 The Navy Act 1957 s 176 (a).

3 The Navy Act 1957 s 176 (b).

4 Ie under the Navy Act 1957 s 176 (a).

5 Ie under the Navy Act 1957 s 176 (b).

6 The Navy Act 1957 s 176 (c).

7 The Navy Act 1957 s 176 (c) proviso.

[1278] Disposal effects not converted into money Where any part of the estate of a deceased officer or sailor consists of effects, securities or other property not converted into money, the certain provisions of the Navy Act 1957[1] with respect to the payment of the surplus shall, extend to the delivery, transmission of transfer of such effects, securities or property. The prescribed person shall have the same power of converting the same into money as a legal representative of the deceased[2].

1 Ie the Navy Act 1957 s 171 (7), s 172 (ii) and s 176; see **[1272]** and **[1277]**.

2 The Navy Act 1957 s 177.

[1279] Termination of liability of commanding officer, committee, prescribed person and the central government Any payment or application of money or delivery sale or other disposition of any property made, or purported to be made by the commanding officer[1], the committee or the prescribed person in good faith in pursuance of certain provisions of the Navy Act 1957[2] shall be valid and shall fully absolve the commanding officer, the committee or the prescribed person, as well as the central government from all liability in respect of the money or property so paid, applied or disposed of. However, nothing contained under this provision shall be deemed to affect the right of any executor or administrator or other legal representative or of any creditor of the deceased against any person to whom any such payment or delivery as aforesaid has been made[3].

1 As to the meaning of 'commanding officer'; see **[0912]**.

2 Ie the Navy Act 1957 s 171-176; see **[1272]** to **[1277]**.

3 The Navy Act 1957 s 178.

[1280] Saving of rights of representative Nothing under the provisions of the Navy Act 1957[1] shall affect the rights and duties of the representative of a deceased sailor[2] or officer[3] or any administrator general, in respect of the property of such deceased sailor or officer not collected by the commanding officer or the committee, and not forming part of the surplus handed over to the prescribed person under the Navy Act 1957[4].

1 Ie under the Navy Act 1957 chapter XIX s 171 to 183.

2 As to the definition of 'sailor'; see **[0933]**.

3 As to the definition of 'officer'; see **[0912]**.

4 Ie the prescribed person under the Navy Act 1957 s 171 (7) or s 172 (ii); The Navy Act 1957 s 179.

[1281] Application of the Navy Act 1957 s 171-179 to person of unsound mind Certain provisions of the Navy Act 1957[1] shall, so far as they can be made applicable, also apply in the case of an officer or sailor[2] subject to naval law[3] who is ascertained in the prescribed manner to be of unsound mind notwithstanding anything contained in the Mental Health Act 1987, or who, while on active service[4], is officially reported missing, as if the said officer or sailor had cited on the day on which his unsoundness of mind is so a ascertained or, as the case may be on the day on which he is officially reported missing[5]. However, in the case of an officer or sailor so reported missing, no action shall be taken to dispose of the property under the Navy Act 1957[6] until such time as a certificate under the Regulations for the Navy 1965, Part II is issued under the authority of the chief of the naval staff or other prescribed person that he is confirmed or presumed to be dead[7].

1 Ie the Navy Act 1957 ss 171-179.

2 As to the definition of 'officer' and 'sailor'; see **[0912]** and **[0933]**.

3 As to the meaning of 'subject to naval law'; see **[0935]**.

4 As to the meaning of 'active service'; see **[0905]**.

5 The Navy Act 1957 s 180.

6 Ie the Navy Act 1957 s 171, 172, and 175.

7 The Navy Act 1957 s 180 proviso.

[1282] Appointment of Standing Committee of Adjustment in certain cases When an officer[1]while subject to naval law[2] dies or is ascertained in the prescribed manner to be of unsound mind or while on active service[3] is officially reported missing, the reference in the forgoing provisions of the Navy Act 1957[4] to the committee shall be construed as references to the Standing Committee of Adjustment, constituted in this behalf in the prescribed manner. Such committee shall alone be entitled to perform all the functions as Standing Committee of Adjustment unless otherwise directed by the chief of the naval staff[5].

1 As to the definition of 'officer'; see **[0912].**

2 As to the meaning of 'subject to naval law'; see **[0935]**.

3 As to the meaning of 'active service'; see **[0905]**.

4 Ie in the Navy Act 1957 ss 171-180; see **[1272]-[1281]**.

5 The Navy Act 1957 s 181.

[1283] Exercise of powers by other persons The functions and powers of the commanding officer under certain provisions of the Navy Act 1957[1] may in any case be performed or exercised by any other person appointed in this behalf by the chief of the naval staff[2].

1 Ie the Navy Act 1957 chapter XIX, ss 171 to 181.

2 The Navy Act 1957 s 182.

[1284] Forfeiture of effect for absence without leave If any person subject to naval law[1] is absent without leave for a period of one month (whether he is guilty of desertion or of improperly leaving his ship or place of duty or not) but is not apprehended or tried for his offence, he shall be liable for forfeiture of pay and allowances and other benefits as the central government from time to time by regulations provide. The chief of the naval staff or the prescribed officer may by an order containing a statement of the absence without leave direct that the clothes and effects, if any, left by absentee on board ship or at his place of duty be forfeited, and the same be sold and the proceeds of the same shall be disposed of as provided in the Regulations for the Navy. Every such order for forfeiture or sale shall be conclusive for the purpose of this provision as to the fact of the absence without leave as therein stated of the person therein named; but in any case the central government may, if it deems fit on sufficient cause being shown at any time after forfeiture and before sale, remit the forfeiture, or after sale pay or dispose of the proceeds of the sale or any part thereof to or for the use of the person to whom the cloths or effects belonged, or his representative[2].

1 As to the meaning of 'person subject to naval law'; see **[0941]**.

2 The Navy Act 1957 s 183.

9. BOARDS OF INQUIRY

CONTENTS

PARA

[1285] Convening of Boards of Inquiry A board of inquiry may be convened by the chief of the naval staff or any administrative authority, or when two or more ships are in company, by the senior naval officer present, whenever any matter arises upon which he requires to be thoroughly informed[1]. An administrative authority or the senior naval officer present shall convene a board of inquiry when so directed by superior authority or when so required by any regulations, government instructions or navy orders[2].

1 The Regulations for the Navy 1965, Part II, regulation 197 (1).

2 The Regulations for the Navy 1965, Part II, regulation 197 (2).

[1286] Constitution of Board of Inquiry The board may consist of any number of officers including officers of the army or the air force or civilian gazetted officers and master chief petty officers, provided the number of such master chief petty officers shall not exceed one half of the members constituting the board[1]. The army and air force officers and civilian gazetted officers, unless they are under the administrative control of the convening authority, shall be appointed only after the concurrence of the appropriate authority superior to the individuals to be appointed[2]. As far as practicable, the president and the members shall be senior or relatively senior to the person whose conduct is under inquiry and persons whose evidence may be required by the board shall not be nominated as members[3]. In selecting members, the convening authority shall have regard to the possibility that a person who has sat on a board of inquiry may, if otherwise qualified to sit on a court martial upon the same subject matter, be objected to and that such objection may be allowed by the court[4].

1 The Regulations for the Navy 1965, Part II, regulation 198 (1).

2 The Regulations for the Navy 1965, Part II, regulation 198 (2).

3 The Regulations for the Navy 1965, Part II, regulation 198 (3).

4 The Regulations for the Navy 1965, Part II, regulation 198 (4).

[1287] President of the board The convening authority may appoint any suitable person to be president of the board[1].

1 The Regulations for the Navy 1965, Part II, regulation 199.

[1288] Duties of the board The board shall perform such duties as may be directed by the authority convening the board[1]. Such directions shall always be made in writing and may in cases of urgency be conveyed by signal and when a board is convened by an administrative authority or senior naval officer present, shall conform to any general directions given in any navy orders[2]. Every order convening the board shall be made in the prescribed form or as near thereto as circumstances permit and where directions are given by signal, it shall be sufficient to make reference to the said form, in respect of the general directions contained therein further directions being added as necessary[3]. A board may be required to collect evidence only, without being required to give any opinion or the board may be required to report fully with regard to any matter, which may be referred to it and to make recommendations[4]. The convening authority shall, when the board is held on a returned prisoner of war or on a prisoner of war who is still absent, direct the board to record its opinion whether the person concerned was taken prisoner through his own willful neglect of duty, or whether he served with or under, or aided the enemy. The convening authority shall also direct the board to record its opinion in the case of a returned prisoner of war, whether he returned as soon as possible to the service and in the case of a prisoner of war still absent whether he failed to return to the service when it was possible for him to do so[5].

1 The Regulations for the Navy 1965, Part II, regulation 200 (1).

2 The Regulations for the Navy 1965, Part II, regulation 200 (2).

3 The Regulations for the Navy 1965, Part II, regulation 200 (3).

4 The Regulations for the Navy 1965, Part II, regulation 200 (4).

5 The Regulations for the Navy 1965, Part II, regulation 200 (5).

[1289] Members of the board not to be sworn or affirmed Members of the board shall not be sworn or affirmed, but when the board is on recovered prisoners of war, the members shall make the following declaration: "I, ...do declare upon my honour that I will duly and impartially inquire into and give my opinion as to the circumstances in which.........became prisoner of war, according to the true spirit and meaning of the Regulations for the Navy"[1].

1 The Regulations for the Navy 1965, Part II, regulation 201.

[1290] Procedure The Board shall be guided by the provisions of the Regulations for the Navy 1965, Part II, and also by the navy orders in force for the time being and the written instructions of the convening authority provided that the navy orders and the written instructions are not consistent with anything contained in the Regulations for the Navy 1965, Part II[1]. The Board may put such questions to a witness as it thinks desirable for testing the truth or accuracy of any evidence he has given and otherwise for eliciting the truth[2].

1 The Regulations for the Navy 1965, Part II, regulation 202 (1).

2 The Regulations for the Navy 1965, Part II, regulation 202 (2).

[1291] Examination of witness Before examination, every witness shall be informed in the following terms which shall be recorded in the minutes: 'You are privileged to refuse to answer any question, the answer to which may tend to expose you any penalty or forfeiture. It will be for you to raise the objection and for the board to decide whether you must answer the question or not"[1]. No one charged with any offence shall be bound to make any statement or answer any questions[2]. The board may be re-assembled as often and with such changes in its composition as the convening authority may direct for the purpose of examining additional witness or further examining any witness, or recording further information[3]. A board shall unless otherwise ordered, sit with closed doors[4]. Except where a board is ordered to inquire into the propriety of a punishment of regulation to a lower rank awarded to a chief petty officer or petty officer, in a case where such chief petty officer or petty officer had elected trial by court martial and due to the exigencies of the service, the commanding officer had exercised his powers under the regulations nevertheless to try the chief petty officer or petty officer summarily, no person shall be present in the character of a prosecutor nor any friend or professional adviser be allowed to assist any person concerned in the inquiry[5]. If the inquiry should have reference to the loss or hazarding a ship, the course directed by the Regulations for the Navy 1965, Part II, regulation 183 shall be adopted mutatis mutandis[6].

1 The Regulations for the Navy 1965, Part II, regulation 203 (1).

2 The Regulations for the Navy 1965, Part II, regulation 203 (2).

3 The Regulations for the Navy 1965, Part II, regulation 203 (3).

4 The Regulations for the Navy 1965, Part II, regulation 203 (4).

5 The Regulations for the Navy 1965, Part II, regulation 203 (5).

6 The Regulations for the Navy 1965, Part II, regulation 203 (6).

[1292] Summoning of witness Any witness whose attendance cannot otherwise be attained may be summoned in accordance with the provisions of the Regulations for the Navy 1965, Part II[1].

1 Ie as contained in the Regulations for the Navy 1965, Part II, regulation 233; see **[1215]**. The Regulations for the Navy 1965, Part II, regulation 204.

[1293] Procedure when character or conduct of a person in government service involved Except in the case of a prisoner of war who is still absent, whenever any inquiry affects the character or reputation of a person in government service or may result in the imputation of liability or responsibility for any loss or damage or is made for the contravention of any regulations or general or local orders, full opportunity shall be accorded to such person of being present throughout the inquiry and of making any statement and of giving any evidence he may wish to make or give and of cross-examining any witness whose evidence in his opinion affects him and producing any witness in his defence[1]. The president of the board shall take such steps as may be necessary to ensure that any such person so affected and not previously notified, receives notice of and fully understands, his rights under the Regulations for the Navy 1965, Part II[2].

1 The Regulations for the Navy 1965, Part II, regulation 205 (1).

2 Also see the Regulations for the Navy 1965, Part II, regulation 209 (b); **[1297]**. The Regulations for the Navy 1965, Part II, regulation 205 (2).

[1294] Evidence when to be taken on oath or affirmation Evidence shall be recorded on oath or affirmation when a board is assembled: (i) on a prisoner of war[1], or (ii) in any other case when so directed by the convening authority[2]. In such cases the board shall administer an oath or affirmation to witness in the following form[3].

> I,.........do swear in the name of God/solemnly affirm, that the evidence which I shall give before this board shall be the truth, the whole truth and nothing but the truth.

1 The Regulations for the Navy 1965, Part II, regulation 206 (1) (a).

2 The Regulations for the Navy 1965, Part II, regulation 206 (1) (b).

3 The Regulations for the Navy 1965, Part II, regulation 206 (2).

[1295] Proceedings of board not admissible in evidence The proceedings of a board or any confession or answer to a question made or given before a board shall not be admissible in evidence against a person subject to naval laws[1] relating to the government of the regular army or air force nor shall any evidence respecting the proceedings of the board be given against any such person except upon the trial of such person for willfully giving false evidence before the board. However, the proceedings of board can be used for the purpose of cross-examining any witness[2].

1 As to the meaning of 'person subject to naval law'; see **[0941]**.

2 The Regulations for the Navy 1965, Part II, regulation 207.

[1296] Minutes of proceedings Subject to the provisions of the Regulations for the Navy 1965, Part II, the proceedings of every board shall be recorded and prepared in accordance with any directions contained in the navy orders in force for the time being and any instructions given by the convening authority[1]. The minutes of such proceedings shall contain a verbatim report of all the evidence given and all questions and answers shall be numbered in one series throughout the minutes[2]. In making up the record of the minutes the sheets shall be securely fastened and numbered consecutively[3]. A list of the witnesses giving the serial number of questions put to each and a list of the exhibits shall be attached to the proceedings[4]. All documentary exhibits shall be placed in the order in which such documents are produced at the inquiry and shall be numbered consecutively and attached to the proceedings, the minutes of which shall be forwarded together with all enclosures to the convening authority in the prescribed form[5]. The written order convening the board shall be returned to the convening officer with the minutes of the proceedings and shall form a part of the record[6]. The convening authority shall, having regard to the fact that copies may have to be supplied to persons concerned in the result of the inquiry, should the proceedings be followed by a court martial arising out of the same subject matter, give directions as to the number of copies of the proceedings which are required and it shall be the duty of the president of the board to see that enough copies of all exhibits are made, one copy to go with such set of papers[7]. The minutes shall be signed by all the members of the board and if a difference of opinion among the members arises then the board is required to make a report or give its findings the grounds of such difference shall be stated fully[8]. On receipt of the minutes of the proceedings including the report from the board, the convening authority shall: (a) take such actions as is within its jurisdiction and as it may deem fit to take[9]; and (b) submit the same together with its comments thereon to the higher authority: (i) if required to do so under the orders issued from time to time by the chief of the naval staff[10]; or (ii) if the convening authority deems it necessary so to do[11]. However, nothing in Regulations for the Navy 1965, Part II, shall be construed as debarring the convening authority from taking appropriate action with his jurisdiction[12].

1 The Regulations for the Navy 1965, Part II, regulation 208 (1).

2 The Regulations for the Navy 1965, Part II, regulation 208 (2).

3 The Regulations for the Navy 1965, Part II, regulation 208 (3).

4 The Regulations for the Navy 1965, Part II, regulation 208 (4).

5 The Regulations for the Navy 1965, Part II, regulation 208 (5).

6 The Regulations for the Navy 1965, Part II, regulation 208 (6).

7 The Regulations for the Navy 1965, Part II, regulation 208 (7).

8 The Regulations for the Navy 1965, Part II, regulation 208 (8).

9 The Regulations for the Navy 1965, Part II, regulation 208 (a).

10 The Regulations for the Navy 1965, Part II, regulation 208 (b) (i).

11 The Regulations for the Navy 1965, Part II, regulation 208 (b) (ii).

12 The Regulations for the Navy 1965, Part II, regulation 208 proviso.

[1297] Right of certain persons to copies of proceedings The following persons shall be entitled to a copy of the proceedings of a board not including any report made by the board: (i) any person subject to naval law who is tried by a court martial in respect of any matter or thing which has been reported on by a board[1]; or (ii) any person in government service whose character, conduct or reputation is, in the opinion of the chief of the naval staff, affected by anything in the evidence before or in the report of a board, unless the chief of the naval staff sees reason to order otherwise[2]. For the purpose of this provision 'proceedings' shall include findings of the board but shall not include recommendations of the board[3].

1 The Regulations for the Navy 1965, Part II, regulation 209 (a).

2 The Regulations for the Navy 1965, Part II, regulation 209 (b).

3 The Regulations for the Navy 1965, Part II, regulation 209 explanation.

9. REGULATIONS

CONTENTS

PARA

[1298] Power to make regulations The Central Government may, by notification in the official Gazette, make regulations[1] for the governance, command, discipline, recruitment, conditions of service and regulation of the naval forces and generally for the purpose of carrying into effect the provisions of the Navy Act 1957[2]. In particular, such regulations may provide for:

1 The rank, precedence, powers of command and authority of officers and sailors in the naval service[3].

2 The relative rank, precedence, powers of command and authority of officers and sailors in the naval service in relation to members of the regular army and the air force[4].

3 The cases in which, and the conditions subject to which, powers of punishment may be exercised under the Navy Act 1957 s 7 (2)[5].

4 The retirement discharge and dismissal of persons in the naval service[6].

5 The authority to which any matter referred to in the Navy Act 1957 s 19A may be refereed and the manner in which an enquiry may be made by that authority[7].

6 The convening and constitution of courts martial and the appointment of prosecutors at trials by court martial[8].

7 The adjournment, dissolution and sitting of courts martial[9].

8 The procedure to be observed in trials by courts martial, the persons by whom an accused may be defended in such trials and the appearance of such persons at court martial[10].

9 The forms of orders to be made under the provisions of the Navy Act 1957 relating to courts martial and the awards and infliction of death, imprisonment and detention[11].

10 The carrying into effect of sentences of courts martial[12].

11 Any matter necessary for the purpose of carrying the Navy Act 1957 into execution as far as it relates to the investigation, arrest, custody, trial and punishment of offences triable or punishable under the aforesaid Act[13].

12 The terms and conditions of service, the pay, the pensions, allowances and other benefits of persons in the naval service, including special provision in this behalf during active service[14].

13 The ceremonials to be observed and marks of respect to be paid in the naval service[15].

14 The convening of, the constitution, procedure and practice of boards of inquiry, the summoning of witnesses before them and the administration of oaths by such boards[16].

15 The computation of time of absence without leave or custody of deserters and absentees without leave[17].

16 Any matter relating to the realization and disposal of the estates of officers or sailors who are deceased, ascertained to be of unsound mind or reported missing on active service[18].

17 The enquiry into the conduct of prisoners of war, and their pay and allowances[19].

18 The provisions to be made for the wives and children of prisoners of war or missing persons[20].

19 The procedure relating to the exercise of powers under Navy Act 1957 s 163[21].

20 The amount required to be prescribed under Navy Act 1957 s 176 (b)[22]

21 Any other matter which is to be, may be, or is required to be, prescribed under the Navy Act 1957[23].

1 The Regulations for the Navy Part I have been issued under the authority of the Government of India and contain provisions of administrative character. The Regulations for the Navy Part II called the Navy (Discipline and Miscellaneous Provisions) Regulations, 1965 are statutory. The Regulations for the Navy Part III are called the Naval Ceremonial, Conditions of Service and Miscellaneous Regulations, 1963. These are statutory and contain issues relating to ceremonials, training and promotion. The Regulations for the Navy Part IV contain the Indian Naval Auxiliary Service Regulations 1973. The Regulations referred under this provision are the Regulations for the Navy 1965, Part II, called the Navy (Discipline and Miscellaneous Provisions) Regulations.

2 The Navy Act 1957 s 184 (1).

3 The Navy Act 1957 s 184 (2) (a).

4 The Navy Act 1957 s 184 (2) (b).

5 The Navy Act 1957 s 184 (2) (c).

6 The Navy Act 1957 s 184 (2) (ca).

7 The Navy Act 1957 s 184 (2) (cb).

8 The Navy Act 1957 s 184 (2) (d).

9 The Navy Act 1957 s 184 (2) (e).

10 The Navy Act 1957 s 184 (2) (f).

11 The Navy Act 1957 s 184 (2) (g).

12 The Navy Act 1957 s 184 (2) (h).

13 The Navy Act 1957 s 184 (2) (i).

14 The Navy Act 1957 s 184 (2) (j).

15 The Navy Act 1957 s 184 (2) (k).

16 The Navy Act 1957 s 184 (2) (l).

17 The Navy Act 1957 s 184 (2) (m).

18 The Navy Act 1957 s 184 (2) (n).

19 The Navy Act 1957 s 184 (2) (o).

20 The Navy Act 1957 s 184 (2) (p).

21 The Navy Act 1957 s 184 (2) (q).

22 The Navy Act 1957 s 184 (2) (qa).

23 The Navy Act 1957 s 184 (2) (r).

[1299] Power to make regulations with retrospective effect The Regulations made under the Navy Act 1957 can be gives retrospective effect, from a date not earlier than the date of commencement of the Navy Act. However, no retrospective effect shall be given to any regulations so as to prejudicially affect the interests of any person to whom such regulation may be applicable[1].

1 The Navy Act 1957 s 184A.

[1300] Laying of Regulations before Parliament Every regulation made under the Navy Act 1957 shall be laid, as soon as may be after it is made, before each House of Parliament, while it is in session for a total period of 30 days which may be comprised in one session or in two or more successive sessions. If, before the expiry of the session immediately following the session or successive sessions, both Houses agree in making any modification in the regulation shall thereafter or both Houses agree that the regulation should not be made, the regulation shall thereafter have effect only in such modified from. However, any such modification or annulment shall be without prejudice to the validity of anything previously done under that regulation[1].

1 The Navy Act 1957 s 185.

V. THE LAW RELATING TO THE COAST GUARD

1. INTRODUCTION

[1301] Introduction The Indian Coast Guard (ICG) came into being on 01 February 1977 on approval of the Cabinet Committee on Parliament Affairs to set up an interim Coast Guard Organization. The service was formally established as an independent organization on 19 August 1978 with the enactment of the Coast Guard Act 1978[1] and a cadre of Coast Guards was created by hiving off a wing of the Indian Navy[2]. The ICG is a maritime armed force operating under the Ministry of Defence and is mandated to protect the maritime and other national interests of India by way of providing protection to offshore and other structures, protection to fishermen and assisting in anti smuggling operations. The ICG, working in co-ordination with other Union agencies, institutions and authorities, safeguards the maritime interests and security of India, assists vessels and fisherman in distress and protects the maritime environment. The ICG is headed by a Director General, an officer of the rank of Vice Admiral of the Indian Navy. The Director General[3] is assisted by other officers who are responsible for different duties and responsibilities.

The establishment of the ICG as a new service was the result of an awareness that had been growing for some time in the Government of India for the requirement to enforce national laws in the waters under national jurisdiction and ensure safety of life and property at sea. It was also considered desirable that these law enforcement responsibilities be undertaken by a service suitably equipped and modelled on the coast guards of advanced nations like the US, the UK, etc leaving the Indian Navy to exercise the fleet for its wartime role. The powers currently vested in the Coast Guard come from: The Criminal procedure Code 1973; The Customs Act 1962; The Maritime Zone of India Act 1981; The Merchant Shipping Act 1958; The Territorial Waters, Continental Shelf, Exclusive Economic Zone, and other Maritime Zones Act 1976; The Maritime Zone of India (Regulation of Fishing by Foreign Vessels) Act 1981. In addition, under special provisions, the Coast Guard can be empowered under any of the following Acts: The Passport (Entry into India) Act 1970, The Emigration Act 1972, The Regulation of Foreigners Act 1939 and The Foreigners Act 1946[4].

The duties of Coast Guard are as follows: (i) ensuring the safety and protection of artificial islands, offshore terminals, installations and other structures and devices in Maritime Zones; (b) providing protection to fishermen including assistance to them at sea while in distress; (iii) taking such measures as are necessary to preserve and protect the maritime environment and to prevent and control marine pollution; (iv) assisting the customs and other authorities in anti-smuggling operations; (v) enforcing the provisions of such enactments as are for the time being in force in the maritime zones; and (vi) such other matters, including measures for the safety of life and property at sea and collection of scientific data, as may be prescribed[5]. The Coast Guard (Discipline) Rules 1983 and the Coast Guard (General) Rules 1986 have been framed under the Coast Guard Act 1978[6].

1 The Ministry of Defence, Annual Report, 2011-12, para 6.1.

2 *Commandant Shamsher Singh Malik v Union of India*, WP (C) Nos 2310/2005 & 12179/2006, Delhi High Court, decided on 19 September 2011.

3 The Director General Coast Guard (DGCG) exercises his command from Coast Guard Headquarters at New Delhi through Commander Coast Guard Regions (COMCG) West, East, North West and Andaman & Nicobar. The Regional Commanders exercise their command through District Commander (COMDIS), CG Stations and CG Air Stations. Most of the ships are under operational control of the COMCG's while some are also under the control of Air Enclave/District Commanders and ICG Stations.

4 Palevi P. (Editor-in-Chief), *Indian Coast Guard: 25 Glorious Years*, Coast Guard Headquarters, New Delhi, pp. 17-19.

5 The Ministry of Defence, Annual Report, 2011-12, para 6.1, 6.2 and 6.3.

6 Ie under the Coast Guard Act 1978 s 123.

2. PRELIMINARY

CONTENTS

[1302] Short title and commencement This statute covering the Coast Guard is the Coast Guard Act 1978[1]. It came into force on 19 August 1978 by notification[2] in the Official Gazette[3].

1 The Coast Guard Act 1978 s 1 (1).

2 Notification No. S.R.O. 10 (E), dated 18 August, 1978. Gazette of India, Pt. II, Sec. 4, page 16

3 The Coast Guard Act 1978 s 1 (2).

(i) Definitions

Certain words and terms as appear in the Coast Guard Act and Coast Guard Rules will need to be understood as they are defined in the Coast Guard Act 1978, the Coast Guard (Discipline) Rules 1983, the Coast Guard (General) Rules 1986, the Coast Guard (Condition of Service) Rules 1986 and the Coast Guard (Seniority and Promotion) Rules 1986.

[1303] Chief Law officer and Law Officer In the Coast Guard Act 1978, unless the context otherwise requires, 'Chief Law Officer' and 'Law Officer' mean, respectively, the chief law officer and a law officer of the Coast Guard appointed under the Coast Guard Act 1978[1].

1 Ie as appointed under the Coast Guard Act 1978 s 115; The Coast Guard Act 1978 s 2 (a).

[1304] Civil Offence In the Coast Guard Act 1978, unless the context otherwise requires, 'civil offence' means an offence which is triable by a criminal court[1].

1 The Coast Guard Act 1978 s 2 (b).

[1305] Civil prison In the Coast Guard Act 1978, unless the context otherwise requires, 'civil prison' means any jail or place used for the detention of any criminal prisoner under the Prisons Act 1894 or under any other law for the time being in force[1].

1 The Coast Guard Act 1978 s 2 (c).

[1306] Coast Guard In the Coast Guard Act 1978, unless the context otherwise requires, 'Coast Guard' means the Coast Guard constituted under the Coast Guard Act 1978[1].

1 The Coast Guard Act 1978 s 2 (d).

[1307] Coast Guard Court In the Coast Guard Act 1978, unless the context otherwise requires, 'Coast Guard Court' means a court convened under the Coast Guard Court 1978 s 64[1].

1 The Coast Guard Act 1978 s 2 (e).

[1308] Coast Guard Custody In the Coast Guard Act 1978, unless the context otherwise requires, 'Coast Guard custody' means the arrest or confinement of member of the Coast Guard according to rules[1].

1 Ie the Coast Guard (Discipline) Rules 1983 r 5 and 6. The Coast Guard Act 1978 s 2 (f).

[1309] Coast Guard Region In the Coast Guard (Condition of Service) Rules 1986, unless the context otherwise requires, 'Coast Guard Region' means: (i) The Coast Guard Region, West, comprising of the coastal areas and the maritime zones of India along the coastal areas of the States of Gujarat, Maharashtra, Karnataka, Kerala and the Union territories of Goa, Daman and Diu and Lakshdweep[1]; (ii) The Coast Guard Region, East, comprising of the coastal areas and the maritime zones of India along the coastal areas of the States of Andhra Pradesh, Orissa, Tamil Nadu, West Bengal and the Union territory of Pondicherry[2]; and (iii) The Coast Guard Region, Andaman and Nicobar Islands, comprising of coastal areas and the maritime zones of India along the coastal areas of the Union territory of Andaman and Nicobar Islands[3].

1 The Coast Guard (Condition of Service) Rules 1986 r 2 (c) (i).

2 The Coast Guard (Condition of Service) Rules 1986 r 2 (c) (ii).

3 The Coast Guard (Condition of Service) Rules 1986 r 2 (c) (iii).

[1310] Commanding officer In the Coast Guard Act 1978, unless the context otherwise requires, 'commanding officer', when used in any provision of the aforesaid Act with reference to any unit or ship of the Coast Guard, means the officer whose duty it is under the rules to discharge with respect to that unit or ship, the functions of a commanding officer in regard to matters of the description referred to in that provision[1]. Commanding officer means the officer or other persons in actual command of a ship[2].

1 The Coast Guard Act 1978 s 2 (g).

2 The Coast Guard (Discipline) Rules 1983 r 2 (d).

[1311] Criminal Court In the Coast Guard Act 1978, unless the context otherwise requires, 'Criminal Court' means a court of ordinary criminal justice in any part of India[1].

1 The Coast Guard Act 1978 s 2 (h).

[1312] Deputy Inspector-General In the Coast Guard Act 1978, unless the context otherwise requires, 'Deputy Inspector-General' means a Deputy Inspector-General of the Coast Guard appointed under Coast Guard Act 1978 s 5[1].

1 The Coast Guard Act 1978 s 2 (i).

[1313] Director-General In the Coast Guard Act 1978, unless the context otherwise requires, 'Director-General' means the Director-General of the Coast Guard appointed under the Coast Guard Act 1978 s 5[1].

1 The Coast Guard Act 1978 s 2 (j).

[1314] Enrolled person In the Coast Guard Act 1978, unless the context otherwise requires, 'enrolled person' means a subordinate officer, sailor or other person enrolled under the Coast Guard Act 1978[1].

1 The Coast Guard Act 1978 s 2 (k).

[1315] Inspector-General In the Coast Guard Act 1978, unless the context otherwise requires, 'Inspector-General' means an Inspector-General of the Coast Guard appointed under the Coast Guard Act 1978 s 5[1].

1 The Coast Guard Act 1978 s 2 (l).

[1316] Maritime zones of India In the Coast Guard Act 1978, unless the context otherwise requires, 'maritime zones of India' means the territorial waters, the contiguous zone, the continental shelf, the exclusive economic zone or any other maritime zone of India[1].

1 The Coast Guard Act 1978 s 2 (m).

[1317] Member of the Coast Guard In the Coast Guard Act 1978, unless the context otherwise requires, 'member of the coast guard' means an officer, a subordinate officer, a sailor or other enrolled person[1].

1 The Coast Guard Act 1978 s 2 (n).

[1318] Notification In the Coast Guard Act 1978, unless the context otherwise requires, 'notification' means a notification published in the Official Gazette[1].

1 The Coast Guard Act 1978 s 2 (o).

[1319] Offence In the Coast Guard Act 1978, unless the context otherwise requires, 'offence' means any act or omission punishable under the Coast Guard Act 1978 and includes a civil offence[1].

1 The Coast Guard Act 1978 s 2 (p).

[1320] Officer In the Coast Guard Act 1978, unless the context otherwise requires, 'officer' means a person appointed or in pay as an officer of the Coast Guard, but does not include a subordinate officer[1], sailor[2] or other enrolled person[3]. In the Coast Guard (General) Rules 1986, unless the context otherwise requires, 'executive officer', means an officer who carries out executive duties of the ship[4].

1 As to the definition of 'subordinate officer'; see **[1326]**.

2 As to the definition of 'sailor'; see **[1323]**.

3 As to the definition of 'enrolled person'; see **[1314]**; The Coast Guard Act 1978 s 2 (q).

4 The Coast Guard (General) Rules 1986 r 2 (f).

[1321] Prescribed In the Coast Guard Act 1978, unless the context otherwise requires, 'prescribed' means prescribed by rules made under the Coast Guard Act 1978[1].

1 The Coast Guard Act 1978 s 2 (r).

[1322] Rules In the Coast Guard Act 1978, unless the context otherwise requires, 'rule' means a rule made under the Coast Guard Act 1978[1].

1 The Coast Guard Act 1978 s 2 (s).

[1323] Sailor In the Coast Guard Act 1978, unless the context otherwise requires, 'sailor' means a member of the Coast Guard other than an officer, a subordinate officer or other enrolled person[1].

1 As to the definition of officer, subordinate officer and enrolled person; see **[1320]**, **[1326]** and **[1314]**. The Coast Guard Act 1978 s 2 (t).

[1324] Ship In the Coast Guard Act 1978, unless the context otherwise requires, 'ship', except in the expression 'on board a ship', means a Coast Guard vessel, and includes any establishment or station belonging to, or under the control of, the Coast Guard whether within or without India[1].

1 The Coast Guard Act 1978 s 2 (u).

[1325] Skipper In the Coast Guard Act 1978, unless the context otherwise requires, 'skipper' means a subordinate officer in command of a ship[1].

1 As to the definition of subordinate officer; see **[1326]**. The Coast Guard Act 1978 s 2 (v).

[1326] Subordinate officer In the Coast Guard Act 1978, unless the context otherwise requires, 'subordinate officer' means a person appointed or in pay as a *Pradhan Adhikari*, a *Pradhan Sahayak* Engineer, an *Uttam Adhikari*, an *Uttam Sahayak* Engineer, an *Adhikari*, a *Sahayak* Engineer or a *Pradhan Yantrik* of the Coast Guard[1].

1 The Coast Guard Act 1978 s 2 (w).

[1327] Superior Officer In the Coast Guard Act 1978, unless the context otherwise requires, 'superior officer', when used in relation to a person subject to the aforesaid Act, means any officer or subordinate officer: (i) who is senior to that person under the rules[1]; or (ii) who is entitled under the Coast Guard Act 1978 or the rules to give a command to that person[2].

1 The Coast Guard Act 1978 s 2 (x) (i).

2 The Coast Guard Act 1978 s 2 (x) (ii).

[1328] Territorial waters, Contiguous zone, Continental shelf and Exclusive economic zone In the Coast Guard Act 1978, unless the context otherwise requires, 'territorial waters, 'contiguous zone', 'continental shelf' and 'exclusive economic zone' shall have the meanings respectively assigned to them in the Territorial Waters, Continental Shelf, Exclusive Economic Zone and other Maritime Zones Act 1976[1]

1 The Coast Guard Act 1978 s 2 (y).

[1329] Words and expressions used and not defined In the Coast Guard Act 1978, unless the context otherwise requires, all words and expressions used and not defined in the aforesaid Act but defined in the Indian Penal Code 1860, shall have the meanings assigned to them in that Code[1].

1 The Coast Guard Act 1978 s 2 (z).

(ii) Persons Subject to the Coast Guard Act

[1330] Persons subject to the Coast Guard Act 1978 The following persons shall be subject to the Coast Guard Act 1978, wherever they may be: (a) officers[1]; (b) subordinate officers and other persons enrolled under the aforesaid Act[2]; (c) persons who have, by a general or special order of the Central Government, been required to serve in a ship, to such extent and subject to such conditions as may be prescribed[3]; and (d) persons ordered to be received, or being passengers, on board any ship or aircraft of the Coast Guard, to such extent and subject to such conditions as may be prescribed[4]. Every person referred to in certain provisions of the Coast Guard Act 1978[5] shall remain so subject until he retires, or he is discharged, released, removed or dismissed from the Coast Guard in accordance with the provisions of the aforesaid Act, and the rules[6].

1 As to the definition of 'officer', 'subordinate officer' and 'enrolled person'; see **[1320]**, **[1326]** and **[1314]**. The Coast Guard Act 1978 s 3 (1) (a). The Central Government may appoint such persons as it considers being suitable as officers in the Coast Guard. Officer shall be recruited in accordance with the recruitment rules for various categories of officers. Procedure for recruitment shall be as promulgated by the Central Government from time to time. The Coast Guard (Condition of Service) Rules 1986 r 3.

2 The Coast Guard Act 1978 s 3 (1) (b).

3 The Coast Guard Act 1978 s 3 (1) (c).

4 The Coast Guard Act 1978 s 3 (1) (d).

5 Ie the Coast Guard Act 1978 s 3 (1) (a) and (b).

6 Ie the Coast Guard (General) Rules 1986; the Coast Guard Act 1978 s 3 (2).

3. CONSTITUTION OF THE COAST GUARD, DUTIES AND FUNCTIONS, CONDITIONS OF SERVICE AND PRIVILEGES

CONTENTS

PARA

A. Constitution of the Coast Guard

B. Duties and Functions

C. Conditions of Service

D. Service Privileges

[1331] Introduction The Indian Coast Guard is patterned on the Indian Navy and has all the characteristics of military service. In exercise of its powers under Article 309 of the Constitution, the Parliament has enacted the Coast Guards Act 1978 and various rules to regulate recruitment and conditions of service of persons appointed in the force. The Coast Guard is an "Armed Force of the Union of India"[1].

1 The Preamble to the Coast Guard Act 1978.

A. Constitution of the Coast Guard

[1332] Constitution of the Coast Guard There shall be an armed force of the Union called the Coast Guard for ensuring the security of the maritime zones of India with a view to the protection of maritime and other national interests in such zones[1]. Subject to the provisions of the Coast Guard Act 1978, the Coast Guard shall be constituted in such manner as may be prescribed and the conditions of service of the members of the Coast Guard shall be such as may be prescribed[2].

1 The Coast Guard Act 1978 s 4 (1).

2 Ie as prescribed under the Coast Guard (Condition of Service) Rules 1986 and the Coast Guard (Seniority and Promotion) Rules 1986. The revised conditions of service in respect of Coast Guard officers have been notified vide SRO 133 dated 17 September 2004 amending various provisions of Coast Guard (Seniority & Promotion) Rules 1987. The Coast Guard Act 1978 s 4 (2).

[1333] Constitution of the Coast Guard The Coast Guard shall consist of officers[1], subordinate officers[2], sailors[3] and other enrolled persons[4], appointed to, or enrolled into, the Coast Guard Service[5]. The Director General[6] shall exercise command through the following authorities: (i) The Commander, Coast Guard Region, West[7]; (ii) The Commander, Coast Guard Region, East[8]; (iii) The Commander, Coast Guard Region, Andaman and Nicobar Islands[9]; and (iv) The Commander, Coast Guard Customs[10]. Certain authorities mentioned at the aforesaid provisions[11], shall be designated as Operational and Administrative Authorities[12]. The Coast Guard Region, West, shall comprise of the Coastal areas and the maritime zones of India along the coastal areas of the States of Gujarat, Maharashtra, Karnataka, Kerala, Goa and the Union Territories of Daman and Diu and Lakshadweep[13]. The Coast Guard Region, East, shall comprise of the coastal areas and the maritime zones of India along the coastal areas of the States of Tamil Nadu, Andhra Pradesh, Orissa, West Bengal and the Union Territory of Pondicherry[14]. The Coast Guard Region, Andaman and Nicobar Islands, shall comprise of coastal areas and the maritime zones along the coastal areas of the Union Territory of Andaman and Nicobar Islands[15]. The Commander, Coast Guard Customs, shall exercise operational and administrative control on all ships assigned to him by the Director General[16].

1 As to the definition of 'officer'; see **[1320]**.

2 As to the definition of 'subordinate officer'; see **[1326]**.

3 As to the definition of 'sailor'; see **[1323]**.

4 As to the definition of 'enrolled person'; see **[1314]**.

5 The Coast Guard (General) Rules 1986 r 4 (1).

6 As to the definition of 'Director-General'; see **[1313]**.

7 The Coast Guard (General) Rules 1986 r 4 (2) (a).

8 The Coast Guard (General) Rules 1986 r 4 (2) (b).

9 The Coast Guard (General) Rules 1986 r 4 (2) (c).

10 The Coast Guard (General) Rules 1986 r 4 (2) (d).

11 Ie the Coast Guard (General) Rules 1986 r 4 (2) (a) to (c).

12 The Coast Guard (General) Rules 1986 r 4 (2) note.

13 The Coast Guard (General) Rules 1986 r 4 (3) (a).

14 The Coast Guard (General) Rules 1986 r 4 (3) (b).

15 The Coast Guard (General) Rules 1986 r 4 (3) (c).

16 The Coast Guard (General) Rules 1986 r 4 (3) (d).

[1334] Coast Guard Districts Each Coast Guard Region shall be further divided into districts and each district shall be under the supervision of the District Commander to be appointed by the Director General[1].

1 The Coast Guard (General) Rules 1986 r 5.

[1335] Coast Guard Stations The Director General shall establish such number of stations and shall assign such number of ships to each Coast Guard Region/district/station as he may think fit depending upon the exigencies of the service from time to time[1].

1 The Coast Guard (General) Rules 1986 r 6.

[1336] Control direction, etc The general superintendence, direction and control of the Coast Guard shall vest in, and be exercised by, the Central Government and subject thereto, and to the provisions of the Coast Guard Act 1978 and the rules, the command and supervision of the Coast Guard shall vest in an officer to be appointed by the Central Government as the Director-General of the Coast Guard[1]. The Director-General shall, in the discharge of his duties under the Coast Guard Act 1978, be assisted by such number of Inspectors-General, Deputy Inspectors-General, Commandant and such other officers as may be appointed by the Central Government[2].

1 The Coast Guard Act 1978 s 5 (1).

2 The Coast Guard Act 1978 s 5 (2). Also see the Coast Guard (Discipline) Rules 1983 r 4.

[1337] Command of Coast Guard Ships Command of Coast Guard Ships, vessels, aircrafts or such establishments as may be promulgated by the Director General will be considered as operational command[1]. Generally officers and enrolled persons of the General Duties Branch shall exercise operational command, or direct any work or undertaking which requires the cooperation of different branches of the Coast Guard Service. It may be conferred on other officers and enrolled persons by appointment or by direction by the Director General.[2] Command of ships/ vessels/aircrafts shall be limited to qualified officers of the General

Duties branch and enrolled persons of seaman specialisation, except when conferred by superior authority on other persons qualified by ability and experience[3]. Command of Coast Guard ships/vessels, establishments and aircrafts may also be exercised by the officers and sailors of the Indian Navy while on deputation to the Coast Guard, when specifically appointed by the Director General[4]. Technical Officers appointed in command of shore establishments may exercise such functions of command as may be necessary for the proper performance of their duties[5]. Officers holding appointments under civil departments of the Government shall not, without the express orders of the Director General, assume any command over, or issue any orders to, the personnel of the Coast Guard, other than to those officers and enrolled persons who are serving under them in their respective departments[6].

1 The Coast Guard (General) Rules 1986 r 10 (1).

2 The Coast Guard (General) Rules 1986 r 10 (2).

3 The Coast Guard (General) Rules 1986 r 10 (3).

4 The Coast Guard (General) Rules 1986 r 10 (4).

5 The Coast Guard (General) Rules 1986 r 10 (5).

6 The Coast Guard (General) Rules 1986 r 10 (6).

[1338] Officer in Command Rank and precedence Officers in command of Coast Guard ships shall take rank and precedence over the officers placed under their command on all occasions, whether on shore or afloat[1].

1 The Coast Guard (General) Rules 1986 r 11.

[1339] Command in temporary absence of commanding officer Except in a shore establishment, the senior general duties officer on board (other than an officer appointed additional for staff or special duties, or an officer not qualified to command ships vessels) shall, in the temporary absence of the commanding officer[1], assume the powers and duties of the commanding officer. In a shore establishment, command shall descend in the branch of the commanding officer. If no officer of the commanding officer's branch is present, then command shall devolve on the senior most officer present; but command shall not devolve on any officer appointed additional for staff or special duties or for courses[2].

1 As to the definition of 'commanding officer'; see **[1310]**.

2 The Coast Guard (General) Rules 1986 r 12.

[1340] Authority of Army, Navy and Air Force Officers An officer of the Army, Navy and Air Force appointed to the Coast Guard shall have and exercise all such powers as are vested in or may be exercised by an officer of the Coast Guard of the corresponding rank or holding a corresponding appointment[1].

1 The Coast Guard (General) Rules 1986 r 18.

[1341] Power of Command Subject to certain provisions of the Coast Guard Act 1978[1], when a person subject to the aforesaid Act is attached to any body, or serving in a unit, or admitted as a patient in a hospital of the regular Army, Navy or Air Force, the Commanding Officer of such body, unit or hospital shall exercise all powers of Command over officers junior to him in rank and all powers of command and punishment over enrolled personnel[2]. Every officer below the rank of the Deputy Inspector General (not being either the Executive Officer or the Commanding Officer of the ship for the time being) and enrolled person shall be subordinate to the officer of the watch, whatever may be his rank, in regard to the performance of the duties with which he is charged[3].

1 Ie the Coast Guard Act 1978 s 57 and 58; see **[1459]** and **[1589]**.

2 The Coast Guard (General) Rules 1986 r 19.

3 The Coast Guard (General) Rules 1986 r 13.

[1342] Classifications and Ranks The officers and other members of the Coast Guard shall be classified in accordance with their ranks in the following categories, namely: (a) Officers: Director General[1]; Inspector General[2]; Deputy Inspector General[3]; Commandant[4]; Commandant (Junior Grade)[5]; Deputy Commandant[6]; and Assistant Commandant[7]. (b) Subordinate Officers: *Pradhan Adhikari/Pradhan Sahayak* Engineer[8]; *Uttam Adhikari/Uttam Sahayak* Engineer[9]; and *Adhikari/Sahayak* Engineer/Pradhan *Yantrik*[10]. (c) Sailors: *Pradhan Navik*[11]; *Uttam Navik/UttamYantrik*[12]; and *Navik/Yantrik*[13].

The officers shall be classified into two branches: general duties and technical. The enrolled persons shall be classified into four branches: general duties, technical, domestic and enrolled followers[14]. Officers and enrolled persons serving afloat or ashore shall be borne on the books of the ship or establishment or station in which they are serving or to which they are attached[15]. When it is desired that an officer borne additional for staff or special duties should practice or gain experience in ship handling and the like, authority for him to take charge of a watch at sea or in harbour may be given by the commanding officer[16]. However, nothing in this provision shall put him in the line of succession to command[17].

1 The Coast Guard (General) Rules 1986 r 7 (a) (i).

2 The Coast Guard (General) Rules 1986 r 7 (a) (ii).

3 The Coast Guard (General) Rules 1986 r 7 (a) (iii).

4 The Coast Guard (General) Rules 1986 r 7 (a) (iv).

5 The Coast Guard (General) Rules 1986 r 7 (a) (v).

6 The Coast Guard (General) Rules 1986 r 7 (a) (vi).

7 The Coast Guard (General) Rules 1986 r 7 (a) (vii).

8 The Coast Guard (General) Rules 1986 r 7 (b) (i).

9 The Coast Guard (General) Rules 1986 r 7 (b) (ii).

10 The Coast Guard (General) Rules 1986 r 7 (b) (iii).

11 The Coast Guard (General) Rules 1986 r 7 (c) (i).

12 The Coast Guard (General) Rules 1986 r 7 (c) (ii).

13 The Coast Guard (General) Rules 1986 r 7 (c) (iii).

14 The Coast Guard (general) Rules 1986 r 8.

15 The Coast Guard (General) Rules 1986 r 14 (1).

16 The Coast Guard (General) Rules 1986 r 14 (2).

17 The Coast Guard (General) Rules 1986 r 14 (2) proviso.

B. Duties and Functions

[1343] Duties and functions of Coast Guard It shall be the duty of the Coast Guard[1] to protect by such measures, as it thinks fit, the maritime and other national interests of India in the maritime zones[3] of India[1]. Without prejudice to the generality of the aforesaid provisions[4], the measures referred to therein may provide for: (i) ensuring the safety and protection of artificial islands, offshore terminals, installations and other structures and devices in any maritime zone[5]; (ii) providing protection to fishermen including assistance to them at sea while in distress[6]; (iii) taking such measures as are necessary to preserve and protect the maritime environment and to prevent and control marine pollution[7]; (iv) assisting the customs and other authorities in anti-smuggling operations[8]; (v) enforcing the provisions of such enactments as are for the time being in force in the maritime zones[9]; and (vi) such other matters, including measures for the safety of life and property at sea and collection of scientific data, as may be prescribed[10]. The Coast Guard shall perform its functions under this provision in accordance with, and subject to such rules, as may be prescribed and such rules may, in particular, make provisions for ensuring that the Coast Guard functions in close liaison with Union agencies, Institutions and authorities so as to avoid duplication of effort[11].

1 As to the definition of 'coast guard'; see **[1306]**.

2 As to the definition of 'maritime zone'; see **[1316]**.

3 The Coast Guard Act 1978 s 14 (1).

4 Ie the Coast Guard Act 1978 s 14 (1).

5 The Coast Guard Act 1978 s 14 (2) (a).

6 The Coast Guard Act 1978 s 14 (2) (b).

7 The Coast Guard Act 1978 s 14 (2) (c).

8 The Coast Guard Act 1978 s 14 (2) (d).

9 The Coast Guard Act 1978 s 14 (2) (e).

10 The Coast Guard Act 1978 s 14 (2) (f).

11 The Coast Guard Act 1978 s 14 (3).

[1344] Powers and duties conferrable and imposable on members of the Coast Guard The Central Government may, by general or special order published in the Official Gazette, direct that, subject to such conditions and limitations, and within the local limits of such inland area adjoining the coast of India, as may be specified in the order, any member of the Coast Guard[1] may: (i) for the purpose of prevention of any offence punishable under the Passport (Entry into India) Act 1920, the Emigration Act 1922, the Registration of Foreigners Act 1939, the Foreigners Act 1946, the Merchant Shipping Act 1958, the Customs Act 1962, the Passports Act 1967, the Foreign Exchange Regulation Act 1973, or the Territorial Waters, Continental Shelf, Exclusive Economic Zone and other Maritime Zones Act 1976, or of any cognizable offence punishable under any other Central Act[2]; or (ii) for the purpose of apprehending any person who has committed any offence referred to in the aforesaid provision[3], exercise or discharge such of the powers or duties under that Act or any other Central Act as may be specified in the said order, being the powers and duties which, in the opinion of the Central Government, an officer of the corresponding or lower rank is by that or such other Act empowered to exercise or discharge for the said purposes[4]. The Central Government may, by general or special order published in the Official Gazette, direct, with the concurrence of the State Government concerned, that any of the powers or duties which may be exercised or discharged under a State Act by a police officer may, subject to such conditions and limitations, and within the local limits of such inland area adjoining the coast of India, as may be specified in the order, be exercised or discharged by a member of the Coast Guard who, in the opinion of the Central Government, holds a corresponding or higher rank[5]. The Central Government may, by general or special order published in the Official Gazette, direct that, subject to such conditions and limitations, and within the local limits of such area in any maritime zone of India, as may be specified in the order, any member of the Coast Guard may: (i) for the purpose of prevention of any offence punishable under any enactment which extends for the time being to such area[6]; or (ii) for the purpose of apprehending any person who has committed any offence referred to in the aforesaid provision, exercise or discharge such of the powers or duties under that enactment, as may be specified in the said order, being the powers and duties which, in the opinion of the Central Government, an officer of the corresponding or lower rank is by that enactment empowered to exercise or discharge for the said purposes[7]. Every order made under this provision[8] shall be laid, as soon as may be after it is made, before each House of Parliament, while it is in session, for a total period of 30 days which may be comprised in one session or in two or more successive sessions. If, before the expiry of the session immediately following the session or the successive sessions aforesaid, both Houses agree in making any modification in the order or both Houses agree that the order should not be made, the order shall thereafter have effect only in such modified form or be of no effect. However, any such modification or annulment shall be without prejudice to the validity of anything previously done under that order[9]

1 As to the definition of 'Coast Guard'; see **[1306]**.

2 The Coast Guard Act 1978 s 121 (1) (i).

3 Ie the Coast Guard Act 1978 s 121 (1) (i).

4 The Coast Guard Act 1978 s 121 (1) (ii).

5 The Coast Guard Act 1978 s 121 (2).

6 The Coast Guard Act 1978 s 121 (3) (i).

7 The Coast Guard Act 1978 s 121 (3) (ii).

8 Ie the Coast Guard Act 1978 s 121.

9 The Coast Guard Act 1978 s 121 (4).

[1345] Protection for acts of members of the Coast Guard In any suit or proceeding against any member of the Coast Guard for any act done by him in pursuance of a warrant or order of a competent authority, it shall be lawful for him to plead that such act was done by him under the authority of such warrant or order[1]. Any such plea may be proved by the production of the warrant or order directing the act, and if it is so proved, the member of the Coast Guard shall thereupon be discharged from liability in respect of the act so done by him, notwithstanding any defect in the jurisdiction of the authority which issued such warrant or order[2]. Notwithstanding anything contained in any other law for the time being in force, any legal proceeding (whether civil or criminal) which may lawfully be brought against any member of the Coast Guard for anything done or intended to be done under the powers conferred by, or in pursuance of any provision of the Coast Guard Act 1978 or the rules, shall be commenced within three months after the act complained of was committed and not otherwise, and notice in writing of such proceeding and of the cause thereof shall be given to the defendant or his superior officer at least one month before the commencement of such proceeding[3].

1 The Coast Guard Act 1978 s 122 (1)

2 The Coast Guard Act 1978 s 122 (2).

3 The Coast Guard Act 1978 s 122 (3).

C. Conditions of Service

[1346] Enrolment The persons to be enrolled to the Coast Guard, the mode of enrolment and the procedure for enrolment shall be such as may be prescribed[1]. Notwithstanding anything contained in the Coast Guard Act 1978 and the rules, every person who has, for a continuous period of three months, been in receipt of pay as a person enrolled under the aforesaid Act and borne on the rolls of the Coast Guard shall be deemed to have been duly enrolled[2].

1 The Coast Guard Act 1978 s 6 (1).

2 The Coast Guard Act 1978 s 6 (2).

[1347] Recruitment, liability for service and transfer of enrolled persons The Director General may recruit enrolled persons required for the service as per the recruitment rules prescribed for various categories of persons[1]. All enrolled persons are liable for service with any other Armed Force of the Union as may be directed by the Director-General. In selecting personnel for such service, preference shall be given to volunteers. If the requisite number of suitable volunteers is not forthcoming, persons may be transferred as considered necessary by the Director-General[2]. All enrolled persons are liable for service in any civil or other appointment whether in India or abroad as may be directed by the Director-General[3]. Enrolled persons shall be liable for transfer within the service[4]. The officer-in-charge BUVIK[5] shall be responsible for issuing transfer orders of enrolled persons and for keeping complete and up-to-date records of the whereabouts of all enrolled persons[6]. No enrolled person shall be prejudiced in his rank by being transferred to another ship, should there be no equivalent rank in the ship to which he was transferred. In such cases, the person shall be borne as additional[7].

1 The Coast Guard (Condition of Service) Rules 1986 r 11.

2 The Coast Guard (Condition of Service) Rules 1986 r 12 (1).

3 The Coast Guard (Condition of Service) Rules 1986 r 12 (2).

4 The Coast Guard (Condition of Service) Rules 1986 r 13 (1).

5 Ie Bureau of Naviks: The Coast Guard (Condition of Service) Rules 1986 r 2 (b).

6 The Coast Guard (Condition of Service) Rules 1986 r 13 (2).

7 The Coast Guard (Condition of Service) Rules 1986 r 13 (3).

[1348] Liability for service outside India Every member of the Coast Guard shall be liable to serve in any part of India as well as outside India[1].

1 The Coast Guard Act 1978 s 7.

[1349] Officers: liability for service All officers are liable for service with any other Armed Force of the Union as may be directed by the Government. In selecting officers for such service, preference may be given to volunteers, but if the requisite number of suitable volunteers, is not forthcoming, officers may be detailed as for any other appointment[1]. All officers are liable for service in any civil or other appointment whether in India or abroad as may be directed by the Central Government[2].

1 The Coast Guard (Condition of Service) Rules 1986 r 6 (1).

2 The Coast Guard (Condition of Service) Rules 1986 r 6 (2).

[1350] Oath of allegiance Every member of the Coast Guard shall, as soon as may be, after appointment or enrolment to the Coast Guard, make and subscribe before his Commanding Officer or other prescribed officer[1], an oath or affirmation in the prescribed form[2].

1 As to the meaning of 'prescribed officer' under the Coast Guard Act 1978 s 8 to administer oath or affirmation: any officer; see the Coast Guard (General) Rules 1986 r 29.

2 The Coast Guard Act 1978 s 8.

[1351] Oath or affirmation Every member of the Coast Guard shall make and subscribed an oath or affirmation in the following form[1]:

Form of Oath/Affirmation

> I,.........do swear in the name of God/solemnly affirm that I will bear true faith and allegiance to the Constitution of India as by law established and that I will as in duty bound, honestly and faithfully serve with Coast Guard and go wherever ordered, by air, land or sea and that I will observe all commands of the President of the Union of India and Commands of any officer set over me even to the peril of my life.

1 The Coast Guard (General) Rules 1986 r 31.

[1352] Tenure of service under the Coast Guard Act 1978 Every member of the Coast Guard shall hold office during the pleasure of the President[1].

1 The Coast Guard Act 1978 s 10.

[1353] Dismissal or removal by Central Government and by other officers Subject to the provisions of the Coast Guard Act 1978 and the rules: (i) the Central Government may dismiss or remove from service any member of the Coast Guard[1]; (ii) the Director-General or any Inspector-General may dismiss or remove from the Coast Guard any person other than an officer[2]; (iii) any prescribed officer not below the rank of a Deputy Inspector-General may dismiss or remove from the Coast Guard any person under his command other than an officer or a subordinate officer[3].

1 The Coast Guard Act 1978 s 11 (a).

2 The Coast Guard Act 1978 s 11 (b).

3 The Coast Guard Act 1978 s 11 (c).

[1354] Dismissal, removal, discharge or release Authorities specified in column 1 shall be competent to authorise dismissal, removal, discharge or release of the members of the Coast Guard specified in column 2, on the grounds stated in the corresponding entries in column 3, in accordance with the procedure specified in column 4 of the Table[1]. Any power conferred by the Coast Guard (General) Rules 1986 on any of the aforesaid authorities may also be exercised by any other authority superior to it[2].

Competent Authority	Member of the Coast Guard	Grounds on which service can be terminated	Procedure for termination of service
1	2	3	4
Central Government	officers	i. Misconduct	As per procedure prescribed under the Coast Guard (General) Rules 1986 r 0
		ii. Unsuitability	-do-
		iii. Unsatisfactory progress in training	The Coast Guard (General) Rules 1986 r 24.
		iv. Furnishing false/wrong information at the time of recruitment	The Coast Guard (General) Rules 1986 r 25.
		v. Unfitness on medical grounds	The Coast Guard (General) Rules 1986 r 26.
		vi. On own request	The Coast Guard (General) Rules 1986 r 27.
Deputy Director General	Subordinate Officers and sailors	i. Misconduct	The Coast Guard (General) Rules 1986 r 23.
		ii. Unsuitability	-do-
		iii. Unsatisfactory progress in training	The Coast Guard (General) Rules 1986 r 24.
		iv. Furnishing false/wrong information at the time of recruitment	The Coast Guard (General) Rules 1986 r 25.
		v. Unfitness on medical grounds	The Coast Guard (General) Rules 1986 r 26.
		vi. On own request	The Coast Guard (General) Rules 1986 r 27.

1 The Coast Guard (General) Rules 1986 r 21 (1).

2 The Coast Guard (General) Rules 1986 r 21(2).

[1355] Procedure for dismissal/removal of officers When it is proposed to dismiss/remove an officer[1] under the certain provision of the Coast Guard Act 1978[2], he shall be given an opportunity to show cause in the manner specified in the following provision[3]. However, the aforesaid provision shall not apply (i) where the officer is dismissed/removed from the service on the grounds of misconduct which has led to his conviction by the criminal court[4]; and (ii) where the Central Government is satisfied that, for reasons to be recorded, it is not expedient or reasonably practicable to give the officer an opportunity of showing cause[5]. When after considering the reports of the officer's misconduct, the Director-General is satisfied that the trial of the officer by a Coast Guard Court[6] is not expedient or not practicable and is of the opinion that the further retention of the officer in the service is not desirable, the Director-General shall so inform the officer together with all the reports adverse to him, and he shall be called upon to submit in writing his explanation and defence[7]. However, the Director

General may, with the prior approval of the Central Government, withhold from disclosure any such reports, or portion thereof, if its disclosure is not in the interest of the security of the State[8].

In the event of the explanation of the officer being considered unsatisfactory by the Director General, or when so directed by the Central Government, the case shall be submitted to the Government with the officer's defence and the recommendations of the Director General as to the termination of officer's service in the manner specified in certain provisions of the Coast Guard (General) Rules 1986[9]. Where, upon the conviction of an officer by a criminal court[10], the Central Government or the Director General considers that the conduct of the officer which has led to his conviction renders his further retention in the service undesirable, a certified copy of the judgement of the criminal court convicting him shall be submitted to the Central Government with the recommendations of the Director General as to termination of the Officer's service in the manner specified in the following provisions of the Coast Guard (General) Rules 1986[11]. When submitting a case to the Central Government under the aforesaid provisions[12], the Director General shall make his recommendation whether the officer's service should be terminated and if so, whether the officer should be: (i) dismissed from the service[13]; or (ii) removed from the service[14]. The Central Government, after considering the reports and the officer's defence, if any, or the judgement of the criminal court, as the case may be, and the recommendation of the Director General, may dismiss or remove the officer from the service[15].

When the Director General is satisfied that an officer is unfit to be retained in the service on the grounds of unsuitability, he may, after giving the officer an opportunity to explain his case, recommend to the Central Government that the officer's service be terminated. The Director General shall also forward to the Central Government the reasons for his recommendations and the record of service of the officer[16]. However, where in the interest of security of the State it would be inexpedient to give the officer an opportunity to explain his case, it shall be lawful for the Central Government to pass an order terminating the service of the officer without giving the officer an opportunity to explain his case[17]. The Central Government on receipt of the report under the aforesaid provision[18] may pass an order as it may deem fit for the dismissal or removal of the officer[19]. The Central Government may in suitable cases retire or remove, the officer with or without pension or gratuity[20].

1 As to the definition of 'officer'; see **[1320]**.

2 Ie the Coast Guard Act 1978 s 11.

3 The Coast Guard (General) Rules 1986 r 22 (1).

4 The Coast Guard (General) Rules 1986 r 22 (1) proviso (a).

5 The Coast Guard (General) Rules 1986 r 22 (1) proviso (b).

6 As to the definition of 'coast guard court'; see **[1307]**.

7 The Coast Guard (General) Rules 1986 r 22(2).

8 The Coast Guard (General) Rules 1986 r 22(2) proviso.

9 Ie the Coast Guard (General) Rules 1986 r 25 (5); the Coast Guard (General) Rules 1986 r 22 (3).

10 As to the definition of 'criminal court'; see **[1311]**.

11 Ie the Coast Guard (General) Rules 1986 r 25 (5); The Coast Guard (General) Rules 1986 r 22 (4).

12 Ie the Coast Guard (General) Rules 1986 r 22 (3) and (4).

13 The Coast Guard (General) Rules 1986 r 22 (5) (a).

14 The Coast Guard (General) Rules 1986 r 22 (5) (b).

15 The Coast Guard (General) Rules 1986 r 22 (6).

16 The Coast Guard (General) Rules 1986 r 22 (7).

17 The Coast Guard (General) Rules 1986 r 22 (7) proviso.

18 Ie the Coast Guard (General) Rules 1986 r 22 (7).

19 The Coast Guard (General) Rules 1986 r 22 (8).

20 The Coast Guard (General) Rules 1986 r 22 (9).

[1356] Procedure for dismissal/removal of enrolled persons Where the Commanding Officer[1] is satisfied that an enrolled person[2] is considered unsuitable to be retained in the service on the grounds of misconduct or unsuitability, he may make a recommendation to the Deputy Director General in the Coast Guard Headquarters for the dismissal/removal of such person from the Coast Guard[3]. In all cases of recommendation for dismissal/removal of a person, the Commanding Officer shall establish clearly the fact that the person has been given a suitable warning and sufficient time to improve. Documentary evidence to this effect shall accompany the recommendation[4]. Where, upon the conviction of an enrolled person by a criminal court[5], the Deputy Inspector General under whom the person is serving considers that the conduct of the person which has led to his conviction renders his further retention in the service undesirable, a certified copy of the judgement of the criminal court convicting him shall be submitted to the Deputy Director General in the Coast Guard Headquarters with recommendations of the Deputy Inspector General under whom the person is serving as to the termination of the person's service in the manner specified in the following provision[6]. The Deputy Director General in the Coast Guard Headquarters on receipt of a recommendation under the aforesaid provisions[7] may pass an order dismissing or removing the person concerned from the service[8]. The Deputy Director General in the Coast Guard Headquarters may in suitable cases retire or remove the person with or without pension or gratuity[9].

1 As to the definition of 'commanding officer'; see **[1310]**.

2 As to the definition of 'enrolled person'; see **[1314]**.

3 The Coast Guard (General) Rules 1986 r 23 (1).

4 The Coast Guard (General) Rules 1986 r 23 (2).

5 As to the definition of 'criminal court'; see **[1311]**.

6 Ie as specified in the Coast Guard (General) Rules 1986 r 23 (4); the Coast Guard (General) Rules 1986 r 23 (3).

7 Ie under the Coast Guard (General) Rules 1986 r 23 (1) or (3).

8 The Coast Guard (General) Rules 1986 r 23 (4).

9 The Coast Guard (General) Rules 1986 r 23 (5).

[1357] Procedure for discharge/release on grounds of unsatisfactory progress in training When it is proposed to discharge/release a member of the Coast Guard from the service on account of unsatisfactory progress in training, the Commanding Officer[1] of training establishment, where the person is undergoing training, shall make a recommendation to the Central Government, or the Deputy Director General in the Coast Guard Headquarters as the case may be for the discharge or release of the person[2]. In all cases of recommendations for discharge or release of a person, the Commanding Officer of the training establishment shall establish clearly the fact that the person has been given suitable warning and sufficient time to show progress, documentary evidence to this effect shall accompany the recommendation[3]. The Central Government or as the case may be the Deputy Director General in the Coast Guard Headquarters on receipt of recommendation under the aforesaid provision[4], may discharge or release the person concerned from the service[5].

1 As to the definition of 'commanding officer'; see **[1310]**.

2 The Coast Guard (General) Rules 1986 r 24 (1).

3 The Coast Guard (General) Rules 1986 r 24 (2).

4 Ie the Coast Guard (General) Rules 1986 r 24 (1).

5 The Coast Guard (General) Rules 1986 r 24 (3).

[1358] Procedure for discharge/release on grounds of furnishing false/incorrect information at the time of recruitment The Central Government or as the case may be, the Deputy Director General in the Coast Guard Headquarters may discharge or release a person subject to the Coast Guard Act 1978 on grounds of furnishing false/wrong information at the time of the recruitment of that person in the service. A show cause notice shall be issued to the individual before the person is discharged/released from the service[1].

1 The Coast Guard (General) Rules 1986 r 25.

[1359] Dismissal of deserter A person subject to the Coast Guard Act 1978[1] who being a deserter from service is not apprehended or does not surrender, shall be dismissed from service under the provisions of the aforesaid Act 1978[2], as follows: (1) after five years from the date of desertion in case where desertion is (i) with arms or lethal weapons[3], (ii) due to subversive or espionage activities[4], or (iii) committed in addition to any other offence[5]; (2) after three years from date of desertion in cases other than mentioned above[6].

1 As to the definition of 'person subject to the Coast Guard Act 1978'; see **[1330]**.

2 Ie the Coast Guard Act 1978 s 11; see **[1353]**.

3 The Coast Guard (General) Rules 1986 r 25A (a) (i).

4 The Coast Guard (General) Rules 1986 r 25A (a) (ii).

5 The Coast Guard (General) Rules 1986 r 25A (a) (iii).

6 Ie as mentioned in the Coast Guard (General) Rules 1986 r 25A (a) (i), (ii) and (iii); The Coast Guard (General) Rules 1986 r 25A (b).

[1360] Retirement/release/discharge on grounds of physical unfitness When a person subject to the Coast Guard Act 1978[1] is found to be permanently unfit for the Coast Guard service by a Medical Board constituted under the Regulations for the Medical Services of the Armed Forces, he may be retired, released, or discharged from the service in accordance with the procedure laid down in this provision[2]. The President of the Medical Board, shall immediately after the Medical Board has come to the conclusion that the person is permanently unfit for any form of Coast Guard service, issue a notice specifying the nature of the disease or disability he is suffering from and the finding of the Medical Board and also inform him that in view of the finding he may be retired, released or discharged from the service[3]. However, where in the opinion of the Medical Board the person is suffering from a mental disease and it is unsafe to communicate the nature of the disease or disability to the person, or the person is unfit to look after his interest, the nature of the disease or disability shall be communicated to the person's next of kin who shall have the right to petition under the following provison[4]. Such notice shall also specify that the person may within fifteen days of the date of receipt of the notice prefer a petition against the findings of the Medical Board to the President of the Medical Board[5]. If no petition is preferred within the time specified in the aforesaid provision[6], the person may be retired, released or discharged from the service, by an order to that effect made by the Central Government, in the case of the officers, and by the Deputy Director General in the Coast Guard Headquarters in the case of enrolled persons[7].

If a petition is preferred within the time specified the aforesaid provisions[8], the President, Medical Board shall refer it to an Appeal Medical Board, constituted under the Regulations for the Medical Services of the Armed Forces, for its decision on the petition. The findings of the Appeal Medical Board shall be final. The findings of the Medical Board together with the records concerning the case shall be forwarded to the Director General in the Coast Guard Headquarters. Depending on the findings of the Appeal Medical Board, the person may be retired, released or discharged from the service, by an order to that effect made by the Central Government, in the case of officers, and by the Deputy Director General in the Coast Guard Headquarters in the case of enrolled persons[9].

1 As to the meaning of 'person subject to the Coast Guard Act 1978'; see **[1330]**.

2 The Coast Guard (General) Rules 1986 r 26(1).

3 The Coast Guard (General) Rules 1986 r 26(2)

4 The Coast Guard (General) Rules 1986 r 26(2) proviso

5 The Coast Guard (General) Rules 1986 r 26(3).

6 Ie the Coast Guard (General) Rules 1986 r 26(3).

7 The Coast Guard (General) Rules 1986 r 26(4).

8 Ie the Coast Guard (General) Rules 1986 r 26(3).

9 The Coast Guard (General) Rules 1986 r 26(5).

[1361] Procedure for discharge/release or retirement on own request A member of the Coast Guard may, in exceptional cases, obtain his discharge, release or retirement from the service on extreme compassionate grounds, i.e. in cases where it is clear that undoubted material hardship will be caused to the member of the Coast Guard or his family members by his retention in the service[1]. The Central Government or the Deputy Director General may, having regard to the circumstances of any case, permit discharge, release or retirement of an officer from the service before attaining the age of retirement. The question of discharge, release or retirement shall be a matter within the discretion of the Central Government or Deputy Director General as the case may be[2]. The Deputy Director General in the Coast Guard Headquarters may discharge, release or retire a member of the Coast Guard other than on officer on compassionate grounds[3]. Application for discharge, release or retirement on compassionate grounds shall be forwarded by the Commanding Officer, through the Regional Commander, to Coast Guard Headquarters for further necessary action[4].

1 The Coast Guard (General) Rules 1986 r 27(1)

2 The Coast Guard (General) Rules 1986 r 27(2)

3 The Coast Guard (General) Rules 1986 r 27(3)

4 The Coast Guard (General) Rules 1986 r 27(4)

[1362] Resignation and withdrawal from the post No member of the Coast Guard shall be at liberty: (i) to resign his appointment during the term of his engagement[1]; or (ii) to withdraw himself from all or any of the duties of his appointment, except with the previous permission in writing of the prescribed authority[2].

1 The Coast Guard Act 1978 s 9 (a).

2 As to the meaning of 'prescribed authority' under the Coast Guard Act 1978 s 9 for resignation and withdrawal from the post: (i) The Central Government for the officers above the rank of Deputy Inspector General; (ii) The Director General in case of officers up to the rank of Deputy Inspector General in accordance with laid

down policy of Central Government; and (iii) The Deputy Director General in the Coast Guard Headquarters for enrolled persons; see the Coast Guard (General) Rules 1986 r 29. The Coast Guard Act 1978 s 9 (b).

[1363] Resignation procedure No person subject to the Coast Guard Act 1978[1] shall have a right to resign his appointment or withdraw himself from the duties of his appointment. But in this regard, he may submit an application through proper channel to the Deputy Director General or the Director General at Coast Guard Headquarters or to the Central Government, as the case may be. He shall not be relieved of his duties until the Central Government or the authority empowered by the Central Government has accepted his resignation[2]. A member of the Coast Guard before his application to resign being accepted by the prescribed authority may apply for withdrawal of his application. The Central Government or the authority empowered by Central Government may at its discretion, grant withdrawal of such application[3].

1 As to the meaning of 'person subject to the Coast Guard Act 1978'; see **[1330]**.

2 The Coast Guard (General) Rules 1986 r 27A (1).

3 The Coast Guard (General) Rules 1986 r 27A (2).

[1364] Retirement Retirement age for officers holding a rank higher than that of a Commandant shall be 60 years and for officers of other ranks it shall be 57 years[1]. Retirement age of enrolled persons shall be 57 years[2].

1 The Coast Guard (General) Rules 1986 r 20 (1).

2 The Coast Guard (General) Rules 1986 r 20 (1).

[1365] Certificate of termination of service An enrolled person who retires, or is discharged, released, removed or dismissed from the Coast Guard or permitted to resign, shall be furnished by the officer, to whose command he is subject, with a certificate in the language which is the mother tongue of such person and also in Hindi or English language setting forth: (i) the authority terminating his service[1]; (ii) the reasons for such termination[2]; and (iii) the full period of his service in the Coast Guard[3].

1 The Coast Guard Act 1978 s 12 (a).

2 The Coast Guard Act 1978 s 12 (b).

3 The Coast Guard Act 1978 s 12 (c).

[1366] Discharge Certificate A certificate furnished under the provisions of the Coast Guard Act 1978[1] shall be called Discharge Certificate[2]. A discharge certificate may be delivered in person, or on behalf of the commanding officer to the enrolled person who retires, or is discharged, released, removed or dismissed from the Coast Guard, or is permitted to resign, by registered post[3].

1 Ie the Coast Guard Act 1978 s 12.

2 The Coast Guard (General) Rules 1986 r 27B (1)

3 The Coast Guard (General) Rules 1986 r 27B (2)

[1367] Date from which retirement, dismissal, removal, resignation, discharge or release otherwise than by sentence of a Coast Guard Court or under the Coast Guard Act 1978 s 57 takes effect The retirement, dismissal, removal, resignation, discharge or release of a person subject to the Coast Guard Act 1978[1] shall take effect from the date specified in the order for such retirement, dismissal, removal, resignation, discharge or release[2]. Such date shall not be retrospective[3].

1 As to the meaning of 'person subject to the Coast Guard Act 1978'; see **[1330]**.

2 The Coast Guard (General) Rules 1986 r 28 (1).

3 The Coast Guard (General) Rules 1986 r 28 (2).

[1368] Restrictions respecting right to form association, freedom of speech, etc. No member of the Coast Guard shall, without the previous sanction in writing of the Central Government or of the prescribed authority[1]: (i) be a member of, or be associated in any way with, any trade union, labour union, or political association[2]; or (ii) be a member of, or be associated in any way with, any society, institution, association or organisation that is not recognised as part of the Coast Guard or is not of a purely social, recreational or religious nature[3] ; or (iii) communicate with the press or publish or cause to be published any book, letter or other document except where such communication or publication is in the bona fide discharge of his duties or is of a purely literary, artistic or scientific character or is of a prescribed nature[4]. If any question arises whether any society, institution, association or organisation is of a purely social, recreational or religious nature under certain provisions of the Coast Guard Act 1978[5], the decision of the Central Government thereon shall be final[6]. No member of the Coast Guard shall participate in, or address, any meeting or take part in any demonstration organised by any body of persons for any political purposes or for such other purposes as may be specified in this behalf by the Central Government[7].

1 As to the meaning of 'prescribed authority' under the Coast Guard Act 1978 s 13 (1) for granting previous sanction to form association, etc., under the aforesaid Act s 13 (1) (a), (b) and (c): (i) The Director General for officers; and (ii) The Deputy Director General in the Coast Guard HQs for enrolled persons; see the Coast Guard (General) Rules 1986 r 29.

2 The Coast Guard Act 1978 s 13 (1) (a).

3 The Coast Guard Act 1978 s 13 (1) (b).

4 The Coast Guard Act 1978 s 13 (1) (c).

5 Ie the Coast Guard Act 1978 s 13 (1) (b).

6 The Coast Guard Act 1978 s 13 (1) explanation.

7 The Coast Guard Act 1978 s 13 (2).

D. Service Privileges

[1369] Immunity from attachment The arms, clothes, equipment, accoutrements or necessaries of any person in the Coast Guard service, while subject to the Coast Guard Act 1978, shall not be seized, nor shall the pay and allowances or any part thereof of such person be attached under any process or direction issued, or by the authority of, any court or public servant in respect of any claim, decree or order enforceable against him[1].

1 The Coast Guard (Condition of Service) Rules 1986 r 48.

[1370] Immunity from arrest for debt No person in the Coast Guard Service, shall so long as he is subject to the Coast Guard Act 1978[1], be liable to be arrested for debt under any processor direction issued by, or by the authority of, any court or public servant[2]. If any such person is arrested in contravention of the aforesaid provisions[3], the court or public servant by whom or by whose authority such process or direction was issued shall on complaint by the person arrested or by his superior officers enquire into the case and if satisfied that the arrest was made in contravention to the aforesaid provisions shall make an order for immediate discharge of the person arrested and may award to the complainant the costs of the complaint to be recoverable in the same manner as if such costs were awarded to him by a decree against the person at whose instance such process or direction was issued[4]. No court fee shall be payable on a complaint made under the aforesaid provision[5] or for recovery of the costs that may be awarded under that provision[6].

1 As to the meaning of 'person subject to the Coast Guard Act 1978'; see **[1330]**.

2 The Coast Guard (Condition of Service) Rules 1986 r 49 (1).

3 Ie in contravention to the Coast Guard (Condition of Service) Rules 1986 r 49 (1).

4 Coast Guard (Condition of Service) Rules 1986 r 49 (2).

5 Ie the Coast Guard (Condition of Service) Rules 1986 r 49 (2).

6 The Coast Guard (Condition of Service) Rules 1986 r 49 (3).

[1371] Immunity of persons attending Coast Guard Court from arrest The presiding officer or other member of the Coast Guard Court, law officer, party to any proceedings before a Coast Guard Court or advocate or agent of such party, and witness acting in obedience to a summons to attend a Coast Guard Court, shall not, while proceeding to, attending of returning from a Coast Guard Court, be liable to arrest under any civil or revenue process[1]. If any such person is arrested under any such process, he may be discharged by order of the Coast Guard Court[2].

1 The Coast Guard (Condition of Service) Rules 1986 r 50 (1).

2 As to the definition of 'Coast Guard Court'; see **[1307]**; the Coast Guard (Condition of Service) Rules 1986 r 50 (1).

[1372] Priority for hearing of cases concerning persons in the Coast Guard Service On the presentation to any civil or criminal or revenue court, by a person subject to the Coast Guard Act 1978[1] of a certificate from the proper Coast Guard authority of leave of absence having been granted to him for the purpose of prosecuting or defending any suit in such court, the court shall, on the application of such person, arrange, so far as may be possible for the hearing and final disposal of such suit, or other proceeding within the period of the leave granted or applied for[2]. The certificate from the proper coast guard authority shall state the first and the last day of the leave granted or applied for and set forth a description of the case with respect to which the leave has been granted or applied for and shall be duly signed and authenticated by such authority[3]. No fee shall be payable to the court in respect of the presentation of any such certificate, or in respect of any application by or on behalf of any such person for priority for the hearing of his case and every such certificate shall be conclusive evidence of the correctness of the contents thereof[4]. Where the court is unable to arrange for the hearing and final disposal of the suit or other proceeding within the period of the leave granted or applied for as aforesaid, it shall record its reasons for having been unable to do so, and shall cause a copy thereof to be furnished to such person on his application without any payment whatever by him in respect either of the application for such copy or of the copy itself[5].

1 As to the meaning of 'person subject to the Coast Guard Act 1978'; see **[1330].**

2 The Coast Guard (Condition of Service) Rules 1986 r 51 (1).

3 The Coast Guard (Condition of Service) Rules 1986 r 51 (2).

4 The Coast Guard (Condition of Service) Rules 1986 r 51 (3).

5 The Coast Guard (Condition of Service) Rules 1986 r 51 (4).

[1373] Complaints to higher authorities If an officer[1] or an enrolled person[2] thinks that he has suffered any personal oppression, injustice, or other ill treatment or that he has been treated unjustly in any way or wishes to make a representation affecting his welfare or has any suggestion to make in connection with service, he shall bring it to the notice of his superior officer[3]. It shall be the duty of the superior officer to whom a representation has been given, to forward the same to the higher authorities for appropriate action[4]. Any other method of seeking redressal from the superior officer/authority save those mentioned in these provisions is forbidden[5].

1 As to the definition of 'officer'; see **[1320]**.

2 As to the definition of 'enrolled person'; see **[1314]**.

3 As to the definition of 'superior officer'; see **[1327]**; The Coast Guard (General) Rules 1986 r 32 (1).

4 The Coast Guard (General) Rules 1986 r 32 (2).

5 The Coast Guard (General) Rules 1986 r 32 (3).

[1374] To whom complaint shall be made If the complainant is a commanding officer[1] of the Coast Guard Ship[2], his complaint shall be in writing and shall be addressed to his immediate superior officer[3]. If the complainant is an officer[4] serving in one of the Coast Guard ships his complaint shall be made orally to the Commanding Officer to see him for that purpose. If the complainant is an officer, such request shall be made through the Executive Officer and if the complainant is a head of the department, a request shall be made direct to the Commanding Officer. If the complainant is an officer working in a particular department, the request shall be made in the first place to the head of the department[5]. If the complainant is an enrolled person[6], his complaint shall be made orally to the Commanding Officer. A request to see the Commanding Officer shall be made to the Executive Officer through the complainant's Divisional or Departmental Officer. An enrolled person detached from his ship or his establishment shall make his complaint to the officer in whose command he may be at that time[7].

1 As to the definition of 'commanding officer'; see **[1310]**.

2 As to the definition of 'ship'; see **[1324]**.

3 As to the definition of 'superior officer'; see **[1327]**; The Coast Guard (General) Rules 1986 r 33 (1).

4 As to the definition of 'officer'; see **[1320]**.

5 The Coast Guard (General) Rules 1986 r 33 (2).

6 As to the definition of 'enrolled person'; see **[1314]**.

7 The Coast Guard (General) Rules 1986 r 33 (3).

[1375] Rules to be observed by the complainant The complaint shall be confined to statement of facts on which the complaint is based and to the alleged consequences to the complainant himself[1]. Joint complaints by two or more persons are not allowed. Each individual shall make his own complaint[2]. It shall be an offence against good order and the Coast Guard discipline to make a complaint, either oral or written, which includes a statement of fact which is untrue to the knowledge of the complaint[3]. It shall be an offence against good order and the Coast Guard discipline to make a complaint in terms which comprise language or comments that are disrespectful or insubordinate or subversive or discipline, except in so far as such language or comments are necessary for an adequate statement of the facts[4].

1 The Coast Guard (General) Rules 1986 r 34 (1).

2 The Coast Guard (General) Rules 1986 r 34 (2).

3 The Coast Guard (General) Rules 1986 r 34 (3).

4 The Coast Guard (General) Rules 1986 r 34 (4).

4. OFFENCES

CONTENTS

PARA

[1376] Correspondence, etc., with offenders A person subject to the Coast Guard Act 1978[1], who: (a) treacherously holds correspondence with, or communicates intelligence to, an offender[2]; (b) wilfully fails to make known to the proper authorities any information he may have received from an offender[3]; (c) assists the offender in any manner[4]; or (d) having been captured by an offender, voluntarily serves with or aids him[5], shall, on conviction by a Coast Guard Court, be liable to suffer imprisonment for a term which may extend to seven years or such less punishment as mentioned in the Coast Guard Act[6]. For the purposes of this provision, the term 'offender' includes: (a) all armed mutineers, armed rebels, armed rioters, pirates and any person in arms against whom it is the duty of any person subject to the Coast Guard Act 1978 to take action[7]; and (b) any person or persons engaged in smuggling, unlawful exploration or exploitation or any other unlawful activity in the maritime zones of India[8].

1 As to the meaning of 'person subject to the Coast Guard Act 1978'; see **[1330]**.

2 The Coast Guard Act 1978 s 15 (a).

3 The Coast Guard Act 1978 s 15 (b).

4 The Coast Guard Act 1978 s 15 (c).

5 The Coast Guard Act 1978 s 15 (d).

6 Ie as mentioned in the Coast Guard Act 1978 s 53; The Coast Guard Act 1978 s 15.

7 The Coast Guard Act 1978 s 15 explanation (a).

8 The Coast Guard Act 1978 s 15 explanation (b).

[1377] Deserting post and neglect of duty A person subject to the Coast Guard Act 1978[1], who: (a) deserts his post[2]; (b) sleeps upon his watch[3]; (c) fails to perform, or negligently performs, the duty imposed on him[4]; or (d) wilfully conceals any words, practice or design tending to the hindrance of the Coast Guard[5]; shall, on conviction by a Coast Guard Court, be liable to suffer imprisonment for a term which may extend to two years or such less punishment as mentioned in the Coast Guard Act[6].

1 As to the meaning of 'person subject to the Coast Guard Act 1978'; see **[1330]**.

2 The Coast Guard Act 1978 s 16 (a).

3 The Coast Guard Act 1978 s 16 (b).

4 The Coast Guard Act 1978 s 16 (c).

5 The Coast Guard Act 1978 s 16 (d).

6 Ie as mentioned in the Coast Guard Act 1978 s 53; The Coast Guard Act 1978 s 16.

[1378] Mutiny Any person subject to the Coast Guard Act 1978[1] who commits any of the following offences, that is to say: (a) begins, incites, causes or conspires with any other person to cause any mutiny in the Coast Guard or in the military, naval or air forces of India or any forces co-operating therewith[2]; (b) joins in any such mutiny[3]; (c) being present at any such mutiny, does not use his utmost endeavours to suppress the same[4]; (d) knowing or having reason to believe in the existence of any such mutiny, or of any intention to mutiny or of any such conspiracy, does not, without delay, give information thereof to his Commanding Officer or other superior officer[5]; or (e) endeavours to seduce any person in the Coast Guard or in the military, naval or air forces of India or any forces co-operating therewith from his duty or allegiance to the Union[6]; shall, on conviction by a Coast Guard Court, be liable to suffer death or such less punishment as mentioned in the Coast Guard Act[7]. However, a sentence of death awarded under this provision shall not be carried out unless it is confirmed by the Central Government[8].

1 As to the meaning of 'person subject to the Coast Guard Act 1978'; see **[1330]**.

2 The Coast Guard Act 1978 s 17 (a).

3 The Coast Guard Act 1978 s 17 (b).

4 The Coast Guard Act 1978 s 17 (c).

5 The Coast Guard Act 1978 s 17 (d).

6 The Coast Guard Act 1978 s 17 (e).

7 Ie as mentioned in the Coast Guard Act 1978 s 53; The Coast Guard Act 1978 s 17.

8 The Coast Guard Act 1978 s 17 proviso.

[1379] Persons on board ship or aircraft seducing Coast Guard personnel from allegiance Any person not otherwise subject to the Coast Guard Act 1978 who, being on board any ship or aircraft belonging to or in the service of the Coast Guard endeavours to seduce any person subject to the aforesaid Act from his allegiance to the Constitution or loyalty to the State or duty to his superior officers[1] shall, on conviction by a Coast Guard Court, be liable to suffer imprisonment for a term which may extend to seven years or such less punishment as mentioned in the Coast Guard Act[2].

1 As to the definition of 'superior officer'; see **[1327]**.

2 Ie as mentioned in the Coast Guard Act 1978 s 53; The Coast Guard Act 1978 s 18.

[1380] Striking or threatening superior officers Any person subject to the Coast Guard Act 1978[1] who commits any of the following offences, that is to say: (a) uses criminal force[2] to or assaults his superior officer[3]; (b) uses threatening language to such officer[4]; (c) uses insubordinate language to such officer[5]; or (d) behaves with contempt to such officer[6], shall, on conviction by a Coast Guard Court, be liable to suffer imprisonment for a term which may extend to ten years or such less punishment as mentioned in the Coast Guard Act[7]. However, in the case of offences specified in certain provisions of the Coast Guard Act 1978[8], the imprisonment shall not exceed five years[9].

1 As to the meaning of 'person subject to the Coast Guard Act 1978'; see **[1330]**.

2 As to the definition of 'criminal force'; see the Indian Penal Code 1860 s 350.

3 As to the definition of 'superior officer'; see **[1327]**; The Coast Guard Act 1978 s 19 (a).

4 The Coast Guard Act 1978 s 19 (b).

5 The Coast Guard Act 1978 s 19 (c).

6 The Coast Guard Act 1978 s 19 (d).

7 Ie as mentioned in the Coast Guard Act 1978 s 53; The Coast Guard Act 1978 s 19.

8 Ie the Coast Guard Act 1978 s 19 (c) and (d).

9 The Coast Guard Act 1978 s 19 proviso.

[1381] Disobedience to superior officer Any person subject to the Coast Guard Act 1978[1] who disobeys in such manner as to show a wilful defiance of authority any lawful command given personally by his superior officer[2] in the execution of his office whether the same is given orally, or in writing or by signal or otherwise, shall, on conviction by a Coast Guard Court, be liable to suffer imprisonment for a term which may extend to fourteen years or such less punishment as is in the aforesaid Act mentioned[3]. Any person subject to the Coast Guard Act 1978 who disobeys any lawful command given by his superior officer, shall, on conviction by a Coast Guard Court, be liable to suffer imprisonment for a term which may extend to seven years or such less punishment as mentioned in the Coast Guard Act[4].

1 As to the meaning of 'person subject to the Coast Guard Act 1978'; see **[1330]**.

2 As to the definition of 'superior officer'; see **[1327]**.

3 Ie as mentioned in the Coast Guard Act 1978 s 53; The Coast Guard Act 1978 s 20 (1).

4 Ie as mentioned in the Coast Guard Act 1978 s 53; The Coast Guard Act 1978 s 20 (2).

[1382] Ill-treating subordinate Any person subject to the Coast Guard Act 1978[1] who uses criminal force[2] to or otherwise ill-treats any other person subject to the aforesaid Act, being his subordinate in rank or position, shall, on conviction by a Coast Guard Court, be liable to suffer imprisonment for a term which may extend to seven years or such less punishment as mentioned in the Coast Guard Act[3].

1 As to the meaning of 'person subject to the Coast Guard Act 1978'; see **[1330]**.

2 As to the definition of 'criminal force'; see the Indian Penal Code 1860 s 350.

3 Ie as mentioned in the Coast Guard Act 1978 s 53; The Coast Guard Act 1978 s 21.

[1383] Quarrelling, fighting and disorderly behaviour Any person subject to the Coast Guard Act 1978[1], who: (a) quarrels, fights with or strikes any other person, whether such person is or is not subject to the aforesaid Act[2]; (b) uses reproachful or provoking speeches or gestures tending to make a quarrel or disturbance[3]; or (c) behaves in a disorderly manner[3], shall, on conviction by a Coast Guard Court, be liable to suffer imprisonment for a term which may extend to two years or such less punishment as mentioned in the Coast Guard Act[4].

1 As to the meaning of 'person subject to the Coast Guard Act 1978'; see **[1330]**.

2 The Coast Guard Act 1978 s 22 (a).

3 The Coast Guard Act 1978 s 22 (b).

4 The Coast Guard Act 1978 s 22 (c).

5 Ie as mentioned in the Coast Guard Act 1978 s 53; The Coast Guard Act 1978 s 22.

[1384] Certain forms of disgraceful conduct Any person subject to the Coast Guard Act 1978[1] who commits any of the following offences, that is to say: (a) is guilty of any disgraceful conduct of a cruel, indecent or unnatural kind[2]; (b) malingers, or feigns, or produces disease or infirmity in himself or intentionally delays his cure or aggravates his disease or infirmity[3]; or (c) with intent to render himself or any other person unfit for service, voluntarily causes hurt to himself or that person[4], shall, on conviction by a Coast Guard Court, be liable to suffer imprisonment for a term which may extend to seven years or such less punishment as mentioned in the Coast Guard Act[5].

1 As to the meaning of 'person subject to the Coast Guard Act 1978'; see **[1330]**.

2 The Coast Guard Act 1978 s 23 (a).

3 The Coast Guard Act 1978 s 23 (b).

4 The Coast Guard Act 1978 s 23 (c).

5 Ie as mentioned in the Coast Guard Act 1978 s 53; The Coast Guard Act 1978 s 23.

[1385] Drunkenness Any person subject to the Coast Guard Act 1978[1], who is guilty of drunkenness shall, on conviction by a Coast Guard Court, be liable to suffer imprisonment for a term which may extend to six months or such less punishment as mentioned in the Coast Guard Act[2]. For the purposes of the aforesaid provision[3], a person shall be deemed to be guilty of drunkenness if, owing to the influence of alcohol or any drug whether alone or in combination with any other circumstances, he is unfit to be entrusted with his duty or with any duty which he may be called upon to perform or behaves in a disorderly manner or in a manner likely to bring discredit to the Coast Guard[4].

1 As to the meaning of 'person subject to the Coast Guard Act 1978'; see **[1330]**.

2 Ie as mentioned in the Coast Guard Act 1978 s 53; The Coast Guard Act 1978 s 24 (1).

3 Ie the Coast Guard Act 1978 s 24 (1).

4 The Coast Guard Act 1978 s 24 (2).

[1386] Desertion and aiding desertion Any person subject to the Coast Guard Act 1978[1], who absents himself from his ship or from the place where his duty requires him to be, with an intention of not returning to such ship or place, or who, at any time and under any circumstances when absent from his ship or place of duty does any act which shows that he has an intention of not returning to such ship or place is said to desert[2]. Every person who deserts or attempts to desert the Coast Guard shall, on conviction by a Coast Guard Court, be liable to suffer imprisonment for a term which may extend to seven years or such less punishment as mentioned in the Coast Guard Act[3] and in every such case he shall forfeit: (i) all pay, salvage, prize money and allowances that have been earned by him[4]; (ii) pension and gratuity, medals and decorations that have been granted to him[5]; and (iii) all clothes and effects which he may have left on board the ship or the place from which he deserted, unless the Tribunal by which he is tried or the Central Government or the Director-General otherwise directs[6]. For the purposes of this provision, all pay, salvage, prize money and allowances shall be deemed to have been earned by a person when such pay, salvage, prize money and allowances have become due but have not been paid to him[7]. Any person subject to the Coast Guard Act 1978, who knowingly harbours any such deserter, shall, on conviction by a Coast Guard Court, be liable to suffer imprisonment for a term which may extend to three years or such less punishment as mentioned in the Coast Guard Act[8].

1 As to the meaning of 'person subject to the Coast Guard Act 1978'; see **[1330]**.

2 The Coast Guard Act 1978 s 25 (1).

3 Ie as mentioned in the Coast Guard Act 1978 s 53.

4 The Coast Guard Act 1978 s 25 (2) (a).

5 The Coast Guard Act 1978 s 25 (2) (b).

6 The Coast Guard Act 1978 s 25 (2) (c).

7 The Coast Guard Act 1978 s 25 (2) explanation.

8 Ie as mentioned in the Coast Guard Act 1978 s 53; The Coast Guard Act 1978 s 25 (3).

[1387] Breaking out of ship and absence without leave Any person subject to the Coast Guard Act 1978[1], who without being guilty of desertion improperly leaves his ship or place of duty or is absent without leave shall, on conviction by a Coast Guard Court, be liable to suffer imprisonment for a term which may extend to two years or such less punishment as mentioned in the Coast Guard Act[2], and shall also be punished by such mulcts of pay and allowances as may be prescribed[3].

1 As to the meaning of 'person subject to the Coast Guard Act 1978'; see **[1330]**.

2 Ie as mentioned in the Coast Guard Act 1978 s 53.

3 The Coast Guard Act 1978 s 26.

[1388] Losing ship or aircraft Any person subject to the Coast Guard Act 1978[1], who wilfully loses, strands or hazards or suffers to be lost, stranded or hazarded any ship belonging to or in the service of the Coast Guard, or loses or suffers to be lost any aircraft belonging to or in the service of the Coast Guard shall, on conviction by a Coast Guard Court, be liable to suffer imprisonment for a term which may extend to seven years or such less punishment as mentioned in the Coast Guard Act[2]. Any person subject to the Coast Guard Act 1978, who negligently or by any default loses, strands or hazards or suffers to be lost, stranded or hazarded any ship belonging to or in the service of the Coast Guard, or loses or suffers to be lost any aircraft belonging to or in the service of the Coast Guard shall, on conviction by a Coast Guard Court, be liable to suffer imprisonment for a term which may extend to two years or such less punishment as mentioned in the Coast Guard Act [3].

1 As to the meaning of 'person subject to the Coast Guard Act 1978'; see **[1330]**.

2 Ie as mentioned in the Coast Guard Act 1978 s 53; The Coast Guard Act 1978 s 27 (1).

3 Ie as mentioned in the Coast Guard Act 1978 s 53; The Coast Guard Act 1978 s 27 (2).

[1389] Dangerous unauthorised flying Any person subject to the Coast Guard Act 1978[1], who is guilty of any act or neglect in flying or in the use of any aircraft belonging to or in the service of the Coast Guard, or in relation to any such aircraft or aircraft material, which causes or is likely to cause loss of life or bodily injury to any person shall, on conviction by a Coast Guard Court: (a) if he acts wilfully or with wilful neglect, be liable to suffer imprisonment for a term which may extend to seven years or such less punishment as mentioned in the Coast Guard Act[2]; and (b) in any other case, be liable to suffer imprisonment for a term which may extend to two years or such less punishment as mentioned in the Coast Guard Act[3].

1 As to the meaning of 'person subject to the Coast Guard Act 1978'; see **[1330]**.

2 Ie as mentioned in the Coast Guard Act 1978 s 53; The Coast Guard Act 1978 s 28 (a).

3 Ie as mentioned in the Coast Guard Act 1978 s 53; The Coast Guard Act 1978 s 28 (b).

[1390] Inaccurate certificate Any person subject to the Coast Guard Act 1978[1], who signs any certificate in relation to an aircraft belonging to or in the service of the Coast Guard or to any, material thereof without ensuring its accuracy shall, on conviction by a Coast Guard Court, be liable to suffer imprisonment for a term which may extend to two years or such less punishment as mentioned in the Coast Guard Act[2].

1 As to the meaning of 'person subject to the Coast Guard Act 1978'; see **[1330]**.

2 Ie as mentioned in the Coast Guard Act 1978 s 53; The Coast Guard Act 1978 s 29.

[1391] Low flying and annoyance by flying Any person subject to the Coast Guard Act 1978[1], being the pilot of an aircraft belonging to or in the service of the Coast Guard, who: (a) flies it at a height lower than the minimum height authorised by his commanding officer except while taking off or landing[2]; or (b) flies it so as to cause or likely to cause unnecessary annoyance to any person[3], shall, on conviction by a Coast Guard Court, be liable to suffer imprisonment for a term which may extend to two years or such less punishment as mentioned in the Coast Guard Act[4].

1 As to the meaning of 'person subject to the Coast Guard Act 1978'; see **[1330]**.

2 The Coast Guard Act 1978 s 30 (a).

3 The Coast Guard Act 1978 s 30 (b).

4 Ie as mentioned in the Coast Guard Act 1978 s 53; The Coast Guard Act 1978 s 30.

[1392] Disobedience of lawful command of captain of an aircraft Any person subject to the Coast Guard Act 1978[1], who while he is in an aircraft belonging to or in the service of the Coast Guard, disobeys any lawful command given by the captain of the aircraft whether such captain is subject to the aforesaid Act or not, in relation to all matters relating to flying or handling of the aircraft or affecting the safety thereof, shall, on conviction by a Coast Guard Court, be liable to suffer imprisonment for a term which may extend to seven years or such less punishment as mentioned in the Coast Guard Act[2].

1 As to the meaning of 'person subject to the Coast Guard Act 1978'; see **[1330]**.

2 Ie as mentioned in the Coast Guard Act 1978 s 53; The Coast Guard Act 1978 s 31.

[1393] False accusations Any person subject to the Coast Guard Act 1978[1], who commits any of the following offences, that is to say: (a) makes a false accusation against any person subject to the aforesaid Act, knowing or having reason to believe such accusation to be false[2]; or (b) in making a complaint against any person subject to the Coast Guard Act 1978 makes any statement affecting the character of such person, knowing or having reason to believe such statement to be false or knowingly or wilfully suppresses any material facts[3], shall, on conviction by a Coast Guard Court, be liable to suffer imprisonment for a term which may extend to three years or such less punishment as mentioned in the Coast Guard Act[4].

1 As to the meaning of 'person subject to the Coast Guard Act 1978'; see **[1330]**.

2 The Coast Guard Act 1978 s 32 (a).

3 The Coast Guard Act 1978 s 32 (b).

4 Ie as mentioned in the Coast Guard Act 1978 s 53; The Coast Guard Act 1978 s 32.

[1394] Falsifying official documents and false declarations Any person subject to the Coast Guard Act 1978[1], who commits any of the following offences: (a) in any report, return, list, certificate, book or other document made or signed by him, or of the contents of which it is his duty to ascertain the accuracy, knowingly make, or is privy to the making of, any false or fraudulent statement[2]; (b) in any document of the description mentioned in the aforesaid provision[3] knowingly makes, or is privy to the making of, any omission, with intent to defraud[4]; (c) knowingly and with intent to injure any person, or knowingly and with intent to defraud, suppresses, defaces, alters or makes away with any document which it is his duty to preserve or produce[5]; (d) where it is his official duty to make a declaration respecting any matter, knowingly makes a false declaration[6]; or (e) obtains for himself, or for any other person, any pension, allowance or other advantage or privilege by a statement which is false, and which he either knows or believes to be false, or does not believe to be true, or by making or using a false entry in any book or record, or by making any document containing a false statement, or by omitting to make a true entry or document containing a true statement[7], shall, on conviction by a Coast Guard Court, be liable to suffer imprisonment for a term which may extend to 10 years or such less punishment as mentioned in the Coast Guard Act[8].

1 As to the meaning of 'person subject to the Coast Guard Act 1978'; see **[1330]**.

2 The Coast Guard Act 1978 s 33 (a).

3 Ie the Coast Guard Act 1978 s 33 (a).

4 The Coast Guard Act 1978 s 33 (b).

5 The Coast Guard Act 1978 s 33 (c).

6 The Coast Guard Act 1978 s 33 (d).

7 The Coast Guard Act 1978 s 33 (e).

8 Ie as mentioned in the Coast Guard Act 1978 s 53; The Coast Guard Act 1978 s 33.

[1395] Offences in respect of property Any person subject to the Coast Guard Act 1978[1], who commits any of the following offences: (a) commits theft of any property belonging to the Government or to any Coast Guard mess, or institution, or to any person subject to the aforesaid Act[2]; (b) dishonestly misappropriates or converts to his own use any such property[3]; (c) commits criminal breach of trust in respect of any such property[4]; (d) dishonestly receives or retains any such property in respect of which any of the offences under the Coast Guard Act 1978[5] has been committed, knowing or having reason to believe the commission of such offence[6]; (e) wilfully destroys or damages any property of the Government entrusted to him[7]; or (f) does any other thing with intent to defraud or to cause wrongful gain to one person or wrongful loss to another person[8], shall, on conviction by a Coast Guard Court, be liable to suffer imprisonment for a term which may extend to 10 years or such less punishment as mentioned in the Coast Guard Act[9].

1 As to the meaning of 'person subject to the Coast Guard Act 1978'; see **[1330]**.

2 The Coast Guard Act 1978 s 34 (a).

3 The Coast Guard Act 1978 s 34 (b).

4 The Coast Guard Act 1978 s 34 (c).

5 Ie the Coast Guard Act 1978 s 34 (a), (b) and (c).

6 The Coast Guard Act 1978 s 34 (d).

7 The Coast Guard Act 1978 s 34 (e).

8 The Coast Guard Act 1978 s 34 (f).

9 Ie as mentioned in the Coast Guard Act 1978 s 53; The Coast Guard Act 1978 s 34.

[1396] Damage to property Any person subject to the Coast Guard Act 1978[1], who commits any act which causes damage to, or destruction of, any property of the Government shall, on conviction by a Coast Guard Court, be liable to suffer imprisonment for a term which may extend to seven years or such less punishment as mentioned in the Coast Guard Act[2].

1 As to the meaning of 'person subject to the Coast Guard Act 1978'; see **[1330]**.

2 Ie as mentioned in the Coast Guard Act 1978 s 53; The Coast Guard Act 1978 s 35.

[1397] Taking unauthorised goods on board Every officer or subordinate officer in command of any ship belonging to or in the service of the Coast Guard who receives on board or permits to be received on board such ship, any goods or merchandise whatsoever other than for the sole use of the ship or persons belonging to the ship, except goods and merchandise on board any ship which may be shipwrecked or in imminent danger either on the high seas or in some port, creek or harbour for the purpose of preserving them for their proper owners, or except such goods or merchandise as he may, at any time be ordered to take or receive on board by order of the Central Government or his superior officer[1], shall, on conviction by a Coast Guard Court, be liable to suffer dismissal from the Coast Guard or such less punishment as mentioned in the Coast Guard Act[2].

1 As to the definition of 'officer', 'subordinate officer', 'ship' and 'superior officer'; see **[1320]**, **[1326]**, **[1324]** and **[1327]** respectively.

2 Ie as mentioned in the Coast Guard Act 1978 s 53; The Coast Guard Act 1978 s 36.

[1398] Offences in respect of papers relating to vessel, craft or aircraft taken into custody All the papers, charter parties, bills of lading, passports and other documents that shall be taken, seized or found on board any vessel, craft or aircraft taken into custody by the Coast Guard shall be duly preserved and the Commanding Officer or skipper shall send the same to his immediate superior[1]. Every Commanding Officer or skipper who fails to send the documents as required under the aforesaid provision[2] shall, on conviction by a Coast Guard Court, be liable to suffer dismissal from the Coast Guard or such less punishment as mentioned in the Coast Guard Act[3].

1 As to the definition of 'commanding officer' and 'skipper'; see **[1310]** and **[1325]**. The Coast Guard Act 1978 s 37 (1).

2 Ie as required under the Coast Guard Act 1978 s 37 (1).

3 Ie as mentioned in the Coast Guard Act 1978 s 53; The Coast Guard Act 1978 s 37 (2).

[1399] Offences in respect of vessel, craft or aircraft taken into custody Any person subject to the Coast Guard Act 1978[1], who commits any of the following offences, that is to say: (a) takes out without proper authority from any vessel, craft or aircraft taken into custody, any money or goods[2]; (b) pillages, beats or ill-treats persons on board the said vessel, craft or aircraft[3]; or (c) breaks bulk on board any such vessel, craft or aircraft with intent dishonestly to misappropriate anything therein or belonging thereto[4] shall, on conviction by a Coast Guard Court, be liable to suffer imprisonment for a term which may extend to two years or such less punishment as mentioned in the Coast Guard Act[5].

1 As to the meaning of 'person subject to the Coast Guard Act 1978'; see **[1330]**.

2 The Coast Guard Act 1978 s 38 (a).

3 The Coast Guard Act 1978 s 38 (b).

4 The Coast Guard Act 1978 s 38 (c).

5 Ie as mentioned in the Coast Guard Act 1978 s 53; The Coast Guard Act 1978 s 38.

[1400] Unlawful taking of ransom Every commanding officer[1] or skipper[2] of a ship[3] who: (a) unlawfully agrees with any person for the ransoming of any vessel, craft, aircraft, goods or things taken into custody by the

Coast Guard[4]; or (b) in pursuance of any unlawful agreement for ransoming or otherwise by collusion actually quits or restores any vessel, craft, aircraft, goods or things taken into custody by the Coast Guard[5], shall, on conviction by a Coast Guard Court[6], be liable to suffer imprisonment for a term which may extend to two years or such less punishment as mentioned in the Coast Guard Act[7].

1 As to the definition of 'commanding officer'; see **[1310]**.

2 As to the definition of 'skipper'; see **[1325]**.

3 As to the definition of 'ship'; see **[1324]**.

4 The Coast Guard Act 1978 s 39 (a).

5 The Coast Guard Act 1978 s 39 (b).

6 As to the definition of 'Coast Guard Court'; see **[1307]**.

7 Ie as mentioned in the Coast Guard Act 1978 s 53; The Coast Guard Act 1978 s 39.

[1401] Offences relating to Coast Guard Courts Any person subject to the Coast Guard Act 1978[1], who commits any of the following offences: (a) being duly summoned or ordered to attend as a witness before a Coast Guard Court, wilfully or without reasonable excuse, makes default in attending[2]; (b) refuses to take an oath or make an affirmation legally required by a Coast Guard Court to be taken or made[3]; (c) refuses to produce or deliver any document in his power or control legally required by a Coast Guard Court to be produced or delivered by him[4]; (d) refuses, when a witness, to answer any question which he is by law bound to answer[5]; or (e) is guilty of contempt of a Coast Guard Court by using insulting or threatening language, or by causing any interruption or disturbance in the proceedings of such Court[6], shall, on conviction by a Coast Guard Court, be liable to suffer imprisonment for a term which may extend to three years or such less punishment as is in the Coast Guard Act 1978 mentioned[7].

1 As to the meaning of 'person subject to the Coast Guard Act 1978'; see **[1330]**.

2 As to the definition of 'coast guard court'; see **[1307]**.The Coast Guard Act 1978 s 40 (a).

3 The Coast Guard Act 1978 s 40 (b).

4 The Coast Guard Act 1978 s 40 (c).

5 The Coast Guard Act 1978 s 40 (d).

6 The Coast Guard Act 1978 s 40 (e).

7 Ie as mentioned in the Coast Guard Act 1978 s 53; The Coast Guard Act 1978 s 40.

[1402] Escape from custody Any person subject to the Coast Guard Act 1978[1], who, being in lawful custody, escapes or attempts to escape, shall, on conviction by a Coast Guard Court, be liable to suffer imprisonment for a term which may extend to three years or such less punishment as mentioned in the Coast Guard Act[2].

1 As to the meaning of 'person subject to the Coast Guard Act 1978'; see **[1330]**.

2 Ie as mentioned in the Coast Guard Act 1978 s 53; The Coast Guard Act 1978 s 41.

[1403] Violation of the Act, rules and orders Any person subject to the Coast Guard Act 1978[1], who neglects to obey, or contravenes any provision of the aforesaid Act or any rule or any order issued by any lawful authority under the Coast Guard Act 1978, shall, if no other punishment is provided in the aforesaid Act for such neglect or contravention, on conviction by a Coast Guard Court, be liable to suffer imprisonment for a term which may extend to two years or such less punishment as mentioned in the Coast Guard Act[2].

1 As to the meaning of 'person subject to the Coast Guard Act 1978'; see **[1330]**.

2 Ie as mentioned in the Coast Guard Act 1978 s 53; The Coast Guard Act 1978 s 42.

[1404] False answers on enrolment Any person having become subject to the Coast Guard Act 1978[1], who is discovered to have made at the time of enrolment, a wilfully false answer to any question set forth in the prescribed form of enrolment which has been put to him by the enrolling officer before whom he appears for the purpose of being enrolled, shall, on conviction by a Coast Guard Court, be liable to suffer imprisonment for a term which may extend to five years or such less punishment as mentioned in the Coast Guard Act[2].

1 As to the meaning of 'person subject to the Coast Guard Act 1978'; see **[1330]**.

2 Ie as mentioned in the Coast Guard Act 1978 s 53; The Coast Guard Act 1978 s 43.

[1405] Offences against good order and discipline Any person subject to the Coast Guard Act 1978[1] who is guilty of any act or omission or disorder or neglect, which, though not specified in the aforesaid Act, is prejudicial to good order and discipline of the Coast Guard shall, on conviction by a Coast Guard Court, be liable to suffer imprisonment for a term which may extend to three years or such less punishment as mentioned in the Coast Guard Act[2].

1 As to the meaning of 'person subject to the Coast Guard Act 1978'; see **[1330]**.

2 Ie as mentioned in the Coast Guard Act 1978 s 53; The Coast Guard Act 1978 s 44.

[1406] Attempt Any person subject to the Coast Guard Act 1978[1], who attempts to commit any of the offences specified in the provisions of the aforesaid Act[2] and in such attempt does any act towards the commission of the offence shall, on conviction by a Coast Guard Court, where no express provision is made by the Coast Guard Act 1978 for the punishment of such attempt, be liable: (a) if the offence attempted to be committed is punishable with death, to suffer imprisonment for a term which may extend to 14 years or such less punishment mentioned in the Coast Guard Act[3]; and (b) if the offence attempted to be committed is punishable with imprisonment, to suffer imprisonment for a term which may extend to one-half of the longest term provided for that offence or such less punishment as mentioned in the Coast Guard Act[4].

1 As to the meaning of 'person subject to the Coast Guard Act 1978'; see **[1330]**.

2 Ie as specified under the Coast Guard Act 1978 s 15 to 44 (both inclusive).

3 Ie as mentioned in the Coast Guard Act 1978 s 53; The Coast Guard Act 1978 s 45 (a).

4 Ie as mentioned in the Coast Guard Act 1978 s 53; The Coast Guard Act 1978 s 45 (b).

[1407] Abetment of offences that have been committed Any person subject to the Coast Guard Act 1978[1], who abets the commission of any of the offences specified in the provisions of the aforesaid Act[2], shall, on conviction by a Coast Guard Court, if the act abetted is committed in consequence of the abetment and no express provision is made by the Coast Guard Act 1978 for the punishment of such abetment, be liable to suffer imprisonment provided for that offence or such less punishment as mentioned in the Coast Guard Act[3].

1 As to the meaning of 'person subject to the Coast Guard Act 1978'; see **[1330]**.

2 Ie as specified under the Coast Guard Act 1978 s 15 to 44 (both inclusive).

3 Ie as mentioned in the Coast Guard Act 1978 s 53; The Coast Guard Act 1978 s 46.

[1408] Abetment of offence punishable with death and not committed Any person subject to the Coast Guard Act 1978[1], who abets the commission of an offence punishable with death under the Coast Guard Act

1978[2] shall, on conviction by a Coast Guard Court, if that offence has not been committed in consequence of that abetment, be liable to suffer imprisonment for a term which may extend to 14 years or such less punishment as mentioned in the Coast Guard Act[3].

1 As to the meaning of 'person subject to the Coast Guard Act 1978'; see **[1330]**.

2 Ie the Coast Guard Act 1978 s 17; see **[1378]**.

3 Ie as mentioned in the Coast Guard Act 1978 s 53; The Coast Guard Act 1978 s 47.

[1409] Abetment of offences punishable with imprisonment and not committed Any person subject to the Coast Guard Act 1978[1], who abets the commission of any of the offences specified in the Coast Guard Act 1978[2] and punishable with imprisonment shall, on conviction by a Coast Guard Court, if that offence has not been committed in consequence of the abetment, and no express provision is made by the aforesaid Act for the punishment of such abetment, be liable to suffer imprisonment for a term which may extend to one-half of the longest term provided for that offence or such less punishment as mentioned in the Coast Guard Act[3].

1 As to the meaning of 'person subject to the Coast Guard Act 1978'; see **[1330]**.

2 Ie specified in the Coast Guard Act 1978 s 15 to 44 (both inclusive).

3 Ie as mentioned in the Coast Guard Act 1978 s 53; The Coast Guard Act 1978 s 48.

[1410] Civil offences Subject to the provisions of the Coast Guard Act 1978 s 50, any person subject to the Coast Guard Act 1978[1] who at any place in, or beyond, India commits any civil offence shall be deemed to be guilty of an offence against the aforesaid Act and, if charged under this provision shall be liable to be tried, by a Coast Guard Court[2], and, on conviction, be punishable as follows: (a) if the offence is one which would be punishable under any law in force in India with death, he shall be liable to suffer any punishment, assigned for the offence, by the aforesaid law or such less punishment as mentioned in the Coast Guard Act[3]; and (b) in any other case, he shall be liable to suffer any punishment, assigned for the offence by the law in force in India, or imprisonment for a term which may extend to seven years, or such less punishment as mentioned in the Coast Guard Act[4].

1 As to the meaning of 'person subject to the Coast Guard Act 1978'; see **[1330]**.

2 As to the definition of 'coast guard court; see **[1307]**.

3 Ie as mentioned in the Coast Guard Act 1978 s 53; The Coast Guard Act 1978 s 49 (a).

4 Ie as mentioned in the Coast Guard Act 1978 s 53; The Coast Guard Act 1978 s 49 (b).

[1411] Civil offences not triable by a Coast Guard Court A person subject to the Coast Guard Act 1978[1], who commits an offence of murder or of culpable homicide not amounting to murder against, or of rape in relation to, a person not subject to the aforesaid Act shall not be deemed to be guilty of an offence against the Coast Guard Act 1978 and shall not be tried by a Coast Guard Court[2], unless he commits any of the said offences: (a) at any place outside India[3]; or (b) at any place specified by the Central Government by notification in this behalf[4].

1 As to the meaning of 'person subject to the Coast Guard Act 1978'; see **[1330]**.

2 As to the definition of 'coast guard court'; see **[1307]**.

3 The Coast Guard Act 1978 s 50 (a).

4 The Coast Guard Act 1978 s 50 (a).

[1412] Period of limitation for trial of offences under the Coast Guard Act 1978 and Trial of a person who ceases to be subject to the Act No person unless he is an offender who has avoided apprehension or escaped arrest or committed the offence of desertion or of giving false entry on enrolment or the offence of mutiny shall be tried or punished in pursuance of the Coast Guard Act 1978 for any offence committed by him unless such trial commences within a period of three years from the commission of such offence and such period shall commence: (i) on the date of the offence[1]; (ii) where the commission of the offence was not known to the person aggrieved by the offence or to the authority competent to initiate action, the first day on which such offence comes to the knowledge of such person or authority[2]; or (iii) where it is not known by whom the offence was committed, on the first day on which the identity of the offender becomes known to the person aggrieved by the offence or to the authority competent to initiate action, whichever is earlier[3]. For the purposes of this provision, in the computation of the period of time mentioned in this provision, any time spent by such person, as a prisoner of war in the enemy territory, or in evading arrest, after the commission of the offence, shall be excluded[4]. Where a proceeding in respect of an offence has been stayed by an injunction or an order of a court, then, in computing the period of limitation under this section, the period of the continuance of the injunction or order, the day on which it was issued or made, and the day on which it was withdrawn shall be excluded[5]. No trial for an offence of desertion or of giving false entry on enrolment shall be commenced if the person in question, not being an officer[6], has subsequent to the commission of the offence served continuously in an exemplary manner for not less than three years in the Coast Guard[7].

Where an offence under the Coast Guard Act 1978 had been committed by any person while subject to the aforesaid Act 1978[8], and such person has since the commission of the offence ceased to be subject to the Coast Guard Act 1978, he may be taken into and kept in the Coast Guard custody, and tried and punished for such offence as if he had continued to be so subject[9]. No such person shall be tried for an offence, unless his trial commences within a period of two years after he has ceased to be subject to the Coast Guard Act 1978; and in computing such period, the time during which such person has avoided arrest by absconding or concealing himself or where a proceeding in respect of an offence has been stayed by an injunction or order, the period of the continuance of the injunction or order, the day on which it was issued or made and the day on which it was withdrawn, shall be excluded[10]. However, nothing contained in the aforesaid provision[11] shall apply to the trial of any such person for an offence of mutiny or desertion[12].

1 The Coast Guard Act 1978 s 51(1) (a).

2 The Coast Guard Act 1978 s 51(1) (b).

3 The Coast Guard Act 1978 s 51(1) (c).

4 The Coast Guard Act 1978 s 51(1) explanation.

5 The Coast Guard Act 1978 s 51(1A).

6 As to the definition of the term 'officer'; see **[1320]**.

7 The Coast Guard Act 1978 s 51 (2).

8 As to the meaning of 'person subject to the Coast Guard Act 1978'; see **[1330]**.

9 The Coast Guard Act 1978 s 52 (1).

10 The Coast Guard Act 1978 s 52 (2).

11 Ie the Coast Guard Act 1978 s 52 (2).

12 As to the offences of 'mutiny' and 'desertion'; see **[1378]** and **[1377]**; The Coast Guard Act 1978 s 52 (2) proviso.

[1413] Offences by witnesses and others When a court[1] is of the opinion that there is ground for inquiring into any offence specified in the Coast Guard Act 1978[2] and committed before it or brought to its notice in the course of proceedings, which would if done by a person subject to the aforesaid Act, have constituted such an offence, such court may proceed as follows: (i) If the person who appears to have committed the offence is subject to the Act, the court may bring his conduct to the notice of his commanding officer[3]; (ii) If the person who appears to have done the act is amenable to army, naval, air force or any other armed forces laws, may bring his conduct to the notice of the proper army, naval, air force, or the concerned other armed force authority[4]; and (iii) In other cases, the officer who summoned the witness to appear or the presiding officer may forward a written complaint to the nearest Judicial Magistrate of the First Class or Metropolitan Judicial Magistrate having jurisdiction. In the case of acts which would if done by a person subject to the Coast Guard Act have constituted an offence under s 40 (e) of the Act, the coast guard court after making preliminary inquiry that may be necessary may send the case to the nearest Judicial Magistrate of the First Class having jurisdiction for inquiry or trial under the Code of Criminal Procedure 1973 s 340[5].

1 Ie the Coast Guard Court; see **[1307]**.
2 Ie offences relating to the coast guard courts and specified in the Coast Guard Act 1978 s 40; see **[1401]**.
3 The Coast Guard (Discipline) Rules 1983 r 124 (a).
4 The Coast Guard (Discipline) Rules 1983 r 124 (b).
5 The Coast Guard (Discipline) Rules 1983 r 124 (c).

5. ARREST AND PROCEEDINGS BEFORE TRIAL, CHIEF LAW OFFICER, LEGAL ADVICE

CONTENTS

PARA

A. Arrest and Custody

A. Arrest and Custody

[1414] Custody of offenders Any person subject to the Coast Guard Act 1978[1], who is charged with an offence[2], may be taken into coast guard custody[3], under the order of any superior officer[4]. An officer[5] may order into coast guard custody any other officer engaged in a quarrel, affray or disorder, though such other officer may be of a higher rank[6].

1 As to the meaning of 'person subject to the Coast Guard Act 1978'; see **[1330]**.

2 As to the definition of 'offence'; see **[1319]**.

3 As to the definition of 'coast guard custody'; see **[1308]**.

4 As to the definition of 'superior officer'; see **[1327]**; the Coast Guard Act 1978 s 59 (1).

5 As to the definition of 'officer'; see **[1320]**.

6 The Coast Guard Act 1978 s 59 (2).

[1415] Forms of arrest Arrest may be either open arrest or close arrest[1]. An arrest, unless specified, shall mean an open arrest[2]. An order imposing arrest may be communicated to the person to be arrested either orally or in writing[3].

1 The Coast Guard (Discipline) Rules 1983 r 5 (1).

2 The Coast Guard (Discipline) Rules 1983 r 5 (2).

3 The Coast Guard (Discipline) Rules 1983 r 5 (3).

[1416] Authority to order arrest No person subject to the Coast Guard Act 1978[1] shall be arrested on a charge under the aforesaid Act except under and in accordance with the orders of a superior officer[2] having power of command over him[3]. A person subject to the Coast Guard Act 1978 may be placed under arrest by any superior officer: (i) if he commits an offence against such superior officer[4], (ii) if he commits an offence in the view of superior officer[5], or (iii) If he is behaving in a disorderly manner and the said superior officer considers it necessary to place such a person under arrest with a view to stop such disorderly behaviour[6]. A superior officer effecting arrest under the aforesaid provisions[7] shall, as soon as possible, and in any case within 24 four hours of such arrest send a report to the commanding officer[8] of the arrested person and in case of the arrest of an officer of and above the rank of commandant, to his immediate superior officer[9].

1 As to the meaning of person subject to the Coast Guard Act 1978'; see **[1330]**.

2 As to the definition of 'superior officer'; see **[1327]**.

3 The Coast Guard (Discipline) Rules 1983 r 6 (1).

4 The Coast Guard (Discipline) Rules 1983 r 6 (2) (a).

5 The Coast Guard (Discipline) Rules 1983 r 6 (2) (b).

6 The Coast Guard (Discipline) Rules 1983 r 6 (2) (c).

7 Ie the Coast Guard (Discipline) Rules 1983 r 6 (2).

8 As to the definition of 'commanding officer'; see **[1310]**.

9 The Coast Guard (Discipline) Rules 1983 r 6 (3).

[1417] Arrest how imposed (A) Close Arrest: Close arrest in the case of sailors[1] and enrolled followers shall be imposed by informing the person to be arrested and ordering him to be marched to the place of confinement under an escort of person of similar or superior rank[2]. Where no such escort is available the person arrested shall be ordered to report himself immediately to the Coast Guard Police Officer or in his absence to the duty officer of his ship or station or other place of confinement[3]. Close arrest in the case of officers[4] and subordinate officers[5] shall be imposed by placing such officer or subordinate officer under the custody of another person of similar or superior rank and wherever considered necessary such officer, or subordinate officer may be confined under charge of a guard[6]. The person under arrest shall not leave his quarter or place of confinement without the permission of his commanding officer[7], or the superior officer designated by his commanding officer in this behalf[8].

(B) Open Arrest: Open arrest shall be imposed by informing the person to be arrested (whether he is an officer, subordinate officer, sailor or any other enrolled person) that he is under open arrest and that he shall confine himself within such limits as may be specified in this behalf by the commanding officer or the concerned superior officer effecting such arrest[9]. The commanding officer may, from time to time, vary the limits referred to in the aforesaid provision[10].

1 As to the definition of 'sailor'; see **[1323]**.

2 The Coast Guard (Discipline) Rules 1983 r 7 (1) (a).

3 The Coast Guard (Discipline) Rules 1983 r 7 (1) (b).

4 As to the definition of 'officer'; see **[1320]**.

5 As to the definition of 'subordinate officer'; see **[1326]**.

6 The Coast Guard (Discipline) Rules 1983 r 7 (2) (a).

7 As to the definition of 'commanding officer'; see **[1310]**.

8 The Coast Guard (Discipline) Rules 1983 r 7 (2) (b).

9 The Coast Guard (Discipline) Rules 1983 r 7 (3) (a).

10 The Coast Guard (Discipline) Rules 1983 r 7 (3) (b).

[1418] Investigation after arrest The charge made against any person subject to the Coast Guard Act 1978[1] taken into custody shall, without any delay, be investigated by the proper authority and as soon thereafter as may be, either proceeding shall be taken for the trial of such person, or he shall be released from custody[2].

1 As to the meaning of 'person subject to the Coast Guard Act 1978'; see **[1330]**.

2 The Coast Guard (Discipline) Rules 1983 r 8.

[1419] Release from arrest during investigation Any person arrested under the Coast Guard (Discipline) Rules 1983[1] may be released from arrest under the order of the commanding officer[2] or an officer superior to the commanding officer[3]. Subject to certain provisions of the Coast Guard (Discipline) Rules 1983[4], no person except on the basis of fresh evidence against him to be re-arrested[5].

1 Ie the Coast Guard (Discipline) Rules 1983 r 7; see **[1417]**.

2 As to the definition of 'commanding officer'; see **[1310]**.

3 The Coast Guard (Discipline) Rules 1983 r 9 (1).

4 Ie the Coast Guard (Discipline) Rules 1983 r 10; see **[1420]**.

5 The Coast Guard (Discipline) Rules 1983 r 9 (2).

[1420] Release without prejudice to re-arrest Pending the completion of the investigation or convening of a coast guard court, any person who has been placed under arrest may without prejudice to a re-arrest be released by his commanding officer or by any officer superior to his commanding officer[1].

1 As to the definition of 'coast guard court'; see **[1307]**. The Coast Guard (Discipline) Rules 1983 r 10.

[1421] Arrest when to be imposed Any person charged with (a) an offence under the Coast Guard Act 1978 ss 19, 20, 21 or 22[1]; (b) a civil offence punishable with death or imprisonment for life[2]; (c) any other offence under the Coast Guard Act 1978: (i) if the interest of discipline so require[3], (ii) if the person concerned deliberately undermines discipline[4], (iii) if the person concerned is of violent disposition[5], (iv) if the person concerned is likely to absent himself with a view to avoid trial[6], or (v) if the person concerned is likely to interfere with witnesses or temper evidence[7], shall be placed under arrest[8]. Where any person arrested shows symptoms of sickness, medical assistance shall be provided for such person[9].

1 The Coast Guard (Discipline) Rules 1983 r 11 (1) (a).

2 The Coast Guard (Discipline) Rules 1983 r 11 (1) (b).

3 The Coast Guard (Discipline) Rules 1983 r 11 (1) (c) (i).

4 The Coast Guard (Discipline) Rules 1983 r 11 (1) (c) (ii).

5 The Coast Guard (Discipline) Rules 1983 r 11 (1) (c) (iii).

6 The Coast Guard (Discipline) Rules 1983 r 11 (1) (c) (iv).

7 The Coast Guard (Discipline) Rules 1983 r 11 (1) (c) (v).

8 The Coast Guard (Discipline) Rules 1983 r 11 (1).

9 The Coast Guard (Discipline) Rules 1983 r 11 (2).

[1422] Special provision in case of arrest of intoxicated persons Where any intoxicated person has been arrested he shall, as far as possible be confined separately and shall be visited by the duty officer, or the duty subordinate officer or the person in charge of the guard, once every two hours[1]. An intoxicated person shall not be taken before a superior officer for investigation of his case until he has become sober[2].

1 The Coast Guard (Discipline) Rules 1983 r 12 (1).

2 The Coast Guard (Discipline) Rules 1983 r 12 (2).

[1423] Arrest in case of person whose trial has been ordered Unless the convening authority has otherwise directed, on the commencement of the trial of a person by the coast guard court, the said person shall be placed under arrest and shall remain under arrest during the trial[1]. Where a sentence lower than detention is passed by a coast guard court, the arrested person shall be released by his commanding officer[2]. However, a person who has been sentenced to be dismissed shall also not be put on any duty[3].

1 As to the definition of 'coast guard court'; see **[1307]**. The Coast Guard (Discipline) Rules 1983 r 13 (1).

2 The Coast Guard (Discipline) Rules 1983 r 13 (2).

3 The Coast Guard (Discipline) Rules 1983 r 13 (2) proviso.

[1424] Rights of a person under arrest Any person placed under arrest shall, at the time of being placed under arrest, be given in writing by the officer effecting the arrest, particulars of the charges against him[1]. The said particulars shall be rendered in simple language and also explained to the accused[2]. Notwithstanding anything contained in the aforesaid provision[3] where during the investigation other offences committed by the accused are discovered, it shall be lawful to charge such person with those offences[4]. The duty officer or duty subordinate officer shall every day make a visit to the person under arrest and take the orders of the commanding officer on any request or representation made by the person under arrest[5]. The request or representation made by the person under arrest shall be entered in the form set out in the Coast Guard (Discipline) Rules 1983[6].

1 The Coast Guard (Discipline) Rules 1983 r 15 (1) (a).

2 The Coast Guard (Discipline) Rules 1983 r 15 (1) (b).

3 Ie the Coast Guard (Discipline) Rules 1983 r 15 (1) (a).

4 The Coast Guard (Discipline) Rules 1983 r 15 (1) (c).

5 The Coast Guard (Discipline) Rules 1983 r 15 (2) (a).

6 Ie the Coast Guard (Discipline) Rules 1983 appendix II, the Coast Guard (Discipline) Rules 1983 r 15 (2) (b).

[1425] Duty of Commanding Officer in regard to detention It shall be the duty of every commanding officer[1] to take care that a person under his command when charged with an offence is not detained in custody for more than 48 hours after the committal of such person into custody is reported to him, without the charge being investigated, unless investigation within that period seems to him to be impracticable having regard to the public service[2]. The case of every person being detained in custody beyond a period of 48 hours, and the reasons therefore, shall be reported by the commanding officer to the Deputy Inspector-General under whom he is serving or such other officer to whom an application may be made to convene a coast guard court for the trial of the person charged[3]. In reckoning the period of 48 hours specified in the provisions of the Coast Guard Act 1978[4], Sundays and other public holidays shall be excluded[5]. Subject to the provisions of the Coast Guard Act 1978, the Central Government may make rules providing for the manner in which and the period for which any person subject to the Coast Guard Act 1978[6] may be taken into and detained in coast guard custody[7], pending the trial by any competent authority for any offence committed by him[8].

1 As to the definition of 'commanding officer'; see **[1310]**.

2 The Coast Guard Act 1978 s 60 (1).

3 The Coast Guard Act 1978 s 60 (2).

4 Ie the Coast Guard Act 1978 s 60 (1).

5 The Coast Guard Act 1978 s 60 (3).

6 As to the meaning of 'person subject to the Coast Guard Act 1978'; see **[1330]**.

7 As to the definition of 'coast guard custody'; see **[1308]**.

8 The Coast Guard Act 1978 s 60 (4).

[1426] Delay Reports Where a person subject to the Coast Guard Act 1978[1] is being detained in Coast Guard custody[2] for a period beyond 48 hours without issuing orders for convening a coast guard court for his trial or awarding him punishment under the Coast Guard Act 1978[3], the report as required under the aforesaid Act[4] for such delay, shall be submitted by the commanding officer[5] to the District Commander or the Regional Commander, in the prescribed form[6]. The said report shall continue to be submitted at an interval of every eighth day until the coast guard court is ordered to assemble or punishment under the Coast Guard Act 1978[7] is awarded or, such person is released from the coast guard custody[8]. A copy of every such delay report shall, on or after the 48 day of such custody, be also sent by the commanding officer directly to the Chief Law Officer and to the Regional Commander of the Region in which such person is held in custody[9]. Where the period of custody exceeds two months, the sanction of the Director General shall be required, who may grant such sanction from time to time, such period as he may deem necessary but not exceeding a total period of three months[10]. Where the period of custody referred to these provisions[11] exceeds three months, the sanction of the Central Government shall be required[12].

1 As to the meaning of 'person subject to the Coast Guard Act 1978'; see **[1330]**.

2 As to the meaning of 'Coast Guard custody'; see **[1308]**.

3 Ie the Coast Guard Act 1978 s 57 or 57A; see **[1459]** and **[1461]**.

4 Ie the Coast Guard Act 1978 s 60; see **[1425]**.

5 As to the definition of 'commanding officer'; see **[1310]**.

6 Ie the Coast Guard (Discipline) Rules 1983 appendix-I; The Coast Guard (Discipline) Rules 1983 r 14 (1).

7 Ie the Coast Guard Act 1978 s 57 and 57A.

8 The Coast Guard (Discipline) Rules 1983 r 14 (2).

9 The Coast Guard (Discipline) Rules 1983 r 14 (3).

10 The Coast Guard (Discipline) Rules 1983 r 14 (4).

11 Ie the Coast Guard (Discipline) Rules 1983 r 14 (1).

12 The Coast Guard (Discipline) Rules 1983 r 14 (5).

[1427] Arrest by civil authorities Whenever any person subject to the Coast Guard Act 1978[1], who is accused of an offence under the aforesaid Act, is within the jurisdiction of civil authority[2], such authority shall aid in the apprehension and delivery to coast guard custody of such person upon receipt of a written application to that effect signed by his commanding officer[3].

1 As to the meaning of 'person subject to the Coast Guard Act 1978'; see **[1330]**.

2 The term 'civil authority' includes 'magistrate or police officer'. As to the definition of 'coast guard custody'; see **[1308]**.

3 As to the definition of 'commanding officer'; see **[1310]**. The application can also be signed by an officer authorised by the commanding officer in that behalf. The Coast Guard Act 1978 s 61.

[1428] Capture of deserters Whenever any person subject to the Coast Guard Act 1978[1] deserts, the commanding officer[2] of the unit or ship[3] to which he belongs, shall give information of the desertion to such civil authorities as, in his opinion, may be able to afford assistance towards the capture of the deserter; and such authorities shall take steps for the apprehension of the said deserter in like manner as if he was a person for whose apprehension a warrant had been issued by a Magistrate, and shall deliver the deserter, when apprehended, into coast guard custody[4]. Any police officer may arrest without warrant any person reasonably believed to be subject to the Coast Guard Act 1978, and to be a deserter or to be travelling without authority, and shall bring him without delay before the nearest Magistrate, to be dealt with according to law[5].

1 As to the meaning of 'person subject to the Coast Guard Act 1978'; see **[1330]**.

2 As to the definition of 'commanding officer'; see **[1310]**.

3 As to the definition of 'ship'; see **[1324]**.

4 As to the definition of 'coast guard custody'; see **[1308]**; the Coast Guard Act 1978 s 62 (1).

5 The Coast Guard Act 1978 s 62 (2).

[1429] Coast Guard police officers The Director-General[1] or any prescribed officer[2] may appoint persons for discharging the functions specified in the following provisions[3]. The duties of a person appointed under the aforesaid provision, are to take charge of persons confined for any offence, to preserve good order and discipline and to prevent breaches of the same by persons serving in, or attached to, the Coast Guard[4]. Notwithstanding anything contained in certain provisions of the Coast Guard Act 1978[5], a person appointed under the provisions of the aforesaid Act[6] may, at any time, arrest and detain for trial any person subject to the Coast Guard Act 1978[7] who commits, or is charged with an offence. He may also carry into effect any punishment to be inflicted in pursuance of a sentence awarded by a coast guard court[8] or by an officer exercising authority under the provisions of the aforesaid Act[9] but shall not inflict any punishment on his own authority[10]. However, no officer[11] shall be so arrested or detained otherwise than on the order of another officer[12].

1 As to the definition of 'director-general'; see **[1313]**.

2 As to the meaning of 'prescribed officer' under the Coast Guard Act 1978 s 63 (1) to appointment of Coast Guard Police officers: Commanders, Regional Headquarters; see the Coast Guard (General) Rules 1986 r 29.

3 Ie as specified in the Coast Guard Act 1978 s 63 (2) and (3); the Coast Guard Act 1978 s 63 (1).

4 As to the definition of 'coast guard'; see **[1306]**; the Coast Guard Act 1978 s 63 (2).

5 Ie the Coast Guard Act 1978 s 59; see **[1414]**

6 Ie the Coast Guard Act 1978 s 63 (1).

7 As to the meaning of 'person subject to the Coast Guard Act 1978'; see **[1330]**.

8 As to the definition of 'coast guard court'; see **[1307]**.

9 Ie the Coast Guard Act 1978 s 57.

10 The Coast Guard Act 1978 s 63 (3).

11 As to the definition of 'officer'; see **[1320]**.

12 The Coast Guard Act 1978 s 63 (3) proviso.

B. Law Officers

[1430] Appointment of Chief Law Officer and Law Officers The Central Government may appoint, a Chief Law Officer and as many Law Officers as deemed necessary[1]. A person shall not be qualified for appointment as Chief Law Officer unless he: (i) is a citizen of India[2]; and (ii) has for at least ten years held a judicial office in the territory of India[3]; or (iii) has for at least ten years been an advocate of a high court or two or more such courts in succession[4]. However, the Central Government may, if it is of opinion that it is necessary or expedient so to do in the exigencies of service, relax, for reasons to be recorded in writing, the qualification specified in the aforesaid provisions[5] in respect of any person[6]. A person shall not be qualified for appointment as Law Officer unless he is: (i) a citizen of India[7], and (ii) qualified for enrolment as an advocate of a high court[8]. For the purposes of this provision: (i) in computing the period during which a person has been an advocate of a high court, there shall be included any period during which the person has held a judicial office after he became an advocate[9]; (ii) the expression 'judicial office' shall be deemed to include the post of Law Officer[10].

1 The Coast Guard Act 1978 s 115 (1).

2 The Coast Guard Act 1978 s 115 (2) (a).

3 The Coast Guard Act 1978 s 115 (2) (b).

4 The Coast Guard Act 1978 s 115 (2) (c).

5 Ie the Coast Guard Act 1978 s 115 (2) (b) or (c).

6 The Coast Guard Act 1978 s 115 (2) proviso.

7 The Coast Guard Act 1978 s 115 (3) (a).

8 The Coast Guard Act 1978 s 115 (3) (b).

9 The Coast Guard Act 1978 s 115 (3) explanation (a).

10 The Coast Guard Act 1978 s 115 (3) explanation (b).

[1431] Functions of Chief Law Officer It shall be the duty of the Chief Law Officer to perform such duties of a legal and judicial character pertaining to the Coast Guard[1] as may, from time to time, be referred or assigned to him by the Central Government or the Director-General[2], and to discharge the functions conferred on him by or under the Coast Guard Act 1978[3]. The functions of the Chief Law Officer shall, in his absence or otherwise, be performed by such Law Officer as may be designated in this behalf by the Director-General[4].

1 As to the definition of 'coast guard'; see **[1306]**.

2 As to the definition of 'Director-General'; see **[1313]**.

3 The Coast Guard Act 1978 s 116 (1).

4 The Coast Guard Act 1978 s 116 (2).

C. Legal Advice, Engagement of Counsel and Defence of Personnel in Criminal Courts and Coast Guard Courts

[1432] Cases in which Coast Guard interested in prosecution The cases in which the Coast Guard[1] is directly interested financially or otherwise in the prosecution of an offender in a Criminal Court (whether subject to the Coast Guard Act 1978 or not), the following procedure shall be followed: (i) either the Advocate General of the State Government where the accused is prosecuted or, when the prosecution is directly controlled from the Coast Guard Headquarters, the Advocate/Counsel to the Government of India should be employed, who will if necessary, take further advice from the Advocate General, or the Government Advocate, according to the State in which the prosecution is being conducted[2]; (ii) no prosecution shall be instituted without adequate legal advice being taken in writing and that no prosecution shall be instituted or withdrawn in any manner contrary to such legal advice without reference to the Central Government[3].

1 As to the definition of 'coast guard'; see **[1306]**.

2 The Coast Guard (Condition of Service) Rules 1986 r 41 (a).

3 The Coast Guard (Condition of Service) Rules 1986 r 41 (b).

[1433] Cases where Government Advocate cannot undertake the prosecution When the employment of a Government Advocate or other Law Officer of the State Government concerned is not feasible owing to the nature of the case or for any other reason and the Government Advocate, who is consulted, advises the employment of special counsel; the fees, travelling and daily allowances of the latter may, on the advice of the Government Advocate concerned, be sanctioned by the Director-General who formally engages counsel. The Director-General is also empowered to meet expenditure on court fees, process fees, and the like, on a requisition to be made by the Advocate General or Central Government Advocate etc[1].

1 The Coast Guard (Condition of Service) Rules 1986 r 43.

[1434] Procedure for defence of enrolled persons The following are the provisions for the defence of enrolled persons charged with criminal offences, and prosecuted by Government in criminal courts: (a) When enrolled persons are to be tried by a criminal court upon any criminal charges, the Director-General or the Regional Commander shall consult the Chief Metropolitan /Chief Judicial Magistrate and arrange with him for the selection and remuneration of advocate[1]. Except in cases in which the Central Government is interested, the maximum amount that may be paid to the advocate shall not exceed the amount payable to the Government Advocate fixed by the Central Government[2]. In a joint trial when the Director-General or the Regional Commander is satisfied that the accused require different lines of defence, he may authorise separate payment of fees for each accused so defended[3]. The Director-General or the Regional Commander, shall appoint an advocate only in cases where he thinks desirable. The amount to be paid to advocate shall be settled before hand, subject to the above maximum. If suitable advocate cannot be obtained for the remuneration admissible under these provisions the case shall be reported to the Central Government with a view to their orders being obtained thereon[4]. In high courts in which advocate may not plead unless instructed by a solicitor, a solicitor may be employed and his bill of costs, which should include advocate's fees, shall be submitted to the Central Government advocate and his certificate obtained that the amount of the bill is reasonable before it is submitted for the orders of the Government[5]. When advocate is provided for the defence of an enrolled person at the first trial in a criminal court, counsel can also be provided, when considered necessary on appeal, subject to the limitation laid down in the aforesaid provisions[6].

1 The Coast Guard (Condition of Service) Rules 1986 r 45 (a).

2 The Coast Guard (Condition of Service) Rules 1986 r 45 (b).

3 The Coast Guard (Condition of Service) Rules 1986 r 45 (c).

4 The Coast Guard (Condition of Service) Rules 1986 r 45 (d).

5 The Coast Guard (Condition of Service) Rules 1986 r 45 (e).

6 Ie the Coast Guard (Condition of Service) Rules 1986 r 45 (b) and (d); The Coast Guard (Condition of Service) Rules 1986 r 45 (f).

[1435] Procedure for defence of officers When an officer is to be tried by a criminal court upon any criminal charge and the defence of the officer is considered desirable, the case shall be reported to the Director-General for obtaining the orders of the Central Government[1].

1 The Coast Guard (Condition of Service) Rules 1986 r 46.

[1436] Engagement of Counsel for Prosecution in Coast Guard Courts If the Director-General[1] or Regional Commander, who convenes a coast guard court[2] consider it necessary to engage a counsel for prosecution of an accused a suitable counsel shall be appointed as per the provisions contained in the Coast Guard (Condition of Service) Rules 1986[3].

1 As to the definition of 'director-general'; see **[1313]**.

2 As to the definition of 'coast guard court'; see **[1307]**.

3 Ie the Coast Guard (Condition of Service) Rules 1986 r 41 to 46; The Coast Guard (Condition of Service) Rules 1986 r 47.

[1437] Right of the Director-General or Commanding Officer to obtain copies of judgement or orders made by a criminal court A criminal court before which any proceedings have been taken against a person in the coast guard service whilst subject to the Coast Guard Act 1978[1] shall, on application by the Director-General or the commanding officer[2] of the person, grant Copies of the judgement and final orders in the case free of cost and without delay[3].

1 As to the meaning of 'person subject to the Coast Guard Act 1978'; see **[1330]**.

2 As to the definition of 'commanding officer'; see **[1310]**.

3 The Coast Guard (Condition of Service) Rules 1986 r 52.

D. Choice of Jurisdiction between Coast Guard Court and Criminal Court

[1438] Choice between criminal court and Coast Guard Court When a criminal court[1] and a coast guard court[2] have each jurisdiction in respect of an offence, it shall be in the discretion of the Director-General, the Inspector-General or the Deputy Inspector-General within whose command the accused person is serving or such other officer as may be prescribed[3], to decide before which court the proceedings shall be instituted, and, if that officer decides that they shall be instituted before a coast guard court, to direct that the accused person shall be detained in Coast Guard custody[4].

1 As to the definition of 'criminal court'; see **[1311]**.

2 As to the definition of 'Coast Guard Court'; see **[1307]**.

3 As to the meaning of 'prescribed officer' under the Coast Guard Act 1978 s 71 to decide the choice of criminal court or Coast Guard Court for initiation of proceedings under the Coast Guard Act 1978: The Commanding Officer under whose Command the accused is serving; see the Coast Guard (General) Rules 1986 r 29.

4 As to the definition of 'coast guard custody'; see **[1308]**; the Coast Guard Act 1978 s 71.

[1439] Trial of cases either by Coast Guard Court or Criminal Court Where an offence is triable by a criminal court[1] and coast guard court[2], an officer referred to in the Coast Guard Act 1978[3], may: (i) where the offence is committed by the accused in the course of the performance of his duty as a member of the coast guard[4]; (ii) where the offence is committed in relation to property belonging to the Government or coast guard or a person subject to the Coast Guard Act 1978[5]; or (iii) Where the offence is committed against a person subject to the Coast Guard Act 1978[6]; direct that any person subject to the aforesaid Act, who is alleged to have committed such an offence, be tried by a Court[7]; and in any other case, decide whether or not it would be necessary in the interests of discipline to claim[8] trial by a coast guard court of any person subject to the Coast Guard Act 1978[9] who is alleged to have committed such an offence[10]. In taking a decision to claim an offender for trial by a coast guard court, an officer referred in the Coast Guard Act 1978[11] may take into account all or any of the following factors: (i) the offender is on active duty or has been warned for active duty and it is felt that he is trying to avoid such duty[12]; (ii) the offender is a young person undergoing training and the offence is not a serious one and the trial of the offender by a criminal court would materially affect his training[13]; (iii) the offender can, in view of the nature of the case be dealt with summarily under the Coast Guard Act 1978[14].

1 As to the definition of 'criminal court'; see **[1311]**.

2 As to the definition of 'coast guard court'; see **[1307]**.

3 Ie the Coast Guard Act 1978 s 71; see **[1438]**.

4 The Coast Guard (Discipline) Rules 1983 r 16 (1) (a) (i).

5 The Coast Guard (Discipline) Rules 1983 r 16 (1) (a) (ii).

6 The Coast Guard (Discipline) Rules 1983 r 16 (1) (a) (iii).

7 The Coast Guard (Discipline) Rules 1983 r 16 (1) (a).

8 See the Coast Guard (Discipline) Rules 1983 appendix IIA: 'Form for claiming offender for trial under the Coast Guard Act 1978'.

9 As to the meaning of 'person subject to the Coast Guard Act 1978'; see **[1330]**.

10 The Coast Guard (Discipline) Rules 1983 r 16 (1) (b).

11 Ie the Coast Guard Act 1978 s 71.

12 The Coast Guard (Discipline) Rules 1983 r 16 (2) (a).

13 The Coast Guard (Discipline) Rules 1983 r 16 (2) (b).

14 The Coast Guard (Discipline) Rules 1983 r 16 (2) (c).

[1440] Power of criminal court to require delivery of an offender When a criminal court[1] having jurisdiction is of opinion that proceedings shall be instituted before itself in respect of any alleged offence, it may, by written notice, require the officer referred to in the provisions of the Coast Guard Act 1978[2] at his option either to deliver over the offender to the nearest magistrate to be proceeded against according to law, or to postpone proceedings, pending a reference to the Central Government[3]. In every such case, the said officer shall either deliver over the offender in compliance with the requisition, or shall forthwith refer the question as to the court before which the proceedings are to be instituted, for the determination of the Central Government whose order upon such reference shall be final[4].

1 As to the definition of 'criminal court'; see **[1311]**.

2 Ie the Coast Guard Act 1978 s 71.

3 The Coast Guard Act 1978 s 72 (1).

4 The Coast Guard Act 1978 s 72 (2).

[1441] Cases not to be tried by Coast Guard Court Without prejudice to certain provisions of the Coast Guard (Discipline) Rules 1983[1] an offender may not be claimed for trial by a coast guard court: (i) where the offence is committed by him along with any other person not subject to the Coast Guard Act 1978 whose identity is known[2]; or (ii) where the offence is committed by him while on leave or during absence without leave[3].

1 Ie the Coast Guard (Discipline) Rules 1983 r 16 (1).

2 The Coast Guard (Discipline) Rules 1983 r 17 (a).

3 The Coast Guard (Discipline) Rules 1983 r 17 (b).

[1442] Suspension Notwithstanding anything contained in the Coast Guard (Discipline) Rules 1983, the appointing authority may, as its discretion, place a person subject to the Coast Guard Act 1978, under suspension; (i) where a disciplinary action under the aforesaid Act against him is contemplated or is pending[1]; or (ii) where in the opinion of such authority, he has engaged himself in activities prejudicial to the interests or the security of the State[2]. However, the Director General may exercise the power of suspension in respect of personnel up to the rank of Commandant (Junior Grade)[3]. Further that the Director General shall report the facts of each case of suspension under the aforesaid provision immediately to the Central Government and all such orders of suspension shall not be valid unless confirmed by the Central Government within a period of one month from the date of the said order[4].

A person subject to the Coast Guard Act 1978 shall be deemed to have been placed under suspension by an order of the appointing authority: (i) with effect from the date of his detention where his detention by the civil police on a criminal charge or otherwise exceeds a period of 24 hours[5]; or (ii) with effect from the date of his conviction if he is convicted by any court on a criminal charge and awarded a sentence of imprisonment for a term exceeding 48 hours[6]. An order of suspension made or deemed to have been made under this provision shall continue to remain in force until it is modified or revoked by the competent authority[7]. An order of suspension made or deemed to have been made under this provision may, at any time, be modified or revoked by the authority, which made the order or by any authority to which that authority is subordinate[8]. When a person remains under suspension for more than 90 days, a report, giving reasons for delay in the finalization of his case, shall be submitted to the Director General by the Commanding Officer of the accused, and thereafter, subsequent reports shall be submitted every month till the case is finalized or the order of suspension is revoked, whichever is earlier[9].

1 The Coast Guard (Discipline) Rules 1983 r 15A (1) (i).

2 The Coast Guard (Discipline) Rules 1983 r 15A (1) (ii).

3 The Coast Guard (Discipline) Rules 1983 r 15A (1) proviso.

4 The Coast Guard (Discipline) Rules 1983 r 15A (1) additional proviso.

5 The Coast Guard (Discipline) Rules 1983 r 15A (2) (i).

6 The Coast Guard (Discipline) Rules 1983 r 15A (2) (ii).

7 The Coast Guard (Discipline) Rules 1983 r 15A (3).

8 The Coast Guard (Discipline) Rules 1983 r 15A (4).

9 The Coast Guard (Discipline) Rules 1983 r 15A (5).

6. INVESTIGATION, CHARGES AND SUMMARY DISPOSAL

CONTENTS

A. Investigation

[1443] Offence Report Where it is alleged that a person subject to the Coast Guard Act 1978[1] has committed an offence punishable under it, the allegation shall be reduced to writing[2].

1 As to the meaning of 'person subject to the Coast Guard Act 1978'; see **[1330]**.

2 Ie in the form set out in the Coast Guard (Discipline) Rules 1983, appendix III; The Coast Guard (Discipline) Rules 1983 r 18.

[1444] Hearing by the officer of the day/officer of the watch and the executive officer In the case of a person subject to the Coast Guard Act 1978[1], other than an officer, the case may, in the first instance, be heard by the officer of the day/officer of the watch and then by the executive officer[2]. The witnesses shall give evidence in the presence of the accused who shall have the right to cross-examine them[3]. The accused shall have the right to call witnesses in defence and to make a statement[4]. After hearing the charge under the aforesaid provision[5], the officer of the day/officer of the watch or the executive officer may: (i) award any punishment which he is empowered to award[6], (ii) dismiss the charge when the charge is not proved[7], or (iii) refer the case to the commanding officer[8]. However, he shall not dismiss the charge or award a punishment: (i) if the case has been reserved by the commanding officer for disposal by himself[9]; or (ii) if the accused is under close arrest[10].

1 As to the meaning of 'person subject to the Coast Guard Act 1978'; see **[1330]**.

2 The Coast Guard (Discipline) Rules 1983 r 19 (1) (a).

3 The Coast Guard (Discipline) Rules 1983 r 19 (1) (b).

4 The Coast Guard (Discipline) Rules 1983 r 19 (1) (c).

5 Ie the Coast Guard (Discipline) Rules 1983 r 19 (1).

6 The Coast Guard (Discipline) Rules 1983 r 19 (2) (a). As to the power of punishment; see [1460].

7 The Coast Guard (Discipline) Rules 1983 r 19 (2) (b).

8 The Coast Guard (Discipline) Rules 1983 r 19 (2) (c).

9 The Coast Guard (Discipline) Rules 1983 r 19 (2) proviso (a).

10 The Coast Guard (Discipline) Rules 1983 r 19 (2) proviso (b).

[1445] Hearing of charge by commanding officer Every charge against a person subject to the Coast Guard Act 1978 shall be heard by the commanding officer[1] in the presence of the accused, who shall have full liberty to cross-examine any witness against him, and to call such witness and make such statement as may be necessary for his defence[2]. However, where the charge against the accused arises as a result of investigation by a Board of Inquiry convened under the Coast Guard (General) Rules 1986[3] and where certain provisions of the said Rules[4] have been complied with, the commanding officer may dispense with the above procedure[5].

The commanding officer shall dismiss a charge brought before him, if, in his opinion, the evidence does not show that an offence under the Coast Guard Act 1978 has been committed, or if he is satisfied that the charge ought not to be proceeded with[6]. However, the commanding officer shall not dismiss a charge under any of the circumstances contained in the Coast Guard (Discipline) Rules 1983[7] or for any offence contained in the Coast Guard (Discipline) Rules 1983[8].

After compliance of the above provisions[9], if the commanding officer is of opinion that the charge ought to be proceeded with, he shall, within a reasonable time: (i) award any of the punishment which he is empowered to award[10]: or (ii) remand the accused for preparing a record of evidence or an abstract of evidence against him[11]. However, where the commanding officer proposes to award any of the punishments under the Coast Guards Act 1978[12], which requires approval, he shall prepare a record of evidence or abstract of evidence and forward the same along with the punishment approval form[13].

1 As to the definition of 'commanding officer'; see **[1310]**.

2 The Coast Guard (Discipline) Rules 1983 r 20 (1). For details of charge-sheet; see **[1452]-1457]**.

3 Ie the Coast Guard (General) Rules 1986 r 36. As to the provisions relating to 'Board of Inquiry'; see **[1623]-[1627]**.

4 Ie the Coast Guard (General) Rules 1986 r 39 (4).

5 The Coast Guard (Discipline) Rules 1983 r 20 (1) proviso.

6 The Coast Guard (Discipline) Rules 1983 r 20 (2).

7 Ie the Coast Guard (Discipline) Rules 1983 r 21.

8 Ie the Coast Guard (Discipline) Rules 1983 r 22.

9 Ie the Coast Guard (Discipline) Rules 1983 r 20 (1).

10 The Coast Guard (Discipline) Rules 1983 r 20 (3) (a). As to the power of punishment; see [1453] and [1454].

11 The Coast Guard (Discipline) Rules 1983 r 20 (3) (b).

12 Ie the Coast Guards Act 1978 s 57.

13 Ie the punishment approval form as contained in the Coast Guard (Discipline) Rules 1983 appendix B; The Coast Guard (Discipline) Rules 1983 r 20 (3) proviso.

[1446] Attachment to another unit The commanding officer[1] shall not deal with a case: (i) where the offence with which the accused is charged is against the commanding officer himself[2]; (ii) where the commanding officer is himself a witness in the case against the accused[3]; or (iii) where the commanding officer is otherwise personally interested in the case[4]. The accused in the above cases shall be attached to another ship or station for the disposal of the charge under the orders of the District Commander or the Regional Commander[5]. However, a commanding officer shall not be disqualified from hearing a charge merely because the offence was committed against the property of a coast guard mess or band or institution of which the commanding officer is a member or trustee or because the offence is one of disobedience of such commanding officer's orders[6].

1 As to the definition of 'commanding officer'; see **[1310]**.

2 The Coast Guard (Discipline) Rules 1983 r 21 (a).

3 The Coast Guard (Discipline) Rules 1983 r 21 (b).

4 The Coast Guard (Discipline) Rules 1983 r 21 (c).

5 The Coast Guard (Discipline) Rules 1983 r 21.

6 The Coast Guard (Discipline) Rules 1983 r 21 proviso.

[1447] Charges not to be dealt with summarily A charge for an offence under certain provisions of the Coast Guard Act 1978[1] shall not be dealt with summarily[2].

1 Ie the charge under the Coast Guard Act 1978 ss 17, 19 (a), 23 (a), or 49 (other than that for simple hurt or theft) or a charge for abetment of or an attempt to commit, any of these offences. For details of charge-sheet; see **[1452]-[1457]**.

2 The Coast Guard (Discipline) Rules 1983 r 22.

[1448] Record of Evidence The commanding officer[1] may either prepare the record of evidence himself or detail another officer to do so[2]. The witnesses are to be summoned in accordance with the provisions of the Coast Guard Act 1978[3]. The witnesses give their evidence in the presence of the accused and the accused shall have the right to cross-examine all witnesses who give evidence against him[4]. After all the witnesses against the accused have been examined, he shall be cautioned in the following terms: "You may make a statement if you wish to do so, you are not bound to make one and whatever you state shall be taken down in writing and may be used in evidence[5]." The accused may call witnesses in his defence and the officer recording the evidence may ask any question that may be necessary to clarify the evidence given by such witnesses[6]. All witnesses shall give evidence on oath or affirmation[7]. However, no oath or affirmation shall be given to the accused nor shall he be cross-examined[8]. The statement given by witness shall ordinarily be recorded in narrative form and the officer recording the evidence may, at the request of the accused, permit any portion of the evidence to be recorded in the form of question and answer[9]. The witnesses shall sign their statements after the same have been read over and explained to them[10]. Where a witness cannot be compelled to attend or is not available or his attendance cannot be procured without an undue expenditure of time or money and after the officer recording the evidence has given a certificate in this behalf, a written statement signed by such witness may be read to the accused and included in the record of evidence[11]. After the recording of evidence is completed, the officer recording the evidence shall give a certificate in the following form: "Certified that the record of evidence ordered by…….. was made in the presence and hearing of the accused and the provisions of The Coast Guard (Discipline) Rules 1983 r 23 have been complied with[12]."

1 As to the definition of 'commanding officer'; see **[1310]**.

2 The Coast Guard (Discipline) Rules 1983 r 23 (1).

3 Ie the Coast Guard Act 1978 s 79; The Coast Guard (Discipline) Rules 1983 r 23 (2).

4 The Coast Guard (Discipline) Rules 1983 r 23 (3).

5 The Coast Guard (Discipline) Rules 1983 r 23 (4).

6 The Coast Guard (Discipline) Rules 1983 r 23 (5).

7 The Coast Guard (Discipline) Rules 1983 r 23 (6).

8 The Coast Guard (Discipline) Rules 1983 r 23 (6) proviso.

9 The Coast Guard (Discipline) Rules 1983 r 23 (7) (a).

10 The Coast Guard (Discipline) Rules 1983 r 23 (7) (b).

11 The Coast Guard (Discipline) Rules 1983 r 23 (8).

12 The Coast Guard (Discipline) Rules 1983 r 23 (9).

[1449] Abstract of evidence An abstract of evidence shall be prepared either by the commanding officer[1] or an officer[2] detailed by him[3]. The abstract of evidence shall include: (i) signed statement of witnesses wherever available or a precise thereof[4]; (ii) copies of all documents intended to be produced at the trial[5]; (iii) a précis of the evidence where signed statements of any witnesses are not available[6]. A copy of the abstract of evidence shall be given by the officer making the same to the accused and the accused shall be given an opportunity to make a statement if he so desires after he has been cautioned[7]. However, the accused shall be given such time as may be reasonable in the circumstances but in no case less than 24 hours after receiving the abstract of evidence to make his statement[8].

1 As to the definition of 'commanding officer'; see **[1310]**.

2 As to the definition of 'officer'; see **[1320]**.

3 The Coast Guard (Discipline) Rules 1983 r 24 (1).

4 The Coast Guard (Discipline) Rules 1983 r 24 (2) (i).

5 The Coast Guard (Discipline) Rules 1983 r 24 (2) (ii).

6 The Coast Guard (Discipline) Rules 1983 r 24 (2) (iii).

7 Ie as laid down in the Coast Guard (Discipline) Rules 1983 r 23 (4); see **[1448]**. The Coast Guard (Discipline) Rules 1983 r 24 (3).

8 The Coast Guard (Discipline) Rules 1983 r 24 (3) proviso.

[1450] Investigation of cases by police Where the commanding officer[1] considers it necessary, he may lodge a report with the police for investigation of any case[2].

1 As to the definition of 'commanding officer'; see **[1310]**.

2 The Coast Guard (Discipline) Rules 1983 r 25.

[1451] Disposal of case by commanding officer after record or abstract of evidence Where an officer[1] has been detailed to prepare the record of evidence or to make an abstract thereof he shall forward the same to the commanding officer[2]. The commanding officer may, after going through the record or abstract of evidence dismiss the charge, or rehear the charge and award one of the summary punishments, or apply to the convening authority to convene a coast guard court[3] for the trial of the accused[4].

1 As to the definition of 'officer'; see **[1320]**.

2 As to the definition of 'commanding officer'; see **[1310]**; The Coast Guard (Discipline) Rules 1983 r 26 (1).

3 As to the definition of 'coast guard court'; see **[1307]**.

4 The Coast Guard (Discipline) Rules 1983 r 26 (2).

B. Charges

[1452] Charge-sheet A charge-sheet shall contain the issue(s) to be tried at one time and may contain more than one charge, if the charges are founded on the same facts or form part of series of offences of same or similar[1]. However, a charge under certain provisions of the Coast Guard Act 1978[2] may be included in any charge-sheet notwithstanding that other charges in that charge-sheet are not founded on the same facts or do not form part of series of offences of the same or similar character[3]. Every charge-sheet shall follow the layout set out in the Coast Guard (Discipline) Rules 1983[4].

1 The Coast Guard (Discipline) Rules 1983 r 45 (1).

2 Ie the Coast Guard Act 1978 ss 25, 26 and 41.

3 The Coast Guard (Discipline) Rules 1983 r 45 (1) proviso.

4 Ie the Coast Guard (Discipline) Rules 1983, appendix V; The Coast Guard (Discipline) Rules 1983 r 45 (2).

[1453] Charges There shall be a separate charge for each offence[1]. If a single act or series of acts is of such nature that it is doubtful which of several offences the facts which can be proved will constitute, the accused may be charged with having committed all or any such offences, and any number of such charges may be tried at once or he may be charged in the alternative with having committed some one of the said offences[2]; the charge for the more serious offences shall precede the one for the less serious offence[3]. Each charge consists of two parts, namely: statement of the offence[4], and particulars of the offence[5]. The offence shall be stated, if not a civil offence, as nearly as practicable, in the words of the Coast Guard Act 1978, and if a civil offence, in such words as would sufficiently describe that offence[6]. The particulars shall state the time and place of the alleged offence and the person (if any) against whom, or the thing (if any) in respect of which, it was committed and these should be sufficient to give the accused notice of the matter with which he is charged[7]. In case such particulars are not sufficient to give the accused notice of the matter with which he is charged, the charge shall also contain such particulars of the manner in which the offence was committed as will be sufficient for that purpose[8].

1 The Coast Guard (Discipline) Rules 1983 r 46 (1).

2 The Coast Guard (Discipline) Rules 1983 r 46 (2) (a).

3 The Coast Guard (Discipline) Rules 1983 r 46 (2) (b).

4 The Coast Guard (Discipline) Rules 1983 r 46 (3) (a).

5 The Coast Guard (Discipline) Rules 1983 r 46 (3) (a).

6 The Coast Guard (Discipline) Rules 1983 r 46 (4).

7 The Coast Guard (Discipline) Rules 1983 r 46 (5) (a).

8 The Coast Guard (Discipline) Rules 1983 r 46 (5) (b).

[1454] Joint Charges Any number of accused may be charged jointly and tried together for an offence averred to have been committed jointly by them[1]. Any number of accused though not charged jointly may also be tried together for an offence averred to have been committed by one or more of them and abetted by other or others[2]. Where the accused are so charged under the aforesaid provisions[3] any one or more of them may be charged with, and tried for any other offence with which they could have been charged under certain provisions of the Coast Guard (Discipline) Rules 1983[4].

1 The Coast Guard (Discipline) Rules 1983 r 47 (1).

2 The Coast Guard (Discipline) Rules 1983 r 47 (2).

3 Ie the Coast Guard (Discipline) Rules 1983 r 47 (1) or (2).

4 Ie the Coast Guard (Discipline) Rules 1983 r 45 (1); The Coast Guard (Discipline) Rules 1983 r 47 (3).

[1455] Validity of charge-sheet A charge-sheet shall not be invalid merely by reason that it contains any mistake in the name or description of the accused. In the construction of a charge-sheet these shall be presumed in favour of supporting every proposition which may reasonably be presumed to be impliedly included, and the statement of the offence and the particulars of the offence shall be read and construed together[1].

1 The Coast Guard (Discipline) Rules 1983 r 48. As to the amendment of charge-sheet; see **[1456]** and **[1457]**.

[1456] Amendment of the charge by the coast guard court At any time during the trial by a coast guard court[1] if it appears to the court that there is a mistake in the charge-sheet: (i) in the name or description of the accused[2], or (ii) which is attributable to a clerical error or omission[3], the Court may amend the charge-sheet so as to correct the mistake[4]. If at any time during a trial it appears to the Coast guard court before it closes to deliberate on its findings that it is desirable in the interests of justice to make any addition to, omission from, or alteration in a charge which cannot be made under the aforesaid provision[5], it may, if such addition, omission, or alteration can be made without unfairness to the accused, and with the concurrence of the Law Officer so amend the charge[6].

1 As to the definition of 'coast guard court'; see **[1307]**.

2 The Coast Guard (Discipline) Rules 1983 r 49 (1)(a).

3 The Coast Guard (Discipline) Rules 1983 r 49 (1)(b).

4 The Coast Guard (Discipline) Rules 1983 r 49 (1).

5 Ie the Coast Guard (Discipline) Rules 1983 r 49 (1).

6 The Coast Guard (Discipline) Rules 1983 r 49 (2).

[1457] Amendment to charge by convening authority When a Coast guard court[1] reports to the convening authority under certain provisions of the Coast Guard (Discipline) Rules 1983[2], the convening authority may amend the charge in the respect of which, the Court has reported to such authority. The convening authority may make any addition to, omission from or alteration in the charge which, in its opinion is desirable in the interest of justice and which can be made without unfairness to the accused[3].

1 As to the definition of 'coast guard court'; see **[1307]**.

2 Ie the Coast Guard (Discipline) Rules 1983 r 64.

3 The Coast Guard (Discipline) Rules 1983 r 50.

C. Summary Disposal: Punishments

[1458] Punishments otherwise than by coast guard courts Punishments may also be inflicted in respect of offences committed by persons subject to the Coast Guard Act 1978[1] without the intervention of a coast guard court in the manner stated in certain provision of the Coast Guard Act 1978[2].

1 As to the meaning of 'person subject to the Coast Guard Act 1978'; see **[1330]**.

2 Ie the Coast Guard Act 1978 s 57 and 57A; The Coast Guard Act 1978 s 56.

[1459] Minor punishments Subject to certain provisions of the Coast Guard Act 1978[1], a commanding officer[2] or other authorized officer, with the consent of the Central Government, specified by the Director-General may, proceed against a person subject to the aforesaid Act, otherwise than as an officer, who is charged with an offence under the Coast Guard Act 1978 and award one or more of the following punishments: (a) imprisonment for a period not exceeding three months[3]; (b) dismissal from the Coast Guard[4]; (c) detention in coast guard custody for a period not exceeding three months[5]; (d) reduction to the ranks or to a lower rank in the case of sailors[6]; (e) fine, in respect of civil offences[7]; (f) mulcts of pay and allowances[8]; (g) deprivation of good conduct badges[9]; (h) reprimand[10]; (i) extra work and drill for a period not exceeding fourteen days in the case of persons below the rank of an *Uttam Navik* or *Uttam Yantrik*[11]; (j) stoppage of leave for a period not exceeding 60 days[12]; (k) admonition[13]. However, no punishments specified in the aforesaid provision[14] shall be inflicted: (a) in the case of a subordinate officer, unless it is approved by an officer not below the rank of an Inspector-General[15]; and (b) in the case of others, unless it is approved by an officer not below the rank of a Deputy Inspector-General[16].

1 Ie the Coast Guard Act 1978 s 58; see **[1589]**.

2 As to the definition of 'commanding officer'; see **[1310]**.

3 The Coast Guard Act 1978 s 57 (a).

4 The Coast Guard Act 1978 s 57 (b).

5 The Coast Guard Act 1978 s 57 (c).

6 The Coast Guard Act 1978 s 57 (d).

7 The Coast Guard Act 1978 s 57 (e).

8 The Coast Guard Act 1978 s 57 (f).

9 The Coast Guard Act 1978 s 57 (g).

10 The Coast Guard Act 1978 s 57 (h).

11 The Coast Guard Act 1978 s 57 (i).

12 The Coast Guard Act 1978 s 57 (j).

13 The Coast Guard Act 1978 s 57 (k).

14 Ie as specified in the Coast Guard Act 1978 s 57 (a) to (d).

15 As to the definition of 'subordinate officer'; see **[1326]**. The Coast Guard Act 1978 s 57 proviso (a).

16 The Coast Guard Act 1978 s 57 proviso (b).

[1460] Authorities empowered to award of Summary Punishments For the purpose of the Coast Guard Act 1978 s 57, the authorities mentioned in column (1) and holding ranks mentioned in column (2) shall have the power to award punishment to the extent mentioned in column (3) of the Table below[1].

Authority	Rank	Extent to which punishment could be awarded
1	2	3
1. The Commanding Officer	All ranks	All punishments
2. Executive Officer	Commandant	(i) Mulcts of pay and allowances for first offence of leave breaking up to 72 hours, and one day's mulcts of pay and allowances for an offence of drunkenness to all enrolled persons in both the cases. (ii) Extra work and drill for a period not exceeding 14 days to Naviks. (iii) Stoppage of leave for a period not exceeding 30 days to all enrolled persons. (iv) Admonition to all enrolled persons.
	Commandant (Junior Grade)	(i) Mulcts of pay and allowances for first offence of leave breaking up to 48 hours, and one day's mulcts of pay and allowances for an offence of drunkenness to all enrolled persons in both the cases. (ii) Extra work and drill for a period not exceeding 14 days to Naviks. (iii) Stoppage of leave for a period not exceeding 21 days to all enrolled persons. (iv) Admonition to all enrolled persons.
	Deputy Commandant	(i) Mulcts of pay and allowances for the first offence of leave breaking up to 36 hours to all enrolled persons. (ii) Extra work and drill for a period not exceeding 7 days to Naviks. (iii) Stoppage of leave for a period not exceeding 15 days to all enrolled persons. (iv) Admonition to all enrolled persons.
	Assistant Commandant	(i) Extra work and drill for a period not exceeding 7 days to Naviks. (ii) Stoppage of leave for a period not exceeding 15 days to other than subordinate officers. (iii) Admonition to persons other than subordinate officers.
3. Officers of the Watch/ Officer of the Day		(i) Extra work and drill for 1 day to Naviks. (ii) Admonition to Naviks.

1 The Coast Guard (General) Rules 1986 r 30.

[1461] Punishment for officers below the rank of commandant The Director-General or an officer not below the rank of Deputy Inspector-General who is appointed as commander of a region or such other officer, with the consent of the Central Government, specified by the Director-General, may in the prescribed manner proceed against an officer below the rank of commandant, who is charged with an offence under the Coast Guard Act 1978 and award such person one or more of the following punishments: (i) forfeiture of seniority of rank or in the case of any of them whose promotion depends upon length of service, forfeiture of service for the purpose of promotion, for a period not exceeding twelve months, but subject to the right of the accused, previous to the award, to elect to be tried by a Coast guard court[1]; (ii) forfeiture of seniority of rank, or in the case of any of them whose promotion depends upon length of service, forfeiture of service for the purpose of promotion for a period not exceeding six months, but subject to the right of the accused, previous to the award, to elect to be tried by a Coast guard court[2]; (iii) mulcts of pay and allowances[3]; (iv) severe reprimand[4]. However, no punishment specified in the aforesaid provision[5] shall be inflicted by an officer other than the Director-General[6]. Further, no punishment specified in the certain provision[7] shall be inflicted by an officer below the rank of Deputy Inspector-General who is appointed as the commander of a region[8].

1 As to the definition of 'director general' and 'deputy inspector-general; see **[1313]** and **[1312]**. The Coast Guard Act 1978 s 57A (a).

2 The Coast Guard Act 1978 s 57A (b).

3 The Coast Guard Act 1978 s 57A (c).

4 The Coast Guard Act 1978 s 57A (d).

5 Ie the Coast Guard Act 1978 s 57A (a).

6 The Coast Guard Act 1978 s 57A first proviso.

7 Ie the Coast Guard Act 1978 s 57A (b).

8 The Coast Guard Act 1978 s 57A second proviso.

[1462] Summary Punishments Punishments enumerated in the Coast Guard Act 1978[1] may be awarded summarily as follows:

(i) An order for the dismissal of a person from Coast Guard Service whether accompanied by other punishments or not shall be made only with the approval of the Director General[2].

(ii) Punishments specified in the Coast Guard Act 1978[3] shall not have effect unless the punishment approval form is approved by the Inspector General or Deputy Inspector General as the case may be, under whom the offender is serving[4].

(iii) The punishment approval form for award of punishments of imprisonment, dismissal, detention and reduction to the ranks or to a lower rank shall be accompanied by a record or abstract of evidence[5].

(iv) If an officer having power to approve a punishment may consider for any reason that the punishment proposed is illegal, unjust, or excessive he may cancel, vary or remit the punishment within the limits of the powers of punishment of a commanding officer[6] and the punishment so altered shall be the punishment awarded[7].

(v) At any time before the sentence is announced, the commanding officer may modify or withdraw the sentence if on further consideration it appears to him desirable to do so provided that if the punishment approval form has been approved by the appropriate authority, the sentence shall not be modified or withdrawn without the consent of that authority[8].

(vi) After signature and approval where necessary, the punishment approval form shall be dated and formally read forthwith to the offender by the commanding [9].

(vii) The date of punishment approval form and the date of reading it shall always be the same. Where there is an unreasonable interval between the dates of commission of the offence and the reading of punishment approval form, the reason for such interval shall be stated in the form[10].

(viii) When an offender whose case has been fully investigated has been sent to a hospital the punishment approval form shall be formally read to him in the hospital unless the medical officer certifies that the offender is medically unfit to have the punishment approval form read to him in which case the formal reading may be carried out by the commanding officer in his office in the absence of the offender and such formal reading of the punishment approval form shall have same effect as if it had been read to the offender[11].

(ix) The fact of the punishment approval form having formally been read in the absence of the offender shall be recorded on the punishment approval form and shall be intimated to the offender as soon as he is in a fit state to receive such intimation[12].

(x) The punishment of imprisonment or detention if not suspended, shall commence on the day on which the punishment approval form is formally read over to the offender[13]. However, where the offender has been kept in custody from the date on which the authority who tried him signed the punishment approval form, the sentence shall begin to run from that date[14]

(xi) The other punishments shall take effect on the date on which the punishment approval form is formally read over to the offender[15].

(xii) Notwithstanding that the state of health of the offender is such as renders him unable to undergo the whole or any part of the punishment to which he may have rendered himself liable and it appears probable that he will be invalidated from the service or remains unfit for punishment for a considerable period of time, the punishment meted out for his offence shall be awarded and if it requires a punishment approval form, it is to be completed and duly signed and read over, where necessary, in the absence of the offender in order that he may not escape the consequences of the other punishments such as loss of pay, stoppage of leave, etc[16].

1 Ie the Coast Guard Act 1978 s 57; see **[1459]**.

2 The Coast Guard (Discipline) Rules 1983 r 28 (a).

3 Ie as specified in the Coast Guard Act 1978 s 57 (c) and (d); relating to detention up to three months and reduction to ranks.

4 Coast Guard (Discipline) Rules 1983 r 28 (b).

5 The Coast Guard (Discipline) Rules 1983 r 28 (c).

6 As to the definition of 'commanding officer'; see **[1310]**.

7 The Coast Guard (Discipline) Rules 1983 r 28 (d).

8 The Coast Guard (Discipline) Rules 1983 r 28 (e).

9 The Coast Guard (Discipline) Rules 1983 r 28 (f).

10 The Coast Guard (Discipline) Rules 1983 r 28 (g).

11 The Coast Guard (Discipline) Rules 1983 r 28 (h).

12 The Coast Guard (Discipline) Rules 1983 r 28 (i).

13 The Coast Guard (Discipline) Rules 1983 r 28 (j).

14 The Coast Guard (Discipline) Rules 1983 r 28 (j) proviso.

15 The Coast Guard (Discipline) Rules 1983 r 28 (k).

16 The Coast Guard (Discipline) Rules 1983 r 28 (l).

[1463] Reduction to the ranks or to a lower rank in the case of sailors A sailor[1] may be reduced to any rank or to a lower rank provided that no sailor shall be reduced to rank: (i) below the rank of *Navik* or *Yantrik*[2]; (ii) below the rank in which he joined the coast guard[3]

1 As to the definition of 'sailor'; see [1323].

2 The Coast Guard (Discipline) Rules 1983 r 29 (a).

3 The Coast Guard (Discipline) Rules 1983 r 29 (b).

[1464] Fine in respect of civil offences A fine not exceeding Rs 250 may be imposed summarily when a subordinate officer[1], sailor[2] or other enrolled person[3] is found guilty of a civil offence[4].

1 As to the definition of 'subordinate officer'; see **[1326]**.

2 As to the definition of 'sailor'; see **[1323]**.

3 As to the definition of 'enrolled person'; see **[1314]**.

4 As to the definition of 'civil offence'; see **[1304]**; The Coast Guard (Discipline) Rules 1983 r 30.

[1465] Mulcts of pay and allowances for improper absence Every subordinate officer[1], sailor[2] or other enrolled person[3] who is guilty of absence without leave or improperly leaving his ship or place of duty shall be punished with mulcts of pay and stoppage of leave in accordance with the following scale: (i) where the period of absence does not exceed three hours, one day's pay and one day's leave[4]; (ii) where the period of absence exceeds three hours, but does not exceed 36 hours, one day's pay and one day's leave for every three hours of absence or part thereof[5]; (iii) where the period of absence exceeds 36 hours, one day's pay and one day's leave for every three hours up to 36 hours and one day's pay and one day's leave for each subsequent period of six hours or part of six hours, so, however, that the stoppage of leave, shall in no case exceed 60 days[6]; (iv) if the period of absence is trivial or if there are extenuating circumstance and period of improper absence does not exceed 36 hours, the commanding officer may at his discretion reduce the mulcts by such an amount as he may consider reasonable the stoppage of leave being reduced to a corresponding extent[7]; (v) certain provision of the Coast Guard (Discipline) Rules 1983[8] shall apply to leave breaking up to 36 hours dealt with in conjunction with other offences[9]; (vi) if the period of absence exceeds 36 hours or the offence is aggravated or repeated, any other punishment permitted by these provisions may be awarded according to the degree of the offence in addition to the mulcts of pay and stoppage of leave on the scale mentioned in the Coast Guard (Discipline) Rules 1983[10]. If there are mitigating circumstances justifying exceptional treatment the commanding officer may at his discretion reduce the mulcts, provided that the actual mulcts (i.e. excluding detention) shall not be reduced to less than one day's pay for each day's absence and where the stoppage of leave according to the said scale would amount to 30 days or less it may also be correspondingly reduced[11]; (vii) if the number of days mulcts in accordance with the aforesaid provision[12] or if the period of sentence to which a leave breaker is confined by reason of the punishment of detention plus the number of days mulcts, would amount to a total of more than 60 days, any excess mulcts shall be remitted provided that in no case shall the actual mulcts (i.e. excluding the punishment of detention) be reduced to less than one day's pay or each day's absence[13].

1 As to the definition of 'subordinate officer'; see **[1326]**.

2 As to the definition of 'sailor'; see **[1323]**.

3 As to the definition of 'enrolled person'; see **[1314]**.

4 The Coast Guard (Discipline) Rules 1983 r 31(a).

5 The Coast Guard (Discipline) Rules 1983 r 31 (b).

6 The Coast Guard (Discipline) Rules 1983 r 31 (c).

7 The Coast Guard (Discipline) Rules 1983 r 31 (d).

8 Ie the Coast Guard (Discipline) Rules 1983 r 31 (b).

9 The Coast Guard (Discipline) Rules 1983 r 31 (e).

10 Ie the Coast Guard (Discipline) Rules 1983 r 31 (a).

11 The Coast Guard (Discipline) Rules 1983 r 31 (f).

12 Ie the Coast Guard (Discipline) Rules 1983 r 31 (f).

13 The Coast Guard (Discipline) Rules 1983 r 31 (g).

[1466] General Provision regarding mulcts For the purpose of these provisions a day's pay shall include full pay and allowances but shall not include the composite personal maintenance hygiene allowance, extra pay, special pay or kindred pay[1]. The scale of mulcts shall not apply to in case of persons charged with desertion[2]. Where mulcts of pay and allowances are awarded for absence without leave, the period shall be treated as regularised for all purposes[3].

1 The Coast Guard (Discipline) Rules 1983 r 32 (1).

2 The Coast Guard (Discipline) Rules 1983 r 32 (2).

3 The Coast Guard (Discipline) Rules 1983 r 32 (3).

[1467] Limits of punishment under the Coast Guard Act s 26 The maximum summary punishment for leave breaking that should as a rule be awarded shall be detention and except for an aggravated offence such punishment shall not exceed 36 days[1]. The act of not returning on duty at the time ordered shall constitute the main offence against discipline and the aggravation of the offence shall depend upon the time for which a person remains absent which shall be dealt with on its merits in each case[2]. Leave breaking offences shall be recorded on the offence report as follows: "Did remain absent over leave.......hours......minutes, namely from...... to......[3]"

1 The Coast Guard (Discipline) Rules 1983 r 33 (1).

2 The Coast Guard (Discipline) Rules 1983 r 33 (2).

3 The Coast Guard (Discipline) Rules 1983 r 33 (3).

[1468] Application of the Coast Guard (Discipline) Rules 1983 r 32 and 33 The provisions of the Coast Guard (Discipline) Rules 1983 r 32 and 33 shall apply to breaking out of ship, breaking away from a landing party and other cases of improper absence other than desertion, except that any punishment applicable to the offence may be awarded in addition to mulcts of pay and stoppage of leave and it shall not be necessary to limit the period of detention for offences of this description in ordinary cases[1].

1 The Coast Guard (Discipline) Rules 1983 r 34.

[1469] Calculation of period of absence The period of improper absence included in the charge shall be computed from the time when leave expires (or the time of breaking out) until the time of return to the ship or place of duty[1]. When a person surrenders or is apprehended as an absentee away from the locality in which his leave expires, the commanding officer may, having regard to the circumstances, consider the absence as having terminated at the time of such surrender or apprehension. If a lengthy journey is involved in returning to the place where leave expired, the time involved in such journey may be included in computing the period of absence[2]. When an absentee is arrested by the civil authority on another charge and is subsequently handed over to the coast guard authorities, his absence without leave shall be regarded as ceasing from the time of his arrest by the civil authority[3].

1 The Coast Guard (Discipline) Rules 1983 r 35 (1).

2 The Coast Guard (Discipline) Rules 1983 r 35 (2).

3 The Coast Guard (Discipline) Rules 1983 r 35 (3).

[1470] Simple leave breaking and aggravated offence of leave-breaking Unless an offence of leave breaking is a repeated or aggravated offence, the punishment for the offence of leave-breaking involving improper absence of not more than 36 hours shall be confined to mulcts of pay and stoppage of leave, but if the offence was the sequel to an offence of improperly leaving a ship or place of duty, other punishments may be awarded in addition[1].

For the purpose of above and certain other provisions of the Coast Guard (Discipline) Rules 1983[2] an offence of leave breaking shall be deemed to be aggravated: (i) if the absence exceeds 36 hours[3]; (ii) if the absentee misses his ship or transfer[4]; (iii) if, when leave was granted, a warning was given that the ship was under sailing orders[5]; (iv) if the offender was undergoing any form of punishment at the time[6]; (v) if there are any other serious circumstances[7]. The charge in a case of aggravated leave breaking may refer to the offence as aggravated, but the charge shall not contain anything which directly or indirectly refers to a previous offence[8].

1 The Coast Guard (Discipline) Rules 1983 r 36.

2 Ie the Coast Guard (Discipline) Rules 1983 r 31 to 36; see **[1465]** to **[1469]**.

3 The Coast Guard (Discipline) Rules 1983 r 37 (1) (a).

4 The Coast Guard (Discipline) Rules 1983 r 37 (1) (b).

5 The Coast Guard (Discipline) Rules 1983 r 37 (1) (c).

6 The Coast Guard (Discipline) Rules 1983 r 37 (1) (d).

7 The Coast Guard (Discipline) Rules 1983 r 37 (1) (e).

8 The Coast Guard (Discipline) Rules 1983 r 37 (2).

[1471] Repeated offence A repeated offence of leave breaking is one committed in the same ship or station within six months of a previous leave breaking offence[1].

1 The Coast Guard (Discipline) Rules 1983 r 38.

[1472] Drunkenness A mulct of one day's pay shall be inflicted for all offences of drunkenness in a ship or while absent on duty, or on returning from shore, whether such return is voluntary or otherwise and a similar mulct shall be inflicted upon persons who are drunk when received in the coast guard or other custody, whether from leave or not, and, if from leave, whether their leave has expired or not, unless the offender has already been dealt with by the civil authority[1]. For the offence of drunkenness in a ship or while absent on duty, punishment by way of imprisonment or detention may be awarded at the discretion of the commanding officer[2]. In awarding punishments for drunkenness on leave, the commanding officer shall take into consideration the circumstances of each case as regards the disgrace or discredit brought to the Coast Guard service[3].

1 The Coast Guard (Discipline) Rules 1983 r 39 (1).

2 The Coast Guard (Discipline) Rules 1983 r 39 (2).

3 As to the definition of 'commanding officer'; see **[1310]**. The Coast Guard (Discipline) Rules 1983 r 39 (3).

[1473] Deprivation of good conduct badges A person who is sentenced to imprisonment or detention or a sailor reduced to any ranks or to a lower rank shall be deprived of any good conduct badge he may hold[1]. One badge lost may be regained by six months 'very good' conduct, and additional badges by further periods of six months reckoned in each case from the date of preceding restoration[2]. If, however, a person has been sentenced to deprivation a second time within three years of actual service, the qualification for restoration shall be twelve months for the first restoration and six months for each subsequent restoration[3]. Time which does not count for purpose of award shall not be reckoned towards restoration of badges[4]. Restoration shall be made when they become due whether the person prefers his claim or not[5].

1 The Coast Guard (Discipline) Rules 1983 r 40 (1).
2 The Coast Guard (Discipline) Rules 1983 r 40 (2).
3 The Coast Guard (Discipline) Rules 1983 r 40 (3).
4 The Coast Guard (Discipline) Rules 1983 r 40 (4).
5 The Coast Guard (Discipline) Rules 1983 r 40 (5).

[1474] Reprimand The punishment of reprimand shall be awarded only to *Uttam Naviks*, *Yantriks* and above[1].

1 The Coast Guard (Discipline) Rules 1983 r 41.

[1475] Extra work and drill Naviks and enrolled followers may be awarded the punishment of extra work and drill up to 14 days. When so punished they shall be subject to the following routines: (i) leave to be stopped[1]; (ii) to do extra work or drill during non-working hours i.e. (from 1700 to 1830) for one and a half hour[2]; (iii) to be mustered frequently[3]; (iv) when a person is under punishment of extra work and drill, he shall be allowed to leave the ship or station only on duty though he may be allowed to proceed on long leave at the discretion of the commanding officer[4]; and (v) the punishment shall be suspended on Sundays and holidays, but these days shall count as part of the period for which any sentence is awarded[5].

1 The Coast Guard (Discipline) Rules 1983 r 42 (a).
2 The Coast Guard (Discipline) Rules 1983 r 42 (b).
3 The Coast Guard (Discipline) Rules 1983 r 42 (c).
4 The Coast Guard (Discipline) Rules 1983 r 42 (d).
5 The Coast Guard (Discipline) Rules 1983 r 42 (e).

[1476] Stoppage of leave When stoppage of leave is awarded for leave-breaking, it shall not exceed the scale laid down except for aggravated or repeated offence[1]. Stoppage of leave may also be awarded in appropriate cases for any other offence either as the only punishment or with another punishment[2]. While under stoppage of leave, a person shall not be allowed to leave the ship or station except on duty, he may, however, be allowed to proceed on leave at the discretion of the commanding officer[3].

1 The Coast Guard (Discipline) Rules 1983 r 43 (1).
2 The Coast Guard (Discipline) Rules 1983 r 43 (2).
3 The Coast Guard (Discipline) Rules 1983 r 43 (3).

[1477] Admonition When a person is found guilty of an offence which of itself or in view of the mitigating circumstances is not considered to deserve any more serious punishment, he shall be awarded the punishment of admonition[1].

1 The Coast Guard (Discipline) Rules 1983 r 44.

[1478] Effect of conviction by civil authorities When an enrolled person[1] is convicted by a civil authority and receives any punishment for an offence which has brought disgrace or discredit on the uniform, the service or the position which the person holds, he may be awarded the following penalties with the prior approval of the Inspector-General in Coast Guard headquarters namely: (i) Break in continuity of very Good Conduct (The date of break in such cases shall be the date of conviction)[2]; (ii) Award of inferior character on the next occasion of assessment[3].

1 As to the definition of 'enrolled person'; see **[1314]**.

2 The Coast Guard (Condition of Service) Rules 1986 r 18 (a).

3 The Coast Guard (Condition of Service) Rules 1986 r 18 (b).

[1479] Punishment of officers below the rank of commandant Where an officer below the rank of commandant is remanded for disposal of a charge against him by an authority empowered to deal summarily under the provisions of the Coast Guard Act 1978[1], the copies of record of evidence[2] and the charge-sheet[3] shall be delivered to him as soon as practicable, but in any case not less than 24 hours before the summary trial[4]. The authority empowered under the Coast Guard Act 1978[5] shall, unless the charge is dismissed or the accused consents to in writing to dispense with the attendance of witnesses, hear the evidence in his presence and he shall have full liberty to cross-examine any witness against him, and to make statement and examine witnesses in his defence[6]. The trial proceedings shall, as far as practicable, be recorded in accordance with the form set out in the Coast Guard (Discipline) Rules 1983[7]. In every case where the trial is conducted by an authority other than the Director General, the proceedings together with the conduct sheet, record of evidence and written consent of the accused to dispense with the attendance of witnesses (if any), shall be forwarded to the Director General[8].

1 Ie the Coast Guard Act 1978 s 57A; see **[1461]**.

2 As to the 'record of evidence'; see **[1448]**.

3 As to the provisions relating to 'charge and charge-sheet'; see **[1452]** and **[1457]**.

4 The Coast Guard (Discipline) Rules 1983 r 44A (1).

5 Ie the Coast Guard Act 1978 s 57A.

6 The Coast Guard (Discipline) Rules 1983 r 44A (2).

7 Ie the Coast Guard (Discipline) Rules 1983 appendix IVA.

8 The Coast Guard (Discipline) Rules 1983 r 44A (3).

7. COAST GUARD COURTS: CONVENING, POWER, PROCEDURE AND INCIDENTAL MATTERS

CONTENTS

PARA

A. Convening of Coast guard court and Power

B. Procedure of Coast guard court

A. Convening of Coast guard court

[1480] Power to convene a coast guard court A coast guard court[1] may be convened by the Central Government or the Director-General[2] or by any officer empowered in this behalf by warrant of the Director-General (referred to as the convening authority)[3]. A warrant issued under the aforesaid provision may contain such restrictions, reservations or conditions as the Director-General may think fit[4].

1 As to the definition of 'coast guard court'; see **[1307]**.

2 As to the definition of 'Director-General'; see **[1313]**.

3 The Coast Guard Act 1978 s 64 (1).

4 The Coast Guard Act 1978 s 64 (2).

[1481] Action by the Convening Authority on receiving an application for convening a coast guard court As soon as the Convening Authority receives an application[1] for convening a coast guard court[2], it shall scrutinise the charge and the evidence against the accused where necessary in consultation with the Chief Law Officer or a Law Officer, and (i) shall direct the commanding officer[3] to dismiss the charge where the evidence against the accused is insufficient and further evidence is not likely to be available and may direct him to do so if considered inadvisable to proceed with the trial[4]; or (ii) may return the case to the commanding officer for being dealt with summarily if it is considered that the same can be adequately dealt with[5]; or (iii) may return the case for recording further evidence if it is considered that the evidence already recorded is insufficient and further evidence may be available[6].

1 As to the 'application for trial by a coast guard court'; see **[1538]**.

2 As to the definition of 'coast guard court'; see **[1307]**.

3 As to the definition of 'commanding officer'; see **[1310]**.

4 The Coast Guard (Discipline) Rules 1983 r 51 (i).

5 The Coast Guard (Discipline) Rules 1983 r 51 (ii).

6 The Coast Guard (Discipline) Rules 1983 r 51 (iii).

[1482] Disqualification of officers for serving on coast guard court An officer shall be disqualified from serving on a coast guard court[1] if he: (i) is an officer who convened the coast guard court[2], (ii) is the prosecutor or a witness for the prosecution[3], (iii) has taken any part in the investigation of the case, which would have necessitated in applying his mind to any part of the evidence or to the facts of the case[4], (iv) is the commanding officer of the accused, or the commanding officer of the ship to which the accused belonged at the time of commission of the alleged offence[5], or (v) has a personal interest in the case[6]. An individual who has acted as presiding officers in the board of enquiry can be appointed as prosecutor and this will not disqualify him to serve in the coast guard court[7].

1 As to the definition of 'coast guard court'; see **[1307]**.

2 The Coast Guard (Discipline) Rules 1983 r 52 (a).

3 The Coast Guard (Discipline) Rules 1983 r 52 (b).

4 The Coast Guard (Discipline) Rules 1983 r 52 (c).

5 The Coast Guard (Discipline) Rules 1983 r 52 (d).

6 The Coast Guard (Discipline) Rules 1983 r 52 (e).

7 *S K Singh v The Director General Coast Guard*, Writ Petition No.13059 of 2006 and WP M.P. No.14645 of 2006, Madras High Court, decided on 9 June 2010.

[1483] Composition of coast guard court A coast guard court shall consist of not less than five officers[1] each of whom has held the post of Assistant Commandant for not less than three years[2]. For the purposes of the aforesaid provision 'Assistant Commandant' includes any post of higher rank and any post declared by the Central Government by notification to be an equivalent post as also any post higher in rank than the post so declared[3]. At every coast guard court, the senior member shall be the presiding officer[4]. A coast guard court shall not be duly constituted unless the members thereof are drawn from at least two ships[5]. No coast guard court for the trial of an officer shall be duly constituted unless the presiding officer and at least two members of the court are of the same rank as the accused or of a higher rank[6].

1 As to the definition of 'officer'; see **[1320]**.

2 The Coast Guard Act 1978 s 65 (1).

3 The Coast Guard Act 1978 s 65 (1) explanation.

4 The Coast Guard Act 1978 s 65 (2).

5 The Coast Guard Act 1978 s 65 (3).

6 The Coast Guard Act 1978 s 65 (4).

[1484] Composition of the coast guard court: Details A prosecutor shall not be qualified to sit on the coast guard court[1] for the trial of the person he prosecutes[2]. The officer ordering the coast guard court, the officer who was the commanding officer[3] of the ship to which the accused belonged at the time of the commission of the alleged offence and the officer investigating the offence shall not be qualified to sit on a coast guard court for the trial of such accused[4]. Except as otherwise provided in these provisions, officers of the Coast Guard shall be eligible to sit as members of a coast guard court irrespective of the branch of the Coast Guard service to which they belong[5]. However, (a) the majority of the members of the coast guard court, including the Presiding Officer, shall be officers of the general duty branch of the Coast Guard service[6], and (b) at trials for offences under certain provisions of the Coast Guard Act 1978[7], officers other than officers of the General Duty Branch of the Coast Guard shall not be eligible to sit[8].

The Presiding Officer of a coast guard court shall be the senior member[9]. No coast guard court for the trial of a Deputy Inspector General shall be duly constituted unless the Presiding Officer is a Deputy Inspector General or of a higher rank and the other officers comprising the court are Commandants or officers of higher rank(s)[10]. No coast guard court for the trial of a Commandant shall be duly constituted unless the Presiding Officer is a Commandant or of a higher rank and two other members are Commandants or officers of higher rank(s)[11]. No coast guard court for a person below the rank of Commandant shall be duly constituted unless the Presiding Officer is a substantive or acting commandant or of higher rank[12].

No Commandant or Deputy Commandant or Assistant Commandant shall be required to sit as a member of a coast guard court when four officers of higher rank and junior to the Presiding Officer can be assembled at the place where the Coast guard court is to be held, but the regularity or validity of any coast guard court or of the proceedings thereof shall not be affected by any Commandant, Deputy Commandant or Assistant Commandant being required to sit or sitting thereon under any circumstances and when any Commandant, Deputy Commandant or Assistant Commandant sits on any Coast guard court, the Members of it shall not be less than Five[13]. No coast guard court shall be deemed to have constituted unless attended by the Law Officer designated for that purpose by the Chief Law Officer[14].

1 As to the definition of 'coast guard court'; see **[1307]**.

2 The Coast Guard (Discipline) Rules 1983 r 53 (1).

3 As to the definition of 'commanding officer'; see **[1310]**.

4 The Coast Guard (Discipline) Rules 1983 r 53 (2).

5 The Coast Guard (Discipline) Rules 1983 r 53 (3).

6 The Coast Guard (Discipline) Rules 1983 r 53 (3) proviso (a).

7 Ie the Coast Guard Act 1978 ss 27, 28, 29, 30 and 31.

8 The Coast Guard (Discipline) Rules 1983 r 53 (3) proviso (b).

9 The Coast Guard (Discipline) Rules 1983 r 53 (4).

10 The Coast Guard (Discipline) Rules 1983 r 53 (5).

11 The Coast Guard (Discipline) Rules 1983 r 53 (6).

12 The Coast Guard (Discipline) Rules 1983 r 53 (7).

13 The Coast Guard (Discipline) Rules 1983 r 53 (8).

14 The Coast Guard (Discipline) Rules 1983 r 53 (9).

[1485] Duties of convening officer when convening coast guard courts When an officer convenes a coast guard court[1] he shall: (i) issue a convening order in the form set out the Coast Guard (Discipline) Rules 1983[2]; (ii) direct upon what charges the accused is to be tried and ensure that the accused has been remanded for trial by a Coast guard court upon these charges by his commanding officer[3]; (iii) if he is of the opinion that charges shall be put in separate charge-sheets, so direct and shall also direct the order in which they are to be tried[4]; (iv) direct, if there is more than one accused, whether the accused are to be tried jointly or separately[5]; (v) appoint members of the court and any waiting members[6]; (vi) appoint an officer, subject to the Coast Guard Act 1978 or a counsel assisted by such an officer to prosecute or direct his commanding officer to appoint an officer subject to the aforesaid Act, to prosecute[7]. However, the Convening Authority may appoint more than one such officer to prosecute if he thinks fit[8]; (vii) appoint an interpreter where necessary[9]; (viii) send to the Presiding Officer the charge-sheet, the convening order[10]; (ix) to appoint an officer to perform the duties mentioned in the Coast Guard (Discipline) Rules 1983[11] and such other duties as may be directed by the Presiding Officer or the Law Officer to perform for the due transaction of the administrative business of the Coast guard court[12]; (x) forward to the Law Officer, each member of the Coast guard court and to each waiting member thereof a copy of the charge-sheet and convening order[13]; (xi) forward to the prosecutor copies of the charge-sheet and convening order and the original record or abstract of evidence together with an unexpurgated copy thereof showing the passage (if any)[14]; (xii) ensure that the Commanding Officer has summoned all prosecution witnesses and defence witnesses as the accused may have requested to, be summoned under the Coast Guard (Discipline) Rules 1983[15].

1 As to the definition of 'coast guard court'; see **[1307]**.

2 As set out in the Coast Guard (Discipline) Rules 1983 appendix VI; The Coast Guard Discipline) Rules 1983 r 54 (a).

3 The Coast Guard (Discipline) Rules 1983 r 54 (b).

4 The Coast Guard (Discipline) Rules 1983 r 54 (c).

5 The Coast Guard (Discipline) Rules 1983 r 54 (d).

6 The Coast Guard (Discipline) Rules 1983 r 54 (e).

7 The Coast Guard (Discipline) Rules 1983 r 54 (f).

8 The Coast Guard (Discipline) Rules 1983 r 54 (f) proviso.

9 The Coast Guard (Discipline) Rules 1983 r 54 (g).

10 The Coast Guard (Discipline) Rules 1983 r 54 (h).

11 Ie as mentioned in the Coast Guard (Discipline) Rules 1983 r 118.

12 The Coast Guard (Discipline) Rules 1983 r 54 (i).

13 The Coast Guard (Discipline) Rules 1983 r 54 (j).

14 The Coast Guard (Discipline) Rules 1983 r 54 (k).

15 Ie the Coast Guard (Discipline) Rules 1983 r 56; The Coast Guard (Discipline) Rules 1983 r 54 (l).

[1486] Dissolution of a coast guard court If a coast guard court after the commencement of a trial is reduced below the minimum number of officers required by the Coast Guard Act 1978, it shall be dissolved[1]. If, on account of the illness of the Law Officer[2] or of the accused before the finding, it is impossible to continue the trial, a Coast guard court shall be dissolved[3]. The convening authority of a coast guard court may dissolve the same if it considers that the exigencies of the service or necessities of discipline render it impossible or inexpedient to continue the said coast guard court[4]. Where a coast guard court is dissolved under this provision, the accused may be tried again[5].

1 For composition of 'coast guard court'; see **[1485]**. The Coast Guard Act 1978 s 66 (1).

2 As to the power, duties and disqualification of 'law officer'; see **[1491], [1529] and [1530].**

3 The Coast Guard Act 1978 s 66 (2).

4 The Coast Guard Act 1978 s 66 (3).

5 The Coast Guard Act 1978 s 66 (4).

[1487] Powers of a coast guard court Every coast guard court[1] shall have the power to try any person subject to the Coast Guard Act 1978[2] for any offence punishable under the Act, and to pass any sentence authorised by the Coast Guard Act 1978[3].

1 As to the definition of 'coast guard court'; see **[1307]**.

2 As to the meaning of 'person subject to the Coast Guard Act 1978'; see **[1330]**.

3 The Coast Guard Act 1978 s 67.

[1488] Prohibition of second trial When any person subject to the Coast Guard Act 1978[1] has been acquitted or convicted of an offence by a coast guard court[2] or by a criminal court[3] or has been dealt with under the Coast Guard Act 1978[4], he shall not be liable to be tried again for the same offence by a coast guard court again[5]. When any person subject to the Coast Guard Act 1978, has been acquitted or convicted of an offence by a coast guard court or has been dealt with under the Coast Guard Act 1978[6], he shall not be liable to be tried again by a criminal court for the same offence or on the same facts[7].

1 As to the meaning of 'person subject to the Coast Guard Act 1978'; see **[1330]**.

2 As to the definition of 'coast guard court'; see **[1307]**.

3 As to the definition of 'criminal court'; see **[1311]**.

4 Ie under the Coast Guard Act 1978 s 57; see **[1459]**.

5 The Coast Guard Act 1978 s 68 (1).

6 Ie under the Coast Guard Act 1978 s 57.

7 The Coast Guard Act 1978 s 68 (2).

[1489] Application of the Coast Guard Act 1978 during term of sentence When a person subject to the Coast Guard Act 1978[1] is sentenced by a coast guard court[2] to imprisonment, the aforesaid Act shall apply to him during the term of his sentence, though he is dismissed from the Coast Guard, or has otherwise ceased to be subject to the Coast Guard Act 1978. He may be kept, removed, imprisoned and punished as if he continued to be subject to the Coast Guard Act[3]. When a person subject to the Coast Guard Act 1978 is sentenced by a Coast guard court to death, the aforesaid Act shall apply to him till the sentence is carried out[4].

1 As to the meaning of 'person subject to the Coast Guard Act 1978'; see **[1330]**.

2 As to the definition of 'coast guard court'; see **[1307]**.

3 The Coast Guard Act 1978 s 69 (1).

4 The Coast Guard Act 1978 s 69 (2).

[1490] Place of trial A coast guard court[1] may be held on shore or afloat[2].

1 As to the definition of 'coast guard court'; see **[1307]**.

2 The Coast Guard Act 1978 s 70.

B. Procedure of Coast guard court

[1491] Law officer Every coast guard court shall be attended by a Law Officer, or if no such officer is available, an officer approved by the Chief Law Officer or a Law Officer[1].

1 As to the power, duties and disqualification of Law Officer; see **[1529]** and **[1530]**. The Coast Guard Act 1978 s 73.

[1492] Challenges At all trials by a coast guard court[1], as soon as the court is assembled, the names of the presiding officer and members shall be read over to the accused, who shall thereupon be asked whether he objects to being tried by any officer sitting on the court[2]. If the accused objects to such officer, his objection and also the reply thereto of the officer objected to shall be heard and recorded, and the remaining officers of the court shall, in the absence of the challenged officer, decide on the objection[3]. If the objection is allowed by one-half or more of the votes of the members entitled to vote, the objection shall be allowed, and the member objected to shall retire, and his vacancy may be filled in the prescribed manner, by another officer subject to the same right of the accused to object[4]. Where no challenge is made or when a challenge has been made and disallowed, or the place of every officer successfully challenged has been filled by another officer to whom no objection is made or allowed, the court shall proceed with the trial[5].

1 As to the definition of 'coast guard court'; see **[1307]**.

2 The Coast Guard Act 1978 s 74 (1).

3 The Coast Guard Act 1978 s 74 (2).

4 The Coast Guard Act 1978 s 74 (1).

5 The Coast Guard Act 1978 s 74 (2).

[1493] Oaths of member, Law Officer and witness An oath or affirmation in the prescribed manner shall be administered to every member of a coast guard court[1] and to the Law Officer[2] by the officer approved under the Coast Guard Act 1978[3], before the commencement of the trial[4]. Every person giving evidence before a coast guard court shall be examined after being duly sworn or affirmed in the prescribed form[5]. The aforesaid provisions shall not apply where the witness is a child under 12 years of age and the coast guard court is of opinion that though the witness understands the duty of speaking the truth, he does not understand the nature of an oath or affirmation[6]

1 As to the definition of 'coast guard court'; see **[1307]**.

2 As to the details of 'law officer'; see **[1491]**.

3 Ie the Coast Guard Act 1978 s 73; see **[1494]**.

4 The Coast Guard Act 1978 s 75 (1).

5 The Coast Guard Act 1978 s 75 (2).

6 The Coast Guard Act 1978 s 75 (3).

[1494] Swearing or affirming of members, law officers and other officers As soon as the court is constituted with the proper number of officers who are not objected to or objections in respect of whom have been overruled, an oath or affirmation shall be administered to the Presiding Officer and every member in the order of their seniority by the Law Officer in the presence of the accused in one of the following forms or in such other form to the same purport as the court ascertains to be according to the religion of the concerned officer or otherwise binding on his conscience[1].

Form of Oath

> I, ...swear by Almighty God, that I will well and truly try the accused (or accused persons) before the court, according to the evidence, and that I will, duly administer justice according to the Coast Guard Act 1978 without partiality, favour or affection; and I do further solemnly, sincerely and truly declare and affirm that I will not, on any account, at any time, whatsoever, discover, the vote or opinion of any particular member of the Court unless required to give evidence thereof by a court of law.

Form of Affirmation

> I, ...do solemnly, sincerely and truly declare and affirm, that I will well and truly try the accused (or accused persons) before the court, according to the evidence, and that I will duly administer justice according to the Coast Guard Act 1978 without partiality, favour or affection, and I do further solemnly sincerely and truly declare and affirm that I will not on any account at any time whatsoever, disclose or discover, the vote or opinion of any particular member of this court unless required to give evidence thereof by court of law.

After the members of the Court are all sworn or have made affirmation, an oath or affirmation shall be administered to the following persons or such of them as are present at the court in such of the following forms as shall be appropriate, or in such other form to the same purport as the Court ascertains to be according to the religion or otherwise binding on the conscience of the persons to be sworn or affirmed[2].

(A) Law Officer

Form of Oath

> I, ...swear by Almighty God that I will, to the best of my ability, carry out the duties of Law Officer, in accordance with the Coast Guard Act 1978 and the rules made thereunder without partiality, favour or affection, and I do further swear that I will not, on any account at any time whatsoever, disclose or discover the vote or opinion on any matter of any particular member of this Court, unless required to give evidence thereof by a court of law.

Form of Affirmation

I, ...do hereby, solemnly, sincerely and truly declare and affirm that I will, to the best of my ability, carry out the duties of Law Officer in accordance with the Coast Guard Act 1978 and the rules made thereunder without partiality, favour or affection, and I do further solemnly, sincerely, and truly declare and affirm, that I will not, on any account, at any time, whatsoever, disclose or discover the vote or opinion, on any matter of any particular member of this Court, unless, required to give evidence thereof by a court of law.

(B) Officers attending for the Purpose of Instruction

Form of Oath

I, ... swear by Almighty God that I will not on any account; at any time whatsoever disclose or discover the vote or opinion of any particular member or this Court unless required to give evidence thereof by a court of law.

Form of Affirmation

I,.........do solemnly, sincerely and truly, declare and affirm that I will not on any account, at any time whatsoever, disclose or discover the vote or opinion of any particular member of this Court unless required to give evidence thereof by a court of law.

(C) Shorthand Writer

Form of Oath

I,......... swear by Almighty God that I will truly take down to the best of my power, the evidence to be given before this Court and such other matters as I may be required to take down and will, when required, deliver to the Court a true transcript of the same.

Form of Affirmation

I,.........do solemnly, sincerely and truly, declare and affirm, that I will truly take down to the best of my power the evidence to be given before this Court and such other matters as I may be required to take down and will, when required, deliver to the Court a true transcript of the same.

(D) Interpreter

Form of Oath

I,.......swear by Almighty God that I will faithfully, interpret and translate, as I shall be required to do, touching the matter before this Court.

Form of Affirmation

I,........do solemnly, sincerely and truly, declare and affirm that I will faithfully interpret and translate, as I shall be required to do, touching the matter before this Court.

1 The Coast Guard (Discipline) Rules 1983 r 59.

2 The Coast Guard (Discipline) Rules 1983 r 60.

[1495] Voting by members Subject to certain provisions of the Coast Guard Act 1978[1], every decision of a coast guard court[2] shall be passed by an absolute majority of votes; and where there is an equality of votes on either the finding or the sentence, the decision shall be in favour of the accused[3]. No sentence of death shall be passed by a coast guard court without the concurrence of at least two-thirds of the members of the court[4]. In matters, other than a challenge or the finding or sentence, the presiding officer shall have a casting vote[5].

1 Ie the Coast Guard Act 1978 s 76 (2) and (3).

2 As to the definition of 'coast guard court'; see **[1307]**.

3 The Coast Guard Act 1978 s 76 (1).

4 The Coast Guard Act 1978 s 76 (2).

5 The Coast Guard Act 1978 s 76 (3).

[1496] General rule as to evidence The Indian Evidence Act 1872, shall, subject to the provisions of the Coast Guard Act 1978, apply to all proceedings before a coast guard court[1].

1 The Coast Guard Act 1978 s 77.

[1497] Judicial notice A coast guard court[1] may take judicial notice of any matter within the general knowledge of the members as officers of the Coast Guard[2].

1 As to the definition of 'coast guard court'; see **[1307]**.

2 The Coast Guard Act 1978 s 78.

[1498] Summoning of witnesses The convening authority, the presiding officer of a coast guard court[1], the law officer or the commanding officer[2] of the accused person may, by summons under his hand, require the attendance, at a time and place to be mentioned in the summons, of any person either to give evidence or to produce any document or other thing[3]. In the case of a witness who is subject to the Coast Guard Act 1978, the summons shall be sent to his commanding officer and such officer shall serve it upon him accordingly[4]. In the case of any other witness, the summons shall be sent to the Magistrate within whose jurisdiction he may be, or resides, and such Magistrate shall give effect to the summons as if the witness were required in the court of such a Magistrate[5]. When a witness is required to produce any particular document or other thing in his possession or power, the summons shall describe it with reasonable precision[6].

1 As to the definition of 'coast guard court'; see **[1307]**.

2 As to the definition of 'commanding officer'; see **[1310]**.

3 The Coast Guard Act 1978 s 79 (1).

4 The Coast Guard Act 1978 s 79 (1).

5 The Coast Guard Act 1978 s 79 (1).

6 The Coast Guard Act 1978 s 79 (1).

[1499] Arranging attendance of witness In case of trial by a coast guard court[1], the commanding officer[2] of the accused, convening authority or, after assembly of the court, the presiding officer or the law officer appointed for the trial, shall take proper steps for arranging attendance of a witness whom the accused or the prosecutor wishes to call and whose attendance can reasonably be arranged[3]. However, the person requesting such attendance may be required to defray the cost, if any[4]. The appropriate coast guard authority shall order the attendance of a witness subject to the Coast Guard Act 1978 without issuance of formal summons[5]. The attendance of persons belonging to Army, Navy and Air Force shall be arranged through appropriate authorities in accordance with any law for the time being in force[6].

1 As to the definition of 'coast guard court'; see **[1307]**.

2 As to the definition of 'commanding officer'; see **[1310]**.

3 The Coast Guard (Discipline) Rules 1983 r 50A (1).

4 The Coast Guard (Discipline) Rules 1983 r 50A (1) proviso.

5 The Coast Guard (Discipline) Rules 1983 r 50A (2).

6 The Coast Guard (Discipline) Rules 1983 r 50A (3).

[1500] Documents exempted from production Nothing in the aforesaid provision[1] shall be deemed to affect the operation of the Indian Evidence Act 1872[2], or to apply to any letter, post card, telegram or other document in the custody of the postal or telegraph authorities[3]. If any document in such custody is, in the opinion of any Chief Judicial Magistrate, Chief Metropolitan Magistrate, Court of Session or High Court, wanted for the purpose of any coast guard court[4], such Magistrate or Court may require the postal or telegraph authorities, as the case may be, to deliver such document to such person as such Magistrate or Court may direct[5]. If any such document is, in the opinion of any other Magistrate or of any Commissioner of Police or District Superintendent of Police wanted for any such purpose, he may require the postal or telegraph authorities, as the case may be, to cause such search to be made for, and to detain such document pending the orders of any such Chief Judicial Magistrate, Chief Metropolitan Magistrate, Court of Session or High Court[6].

1 Ie the Coast Guard Act 1978 s 79; see **[1498]**.

2 Ie the Indian Evidence Act 1872 s 123 and 124.

3 The Coast Guard Act 1978 s 80 (1).

4 As to the definition of 'coast guard court'; see **[1307]**.

5 The Coast Guard Act 1978 s 80 (2).

6 The Coast Guard Act 1978 s 80 (3).

[1501] Commissions for examination of witnesses Whenever, in the course of a trial by a coast guard court[1], it appears to the court that the examination of a witness is necessary for the ends of justice, and that the attendance of such witness cannot be procured without an amount of delay, expense or inconvenience which, in the circumstances of the case, would be unreasonable, such court may address the Chief Law Officer in order that a commission to take the evidence of such witness may be issued[2]. The Chief Law Officer may then, if he thinks necessary, issue a commission to any Metropolitan Magistrate or Judicial Magistrate of the first class, within the local limits of whose jurisdiction such witness resides, to take the evidence of such witness[3]. The Magistrate to whom the commission is issued[4], shall proceed to the place where the witness is, or shall summon the witness before him and shall take down his evidence in the same manner, and may, for this purpose, exercise the same powers, as in the trials of warrant-cases under the Code of Criminal Procedure 1973[5]. When the witness resides in any place outside India, the commission may be issued as specified in the Code of Criminal Procedure 1973[6].

1 As to the definition of 'coast guard court'; see **[1307]**.

2 The Coast Guard Act 1978 s 81 (1).

3 The Coast Guard Act 1978 s 81 (2).

4 Or, if he is the Chief Metropolitan Magistrate or Chief Judicial Magistrate, he or such Metropolitan Magistrate or Judicial Magistrate of the first class as he appoints in this behalf; see The Coast Guard Act 1978 s 81 (3).

5 The Coast Guard Act 1978 s 81 (3).

6 Ie the Code of Criminal Procedure 1973 s 285 (3); The Coast Guard Act 1978 s 81 (4).

[1502] Examination of a witness on commission The prosecutor and the accused person in any case in which a commission is issued under the aforesaid provision[1] may respectively forward any interrogatories in writing which the court may think relevant to the issue, and the Magistrate executing the commission shall examine the witness upon such interrogatories[2]. The prosecutor and the accused person may appear before such Magistrate by counsel, or except in the case of an accused person in custody, in person, and may examine, cross-examine and re-examine, as the case may be, the said witness[3]. After a commission issued under the Coast Guard Act 1978[4] has been duly executed, it shall be returned together with the deposition of the witness examined there under to the Chief Law Officer[5]. On receipt of a commission, and deposition returned under the aforesaid provision[6], the Chief Law Officer shall forward the same to the coast guard court at whose instance the commission was issued or, if such court has been dissolved, to any other court convened for the trial of the accused person; and the commission, the return thereto and the deposition shall be open to inspection by the prosecutor and the accused person, and may, subject to all just exceptions, be read in evidence in the case by either the prosecutor or the accused, and shall form part of the proceedings of the court[7]. In every case in which a commission is issued under the Coast Guard Act 1978[8], the trial may be adjourned for a specified time reasonably sufficient for the execution and return of the commission[9].

1 Ie The Coast Guard Act 1978 s 81; see **[1501]**.

2 The Coast Guard Act 1978 s 82 (1).

3 The Coast Guard Act 1978 s 82 (2).

4 Ie the Coast Guard Act 1978 s 81.

5 The Coast Guard Act 1978 s 82 (3).

6 Ie the Coast Guard Act 1978 s 82 (3).

7 The Coast Guard Act 1978 s 82 (4).

8 Ie The Coast Guard Act 1978 s 81.

9 The Coast Guard Act 1978 s 82 (5).

[1503] Alternative findings If an accused is charged before a coast guard court[1] with one offence and it appears in evidence that he committed a different offence, he may be convicted of the offence which he is shown to have committed although he was not charged with it[2].

1 As to the definition of 'coast guard court'; see **[1307]**.

2 The Coast Guard Act 1978 s 83.

[1504] Presumption as to signatures In any proceeding under the Coast Guard Act 1978, any application, certificate, warrant, reply or other document purporting to be signed by an officer in the service of the

Government shall, on production, be presumed to have been duly signed by the person by whom and in the character in which it purports to have been signed, until the contrary is shown[1].

1 The Coast Guard Act 1978 s 84.

[1505] Enrolment paper Any enrolment paper purporting to be signed by an enrolling officer shall, in proceedings under the Coast Guard Act 1978, be evidence of the person enrolled having given the answers to questions which he is therein represented as having given[1]. The enrolment of such person may be proved by the production of the original or a copy of his enrolment paper purporting to be certified to be a true copy by the officer having the custody of the enrolment paper[2].

1 The Coast Guard Act 1978 s 85 (1).

2 The Coast Guard Act 1978 s 85 (2).

[1506] Presumption as to certain documents A letter, return or other document respecting the service of any person in, or the dismissal or discharge of any person from, any unit or ship of the Coast Guard, or respecting the circumstances of any person not having served in, or belonged to, any unit or ship, if purporting to be signed by or on behalf of the Central Government or the Director-General, or by any prescribed officer[1], shall be evidence of the facts stated in such letter, return or other document[2]. A Coast Guard List or Gazette purporting to be published by authority shall be evidence of the status and rank of the officers therein mentioned, and of any appointment held by them and of the unit or ship of the Coast Guard to which they belong[3]. Where a record is made in the books of a ship in pursuance of the Coast Guard Act 1978 or any rule or otherwise in the discharge of official duties, and purports to be signed by the commanding officer[4] or by the officer whose duty it is to make such record, such record shall be evidence of the facts therein stated[5]. A copy of any record in the books of a ship purporting to be certified to be a true copy by the officer having custody of such books shall be evidence of such record[6]. Where any person subject to the Coast Guard Act 1978 is being tried on a charge of desertion or of absence without leave, and such person has surrendered himself into the custody of any officer or other person subject to the aforesaid Act or any unit or ship of the Coast Guard, or has been apprehended by such officer or person, a certificate purporting to be signed by such officer, or by the Commanding Officer of the unit or ship to which such person belongs, as the case may be, and stating the fact, date and place of such surrender or apprehension, and the manner in which he was dressed shall be evidence of the matters so stated[7]. Where any person subject to the Coast Guard Act 1978 is being tried on a charge of desertion or of improperly leaving a ship or of absence without leave and such person has surrendered himself into the custody of, or has been apprehended by, a police officer not below the rank of an officer in charge of a police station, a certificate purporting to be signed by such police officer and stating the fact, date and place of such surrender or apprehension and the manner in which he was dressed shall be evidence of the matters so stated[8]. Any document purporting to be a report under the hand of a Chemical Examiner or Assistant Chemical Examiner to Government or any of the Government scientific experts, namely, the Chief Inspector of the Explosives, the Director of the Fingerprint Bureau, the Director, Haffkeine Institute, Mumbai, the Director of a Central Forensic Science Laboratory or a State Forensic Science Laboratory and the Serologist to the Government upon any matter or thing duly submitted to him for examination or analysis and report, may be used as evidence in any proceeding under the Coast Guard Act 1978[9]. In this provision, the term 'books of a ship' shall include any official book, document or list purporting to contain the name or names of persons appointed to the ship[10].

1 As to the meaning of 'prescribed officer' under the Coast Guard Act 1978 s 86 (1) to sign letters, returns or other

documents: The Director (Personnel) Coast Guard Headquarters and Officer in-Charge, Bureau of Naviks; see the Coast Guard (General) Rules 1986 r 29.

2 The Coast Guard Act 1978 s 86 (1).

3 The Coast Guard Act 1978 s 86 (2).

4 As to the definition of 'commanding officer'; see **[1310]**.

5 The Coast Guard Act 1978 s 86 (3).

6 The Coast Guard Act 1978 s 86 (4).

7 The Coast Guard Act 1978 s 86 (5).

8 The Coast Guard Act 1978 s 86 (6).

9 The Coast Guard Act 1978 s 86 (7).

10 The Coast Guard Act 1978 s 86 explanation.

[1507] Evidence of previous convictions and general character When any person subject to the Coast Guard Act 1978[1] has been convicted by a coast guard court[2] of any offence, such court may inquire into, and receive, and record evidence of any previous convictions of such person, either by a coast guard court or by a criminal court[3] or any previous award of punishment under the provisions of the Coast Guard Act 1978[4]. The Court may further inquire into and record the general character of such person and such other matters as may be prescribed[5]. Evidence received under this provision may be either oral, or in the shape of entries in, or certified extracts from, books of coast guard courts or other official records ; and it shall not be necessary to give notice before trial to the person tried, that evidence as to his previous convictions or character will be received[6].

1 As to the meaning of 'person subject to the Coast Guard Act 1978'; see **[1330]**.

2 As to the definition of 'coast guard court'; see **[1310]**.

3 As to the definition of 'criminal court'; see **[1311]**.

4 Ie the Coast Guard Act 1978 s 57 or 57A; see **[1459]** and **[1461]**.

5 The Coast Guard Act 1978 s 87 (1).

6 The Coast Guard Act 1978 s 87 (2).

[1508] Lunacy of accused Whenever, in the course of a trial by a coast guard court[1], it appears to the court that the person charged is by reason of unsoundness of mind incapable of making his defence, or that he committed the act alleged but was by reason of unsoundness of mind incapable of knowing the nature of the act or knowing that it was wrong or contrary to law, the court shall record a finding accordingly[2]. The presiding officer of the coast guard court shall forthwith report the case to the convening authority[3]. The convening authority to whom the finding of a coast guard court is reported under the aforesaid provision[4] shall order the accused person to be kept in custody in the prescribed manner and shall report the case for the orders of the Central Government[5]. On receipt of a report under the aforesaid provision[6], the Central Government may order the accused person to be detained in a lunatic asylum or other suitable place of safe custody[7].

1 As to the definition of 'coast guard court'; see **[1307]**.

2 The Coast Guard Act 1978 s 88 (1).

3 The Coast Guard Act 1978 s 88 (2).

4 Ie the Coast Guard Act 1978 s 88 (2).

5 The Coast Guard Act 1978 s 88 (3).

6 Ie the Coast Guard Act 1978 s 88 (3).

7 The Coast Guard Act 1978 s 88 (4).

[1509] Subsequent fitness of lunatic accused for trial Where any accused person, having been found by reason of unsoundness of mind to be incapable of making his defence, is in custody or under detention under the aforesaid provision[1], any officer prescribed[2] in this behalf, may: (i) if such person is in custody under the Coast Guard Act 1978[3], on the report of a medical officer that he is capable of making his defence[4], or (ii) if such person is detained in jail under certain provisions of the Coast Guard Act 1978[5] , on a certificate of the Inspector-General of Prisons, and if such person is detained in a lunatic asylum under the said provision, on a certificate of any two or more of the visitors of such asylum and if he is detained in any other place under that sub-section, on a certificate of the prescribed authority, that he is capable of making his defence, take steps to have such person tried by the same or another coast guard court[6] for the offence with which he was originally charged, or, if the offence is a civil offence, by a criminal court[7].

1 Ie the Coast Guard Act 1978 s 88; see **[1508]**.

2 As to the meaning of 'prescribed officer' under the Coast Guard Act 1978 s 89 for taking steps for trial of a person of unsound mind: the officers who ordered original trial by the coast guard court. The prescribed authority under the Coast Guard Act 1978 s 89 for issue of certificate of fitness to attend trial: Medical Officer of the lunatic asylum or other place of safe custody where the person is kept; see the Coast Guard (General) Rules 1986 r 29.

3 Ie the Coast Guard Act 1978 s 88 (3).

4 The Coast Guard Act 1978 s 89 (a).

5 Ie the Coast Guard Act 1978 s 88 (4).

6 As to the definition of 'coast guard court'; see **[1307]**.

7 As to the definition of 'criminal court'; see **[1311]**; The Coast Guard Act 1978 s 89 (b).

[1510] Transmission to Central Government of orders under the Coast Guard Act 1978 s 89 A copy of every order made by an officer under the aforesaid provision[1] for the trial of the accused shall forthwith be sent to the Central Government[2].

1 Ie the Coast Guard Act 1978 s 89; see **[1509]**.

2 The Coast Guard Act 1978 s 90.

[1511] Release of lunatic accused Where any person is in custody or detention under the Coast Guard Act 1978[1]: (i) if such person is in custody, on the report of the medical officer[2], or (ii) if such person is detained, on a certificate from any of the authorities mentioned in the provisions of the Coast Guard Act 1978[3] that in the judgment of such officer or authority such person may be released without danger of his doing injury to himself or to any other person[4], the Central Government may order that such person be released or detained in custody, or transferred to a public lunatic asylum if he has not already been sent to such asylum[5].

1 Ie in custody or detention under the Coast Guard Act 1978 s 88 (3) or s 88 (4) respectively; see **[1508]**.

2 The Coast Guard Act 1978 s 91 (a).

3 Ie the Coast Guard Act 1978 s 89 (b).

4 The Coast Guard Act 1978 s 91 (b).

5 The Coast Guard Act 1978 s 91.

[1512] Delivery of lunatic accused to relatives Where any relative or friend of any person who is in custody or detention under the Coast Guard Act 1978[1] desires that he should be delivered to his care and custody, the Central Government may, upon application by such relative or friend and, on his giving security to the satisfaction of that Government that the person delivered shall be properly taken care of, and, prevented from doing injury to himself or to any other person, and be produced for the inspection of such officer, and at such times and places, as the Central Government may direct, order such person to be delivered to such relative or friend[2].

1 Ie in custody or detention under the Coast Guard Act 1978 s 88 (3) or s 88 (4) respectively; see **[1508]**.

2 The Coast Guard Act 1978 s 92.

[1513] Order for custody and disposal of property pending trial When any property regarding which any offence appears to have been committed, or which appears to have been used for the commission of any offence, is produced before a Coast guard court[1] during a trial, the court may make such order as it thinks fit for the proper custody of such property pending the conclusion of the trial, and if the property is subject to speedy or natural decay may, after recording such evidence as it thinks necessary, order it to be sold or otherwise disposed of[2].

1 As to the definition of 'coast guard court'; see **[1307]**.

2 The Coast Guard Act 1978 s 93.

[1514] Order for disposal of property regarding which offence is committed After the conclusion of a trial before a coast guard court[1], an officer not below the rank of a Deputy Inspector-General within whose command the trial was held, may make such order for the disposal by destruction, confiscation, delivery to any person claiming to be entitled to possession thereof, or otherwise, of any property or document produced before the court or in its custody, or regarding which any offence appears to have been committed or which has been used for the commission of any offence[2]. Where any order has been made under the aforesaid provision in respect of property regarding which an offence appears to have been committed, a copy of such order signed, and certified by the authority making the same may, whether the trial was held within India or not, be sent to a Magistrate within whose jurisdiction such property is situated. Such Magistrate shall thereupon cause the order to be carried out into effect as if it were an order passed by him under the provisions of the Code of Criminal Procedure 1973[3]. In this provision, the term 'property' includes, in the case of property regarding which an offence appears to have been committed, not only such property as has been originally in the possession or Under the control of any person, but also any property into or for which the same may have been converted or exchanged, and anything acquired by such conversion or exchange whether immediately or otherwise[4].

1 As to the definition of 'coast guard court'; see **[1307]**.

2 The Coast Guard Act 1978 s 94 (1).

3 The Coast Guard Act 1978 s 94 (2).

4 The Coast Guard Act 1978 s 94 (3).

[1515] Powers of coast guard court in relation to proceedings under the Coast Guard Act 1978 Any trial by a coast guard court[1] under the provisions of the Coast Guard Act 1978 shall be deemed to be a judicial proceeding within the meaning of the Indian Penal Code 1860[2] and the coast guard court shall be deemed to be a court within the meaning of the Code of Criminal Procedure 1973[3].

1 As to the definition of 'coast guard court'; see **[1307]**.

2 Ie the Indian Penal Code 1860 s 193 and 228.

3 Ie the Code of Criminal Procedure 1973 s 345 and 346; The Coast Guard Act 1978 s 95.

C. Coast guard courts: Incidental Matters

[1516] Seating of Members The members of a coast guard court shall take their seats according to their seniority[1].

1 The Coast Guard (Discipline) Rules 1983 r 98.

[1517] Responsibility of Presiding Officer The Presiding Officer together with the Law Officer is responsible for the trial being conducted in proper order, and in accordance with the Coast Guard Act 1978, the Coast Guard Rules and in a manner befitting a court of justice[1]. It is the duty of the Presiding Officer to see that the accused has a fair trial, and that he does not suffer any disadvantage in consequences of his position as a person under trial, or of his incapacity to examine or cross-examine witnesses or otherwise[2].

1 The Coast Guard (Discipline) Rules 1983 r 99 (1).

2 The Coast Guard (Discipline) Rules 1983 r 99 (2).

[1518] Power of court over address of prosecutor and accused It is the duty of the prosecutor to assist the court in the administration of justice, to behave impartially, to bring the whole of the transaction before the court and not to take any unfair advantage of, or suppress any evidence in favour of the accused[1]. The prosecutor may not refer to any matter, not relevant to the charge or charges, than before the court and it is the duty of the court to stop him from so doing and also to restrain any undue violence or want of fairness or moderation on the part of the prosecutor[2]. The court shall give reasonable facilities to the accused, in making his defence the accused must abstain from any remarks contemptuous or disrespectful towards the court, and from coarse and insulting language towards others, but he may for the purpose of his defence impeach the evidence and charge other persons with blame and even criminality, subject, if he does so, to any liability which he may thereby incur. The court may caution the accused as to the irrelevance of his defence, but shall not, unless in special cases stop his defence solely on ground of such irrelevance[3].

1 The Coast Guard (Discipline) Rules 1983 r 100 (1).

2 The Coast Guard (Discipline) Rules 1983 r 100 (2).

3 The Coast Guard (Discipline) Rules 1983 r 100 (3).

[1519] Sitting in closed court A court shall, where it is so directed by these provisions, and may in any other case on any deliberation amongst the members, sit in closed court[1]. No person shall be present in closed court except the members of the court, the Law Officer and any other officer under instruction[2]. For this purpose[3], a Court may either retire or cause the place where it sits to be cleared of all other persons not entitled to be present[4]. Except as mentioned above, all proceedings including the view of any place shall be in open court and in the presence of the accused[5]. However, the court shall have the power to exclude from the court any witness who has yet to give evidence or any other person, other than the accused, who interferes with its proceedings[6].

1 The Coast Guard (Discipline) Rules 1983 r 101 (1).

2 The Coast Guard (Discipline) Rules 1983 r 101 (2).

3 Ie the Coast Guard (Discipline) Rules 1983 r 101 (1) and (2).

4 The Coast Guard (Discipline) Rules 1983 r 101 (3).

5 Ie the Coast Guard (Discipline) Rules 1983 r 101 (5); The Coast Guard (Discipline) Rules 1983 r 101 (4).

6 The Coast Guard (Discipline) Rules 1983 r 101 (5).

[1520] Continuity of trial and adjournment of court When a court is once assembled and the accused has been arraigned, the court shall continue the trial from day to day in accordance with these provisions unless it appears to the court that an adjournment is necessary for the ends of justice or that such continuance is impracticable[1]. A court may from time to time adjourn its proceedings and meet at such place as may be convenient[2], and where necessary, visit the scene of occurrence[3]. A court in the absence of a Law Officer shall not proceed and shall adjourn[4]. If the time to which an adjournment is made is not specified, the adjournment shall be until further orders from the Presiding Officer, and, if the place to which an adjournment is made is not specified, the adjournment shall be to the same place or to such other place as may be specified in further orders from the Presiding Officer[5]. On all working days a coast guard court may sit at such times and for such period between sunrise and sunset for reasonable hours to conduct the proceedings[6]. However, in cases where the court or the convening authority thinks that the service exigencies or the interest of discipline so require, the court may also sit on Sundays or gazetted holidays, as deemed necessary[7].

1 The Coast Guard (Discipline) Rules 1983 r 102 (1).

2 The Coast Guard (Discipline) Rules 1983 r 102 (2) (a).

3 The Coast Guard (Discipline) Rules 1983 r 102 (2) (b).

4 The Coast Guard (Discipline) Rules 1983 r 102 (3).

5 The Coast Guard (Discipline) Rules 1983 r 102 (4).

6 The Coast Guard (Discipline) Rules 1983 r 102 (5).

7 The Coast Guard (Discipline) Rules 1983 r 102 (5) proviso.

[1521] Suspension of trial Where, in consequence of anything arising while the court is sitting, the court is unable by reasons of dissolution as specified in the Coast Guard Act 1978, the Coast Guard (Discipline) Rules 1983 or otherwise, to continue the trial, the Presiding Officer or in his absence the senior member present, shall immediately report the facts to the convening authority[1].

1 The Coast Guard (Discipline) Rules 1983 r 103.

[1522] Death, retirement or absence of Presiding Officer and Proceedings on death or illness of accused In the case of the death, retirement on challenge or unavoidable absence of the Presiding Officer the next senior officer shall take the place of the Presiding Officer and the trial shall proceed if the court is still composed of not less than the minimum number of officers required by the Coast Guard Act 1978[1].

In case of the death of the accused or of such illness of the accused as renders it impossible to continue the trial, the court shall ascertain the fact of the death or illness by evidence and record the same and adjourn and transmit the proceedings to the Convening Authority[2].

1 The Coast Guard (Discipline) Rules 1983 r 105.

2 The Coast Guard (Discipline) Rules 1983 r 104.

[1523] Presence throughout of all members of court A member of a court who has been absent while any part of the evidence on the trial of an accused person is taken, shall take no further part in the trial by that court of that person, but the court will not be affected unless it is reduced below the legal minimum[1].

1 The Coast Guard (Discipline) Rules 1983 r 106.

[1524] Taking of opinions of members of Court Every member of a coast guard court must give his opinion by word of mouth on every question which the court has to decide, and must give his opinion as to the sentence notwithstanding that he has given his opinion in favour of acquittal[1]. The opinions of the members of the court shall be taken in succession, beginning with the member junior most in seniority[2].

1 The Coast Guard (Discipline) Rules 1983 r 107 (1).

2 The Coast Guard (Discipline) Rules 1983 r 107 (2).

[1525] Procedure on incidental question If any objection is raised on any matter of law, evidence or procedure, by the prosecutor or by or on behalf of the accused during the trial, the prosecutor or the accused or counsel or the defending officer, as the case may be, shall have a right to answer the same and the person raising the objection shall have right to reply[1].

1 The Coast Guard (Discipline) Rules 1983 r 108.

[1526] Evidence when to the translated When any evidence is given in a language which any of the officers composing the court, the accused or the Law Officer does not understand, it shall be translated into a language which is understood by all concerned[1].

1 The Coast Guard (Discipline) Rules 1983 r 109.

[1527] Defending Officer, Friend of Accused and Counsel At any coast guard court, an accused person may be represented by a counsel or by an officer subject to the Act who shall be called the 'defending officer' or assisted by any person whose services he may be able to procure and who shall be called the 'friend of the accused'[1]. The defending officer shall have the same rights and duties as pertain to a counsel under these provisions and shall be under the same like obligation[2]. The friend of the accused may advise the accused on all points and suggest the questions to be put to the witnesses, but he shall not examine or cross-examine the witnesses or address the Court[3].

1 The Coast Guard (Discipline) Rules 1983 r 114 (1).

2 The Coast Guard (Discipline) Rules 1983 r 114 (2).

3 The Coast Guard (Discipline) Rules 1983 r 114 (3).

[1528] Requirements for Appearance of Counsel An accused person intending to be represented by a counsel shall give notice of such intention to his commanding officer or the Convening Authority. If notice has not been given, the Court may, if it thinks fit, on the application of the prosecutor, adjourn to enable him to obtain a counsel on behalf of the prosecutor at the trial[1]. Where the Convening Authority so directs, counsel may appear along with the prosecutor, but in that case, unless the notice referred in the aforesaid provision[2] has been given by the accused, notice of the direction or counsel to appear shall be given to the accused at such time (not in any case less than seven days) before the trial as would, in the opinion of the Court, have enabled the accused to obtain counsel to assist him at the trial[3].

The counsel who appears before a Court on behalf of the prosecutor or accused, shall have the same rights, as the prosecutor or the accused, for whom he appears. He shall have the right to call, and orally examine, cross-examine, and re-examine witnesses, to put in any plea and to inspect the proceedings and the right otherwise to act in the course of the trial in place of the person on whose behalf he appears. The counsel shall comply with these provisions as if he were that person and in such a case that person shall have no right himself to do any of the aforesaid matters except as regards the statement allowed by certain provisions of the Coast Guard (Discipline) Rules 1983[4] or except so far as the Court permits him so to do[5].

1 The Coast Guard (Discipline) Rules 1983 r 115 (1).

2 Ie the Coast Guard (Discipline) Rules 1983 r 115 (1).

3 The Coast Guard (Discipline) Rules 1983 r 115 (2).

4 Ie the Coast Guard (Discipline) Rules 1983 r 87 (2) and 95 (4).

5 The Coast Guard (Discipline) Rules 1983 r 115 (3).

[1529] Disqualification of Law Officer An officer who is disqualified for sitting on a Court, shall be disqualified for acting as a Law Officer at that Court[1].

1 The Coast Guard (Discipline) Rules 1983 r 116.

[1530] Powers and Duties of Law Officer The Law Officer shall: (i) give his opinion on any question of law relating to the charge (s) or trial, whenever so required by the Court, the prosecutor or the accused[1]; (ii) inform the Court of any irregularity or other infirmity in the proceedings[2]; (iii) inform the Convening Authority and the Court of any infirmity or defect in the charge or in the constitution of the Court[3]; (iv) sum up the evidence and give his opinion on any question of law, before the court proceeds to deliberate upon its findings[4]. It shall be duty of the Law Officer to ensure that the accused does not suffer any disadvantage in consequence of his position as such, or because of ignorance or incapacity to examine or cross-examine the witnesses and for this purpose the Law Officer may with the permission of the Court, call witnesses and put questions to them which appear to him necessary or desirable[5]. During any trial by coast guard court, it is the duty of the Law Officer to decide all questions of law, including questions as to the relevancy of facts and admissibility of oral and documentary evidence[6]. Whenever during trial, it appears to the Law Officer that any argument as to the admissibility of the evidence or on application for separate trials or on any other question of law, should not be heard in the presence of the court, he may advise the Presiding Officer of the court accordingly and the Presiding Officer shall thereupon, make an order for the court to retire and thereafter, the Law Officer shall hear the arguments and give his opinion[7]. Where any opinion has been given by the Law Officer to the court on any matter before it, it may be recorded in the proceedings[8]. In the discharge of his duties, the Law Officer shall maintain a strict impartial position[9].

1 The Coast Guard (Discipline) Rules 1983 r 117 (1) (a).

2 The Coast Guard (Discipline) Rules 1983 r 117 (1) (b).

3 The Coast Guard (Discipline) Rules 1983 r 117 (1) (c).

4 The Coast Guard (Discipline) Rules 1983 r 117 (1) (d).

5 The Coast Guard (Discipline) Rules 1983 r 117 (2)

6 The Coast Guard (Discipline) Rules 1983 r 117 (3)

7 The Coast Guard (Discipline) Rules 1983 r 117 (4)

8 The Coast Guard (Discipline) Rules 1983 r 117 (5)

9 The Coast Guard (Discipline) Rules 1983 r 117 (6)

[1531] Duties of the officer of the court The officer of court appointed under the provisions of the Coast Guard (Discipline) Rules 1983[1] shall perform the following duties: (i) He shall be responsible for making due arrangements for the sitting of the court under the directions of the Law Officer and shall obtain from the proper source the furniture and fittings and supply stationery required for use of the court[2]; (ii) He shall muster the witnesses outside the court-room and as soon as the coast guard court is assembled he shall report to the Presiding Officer that they are in attendance[3]; (iii) When so directed by the Presiding Officer, he shall cause the accused to be brought in and to admit the prosecutor and audience[4]; (iv) He shall ensure that no witness enters the court unless called upon to give evidence, except by the permission of the court[5]; (v) He shall ensure that witnesses leave the court as soon as they have been examined and are not allowed to communicate with other witnesses who have yet to give evidence[6]; (vi) He shall ensure that no witness, duly summoned, leaves the vicinity of the court[7]; (vii) When the court is cleared for deliberations, he shall ensure that no one is allowed to remain within the court's vicinity[8].

1 Ie the Coast Guard (Discipline) Rules 1983 r 54 (i).

2 The Coast Guard (Discipline) Rules 1983 r 118 (1) (a).

3 The Coast Guard (Discipline) Rules 1983 r 118 (1) (b).

4 The Coast Guard (Discipline) Rules 1983 r 118 (1) (c).

5 The Coast Guard (Discipline) Rules 1983 r 118 (1) (d).

6 The Coast Guard (Discipline) Rules 1983 r 118 (1) (e).

7 The Coast Guard (Discipline) Rules 1983 r 118 (1) (f).

8 The Coast Guard (Discipline) Rules 1983 r 118 (1) (g).

[1532] Findings of Insanity Where the Court finds either that the accused by reason of unsoundness of mind is incapable of making his defence, or that he committed the act alleged but was by reason of unsoundness of mind incapable of knowing the nature of the act or that it was wrong or contrary to law, the Presiding Officer shall affix his signature and the date on the findings which shall also be signed by the Law Officer and thereupon the proceedings shall at once be transmitted to the convening authority or in the case of summary trial to the Inspector General or Deputy Inspector General empowered to approve them[1].

1 As to the lunacy of the accused; see the Coast Guard Act 1978 s 88: **[1508]**. The Coast Guard (Discipline) Rules 1983 r 119.

[1533] Preservation of Proceedings The proceedings of every coast guard court shall, after promulgation, be forwarded, to the office of the Chief Law Officer and be preserved there for not less than seven years, or until the sentence awarded by the Court has expired, whichever is later[1]. The proceedings of every summary trial shall, after promulgation, be forwarded to the Officer-in-Charge, Bureau of Naviks, who shall preserve these proceedings for a period not less than seven years[2].

1 The Coast Guard (Discipline) Rules 1983 r 120 (1).

2 The Coast Guard (Discipline) Rules 1983 r 120 (1).

[1534] Right of person tried to copies of proceedings Every person tried by a coast guard court shall be entitled to obtain on demand at any time after the verdict of the court is announced and before the proceedings are destroyed, from the Chief Law Officer a copy thereof[1].

1 The Coast Guard (Discipline) Rules 1983 r 121.

[1535] Copy of proceedings not to be given in certain cases Notwithstanding anything contained in the aforesaid provision[1], if the Central Government is satisfied for reasons to be recorded that it is against the interests of the Security of the State or friendly relations with foreign states to supply a copy of the proceedings or any part thereof, the accused shall not be furnished with such a copy[2]. However, if the Central Government is satisfied that the person demanding the copy is desirous of submitting a petition in accordance with the Coast Guard Act 1978 or instituting any action in the court of law in relation to the findings or sentence by a Court it shall permit inspection of the proceedings by such person or his legal Adviser, if any, on the following conditions: (a) The inspection shall be made at such time and such places as the Central Government or any authority authorised by it may direct[3], and (b) the person allowed to inspect the proceedings shall before such inspection, furnish: (i) an undertaking, in writing that he shall not make copies of the proceedings or any part thereof and that the information or documents contained in such proceedings shall not be used by him, for the purpose of submitting a petition in accordance with the Coast Guard Act 1978 or instituting an action in a court of law in relation to the said finding or sentence[4]; and (ii) a certificate that he is aware that he may render himself liable to prosecution under the Indian Official Secrets Act 1923 s 3 and 5 if he commits any act specified in the said provisions in relation to the documents or information contained in the said proceedings[5].

1 Ie the Coast Guard (Discipline) Rules 1983 r 121; see **[1534]**.

2 The Coast Guard (Discipline) Rules 1983 r 122.

3 The Coast Guard (Discipline) Rules 1983 r 122 proviso (a).

4 The Coast Guard (Discipline) Rules 1983 r 122 proviso (b) (i).

5 The Coast Guard (Discipline) Rules 1983 r 122 proviso (b) (ii).

[1536] Loss of Proceedings If the original proceedings or any part thereof are lost, and there is sufficient evidence of the charge, findings, sentence and transactions of the Court, that evidence shall be a valid and sufficient record of trial for all purposes[1].

1 The Coast Guard (Discipline) Rules 1983 r 123.

[1537] Offences by witnesses and others[1]

1 See **[1413]**.

8. THE COAST GUARD COURT: GENERAL

CONTENTS

PARA

Coast Guard Courts: General

[1538] Application for trial by a coast guard court An application for trial by a coast guard court[1] shall be made by the commanding officer[2] in the form set out in the Coast Guard (Discipline) Rules 1983 Appendix IV and shall be accompanied by five copies of the record or abstract of evidence, charge sheet and other documents as mentioned in the application form[3].

1 As to the definition of 'coast guard court'; see **[1307]**.

2 As to the definition of 'commanding officer'; see **[1310]**.

3 The Coast Guard (Discipline) Rules 1983 r 27.

[1539] Assembly and swearing of coast guard courts Upon assembling the coast guard court shall, before beginning the trial, satisfy in closed court that the: (a) court has been convened in accordance with the Coast Guard Act 1978 and the Coast Guard (Discipline) Rules 1983[1]; (b) court consists of not less than the minimum number of officers specified in Act[2]; (c) members are of the required rank[3]; (d) that members have been duly appointed and are not disqualified under the Coast Guard Act 1978[4]; (e) law officer has been duly appointed[5]; (f) accused appears from the charge-sheet, to be subject to the Coast Guard Act 1978 and to be subject to the jurisdiction of the court[6]; and (g) charge is correct in law and framed in accordance with the Coast Guard (Discipline) Rules 1983[7]. Where a vacancy occurs by reason of disqualification of a member of the court under the Coast Guard Act 1978 or being absent when the court assembles, the Presiding Officer may appoint a duly qualified waiting member to fill that vacancy[8]. The Presiding Officer may, if the interests of justice so require, substitute a duly qualified waiting member for a member appointed by the Convening Authority[9]. If the court is not satisfied on any of the matters mentioned in the Coast Guard (Discipline) Rules 1983[10] and is not competent to rectify such matter itself under the Coast Guard Act 1978 or the aforesaid Rules, it shall, before commencing the trial, report thereon to the Convening Authority[11]. When the court has complied with these provisions and is ready to proceed with the trial, the Presiding Officer shall open the court and the trial shall begin[12].

1 The Coast Guard (Discipline) Rules 1983 r 57 (1) (a).

2 The Coast Guard (Discipline) Rules 1983 r 57 (1) (b).

3 The Coast Guard (Discipline) Rules 1983 r 57 (1) (c).

4 The Coast Guard (Discipline) Rules 1983 r 57 (1) (d).

5 The Coast Guard (Discipline) Rules 1983 r 57 (1) (e).

6 The Coast Guard (Discipline) Rules 1983 r 57 (1) (f).

7 The Coast Guard (Discipline) Rules 1983 r 57 (1) (g).

8 The Coast Guard (Discipline) Rules 1983 r 57 (2) (a).

9 The Coast Guard (Discipline) Rules 1983 r 57 (2) (b).

10 Ie the Coast Guard (Discipline) Rules 1983 r 57 (1).

11 The Coast Guard (Discipline) Rules 1983 r 57 (3).

12 The Coast Guard (Discipline) Rules 1983 r 57 (4).

[1540] Commencement of trial As soon as the Court has been opened, the accused shall be brought before it and the prosecution, the person(s), if any defending the accused and the audience admitted[1]. The order convening the court and the names of the officers appointed to try the accused shall be read over to the accused by the Law Officer and the accused shall be given an opportunity to object to any of the officers in accordance with the Coast Guard Act 1978[2]. When a court is to try more than one accused whether separately or jointly, each accused shall be given an opportunity to object to any officer on the court in accordance with the foregoing provision and shall be asked separately whether he has any such objection[3]. An accused shall state the names of all the officers to whom he objects before any objection is disposed of[4]. If more than one officer is objected to, the objection to each officer shall be disposed of separately and the objection to the lowest in rank shall be disposed of first[5]. An accused may make a statement and call any person to make a statement in support of his objection[6]. An officer to whom the accused has objected may state in open court anything relevant to the objection of the accused whether in support or in rebuttal thereof[7]. An objection to an officer shall be considered in closed court by all the other officers on the court and the officer objected to shall not be present at that time[8]. When an officer objected to retires and there is a duly qualified waiting member in attendance, the Presiding Officer shall immediately appoint him to take the place of the officer who has retired[9]. The court shall satisfy itself that a waiting member who takes the place of a member of the court is of the required rank and not disqualified under the Coast Guard Act 1978 and shall give the accused an opportunity to object to him and shall deal with any such objection in accordance with the Coast Guard Act 1978 and the Coast Guard (Discipline) Rules 1983[10]. If as a result of the allowance of an objection to a member there are insufficient officers available to form a court in compliance with the Coast Guard Act 1978, the court shall report to the Convening Authority without proceeding further with the trial and the Convening Authority may either appoint another officer as a member to fill the vacancy or convenes a fresh court to try the accused[11].

1 The Coast Guard (Discipline) Rules 1983 r 58 (1).

2 Ie the Coast Guard Act 1978 s 74; The Coast Guard (Discipline) Rules 1983 r 58 (2).

3 The Coast Guard (Discipline) Rules 1983 r 58 (3).

4 The Coast Guard (Discipline) Rules 1983 r 58 (4).

5 The Coast Guard (Discipline) Rules 1983 r 58 (5).

6 The Coast Guard (Discipline) Rules 1983 r 58 (6).

7 The Coast Guard (Discipline) Rules 1983 r 58 (7).

8 The Coast Guard (Discipline) Rules 1983 r 58 (8).

9 The Coast Guard (Discipline) Rules 1983 r 58 (9).

10 The Coast Guard (Discipline) Rules 1983 r 58 (10).

11 The Coast Guard (Discipline) Rules 1983 r 58 (11).

[1541] Objection to interpreter or shorthand writer A person shall not be sworn or affirmed as an interpreter or shorthand writer, if he is objected to by the accused unless the court after hearing the accused and the prosecutor disallows such objection as being unreasonable[1].

1 The Coast Guard (Discipline) Rules 1983 r 61.

[1542] Arraignment When the court and the law officer have been sworn, the charge shall be read to the accused and he shall be asked whether he pleads guilty or not guilty to the charge or charges[1]. If there is more than one charge against the accused he shall be required to plead separately to each charge[2]. If there is more than one charge against the accused before the court, the court shall proceeds with the charges in the first of such charge sheets and shall announce its finding thereon and if the accused has pleaded guilty comply with the provisions of the Coast Guard (Discipline) Rules 1983[3] before it arraigns him upon the charges in any subsequent charge sheet[4].

1 The Coast Guard (Discipline) Rules 1983 r 62 (1).

2 The Coast Guard (Discipline) Rules 1983 r 62 (2).

3 Ie the Coast Guard (Discipline) Rules 1983 r 69.

4 The Coast Guard (Discipline) Rules 1983 r 62 (3).

[1543] Plea to jurisdiction The accused, before pleading to the charge may offer a plea regarding the jurisdiction of the court, and in such case: (i) the accused may adduce evidence in support of the plea and the prosecutor may adduce evidence in answer thereto[1]; and (ii) the prosecutor may address the court in answer to the plea and the accused may reply to the prosecutor's address[2]. If the court allows the plea it shall adjourn and report to the Convening Authority[3]. When the court reports to the Convening Authority under this provision, the Convening Authority shall dissolve the court[4].

1 The Coast Guard (Discipline) Rules 1983 r 63 (1) (a).

2 The Coast Guard (Discipline) Rules 1983 r 63 (1) (b).

3 The Coast Guard (Discipline) Rules 1983 r 63 (2).

4 The Coast Guard (Discipline) Rules 1983 r 63 (3).

[1544] Objection to the charges An accused before pleading to a charge may object to it on grounds that it is not correct in law or is not framed in accordance with the Coast Guard (Discipline) Rules 1983. If the accused does so, the prosecutor may address the court in answer to the objection and the accused may reply to the prosecutor's address[1]. If the court upholds the objection, it shall either amend the charge if permissible under the Coast Guard (Discipline) Rules 1983[2] or adjourn and report to the Convening Authority[3]. However, if there is another charge-sheet before the court, the court may, before adjourning under this provision, proceed with the trial on such other charge or other charge-sheet[4]. When the court reports to the Convening Authority under this provision, the Convening Authority shall if he approves the decision of the court to allow the objection: (i) dissolve the court[5]; (ii) where there is another charge or another charge-sheet before the court to which the objection does not relate and which the court has not tried, direct the court to proceed with the trial of such other charge or charge-sheet only[6]; or (iii) amend the charge to which the objection relates if permissible under the Coast Guard (Discipline) Rules 1983[7] and direct the court to try it as amended[8].

1 The Coast Guard (Discipline) Rules 1983 r 64 (1).

2 Ie the Coast Guard (Discipline) Rules 1983 r 49; see **[1456]**.

3 The Coast Guard (Discipline) Rules 1983 r 64 (2).

4 The Coast Guard (Discipline) Rules 1983 r 64 (2) proviso.

5 The Coast Guard (Discipline) Rules 1983 r 64 (3) (i).

6 The Coast Guard (Discipline) Rules 1983 r 64 (3) (i).

7 Ie the Coast Guard (Discipline) Rules 1983 r 50; see **[1457]**.

8 The Coast Guard (Discipline) Rules 1983 r 64 (3) (i).

[1545] Plea in bar of trial An accused before pleading to a charge may offer a plea that the trial is barred under the provisions of the Coast Guard Act 1978[1]. If he does so: (i) the accused may adduce evidence in support of the plea and the prosecutor may adduce evidence in answer thereto[2], and (ii) the prosecutor may address the court in answer to the plea and the accused may reply to the prosecutor's address[3]. If the court allows the plea, it shall adjourn and report to the Convening Authority[4]. However, if there is another charge or another charge-sheet before the court, the court may, before adjourning under this rule, proceed with the trial of such other charge, or other charge-sheet[5]. When a court reports to the Convening Authority under this provision, the Convening Authority shall: (i) dissolve the court[6]; or (ii) where there is another charge or another charge-sheet before the court to which the plea does not relate and which the court has not tried, direct the court to proceed with the trial of such other charge or charge-sheet only[7].

1 Ie the Coast Guard Act 1978 s 51 or 68; see **[1548]**.

2 The Coast Guard (Discipline) Rules 1983 r 65 (1) (a).

3 The Coast Guard (Discipline) Rules 1983 r 65 (1) (b).

4 The Coast Guard (Discipline) Rules 1983 r 65 (2).

5 The Coast Guard (Discipline) Rules 1983 r 65 (2) proviso.

6 The Coast Guard (Discipline) Rules 1983 r 65 (3) (i).

7 The Coast Guard (Discipline) Rules 1983 r 65 (3) (ii).

[1546] Application for separate trial Where two to more accused are charged jointly, any one of the accused may, before pleading to the charge, apply to the court to be tried separately on the ground that he would be prejudiced in his defence if he was not tried separately[1]. Where the accused makes such an application, the prosecutor may address the court in answer thereto and the accused may reply to the prosecutor's address[2]. Where the court is of the opinion that the interests of justice so require, it shall allow the application and try separately the accused who made it[3].

1 The Coast Guard (Discipline) Rules 1983 r 66 (1).

2 The Coast Guard (Discipline) Rules 1983 r 66 (2).

3 The Coast Guard (Discipline) Rules 1983 r 66 (3).

[1547] Application for trial on separate charge-sheet When a charge-sheet contains more than one charge, the accused may, before pleading to the charges apply to the court to be tried separately on any charge in the charge-sheet on the ground that he would be prejudiced in his defence if he were not tried separately on that charge[1]. Where the accused makes such an application, the prosecutor may address the Court in answer thereto and the accused may reply to the prosecutor's address[2]. Where the Court is of the opinion that interests of justice so require, it shall allow the application and try the accused separately of the charge to which it relates as if that charge had been inserted in a separate charge-sheet[3].

1 The Coast Guard (Discipline) Rules 1983 r 67 (1).

2 The Coast Guard (Discipline) Rules 1983 r 67 (2).

3 The Coast Guard (Discipline) Rules 1983 r 67 (3).

[1548] Pleading to the charge After any plea under the Coast Guard (Discipline) Rules 1983[1] have been dealt with, the accused shall be required subject to the following provision[2] to plead either guilty or not guilty to each charge on which he is arraigned[3]. Where a court is empowered by certain provision of the Coast Guard Act 1978[4] to find an accused guilty of an offence other than that charged or guilty of committing the offence, in circumstances involving a less degree of punishment or where it could after hearing the evidence, make a special finding of guilty subject to exception or variation in accordance with rules. The accused may plead guilty to such other offence, or to the offence charged as having been committed in the circumstances involving a less degree of punishment or to the offence charged subject to such exception or variations[5].

1 Ie the Coast Guard (Discipline) Rules 1983 r 63 and 65; see **[1543]** and **[1545]**.

2 Ie the Coast Guard (Discipline) Rules 1983 r 68 (2).

3 The Coast Guard (Discipline) Rules 1983 r 68 (1).

4 Ie the Coast Guard Act 1978 s 83; see **[1503]**.

5 The Coast Guard (Discipline) Rules 1983 r 68 (2).

[1549] Acceptance of plea of guilty Where an accused pleads guilty to a charge under the Coast Guard (Discipline) Rules 1983[1] the Law Officer shall, before the court decides to accept the plea, explain to the accused the nature of the charge and the general effect of his plea and in particular the difference in procedure when an accused pleads guilty and when an accused pleads not guilty[2]. A court shall not accept a plea of guilty[3] if: (i) the court is not satisfied that the accused understands the nature of the charge or the effect of his plea[4]; (ii) the Presiding Officer having regard to all the circumstances, considers that the accused shall plead not guilty[5]; or (iii) the accused is liable, if convicted, to be sentenced to death[6]. In the case of a plea of guilty under the Coast Guard (Discipline) Rules 1983[7] court shall not accept the plea unless the Convening Authority concurs and it is satisfied of the justice of such course[8]. The concurrence of the Convening Authority may be signified by the prosecutor[9]. When a plea of guilty[10] has been accepted, the Court shall record a finding of guilty in respect thereof[11].

1 Ie under the Coast Guard (Discipline) Rules 1983 r 68 (1) or (2); see **[1548]**.

2 The Coast Guard (Discipline) Rules 1983 r 69 (1).

3 Ie under the Coast Guard (Discipline) Rules 1983 r 68 (1) or (2).

4 The Coast Guard (Discipline) Rules 1983 r 69 (2) (a).

5 The Coast Guard (Discipline) Rules 1983 r 69 (2) (b).

6 The Coast Guard (Discipline) Rules 1983 r 69 (2) (c).

7 Ie the Coast Guard (Discipline) Rules 1983 r 70; see [1550].

8 The Coast Guard (Discipline) Rules 1983 r 69 (3) (a).

9 The Coast Guard (Discipline) Rules 1983 r 69 (3) (b).

10 Ie under the Coast Guard (Discipline) Rules 1983 r 68 (1) or (2); see **[1548]**.

11 The Coast Guard (Discipline) Rules 1983 r 69 (4).

[1550] Plea of alternative charge When an accused pleads guilty to the first of two or more alternative charges, the court, if it accepts the accused's plea of guilty, shall record a finding of guilty in respect of the first charge and the prosecutor shall withdraw any alternative charge before the accused is arraigned on it[1].

When an accused pleads guilty to one of two or more charges which are laid in the alternative other than the first of such charges, the court may proceed as if the accused had pleaded not guilty to all the charges[2]. The Court with concurrence of the convening authority (which may be signified by the prosecutor) record a finding of guilty on the charge to which the accused has pleaded guilty and a finding of not guilty on any alternative charge which is placed before it in the charge-sheet[3]. Where the court records such findings the prosecutor shall before the accused is arraigned on it withdraw any charge which is alternative to the charge of which the court has found the accused guilty and which is placed after it in the charge-sheet[4].

1 The Coast Guard (Discipline) Rules 1983 r 70 (1).

2 The Coast Guard (Discipline) Rules 1983 r 70 (2) (a).

3 The Coast Guard (Discipline) Rules 1983 r 70 (2) (b) (i).

4 The Coast Guard (Discipline) Rules 1983 r 70 (2) (b) (ii).

[1551] Order of trial in the case of plea of guilty and not guilty After the court has recorded a finding of guilty, if there is no other charge in the same charge sheet to which the accused has pleaded not guilty to a charge in that charge sheet, it shall proceed with the trial[1]. Where there is another charge in the charge-sheet to which the accused has pleaded not guilty or there is another accused who has pleaded not guilty to a charge in that charge-sheet, the court shall not comply with the provisions of the Coast Guard (Discipline) Rules 1983[2] until after it has dealt with such other charge or tried such other accused and has announced and record its finding in respect thereof[3].

1 Ie as directed by the Coast Guard (Discipline) Rules 1983 r 72; The Coast Guard (Discipline) Rules 1983 r 71 (1).

2 Ie the Coast Guard (Discipline) Rules 1983 r 70; see **[1550]**.

3 The Coast Guard (Discipline) Rules 1983 r 71 (2).

[1552] Procedure on plea of guilty When the court has recorded a finding of a guilty in respect of a charge to which an accused has pleaded guilty the prosecutor shall read the record or abstract of evidence to the court or inform the court of the facts contained therein[1] Where there is no record or abstract of evidence the court shall record in accordance with these provisions sufficient evidence to enable it to determine the sentence[2]. After the aforesaid provisions[3] have been complied with, the accused may (i) adduce evidence of character and in mitigation of punishment[4] and (ii) address the court in mitigation of punishment[5]. After the aforesaid provision[6] has been complied with the court shall proceed as directed in the Coast Guard (Discipline) Rules 1983[7].

1 The Coast Guard (Discipline) Rules 1983 r 72 (1).

2 The Coast Guard (Discipline) Rules 1983 r 72 (2).

3 Ie the Coast Guard (Discipline) Rules 1983 r 72 (1) and (2).

4 The Coast Guard (Discipline) Rules 1983 r 72 (3) (a).

5 The Coast Guard (Discipline) Rules 1983 r 72 (3) (b).

6 Ie the Coast Guard (Discipline) Rules 1983 r 72 (3).

7 Ie as directed in the Coast Guard (Discipline) Rules 1983 r 95; see **[1579]**. The Coast Guard (Discipline) Rules 1983 r 72 (4).

[1553] Change of plea A accused who has pleaded not guilty may at any time before the court closes to deliberate on its finding withdraw his plea of not guilty and substitute a plea of guilty (including plea of guilty under the Coast Guard (Discipline) Rules 1983 r 70). In such a case the court shall, if it is satisfied that it can accept the accused's changed plea under these provisions, record a finding in accordance with accused's changed plea and so far as is necessary proceed as directed by the aforesaid provision[1]. Where at any time during the trial it appears to the court that an accused who has pleaded guilty does not understand the effect of his plea or the nature of the charge the court shall enter a plea of not guilty and proceed with the trial accordingly[2]. When the court records a plea of not guilty in respect of any charge under the aforesaid provision[3], it shall, if there was a charge laid in the alternative thereto which the prosecutor withdrew [4] reinstate such alternative charge, arraign the accused thereon and proceed with the trial as if it had never been withdrawn[5].

1 Ie the Coast Guard (Discipline) Rules 1983 r 72; see **[1553]**. The Coast Guard (Discipline) Rules 1983 r 73 (1).

2 The Coast Guard (Discipline) Rules 1983 r 73 (2).

3 Ie the Coast Guard (Discipline) Rules 1983 r 73 (2).

4 Ie under the provisions of the Coast Guard (Discipline) Rules 1983 r 70; see **[1550]**.

5 The Coast Guard (Discipline) Rules 1983 r 73 (3).

[1554] Procedure on plea of not guilty After a plea of not guilty to any charge has been recorded, the court shall ask the accused whether he wishes to apply for an adjournment on the ground that any of these provisions relating to procedure before trial have not been complied with and that he has been prejudiced thereby or on the ground that he has not had sufficient opportunity for preparing his defence[1]. Where the accused applies for an adjournment: (i) the accused may adduce evidence in support of his application and the prosecutor may adduce evidence in answer thereto[2]; and (ii) the prosecutor may address the court in answer to the application and the accused may reply to the prosecutor's address[3]. The court may grant an adjournment if it thinks the interests of justice so require[4].

1 The Coast Guard (Discipline) Rules 1983 r 74 (a).

2 The Coast Guard (Discipline) Rules 1983 r 74 (b) (i).

3 The Coast Guard (Discipline) Rules 1983 r 74 (b) (ii).

4 The Coast Guard (Discipline) Rules 1983 r 74 (c).

[1555] Opening address The prosecutor may if he so desire and shall if required by the court make an opening address explaining the charge and the nature and general effect of the evidence which he proposes to adduce[1]. The witnesses for the prosecution shall then be called and give their evidence[2].

1 The Coast Guard (Discipline) Rules 1983 r 75 (1).

2 The Coast Guard (Discipline) Rules 1983 r 57 (2).

[1556] Additional witnesses Where the prosecutor intends to adduce evidence which is not contained in any record or abstract of evidence given to the accused, notice of such intention together with the particulars of the evidence shall, when practicable, be given to the accused within a reasonable time before the evidence is adduced. If such evidence is adduced without such notice or particulars having been given, the court may if the accused so desires either adjourn after receiving the evidence or allow any cross-examination arising out of that evidence to be postponed, and the court shall inform the accused of his right to apply for such an adjournment[1].

1 The Coast Guard (Discipline) Rules 1983 r 76.

[1557] Dropping witness The prosecution shall not be bound to call all the witnesses against the accused whose evidence is contained in the record or abstract of evidence, nor a witness when he has notified the accused that he intends to call under the aforesaid provision[1]. In case the prosecutor does not intend to call such witness to give evidence, he shall either tender him for cross-examination by the accused, or give the accused reasonable notice that he does not intend to call the witness and that the accused will be allowed to communicate with him to call him as a witness for the defence, if he so desires and if the witness is available[2].

1 Ie the Coast Guard (Discipline) Rules 1983 r 76; see **[1556]**.

2 The Coast Guard (Discipline) Rules 1983 r 77.

[1558] Withdrawal of witness During a trial, a witness other than the prosecutor or accused shall not, except by leave of the court, be in court while not under examination. While he is under examination, in case a discussion arises as to whether a question is to be allowed or not with regard to his evidence, the court may direct the witness to withdraw during such discussions[1].

1 The Coast Guard (Discipline) Rules 1983 r 78.

[1559] Examination of witnesses A witness may be examined by the person calling him and may be cross-examined by the opposite party to the proceedings and on the conclusion of any such cross-examination may be re-examined by the person who called him on matters arising out of the cross-examination[1]. The person examining a witness shall put his question to his witness orally and unless an objection is made by the witness, the court, the Law Officer, the prosecutor or by the accused the witness shall reply forthwith[2]. Where such an objection is made the witness shall not reply until the objection has been disposed of[3]. The court may allow the cross-examination or re-examination of a witness to be postponed[4]. Before the examination of a witness, he shall be administered an oath or affirmation in the following form or in such other form to the same purport as the court ascertains to be in accordance with his religion or otherwise binding on his conscience[5].

Form of Oath

> I,...........swear by Almighty God that whatever I shall state shall be the truth, the whole truth and nothing but the truth.

Form of Affirmation

> I,..........do solemnly, truly and sincerely declare and affirm that whatever I shall state, shall be the truth, the whole truth and nothing but the truth.

1 The Coast Guard (Discipline) Rules 1983 r 79 (1).

2 The Coast Guard (Discipline) Rules 1983 r 79 (2) (a).

3 The Coast Guard (Discipline) Rules 1983 r 79 (2) (b).

4 The Coast Guard (Discipline) Rules 1983 r 79 (3).

5 The Coast Guard (Discipline) Rules 1983 r 79 (4).

[1560] Questioning by the court The Presiding Officer, the Law Officer and any member of the court may put questions to a witness[1]. Upon any such question being answered the prosecutor and the accused may put to the witness question arising from the answer which he has given as the court may think proper[2].

1 The Coast Guard (Discipline) Rules 1983 r 80 (1).

2 The Coast Guard (Discipline) Rules 1983 r 80 (2).

[1561] Reading over of evidence The record which has been made of the evidence given by a witness shall be read back to him before he leaves the court and when this is done he may ask for the record to be corrected or explain the evidence which he has given[1]. Where any such correction is made or explanation given, the prosecutor and the accused may put such questions to the witness respecting the correction or explanation as seem proper to the court[2]. When a shorthand writer is employed, it shall not be necessary to comply with the aforesaid provision, if in the opinion of the court and the Law Officer, it is unnecessary to do so. However, if any witness so demands, aforesaid provisions[3] shall be complied with[4].

1 The Coast Guard (Discipline) Rules 1983 r 81 (1) (a).

2 The Coast Guard (Discipline) Rules 1983 r 81 (1) (b).

3 Ie the Coast Guard (Discipline) Rules 1983 r 81 (1).

4 The Coast Guard (Discipline) Rules 1983 r 81 (2).

[1562] Calling or recalling witness by the court The court may at any time before it closes to deliberate on its finding or before the Law Officer begins to sum up, call a witness or recall a witness, if in the opinion of the Court it is in the interest of justice to do so[1]. Where the court calls a witness or recalls a witness under this rule, the prosecutor and the accused may put such questions to the witness as the court may think proper[2]. The prosecutor and the accused may, at any time before the court closes to deliberate on its finding or before the Law Officer begins to sum up recall a witness by leave of the court and the prosecutor and the accused may put such questions to the witness as the court may think proper[3].

1 The Coast Guard (Discipline) Rules 1983 r 82 (1) (a).

2 The Coast Guard (Discipline) Rules 1983 r 82 (1) (b).

3 The Coast Guard (Discipline) Rules 1983 r 82 (2).

[1563] Submission of no case to answer and stopping of cases At the close of the case for the prosecution the accused may submit to the court in respect of any charge that the prosecution has failed to establish a prima facie case for him to answer and that he should not be called upon to make his defence to that charge[1]. Where the accused makes such submission the prosecutor may address the court in answer thereto and the accused may reply to the prosecutor's address[2]. The court shall not allow the submission unless it is satisfied that: (i) the prosecution has not established a prima-facie case on the charge as laid[3]; and (ii) it is open to it on the evidence to make a special finding[4]. Where the court allows the submission, it shall find the accused not guilty of the charge to which it relate and finding shall forthwith be announced in open court[5]. Where the court disallows the submission it shall proceed with the trial of the offence as charged[6]. The court may, of its own motion, after the close of the hearing of the case for the prosecution, and after hearing the prosecutor find the accused not guilty of the charge and the finding shall forthwith be announced in open court[7].

1 The Coast Guard (Discipline) Rules 1983 r 83 (1) (a).

2 The Coast Guard (Discipline) Rules 1983 r 83 (1) (b).

3 The Coast Guard (Discipline) Rules 1983 r 83 (2) (a).

4 Ie under the Coast Guard Act 1978 s 83 or the Coast Guard (Discipline) Rules 1983 r 93 (3); see **[1503]** and **[1576]**. The Coast Guard (Discipline) Rules 1983 r 83 (2) (b).

5 The Coast Guard (Discipline) Rules 1983 r 83 (3) (a).

6 The Coast Guard (Discipline) Rules 1983 r 83 (3) (b).

7 The Coast Guard (Discipline) Rules 1983 r 83 (4).

[1564] Evidence on navigational matters (A) Documents to be made available in navigational cases: All trials at which evidence is to be given on the navigation of one of the ships, the prosecutor on opening his case shall lay before the court such of the following documents as exist and apply to the case namely: the ship's log[1]; the rough and fair engine room registers[2]; control room log[3]; the chart or charts and sailing directions by which the ship was navigated[4]; the last table of compass deviations[5]; the navigational data book and the gyro-compass log[6]; the Captain's night order book[7]; the Navigating Officer's note book and work book[8]; the engine room log book[9]; the Officer of the Watch work book[10]; the echo sounder log book[11]; the Navigating Yeoman's note book[12]; the Navigating Officer's nigh order[13]; the Navigating Officer's sight forms[14]; and the wheel and engine order book[15].

(B) After the prosecutor has opened his case, the Presiding Officer shall, unless he considers the circumstances so exceptional that such procedure would be a waste of time, order the documents referred to in the aforesaid proviison[16] to be handed to one or more Navigation Direction Officer or other competent officers who shall work up the ship's reckoning throughout the material time, and the result, together with such other details as may be required, being delivered to the court in the form set out in the Rules[17] completed in all relevant respects and attested by the signatures of the officer or officers so directed, and such officer or officers shall be sworn and be subject to cross-examination by both prosecution and defence as to its accuracy[18].

(C) The Presiding Officer shall endorse such reports as approved, if the court concurs, and if not, an expression of its dissent shall be added, signed by the Presiding Officer, showing in what respects and for what reasons it dissents[19]. With the said report such officer or officers shall also deliver to the court a copy or tracing of the chart by which the ship was navigated on which the position of the ship so determined have been laid-off, and also the determined position when ashore or in danger, as not in the log book[20]. The date and direction of the current and of the tidal stream and the state of the tide should also, if possible, be ascertained, stated, and verified on oath[21]. The report in the form set out in the Rules[22] and the prepared chart, as well as an attested copy of the ship's log book and the engine room register or of the control room log, commencing from at least 48 hours before the ship took the ground or was endangered, if so long from a known anchorage, shall accompany the minutes[23]. At trials at which evidence may be required on the navigation of an aircraft such documents as exist and may be available to serve a similar purpose to those set out in the Coast Guard (Discipline) Rules 1983[24] shall be made available by the commanding officer of the aircraft and the court may follow, with such variation as may be necessary or desirable, the procedure prescribed in this provision[25].

1 The Coast Guard (Discipline) Rules 1983 r 84 (1) (a).

2 The Coast Guard (Discipline) Rules 1983 r 84 (1) (b).

3 The Coast Guard (Discipline) Rules 1983 r 84 (1) (c).

4 The Coast Guard (Discipline) Rules 1983 r 84 (1) (d).

5 The Coast Guard (Discipline) Rules 1983 r 84 (1) (e).

6 The Coast Guard (Discipline) Rules 1983 r 84 (1) (f).

7 The Coast Guard (Discipline) Rules 1983 r 84 (1) (g).

8 The Coast Guard (Discipline) Rules 1983 r 84 (1) (h).

9 The Coast Guard (Discipline) Rules 1983 r 84 (1) (i).

10 The Coast Guard (Discipline) Rules 1983 r 84 (1) (j).

11 The Coast Guard (Discipline) Rules 1983 r 84 (1) (k).

12 The Coast Guard (Discipline) Rules 1983 r 84 (1) (l).

13 The Coast Guard (Discipline) Rules 1983 r 84 (1) (m).

14 The Coast Guard (Discipline) Rules 1983 r 84 (1) (n).

15 The Coast Guard (Discipline) Rules 1983 r 84 (1) (o).

16 Ie the Coast Guard (Discipline) Rules 1983 r 84 (1).

17 Ie the Coast Guard (Discipline) Rules 1983 appendix VII.

18 The Coast Guard (Discipline) Rules 1983 r 84 (2).

19 The Coast Guard (Discipline) Rules 1983 r 84 (3).

20 The Coast Guard (Discipline) Rules 1983 r 84 (4).

21 The Coast Guard (Discipline) Rules 1983 r 84 (5).

22 Ie the Coast Guard (Discipline) Rules 1983 Appendix VII.

23 The Coast Guard (Discipline) Rules 1983 r 84 (6).

24 Ie the Coast Guard (Discipline) Rules 1983 r 84 (1).

25 The Coast Guard (Discipline) Rules 1983 r 84 (7).

[1565] Absence of documents Should the absence of any of the documents mentioned in the aforesaid provision[1] be likely to render it difficult for the officers mentioned therein to complete their task to the satisfaction of the court, it shall be permissible for the prosecution to call an expert witness (if possible a qualified Navigation Direction Officer) to assist the court[2]. Such a witness shall not be called under the Rules[3] and shall, with the permission of the court, be present to hear the evidence and shall then lay out the resulting courses on the chart[4]. Such witness shall be subject to unrestricted cross-examination[5].

1 Ie the Coast Guard (Discipline) Rules 1983 r 84; see **[1564]**.

2 The Coast Guard (Discipline) Rules 1983 r 85 (1).

3 Ie the Coast Guard (Discipline) Rules 1983 r 84.

4 The Coast Guard (Discipline) Rules 1983 r 85 (2).

5 The Coast Guard (Discipline) Rules 1983 r 85 (3).

[1566] Navigation Direction Officer examination and cross-examination The examination and cross-examination of the Navigation Direction Officer or other competent officers who have been directed to perform the duty mentioned in the Coast Guard (Discipline) Rules 1983[1] shall be limited to ascertaining the accuracy or inaccuracy of the document laid before the court[2].

1 Ie the Coast Guard (Discipline) Rules 1983 r 84; see **[1564]**.

2 The Coast Guard (Discipline) Rules 1983 r 86.

[1565] Case for the defence After the close of the case for the prosecution, the Law Officer shall explain to the accused that: (i) if he wishes, he may give evidence on oath as a witness or make a statement without being sworn but that he is not obliged to do either[1]; (ii) if he gives evidence on oath, he shall be liable to be cross-examined by the prosecutor and to be questioned by the court[2]. For the purpose of enabling the accused to explain in any circumstances appearing in the evidence against him, the court may, at any stage of the trial, without previously warning the accused, put such question to him as the court considers necessary, and shall for the purpose aforesaid, question him generally on the case after the witness for the prosecution have been examined and before he is called on for his defence[3]. The accused shall not render himself liable to punishment by refusing to answer such questions or by giving false answers to them[4]. The answers given by the accused may be taken into consideration in such trial and put in evidence for or against him in any other inquiry into or trial for any other offence which such answers may tend to show he has committed[5]. If the accused intends to call a witness to the facts of the case other than himself, he may make an opening address outlining the case for the defence before the evidence for the defence is given[6].

1 The Coast Guard (Discipline) Rules 1983 r 87 (1) (a).

2 The Coast Guard (Discipline) Rules 1983 r 87 (1) (b).

3 The Coast Guard (Discipline) Rules 1983 r 87 (2).

4 The Coast Guard (Discipline) Rules 1983 r 87 (3).

5 The Coast Guard (Discipline) Rules 1983 r 87 (4).

6 The Coast Guard (Discipline) Rules 1983 r 87 (5).

[1568] Preparation of defence by the accused An accused, who has been remanded for trial, shall be afforded proper opportunity for preparing his defence and shall be allowed proper facilities with his defending officer or counsel and with his witnesses[1]. A defending officer shall be appointed to defend an accused who has been remanded for trial unless the accused states in writing that he does not wish an appointment to be made[2]. If the prosecution is to be undertaken by a legally qualified officer or by a counsel the accused shall be notified of the fact in sufficient time to enable him, if he so desires, to make arrangements for a legally qualified officer or a counsel to defend him[3]. As soon as practicable after a decision has been taken to place the accused on trial and in any case not less than seven days before his trial, he shall be given: (i) a copy of the charge-sheet[4]; (ii) an unexpurgated copy of the record or abstract of evidence showing the passages (if any) which have been expurgated[5]; (iii) notice of any additional evidence which the prosecution intends to adduce[6]; and (iv) if the accused so requires, a list of the ranks, names and ships of the members who are to form the coast guard court and of any waiting member[7]. When an accused is given a copy of the charge-sheet and of the record or abstract of evidence in accordance with this rule, he shall: (i) have the charge explained to him[8], and (ii) be informed that upon his making a written request to his commanding officer not less than 24 hours before his trial requiring the attendance of a witness (other than the witness for the prosecution) whom he desires to call in his defence (such witness to be named by him), reasonable steps will be taken in accordance with these provisions to procure the attendance of any such witness at his trial[9].

1 The Coast Guard (Discipline) Rules 1983 r 55 (1).

2 The Coast Guard (Discipline) Rules 1983 r 55 (2).

3 The Coast Guard (Discipline) Rules 1983 r 55 (3).

4 The Coast Guard (Discipline) Rules 1983 r 55 (4) (a).

5 The Coast Guard (Discipline) Rules 1983 r 55 (4) (b).

6 The Coast Guard (Discipline) Rules 1983 r 55 (4) (c).

7 The Coast Guard (Discipline) Rules 1983 r 55 (4) (d).

8 The Coast Guard (Discipline) Rules 1983 r 55 (5) (a).

9 The Coast Guard (Discipline) Rules 1983 r 55 (5) (b).

[1569] Witness for defence After the aforesaid provision[1] has been complied with, the witnesses for the defence shall be called to give their evidence[2]. Certain provisions of the Coast Guard (Discipline) Rules 1983[3] shall apply to the witnesses for the defence as they apply to the evidence of witnesses for the prosecution[4].

1 Ie the Coast Guard (Discipline) Rules 1983 r 87; see **[1567]**.

2 The Coast Guard (Discipline) Rules 1983 r 88 (1).

3 Ie the Coast Guard (Discipline) Rules 1983 r 79, 80, and 81; see **[1559]**, **[1560]** and **[1561]**.

4 The Coast Guard (Discipline) Rules 1983 r 88 (2).

[1570] Summoning of defence witnesses Subject to certain provision of the Coast Guard (Discipline) Rules 1983[1] the commanding officer shall be requested in this behalf by the accused, summon such witnesses as are specified by the accused[2]. Where the commanding officer is satisfied that the evidence to be given by any witness is not likely to be of material assistance at the trial, he may refuse to summon such witness[3]. Where the commanding officer has refused to summon the witnesses under the aforesaid provision[4] the accused may make an application to the coast guard court for the summoning of such witness or such witnesses and the court may, if it considers it to be expedient in the interest of justice, order the summoning of such witness and, if necessary, adjourn the proceedings, for the attendance of such witnesses[5].

1 Ie the Coast Guard (Discipline) Rules 1983 r 56 (2).

2 The Coast Guard (Discipline) Rules 1983 r 56 (1). As to the issue of summon to witnesses; see **[1498]** and **[1499]**.

3 The Coast Guard (Discipline) Rules 1983 r 56 (2).

4 Ie the Coast Guard (Discipline) Rules 1983 r 56 (2).

5 The Coast Guard (Discipline) Rules 1983 r 56 (3).

[1571] Witness in reply After the witnesses for the defence have given their evidence, the prosecutor may by leave of the court call a witness or recall to give evidence on any matter raised by the accused in his defence which the prosecution could not properly have mentioned to the court before the accused disclosed his defence or which the prosecutor could not reasonably have foreseen[1].

1 The Coast Guard (Discipline) Rules 1983 r 89.

[1572] Closing address After all the evidence has been given, the prosecutor and the accused may each make a closing address to the court[1]. The accused shall be entitled to make his closing address after the closing address by the prosecutor unless the accused has called a witness to facts other than himself in which case, the prosecutor shall be entitled, subject to following provisions[2], to make his closing address after the accused has made the closing address[3]. However, where any question of law is raised by the accused, the prosecutor may, with the permission of the court, make additional address[4]. Where two or more accused are tried jointly, anyone of them who has called no such witness shall be entitled to make his closing address after the prosecutor has made the closing address[5]. Where two or more accused are represented by the same defending officer or counsel he may make one closing address only[6]. Where any one of the accused for whom he appears has called no witnesses to facts other than himself such defending officer or counsel shall be entitled to make his closing address after the prosecutor has made the closing address[7].

1 The Coast Guard (Discipline) Rules 1983 r 90 (1).

2 Ie the Coast Guard (Discipline) Rules 1983 r 90 (3) and (4).

3 The Coast Guard (Discipline) Rules 1983 r 90 (2).

4 The Coast Guard (Discipline) Rules 1983 r 90 (2) proviso.

5 The Coast Guard (Discipline) Rules 1983 r 90 (3).

6 The Coast Guard (Discipline) Rules 1983 r 90 (4) (a).

7 The Coast Guard (Discipline) Rules 1983 r 90 (4) (b).

[1573] Summing up by Law Officer After the closing address, the Law Officer shall sum up the evidence and advise the court on the law relating to the case in open court[1].

1 The Coast Guard (Discipline) Rules 1983 r 91.

[1574] Deliberation on finding The court shall deliberate on its finding in closed court in the presence of the Law Officer[1]. The opinion of each member of the court as to the finding shall be given by word of mouth on each charge separately starting with the junior most rank[2].

1 The Coast Guard (Discipline) Rules 1983 r 92 (1).

2 The Coast Guard (Discipline) Rules 1983 r 92 (2).

[1575] Recording of findings The finding on every charge upon which the accused is arraigned shall be recorded and except as provided in the following provisions, shall be recorded simply as a finding of 'Guilty' or of 'Not guilty'[1]. The reasons for finding of 'Guilty' or 'Not Guilty', including cases where the court accepts the defence submission of 'no case' to answer on charges under the Coast Guard Act 1978[2], shall be recorded[3]. Where the court is of the opinion as regards any charge that the facts proved do not disclose the offence charged or any offence of which the accused might under the Coast Guard Act 1978 legally be found guilty on the charge as laid, the court shall acquit the accused of that charge[4].

1 The Coast Guard (Discipline) Rules 1983 r 93 (1). The Coast Guard (Discipline) Rules 1983 r 93(1) expressly dispenses with the requirement of recording reasons while stipulating that only a finding of either "guilty" or "not guilty" is required to be specified. *Ex.Uttam Navik Dalbir Singh v. Union of India*, WP (C) No. 496/2004, Delhi High Court, decided on 21 March 2012.

2 Ie the Coast Guard Act 1978 s 27 and 28; see **[1388]** and **[1389]**.

3 The Coast Guard (Discipline) Rules 1983 r 93 (1A).

4 The Coast Guard (Discipline) Rules 1983 r 93 (2).

[1576] Special findings Where the court is of the opinion as regards any charge that the facts which it finds to be proved in evidence differ materially from the facts alleged in the statement of particulars in the charge but are nevertheless sufficient to prove the offence stated in the charge, and that the difference is not so material as to have prejudiced the accused in his defence, it may, instead of a finding of 'not guilty' record a special finding[1]. The special finding may find the accused guilty on a charge subject to the statement of exceptions or variation specified therein[2]. Where there are alternative charges, and the facts proved appear to the court not to constitute the offence mentioned in any of those alternative charges, the court shall record a finding of 'not guilty', on that charge[3]. The court shall not find the accused guilty on more than one of two or more charges laid in the alternative, even if conviction upon one charge necessarily connotes guilty upon the alternative charge or charges[4].

1 The Coast Guard (Discipline) Rules 1983 r 93 (3).

2 The Coast Guard (Discipline) Rules 1983 r 93 (4).

3 The Coast Guard (Discipline) Rules 1983 r 93 (5).

4 The Coast Guard (Discipline) Rules 1983 r 93 (6).

[1577] Announcement of finding The finding on each charge shall be announced forthwith in the open court[1]. There is no requirement to record reasons by the administrative authority in its decision as long as it has been expressly or by necessary implication been excluded by the statutory provisions that govern its functioning. The Coast Guard (Discipline) Rules 1983[2] prescribe the procedure for the coast guard courts, wherein, specifically r 92 and 93 deal with the aspect of the finding pursuant to trial by the court. The Coast Guard (Discipline) Rules 1983 expressly dispenses with the requirement of recording reasons while stipulating that only a finding of either "guilty" or "not guilty" is required to be specified[3].

1 The Coast Guard (Discipline) Rules 1983 r 93 (7).

2 Ie the Coast Guard (Discipline) Rules 1983 r 57 to 97.

3 *Ex.Uttam Navik Dalbir Singh v. Union of India*, WP (C) No. 496/2004, Delhi High Court, decided on 21 March 2012.

[1578] Procedure on acquittal If the finding on all the charges is 'not guilty' the Presiding Officer shall affix his signature and date on the finding and such signature shall authenticate the whole of the proceedings. The proceedings upon being signed by the Law Officer shall at once be transmitted to the Convening Authority[1].

1 The Coast Guard (Discipline) Rules 1983 r 94.

[1579] Procedure on conviction If the finding on any charge is 'guilty' then for the guidance of the court in determining its sentence, the court before deliberating on the sentence, shall, wherever possible, take evidence of and record the general character, age, service, rank, any recognised acts of gallantry or distinguished conduct of the accused, any previous convictions of the accused either by a coast guard court[1] or a criminal court[2] and any decoration or reward, of which he may be in possession or to which he is entitled[3]. Evidence under the aforesaid provision[4] may be given by a witness producing a document containing information as set out in the Coast Guard (Discipline) Rules 1983[5] and identifying the accused as the person referred to in that document[6]. The accused may cross-examine any such witness and may call witnesses to rebut such evidence. If the accused requests the service book or a certified copy of the material entries therein shall be produced and if the accused alleges that the summary is in any respect not in accordance with the service book, or such certified copy, as the case may be, the court shall compare the summary with service book or copy. If the Court finds that the entry is not in accordance therewith, it shall cause the summary to be corrected or the objection of the accused to be recorded[7]. When all the evidence on the above matter has been given, the accused may address the court in mitigation of the punishment[8].

1 As to the definition of 'coast guard court'; see **[1307]**.

2 As to the definition of 'criminal court'; see **[1311]**.

3 The Coast Guard (Discipline) Rules 1983 r 95 (1).

4 Ie the Coast Guard (Discipline) Rules 1983 r 95 (1).

5 Ie as set out in the Coast Guard (Discipline) Rules 1983 appendix-VIIA.

6 The Coast Guard (Discipline) Rules 1983 r 95 (2).

7 The Coast Guard (Discipline) Rules 1983 r 95 (3).

8 The Coast Guard (Discipline) Rules 1983 r 95 (4).

[1580] Sentence The court shall award a single sentence in respect of all the offences of which the accused is found guilty, and such sentence shall be deemed to be awarded in respect of which it can be legally given and not to be awarded in respect of which it cannot be legally given[1].

1 The Coast Guard (Discipline) Rules 1983 r 96.

[1581] Announcement of sentence, signing and transmission of proceedings The sentence shall be announced in open court. Upon the court awarding the sentence, the Presiding Officer shall affix his signature and date the sentence and such signatures shall authenticate the whole of the proceedings. The proceedings upon being signed by the Law Officer shall at once be transmitted to the Convening Authority[1].

1 The Coast Guard (Discipline) Rules 1983 r 97.

[1582] Record in proceedings of transactions of a coast guard court At a coast guard court the Law Officer shall record or cause to be recorded all transactions of the Court, and shall be responsible for the accuracy of the record (in these provisions referred to as the proceedings). If the Law Officer is called as a witness by the accused, the Presiding Officer shall be responsible for the accuracy of the record in the proceedings of the evidence of the Law Officer[1]. The evidence shall be taken down in a narrative form in as nearly as possible the words used, but in any case where the prosecutor, the accused, the Law Officer, or the Court considers it material, the question and answer shall be taken down verbatim[2]. Where an objection has been taken to any question or to the admission of any evidence or to the procedure of the Court, such objection shall if the prosecutor or accused so requests or the Court thinks fit, be entered upon the proceedings together with the grounds of the objection and the decision of the Court thereon[3]. Where any address by, or on behalf of the prosecutor or the accused, is not in writing, it shall not be necessary to record the same in the proceedings further or otherwise than the Court thinks proper, except that: (i) the Court shall, in every case, make such record of the defence made by the accused as will enable the reviewing authority to judge of the reply made by, or on behalf of, the accused to each charge against him[4], and; (ii) the Court shall also record any particular matters in the address by or on behalf of, the prosecutor or the accused which the prosecutor or the accused, as the case may be, may require[5]. The Court shall not enter in the proceedings any comment or anything not before the Court, or any report of any fact not forming part of the trial, but if any such comment or report seems to the Court necessary, the Court may forward it to the proper authority in a separate document, signed by the Presiding Officer[6].

1 The Coast Guard (Discipline) Rules 1983 r 110 (1).

2 The Coast Guard (Discipline) Rules 1983 r 110 (2).

3 The Coast Guard (Discipline) Rules 1983 r 110 (3).

4 The Coast Guard (Discipline) Rules 1983 r 110 (4) (a).

5 The Coast Guard (Discipline) Rules 1983 r 110 (4) (b).

6 The Coast Guard (Discipline) Rules 1983 r 110 (5).

[1583] Custody and Inspection of proceedings The proceedings shall be deemed to be in the custody of the Law Officer but may, with proper precaution for their safety, be inspected by the member of the Court, the prosecutor and the accused, at all reasonable times before the Court is closed to consider the findings[1].

1 The Coast Guard (Discipline) Rules 1983 r 111.

[1584] Transmission of proceedings The proceedings shall, at once, be sent by the person having the custody thereof to such person as may be directed by the convening order or, in default of any such direction, to the convening authority[1]. Sufficient copies of the proceedings shall be made to enable one to be supplied to each of the accused in the event of an application being made therefor[2].

1 The Coast Guard (Discipline) Rules 1983 r 112 (1).

2 The Coast Guard (Discipline) Rules 1983 r 112 (2).

[1585] Report by the Presiding Officer to Convening Authority As soon as the court has been dissolved, the presiding officer shall inform the convening authority the findings and the sentence, punishment awarded by the Court to the accused[1].

1 The Coast Guard (Discipline) Rules 1983 r 113.

9. PUNISHMENTS AND DEDUCTION FROM PAY AND ALLOWANCES

CONTENTS

PARA

A. Punishments

B. Deduction from Pay and Allowances

A. Punishments

[1586] Punishments awardable by coast guard courts Punishments may be inflicted in respect of offences committed by persons subject to the Coast Guard Act 1978[1] and convicted by coast guard courts according to the scale following: death[2]; imprisonment which may be for the term of life or any other lesser term[3]; dismissal from the Coast Guard[4]; detention in Coast Guard custody for a period not exceeding two years[5]; reduction to the ranks or to a lower rank in the case of sailors[6]; forfeiture of seniority of rank, forfeiture of all or any part of the service for the purpose of promotion[7]; forfeiture of service for the purpose of increased pay, pension or any other prescribed purpose[8]; fine, in respect of civil offences[9]; mulcts of pay and allowances[10]; severe reprimand or reprimand except in the case of persons below the rank of an *Uttam Navik* or *Uttam Yantrik*[11]. Each of the punishments specified in the aforesaid provision[12] shall be deemed to be inferior in degree to every punishment preceding it in the above scale[13].

1 As to the meaning of 'persons subject to the Coast Guard Act 1978'; see **[1330]**.

2 The Coast Guard Act 1978 s 53 (1) (a).

3 The Coast Guard Act 1978 s 53 (1) (b).

4 The Coast Guard Act 1978 s 53 (1) (c).

5 The Coast Guard Act 1978 s 53 (1) (d).

6 The Coast Guard Act 1978 s 53 (1) (e).

7 The Coast Guard Act 1978 s 53 (1) (f).

8 The Coast Guard Act 1978 s 53 (1) (g).

9 The Coast Guard Act 1978 s 53 (1) (h).

10 The Coast Guard Act 1978 s 53 (1) (i).

11 The Coast Guard Act 1978 s 53 (1) (j).

12 Ie the Coast Guard Act 1978 s 53 (1).

13 The Coast Guard Act 1978 s 53 (2).

[1587] Alternative punishments awardable by coast guard courts Subject to the provisions of the Coast Guard Act 1978, a coast guard court may, on convicting a person subject to the aforesaid Act of any of the offences specified[1] award either the particular punishment with which the offence is stated in the said provision to be punishable, or in lieu thereof, any one of the punishments lower in the scale[2] regard being had to the nature and degree of the offence[3].

1 Ie the offences specified in the Coast Guard Act 1978 ss 15 to 48 (both inclusive).

2 Is as set out in the Coast Guard Act 1978 s 53.

3 The Coast Guard Act 1978 s 54.

[1588] Combination of punishments Subject to certain provisions of the Coast Guard Act 1978[1], a coast guard court may award punishment in addition to the punishment specified[2] and any one or more of the punishments[3].

1 Ie the Coast Guard Act 1978 s 58; see **[1589]**.

2 Ie as specified in the Coast Guard Act 1978 s 53 (1) (c)

3 Ie the Coast Guard Act 1978 s 53 (1) (e) to (j) (both inclusive). The Coast Guard Act 1978 s 55.

[1589] Provisions as to award of punishments The punishments that may be inflicted under Coast Guard Act 1978 shall be awarded in accordance with the following provisions[1]. A sentence of imprisonment under Coast Guard Act 1978 shall in all cases be accompanied by a sentence of dismissal[2]. A sentence of imprisonment may be rigorous or simple or partly rigorous and partly simple[3]. No officer shall be subject to detention for any offence under the Coast Guard Act 1978[4]. No subordinate officer shall be sentenced to detention except for desertion[5]. A sentence of detention shall not be accompanied by a sentence of dismissal from the Coast Guard[6]. A sentence of detention for a period exceeding 14 days shall in all cases be accompanied by stoppage of pay and allowances during the period of detention[7]. Where mulcts of pay and allowances are awarded for absence without leave, the absence shall be treated as regularised for all purposes[8].

1 The Coast Guard Act 1978 s 58 (1).

2 The Coast Guard Act 1978 s 58 (2).

3 The Coast Guard Act 1978 s 58 (3).

4 The Coast Guard Act 1978 s 58 (4).

5 The Coast Guard Act 1978 s 58 (5).

6 The Coast Guard Act 1978 s 58 (6).

7 The Coast Guard Act 1978 s 58 (7).

8 The Coast Guard Act 1978 s 58 (8).

[1590] Application of the Coast Guard Act 1978 during term of sentence When a person subject to the Coast Guard Act 1978[1] is sentenced by a coast guard court[2] to imprisonment, the aforesaid Act shall apply to him during the term of his sentence, though he is dismissed from the Coast Guard, or has otherwise ceased to be subject to the Coast Guard Act 1978, and he may be kept, removed, imprisoned and punished as if he continued to be subject to the aforesaid Act[3]. When a person subject to the Coast Guard Act 1978 is sentenced by a coast guard court to death, the aforesaid Act shall apply to him till the sentence is carried out[4].

1 As to the meaning of 'person subject to the Coast Guard Act 1978'; see **[1330]**.

2 As to the definition of 'coast guard court'; see **[1307]**.

3 The Coast Guard Act 1978 s 69 (1).

4 The Coast Guard Act 1978 s 69 (2).

B. Deduction from Pay and Allowances

[1591] Deduction from pay etc. not to be made unless authorized No deduction other than those authorised by the Coast Guard (Condition of Service) Rules 1986 shall be made from the pay, pension, gratuities, allowances and other benefits due to officers[1] and enrolled persons[2] of the Coast Guard[3].

1 As to the definition of 'officer'; see **[1320]**.

2 As to the definition of 'enrolled persons'; see **[1314]**.

3 The Coast Guard (Condition of Service) Rules 1986 r 53.

[1592] Deduction from pay and allowances The following deductions may be made from the pay and allowances of a person subject to the Coast Guard Act 1978[1] without recourse to trial by a coast guard court[2] or by the commanding officer[3]: All pay and allowances for every day of absence without leave unless an explanation is given to the satisfaction of his commanding officer for such absence and approved by Director-General in the case of officers and others by the Deputy Inspector-General under whom the enrolled person is serving[4]. However, the person is not dealt with by a coast guard court or by the Commanding Officer of the person for the said absence[5]. All pay and allowances for every day while he is in civil, criminal or Coast Guard custody on a charge for an offence of which he is afterwards convicted by a Commanding Officer or coast guard court or criminal court[6] and sentenced to imprisonment or detention[7]. All pay and allowances for every day while he is in hospital on account of sickness certified by the commanding officer or the medical officer-in-charge of the hospital where the individual was hospitalised to have been caused by an act amounting to an offence punishable under the Coast Guard Act 1978[8]. However, such certificate is to be accepted by the Director-General in the case of officers and by the Deputy Director-General in the case of enrolled persons[9]. Any sum required to make good the pay and allowances of any person subject to the Coast Guard Act 1978 which he has unlawfully retained or refused to pay[10]. Any sum required to make good any loss, damage or destruction of any Government property or property belonging to a Coast Guard or defence services mess, band or institution which after due investigation appears to the Central Government or the Director-General to have been occasioned by the wrongful act or negligence on the part of the person[11]. Any sum required to be paid for the maintenance of his wife or legitimate or illegitimate children under the provisions of the Coast Guard (Condition of Service) Rules 1986[12]. Any sum which after due investigation appears to the Director-General or the Deputy Director-General under whom the person is serving to be due to a Coast Guard or defence services mess, canteen, or any other institution[13].

1 As to the meaning of 'person subject to the Coast Guard Act 1978'; see **[1330]**.

2 As to the definition of 'coast guard court'; see **[1307]**.

3 As to the definition of 'commanding officer'; see **[1310].**

4 The Coast Guard (Condition of Service) Rules 1986 r 54 (1).

5 The Coast Guard (Condition of Service) Rules 1986 r 54 (1) proviso.

6 As to the definition of 'criminal court'; see **[1311].**

7 The Coast Guard (Condition of Service) Rules 1986 r 54 (2).

8 The Coast Guard (Condition of Service) Rules 1986 r 54 (3).

9 Coast Guard (Condition of Service) Rules 1986 r 54 (3) proviso.

10 The Coast Guard (Condition of Service) Rules 1986 r 54 (4).

11 The Coast Guard (Condition of Service) Rules 1986 r 54 (5).

12 Ie the Coast Guard (Condition of Service) Rules 1986 r 56; The Coast Guard (Condition of Service) Rules 1986 r 54 (6).

13 The Coast Guard (Condition of Service) Rules 1986 r 54 (7).

[1593] Deductions awarded by coast guard courts and other authorities Deductions may be made from the pay and allowances of a person subject to the Coast Guard Act 1978[1] in respect of any sentence of fine, forfeiture or mulcts of pay and allowances awarded in pursuance of the aforesaid Act by a coast guard court[2] or by the commanding officer[3].

1 As to the meaning of 'person subject to the Coast Guard Act 1978'; see **[1330]**.

2 As to the definition of 'coast guard court'; see **[1307].**

3 As to the definition of 'commanding officer'; see **[1310]**; the Coast Guard (Conditions of Service) Rules 1986 r 55.

[1594] Liability for maintenance of wife and children A person subject to the Coast Guard Act 1978[1] shall be liable to maintain his wife and his legitimate or illegitimate children to the same extent as if he were not so subject; but the execution or enforcement of any decree or order for maintenance passed or made against such personal shall not be directed against his personal pay, arms, ammunition, equipment, instruments or clothing[2]. Notwithstanding anything contained in the aforesaid provision[3]: (i) where it appears to the satisfaction of the Central Government or the Director-General that a person subject to the Coast Guard Act 1978 without reasonable cause deserted or left in destitute circumstances his wife or legitimate children unable to maintain themselves or has by reason of contracting a second marriage become liable to provide separate maintenance to his first wife[4], or (ii) Where any decree or order is passed under any law against a person who is, or subsequently becomes, subject to the Act for the maintenance of his wife or his legitimate or illegitimate children and a copy of the decree or order is sent to the Central Government or the Director-General[5]; the Central Government or the Director-General may direct a portion of the pay of the person so subject to the Coast Guard Act 1978 to be deducted from such pay and appropriated in the manner as decided by the Director-General towards the maintenance of wife or children, but the amount deducted shall not exceed the amount fixed by the decree or order[6]. However, in the case of a decree or order for maintenance referred to in the aforesaid provision[7] no deduction from pay shall be directed unless the Central Government or the Director-General is satisfied that the person against whom such decree or order has been passed or made, has had a reasonable opportunity of appearing or has actually appeared either in person or through a duly appointed legal practitioner, to defend the case before the court by which the decree or order was passed or made[8].

Where arrears of maintenance under a decree or order referred to in the aforesaid provision[9] have accumulated while the person against whom the decree or order has been made is subject to the Coast Guard Act 1978 whether or not deductions in respect thereof have been made from his pay under this provision, no step for the recovery of these arrears shall be taken in any court after such person has ceased to be so subject unless the court is satisfied that he has, since he ceased to be subject to the aforesaid Act, the ability to pay the arrears or part thereof and has failed to do so[10]. Notwithstanding anything contained in any other law, where a proceeding for obtaining a decree or order for maintenance is started against a person subject to the Coast Guard Act 1978 the court may send the process for service on that person to the commanding officer[11] of such person provided that such service shall not be valid unless there is sent along with the process such sum of money as may be prescribed to enable that person to attend the hearing of the proceeding and to return to his ship after such attendance[12]. If a decree or order is passed or made in the proceeding against the person on whom the process is served, the sum sent along with the process shall be awarded as costs of the proceeding against that person[13]. No process in any proceeding under this provision shall be valid against a person subject to the Coast Guard Act 1978 if served on him after he is under orders for service at a foreign station or beyond Indian waters[14]. The production of a certificate of the receipt of the process purporting to be signed by such commanding officer as aforesaid shall be evidence that the process has been duly served, unless the contrary to proved[15].

Whereby a decree or order, a copy whereof has been sent to the Central Government or the Director-General under the provision of the Coast Guard (Condition of Service) Rules 1986[16] the person against whom the decree or order has been passed or made is directed to pay as costs any sum sent along with the process, the Central Government may pay to the person entitled an amount in full satisfaction of that sum and the amount so paid by the Central Government shall be deemed to be a public demand recoverable from the person against whom the decree or order has been passed or made, and without prejudice to any other mode of recovery, may be recoverable by deduction from his pay, in addition to the deduction authorised by the Coast Guard (Condition of Service) Rules 1986[17]. Where any person subject to the Coast Guard Act 1978 has made an allotment of any part of his pay and allowances for the benefit of his wife, that allotment shall not be discontinued or reduced until the Central Government or the Director-General or the commanding officer is satisfied that the allotment should no longer be made or should be reduced[18]. In this provision, the expression 'pay' includes all sums payable to a person subject to the Coast Guard Act 1978 in respect of his service other than allowances in lieu of lodgings, rations/provisions, clothing and traveling allowances[19].

1 As to the meaning of 'person subject to the Coast Guard Act 1978'; see **[1330]**.

2 The Coast Guard (Condition of Service) Rules 1986 r 56 (1).

3 Ie the Coast Guard (Condition of Service) Rules 1986 r 56 (1).

4 The Coast Guard (Condition of Service) Rules 1986 r 56 (2) (a).

5 The Coast Guard (Condition of Service) Rules 1986 r 56 (2) (b).

6 The Coast Guard (Condition of Service) Rules 1986 r 56 (2).

7 Ie the Coast Guard (Condition of Service) Rules 1986 r 56 (2).

8 The Coast Guard (Condition of Service) Rules 1986 r 56 (2) proviso.

9 Ie the Coast Guard (Condition of Service) Rules 1986 r 56 (2).

10 The Coast Guard (Condition of Service) Rules 1986 r 56 (3).

11 As to the definition of 'commanding officer'; see **[1310]**.

12 The Coast Guard (Condition of Service) Rules 1986 r 56 (4).

13 The Coast Guard (Condition of Service) Rules 1986 r 56 (5).

14 The Coast Guard (Condition of Service) Rules 1986 r 56 (6).

15 The Coast Guard (Condition of Service) Rules 1986 r 56 (7).

16 Ie the Coast Guard (Condition of Service) Rules 1986 r 56 (2).

17 Ie the Coast Guard (Condition of Service) Rules 1986 r 56 (2); The Coast Guard (Condition of Service) Rules 1986 r 56 (8).

18 The Coast Guard (Condition of Service) Rules 1986 r 56 (9).

19 The Coast Guard (Condition of Service) Rules 1986 r 56 (10).

[1595] Limit of certain deductions Except when the deductions are made under certain provisions of the Coast Guard (Condition of Service) Rules 1986[1], the total deduction from the pay and allowances of an officer or an enrolled person shall not exceed in any one month one-half of his pay and allowances for that month[2].

1 Ie the Coast Guard (Condition of Service) Rules 1986 r 55 (1), (2) and (3).

2 The Coast Guard (Condition of Service) Rules 1986 r 57.

[1596] Remission of deductions Any deductions from the pay and allowances authorised by the Coast Guard (Condition of Service) Rules 1986 may be remitted by the Director-General in his discretion[1].

1 The Coast Guard (Condition of Service) Rules 1986 r 58.

10. PETITIONS AND JUDICIAL REVIEW

CONTENTS

A. APPLICATIONS AND PETITIONS

[1597] Applications and Petitions against findings and sentence of a coast guard court A person subject to the Coast Guard Act 1978, who has been tried by a coast guard court, may make an application to the Chief Law Officer for review of the proceedings of the Court[1]. A petition shall also be allowed to be made to any authority mentioned in the Coast Guard Act 1978 s 119[2].

1 Ie under the Coast Guard Act 1978 s 117; see **[1600]**. The Coast Guard (General) Rules 1986 r 43 (1).

2 The Coast Guard (General) Rules 1986 r 43 (2).

[1598] Period of Limitation An application for judicial review shall be submitted within 21 days of the date on which the sentence was passed by the coast guard court. A petition shall be submitted within three months[1] of the date of the order of the Director General on the Judicial Review by the Chief Law Officer of the proceedings of the trial by the coast guard court[2]. However, the time taken by such person to obtain a copy of the proceedings or the orders of the Director General on the Judicial Review of the proceedings by the Chief Law Officer shall be excluded in calculating the period of 21 days or 3 months as the case may be[3]. Further that an application received after the expiration of the aforesaid period may be entertained by the Director General or the Central Government as the case may be if he or it is satisfied that the delay was due to reasons beyond the control of the applicant[4].

1 Ie under the Coast Guard Act 1978 s 119; see **[1602]**.

2 The Coast Guard (General) Rules 1986 r 44.

3 The Coast Guard (General) Rules 1986 r 44 proviso.

4 The Coast Guard (General) Rules 1986 r 44 additional proviso.

[1599] Mode of submitting application and petition An application or a petition may be presented in person or sent by a registered post. It shall be in duplicate and shall be signed by the applicant. It shall state succinctly and clearly all grounds on which the conviction or sentence is sought to be impugned. The applicant should also state whether he desires to be heard in person or through a legal practitioner or an officer of the Coast Guard if the application is under certain provision of the Coast Guard Act 1978[1]. No personal hearing is required to be given if the petition is under the Coast Guard Act 1978 s 119[2]. An application under the Coast Guard Act 1978 s 117 is to be submitted directly to the Chief Law Officer. A petition under the Coast Guard Act 1978 s 119 is to be submitted through the Commander Coast Guard Region in whose command the trial was held. The Commander Coast Guard Region shall forward it to the Director General with his remarks within a period of one month[3]. A petition against summary award of punishment shall not be entertained. If there are exceptional circumstances warranting interference with the finding or sentence awarded summarily, the case is to be forwarded to the Coast Guard Headquarters through proper channel with full details necessitating the exercise of plenary powers of the Director General or the Central Government as the case may be. As in the case of a petition under the Coast Guard Act 1978 s 119, the period of limitation shall be 3 months from the date on which the summary punishment was awarded[4].

1 Ie under the Coast Guard Act 1978 s 117; see **[1600]**.

2 The Coast Guard (General) Rules 1986 r 45 (1).

3 The Coast Guard (General) Rules 1986 r 45 (2).

4 The Coast Guard (General) Rules 1986 r 45 (3).

B. Judicial Review of Proceedings of Coast guard court

[1600] Judicial review by the Chief Law Officer All proceedings of trials by coast guard courts[1] shall be reviewed by the Chief Law Officer either on his own motion or on application made to him within the prescribed time by any person aggrieved by any sentence or finding, and the Chief Law Officer shall transmit the report of such review together with such recommendations as may appear to him just and proper to the Director-General[2] for his consideration and for such action as the Director-General may think fit[3]. Where any person aggrieved has made an application under the aforesaid provision[4], the Chief Law Officer may, if the circumstances of the case so require, give him an opportunity of being heard either in person or through a legal practitioner or an officer of the Coast Guard[5].

1 As to the definition of 'coast guard court'; see **[1307]**.

2 As to the definition of 'Director-General'; see **[1313]**.

3 The Coast Guard Act 1978 s 117 (1).

4 Ie the Coast Guard Act 1978 s 117 (1).

5 The Coast Guard Act 1978 s 117 (2)

[1601] Consideration by the Director General On receipt of the report and recommendations, if any, from the Chief Law Officer[1], the Director-General[2] shall in all cases of sentences of death, and in all cases where the coast guard court[3] is convened by the Central Government, and may, in other cases, transmit the proceedings and the report to the Central Government together with such recommendations as he may deem fit to make[4]. Nothing in the provisions of the Coast Guard Act 1978[5] shall authorise the Chief Law Officer or the Director-General to make any recommendation for setting aside, or the Central Government to set aside, an order of acquittal passed under the Coast Guard Act 1978[6].

1 Ie under the Coast Guard Act 1978 s 117; see **[1600]**.

2 As to the definition of 'Director-General'; see **[1313]**.

3 As to the definition of 'coast guard court'; see **[1307]**.

4 The Coast Guard Act 1978 s 118 (1).

5 Ie the Coast Guard Act 1978 s 117 or 118.

6 The Coast Guard Act 1978 s 118 (2).

C. Modification of Finding and Sentence, Pardons, Commutation and Remission of Sentence

[1602] Petitions to Central Government or Director-General against findings and sentences Any person subject to the Coast Guard Act 1978[1], who considers himself aggrieved by a finding or sentence of any coast guard court[2] may present a petition to the Central Government or to the Director-General[3]. The Central Government or the Director-General, as the case may be, may pass such orders thereon as it or he may think fit[4]. The reasons are not required to be recorded for an order passed by the confirming authority confirming the findings and sentence recorded by the coast guard court martial as well as for the order passed by the Central Government dismissing the post-confirmation petition[5].

1 As to the meaning of 'person subject to the Coast Guard Act 1978'; see **[1330]**.

2 As to the definition of 'coast guard court'; see **[1307]**.

3 As to the definition of 'Director-General'; see **[1313]**.

4 The Coast Guard Act 1978 s 119. As to the powers of Central Government and Director-General in respect of

findings and sentences; see **[1603]**.

5 *S K Singh v The Director General Coast Guard*, Writ Petition No.13059 of 2006 and WP MP No.14645 of 2006, Madras High Court, decided on 9 June 2010.

[1603] Powers of Central Government and Director-General in respect of findings and sentences Where any person is tried under the provisions of the coast Guard Act 1978, the Central Government or the Director-General[1] may, in the case of a conviction: (i) set aside the finding and sentence and acquit or discharge the accused or order him to be re-tried[2]; (ii) alter the finding without modifying the sentence if such sentence may be legally passed on the altered finding[3]; (iii) with or without altering the finding, reduce the sentence or commute the punishment awarded for any punishment inferior in scale[4]; (iv) either with or without conditions, pardon the person or remit the whole or any part of the punishment awarded[5]; or (v) with or without conditions release the person on parole[6]. However, a sentence of imprisonment shall not be commuted for a sentence of detention for a term exceeding the term of imprisonment awarded[7]. Further, under the above provisions[8] the Central Government or the Director-General are not authorized to enhance the sentence[9]. Any sentence modified under the provisions of the Coast Guard Act 1978[10] shall be carried into execution as if it had been originally passed[11]. If any condition on which a person has been pardoned or has been released on parole or a punishment has been remitted is in the opinion of the authority which granted the pardon, release or remission not fulfilled, such authority may cancel the pardon or release or remission and thereupon the sentence awarded shall be carried into effect as if such pardon, release or remission had not been granted[12]. However, in the case of a person sentenced to imprisonment or detention, such person shall undergo only the unexpired portion of the sentence[13].

1 As to the definition of 'Director-General'; see **[1313]**.

2 The Coast Guard Act 1978 s 120 (1) (a).

3 The Coast Guard Act 1978 s 120 (1) (b).

4 The Coast Guard Act 1978 s 120 (1) (c).

5 The Coast Guard Act 1978 s 120 (1) (d).

6 The Coast Guard Act 1978 s 120 (1) (e).

7 The Coast Guard Act 1978 s 120 (1) proviso

8 Ie the Coast Guard Act 1978 s 120 (1) (a) to (e).

9 The Coast Guard Act 1978 s 120 (1) additional proviso.

10 The Coast Guard Act 1978 s 120 (1).

11 Coast Guard Act 1978 s 120 (2).

12 The Coast Guard Act 1978 s 120 (3)

13 The Coast Guard Act 1978 s 120 (3) proviso.

11. EXECUTION AND SUSPENSION OF SENTENCE

CONTENTS

[1604] Form of sentence of death In awarding a sentence of death, a coast guard court[1] shall, in its discretion, direct that the offender shall suffer death by being hanged by the neck until he be dead or shall suffer death by being shot to death[2].

1 As to the definition of 'coast guard court'; see **[1307]**.

2 The Coast Guards Act 1978 s 96.

[1605] Interim custody until execution of sentence of death A person sentenced to death may be detained in Coast Guard custody[1] or may be removed to a civil prison to be kept in custody until further orders are received from the Central Government, the Director-General[2] or the convening authority of the coast guard court[3] by which he was sentenced to death or other prescribed officer[4], and the order of the Central Government, the Director-General or the convening authority or such officer shall be sufficient warrant for detaining the person in custody[5].

1 As to the definition of 'coast guard custody'; see **[1308]**.

2 As to the definition of 'Director-General'; see **[1313]**.

3 As to the definition of 'coast guard court'; see **[1307]**.

4 As to the meaning of 'prescribed officer' under the Coast Guard Act 1978 s 97 to order interim custody of a person sentenced to death: the commanding officer under whose command the accused person was serving; see the Coast Guard (General) Rules 1986 r 29.

5 The Coast Guards Act 1978 s 97.

[1606] Execution of sentence of death When a sentence of death is to be executed, the Director-General[1], the convening authority or the prescribed officer[2] shall give directions as to the time, place and manner in which such sentence is to be carried out and the order of such officer or authority in the prescribed form shall be sufficient warrant for the execution of such sentence[3]. There shall be attached to the prescribed form, an order of the Central Government certifying the confirmation of the sentence by the Central Government[4].

1 As to the definition of 'Director-General'; see **[1313]**.

2 As to the meaning of 'prescribed officer' under the Coast Guard Act 1978 s 98 to give directions for execution of sentence to death: the Commanding Officer under whose command the accused was serving; see the Coast Guard (General) Rules 1986 r 29.

3 The Coast Guards Act 1978 s 98 (1).

4 The Coast Guards Act 1978 s 98 (2).

[1607] Commencement of sentence of imprisonment or detention Whenever any person is sentenced under the Coast Guards Act 1978 to imprisonment or detention, the term of the sentence shall be reckoned to commence on the date on which the sentence was awarded[1].

1 The Coast Guards Act 1978 s 99.

[1608] Execution of sentence of imprisonment Whenever any sentence of imprisonment is passed under the Coast Guards Act 1978 or whenever any sentence of death is commuted to imprisonment, the presiding officer of the coast guard court[1] which passed the sentence or such other officer as may be prescribed[2] shall direct that the sentence shall be carried out by confinement in a civil prison[3]. When a direction has been made under the aforesaid provision[4], the commanding officer[5] of the person under sentence or a prescribed officer[6] shall forward a warrant in the prescribed form to the officer in charge of the prison in which such person is to be confined and shall arrange for his dispatch to such prison with the warrant[7].

1 As to the definition of 'coast guard court'; see **[1307]**.

2 As to the meaning of 'prescribed officer' under the Coast Guard Act 1978 s 100 (1) to give directions for confinement in a Civil prison: the officer who ordered trial by the Coast guard court; see the Coast Guard (General) Rules 1986 r 29.

3 The Coast Guards Act 1978 s 100 (1).

4 Ie the Coast Guards Act 1978 s 100 (1).

5 As to the definition of 'commanding officer'; see **[1310]**.

6 Prescribed officer under the Coast Guard Act 1978 s 100 (1) to issue, warrant for confinement of a person to a civil prison: the Executive Officer of the person under sentence; see the Coast Guard (General) Rules 1986 r 29.

7 The Coast Guards Act 1978 s 100 (2).

[1609] Temporary custody of offender Where a sentence of imprisonment is directed to be undergone in a civil prison, the offender may be kept in coast guard custody[1] or in any other fit place, till such time as it is possible to send him to a civil prison[2].

1 As to the definition of 'coast guard custody'; see **[1308]**.

2 The Coast Guards Act 1978 s 101.

[1610] Conveyance of prisoner from place to place A person under sentence of imprisonment may during his conveyance from place to place, or when on board a ship, aircraft or otherwise, be subject to such restraint as is necessary for his safe conduct and removal[1].

1 The Coast Guards Act 1978 s 102.

[1611] Communication of certain orders to prison officers Whenever an order is duly made under the Coast Guards Act 1978 setting aside or varying any sentence, order or warrant under which any person is confined in a civil prison, a warrant in accordance with such order shall be forwarded[1], to the officer in charge of the prison in which such person is confined[2].

1 The order can be made by a commanding officer of the person under sentence or a staff officer; see the Coast Guard (General) Rules 1986 r 29: **[1463]**.

2 The Coast Guards Act 1978 s 103.

[1612] Execution of sentence of fine When a sentence of fine is imposed by a coast guard court[1] under the provision of the Coast Guard Act 1978[2], a copy of such sentence signed and certified by the presiding officer of the court may be sent to any Magistrate in India. Such Magistrate shall thereupon cause the fine to be recovered in accordance with the provisions of the Code of Criminal Procedure 1973, as if it were a sentence of fine imposed by such Magistrate[3].

1 As to the definition of 'coast guard court'; see **[1307]**.

2 Ie the Coast Guard Act 1978 s 53; see **[1586]**.

3 The Coast Guards Act 1978 s 104.

[1613] Informality or error in the order or warrant Whenever any person is sentenced to imprisonment under the Coast Guards Act 1978, and is undergoing the sentence in any place or manner in which he might be confined under a lawful order or warrant in pursuance of the aforesaid Act, the confinement of such person shall not be deemed to be illegal only by reason of any informality or error in the order, warrant or other document. The authority by which, or in pursuance whereof such person was brought into, may amend such order, warrant or document accordingly[1].

1 The Coast Guards Act 1978 s 105.

[1614] Imprisonment or detention of offender already under sentence Whenever a sentence is passed by a coast guard court[1] on a person already under sentence of imprisonment or detention passed on him under the Coast Guards Act 1978 for a former offence, the court may award a sentence of imprisonment or detention for the offence for which he is under trial to commence at the expiration of the sentence of imprisonment/ detention to which he has been previously sentenced[2]. However, the extent of any term of detention imposed on a person by a sentence in pursuance of this provision as will prolong the total term of detention beyond two years shall be deemed to be remitted[3].

1 As to the definition of 'coast guard court'; see **[1307]**.

2 The Coast Guards Act 1978 s 106.

3 The Coast Guards Act 1978 s 106 proviso.

[1615] Suspension of sentence of imprisonment or detention Where a person subject to the Coast Guards Act 1978 is sentenced to imprisonment or detention, the prescribed authority or officer[1] may suspend the sentence whether or not the offender has already been committed to prison or to Coast Guard custody[2]. The authority or officer specified[3] may, in the case of an offender so sentenced, direct that until the orders, of such authority or officer have been obtained, the offender shall not be committed to prison or to Coast Guard custody[4]. The powers conferred by the aforesaid provisions[4] may be exercised in the case of any such sentence which has been reduced or commuted[6].

1 Ie the Central Government, the Director-General, the commanding officer imposing the sentence or any prescribed officer; see the Coast Guards Act 1978 s 107 (1).

2 The Coast Guards Act 1978 s 107 (1).

3 Ie as specified in the Coast Guards Act 1978 s 107 (1).

4 The Coast Guards Act 1978 s 107 (2).

5 Ie the Coast Guards Act 1978 s 107 (1) and (2).

6 The Coast Guards Act 1978 s 107 (3).

[1616] Release on suspension Where a sentence is suspended under the provision of the Coast Guards Act 1978[1], the offender shall forthwith be released from custody[2].

1 Ie the Coast Guards Act 1978 s 107; see **[1615]**.

2 The Coast Guards Act 1978 s 108.

[1617] Computation of period of suspension Any period during which the sentence is under suspension shall be reckoned as part of the term of such sentence[1].

1 The Coast Guards Act 1978 s 109.

[1618] Order after suspension The authority or officer specified in the provision of the Coast Guards Act 1978[1] may, at any time while a sentence is suspended, order: (i) that the offender be committed to undergo the unexpired portion of the sentence[2]; or (ii) that the sentence be remitted[3].

1 Ie the Coast Guards Act 1978 s 107; see **[1615]**.

2 The Coast Guards Act 1978 s 110 (a).

3 The Coast Guards Act 1978 s 110 (b).

[1619] Reconsideration of case after suspension Where a sentence has been suspended, the case may at any time, and shall at intervals of not more than four months, be reconsidered by the authority or officer specified the Coast Guards Act 1978[1], or by any officer not below the rank of a Deputy Inspector-General duly authorised by the authority or officer specified in the aforesaid provision[2]. Where on such reconsideration by the officer so authorised it appears to him that the conduct of offender since his conviction has been such as to justify a remission of the sentence, he shall refer the matter to the authority or officer specified in the Coast Guards Act 1978[3].

1 Ie the Coast Guards Act 1978 s 107; see **[1615]**.

2 The Coast Guards Act 1978 s 111 (1).

3 Ie as specified in the Coast Guards Act 1978 s 107; The Coast Guards Act 1978 s 111 (2).

[1620] Fresh sentence after suspension Where an offender, while a sentence on him is suspended under the Coast Guards Act 1978, is sentenced for any other offence, then: (i) if the further sentence is also suspended under the aforesaid Act the sentence shall run concurrently[1]; (ii) if the further sentence is for a period of three months or more and is not suspended under the Coast Guards Act 1978, the offender shall also be committed to prison or Coast Guard custody[2] for the unexpired portion of the previous sentence, but both sentences shall run concurrently[3]; and (iii) if the further sentence is for a period of less than three months and is not suspended under the aforesaid Act, the offender shall be so committed on that sentence only, and the previous sentence shall, subject to any order which may be passed under certain provisions of the Coast Guards Act 1978[4] continue to be suspended[5].

1 Ie as suspended under the Coast Guards Act 1978 s 107; see **[1615]**.The Coast Guards Act 1978 s 112 (a).

2 As to the definition of 'coast guard custody'; see **[1308]**.

3 The Coast Guards Act 1978 s 112 (b).

4 Ie the Coast Guards Act 1978 s 110 or 111.

5 The Coast Guards Act 1978 s 112 (c).

[1621] Scope of power of suspension The powers conferred by certain provision of the Coast Guard Act 1978[1] shall be in addition to, and not in derogation of, the power of mitigation, remission and commutation[2].

1 Ie the Coast Guard Act 1978 s 107 and 110; see **[1615]** and **[1618]**.

2 The Coast Guards Act 1978 s 113.

[1622] Effect of suspension and remission on dismissal Where in addition to any other sentence, the punishment of dismissal has been awarded under the Coast Guards Act 1978 and such other sentence is suspended under the provisions of the Coast Guards Act 1978[1], then, such dismissal shall not take effect until so ordered by the authority or officer specified in the aforesaid provision[2]. If such other sentence is remitted under the provision of the Coast Guards Act 1978[3], the punishment of dismissal shall also be remitted[4].

1 Ie under the Coast Guards Act 1978 s 107; see **[1615]**.

2 Ie the Coast Guards Act 1978 s 107; The Coast Guards Act 1978 s 114 (1).

3 Ie the Coast Guards Act 1978 s 110.

4 The Coast Guards Act 1978 s 114 (2).

12. BOARD OF INQUIRY

CONTENTS

PARA

[1623] Duties of the Board Board[1] shall perform such duties as may be directed by the authority convening the board[2]. Such directions shall always be made in writing and may in case of urgency be conveyed by signal[3]. However, the order convening the Board shall be made in the format given in the provisions of the Coast Guard (General) Rules 1986[4].

1 'Board' means the board of inquiry convened under the Coast Guard (General) Rules 1986. The Coast Guard (General) Rules 1986 r 2 (c).

2 The Coast Guard (General) Rules 1986 r 38 (1).

3 The Coast Guard (General) Rules 1986 r 38 (2).

4 As given in the Coast Guard (General) Rules 1986 annexure.

[1624] Procedure for Board of Inquiry The board shall be guided by the provisions of the Coast Guard (General) Rules 1986 and also by the Coast Guard Orders, for the time being in force, and the written instructions of the convening authority. However, the Coast Guard Orders and the written instructions must not be inconsistent with the provisions of the aforesaid Rules[1]. The proceedings of the board of inquiry shall not be open to the public. Only such persons may attend the proceedings as are permitted by the board to do so[2]. Every witness examined by the Board shall be informed in the following terms which shall be recorded in the minutes: "You are privileged to refuse to answer any question, the answer to which may tend to expose you to any penalty or forfeiture. It will be for you to raise the objection and for the board to decide whether you must answer the question or not[3]."

Whenever an enquiry affects the character or reputation of a person serving in the Coast Guard or may result in the imputation of liability or responsibility for any loss or damage, or is made for the contravention of any rules or general or local orders, the board shall afford full opportunity: (i) to such person for being present throughout the enquiry, (ii) of making any statement and of giving any evidence he may wish to make or give, (iii) of cross-examining any witness whose evidence in its opinion affects him, and (iv) of producing any witness in his defence. The Presiding Officer of the board shall take such steps as may be necessary to ensure that any such person so affected and not previously notified receives notice of, and fully understands, his rights under the Coast Guard (General) Rules 1986[4]. The proceedings of the board shall be recorded in accordance with any directions contained in the Coast Guard Orders for the time being in force and any instructions given by the convening authority. The minutes of such proceedings shall contain a verbatim report of all evidence given, and all questions and answers shall be numbered in one series throughout the minutes[5].

The proceedings of the board or any confession, statement, or answer to a question made or given before the board, shall not be admissible in evidence against a person subject to the laws relating to any armed forces of the Union nor shall any evidence respecting the proceedings of the board be given against any such person[6]. However, nothing in these provisions shall prevent proceedings from being used for the purpose of cross-examining any witness[7]. No counsel or legal practitioner shall be permitted to appear before a board of inquiry[8]. The board may put such questions to a witness as it thinks desirable for testing the truth or accuracy of any evidence he has given and otherwise for eliciting the truth[9]. A board shall, unless otherwise ordered by the convening authority, sit within closed doors[10].

1 The Coast Guard (General) Rules 1986 r 39 (1).

2 The Coast Guard (General) Rules 1986 r 39 (2).

3 The Coast Guard (General) Rules 1986 r 39 (3).

4 The Coast Guard (General) Rules 1986 r 39 (4).

5 The Coast Guard (General) Rules 1986 r 39 (5).

6 The Coast Guard (General) Rules 1986 r 39 (6).

7 The Coast Guard (General) Rules 1986 r 39 (6) proviso.

8 The Coast Guard (General) Rules 1986 r 39 (7).

9 The Coast Guard (General) Rules 1986 r 39 (8).

10 The Coast Guard (General) Rules 1986 r 39 (9).

[1625] Board of Inquiry when to be held A board of inquiry shall be convened to investigate into any matter of importance such as: (i) loss, stranding or hazarding of Coast Guard Ships, Vessels, or Air Craft[1]; (ii) accidental death of, or serious bodily injury to, any person on board a Ship/Establishment/Aircraft[2]; (iii) loss of classified books or publication involving breach of security[3]; (iv) damage to or loss of Government property or stores, or loss of public money[4]; (v) damage to private persons or property, in respect of which there is likely to be a claim against the Central Government or the Coast Guard[5].

1 The Coast Guard (General) Rules 1986 r 40 (a).

2 The Coast Guard (General) Rules 1986 r 40 (b).

3 The Coast Guard (General) Rules 1986 r 40 (c).

4 The Coast Guard (General) Rules 1986 r 40 (d).

5 The Coast Guard (General) Rules 1986 r 40 (e).

[1626] Action on the proceedings of board of inquiry The proceedings of the board of inquiry shall be submitted by the Presiding Officer of the board to the convening authority. On receipt of the proceedings the convening authority shall: (i) take such action as is within its jurisdiction and as it may deem fit to take[1], and (ii) submit the same together with its comments thereon to the higher authority, if required to do so under the orders of such authority[2].

1 The Coast Guard (General) Rules 1986 r 41 (i).

2 The Coast Guard (General) Rules 1986 r 41 (ii).

[1627] Right of certain persons to copies of statements and documents Any person who is tried by a coast guard court shall be entitled to copies of such statements and documents contained in the proceedings of a Board of Inquiry, as are relevant to his prosecution or defence at his trial[1]. Any person whose character or reputation is affected by the evidence before a Board of Inquiry shall be entitled to copies of such statements and documents as have a bearing on his character or reputation as aforesaid unless the Director General for reasons recorded by him in writing, orders otherwise[2]. For the purpose of the provisions proceedings shall include findings of the Board but shall not include recommendations of the Board[3].

1 The Coast Guard (General) Rules 1986 r 42 (1).

2 The Coast Guard (General) Rules 1986 r 42 (2).

3 The Coast Guard (General) Rules 1986 r 42 explanations.

13. RULES

[1628] Power to make rules The Central Government may, by notification, make rules for the purpose of carrying into effect the provisions of the Coast Guard Act 1978[1]. In particular, such rules may provide for: (i) the constitution, governance, command and discipline of the Coast Guard[2]; (ii) the enrolment of persons to the Coast Guard and the recruitment of other members of the Coast Guard[3]; (iii) the conditions of service (including service privileges and deductions from pay and allowances) of members of the Coast Guard[4]; (iv) the rank, precedence, powers of command and authority of the officers, subordinate officers and other enrolled persons[5]; (v) the removal, retirement, release or discharge from the service of officers, subordinate officers and other enrolled persons[6]; (vi) the purposes and other matters required to be prescribed under the Coast Guard Act 1978 s 13[7]; (vii) the manner in which proceedings may be initiated under section 57A[8]; (viii) the additional matters in respect of which the Coast Guard may undertake measures in the performance of its functions[9]; (ix) the convening, constitution, adjournment, dissolution and sittings of Coast guard courts, the procedure to be observed in trials by such courts, the persons by whom an accused may be defended in such trials and the appearance of such persons thereat[10]; (x) the forms of orders to be made under the provisions of this Act relating to Coast guard courts and the awards and infliction of death, imprisonment and detention[11]; (xi) the carrying into effect of sentences of Coast guard courts[12]; (xii) any matter necessary for the purpose of carrying the Coast Guard Act 1978 into execution, as far as it relates to the investigation, arrest, custody, trial and punishment of offences triable or punishable under the Coast Guard Act 1978[13]; (xiii) the procedure relating to the exercise of powers under the Coast Guard Act 1978 s 120[14]; (xiv) the ceremonials to be observed and marks of respect to be paid in the Coast Guard[15]; (xv) any other matter which is to be, or may be prescribed or in respect of which this Act makes no provision or makes insufficient provision and provision is, in the opinion of the Central Government, necessary for the proper implementation of the Coast Guard Act 1978[16].

Every rule made under the Coast Guard Act 1978 shall be laid, as soon as may be after it is made, before each House of Parliament, while it is in session, for a total period of thirty days which may be comprised in one session or in two or more successive sessions, and if, before the expiry of the session immediately following the session or the successive sessions aforesaid, both Houses agree in making any modification in the rule or both Houses agree that the rule should not be made, the rule shall thereafter have effect only in such modified form or be of no effect, as the case may be; so, however, that any such modification or annulment shall be without prejudice to the validity of anything previously done under that rule[17].

1 The Coast Guard Act 1978 s 123 (1). The government has made the following rules: The Coast Guard (Discipline) Rules 1983, The Coast Guard (General) Rules 1986, The Coast Guard (Conditions of Service) Rules 1986, and The Coast Guard (Seniority and Promotion) Rules 1987.

2 The Coast Guard Act 1978 s 123 (2) (a).

3 The Coast Guard Act 1978 s 123 (2) (b).

4 The Coast Guard Act 1978 s 123 (2) (c).

5 The Coast Guard Act 1978 s 123 (2) (d).

6 The Coast Guard Act 1978 s 123 (2) (e).

7 The Coast Guard Act 1978 s 123 (2) (f).

8 The Coast Guard Act 1978 s 123 (2) (fa).

9 The Coast Guard Act 1978 s 123 (2) (g).

10 The Coast Guard Act 1978 s 123 (2) (h).

11 The Coast Guard Act 1978 s 123 (2) (i)

12 The Coast Guard Act 1978 s 123 (2) (j).

13 The Coast Guard Act 1978 s 123 (2) (k).

14 The Coast Guard Act 1978 s 123 (2) (l).

15 The Coast Guard Act 1978 s 123 (2) (m).

16 The Coast Guard Act 1978 s 123 (2) (n).

17 The Coast Guard Act 1978 s 123 (3).

VI. THE CRIMINAL COURTS AND COURT MARTIAL (ADJUSTMENT OF JURISDICTION) RULES 1978

CONTENTS

A. THE CRIMINAL COURTS AND COURT MARTIAL (ADJUSTMENT OF JURISDICTION) RULES 1978

[1629] Introduction In exercise of the powers conferred by the Code of Criminal Procedure 1973[1], the Government has made the Criminal Courts and Court Martial (Adjustment of Jurisdiction) Rules 1978. The Rules provides the procedure to resolve any dispute concerning the trial of the persons subject to military, naval, air force or coast guard law, under the respective service law by a court martial/coast guard court or a criminal court[2]. The Criminal Courts and Court Martial (Adjustment of Jurisdiction) Rules 1978 empowers the magistrate, on coming to know that a person has committed an offence and proceedings in respect of which ought to be instituted before him and that the presence of such person cannot be procured except through military, navel, air force or coast guard authorities, to require the commanding officer of such person either to deliver such person to a magistrate for trial or to stay the proceedings against such person before the court martial if since instituted, and to make a reference to the Central Government for determination as to the court before which the proceedings should be instituted[3].

1 Ie the Code of Criminal Procedure 1973 s 475 (1).

2 Ie person subject to the Army Act 1950, the Air Force Act 1950, the Navy Act 1957 or the Coast Guard Act 1978.

3 *Union of India v Major SK Sharma* 1987 AIR 1878, 1987 SCR (3) 456.

[1630] Short title This statute relating the adjustment of jurisdiction between a court martial and criminal court is called the Criminal Courts and Court Martial (Adjustment of Jurisdiction) Rules 1978[1].

1 The Criminal Courts and Court Martial (Adjustment of Jurisdiction) Rules 1978 r 1. It supersedes the Criminal Courts and Court Martial (Adjustment of Jurisdiction) Rules 1952.

B. DEFINITIONS AND MEANING

[1631] Commanding officer In the Criminal Courts and Court Martial (Adjustment of Jurisdiction) Rules 1978, unless the context otherwise requires, the term 'commanding officer', (i) in relation to a person subject to military law, means the officer commanding the unit to which such person belongs or is attached[1]; (ii) in relation to a person subject to naval law, means the commanding officer of the ship or naval establishment or unit to which such person belongs or is attached[2]; (iii) in relation to a person subject to air force law, means the officer for the time being in command of the unit to which such person belongs or is attached[3]; and (iv) in relation to a person subject to the coast guard law, means the commanding officer of the coast guard ship or establishment or unit to which such person belongs or is attached[4].

1 The Criminal Courts and Court Martial (Adjustment of Jurisdiction) Rules 1978 r 2 (a) (i); as to the definition of 'commanding officer' under the Army Act 1950; see **[0013]**.

2 The Criminal Courts and Court Martial (Adjustment of Jurisdiction) Rules 1978 r 2 (a) (ii); as to the definition of 'commanding officer' under the Navy Act 1957; see **[0912]**.

3 The Criminal Courts and Court Martial (Adjustment of Jurisdiction) Rules 1978 r 2 (a) (iii); as to the definition of 'commanding officer' under the Air Force Act 1950; see **[0506]**.

4 The Criminal Courts and Court Martial (Adjustment of Jurisdiction) Rules 1978 r 2 (a) (iv); as to the definition of 'commanding officer' under the Coast Guard Act 1978; see **[1310]**.

[1632] Competent air force authority In the Criminal Courts and Court Martial (Adjustment of Jurisdiction) Rules 1978, unless the context otherwise requires, 'competent air force authority' means the chief of the air staff, the air or other officer commanding any command, wing or station in which the accused person is serving, or where such person is serving in field area, the officer commanding the forces or the air forces in the field[1].

1 The Criminal Courts and Court Martial (Adjustment of Jurisdiction) Rules 1978 r 2 (b).

[1633] Competent military authority In the Criminal Courts and Court Martial (Adjustment of Jurisdiction) Rules 1978, unless the context otherwise requires, 'competent military authority' means the chief of army staff or officer commanding the army, army corps, division, area, sub-area or independent brigade in which the accused person is serving, and except in cases falling under the Army Act, 1950 s 69 in which death has resulted, the officer commanding the brigade or sub-area or station in which the accused person is serving[1].

1 The Criminal Courts and Court Martial (Adjustment of Jurisdiction) Rules 1978 r 2 (c).

[1634] Competent naval authority In the Criminal Courts and Court Martial (Adjustment of Jurisdiction) Rules 1978, unless the context otherwise requires, 'competent naval authority' means the chief of the naval staff or the flag officer, commanding-in-chief, Western Naval Command Bombay or the flag officer commanding-in-chief, Eastern Naval Command Vishakhapatnam or the flag officer commanding, Southern Naval Area, Cochin or the flag officer commanding, Western Fleet or the flag officer commanding, Eastern Fleet or senior naval officer where the accused person is serving[1].

1 The Criminal Courts and Court Martial (Adjustment of Jurisdiction) Rules 1978 r 2 (d).

[1635] Competent coast guard authority In the Criminal Courts and Court Martial (Adjustment of Jurisdiction) Rules 1978, unless the context otherwise requires, 'competent coast guard authority' means the director general or inspector general or deputy inspector general within whose command the accused person is serving[1].

1 The Criminal Courts and Court Martial (Adjustment of Jurisdiction) Rules 1978 r 2 (e).

C. JURISDICTION

[1636] Cognizance by Magistrate Where a person subject to military, naval, air force or coast guard law, is brought before a magistrate and charged with an offence for which he is also liable to be tried by a court martial or coast guard court, such magistrate shall not proceed to try such person or to commit the case to the court of session, unless: (i) he is moved thereto by a competent military, naval, air force or coast guard authority[1]; or (ii) he is of opinion, for reasons to be recorded, that he should so proceed or to commit without being moved thereto by such authority[2].

There is no bar for taking cognisance by a magistrate, and to proceed to issue summons to the accused, after following the provisions contained in the Code of Criminal Procedure 1973 s 200 to 204. Likewise, for taking cognizance on a police report under the Code of Criminal Procedure 1973 s 190 also, there is no bar for the magistrate in respect of an offence committed by any person who is subject to either the Army Act 1950, the Navy Act 1957 or the Air Force Act 1950, in respect of civil offence as defined in the respective Acts. It is only after taking cognizance; the magistrate is required to follow the procedure contained in Criminal Courts and Court Martial (Adjustment of Jurisdiction) Rules 1978[3]. The option as to whether the accused be tried before the criminal court or by a court martial could be exercised only after the police had completed the investigation and submitted the charge-sheet and these provisions could not be invoked in a case where the police had merely started an investigation against a personnel subject to military, naval or air force law[4].

1 The Criminal Courts and Court Martial (Adjustment of Jurisdiction) Rules 1978 r 3 (a).

2 The Criminal Courts and Court Martial (Adjustment of Jurisdiction) Rules 1978 r 3 (b).

3 *Union of India v S K Sharma* 1987 AIR 1878, 1987 SCR (3) 456.

4 *Som Datt Datta v Union of India* AIR 1969 SC 414, [1969] 2 SCR 177, (1969) Cr LJ 663; *Commodore SK Jha v State of Kerala* [2011] 1 SCR 295.

[1637] Notice by the Magistrate Before proceeding under the aforesaid provision[1], the magistrate shall give a written notice to the commanding officer or the competent military, naval, air force or coast guard authority, of the accused and until the expiry of a period of 15 days from the date of service of the notice he shall not: (i) convict or acquit the accused under the Code of Criminal Procedure 1973 s 252, s. 255 (1) and (2), s. 256 (1), or 257, or hear him in his defence under the Code of Criminal Procedure 1973 s 254[2]; (ii) frame in writing a charge against the accused under the Code of Criminal Procedure 1973 ss 240 or 246 (1)[3]; (iii) make an order committing the accused for trial to the Court of Session under the Code of Criminal Procedure 1973 s 209[4]; or (iv) make over the case for inquiry or trial under the Code of Criminal Procedure 1973 s 192[5].

The provision mandatorily requires the magistrate to give a written notice to the commanding officer or the competent military, naval or air force authority, as the case may be and until the expiry of a period of 15 days from the date of service of notice, he shall not either frame charges or make over the case for inquiry, or commit the case for trial[6].

1 Ie the Criminal Courts and Court Martial (Adjustment of Jurisdiction) Rules 1978 r 3 (b); see **[1636]**.

2 The Criminal Courts and Court Martial (Adjustment of Jurisdiction) Rules 1978 r 4 (a).

3 The Criminal Courts and Court Martial (Adjustment of Jurisdiction) Rules 1978 r 4 (b).

4 The Criminal Courts and Court Martial (Adjustment of Jurisdiction) Rules 1978 r 4 (c).

5 The Criminal Courts and Court Martial (Adjustment of Jurisdiction) Rules 1978 r 4 (d).

6 *R K Yadav v State* (2007) 2 MLJ 1754 (BMM).

[1638] Procedure on notice to the Magistrate Where a magistrate has been moved by the competent military, naval, air force or coast guard authority, under the provisions of the Criminal Courts and Court Martial (Adjustment of Jurisdiction) Rules 1978[1], and such authority, subsequently gives notice to such magistrate that, in opinion of such authority, the accused should be tried by a court martial/coast guard court, such magistrate if he has not taken any action or made any order under the aforesaid provision[2], before receiving the notice shall stay the proceedings and if the accused is in his power or under his control, shall deliver him together with a statement of offence[3] to the commanding officer for trial by a court martial[4].

1 Ie the Criminal Courts and Court Martial (Adjustment of Jurisdiction) Rules 1978 r 3 (a).

2 Ie under the Criminal Courts and Court Martial (Adjustment of Jurisdiction) Rules 1978 r 4.

3 Ie as referred to in the Code of Criminal Procedure 1973 s 475 (1); see **[1685]**.

4 The Criminal Courts and Court Martial (Adjustment of Jurisdiction) Rules 1978 r 5.

[1639] Delivery of the accused Where within the period of 15 days[1], or at any time thereafter but before the magistrate takes any action or makes any order referred to in that provision, the commanding officer of the accused or the competent military, naval, air force or coast guard authority, gives notice to the magistrate that in the opinion of such officer or authority, the accused should be tried by a court martial or coast guard court the magistrate shall stay the proceedings, and if the accused is in his power or under his control, shall deliver him together with the statement of offence[2] to the commanding officer[3].

1 Ie as mentioned in the Criminal Courts and Court Martial (Adjustment of Jurisdiction) Rules 1978 r 4; see **[1637]**.

2 Ie as referred to in the Code of Criminal Procedure 1973 s 475 (1); see **[1685]**.

3 The Criminal Courts and Court Martial (Adjustment of Jurisdiction) Rules 1978 r 6.

[1640] Intimation regarding trial of accused When an accused has been delivered by the magistrate[1], the commanding officer of the accused or the competent military, naval, air force or coast guard authority, shall as soon as may be, inform the magistrate whether the accused has been tried by a court martial or coast guard court or other effectual proceedings have been taken or ordered to be taken against him[2]. When the magistrate has been informed under the aforesaid provision that the accused has not been tried or other effectual proceedings have not been taken or ordered to be taken against him, the magistrate shall report the circumstances to the State government which may, in consultation with the Central Government, take appropriate steps to ensure that the accused person is dealt with in accordance with law[3].

When a magistrate has taken cognizance of an offence committed by a member of the armed forces and thereafter transferred the case for trial under the Army Act 1950 and the Army Rules 1964, it is not open to the competent authority to hold an inquiry for determining whether there is any case for trying the accused. It must proceed to hold the court martial or take such other 'effectual proceedings' as is contemplated by the Criminal Courts and Court Martial (Adjustment of Jurisdiction) Rules 1978 r. 7(1)[4].

1 Ie under the provisions of the Criminal Courts and Court Martial (Adjustment of Jurisdiction) Rules 1978 r 5 or 6.

2 The Criminal Courts and Court Martial (Adjustment of Jurisdiction) Rules 1978 r 7(1).

3 Criminal Courts and Court Martial (Adjustment of Jurisdiction) Rules 1978 r 7 (2).

4 *Union of India v Major SK Sharma* 1987 AIR 1878, 1987 SCR (3) 456.

[1641] Reference to Central Government for determination of court of trial Notwithstanding anything in the foregoing provisions[1], where it comes to the notice of a magistrate that a person subject to military, naval, air force or coast guard law, has committed an offence, proceedings in respect of which ought to be instituted before him and that the presence of such person cannot be procured except through military, naval, air force or coast guard authorities, the magistrate may by a written notice require the commanding officer of such person either to deliver such person to a magistrate to be named in the said notice for being proceeded against according to law, or to stay the proceedings against such person before the court martial or coast guard court, as the case may be if since instituted, and to make a reference to the Central Government for determination as to the court before which proceedings should be instituted[2].

1 Ie the Criminal Courts and Court Martial (Adjustment of Jurisdiction) Rules 1978 r 1-7; see **[1630]-[1640]**.

2 The Criminal Courts and Court Martial (Adjustment of Jurisdiction) Rules 1978 r 8.

[1642] Delivery of accused to the Magistrate Where a person subject to military, naval, air force or coast guard law, has committed an offence which in the opinion of competent military, naval, air force or coast guard authority, ought to be tried by a magistrate in accordance with the civil law in force or where the Central Government has, on a reference mentioned in the aforesaid provision[1], decided that proceedings against such person should be instituted before a magistrate, the commanding officer of such person shall after giving a written notice to the magistrate concerned, deliver such person under proper escort to that magistrate[2].

1 Ie the Criminal Courts and Court Martial (Adjustment of Jurisdiction) Rules 1978 r 8; see **[1641]**.

2 The Criminal Courts and Court Martial (Adjustment of Jurisdiction) Rules 1978 r 9.

D. CONCURRENT JURISDICTION

[1643] Choice between criminal court and court martial When a criminal court[1] and a court martial[2] have each jurisdiction[3] in respect of an offence, it shall be in the discretion of the competent authority[4] to decide before which court the proceedings shall be instituted, and, if that officer decides that they should be instituted before a court martial, to direct that the accused person shall be detained in military or air force custody[5].

Under the aforesaid provision[6], both court martial as well the criminal court as defined in the Act[7] have got concurrent jurisdiction to try an offender who has committed a civil offence as defined in the Army Act or the Air Force Act. Thus there is an express provision indicating that the jurisdiction of the criminal court is not ousted. However, under the Army Act, or the Air Force 1950, discretion has been given to the competent authority[8] to decide before which court the proceedings shall be instituted. For any reason if the officer decides that they should be instituted before a court martial he may direct that the accused person shall be detained in military/air force custody[9].

1 As to the definition of 'criminal court'; see the Army Act 1950 s 3 (viii) or the Air Force Act 1950 s 4 (xvii).

2 As to the definition of 'court martial'; see the Army Act 1950 s 3 (vii) or the Air Force Act 1950 s 4 (xvi).

3 The word 'jurisdiction' in this provision really signifies the initial jurisdiction to take cognisance of a case. It refers to a state at which proceedings are instituted in a court and not to the jurisdiction of the ordinary criminal court and court martial to decide the case on merits. The provision of the Code of Criminal Procedure s 475 (1) should be construed in the light of the provision of the Army Act 1950 s 125. Both the provisions have in mind the object of avoiding a collision between the ordinary criminal court and the court martial. Therefore, both of them should receive a similar construction. *Delhi Special Police Establishment v Lt Col SK Loraiya* (1972) 2 SCC 692; 1973 Cr LJ 33, AIR 1973 SC 2548.

4 Ie the officer commanding the army, army corps, division or independent brigade in which the accused person is serving or such other officer as may be prescribed; see the Army Act 1950 s 125, the Air Force Act 1950 s 124.

5 The Army Act 1950 s 125; the Air Force Act s 124.

6 Ie the Army Act 1950 s 125,

7 Ie the Army Act 1950 s 3 (viii) and 3 (vii) or the Air Force Act 1950 s 4 (xvi) and (xvii) respectively.

8 Ie officer commanding army corps, division or independent brigade in which the accused person is serving or such other officer as may be prescribed; or the chief of the air staff, the officer commanding a command, wing or station; see the Army Act 1950 s 125 and the Air Force Act s 124.

9 *R K Yadav v State* (2007) 2 MLJ 1754 (BMM).

[1644] Power of criminal court to require delivery of offender When a criminal court having jurisdiction is of opinion that proceedings shall be instituted before itself in respect of any alleged offence, it may, by written notice, require the specified officer[1] at his option, either to deliver over the offender to the nearest magistrate to be proceeded against according to law, or to postpone proceedings pending a reference to the

Central Government[2]. In every such case the said officer shall either deliver over the offender in compliance with the requisition, or shall forthwith refer the question as to the court before which the proceedings are to be instituted for the determination of the Central Government, whose order upon such reference shall be final[3].

A close scrutiny of the aforesaid provision shows that if a criminal court having jurisdiction is of the opinion, that the proceedings shall be instituted before itself, it requires a written notice from the said court to the officer referred to in the Army Act 1950 s 125 or the Air Force Act 1950 s 124 either to deliver the offender to the nearest Magistrate to be proceeded against him according to law, or to postpone proceedings pending a reference to the Central Government. A conjoint reading of the provisions of the Army Act/ the Air Force Act 1950[4], makes it manifestly clear that the ordinary criminal court as well as the court martial have got concurrent jurisdiction to try an offender who has committed a civil offence and power has been given to an officer referred to in these two provisions to choose between the court martial and the criminal court. A close scrutiny of the Code of Criminal Procedure 1973[5]and the rules[6] lead to the conclusion that in respect of civil offences under the Navy Act 1957 also, the criminal courts and court martial have got concurrent jurisdiction and the jurisdiction of the criminal courts has not been ousted[7].

A close reading of the Criminal Courts and Court Martial (Adjustment of jurisdiction) Rules 1978[8], which govern all the three forces namely, army, navy and air force, makes it undoubtedly clear that with reference to any civil offence committed by any person, who is subject to the Army Act 1950, the Navy Act 1957, and the Air Force Act 1950, the accused could be tried either by the ordinary criminal court or by a court martial. The jurisdiction of the criminal court in respect of civil offences as defined in all the three Acts has not been ousted either expressly or impliedly. But at the same time, the ordinary criminal courts cannot try an offender on their own without following the above procedure contained in the Criminal Courts and Court Martial (Adjustment of jurisdiction) Rules 1978 r 3-7, which are mandatory in nature[9].

Once the criminal court determines that there is a case for trial, and pursuant to the Criminal Courts and Court Martial (Adjustment of jurisdiction) Rules 1978, delivers the accused to the commanding officer or the competent military, naval or air force authority, the law intends that the accused must either be tried by a court martial or some other effectual proceedings must be taken against him. To ensure that proceedings are taken against the accused the Criminal Courts and Court Martial (Adjustment of jurisdiction) Rules 1978 require the commanding officer or the competent authority to inform the Magistrate of what has been done[10].

1 Ie as referred to in the Army Act 1950 s 125 or the Air Force Act 1950 s 124; see **[1643]**.

2 The Army Act 1950 s 126 (1); the Air Force Act 1950 s 125 (1).

3 The Army Act 1950 s 126 (2); the Air Force Act 1950 s 125 (2).

4 Ie the Army Act 1950 ss 125 and 126; and the Air Force Act 1950 ss 124, 125.

5 Ie the Code of Criminal Procedure 1973 s 475.

6 Ie the Criminal Courts and Court Martial (Adjustment of jurisdiction) Rules 1978.

7 The Regulations for the Navy 1965, part II, regulations 114A.

8 Ie the Criminal Courts and Court Martial (Adjustment of jurisdiction) Rules 1978 r 3-7.

9 *R K Yadav v State* (2007) 2 MLJ 1754 (BMM).

10 *Union of India v Major SK Sharma* 1987 AIR 1878, 1987 SCR (3) 456.

VII. THE ARMY AND AIR FORCE (DISPOSAL OF PRIVATE PROPERTY) ACT 1950

CONTENTS

A. Introduction

[1645] Introduction This statute provides for the disposal of the private property of persons subject to the Army Act 1950 or the Air Force Act 1950, who die or desert or are ascertained to be of unsound mind or while on active service are officially reported to be missing.

B. Short title, extent and commencement

[1646] Short title, extent and commencement This statute dealing with the disposal of the private property of certain categories of persons belonging to the army and the air force is called the Army and Air Force (Disposal of Private Property) Act 1950[1]. It extends to the whole of India, and is applicable to the citizens of India and persons subject to the Army Act 1950, or the Air Force Act 1950[2]. It came into force on 22 July 1950 by notification[3] in the official gazette[4].

1 The Army and Air Force (Disposal of Private Property) Act 1950, s 1 (1).

2 The Army and Air Force (Disposal of Private Property) Act 1950, s 1 (2). As to the 'persons subject to the' Army Act 1950 and the Air Force Act 1950; see **[0013]** and **[0506]**.

3 See Notification No SRO 123, dated 22 July 1950, Gazette of India 1950, Part II, Section 3, p 87.

4 The Army and Air Force (Disposal of Private Property) Act 1950, s 1 (3).

C. Meaning and definitions

[1647] Committee In the Army and Air Force (Disposal of Private Property) Act 1950, unless the context otherwise requires, 'committee' means the committee of adjustment constituted under the aforesaid Act[1].

1 Ie the Army and Air Force (Disposal of Private Property) Act 1950 s 4; the Army and Air Force (Disposal of Private Property) Act 1950 s 2 (1).

[1648] Prescribed In the Army and Air Force (Disposal of Private Property) Act 1950, unless the context otherwise requires, 'prescribed' means person prescribed by rules under the aforesaid Act[1].

1 The Army and Air Force (Disposal of Private Property) Act 1950 s 2 (2). Prescribed person for the purposes of the Army and Air Force (Disposal of Private Property) Act 1950 ss 3, 4, 5, 7, 8, 9, 11, 12 and 13: (i) in relation to the estate of 'officers' subject to the Army Act 1950 and the 'officers' subject to the Air Force Act 1950 shall be the secretary, ministry of defence; (ii) in relation to the estate of persons other than officers subject to the Army Act 1950 brigade or equivalent commander; (iii) in relation to the estate of persons other than officers subject to

the Air Force Act 1950 the air officer in charge of a command under their respective command and the director of personnel services at air headquarters. See for further details: the Army and Air Force (Disposal of Private Property) Rules 1953 r 24.

[1649] Regimental and other debts in camp or quarters In the Army and Air Force (Disposal of Private Property) Act 1950, unless the context otherwise requires, 'regimental and other debts in camp or quarters' includes: (a) in relation to any person subject to the Army Act 1950 moneys due as military debts, namely, sums due in respect of or of any advance in respect of: (i) quarters[1]; (ii) mess, band and other regimental accounts[2]; (iii) military clothing, appointments and equipments, not exceeding a sum equal to three months' pay of the deceased and having become due within eighteen months before the date of his death[3]; and (b) in relation to any person subject to the Air Force Act 1950 moneys due as air force debts, namely, sums due in respect of or of any advance in respect of: (i) quarters[4]; (ii) mess, band and other service accounts[5]; (iii) air force clothing, appointments and equipments, not exceeding a sum equal to three months' pay of the deceased and having become due within eighteen months before the date of his death[6].

1 The Army and Air Force (Disposal of Private Property) Act 1950 s 2 (3) (i) (a).

2 The Army and Air Force (Disposal of Private Property) Act 1950 s 2 (3) (i) (b).

3 The Army and Air Force (Disposal of Private Property) Act 1950 s 2 (3) (i) (c).

4 The Army and Air Force (Disposal of Private Property) Act 1950 s 2 (3) (ii) (a).

5 The Army and Air Force (Disposal of Private Property) Act 1950 s 2 (3) (ii) (b).

6 The Army and Air Force (Disposal of Private Property) Act 1950 s 2 (3) (ii) (c).

[1650] Representation In the Army and Air Force (Disposal of Private Property) Act 1950, unless the context otherwise requires, 'representation' includes probate, letters of administration, with or without the will annexed and a succession certificate, constituting a person executor or administrator of the estate of a deceased person or authorising him to receive or realise the assets of a deceased person[1].

1 The Army and Air Force (Disposal of Private Property) Act 1950 s 2 (4).

[1651] Representative In the Army and Air Force (Disposal of Private Property) Act 1950, unless the context otherwise requires, 'representative' means any person who has taken out representation, but does not include in administrator general[1].

1 The Army and Air Force (Disposal of Private Property) Act 1950 s 2 (5).

[1652] Words and expressions used Unless the context otherwise requires, all words and expressions used and defined in the Army Act 1950 or the Air Force Act 1950 and not defined in the Army and Air Force (Disposal of Private Property) Act 1950, shall be deemed to have the meanings respectively attributed to them by those Acts[1].

1 The Army and Air Force (Disposal of Private Property) Act 1950 s 2 (6).

D. Disposal of property

[1653] Property of deceased persons and deserters other than officers

1 On the death or desertion of any person, not being an officer[1], subject to the Army Act 1950 or the Air Force Act 1950, the commanding officer[2] of the corps, department, detachment or unit to which the deceased or deserter belonged, shall: (i) secure all the movable property belonging to the deceased or deserter that is in camp or quarters, and cause an inventory thereof to be made[3]; (ii) draw the pay and allowances due to such person[4], (iii) make due provision for the payment of regimental and other debts in camp or quarters, if any, of such persons[5].

2 In the case of a deceased person, the commanding officer: (i) if it appears to him to be necessary to make provision for the payment of regimental and other debts in camp or quarters, the funeral expenses of the deceased and the expenses incurred in respect of the estate of the deceased, shall[6], and (ii) in any other case, may[7],-- collect all moneys left by the deceased in any bank (including any post office savings bank, co-operative bank or society or any other institution receiving deposits in money however named). For this purpose, he may require the agent or manager of such bank, society or other institution to pay the moneys to the commanding officer forthwith, notwithstanding anything in the rules of the bank, society or other institution, and such agent, manager or other officer shall be bound to comply with the requisition[8].

3 Where any money has been paid by a bank, society or other institution in compliance with a requisition made under the aforesaid provision, no person shall have any claim against the bank, society or other institution in respect of such money[9].

4 Where the representative of a deceased has given security to the satisfaction of the commanding officer for the payment of the regimental and other debts in camp or quarters, and expenses incurred by the commanding officer in respect of the estate of the deceased, the commanding officer shall deliver over the property received by him under the aforesaid provisions[10] to that representative, whereupon his responsibility for the administration of the estate of the deceased shall cease[11].

5 In the case of a deceased whose estate has not been dealt with under the aforesaid provision, or under the Army and Air Force (Disposal of Private Property) Act 1950 s 10, and in the case of a deserter, the commanding officer: (i) if in any case it is necessary in his opinion so to do for the purpose of securing the payment of the regimental and other debts in camp or quarters of the deceased or deserter, the funeral expenses of the deceased, if any, and the expenses, if any, incurred by the commanding officer in respect of the estate of the deceased or deserter, shall[12], and (ii) in any other case, may cause the movable property of the deceased or deserter, as the case may be, to be sold or converted into money[13].

6 The commanding officer shall, out of the moneys received, collected or realised[14] pay the regimental and other debts in camp or quarters, of the deceased or deserter, the expenses, incurred by the commanding officer in respect of the estate of the deceased or deserter, and in the case of a deceased his funeral expenses in cases where no provision for the payment of such expenses has been made otherwise[15].

7 The surplus, if any, after payment of the debts and expenses specified in the aforesaid provision, shall: (i) in the case of a deceased, be paid to his representative, if any, or in the event of no claim to such

surplus being established within twelve months after the death, to the prescribed person[16]; and (ii) in the case of a deserter, be forthwith paid to the prescribed person, and shall, on the expiry of three years from the date of desertion, be forfeited to the central government, unless the deserter has surrendered or apprehended[17]. However, the prescribed person may, if the deserter has not surrendered or been apprehended in the meantime, pay the whole or any part of the surplus received by him under aforesaid provision (ii) to the wife or children or any other dependent of the deserter at any time during the said period of three years[18].

8 In this provision and in the Army and Air Force (Disposal of Private Property) Act 1950 s 4, the word 'officer' with reference to persons subject to the Air Force Act 1950 includes a warrant officer who has died or deserted[19].

1 The word 'officer', in this provision and in the Army and Air Force (Disposal of Private Property) Act 1950 s 4, with reference to persons subject to the Air Force Act 1950 includes a warrant officer who has died or deserted. As to the meaning of the term 'officer' under the Army Act 1950; see **[0029]**.

2 As to the definition of 'commanding officer' under the Army Act 1950 and the Air Force Act 1950; see **[0013]** and **[0485]** respectively.

3 The Army and Air Force (Disposal of Private Property) Act 1950 s 3 (1) (a).

4 The Army and Air Force (Disposal of Private Property) Act 1950 s 3 (1) (b).

5 The Army and Air Force (Disposal of Private Property) Act 1950 s 3 (1) (c).

6 The Army and Air Force (Disposal of Private Property) Act 1950 s 3 (2) (a).

7 The Army and Air Force (Disposal of Private Property) Act 1950 s 3 (2) (b).

8 The Army and Air Force (Disposal of Private Property) Act 1950 s 3 (2).

9 The Army and Air Force (Disposal of Private Property) Act 1950 s 3 (3).

10 Ie under the Army and Air Force (Disposal of Private Property) Act 1950 s 3 (1) and (2)

11 The Army and Air Force (Disposal of Private Property) Act 1950 s 3 (4).

12 The Army and Air Force (Disposal of Private Property) Act 1950 s 3 (5) (i).

13 The Army and Air Force (Disposal of Private Property) Act 1950 s 3 (5) (ii).

14 Ie the Army and Air Force (Disposal of Private Property) Act 1950 s 3 (1), (2) and (5).

15 The Army and Air Force (Disposal of Private Property) Act 1950 s 3 (6).

16 The Army and Air Force (Disposal of Private Property) Act 1950 s 3 (7) (a).

17 The Army and Air Force (Disposal of Private Property) Act 1950 s 3 (7) (b).

18 The Army and Air Force (Disposal of Private Property) Act 1950 s 3 (7) proviso.

19 The Army and Air Force (Disposal of Private Property) Act 1950 s 3 explanation.

[1654] Property of officers who die or desert The aforesaid provision[1] shall also apply to the disposal of the property of any officer subject to the Army Act 1950 or the Air Force Act 1950 who dies or deserts, but with the following modifications: (a) the functions of the commanding officer under the Army and Air Force (Disposal of Private Property) Act 1950 s 3 shall be performed by a Committee of Adjustment constituted in this behalf in the prescribed manner[2]; (b) the surplus, if any, after payment of the debts and expenses specified in the Army and Air Force (Disposal of Private Property) Act 1950 s 3 (6), shall in the case of a deceased officer, be paid to the prescribed person[3].

1 Ie the Army and Air Force (Disposal of Private Property) Act 1950 s 3; see **[1653]**.

2 The Army and Air Force (Disposal of Private Property) Act 1950 s 4 (i).

3 The Army and Air Force (Disposal of Private Property) Act 1950 s 4 (ii).

[1655] Decision of questions as to regimental and other debts in camp quarters If in any case a doubt or difference arises as to what are the regimental and other debts in camp or quarters of a deceased or deserter or as to the amount payable in respect thereof, the decision of the prescribed person shall be final and shall be binding on all persons for all purposes[1].

1 The Army and Air Force (Disposal of Private Property) Act 1950 s 5.

[1656] Representative powers of commanding officer or committee For the purpose of the exercise of his or its duties under certain provisions of the Army and Air Force (Disposal of Private Property) Act 1950[1], the commanding officer[2] or the committee, as the case may be, shall, to the exclusion of all other persons and authorities whomsoever or whatsoever, have the same rights and powers as if he or it had taken out representation to the estate of the deceased, and any receipt given by the commanding officer or the committee, as the case may be, shall have effect accordingly[3].

1 Ie the Army and Air Force (Disposal of Private Property) Act 1950 s 3 or 4.

2 As to the definition of 'commanding officer' under the Army Act 1950 and the Air Force Act 1950; see **[0013]** and **[0485]** respectively.

3 The Army and Air Force (Disposal of Private Property) Act 1950 s 6.

[1657] Power of central government to hand over estate of deceased person to the administrator general

1 Notwithstanding anything contained in the Administrator General's Act 1963, an administrator general shall not interpose in any manner in relation to any property of a deceased which has been dealt with under the provisions of the Army and Air Force (Disposal of Private Property) Act 1950 s 3 or 4, except in so far as he is expressly required or permitted to do so by or under the provisions of the Administrator General's Act[1].

2 The central government may, at any time and in such circumstances as it thinks fit, direct that the estate of a deceased shall be handed over by the commanding officer[2] or the Committee, to the administrator general of a State for administration, and thereupon the commanding officer or the committee, as the case may be, shall make over the estate to such administrator general[3].

3 Where any estate is handed over to the administrator general, the administrator general shall administer such estate in accordance with the provisions of the Administrator General' s Act 1963, or, if that Act is not in force in any State, of the corresponding law in force in that State[4]. However, the regimental and other debts in camp or quarters of the deceased, if any, shall be paid by the administrator general in priority to any other debts due by the deceased[5].

4 The administrator general shall pay the surplus, if any, remaining in his hands after discharging all debts and charges, to the heirs of the deceased, and, if no heir is traceable, shall make over the surplus in the prescribed manner to the prescribed person[6].

5 The administrator general shall not charge in respect of his duties under this provision any fee exceeding

three per cent of the gross amount coming to or remaining in his hands after payment of the regimental and other debts in camp or quarters[7].

1 The Army and Air Force (Disposal of Private Property) Act 1950 s 7 (1).

2 As to the definition of 'commanding officer' under the Army Act 1950 and the Air Force Act 1950; see **[0013]** and **[0485]** respectively.

3 The Army and Air Force (Disposal of Private Property) Act 1950 s 7 (2).

4 The Army and Air Force (Disposal of Private Property) Act 1950 s 7 (3).

5 The Army and Air Force (Disposal of Private Property) Act 1950 s 7 (3) proviso.

6 The Army and Air Force (Disposal of Private Property) Act 1950 s 7 (4).

7 The Army and Air Force (Disposal of Private Property) Act 1950 s 7 (5).

[1658] Disposal of surplus by prescribed persons On receipt of the surplus referred to in certain provisions of the Army and Air Force (Disposal of Private Property) Act 1950[1], the prescribed person shall: (i) if he knows of a representative of the deceased, pay the surplus to that representative[2]; (ii) if he does not know of any such representative and the surplus has not been disposed of under the Army and Air Force (Disposal of Private Property) Act 1950 s 10, publish every year a notice in the prescribed form and manner for six consecutive years and if no claim to the surplus is made by a representative of the deceased within six months even after the publication of the last of such notices, the prescribed person shall deposit the surplus together with any income or accumulation of income accrued therefrom to the credit of the central government[3]. However, such deposit shall not bar the claim of any person to such surplus or any part thereof, if he is otherwise entitled to it[4].

1 Ie the Army and Air Force (Disposal of Private Property) Act 1950 s 3 (7), s 4 (ii) or s 7 (4)

2 The Army and Air Force (Disposal of Private Property) Act 1950 s 8 (a).

3 The Army and Air Force (Disposal of Private Property) Act 1950 s 8 (b).

4 The Army and Air Force (Disposal of Private Property) Act 1950 s 8 (b) proviso.

[1659] Disposal of effects, not money Where any part of the estate of a deceased person consists of effects, securities or other property not converted into money, the provisions of the Army and Air Force (Disposal of Private Property) Act 1950[1], with respect to the payment of the surplus, shall extend to the delivery, transmission or transfer of such effects, securities or property. The prescribed person shall have the same power of converting the effects, securities or other property into money as a representative of the deceased[2].

1 Ie the Army and Air Force (Disposal of Private Property) Act 1950 s 3 (7), s 4 (ii) and s 8.

2 The Army and Air Force (Disposal of Private Property) Act 1950 s 9.

[1660] Disposal of certain property without production of probate, etc Property deliverable and money payable to the representative of a deceased under certain provisions of the Army and Air Force (Disposal of Private Property) Act 1950[1] may, if the total amount or value thereof does not exceed Rs 200,000 and if the prescribed person thinks fit, be delivered or paid to any person appearing to him to be entitled to receive it or to administer the estate of the deceased without requiring such person to produce any probate, letters of administration, succession certificate or other such conclusive evidence of title[2].

1 Ie the Army and Air Force (Disposal of Private Property) Act 1950 s 3 or 4 or 8.

2 The Army and Air Force (Disposal of Private Property) Act 1950 s 10.

[1661] Discharge of commanding officer, committee, prescribed person and the central government Any payment or application of money or application, delivery, sale or other disposition of any property made, or purported to be made, by the commanding officer, the committee or the prescribed person in good faith in pursuance of certain provisions of the Army and Air Force (Disposal of Private Property) Act 1950[1] shall be valid and shall be a full discharge to the commanding officer, the committee or the prescribed person, as the case may be, and to the central government from all further liability in respect of that money or property; but nothing herein contained shall affect the right of any executor or administrator or other representative, or of any creditor of the deceased against any person to whom such payment or delivery has been made[2].

1 Ie the Army and Air Force (Disposal of Private Property) Act 1950 s 3, 4, 8, 9 or 10.

2 The Army and Air Force (Disposal of Private Property) Act 1950 s 11.

[1662] Property in the hands of commanding officer, committee or prescribed person not to be assets where commanding officer, committee or prescribed person is stationed Any property coming into the hands of the commanding officer[1] or the committee or the prescribed person[2] shall not, be deemed to be assets or effects at the place in which that commanding officer or the committee is stationed, and it shall not be necessary that representation be taken out in respect of the property for that place[3].

1 As to the definition of 'commanding officer' under the Army Act 1950 and the Air Force Act 1950; see **[0013]** and **[0485]** respectively.

2 Ie under the Army and Air Force (Disposal of Private Property) Act 1950 s 3, 4, or 7 (4).

3 The Army and Air Force (Disposal of Private Property) Act 1950 s 12.

[1663] Saving of rights of representative After the commanding officer[1], or the committee has paid to the prescribed person the surplus of the property of any deceased[2], any representative of the deceased or any administrator general, shall, as regards any property of the deceased not collected by the commanding officer or the committee, and not forming part of the aforesaid surplus, have the same rights and duties as if the Army and Air Force (Disposal of Private Property) Act 1950 s 3 and 4 had not been enacted[3].

1 As to the definition of 'commanding officer' under the Army Act 1950 and the Air Force Act 1950; see **[0013]** and **[0485]** respectively.

2 Ie under the Army and Air Force (Disposal of Private Property) Act 1950 s 3 (7) or s 4 (ii).

3 The Army and Air Force (Disposal of Private Property) Act 1950 s 13.

[1664] Application of the Army and Air Force (Disposal of Private Property) Act 1950 s 3 to 13 to persons of unsound mind or to persons reported missing on active service Certain provisions of the Army and Air Force (Disposal of Private Property) Act 1950[1] shall, so far as they can be made applicable, also apply in the case of a person subject to the Army Act 1950 or the Air Force Act 1950, who, notwithstanding anything contained in the Mental Health Act 1987 is ascertained to be of unsound mind, or who, while on active service, is officially reported missing, as if he had died on the day on which his unsoundness of mind is so ascertained, on the day on which he is officially reported missing. However, in the case of a person so reported missing, no action shall be taken under the provisions of the Army and Air Force (Disposal of Private Property) Act 1950[2] until such time as he is officially presumed to be dead[3].

1 Ie the Army and Air Force (Disposal of Private Property) Act 1950 s 3 to 13.

2 Ie under the Army and Air Force (Disposal of Private Property) Act 1950 s 3 (2) to (6), s 4 or s 7.

3 The Army and Air Force (Disposal of Private Property) Act 1950 s 14.

[1665] Appointment of Standing Committee of Adjustment in certain cases When an officer dies or deserts or is ascertained in the prescribed manner to be of unsound mind or while on active service[1] is officially reported missing, the references in the foregoing provisions of the Army and Air Force (Disposal of Private Property) Act 1950 to the Committee shall be construed as references to the Standing Committee of Adjustment[2], constituted in this behalf in the prescribed manner. Such Standing Committee shall alone be entitled to perform all the functions of the committee under the aforesaid provision[3].

1 As to the definition of 'active service' under the Army Act 1950; see **[0008]**.

2 The Standing Committee of Adjustment can be constituted under the Army and Air Force (Disposal of Private Property) Rules 1953 r 19.

3 The Army and Air Force (Disposal of Private Property) Act 1950 s 15.

E. Rules

[1666] Power to make rules The central government may, by notification in the official gazette, make rules for the purpose of carrying into effect the purposes of the Army and Air Force (Disposal of Private Property) Act 1950[1]. In particular, such rules may: (i) prescribe the manner in which any property belonging to a deceased or deserter may be secured or collected and his regimental and other debts in camp or quarters paid[2]; (ii) provide for the payment of the funeral expenses of any deceased[3]; (iii) provide for the constitution of the Committee of Adjustment or any Standing Committee of Adjustment under the Army and Air Force (Disposal of Private Property) Act 1950[4]; (iv) specify the person who shall be regarded as the prescribed person for the purposes of the Army and Air Force (Disposal of Private Property) Act 1950[5]; (v) prescribe the circumstances in which the estate of any deceased shall be handed over to the administrator general[6]; (vi) prescribe the form and manner in which a notice under the Army and Air Force (Disposal of Private Property) Act 1950 s 8 shall be published[7]; and (vii) prescribe the procedure by which any person may be ascertained to be of unsound mind[8].

Every rule made by the central government under the Army and Air Force (Disposal of Private Property) Act 1950 shall be laid, as soon as may be after it is made, before each House of Parliament while it is in session, for a total period of 30 days which may be comprised in one session or in two or more successive sessions, If, before the expiry of the session immediately following the session or the successive sessions aforesaid, both Houses agree in making any modification in the rule or both Houses agree that the rule should not be made, the rule shall thereafter have effect only in such modified form or be of no effect; so, however, that any such modification or annulment shall be without prejudice to the validity of anything previously done under that rule[9].

1 The Army and Air Force (Disposal of Private Property) Act 1950 s 16 (1). See the Army and Air Force (Disposal of Private Property) Rules 1953.

2 The Army and Air Force (Disposal of Private Property) Act 1950 s 16 (2) (a).

3 The Army and Air Force (Disposal of Private Property) Act 1950 s 16 (2) (b).

4 The Army and Air Force (Disposal of Private Property) Act 1950 s 16 (2) (c).

5 The Army and Air Force (Disposal of Private Property) Act 1950 s 16 (2) (d).

6 The Army and Air Force (Disposal of Private Property) Act 1950 s 16 (2) (e).

7 The Army and Air Force (Disposal of Private Property) Act 1950 s 16 (2) (f).

8 The Army and Air Force (Disposal of Private Property) Act 1950 s 16 (2) (g).

9 The Army and Air Force (Disposal of Private Property) Act 1950 s 16 (3).

VIII. INDIAN PENAL CODE AND CODE OF CRIMINAL PROCEDURE

1. THE INDIAN PENAL CODE 1860: PROVISIONS RELATING TO THE ARMED FORCES

CONTENTS

[1667] Public servant Every commissioned officer in the military, naval or air forces of India is a 'public servant' within the meaning of the Indian Penal Code 1860[1].

1 The Indian Penal Code 1860 s 21, clause second. As to the definition of 'officer' in the military, naval or air forces of India; see **[0029]**, **[0927]** and **[0494]**.

[1668] Construction of reference to transportation Subject to certain provisions of the Indian Penal Code 1860[1], any reference to 'transportation for life' in any other law for the time being in force or in any instrument or order having effect by virtue of any such law or of any enactment repealed shall be construed as a reference to 'imprisonment for life'[2]. In every case in which a sentence of transportation for a term has been passed before the commencement of the Code of Criminal Procedure (Amendment) Act 1955, the offender shall be dealt with in the same manner as if sentenced to rigorous imprisonment for the same term[3]. Any reference to transportation for a term or to transportation for any shorter term (by whatever name called) in any other law for the time being in force shall be deemed to have been omitted[4]. Any reference to 'transportation' in any other law for the time being in force shall: (i) if the expression means transportation for life, be construed as a reference to imprisonment for life[5]; and (ii) if the expression means transportation for any shorter term, be deemed to have been omitted[6].

1 The Indian Penal Code 1860 s 53A (2) and (3)

2 The Indian Penal Code 1860 s 53A (1).

3 The Indian Penal Code 1860 s 53A (2).

4 The Indian Penal Code 1860 s 53A (3).

5 The Indian Penal Code 1860 s 53A (4) (a).

6 The Indian Penal Code 1860 s 53A (4) (b).

[1679] Abetting mutiny, or attempting to seduce soldiers, sailors or airmen from duty Whoever abets[1] the committing of mutiny[2] by an officer, soldier, sailor or airman in the army, navy or air force of the Government of India or attempts to seduce any such officer, soldier, sailor or airman from his allegiance or his duty, shall be punished with imprisonment for life, or with imprisonment of either description for a term which may extend to 10 years, and shall also be liable to fine[3]. In this provision, the words 'officer', 'soldier', 'sailor' and 'airman' include any person subject to the Army Act 1950, the Navy Act 1957, and the Air Force Act 1950[4]. This provision supplements and extends to civilians, the penal provisions relating to mutiny and desertion[5].

1 As to the meaning of 'abetment' see The Indian Penal Code 1860 s 107.

2 The term 'mutiny' has been defined under the Navy Act 1957 s 42; see **[0993]**.

3 Indian Penal Code 1860 s 131.

4 The Indian Penal Code 1860 s 131 explanation. As to the meaning of 'persons' subject to the Army Act 1950, the Navy Act 1957, and the Air Force Act 1950; see **[0039]**, **[0941]** and **[0506]**.

5 *Pindi Das v Emperor* (1907) 6 Cr LJ 411 (Lah).

[1670] Statements conducting to public mischief Whoever makes, publishes or circulates any statement, rumour or report: (i) with intent to cause, or which is likely to cause, any officer, soldier, sailor or airman in the Army, Navy or Air Force of India to mutiny or otherwise disregard or fail in his duty as such[1]; or (ii) with intent to cause, or which is likely to cause, fear or alarm to the public, or to any section of the public whereby any person may be induced to commit an offence against the State or against the public tranquility[2]; or (iii) with intent to incite, or which is likely to incite, any class or community of persons to commit any offence against any other class or community, shall be punished with imprisonment which may extend to three years, or with fine, or with both[3].

1 The Indian Penal Code 1860 s 505 (1)(a).

2 The Indian Penal Code 1860 s 505 (1)(b).

3 The Indian Penal Code 1860 s 505 (1)(c).

[1671] Abetment of mutiny, if mutiny is committed in consequence thereof Whoever abets the committing of mutiny by an officer, soldier, sailor or airman, in the army, navy or air force of the Government of India, shall, if mutiny be committed in consequence of that abetment, be punished with death or with imprisonment for life, or imprisonment of either description for a term which may extend to ten years, and shall also be liable to fine[1].

1 The Indian Penal Code 1860 s 132.

[1672] Abetment of assault by soldiers, sailors or airmen on superior officers in execution of office Whoever, abets an assault by an officer, soldier, sailor or airman, in the army, navy or air force of the Government of India, on any superior officer being in the execution of his office, shall be punished with imprisonment of either description for a term which may extend to three years, and shall also be liable to fine[1].

1 The Indian Penal Code 1860 s 133.

[1673] Abetment of assault by soldiers, sailors or airmen on superior officers if committed Whoever abets an assault by an officer, soldier, sailor or airman in the army, navy or air force of the Government of India, on any superior officer being in the execution of his office, shall, if such assault be committed in consequence of that abetment, be punished with imprisonment of either description for a term which may extend to seven years, and shall also be liable to fine[1].

1 The Indian Penal Code 1860 s 134.

[1674] Abetment of desertion of soldiers, sailors or airmen Whoever abets the desertion of any officer, soldier, sailor or airman in the army, navy or air force of the Government of India, shall be punished with imprisonment of either description for a term which may extend to two years, or with fine, or both[1].

1 The Indian Penal Code 1860 s 135.

[1675] Harbouring deserter Whoever, knowing or having reason to believe[1] that an officer, soldier, sailor or airman, in the army, navy or air force of the Government of India, has deserted, harbours[2] such officer, soldier, sailor or airman, shall be punished with imprisonment of either description for a term, which may extend to two years, or with fine, or with both[3]. However, this provision does not extend to the case in which the harbour is given by a wife to her husband[4].

1 As to the meaning of 'reason to believe'; see the Indian Penal Code 1860 s 26.

2 As to the meaning of 'harbour' see the Indian Penal Code 1860 s 52A.

3 The Indian Penal Code 1860 s 136.

4 The Indian Penal Code 1860 s 136 explanation.

[1676] Deserter concealed on board merchant vessels through negligence of masters The master or person in charge of a merchant vessel, on board of which any deserter from the army, navy or air force of the Government of India is concealed, shall, though ignorant of such concealment, be liable to a penalty not exceeding Rs 500, if he might have known of such concealment but for some neglect of his duty as such master or person in charge, or but for some want of discipline on board of the vessel[1].

1 The Indian Penal Code 1860 s 137.

[1677] Abetment of acts of insubordination by soldiers, sailors or airmen Whoever abets what he knows to be an act of insubordination by an officer, soldier, sailor or airman, in the army, navy or air force, of the Government of India, shall, if such act of insubordination be committed in consequence of that abetment[1], be punished with imprisonment of either description for a term which may extend to six months, or with fine, or both[2].

1 As to the meaning of 'abetment'; see the Indian Penal Code 1860 s 107.

2 The Indian Penal Code 1860 s 138.

[1678] Persons subject to certain legislations No person subject to the Army Act 1950, the Navy Act 1957, the Air Force Act 1950[1], is subject to punishment for any of the offences defined in certain provisions of the Indian Penal Code 1860[2].

1 As to the meaning of 'persons' subject to the Army Act 1950, the Navy Act 1957, and the Air Force Act 1950; see **[0039]**, **[0941]** and **[0506]**.

2 Ie as defined in the Indian Penal Code 1860 Ch VII, ss 131-140: see the Indian Penal Code 1860 s 139.

[1679] Wearing garb or carrying token used by soldiers, sailors or airmen Whoever, not being a soldier, sailor or airman in the military, naval or air service of the Government of India, wears any garb or carries any token resembling any garb or token used by such a soldier, sailor or airman with the intention that it may be believed that he is such a soldier, sailor or airman shall be punished with imprisonment of either description for a term which may extend to three months, or with fine which may extend to Rs 500, or both[1].

1 The Indian Penal Code 1860 s 140.

2. THE CODE OF CRIMINAL PROCEDURE 1973: PROVISIONS RELATING TO THE ARMED FORCES

CONTENTS

[1680] Maintenance of Public Order and Tranquility The law governing the dispersal of unlawful assemblies is contained in the Criminal Procedure Code 1973[1]. Any executive magistrate or a police officer of designated rank may command any unlawful assembly likely to cause a disturbance of the public peace, to disperse. In such a situation, it becomes the duty of every member of such an assembly to disperse accordingly. When the civil authorities are incapable of dispersing such an unlawful assembly by the use of all the resources at their disposal, they can seek the aid of the armed forces, if it is necessary for the public security that such assembly should be dispersed. Every officer of the armed forces is required to obey the requisition of the magistrate in such manner as he thinks fit but in doing so, he is to use as little force and do as little injury to person and property as may be consistent with dispersing the assembly and arresting and detaining such persons.

1 Ie the Criminal Procedure Code 1973, chapter X, ss 129-132.

[1681] Dispersal of assembly by use of civil force Any executive magistrate or officer in-charge of a police station or, in the absence of such officer in-charge, any police officer, not below the rank of a sub-inspector, may command any unlawful assembly[1], or any assembly of five or more persons likely to cause a disturbance of the public peace, to disperse; and it shall thereupon be the duty of the members of such assembly to disperse accordingly[2]. If, upon being so commanded, any such assembly does not disperse, or if, without being so commanded, it conducts itself in such a manner as to show a determination not to disperse, any executive magistrate or police officer referred to in the aforesaid provision, may proceed to disperse such assembly by force, and may require the assistance of any male person, not being an officer or member of the armed forces and acting as such, for the purpose of dispersing such assembly, and, if necessary, arresting and confining the persons who form part of it, in order to disperse such assembly or that they may be punished according to law[3].

1 As to the definition of 'unlawful assembly' see the Indian Penal Code 1860 s 141. Article 19 (1) of the India Constitution confers upon all citizens of India the right to assemble peacefully and without arms. This right is subject to reasonable restrictions in the interests of the sovereignty of India and public order.

2 Criminal Procedure Code 1973 s 129 (1).

3 Criminal Procedure Code 1973 s 129 (2).

[1682] Use of armed forces to disperse assembly If any such assembly[1] cannot be otherwise dispersed, and if it is necessary for the public security that it should be dispersed, the executive magistrate of the highest rank who is present may cause it to be dispersed by the armed force[2]. Such magistrate may require any officer in command of any group of persons belonging to the armed forces to disperse the assembly with the help of the armed forces under his command, and to arrest and confine such persons forming part of it as the magistrate may direct, or as it may be necessary to arrest and confine in order to disperse the assembly or to have them punished according to law[3]. Every such officer of the armed forces shall obey such requisition in such manner as he thinks fit, but in so doing he shall use as little force, and do as little injury to person and property, as may be consistent with dispersing the assembly and arresting and detaining such persons[4].

1 Ie an 'unlawful assembly' as referred in the Criminal Procedure Code 1973 s 129 (1). As to the definition of 'unlawful assembly' see the Indian Penal Code 1860 s 141.

2 Criminal Procedure Code 1973 s 130 (1). Where the police fired without lawful orders from the authorities on the members of an unlawful assembly and caused the death of one person, it was held that the state government was vicariously liable and had to pay compensation to the dependents of the deceased. *State of Karnataka v B Padmanabha Beliya* 1992 Cr LJ 634 (Knt).

3 Criminal Procedure Code 1973 s 130 (2).

4 Criminal Procedure Code 1973 s 130 (3). In reference to the situations requiring the use of armed force in aid of civil power, the provisions of the Criminal Procedure Code 1973 s 130 and 131 are not adequate to deal with the situations. *Naga People's Movement of Human Rights v Union of India* (1998) 2 SCC 109, AIR 1998 SC 431. The request by the Magistrate should preferably in writing, but if made verbally, the officer commanding troops should ask the magistrate to repeat the request in the presence of two military personnel. The requisition will be complied with

immediately. The strength and composition of the fore, the amount of ammunition to be taken and the manner of carrying out the task are matters of the decision of the military authorities alone. Defence Services Regulations, Regulations for the Army, volume I, paragraph 305.

[1683] Power of certain armed force officers to disperse assembly When the public security is manifestly endangered by any such assembly and no executive magistrate can be communicated with, any commissioned or gazetted officer of the armed forces may disperse such assembly with the help of the armed forces under his command, and may arrest and confine any persons forming part of it, in order to disperse such assembly or that they may be punished according to law. While such commissioned or gazetted officer is acting under this provision, it becomes practicable for him to communicate with an executive magistrate, he shall do so, and shall thereafter obey the instructions of the magistrate, as to whether he shall or shall not continue such action[1].

1 Criminal Procedure Code 1973 s 131. In reference to the situations requiring the use of armed force in aid of civil power, the provisions of the Criminal Procedure Code 1973 s 130 and 131 are not adequate to deal with the situations. *Naga People's Movement of Human Rights v Union of India* (1998) 2 SCC 109, AIR 1998 SC 431. When officer commanding the troops decides that it is necessary to disperse an unlawful assembly by force, he will, before taking action, adopt the most effective measure possible to explain to the people concern that the fire of the troop will be effective. Defence Services Regulations, Regulations for the Army, volume I, paragraph 306.

[1684] Protection against prosecution for acts done under the Criminal Procedure Code 1973 s 131

1 No prosecution against any person for any act purporting to be done under certain provisions of the Criminal Procedure Code 1973[1] shall be instituted in any Criminal Court except: (i) with the sanction of the Central Government where such person is an officer or member of the armed forces[2]; (ii) with the sanction of the State Government in any other case[3].

2 No executive magistrate or police officer acting under any of the stated provisions[4] in good faith[5]; (ii) no person doing any act in good faith in compliance with a requisition under the Criminal Procedure Code 1973 s 129 or 130[6]; (iii) no officer of the armed forces acting under the Criminal Procedure Code 1973 in good faith[7]; (iv) no member of the armed forces doing any act in obedience to any order which he was bound to obey[8]; shall be deed to have thereby committed an offence[9].

3 In the Criminal Procedure Code 1973 s 129, 130, 131 and 132: (i) the expression 'armed forces' means the military, naval and air forces, operating as land forces and includes any other Armed Forces of the Union so operating[10]; (ii) 'officer', in relation to the armed forces, means a person commissioned, gazetted or in pay as an officer of the armed forces and includes a junior commissioned officer, a warrant officer, a petty officer, a non-commissioned officer and a non-gazetted officer[11]; (iii) 'member', in relation to the armed forces, means a person in the armed forces other than an officer[12].

1 Ie under the Criminal Procedure Code 1973 s 129, 130 or 131.

2 Criminal Procedure Code 1973 s 132 (1) (a).

3 Criminal Procedure Code 1973 s 132 (1) (b).

4 Ie under the Criminal Procedure Code 1973 s 129, 130 or 131.

5 As to the meaning of 'good faith' see the Indian Penal Code 1860 s 52; the Criminal Procedure Code 1973 s 132 (2) (a).

6 Criminal Procedure Code 1973 s 132 (2) (b).

7 Ie under the Criminal Procedure Code 1973 s 131; Criminal Procedure Code 1973 s 132 (2) (c).

8 Criminal Procedure Code 1973 s 132 (2) (d).

9 Criminal Procedure Code 1973 s 132 (2).

10 Criminal Procedure Code 1973 s 132 (3) (a).

11 Criminal Procedure Code 1973 s 132 (3) (b).

12 Criminal Procedure Code 1973 s 132 (3) (b). As to the meaning of 'persons' subject to the Army Act 1950, the Navy Act 1957, and the Air Force Act 1950; see **[0039]**, **[0941]** and **[0506]**.

[1685] Delivery to commanding officers of persons liable to be tried by court martial The Central Government is empowered to make rules consistent with the Code of Criminal Procedure 1973, the Army Act 1950, the Navy Act 1957, and the Air Force Act 1950, and any other law, relating to the Armed Forces of the Union, as to the cases in which persons subject to such military, naval or air force, or such other law, shall be tried by a court to which the Code of Criminal Procedure 1973 applies or by a court martial[1]. When any person is brought before the magistrate and charged with an offence for which he is liable to be tried either by a court to which the Code of Criminal Procedure 1973 applies or by a court martial, such magistrate shall have regard[2] to such rules, and shall in proper cases deliver him, together with a statement of offence of which he is accused, to the commanding officer of the unit[3] to which he belongs, or to the commanding officer[4] of the nearest military, naval or air force station, for the purpose of being tried by a court martial[5]. Every magistrate shall on receiving an application on receiving a written application for that purposes by the commanding officer of any unit or body of soldiers, sailors or airmen stationed or employed at any such place, use his utmost endeavours to apprehend and secure any person accused of such offence[6]. A high court may, if it thinks fit, direct that a prisoner detained in any jail situated within the State to be brought before a court-martial for trial or to be examined touching any matter pending before the court martial[7].

In exercise of the powers conferred by the aforesaid provision[8], for avoidance of conflict of jurisdiction between the criminal courts and court martial, the Central Government has made the rules[9] for the trial of the persons subject to military, naval, air force or coast guard law, by a criminal court or by a court martial/ coast guard court. Under the Army Act 1950[10], the discretion is given to the officer mentioned therein to decide the question where the proceedings should be instituted; but if the designated officer does not exercise his discretion, it will be open to the criminal court to exercise its jurisdiction as provided by law[11]. If a magistrate proceeds in the matter, or even commits the case to the court of sessions, without giving such notice to the designated authorities, the entire proceedings shall be void and *non-est*[12]. Where the naval authorities requested the magistrate to allow the accused to be tried under the naval law, the magistrate had no choice but to stay the proceedings and deliver the accused to the naval authorities and there was no necessity to record reasons thereof[13].

1 The term 'court martial' includes any tribunal with the powers similar to those of a court martial constituted under the relevant law applicable to the armed forces of the Union; the Code of Criminal Procedure 1973 s 475, explanation (b).

2 The phrase 'magistrate shall have regard' is mandatory. *Delhi Special Police Establishment v S K Loraiya* AIR 1972 SC 2548; 1973 Cr LJ 33.

3 The term 'unit' includes a regiment, corps, ship, detachment, group, battalion or company; the Code of Criminal Procedure 1973 s 475, explanation (a).

4 As to the definition of 'commanding officer' under the Army Act 1950, the Navy Act 1957, and the Air Force Act 1950; see **[0013]**, **[0912]** and **[0485]** respectively.

5 The Code of Criminal Procedure 1973 s 475 (1).

6 The Code of Criminal Procedure 1973 s 475 (2).

7 The Code of Criminal Procedure 1973 s 475 (3). This provision gives discretionary powers to the High Court to direct that a prisoner detained in any jail situated within the State be sent to court martial either for trial or for his examination regarding any matter pending before the court martial. *Umesh Singh v State of Bihar*, 2003, Cr LJ 2215 (Pat).

8 Ie the Code of Criminal Procedure 1976 s 475 (1).

9 Ie the Criminal Courts and Court Martial (Adjustment of Jurisdiction) Rules 1978; see **[1629] to [1642]**.

10 Ie the Army Act 1950 s 125; also see the Air Force Act 1950 s 124, the Regulations for the Navy 1965, part II, regulation 114A and appendix IV.

11 *Joginder Singh v State of Himachal Pradesh* AIR 1971 SC 500; 1971 Cr LJ 33.

12 *Gajendra Singh v State of Rajasthan* 1995 Cr LJ 3347 (Raj).

13 *Mangal Singh Bhatti v Union of India*, 1993 Cr LJ 3070 (Ker).

IX. THE ARMED FORCES TRIBUNAL LAW

1. INTRODUCTION

[1686] Introduction The Supreme Court of India in the case of *Lt Col PPS Bedi v Union of India*[1] observed that military trials are subject to varying degrees of command influence and there was absence of even one appeal with an appellate forum having power to review evidence, legal formulations, conclusions and adequacy or otherwise of punishment. The Supreme Court opined that the same to be not in sync with democratic principles and expressed a pious hope that the legislature should earnestly consider creating an appellate forum for members of armed forces, which should be free from the command influence. The Court suggested the need of a judicial review forum for the members of the armed forces to question the verdicts against them at a court martial[2].

Having regard to the fact that a large number of cases relating to service matters of the members of the three armed forces of Union were pending in the higher courts for a long time, the government proposed to enact a new legislation by constituting an armed forces tribunal for the adjudication of complaints and dispute regarding service matters and appeals arising out of the verdicts of the courts martial of the members of the three services (the Army, Navy and the Air Force). The proposal of Ministry of Defence was approved by the Cabinet on 29 September 2005 and the Armed Forces Tribunal Bill 2005 was introduced in Rajya Sabha on 20 December, 2005. The Armed Forces Tribunal Act 2007 was passed by the Parliament in December 2007[3].

The formation of the Armed Forces Tribunal by virtue of the 2007 Act was for the creation of an efficacious, inexpensive and speedy dispute resolution mechanism[4]. The object of the establishment of an independent Armed Forces Tribunal was to provide for a speedy and less expensive dispensation of justice to the members of the three armed forces of the union[5]. The Armed Force Tribunal Act 2007 aims to provide, for the adjudication or trial, by Armed Forces Tribunal, of disputes and complaints with respect to commission, appointment, enrollment and conditions of service in respect of persons subject to the Army, Navy and Air Force Act and additionally to provide for appeals arising out of orders, findings or sentences of court martial held under the said three service Acts. In other words, the Tribunal exercises original jurisdiction with respect to service disputes[6] and appellate jurisdiction with respect to orders, findings or sentences of court martial[7].

The Armed Forces Tribunal, being manned by personnel appointed by the executive, albeit in consultation with the Chief Justice of India cannot be said to be truly a judicial review forum as a substitute to High Courts which are constitutional courts and the power of judicial review, being a basic feature of the Constitution, under Article 226 and Article 227 of the Constitution of India is unaffected by the constitution of the Armed Forces Tribunal. Article 227(4) of the Constitution of India takes away only the administrative supervisory jurisdiction of High Court over the Armed Forces Tribunal and does not impact the judicial supervisory jurisdiction over the Armed Forces Tribunal. Thus, decisions by the Armed Forces Tribunal would be amenable to judicial review by High Court under Article 226 as also Article 227 of the Constitution of India[8]. The Armed Forces Tribunal Act 2007 does not take away or violate the right of judicial review under Article 226/227 and Article 32 of the Constitution of India[9].

1 *Lt Col PPS Bedi v Union of India* AIR 1982 SC 1414.

2 *Colonel AD Nargolkar v Union of India* decided 26 April 2011, ILR (2011) IV Delhi, 114.

3 The Armed Forces Tribunal has been set up under Article 246 of the Constitution read with Entry 2 of List-1 (Union List) in the Seventh Schedule to the Constitution.

4 *Major Saurabh Saharan v Union of India*, WP(C) No1755 of 2013 and CM No 3355 of 2013, decided by the Delhi High Court on 19 March 2013.

5 The Statement of Objects and Reasons, the Armed Forces Tribunal Bill, 2005.

6 Ie under the Armed Forces Tribunal Act s 14.

7 Ie under the Armed Forces Tribunal Act s 15.

8 *Colonel AD Nargolkar v Union of India* decided 26 April 2011, ILR (2011) IV Delhi, 114.

9 The writ petitions under Article 226 of the Constitution of India would be maintainable, where: (i) it pertains to challenge against the constitutional validity of any of the provisions of the Armed Forces Tribunal Act 2007, (ii) in the matters relating to armed forces exempted from the jurisdiction of the Armed Forces Tribunal Act 2007 under s 3(o), and (iii) in the matters of interlocutory orders passed by the Armed Forces Tribunal. However no writ will lie to the High Court: (i) in contempt matters, where statutory appeal is provided to the Supreme Court under the Armed Forces Tribunal Act 2007 s 30(2), (ii) against final orders of the Armed Forces Tribunal, in which an appeal lies to Supreme Court under Armed Forces Tribunal Act 2007 s 31(1), and (iii) under Article 227 of the Constitution of India. *Surendra Bahadur Singh v Armed Force Tribunal, Regional Bench Lucknow*, WP No 20294 of 2012, Allahabad High Court decided on 2 May 2012.

2. PRELIMINARY

CONTENTS

A. Short title

[1687] Short title and commencement This statue having power to review decisions and orders of court martial and grievances of the persons subject to the Army Act 1950, the Air Force Act 1950 and the Navy Act 1957 is called the Armed Forces Tribunal Act 2007[1]. It came into force on 10 August 2009 by notification[2] in the official gazette[3].

1 The Armed Forces Tribunal Act 2007 s 1 (1).

2 The Ministry of Defence Notification SRO 9 (E): In exercise of power conferred by the Armed Forces Tribunal Act 2007 s 4, the central Government established the Armed Forces Tribunal with effect from 10 August 2009, which shall be the appointed day within the meaning of this provision. The Gazette of India, Part II, Section 4, 7 August 2009.

3 The Armed Forces Tribunal Act 2007 s 1 (2).

B. Applicability

[1688] Applicability of the Armed Forces Tribunal Act 2007 The provisions of the Armed Forces Tribunal Act 2007 apply to all persons subject to the Army Act 1950, the Navy Act 1957 and the Air Force Act 1950[1]. The Armed Forces Tribunal Act 2007 is also applicable to retired personnel subject to the Army Act 1950 or the

Navy Act 1957 or the Air Force Act 1950 including their dependants, heirs and successors, in so far as it relates to their service matters[2].

1 The Armed Forces Tribunal Act 2007 s 2 (1). A combined reading of the Armed Forces Tribunal Act 2007 s 2 and s 3(o) shows that the Tribunal has limited jurisdiction to deal with the service conditions under the Army Act 1950 and the Army Rules 1957. The issue relating to non-selection of the petitioner by the Defence Research and Development Organization (DRDO) for the rank of Lt Gen was under the DRDO Rules of the Office Memorandum dated 23 November 1989 and not supersession under the Army Act 1950 or Army Rules 1957. As such, the Tribunal cannot sit over the selection by DRDO to decide the issue whether petitioner has been correctly superseded or not, since the service conditions of the seconded officers under the DRDO is regulated by Office Memorandum. Therefore, the Tribunal does not have the jurisdiction to decide the case of supersession of petitioner for promotion to the rank of Lt Gen. *Major General SB Akali v Union of India*, TA No. 125 and 221 of 2010, The Armed Forces Tribunal, Principal Bench New Delhi, decided on 9 April 2010. As to the meaning of 'persons' subject to the Army Act 1950, the Navy Act 1957, and the Air Force Act 1950; see **[0039]**, **[0941]** and **[0506]**.

2 The Armed Forces Tribunal Act 2007 s 2 (2).

C. Definitions

Certain word and terms that appear in the Armed Forces Tribunal Act, the Armed Forces Tribunal (Procedure) Rules, and the Armed Forces Tribunal (Practice) Rules will need to be understood as they are defined in the Armed Forces Tribunal Act 2007, the Armed Forces Tribunal (Procedure) Rules 2008, and the Armed Forces Tribunal (Practice) Rules 2009.

[1689] Administrative member In the Armed Forces Tribunal Act 2007, unless the context otherwise requires, 'administrative member' means a member of the Tribunal who is not a judicial member[1] within the meaning of certain provisions[1] of the aforesaid Act[2].

1 As to the definition of 'judicial member'; see the Armed Forces Tribunal Act 2007 s 3 (g): **[1698]**.

2 The Armed Forces Tribunal Act 2007 s 3 (a).

[1690] Agent In the Armed Forces Tribunal (Procedure) Rules 2008, unless the context otherwise requires, 'agent' means a person duly authorized by a party to present an application, written reply, rejoinder or any other document on its behalf before the Armed Forces Tribunal[1].

1 The Armed Forces Tribunal (Procedure) Rules 2008 r 2 (ii).

[1691] Applicant In the Armed Forces Tribunal (Procedure) Rules 2008, unless the context otherwise requires, 'applicant' means a person making an application to the Tribunal[1].

1 Ie making an application under the Armed Forces Tribunal Act 2007 s 14 (2) or an appeal under s 15 (2). The Armed Forces Tribunal (Procedure) Rules 2008 r 2 (iii).

[1692] Application In the Armed Forces Tribunal Act 2007, unless the context otherwise requires, 'application' means an application made under certain provisions[1] of the Armed Forces Tribunal Act 2007[2]. The term 'application' includes Original Application (OA), Review Application (RA), Transferred Application (TA), Miscellaneous Application (MA), Application for Transfer (AT) and Contempt Application (CA), filed before the Armed Forces Tribunal[3]. Transferred application means the suit or other proceeding which has been transferred to the tribunal under certain provisions of the Armed Forces Tribunal Act 2007[4].

1 Ie under the Armed Forces Tribunal Act 2007 s 14 (2).

2 The Armed Forces Tribunal Act 2007 s 3 (b).

3 The Armed Forces Tribunal (Procedure) Rules 2008 r 2 (iv).

4 Ie under the Armed Forces Tribunal Act 2007 s 34 (1) or (2). The Armed Forces Tribunal (Procedure) Rules 2008 r 2 (xviii).

[1693] Appointed day In the Armed Forces Tribunal Act 2007, unless the context otherwise requires, 'appointed day' means the date with effect from which the Tribunal is established by notification under Armed Forces Tribunal Act 2007 s 4[1].

1 The Armed Forces Tribunal Act 2007 s 3 (c). The Ministry of Defence Notification SRO 9 (E): In exercise of power conferred by the Armed Forces Tribunal Act 2007 s 4, the central Government established the Armed Forces Tribunal with effect from 10 August 2009, which shall be the appointed day within the meaning of this provision. The Gazatte of India, Part II, Section 4, 7 August 2009.

[1694] Bench In the Armed Forces Tribunal Act 2007, unless the context otherwise requires, 'bench' means a bench of the Armed Forces Tribunal[1].

1 The Armed Forces Tribunal Act 2007 s 3 (d).

[1695] Chairperson In the Armed Forces Tribunal Act 2007, unless the context otherwise requires, 'chairperson' means the chairperson of the Armed Forces Tribunal[1].

1 The Armed Forces Tribunal Act 2007 s 3 (e).

[1696] Court martial In the Armed Forces Tribunal Act 2007, unless the context otherwise requires, 'court martial' means a court martial held under the Army Act 1950[1] or the Navy Act 1957 including the disciplinary courts constituted under the Navy Act 1957[2] or the Air Force Act 1950[1].

1 As to the definition of 'court martial' under the Army Act 1950; see **[0016]**.

2 As to the definition of 'court martial' under the Navy Act 1957; see **[0915]**. Under the Navy Act, 'disciplinary court' means a tribunal constituted under s 95 of the Act.

3 As to the definition of 'court martial' under the Air Force Act 1950; see **[0486]**. The Armed Forces Tribunal Act 2007 s 3 (f).

[1697] Judgment In the Armed Forces Tribunal (Practice) Rules 2009, unless the context otherwise requires, 'judgment' includes decree, order, sentence or determination of any court, tribunal, judge, judicial officer or authority[1].

1 The Armed Forces Tribunal (Practice) Rules 2009 r 2 (ix).

[1698] Judicial member In the Armed Forces Tribunal Act 2007, unless the context otherwise requires, 'judicial member' means a member of the Armed Forces Tribunal appointed as such under the aforesaid Act, and includes the chairperson, who possesses any of the qualifications specified in certain provisions of the aforesaid Act[1].

1 Ie as specified in the Armed Forces Tribunal Act 2007 s 6 (2); The Armed Forces Tribunal Act 2007 s 3 (g).

[1699] Legal representative In the Armed Forces Tribunal (Practice) Rules 2009, unless the context otherwise requires, 'legal representative' means a person who represents the estate of a serving or deceased person and includes a person or persons in whom the right to receive pensionary, retirement, terminal, disability or other benefits or family pension vests under any law for the time being in force[1].

1 The Armed Forces Tribunal (Practice) Rules 2009 r 2 (xi).

[1700] Member In the Armed Forces Tribunal Act 2007, unless the context otherwise requires, 'Member' means a member (whether judicial or administrative) of the Armed Forces Tribunal and includes the chairperson[1].

1 The Armed Forces Tribunal Act 2007 s 3 (h).

[1701] Military custody In the Armed Forces Tribunal Act 2007, unless the context otherwise requires, 'military custody' means the arrest or confinement of a person according to the usages of the service and includes naval or air force custody[1].

1 The Armed Forces Tribunal Act 2007 s 3 (i). As to the definition of 'military custody', 'naval custody' and 'air force custody'; see [22.024], [22.912] and [22.475].

[1702] Notification In the Armed Forces Tribunal Act 2007, unless the context otherwise requires, 'notification' means a notification published in the Official Gazette[1].

1 The Armed Forces Tribunal Act 2007 s 3 (j).

[1703] Officer of the judge advocate general's department In the Armed Forces Tribunal (Practice) Rules 2009, unless the context otherwise requires, 'officer of the judge advocate general's department' means an officer commissioned into the judge advocate general's department of the army or an officer permanently transferred to that department after qualifying at the judge advocate general's departmental examination and includes an officer of judge advocate general's department of navy and air force[1].

1 The Armed Forces Tribunal (Practice) Rules 2009 r 2 (xii).

[1704] Prescribed In the Armed Forces Tribunal Act 2007, unless the context otherwise requires, 'prescribed' means prescribed by rules made under the Armed Forces Tribunal Act 2007[1].

1 The Armed Forces Tribunal Act 2007 s 3 (k).

[1705] President In the Armed Forces Tribunal Act 2007, unless the context otherwise requires, 'President' means the President of India[1].

1 The Armed Forces Tribunal Act 2007 s 3 (l).

[1706] Registrar In the Armed Forces Tribunal (Procedure) Rules 2008, unless the context otherwise requires, 'registrar' means Registrar of the Armed Forces Tribunal or its Benches and shall include Registrar General,

Principal, Additional, Joint and Deputy Registrars, authorized to discharge the functions of the Registrar[1].

1 The Armed Forces Tribunal (Procedure) Rules 2008 r 2 (xiii). The functions, powers and duties of the Registrar are contained in r 30 and 31.

[1707] Rules In the Armed Forces Tribunal Act 2007, unless the context otherwise requires, 'rules' means the rules made under Armed Forces Tribunal Act 2007[1].

1 The Armed Forces Tribunal Act 2007 s 3 (m). The following rules have been made so far under the provisions of the Armed Forces Tribunal Act 2007: (i) The Armed Forces Tribunal (Procedure) Rules 2008; (ii) The Armed Forces Tribunal (Procedure for appointment of Vice-Chairperson and other Members) Rules 2008; (iii) the Armed Force Tribunal (Procedure for investigation of misbehaviour or incapacity of Chairperson and other Members) Rules 2008; (iv) The Armed Forces Tribunal (Financial and Administrative Powers) Rules 2008; (v) The Armed Forces Tribunal (Procedure) Rules 2008; (vi) The Armed Forces Tribunal (Practice) Rules 2009; and (vii) The Armed Forces Tribunal (Salaries, Allowances and Conditions of Service of Chairperson and Members) Rules 2009.

[1708] Service In the Armed Forces Tribunal Act 2007, unless the context otherwise requires, 'service' means the service within or outside India[1].

1 The Armed Forces Tribunal Act 2007 s 3 (n).

[1709] Service matters In the Armed Forces Tribunal Act 2007, unless the context otherwise requires, 'service matters', in relation to the persons subject to the Army Act 1950, the Navy Act 1957 and the Air Force Act 1950 mean all matters relating to the conditions of their service and shall include: (a) remuneration (including allowances), pension and other retirement benefits[1]; (b) tenure, including commission, appointment, enrolment, probation, confirmation, seniority, training, promotion, reversion, premature retirement, superannuation, termination of service and penal deductions[2]; (c) summary disposal and trials where the punishment of dismissal is awarded[3]; (d) any other matter, whatsoever[4]. However, the term 'service matters', shall not include matters relating to: (a) orders issued under doctrine of the pleasure of the President[5]; (b) transfers and postings including the change of place or unit on posting whether individually or as a part of unit, formation or ship in relation to the persons subject to the Army Act 1950, the Navy Act 1957 and the Air Force Act 1950[6]; (c) leave of any kind[7]; and (d) summary court martial except where the punishment is of dismissal or imprisonment for more than three months[8].

1 The Armed Forces Tribunal Act 2007 s 3 (o) (i).

2 The Armed Forces Tribunal Act 2007 s 3 (o) (ii).

3 The Armed Forces Tribunal Act 2007 s 3 (o) (iii). The award of summary punishments to a sailor; i.e., reduction in rank, deprivation of first good conduct badge, mulcts of pay and allowances for 31 days, and stoppage of leave for 60 days, under the Navy Act 1957 was not under the covered by the Armed Forces Tribunal Act 2007 s 3(o) and the Tribunal had no jurisdiction to deal with the matter. The delinquent has the right to approach the High Court under Article 226 of Indian Constitution. *Abhinandan Kumar v Union of India*, OA No 39 of 2010, the Armed Forces Tribunal, Regional Bench Kochi, decided on 4 June 2010.

4 The Armed Forces Tribunal Act 2007 s 3 (o) (iv).

5 Ie under the Army Act 1950 s 18, the Navy Act 1957 s 15 (1) and the Air Force Act 1950 s 18; The Armed Forces Tribunal Act 2007 s 3 (o) proviso (i).

6 The Armed Forces Tribunal Act 2007 s 3 (o) proviso (ii). Transfer and posting is not covered in the definition of

'service matters'. *Subedar/Clerk Pawan Kumar v Chief of the Army Staff*, OA No. 05 of 2011, Armed Forces Tribunal, Regional Bench Lucknow, decided on 23 September 2011. A matter of differences arising due to posting, and subsequent compensation for the harassment, humiliation and financial loss, the matter is not covered under the definition of service matters as given in the Armed Forces Tribunal Act 2007 s 3(o). *Sukhdev Singh v Union of India*, OA No 303 of 2013, Armed Forces Tribunal, Regional Bench Chandigarh, decided on 13 February 2013. Shifting from one Regiment to another Regiment would amount to transfer and the same falls within the ambit of word 'transfer' as defined under the Armed Forces Tribunal Act 2007 s 3(o) and the tribunal lacks jurisdiction to adjudicate upon the matter. *Lt Col SK Goswami v Union of India*, OA No. 279 of 2011, Armed Forces Tribunal, Regional Bench, Lucknow, decided on 6 January 2012; *Subedar/Clerk Pawan Kumar v Chief of the Army Staff*, OA No 5 of 2011, decided by the Armed Forces Tribunal, Regional Bench, Lucknow on 23 September 2011.

7 The Armed Forces Tribunal Act 2007 s 3 (o) proviso (iii).

8 The Armed Forces Tribunal Act 2007 s 3 (o) proviso (vi).An order other than dismissal or imprisonment of three months awarded by a summary court martial is outside the ambit of the Tribunal by virtue of this provision. *Ex Hav Sukhwinder Singh v Union of India*, TA No 305 of 2009, decided by Armed Forces Tribunal, Principal Bench New Delhi on 24 February 2010.

[1710] Services In the Armed Forces Tribunal (Practice) Rules 2009, unless the context otherwise requires, 'services' means the army, navy and air force, as applicable[1].

1 The Armed Forces Tribunal (Practice) Rules 2009 r 2 (xviii).

[1711] Standing counsel In the Armed Forces Tribunal (Practice) Rules 2009, unless the context otherwise requires, 'standing counsel" means as advocate authorized to act; represent and accept the service for the army, navy or air force for the Union of India[1].

1 The Armed Forces Tribunal (Practice) Rules 2009 r 2 (xix).

[1712] Summary disposals and trials In the Armed Forces Tribunal Act 2007, unless the context otherwise requires, 'summary disposals and trials' means summary disposals and trials held under the Army Act 1950, the Navy Act 1957 and the Air Force Act, 1950[1].

1 The Armed Forces Tribunal Act 2007 s 3 (p).

[1713] Tribunal In the Armed Forces Tribunal Act 2007, unless the context otherwise requires 'tribunal' means the Armed Forces Tribunal established under the aforesaid Act[1].

1 Ie under the Armed Forces Tribunal Act 2007 s 4; The Armed Forces Tribunal Act 2007 s 3 (q).

3. TRIBUNAL AND ITS BENCHES

CONTENTS

PARA

[1714] Establishment of Armed Forces Tribunal The Central Government has established[1] the Armed Forces Tribunal to exercise the jurisdiction, powers and authority conferred on it by or under the Armed Forces Tribunal 2007[2].

1 By the Ministry of Defence Notification SRO 9 (E): In exercise of power conferred by the Armed Forces Tribunal Act 2007 s 4, the central Government established the Armed Forces Tribunal with effect from 10 August 2009, which shall be the appointed day within the meaning of the Armed Forces Tribunal Act 2007 s 3 (c). The Gazette of India, Part II, Section 4, 7 August 2009.

2 The Armed Forces Tribunal Act 2007 s 4.

[1715] Composition of tribunal and its benches The Tribunal consists of a chairperson and such number of judicial and administrative members as the Central Government may deem fit. Subject to the provisions of the Armed Forces Tribunal Act, the jurisdiction, powers and authority of the Tribunal may be exercised by its benches[1]. A bench shall consist of one judicial member and one administrative member[2]. However, the chairperson may, for the purpose of securing that any case(s), which having regard to the nature of the questions involved, requires to be decided by a bench composed of more than two members, issue such general or special orders, as he may deem fit[3]. Every such bench constituted in pursuance of the aforesaid provision shall include at least one judicial member and one administrative member[4]. The chairperson may: (i) in addition to discharging the functions of a judicial member of the bench, to which he is appointed, discharge the functions of an administrative member of any other bench[5]; and (ii) transfer a member from one bench to another bench[6]. Subject to the other provisions[7], the benches of the tribunal shall ordinarily sit at Delhi (which shall be known as the Principal Bench), and at such other places as the Central Government may specify by a notification[8].

1 The Armed Forces Tribunal Act 2007 s 5 (1).

2 The Armed Forces Tribunal Act 2007 s 5 (2).

3 The Armed Forces Tribunal Act 2007 s 5 (3) (c).

4 The Armed Forces Tribunal Act 2007 s 5 (3) (c) proviso

5 The Armed Forces Tribunal Act 2007 s 5 (3) (a).

6 The Armed Forces Tribunal Act 2007 s 5 (3) (b).

7 Ie the Armed Forces Tribunal (Financial and Administrative Powers) Rules 2008 r 3; see **[1716]**.

8 The Armed Forces Tribunal Act 2007 s 5 (4). A total of 15 benches have been created across India. These are:

Delhi (Principal Bench) 3 benches, Chandigarh 3 benches, Lucknow 3 benches, Kolkata 1 bench, Guwahati 1 bench, Mumbai 1 bench, Kochi 1 bench, Chennai 1 bench, and Jaipur 1 bench.

[1716] Sitting of an additional bench at place other than the place where it shall ordinarily sit If at any time the vice-chairperson of any additional bench is satisfied that circumstances exist which render it necessary to have sitting of the said bench at any place falling within its territorial jurisdiction, other than the place falling within its territorial jurisdiction, other than the place or places at which it ordinarily sits, he may with the previous consent of the chairperson direct that the additional bench shall hold its sittings as any such appropriate place[1].

1 The Armed Forces Tribunal (Financial and Administrative Powers) Rules 2008 r 3.

[1717] Qualifications for appointment of chairperson and other members

1 A person shall not be qualified for appointment as the chairperson unless he is a retired judge of the Supreme Court or a retired chief justice of a High Court[1].

2 A person shall not be qualified for appointment as a judicial member unless he is or has been a judge of a High Court[2].

3 A person shall not be qualified for appointment as an administrative member unless: (i) he has held or has been holding the rank of major general or above for a total period of at least three years in the Army or equivalent rank in the Navy or the Air Force[3]; or (ii) he has served for not less than one year as judge advocate general in the Army or the Navy or the Air Force, and is not below the rank of major general, commodore and air commodore respectively[4].

4 When a serving person is appointed as an administrative member, he shall have retired from service prior to assuming such appointment[5].

1 The Armed Forces Tribunal Act 2007 s 6 (1).

2 The Armed Forces Tribunal Act 2007 s 6 (2).

3 The Armed Forces Tribunal Act 2007 s 6 (3) (a).

4 The Armed Forces Tribunal Act 2007 s 6 (3) (b).

5 The Armed Forces Tribunal Act 2007 s 6 (3) explanation.

[1718] Appointment of chairperson and other members The chairperson and other members of the tribunal shall be appointed by the President of India[1], after consultation with the Chief Justice of India[2]. The President may appoint one or more members of the tribunal to be the vice-chairperson(s) of the tribunal[3].

1 The Armed Forces Tribunal Act 2007 s 7 (1). See: the Armed Forces Tribunal (Procedure for appointment of Vice-Chairperson and other Members) Rules, 2008.

2 The Armed Forces Tribunal Act 2007 s 7 (1) proviso.

3 The Armed Forces Tribunal Act 2007 s 7 (2).

[1719] Term of office The chairperson or a member shall hold office for a term of four years from the date on which he enters upon his office and shall be eligible for re-appointment[1]. However, no chairperson shall hold office as such after he has attained: (i) in case he has been a judge of the Supreme Court, the age of 70[2]; and (ii) in case he has been the chief justice of a high court, the age of 65 years[3]. Further no other member shall hold office as such member after he has attained the age of 65 years[4].

1 The Armed Forces Tribunal Act 2007 s 8.

2 The Armed Forces Tribunal Act 2007 s 8 proviso (a).

3 The Armed Forces Tribunal Act 2007 s 8 proviso (b).

4 The Armed Forces Tribunal Act 2007 s 8 additional proviso.

[1720] Resignation and removal The chairperson or a member may, by notice in writing under his hand addressed to the President, resign his office[1]. However, the chairperson or a member shall, unless he is permitted by the President to relinquish his office sooner, continue to hold office until the expiry of three months from the date of receipt of such notice or until a person duly appointed as his successor enters upon his office or until the expiry of his term of office, whichever is the earliest[2]. The chairperson or a member shall not be removed from his office except by an order made by the President on the ground of proved misbehaviour or incapacity after an inquiry made by a sitting judge of the Supreme Court in which such chairperson or other member had been informed of the charges against him and given a reasonable opportunity of being heard in respect of those charges[3]. The Central Government may, by rules, regulate the procedure for the investigation of misbehaviour or incapacity of the chairperson or other member referred to in the aforesaid provision[4].

1 The Armed Forces Tribunal Act 2007 s 9 (1).

2 The Armed Forces Tribunal Act 2007 s 9 (1) proviso.

3 The Armed Forces Tribunal Act 2007 s 9 (2).

4 The Armed Forces Tribunal Act 2007 s 9 (3). The Central Government has made the Armed Force Tribunal (Procedure for investigation of misbehaviour or incapacity of Chairperson and other Members) Rules 2008.

[1721] Salaries, allowances and other terms and conditions of service of chairperson and other members The salaries and allowances payable to, and the other terms and conditions of service (including pension, gratuity and other retirement benefits) of, the chairperson and other members shall be such as may be prescribed[1] by the Central Government[2]. However, neither the salary and allowances nor the other terms and conditions of service of the chairperson and other members shall be varied to their disadvantage after their appointment[3].

1 As prescribed in the Armed Forces Tribunal (Salaries, Allowances and Conditions of Service of Chairperson and Members) Rules 2009.

2 The Armed Forces Tribunal Act 2007 s 10.

3 The Armed Forces Tribunal Act 2007 s 10 proviso.

[1722] Prohibitions as to holding of offices, etc., by chairperson or member on ceasing to be such chairperson or member On ceasing to hold office: (i) the chairperson shall be ineligible for further employment either under the Government of India or under the Government of a State[1]; (ii) a member other than the chairperson shall, subject to the provisions of the Armed Forces Tribunal Act 2007, be eligible for appointment as a member of any other tribunal but not for any other employment either under the Government of India or under the Government of a State[2]; and (iii) the chairperson or other members shall not appear, act or plead before the tribunal[3].

1 The Armed Forces Tribunal Act 2007 s 11 (a).

2 The Armed Forces Tribunal Act 2007 s 11 (b).

3 The Armed Forces Tribunal Act 2007 s 11 (c).

[1723] Financial and administrative powers of chairperson The chairperson shall exercise such financial and administrative powers over the benches as may be prescribed[1]. However, the chairperson shall have the authority to delegate such of his financial and administrative powers as he may think fit to any other member or any officer of the tribunal, subject to the conditions that such member or officer shall, while exercising such delegated powers, continue to act under the direction, control and supervision of the chairperson[2].

1 The Armed Forces Tribunal Act 2007 s 12. See: the Armed Forces Tribunal (Financial and Administrative Powers) Rules 2008.

2 The Armed Forces Tribunal Act 2007 s 12 proviso.

[1724] Powers of chairperson The Chairperson shall have the same powers as are conferred on a Department of the Central Government in respect of the delegation of Financial Powers Rules 1978, the General Financial Rules 1963, the Fundamental and Supplementary Rules, the Central Civil Services (Leave) Rules 1972, the Central Civil Services (Joining Time) Rule 1979, the Central Civil Services (Conduct) Rules 1964, the Central Civil Services (Classification, Control and Appeal) Rules 1965 and the General Provident Fund (Central Services) Rules 1960[1]. However, the exercise of the financial powers shall be subject to any procedural or other instructions issued from time to time by the government and after obtaining the advice of the financial adviser and chief accounts officer of the tribunal[2]. Further, in respect of matters not within the competence of the chairperson, concurrence of the Ministry of Finance or any other authority shall obtained by the chairperson through the Ministry of Defence[3].

1 The Armed Forces Tribunal (Financial and Administrative Powers) Rules 2008 r 4.

2 The Armed Forces Tribunal (Financial and Administrative Powers) Rules 2008 r 4 proviso.

3 The Armed Forces Tribunal (Financial and Administrative Powers) Rules 2008 r 4 additional proviso.

[1725] Staff of the Tribunal The Central Government shall determine the nature and categories of the officers and other employees required to assist the tribunal in the discharge of its functions and provide the tribunal with such officers and other employees as it may think fit[1]. The salaries and allowances payable to, and the other terms and conditions of service of the officers and other employees of the tribunal shall be such as may be prescribed[2]. The officers and other employees of the tribunal shall discharge their functions under the general superintendence of the Chairperson[3].

1 The Armed Forces Tribunal Act 2007 s 13 (1).

2 The Armed Forces Tribunal Act 2007 s 13 (2).

3 The Armed Forces Tribunal Act 2007 s 13 (3).

4. JURISDICTION, POWER AND AUTHORITY

CONTENTS

PARA

[1726] Jurisdiction, powers and authority in service matters

1 Except as otherwise expressly provided in the Armed Forces Tribunal Act 2007[1], the tribunal shall exercise, all the jurisdiction, powers and authority, in relation to all service matters[2].

2 Subject to certain other provisions of the Armed Forces Tribunal Act 2007, a person aggrieved by an order pertaining to any service matter may make an application to the tribunal in prescribed form and accompanied by documents or other evidence and on payment of prescribed fee[3].

3 On receipt of an application relating to service matters, the tribunal shall, if satisfied after due inquiry, as it may deem necessary, that it is fit for adjudication by it, admit such application. In cases where the tribunal is not so satisfied, it may dismiss the application after recording its reasons in writing[4].

4 For the purpose of adjudicating an application, the Tribunal shall have the same powers as are vested in a civil court under the Code of Civil Procedure 1908 while trying a suit in respect of the following matters: (i) summoning and enforcing the attendance of any person and examining him on oath[5]; (ii) requiring the discovery and production of documents[6]; (iii) receiving evidence on affidavits[7]; (iv) subject to certain provisions of the Indian Evidence Act 1872[8], requisitioning any public record or document or copy of such record or document from any office[9]; (v) issuing commissions for the examination of witnesses or documents[10]; (vi) reviewing its decisions[11]; (vii) dismissing an application for default or deciding it ex-parte[12]; (viii) setting aside any order of dismissal of any application for default or any order passed by it ex-parte[13]; and (ix) any other matter which may be prescribed by the Central Government[14].

5 The Tribunal shall decide both questions of law and facts that may be raised before it[15].

1 The term 'service matter' has been defined under the Armed Forces Tribunal Act 2007 s 3 (o). The tribunal therefore shall not have jurisdiction in matters relating to: (a) orders issued under the Army Act 1950 s 18, the Navy Act 1957 s 15 (1) and the Air Force Act 1950 s 18[5]; (b) transfers and postings including the change of place or unit on posting whether individually or as a part of unit, formation or ship in relation to the persons subject to the Army Act 1950, the Navy Act 1957 and the Air Force Act; (c) leave of any kind; and (d) summary court martial except where the punishment is of dismissal or imprisonment for more than three months. See: **[1709]**.

2 The Armed Forces Tribunal Act 2007 s 14 (1).

3 The Armed Forces Tribunal Act 2007 s 14 (2). The procedure for filing an application is contained in the Armed Forces Tribunal (Procedure) Rules 2008 r 4.

4 The Armed Forces Tribunal Act 2007 s 14 (3).

5 The Armed Forces Tribunal Act 2007 s 14 (4) (a).

6 The Armed Forces Tribunal Act 2007 s 14 (4) (b).

7 The Armed Forces Tribunal Act 2007 s 14 (4) (c).

8 Ie the Indian Evidence Act 18725 s 123 and 124.

9 The Armed Forces Tribunal Act 2007 s 14 (4) (d).

10 The Armed Forces Tribunal Act 2007 s 14 (4) (e).

11 The Armed Forces Tribunal Act 2007 s 14 (4) (f).

12 The Armed Forces Tribunal Act 2007 s 14 (4) (g).

13 The Armed Forces Tribunal Act 2007 s 14 (4) (h).

14 The Armed Forces Tribunal Act 2007 s 14 (4) (1).

15 The Armed Forces Tribunal Act 2007 s 14 (5).

[1727] Commission for local inquiry and accounts Whenever it becomes necessary in the course of proceedings before the tribunal to appoint a commission to make a local inquiry or to examine documents or accounts, the chairperson or the vice-chairperson may issue orders for such appointments, specifying therein: (i) the precise matter of the inquiry[1]; and (ii) the reason asking why the evidence bearing on that matter could not reasonably have been taken in the usual way in the proceedings in the tribunal[2]. Commissioners to examine accounts may be selected from persons competent in the particular form of accounts[3]. The tribunal shall exercise great care in selecting persons for appointment as commissioners for the purpose of making inquiries. The habitual employment of the same person should be avoided[4]. The tribunal shall for the said purpose, maintain a list of legal practitioner's whom the chairperson or vice-chairperson may select, from time to time, as fit to be employed in such cases[5]. The legal practitioner so appointed shall receive prescribed fee[6]. The certificate for the hearing shall be signed by the registrar and the payment shall be made by the government on production of the said certificate[7].

1 The Armed Forces Tribunal (Procedure) Rules 2008 r 26 (1) (i).

2 The Armed Forces Tribunal (Procedure) Rules 2008 r 26 (1) (ii).

3 The Armed Forces Tribunal (Procedure) Rules 2008 r 26 (2).

4 The Armed Forces Tribunal (Procedure) Rules 2008 r 26 (3).

5 The Armed Forces Tribunal (Procedure) Rules 2008 r 26 (4).

6 The legal practitioner so appointed shall receive a fee of Rs. 800/- for the first effective hearing and Rs. 500/- for every subsequent effective hearing in the same or similar matters or for non-effective hearing. In criminal cases including murder appeals, the fee shall be Rs. 2000/- for preparation of the case, Rs. 12000/- per effective hearing and Rs. 500/- per non-effective hearing. The Armed Forces Tribunal (Procedure) Rules 2008 r 26 (5).

7 The Armed Forces Tribunal (Procedure) Rules 2008 r 26 (6).

[1728] Jurisdiction powers and authority in matters of appeal against court martial:

1 Except as otherwise expressly provided in the Armed Forces Tribunal Act 2007, the tribunal shall exercise, on and from the appointed day, all the jurisdiction, powers and authority exercisable under the aforesaid Act in relation to appeal against any order, decision, finding or sentence passed by a court martial or any matter connected therewith or incidental thereto[1].

2 Any person aggrieved by an order, decision, finding or sentence passed by a court martial may prefer an appeal in such form, manner and within such time as may be prescribed[2].

3 The tribunal shall have power to grant bail to any person accused of an offence and in military custody, with or without any conditions which it considers necessary[3]. However, no accused person shall be so released if there appears reasonable ground for believing that he has been guilty of an offence

punishable with death or imprisonment for life[4].

4 The Tribunal shall allow an appeal against conviction by a court martial where: (i) the finding of the court martial is legally not sustainable due to any reason whatsoever[5]; (ii) the finding involves wrong decision on a question of law[6]; or (iii) there was a material irregularity in the course of the trial resulting in miscarriage of justice[7]. But, in any other case, may dismiss the appeal where the tribunal considers that no miscarriage of justice is likely to be caused or has actually resulted to the appellant[8]. However, no order dismissing the appeal by the tribunal shall be passed unless such order is made after recording reasons in writing[9].

5 The Tribunal may allow an appeal against conviction, and pass appropriate order thereon[10].

6 Notwithstanding anything contained in the aforesaid provisions the tribunal shall have the power to: (a) substitute for the findings of the court martial, a finding of guilty for any other offence for which the offender could have been lawfully found guilty by the court martial and pass a sentence afresh for the offence specified or involved in such findings under the provisions of the Army Act 1950, the Navy Act 1957 or the Air Force Act 1950, as the case may be[11]; or (b) if sentence is found to be excessive, illegal or unjust, the tribunal may: (i) remit the whole or any part of the sentence, with or without conditions[12]; (ii) mitigate the punishment awarded[13]; (iii) commute such punishment to any lesser punishment or punishments mentioned in the Army Act 1950, the Navy Act 1957 and the Air Force Act 1950, as the case may be[14]; (c) enhance the sentence awarded by a court martial[15]. However, no such sentence shall be enhanced unless the appellant has been given an opportunity of being heard[16]; (d) release the appellant, if sentenced to imprisonment, on parole with or without conditions[17]; (e) suspend a sentence of imprisonment[18]; (f) pass any other order as it may think appropriate[19].

7 Notwithstanding any other provisions in the Armed Forces Tribunal Act 2007, for the purposes of this provision, the tribunal shall be deemed to be a criminal court for the purposes of the Indian Penal Code 1860[20] and the Code of Criminal Procedure 1973[21].

1 The Armed Forces Tribunal Act 2007 s 15 (1). The terminology used in this provision makes it clear that the Armed Forces Tribunal shall exercise all jurisdiction, powers and authorities in relation to appeal against any order, decision, finding or sentence passed by a court martial or any matter connected therewith or incidental thereto. *Major Saurabh Saharan v Union of India*, WP(C) No1755 of 2013 and CM No 3355 of 2013, decided by the Delhi High Court on 19 March 2013.

2 The Armed Forces Tribunal Act 2007 s 15 (2).

3 The Armed Forces Tribunal Act 2007 s 15 (3). The power conferred under this provision is not constrained by any consideration of pendency of statutory remedies or procedures contained in the Army Act 1950 s 153 and 164. The Tribunal possesses the jurisdiction to decide upon the legality of the proceedings and procedure adopted by the court martial, irrespective of whether or not confirmation had taken place. *Major Saurabh Saharan v Union of India*, WP(C) No1755 of 2013 and CM No 3355 of 2013, decided by the Delhi High Court on 19 March 2013.

4 The Armed Forces Tribunal Act 2007 s 15 (3) proviso.

5 The Armed Forces Tribunal Act 2007 s 15 (4) (a).

6 The Armed Forces Tribunal Act 2007 s 15 (4) (b).

7 The Armed Forces Tribunal Act 2007 s 15 (4) (c).

8 The Armed Forces Tribunal Act 2007 s 15 (4) proviso.

9 The Armed Forces Tribunal Act 2007 s 15 (4) additional proviso.

10 The Armed Forces Tribunal Act 2007 s 15 (5).

11 The Armed Forces Tribunal Act 2007 s 15 (6) (a).

12 The Armed Forces Tribunal Act 2007 s 15 (6) (b) (i)

13 he Armed Forces Tribunal Act 2007 s 15 (6) (b) (ii)

14 The Armed Forces Tribunal Act 2007 s 15 (6) (b) (iii)

15 The Armed Forces Tribunal Act 2007 s 15 (6) (c).

16 The Armed Forces Tribunal Act 2007 s 15 (6) (c) proviso.

17 The Armed Forces Tribunal Act 2007 s 15 (d).

18 The Armed Forces Tribunal Act 2007 s 15 (e).

19 The Armed Forces Tribunal Act 2007 15 (f)

20 Ie the Indian Penal Code 1860 ss 175, 178, 179, 180, 193, 195, 196 or 228.

21 Ie the Code of Criminal Procedure 1973 chapter XXVI; the Armed Forces Tribunal Act 2007 s 15 (7).

[1729] Re-trial

1 Except as provided by the Armed Forces Tribunal Act 2007, where the conviction of a person by court martial for an offence has been quashed, he shall not be liable to be tried again for that offence by a court martial or by any other court[1].

2 The tribunal shall have the power on quashing a conviction, to make an order authorising the appellant to be retried by court martial, but shall only exercise this power when the appeal against conviction is allowed by reasons only of evidence received or available to be received by the tribunal under the Armed Forces Tribunal Act 2007 and it appears to the tribunal that the interests of justice require that an order under this section should be made[2]. However, an appellant shall not be retried under this section for an offence other than: (i) the offence for which he was convicted by the original court martial and in respect of which his appeal is allowed[3]; (ii) any offence for which he could have been convicted at the original court martial on a charge of the first-mentioned offence[4]; (iii) any offence charged in the alternative in respect of which the court martial recorded no finding in consequence of convicting him of the first-mentioned offence[5].

3 A person who is to be retried under this section for an offence shall, if the tribunal or the Supreme Court so directs, whether or not such person is being tried or retried on one or more of the original charges, no fresh investigation or other action shall be taken under the relevant provision of the Army Act 1950, the Navy Act 1957 or the Air Force Act 1950 as the case may be, or rules and regulations made there under, in relation to the said charge or charges on which he is to be retried[6].

1 The Armed Forces Tribunal Act 2007 s 16 (1).

2 The Armed Forces Tribunal Act 2007 s 16 (2). *Ex Lt Col Ranjodg Singh v. Union of India*, TA No. 68 of 2010, decided on 5 October 2010.

3 The Armed Forces Tribunal Act 2007 s 16 (2) proviso (a).

4 The Armed Forces Tribunal Act 2007 s 16 (2) proviso (b).

5 The Armed Forces Tribunal Act 2007 s 16 (2) proviso (c).

6 The Armed Forces Tribunal Act 2007 s 16 (3).

[1730] Powers of the Tribunal on appeal under the Armed Forces Tribunal Act 2007 s 15 The tribunal, while hearing and deciding an appeal under the Armed Forces Tribunal Act 2007[1], shall have the power: (i) to order production of documents or exhibits connected with the proceedings before the court martial[2]; (ii) to order the attendance of the witnesses[3]; (iii) to receive evidence[4]; (iv) to obtain reports from court martial[5]; (v) order reference of any question for enquiry[6]; (vi) appoint an expert[7] to act as an assessor[8]; and (vii) to determine any question which is necessary to do justice in the case[9].

1 Ie under the Armed Forces Tribunal Act 2007 s 15; see **[1728]**.

2 The Armed Forces Tribunal Act 2007 s 17 (a).

3 The Armed Forces Tribunal Act 2007 s 17 (b).

4 The Armed Forces Tribunal Act 2007 s 17 (c).

5 The Armed Forces Tribunal Act 2007 s 17 (d).

6 The Armed Forces Tribunal Act 2007 s 17 (e).

7 An expert is one who has devoted his time and study to a special branch of learning, and thus is especially skilled on those points on which he is asked to state his opinion. The Indian Evidence Act 1872 s 45 deals with opinions of expert.

8 The Armed Forces Tribunal Act 2007 s 17 (f).

9 The Armed Forces Tribunal Act 2007 s 17 (g).

[1731] Cost While disposing of the application under the provisions of the Armed Forces Tribunal Act 2007[1], the Tribunal shall have power to make such order as to costs as it may deem just[2].

1 Ie under The Armed Forces Tribunal Act 2007 s 14 or an appeal under s 15.

2 The Armed Forces Tribunal Act 2007 s 18.

[1732] Power to punish for contempt Any person who is guilty of contempt of the tribunal by using any insulting or threatening language, or by causing any interruption or disturbance in the proceedings of such tribunal shall, on conviction, be liable to suffer imprisonment for a term which may extend to three years[1]. For the purposes of trying an offence under this provision, certain provisions of the Contempt of Courts Act 1971[2] shall mutatis mutandis apply, as if a reference therein to: (i) Supreme Court or High Court were a reference to the tribunal[3]; (ii) Chief Justice were a reference to the chairperson[4]; (iii) Judge were a reference to the judicial or administrative member of the tribunal[5]; (iv) Advocate-General were a reference to the prosecutor[6]; and (v) Court were a reference to the Tribunal[7].

1 The Armed Forces Tribunal Act 2007 19 (i).

2 Ie the Contempt of Courts Act 1971 ss 14, 15, 17, 18 and 20.

3 The Armed Forces Tribunal Act 2007 s 19 (2) (a).

4 The Armed Forces Tribunal Act 2007 s 19 (2) (b).

5 The Armed Forces Tribunal Act 2007 s 19 (2) (c).

6 The Armed Forces Tribunal Act 2007 s 19 (2) (d).

7 The Armed Forces Tribunal Act 2007 s 19 (2) (e). The Armed Forces Tribunal, however, does not have any power of 'civil contempt'.

[1733] Distribution of business among the benches The chairperson may make provisions as to the distribution of the business of the tribunal among its benches[1].

1 The Armed Forces Tribunal Act 2007 s 20.

5. PROCEDURE

CONTENTS

PARA

[1734] Application not to be admitted unless other remedies exhausted The Tribunal shall not ordinarily admit an application unless it is satisfied that the applicant had availed of the remedies available to him under the Army Act 1950, the Navy Act 1957 or the Air Force Act 1950, and respective rules and regulations made thereunder[1]. For the purposes of the aforesaid provision, a person shall be deemed to have availed of all the remedies available to him under the Army Act 1950, the Navy Act 1957 or the Air Force Act 1950 and respective rules and regulations: (i) if a final order has been made by the Central Government or other authority or officer competent to pass such order under the said provisions, rejecting any petition preferred or representation made by such person[2]; (ii) where no final order has been made by the Central Government, other authority or officer competent to pass such order with regard to the petition preferred or representation made by such person, if a period of six months from the date on which such petition was preferred or representation was made has expired[3].

1 The Armed Forces Tribunal Act 2007 s 21 (1).

2 The Armed Forces Tribunal Act 2007 s 21 (2) (a).

3 The Armed Forces Tribunal Act 2007 s 21 (2) (b).

[1735] Place of filing application An application shall ordinarily be filed by the applicant with the registrar of the bench within whose jurisdiction: (i) the applicant is posted for the time being, or was last posted or attached[1]; or (ii) where the cause of action, wholly or in part, has arisen[2]. However, with the leave of the chairperson the application may be filed with the registrar of the principal bench and subject to the orders under certain provisions of the Armed Forces Tribunal Act 2007[3], such application shall be heard and disposed of by the bench which has jurisdiction over the matter[4]. A person who has ceased to be in service by reason of his retirement, dismissal, discharge, cashiering, release, removal, resignation or termination of service may, at his option, file an application with the registrar of the bench within whose jurisdiction such person is ordinarily residing at the time of filling of the application[5].

1 The Armed Forces Tribunal (Procedure) Rules 2008 r 6 (1) (i).

2 The Armed Forces Tribunal (Procedure) Rules 2008 r 6 (1) (ii). The cause of action to the petitioner has arisen at Mumbai as he was posted at Mumbai, therefore, Mumbai Regional Bench of Armed Forces Tribunal will have territorial jurisdiction to entertain the petition, or if the petitioner joins at Vishakhapatnam and challenges his non promotion then Chennai Bench will have jurisdiction. The petition was dismissed for want of territorial jurisdiction. *Lt Cdr Srimali Venkiteela v Union of India*, OA No. 165 of 2012, the Armed Forces Tribunal, Principal Bench, New Delhi, decided on 7 August 2012.

3 Ie the Armed Forces Tribunal Act 2007 s14 or 15.

4 The Armed Forces Tribunal (Procedure) Rules 2008 r 6 (1) (ii) proviso.

5 The Armed Forces Tribunal (Procedure) Rules 2008 r 6 (2).

[1736] Limitation The tribunal shall not admit an application: (i) in a case where a final order such as is mentioned in the aforesaid provision[1] has been made unless the application is made within six months from the date on which such final order has been made[2]; (ii) in a case where a petition or a representation such as mentioned in certain provisions[3] has been made and the period of six months has expired thereafter without such final order having been made[4]; (iii) in a case where the grievance in respect of which an application is made had arisen by reason of any order made at any time during the period of three years immediately preceding the date on which jurisdiction, powers and authority of the Tribunal became exercisable under the Armed Forces Tribunal Act 2007, in respect of the matter to which such order relates and no proceedings for the redressal of such grievance had been commenced before the said date before the High Court[5]. Notwithstanding anything contained in the aforesaid provision, the tribunal may admit an application after the period of six months referred in certain provisions[6] or prior to the period of three years specified in certain other the provision[7], if the tribunal is satisfied that the applicant had sufficient cause for not making the application within such period[8].

1 Ie the Armed Forces Tribunal Act 2007 s 21 (2) (a); see **[1734]**.

2 The Armed Forces Tribunal Act 2007 s 22 (1) (a).

3 Ie the Armed Forces Tribunal Act 2007 s 21 (2) (b).

4 The Armed Forces Tribunal Act 2007 s 22 (1) (b).

5 The Armed Forces Tribunal Act 2007 s 22 (1)(c).

6 Ie the Armed Forces Tribunal Act 2007 s 22 (1) (a) and (b).

7 Ie the Armed Forces Tribunal Act 2007 s 22 (1) (c).

8 The Armed Forces Tribunal Act 2007 s 22 (2).

[1737] Procedure and powers of the tribunal The tribunal shall not be bound by the procedure laid down in the Code of Civil Procedure 1908 but shall be guided by the principles of natural justice. The tribunal shall have the power to lay down and regulate its own procedure including the fixing of place and time of its inquiry and deciding whether to sit in public or in camera[1]. The Tribunal shall decide every application made to it as expeditiously as possible after a perusal of documents, affidavits and written representations and after hearing such oral arguments as may be advanced[2]. However, where the tribunal deems it necessary, for reasons to be recorded in writing, it may allow oral evidence to be adduced[3]. No adjournment shall be granted by the tribunal without recording the reasons justifying the grant of such adjournment and cost shall be awarded, if a party requests for adjournment more than twice[4].

1 The Armed Forces Tribunal Act 2007 s 23 (1).

2 The Armed Forces Tribunal Act 2007 s 23 (2).

3 The Armed Forces Tribunal Act 2007 s 23 (2) proviso.

4 The Armed Forces Tribunal Act 2007 s 23 (3).

[1738] Term of sentence and its effect on appeal The term of any sentence passed by the tribunal under certain provision[1] of the Armed Forces Tribunal Act 2007 shall, unless the tribunal otherwise directs, be reckoned to commence on the day on which it would have commenced under the Army Act 1950, the Navy Act 1957 or the Air Force Act 1950, under which the court martial against which the appeal was filed, had been held[2]. Subject to the following provision[3], any sentence passed on an appeal from the tribunal to the Supreme Court in substitution for another sentence shall, unless the Supreme Court otherwise directs, be reckoned to commence on the day on which the original sentence would have commenced[4]. Where a person who is undergoing sentence is granted stay of the operation of the said sentence, either by suspension or otherwise, pending an appeal, the period during which he is so released due to the sentence having been so stayed, shall be excluded in computing the term for which he is so sentenced by the Tribunal or the Supreme Court[5].

1 Ie under the Armed Forces Tribunal Act 2007 s 15 (6) (a); see **[1728]**.

2 The Armed Forces Tribunal Act 2007 s 24 (1).

3 Ie the Armed Forces Tribunal Act 2007 s 24 (3).

4 The Armed Forces Tribunal Act 2007 s 24 (2).

5 The Armed Forces Tribunal Act 2007 s 24 (3).

[1739] Right of applicant or of appellant to take assistance of a legal practitioner and of Government, etc., to appoint counsel A person making an application or preferring an appeal to the Tribunal may either appear in person or take the assistance of a legal practitioner[1] of his choice to present his case before the tribunal[2]. The Central Government or the competent authority may authorise one or more legal practitioners or its law officers to act as counsel. Every person so authorized, may present its case with respect to any application or appeal before the tribunal[3].

1 The term 'legal practitioner' shall have the same meaning as assigned to it in the Advocates Act 1961 and includes a standing counsel authorized or appointed by the Central Government to accept the service for any department or organisation of Union of India. The Armed Forces Tribunal (Procedure) Rules 2008 r 2 (ix).

2 The Armed Forces Tribunal Act 2007 s 25 (1).

3 The Armed Forces Tribunal Act 2007 s 25 (2).

[1740] Condition as to making of interim order

1 Notwithstanding anything contained in any other provisions of the Armed Forces Tribunal Act 2007 or in any other law for the time being in force, no interim order (whether by way of injunction or stay or in any other manner) shall be made on an application or appeal, or in any proceeding relating thereto, unless: (i) copies of such application or appeal, as the case may be, and all documents in support of the plea for such interim order are furnished to the party against whom such application or appeal, as the

case may be, is made or proposed to be made[1]; and (ii) opportunity of being heard is given to the other party in the matter[2]. However, the Tribunal may dispense with the requirements under the aforesaid provisions and make an interim order as an exceptional measure if it is satisfied, for reasons to be recorded in writing, that it is necessary so to do for preventing any loss being caused to the applicant or to the appellant, as the case may be[3].

2 Where any party against whom an interim order (injunction or stay), is made on an application or appeal or in any proceeding under the aforesaid provision[4], without: (i) furnishing to such party copies of such application or appeal, and all documents in support of the plea for such interim order[5]; and (ii) giving such party an opportunity of being heard, and making an application to the tribunal for the vacation of such order and furnishing a copy of such application or appeal, to the party in whose favour such order has been made or the counsel of such party[6]; the tribunal shall dispose of the application within a period of 14 days from the date on which it is received or from the date on which the copy of such application is so furnished, whichever is later, or where the tribunal is closed on the last day of that period, before the expiry of the next working day; and if the application is not so disposed of, the interim order shall, on the expiry of that period, or, as the case may be, the expiry of the said next working day, stand vacated[7].

1 The Armed Forces Tribunal Act 2007 s 26 (1) (a).

2 The Armed Forces Tribunal Act 2007 s 26 (1) (b).

3 The Armed Forces Tribunal Act 2007 s 26 (1) (b) proviso.

4 Ie under the Armed Forces Tribunal Act 2007 s 26 (1).

5 The Armed Forces Tribunal Act 2007 s 26 (2) (a).

6 The Armed Forces Tribunal Act 2007 s 26 (2) (b).

7 The Armed Forces Tribunal Act 2007 s 26 (2).

[1741] Power of Chairperson to transfer cases from one bench to another On the application of any of the parties and after notice to the parties concerned, and after hearing such of them as he may desire to be heard, or on his own motion without such notice, the chairperson may transfer any case pending before one bench for disposal, to, any other bench[1].

1 The Armed Forces Tribunal Act 2007 s 27.

[1742] Decision to be by majority If the members of a bench differ in opinion on any point, the point shall be decided according to the opinion of the majority, if there is a majority. If the members are equally divided, they shall state the point(s) on which they differ and make a reference to the chairperson who shall either hear the point(s) himself or refer the case for hearing on such point(s) by one or more of the members of the tribunal. Such point(s) shall be decided according to the opinion of the majority of the members of the tribunal who have heard the case, including those who first heard it[1].

1 The Armed Forces Tribunal Act 2007 s 28.

[1743] Execution of order of Tribunal Subject to the other provisions of the Armed Forces Tribunal Act 2007, the order of the tribunal disposing of an application shall be final and shall not be called in question in any court and such order shall be executed accordingly[1].

1 The Armed Forces Tribunal Act 2007 s 29.

6. APPEAL

CONTENT

[1744] Appeal to Supreme Court Subject to certain provisions of the Armed Forces Tribunal Act 2007[1], an appeal shall lie to the Supreme Court against the final decision or order of the tribunal (other than an order passed under certain provisions[2] of the aforesaid Act)[3]. However, such appeal is to be preferred within a period of 90 days of the said decision or order[4]. Further, there shall be no appeal against an interlocutory order of the tribunal[5]. An appeal shall lie to the Supreme Court as of right from any order or decision of the tribunal in the exercise of its jurisdiction to punish for contempt[6]. However, an appeal under the aforesaid provision shall be filed in the Supreme Court within 60 days from the date of the order appealed against[7]. Pending any appeal under the aforesaid provision[8], the Supreme Court may order that (i) the execution of the punishment or the order appealed against be suspended[9]; or (ii) if the appellant is in confinement, he be released on bail[10].

However, where an appellant satisfies the tribunal that he intends to prefer an appeal, the tribunal may also exercise any of the powers conferred under the aforesaid provisions[11], as the case may be[12]. There is a clear distinction between cases where an appeal lies as a matter of right and others where it lies subject to the provisions of the Armed Forces Tribunal Act 2007[13].

1 Ie the Armed Forces Tribunal Act 2007 s 31; see **[1745]**.

2 Ie the Armed Forces Tribunal Act 2007 s 19; see **[1732]**.

3 The Armed Forces Tribunal Act 2007 s 30 (1).

4 The Armed Forces Tribunal Act 2007 s 30 (1) proviso.

5 The Armed Forces Tribunal Act 2007 s 30 (1) additional proviso.

6 The Armed Forces Tribunal Act 2007 s 30 (2). There is no vested right of appeal against a final order or decision of the tribunal to the Supreme Court other than those falling under the Armed Forces Tribunal Act 2007 s 30(2) (i.e., against an order or decisions of the Tribunal to punish for contempt). *Union of India v Brigadier P S Gill*, AIR 2012 SC 1280.

7 The Armed Forces Tribunal Act 2007 s 30 (2) proviso.

8 Ie the Armed Forces Tribunal Act 2007 s 30 (2).

9 The Armed Forces Tribunal Act 2007 s 30 (3) (a).

10 The Armed Forces Tribunal Act 2007 s 30 (3) (b).

11 Ie the Armed Forces Tribunal Act 2007 s 30 (3) (a) or (b).

12 The Armed Forces Tribunal Act 2007 s 30 (3) proviso.

13 Ie the Armed Forces Tribunal Act 2007 s 31. *Union of India v Brigadier P S Gill*, AIR 2012 SC 1280.

[1745] Leave to appeal An appeal to the Supreme Court shall lie with the leave of the tribunal; and such leave shall not be granted unless it is certified by the tribunal that a point of law of general public importance is involved in the decision, or it appears to the Supreme Court that the point is one which ought to be considered by that Court[1]. An application to the tribunal for leave to appeal to the Supreme Court shall be made within a period of 30 days beginning with the date of the decision of the tribunal and an application to the Supreme Court for leave shall be made within a period of 30 days beginning with the date on which the application for leave is refused by the tribunal[2]. An appeal shall be treated as pending until any application for leave to appeal is disposed of and if leave to appeal is granted, until the appeal is disposed of; and an application for leave to appeal shall be treated as disposed of at the expiration of the time within which it might have been made, but it is not made within that time[3].

This provision does not create a vested, indefeasible or absolute right of filing an appeal to the Supreme Court against a final order or decision of the tribunal to the Court. Such an appeal must be preceded by the leave of the tribunal and such leave must in turn be preceded by a certificate by the tribunal that a point of law of general public importance is involved in the appeal. A conjoint reading of the Armed Forces Tribunal Act s 30 and 31 leads to conclusion that only mode to appeal against an order of the tribunal is: (i) by way of certificate obtained from the tribunal that decided the matter that 'a point of law of general public importance is involved in the decision', or (ii) by obtaining leave of the Supreme Court under the Armed Forces Tribunal Act 2007 s 31 for filing an appeal that 'the point is one which ought to be considered by the Supreme Court'[4].

1 The Armed Forces Tribunal Act 2007 s 31 (1). Where there was no serious legal issue of public importance involved in the matter, the prayer for leave to appeal was rejected. *Lt Cdr Srimali Venkiteela v Union of India*, OA No. 165 of 2012, the Armed Forces Tribunal, Principal Bench, New Delhi, decided on 7 August 2012. The Armed Forces Tribunal Act 2007 s 31(1) in no uncertain terms forbids grant of leave to appeal to the Supreme Court unless the Tribunal certifies that a point of law of general public importance is involved in the decision. This implies that s 31 does not create a vested, indefeasible or absolute right of filing an appeal to this Court against a final order or decision of the Tribunal to the Supreme Court. Such an appeal must be preceded by the leave of the Tribunal and such leave must in turn be preceded by a certificate by the Tribunal that a point of law of general public importance is involved in the appeal. *Union of India v Brigadier PS Gill* AIR 2012 SC 1280, (2012) 4 SCC 463, 2012 STPL(Web) 190 SC.

2 The Armed Forces Tribunal Act 2007 s 31 (2); see [1746].

3 The Armed Forces Tribunal Act 2007 s 31 (3). An appeal is presumed to be pending under this provision until an application for leave to appeal is disposed of and if the leave is granted until the appeal is disposed of. *Union of India v Brigadier PS Gill* AIR 2012 SC 1280, (2012) 4 SCC 463, 2012 STPL(Web) 190 SC.

4 *Union of India v Brigadier PS Gill* AIR 2012 SC 1280, (2012) 4 SCC 463, 2012 STPL (Web) 190 SC.

[1746] Condonation The Supreme Court may, upon an application made at any time by the appellant, extend the time within which an appeal may be preferred by him to that Court under certain provisions of the Armed Forces Tribunal Act 2007[1]. The provisions of the Armed Forces Tribunal Act 2007 ss 30 to 32 could not be considered as violative of the basic structure of the Constitution[2].

1 Ie under the Armed Forces Tribunal Act 2007 s 30 or 31 (2); the Armed Forces Tribunal Act 2007 s 32.

2 *Suresh Kumar K v Union of India*, WP(C) No 21772 of 2009(N), decided by Kerala High Court on 15 October 2009.

7. MISCELLANEOUS PROVISIONS

CONTENTS

PARA

[1747] Exclusion of jurisdiction of civil courts The date from which the jurisdiction, powers and authority becomes exercisable by the tribunal in relation to service matters under the Armed Forces Tribunal Act 2007, no civil court shall be entitled to exercise, such jurisdiction, power or authority in relation to those service matters[1].

1 The Armed Forces Tribunal Act 2007 s 33.

[1748] Transfer of pending cases

1 Every suit, or other proceeding pending before any court including a high court or other authority immediately before the date of establishment of the tribunal under the Armed Forces Tribunal Act 2007, being a suit or proceeding the cause of action whereon it is based, is such that it would have been within the jurisdiction of the tribunal, if it had arisen after such establishment within the jurisdiction of such tribunal, stand transferred on that date to such tribunal[1].

2 Where any suit, or other proceeding stands transferred from any court including a high court or other authority to the tribunal under the aforesaid provision: (i) the court or other authority shall, as soon as may be, after such transfer, forward the records of such suit, or other proceeding to the tribunal[2]; (ii) the tribunal may, on receipt of such records, proceed to deal with such suit or proceeding, in the same manner as in the case of an application made under the Armed Forces Tribunal Act 2007[3], from the stage which was reached before such transfer or from any earlier stage or de novo as the tribunal may deem fit[4].

1 The Armed Forces Tribunal Act 2007 s 34 (1).

2 The Armed Forces Tribunal Act 2007 s 34 (2) (a).

3 Ie the Armed Forces Tribunal Act 2007 s 14 (2); see **[1726]**.

4 The Armed Forces Tribunal Act 2007 s 34 (2) (b).

[1749] Provision for filing of certain appeals Where any decree or order has been made or passed by any court (other than a high court) or any other authority in any suit or proceeding before the establishment of the tribunal, being a suit or proceeding the cause of action whereon it is based, is such that it would have been, if it had arisen after such establishment, within the jurisdiction of the tribunal, and no appeal has been preferred against such decree or order before such establishment or if preferred, the same is pending for disposal before any court including high court and the time for preferring such appeal under any law for the time being in force had not expired before such establishment, such appeal shall lie to the tribunal, within 90 days from the date on which the tribunal is established, or within 90 days from the date of receipt of the copy of such decree or order, whichever is later[1].

1 The Armed Forces Tribunal Act 2007 s 35.

[1750] Proceedings before tribunal to be judicial proceedings All proceedings before the Tribunal shall be deemed to be judicial proceedings within the meaning of certain provisions of the Indian Penal Code 1860[1].

1 Ie the Indian Penal Code 1860 ss 193, 219 and 228; the Armed Forces Tribunal Act 2007 s 36.

[1751] Members and staff of tribunal to be public servants The chairperson, members, the officers and other employees[1] of the Tribunal shall be deemed to be public servants within the meaning of the Indian Penal Code 1860[2].

1 Ie provided under the Armed Forces Tribunal Act 2007 s 13; see **[1725]**.

2 Ie the Indian Penal Code 1860 s 21; the Armed Forces Tribunal Act 2007 s 37.

[1752] Protection of action taken in good faith No suit, prosecution or other legal proceeding shall lie against the Central Government or against the chairperson or other member for anything which is done in good faith or intended to be done in pursuance of the Armed Forces Tribunal Act 2007 or any rule or order made in the discharge of official duties[1].

1 The Armed Forces Tribunal Act 2007 s 38.

[1753] Act to have overriding effect The provisions of the Armed Forces Tribunal Act 2007 shall have effect notwithstanding anything inconsistent therewith contained, in any other law for the time being in force or in any instrument having effect by virtue of any law other than the aforesaid Act[1].

1 The Armed Forces Tribunal Act 2007 s 39.

[1754] Power to remove difficulties If any difficulty arises in giving effect to the provisions of the Armed Forces Tribunal Act 2007, the Central Government may, by order published in the Official Gazette, make such provisions, not inconsistent with the provisions of the aforesaid Act as appear to it to be necessary or expedient for removing the difficulty[1]. However, no order shall be made under this provision after the expiry of two years from the date of commencement of the Armed Forces Tribunal Act 2007[2]. Every order made under this provision shall, as soon as may be after it is made, be laid before each House of Parliament[3].

1 The Armed Forces Tribunal Act 2007 s 40 (1).

2 The Armed Forces Tribunal Act 2007 s 40 (1) proviso.

3 The Armed Forces Tribunal Act 2007 s 40 (2).

[1755] Power of Central Government to make rules The Central Government may, by notification, make rules for the purposes of carrying out the provisions of the Armed Forces Tribunal Act 2007[1]. Such rules may provide for all or any of the following matters:

1 The case or cases which shall be decided by a bench composed of more than two members under the Armed Forces Tribunal Act 2007 s 5 (3) (c)[2].

2 The procedure under the Armed Forces Tribunal Act 2007 s 9 (3) for the investigation of misbehaviour or incapacity of chairperson or other member[3].

3 The salaries and allowances payable to, and the other terms and conditions of service of the chairperson and other members under the Armed Forces Tribunal Act 2007 s 10[4].

4 The financial and administrative powers which the Chairperson may exercise over the benches of the tribunal under the Armed Forces Tribunal Act 2007 s 12[5].

5 The salaries and allowances payable to, and other terms and conditions of service of the officers and other employees of the Armed Forces Tribunal under the Armed Forces Tribunal Act 2007 s 13 (2)[6].

6 The form in which an application may be made under the Armed Forces Tribunal Act 2007 s 14 (2), the documents and other evidence by which such application shall be accompanied and the fee payable in respect of the filing of such application or for the service of execution of processes[7].

7 The other matter which may be prescribed under Armed Forces Tribunal Act 2007 s 14 (4) (i)[8].

8 The form and manner in which an appeal may be filed, the fee payable thereon and the time within which such appeal may be filed under the Armed Forces Tribunal Act 2007 s 15 (2)[9].

9 The rules subject to which the Tribunal shall have power to regulate its own procedure under the Armed Forces Tribunal Act 2007 s 23 (1)[10].

10 Competent authority who may authorise legal practitioners or law officers to act as counsel under the Armed Forces Tribunal Act 2007 s 25 (2)[11].

11 Any other matter which may be prescribed or in respect of which rules are required to be made by the Central Government[12].

1 The Armed Forces Tribunal Act 2007 s 41 (1). In exercise of the powers conferred by this provision the following rules have been made so far: (i) The Armed Forces Tribunal (Procedure) Rules 2008; (ii) The Armed Forces Tribunal (Procedure for appointment of Vice-Chairperson and other Members) Rules 2008; (iii) the Armed Force Tribunal (Procedure for investigation of misbehaviour or incapacity of Chairperson and other Members) Rules 2008; (iv) The Armed Forces Tribunal (Financial and Administrative Powers) Rules 2008; (v) The Armed Forces Tribunal (Procedure) Rules 2008; (vi) The Armed Forces Tribunal (Practice) Rules 2009; and (vii) The Armed Forces Tribunal (Salaries, Allowances and Conditions of Service of Chairperson and Members) Rules 2009.

2 The Armed Forces Tribunal Act 2007 s 41 (2) (a).

3 The Armed Forces Tribunal Act 2007 s 41 (2) (b). In exercise of the powers conferred by this provision of the Armed Forces Tribunal Act 20007 the Central Government has made the Armed Force Tribunal (Procedure for investigation of misbehaviour or incapacity of Chairperson and other Members) Rules 2008.

4 The Armed Forces Tribunal Act 2007 s 41 (2) (c). In the exercise of powers conferred by this provision, the Central Government has made the Armed Forces Tribunal (Salaries, Allowances and Conditions of Service of Chairperson and Members) Rules 2009.

5 The Armed Forces Tribunal Act 2007 s 41(2) (d).

6 The Armed Forces Tribunal Act 2007 s 41 (2) (e).

7 The Armed Forces Tribunal Act 2007 s 41 (2) (f). In exercise of the powers conferred by this provision the Central Government has made the Armed Forces Tribunal (Procedure) Rules 2008, the Armed Forces Tribunal (Practice) Rules 2009.

8 The Armed Forces Tribunal Act 2007 s 41 (2) (g). In exercise of the powers conferred by this provision the Central Government has made the Armed Forces Tribunal (Procedure) Rules 2008, the Armed Forces Tribunal (Practice) Rules 2009.

9 The Armed Forces Tribunal Act 2007 s 41 (2) (h).

10 The Armed Forces Tribunal Act 2007 s 41 (2) (i).

11 The Armed Forces Tribunal Act 2007 s 41 (2) (j).

12 The Armed Forces Tribunal Act 2007 s 41 (2) (k). In exercise of the powers conferred by this provision the Central Government has made the Armed Forces Tribunal (Procedure) Rules 2008, the Armed Forces Tribunal (Procedure for appointment of Vice-Chairperson and other Members) Rules 2008 to regulate the procedure of appointment of vice-chairperson or other members of the Armed Forces Tribunal, and the Armed Forces Tribunal (Practice) Rules, 2009.

[1756] Power to make rules retrospectively The powers to make rules under certain provision of the Armed Forces Tribunal Act 2007[1] shall include the power to make such rule(s) retrospectively from a date not earlier than the date on which the aforesaid Act shall come into operation. However, no such retrospective effect shall be given to any such rule so as to prejudicially affect the interests of any person to whom such rule may be applicable[2].

1 Ie the Armed Forces Tribunal Act 2007 s 41.

2 The Armed Forces Tribunal Act 2007 s 42.

[1757] Laying of rules Every rule made under the Armed Forces Tribunal Act 2007 shall be laid, as soon as may be after it is made, before each House of Parliament while it is in session, for a total period of 30 days which may be comprised in one session or in two or more successive sessions. If, before the expiry of the session immediately following the session or the successive sessions aforesaid, both Houses agree in making any modification in the rule or both Houses agree that the rule should not be made, the rule shall thereafter have effect only in such modified form or be of no effect. However, any such modification or annulment shall be without prejudice to the validity of anything previously done under that rule[1].

1 The Armed Forces Tribunal Act 2007 s 43.

X. THE ARMED FORCES (SPECIAL POWERS) ACT

CONTENTS

PARA

A. The Armed Forces (Special Powers) Act 1958

[1758] Introduction The President of India promulgated the Armed Forces (Assam and Manipur) Special Powers Ordinance on 22 May 1958 to confer 'special powers' on the armed forces and to provide them the legal framework to function in the 'disturbed areas' of Assam and the Union Territory of Manipur. It was based on the Armed Forces Special Powers Ordinance 1942. In 1958, the Parliament adopted the Armed Forces (Special Powers) Act 1958. In the decade that followed, the northeast was divided into separate states to accommodate the ethnic claims of various tribal and other ethnic groups. In 1972, the Armed Forces (Special Powers) Act was amended to extend to cover the states of Assam, Manipur, Meghalaya, Nagaland and Tripura and the Union Territories of Arunachal Pradesh. In 1986, the Act was further amended to cover the states of 'Arunachal Pradesh, Assam, Manipur, Meghalaya, Mizoram, Nagaland and Tripura' for 'Assam, Manipur, Meghalaya, Mizoram, Nagaland and Tripura and the Union Territory of Arunachal Pradesh'. This Act is called the Armed Forces (Special Powers) Act 1958[1] and now extends to the whole of the State of Arunachal Pradesh, Assam, Manipur, Meghalaya, Mizoram, Nagaland and Tripura[2].

1 The Armed Forces (Special Powers) Act 1958 s 1 (1).

2 The Armed Forces (Special Powers) Act 1958 s 1 (2).

[1759] Armed forces Unless the context otherwise requires, 'armed forces' means the military forces and the air forces of the Union so operating[1].

1 The Armed Forces (Special Powers) Act 1958 s 2(a).

[1760] Disturbed area Unless the context otherwise requires, 'disturbed area' means an area which is for the time being declared by notification[1], to be a disturbed area[2]. The lack of precision in the definition of a 'disturbed area' is not an issue since the government and the people of India understand its meaning. The term 'disturbed area' defies any definition—it has to be adjudged according to the location, situation and circumstances of a particular case[3].

1 Ie declared by notification under the Armed Forces (Special Powers) Act 1958 s 3; see **[1762]**.

2 The Armed Forces (Special Powers) Act 1958 s 2(b).

3 *Indrajit Barua v State of Assam* AIR 1983 Del 54.

[1761] Words and expressions not defined Unless the context otherwise requires, all the words and expressions used in the Armed Forces (Special Powers) Act 1958, but not defined and defined in the Air Force Act 1950, or the Army Act 1950 shall have meanings respectively assigned to them in those Acts[1].

1 The Armed Forces (Special Powers) Act 1958 s 2(c).

[1762] Power to declare areas to be disturbed areas If, in relation to any State or Union territory of which the Armed Forces (Special Powers) Act 1958 extends, the Governor of that State or the Administrator of that Union Territory or the Central Government, in either case, if of the opinion that the whole or any part of such State or Union Territory, is in such a disturbed or dangerous condition that the use of armed forces in aid of the civil powers in necessary, the Governor of that State or the Administrator of that Union Territory or the Central Government, may, by notification in the Official Gazette, declare the whole or such part of such State or Union Territory to be a disturbed area[1].

The Governor is empowered to declare any area of the state as 'disturbed area'. It could not be arbitrary on the grounds of absence of legislative guidelines[2]. This provision cannot be construed as conferring a power to issue a declaration without any time-limit. There should be periodic review of the declaration before the expiry of six months. Although a declaration under this provision can be made by the Central Government *suo moto* without consulting the concerned State Government, but it is desirable that the State Government should be consulted by the Central Government while making the declaration. The conferment of the power to make a declaration under this provision on the Central Government is not violative of the federal scheme as envisaged by the Constitution.[3]

1 The Armed Forces (Special Powers) Act 1958 s 3.

2 *Indrajit Barua v State of Assam AIR* 1983 Del 54.

3 *Naga People's Movement of Human Rights v Union of India* (1998) 2 SCC 109, AIR 1998 SC 431.

[1763] Special powers of the armed forces Any commissioned officer[1], warrant officer[2], non-commissioned officer[3] or any other person of equivalent rank in the armed forces may, in a disturbed area[4],

(1) if he is of opinion that it is necessary so to do for the maintenance of public order, after giving such due warning as he may consider necessary, fire upon or otherwise use force[5], even to the causing of death, against any person who is acting in contravention of any law or order for the time being in force in the disturbed area prohibiting the assembly of five or more persons or the carrying of weapons or of things capable of being used as weapons or of fire-arms, ammunition or explosive substances[6];

(2) if he is of opinion that it is necessary so to do, destroy any arms dump, prepared or fortified position or shelter from which armed attacks are made or are likely to be made or are attempted to be made, or any structure used as a training camp for armed volunteers or utilised as a hide-out by armed gangs or absconders wanted for any offence[7];

(3) arrest, without warrant, any person who has committed a cognisable offence or against whom a reasonable suspicion exists that he has committed or is about to commit a cognisable offence and may use such force as may be necessary to effect the arrest[8];

(4) enter and search without warrant any premises to make any such arrest as aforesaid or to recover any person believed to be wrongfully restrained or any arms, ammunition or explosive substances believed to be unlawfully kept in such premises and may for that purpose use such force as may be necessary[9].

The armed forces must act in cooperation with the district administration and not as an Independent body. Armed Forces could work in harmony when they deployed in disturbed area[10]. The powers conferred under the

Armed Forces (Special Powers) Act 1958 s 4 on the officers of the armed forces, including a non-commissioned Officer are not arbitrary and unreasonable and are not violative of the provisions of art 14, 19 or 21 of the Constitution[11].

1 As to the definition of 'officer' under the Army Act 1950; see **[0029]**.

2 As to the definition of 'warrant officer' under the Army Act 1950; see **[0037]**.

3 As to the definition of 'non-commissioned officer' under the Army Act 1950; see **[0026]**. Conferment of power on non-commissioned officer like a havildar cannot be said to be bad and unjustified. *Indrajit Barua v State of Assam* AIR 1983 Del 54.

4 The term 'disturbed area' has not been defined. The lack of precision in the definition of was not an issue since the government and the people of India understand its meaning. *Indrajit Barua v State of Assam* AIR 1983 Del 54.

5 The 'use of force' is governed by Manual of Military Law, Vol. I, Chapter VII, para 8: Principles governing use of force: The use of force in dispersal of unlawful assemblies is governed by the following principles (a) Necessity (i) There must be justification for each separate act; (ii) Action should not be taken in one place with the object of creating effect in another place; (iii) There should be no reprisals; and (iv) Action should be preventive and not punitive. (b) Minimum force: No more force is to be used than is necessary to achieve the immediate object. This refers to the actual amount of force used and not to the number of troops employed. (c) Impartiality: Officers and other persons must be impartial in communal disturbances or labour strikes. They should not accept gifts or show favours. (d) Good faith; Officers and other persons must act in good faith. Nothing is said to be done or believed in good faith which is done or believed without due care and attention (The Indian Penal Code 1860 s 52).

6 The Armed Forces (Special Powers) Act 1958 s 4(a).

7 The Armed Forces (Special Powers) Act 1958 s 4(b).

8 The Armed Forces (Special Powers) Act 1958 s 4(c). The power conferred under this provision read with the Armed Forces (Special Powers) Act s 5 has to be exercised in consonance with the overriding requirements of Article 22 clauses (1) and (2) of the Constitution which means that the person who is arrested by an officer has to be made over to the officer in charge of the nearest police station together with a report of the circumstances occasioning the arrest with the least possible delay so that the person arrested can be produced before the nearest magistrate within a period of 24 hours of such arrest excluding the time necessary for the journey from the place of arrest to the court of the magistrate and no such person can be detained in custody beyond the said period without the authority of a magistrate. *Naga People's Movement of Human Rights v Union of India* (1998) 2 SCC 109.

9 The Armed Forces (Special Powers) Act 1958 s 4(d). The power conferred under this provision should be exercised in accordance with the provisions relating to search and seizure contained in the Cr PC 1973 and the property or the arms ammunitions, etc., that is seized during the course of search under must be handed over to the officer in charge of the nearest police station with the least possible delay together with a report of the circumstances occasioning the search and seizure. *Naga People's Movement of Human Rights v Union of India* (1998) 2 SCC 109.

10 *Luithukia v Rishang Keishing* (1988) 2 Gau LR 159.

11 *Naga People's Movement of Human Rights v Union of India* (1998) 2 SCC 109.

[1764] Arrested persons to be made over to the police Any person arrested and taken into custody under the Armed Forces (Special Powers) Act 1958 shall be made over to the officer-in-charge of the nearest police station with the least possible delay[1], together with a report of the circumstances occasioning the arrest[2]. In case of arrest of any person, army authority is duty bound to handover to the officer-in-charge of the nearest police station with least possible delay[3]. What is the least possible delay in a case depends upon the facts, that is to say, how, where and in what circumstances the arrest was affected. The difficulty of the terrain, the presence of hostile elements in the area must be considered in this connection. The handing over of the delinquent to the civil authorities after two months was considered as not 'too much delay'[4]. The powers conferred under this provision on the officers of the armed forces, including a non-commissioned officer are not arbitrary and unreasonable and are not violative of the provisions of art 14, 19 or 21 of the Constitution[5].

There is no ambiguity in this provision[6], it requires in clear terms that any person arrested under the Act has to be made over to the nearest police station without delay. The provision does not permit the arresting armed force to keep the arrested person in custody for the purpose of interrogation, or to be fully satisfied whether the concerned person was really involved in the matter which had led to his (her) arrest. This satisfaction has to precede the arrest, and not to follow it. Any power given beyond the aforesaid provisions would amount to giving untrammelled power of arrest to the armed forces beyond what is permitted by the Armed Forces (Special Powers) Act 1958[7].

1 The words 'least possible delay' means 'within the shortest possible time' though no arbitrary time limit can be set down as it may not be possible in many cases to precisely quantify the period of time by reference to hours, dates or months. Therefore, whenever the question of 'least possible delay' arises for decision in computing the period of time the Court has to have regard to the particular circumstances of the case, for example, physical impossibility or otherwise to make over the arrested person to the nearest police station, and how, where and in what circumstances the arrest was effected. *Bacha Bora v. State of Assam* (1991) 2 GLR 119.

2 The Armed Forces (Special Powers) Act 1958 s 5.

3 *Horendi Gogoi v. Union of India* (1991) Gau CR 3081.

4 *VL Rohlua v Dy Commr, Aizol, District Mizo* decided on 29 September 1970.

5 *Naga People's Movement of Human Rights v Union of India* (1998) 2 SCC 109.

6 Ie the Armed Forces (Special Powers) Act 1958 s 5.

7 Ie the Armed Forces (Special Powers) Act 1958 s 4(c). *Naosam Ningol Chandam Ongbi Nungshitombi Devi v. Rishang Keishing, Chief Minister of Manipur* 1983 Cri LJ 574; *The Civil Liberties and Human Rights Organisation v P L Kukrery, GOC 'M' Sector, Assam Rifles* (1988) 2 Gau LR 137.

[1765] Protection of persons acting under the Armed Forces (Special Powers) Act No prosecution, suit or other legal proceeding shall be instituted, except with the previous sanction of the Central Government against any person in respect of anything done or purported to be done in exercise of the powers conferred by the Armed Forces (Special Powers) Act 1958[1]. This provision only gives protection in the form of previous sanction of the Central Government before a criminal prosecution of a suit or other civil proceeding is instituted against such person. In so far as such protection against prosecution is concerned, the provision is similar to that contained in the Code of Criminal Procedure 1973 s 197 which covers an offence alleged to have been committed by a public servant 'while acting or purporting to act in the discharge of his official duty'. The provision only extends this protection in the matter of institution of a suit or other legal proceeding. Since the order of the Central Government refusing or granting the sanction under the Armed Forces (Special Powers) Act 1958 s 6 is subject to judicial review, the Central Government shall pass an order giving reasons[2]. The provision prevents the filing of 'frivolous claims'[3].

1 The Armed Forces (Special Powers) Act 1958 s 6.

2 *Naga People's Movement of Human Rights v Union of India* (1998) 2 SCC 109.

3 *Indrajit Barua v State of Assam* AIR 1983 Del 54.

B. The Armed Forces (Punjab and Chandigarh) Special Power Act 1983

[1766] Introduction The 1980s in Punjab witnessed a decade-long militancy fueled by failed attempts at procuring greater autonomy. Militants were responsible for numerous human rights abuses during the violent separatist struggle, including the killings of civilians, assassinations of political leaders, and the indiscriminate use of bombs leading to a large number of civilian deaths in Punjab and other parts of India. Under the cover of militancy, criminals began to coerce businessmen and landowners, demanding protection money. In order to counter militancy in Punjab state, the Government of India enacted the Armed Forces (Punjab and Chandigarh) Special Power Act 1983, which came into force from 15 October 1983. The Act enabled certain special powers to be conferred upon members of the armed forces in the disturbed areas in the State of Punjab and the Union territory of Chandigarh. This Act was allowed to lapse in Punjab once violence ended.

[1767] Short title, extent and commencement This statute dealing with special powers to the armed forces is called the Armed Forces (Punjab and Chandigarh) Special Power Act 1983[1]. It came into force on 15 October 1983 and extended to the whole of the state of Punjab and the Union Territory of Chandigarh[2]

1 The Armed Forces (Punjab and Chandigarh) Special Power Act 1983 s 1 (1).

2 The Armed Forces (Punjab and Chandigarh) Special Power Act, 1983 s 1(2) and (3).

[1768] Armed forces In the Armed Forces (Punjab and Chandigarh) Special Power Act 1983, unless the context otherwise requires 'armed forces' means the military forces and the air forces operating as land forces, and includes any other armed forces of the Union so operating[1].

1 The Armed Forces (Punjab and Chandigarh) Special Power Act, 1983 s 2(a).

[1769] Disturbed area In the Armed Forces (Punjab and Chandigarh) Special Power Act 1983, unless the context otherwise requires 'disturbed area' means an area which is for the time being declared by notification under the provisions of the aforesaid Act[1] to be a disturbed area[2].

1 Ie under the Armed Forces (Punjab and Chandigarh) Special Power Act 1983 s 3.

2 Armed Forces (Punjab and Chandigarh) Special Power Act 1983 s 2 (b).

[1770] Word and expressions not defined In the Armed Forces (Punjab and Chandigarh) Special Power Act 1983, unless the context otherwise requires, all other words and expressions used therein, but not defined and defined in the Air Forces Act 1950, or the Army Act 1950, shall have the meanings respectively assigned to them in those Acts[1].

1 The Armed Forces (Punjab and Chandigarh) Special Power Act, 1983 s 2(c).

[1771] Power to declare areas to be disturbed area If, the Governor of the State of Punjab or the Administrator of the Union Territory of Chandigarh, or the Central Government, is of the opinion that the whole or any part of such State or Union Territory, is in such a disturbed or dangerous condition that the use of armed forces in aid of the civil power is necessary, the Governor of the State or the Administrator of the Union territory or the Central Government, by notification in the Official Gazette, declare the whole or such part of that State or Union territory to be disturbed area[1].

1 As to the meaning of 'disturbed area'; see **[1762];** The Armed Forces (Punjab and Chandigarh) Special Power Act 1983 s 3.

[1772] Special power of the armed forces Any commissioned officer[1], warrant officer[2], non-commissioned officer[3] or any other person of equivalent rank in the armed forces may, in a disturbed area:

(1) If he is of opinion that it is necessary so to do for the maintenance of public order, after giving such due warning as he may consider necessary, fire upon or otherwise use forces[4], even to the causing of death, against any person who is acting in contravention of any law or order for the time being in force in the disturbed area prohibiting the assembly of five or more persons or the carrying of weapons or of things capable of being used as weapons or firearms, ammunition or explosive substances[5].

(2) If he is of opinion that it is necessary so to do, destroy any arms dump, prepared or fortified position or shelter from which armed attacks are made or likely to be made or are attempted to be made, of any structure used as a training camp for armed volunteers or utilized as a hide- out by armed gangs or absconders wanted for any offence[6].

(3) Arrest, without warrant, any person who has committed a cognizable offence or against whom a reasonable suspicion exists that he has committed or is about to commit a cognizable offence any may use such force as may be necessary to effect the arrest[7].

(4) Enter and search, without warrant, any premises to make any such arrest as aforesaid or to recover any person believed to be wrongfully restrained or confined or any property reasonably suspected to be stolen property or any arms, ammunition or explosive substances believed to be unlawfully kept in such premises, and may for that purpose use such forces as may be necessary, and seize any such property, arms ammunition or explosive substances[8].

(5) Stop, search and seize any vehicle or vessel reasonably suspected to be carrying any person who is a proclaimed offender, or any person who has committed a non-cognizable offence, or against whom a reasonable suspicion exists that he has committed or is about to commit a non-cognizable offence, or any person who is carrying any arms, ammunition or explosive substance believed to be unlawfully held by him, and may, for that purpose, use such forces as may be necessary to effect such stoppage, search or seizure, as the case may be[9].

1 As to the meaning of 'commissioned officer'; see **[0029]**.

2 As to the meaning of 'warrant officer'; see **[0037]**.

3 As to the meaning of 'non-commissioned officer'; see **[0026]**.

4 As to the use of force, see **[1763]** note 5.

5 The Armed Forces (Punjab and Chandigarh) Special Power Act, 1983 s 4 (a).

6 The Armed Forces (Punjab and Chandigarh) Special Power Act, 1983 s 4 (b).

7 The Armed Forces (Punjab and Chandigarh) Special Power Act, 1983 s 4 (c).

8 The Armed Forces (Punjab and Chandigarh) Special Power Act, 1983 s 4 (d).

9 The Armed Forces (Punjab and Chandigarh) Special Power Act, 1983 s 4 (e).

[1773] Power of search to include powers to break open locks, etc. Every person making a search under the Armed Forces (Punjab and Chandigarh) Special Power Act 1983[1], shall have the power to break open the lock of any door, almirah, safe, box, cupboard, drawer, package or other thing, if the key thereof is withheld[2].

1 Ie under the Armed Forces (Punjab and Chandigarh) Special Power Act, 1983 s 4 (d) and (e).

2 The Armed Forces (Punjab and Chandigarh) Special Power Act 1983 s 5.

[1774] Arrested person and seized property to be made over to the police Any person arrested and taken into custody under the Armed Forces (Punjab and Chandigarh) Special Power Act 1983 and every property, arm and ammunition, or explosive substance or any vehicle or vessel seized under the aforesaid Act, shall be made over to the officer-in-charge of the nearest police station with the least possible delay[1], together with a report of the circumstances occasioning the arrest, or, as the case may be, occasioning the seizure of such property, arm, ammunition or explosive substance or any vehicle or vessel, as the case may be[2].

1 As to the meaning of 'least possible delay'; see **[1764]**. *Horendi Gogoi v. Union of India* (1991) Gau CR 3081.

2 The Armed Forces (Punjab and Chandigarh) Special Power Act, 1983 s 6.

[1775] Protection of person acting in good faith under the Armed Forces (Punjab and Chandigarh) Special Power Act 1983 No prosecution, suit or other legal proceeding shall be instituted, except with the previous sanction of the Central Government, against any person in respect of anything done or purported to be done in exercise of the powers conferred by the Armed Forces (Punjab and Chandigarh) Special Power Act 1983[1].

1 The Armed Forces (Punjab and Chandigarh) Special Power Act 1983 s 7.

[1776] Repeal and saving The Armed Forces (Punjab and Chandigarh) Special Powers Ordinance 1983 is hereby repealed[1]. Notwithstanding such repeal, anything done or any action taken under the said Ordinance shall be deemed to have been done or taken under the corresponding provisions of the Armed Forces (Punjab and Chandigarh) Special Power Act 1983[3].

1 The Armed Forces (Punjab and Chandigarh) Special Power Act 1983 s 8 (1).

2 The Armed Forces (Punjab and Chandigarh) Special Power Act, 1983 s 8 (2).

C. The Armed Forces (Jammu and Kashmir) Special Powers Act 1990

[1777] Introduction The Central Government, on 11 September 1990 enacted the Armed Forces (Jammu and Kashmir) Special Powers Act and enforced it retrospectively from 5 July 1990. It enables certain special powers to be conferred upon members of the armed forces in the disturbed areas in the State of Jammu and Kashmir. This Act may be called the Armed Forces (Jammu and Kashmir) Special Powers Act, 1990[1]. It extends to the whole of the State of Jammu and Kashmir[2] and shall be deemed to have come into force on 5 July 1990[3].

1 The Armed Forces (Jammu and Kashmir) Special Powers Act 1990 s 1(1).

2 The Armed Forces (Jammu and Kashmir) Special Powers Act 1990 s1 (2).

3 The Armed Forces (Jammu and Kashmir) Special Powers Act 1990 s 1 (3).

[1778] Armed forces In the Armed Forces (Jammu and Kashmir) Special Powers Act 1990, unless the context otherwise requires, 'armed forces' means the military forces and the air forces operating as land forces and includes any other armed forces of the Union so operating[1].

1 The Armed Forces (Jammu and Kashmir) Special Powers Act 1990 s 2 (a).

[1779] Disturbed area In the Armed Forces (Jammu and Kashmir) Special Powers Act 1990, unless the context otherwise requires, 'disturbed area' means an area which is for the time being declared by notification under the provisions of the Armed Forces (Jammu and Kashmir) Special Powers Act 1990,[1] to be a disturbed area[2].

1 Ie under the Armed Forces (Jammu and Kashmir) Special Powers Act 1990 s 3; see **[1760]**.

2 The Armed Forces (Jammu and Kashmir) Special Powers Act 1990 s 2 (b).

[1780] Meaning of words and expressions In the Armed Forces (Jammu and Kashmir) Special Powers Act 1990, unless the context otherwise requires, all other words and expressions used herein, but not defined and defined in the Air Force Act, 1950, or the Army Act, 1950, shall have the meanings respectively assigned to them in those Acts[1].

1 The Armed Forces (Jammu and Kashmir) Special Powers Act 1990 s 2(c).

[1781] Power to declare areas to be disturbed areas If, the Governor of the State of Jammu and Kashmir, or the Central Government, is of opinion that the whole or any part of the State is in such a disturbed and dangerous condition that the use of armed forces in aid of the civil power is necessary to prevent:

(1) activities involving terrorist acts directed towards overawing the Government as by law established or striking terror in the people or any section of the people or alienating any section of the people or adversely affecting the harmony amongst different sections of the people[1];

(2) activities directed towards disclaiming, questioning or disrupting the sovereignty and territorial integrity of India or bringing about cession of a part of the territory of India or secession of a part of the territory of India front the Union or causing insult to the Indian National Flag, the Indian National Anthem and the Constitution of India[2];

the Governor of the State or the Central Government, may, by notification in the Official Gazette, declare the whole or any part of the State to be a disturbed area[3]. Under this provision[4], 'terrorist act' has the same meaning as in e*xplanation* to art 248 of the Constitution of India as applicable to the State of Jammu and Kashmir[5].

1 The Armed Forces (Jammu and Kashmir) Special Powers Act 1990 s 3 (a).

2 The Armed Forces (Jammu and Kashmir) Special Powers Act 1990 s 3 (b).

3 The Armed Forces (Jammu and Kashmir) Special Powers Act 1990 s 3.

4 Ie under the Armed Forces (Jammu and Kashmir) Special Powers Act 1990 3.

5 The Armed Forces (Jammu and Kashmir) Special Powers Act 1990 s 3 explanation.

[1782] Special powers of the armed forces Any commissioned officer[1], warrant officer[2], non-commissioned officer[3] or any other person of equivalent rank in the armed forces may, in a disturbed area:

(1) if he is of opinion that it is necessary so to do for the maintenance of public order, after giving such due warning as he may consider necessary, fire upon or otherwise use force[4], even to the causing of death, against any person who is acting in contravention of any law or order for the time being in force in the disturbed area prohibiting the assembly of five or more persons or the carrying of weapons or of things capable of being used as weapons or of firearms, ammunition or explosive substances[5];

(2) if he is of opinion that it is necessary so to do, destroy any arms-dump, prepared or fortified position or shelter from which armed attacks are made or are likely to be made or are attempted to be made, or any structure used as training camp for armed volunteers or utilized as a hide-out by armed gangs or absconders wanted for any offence[6];

(3) arrest, without warrant, any persons who has committed a cognizable offence or against whom a reasonable suspicion exists that he has committed or is about to commit a cognizable offence and may use such force as may be necessary to effect the arrest[7];

(4) enter and search, without warrant, any premises to make any such arrest as aforesaid or to recover any person believed to be wrongful restrained or confined or any property reasonably suspected to be stolen property or any arms, ammunition or explosive substances believed to be unlawful kept in such premises, and may for that purpose use such force as may be necessary, and seize any such property, arms, ammunition or explosive substances[8];

(5) stop, search and seize any vehicle or vessel reasonably suspected to be carrying any person who is a proclaimed offender, or any persons who has committed a non-cognizable offence, or against whom a reasonable suspicion exists that he has committed or is about to commit a non-cognizable offence, or any person who is carrying any arms, ammunition or explosive substance believed to be unlawfully held by him, and may, for that purpose, use such force as may be necessary to effect such stoppage, search or seizure, as the case may be[9].

1 As to the meaning of 'commissioned officer'; see **[0029]**.

2 As to the meaning of 'warrant officer'; see **[0037]**.

3 As to the meaning of 'non-commissioned officer'; see **[0026]**.

4 As to the use of force, see **[1763]** note 5.

5 The Armed Forces (Jammu and Kashmir) Special Powers Act 1990 s 4(a).

6 The Armed Forces (Jammu and Kashmir) Special Powers Act 1990 s 4(b).

7 The Armed Forces (Jammu and Kashmir) Special Powers Act 1990 s 4(c).

8 The Armed Forces (Jammu and Kashmir) Special Powers Act 1990 s 4(d).

9 The Armed Forces (Jammu and Kashmir) Special Powers Act 1990 s 4(e).

[1783] Power of search to include powers to break open locks, etc. Every person making a search under the Armed Forces (Jammu and Kashmir) Special Powers Act 1990[1] shall have the power to break open the lock of any door, almirah, safe, box, cupboard, drawer, package or other thing, if the key thereof is withheld[2].

1 Ie under the Armed Forces (Jammu and Kashmir) Special Powers Act 1990 s 4.

2 The Armed Forces (Jammu and Kashmir) Special Powers Act 1990 s 5.

[1784] Arrested persons and seized property to be made over to the police Any person arrested and taken into custody under the Armed Forces (Jammu and Kashmir) Special Powers Act 1990 and every property, arms, ammunition or explosive substance or any vehicle or vessel seized under the aforesaid Act, shall be made over to the officer-in-charge of the nearest police station with the least possible delay[1], together with a report of the circumstances occasioning the arrest, or as the case may be, occasioning the seizure of such property, arms, ammunition or explosive substance or any vehicle or vessel, as the case may be[2].

1 As to the meaning of 'least possible delay'; see **[1764]**. When a person has been detained (by the army authorities), and his interrogation had revealed the presence of arms and ammunition, the first priority would have been to recover the weapons as to cause any delay could lead to a failure of the operation….in the short time available to the army patrol it was perhaps not feasible nor practicable to first inform police station....the fact that prompt action by the army in such matters is the key to success and any delay can result in the leakage of information which would frustrate the very purpose of the army action. *Masooda Parveen v. Union of India* AIR 2007 SC 1840.

2 The Armed Forces (Jammu and Kashmir) Special Powers Act 1990 s 6.

[1785] Protection of persons acting in good faith under the Armed Forces (Jammu and Kashmir) Special Powers Act 1990 No prosecution, suit or other legal proceeding shall be instituted, except with the previous sanction of the Central Government, against any person in respect of anything done or purported to be done in exercise of the powers conferred by the Armed Forces (Jammu and Kashmir) Special Powers Act 1990[1].

Use of words like 'no' and 'shall' [2] denotes the mandatory requirement of obtaining prior sanction of the Central Government before institution of the prosecution, suit or legal proceedings. From the conjoint reading of this provision and the Code of Criminal Procedure 1973 s 197(2), it is clear that prior sanction is a condition precedent before institution of any legal proceedings[3]. The Armed Forces J & K (Special Powers) Act 1990 puts an embargo on the complainant/investigating agency/person aggrieved to file a suit, prosecution etc. in respect of anything done or purported to be done by army personnel, in good faith, in exercise of power conferred by the aforesaid Act, except with the previous sanction of the Central Government[4].

1 The Armed Forces (Jammu and Kashmir) Special Powers Act 1990 s 7.

2 Ie in the Armed Forces (Jammu and Kashmir) Special Powers Act 1990 s 7.

3 *General Officer Commanding v Central Bureau of Investigation* AIR 2012 SC 1890.

4 *General Officer Commanding v Central Bureau of Investigation* AIR 2012 SC 1890.

[1786] Repeal and saving The Armed Forces (Jammu and Kashmir) Special Powers Ordinance, 1990, is hereby repealed[1]. Notwithstanding such repeal, anything done or any action taken under the said Ordinance shall be deemed to have been done or taken under the corresponding provisions of the Armed Forces (Jammu and Kashmir) Special Powers Act 1990[2].

1 The Armed Forces (Jammu and Kashmir) Special Powers Act 1990 s 8 (1).

2 The Armed Forces (Jammu and Kashmir) Special Powers Act 1990 s 8 (2).

CORRESPONDING PROVISIONS

ARMY ACT, AIR FORCE ACT, NAVY ACT AND COAST GUARD ACT

Provisions	Army Act 1950 section	Air Force Act 1950 section	Navy Act 1957 section	Coast Guard Act 1978 section
Short title and commencement	1	1	1	1
Persons subject to the Act	2	2, 3	2	3
Definitions	3	4	3	2
Power of central government to raise and maintain naval forces	-	-	5	-
Application of Act to certain forces under central government	4	5	-	-
Special provision as to rank	6	6	6	-
Commanding officer of persons subject to military law in certain cases	7	7	-	-
Officers exercising powers in certain cases	8	8	-	-
Power to declare persons to be on active service	9	9	-	-
Commission and appointment	10	10	10	-
Ineligibility of aliens for enrolment	11	11	9	6
Ineligibility of females for enrolment or employment	12	12	9	-
Procedure before enrolling officer	13	13	11	6
Mode of enrolment	14	14	11	6
Validity of enrolment	15	15	12	6
Persons to be attested	16	16	-	-
Mode of attestation	17	17	13	8
Tenure of service under the Act	18	18	15	10
Termination of service by Central Government	19	19	15 (2)	11

Provisions	Army Act 1950 section	Air Force Act 1950 section	Navy Act 1957 section	Coast Guard Act 1978 section
Dismissal, removal or reduction by Chief of the Staff and by other officers	20	20	15	11
Power to modify certain fundamental rights in their application to persons subject to the Act	21	21	4, 19	13
Retirement, release or discharge	22	22	16	-
Certificate on termination of service	23	23	17 (4)	12
Discharge or dismissal when out of India	24	24	17(1)(2)	-
Authorized deductions only to be made from pay	25	25	27	-
Remedy of aggrieved persons other than officers	26	26	23	-
Remedy of aggrieved officers	27	27	23	-
Immunity from attachment	28	28	20	-
Immunity from arrest for debt	29	29	21	-
Immunity of persons attending courts-martial from arrest	30	30	22	-
Privileges of reservists	31	31	-	-
Priority in respect of litigation	32	32	24	-
Saving of rights and privileges under other laws	33	33	26	-
Offences in relation to the enemy and punishable with death	34	34	34(c), 36, 39	15
Offences in relation to the enemy and not punishable with death	35	35	40	15
Offences punishable more severely on active service than at other times	36	36	-	-
Mutiny	37	37	42	17
Desertion and aiding desertion	38	38	49, 50	16
Absence without leave	39	39	51	26
Striking or threatening superior officers	40	40	45, 47	19
Disobedience to superior officer	41	41	47	20
Insubordination and obstruction	42	42	42, 68	-
Fraudulent enrolment	43	43	-	-
False answers on enrolment	44	44	70	43

Provisions	Army Act 1950 section	Air Force Act 1950 section	Navy Act 1957 section	Coast Guard Act 1978 section
Unbecoming conduct	45	45	54 (2)	-
Certain forms of disgraceful conduct	46	46	53 (b), 54 (1), 61	23
Ill-treating a subordinate	47	47	46	21
Intoxication	48	48	52	24
Permitting escape of person in custody	49	49	-	-
Irregularity in connection with arrest or confinement	50	50	-	-
Escape from custody	51	51	71	41
Offences in respect of property	52	52	29	-
Extortion and corruption	53	53	56 (d)	-
Making away with equipment	54	54	-	27
Injury to property	55	55	59	35
False accusations	56	56	-	32
Falsifying official documents and false declaration	57	57	60	33
Signing in blank and failure to report	58	58	-	-
Offences relating to courts-martial	59	59	69	40
False evidence	60	60	-	-
Unlawful detention of pay	61	61	-	-
Offences in relation to aircraft and flying	62	62	55	28, 30
Other offences relating to aircraft and flying	-	63	-	-
Disobedience of lawful command of captain of aircraft	-	63	-	-
Violation of good order and discipline	63	65	74	44
Miscellaneous offences	64	66	-	-
Attempt	65	67	75	45
Abetment of offences that have been committed	66	68	76	46
Abetment of offences punishable with death and not committed	67	69	76	47

Provisions	Army Act 1950 section	Air Force Act 1950 section	Navy Act 1957 section	Coast Guard Act 1978 section
Abetment of offences punishable with imprisonment and not committed	68	70	77, 78	49
Civil offences	69	71	78 (1), 77	49
Civil offence not triable by court-martial	70	72	78 (2)	50
Punishments awardable by courts-martial	71	73	81	53
Alternative punishments awardable by court-martial	72	74	82	54
Combination of punishments	73	75	-	55
Cashiering of officers	74	76	82	-
Field Punishment	-	77	-	-
Position of field punishment in scale of punishment	-	78	-	-
Result of certain punishments in the case of a warrant officer or non-commissioned officer	77	79	-	-
Retention in the ranks of a person convicted on active service	78	80	-	-
Punishments otherwise than by court-martial	79	81	-	56
Punishment of persons other than officers, junior commissioned officers and warrant officers	80	82	93 (2)	57
Requirement of sanction in certain cases	-	83	-	-
Limit of punishments	81	84	93 (2)	58
Punishments in addition to those specified in the Army Act s 80/Air Force Act s. 82	82	85	-	-
Punishment of officers, junior commissioned officers and warrant officers by brigade commanders and others	83	86	-	-
Punishment of officers, junior commissioned officers and warrant officers by area commanders and others	84	86	94	-
Punishment of junior commissioned officers	85	-	-	57
Transmission of proceedings	86	87	-	-
Review of proceedings	87	88	-	-
Superior military/air force authority	88	89	-	-

Provisions	Army Act 1950 section	Air Force Act 1950 section	Navy Act 1957 section	Coast Guard Act 1978 section
Collective fines	89	90	-	-
Deductions from pay and allowances of officers	90	91	28	-
Deductions from pay and allowances of persons other than officers	91	92	29	-
Computation of time of absence or custody	92	93	-	-
Pay and allowances during trial	93	94	-	-
Limit of certain deductions	94	95	32	-
Deduction from public money due to a person	95	96	-	-
Pay and allowances of prisoner of war during inquiry into his conduct	96	97	-	-
Remission of deductions	97	98	33	-
Provision for dependants of prisoner of war from remitted deductions	98	99	-	-
Provision for dependants of prisoner war from his pay and allowances	99	100	-	-
Period during which a person is deemed to be a prisoner of war	100	101	-	
Custody of offenders	101	102	84	59
Duty of commanding officer in regard to detention	102	103	85, 86	60
Interval between committal and court-martial	103	104	-	-
Arrest by civil authorities	104	105	83	61
Capture of deserters	105	106	-	62
Inquiry into absence without leave	106	107	-	-
Provost-marshals	107	108	89	63
Kinds of courts-martial (differ in different armed forces)	108	109	-	-
Power to convene a general court-martial	109	110	97 (2)	64
Power to convene a district court-martial	110	111	-	-
Contents of warrants issued under the Army Act s 109 and 110/ Air Force Act s110 and 111	111	112	-	64 (2)

Provisions	Army Act 1950 section	Air Force Act 1950 section	Navy Act 1957 section	Coast Guard Act 1978 section
Power to convene a summary general court-martial	112	113	95-96 Disciplinary courts	-
Composition of general court-martial	113	114	97	65
Composition of district court-martial	114	115	-	-
Composition of summary general court-martial	115	116	96	-
Summary court-martial	116	-	-	-
Dissolution of courts-martial	117	117	123	66
Powers of general and summary general courts-martial	118	118	96 (3)	67
Powers of district courts-martial	119	119	-	-
Powers of summary courts-martial	120	-	-	-
Prohibition of second trial	121	120	-	68
Period of limitation for trial	122	121	179	51
Liability of offender who ceases to be subject to Act	123	122	80	52
Place of trial	124	123	78 (a)	70
Choice between criminal court and court-martial	125	124	Regulations	71
Power of criminal court to require delivery of offender	126	125	Regulations	72
Successive trials by a criminal court and a court martial	-	126	-	-
Presiding officer	128	127	97 (12)	65
Judge advocate	129	128	99	73
Challenges	130	129	102, 103	74
Oaths of member, judge advocate and witness	131	130	104, 110	75
Voting by members	132	131	124	76
General rule as to evidence	133	132	130	77
Judicial notice	134	133	132	78
Summoning witnesses	135	134	134, 137	79
Documents exempted from production	136	135	-	80

Provisions	Army Act 1950 section	Air Force Act 1950 section	Navy Act 1957 section	Coast Guard Act 1978 section
Commissions for examination of witnesses	137	136	135	81
Examination of a witness on commission	138	137	136	82
Conviction of offence not charged	139	138	125, 126, 127	83
Presumption as to signatures	140	139	-	84
Enrolment paper	141	140	-	85
Presumption as to certain documents	142	141	133	86
Reference by accused to government officer	143	142	-	-
Evidence of previous convictions and general character	144	143	119	87
Lunacy of accused	145	144	143, 144	88
Subsequent fitness of lunatic accused for trial	146	145	143	89
Transmission to Central Government of orders under the Army Act s 146/ Air Force Act s 145	147	146	-	90
Release of lunatic accused	148	147	-	91
Delivery of lunatic accused to relatives	149	148	-	92
Order for custody and disposal of property pending trial	150	149	145	93
Order for disposal of property regarding which offence is committed	151	150	146	94
Powers of court-martial in relation to proceedings under the Act	152	151	142	95
Finding and sentence not valid, unless confirmed	153	152	-	-
Power to confirm finding and sentence of general court- martial	154	153	-	-
Power to confirm finding and sentence of district court-martial	155	154	-	-
Limitation of powers of confirming authority	156	155	-	-
Power to confirm finding and sentence of summary general court-martial	157	156	-	-
Power of confirming authority to mitigate, remit or commute sentences	158	157	-	-
Confirming of findings and sentences on board a ship	159	158	-	-

Provisions	Army Act 1950 section	Air Force Act 1950 section	Navy Act 1957 section	Coast Guard Act 1978 section
Revision of finding or sentence	160	159	-	-
Finding and sentence of a summary court-martial	161	-	-	-
Transmission of proceedings of summary court-martial	162	-	-	-
Alteration of finding or sentence in certain cases	163	160	-	-
Remedy against order, finding or sentence of court-martial	164	161	162	119
Annulment of proceedings	165	162	-	-
Form of sentence of death	166	163	147	96
Commencement of sentence of life imprisonment or imprisonment	167	164	151	99
Execution of sentence of life imprisonment	168	165	150	-
Execution of sentence of imprisonment	169	166	150	100
Period of custody undergone by the officer or person to be set off against the imprisonment	169A	-	151 (3)	-
Temporary custody of offender	170	167	150 (3)	101
Execution of sentence of imprisonment in special cases	171	168	-	-
Conveyance of prisoner from place to place	172	169	153	102
Execution of sentence of detention	-	170	-	-
Communication of certain orders to prison officers	173	171	-	103
Execution of sentence of fine	174	172	158	104
Establishment and regulation of military prisons	175	173	157	-
Informality or error in the order or warrant	176	174	-	105
Power to make rules in respect of prisons and prisoners	177	175	159	-
Restriction of rule making power in regard to corporal punishment	178	176	159 (3)	-
Pardon and remission	179	177	163 (1)	120 (1)
Cancellation of conditional pardon, release on parole or remission	180	178	163 (3)	120 (3)

Provisions	Army Act 1950 section	Air Force Act 1950 section	Navy Act 1957 section	Coast Guard Act 1978 section
Reduction of warrant officer or non-commissioned officer	181	179	-	-
Suspension of sentence of life imprisonment or imprisonment	182	180	164 (1)	107
Orders pending suspension	183	181	-	-
Release on suspension	184	182	164 (2)	108
Computation of period of suspension	185	183	164 (1)(b)	109
Order after suspension	186	184	164	110
Reconsideration of case after suspension	187	185	164(1)(b)	111
Fresh sentences after suspension	188	186	164(1)(d)	112
Scope of power of suspension	189	187	-	113
Effect of suspension and remission on dismissal	190	188	-	114
Power to make rules	191	189	184	123
Power to make regulations	192	190	184A	-
Publication of rules and regulations in Gazette	193	191	-	-
Rules and regulations to be laid before Parliament	193A	191A	185	123 (3)

www.ingramcontent.com/pod-product-compliance
Lightning Source LLC
Chambersburg PA
CBHW080929240926
51849CB00003BA/417
* 9 7 8 9 3 8 2 6 5 2 8 7 8 *